France

a photo essay

1 Château du Rivau, Loire Valley

2 Château de Chavaniac-Lafayette, Auvergne
3 Château de Montreuil-Bellay, Loire Valley
4 Château de Josselin, Brittany
5 Château de Biron, Dordogne

3

5

6 vineyards near Dijon, Burgundy

CHÂTEAU LÉOVILLE BARTON

ST-JULIEN-MEDOC

12 B\ˡˡᵉˢ   L.0011   1996

CHATEAU-FIGEAC

SAINT-ÉMILION

FRANCE   1996

CHATEAU
GRAND MAYNE

GRAND CRU CLASSE

SAINT-EMILION

12 B\ˡˡᵉˢ   1996

CHATEAU SOUTARD

8

7 wine crates, St-Emilion, the Southwest
8 marzipan fruits, Périgueux, the Southwest

9

9 Fayence, Provence

13 Château d'Ainay-le-Vieil, Loire Valley
14 Rouen cathedral, Normandy

15 Notre-Dame-la-Grande, Poitiers,
   Atlantic Coast
16 Place des Vosges, Paris
17 church, Aulnay, Atlantic Coast

16

17

18 timberframe house, Auxerre, Burgundy
19 street corner, Lyon, Rhône Valley
20 Angles-sur-l'Anglin, Atlantic Coast
21 Fourvière hillside and Palais de Justice,
   Lyon, Rhône Valley

22

22 Reims cathedral, the Northeast
23 Moselle, the Northeast

24, 25 and 26 around Mont Blanc, Alps

27

27 Pra-Loup, Alps

28 church, Thaon, Normandy
29 neolithic tumulus, Bougon, Atlantic Coast
30 neolithic stones, St-Just, Brittany
31 Marais Poitevin, Atlantic Coast

31

32 harbour, La Rochelle, Atlantic Coast

34

33 and 34 mussel-farming in the Bay of
   Mont-St-Michel, Brittany
35 Sept Iles, Brittany
36 Fort National, St-Malo, Brittany

36

37

37 Nice, Côte d'Azur

Philippe Barbour,
Dana Facaros and Michael Pauls

FRANCE

'Black is the colour of Clermont-
Ferrand's gorgeous heart, and of its
cathedral, dwarfed by the silhouettes
of the spectacular Monts Dômes.
It is also the colour of the rubber tyres
indelibly linked with the city's growth.'

CADOGANguides

Contents

About the Authors

Philippe Barbour (*Normandy, Brittany, the Loire Valley, the Atlantic Coast, the Limousin, the North, the Northeast, Burgundy and Beyond, the Rhône Valley, the Auvergne, the Alps and Jura*) is totally in love with France. Both Petit Breton and Grand Breton, being half-Breton and half-British, he studied French literature at Oxford University, but has learnt a great deal more about French culture on his touristic Tour de France researching Cadogan's French guides. Among the other major books he has written for Cadogan are their regional guides to *Brittany* and to the *Loire*. *Flying Visits France*, which Philippe put together with Dana Facaros, Michael Pauls and editor Linda McQueen, focuses on the country's great cities now easily reached via budget airlines, ferries and superfast train links. His latest Cadogan guide, out in 2005, is on the *Rhône-Alpes* region, with which he has become infatuated in recent times.

The author's acknowledgements can be found at the end of the guide.

Dana Facaros and Michael Pauls (*Paris and the Ile de France, the Southwest, Gascony, the Basque Lands and the Pyrenees, Provence and the Côte d'Azur, Languedoc-Roussillon*) lived for eight years in a leaky old farmhouse in southwest France, and now they're back...at least for a while. They have written over 40 guides for Cadogan.

Updated 2004 by Philippe Barbour, Robert Harneis, Kate Read, Linda Rano, Robin Pridy, Anselm Eustace and Jacqueline Chnéour.

Cadogan Guides
Highlands House, 165 The Broadway,
London SW19 1NE
info.cadogan@virgin.net
www.cadoganguides.com

The Globe Pequot Press
246 Goose Lane, PO Box 480, Guilford,
Connecticut 06437–0480

Copyright © Philippe Barbour, Dana Facaros and
    Michael Pauls 2001, 2004

Cover and photo essay design by Sarah Gardner
Book design by Andrew Barker
Cover photographs © Philippe Barbour
Photo essay © Philippe Barbour (2, 3, 10, 13, 14, 15, 17,
    18, 19, 20, 21, 24, 25, 26, 28, 29, 30, 31, 32, 33, 34, 35,
    36) and © John Ferro Sims (4, 5, 6, 7, 8, 9, 11, 12, 16,
    22, 23, 27, 37); image (1) © Patricia Laigneau
Maps © Cadogan Guides, drawn by Map Creation
    Ltd; Paris metro map © TCS
Editor: Linda McQueen
Proofreading: Catherine Charles, Jacqueline
    Chnéour and Susannah Wight
Indexing: Isobel McLean
Production: Navigator Guides

Printed in Italy by Legoprint
A catalogue record for this book is available
    from the British Library
ISBN 1-86011-881-X

Introduction

'As happy as God in France,' is an old German saying, one with which so many of us merrily concur. The country's charms are legion, from Champagne and *haute couture* to a country market or a sandy Breton beach, from the otherworldly meringue of Mont Blanc to a sliver of truffle in a *foie gras*. France was lucky enough to be born with every grace geography could bestow. Atlantic, Mediterranean, and Continental climates, abundant rivers, rich plains and sunlit hills make it the most fertile country in Europe, producing the ingredients for its world-famous cuisine and wines.

On these lovely landscapes, the French have developed a way of life that is marked with a style and *savoir faire* that make other countries seem like amateurs. On top of that, wealth and talent have left an artistic legacy second only to Italy's, with a prehistoric head start in the painted caves of the south and the Neolithic stone alignments of the north. Celtic metalwork and the Gallo-Roman monuments scattered around the country are a prelude to Romanesque works of pure imagination, followed by perhaps France's greatest invention, soaring Gothic cathedrals with walls of stained glass. Enchanting châteaux in late-Gothic and Renaissance variations around the Loire Valley give way to the classical and rococo styles of the kings Louis.

In the 19th century Paris was remade as Europe's first modern city, where Impressionism and its aftershocks brought the old art world to the ground. The five-sixths of the French population who don't live in Paris have countless beautiful village, towns and cities to call home: Avignon and Aix, Tours and Nantes, Bordeaux and Toulouse, Dijon and Besançon, Nancy and Strasbourg, to name just a few, many now made more accessible by a flurry of low-cost airlines.

As heirs of the highly individualistic tribes of Gaul, picked off one by one by Caesar, the French like to do as they please. De Gaulle got it right when he said that 'The French will only be united under the threat of danger. Nobody can simply bring together a country that has 265 kinds of cheese' – only, as has often been noted, he grossly underestimated the number of cheeses. The compulsion to melt the French down into some kind of centrally controlled fondue is a constant throughout the monarchy, the Revolution, the Napoleons, and the old-style *classe politique*: France, after all, wrote the book on centralization. There is, however, a growing restlessness with the schoolbook image of a culturally and politically homogenous France. You only need to look into the corners of the Hexagon, as France is often nicknamed, to see how unFrench France can be. In Alsace, German is still widely spoken. In the northwest, the Bretons cling on to their Celtic roots. In the far southwest, the Basque country retains its language, culture and fierce nationalists, even if the Catalans, another group scooped up by the Pyrenees, tend to be more pragmatic. In the southeast, Savoy and Nice only voted to become a part of France (rather than Italy) in 1860. Not forgetting Corsica, the biggest political thorn in the national side, recently, momentously, given a measure of autonomy.

Change is in the air, and, as power devolves from Paris, France may well become even more colourful, even more fun to visit and even more enjoyable to live in. Already it is more determined than most countries to dig in its heels to save its soul. If anyone can resist the bland siren song of globalization, it'll be the French. After all, ensconced in their earthly paradise, they have the most to lose.

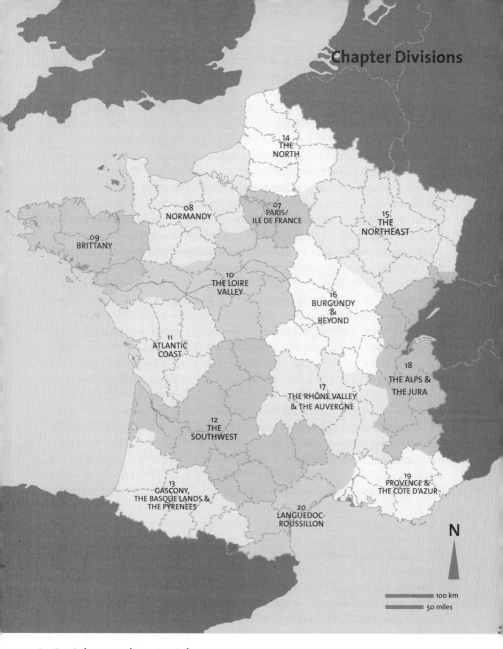

14
THE
NORTH

08
NORMANDY

07
PARIS/
ILE DE FRANCE

15
THE
NORTHEAST

09
BRITTANY

10
THE LOIRE
VALLEY

16
BURGUNDY
&
BEYOND

11
ATLANTIC
COAST

18
THE ALPS &
THE JURA

17
THE RHÔNE VALLEY
& THE AUVERGNE

12
THE
SOUTHWEST

13
GASCONY,
THE BASQUE LANDS &
THE PYRENEES

19
PROVENCE &
THE CÔTE D'AZUR

20
LANGUEDOC-
ROUSSILLON

N

100 km
50 miles

A Guide to the Guide

Paris and the Ile de France: The City of Light glitters brighter than ever at the dawn of the 21st century, spruced up and bursting with the lion's share of France's art and culture, restaurants, shops and myths, plus Versailles and Disneyland Paris.

Normandy: Explore the appley interior as well as the coastal high drama of Honfleur and Deauville, the D-Day landing beaches, the Bayeux tapestry, and Mont-St-Michel.

Brittany: Even Neolithic men couldn't resist the region's tough granite charms, as Carnac most memorably recalls. Virtually every inch of the Breton shore can still seduce you; inland, up the river estuaries, hide delightful historic towns and chapels.

Loire Valley: With its pure French accent and its plethora of fantasy châteaux, the Loire sums up refined French living. It also boasts numerous wine villages, and a whole underground world from which the region's white stone was quarried.

Atlantic Coast: A dark horse, concealing gorgeous islands; the splendid old ports of La Rochelle and Rochefort; the pilgrimage churches of inland Poitou; the Marais Poitevin, knocking spots off the Camargue; and the shock of Futuroscope cinema park.

The Southwest: A gentle land of rivers, from the quiet wooded Limousin through the honeyed villages, châteaux and prehistoric caves of the Dordogne and Lot to Bordeaux, wine capital of the world, and its upriver dynamic rival, Toulouse.

Gascony and the Pyrenees: Under the snowy citadels of the Pyrenees, the land of the Gascons and Basques offers *la France profonde* at its most genial, with the cathedral of Auch and the lively cities of Biarritz, St-Jean-de-Luz, Bayonne and Pau.

The North: Head for pretty St-Omer, Montreuil and Bergues, or, further inland, the high drama of Lille and Arras, the cathedral cities of Amiens and Senlis, or the many grand castles. More moving than all these are the war cemeteries of the Somme.

The Northeast: Champagne and its wine route fills many a visitor with joy; Troyes, old capital of the region, conceals startling artistic riches. In the fortified territories of French Ardenne, Charleville's Place Ducale proves more than a match for Paris' Place des Vosges. In Lorraine, with its lashings of splendid countryside, Nancy screeches style, both Ancien Régime and Art Nouveau. The beautiful, forested, ruddy Vosges mountains separate Lorraine from Alsace, which looks sweetly across the Rhine to Germany, while offering splendid cities such as Strasbourg, Colmar and Mulhouse.

Burgundy and Beyond: Renowned above all for its wine and its religious legacy, in Burgundy you'll also find endless rustic hilltop villages, ancient sites such as Alésia and Autun, and ducal Dijon and Beaune in the winey east. We add misunderstood Vichy and Moulins; the religious Brionnais; bibulous Beaujolais and the calmer Bresse.

Rhône Valley and the Auvergne: These are sensational, little-explored areas, hiding the weird and wonderful volcanic landscapes of the Auvergne; the secretive upper Loire and upper Allier valleys; staggering Le Puy-en-Velay and its stairways to heaven; the hillside paradise of the Ardèche and the Drôme; and the glorious city of Lyon.

The Alps and the Jura: Mont Blanc is the crowning glory of the Savoy Alps. The most famous ski resorts lie way up above the Isère valley, circling the great Vanoise range. The southern Alps of the Dauphiné, centred on the Ecrins mountains, come as an exceptionally sunny surprise. North of genteel Lake Geneva, the Jura mountains are a better-kept secret, along with Besançon and the Franche-Comté wine and salt routes.

Provence and Côte d'Azur: This region attracts tourists like bees to a honeypot with its glittering resorts, modern art, Roman monuments, landscapes painted by Cézanne and Matisse, and *villages perchés*. Off the coast lies **Corsica**, the Ile de Beauté.

Languedoc-Roussillon: France's other, less-visited Mediterranean region, with bigger and better beaches, plus the fascinating cities of Narbonne, Montpellier, Nîmes, Carcassonne and Perpignan, and the vertiginous castles of the Cathars.

France Past and Present

History

–AD 260
A precocious prehistory, followed by Celts and Romans

Cro-Magnon is the name of a hamlet in the Dordogne, only one of many terms to describe early man that come from finds in France. Someone was tramping around these green valleys around a million years ago, and the upper Palaeolithic cultures called the **Perigordian** (from Périgord), the **Aurignacian** (from Aurignac, near Toulouse) and the **Magdalenian** (from a cave in the Tarn; 15000–9000 BC) left the famous cave paintings that are the world's oldest art. France continued its precocious start in Europe's first real civilization, the **Neolithic** (4500–2000 BC), a period that saw the beginnings of agriculture, astronomy and architecture. Situated at the heart of the Neolithic world, the country has more than its share of dolmens, tumuli and menhirs, as well as the spectacular alignments at Carnac in Brittany.

After a rather sleepy millennium, things picked up again *c.* 1000 BC with the beginnings of the 'Iron Age'; this, probably not coincidentally, is also the earliest date proposed for the arrival of the **Celts** from central Europe. These 'Gauls', as the Romans would call them, were not as backward as is often believed. They developed a prosperous land, supporting millions. Though the Celts never cared much for urban life, some of their *oppida* (trading centres) grew into little towns. Gaul was never exclusively Gaulish. The Celts had to share the land with earlier inhabitants in the south: the Iberians and Basques in the southwest, and the Ligurians in the southeast. The **Greeks** arrived in *c.* 600, with the founding of Marseille, which became the mother to a string of towns along the coast. The Greeks introduced the olive and vine, and probably roses from Persia to give Provence's perfume industry a start. **Rome** became interested in Gaul from its need to control a land route to Spain, newly acquired in the Punic Wars. With the support of its long-time ally Marseille, Rome occupied southeastern Gaul in 121 BC, and the region became Rome's first 'province' outside Italy, hence **Provence**. It assimilated so rapidly that the Romans liked to call it *Gallia Togata* ('Gaul with the toga on'), as opposed to *Gallia Comata* ('Hairy Gaul') further north.

By the 1st century BC, the first Germanic tribes were already infiltrating across the Rhine, and worries about these fierce warriors were one factor that spurred Rome to complete the conquest. Another was the ambition of **Julius Caesar**. Starting in 58 BC, he did the job with impressive brutality, tackling one Celtic tribe at a time. When the Gauls finally united under **Vercingétorix**, their last revolt was crushed at the siege of Alésia (Alise-Ste-Reine in Burgundy) in 52. Caesar sold a tenth of the Gauls into slavery.

For all that, Hairy Gaul proved remarkably receptive to Roman language, religion and ways of life. Old Celtic centres, such as *Lutetia* (Paris), grew into modest provincial capitals, while the greatest city of all was *Lugdunum* (Lyon), a key crossroads both for trade and defence. Rome's enormous investment in maintaining the Rhine frontier against the Germans was always a key factor in eastern Gaul's prosperity.

AD 260–687

Gaul becomes a Teutonic playground

The Roman 'crisis of the 3rd century' was felt in Gaul as much as any part of the Empire. Troubles started when two German tribes, the Franks and Alemanni, broke through the Rhine frontier in 260. It took 16 years to chase them out, and after that a series of civil wars and imperial pretenders raised by the legions kept the land in turmoil. Many rural districts became depopulated and the hard-pressed cities had to build defensive walls.

By the 4th century, Gaul had become a very different place. The old Gallo-Roman aristocracy had been replaced by a class of new men, mostly Romans with ties to the emperor. They owned nearly everything, including the people, as free farmers and tradesmen came under increasing pressure to sell themselves into serfdom to escape worse fates. The small élite lived in luxury in their palatial rural villas and supported a last flowering of Latin culture, centred on the famous school of *Bordigala* (Bordeaux); many among the élite also converted to Christianity.

The Rhine frontier finally collapsed in 406, Gaul overrun by **Franks**, **Burgundians** and **Visigoths**. These 'barbarians' had not come to pull down the temples and rape the women. Pushed from behind by other Germans, themselves pushed by rampaging Huns, they chiefly wanted a safe place to settle; all of them made their arrangements with Rome, and with the landowners, who kept considerable control by means of their wealth and their monopoly of positions in the now-established Church. The Visigoths in Provence, along with the Burgundians, were the most advanced Germans, and accepted Roman culture and Christianity easily. Up north, the Franks and Alemanni stayed pagan and continued to coat their bodies in bear grease. No doubt that is what gave the Franks the extra power they needed to gain ascendency over all of Gaul. One Frankish tribe, at Tournai, was ruled by a formidable chieftain named **Merovech**, and he and his sons first unified the Franks and then went after their German cousins. **Clovis** (ruled 482–511) devoured the Alemanni, snuffed out the Roman 'King' Syagrius, conquered Aquitania (the southwest) and drove the Visigoths into Spain. He also converted to Christianity, with the aid of a nagging pious wife and St Remigius, bishop of Reims. When Remigius told him the story of Christ's crucifixion, Clovis sighed and said, 'Ah, if only my Franks had been there!' One more fateful decision of Clovis's – he made a little town on the Seine called **Paris** his capital. The advantages of the strategically located, fertile and defensible Ile-de-France were becoming apparent, and as the centre of Frankish power the region came to be called *Francia*, and its dialect *Francien*, the embryo of modern French. For a time, the Merovingians prevailed over their enemies, though their own custom of dividing up inheritances made the job difficult. Two new peoples, beyond Frankish control, appear in this period to add complications: British refugees fleeing from Angles and Saxons to make **Brittany** a Celtic redoubt, and the **Gascons**, or Vascones – slightly Romanized Basques, come to reclaim lands between the Pyrenees and the Garonne.

687–1000
A short-lived Carolingian Empire, followed by feudal anarchy

The Merovingians were slipping. Not the least of their mysteries is how such a virile dynasty could decline so rapidly into the line of 'do-nothing kings', the *rois fainéants*. By the mid-7th century, real power in the Frankish courts was held by the 'mayors of the palace', the kings' chief ministers. Strongest of these was **Pépin II** of Herstal, who was boss of nearly all the Frankish lands by 687; from then on his descendants ruled, and the anointed kings were their puppets. Pépin's grandson **Charles Martel** – the 'Hammer' – took power at a time when the Franks were facing their greatest threats. Charles was equal to the challenge. He reasserted control over Aquitaine, pushed the invading Saxons back into Saxony and, most importantly, defeated the hitherto invincible Arabs, rolling northwards after their conquest of Spain, at Poitiers in 732.

It was left to Charles' son **Pépin III le Bref** (the Short) to take the logical final step: disposing of the last feeble Merovingian and having himself proclaimed king. This was accomplished with the aid of the pope, and in return Pépin had to cross the Alps and sort out the Lombards in Italy. Pépin the Short's son and successor in the new Carolingian dynasty, apparently legitimate, was a seven-foot cracker who has gone down in history as **Charlemagne**, though he might have answered as readily to Karl der Grosse – half of Charles/Karl's lands were in Germany and his preferred capital was at Aachen. Above all, Charlemagne was a warrior. He made his authority felt in every part of old Gaul, intervened in Spain, destroyed the Lombards and seized all northern Italy, and pushed his frontiers far out into the German lands, treating any tribes who refused conversion to Christianity with a policy tantamount to genocide. At home, he was a loving paterfamilias and a great patron of learning, though all the efforts of his learned English culture minister Alcuin were not quite enough to teach him how to write his own name. He ruled his vast kingdom like a paterfamilias too, sending agents called the *missi domenici* to every corner to see if officials were doing their jobs and justice was secure. Something very significant in the history of the west was happening, though Charlemagne may not have realized it until Christmas Eve in Rome in the year 800. While he was kneeling at Mass, a scheming Pope Leo III sneaked up behind him and placed an imperial crown on his head. Whether or not he expected it to happen, or even desired it, the Empire of the West had been reborn, and the papacy had created the pretension that the crown was theirs to give.

Unfortunately, all this new Carolingian empire was good for was falling apart. Poor communications, a lack of resources and a lack of ingrained unity ensured that the vast areas tied together by Charlemagne's conquests could never be held together for long. Even while Charlemagne was alive, the **Vikings** had begun their raids, and there was little he could do about it. A speedy dissolution was made certain by the old Germanic habit of dividing everything between one's sons. Thus, after the death of Charlemagne's only son **Louis the Pious** in 840, the empire was split into three kingdoms for each of Louis' sons. The arrangement was confirmed at the **Treaty of Verdun** in 843. **Charles the Bald** got the west, *Francia Occidentalis*, the lands that would one day be France.

The 9th century, which had started with such promise, turned out to be the very darkest stretch of the Dark Ages. Other bugbears, notably the Magyars, came roaring through the land, but it was the Vikings who provided the greatest menace, repeatedly ravaging the country. One of their favourite raiding grounds was the Seine valley. In 885 they besieged Paris, but **Count Eudes** held them off – the first time anyone had ever managed to do so. Eudes' heirs, the **Counts of Paris** (later dukes), would for the next century be the most powerful lords of France.

After thoroughly wrecking the lower Seine, about 896 the Vikings began to settle it. The 'northmen' were becoming **Normans**, and in 911 under their chief Rollo they turned Christian in exchange for recognition of their right to what is now Normandy. Elsewhere, great lords were finding opportunity in disorder, carving out effectively independent states: besides Paris, **Aquitaine**, **Provence**, **Burgundy** and **Toulouse** were the strongest. In one sense it was the triumph of Germanic law and customs over Roman, personal relations over state control – in short, feudalism. Nor was the atomization of society limited to the few grandees. The castellans, originally royal or ducal agents, began everywhere to think of themselves as lords in their own right.

Still, feudalism gave the country a paradoxical stability in the midst of the chaos of battling barons, and the 10th century was a time of slow, gradual recovery. One of the Counts of Paris, **Hugues Capet**, became king in 987. His royal domain was limited to a thin strip between Paris and Orléans, and passing from one town to the other he had to worry about ambushes from any castle along the way.

1000–1328
Paris becomes the capital of the Middle Ages, and France a nation

No one at the time could have noticed that something important had begun, but Hugues' **Capetian descendants** would hold that throne for the next 805 years. The year 1000 found the first French pope, the learned Sylvester II, ruling at Rome, the Ottonian dynasty (inheritors of Charlemagne's imperial title) bringing prosperity to Germany, and the new Europe's first commercial cities in Flanders and Italy providing an impetus to trade. The lands that were coming to be known as 'France' shared fully in the ascent. Cities were growing here too, and by 1050 some, such as Laon and Le Mans, were asserting their independence. New wealth brought new life to the Church; 'the world was clothing itself in a white mantle of churches', as one chronicler put it, while the great abbey of Cluny, founded in 910, contributed much to the growth of education. The revival of learning gathered momentum at Laon, at the cathedral school of Chartres, and in Paris, with its school that would develop into the most renowned of Europe's new universities.

While the feudal order permitted such progress, it continued to have its drawbacks – most of all, a simple overabundance of knights, all striving to impress. Constant feudal warfare was the curse of the age. The Church responded with such initiatives as the late 10th-century Truce of God and the 1120 Peace of God, but the problem was partly resolved by the Crusades. Pope Urban II proclaimed the **First Crusade** in 1095 not in Rome, but in Clermont-Ferrand, and he was correct in his assumption that French knights would be the most numerous and enthusiastic Crusaders. France, this chaotic new country without a central government to speak of, had quite suddenly become a powerhouse in European affairs. In 1066, 30 years before the Crusaders sailed off to found 'Frankish' states in the Middle East, **Duke William of Normandy** had conquered England at a blow, and Norman knights who missed out on that escapade would later carve out a kingdom for themselves in southern Italy and Sicily.

If the new powerhouse did not have a head, at least it was developing a worthy capital. By organizing the towns of northern France into a powerful economic unit, **Paris** in the 12th century surpassed Venice to become the biggest city in Europe. Besides its university, the intellectual centre of Christendom, and its revolutionary Gothic architecture, Paris also created the schools of painting, sculpture and music that developed so much of the exquisite style of the Middle Ages.

For all its energy, this 'France' was still more a geographical expression than a political reality, and the 'king' in Paris only one player on an extremely complicated chessboard. Louis VI, in 1137, thought he had achieved a master stroke by marrying off his son, the future Louis VII, to **Eleanor of Aquitaine**, heiress to the biggest state in the land. But Eleanor was a lively girl, and she found life with the pious, slow-witted Louis intolerable. From this family soap opera came a conflict that would spring the plot of French history for the next 300 years. In 1152 they divorced; Eleanor had found someone she liked better – Henri Plantagenet of Anjou, also Duke of Normandy and soon to be **King Henry II of England**. It was the ultimate nightmare for the king in Paris, now nearly surrounded by the possessions of a far more powerful vassal.

Louis VII wasn't up to the challenge, but he did leave an heir who would be. **Philippe Auguste** battled with the Plantagenets for three decades, first against Henry and then his sons Richard the Lionheart and John. He manoeuvered the hapless John into appearing a disloyal vassal (as Duke of Normandy, Philippe was his lord) and used that as an excuse to confiscate the fief. Success in battle made it stick. The Plantagenets gathered a formidable European coalition of allies, but Philippe whipped them all at the **Battle of Bouvines** (1214); Paris celebrated with a week-long party in the streets.

No one did more to build France. By the end of his reign Philippe had gained for the crown not only Normandy, but also Touraine, Anjou and Poitou besides; for the first time, there was enough land, and enough men, under direct royal control to make Paris' ruler a king not only in name but in fact. Philippe reformed and reorganized his state along Norman lines; with a strong and capable bureaucracy, he chartered cities and fostered commerce and learning. Fittingly, in his own time he was the first to be called not 'King of the Franks', but King of France.

This new France was still largely limited to the north. No one in the south thought of themselves as French at all. They didn't even speak the same language, but the various related tongues (Languedocien, Provençal, Gascon) that are now called **Occitan** – the language of the troubadours, and of an accomplished civilization that looked more to the Mediterranean than to Paris. One of Occitania's peculiarities was its tolerance for religious heresy, especially the dualistic faith of the **Cathars**, imported from the Balkans. The growth of this sect, with its own bishops and church organization in the southwest, was the excuse for the **Albigensian Crusade** of 1209, in which the pope and the French combined to conquer much of the south, notably the powerful County of Toulouse. Mass slaughters of Cathars and the introduction of the Inquisition accompanied a vast and blatant land-grab by the northern knights.

Philippe Auguste's son Louis IX (1226–70) mopped up the remaining heretics, and became **Saint Louis** for his trouble. But while he may look something of a thug from the southern point of view, the French regard him with some justification as their all-time model monarch. Louis' obsession with crusading abroad detracted from the good he did at home, but he did show a sincere concern for the welfare of his people.

Saint Louis also continued his father's policy of building a strong, centralized state, and this trend would reach its culmination in the reign of his grandson, **Philippe IV le Bel** (1285–1314). In 1302 he called the first **Estates-General**, a national parliament divided into the three 'estates' of nobles, clergy and bourgeois. What he wanted from them was, of course, money. Philippe always needed more, especially for his epic battle with the papacy, which had been meddling in French affairs for centuries. All Europe was fed up with the impostures of the most arrogant and grasping of all popes, Boniface VIII, and Philippe beat him off, gaining considerable control over the French Church and its revenues, as well as having the papacy in his pocket; a French pontiff, Clement V, fled Roman anarchy in 1309 for Provence – not part of France until 1481, but still close enough for Philippe to keep an eye on him. The 'Babylonian Captivity', as Italians called it, would keep the popes in Avignon until 1377.

1328–1453
A century of war, and the ruin of medieval France

Medieval France was the richest and most populous country in Europe, the land of chivalry, scholarly authority and artistic innovation – and, quite suddenly, it all started to come apart. France had beaten the English under Philippe Auguste, and now the old National Enemy was coming back for its revenge. King Charles le Bel, last of the direct line of Hugues Capet, died in 1328. A cousin, Philippe de Valois, had a reasonable claim to the throne, but so did Edward III of England, and the result would be the **Hundred Years War**. At first, the war proceeded fitfully in the southwest, in Aquitaine, held by England since the days of the Plantagenets. In 1346, however, Edward invaded France proper, and he brought his Welsh and English archers with him. Though the French took a very long time to realize it, a revolution in warfare was occurring, and Edward's bowmen chopped down French knights like grass at the **Battle of Crécy**. Ten years later, they repeated the performance at Poitiers, and took King Jean II prisoner.

France was down, and leaderless. The war played hell with commerce and culture in the cities, while an epochal change in Europe's main trade route helped finish off France's medieval prosperity; where once merchants linked Italy and Flanders by way of Lyon and the great fairs of Champagne, now the fighting made them take a new route, over the Alps and down the Rhine. In the country things were even worse. Every region of France was devastated in the war, and the mercenary companies that sprung up spread terror when no king was paying them. Add to that the waves of peasant rebellions, the *jacqueries* in Picardy and elsewhere, and the **Black Death** of 1347–8, which carried off a third of the population, and France's misery was complete.

France nearly had a real revolution in these dark times, one that might have set the nation on the same course of constitutional evolution as England. In 1356 the provost of the Paris merchants, **Etienne Marcel**, proposed to the Estates-General that they meet on a regular basis, and assume more power over the king's government and his purse. Royal resistance led to a revolt, and Marcel ruled Paris, with some help from the English, until his assassination in 1358.

The dauphin who put down Paris' revolt (while his father was imprisoned in London) became **Charles V** (1364–80), and despite this unpromising start he ruled with caution and skill, even winning some territories back from the English with his talented commander Bertrand du Guesclin. For the French, it would be only the eye of the hurricane in the endless war.

In the next round, most of France's injuries would be self-inflicted. It did not help that the next king, **Charles VI**, went mad, but while the English waited in the wings the French, quite irresponsibly, collapsed into a bitter and pointless civil war. The two sides were called 'Armagnacs' and 'Bourguignons' after their noble leaders, and as they tore up the country the English came back. They played one faction off against the other, and in 1415 crushed the French army once again at the **Battle of Agincourt**. When Charles VI died in 1422, most of France recognized **Henry V of England** as king. His brother, the Duke of Bedford, ran the occupation government from a half-abandoned Paris, while the rightful king, young, indecisive **Charles VII**, held on to parts of central France; contemporaries mocked him as the 'Little King of Bourges'.

At France's darkest hour, history seems to dissolve into myth with the appearance of **Joan of Arc**, the shepherd girl from Lorraine who came to tell the king of her visions, gained a horse and some men from a sympathetic commander, and chased the English out of Orléans in 1429. Captured by the Bourguignons at Compiègne in 1430, she was sold to the English, who burned her as a witch the following year (while King Charles did nothing to help her). But the revival of the French spirit she began soon swept all before it. In 1436 Paris fell, and by 1453 the English had lost all of their possessions in France, save only the town of Calais.

1453–1562
Recovery, and a touch of royal Renaissance opulence

Much of France, including Paris, was a desolation, but economic recovery came with surprising pace, speeded along by Charles' son, **Louis XI** (1461–83). Eccentric and miserly, often living in near solitude at Tours by the Loire, his huge nose and dusty felt hat made him a butt of jokes in Europe's courts, but Louis attended to business with wily tenacity. England, preoccupied with the Wars of the Roses, was no longer a threat, but a powerful new foe appeared in **Burgundy**, which had taken advantage of French setbacks in the Hundred Years War to become a kingdom in all but name. Duke

Charles le Téméraire even managed once to capture Louis in battle, but after he had died on the field in 1477, without a male heir, Burgundy and Picardy reverted to the king. Three years later, Louis acquired Provence, Maine and Anjou by similar fortune.

By the late 15th century France was back on its feet and making trouble for its neighbours. Charles VIII (1483–98), Louis XII (1498–1515) and François Ier (1515–47), all brought up along the Loire, spent most of their time meddling south of the Alps, trying to assert their inheritance claims there. But instead of conquering Italy the Renaissance Italians conquered France – with their music, poetry, clothes, cuisine, art and architecture. A host of exquisite castles built along the Loire and its tributaries was one fabulous legacy. In these and the palaces of the Marais in Paris and suburban digs such as Fontainebleau, François Ier and his son Henri II held the showiest courts France had yet seen – also the most expensive; besides the innumerable scrimmaging nobles François supported 12,000 hunting dogs and 12,000 horses.

The long Italian Wars proved a waste of effort, and at the Battle of Pavia in 1525 François himself became the third French king in two centuries to be captured in battle. This time, the tormentor was Charles V, Holy Roman Emperor and King of Spain, who had amassed the largest European empire since Charlemagne. The French were lucky to hold their own against him and his ally Henry VIII of England, and although they gave up their designs in Italy in 1559 they managed to snatch Calais from the English, and also pick up some imperial territories in the east (Metz and Verdun) by paying German barons to oppose the emperor.

Also in 1559, Henry II took a shot through the visor at a mock tournament, and France came under the rule of a queen-regent, the unstable but always interesting Catherine de Médicis (de' Medici). This was a woman who took her political advice from sorcerers and seers (Nostradamus among them); and whose actions were largely expressed in plots, poison and intrigues. After bringing up three boys who would each be untalented, unfortunate and short-lived kings (François II, Charles IX and Henri III), Catherine often continued to pull all the strings.

1562–1610
In the Wars of Religion, France nearly destroys itself again

It was not a propitious time for France to be without a strong king. The Reformation was turning once-calm souls into partisan zealots, especially after French-born Jean Calvin made Geneva the main centre for exiled Protestants in 1541. François Ier, that perfect Renaissance prince, had done much to turn religious difference into a mortal struggle; he incinerated whatever Protestants he could catch, and sent an army into Provence to destroy the communities of Waldensian dissenters who had been living peacefully there for centuries. Meanwhile, mobs of peasants and labourers would occasionally sack a church and smash the images of the Virgin and saints, and powerful princes, even some close to the royal family, were lining up on the Protestant side. France divided into two parties, the Catholics under the Duc de Guise (who had been the liberator of Calais), supported by Spain; and the Protestants (or

Huguenots, from the German word *eidgenossen*, or 'comrades') under Antoine de Bourbon, king of the small Pyrenean state of Navarre, supported by England.

In 1562, three years after the death of Henri II, the long-threatened **civil war** broke out. Factional armies, some little more than thugs, roamed the countryside, while both sides strove to outdo the other in atrocities, particularly in the Midi. Paris lay in the grip of fear, in good part due to the dreaded Catholic de Guise family. A truce was agreed in 1570, and many of the principal Protestant leaders, including Amiral de Coligny, returned to the capital. Two nervous years later, Queen Catherine, who had once sincerely worked for peace and accommodation, arranged the **St Bartholomew's Day Massacre**, which 'took care' of the moderate Protestant leaders and some 10,000 followers across France, and guaranteed another 26 years of war.

For most of this time Paris continued to be dominated by the Guises, who hoped to be kings themselves, and fanatically kept the wars going. The decadent court of **Henri III** and his male favourites shocked both sides; Henri at first played little part in events, but he showed some steel when the designs of the Duc de Guise became apparent. He finally ordered the de Guises' assassination at Blois, only to be assassinated in turn by one of their followers. The Valois dynasty had come to a bloody end. As luck would have it, the rightful heir to the throne was now Henri of Navarre, son of Antoine, leader of the Protestant cause, and France's first Bourbon king.

And as luck would have it, **Henri IV** turned out to be just the man France needed. A courageous commander, tried in over a decade of campaigns, his kindness, natural charm and good sense made him popular even among Catholics. While the Catholic League, propped up by the money and troops of Philip II of Spain, still held Paris and plotted to give the crown to one of their own, Henri marched north with a small force, beat the Catholics in Normandy, and besieged Paris. His conversion to Catholicism in 1593 – in fact, his third conversion to the old faith in the course of a busy life – removed the last obstacles to peace. After the four years it took him to chase the Spaniards out of France, he issued the **Edict of Nantes**, decreeing religious tolerance, and allowing Protestants the control of the 150 towns and forts they already held. Rebuilding a devastated country proved more difficult, but again Henri was fortunate to have the model for that stock character of French history, the wise and prudent minister. His friend Maximilien de Béthune, whom he made **Duc de Sully**, squeezed corrupt officials, reformed the administration, rebuilt bridges and roads, worried the nobles and defended the peasants, and went far to realize Henri's wish for every Frenchman to 'have a chicken in the pot' every Sunday. Sully started the gracious French habit of planting avenues of trees by roadsides, and he built the nation a silk industry, beginning a tradition of state initiative and state control.

1610–1715
France's Grand Siècle, in which all was not as grand as it seemed

Henri ended his reign tragically, knifed by a Catholic fanatic named Ravaillac in 1610 while his carriage was caught in a Paris traffic jam. His son, **Louis XIII**, took the throne at the age of 11. Louis' mother, fat and silly Marie de Médicis (immortalized by an incredible cycle of paintings by Rubens in the Louvre) controlled the government at first. Lacking any idea of how to govern, Marie called the Estates-General in 1614. The third estate, the bourgeoisie, demanded lower taxes and reforms so loudly that the Estates were sent home and not called again for another 175 years. Finally, in 1624, after a bizarre attempted maternal *coup d'état* that has gone down in history as the 'Day of the Dupes', the weak-willed king was finally able to ease Mum out of power, with the help of his immensely capable and devoted minister, **Cardinal Richelieu**.

Sully's heir concentrated less on economics than on control, making sure that the nobles would never again challenge the king's power. He knocked down their castles wherever he could manage it, and set middle-class *intendants* to watch over every corner of the kingdom, all of whom were directly responsible to him. Richelieu also put an end to the strongholds Henri IV had left the Protestants, which were beginning to look like a state within the state. The climactic event was a dramatic and successful siege of La Rochelle (1628). Both king and minister died in 1642; they left France the strongest and most intelligently run state in Europe.

Louis XIV (1643–1715) became king at the age of five; the regent was his mother, Anne of Austria, and the minister was Richelieu's protégé, **Cardinal Mazarin**, whose father had been a Roman butler. Though corrupt to the core, Mazarin did well by France in extremely perilous times, beating back a Spanish invasion, organizing the peace of Europe, and surviving the civil wars of the Fronde (1648). '*Fronde*' means a slingshot, a children's toy; this name, which the Parisians conferred on the affair, captures its lack of seriousness. In succession, the useless Parlement de Paris, a cabal of scheming court ladies called the 'Amazons', the greedy nobility, and the long-oppressed bourgeoisie of Paris tried to take advantage of the child-king's weakness. Though briefly forced to flee Paris, Mazarin and the royal cause prevailed by 1661.

Young Louis, enjoying total, personal power over France when he reached his majority, chose as his new minister **Jean-Baptiste Colbert**. A relentless overachiever, Colbert assumed control of the economy and tried to reform everything. None of the money Colbert made for Louis rested in the king's pocket for long. As Louis grew older, his conceit and ambitions ballooned to incredible proportions, disturbing Europe with wars of aggression for almost 50 years.

At home, meanwhile, Louis had put an end to the independence of the nobles once and for all. Following the example of Henri IV, he simply lavished money upon them, bribing them to spend all their time at court, where he could hold the chits for their gambling debts. Turning the entire ruling class into complacent, mincing lapdogs ensured unity and civil peace. But surrounded by sycophants – some 10,000 of them – Louis rapidly lost all touch with reality. Perhaps he never really believed himself to be the Sun incarnate, illuminating this poor planet all by himself, but he did act the part, every hour of every day, and seemed to enjoy it. The bottom line for all the expenses of his court, and the insane new playpen that Louis built for it at Versailles, plus the costs of the wars, is simple – France nearly went bust again.

The realm of the Roi-Soleil had never exactly been paradise for the poor. Besides the grinding taxes and forced labour, Colbert locked up the indigent in workhouses to provide slave labour for his new industries, and even religious pilgrims without expensive permits from the police were likely to get pressed into the navy. By the end of Louis' long reign, misery was widespread and terrible famines gripped town and country alike. As if this wasn't enough, Louis also destroyed Henri IV's religious compromise: the Edict of Nantes was revoked in 1685.

1715–89
The Enlightenment, and the twilight of the Ancien Régime

Another century, another Louis. After 72 years of the Roi-Soleil, his great-grandson **Louis XV** ascended the throne in 1715, at the age of five; this time the regent was the Duke of Orléans, who allowed France a refreshing interlude of Edwardian decadence after the Victorian coma of the 'Great Reign'. The regent fell for John Law's speculative schemes, and the bursting of his 'Mississippi Bubble' in 1720 nearly bankrupted the entire nation. When Louis XV began to reign in his own right, his people called him *le bien-aimé*, 'the well-beloved'. Unfortunately, no. Louis XV turned out to be an indolent, pleasure-loving fool, who allowed France to be governed by flouncing favourites and court ladies, most notably the famous Madame de Pompadour.

France was stirring. This was the age of the *salons* and the *philosophes*: Voltaire, Diderot and Montesquieu, importing English political thought and common sense to the continent. The ills of France were discussed endlessly. Most flagrant of these were the incredible privileges of the all-devouring nobility and Church. The middle classes were exasperated by the economic oppression of every productive effort, and the total lack of justice, fairness and political rights.

Despite high taxes and forced labour, France hovered near bankruptcy for most of Louis' reign. Military defeats, notably the loss of the American empire in the **Seven Years' War** (1756–63), added to the disturbing sense that the France which had loomed so large under Louis XIV no longer counted for much. The solutions were obvious, but reform depended on the king, and he wasn't having any of it. Louis really did say, '*Après moi, le déluge.*' When he finally died in 1774, curses and rotten vegetables followed his coffin to St-Denis. Voltaire died four years later, regretting the coming Revolution he would not live to enjoy.

Under **Louis XVI** (1774–92) the last years of the Ancien Régime saw well-intentioned ministers try to push through reforms, only to be let down by the weak-willed, slow-witted king. Louis did allow his ministers to give the crucial support that led to the success of the American Revolution. Beating the Brits lifted national morale, but it also gave the French a dangerous whiff of liberty. And it left the nation in the poorhouse. By 1789 the financial situation was desperate; Louis, having failed miserably on his own, made the fatal step of doing what every Frenchman demanded – he called the Estates General. They met at Versailles on 5 May 1789, for the first time in 179 years.

1789–1815
History's noisiest revolution, followed by a Man on Horseback

As was traditional, the Estates voted by orders, not by individuals, and the noble and Church delegates at first stymied the reforms proposed by the Third Estate, the bourgeoisie. On 20 June the king ordered the Third Estate locked out of the sessions, whereupon they assembled at the real tennis court and swore the 'Tennis Court Oath', declaring themselves the **National Assembly** and promising not to break up until they gave France a constitution. After some typical indecision, the king surrounded Versailles with foreign troops, mostly Swiss and German. But things were already getting out of hand. Radical agitators in Paris had inflamed the population, and on 12 July the mob sacked the customs barriers on the hated Farmers-General wall around the city. Two days later, they took the **Bastille**, the prime symbol of arbitrary authority, even though it was nearly empty and scheduled for demolition. After that, the Parisians formed a militia, commanded by the **Marquis de Lafayette**, and invented the tricolour, taking Paris' red and blue, and adding the white of the royal flag (Lafayette's idea).

More and more liberal-minded nobles and clergy were joining the Assembly and accepting its principles. On the dramatic night of 4 August they spontaneously renounced all their old feudal exemptions and privileges. The **Declaration of the Rights of Man** was voted in, along with a liberal constitution. Meanwhile, the émigrés, reactionary nobles who had fled France, were conspiring with foreign governments to overthrow the Revolution. The king was now obviously on their side. Louis and his family attempted to flee Paris in June 1791 – the 'flight to Varennes' – and after that they were kept as prisoners.

The émigrés' invasion from across the Rhine in June 1792 brought war with their protectors, Austria and Prussia. At first things went badly for the hastily formed citizen army, but they checked the Prussian advance at the Battle of Valmy; the next day the newly elected National Convention declared France a republic. The Convention, led at first by the moderate faction of the Girondins, was captured in 1793 by the radical Jacobins, backed by the Paris mob and the new Paris government, the **Commune**. Its vote to execute Louis was the prelude to the **Reign of Terror**, overseen by the 'incorruptible' **Maximilien Robespierre** from September 1793, until he himself became its last victim in July 1794. The revolutionary orgy of violence had left a trail of destruction across the land.

The government passed to a five-man executive, the **Directoire**, as provided by the new constitution. By 1797 the mood of the nation had changed. Reaction was in the air, and a royalist party began to manoeuvre semi-openly. In Paris few cared for politics after such a glut of it; the workers who had supported the Commune were silent, battered by rampant inflation, and still without the right to vote. The new government had difficulty gaining any authority or respect.

The victorious army had both authority and respect, and its most able general, **Napoleon Bonaparte**, had already saved the Republic from a royalist revolt in Paris. Having beaten the English at Toulon, and conquered northern Italy from the

Austrians in a campaign against overwhelming odds, he was the man of the hour. With his brother Jérôme as speaker of the national legislature, and his ally, the intriguer Siéyès, in control of the Directoire, the road was prepared for a coup that many clever politicians found desirable; like the German conservatives in 1933, they were sure they could 'handle' their man. In November 1799 Napoleon took power, and his control was solid enough for him to declare himself Emperor in 1804.

As long as Napoleon was winning, and loot and art flowed into Paris, there was little need for a heavy hand. His government consolidated the work of the Revolution at home, adopting the metric system and the law code that came to be known as the Code Napoléon, and creating such enduring institutions as the first of the Grandes Ecoles, the Ecole Polytechnique and the Ecole Normale. The real oppression came after 1810, when the economy was in disarray and the cemeteries were starting to fill up. Eight new state prisons, meant for political dissenters, had just opened when the game was stopped in 1814. However, Napoleon made a brief dramatic comeback until his defeat at **Waterloo** on 18 June 1815 put a final end to the megalomaniac's dreams.

1815–71
France tries out every imaginable government, but all fail

The Revolution had shaken France so thoroughly, and created so many opinions and grudges, that no regime of whatever stripe could govern impartially and effectively. The rest of the nineteenth century would be an impossible search for consensus and legitimacy; from 1790 to 1875, the Gallic banana republic/empire/monarchy lurched through 13 regimes and 17 constitutions.

The king imposed by the allies at the Congress of Vienna was Louis XVI's gouty brother, **Louis XVIII** (1814–24): 'partly an old woman, partly a capon, partly a son of France and partly a pedant'. But France as a whole was content, and Louis had mellowed enough in his long exile not to exact too much revenge, even permitting a charter (not quite a constitution) and a parliament. His successor was the youngest brother, **Charles X** (1824–30). As Count of Artois he had been the head of the émigrés, and the most reactionary of the lot, the proverbial Bourbon who 'learned nothing and forgot nothing'. When he tried to gut the charter, in July 1830, Paris revolted. A movement of journalists, secret political societies and Napoleonic veterans seized the Hôtel de Ville, won over the troops, and tossed out the Bourbons once and for all.

The new king, **Louis-Philippe** of the Orléans royal branch, had fought briefly in the Revolutionary army and taught French in Boston. This 'bourgeois king' (his drab coat the prototype for the businessman's uniform of today) entrusted government to Gradgrinds like the liberal Guizot, with his message to the poor: '*Enrichissez-vous!*' ('Get rich!'), and Adolphe Thiers. The rich alone had the right to vote, while the workers were rewarded with laws almost as oppressive as those under the Bourbons.

Increasing prosperity had buoyed the regime since its birth, but the depression of the late 1840s brought discontent into the open. A provocative Washington's Birthday Dinner in Paris started the 'Revolution of Contempt' on 21 February 1848. The next day

students and workers occupied the Place de la Concorde; Louis-Philippe soon abdi-
cated, and the **Second Republic** was proclaimed. The winner of the first presidential
elections turned out to be Napoleon's nephew Louis-Napoléon. Louis made a coup
three years later and declared himself **Emperor Napoléon III**, sending some 26,000
political opponents off to the prison hulks in 1851 alone.

Under the influence of his Spanish wife, the ambitious and reactionary Eugénie, the
new emperor who had previously written a book called *The Extinction of Pauperism*
now found himself pampering a court of *nouveaux-riches*, and presiding over a vulgar
orgy of conspicuous consumption unmatched since Louis XIV's court at Versailles.
Paris, naturally, was the Second Empire's showcase, with the first of the great
Expositions (1867), grandiose new monuments such as the Opéra, and the total
replanning of the city by Napoléon III's prefect of the Seine, Baron Georges
Haussmann. The reign of Napoléon III also saw a new overseas empire based on the
occupation of Algeria (begun 1830, but not finished until 1870), Indochina, and the
intervention in Italy's war of independence that got France Nice and Savoy.

The glitter fell off fast. The 1870 **Franco-Prussian War**, cleverly instigated by
Bismarck, proved no contest; the French army was immediately surrounded at Sedan,
and within three weeks most of it had surrendered, including the emperor. Two weeks
later began the **Siege of Paris**, where a citizens' militia held the city behind its strong
fortifications, while Parisians ate the animals in the zoo and the rats from the sewers.
Léon Gambetta made his dramatic escape by balloon to raise a new army in the
south. A self-proclaimed government at Bordeaux – led by old Adolphe Thiers –
signed an armistice and made a humiliating peace with Bismarck and the Kaiser.
When Thiers tried to disarm the Parisians, the result was the rebellion of the Paris
Commune. 'Bloody Week', the taking of Paris, began in May 1871; the revolutionaries
responded to the bombardments and massacres by murdering the archbishop
among others and burning down the Tuileries Palace. By the end, 50,000 Parisians
had been killed or sent to prison camps in French Guiana. Thomas Cook was organizing special 'Ruins of Paris' tours, while the Germans had annexed Alsace-Lorraine.

1871–1940
A solid Republic prevails in one Great War, and folds up in the next

Despite its bloody start, the **Third Republic** worked with a will to make itself a stable
and popular regime. Given France's turbulent history since the revolution, this was no
mean accomplishment. The new regime had to contend with a strong sentiment for
monarchy – the romantic young pretender who could have been Henri V only lost his
chance when he refused to accept the tricolour as the national flag. France, like the
other major European powers, rushed to increase its colonial empire in Africa and
southeast Asia. Military security and hopes for revenge against Germany filled the
Republic's debates, while in 1888 came the bizarre episode with General Boulanger, a
dummy for rightist factions that at one point seemed ready to make a *coup d'état*.
The Republic survived, and its governments, dominated by the Left under such leaders

as Gambetta, Jules Ferry and Georges Clemenceau, pushed through the first social welfare acts and vastly improved education all over the country.

More tribulations were in store for a regime that still had not entirely won the nation's confidence. The Panama Company, engineer Ferdinand de Lesseps' attempt to duplicate his triumph at Suez by digging a canal through the Isthmus of Panama, collapsed in 1889, leaving investors ruined and angry, and government ministers compromised. Worse, the **Dreyfus Affair** divided the nation on bitter partisan lines after 1894. A false accusation of spying against a Jewish army officer turned into a consuming issue when the army not only tried to cover up its mistakes, but convicted Dreyfus in a new trial against all evidence. Rightists felt compelled to line up on the side of injustice. The Left, aided by Emile Zola's famous *J'accuse*, finally won the fight with Dreyfus' exoneration, recompense and promotion ten years later, but the old leftist parties found themselves increasingly pushed from their left by a burgeoning Socialist movement. France's confederation of trade unions, the CGT, appeared in 1895, and the Socialist party was founded by Jean Jaurès in 1905. Frequent strikes and anarchist terrorism, including the assassination of President Sadi Carnot in 1894, did not seriously disturb the dreams of most Frenchmen in a period of increasing prosperity and contentment which became known as the **Belle Epoque**.

While 1904 saw France and Britain's sealing of the **Entente Cordiale**, settling colonial issues, few doubted that the showdown with Germany would soon come. French politicians made a cult out of 'martyred' Alsace and Lorraine, while schools reminded children that some day they would have to be good soldiers to redeem them. When the **First World War** was sparked off in 1914, the long-prepared German attack was only stopped outside Paris at the 'Miracle of the Marne', the battle that saw the famous ride of the Paris taxis carrying the reserves up to the front. Then followed the heartbreaking years of trench warfare, with the familiar names of terrible failed offensives: Ypres, the Somme, Verdun, and in 1917 Chemin des Dames, a French attack so bloody and pointless it caused resistance all across the line; order was restored, barely, by Marshal **Philippe Pétain**. **Georges Clemenceau**, the 76-year-old 'Tiger', rallied the nation. In 1918 German exhaustion and the arrival of fresh American divisions won the war, but. in all, France had contributed more than any nation to the victory.

The nation had restored its honour, and its two lost provinces, but at a cost proportionally greater than that of any country except Serbia, some 1,400,000 dead. The war left France with a stricken economy and huge debts. Paris may have had one of its most colourful decades in the 1920s, jumping with avant-garde painters, Dadaist pranksters and expatriate Americans, but under the façade lay an exhausted nation. The **Depression** made things still worse, the 1930s a grim time indeed, with strikes and agitation coming from the powerful Communists, and at the other extreme from an increasingly venomous Right, which found its inspiration in Italy and Germany.

To defend the Republic, the leftist parties combined in a **Popular Front** to win the elections of 1936 under Léon Blum. But, lacking enough unified support, Blum was unable to push through promised reforms (or aid Loyalist Spain in the Civil War) and his government fell before the year was out. Divided, disgruntled and confused, France drifted towards its appointment with Hitler as if in a dream.

1940–the present
Convalescence, European union, and a complex wider world

Some nations suffered more death and destruction in the **Second World War**, but France's experience contained a unique dose of humiliation. Europe's biggest army was annihilated in four weeks, as refugees clogged every road of northeastern France, making counterattacks nearly impossible. The dithering government decamped to Tours, then Bordeaux. **Charles de Gaulle** had more vision, fleeing to London, from where he made his famous speech over the BBC on 18 June 1940, four days before France's formal surrender, calling on the French to join him in resisting the Nazis.

In the armistice, the German authorities made all of northern France and a strip along the Atlantic coast into their occupied zone, leaving the rest to be governed from **Vichy** by Marshal Pétain, who had been granted dictatorial powers by what was left of the Assembly. Pétain and the rest of the old anti-Dreyfus Right now created a model Fascist 'French State', and efficiently aided the Nazis in the deportation of Jews and political opponents. After the North African landings in 1942 the Nazis put an end to Vichy and occupied all of France, although the **Résistance**, its strongest units dominated by the Communists, became an effective rebellious force. However, significant numbers of French people collaborated with the occupying Germans. The US and UK military meanwhile set about preparing one of the most audacious large-scale attacks in history from the start of 1943. **Liberation** came with the Normandy invasions in June 1944. Eisenhower's army graciously stepped aside to let the French under General Leclerc be the first to enter Paris, on 24 August. At the same time, an efficient landing in Provence allowed the rapid liberation of most of the Midi.

Following a jittery moment immediately after the war, when it seemed France might turn red as the world was dividing between capitalists and communists, economic recovery began to make swift progress. And instead of seeking crippling punitive restoration from Germany, with the US spending a fortune on the Marshall Plan to reconstruct Europe, enlightened French politicians, notably Robert Schuman and Jean Monnet, began helping to build co-operative ventures between Western European states. In one of the most significant shifts in European history, after centuries upon centuries of war-mongering leaderships, the French government and its neighbouring counterparts began working together, peaceably. While there are plenty of healthy arguments to be had over the bureaucracies and regulations that have been created, the principle behind this co-operation has helped bring Western Europe unprecedented stability. The 1951 European Coal and Steel Community was the first rather unexciting-sounding joint enterprise, which grew into the European Economic Community, forerunner of the **European Union** (EU).

However, back with the postwar **Fourth Republic** and its Italian-style revolving-door governments, France cut a poor figure on the wider international stage. Its attempts to maintain its colonial empire led to awful disasters, first in **Vietnam**, with total military defeat at Dien Bien Phu in 1954, and next in **Algeria**, at the time treated as a part of metropolitan France, with over a million French settlers. The French army's use of torture and civilian massacres in the Guerre d'Algérie has recently become public knowledge. When the government seemed ready to negotiate with the Algerians in 1958 the army nearly staged a coup, and all sides turned to de Gaulle as the only hope.

So the **Fifth Republic** was born, with the strong executive that de Gaulle had always believed necessary. Instead of indulging the army, the old general worked to end the war, although the sinister OAS, the 'Secret Army' formed by French officers in Algeria, staged a revolt in 1961 and made attempts on de Gaulle's life. He survived this crisis with the help of a referendum that turned out a huge 'yes' vote for Algerian independence. De Gaulle saved French democracy, but his years in the presidency were a grim and nervous time for France, with a government run by colourless technocrats, a state-run radio and television worthy of a dictatorship, and an erratic, independent foreign policy that often irritated France's allies, with the French government leaving NATO and adopting its own active policies on nuclear weapons and nuclear energy.

Many Frenchmen, especially the leftists and old Resistance members, had hoped for a freer, more modern society in the postwar era. Gaullism frustrated them, and the lid blew off in **May 1968** with the students' revolt in Paris, joined by nine million striking workers. With control over the media, de Gaulle mobilized the 'silent majority' and survived, though he torpedoed his own presidency soon after on a trivial referendum that failed. The urge to reform died on the vine under the tedious reigns of Gaullist Georges Pompidou and UDF (centrist) Valéry Giscard d'Estaing.

Hopes revived with the election of Socialist **François Mitterrand** in 1981, bringing the left to power for the first time since the late 1940s. Mitterrand's years produced some welcome initiatives, notably the supporting of **regional governments**, part of the process of reversing the centuries-old habit of Parisian centralism. His pharaonic building projects in Paris, the *Grands Projets*, put a veneer of modernist gloss on what turned out to be a 14-year reign of corruption and sleaze; an honest Socialist prime minister, Pierre Bérégovoy, shot himself in 1993 when the details started leaking out.

The Gaullist party, the RPR, took over in parliament, but Mitterrand clung on to the presidency in a strange left–right split in leadership termed *cohabitation*. While France had become a more open society under Mitterrand, it emerged at the end of his life that the two-timing old cynic had briefly served Vichy, and protected war criminals while in office. His place in the Socialist leadership was taken by the decidedly non-sleazy Protestant **Lionel Jospin**, although the wily former RPR mayor of Paris **Jacques Chirac** grabbed the presidency in 1995. The RPR also won parliamentary elections that year, but in 1997 Jospin became prime minister in a new period of *cohabitation*. The Right had had sleaze problems of its own, and Chirac was caught up in them. The French judiciary has been showing increasing independence in bringing corrupt politicians and businessmen to trial in recent years.

Jospin pitted himself against Chirac in the first round of the 2002 presidential elections, but his campaign ended in humiliation, as the loud-mouthed extreme-right-wing Front National candidate, **Jean-Marie Le Pen**, beat him to the final round of voting; the Socialists were forced to give their votes to much-despised Chirac to stop the unthinkable. The shock of Le Pen's relative success led to mass demonstrations in support of a tolerant society. Various centre-right parties, including the RPR, merged to form the UMP, which won a large majority in parliamentary elections following Jospin's resignation, **Jean-Pierre Raffarin** becoming prime minister.

Major French sporting successes around the turn of the millennium, notably victory in the football World Cup, won by a team of an extraordinarily uplifting mix of colours, had lulled few into a sense of harmonious security. Sadly, extremism had been growing at the ends of the racial spectrum, the Front National winning increasing support, extreme Islamists finding converts to their evil fanaticism. When Algeria descended into horrific civil war in the 1990s, with sickening violence on both sides, extreme Islamists also exported terrorism to France. The French government has also long had home-grown terrorism to deal with; while Breton and Basque autonomist violence has only rarely flared up, the sustained problems are in Corsica, with more violence than Northern Ireland over past decades.

The vile targeting of the innocent puts in the shade the truculent protests of French farmers, fishermen and truckers who periodically organize annoyingly well-targeted protests to defend their livelihoods. While France has been suffering from much worse unemployment than Britain or the USA in the past few years, this is in part because egalitarian social provisions, for example in health and transport, have been far more respected. But the introduction of the EU's 35-hour working week has been regarded as folly by many in business, who fear loss of competitivity and do not believe the policy will create new jobs. As to tackling the massively bloated French civil service, that is a major stumbling block capable of bringing any French government to its knees. Many sectors of French society are willing to protect their interests vociferously, and there is widespread anxiety and debate about the influence of American-style business, culture, and even cuisine.

Of course, all sorts of tensions bubble away within French society. If gay couples have managed to put themselves on the same legal footing as straight couples in law, the issue of the wearing of the Islamic veil in French schools or in the civil service, and anti-Semitic attacks, have caused terrible stirs recently, major headaches for a state which cherishes the principle that religion should be a private matter and not expressed in state-run establishments. For all the sleaze surrounding Chirac, he has long spoken out in support of an inclusive society which embraces all French citizens.

Not that this always gets a leader far when taking on terrorism, or standing up to George W. Bush's decision to bypass the United Nations. Disagreements in 2003 over whether to attack Saddam Hussein's dictatorship in Iraq descended into crude nationalistic attacks. Hearteningly, wise commentators from all sides wrote articles highlighting the co-operation that there has been over the past couple of centuries, not just in world wars, but, with America, in the War of Independence, in which French troops secured that nation's vital victory. Looking to the immediate future, with the expansion of the EU, France's role in Europe and its partnership with Germany are perhaps the French government's top priority. While some describe Chirac as a frustrated leader of Europe, and while Britain's government makes clear its allegiance to the USA, 2004 sees the centenary celebration of France and Britain's Entente Cordiale. Intelligent tourism too should rise above crass nationalism, and be a positive force for enjoying the variety and wealth of each other's culture.

Culture: Architecture and the Arts

Palaeolithic and Neolithic

The world's art, as far as has yet been discovered, begins in France, with Palaeolithic cave paintings, some 35,000 years old. These startling, sophisticated works have been aptly described as 'the infancy of art, not an art of infancy' (Chauvet, Lascaux, Font-de-Gaume, Pech Merle around the Dordogne, Niaux in the Ariège). The over-voluptuous 'fertility goddesses' common throughout the era also turn up in many of France's museums. Culture seems to take a nap – at least from the archaeological evidence – until the advent of Neolithic civilization c. 5000 BC. Neolithic peoples, with a cultural continuity that stretched for over 3,000 years along Europe's western coasts, were the first serious builders; in France their most enigmatic monuments are the stone avenues of Brittany (Carnac), though their dolmens and menhirs, as well as some passage-grave tombs, can be seen at innumerable sites, mostly in the west and south.

Roman Gaul to Romanesque

In Roman times, the south was the richest and most cultured part of Gaul, with amazing monuments that have survived: the Pont du Gard, one of the greatest of all works of Roman engineering; the theatre of Orange, with the only intact stage building in the West; the Maison Carrée and amphitheatre at Nîmes; the amphitheatre and cryptoporticus in Arles; the elegant 'Antiques' of St-Rémy; the Pont Flavien at St-Chamas; the trophy at La Turbie; the excavated towns at Vaison-la-Romaine and *Glanum* (St-Rémy); the theatres of Lyon; the sumptuous mosaics of Vienne... But many northern towns also come up with a surprising number of Gallo-Roman remains.

Most of the early Christian buildings that remain are baptistries (Poitiers, Grenoble, Fréjus, Aix-en-Provence, Marseille), all from the 5th century. Such art as was possible in the centuries after the Germanic invasions mixed classical Roman styles with a Germano-Celtic fancy for abstract geometric and floral patterns. Like most barbarians of the time, France's were interested in jewellery; a few illustrated manuscripts and *objets d'art* have survived, but precious little architecture or sculpture, though Merovingian carved stones can often be found recycled into later churches.

Charlemagne's dream of recreating the empire was accompanied by a style of art and architecture that closely copied surviving Roman examples. Carolingian artists did well at ivories, metalwork and manuscript illumination (there was an important workshop at Reims). They also tried their hand at painting and mosaic; little survives, apart from a rare, lovely apse mosaic (c. 800) at Germigny-des-Près, near Orléans.

'Romanesque' is a catch-all term that covers a wide variety of styles, all born with the great upsurge of culture and wealth that created medieval Europe after the year 1000. Its sources are more complex than simple copying of the monuments left by ancient Rome. Influences range from the court architecture of Charlemagne to early churches in the east, in Syria and Armenia, and buildings of the Byzantine and the

Islamic world. Wealthy, cultured Burgundy was one of the places where the new architecture and sculpture made their greatest advances, including the stone barrel vault. Cluny created a church style (Cluny II) that proved equally influential; it provided the model for other Burgundian churches, notably at Autun, Paray-le-Monial, Tournus and Vézelay, all begun in the early 12th century. Cluny was soon rebuilt, as the biggest church ever attempted in medieval Europe (Cluny III, 1088, demolished in 1810). Other important early Romanesque churches survive at Toulouse (St-Sernin), Reims (St-Rémi) and Conques in the Aveyron (Ste-Foy). The Loire valley has several, including those at La Charité-sur-Loire, Nevers and St-Benoît-sur-Loire.

As the Romanesque developed, distinctive regional styles rapidly appeared all over France: ornate, domed churches in Périgord (St-Front at Périgueux, also Angoulême cathedral); in the Auvergne, octagonal crossing towers and delicately patterned exterior decoration in coloured stone (St-Nectaire, Clermont-Ferrand, Orcival, Issoire). In Poitou and the Loire, the fashion was 'hall churches' with narrow, steep naves (St-Savin-sur-Gartempe, Talmont, Cunault); other southern buildings show a great liberty, even eccentricity of styles, as at the round church of Rieux-Minervois in Languedoc, or the fortress-like Stes-Maries-de-la-Mer in the Camargue. In Roussillon, then part of Catalunya, churches and monasteries naturally followed the heavy, yet graceful Catalan Romanesque (St-Michel-de-Cuxa, St-Martin-du-Canigou).

While most of the new architecture appeared in the service of the Church, secular building also participated in the great revival. Early medieval architects created engineering works to compete with the ancient Romans, such as the bridge across the Rhône at Avignon. It was also a great age for castle-building, witnessing the development of the residential keep. Château-Gaillard in Normandy, the Key of France, was contested by Capetians and Plantagenets; other large concentrations are in the Loire valley and in western Languedoc.

From the beginning, architecture and **sculpture** were inseparable. French Romanesque sculpture, a mixture of transcendent spirituality and fairy-tale strangeness, had its beginnings in Burgundy and the Pyrenees, and it sprouted somewhat magically as a fully mature art in the early 1100s. Burgundy, under the influence of Cluny, and Poitou, often thriving in the period, developed the most wonderfully distinctive styles. The greatest works were the unearthly Christs in Majesty and ferocious Last Judgements, as on the spectacular façades at Autun, Vézelay, or Poitiers. A similar, brilliant style was evolved by the 'School of Toulouse'; its finest works can be seen there and at Moissac and Souillac in the Lot.

There is more to Romanesque sculpture than the tremendous scenes on the great portals. The period witnessed the rebirth of tomb sculpture, as at Fontrevault, the Plantagenet pantheon where Henry II, Eleanor of Aquitaine and Richard the Lionheart are buried. Even in some of the less ambitious village churches, you will see good sculptural work on capitals, on the modillons around the cornice of an apse, and hidden in unexpected places where you have to look twice to find them. Here you will meet all the monsters of the medieval bestiary, allegorical figures that often defy explanation, or occasionally illustrate a medieval joke; the freshness and freedom of subject matter in sculptural decoration gives Romanesque buildings great charm.

Romanesque wall paintings, while heavily stylized, also left powerful images from the Bible on many churches around the land. As to the St-Savin in Poitou, it has been nicknamed the Sistine Chapel of Romanesque art.

Gothic

The word 'Gothic' itself is a disparagement invented by 16th-century Italian critics, an attempt to make the most technically sophisticated architecture the world had ever seen seem somehow barbarous. 'Gothic' might better be called the 'Parisian' style, since Paris and the Ile-de-France is where it was developed.

The transition from early medieval civilization to the great world of the High Middle Ages was accompanied by a rapid evolution of architecture. The landmarks along the way included technical advances such as the ribbed vault, the pointed arch and the flying buttress. Never before could so much space, so much height, be enclosed with so little stonework; the walls, no longer required to carry the load, offered great opportunities to the medium of stained glass.

The first complete 'Gothic' church was St-Denis, the traditional resting place of the Capetian kings outside Paris, begun in 1140. The new system of building spread rapidly; among the early Gothic cathedrals, Sens' was begun the same year as St-Denis, followed by Noyon (1145), Notre-Dame-de-Paris (1163), and Laon (1165). High Gothic – more elaborate vaulting, carved stone traceries and crockets, flying buttresses to make possible even greater height, and greater areas of glass – began with Chartres, rebuilt beginning in 1194, and Bourges (begun roughly the same time) and continued through Reims (1211), Amiens (1220) and Troyes (1262). Aspirations culminated at Beauvais, with the tallest nave ever attempted, 155ft – though its collapse while still under construction dampened enthusiasm somewhat.

Replacing the diversity of Romanesque, this first national style imposed itself everywhere just as the French monarchy was imposing its rule over the lands that now make up France. Only very slight regional variations ever appeared, in Anjou and Poitou, and in the south at the extraordinary cathedral of Albi (1282).

In the 13th century Gothic evolved more in decoration than structure. The period roughly from 1230 to 1350 is called the **Rayonnant** ('Decorated Style' in Britain), applying increasingly complex decoration in pinnacles and window traceries, including the great rose windows. This was the style of one of the greatest Gothic achievements, Sainte-Chapelle in Paris (1241). The **Flamboyant** (roughly 1350–1500, the equivalent of the English Perpendicular) brought even more elaborate traceries, carved stonework on as many surfaces as possible, a love of sinuous curves in stonecarving, and ornate, web-like rib vaulting – Gothic taken to its extremes, at its best in Rouen (the Tour de Beurre of the cathedral, St-Ouen, St-Maclou).

In Gothic the marriage of architecture and sculpture begun in the Romanesque was perfected. The two arts evolved hand in hand, and Gothic sculpture presents an increasing confidence and skill, and a new delight in nature, as in the motifs of buttercup and lettuce leaves that adorn windows and columns. A complex, detailed iconography grew up, dictated by the Church, in which all the universe was the sculptor's province; scenes of everyday life (the Labours of the Months), and a love of fantasy continued from the Romanesque, as in the monsters atop Notre-Dame. Some of the finest sculpture can be seen in the cathedrals of Reims and Amiens.

Gothic architecture ironically retarded the art of painting in France; even had painters wanted to compete with stained glass, in the important churches, there simply wasn't much wall surface. In Avignon, however, the 14th-century papal court attracted some of Italy's finest artists, especially Simone Martini of Siena and Matteo Giovanetti of Viterbo, whose frescoes inspired the graceful, colourful style known as International Gothic. A distinct school of painting developed from International Gothic and the influence of Flemish painters favoured by the last popes: the early 15th-century **School of Avignon**. The school's greatest masters were from the north: the exquisite **Enguerrand Quarton** (*c.* 1415–66) from Laon, and **Nicolas Froment**. The little that has come down from the 15th century continues to show a strong Flemish influence, as in court painter **Jean Fouquet** (*c.* 1420–75), and in the so-called 'Maître de Moulins'; it was Flemish miniaturist monks who illuminated one of the masterpieces of the century, the little book called the ***Très Riches Heures du Duc de Berry*** (1416).

Medieval Literature

Written French (really *Francien*, the dialect of the Franks around Paris) traditionally begins in 842 with the Oath of Strasbourg, signed by Charles the Bald and Louis the German, both grandsons of Charlemagne, though Latin remained the unchallenged language of scholars at the Sorbonne and elsewhere all through the Middle Ages. Already, the *jongleurs*, itinerant minstrels, were developing an oral tradition of narrative poetry, consisting mostly of stirring tales of feudal valour and the lives of saints. Some of these were written down *c.* 1100: the *Chansons de Geste*, many dealing with the deeds of Charlemagne and his knights. The most famous of them, the ***Chanson de Roland***, is still read for pleasure today.

By the early Middle Ages, the old Latin vernacular of Gaul had divided into two distinct languages, the northern *langue d'oïl* and southern *langue d'oc* (from their two ways of saying 'yes'). The southerners, who would have laughed to hear themselves called 'French', were closer to the Muslim world, which provided much of the inspiration for the first European poetry, and they produced the *troveres*, or **troubadours**. One of the first was a powerful duke, William IX of Aquitaine (1071–1127); other notables included Bertran de Born, Jaufré Rudel, Peire Vidal and Bernard de Ventadour.

The 'Courts of Love' in which this ideal of chivalry was perfected were brought to the north by Eleanor of Aquitaine, granddaughter of William IX. The subject of chivalry found its most mature expression in the high medieval masterpiece, the ***Romaunt de la Rose***, begun by Guilaume de Lorris *c.* 1230 and finished by the more cynical Jean de Meun. Much later, the proto-feminist writer **Christine de Pisan** (1364–1430) would speak up for women (*Le Livre de la Cité des Dames*) in a time when the chivalric ideal had become an occasion for literary argument more than inspiration.

The 12th century also witnessed an increasing interest in the legends of the Celts; these too had always been present in the oral tradition. Chrétien de Troyes gave form to the **Arthurian cycle** in the 1160s and '70s, with *Lancelot*, *Erec et Enide*, and *Perceval*, in which the legend of the Holy Grail first appears. Medieval France always enjoyed a laugh, and the *fabliaux*, verse satires on everyday life, on haughty nobles and grasping friars, became increasingly popular. The love of **animal fables** created one master-piece, the stories of Reynard the Fox, the *Roman de Renart*, begun c. 1175 by Pierre de St-Cloud and carried on by other hands over the next 200 years until it became a veri-table epic cycle.

In the late Middle Ages, literature became less fantastical and more down-to-earth, especially as France suffered the continuing disaster of the Hundred Years War. That period also saw the beginnings of French **historical writing**; **François Villon** (b. 1431), the Baudelaire of his day, left an intensely personal, topical, mocking portrait of life in medieval Paris. This was also a great age for the **theatre**, not only the mystery plays and miracle plays (dramatized lives of the saints) acted out inside churches, but secular theatre – farces, tragedies and morality plays put on by *confréries* or the guilds of lawyers and clerks, or (in Paris) the goldsmiths.

The Renaissance

To most people, the term 'French Renaissance' conjures up visions of the great châteaux of the Loire. Dating from the early 16th century, these were architectural hybrids, combining traditional French ideas with an emphasis on turrets and gables, and some elements of new Italian architecture (Blois, Chambord, Azay-le-Rideau, as well as some *hôtels particuliers* in the Marais, Paris).

The onset of the Wars of Religion retarded the progress of the new art in France. It did produce a few exceptional architects: **Pierre Lescot**, who designed the Cour Carrée of the Louvre (1546); **Philibert Delorme** (1514–70), whose few surviving works include the Château d'Anet, made for Diane de Poitiers; **Jean Bullant** (Petit Château at Chantilly, Château d'Ecouen); and **Jacques du Cerceau** and his son **Baptiste**.

Paralleling the arts, the classical revival begins in the 16th century with the poets called the *grands rhétoriqueurs*, especially with the most famous of them, **Clément Marot** (1496–1544). A humanist and a Protestant, Marot wrote classical allegories and lyrics, and was constantly in trouble with the Church authorities and the Sorbonne. Love poetry, though increasingly precious, was never out of fashion (Marot once wrote a sonnet in honour of his lady's nipple); something beyond came from the group of poets that came to be known as **La Pléiade**, refined, scholarly Humanists with a clas-sical bent, including the supremely lyrical **Pierre de Ronsard** (*Odes* 1550), and **Joachim du Bellay**, remembered for his poems mourning the lost glories of ancient Rome (*Regrets*, 1558).

In prose, a bitter century produced two refreshingly sane writers: **François Rabelais** (1494–1553), a mocker and a scholarly sceptic in an age when both were dangerous, concealed his talent behind a career as a Franciscan friar. Later in life, he dropped out and became a physician, while writing his *Pantagruel* and *Gargantua* under the pen name Alcofribas Nasier. French literature before or since has produced nothing like this rare spirit, capable of mixing spectacular scatological humour and the praise of drink (on one level, the thirst is for wisdom), with a vision of the Abbey of Thélème, the ideal of a civilized, tolerant community. Another great voice for good sense and tolerance was **Michel de Montaigne** (1533–92), who invented the term 'essay' and developed its literary form. From his book-lined tower on the family estate, Montaigne restated classical stoicism in a wholly original form.

17th-century Literature

The early 17th century was a turning point in French cultural life, a time that first expressed a national craving for order, authority and common sense after the tumults of the Wars of Religion. The tone for a restrained, reasonable (though oft over-decorated) literature was set by **François de Malherbe**, a mediocre and pedantic poet, and later by **Jean Chapelain**, critic and habitué of the *salons*, who came to control the pensions handed out by Louis XIV to favoured writers. So began the classical ideal of harmony and order that was to dominate the nation's cultural life for 200 years.

This was the age of alexandrines and well-polished clichés, and of the 'three unities' (time, place and action). Famously, the ultra-controlling Cardinal Richelieu created the **Académie Française** in 1634, which oversaw literary output with a hawkish eye. While the theatres of England and Spain were enjoying liberated golden ages, France made do with the more formal, measured drama of **Pierre Corneille** (*Le Cid*, 1637, and a string of well-received plays in the 1640s), capturing the 'heroic ideal' of the time as an alternative to true tragedy.

Popular opinion was more in tune with works like the worldly, cynical *Maximes* of **François de la Rochefoucauld** (1665). The influence of women, both in the *salons* and as writers, such as **Madame de Sévigné** and the novelist **Madame de Lafayette**, brought delicacy and urbanity, as well as a bit of new freedom. A great variety of miscellaneous literature appeared, from the sonorous volumes of sermons of the conservative **Bishop Bossuet** to **Jean de la Fontaine**'s delightful verse fables. **Charles Perrault**, a protagonist in the great literary battle of the day, the 'Quarrel of the Ancients and Moderns', also gave the world the first collection of *Contes de ma mère l'oie* – *Mother Goose*, including fairy tales such as *Little Red Riding Hood*, *Sleeping Beauty* and *Puss-in-Boots*. One of the most popular figures of the day was poet and critic **Nicolas Boileau**, whose 'Le Lutrin' was the model for Pope's 'Rape of the Lock'.

Jean Racine (1639–99) restored tragedy from the formalism of Corneille. Racine took his themes from Greek mythology (*Iphigénie*, and *Phèdre*, his greatest work), from classical history (*Britannicus*, *Mithridate*), the Bible (*Esther*), and even from the contemporary Turks (*Bajazet*); all his dramas are noted for their strongly drawn characters with tragic flaws. The best-loved Grand Siècle name of all is **Molière** (Jean-Baptiste Poquelin, 1622–73), the master of farces and comedies of manners, and a breath of fresh air in an overdecorous age. Molière spent most of his life with his theatre troupes, like Shakespeare, whom he rivals in the rich humanity and wit of his comedies (*Tartuffe*, *Le Misanthrope*, *Le Médecin malgré lui*).

For all its fussiness, the age of Louis XIV maintained a strong interest in science – *Provinciales* and *Pensées* by **Blaise Pascal** (1623–62), scientist and philosopher, found a wide audience despite their tacit condemnation of the worldliness and watered-down piety of the court and aristocracy. Then there was Pascal's contemporary, **René Descartes** (1596–1650). Besides his contributions to mathematics, his analytic philosophy and logic have influenced everything written and thought in France since the publication of his *Discours de la méthode* in 1637.

French Baroque and Art in the Grand Siècle

The massive rebuilding of Paris in the 17th century created a tremendous demand for art of all kinds. The first of the remarkable *places royales* (squares built as unified architectural ensembles) emerged in the 1610s – Place des Vosges and Place Dauphine – while Henri IV had made it easy to find talented painters by converting the Long Gallery of the Louvre into lodgings and studios for artists. Patrons, however, continued to regard them as their servants, and imposed on them not only the subject matter but their own taste. The greatest French painters of the day, **Claude Lorrain** (1600–82) and **Nicolas Poussin** (1594–1665), fled Paris like the plague and spent most of their lives in Italy. Louis XIII and Richelieu commissioned the likes of **Simon Vouet** (1590–1649) and **Philippe de Champaigne** (1602–74) for their self-glorifying pieces. All the court artists who followed – **Le Sueur**, **Mignard** and **Lebrun** – painted in Vouet's workshop. The greatest artist to work in Paris under Louis XIII had been **Rubens**, in town to do the queen-sized scenes of Marie de Médicis' life for the Palais de Luxembourg (now in the Louvre). Some of his Flemish and Dutch assistants stayed behind; they influenced a notable set of non-court painters to tackle similar everyday subjects, especially the **Le Nain** brothers – Antoine, Louis and Mathieu. An even greater realistic artist was **Georges de La Tour** (1593–1652), whose solemn figures captured in candlelight and shadow are the most distinctive of the period. But Louis XIV's opinion of the Flemish and realist painters was well known: '*Enlevez-moi ces magots*' ('Get these apes away from me').

Meanwhile the Counter-Reformation Church was promoting a new wave of religious building; with St-Paul-St-Louis in the Marais (1627) began the fashion for tepid reworkings of Roman Baroque, and Italianate domes began springing up all over Paris. In secular buildings, imported Baroque translated into a more restrained, more French manner; its leading exponents were **François Mansart** (1598–1666, Château de Blois) and **Louis le Vau** (Vaux-le-Vicomte, 1657–61, the beginnings of Versailles, 1669, and the Institut de France on the left bank of the Seine, 1661).

Together with the painter Lebrun, Le Vau and **Le Nôtre** created the style of the Grand Siècle. For the long-postponed completion of the Louvre, though, Louis XIV and Colbert had called upon the King of Baroque himself, Gianlorenzo Bernini, in 1664. Bernini's foreign ideas and arrogance caused endless disputes; finally his plans were abandoned and the project was entrusted to **Claude Perrault**. The result was a classicist revelation, a remarkably original colonnade that has had a tremendous influence over everything built in France since.

In 1648 the king founded the **Académie Royale de Peinture et de Sculpture** to govern his artists. The Académie lay dormant until 1661, when the indefatigable Colbert took over its direction. Colbert believed that art had but one purpose: to enhance the glory of his master, Louis XIV, and France. To make the propaganda credible, Colbert demanded that the Académie dictate the highest standards to painters and sculptors, and to the weavers and furniture-makers at the the newly established Gobelins. Astute flattery in the right places by **Charles Lebrun** (1619–90) earned him the position as the Académie's first director-dictator, and in 1675 he issued the magnificently flatulent *Tables de Préceptes*, the Académie's rules for art.

At the same time Colbert and Lebrun were snapping up paintings and sculptures for the royal collection (in the Louvre since 1681, where the academicians could study them). Lebrun, *premier peintre du roi*, spent his last 12 years directing the decoration of Versailles – painting the tedious Hall of Mirrors' ceiling with the glory of the Sun King.

The Enlightenment

Even in the last comatose decades of the 'Great Reign', there were stirrings of thought and change. The protestant Pierre Bayle spoke up for religious freedom and toleration (*Dictionnaire historique et critique*, 1697), while his contemporary the Sieur de Fontanelle spread new scientific ideas to the general public with his *Entretiens sur la pluralité des mondes* (1697). Only six years after the Sun King's death, the **Baron de Montesquieu** (1689–1755) wrote a book that would not have much pleased him: the *Lettres persanes* (1721), a satirical critique of French society. In 1748 came *De l'esprit des lois*, expounding a liberal political philosophy that would help inspire the Revolution.

Voltaire (François-Marie Arouet, 1694–1778) embodied the whole of Enlightenment beliefs and aspirations. His admiration for the freer climate and more progressive outlook of England, where he spent two years in the 1720s, resulted in his *Lettres philosophiques* (1734). The eternal enemy of the Church, its dogmas and its privileges, for over sixty years he was the voice of France's intellect and conscience against the rotting, medieval complex of crown, church and aristocracy. Besides his role as social critic and philosopher, he also found time to write volumes of poetry and letters, magisterial histories, and novels (*Candide*, 1759).

In the wake of Voltaire came the other *philosophes*, the men of new ideas, of whom the most prominent was **Denis Diderot** (1713–84), encyclopedist, dramatist, art critic, novelist and philosopher. He oversaw the creation of the famous 28-volume *Encyclopédie* (1772), to which most of the leading figures of the Enlightenment contributed; it was a summation of the scientific knowledge and philosophical speculation of the day, as well as a complete course in the new radical ideas. The other great influence of the age came from **Jean-Jacques Rousseau** (1712–78), a watchmaker's son from Geneva. Rousseau was the eternal opposite to urban, urbane

Voltaire, celebrating nature, and everything in humanity that he naïvely thought could be called 'natural' – simplicity, spontaneity and sincerity – as a remedy for a culture that had been too studied and too artificial for too long. Foreshadowing the Romantic era, he was the champion of the creative spirit over artistic rules. His novels of sensibility (*Julie: ou la nouvelle Héloïse* and *Emile*) caused a sensation, while his *Du Contrat social* applied the same ideas to politics, with an analysis of the artificial bases of inequality and a revolutionary vision of liberty.

As the crisis of society was building up steam, several brilliant, notorious novels exposed the deep levels of evil cunning and artifice that often direct human affairs, notably **Laclos**' *Les Liaisons dangereuses* (1782) and, most notoriously, the works of the **Marquis de Sade** (*Justine, ou les malheurs de la vertu*, 1791).The most influential writer of the lot at this time was **Beaumarchais**, whose *Mariage de Figaro* (1784), showing mocking servants running rings round their masters, came to be viewed as seditious.

Meanwhile, many leading 18th-century painters, like **Boucher** (1703–77) and **Fragonard** (1732–1806) had skipped off into sensual pastoral fantasies. While **Chardin** (1699–1779) concentrated on sublime still lifes, **Greuze** (1725–1805) brought out tear-jerking scenes of the difficulties of real life. One of the most fascinating but most unrecognized of French architects, **Ledoux** (1736–1806), was creating amazing palaces for the aristocracy and an ideal salt-workers' city in Franche-Comté, but also deeply unpopular tax gateways around Paris.

Neoclassicism and the Art of the *Salons*

As the Revolution approached, Paris was full to bursting with hack painters, and in 1791 the National Assembly opened the *salon* to all, bringing in a flood of art. The leading painter and art dictator of the Revolution, **Jacques-Louis David** (1748–1825), closed down the Académie's *salon* the next year and opened up a carbon copy called the **Académie des Beaux-Arts**. It held competitions for Neoclassical patriotic pictures like his own, evocations of austere civic virtue, modelled on a ludicrous fantasy of ancient Rome. He led the government's nationalizing of art from royal palaces, churches (at least the bits that somehow escaped the anti-clerical fury of the *sans-culottes*) and the châteaux of the *émigrés*.

In 1804 Napoleon made himself Emperor, instigating grandiose neoclassical projects in Paris, such as the building of the Arc de Triomphe (1806). He mandated the new **Empire Style** to decorate his residences, and to create political propaganda pieces more repugnant even than Louis XIV's. Besides imitating Louis XIV's use of art to sanctify tyranny, Napoleon shared his mania for the prestige of sheer accumulation. Advised by David, he cleaned out a number of Italian collections and even stripped Venice's San Marco of its famous horses as a prize for Paris; he booted the artists out of the Louvre and made it the Musée Napoléon. But thanks to the little hoodlum, all the artists and art-lovers in Paris could freely go to study the Grand Masters – a crucial first step for the artistic revolutions that were to follow.

The 1819 *salon* was shocked by its first Romantic painting, a barn-burner called the *Radeau de la Méduse* (now in the Louvre) by **Théodore Géricault** (1791–1824). In 1822 **Eugène Delacroix** (1798–1863), putative son of Talleyrand, made his *salon* debut and quickly became the leader of the Romantics. Like Géricault he painted topical subjects that moved him; his *La Liberté guidant le peuple* (in the Louvre), the well-known image of the people of Paris at their barricades, was painted after the Revolution of 1830. Considered as an incitement to riot, it was hidden away until the Exposition of 1855.

The Romantic emphasis on the emotions and the individuality of the artist created the image of the artist as a bohemian, an eccentric outside respectable society. One group of painters – led by **Théodore Rousseau** (1812–67) – went off to paint landscapes in Barbizon, a hamlet in the Forest of Fontainebleau. But the greatest landscape painter of the day was **Camille Corot** (1796–1875). As lyrical as his landscapes are, Corot was also the first painter inspired by photography; by mid-century, when the Académie and *salon public* had tacitly accepted the fact that the best an artist could do was mimic the camera, Corot was extremely popular, and artists were instructed to paint in his style, in various tones of grey.

'Paint what your eyes see' became the slogan of the realist painters who followed, although the first exponent, **Gustave Courbet** (1819–77) carefully composed his pictures to improve on it. Courbet's declarations that his own judgement and appreciation of his art was all that mattered infuriated the *salon* and its public. After Courbet, the *salon* next declared war on **Edouard Manet** (1832–83), who, like Corot, had sufficient means to withstand the thundering hostility his works provoked. When the *salon* jury of 1863 turned out so blatantly conservative that Napoléon III permitted a Salon des Refusés, Manet made Paris howl with outrage at the unclassical naked women in his *Déjeuner sur l'herbe* and *Olympia* (1866). Manet's bold new technique, and his novel but masterful handling of paint, may have offended the smoothies in the *salon*, but it would make him the idol of the Impressionists.

19th-century Literature: Romanticism and Realism

If Rousseau was Romanticism's godfather, the movement in France hung considerably behind Britain and Germany. Exhausted, overstimulated, and confused – suffering its Revolutionary and Napoleonic double hangover – France had little to contribute, except perhaps **André Chénier**, the poet executed under the Terror whose works were not published until 1819. In most writing the prevailing tone was emptiness, loss and regret, the *mal du siècle*: The **Vicomte de Chateaubriand** (1768–1848), who reawakened intellectual interest in Christianity with his *Génie du Christianisme*, also redeemed the Middle Ages, leading to a great age of historical novels: **Stendhal**'s *Chartreuse de Parme* (1839), and **Alexandre Dumas**' *Les Trois Mousquetaires* (1844). The growth of the middle class led naturally to a more popular literature, melodramas that could be serialized in newspapers such as Eugène Sue's *Mystères de Paris* (1842).

The *mal du siècle* did bring forth some incisive historical writing, such as Jules Michelet's seminal *Histoire de France* (1844), though its greatest achievement was dedicated to another land – Alexis de Tocqueville's *De la démocratie en Amérique* (1844), still uncannily up to date after more than a century and a half.

Romanticism, still gathering momentum, eventually spawned native poets in the wake of Byron and Shelley and Schiller. **Victor Hugo** (1802–85) had his first great success with a novel, *Notre-Dame de Paris* (*The Hunchback of Notre-Dame*) in 1831. His *Le roi s'amuse* became the libretto for Verdi's *Rigoletto*. Although politically radical, Hugo nevertheless exerted himself mightily to be elected to the Académie, finally succeeding on the third attempt in 1841. He wrote little else until *Les Misérables* in 1862. Much of his finest poetry also appeared in this late period, when Hugo was in voluntary exile from Napoléon III; by his death he had become a national institution.

Along with Romantic poets came Romantic novelists: **Prosper Mérimée** (1803–70), with his *Carmen* and *Colomba*, specialized in violent passions in exotic settings; **George Sand** (Aurore Dupin, 1804–76) began with socialist and feminist themes, and ended writing rustic romances. **Honoré de Balzac** (1799–1850), like Hugo, was capable of exhausting even the most devoted readers by the sheer volume of his work (*Père Goriot*, 1835, *Les Illusions Perdues*, *Splendeurs et Misères des courtisanes*). An obsessive observer of every detail of contemporary society, Balzac arranged some 90 stories and novels into an all-encompassing overview of society called *La Comédie humaine*.

Under the gilded dictatorship of Napoléon III, many of France's intellectuals turned to the sturdier truths of science, or at least pseudo-science, as in the woolly Positivism of philosophers Auguste Comte and Hippolyte Taine, who sought to rationalize human life into narrow and poorly digested biological concepts. Another alternative was art for art's sake, as in the aestheticism of poet-novelists such as Théophile Gautier. Yet another was disgust and withdrawal; **Charles Baudelaire** (1821–67) a rebellious youth, led a life of drug-fuelled excess, at turns ribald and melancholy. A translator of Poe, a child alone in the modern city, Baudelaire set the pattern for the solitary wrestling with the problem of modern evil. Parts of his *Les Fleurs du Mal* (1857) remained suppressed for obscenity until 1949. Disenchantment on a more down-to-earth level found expression in the novels of **Gustave Flaubert** (1821–80). Haunted by the difference between ideals and reality, between the vast complex façade of modern life and the elemental, Flaubert explored the none-too-flattering motives that govern our behaviour in *Madame Bovary* (1857) and *L'Education sentimentale* (1870). **Guy de Maupassant** (1850–93), protégé of Flaubert, added to the roll of classic 19th-century novels of passion and greed with *Bel-Ami*, though he is better known for his collections of short stories.

The scientific bent of late 19th-century thought reached fiction in a tendency variously called 'realist' or 'naturalist'. **Emile Zola** churned out a cycle of 20 novels called *Les Rougon-Macquart* (1871–93). The subtitle, *Histoire naturelle et sociale d'une famille sous le Second Empire*, gives away Zola's intention to put social relations under a 'scientific' scrutiny. One of the first to interest himself in the tribulations of the new working class, as in *Germinal* and *L'Assommoir*, Zola became the conscience of France when he intervened in the Dreyfus affair with his famous manifesto *J'accuse* (1898).

In Paris, at least, the bohemian idyll was contagious. The *décadents*, heirs of Baudelaire, took in absinthe and turned it into free verse. Mostly self-obsessed types who met bad ends, they shook up the dusty old metres and style of French verse while distilling poetic atmosphere and radiating subjectivity. The best were **Paul Verlaine** (1844–96) and his lover **Arthur Rimbaud** (1854–91) (the affair ended famously with pistol shots). Rimbaud, who preferred to be thought of as a 'Symbolist', was a precocious genius seeking the 'alchemy of word and sense' in poems ('Le Bateau Ivre') and prose poems ('Illuminations'). Rimbaud stopped writing at 20 and became a drunken wreck; Verlaine kept writing and became a Catholic.

Impressionism and Beyond

In 1874 the Société Anonyme des Artistes held its first exhibition – yet another protest against exclusion from the *salon*. What set it apart from other protest shows were the artists exhibiting: **Edgar Degas** (1834–1917), **Auguste Renoir** (1841–1919), **Camille Pissarro** (1830–1903) and **Claude Monet** (1840–1926). Monet's painting of a sunrise entitled *Impression: Soleil Levant* inspired the papers to call the whole group *Impressionnistes* – a name the painters adopted for their next seven exhibitions. The Impressionists were not as interested in the realism of photography as in the science behind it, the discovery that colour completely owes its existence to light, and they made it their goal to record objectively what their eye saw in an instant. Their works achieved considerable critical acceptance by the 1880s – although soreheads at the *salon* made sure that the state never spent any money to purchase their works; nearly all the magnificent paintings in Paris' Musée d'Orsay are later gifts.

The crucial role the south was to play in modern art dates from the 1880s, thanks to the two artists most closely associated with Provence today, **Vincent Van Gogh** (1853–90) and **Paul Cézanne** (1839–1906). Van Gogh was influenced at first by the Impressionists and Japanese prints he saw in Paris; after his move to Arles in 1888 he responded to the heightened colour and light of Provence on such an intense, personal level that colour came less and less to represent form (as it did for the Impressionists), but instead took on a symbolic value; colour became the only medium Van Gogh found powerful enough to express his extraordinary moods and visions. Cézanne's innovations were as important as Van Gogh's, although his response to Provence was analytical rather than emotional, perhaps because he was born in the south. Loosely associated with the Impressionists in the 1860s and '70s, by the 1880s he had undertaken his stated task of 'making Impressionism solid and enduring, like the art of the museums', exploring underlying volumes, planes and structure not through perspective, but through amazingly subtle variations of colour. A third important figure, **Paul Gauguin** (1848–1903) echoed Van Gogh in finding spiri-tuality in colour. After leaving Paris for Pont-Aven in Brittany, his search for the primitive sources of creativity led him off to the South Pacific in 1891.

In these 'Post-impressionist' decades, plenty of artists remained in Paris, including **Georges Seurat** (1859–91), the most scientific of painters, who invented pointillism to bring a new classical structure to art. In 1884 he took part in the founding of the Salon des Indépendants, open to all; those exhibiting included **Henri de Toulouse-Lautrec** (1864–1901), whose portraits of Montmartre and Paris' underworld have so powerfully affected the way the world looks at Paris, and **Henri Rousseau** (1844–1910), the first and greatest of naïve painters. At the same time, the expressive Romantic **Auguste Rodin** (1840–1917) was shaking sculpture awake from its stale neoclassical doldrums, causing furious controversies with his powerful, often radically distorted works.

In the 1890s artists searched for ever more rare, exotic and exquisite stimulation – most interesting of all are the works of **Odilon Redon** (1840–1916), who painted from his pre-Freudian dreams, and was much admired by Mallarmé and the Symbolists. An unfortunate side effect of the 'decadents' with their languid maidens and ambiguous sexuality is that they retarded a genuine renaissance in European design, the **Art Nouveau**. Best known for its long flowing line inspired by plants and the geometry of natural growth, Art Nouveau's complete devotion to craftsmanship put prices out of reach of the masses, and it never caught the popular fancy. The little success Art Nouveau had in France outside of architecture was in vases by Gallé, curvilinear furniture by Prouve, Vallin and Majorelle, and the virtuoso creations of Lalique, whose intricate, fairy-like jewellery, often in the form of dragonflies or beetles, delighted Sarah Bernhardt.

Beaux-Arts, and a Revolution in Iron

As in art, the result of the Revolutionary/Napoleonic experience for architecture was to replace one kind of academicism with another. The opening of the Ecole Polytechnique in 1794 created the new model, entirely separating the engineering side of architecture from the artistic. To be an architect, you had to attend the Ecole des Beaux-Arts, the proud bastion of academicism. The real action was elsewhere. Paris, far ahead of any other European city, was on the verge of beginning a new architectural age, using durable, versatile iron and glass to make buildings fit for the Industrial Revolution and the new century dawning. Glass roofs were being put up over narrow shopping streets as early as 1776; the first of Paris' *passages*, or arcades, were probably built in the 1790s, and the first iron bridges appeared shortly after 1800. Other uses for iron and glass included churches, greenhouses, market buildings and railway stations, prime symbols of the Industrial Revolution that tried to marry the new technology to traditional French monumental architecture. The most surprising application was supplied by the visionary architect **Henri Labrouste** (1801–75) in the main reading room of the Bibliothèque Nationale, an enormous, soaring ceiling of lovely intersecting domes, perching on the slenderest of iron columns.

In the reign of Napoléon III, Paris was transformed under the direction of the brilliant and forceful Prefect of the Seine department, **Georges Haussmann**. To facilitate traffic, to enrich the unsavoury swarm of speculators that buzzed about the imperial throne, and to get the poor out of sight and out of mind, central Paris was nearly obliterated by a gargantuan programme of slum clearance and boulevard-building. It might have been a perfect opportunity for a new architecture to take hold, but despite the new ideas and new advances the Second Empire was the heyday of the Beaux-Arts, with eclectic regime showpieces like the completion of the Louvre wings and **Charles Garnier**'s mammoth Opéra, begun in 1861. Recovery from the disasters of 1870–71 was slow, but by the 1880s the Third Republic was fostering inspired architecture once more. The 1889 Exposition was the apotheosis of iron, producing not only engineer Gustave Eiffel's tower but also the incredible Galerie des Machines (over 1,300ft long), demolished in 1910. The Eiffel Tower was a magical apparition: a symbol for Paris, for its century, for all of modern industrial civilization – a building with no purpose, an ornament, yet one that delights everyone and makes intellectuals discuss and contemplate endlessly.

20th-century Literature

With the turn of the century, ideas of the avant-garde began spreading from the artists and poets to the novelists; a wave of experimentation in style and language was pioneered by **Marcel Proust** (1871–1922), another old Dreyfusard, with his huge rumination on memory and eternity (*A la recherche du temps perdu*, 1913–27), and **André Gide** (1869–1951), whose works sought a 'new humanism' in themes of freedom and commitment. Among the poets of the new century, the most popular was **Paul Valéry** (1871–1945), whose most famous poem 'Le Cimetière marin' was a memory of his home town, Sète. Other poets were breaking moulds: **Guillaume Apollinaire** (1880–1918), friend of Picasso, Derain and other young artists, tried to translate their Cubist inspiration into poetry, and became a fantastical forebear of the Surrealists ('L'Enchanteur pourrissant', 1909; 'Alcools', 1913).

Surrealism, a term Apollinaire invented to describe his play *Les Mamelles de Tirésias* (1917), attempted to subvert a perverse society from within, by attacking its perception and processes of thought. The assault was led by **André Breton** (*Nadja*, 1928), **Louis Aragon** and **Paul Eluard**. Another early Surrealist was **Jacques Prévert** (1900–77) who later became widely popular for his humorous, politically radical poems and song lyrics (*Paroles*, 1950). Eluard and Aragon too came to write more direct poetry, circulated clandestinely during the Occupation. This rare phenomenon – serious poets finding common ground with a mass audience – would lead to the postwar success of the *chanson française*, most memorably in the songs of Georges Brassens and Jacques Brel.

Paris' busy, creative 1920s also saw a revival of **theatre**. Most of the impetus came from **Jean Cocteau** (1889–1963) who not only wrote plays (*Orphée*, 1926) but collaborated on ballets with Satie and Milhaud. **Jean Giraudoux** (1882–1944) added a touch of the absurd, along with some high seriousness and poetic stylization, though in the age-old French tradition his plays dealt with classical themes and subjects as well as modern (*La Guerre de Troie n'aura pas lieu*, 1935; *Ondine*, 1939, *La Folle de Chaillot*, 1946).

Politically and philosophically, French **letters** remained divided along the lines of the Dreyfus case for decades. Put the extremes of Left and Right together, add a good dose of misanthropy, and you get **Louis-Ferdinand Céline** (1894–1961) who caused a sensation in the '30s with his *Voyage au bout de la nuit* (*Journey to the End of Night*) and *Mort à crédit* (*Death on the Instalment Plan*), violent, nihilistic rejections of everything in a rotten modern world.

Interesting theatre picked up directly after the war. The more traditional works of writers such as **Jean Anouilh** (1910–87) maintained favour, though the spotlight soon turned to the more experimental works of **Jean Genet** (*Les Bonnes*, 1947) and especially to the 'theatre of the absurd' pioneered by Romanian-born **Eugène Ionesco** with *La Cantatrice Chauve* (1949, *The Bald Soprano*) and Irishman **Samuel Beckett** (*En attendant Godot*, 1952).

No one mistook **Jean-Paul Sartre** (1905–80) for an absurdist; he first gained attention with plays (*Huis-clos*, 1944) and novels (*La Nausée*, 1938) as misanthropic as anything by Céline. Not content with describing an empty universe, he also developed existentialist philosophy to tell us what to do about it, beginning with *L'Etre et le Néant* (1943). **Albert Camus** (1913–60), who grew up in Algeria, echoed Sartre's conclusions, but caught the dark postwar mood of alienation better with a series of remarkable novels (*L'Etranger*, 1942, *La Peste*, 1947) and plays (*Caligula*, 1945). Sartre's companion and collaborator **Simone de Beauvoir** (1908–86) became an important novelist in her own right, though she is best known for her groundbreaking feminist work *Le Deuxième Sexe* (1949).

Much of the Baroque, relentlessly didactic flavour of French discourse in the postwar decades can be traced to the 'Structuralist' anthropology of **Claude Lévi-Strauss** (*Mythologiques*, 1964–71). His ideas were carried into the realm of contemporary culture by **Roland Barthes** (1915–80) and **Jacques Derrida** (1930–) with his idea of 'deconstruction': concentrating on the 'text' as an object in itself, something to be 'decoded'. The French approach has proved useful in the examination of the hidden codes by which our society operates, especially in the work of **Michel Foucault** (1926–84): studying the history of prisons and madhouses to discover society's 'principles of exclusion', compiling the history of sexuality, and 'archaeologies' of knowledge and science.

Few Frenchmen in the postwar years were moved to serious poetry, or by it, and by the 1970s critics were speaking of the 'crisis of verse'. Such works as did appear were often little more than intellectual word games, as in **Georges Perec**, who wrote a novel (*La Disparition*) without using the letter 'e'. Even in fiction-writing there had to be 'movements', complete with manifestos, and a little of all the ideas of the postwar ferment became grafted on to novel writing. As a counterpart to *nouvelle vague* cinema, there was the *nouveau roman*. Novelists such as **Alain Robbe-Grillet**, **Nathalie Sarrante**, **Marguerite Duras** and **Claude Simon** exploded the traditional framework of fiction, and played games with narrative and time, in settings of intentional vagueness and indeterminate reality. Not all readers were happy with a diet of constant polemics, and the traditional French novel lived on in the works of **Françoise Sagan**, **Jean-Marie Le Clézio**, **Marcel Pagnol**, the historical novels of **Marguerite Yourcenar**, the first woman elected to the Académie, and the endless list of detective novels by **Georges Simenon** (1903–89).

Movements in 20th-century Art

Among the poor bohemians living in Paris at the turn of the 20th century were three painters inspired by the intense, pure colours of Van Gogh and the decorative Nabis group that followed Gauguin. **Henri Matisse** (1869–1954), **André Derain** (1880–1954) and **Maurice de Vlaminck** (1876–1958) first became known to the Paris public at an exhibition in 1905, when a critic labelled them 'wild beasts', or **Fauves**, for their uninhibited use of colour. Although Fauvism only lasted another three years, it was the first great avant-garde movement of the century and, as Matisse said, the one that made all the others possible.

The next movement followed quickly on its heels and lasted longer. In 1907 two hungry artists in Montmartre, admirers of the recently deceased Cézanne, **Pablo Picasso** (1881–1973) and **Georges Braque** (1882–1963), formulated **Cubism**, which liberated form in the same way that the Fauves had liberated colour. They aimed to depict the permanent structure of objects, and not the transitory appearance of the moment, by showing them from a number of angles at the same time. In 1910 **Robert Delaunay** (1885–1941) began his vibrant Cubist paintings of the Eiffel Tower, and two years later went a step further from the austere Cubism of Picasso, Braque and Gris to a lyrical style of brightly coloured, non-representational abstraction which the poet Apollinaire called **Orphism**. Orphism had an influence on German Expressionism and Italian Futurism, if little in Paris. More new influences came with refugees from Eastern Europe: sculptors **Constantin Brancusi** (1876– 1957) and **Osip Zadkine** (1890–1967), who borrowed the multi-faceted aspect of Cubism to create powerful, expressive works; **Marc Chagall** (1887–1985), who with his dreamy Russian-Jewish paintings brought figurative painting into the avant-garde; and the Lithuanian-born Expressionist **Chaïm Soutine** (1893–1943).

Meanwhile, Parisian **Marcel Duchamp** (1887– 1968) made the tradition of shocking the bourgeoisie a goal in itself (most famously at the 1913 New York Armoury Show, America's introduction to modern art). In 1915 he outraged the public even further with his 'ready-mades' – everyday items such as toilet seats displayed as art to challenge the typical attitudes towards taste. His anti-art ideas had followers on both sides of the Atlantic: **Dada**, founded in Zurich in 1916, arrived in Paris after the war with **Francis Picabia** and **Tristan Tzara**.

In 1924 a new manifesto announced that Dadaism was dead and a new movement with deeper aims, known as **Surrealism**, would take its place. As its theoretician, **André Breton**, explained it, Surrealism was 'to resolve the previously contradictory conditions of dream and reality into an absolute reality, a super-reality'. The police had to be called to stop the riots at the first Surrealist show in 1925: exhibitors included the American photographer **Man Ray**, Picasso, the Catalan **Joan Miró** (1893–1983) and **Max Ernst** (1891–1976); in 1929 the group was joined by another Catalan, **Salvador Dalí** (1904–89), whose knack for self-publicity made him famous and controversial.

After the war and occupation, the Paris art scene reflected the grey, postwar malaise. In the 1940s the explosion of Abstract Expressionism in New York stripped Paris of its position in the avant-garde, leaving Paris with pale imitators – but also with refreshing 'anti-artists', such as **Jean Dubuffet** (1901–85), who engaged in open warfare with France's culture czars; in his art he rejected professional technique in favour of spontaneity and authenticity, which he called *art brut* (raw art), inspired by the works of children, prisoners and the insane. In the early 1960s a playful group of artists known as the Nouveaux Réalistes emerged, inspired by the everyday items presented as art in Duchamp's 'ready-mades', and by a disgust for contemporary culture: **Nikki de Saint-Phalle** (b. 1930), **Jean Tinguely** (1925–92), Bulgarian-American **Christo** (b. 1935), **César** (b. 1921), **Ben** and **Arman** (b. 1928) gave Paris in the 1980s some of its most important (and amusing) monuments.

French Cinema

Photography is a field where France has made important contributions since the time of pioneers Niepce (1816) and **Jacques Daguerre**, who perfected daguerrotypy in 1839. It was only natural that the French should also have been at the forefront of the cinema. The **Lumière** brothers of Besançon perfected the first practical film projector, their *cinématographe* (from which the word cinema derives), in 1895.

Their early films inspired **Georges Méliès**, a magician by trade who pioneered in putting actual stories on the screen, beginning in 1896. He made one of cinema's first artistic triumphs with the magical *Voyage dans la lune* (1902), which included animated sequences. The **Pathé Company**, founded in 1896, had the best technology of its time, the first big studio, at Vincennes, and the first specially built luxury theatre, in Paris (1906). Its rival **Gaumont**, founded a year earlier, employed the first woman director, Alice Guy. These studios produced some of the first full-length features, including such international successes as Louis Mercanton's *Les Amours de la Reine Elisabeth*.

Before the First World War, the French film industry was the world's largest along with Italy's. It produced the popular comedian Max Linder, whose persona was the inspiration for Charlie Chaplin's, along with the elegant productions of directors such as **Louis Feuillade** (*Fantômas*, 1914), as well as 'art films', such as Comédie Française productions brought to the screen. The industry nearly closed down during the war because of a film shortage; it never recovered its leading role, though the '20s saw such memorable productions as Abel Gance's epic eight-hour *Napoléon*. Some recovery did take place in the '30s, and at the end of the decade France's industry was second only to America's. Many of the best films of the period were in a manner described as 'poetic realism', as in the works of **Jean Renoir** (1894–1979), son of the painter (*Boudu sauvé des eaux*, 1932, the anti-war *La Grande Illusion*, 1937, *La Règle du jeu*, 1939), as well as those of **René Clair**, who made one of the first important sound movies, *Sous les toits de Paris* (1930), **Julien Duvivier** (*Pépé le Moko*, 1937), **Marcel Carné** (*Le Jour se lève*, 1937, *Hôtel du Nord*, 1938), and **Jean Vigo** (*Zéro de conduite*, 1933).

Ironically, French film-making did better under occupation in the Second World War than it had in the First. Marcel Carné was able to make *Les Enfants du Paradis*, a big-budget spectacular with screenplay by Jacques Prévert, in the middle of the war. Poet

Jean **Cocteau**, who made the Surrealist film, *Sang d'un poète* in 1930, returned to film-making after the war with a French classic, *La Belle et la Bête* (1946). **Robert Bresson** continued a 50-year career of stylish films full of psychological insight (*Le Journal d'un curé de campagne*, 1950). Some of the most popular postwar films were made by Jacques Tati (1907–82), a former rugby player who provided some rare fun in a time when the French were not easily amused (*Les Vacances de Monsieur Hulot*, 1953, *Mon oncle*, 1958, *Playtime*, 1967). **Max Ophüls**, a German who directed sophisticated films in four different countries, gave France *La Ronde* (1950) and *Lola Montès* (1955).

The French began to take cinema more seriously in these years, seeing a necessity for an alternative to the more commercial American approach, and they went about it in a way that was typically French: the establishment of film schools and *cinéma-thèques* (film museums), and the influential review, André Bazin's *Cahiers du Cinéma*, founded in 1951. A conscious 'movement' in cinema could not be far behind. The *nouvelle vague* (new wave) of films that were cheaply made (of necessity), shot on location and with less narrative continuity, made its breakthrough in 1959, with the works of **François Truffaut** (*Les quatre cents coups*, 1959, *Jules et Jim*, 1961), **Alain Resnais** (*Hiroshima mon amour*, 1959), and **Jean-Luc Godard** (*Alphaville*, 1965, and plenty of Marxist-oriented works in the '60s and '70s). Along with these pioneers came a whole generation of directors: **Claude Chabrol**, **Eric Rohmer**, **Agnès Varda** and **Louis Malle**, names that dominated the French cinema for the next three decades, treating audiences to the blank face of Jean-Luc Belmondo and countless hours of Parisians smoking cigarettes and discussing their relationships. In many ways it was the counterpart of the *nouveau roman*, and there was a strong connection between the two; **Alain Robbe-Grillet** wrote screenplays for Alain Resnais (*L'Année dernière à Marienbad*, 1961), and directed films of his own.

The 1970s heralded the rise of a French star system, that aped the Hollywood model with Belmondo and Alain Delon at the outset, giving way to Gérard Depardieu and Isabelle Adjani by its close. With *L'Amour en fuite*, in 1978, François Truffaut completed a remarkable series of four films made over 20 years charting the life of Antoine Doinel – the character played by his alter ego, actor Jean-Pierre Léaud. But with the shock of Truffaut's death in 1984, his spirit of romantic humanism gave way to the more gritty, psychological nature of films by **Maurice Pialat** and **Jacques Doillon**. By contrast, the glossy *cinéma du look*, begun by **Luc Besson** (*Diva*, 1981), took hold in the mid-80s – epitomized by films like **Jean-Jacques Beineix**'s *Betty Blue*, in 1985, and Besson's own first English language hit *The Big Blue* in 1988. It was perceived that the French industry needed to up its budgets to compete with Hollywood, and this led to a series of super-production, heritage films such as **Claude Berri**'s Pagnol adaptations, *Jean de Florette*, and *Manon des Sources*, in 1985–6. French producers were still not averse to taking risks, however, giving one of the new generation of filmmakers, **Léos Carax**, the then biggest French film budget to date to make the modern fable *Les Amants du Pont Neuf*, with Juliette Binoche, in 1990. France scored its biggest domestic success to date with the medieval comedy *Les Visiteurs*, in 1993. More recently, a new breed of young filmmakers have begun to make their mark with widely diverging styles – from **Matthieu Kassovitz**'s angry debut *La Haine* (1995) through **Gilles Mimouni**'s stylishly complex *L'Appartement* (1996) to the poetic naturalism of **Erick Zonca**'s *La Vie rêvée des anges* (1998).

Architecture: from Classicism to the *Grands Projets*

On the whole, it was a miserable century for French architecture, and the best works around are mostly by foreigners. With the turn of the 20th century, instead of carrying bravely on with modern styles, architecture inexplicably decayed into another heavy, tedious classicism – Louis XIV without the frills, as exemplified in the work of **Auguste Perret** (1874–1954; the first Frenchman to fall in love with bare concrete) and in the 1937 Exposition (Palais de Chaillot). France may have invented the term Art Deco, but no French architect ever caught its spirit.

France is largely exempt from blame for the beginnings of architectural Modernism, if only because early pioneer Tony Garnier was rarely allowed to build anything, and because **Le Corbusier** (Charles Jeanneret, 1887–1965) was really Swiss. The great theorist of the movement (*Vers une architecture*, 1923) built several houses in and around Paris in the 1920s and '30s, and the Unité d'habitation in Marseille (1947) before turning to an abstract, curvilinear style (church at Ronchamp, 1950). More influential than his individual buildings were his plans for Paris; his Voisin Project proposed demolishing much of central Paris and replacing it with tidy rows of tower blocks. Paris' élite saved the city for itself, but after the Second World War it imposed Le Corbusier's totalitarian vision on hundreds of thousands of Frenchmen, 'rehoused' in grim suburban concrete wastelands. Today, scenes of the dynamiting of tower blocks are still a regular feature at the end of the French television news, but the damage inflicted on the fabric of France by the Modernist architects and planners will take at least a century to repair.

Until 1968 architects were still being trained almost exclusively in the Beaux-Arts, guaranteeing a maximum of conformity and an allergy to creativity. This shows best in Paris' huge office project of La Défense, begun in 1958. In the 1970s, though, the steadfast modernist President Pompidou stood Paris on its ear by commissioning Richard Rogers' and Renzo Piano's Centre Pompidou, a controversial, high-tech structure that has won fans even among traditionalists.

With the 1980s and President François Mitterrand, both Paris and its tutelary state were desperate to make up for so much lost time. Thus the Pharaonic era of the Grands Projets: the Grande Arche at La Défense, the Bastille Opéra, the Grand Louvre renovation that includes I. M. Pei's Pyramid, the Science Park at La Villette, the museum conversion of the Gare d'Orsay, almost all by foreign architects. For a glimmer of optimism on the state of French architecture, the building that won the widest acclaim in the last two decades has been Jean Nouvel's elegant Institut du Monde Arabe (1987) on the Left Bank.

Topics

The Names on the Pedestal

Every village has one. Some, for reasons that nobody remembers, have two. To any American they will seem familiar, since they closely resemble the monuments that every town in the eastern states erected for the dead of the Civil War. Only instead of a slouch-capped Union or Confederate soldier, the statue on top will be a *poilu* in an iron helmet from the First World War. Some villages could only afford a simple stone plaque, and some chose to commemorate the war with allegories featuring naked ladies, as Frenchmen will do (and at least one village has a stone obelisk with a rooster on top). Still, in the 1920s the studios and foundries of Paris were cranking out bronze or iron *poilus* by the hundred. On the pedestal, usually, will be inscribed the names of the local boys who died in the Marne or the Somme or Verdun or Chemin-des-Dames. Just what all this means to the French may dawn on you, in a little village that scarcely counts two hundred people, when you look at the names and realize that there are over thirty of them.

'Eleven-eleven', Armistice Day, is still observed here. At noon, in almost every village, people will congregate by reflex at the monument to the *poilus*. Only a few years ago, one might still see a stooped old veteran or two, with ribbons on his coat. Today, any one still around would have to be a centenarian at least. The mayor, with or without his sash, will make a short speech, and maybe read a letter from a government minister or the head of a veterans' organization. Then, in our village and many others, comes the part that seems somewhat strange to us outsiders. The mayor reads the list of the soldiers who died, and after each name the assemblage gives the response like a congregation: '*Mort pour la France*'.

As in many nations, Armistice Day has become a day of remembrance for the dead of all the wars. The names listed may include a few from the Second World War, the Resistance, Vietnam or Algeria, but the overwhelming majority will always be from the War to End All Wars. In the beginning, they went off to war in sky-blue uniforms with bright red trousers – a Gallic gesture perhaps designed to impress the enemy in some strange way, but one that instead merely made the *poilus* better targets. The shooting gallery would be open for the next four years, a war conducted by generals on both sides who didn't mind casualties in the tens of thousands, in the cause of trying out some new tactical ideas. When it was over, 1,400,000 Frenchmen were dead – roughly a fifth of the nation's young men.

In the years before the war, France had never seemed more prosperous and content. A stable government, the first since the Revolution, presided over an age of social progress and techological marvels, of ice-cream and the first holidays on the beach and the bright colours of the avant-garde painters, an age epitomized by the Paris of the great World Fairs, the Moulin Rouge and the Eiffel Tower. When it was over, France had been bled white. Besides the sheer loss of life, the wreck of an entire generation, the war left much of the northeast of the country in ruins (in Picardy the farmers are still finding unexploded shells). France's economy was in ruins too; after 1918 business, along with the government's tax revenue, contracted by a sixth; recovery would really only start in the 1950s.

In the 1920s France watched Germany rebuild, and complained that the Americans were giving it better terms on the war debts than her allies. The inter-war decades were filled with strikes and dissension even before the Depression came along to leave the country even lower. When the next war came, France was still dealing with the shocks of the first one. Though not entirely exhausted in a physical sense, emotionally and physically something seemed to have died. When the challenge came, France simply collapsed.

It was definitely a rough century, here as much as any part of Europe. The noted historian André Maurois, however, repeats over and over the fact of his country's 'wonderful powers of recuperation'. There have been other disasters, and worse ones: the Hundred Years War, and the Wars of Religion. Maurois, writing in the 1960s, was no doubt fondly wishing that the charm would work again. Perhaps it has, though these things take time, and the disasters of the early 20th century are the central fact of the nation's life, more so than the long ago age of cathedrals, or the Grand Siècle of Louis XIV, or even the Revolution. So it is entirely fitting that a tiny village, each year, should come out and dedicate a few minutes to the memory of Louis, Laurent, Cyprien, Armand, Auguste, Daniel, Abel, Alphonse, Paul, Omer, Isidore, Jean, Joseph, Germain, Ernest and Charles.

North and South

'Well, what about us?' regionalist partisans of the Bretons, Corsicans, Catalans and Basques might ask. They have a case, but for the moment, let us consider this surprisingly diverse France as essentially two nations. According to most histories, it all started in the Dark Ages, when Gaulish Latin vernacular was evolving, or maybe decomposing, into two languages. Latin didn't have a word for yes, surprisingly (the Romans were never the most agreeable of peoples). To indicate affirmation, they would say *hic*, literally 'thus', and through the prisms of the two opposite ends of Gaul this came out *oc*, in the south, and *oïl* in the north, where people even at this early date showed a deplorable sloppiness about their consonant sounds. Eventually the northern version would be spelled *oui*, but people as early as the Middle Ages came to call the two nations after their languages, the *langue d'oc* and the *langue d'oïl*.

It would, however, be a mistake to say that the north-south division is as old as history. It's older. Recent research (through aerial photography, place names and archaeology) has discovered faint traces of a line of fortifications that once cut a nearly straight line clean across what is now France. It may have been built by the prehistoric Ligurians, an unsuccessful try at keeping out the Celts. The Romans refortified it, as a second line of defence against any Germans who broke through the Rhine frontier, and later it would mark the southern boundary of the Franks. South of the line was always the more civilized part, the *Gallia Togata* of the great Romanized cities: Lyon, Marseille, Arles, Nîmes, Narbonne. To the north lay forests and bears, little Gaulish villages probably quite like Asterix's, and scubby backwater outposts such as *Lutetia* ('Mudville') on the Seine, one day to be Paris.

By one of history's tricks, this wilderness was to give birth to a creative and powerful civilization in the Middle Ages. For the first time, the south was falling behind. Occitania (a word invented only in the 18th century to describe the Provençal-Languedocien-Gascon-Aquitanien-Auvergnat cultural world) was thriving too – this after all was the home of the troubadours. But the north suddenly had bigger ideas, greater resources, and, most important of all, a huge surplus of well-armed knights. These came south to stay in the Albigensian Crusade, in which the pretence of extinguishing Languedoc's Cathar 'heretics' made possible a land-grab of monumental proportions. The Crusaders' leader was northerner Simon de Montfort – grim-visaged, incredibly lucky and always victorious. After his death at the siege of Toulouse other captains took up the fight, and often kept the land they won. For many southerners, the castle of Montségur is the Alamo, the last hurrah of not only the Cathars (1244) but all the tolerant, sophisticated world of medieval Occitania. Other parts fell to Paris later on; Provence did not become part of France until 1481.

The cultural effacement of Occitania came later. Landmarks along the way include the Edict of Villars-Cotterets in 1539 that made French the legal language of all the kingdom, and the dividing of France into homogenous *départements* in the Revolution, erasing all the old regional boundaries and names. Despite these, north and south carried on as essentially separate countries. Until the Revolution, there were actually customs barriers, and tolls to pay, between north and south. In our time, Paris was still treating the south like a conquered province. The new schools of the Third Republic taught in French only, and until very recently students were punished if they were caught speaking their own language in the schoolyard; the Parisians created the myth that the Occitan languages were not languages at all, but mere *patois*. The south's politics were carefully managed by northerners; in radical, Catalan Roussillon, for example, they long manipulated the vote to keep one of their own sitting for the *département* in the National Assembly; no natives need apply.

The south is the Midi, the Noonday, in the same way Italians call their south the Mezzogiorno, and, like the good burghers of Milan and Turin, many northern Frenchmen have always found it unaccountable that they should be sharing a country with such outlandish and foreign-seeming people, that there should be a France where palm trees and lemons grow. The stereotypical view was voiced by Ernest Renan: 'Our foolishness comes from the south, and if France had never drawn Languedoc and Provence into her sphere of activity, we should be a serious, active, Protestant and parliamentary people.'

Today the Occitan/Provençal languages of the troubadours are seeing a modest revival, and even some state schools are teaching them – for the first time ever. Some towns put up street signs in Occitan, and when you see a car with a white oval sticker on the back that says OC instead of F, you've found a partisan for the cause. Contacts between nationalistic Occitans and Catalans have already begun to create a kind of cross-border cultural union – an eastern counterpart to the relationship between French and Spanish Basques.

Especially since the introduction of regional governments in the 1980s, southerners have shown new confidence, and a new willingness to re-examine their identity, their interests and their future. Their olive oil- and duck fat-fuelled cuisine is triumphant everywhere, and even the economy is reviving in many places. Some think that France might have a long-sustained 'sunbelt' boom like America's. Some of the big southern cities, moribund for centuries, are on their way up, notably Toulouse, Montpellier and Nice, while some rural areas that became severely depopulated a century ago are filling up again with people from all over France and Europe, who find them simply delightful places to live or retire. The south, perhaps, shall rise again.

Microtourism

To keep it smaller than a breadbox, this book by necessity concentrates on France's more obvious charms – its Eiffel Towers, the awe-inspiring cathedrals, its most stunning châteaux. While visiting them, however, you may feel swept up in a tide of tourists, of hordes shooting the big-game monuments of France with Nikons or camcorders to add them like trophies to their collections. Behind this dazzling surface, however, is another, less chic and arty place, an eminently rural, slow France, that is far from boring. Getting the most out of it requires learning to look at the country the way the French themselves do – on a small scale. Connoisseurs of every particularity of *village* and *pays*, the French are passionately interested in the detail of traditional life and local history. Painstaking cartographers have compiled maps showing traditional roof styles in France: where they are high-pitched or shallow, and where the boundary is between slate and canal tiles (which roughly corresponds to the boundary between the *langue d'oïl* and *langue d'oc* – it's all connected). Other maps display the types of construction used for *pigeonniers*, or dovecotes.

Get the locals talking about these subjects and they'll go on for hours, explaining how in some areas only nobles were allowed to keep pigeons, which went out every day and ate all the peasants' grain and so caused the Revolution, which allowed everyone to keep pigeons, and farmers let the poo pile up for their daughters' dowries, but later they planted groves of poplars when a girl was born, because the trees would mature just in time for her marriage, by which time chemical fertilizers had made pigeon droppings less valuable than firewood...you get the idea. And by the way, you've probably noticed how the poplars are always planted in orderly quincunxes, but scholars are divided on whether this fashion, invented by King Cyrus of Persia, came into France in the Middle Ages or in the time of Louis XIV...

If you want to play too, the first thing to do is pick up the Cartes IGN: Série Bleue map for the area that interests you. Drawn on a scale of 1:25,000, these are the equivalent of the Ordnance Survey or US Geodetic Survey maps. You'll find them in any good newsagent or bookshop; walkers and mushroom-hunters probably account for much of the demand. From the first glance, you'll get a feeling for the traditional life and the slowly evolving fabric of your area: the villages and hamlets, each with its patch of cleared farmland, like islands in the vast green of the forests, along with the works that kept life going: sawmills, remains of old water mills, *pigeonniers*, sandpits and quarries, sources and fountains.

The map will show you some surprises, even if you think you already know the area well. Naturally it will help you find the nearest swimming hole, and some nice places for a walk in the woods, but there will be other surprises too: maybe a dolmen or menhir, a collection of *gariottes* or a fortified tower, or a medieval chapel in an unlikely place that may turn out to have seven devils frescoed on the walls inside. Ruins by the score are generally marked on the map – without further detail, so take pot luck; ruins can mean anything from bits of a Roman aqueduct to a *routiers'* stronghold destroyed at the end of the Hundred Years War, or a barn abandoned by some poor farmer who gave up when the *phylloxera* hit.

Once you get to know the country and its history better, you'll be able to read these maps like a detective. That village surrounded by a circuit of roadside crosses – it must have been a *sauveté* of the Church in the 1100s; the crosses marked the limits within which knights were forbidden to bash each other or molest the peasants. Crosses of all kinds grow thick along the roadsides. People from Brittany to the Alps have various folk stories to explain them, but in fact many are simply the latest incarnation of markers that go back to Neolithic times.

Not least among the virtues of rural France is modesty. This doesn't mean a lack of pride; on the contrary, nearly everyone here is convinced that their particular coin is Paradise on Earth. But rather, modesty as an outlook, as a way of life. As historian Emmanuel LeRoy Ladurie has noted, France is the country where bars are called *Au Petit Bonheur* or *Au Petit Profit*. Ladurie and others have developed an equally modest and original way of looking at the past. 'Microhistory', studying a single place and time in the minutest detail, not only flushes out unwarranted generalities and clichés, but adds real depth to our understanding. And a little understanding is all that the rural French, the 'provincials' so disdained by the Parisians, ask of the visitor. Deeply in love with their country, they are concerned that we learn to appreciate it as they do. With understanding, the *petits bonheurs* and sweet surprises begin to add up, secret doors into a country where the roots of life are rich and deep.

Big Mac Attack

José Bove and his nine co-defendants absolutely denied that they 'wrecked' that McDonald's in Millau, in the Aveyron, back in August 1999. Rather, they called it 'a festive dismantling with collateral damage'. Whatever that means, they did a pretty thorough job of it, over $100,000 worth of damage and entirely without the use of any such potential pollutants as dynamite or nitroglycerin. The leader of *Confédération Paysanne* and his followers were out to make a point, and no one doubts they succeeded. Now everybody in France knows who they are, and 20,000 people came out to show their support when Mr Bove went on trial.

Though festively dismantling a McDonald's might seem like good clean family fun, opinions in the Anglophone world found the whole exercise a bit immature. The French, it was often claimed, just couldn't understand 'globalization', and it was all a matter of some grumpy peasants venting some steam at a common symbol of American hegemony. Thanks to the congenital laziness of most of the media, though (especially television), most Americans in particular never got to hear the real story. It's about cows, all right, but not about the indisputably Gallic ones that get turned into McDo's burgers here. The cows in question are American, nice fat ones pumped full of growth hormones. France, and Europe, won't let them into their markets. They believe in the precautionary principle – that more should be known about the health effects of artificially juiced-up food before they are put on sale. America says rather, you've got to eat our beef whether you like it or not, and it's none of your business what we put in it. That's what free markets are all about.

The US has invented a nice new shiny World Trade Organization, where it can sue countries that let health, environmental or social concerns get in its way. But in the meantime, while the issue of hormone-laced cows is being fought out there, Washington has used its favourite tactic of 'revolving sanctions' against France, cleverly designed to annoy as many Frenchmen as possible. For a year it might be 100 per cent tariffs on champagne, and then on perfume, or perhaps Roquefort cheese. That, in fact is what it was. Mr Bove's sheep happen to be signed up with the Société Roquefort, and he has been getting screwed by Uncle Sam over a quarrel that has nothing to do with him.

French politicians do not like to argue with Mr Bove, or with any farmer. This is after all the country where every new president traditionally forgives all outstanding traffic fines on his first day in office, a country where the art of governance has become almost all carrot and no stick. Like the truckers who can now shut down France any time they feel like when fuel prices go up, and the trade unions that stop the railroads every now and then just to remind the government that they can do it, France's farmers are politically unassailable. They can close borders, tie up roads, or trash warehouses full of imported wine while the *gendarmes* stand and watch. Local officials are always in their corner; farmers do vote, and besides, no mayor really needs ten tons of manure dumped on the steps of his *mairie*.

For decades now, France's farmers have had the temerity to demand that they be allowed to make a good living in the old-fashioned way, in the face of all the trends, and defying all the economists' prattle about markets and the inevitability of more efficient means of production. While fighting for their livelihoods, they have also been fighting to keep their communities alive – as when the government tries to close village schools or cut transport services. In trying to preserve a way of life, they have suffered a good deal of condecension from the economic planners, but things are changing fast. In a time when issues of food seem to crystallize the big issues, the farmers of *Confédération Paysanne* suddenly look very much like the cutting edge. They have made the connection between healthy food, a healthy environment, and healthy communities. Europe's 'mad cow' crisis, very much in the public eye, is their Exhibit A. France's record of protecting consumers, like that of most European countries, is hardly more virtuous that America's; fate just led the two systems to foul up in different ways. The framers point out that whenever agriculture is corporatized and industrialized, this is what happens: chemical, potentially fatal food, a poisoned environment, and dying villages. Now they have a philosophy, and they know who the enemy is. France and the rest of the world will be hearing from them again.

That World Record Breaking Spirit

As far as we know, Jean Gimpel in his Medieval Machine was the first to use this expression to describe a key trait of the French, that spirit of *élan*, that shot of Gallic pepper sauce, that daring to go an extra mile, often right over the top, that sets them apart in Europe. No one else does it with such panache. Rugby and football fans know it well. Les Bleus are playing a sloppy game, the other side looks sure to win, when suddenly the French rustle up their old *esprit de corps* with the flair of d'Artagnan, with something of the fire that kindled Jeanne d'Arc or rallied Napoleon's diehards against the odds, and proceed to steamroller the bewildered opposition.

The first true sign of the World Record Breaking Spirit is in Brittany. Alignments of a few dozen menhirs sufficed for other Neolithic folk, but in Carnac there are thousands. Charlemagne was a big one-off spark in the Dark Ages, but in the 11th century the juices really began to flow. Adventure was there. The Normans grabbed it in Britain and southern Italy; in the Crusades, France responded with more enthusiasm than anyone to the papal jihad and set up one of their own, Geoffroy de Bouillon, as king of Jerusalem. The biggest Romanesque churches in the world were built at Cluny (destroyed), followed by Toulouse's St-Sernin (still there); French monasteries sponsored the great pilgrimage routes to Compostela. A century later in the Ile-de-France, Abbot Suger built the first Gothic church at St-Denis. Gothic really ignited the WRBS, in the first romances, in the intellectual challenges of Abelard's dialects, in sheer walls of stained glass, and as the cathedrals grew like the tower of Babel ever closer to God – at least until Beauvais', the tallest ever, which collapsed.

The Hundred Years War, itself something of a record-breaking war, put the kibosh on all that (indeed, the mind boggles to think what France might have done if it hadn't been Europe's favourite battleground). Later the concentration of power in one man – the king – also concentrated the WRBS. The court's Loire châteaux, and François 1er's personal collection of the same, still dazzle today, although it was Louis XIV who created the yardstick for modern megalomania in Europe. So much of the nation's resources were sucked into Versailles that the gilt, the marble vases, the dainty tables might as well be made of blood. A far more useful project of his reign, the linking of the Mediterranean and the Atlantic with the Canal du Midi, was achieved by Paul Riquet, an engineer who spent his own money on his idea when Louis refused to help, and inevitably went broke.

As the sap began to rise again in the 18th century, France was on its way to starting the Industrial Revolution. In 1778 Jouffroy invented the first steam boat, and the French got a steam car on the road in 1792; it immediately crashed into a wall. Instead, France chose to have another kind of Revolution – a World Record Breaking Revolution – before the bottled-up talent and ambition of the nation was hijacked by Napoleon, whose extra private helping of WRBS cost, by his own account, the lives of a million Frenchmen. When the dust settled, the Parisians invented the department store and much of what we call modern society; Eiffel erected his daredevil tower, the tallest structure in the world, and built a skeleton for the Statue of Liberty. The French invented – although they didn't always get to the patent office first – photography, the hot air balloon, automobiles, motion pictures, the phonograph, and the aeroplane. As the 19th century marched on, the restless, feverish impetus to go beyond the limits led to the first great -isms of modern art and literature as French daring and freedom sucked in avant-garde talent from around the world. Even the cancan and the Moulin Rouge were world record breaking in their way.

After a prolonged postwar hangover, France didn't really get back into its groove until the 1970s, when speed became an obsession: high-speed trains, rockets and jets made in Toulouse, followed by two co-productions with Britain, the Concorde supersonic jets and the Channel Tunnel. France Telecom came up with the Minitel before there was an Internet. Pharaonic WRBS *Grands Projets* changed the face of Paris.

The French (wisely, if the Millennium Dome and World Fair in Hanover are any indication) avoided seeing in 2000 with any more *Grands Projets*, but not without WRBS: turning the Eiffel Tower into the world's biggest Roman candle on New Year's Eve was perhaps the most brilliant single image of the world celebrations, and it was followed, on Bastille Day, with the fondest: *L'Incroyable Pique-Nique*, a 1,000km-long picnic straight down the heart of France along the Paris Meridian (which, in 1884, lost its honour of anchoring all the world's lines of longitude to Greenwich). Renamed the Green Meridian for the Millennium, it was planted with trees by children and decorated with plinths by artists. The weather didn't cooperate as it might have, but nothing could dampen a feeling that was mostly a stranger to war-wounded, existential, cynical, deconstructed France in the 20th century: optimism.

The Most Improved Nation

Nearly everybody of a certain age has fond memories of their first trip to France. Trying to buy bread, for example, and mistaking the gender of the word. *'C'est une baguette! Une baguette!'* shrieks the shopkeeper, wagging her finger while the other customers viciously smile. Back in the 1970s, it seemed the streets were full of pinch-faced souls who quite literally, we all found, wouldn't give you the time of day. We learned to appreciate, if only as a kind of surreal comic relief, the jaded bureaucrats who pretended not to understand anything you said, while they tried to think of another piece of paper to send you out hunting for, or the impossible middle-aged women with hairdos from hell and the inevitable poodles whose expressions matched theirs exactly. Many of these belonged to France's unique class of shopkeepers, those desiccated souls who thought of customers only as nuisances who open the door and let in a draught, and who used to hang up *Entrée libre* signs by the door, knowing we would feel honoured by the privilege.

The spirit of the age was captured in the *minuterie*, the arch-French device that, when you turned on the light in the hotel lobby, would give you just enough of it to let you reach your floor in total darkness.

Back in the 1950s, Paris was looking pretty shabby. Culture Minister André Malraux made Paris' building owners clean off all the grimy façades, though it didn't seem to cheer anyone up. It was a difficult time. The music was rotten, nothing got built except concrete monstrosities, and cultural life was dominated by the Stalinist-existentialist spleen of Monsieur Sartre; foreigners were not forgiven for thinking it all looked like boredom and angst masquerading as art and philosophy. Modern art had moved on to New York, and in Paris' galleries nothing much was happening. Even after France finally got fed up with Charles de Gaulle, in 1968, the tone was still set by the National Nose and his governments of nervous grey technocrats with sticks up their heinies, the fellows who built the public housing *cités* and knocked down Les Halles, Paris' beloved market.

When the technocrats built a horrific new home for the state-controlled radio and television on the banks of the Seine, its own employees named the place 'Alphaville', after the cold, clinical and thoroughly sinister fantasy city in the 1965 film of the same name by Jean-Luc Godard. That film made quite an impression on the French; like all the best science fiction, it showed them exactly where they were headed.

It was a common Anglo-American misconception at the time that France's ill-humour came from smoking Gauloises; another is that they were mad at us for liberating them. The fact is, France had reason to be grumpy. The traumas of the early 20th century were murder on a country that has always been rather highly strung. We like to imagine that France in the late 1400s, after the Hundred Years War, was much the same, and the art of the time does hint of neurosis, just like Alphaville on the Seine and the other creations of the postwar decades. The good news is that the fit does seem to be passing. All of us foreigners who have been around a while have noticed it, so it must be true. Now, even Parisians occasionally smile.

What has happened to France's ill-humour? It hasn't all disappeared, and there are still plenty of poodle ladies and reptilian bureaucrats to remind you where you are. And the country still has its share of bizarre habits, like the brown (yes, brown) chrysanthemums people give their dear departed on All Souls' Day, or the beige bathroom tiles with pictures of tropical fish on them, which in *la France profonde* are the only kind you can get. Even *bal musette* music (cue the accordions) is making a comeback, though considering the musical alternatives in this country that might not be such a bad thing.

The signs are everywhere. A French director has made a successful comedy. The *cités*, the poverty traps that became the sites of so much violence and *anomie* in the last thirty years, are dynamited almost daily. Following the political sleaze is delicious; everyone seems to enjoy it, and this is one area where the French know they can successfully compete with the Americans. The French are more open to new ideas than they have been for a long time, and they definitely seem happier and more relaxed. Shame about the bathroom tiles.

Food and Drink

04

Eating Out in France

Restaurants, especially the cheaper ones in rural areas, presume everyone has the appetite of Gargantua. A full meal consists of: an apéritif, *hors-d'œuvre* and/or a starter (typically, soup, pâté or *charcuterie*), an *entrée* (usually fish or an omelette), a main course (usually meat, poultry, game or offal, *garni* with a vegetable, rice or potatoes), often followed by a green salad (to 'lighten' the stomach), then cheese, then dessert, coffee, chocolates and *mignardises* (or *petits fours*) and perhaps a *digestif* to round things off. Most people only devour the whole whack on Sunday afternoons.

When looking for a restaurant, homing in on the one place crowded with locals is as sound a policy in France as anywhere. Don't overlook **hotel restaurants**, some of which are absolutely top notch even if a certain red book refuses on some obscure principle to give them more than two stars. To avoid disappointment, call ahead in the morning to **reserve**, especially at the smarter restaurants, and particularly in the summer.

Cities and resorts have a plethora of ethnic restaurants, mostly North African (a favourite for couscous), Asian (usually Vietnamese, sometimes Chinese, Cambodian or Thai) and Italian. **Vegetarians** will have a hard time in France, especially if they don't eat fish or eggs, but most establishments will try to accommodate them somehow. Pizzas, salads and bushels of *frites* are the old stand-bys.

Each region of France is proud of its local cuisine, or *cuisine de terroir*. Some of these are so popular that you'll find them throughout France: Breton *crêperies* or *galetteries* (with buckwheat pancakes); restaurants from Alsace serving *choucroute* (sauerkraut and sausage); Périgordin restaurants featuring duck, *foie gras* and truffles; and Lyonnaise *haute cuisine*. Boxes at the beginning of and throughout the main area chapters explore local specialities, wines and cheeses.

Markets, Picnic Food and Snacks

The food markets of France are justly celebrated for the colour and perfumes of their produce and flowers. They are fun to visit, and become even more interesting if you're cooking or gathering the ingredients for a picnic. In the larger cities, markets take place every day, while smaller towns and villages have markets once a week which double as a social occasion for the locals. Most finish around noon.

Other good sources for picnic food are the *charcuteries* or *traiteurs*, both of which sell prepared dishes sold by weight in cartons or tubs, a service also provided by the larger supermarkets. Cities are snack-food wonderlands, with outdoor counters selling pastries, *crêpes*, pizza slices, *frites*, *croque-monsieur* (toasted ham and cheese sandwiches) and a wide variety of sandwiches made from baguettes.

Restaurant Practicalities

French **restaurants** generally serve between noon and 2pm and in the evening from 7 to 10pm, with later summer hours; *brasseries* in the cities often stay open continuously. Most post menus outside the door so you know what to expect, and offer a choice of set-price (*prix fixe*) menus; if prices aren't listed, it's usually not because they're a bargain. If you summon up the appetite to eat the biggest meal of the day at

noon, you'll spend a lot less money, as many restaurants offer special **lunch menus** –
an economical way to experience some of the finer gourmet temples. Some of these
offer a set-price gourmet *menu dégustation* – a selection of chef's specialities, which
can be a great treat. At the humbler end of the scale, bars and brasseries often serve a
simple *plat du jour* (daily special) and the no-choice *formule*, which is more often than
not steak and *frites*. Eating *à la carte* anywhere will always be more expensive. *See* p.81
for the price ranges used in this guide.

Menus sometimes include the **house wine** (*vin compris*). If you choose a better wine
anywhere, expect a big mark-up.

Drink

Café Society

You can order any kind of drink at any bar or café – except cocktails, unless the bar
has a certain cosmopolitan flair. Cafés are also a home from home, places to read the
papers, play cards, meet friends, and just unwind, sit back and watch the world go by.
Prices are listed on the *tarif des consommations*: note they are progressively more
expensive depending on whether you're served at the bar (*comptoir*), at a table
(*la salle*) or outside (*la terrasse*).

French **coffee** is strong and black, but lacklustre next to the aromatic brews of Italy
or Spain (you'll notice an improvement in the coffee near their respective frontiers). If
you order *un café* you'll get a small black espresso; if you want milk, order *un crème*. If
you want more than a few drops of caffeine, ask them to make it *grand*. For decaf-
feinated, the word is *déca*. Some bars offer cappuccinos, but again they're only really
good near the Italian border. In the summer, try a *frappé* (iced coffee). The French only
order *café au lait* (a small coffee topped off with lots of hot milk) when they stop in
for breakfast, and, if what your hotel offers is expensive, consider joining them. There
are baskets of croissants and pastries, and some bars will make you a baguette with
butter, jam or honey. If you want to go native, try the Frenchman's Breakfast of
Champions: a *pastis* or two, and five non-filter Gauloises. *Chocolat chaud* (**hot chocolate**) is usually good. If you order *thé* (**tea**), you'll get an ordinary bag. An *infusion* is a
herbal tea – *camomille*, *menthe* (mint), *tilleul* (lime or linden blossom) or *verveine*
(verbena). These are kind to the all-precious *foie*, or liver, after you've over-indulged.

Mineral water (*eau minérale*) can be addictive, and comes either sparkling (*gazeuse*
or *pétillante*) or still (*non-gazeuse* or *plate*). The usual international corporate **soft
drinks** are available, and all kinds of bottled fruit juices (*jus de fruits*). Some bars also
do fresh lemon and orange juices (*citron pressé* or *orange pressée*). The French are also
fond of **fruit syrups** – red grenadine and ghastly green *diabolo menthe*.

Beer (*bière*) in most bars and cafés is run-of-the-mill big brands from Alsace,
Germany and Belgium. Draft (*à la pression*) is cheaper than bottled beer. Nearly all
resorts have bars or pubs offering wider selections of drafts, lagers and bottles.

The strong spirit of the Midi comes in a liquid form called *pastis*, first made popular
in Marseille as a plague remedy, now drunk as an apéritif before lunch and in rounds

French Menu Reader

Hors-d'œuvre et Soupes (Starters and Soups)

assiette assortie plate of mixed cold *hors d'œuvre*
bisque shellfish soup
bouchées mini *vol-au-vents*
bouillabaisse famous fish soup of Marseille
bouillon broth
charcuterie mixed cold meats, salami, ham, etc.
consommé clear soup
crudités raw vegetable platter
potage thick vegetable soup
tourrain garlic and bread soup
velouté thick smooth soup, often fish or chicken

Poissons et Coquillages (Crustacés) (Fish and Shellfish)

aiglefin little haddock
alose shad
anchois anchovies
anguille eel
bar sea bass
barbue brill
baudroie anglerfish
belons flat oysters
bigorneau winkle
blanchailles whitebait
brème bream
brochet pike
bulot whelk
cabillaud cod
calmar squid
carrelet plaice
colin hake
congre conger eel
coques cockles
coquillages shellfish
coquilles St-Jacques scallops
crabe crab
crevettes grises/roses shrimp/prawns
daurade sea bream
écrevisse freshwater crayfish
escargots snails

espadon swordfish
esturgeon sturgeon
flétan halibut
friture deep-fried fish
fruits de mer seafood
gambas giant prawns
gigot de mer a large fish cooked whole
grondin red gurnard
hareng herring
homard Atlantic (Norway) lobster
huîtres oysters
lamproie lamprey
langouste spiny Mediterranean lobster
langoustines Norway lobster (often called Dublin Bay prawns or scampi)
limande lemon sole
lotte monkfish
loup (de mer) sea bass
maquereau mackerel
merlan whiting
morue salt cod
moules mussels
oursin sea urchin
pagel sea bream
palourdes clams
poulpe octopus
praires small clams
raie skate
rascasse scorpion fish
rouget red mullet
saumon salmon
St-Pierre John Dory
sole (meunière) sole (with butter and lemon)
stockfisch stockfish (wind-dried cod)
telline tiny clam
thon tuna
truite trout
truite saumonée salmon trout

Viandes et Volailles (Meat and Poultry)

agneau (de pré-salé) lamb (grazed in fields by the sea)
aloyau sirloin
andouillette chitterling (tripe) sausage
biftek beefsteak
blanc breast or white meat

after work. Most people drink their '*pastaga*' with lots of water and ice (*glaçons*), which makes it almost palatable. **Spirits** include the familiar cognac and armagnac brandies, liqueurs and *digestifs* made from walnuts, cherries, pears and herbs (these are a speciality of the Alps), and fiery *marc*, the grape spirit that is the same as Italian grappa (but usually better).

blanquette stew of white meat
bœuf beef
boudin blanc sausage of white meat
boudin noir black pudding
brochette meat (or fish) on a skewer
caille quail
canard, caneton duck, duckling
carré the best end of a cutlet or chop
cassoulet haricot bean stew with sausage,
    duck, goose, etc.
cervelle brains
chapon capon
châteaubriand porterhouse steak
cheval horsemeat
chevreau kid
civet meat (usually game) stew, in wine and
    blood sauce
cœur heart
confit meat cooked and preserved in its
    own fat
côte, côtelette chop, cutlet
cou d'oie farci goose neck stuffed with pork,
    foie gras and truffles
crépinette small sausage
cuisse thigh or leg
dinde, dindon turkey
épaule shoulder
estouffade a meat stew marinated, fried
    and then braised
faisan pheasant
faux-filet sirloin
foie liver
frais de veau veal testicles
fricadelle meatball
gésier gizzard
gibier game
gigot leg of lamb
graisse or *gras* fat
grillade grilled meat, often a mixed grill
grive thrush
jambon ham
jarret knuckle
langue tongue
lapereau young rabbit
lapin rabbit
lard (lardons) bacon (diced bacon)
lièvre hare

maigret (or magret) (de canard) breast
    (of duck)
manchons duck or goose wings
marcassin young wild boar
merguez spicy red sausage
moelle bone marrow
mouton mutton
museau muzzle
navarin lamb stew with root vegetables
noix de veau (agneau) topside of veal (lamb)
oie goose
os bone
perdreau (or perdrix) partridge
petit salé salt pork
pieds trotters
pintade guinea fowl
plat-de-côtes short ribs or rib chops
porc pork
pot au feu meat and vegetables in stock
poulet chicken
poussin baby chicken
quenelle poached dumplings made of fish,
    fowl or meat
queue de bœuf oxtail
ris (de veau) sweetbreads (veal)
rognons kidneys
rosbif roast beef
rôti roast
sanglier wild boar
saucisses sausages
saucisson dry sausage, like salami
selle (d'agneau) saddle (of lamb)
steak tartare raw minced beef, often topped
    with a raw egg yolk
suprême de volaille fillet of chicken breast
    and wing
taureau bull's meat
tête (de veau) head (calf's), fatty and usually
    served with a mustardy vinaigrette
tournedos thick round slices of beef fillet
veau veal
venaison venison

Légumes, Herbes, etc.
(Vegetables, herbs, etc.)
ail garlic
aïoli garlic mayonnaise

Wine

One of the pleasures of travelling in France is drinking great wines for a fraction of what you pay at home, and discovering new ones you've never seen in your local shop. Wines labelled AOC (*Appellation d'Origine Contrôlée*) come from a certain defined area and are made from certain varieties of grapes, guaranteeing a standard

algue seaweed
aneth dill
artichaut artichoke
asperges asparagus
avocat avocado
basilic basil
betterave beetroot
blette Swiss chard
cannelle cinnamon
céleri (-rave) celery (celeriac)
cèpes ceps, wild boletus mushrooms
champignons mushrooms
chanterelles wild yellow mushrooms
chicorée curly endive
chou cabbage
chou-fleur cauliflower
choucroute sauerkraut
choux de bruxelles Brussels sprouts
ciboulette chives
citrouille pumpkin
clou de girofle clove
cœur de palmier heart of palm
concombre cucumber
cornichons gherkins
courgettes courgettes (zucchini)
cresson watercress
échalote shallot
endive chicory (endive)
épinards spinach
estragon tarragon
fenouil fennel
fèves broad (fava) beans
flageolets white beans
fleurs de courgette courgette blossoms
frites chips (French fries)
genièvre juniper
gingembre ginger
haricots (rouges, blancs) beans (kidney, white)
haricot verts green (French) beans
jardinière with diced garden vegetables
laitue lettuce
laurier bay leaf
lentilles lentils
maïs (épis de) sweetcorn (on the cob)
marjolaine marjoram
menthe mint
mesclun salad of various leaves

morilles morel mushrooms
moutarde mustard
navet turnip
oignon onion
oseille sorrel
panais parsnip
persil parsley
petits pois peas
piment pimento
pissenlits dandelion greens
poireau leek
pois chiches chickpeas
pois mange-tout sugar peas or mangetout
poivron sweet pepper (capsicum)
pomme de terre potato
potiron pumpkin
primeurs young vegetables
radis radishes
raifort horseradish
riz rice
romarin rosemary
roquette rocket
safran saffron
salade verte green salad
salsifis salsify
sarriette savory
sarrasin buckwheat
sauge sage
seigle rye
serpolet wild thyme
thym thyme

Fruits et Noix (Fruit and Nuts)

abricot apricot
amandes almonds
ananas pineapple
banane banana
bigarreau black cherries
brugnon nectarine
cacahouètes peanuts
cassis blackcurrant
cerise cherry
citron lemon
citron vert lime
coco (noix de) coconut
coing quince
dattes dates

of quality. *Cru* on the label means vintage; a *grand cru* is a great, noble vintage. Descending in the vinous hierarchy are those labelled VDQS (*Vin de Qualité Supérieure*), followed by *Vin de Pays* (guaranteed to originate in a certain region; some are excellent), with *Vin Ordinaire* (or *Vin de Table*) at the bottom, which may not send you to seventh heaven but is usually drinkable and cheap. In a restaurant if you order

figue (de Barbarie) fig (prickly pear)
fraise (des bois) strawberry (wild)
framboise raspberry
fruit de la passion passion fruit
grenade pomegranate
groseille redcurrant
mandarine tangerine
mangue mango
marron chestnut
mirabelle mirabelle plum
mûre (sauvage) mulberry, blackberry
myrtille bilberry
noisette hazelnut
noix walnut
noix de cajou cashew
pamplemousse grapefruit
pastèque watermelon
pêche (blanche) peach (white)
pignons pine nuts
pistache pistachio
poire pear
pomme apple
prune plum
pruneau prune
raisins (secs) grapes (raisins)
reine-claude greengage plum

Desserts

Bavarois mousse or custard in a mould
biscuit biscuit, cracker, cake
bombe ice-cream dessert in a round mould
chausson turnover
clafoutis batter fruit cake
compôte stewed fruit
corbeille de fruits basket of fruit
coulis thick fruit sauce
coupe ice-cream: a scoop or in cup
crème anglaise egg custard
gaufre waffle
génoise rich sponge cake
glace ice-cream
miel honey
œufs à la neige floating island/meringue on a
    bed of custard
pain d'épice gingerbread
sablé shortbread
savarin a filled cake, shaped like a ring

tarte tropézienne sponge cake filled with
    custard and topped with nuts
truffes chocolate truffles

Cooking Terms and Sauces

à point medium steak
bien cuit well-done steak
bleu very rare steak
aigre-doux sweet and sour
aiguillette thin slice
à l'anglaise boiled
à la bordelaise cooked in wine and diced
    vegetables (usually)
à la châtelaine with chestnut purée and
    artichoke hearts
à la diable in spicy mustard sauce
à la grecque cooked in olive oil and lemon
à la jardinière with garden vegetables
à la périgourdine in a truffle and *foie gras*
    sauce
à la provençale cooked with tomatoes, garlic
    and olive oil
allumettes strips of puff pastry
au feu de bois cooked over a wood fire
au four baked
auvergnat with sausage, bacon and cabbage
barquette pastry boat
beignets fritters
béarnaise sauce of egg yolks, shallots and
    white wine
bordelaise red wine, bone marrow and
    shallot sauce
broche roasted on a spit
chaud hot
cru raw
cuit cooked
diable spicy mustard or green pepper sauce
émincé thinly sliced
en croûte cooked in a pastry crust
en papillote baked in buttered paper
épices spices
farci stuffed
feuilleté flaky pastry
flambé set aflame with alcohol
forestière with bacon and mushrooms
fourré stuffed
frit fried

a *rouge* (red), *blanc* (white) or *rosé* (pink), this is what you'll get, either by the glass (*un verre*), by the quarter-litre (*un pichet*) or bottle (*une bouteille*). *Brut* is very dry, *sec* dry, *demi-sec* and *moelleux* sweetish, *doux* sweet, and *méthode champenoise* is sparkling.

If you're buying direct from the producer (or a wine co-operative, or *syndicat*, a group of producers), you'll be offered glasses to taste, each wine older than the previous one

froid cold
fumé smoked
galantine cooked food served in cold jelly
galette flaky pastry case or pancake
garni with vegetables
(au) gratin topped with browned cheese
    and breadcrumbs
haché minced
marmite casserole
médaillon round piece
mornay cheese sauce
pané breaded
pâte pastry, pasta
pâte brisée shortcrust pastry
pâte à chou choux pastry
pâte feuilletée flaky or puff pastry
paupiette rolled and filled thin slices of fish
    or meat
parmentier with potatoes
pavé slab
poché poached
pommes allumettes thin chips (fries)
raclette melted cheese with potatoes, onions
    and pickles
sanglant rare steak
salé salted, spicy
sucré sweet
timbale pie cooked in a dome-shaped
    mould
tranche slice
véronique green grapes, wine and cream
    sauce

Miscellaneous

addition bill (check)
beurre butter
carte menu
confiture jam
couteau knife
crème cream
cuillère spoon
formule à €12 €12 set menu
fourchette fork
fromage cheese
lait milk
menu set menu
nouilles noodles

pain bread
œuf egg
poivre pepper
sel salt
sucre sugar
vinaigre vinegar

Snacks

chips crisps
crêpe thin pancake
croque-madame toasted ham and cheese
    sandwich with fried egg
croque-monsieur toasted ham and cheese
    sandwich
croustade small savoury pastry
frites chips (French fries)
gaufre waffle
pissaladière a kind of pizza with onions,
    anchovies, etc.
sandwich canapé open sandwich

Boissons (Drinks)

bière (pression) beer (draught)
bouteille (demi) bottle (half)
brut very dry
doux sweet (wine)
eau-de-vie brandy
eau potable drinking water
glaçons ice cubes
infusion/tisane herbal tea
jus juice
lait milk
menthe à l'eau peppermint cordial
moelleux semi-dry
mousseux sparkling (wine)
pastis anis liqueur
pichet pitcher
citron pressé/orange pressée fresh
    lemon/orange juice
pression draught
ratafia home-made liqueur made by steeping
    fruit or green walnuts in alcohol or wine
sec dry
sirop d'orange/de citron orange/lemon squash
thé tea
verre glass
vin blanc/rosé/rouge white/rosé/red wine

until you are feeling quite jolly and ready to buy the oldest (and most expensive)
vintage. On the other hand, some sell loose wine *à la* petrol pump, *en vrac*; many caves
even sell the little plastic barrels to put it in.

Travel

05

Getting There

By Air

From the UK and Ireland

The main international airports are in Paris (Roissy-Charles de Gaulle and Orly), Bordeaux, Brest, Grenoble, Lille, Lyon, Marseille, Montpellier, Nantes, Nice, Rennes, Strasbourg and Toulouse. It takes around 50mins to fly from London to Paris, or a mere 90mins to Nice, deep in the south of France. Prices depend on how and when you wish to travel. To be sure of a seat and to save money (especially in the summer and during the Easter holidays), it's well worth shopping around and trying to book ahead.

Airline Carriers

UK and Ireland

Major Carriers

Air France, t 0845 359 1000, *www.airfrance. co.uk*. Regular flights from Heathrow, London City, Birmingham, Edinburgh, Glasgow, Aberdeen, Manchester, Newcastle, Southampton and Bristol to Paris Charles de Gaulle. Also flies from Heathrow to Lyon, Toulouse and Nice; and from Gatwick to Brest, Nantes, Bordeaux and Strasbourg.

British Airways, t 0870 850 9850, *www.ba. com*. Direct flights to Paris from Belfast, Birmingham, Bristol, Edinburgh, Glasgow, London City, Gatwick, Heathrow and Manchester; to Nice from Birmingham, Gatwick, Heathrow and Manchester; to Lyon from Birmingham, Edinburgh, Heathrow and Manchester; and to Bordeaux or Toulouse from Birmingham and Gatwick. From Gatwick you can also fly to Marseille, Montpellier, Nantes and Toulon. Connecting flights to and from smaller UK airports.

British Midland, t 0870 6070 555, *www. flybmi.com*. Flights to Nice from Belfast, Dublin, Edinburgh, Glasgow, Heathrow, Leeds, Manchester and Teesside; flights to Paris Charles de Gaulle from all of above plus Cork; to Toulouse from Aberdeen, Edinburgh, Glasgow and Manchester.

Low-cost Carriers

Aurigny, t (01481) 822 886, *www.aurigny.com*. The Channel Islands airline, with flights to Dinard from Alderney, Bournemouth, Bristol, East Midlands, Guernsey, Jersey, Gatwick, Stansted and Manchester.

Flyglobespan.com, t 08705 561 522, *www. flyglobespan.com*. Flights to Nice from Prestwick, Edinburgh and Glasgow.

bmibaby, t 0870 264 2229, *www.bmibaby.com*. Flights to Paris, Nice and Toulouse from East Midlands Airport, and to Paris and Toulouse from Cardiff.

Flybe, t 08708 890 908, *www.flybe.com*. Flights to Paris from Aberdeen, Bristol, Edinburgh, Glasgow, London City, Heathrow, Manchester and Southampton; to Toulouse from Belfast, Birmingham, Bristol, Edinburgh, Glasgow, Guernsey, Jersey and Southampton; to Bergerac from Guernsey, Jersey and Southampton; and to Bordeaux or Nantes from Gatwick. You can also fly to Chambéry from Southampton.

Lyddair, t (01797) 320 000, *www.lyddair.com*. Daily flights from Lydd Airport in Kent to Le Touquet.

easyJet, t 08717 500 100 , *www.easyjet.com*. Daily flights to Nice from Bristol, Liverpool, Gatwick, Luton and Stansted; to Paris from Liverpool, Luton and Newcastle, and to Lyon from Stansted. You can also fly to Marseille and Toulouse from Gatwick.

Ryanair, t 0905 566 0000 (peak rate help desk), *www.ryanair.com*. Regular flights from Stansted to Bergerac, Biarritz, Brest, Carcassonne, Dinard, La Rochelle, Limoges, Montpellier, Nîmes, Pau, Perpignan, Poitiers, Rodez, St-Etienne and Tours; also from Glasgow, Dublin and Shannon to Paris.

USA and Canada

Major Carriers

Air France, t 800 237 2747, Canada **t** 800 667 2747, *www.airfrance.com*. Regular services to Paris from Atlanta, Boston, Chicago, Cincinnati, Houston, Los Angeles, Miami, New York, Philadelphia, San Francisco and Washington. In Canada, from Montreal (3 daily flights), Toronto (1 daily flight) and Ottawa.

There are a number of **budget airlines** flying from London and an increasing number of UK regional cities such as Birmingham to a volatile variety of France's regional airports. These are usually cheaper booked online, and the earlier the better; fares booked at the last minute are, in fact, not much cheaper than those of the major carriers. Fares are one-way and times can be inconvenient, but there are some real bargains to be had, if you can do without the frills. All services may be less frequent in the winter, and some routes, such as to the Alps, will shut down in summer. Major carriers such as BA have begun to get in on the act too, by offering one-way reservations and online discounts.

Though the likes of Ryanair and easyJet are slightly cheaper, **charter flights** can be good

American Airlines, **t** 800 433 7300, *www.aa. com*. Flights from Boston, Chicago, Dallas, JFK, Miami, San Diego and San Francisco.
British Airways, **t** 800 AIRWAYS or **t** 800 403 0882, *www.britishairways.com*.
Continental, **t** 800 231 0856 , **t** 800 343 9195 (hearing impaired), *www.continental.com*. Flights from Houston and Newark.
Delta, **t** 800 221 1212, **t** 800 831 4488 (hearing impaired), *www.delta.com*. Flights from Atlanta, Boston, Chicago, Cincinnati, Houston, Los Angeles, New York, Philadelphia and San Francisco to Paris.
Northwest Airlines, **t** 800 225 2525 or **t** 800 328 2298 (hearing impaired), *www.nwa.com*. Flights from Detroit to Paris.
Icelandair, **t** 800 223 5500 ext 2 prompt 1, *www.icelandair.com*. Flights to Paris from Baltimore, Boston, Minneapolis, Orlando and Philadelphia, with a stopover in Reykjavik.
United Airlines, **t** 800 864 8331 or **t** 800 323 0170 (hearing impaired), *www.united.com*. Direct flights to Paris from Chicago, Denver, Los Angeles, Miami, Philadelphia, San Francisco and Washington.

Students, Discounts and Special Deals

UK and Ireland
Besides saving 25% on regular flights, young people under 26 have the choice of flying on special discount charters. Students with the relevant ID cards are eligible for considerable reductions, not only on flights but also on trains and admission fees to museums, concerts and more. Agencies specializing in student and youth travel can supply ISIC cards.
STA, Priory House, 6 Wright's Lane, London W8 6TA, *www.statravel.com*, **t** (020) 7361 6100; Bristol, **t** 08701 676 777; Leeds, **t** 0870 168 6878; Manchester, **t** (0161) 839 3253; Oxford, **t** 08701 636 373; Cambridge, **t** (01223) 366 966; and many other branches.
Trailfinders, 215 Kensington High St, London W8 6BD, **t** (020) 7937 1234, *www.trailfinder. com*. Itineraries and discounted flights.
Europe Student Travel, 6 Campden St, London W8, **t** (020) 7727 7647. Kindly travel agency, catering to non-students as well.

USA and Canada
If you're resilient, flexible and/or youthful and prepared to shop around for budget deals on standbys or even courier flights (you can usually only take hand luggage on the latter), you should be able to get yourself some rock-bottom prices. Check out the *Yellow Pages* for courier companies. For discounted flights, try the small ads in newspaper travel pages (e.g. *New York Times, Chicago Tribune, Toronto Globe and Mail*). Numerous travel clubs and agencies also specialize in discount fares, but may require an annual membership fee. Also see the websites at *www.xfares.com* (carry-on luggage only) and *www.smarterliving.com*.
Airhitch, 481 Eighth Avenue, Suite 1771, New York NY 10001-1820, **t** 877 247 4482, *www.airhitch.org*. Last-minute tickets to Europe from around $195.
STA, **t** 800 781 4040, *www.statravel.com*, with branches at most universities and also at 10 Downing St, New York, NY 10014, **t** (212) 627 3111, and ASUC Building, Telegraph at Bancroft Way, 1st Floor, University of California, Berkeley, CA 94720, **t** (510) 642 3000.
TFI, 34 West 32nd St, New York, NY 10001, **t** 800 745 8000, **t** (212) 736 1140, *www. lowestairprice.com*.
Travel Cuts, 187 College St, Toronto, Ontario M5T 1P7, **t** (416) 979 2406, *www.travelcuts. com*. Canada's largest student travel specialists; branches in most provinces.

value, and offer the added advantage of departing from a wider range of regional airports. Companies such as Thomson (*www.thomson.co.uk*), Airtours (*www.airtours.co.uk*) and Unijet (*www.unijet.com*) can offer return flights from as little £80. Check out your local travel agency, the Sunday papers, TV Teletext and websites such as *www.flightline.co.uk, www.cheaponlineflights.com* and *www.charterflights.co.uk*. In London, look in the *Evening Standard* and *Time Out*. Remember, there are no refunds for missed flights – most travel agencies sell insurance so that you don't lose all your money if you become ill.

To get an idea of the lowest fares available you could also take a look on the Internet at the useful sites found at: *www.flightmapping.com, www.cheapflights.co.uk, www.travelocity.co.uk, www.lastminute.com, www.opodo.co.uk*.

From the USA and Canada

There are frequent flights to Paris, the gateway to France, on most of the major airlines. During off-peak periods (the winter months and fall) you should be able to get a scheduled economy flight from New York to Paris from as little as around $320–750, and for an extra $130 or so a transfer to one of the regional airports.

Check the Sunday paper travel sections for the latest deals, and if possible research your fare initially on some of the US cheap-flight websites: *www.priceline.com* (bid for tickets), *www.expedia.com, www.orbitz.com, www.flights.com, www.hotwire.com, www.bestfares.com, www.lowestfare.com, www.onetravel.com, www.travelocity.com, www.travelnow.com, www.eurovacations.com, www.cheaptrips.com, www.courier.org* (courier flights), *www.fool.com/travel/* (advice on booking over the net), *www.ricksteves.com* (travel advice).

It is also possible for North Americans to take advantage of the explosion of budget European flights, by taking a charter flight to London, and booking a London–France flight with a low-cost carrier like Ryanair or easyJet on the airline's website. This will need careful planning: you will be faced with an 8hr flight followed by a 3hr journey across London to a different airport up to 55 miles out of the centre, and another 1½–2hr hop to France; but it can be done, and you may prefer to spend a night or two in London.

By Sea

The ferry is a good option if you're travelling by car or with young children (children of four–15 get reduced rates; under-fours go free), or if you want to nip across the Channel to do some shopping (it takes 50mins from Dover to Calais by Seacat). Fares can be expensive and vary according to season and demand (these days, annoyingly, brochures will only print a rough 'price guide'). The most expensive booking period runs from the first week of July to mid-August; other pricey times

Ferry Operators

Brittany Ferries, Millbay, Plymouth PL1 3EW, t 08703 665 333 , *www.brittany-ferries.com*. Sailings from Portsmouth to Caen (6hrs), Cherbourg (4½–7hrs) and St-Malo (8¾hrs), from Poole to Cherbourg (2¼–4¼hrs), from Plymouth to Roscoff (6hrs), Cherbourg and St Malo, and from Cork to Roscoff (14hrs).

Condor Ferries, Ferry Terminal Building, Weymouth, Dorset DT4 8DX, t (01305) 761551, *www.condorferries.co.uk*. Sails from Poole and Weymouth to St-Malo, and Portsmouth and Poole to Cherbourg in season.

Hoverspeed Ferries, International Hoverport, Dover CT17 9TG, t 0870 240 8070, *www.hoverspeed.co.uk*. Seacats Dover–Calais (35mins) and Newhaven–Dieppe (2hrs).

Norfolkline, Export Freight Plaza,Eastern Dock, Dover CT16 1JA, t (01304) 218 400, *www.norfolkline.com*. An alternative option to consider between Dover and Dunkerque, but for cars only, not foot passengers.

P&O Portsmouth, Peninsular House, Wharf Rd, Portsmouth PO2 8TA, t 08705 20 20 20, *www.poportsmouth.com*. Day and night sailings from Portsmouth to Le Havre (5½–8hrs) and Cherbourg (2¾–9½hrs).

P&O Ferries, Channel House, Channel View Rd, Dover CT17 9TJ, t 08705 20 20 20, *www.poferries.com*. Ferry and superferry from Dover to Calais (75–90mins).

SeaFrance, Eastern Docks, Dover, Kent CT16 1JA, t 08705 711 711, *www.seafrance.com*. Sailings from Dover to Calais (70–90 mins).

Southern Ferries/SNCM, 179 Piccadilly, London W1V 9DB, t (020) 7491 4968, *www.sncm.fr*. Sailings from Marseille/Nice/Toulon to Corsica/Sardinia/Livorno/Genoa/Algeria.

include Easter and the school holidays. Book as far ahead as possible and keep your eyes peeled for special offers. Some good-value five-day mini breaks for a car and up to nine people (Le Havre from £50, for example) are available. **Cheapest Offer Ltd**, t 07092 316 745, www.cheapest-channel-crossing.co.uk, gives concise information about ferry companies and a link to www.ferrysavers.com for best-price comparisons.

Weather forecasts: www.onlineweather.com, www.meteo.fr.

Weather forecast for Dover: t 09061 444 069.
Weather forecast for France: t 09061 444 070 .

By Train

Air prices and the sheer brain-mushing awfulness of airports make travelling by high-speed train an attractive alternative. **Eurostar** (t 08705 186 186, www.eurostar.com) trains leave from London Waterloo or Ashford International, in Kent, and there are direct connections to Paris (Gare du Nord; 2hrs 35mins), Brussels (2hrs 20mins) and Lille (1hr 40mins). Eurostar also goes directly to Disneyland Paris (3hrs); in winter, look out for direct trains to the French Alps, in summer to Avignon. Fares are cheaper if booked at least seven days in advance and you include a Saturday night away; expect to pay £79–240, but check the website for special offers. Check in 20mins before departure, or you will not be allowed on to the train.

When they're not breaking world records, France's legendary TGVs (trains à grande vitesse) zip along at an average speed of 180mph; from Paris there are connections to Avignon, Nice and Montpellier in the south; Limoges, Bordeaux, Biarritz and Lourdes in the southwest; and Reims, Nancy and Strasbourg in the east. The journey from Paris's Gare de Lyon to Marseille takes only 3hrs; to Poitiers 1hrs 25mins; to Avignon 2hrs 40mins; to Montpellier 3hrs 15mins; to Nice 5hrs 35mins. Ticket prices from London range from £150 to

Rail Passes

If you're planning on taking some long train journeys, it may be worth investing in a rail pass available only in your home country.

Available in the UK and Ireland

The excellent-value **Euro Domino** pass entitles EU citizens to unlimited rail travel through France for 3–8 days in a month for £122–306, or £88–173 for 12–25-year-olds.

These days, EU citizens of any age and non-EU citizens who've been resident in Europe for more than six months are all eligible for the **InterRail** pass (currently £219 if you're over 26, or £149 if you're under 26). Passes entitle holders to 22 days' unlimited second-class travel through France, Belgium, Luxembourg and Holland (one zone), plus 50% off travel from Dover to Calais with P&O or Hoverspeed, or returns on Eurostar from £60. InterRail cards are not valid on trains in the UK. Contact Rail Europe, see above.

Available in the USA and Canada

The North American **Eurail** pass allows unlimited first-class travel through 17 European countries for 15-, 21-, 30-, 60- or 90-day periods; it saves the hassle of buying numerous tickets, but will only pay for itself if you use it a lot. It is not valid in the UK, Morocco or countries outside the European Union. Two weeks' travel is $414 for those under 26; those over 26 can get a 15-day pass for $588, a 21-day pass for $762, 30 days for $946 or three months for $1,654.

Other passes for North Americans include the **France Railpass**, which gives four days of unlimited travel throughout the country in a one-month period for $218, or $252 first class (reducing to $186, or $215, per person for two people travelling together). The equivalent **France Youthpass** gives under-26s the same benefits for $164, or $189 first class. All three passes include reduced rates on Eurostar. The **Eurail Selectpass** gives unlimited first-class travel through 3–5 adjoining Eurail countries for 5, 6, 8, 10 and 15 days in a two-month period for $356–794, or $249–556 (second class) if you're under 26. You may also wish to invest in a Paris Museum Pass ($22 for one day), a Bus and Métro Paris Pass ($41 for two days) or a six-day **Rail 'n' Drive** pass giving four days' unlimited rail travel through France and two days' car rental for $215–485. Contact Rail Europe, see above.

Dijon, to £165 to Nice. Another pleasant if slower way of getting deep into France is by overnight sleeper after dinner in Paris.

People under 26 are eligible for a 30 per cent discount on fares (*see* the travel agencies in the box on p.67) and there are discounts if you're 60 or over, available from major travel agencies. Details, advance reservations and car hire information are available at:

Rail Europe, 178 Piccadilly, London W1,
t 08705 848 848, *www.raileurope.co.uk*.
Rail Europe, t 877 257 2887,
www.raileurope.com. Take your passport.

By Coach

Eurolines, part of National Express, has regular coach services from London to over 65 destinations, including Paris, Bordeaux, Chamonix, Grenoble, Perpignan and Strasbourg. If you book a week in advance, return tickets to Paris are as low as £35. The journey to Paris takes around 9hrs, to Avignon 17hrs 30mins, to Marseille 19hrs 30mins, and to Toulouse 20hrs 45mins. There are discounts for anyone under 26, senior citizens, and children under 12; infants under two go free if they're not occupying a seat.

Eurolines, National Express Limited, Ensign Court, 4 Vicarage Road, Edgbaston, Birmingham B15 3ES , t 08705 80 80 80 or t (0121) 455 0086 (hearing impaired), *www.eurolines.co.uk*.

By Car

Putting your car on a **Eurotunnel** train is the most convenient way of crossing the Channel. It takes only 35mins to get through the tunnel from Folkestone to Calais, and there are up to four departures an hour 365 days of the year. In low season, tickets for a car and passengers should cost around £170 return, rising to over £300 return at peak times, or for longer stays. If you travel at night (*10pm–6am*), it will be slightly cheaper. Special-offer day returns (look for them on the website) range from £15 to £50. The price for all tickets is per car less than 6.5m in length, plus the driver and all passengers. Book well in advance for cheaper fares.

Eurotunnel, t 08705 35 35 35,
www.eurotunnel.com.

A fairly comfortable but costly option is to put your car on a Motorail train. Accommodation is compulsory, in a two- or four-berth (1st class) or six-berth (2nd class) carriage. Linen is provided, along with washing facilities and breakfast. Compartments are not segregated by sex. The Motorail services operate from May to September running from Calais to Avignon, Biarritz, Bordeaux, Brive, Narbonne, Nice and Toulouse.

Rail Europe, *see* 'By Train', above.
French Motorail, t 08702 415 415,
www.frenchmotorail.com.

If you prefer a dose of bracing sea air, you've plenty of choice, although changes and mergers may be on the horizon. Short ferry crossings currently include Dover–Calais with P&O, SeaFrance, or Hoverspeed, which offers the fastest crossing, at 35mins. *See* 'By Sea', above, for contact details and information on other routes.

For information on rules and regulations when driving in France, *see* 'Getting Around', pp.69–70.

Entry Formalities

Passports and Visas

Holders of full, valid EU, US, Canadian, Australian and New Zealand passports do not need a visa to enter France for stays of up to three months. If you intend to stay longer, the law says you need a *carte de séjour*, a requirement EU citizens can easily get around as passports are rarely stamped. Non-EU citizens had best apply for an extended visa before leaving home, a complicated procedure requiring proof of income, etc. You can't get a *carte de séjour* without the visa, and obtaining that is a trial run in the *ennui* you'll undergo in applying for a *carte de séjour* at your local *mairie*. For further information contact your nearest French consulate (p.78).

Customs

Those arriving from another EU country do not have to declare goods imported into France for personal use if they have paid duty on them in the country of origin. You are allowed to bring in, duty paid, or take home from France to the UK, up to 800 cigarettes or 400 cigarillos, 200 cigars or 1kg of tobacco;

plus 10 litres of spirits, 90 litres of wine and 110 litres of beer.

Travellers from outside the EU are meant to pay duty on goods worth over €175 which they import into France.

Travellers from the USA are allowed to bring home, duty-free, goods to the value of $800, including 200 cigarettes or 100 cigars; plus 1 litre of alcohol. For more information, telephone the US Customs Service at **t** (202) 354 1000, or see the pamphlet *Know Before You Go* available from *www.customs.gov*. You're not allowed to bring back absinthe or Cuban cigars.

French Customs, *www.douane.gouv.fr*.
UK Customs, *www.hmce.gov.uk*.
US Customs, *www.customs.gov*.

Getting Around

By Air

Air France (in the UK, **t** 0845 359 1000) has a very extensive nationwide network with daily connections to 27 cities from Paris Orly, and another 17 cities from Paris Charles de Gaulle. Show-up-and-fly '*navette*' shuttles leave Orly at frequent intervals: every 30mins for Marseille and Toulouse, every hour for Nice, several times a day for Bordeaux.

Scheduled domestic flights on Corsair, France's second national carrier, can be booked online at *www.corsair.fr*, or by phone (France): **t** 0820 042 042 (€0.12/min). To get the best prices be sure to book at least 14 days in advance and include a Saturday night. Ask about reduced prices for under-26s and over-60s, and discount family fares for anyone who has a husband, wife or children.

By Train

The SNCF's France-wide information number is **t** 08 91 67 68 69 (€0.23/min), or check out *www.sncf.com* (you can book advance tickets from the USA or UK prior to departure on this website, and pay by credit card at an SNCF machine in France).

The SNCF runs a decent and efficient network of trains through all the major cities. If you plan on making only a few long hauls

Rail Discounts (France)

Découverte Séjour If you book a return ticket in advance, depart in a *période bleue* and travel at least 200km and stay away a Saturday night, you get a 25% discount.

Découverte à Deux If up to nine people (related or not) book a return trip together in advance, they are eligible for a 25% discount in first or second class for journeys begun in blue periods.

Découverte Enfant+ This is free, issued in the name of a child aged 4–12, and allows a 25% discount for the child and up to four others on trains departing in a *période bleue* as long as the tickets are booked in advance, subject to limited availability.

Découverte 12–25 Young people are eligible for a 25% discount if they buy their ticket in advance and begin travel in a *période bleue*.

Découverte Senior 25% off the journey for those over 60, travelling in *période bleue*; tickets must be booked in advance.

Carte Enfant+ This is purchased in the name of a child aged 4–12, and allows the child and up to four people who travel with him or her 50% discount on daytime TGVs and night berths on *trains Corail* (subject to limited availablity), plus also 50% discount on seats on daytime *trains Corail*, sleeping cars and TERs departing in a *période bleue* and booked in advance; or 25% when the 50% seats are gone, or when departing in a *période blanche*, or when tickets are purchased on the train.

Carte 12–25 Young people aged 12–25 can purchase this annual card (€43) giving 50% discount on daytime TGVs and night berths on *trains Corail* (subject to limited availability), plus also 50% discount on seats on daytime *trains Corail*, sleeping cars and TERs departing in a *période bleue* and booked in advance; or 25% when the 50% seats are gone, or when departing in a *période blanche*, or when tickets are purchased on the train. This card offers 25% off train journeys from France to 27 countries in Europe, plus other perks.

Carte Senior People over 60 can purchase a senior citizens' card (€45), valid for a year, offering the same discounts as the Carte 12–25, above.

Major Rail Routes

Amsterdam

NETHER-LANDS

London

ENGLAND

Dover

Calais

Boulogne

Dunkerque

Brussels

Lille

Lens

GERMANY

LUX.

English Channel

Dieppe

Amiens

Arras

Cambrai

St-Quentin

Charleville-Mézières

Cherbourg

Le Havre

Rouen

Reims

Thionville

Metz

Channel Is

Granville

Caen

Evreux

Mantes

PARIS

Epernay

St-Dizier

Nancy

Sarrebourg

Brest

Morlaix

St-Brieuc

Alençon

Chartres

Fontainebleau

Sens

Strasbourg

Quimper

Rennes

Châteaudun

Montargis

Epinal

Colmar

Lorient

Vannes

Le Mans

Vendôme

Orléans

Auxerre

Mulhouse

Angers

Blois

Dijon

Vesoul

Belfort

St-Nazaire

NANTES

Tours

Bourges

Nevers

Besançon

SWITZER-LAND

La Roche-sur-Yon

Poitiers

Châteauroux

Montceau-les-Mines

Chalon-sur-Saône

Mâcon

Bourg-en-Bresse

Geneva

La Rochelle

Niort

Vichy

Roanne

Rochefort

Gironde

Royan

Cognac

Limoges

CLERMONT-FERRAND

St-Etienne

LYON

Chambéry

Angoulême

Périgueux

Brive-la-Gaillarde

Grenoble

ITALY

BORDEAUX

Valence

Arcachon

Villeneuve-sur-Lot

Rodez

Montélimar

BIARRITZ

Montauban

Alès

Orange

AVIGNON

NIMES

NICE

MONTE-CARLO

Pau

Tarbes

TOULOUSE

MONTPELLIER

MARSEILLE

Lourdes

NARBONNE

TOULON

SPAIN

PERPIGNAN

N

TGV rail network

100 km

50 miles

the Euro Domino or France Railpass (*see* 'Rail Passes', p.65) will save you money. Other possible discounts hinge on the exact time of your departure. For ordinary trains (excluding TGVs and *couchettes*), SNCF has divided the year into blue (off-peak) and white (peak) periods, which are described in little calendars given out by all stations. Various discounts and travel cards are available, *see* box. *Découverte* discounts are free; the *cartes* must be paid for. Ask about extra perks with the *cartes*, such as Avis car hire, hotel discounts, and discounts on Corsica ferries.

Tickets must be stamped in the little orange machines by the entrance to the lines that say *Compostez votre billet* (this puts the date on the ticket, to keep you from using the same one over and over again). Any time you interrupt a journey until another day, you have to re-compost your ticket. Long-distance trains (*trains Corail*) have snack trolleys and bar-cafeteria cars.

By Coach

There is no national bus network. Though local services can work out, do not count on seeing any part of rural France by public transport. The bus network is just about adequate between major cities and towns (places often already well served by rail), but can be rotten in rural areas – where the one bus a day fits the school schedule, leaving at the crack of dawn and returning in the afternoon. More remote villages are linked to civilization only once a week.

Buses are run either by the SNCF (replacing discontinued rail routes) or private firms. Rail passes are valid on SNCF lines, and buses generally coincide with trains. Private bus firms, especially when they have a monopoly, tend to be more expensive than trains. Some towns have a *gare routière* (coach station), usually near the train station, though many lines start from anywhere in town.

By Car

Unless you plan to stick to the major cities or the coast, a car is the only way to see some of the remoter parts of France. This has its drawbacks: expensive petrol and car hire rates, and an accident rate double that of the UK (and much higher than in the USA).

Roads are generally excellentely maintained, but anything less than a departmental route (D road) may be uncomfortably narrow. Mountain roads are reasonable except in the vertical *département* of Alpes-Maritimes, where they inevitably follow old mule tracks. Conditions vary widely: in rural Languedoc you may catch up on your sleep while you drive; traffic in the Côte d'Azur, the 'California of Europe', can be diabolically Californian, and parking a nightmare; in Paris, parking is forbidden in many streets in the centre. Many towns now have pricey guarded car parks underneath their very heart, spectacularly so in Nice. Everywhere else, the blue 'P' signs infallibly direct you to a village or town's already full car park.

Car hire in France can be an expensive proposition. To save money, look into air and holiday package deals as well as combination 'Train and Auto' rates (*see* 'Rail Passes', p.65).

Car Hire

UK and Ireland

Avis, t 08700 100 287, *www.avis.co.uk*.
Budget, t 08701 56 56 56, *www.budget.com*.
easyCar, *www.easycar.com*.
Europcar, t 0870 607 5000,
  www.europcar.com.
Hertz, t 08708 44 88 44, *www.hertz.co.uk*.
Thrifty, t (01494) 751 600, *www.thrifty.co.uk*.

USA and Canada

Auto Europe, 39 Commercial St, PO Box 7006, Portland, ME 04112, t 1 888 223 5555 , t (207) 842 2000, *www.autoeurope.com*.
Auto France, PO Box 760, 211 Shadyside Rd, Ramsey, NJ 07446, t 800 572 9655, *www. auto-france.com*.
Avis Rent a Car, t 800 230 4898 (USA), t 800 272 5871 (Canada), t 800 331 2323 (hearing impaired), *www.avis.com*.
Europe by Car, t 800 223 1516 (nationwide), t (212) 581 3040 (NY), *www.europebycar.com*.
Europcar, t 877 940 69 00, *www.europcar.com*.
Hertz, t 800 654 3131, t 800 654 3001 (international), t 800 654 2280 (hearing impaired), t 800 263 0600 (Canada), t 800 654 2260 (hearing impaired), *www.hertz.com*.

Prices vary widely from firm to firm: beware the small print about service charges and taxes. The minimum age for hiring a car in France is around 21 to 25, and the maximum around 70.

Rules and Regulations

You will need your vehicle registration document, full driving licence and an up-to-date insurance certificate. Green cards are no longer compulsory, but are worth getting as they give fully comprehensive cover – your home insurance may only provide minimum cover. If you're coming from the UK or Ireland, you'll need headlight converters to adjust the dip of the headlights to the right. Carrying a warning triangle is mandatory if you don't have hazard lights, and advisable even if you do. In the mountains you may need to buy (or hire from a garage) snow chains. Drivers with a valid licence from an EU country, Canada, the USA or Australia do not need to have an international driving licence.

France has over 8,000km of motorways and most of these are privately run toll roads or *autoroutes à péage* which can be paid for by cash or credit card. Speed limits are 130km/80mph (110km/h in wet weather) on the *autoroutes* (toll motorways); 110km/69mph on dual carriageways (divided highways and motorways without tolls); 90km/55mph on other roads; 50km/30mph in an 'urbanized area'. Fines for speeding, payable on the spot, begin at €135 and can reach an astronomical €4,500 if you fail the breathalyser.

If you wind up in an accident, the procedure is to fill out and sign a *constat amiable*. If your French isn't sufficient to deal with this, hold off until you find someone to translate for you. If you break down and are a member of a motoring club affiliated with the Touring Club de France, ring the latter; if not, ring the police.

The French have one delightfully civilized custom of the road: if oncoming drivers unaccountably flash their headlights at you, it means that the *gendarmes* are lurking.

France used to have a rule of giving priority to the right at every intersection. This has somewhat disappeared, although there may still be intersections, usually in towns, where it applies – these will be marked. Watch out for the *Cédez le passage* (Give way) signs and be careful. Generally, as you'd expect, give priority to the main road, and to the left on roundabouts. Watch out for Byzantine street-parking rules (be especially careful about village centres on market days). When you (inevitably) get lost in a town or city, the *Toutes directions* or *Autres directions* signs are like Get Out of Jail Free cards. Watch out for the tiny signs indicating which streets are meant for pedestrians only.

Petrol (*essence*) at the time of writing is €1.02 a litre for unleaded, €1.09 a litre leaded, €0.77 for diesel (*gasoil*), but varies considerably, with motorways always more expensive. Petrol stations keep shop hours (most close Sunday and/or Monday) and are rare in rural areas, so consider your fuel supply while planning any forays. If you come across a garage with petrol-pump attendants, they will expect a tip for oil, windscreen-cleaning or air.

Europ Assistance, Sussex House, Perrymount Rd, Haywards Heath, West Sussex RH16 1DN, t 0870 737 5720, *www.europ-assistance.co.uk*. Help with car insurance for abroad.

Useful Websites

Mappy, route planner: *www.iti.fr*.
Autoroute information: *www.route.equipement.gouv.fr*, *www.equipement.gouv.fr*.
Roads and traffic information: *www.autoroutes.fr, www.asf.fr, www.saprr.fr*.

By Bicycle

Cycling signals more pain than pleasure in most French minds. That said, one of the hazards of driving in the Alps and Pyrenees is suddenly coming upon bands of cyclists pumping up the kinds of inclines that most people require escalators for. If you mean to cycle in the south during the summer, start early and stop early to avoid heatstroke. French drivers, not always courteous to fellow motorists, usually give cyclists a wide berth; and yet, on any given summer day, half the patients in a French hospital are from accidents on two-wheeled transport. Consider a helmet. Also be aware that bike thefts are fairly common, so make sure your insurance covers your bike or the one you hire.

Getting your own bike to France from the UK and Ireland is fairly easy: Air France, British Airways and some of the ferry operators will carry them free. From the USA or Australia most airlines will carry them as long as they're boxed and are included in your total baggage weight. In all cases, telephone ahead. Certain French trains (called *autotrains*, with a bicycle symbol in the timetable) carry bikes free; otherwise you have to send it as registered luggage, and pay a €49 fee, with delivery 'guaranteed' within 48 hours. Delays are common, however.

You can hire bikes of varying quality at most SNCF stations and in major towns. The advantage of hiring from a station means that you can drop it off at another, as long as you specify where when you hire it. Rates run at around €7.5 a day, with a deposit of €45–60 or a credit card number. Private firms hire mountain bikes (VTTs or *vélos tout terrain*) and racing bikes. There are cycling paths and shelters in most French towns, and cycle hire points in some car parks. Those aged between 14 and 16 need to pass a road safety test before they can ride a moped up to 50cc.

For more information on cycle touring abroad contact:

Cyclists' Touring Club, Cotterell House, 69 Meadrow, Godalming, Surrey GU7 3HS, **t** 0870 873 0060, *www.ctc.org.uk*.

Fédération Française des Usagers de la Bicyclette, 7 rue Sédillot, 67000 Strasbourg, **t** 03 88 75 71 90, *www.fubicy.org*.

On Foot

A massive 40,000km network of long-distance paths, or Sentiers de Grandes Randonnées, **GRs** for short (marked by distinctive red and white signs), takes in some of France's most spectacular scenery.

Each GR is described in a *Topoguide*, with maps and details about campsites, refuges and so on, available in area bookshops or from the **Fédération Française de la Randonnée Pédestre,** 14 Rue Riquet, 75019 Paris, **t** 01 44 89 93 93, *www.ffrp.asso.fr*. The complete set, plus English translations covering GRs in Alsace and Provence, is available from **Stanfords,** 12–14 Long Acre, London WC2, **t** (020) 7836 1321, *www.stanfords.co.uk*. Otherwise, the best maps for local excursions, based on ordnance surveys, are put out by the Institut Géographique National (1:50,000 or 1:100,000).

Of special interest are: GR5 from Holland to Nice; GR3 following the entire length of the Loire; GR65, the Chemin de St-Jacques, from Le Puy-en-Velay to Santiago de Compostela (in Spain); GR52 from Menton up to Sospel, the Vallée des Merveilles to St-Dalmas-Valdeblore (in the Provençal Alps); GR52a and GR5 through Mercantour National Park (*both of which are only open end of June–beginning Oct*); GR51, nicknamed 'the balcony of the Côte d'Azur', from Castellar (near Menton), taking in the Esterel and Maures before ending at Bormes-les-Mimosas; GR9, beginning in St-Tropez and crossing over the region's most famous mountains – Ste-Baume, Ste-Victoire, the Luberon and Ventoux; GR4, which crosses the Dentelles de Montmirail and Mont Ventoux en route to Grasse; and GR42, which descends the west bank of the Rhône from near Bagnols-sur-Cèze to Beaucaire.

For a description in French of the *Sentier Cathare* (which is well marked and well endowed with places to eat and stay en route) via the famous Cathar citadels of Padern, Peyrepertuse and Puilaurens to Montségur, *see* Louis Salavy's excellent *Le Sentier Cathare*.

For other walks in the Pyrenees you could also consult the excellent *Randonnées Pyrénéennes* by J. L. Sarret.

By Boat

France has around 8,000km of navigable waterways; travelling along the network of rivers and canals at an average speed of 6km/h can be the best of all ways of getting to the heart of some ravishing French countryside (especially in the south). The main barging areas are in Brittany, Anjou (the beautiful Canal de Nantes à Brest), Burgundy, Nivernais and Franche-Comté in central France (you can riverbathe and fish, and cross the Loire via Eiffel's aqueduct at Briare); Alsace and the Ardennes in the east; Charentes and Périgord in the southwest; and the Lot et Garonne, Camargue and Midi in the south (where the Canal du Midi takes you past the 549m aqueduct at Agen and the towers of Carcassonne). It's possible, though complicated, to get by water from the Channel to the Mediterranean, via Le Havre, Paris, Burgundy and the Camargue.

Yacht, motorboat and sailing-boat charters are big business (France has the longest coastline – nearly 2,000 miles – of any European country). Companies hire boats out by the hour or day, or, in the case of yachts, by the week or fortnight. The average cost per week for a 16m yacht that sleeps six, including food, drink and all expenses, is about what six people would pay for a week in a luxury hotel. If things are slow you may barter the price down. For a 20m crewed yacht, you would be looking at paying a cool $25,000 for a week.

Contact individual tourist offices for boat-hire companies in their area. For a full list of companies contact the **Syndicat National des Loueurs de Bateaux de Plaisance,** Port de la Bourdonnais, 75007 Paris, **t** 01 45 55 10 49. For crewed yachts try **Camper & Nicholsons,** 25 Bruton St, London W1J 6QH, **t** (020) 7491 2950, *www.cnconnect.com*. For canal boats and barges, contact **Locaboat Plaisance,** Port au Bois, B.P. 150, 89303 Joigny Cedex, **t** 03 86 91 72 72, *www.locaboat.com*.

Special-interest Holidays

For a complete list of tour operators, see the Maison de France website, *www.franceguide.com* or the US website at *www.francetourism.com*, or get in touch with a tourist office. Other sources of information are **The French Centre**, 164–168 Westminster Bridge Rd, London SE1 7RW, **t** (020) 7960 26 00, *www.cei-frenchcentre.com*, or the **Cultural Services of the French Embassy**, 23 Cromwell Rd, London SW7 2EL, **t** (020) 7073 1300, *www.ambafrance-uk.org*, or at 972 Fifth Avenue, New York, NY 10021, **t** (212) 439 1400, *www.info-france-usa.org*. Check out *www.fr-holidaystore.co.uk*, *www.aito.co.uk* or *www. holidayfrance.org.uk*.

France

Atelier du Safranier, 2 bis Rue du Cannet, 06600 Vieil Antibes, **t** 04 93 34 53 72, *www.chez.com/ateliersafranier/*. Year-round courses in painting, engraving, lithography.

Champagne Air Show, 9 Rue Thiers, 51100 Reims, **t** 03 26 87 89 19, *www.champagne-connection.com*. Deluxe ballooning trips in Champagne, Alsace, Chantilly and the Bourgogne and the Loire; also vintage car and helicopter tours.

Ecole du Moulin, Restaurant L'Amandier, Mougins 06250, **t** 04 93 75 78 24, *www.moulin-mougins.com*. Year-round week-long Cuisine du Soleil cookery courses.

Ecole Ritz Escoffier, 15 Place Vendôme, 75041 Paris Cedex, **t** 01 43 16 30 50, *www.ritzparis.com*. Cookery courses at the Ritz.

Fédération Nationale Ânes et Randonnées, 16 Route de Canlers, 62310 Ruisseauville, **t** 03 21 41 21 97, *www.ane-et-rando.com*. Treks available throughout France.

Institut de Paléontologie Humaine, M. Henry de Lumley, 1 Rue René Panhard, 75013 Paris, **t** 01 43 31 62 91. Palaeontology students or fans can spend a minimum of 15 or 30 days excavating caves in southeast France.

Vedel – Cuisine et Tradition School of Provençal Cuisine, 30 Rue Pierre Euzeby, 13200 Arles, **t** 04 90 49 69 20, *www.cuisineprovencale.com*. Courses in Provençal cuisine.

Language

Alliance Française, 2 Rue Paris, 06000 Nice, **t** 04 93 62 67 66, *www.alliance-francaise-nice.com*. French classes at all levels. Courses last a month but they will tailor.

Accord, 4, Bd Poissonnière, 75009 Paris, **t** 01 55 33 52 33, *www.accord-langues.com*. Year-round intensive language courses.

Centre International d'Etude des Langues, Rue du Gué Fleuri, B.P. 35, 29480 Le Relecq-Kerhuon, **t** 02 98 30 57 57, *www.ciel.fr*. Language courses in Brittany, accommodation provided.

Cercle d'Echanges Interculturels et Linguistiques Avignon 16 Impasse Jean-Pierre Gras, 84000 Avignon, **t** 04 32 76 39 94, *www.avignon-et-provence.com/ceila/*.

Eurocentres Foundation, 56 Eccleston Square , London SW1V 1PQ, **t** (020) 7834 4155; in the US **t** (703) 684 1494, *www.eurocentres.com*. Non-profit organization: intensive general and business French in professionally equipped centres.

UK and Ireland

Abercrombie & Kent, St George's House, Ambrose Street, Cheltenham, Glos GL50 3LG, **t** 0845 070 0610, *www.abercrombiekent.co.uk*. Quality city breaks. Also barges and houseboats.

Allez France, 27 West St, Storrington, West Sussex RH20 4DZ, **t** 0870 160 5743, *www.allezfrance.com*. Apartment holidays and Center Parcs cottages, self-catering houses, short breaks, and hotel touring.

Alternative Travel Group, 69–71 Banbury Rd, Oxford OX2 6PJ, **t** (01865) 315 678, *www.atg-oxford.co.uk*. Walking and cycling holidays.

Andante Travels, The Old Barn, Old Road, Alderbury, Salisbury, Wilts SP5 3AR, **t** (01722) 713 800, *www.andantetravels.co.uk*. Guided archaeological tours.

Arblaster & Clarke, Clarke House, Farnham Rd, West Liss, GU33 6JQ, **t** (01730) 893 344, *www.arblasterandclarke.com*. Escorted wine tours of major wine regions: Alsace, Burgundy, Loire, Champagne-Ardennes, Languedoc-Roussillon, Provence, Rhône-Alps, Corsica.

Chalfont Line Ltd, 4 Providence Rd, West Drayton, Middlesex UB7 8HJ, **t** (01895) 459 540, *www.chalfont-line.co.uk*. Holidays for the slow walker and wheelchair-user.

Crown Blue Line, The Port House, Port Solent, Portsmouth, Hants PO6 4TH, **t** 0870 160

5630, *www.crownblueline.com*. Cruise down the canals of France.

French Country Cruises, 29a Main Street, Lyddington, Oakham, Rutland LE15 9LR, t (01572) 821 330, *www.andrewbrocktravel. co.uk*. Canal and river cruises.

Headwater Holidays, The Old School House, Chester Road, Castle, Northwich, Cheshire, CW8 1LE, t (01606) 720 099, *www.head water.com*. Accompanied and independent cycling, walking, canoeing and rafting.

Holts Tours Ltd, The Old Plough, High Street, Eastry, Sandwich, Kent CT13 0HF, t (01304) 612 248, *www.battletours.co.uk*. Battlefield tours guided by military historians.

InnTravel, Hovingham, York YO62 4JZ, t (01653) 629 000, *www.inntravel.co.uk*. Walking, skiing and cycling holidays.

J.M.B. Travel, Suite Four, High Tree House, 4 Cromwell Road, Powick, Worcester WR2 4QJ, t (01905) 830 099, *www.jmb-travel.co. uk*. Opera and music festivals.

Kirker Holidays, 3 New Concordia Wharf, Mill St, London SE1 2BB, t (020) 7231 3333, *www. kirkerholidays.com*. Tailor-made itineraries and packages.

Martin Randall, Voysey House, Barley Mow Passage, London W4 4GF, t (020) 8742 3355, *www.martinrandall.com*. Lecturer-accompanied cultural tours.

Page & Moy, 136–40 London Rd, Leicester LE2 1EN, t 08700 106 212, *www.page-moy. com*. City breaks, river cruises and cultural tours throughout France.

Prospect Music and Art Tours, 36 Manchester Street, London W1U 7LH, t (020) 7486 5704, *www.prospecttours.com*. Cultural breaks and cruises throughout France.

Sherpa Expeditions, 131a Heston Rd, Hounslow, Middlesex TW5 0RF, t (020) 8577 2717, *www.sherpa-walking-holidays.co.uk*. Walks, cycling and treks.

Susi Madron's Cycling for Softies, 2–4 Birch Polygon, Rusholme, Manchester M14 5HX, t (0161) 248 8282, *www.cycling-for-softies. co.uk*. Easy cycling.

Language

Euro Academy, 67–71 Lewisham High Street, London SE13 5JX, t (020) 8297 0505, *www. euroacademy.co.uk*. French courses with activities or sports options.

Languages Abroad (C.E.S.A.), CESA House, Pennance Road, Lanner, Cornwall TR16 5TQ, t (01209) 211 800, *www.cesalanguages.com*. Language courses in group classes, with accommodation in college residences or with host families.

USA and Canada

Abercrombie & Kent, 1520 Kensington Rd, Oak Brook, IL 60523-2156, t 800 554 7016, t (630) 954 2944, *www.abercrombiekent.com*. Quality city and country breaks throughout France. Barges and river cruises.

Adventure Sport Holidays, 815 North Rd, Westfield, MA 01085, t 800 628 9655, t (413) 568 2855, *www.advonskis.com*. Skiing, biking, hiking, mountaineering, canal-barging and mountain biking throughout France.

Archaeological Tours, 271 Madison Avenue Suite 904, New York, NY 10016, t (866) 740 5130, *www.archaeologicaltrs.com*. Caves, castles and megaliths in the Pyrenees and Brittany.

Art Horizons, 330 W. 58th St, Suite 608, New York, NY 10019, t (212) 969 9410, *www. art-horizons.com*. Art and history tours.

Backroads, 801 Cedar St, Berkeley, CA 94701-1800, t 800 462 2848, *www.backroads.com*. Bicycling, hiking and multisport holidays in Burgundy, the Loire Valley, Dordogne, Brittany, Normandy, Provence, etc.

The Barge Connection, 12036 Nevada City Highway, #311, Grass Valley, California 95945, t 888 550 8580 or t (530) 274 0764, *www. bargeconnection.com*. Luxury hotel or self-pilot barges, plus themed holidays – walking, biking, golfing, or wine-tasting.

The Bombard Society, 333 Pershing Way, West Palm Beach, FL 33401, t 800 862 8537, t (561) 837 6610, *www.bombardsociety.com*. Five-day luxury ballooning 'adventures' in Burgundy and the Loire.

Breakaway Adventures, 1312 18th Street NW, Suite 401, Washington, DC 20036, t 800 567 6286, *www.breakaway-adventures.com*. Self-guided walking and cycling trips staying in small country inns, with full vehicle support; destinations include Provence, the Dordogne, the Loire and Burgundy.

Brooks Country Cycling Tours, PO Box 20792 New York NY 10025, t (212) 874 5151, *www.brookscountrycycling.com*. Guided cycling tours in Brittany, Normandy, the Dordogne and the Loire Valley.

CBT Tours, 2506 N. Clark St #150, Chicago, IL 60614, t 800 736 2453, t (773) 871 5510, *www.cbttours.com*. Hiking, biking, mountain biking and skiing tours for all abilities.

Country Walkers, PO Box 180, Waterbury, VT 05676, t 800 464 9255, t (802) 244 1387, *www.countrywalkers.com*. Walking holidays during the summer, in the Pyrenees, Dordogne and Provence, led by expert local guides.

Cross Country International, PO Box 1170, Millbrook, NY 12545, t 800 828 8768, *www.equestrianvacations.com*. Horse-riding in Provence, the Dordogne, Bordeaux, the Loire and the Camargue.

Dailey Thorp Travel, PO Box 670, Big Horn, Wyoming 82833, t (307) 673 1555 or t 800 998 4677, *www.daileythorp.com*. Luxury escorted tours to opera and music festivals.

DuVine Adventures, 124 Holland Street, Suite 2, Somerville, MA 02144, t 888 396 5383, t (617) 776 4441, *www.duvine.com*. Bicycling tours through French vineyards: Burgundy, Provence, the Loire, Bordeaux, and following the Tour de France.

Elderhostel, 11 Avenue de Lafayette, Boston, MA 02111-1746, t 877 426 8056 or from outside US and Canada t 978 323 4141, *www.elderhostel.org*. Courses in art, history, language, music, wine, etc. for older adults.

Elegant Cruises and Tours, 24 Vanderventer Ave, Port Washington, NY 11050, t 800 683 6767, t (516) 767 9302, *www.elegantcruises. com*. River cruises on the Rhône and Seine, plus barges.

Elite Golf Tours, PO Box 1091, Commack, NY 11725 1091, t 800 711 8089, t (631) 462 1946, *www.elitegolftours.com*. Luxury golf tours.

Europe Train Tours, 2485 Jennings Road, Olin, NC 28660, t 800 551 2085 or t (704) 876 9081, *www.etttours.com*. Escorted tours by train and car in Provence and the Riviera.

Expo Garden Tours, 33 Fox Crossing, Litchfield, CT 06759, t 860 567 0322, *www.expogarden tours.com*. Fully escorted tours.

French Country Waterways, PO Box 2195, Duxbury, MA 02331, t 800 222 1236, t (781) 934 2454, *www.fcwl.com*. Hotel barges in Alsace, Burgundy, Champagne and the Loire.

Historic Tours, 1281 Paterson Plank Road, Secaucus, New Jersey 07094, t 877 992 8687, *www.ww2tours.com*. Second World War veterans' tours.

La Varenne, PO Box 25574, Washington, DC 20007, t 800 537 6486, *www.lavarenne. com*. Cookery school in a château in Burgundy.

Lindenmeyr Travel, 19 E. 37th St, New York, NY 10016, t 800 248 2807, t (212) 725 2807, *www.lindenmeyrtravel.com*. Ski vacations staying in family-run hotels and inns.

Maupintour, 10650 W. Charleston Blvd. Summerlin, NV 89135, t 800 255 4266, *www.maupintour.com*. Barge cruises and escorted tours.

New Frontiers, 5757 West Century Blvd, Suite 650, Los Angeles, CA 90045, t 800 677 0720, t (310) 670 7318, *www.newfrontiers.com*. Hotels, flights, entertainment and car hire.

Ski Europe, 1535 W. Loop St, Suite 319, Houston, TX 77027, t 800 333 5533, t (713) 960 0900, *www.ski-europe.com*. Group tours to the French Alps.

Snow Tours, 1281 Paterson Plank Rd, Secaucus, NJ 07094, t 800 222 1170, t (201) 348 2244, *www.snowtour.com*. Organized by ski professionals, and staying in quality hotels.

Sportstours, PO Box 457, New York, NY 10185-0457, t 800 879 8647, t (772) 335 4855, *www.sportstours.com*. Racing, tennis, Formula One, Tour de France, etc.

Walking Softly Adventures, PO Box 86250, Portland, OR 97286, t 888 743 0723, t (503) 788 9017, *www.wsadventures.com*. Wildflowers, glaciers and canyon-walking.

Language

Accent, 870 Market St, Suite 1026, San Francisco, CA 94102, t 800 869 9291, *www.accentintl.com*. Semester/year-long programmes at the Sorbonne for all abilities.

International Studies Abroad, 901 West 24th Street, Austin, TX 78705, t 800 580 8826, t (512) 480 8522, *www.studiesabroad.com*. Courses in Paris.

National Registration Centre for Study Abroad, 207 E. Buffalo St, Suite 610, PO Box 1393, Milwaukee, WI 53201, t (414) 278 0631 or t (414) 278 7410, *www.nrcsa.com*. Language and culture courses.

Practical A–Z

06

Children

France is a very child-friendly country, and there are few places – mostly very hoity-toity bars and restaurants – where children aren't welcome. Under-fours travel for free on the trains and most buses, and four- to eleven-year-olds go for half-price; long-distance trains often have a special play area.

Hotels will put a cot (child's bed) in a room for a small fee, and family-orientated ones often provide an array of special activities, watersports and baby-sitting services. Most restaurants offer a low-cost *menu enfant* with kid-pleasing dishes (invariably including *frites*), although high chairs are still rare outside family resort areas.

Although all baby supplies are available in supermarkets and pharmacies, you may want to bring powdered formulas and prepared foods along if exact matches are important to you (or the pipsqueak).

Climate and When to Go

France has a full deck of climates. Continental cold winters and hot summers prevail in the east and centre; the north is as changeable as Britain, while the west is tempered and wettened by the Atlantic. Provence, Languedoc and Corsica have a Mediterranean climate, cooled by the mistral and other winds. The Pyrenees get more rain than most places on the planet – nearly 7ft a year – while the Camargue gets the least in France. In an average year, it rains as much in Nice as in Brest, and more in Marseille than Paris, but in Provence it tends to come down all at once, especially in the autumn.

France is the world's top tourist destination, and avoiding the crowds can be a prime consideration when deciding when you go. The Easter school break in April and the months of July and August are the busiest, when temperatures and prices soar, tempers

Average Daily High Temperatures in °C (°F)

	Jan	Feb	Mar	April	May	June	July	Aug	Sept	Oct	Nov	Dec
Ajaccio (Corsica)	13 (55)	14 (56)	15 (59)	17 (63)	20 (70)	24 (75)	27 (81)	27 (81)	25 (77)	21 (70)	17 (63)	14 (56)
Biarritz	13 (55)	14 (56)	16 (61)	18 (64)	21 (70)	25 (77)	28 (82)	27 (81)	26 (79)	24 (75)	19 (66)	13 (55)
Grenoble	3 (37)	3 (37)	8 (45)	14 (56)	16 (61)	22 (71)	27 (81)	26 (79)	22 (71)	16 (61)	11 (51)	6 (42)
La Rochelle	10 (50)	9 (48)	12 (54)	18 (64)	16 (61)	22 (71)	25 (77)	25 (77)	22 (71)	18 (64)	14 (56)	10 (50)
Lyon	7 (44)	6 (42)	11 (51)	16 (61)	17 (63)	25 (77)	27 (81)	27 (81)	24 (75)	17 (63)	10 (50)	8 (45)
Nice	12 (54)	12 (54)	14 (56)	18 (64)	21 (70)	26 (79)	27 (81)	28 (82)	25 (77)	22 (71)	16 (61)	14(56)
Paris	7 (44)	7 (44)	10 (50)	16 (61)	17 (63)	24 (75)	25 (77)	26 (79)	21 (70)	17 (63)	12 (54)	8 (45)
Périgueux	10 (50)	12 (54)	14 (56)	17 (63)	19 (66)	23 (73)	25 (77)	26 (79)	22 (71)	18 (64)	15 (59)	12 (54)
Rennes	9 (48)	9 (48)	11 (51)	17 (63)	16 (61)	23 (73)	25 (77)	24 (75)	21 (70)	16 (61)	12 (54)	9 (48)
Strasbourg	5 (41)	5 (41)	9 (48)	13 (55)	16 (61)	23 (73)	24 (75)	26 (79)	21 (70)	15 (59)	8 (45)	4(39)

flare, and weekend traffic is abominable, but it's also the season of the great festivals.

From December to March most of the tourists are in the mountains; in February the mimosa and almonds bloom on the Côte d'Azur. By April and May you can sit outside at restaurants in most places and start to swim in the Med. June is usually warm and a relatively quiet month, and the beginning of the walking season in the mountains. In August, the cities empty out except for tourists; shops and restaurants close, while getting any kind of room on the coast can be impossible if you haven't booked well ahead.

Once French school holidays end in early September, prices and crowds decrease with the temperature. In October the weather is often mild on the coast, although torrential downpours and floods are not unknown; the first snows fall in the Pyrenees and Alps. November is generally a bad month to visit: it rains, and many museums, hotels and restaurants close down.

For day-to-day information, see the comprehensive Météo France website at *www.meteo.fr.*

Crime and the Police

France is a safe and very policed country, but it's important to be aware that thieves target visitors, especially their holiday homes and cars – they see foreign numberplates or a rental car as easy pickings. Leave anything you'd really miss at home, carry travellers' cheques, insure your property, and be especially careful in large cities or on the Côte d'Azur. Report thefts to the nearest *gendarmerie* or *police nationale* – it's not a pleasant task but the reward is the bit of paper you need for an insurance claim. If your passport is stolen, contact the police and your nearest consulate for emergency travel documents. Carry photocopies of your passport, driver's licence, etc. – it makes it easier when reporting a loss.

By law, the police in France can stop anyone anywhere and demand to see ID; in practice, they tend to do it only to harass minorities, the homeless and the scruffy (the Paris police are notorious for this). The drug situation is the same in France as anywhere in Western Europe: soft and hard drugs are widely available, and the police only make an issue of victimless crime when it suits them – being a foreigner may be reason enough, and there is little that your consulate can or will do.

Disabled Travellers

When it comes to providing access for all, France is not exactly in the vanguard of nations, but things are beginning to change. The SNCF, for instance, now publishes a pamphlet, *Mémento du voyageur à mobilité réduite*, covering travel by train for the disabled – contact the French Railways office in your country for details, or in France **t** 08 00 15 47 53. All TGVs are equipped and, on non-TGV trains, if in a wheelchair, you can use the designated areas in first-class carriages, even if you have a second-class ticket – provided you book in advance. The Channel Tunnel is a good way to travel by car since disabled passengers are allowed to stay in their vehicle. By train, Eurostar gives wheelchair passengers firstclass travel for second-class fares. Most ferry companies will offer facilities if contacted beforehand. Vehicles fitted to accommodate transport for disabled people pay reduced tolls on *autoroutes*. An *autoroute* guide for disabled travellers is available free from the **Ministère des Transports**, Grande Arche, Paroi Sud, 92055 La Défense Cedex, Paris, **t** 01 40 81 21 22, *www.transports. equipement.gouv.fr*. The *Gîtes accessibles aux personnes handicapées*, published by Gîtes de France, lists self-catering possibilities (*see* p.88 for their address). Other useful contacts:

Access Ability, *www.access-ability.co.uk*. Information on travel agencies catering specifically to disabled people.

Access-Able Travel Source, *www.access-able. com*. Web-based database of information, travel operators, cruise lines, hotels, equipment hire, etc. for the disabled traveller.

Access Travel, 6 The Hillock, Astley, Lancashire M29 7GW, **t** (01942) 888 844, *www.access-travel.co.uk*. Travel agent for disabled people: special air fares, car hire and wheelchair-accessible *gîtes* in Calais, Normandy, Champagne and the Loire.

Association des Paralysés de France, Siège National, 17 Bd Auguste Blanqui, 75013 Paris,

t 01 40 78 69 00, *www.apf.asso.fr*. A national
organization with an office in each *département*, with in-depth local information;
headquarters are in Paris.

**Australian Council for Rehabilitation of the
Disabled** (ACRODS), PO Box 60, Curtin, ACT
2605, Australia, t (02) 6283 3200, t (TTY) (02)
6282 4333, *www.acrod.org.au*. Information
and contact numbers for specialist travel
agencies.

**Comité National Français de Liaison pour la
Réadaptation des Handicapés**, 236B Rue
Tolbiac, 75013 Paris, t 01 53 80 66 66. Provides
information on access, and produces useful
guides to various regions in France.

Emerging Horizons, *www.emerging
horizons.com*. International online (or
mailed) quarterly travel newsletter for
people with disabilities. Subscription-based.

Global Access, *www.geocities.com/Paris/1502/*.
Online network for disabled travellers, with
links, archives and information on travel
guides for the disabled, etc.

Holiday Care Service, 7th Floor, Sunley House,
4 Bedford Park, Croydon, Surrey CR0 2AP,
t 0845 124 9971, t (020) 8760 0072, Minicom
t 0845 124 9976, *www.holidaycare.org.uk*.
Publishes an information sheet on holidays
for disabled and older people (£5).

Mobility International USA, PO Box 10767,
Eugene, OR 97440, USA, t/TTY (541) 343 1284,
www.miusa.org. Information on international educational exchange programmes
and volunteer service overseas for the
disabled.

RADAR (Royal Association for Disability and
Rehabilitation), 12 City Forum, 250 City Rd,
London EC1V 8AF, t (020) 7250 3222, Minicom
t (020) 7250 4119, *www.radar.org.uk*.
Campaigning organization with some infor-
mation about travel.

SATH (Society for Accessible Travel and
Hospitality), 347 5th Av, Suite 610, New York,
NY 10016, t (212) 447 7284, *www.sath.org*.
Travel and access information.

Electricity

France is all 220v. British and Irish appliances
will need an adapter with two round prongs;
North American appliances usually need a
transformer as well.

Embassies and Consulates

In France

Australia: 4 Rue Jean Rey, 75724 Paris Cedex 15,
t 01 40 59 33 00, *www.austgov.fr*.

Canada: 35 Av Montaigne, 75008 Paris, t 01 44
43 29 00, *www.amb-canada.fr*; 21 Rue
Bourgelat, 69002 Lyon, t 04 72 77 64 07; 10
Rue Lamartine, 06000 Nice, t 04 93 92 93 22.

Ireland: 4 Rue Rude, 75116 Paris, t 01 44 17 67 00,
irembparis@wanadoo.fr; Monaco t 07 93 15
70 00.

New Zealand: 7 Rue Léonard de Vinci, 75116
Paris, t 01 45 01 43 43, *www.nzembassy.com*.

UK: 18 bis Rue d'Anjou, 75008 Paris, t 01 44 51
31 02, *www.amb-grandebretagne.fr*; also
24 Av du Prado, 13006 Marseille, t 04 91 15
72 10; 353 Bd du Président Wilson, 33073
Bordeaux Cedex, t 05 57 22 21 10; 11 square
Dutilleul, 59800 Lille, t 03 20 12 82 72; and 24
Rue Childebert, 69002 Lyon, t 04 72 77 81 70.

USA: 2 Rue St-Florentin, 75382 Paris Cedex 08,
t 01 43 12 22 22, *www.amb-usa.fr*; Place
Varian Fry, 13086 Marseille, t 04 91 54 92 00;
15 Av d'Alsace, 67082 Strasbourg, t 03 88 35
31 04; 7 Av Gustave V, 3rd floor, 06000 Nice,
t 04 93 88 89 55.

Abroad

Canada: 42 Promenade Sussex, Ottawa,
Ontario, K1M 2C9, t (613) 789 1795,
www.ambafrance-ca.org;25 Rue St Louis,
Québec, QC G1R 3Y8, t (418) 694 2294,
www.consulfrance-quebec.org; Suite #
1100–1130, West Pender St, Vancouver, BC,
V6E 4A4, t (604) 681 4345, *www.consul
france-vancouver.org*.

Ireland: 36 Ailesbury Rd, Ballsbridge, Dublin 4,
t (01) 277 5002.

UK: 21 Cromwell Rd, London SW7 2EN, t (020)
7073 1200, *www.ambafrance-uk.org*;
11 Randolph Crescent, Edinburgh EH3 7TT,
t (0131) 225 7954, *www.consulfrance-
edimbourg.org*.

USA: 4101 Reservoir Rd NW, Washington, DC
20007-2185, t (202) 944 6202; 205 North
Michigan Avenue, Suite 3700, Chicago, IL
60601, t (312) 327 5200; 10990 Wilshire Bd,
Suite 300, Los Angeles, CA 90024, t (310) 235
3200; 934 Fifth Av, New York, NY 10021,
t (212) 606 3680, *www.ambafrance-us.org*,
www.france-consulat.org.

Festivals and Events

Festivities in France range from the village fête, celebrating the patron saint, with feasting, dancing, music, various amounts of *animations* (jumping motorbikes, dogs pulling sleds on wheels, etc.) and fireworks, to the glittering Cannes film festival. Traditional events, however, are rare outside Brittany, Corsica and a few places in the south. Local tourist offices will be happy to give you precise dates.

Besides **Bastille Day**, another nationally celebrated affair is the **Fête de la Musique** on 21 June. The first three weeks of July are taken up with the **Tour de France**. Then there's the **Fête du Patrimoine**, which throws open the doors of usually inaccessible monuments and offers free admission to museums.

Calendar of Major Events

January
Late Jan International Comic Strip Festival, Angoulême
Late Jan–early Feb Festival of short films, Clermont-Ferrand; *La Folle Journée*, classical music at Nantes

February
Late Feb Nice has the most famous Mardi Gras in France; *Féria du Carnival*, Nîmes
Last fortnight *Fête du Citron*, Menton

March
Throughout month Strasbourg film festival
Late March *Salon du Livre* bookfair, Paris
End of March *Bénédiction des Chevaux* at Cabriès-Calas (annual blessing of 600 horses, with races and games)

April
Good Friday Traditional processions in Corsica, especially Bonifacio, Sartène and Bastia
Easter Bullfights in Arles
Early April Paris marathon; ham fair, Bayonne
Late April *Le Printemps de Bourges*, international contemporary music festival; *Fêtes Musicales*, classical music at Biarritz

May
Start of May *Fête des Gardians*, traditional rodeo in Arles
Early May Festival of French song, Montauban; *Fêtes Johanniques*, Orléans
Mid-month Cannes International Film Festival
16–17 *Bravade de St-Torpes*, St-Tropez
24–25 Gypsy pilgrimage, Stes-Maries-de-la-Mer
Mid-May Monte Carlo Grand Prix; *Fête de la Morue*, Bègles
Whitsun *Féria de Pentecôte*, Nîmes
Last week–early June Roland Garros tennis tournament, Paris

June
Start of June *Nuits de Feu* – fireworks at Chantilly
Throughout month Saint Denis Music Festival
Mid-month Le Mans 24-hour rally; *Prix de Diane Hermès* horse-racing, Chantilly
Last fortnight Jazz and chamber music, Aix; *Festival de la Nouvelle Danse*, Uzès
20 *Courses landaises*, L'Aire-sur-Adour
21 Summer equinox gatherings, Montségur; *Fête de la Musique*, nationwide music festival
23–24 St Jean: bonfires, dancing and fireworks in Perpignan and Céret
End of June Wine festival, Bordeaux (3 days), Gay Pride, Paris
Late June–early July *Festival International de Danse*, Montpellier; Quinzaine Celtique, Nantes; Festival de Pau; international film festival, La Rochelle; festival of the giants, Douai, Aix en Musique, Aix
Late June–mid-July Jazz à Vienne

July
Early July Flamenco festival, Mont-de-Marsan; festival of European theatre, Grenoble; Tour de France; International jazz festival, Juan-les-Pins (10 days); Formula One Grand Prix, Magny-Cours; International Music and Opera Festival, Aix (3 weeks), classical and chamber music festival, Evian
1st Sunday after 5 July Parade of the Giants, Douai
1st 10 days *Tombées de la Nuit* theatre and music festival, Rennes
Last Sunday *Fête de la Tarasque*, Tarascon

Useful Websites

Music festivals throughout France:
www.francefestivals.com
General information about festivals:
www.whatsonwhen.com
www.culture.fr
www.franceguide.com
Also check local tourist office sites for more detailed information.

Food and Drink

French restaurants generally serve between noon and 2pm and in the evening from 7 to 10pm, with later summer hours; *brasseries* in the cities often stay open continuously.

If service is included it will say *service compris* or s.c.; if not, *service non compris* or s.n.c, and you should tip between 10 and 15%,

July–August International fireworks festival, Monaco; modern music festival, St-Paul-de-Vence

Throughout month International music festival, Vence; music festival, Carcassonne

Mid-month Aix international dance festival; world music and gypsy festival, Arles; blues festival, Cahors; International Festival of the Sea and Sailors, quadrennial festival at Brest (2004); *son et lumière* festival, Montgothier

Mid-July–mid-Aug *Festival Pablo Casals*, Prades; dance festival, Vaison-la-Romaine

13 Grand Paris Ball, Place de la Bastille, Paris

14 Fireworks in many places for Bastille Day: Paris, Cap d'Agde, Avignon, Arcachon and Carcassonne put on excellent shows

Third week End of the Tour de France, in Paris; Basque festival and surfing, Biarritz; *Festival de Cornouaille*, Quimper; Vannes Festival de Jazz; national festival of street artists, Chalon-sur-Saône; jazz festival, Souillac

Early July–end of month Dance and drama festival, Avignon

Late July Nice Jazz Festival

Late July–early Aug Theatre festival, Sarlat; *Festival de Radio France*, classical music and jazz in Montpellier

August

Throughout month *Tournois de Joutes*, nautical jousts at Sète; chamber music festival, Menton

First two weeks *Festival Interceltique*, Lorient; jousts and medieval costumes, Carcassonne; international mime festival, Périgueux

Mid-month Bullfights at Béziers; Twins Festival, Pleucadeuc

Second week Medieval festival, Foix; *Grande Fête des Menhirs*, Carnac

Second and third week Jazz in Marciac; *La Route du Rock*, St-Malo

End of August *Fête de St Louis*, with historical re-enactment, at Aigues-Mortes; street theatre festival, Aurillac

September

Throughout month Sigma theatre, dance and music festival, Bordeaux

First week Dijon wine and folk festival

6–8 *Santa di U Niolu*, with traditional songs and fair, Casamaccioli (Corsica)

Mid-month *Festival du Roi de l'Oiseau*, Le Puy-en-Velay; Napoleon Days, Ajaccio

Third week *Féria des Vendanges*, bullfights at Nîmes

Last week–first week Oct *Nioulargue*, yacht race in St-Tropez

Sun nearest the 29th *Festival de St Michel*, Mont-St-Michel

3rd weekend (2 days) *Journées du Patrimoine* – open house for usually closed monuments

October

Throughout month Jazz festival, Paris

Early Oct Montmartre grape harvest, Paris

Mid-month International theatre festival, Bayonne

Last week *Festiventu*, Calvi (Corsica), a popular event dedicated to the wind

November

Throughout month International mime and clown festival, Strasbourg

Mid-month International contemporary music festival, Metz

Late November Paris Gay and Lesbian Film Festival

December

Throughout month Music festival, Marseille; traditional Christmas markets, Alsace

Second week *Les Transmusicales* rock festival, Rennes

For more information about food, wine, and eating out in France, and some general help in ordering, *see* **Food and Drink**, pp.53–60.

Health and Emergencies

Ambulance (SAMU) **t** *15*
Police and ambulance **t** *17*
Fire **t** *18*

France has one of the best healthcare systems in the world. Local hospitals are the place to go in an emergency (*urgence*). Doctors take turns going on duty at night and on holidays: ring any surgery to listen to the recorded message to find out what to do.

To be on the safe side, always carry a phone card. If it's not an emergency, pharmacists are trained to administer first aid, and dispense advice for minor problems. In rural areas there is always someone on duty if you ring the bell of a pharmacy; in cities, pharmacies are open on a rota and addresses are posted in their windows and in the local newspaper.

In France, however you're insured, you pay up front for everything, unless it's an emergency, when you will be billed later. Doctors will give you a brown and white *feuille de soins* with your prescription; take both to the pharmacy and keep the *feuille*, the various medicine stickers (*vignettes*) and prescriptions for insurance purposes at home. *See* 'Insurance', below.

Insurance

Citizens of the EU should bring an E111 form (available from post offices before you travel), entitling you to the same emergency health services and treatments as French citizens. This means paying up front for medical care and prescriptions, of which 70 to 75 per cent of the costs of doctors' fees, and 35 to 65 per cent of the cost of most medicines, are reimbursed about two months later. Keep copies of all documents and make sure you obtain receipts. In the UK, see the Department of Health website at *www.doh.gov.uk/traveladvice*.

Many of the larger credit card companies will also offer free travel insurance for health and theft, etc., when you use them to book a package holiday or aeroplane/train tickets. Read the small print very carefully, especially if you're travelling with expensive equipment (laptops, cameras, etc.).

If you're not covered on your credit card, you may want to consider taking out extra insurance, covering theft and losses and offering 100 per cent medical refund and emergency repatriation if necessary; check to see if it covers extra expenses should you get bogged down in airport or train strikes. Be aware that accidents resulting from sports are rarely covered by ordinary insurance.

Canadians may or may not be covered in France by their provincial health coverage; Americans and others should check their individual policies.

Maps

If you plan to cover a lot of territory in France by car, you can't do better than the Michelin *Atlas Routier* (1:200 000), which binds together Michelin's yellow regional maps. Michelin also does one of the best sheet maps for the entire country, No.989. These are all readily available in French service stations or newsagents.

Walkers, cyclists and micro-tourists (*see* pp.47–8) who are serious about exploring a certain patch of France should have a look at the IGN ordnance survey maps; the most common blue series (1:25 000), almost always carried by local newsagents or stationers, marks every path, building and roadside cross.

Money and Banks

The **euro** has been the currency in France since 2002. Banknotes come in denominations of €5, €10, €20, €50, €100, €200 and €500; coins in 1, 2, 5, 10, 20 and 50 cents, €1 and €2. If you're travelling across European border, you can use your euros in any EU country in the euro zone, including Italy, Spain, Germany and Belgium but not Switzerland.

Travellers' cheques are the safest way of carrying money, but the wide acceptance of credit or debit cards and the presence of **ATMs** (*distributeurs de billets*) even in small villages make them a convenient alternative. Major international **credit cards** are widely used in France; Visa (in French, Carte Bleue) is the most readily accepted, although, for the French, Carte Bleue is a direct-debit bank card. American Express is often not accepted, however. Smaller hotels and restaurants and bed and breakfasts may not accept cards at all. For debit/cash cards, ask at your bank before you leave. In any case, bring some travellers' cheques in case you lose your card or go over its daily or weekly limits. Some shops and supermarkets experience difficulties reading UK-style magnetic strips (French credit cards now contain a chip or *puce* containing ID information), so arm yourself with cash in case. However, your card is valid, and the French Government Tourist Office suggests you use the following phrase to explain the problem:

'*Les cartes internationales ne sont pas des cartes à puce, mais à bande magnétique. Ma carte est valable et je vous serais reconnaissant d'en demander la confirmation auprès de votre banque ou de votre centre de traitement.*'

Under the Cirrus system, withdrawals in euros can be made from bank and post office automatic cash machines, using your UK PIN. The specific cards accepted are marked on each machine, and most give instructions in English. Credit card companies charge a fee for cash advances, but rates are often better than those at banks.

In the event of **lost or stolen credit cards**, call the following emergency numbers:
Mastercard t 0800 901 387 or t 01 45 67 84 84.
American Express t 01 47 77 72 00 or t 01 47 77 77 77.
Visa (Carte Bleue) t 01 42 77 11 90.
Diners Club t 01 49 06 17 50 or t 01 47 62 75 00.
Barclaycard t (00 44) 1604 230 230 (UK number).

Banks are generally open 8.30am–12.30pm and 1.30–4pm; they close on Sunday, and most close either on Saturday or Monday as well. Exchange rates vary, and nearly all take a commission of varying proportions. *Bureaux de change* that do nothing but exchange money (and hotels and train stations) usually have the worst rates or take the heftiest commissions.

Opening Hours, Museums and National Holidays

While many **shops and supermarkets** are now open continuously Tuesday–Saturday from 9 or 10am to 7 or 7.30pm, businesses in smaller towns still close down for lunch from 12 or 12.30pm to 2 or 3pm, or in the summer 4pm. There are local exceptions, but nearly everything shuts down on Mondays, except for grocers and *supermarchés* that open in the afternoon. In many towns, Sunday morning is a big shopping period. **Markets** (daily in the cities, weekly in villages) are usually open mornings only, although clothes, flea and antique markets run into the afternoon.

Most **museums** close for lunch, and often all day on Mondays or Tuesdays, and sometimes for all of November or the entire winter. Hours change with the season: longer summer hours begin in May or June and last until the end of September – usually. Most museums close on national holidays. We've done our best to include opening hours in the text, but don't

National Holidays
1 January New Year's Day
Easter Sunday March or April
Easter Monday March or April
1 May Fête du Travail (Labour Day)
8 May VE Day, Armistice 1945
Ascension Day usually end of May
Pentecost (Whitsun) and the following Monday beginning of June
14 July Bastille Day
15 August Assumption of the Virgin Mary
1 November All Saints' Day
11 November Remembrance Day (First World War Armistice)
25 December Christmas Day

sue us if they're not exactly right. Most museums give discounts if you have a student ID card, or are an EU citizen under 18 or over 65 years old; most charge admissions ranging from €2 to €10. National museums are free if you're under 18.

Churches are usually open all day, or closed all day and only open for Mass. Sometimes notes on the door direct you to the *mairie* or priest's house (*presbytère*) where you can pick up the key. There are often admission fees for cloisters, crypts and special chapels.

On French **national holidays** (*see* box), banks, shops, businesses and some museums close; but most restaurants stay open. The French have a healthy approach to holidays: if there is a holiday on a Tuesday or Thursday, they 'make a bridge' (*faire un pont*) to the weekend and make Monday or Friday a holiday too.

Post Offices, Telephones and the Internet

Known as the La Poste, easily discernible by a blue bird on a yellow background, **post offices** are open in the cities Monday–Friday 8am–7pm, and Saturdays 8am until noon. In villages, offices may not open until 9am, then they break for lunch, and close at 4.30 or 5pm. You can receive letters *poste restante* at any of them; the postal codes in this book should help your mail get there in a timely fashion. To collect it, bring ID; you may have to pay a small fee. You can purchase stamps in tobacconists as well as post offices.

Nearly all public telephones have switched over from coins to *télécartes*, which you can purchase at any post office or newsstand for about €7.40 for 50 *unités* or €14.70 for 120 *unités*. The French have eliminated area codes, giving everyone a 10-digit telephone number (Paris and Ile de France region 01, Northwest 02, Northeast 03, Southeast and Corsica 04, and Southwest 05). If **ringing France from abroad**, the international dialling code is 33, and drop the first '0' of the number. For **international calls** from France, dial 00, wait for the change in the dial tone, then dial the country code (UK 44; US and Canada 1; Ireland 353; Australia 61; New Zealand 64), and then the local code (minus the 0 for UK numbers) and number. The easiest way to reverse charges is to spend a few francs ringing the number and giving your number in France, which is always posted by public phones; alternatively, ring your national operator and tell him or her that you want to call reverse charges (for the UK dial 00 33 44; for the USA 00 33 11). For directory enquiries, dial **t** 12, or try your luck and patience on the free, slow, inefficient Minitel electronic directory in every post office, or look it up on *www.pagesjaunes.fr*.

The old saying that it doesn't pay to be first certainly applies to France with its national computer system, the Minitel, which was distributed to every phone subscriber in the 1980s. Next to the internet, it seems a Neanderthal, but its presence considerably slowed French interest in the internet.

This is changing fast: most cities and towns now have cybercafés, and the French have some of the most remarkable websites on the information highway – *www.pagesjaunes.fr* pinpoints every address in Paris, with a photo of the building.

Hotels and tourist offices are creating new websites as we speak; if they're not listed in this guide, try putting the name and the town in a search engine such as Google and see if it comes up.

Racism

Unfortunately, in France the forces of bigotry and reaction are strong enough to make racism a serious concern.

It's especially bad in the south, where Jean-Marie Le Pen's Front National is a powerful political force: in places such as Orange, Marseille, Nice, Toulon and Perpignan, campsites, hotels and restaurants may suddenly have no places if the colour of your skin doesn't suit the proprietor; the bouncers at clubs may say it's really the cut of your hair or trousers they find offensive; police may stop you for no reason and demand to check your papers.

If any place recommended in this book is guilty of such behaviour, please let us know: we will remove it in the next edition and forward your letter to the regional tourist office and relevant authorities in Paris.

Sports and Leisure Activities

Basque Sports

Summer in the Pays Basque is a great time to watch its special sports: tug of war, stone-lifting, or running with 100lb weights. But there's more to the Basques than brute strength: every town has an outdoor *fronton*, or court for *pelote*, the fastest ball game in the world; the indoor version, *cesta punta* or *jaï alaï*, is even more fast and furious.

If you want to get in a little action yourself, you might try to talk your way into it at any village *fronton* when they're practising (they'd be charmed), or else contact the **Fédération Française de Pelote Basque** at the Trinquet Moderne, B.P. 816, 64108 Bayonne, **t** 05 59 59 76 49, *www.ffpb.net*; they set up training courses in summer for beginners. Matches take place at least once a week in towns throughout the Pays Basque, but times and days change, so ring the local tourist office to ask for the most up-to-date schedule.

Boules/Pétanque

Even the smallest village has a rough, hard court for *boules* or *pétanque*. Nearly all players are male and of a certain age, although women are welcome to join in. The object is to get your metal ball closest to the wooden marker (*bouchon* or *cochonnet*). Tournaments are frequent and well attended.

Bullfights

The Roman amphitheatres at Nîmes and Arles had hardly been restored when they once again became venues for *tauromachie*. However, most bullfights in Provence, Languedoc and Gascony are not bloody: the object is to remove a round cockade from between the horns of the bull (or cow) by cutting its ribbons with a blunt razor comb – a sport far more dangerous to the human players than the animals. You will see other types of bullfight advertised: the *corrida*, or traditional Spanish bullfight, in which the bull is put to death, and the *corrida portuguaise*, in which the bullfighter is on horseback but doesn't kill the bull.

Cycling

No country on earth respects cycling more, and the French follow the flying Lycra of the Tour de France with passion. If you find yourself along the route in July, it's fun to see what the fuss is all about. If you do it yourself, you'll get plenty of respect.

Football/Soccer

The dazzling success of the French national team in the World Cup in 1998 and Euro 2000 has given the country a boost of self-confidence and pride, and the fact that its star players came in all shades brought home the fact that a multicultural France is a tremendous asset. At other times, almost all of its stars play outside of the country, where TV deals shower clubs with megatons of money. Nevertheless, the French follow *le foot* with the same passion as everyone else in Europe: Paris St-Germain, Auxerre, Monaco and Olympique Marseille are the most exciting teams in the First Division.

Rugby

Rugby is the national sport of southwest France, which is the cradle of most of the players on the national team, famous for its virtuosity. Although the best teams lately have been Toulouse, Brive, Dax, Agen and Bayonne, you can still see fiery matches in Béziers, long-time champions, and Carcassonne. In some places they play 'Cathar rugby' – 13 to a side instead of 15.

Skiing

The French Alps are famous for their skiing, and the most economical way of joining in is to book a package ski holiday from a local travel agency. Snowfall is less reliable in the Pyrenees, although the atmosphere is generally more relaxed and *sympa*. Here cross-country skiing (*ski de fond*) is as popular as downhill skiing, just as it is in the Massif Central. Contact the **Fédération Française de Ski**, 50 Rue des Marquisats, 74011 Annecy Cedex, **t** 04 50 51 40 34, *www.ffs.fr*. Another useful guide, with information about all the resorts, events, special deals and packages, is **Association Nationale des Maires des Stations de Montagne**, 61 Bd Haussmann, 75008 Paris, **t** 01 47 42 23 32, *www.skifrance.fr*.

Water Sports and Beaches

France has beaches for all tastes: sheltered nooks in Brittany, endless miles of sand and big waves along the Bay of Biscay, long beaches in Languedoc, short ones with paying concessions on the Côte d'Azur. Legally, and often in spite of appearances, all are public up to 15ft of the high-tide mark.

Green flags mean that swimming is permitted and that a lifeguard is on duty (*baignade autorisée et surveillée*). Orange flags mean that swimming is not advised, but that there is a lifeguard on duty (*baignade surveillée mais déconseillée*). Red flags mean that swimming is forbidden and that there is no lifeguard on duty (*baignade interdite*). Topless bathing is accepted every-where; areas are set aside for *les naturistes*, or nudists.

Every town on the coast hires out equipment for water sports, often for hefty prices. Some of the best diving is in the clear waters off Ile Port-Cros National Park and around Corsica.

For a list of diving clubs, contact the **Fédération Française d'Etudes et de Sports Sous-Marins**, 24 Quai de Rive Neuve, 133284 Marseille Cedex, **t** 04 91 33 99 31, *www.ffessm.fr*.

Time

France is usually an hour ahead of the UK and Ireland, and six hours ahead of US Eastern Standard Time.

Tourist Information

Every city and town, and most villages, has a tourist information office, usually called a Syndicat d'Initiative or an Office de Tourisme. In smaller villages this service is provided by the town hall (*mairie*). They distribute free maps and town plans, and hotel, camping and self-catering accommodation lists for their area, and can inform you about sporting events, leisure activities, wine estates open for visits, and festivals. Addresses, websites and telephone numbers are listed in the text, and if you write to them they'll post you their booklets to help you plan your holiday.

French government tourist offices abroad:
Australia: Level 20, 25 Bligh St, Level 22, NSW 2000 Sydney, **t** (02) 9231 5244.
Canada: 1981 Av McGill College, No.490, Montreal H3A 2W9, **t** (514) 876 9881.
Ireland: 10 Suffolk St, Dublin 1, **t** (01) 679 0813, *frenchtouristoffice@tinet.ie*.
UK: 178 Piccadilly, London W1J 9AL, **t** 09068 244 123 (calls charged at 60p/min).
USA: 444 Madison Av, New York, NY 10022, **t** (410) 286 8310;
John Hancock Center, Suite 3214, 875 North Michigan Avenue, Chicago, IL 60611, **t** (312) 751 7800;
9454 Wilshire Bd, Suite 715, Beverly Hills, CA 90212, **t** (310) 271 6665;
1 Biscayne Tower, Suite 1750 – 2 South B Tower, Suite 1750, 2 South Biscayne Blvd; Miami, FL 33131, **t** (305) 373 81 77.

Check *www.franceguide.com* for a compre-hensive list of French tourist offices in these and other countries.

Where to Stay

Hotels and *Chambres d'Hôtes*

In France you can find some of the most splendid hotels in Europe and some genuine fleabags, with the vast majority of establish-ments falling somewhere between. As in most countries, the tourist authorities grade hotels by their facilities (not by charm or location) with stars. Hotels with no stars are not necessarily dives: their owners probably never bothered filling out a form for the tourist authorities.

Most hotels have a wide range of rooms and prices – a very useful and logical way of doing things, once you're used to it. In some the difference in quality and price can be enor-mous: a large room with antique furniture, a television, a balcony over the sea and a bath-

> **Hotel Price Ranges**
> *Note: all prices listed here and elsewhere in this book are for a double room.*
> **luxury** €230 and over
> **very expensive** €150–230
> **expensive** €100–150
> **moderate** €60–100
> **inexpensive** under €60

room will cost much more than a poky back room in the same hotel, with a window overlooking a car park, no antiques, and the WC down the hall. Some proprietors will drag out a sort of menu for you to choose the level of price and facilities you would like.

Standards vary so widely that it's impossible to be more precise, but we can add a few more generalizations. Single rooms are relatively rare, and usually two-thirds the price of a double, and rarely will a hotelier give you a discount if only doubles are available (again, because each room has its own price); on the other hand, if there are three or four of you, triples or quads or adding extra beds to a double room is usually cheaper than staying in two rooms. Flowered wallpaper, usually beige, comes in all rooms with no extra charge – it's an essential part of the French experience. Breakfast (usually coffee, a croissant, bread and jam) is nearly always optional and extra. Rates rise considerable in the busy season (Easter holidays and summer, and in the winter around ski resorts), when many hotels with restaurants will require that you take half-board (*demi-pension* – breakfast and a set lunch or dinner). Many hotel restaurants are superb and described in the text, and non-residents are welcome. At worst the food will be boring, and it can be monotonous eating in the same place every night. In the off-season, board requirements vanish into thin air.

Your holiday will be much sweeter if you **book ahead**, especially in popular areas from May to October when the few reasonably priced rooms are snapped up very early across the board. Phoning a day or two ahead is always a good policy, although hotels will only confirm a room with the receipt of a cheque or a credit card number covering the first night.

Tourist offices have complete lists of accommodation in their given areas or even *département* which come in handy during the peak season; many will even call around and book a room for you on the spot for free or a nominal fee.

Chain hotels (Sofitel, Formula One, etc.) are in most cities, but always dreary and geared to the business traveller, so you won't find them in this book. Don't confuse chains with the various **umbrella organizations**, such as Logis et Auberges de France, Relais du Silence or the prestigious Relais et Châteaux, which promote and guarantee the quality of independently owned hotels. Many are recommended in the text. Larger tourist offices usually stock their booklets, or you can pick them up before you leave from the French National Tourist Office, *www.tourisme.fr.*

Chambres d'hôtes, or bed and breakfasts, are in private homes, châteaux or farms, or may be connected to restaurants or wine estates. Local tourist offices can provide listings. Prices tend to be moderate to inexpensive. Also try **B & B France**, PO Box 66, Bell St, Henley-on-Thames, Oxon RG9 1XS, **t** (01491) 578 803 or toll-free from the USA **t** 800 454 8704, *www.bedbreak.com* (catalogue £15.25).

Association Française BAB France, 9 Rue Jacques Louvel Tessier, 75010 Paris, **t** 01 42 01 34 34 (catalogue £17.99).

Youth Hostels, *Gîtes d'Etapes* and *Refuges*

Most cities and resort areas have youth hostels (*auberges de jeunesse*) which offer simple dormitory accommodation and breakfast to people of any age for €8.50–25 a night. Most offer kitchen facilities as well, or inexpensive meals. They are the best deal if you're travelling on your own; for people travelling together, a one-star hotel can be just as cheap. Another downside is that many are in the most ungodly locations – in the suburbs where the last bus goes by at 7pm, or miles from any transport at all in the country. In the summer the only way to be sure of a room is to arrive early in the day. Most require a Hostelling International card, which you can often purchase on the spot, although regulations say you should buy them in your home country (UK: from YHA, Trevelyan House, Dimple Road, Matlock, Derbyshire DE4 3YH, **t** 0870 770 8868, *www.yha.org.uk*; USA: from HI-USA, 8401 Colesville Road, Suite 600,Silver Spring, MD 20910, **t** (301) 495 1240, *www.hiayh.org*; Canada: from 75 Nicholas St, Ottawa, Ont KIN 7B9, **t** (613) 235 2595; Australia: from AYHA, 11 Rawson Place, Sydney, NSW 2000, **t** (02) 9281 9444, *www.yha.com.au*).

A *gîte d'étape* is a simple shelter with bunk beds and a rudimentary kitchen set up by a village along GR walking paths or a scenic bike route. Again, lists are available for each *département*. In the mountains, similar rough

Self-catering Operators

In France

Agence VVF VACANCES,115 Rue de Rennes, 75006 Paris, **t** 01 49 54 70 70, *www.vvf-vacances.fr*. *Gîtes*, B&B, holiday clubs and youth centres.

Château de la Guillonnière, La Guillonnière, Dienne 86410, **t** 05 49 42 05 46, *www.rent-a-castle.com*. Cottages, B&B and castles in the Loire Valley.

Locaflat, 63 Av de la Motte Picquet, 75015 Paris, **t** 01 43 06 78 79, *www.locaflat.com*. Apartments in central Paris.

Maeva, Pierre et Vacances, L'Artois, Espace Pont de Flandre, 11 Rue de Cambrai, 75947 Paris Cedex 19, **t** 01 58 21 58 21, *www.maeva.com*. Self-catering apartments and other accommodation combined with sports activities such as skiing.

In the UK

Allez France, 27a West St, Storrington, West Sussex RH20 4DZ, **t** 0870 160 5743, *www.allezfrance.com*. Wide variety of accommodation all over France, from cottages to châteaux.

Bowhills, Mayhill Farm, Swanmore, Southampton SO32 2QW, **t** (01489) 872 727, *www.bowhills.co.uk*. Luxury villas and farmhouses, mostly with pools.

Chez Nous, Spring Mill, Earby, Barnoldswick, Lancashire BB94 0AA, **t** 08700 781 400,

www.cheznous.com. Over 3,000 privately owned holiday cottages and B&Bs.

Crystal Holidays, King's Place, Wood St, Kingston-upon-Thames, Surrey KT1 1JY, **t** 0870 888 0262, *www.crystalholidays.co.uk*. Villas and hotels all over France.

CV Travel, 43 Cadogan Street, London SW3 2PR, **t** (020) 7591 2800, *www.cvtravel.net*, *enquiries@cvtravel.net*. Attentive personal service from a company with years of experience and a great range of lovely upmarket villas across France.

Dominique's Villas, 25 Thames House, 140 Battersea Park Rd, London SW11 4NB, **t** (020) 7738 8772, *www.dominiquesvillas.co.uk*. Large villas and châteaux with pools.

French Affair, 5–7 Humbolt Rd, London W6 8QH, **t** (020) 7381 8519, *www.frenchaffair.com*. Traditional cottages, villas, manors and châteaux in the Dordogne, Lot, Languedoc-Roussillon, Pays Basque and Atlantic coast and Corsica.

Meon Villas, Meon House, College St, Petersfield GU32 3JN, **t** (01730) 230 200 or **t** 0870 850 8551, *www.meontravel.co.uk*. Villas with pools.

Palmer and Parker Villa Holidays, Bank Rd, Penn, Bucks 8P10 8LA, **t** (01494) 815 411, *www.palmerparker.com*. Upmarket villas with pools on the Riviera.

The Apartment Service, 5–6 Francis Grove, London SW19 4DT, **t** (020) 8944 1444, *www.apartmentservice.com*. Selected

shelters along the GR paths are called *refuges*, most of them open summer only. Both charge around €9–€15 a night.

Camping

Camping is a very popular among the French themselves, and there's at least one campsite in every town, often an inexpensive, no-frills place run by the town itself (*camping municipal*). Other campsites are graded with stars from four to one: at the top of the line you can expect lots of trees and grass, hot showers, a pool or beach, sports facilities, a grocer's, a bar and/or restaurant, and, on the coast, prices rather similar to one-star hotels (although these, of course, never have all the extras). But be aware that July and August are terrible months to camp near the most popular

beaches, when sites become so overcrowded that the authorities have begun to worry about health problems.

Tourist offices have complete lists of campsites in their regions, or if you plan to move around a lot pick up a *Guide Officiel Camping/Caravanning*, available in French bookshops. A number of UK holiday firms book camping holidays and offer discounts on Channel ferries:

Canvas Holidays, **t** (01383) 629 000, *www.canvasholidays.co.uk*

Eurocamp Travel, **t** (01606) 787 000, *www.eurocamp.co.uk*

Keycamp Holidays, **t** 0870 700 0123, *www.keycamp.co.uk*

apartment accommodation in cities for long or short stays.

VFB Holidays, Normandy House, High St, Cheltenham GL50 3FB, **t** (01242) 240 340, *www.vfbholidays.co.uk*. From rustic *gîtes* to luxurious farmhouses and hotels; also provides river cruises.

In the USA and Canada

At Home in France, PO Box 643, Ashland, OR 97520, **t** (541) 488 9467, *www.athomein france.com*. Apartments, cottages, farm-houses, manor houses and villas; moderate to deluxe.

Doorways Ltd., PO Box 151, Bryn Mawr, PA 19010 2502, **t** 800 261 4460, **t** (610) 520 0806, *www.villavacations.com*. Villas and apart-ments all over France.

Families Abroad, 194 Riverside Drive, New York, NY 10025, **t** (212) 787 2434, **t** (718) 768 6185, *www.familiesabroad.com*. Sabbatical and vacation rentals, in apartments, villas and châteaux in Paris, Normandy, Loire, Provence, the Riviera and elsewhere.

France by Heart, PO Box 614, Mill Valley, CA 94942, **t** (415) 388 3075, *www.franceby-heart.com*. Hundreds of properties throughout the country.

Global Home Network, Bridge Street Corporate Housing Worldwide, **t** 800 528 3549, *www. globalhomenetwork.com*. Apartments, hotels and corporate lodging in Paris and major cities.

Heaven on Earth, 39 Radcliffe Rd, Rochester, NY 14617, **t** 800 466 5605, **t** (585) 342 5550, *www.heavenlyvillas.com*. Properties in Paris, the Riviera, Provence, the Loire and the Dordogne; moderate to luxury.

Hideaways International, 767 Islington St, Portsmouth, NH 03801, **t** 800 843 4433, **t** (603) 430 4433, **f** (603) 430 4444, *www.hideaways.com*. Apartments in Paris, plus villas, farmhouses and châteaux throughout France.

New York Habitat, 307 7th Av, Suite 306, New York, NY 10001, **t** (212) 255 8018, *www. nyhabitat.com*. Over a thousand apartments throughout Paris and the South of France.

Overseas Connection, PO Box 1800, Sag Harbor, New York 11963, **t** (631) 725 9308, *www.overseasvillas.com*. Villas and apart-ments.

Paris Sleeps, PMB 234, 2245 E. Colorado Blvd, Suite 104, Pasadena, CA 91107, **t** (626) 568 3073, *www.paris-sleeps.com*. Fully equipped Paris apartments.

Vacances Provencales, 1425 Bayview Av, Suite 204, Toronto, Ontario M4G 3A9, **t** 800 263 7152, **t** (416) 322 5565, *www.europeanhome rentals.com*. Moderate to luxury villas, country homes, châlets and apartments throughout most of France.

Villas of Distinction, PO Box 55, Armonk, NY 10504, **t** 800 289 0900, **t** (914) 273 3331, *www.villasofdistinction.com*. Private villas, cottages and châteaux.

Gîtes de France and Other Self-catering Accommodation

France offers a vast range of self-catering accommodation: inexpensive farm cottages, history-laden châteaux with gourmet frills, sprawling villas, flats in modern beach resorts or even on board canal boats. The Fédération Nationale des Gîtes de France is a French government service offering inexpensive accommodation by the week in rural areas. Lists with photos arranged by *département* are available from the Maison des Gîtes de France, 59 Rue St-Lazaire, 75439 Paris Cedex 09, **t** 01 49 70 75 75, *www.gites-de-france.fr*, or in the UK from their official agents, Brittany Ferries, **t** 08705 360 360.

If you want to stay in châteaux, request the *Chambres d'Hôtes et Gîtes de Prestige*. Other options are advertised in the Sunday papers, or contact one of the firms listed above. The accommodation they offer will nearly always be more costly than a *gîte*, but the discounts holiday firms can offer on ferries, plane tickets or car hire can make up for the difference.

Paris and the Ile de France

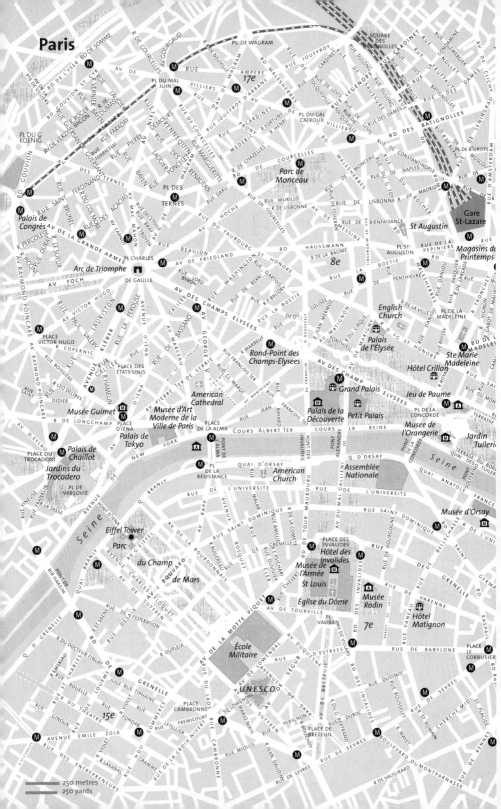

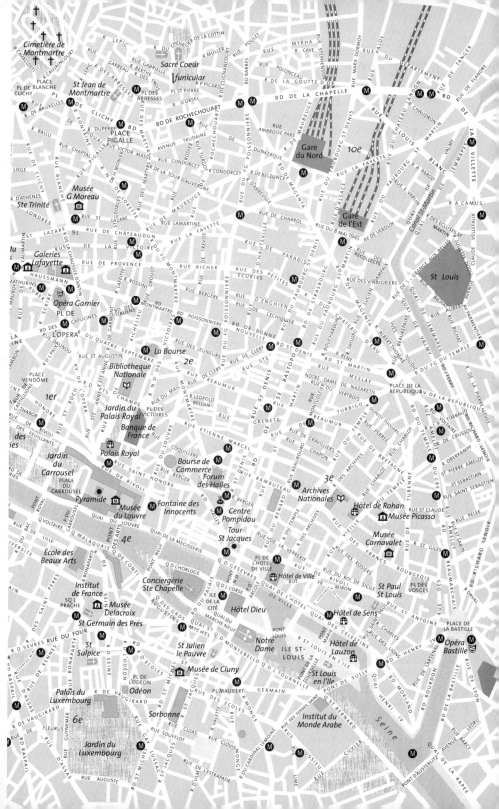

Getting There

You can still fly to Paris, arriving at Roissy airport a 20min RER ride from the centre, but by far the most convenient way is to take the Eurostar (*see* p.65) from London Waterloo.

Getting Around

By Métro and RER

The **Métro** is a godsend to disorientated visitors. To find the right train you'll need to look at the map and remember the name of the station at the *end of the line*. You can change Métro lines as often as you want during the same journey on the same ticket. There is a new automatic line, the *Météor*, Line 14, from Bibliothèque F. Mitterrand to the Gare St-Lazare, super efficient and hi-tech.

The **RER** is Paris' suburban commuter-train system, and you can use Métro tickets on it within the Paris boundaries. It can come in handy for getting across town fast or for visiting places like the Musée d'Orsay or the Jardin du Luxembourg. You can change on to the Métro at most stations. The RER can also take you to Versailles or the airports.

Buy a *carnet* of 10 tickets for bus, Métro and RER, for €9.60, or a *carte orange* weekly pass.

By Bus

An unused Métro ticket is equally valid for the bus, but you'll need a fresh ticket with each bus. Enter from the front of the bus and leave from the middle or the rear; press the *arrêt demandé* button just before your stop; you'll need to stamp (*oblitérer*) your ticket in the machine next to the driver.

Route 29, through the Marais (from Gare St-Lazare to Gare de Lyon), features a modern version of the old Paris buses with open-back platforms. The *Noctambus*, Paris' **night bus** network, can be useful; there are 16 lines, many converging at Place du Châtelet.

Sightseeing: *Paris L'Open Tour*, a system of tourist buses with an open upper deck, follows a circular route of the principal sites with further loops out to Montmartre and to Bercy; *Montmartrobus* (route 64), another circular route, runs up, down and around Montmartre; get on or off anywhere.

By Taxi

There are 14,900 taxis in Paris. You can hail them in the street if their light is on.

By Boat

Bateaux-Mouches de Paris, t 01 42 25 96 10, *www.bateaux-mouches.fr*. From Pont de l'Alma, RER *Pont de l'Alma* (north side, 8e); this one has night tours in summer and a fancy dinner cruise.

Bateaux Parisiens, t 01 44 11 33 55, *www.bateauxparisiens.com*. From the Port de La Bourdonnais, 7e, **M** *Bir-Hakeim/Iéna*.

BatObus, t 01 44 11 33 99, *www.batobus.com*. An April–Oct riverbus service operating up and down the Seine in the heart of Paris.

Canauxrama, t 01 42 39 15 00, *www.location-bateaux.info*. Reserve for 3hr tours of Canal St-Martin.

Paris Canal, t 01 42 40 96 97, *www.pariscanal.com*. From the Musée d'Orsay up the Canal St-Martin to La Villette.

Vedettes du Pont Neuf, t 01 46 33 98 38. From Square du Vert-Galant, Ile de la Cité, 1er.

Tourist Information

Paris: 11 Rue Scribe, 9e, **t** 08 36 68 31 12, near the Opéra, *open Mon–Sat 9–6.30*. Other offices at the Gare du Nord, Gare de Lyon, and in Montmartre, 21 Place du Tertre, 18e, *open daily 10–7*. Plus, from May 2004, a new main office at 25–27 Rue des Pyramides, 1er.

Shopping

You can tackle Paris' huge department stores, or there are endless little speciality shops tucked into nearly every *quartier*. Most shops close on Sundays and Mondays.

The area around the **Opéra** is one of Paris' liveliest shopping districts, where the managers still send hucksters out on to the street to demonstrate vegetable choppers.

Galeries Lafayette, 40 Bd Haussmann, 9e. A bit of Art Nouveau splendour has survived the current management. But, better than anyone, they know what the Parisiennes like. **M** *Chaussée d'Antin*.

Au Printemps, 64 Bd Haussmann, 9e. On the whole, Printemps is a wee bit posher, stuffier and nearer the cutting edge of fashion for women's designer clothes and accessories. Good household and linen departments, and a good view from the café on the top floor. **M** *Havre-Caumartin*.

The area around **Place de la Madeleine** is one of Paris' gourmet paradises, with famous restaurants such as Lucas Carton, and many of the city's finest food shops. There is also a small flower market (*Tues–Sun*).

Ladurée, 16 Rue Royale, 8e, **M** *Madeleine*; 75 Av des Champs-Elysées, **M** *Franklin D. Roosevelt*, www.laduree.fr. Maker of heavenly chocolates.

Au Nain Bleu, 408–10 Rue St-Honoré, 1er, www.au-nain-bleu.com. Paris's oldest and most magical toy store. **M** *Concorde*.

The **Champs-Elysées** is still the street to stroll, to see and be seen, with high-class designer shops and *parfumeries*.

Rue de Rivoli is a long, busy street, lined with imposing buildings, and arcades.

W. H. Smith, 248 Rue de Rivoli, 1er, **t** 01 44 77 88 99. Especially good for English-language magazines and books. **M** *Concorde*.

Louvre des Antiquaires, next to the Louvre, 1er. The poshest, biggest antiques centre and a great place for browsing. **M** *Palais Royal*.

Bazar de l'Hôtel de Ville, 52 Rue de Rivoli, 4e, www.bhv.fr. BHV has been around since 1854 and lacks the pretensions of other department stores. A good bet for practical items not easily found: brake fluid, electric outlets and mixing bowls. **M** *Hôtel de Ville*.

La Samaritaine, 19 Rue de la Monnaie, 1er, www.lasamaritaine.com. The most beautiful department store in Paris, with its Art Nouveau façade, skylight and balconies (in the old building) – though the present management thinks more like Woolworth's than Harrods. The café on its 10th-floor terrace, *open April to September*, has one of the best of all views. **M** *Louvre-Rivoli*.

The **Forum des Halles** is a subterranean labyrinthine 'new town' of shops and fast food outlets. The streets around are full of shops.

FNAC, a Paris institution – the city's biggest and fullest book chain (including some titles in English). Outlets in the Forum des Halles, Rue Pierre-Lescot, **M** *Etienne Marcel*; at 136 Rue de Rennes, **M** *Montparnasse Bienvenüe*; at 109 Rue Saint-Lazare, **M** *St-Lazare*.

Although you'll have to save up your pocket money just to be able to afford a *café au lait* in **St-Germain**, the bustling narrow streets, legendary cafés and trendy bookshops invite you to explore and tempt you to spend. The **Latin Quarter** is the *quartier* of publishers and bookshops.

Le Bon Marché, 24 Rue de Sèvres, 7e, www.lebonmarche.fr. The only department store on the Left Bank, but the grand-daddy of them all – its extraordinary food halls are a gourmet cornucopia. **M** *Sèvres-Babylone*.

Shakespeare and Co., 37 Rue de la Bûcherie, 5e, **t** 01 43 26 96 50. Just what a bookshop should be – a convivial treasure hunt, crammed full of inexpensive second-hand and new books in English. **M** *St-Michel*.

The most ambitious restoration effort in Paris has spruced up the elegant streets and old palaces of the **Marais**, ready for your inspection. The shops are small, exclusive and individual: antiques, jewellery, crafts, books and unusual objects that make it the perfect area for gift-hunting.

Markets

Les Puces de Saint-Ouen, the mother of all flea markets. *Open Sat, Sun and Mon.* **M** *Porte de Clignancourt*.

Les Puces de Montreuil, great junky flea market. *Open Sat, Sun and Mon.* **M** *Porte de Montreuil*.

Marché aux Fleurs, Place de la Madeleine, 8e (*daily except Mon*); Place des Ternes, 8e (*daily except Mon*); and Place Lépine, 4e (*daily*).

Place d'Aligre, 12e. Food market, strong North African presence. **M** *Ledru-Rollin*.

Buci, 6e. One of the liveliest food markets, with a good selection; best Sun am. **M** *Mabillon*.

Mouffetard, 5e. Lower end of Rue Mouffetard, see p.127. **M** *Censier-Daubenton*.

Where to Stay

There are basically three kinds of hotel in the centre of Paris: big luxury grand hotels, mainly on the Right Bank; business hotels, scattered everywhere; and small, privately owned hotels, some very fashionable and some dogged dives. Advance bookings are essential in June, and in September and October when Paris is awash in *salons* and conventions. July and August are low season. A list available from the tourist office indicates all hotels with facilities for the **disabled**.

Postcodes include the *arrondissement*, so an address with the postcode 75004 is in the 4th *arrondissement*.

Ile de la Cité and Ile St-Louis

★★★★**Jeu de Paume**, 54 Rue St-Louis-en-l'Ile, 75004, t 01 43 26 14 18, *www.jeudepaume hotel.com* (*luxury–expensive*). Paris' last real-tennis venue is now the most enchanting little inn on the Seine, complete with a lovely sunny garden. Ⓜ *Pont Marie*.

★★★**Hôtel des Deux Iles**, 59 Rue St-Louis-en-l'Ile, 75004, t 01 43 26 13 35, *www.parishotels. com* (*expensive*). In an 18th-century house, smallish rooms decorated with period pieces and Provençal fabrics. Ⓜ *Pont Marie*.

Henri IV, 25 Place Dauphine, 75001, t 01 43 54 44 53 (*inexpensive*). 400 years old, frumpy flowered wallpaper, and toilets and showers down the hall, but visitors book months in advance to stay in all simplicity in this most serendipitous square (no credit cards). Ⓜ *Pont Neuf, Cité*.

Beaubourg/Les Halles

★★★**St-Merry**, 78 Rue de la Verrerie, 75004, t 01 42 78 14 15, *www.hotel marais.com* (*luxury–expensive*). A stone's throw from the Pompidou Centre, this was once St Merri's presbytery and later a bordello. Its latest metamorphosis as a hotel stands out for the beautiful Gothic rooms. Ⓜ *Hôtel de Ville*.

★★★**Hôtel de la Bretonnerie**, 22 Rue Ste-Croix-de-la-Bretonnerie, 75004, t 01 48 87 77 63, *www.labretonnerie.com* (*expensive*). A very popular small hotel: Louis XIII furnishings and television. Ⓜ *Hôtel de Ville*.

★★**Andréa**, 3 Rue Saint-Bon, 75004, t 01 42 78 43 93, *www.hotelandrearivoli.com* (*moderate*). Decent quiet choice near the Rue de Rivoli. Ⓜ *Hôtel de Ville*.

★**Hôtel de la Vallée**, 84–6 Rue St-Denis, 75001, t 01 42 36 46 99, *hvallee@noos.fr* (*inexpensive*). Excellent bargain choice, between Les Halles and Beaubourg. Ⓜ *Châtelet-Les Halles*.

St-Germain

★★★★**L'Hôtel**, 13 Rue des Beaux-Arts, 75006, t 01 44 41 99 00, *www.l-hotel.com* (*luxury*).

Besides seeing the last of Oscar Wilde, this is one of the most romantic hotels in Paris. Ⓜ *St-Germain-des-Prés*.

★★★★**Le Relais Christine**, 3 Rue Christine, 75006, t 01 40 51 60 80, *www.relais-christine.com* (*luxury*). Luxurious, colourful rooms in a 16th-century Augustinian cloister, a quiet oasis. Ⓜ *Odéon*.

★★★**Hôtel de l'Abbaye**, 10 Rue Cassette, 75006, t 01 45 44 38 11, *www.hotel-abbaye.com* (*luxury–expensive*). One of the swankiest small Left Bank hotels – originally a monastery – and serenely quiet, especially if you get one of the bedrooms over the lovely garden courtyard. Ⓜ *St-Sulpice*.

★★★**Crystal**, 24 Rue St-Benoît, 75006, t 01 45 48 85 14, *hotel.crystal@wanadoo.fr* (*expensive*). Just around the corner from the church of St-Germain, a charming, cosy and lovingly cared-for little hotel. Ⓜ *St-Germain-des-Prés*.

★★★**Les Marronniers**, 21 Rue Jacob, 75006, t 01 43 25 30 60 (*expensive*). An enchanting hotel at the bottom of a courtyard, with a garden at the back. Ⓜ *St-Germain-des-Prés*.

★★**Welcome**, 66 Rue de Seine, 75006, t 01 46 34 24 80 (*moderate*). Renovated, simple, sound-proofed, with a warm welcome. Ⓜ *Mabillon*.

Latin Quarter

★★★**Melia Colbert**, 7 Rue de l'Hôtel-Colbert, 75005, t 01 56 81 19 00, *melia.colbert@solmelia.com* (*luxury*). Elegant, peaceful hotel with tearoom south of Place Maubert. Ⓜ *Maubert-Mutualité*.

★★**Hôtel du Collège de France**, 7 Rue Thénard, 75005, t 01 43 26 78 36, *www.hotel-collegedefrance.com* (*moderate*). Good-value, very popular small hotel offering spacious rooms with all mod cons. Some have views of Notre-Dame and balcony. Dark red *salon* and breakfast room. Ⓜ *Maubert-Mutualité*.

★**Esméralda**, 4 Rue St-Julien-le-Pauvre, 75005, t 01 43 54 19 20 (*moderate*). Endearing, romantic hotel in a 16th-century building with a *classé* stairway and 19th-century furnishings. Ⓜ *St-Michel*.

Mouffetard/Jardin des Plantes

★★★**Hôtel des Grandes Ecoles**, 75 Rue du Cardinal-Lemoine, 75005, t 01 43 26 79 23, *www.hotel-grandes-ecoles.com* (*expensive*). One of the most amazing settings in Paris, a peaceful cream-coloured villa in a beautiful garden courtyard. Reserve weeks ahead. Ⓜ *Cardinal Lemoine.*

✶✶Timhotel Jardin des Plantes, 5 Rue Linné, 75005, t 01 47 07 06 20, *www.timhotel.fr* (*expensive*). The best choice in the area, with its sauna, cheerful décor, and sunbathing on 5th-floor terrace overlooking the botanical gardens. Ⓜ *Jussieu.*

✶✶Hôtel Résidence Les Gobelins, 9 Rue des Gobelins, 75013, t 01 47 07 26 90, *www.hotel-gobelins.com* (*moderate*). Friendly hotel at the bottom of the price range, on a quiet street just a few minutes' walk from Rue Mouffetard. Ⓜ *Les Gobelins.*

✶Hôtel des Alliés, 20 Rue Berthollet, 75005, t 01 43 31 47 52 (*inexpensive*). Simple place in a quiet street by the Val de Grâce. Ⓜ *Censier-Daubenton.*

✶Le Central, 6 Rue Descartes, 75005, t 01 46 33 57 93 (*inexpensive*). Conveniently located, family-run haven. No en-suite bathrooms. Ⓜ *Maubert-Mutualité, Cardinal Lemoine.*

Montmartre/Place de Clichy

Note that, because of the steps, disabled access is very limited.

✶✶✶✶Hôtel Terrass, 12 Rue Joseph-de-Maistre, 75018, t 01 44 92 34 14, *www.terrass-hotel. com* (*luxury–expensive*). The area's most luxurious hotel, overlooking the cemetery and rest of Paris. Also a good restaurant with a terrace. Ⓜ *Place de Clichy.*

✶✶Timhotel Montmartre, 11 Rue Ravignan, 75018, t 01 42 55 74 79, *www.timhotel.fr* (*expensive*). Henry Miller knew it when it was called Paradis. It's still one of the most romantic hotels in Paris, overlooking delightful Place Emile-Goudeau. Ⓜ *Abbesses.*

✶✶Ermitage Hôtel, 24 Rue Lamarck, 75018, t 01 42 64 79 22 (*moderate*). A charming little white hotel under the gardens around Sacré-Cœur. Ⓜ *Lamarck-Caulaincourt.*

✶✶Hôtel des Arts, 5 Rue Tholozé, 75018, t 01 46 06 30 52, *www.arts-hotel-paris.com* (*moderate*). Excellent value, family-run hotel on a quiet street. Ⓜ *Blanche.*

✶✶Régyn's Montmartre, 18 Place des Abbesses, t 01 42 54 45 21, *www.regynsmontmartre. com* (*moderate*). A simple but good address in the heart of Montmartre, with good views over Paris. Ⓜ *Abbesses.*

Marais/Bastille

✶✶✶Caron, 12 Rue Vieille-du-Temple, 75004, t 01 42 72 34 12, *www.carondebeaumarchais. com* (*expensive*). A small, beautifully restored hotel near the Jewish quarter. The lobby sets the tone, with period fireplace and furniture. A much-loved hotel. Ⓜ *Hôtel de Ville.*

✶✶Hôtel de la Place des Vosges, 12 Rue de Birague, 75004, t 01 42 72 60 46, *hotel.place. des.vosges@gofornet.com* (*expensive*). Well restored. Ⓜ *Bastille.*

✶✶Hôtel Jeanne d'Arc, 3 Rue de Jarente, 75004, t 01 48 87 62 11, *information@hoteljeanne darc.com* (*moderate*). Ancient, cute and well run, close to the Place des Vosges; book far ahead. Ⓜ *St-Paul.*

✶✶Sévigné, 2 Rue Malher, 75004, t 01 42 72 76 17, *contact@le-sevigne.com* (*inexpensive*). Nice place around the corner from the Rue des Rosiers. Ⓜ *St-Paul.*

Opéra/Palais Royal

✶✶✶✶Hôtel Meurice, 228 Rue de Rivoli, 75001, t 01 44 58 10 10, *www.meuricehotel.com* (*luxury*). Reopened in July 2000, this is one of Paris' most opulent hotels. Even if you can't stretch to staying here, pop in for tea in the Jardin d'Hiver. Ⓜ *Tuileries.*

✶✶Antin-Trinité Hôtel, 74 Rue de Provence, 75009, t 01 48 74 29 07, *www.paris-hotel-antin.com* (*expensive*). Perfect location for shopaholics, just by the *grands magasins* on Boulevard Haussmann. The small rooms are decorated in pretty colours and have all mod cons. Ⓜ *Chaussée d'Antin-Lafayette.*

Hôtel Chopin, 46 Passage Jouffroy, 75009, t 01 47 70 58 10 (*moderate*). Lovely hotel located at the end of one of Paris' prettiest *passages*. The staff are very friendly. Ⓜ *Grands Boulevards.*

✶Hôtel de Rouen, 42 Rue Croix-des-Petits-Champs, 75001, t 01 42 61 38 21 (*inexpensive*). Old and comfortable, a good choice near the Palais Royal. Ⓜ *Palais Royal.*

Hôtel de Lille, 8 Rue du Pélican, 75001, t 01 42 33 33 42 (*inexpensive*). A rare bargain hotel between the Louvre and Palais Royal. Old and plain. Ⓜ *Palais Royal, Musée du Louvre.*

Montparnasse

✶✶✶Hôtel de l'Orchidée, 65 Rue de l'Ouest, 75014, t 01 43 22 70 50, *orchidee@escapade-*

paris.com (expensive). Up-to-date, with a Jacuzzi, garden and sauna. ⓜ *Gaîté, Pernety*.

★★★**La Villa des Artistes**, 9 Rue de la Grande-Chaumière, 75006, **t** 01 43 26 60 86, *www.villa-artistes.com (expensive)*. Where Samuel Beckett stayed; recent Art Deco facelift – some of Montparnasse's artists had studios across the street. ⓜ *Vavin*.

★★★**Delambre**, 35 Rue Delambre, 75014, **t** 01 43 20 66 31, *www.hotelde lambre.com (moderate)*. André Breton once lived in this house, now a good-value, attractive hotel. Rooms are decorated in bright colours, with all mod cons. ⓜ *Vavin*.

★**Hôtel des Académies**, 15 Rue de la Grande-Chaumière, 75006, **t** 01 43 26 66 44 *(moderate)*. Unpretentious family hotel near the Luxembourg gardens. ⓜ *Vavin*.

Concorde/Faubourg St-Honoré

★★★★★**Hôtel de Crillon**, 10 Pl de la Concorde, 75008, **t** 01 44 71 15 00, *www.crillon.com (luxury)*. Behind the classic 18th-century façade stands the last luxury hotel in Paris to remain completely in French hands. ⓜ *Concorde*.

★★★★ **Hôtel Ritz**, 15 Pl Vendôme, 75001, **t** 01 43 16 30 30, *www.ritz.com (luxury)*. One of the most famous hotels in the world. ⓜ *Opéra*.

★★★**Hôtel des Tuileries**, 10 Rue St-Hyacinthe, 75001, **t** 01 42 61 04 17, *www.hotel-des-tuileries.com (expensive)*. A quiet 18th-century *hôtel particulier* with antiques. ⓜ *Tuileries/Pyramides*.

Faubourg St-Germain: Eiffel Tower/Invalides

★★**La Motte Picquet**, 30 Av de la Motte-Picquet, 75007, **t** 01 47 05 09 57, *www.hotel mottepicquet.com (expensive)*. A small hotel with flowers in window boxes and 18 rooms over three floors. ⓜ *Ecole Militaire*.

★★**Hôtel de la Tulipe**, 33 Rue Malar, 75007, **t** 01 45 51 67 21, *www.hoteldelatulipe.com (expensive)*. Former convent, now a charming, small hotel on two floors around a garden courtyard. The rooms have been designed in a country style with warm colours, fresh flowers and wooden beams; no.24 is the most romantic, in what was once the chapel and overlooking the court-yard. ⓜ *Latour- Maubourg, Invalides*.

★★**La Serre**, 24bis Rue Cler, 75007, **t** 01 47 05 52 33, *www.eiffeltower-hotel-paris.com, laserre@easynet.fr (moderate)*. Old-fashioned hotel on Faubourg St-Germain's liveliest market street, and one of the cheapest in the quarter. ⓜ *Latour-Maubourg*.

Champs-Elysées/Etoile/Passy/Auteuil

★★★★**George V**, 31 Av George-V, 75008, **t** 01 49 52 70 00, *www.fourseasons.com (luxury)*. Recently restored Art Deco hotel minutes from the glittering shops of the Champs-Elysées. ⓜ *George V*.

★★★★**Plaza Athénée**, 25 Av Montaigne, 75008, **t** 01 53 67 66 67, *www.plaza-athenee-paris.com (luxury)*. Mata Hari was arrested in its bar, but the spies have since given way to celebrities and corporate bosses. ⓜ *Franklin D. Roosevelt, Alma-Marceau*.

★★★★**Hôtel de Vigny**, 9–11 Rue Balzac, 75008, **t** 01 42 99 80 80, *www.relaischateaux.fr/ vigny (luxury)*. Transformed in 1990 from a town house into one of Paris's most sump-tuous small hotels, its bar evoking the Paris of the 1930s salons. Soundproof, marble bathrooms, library, cable TV. ⓜ *George V*.

Eating Out

Nearly all the restaurants listed below offer set-price menus, sometimes including wine. Some of the most famous places offer excel-lent bargain lunch menus.

For dinner, bookings are essential – weeks in advance (lunch too) for real gourmet citadels.

Ile de la Cité and Ile St-Louis

L'Orangerie, 28 Rue St-Louis-en-l'Ile, 4e, **t** 01 46 33 93 98 *(expensive)*. One of the most elegant and romantic dining rooms in Paris, founded by actor Jean-Claude Brialy as an after-theatre rendezvous; *cuisine bourgeoise*. Dinner only; book. ⓜ *Pont Marie*.

L'Ilot Vache, 35 Rue St-Louis-en-l'Ile, 4e, **t** 01 46 33 55 16 *(moderate)*. Lovely, old-fashioned and full of flowers, with an honest €33 menu that usually includes lots of seafood. *Evenings only*. ⓜ *Pont Marie*.

Au Rendez-vous des Camionneurs, 72 Quai des Orfèvres, 1er, **t** 01 43 54 88 74 *(moderate–inexpensive)*. Good French-truckers' style cooking. ⓜ *Cité*.

Les Halles/Beaubourg

Benoît, 20 Rue St-Martin, 4e, t 01 42 72 25 76 (*luxury – €90 per head; lunch menus moderate*). Considered by many the most genuine Parisian *bistrot*, devoted to the most perfectly prepared dishes of *la grande cuisine bourgeoise.* ⓜ *Châtelet.*

Ambassade d'Auvergne, 22 Rue du Grenier-St-Lazare, 3e, t 01 42 72 31 22, *www. ambassade-auvergne.com* (*moderate*). Mouthwatering *cuisine de terroir* from the Auvergne. ⓜ *Rambuteau.*

Caveau François Villon, 64 Rue de l'Arbre-Sec, 1er, t 01 42 36 10 92 (*moderate*). A *bistrot* in a 15th-century cellar, with a strumming guitar in the evening; delicious fresh salmon with orange butter. *Closed Sun, and Mon lunch.* ⓜ *Louvre-Rivoli.*

Au Pied de Cochon, 6 Rue Coquillière, 1er, t 01 40 13 77 00 (*moderate*). An institution. Famous for *pied de cochon* and its seafood platter. *Open 24 hours.* ⓜ *Les Halles, Louvre.*

Auberge Nicolas Flamel, 51 Rue de Montmorency, 3e, t 01 42 71 77 78, (*moderate–inexpensive; €12 lunch menus*). In one of the oldest houses in Paris, refined cooking from *maigrets* cooked with cider to seafood raviolis. *Closed Sat lunch and Sun.* ⓜ *Rambuteau.*

Le Pharamond, 24 Rue de la Grande-Truanderie, 1er, t 01 40 28 45 18 (*moderate–inexpensive*). This has been here since 1832. The Belle Epoque interior is a national monument, and the recipes could be as well. *Closed Sun and Aug.* ⓜ *Etienne Marcel, Les Halles.*

Aux Tonneaux des Halles, 28 Rue Montorgueil, 1er, t 01 42 33 36 19 (*inexpensive*). You'd think that the market porters were still alive and well and about to crowd in through the door. Friendly, chaotic and excellent. *Closed Sun.* ⓜ *Etienne Marcel.*

Les Forges, 5 Rue des Forges, 2e, t 01 42 36 40 83 (*cheap*). The true Sentier restaurant: owners, models and drivers all eating together. Fresh fish. *Closed Sat and Sun.* ⓜ *Sentier.*

Marais

L'Ambroisie, 9 Place des Vosges, 4e, t 01 42 78 51 45 (*luxury*). Under the fine touch of master chef Bernard Pacaud, one of the top gastronomic addresses in the country, in the elegant Hôtel de Luynes. *Closed Sun and Mon, Aug and two weeks in Feb.* ⓜ *Bastille.*

Le Train Bleu, Gare de Lyon, first floor, 12e, t 01 43 43 09 06, *www.le-train-bleu.com* (*expensive; lunch menu €42*). After Maxim's, perhaps the most spectacular decoration in Paris; frescoes and gilt everywhere in this showpiece, built for the 1900 World Fair. ⓜ *Gare de Lyon.*

Bofinger, 5 Rue de la Bastille, 4e, t 01 42 72 87 82 (*expensive; menus lunch €21.50, lunch and eves €30.50*). The prettiest of *brasseries,* and an institution for over a century. Oysters by the dozen or half; wonderful seafood specialities. A great place. ⓜ *Bastille.*

Le Petit Bofinger, 6 Rue de la Bastille, 4e, t 01 42 72 05 23 (*moderate*). Cheaper version of Bofinger, across the road. ⓜ *Bastille.*

La Guirlande de Julie, 25 Place des Vosges, 3e, t 01 48 87 94 07 (*moderate*). A memorable lunch and a setting under the arcades. *Closed Mon in winter.* ⓜ *Chemin Vert, Bastille.*

Jo Goldenberg, 7 Rue des Rosiers, 4e, t 01 48 87 20 16 (*moderate–inexpensive*). The Marais branch of Paris' most famous delicatessen. You'll think you're in New York (the ultimate compliment for delis). ⓜ *St-Paul.*

Chez Paul, 13 Rue de Charonne, 11e, t 01 47 00 34 57 (*inexpensive*). Solid family cooking (*rillettes,* duckling with prunes) in an old Paris setting straight out of a Doisneau photo, complete with terrace. ⓜ *Bastille.*

Palais Royal/Bourse

Le Grand Véfour, 17 Rue de Beaujolais, 1er, t 01 42 96 56 27, *www.relaischateaux.com* (*luxury; lunch menu €75*). More a temple than a commercial enterprise, this grandest of grand old restaurants with one of the loveliest dining rooms in Paris maintains a tradition in the Palais Royal that is now 200 years old. *Closed Fri eve, Sat and Sun, and Aug.* ⓜ *Palais Royal, Bourse.*

Le Gavroche, 19 Rue St-Marc, 2e, t 01 42 96 89 70 (*inexpensive; lunch menu €14*). The archetypal family-run *bistrot à vins* of old; authentic without even trying. Very good wines. *Closed Sun.* ⓜ *Bourse.*

Opéra/Madeleine/St-Honoré

Les Ambassadeurs, Hôtel de Crillon, 10 Place de la Concorde, 8e, t 01 44 71 16 16, *www.crillon. com* (*luxury*). The €62 menu is a relative bargain. Book ahead. ⓜ *Concorde.*

Drouant, 18 Place Gaillon, 2e, **t** 01 42 65 15 16, *www.drouant.com (luxury; lunch menu €53, dinner €104).* Since 1914 the seat of the Académie Goncourt, where it bestows France's most sought-after literary prize. Sumptuous Art Deco interior. *Closed Sat and Sun.* The **Café Drouant** has a €30 menu. *Open daily.* Ⓜ *Opéra, Quatre Septembre.*

Lucas Carton, 9 Pl de la Madeleine, 8e, **t** 01 42 65 22 90, *www.lucascarton.com (luxury; menu gastronomique €360, lunch menu €76).* The perfect marriage of tradition, beautiful surroundings and one of the top-rated modern chefs, Alain Senderens. *Closed Sat lunch, Sun, Mon lunch.* Ⓜ *Madeleine.*

Maxim's, 3 Rue Royale, 8e, **t** 01 42 65 27 94, *www.maxims-de-paris.com (luxury).* Still the most beautiful restaurant in the galaxy. Overpriced, though. *Closed Sat lunch, Sun and Mon.* Ⓜ *Concorde.*

La Ferme St-Hubert, 21 Rue Vignon, 8e, **t** 01 47 42 79 20, *www.fermesainthubert.com (inexpensive).* Restaurant annexe to the famous *fromager*, serving a variety of delicious cheese dishes based on country recipes. *Closed Sun.* Ⓜ *Madeleine.*

Le Roi du Pot au Feu, 34 Rue Vignon, 9e, **t** 01 47 42 37 10 *(inexpensive).* Entirely devoted to the most humble and traditional of all French dishes, but here raised to an art form. *Closed Sun, and 15 July–15 Aug.* Ⓜ *Madeleine.*

Montmartre

Beauvilliers, 52 Rue Lamarck, 18e, **t** 01 42 54 54 42 *(expensive).* Montmartre's gourmet restaurant and one of the oldest in France (1787); very romantic. *Closed Sun, and Mon lunch.* Ⓜ *Lamarck-Caulaincourt.*

Le Montagnard, 102ter Rue Lepic, 18e, **t** 01 42 58 06 22 *(inexpensive).* Good-quality traditional country cooking in an old Montmartre grill. Highlights are fondue and other mountain specialities. *Closed Tues.* Ⓜ *Abbesses.*

Latin Quarter

La Tour d'Argent, 15 Quai de la Tournelle, 5e, **t** 01 43 54 23 31, *www.tourdargent.com (luxury; lunch menu €65).* Established in the reign of Henri II and recently brought back to splendour by a new chef. Unforgettable, romantic views of Notre-Dame. *Closed Mon, and Tues lunch.* Ⓜ *Maubert-Mutualité.*

Balzar, 49 Rue des Ecoles, 5e, **t** 01 43 54 13 67 *(moderate).* An institution from the 1930s where stars and Sorbonne *intellectuels* rub shoulders – you might find yourself sitting next to Gwyneth Paltrow. Also has a cheaper *brasserie.* Ⓜ *Maubert-Mutualité.*

Chez Maître Paul, 12 Rue Monsieur-le-Prince, 6e, **t** 01 43 54 74 59 *(moderate).* Ordinary-looking but recommended, with dishes from the Franche-Comté to match. *Closed Sun and Mon in July and Aug.* Ⓜ *Odéon.*

Panthéon/Rue Mouffetard

Perraudin, 157 Rue St-Jacques, 5e, **t** 01 46 33 15 75 *(inexpensive).* Comfortable old-fashioned place; one of the best choices in this *quartier.* Fresh tarts are a speciality. *Closed Sat and Sun. RER Luxembourg.*

St-Germain

Jacques Cagna, 14 Rue des Grands-Augustins, 6e, **t** 01 43 26 49 39, *www.jacques-cagna.com (luxury; lunch menu €80).* One of Paris' most gracious institutions; an unforgettable lunch menu. *Closed Sat lunch, Sun, and Mon lunch.* Ⓜ *Odéon.*

Alcazar, 62 Rue Mazarine, 6e, **t** 01 53 10 19 99, *www.alcazar.fr (expensive; lunch menus €16, €22, €26).* Since 1998 a modern brasserie owned by English *restaurateur*, Terence Conran. Featuring classic English and French dishes. The Az Bar, overlooking the restaurant, has become a pre-clubbing venue par excellence. Ⓜ *Odéon.*

Aux Charpentiers, 10 Rue Mabillon, 6e, **t** 01 43 26 30 05 *(moderate; menus €19–25).* Located in the former carpenters' guildhall (with a little museum about it), serving excellent *pot-au-feu, boudin* and other everyday French basics. Ⓜ *Mabillon.*

Eiffel Tower/Faubourg St-Germain

Le Pied de Fouet, 45 Rue de Babylone, 7e, **t** 01 47 05 12 27 *(cheap).* Le Corbusier's favourite restaurant, with checked table-cloths and long queues for its tasty and very affordable meals. *Closed Sat night, Sun and Aug.* Ⓜ *St-François-Xavier.*

Montparnasse

Dominique, 19 Rue Bréa, 6e, **t** 01 43 27 08 80, *www/dominique-fr.com (expensive; lunch* menus €40 and €55). A favourite of Paris's Russians since the 1920s, with succulent chicken Kiev and Russian cheesecake (*vatrouchka*). *Closed Sun and Mon.* Ⓜ *Vavin*.

La Coupole, 102 Bd du Montparnasse, 14ᵉ, t 01 43 20 14 20 (*expensive–moderate; menus lunch €29, eves €30.50*). Still a sight to behold in full flight. Dancing in the afternoons (*Sat and Sun*). *Open until 2am daily.* Ⓜ *Vavin*.

Bars and Beer Cellars

Cafés are Parisian, bars are not, therefore almost all the bars you will find in this city have one sort of angle or another. Beer is trendy in this city.

Le Comptoir, 14 Rue Vauvilliers, 1ᵉʳ. Fashionable 1950s retro; beers, cocktails and very fancy *tapas. Open until 2am.* Ⓜ *Les Halles*.

Costes Bar, Hôtel Costes, 239 Rue St-Honoré, 1ᵉʳ. A useful address if you need a drink in the middle of the night. Small, with very glamorous crowd. Ⓜ *Tuileries*.

La Champmeslé, 4 Rue Chabanais, 2ᵉ. Very intimate, very feminine and romantic bar. *Open 6–10pm; closed Sun.* Ⓜ *Pyramides, Bourse*.

Harry's Bar, 5 Rue Daunou, 2ᵉ. Since 1911 the most famous American bar in Paris, with 180 different brands of whisky. *Open daily until 4am.* Ⓜ *Opéra*.

Le Fouquet's, 99 Av des Champs-Elysées, 8ᵉ. A Paris institution for the rich and famous. Ⓜ *George V*.

Café de l'Industrie, 16 Rue St-Sabin, 11ᵉ. A Bastille institution. Photos of actors on the walls and corners crammed full of ornaments. A peaceful place in the afternoon, but come evening its fans pile in. Ⓜ *Bastille*.

China Club, 50 Rue de Charenton, 12ᵉ. In an old ice house, one of the most beautiful bars in Paris, with leather sofas and high ceilings; elegant atmosphere, Chinese snacks. *Open until 2am.* Ⓜ *Ledru-Rollin*.

Académie de la Bière, 88bis Bd de Port-Royal, 5ᵉ. German beer specialists, with over 50 different varieties, mussels and *frites. Open until 3am.* RER *Port-Royal*.

La Gueuze, 19 Rue Soufflot, 5ᵉ. Extremely popular café with Paris' most impressive *carte des bières* – over 400 kinds of brew from around the world. RER *Luxembourg*.

La Closerie des Lilas, 171 Boulevard de Montparnasse, 6ᵉ. Unchanged since Verlaine and Hemingway boozed here; cocktails at a price. *Open until 2am.* RER *Port-Royal*.

Cafés, *Salons de Thé, Glaciers*

Angelina, 226 Rue de Rivoli, 1ᵉʳ, *www.angelina. fr*. A Viennese confection, vintage 1903 (when it was called Rumpelmayer), with a special rich African chocolate. Ⓜ *Tuileries*.

Café Marly, in the Louvre courtyard, facing the Pyramid, 1ᵉʳ. New, beautifully designed chic hangout. Especially pretty at night. Ⓜ *Palais Royal-Musée du Louvre*.

A Priori Thé, 35–7 Galerie Vivienne, 2ᵉ. Take a trip back in time over a cup of English tea and cheesecake in the *passage*. Ⓜ *Bourse*.

Berthillon, 31 Rue St-Louis-en-l'Ile, Ile St-Louis, 4ᵉ. Paris' best ice-creams and sorbets with a list of flavours a mile long; you can also enjoy them sitting down in most of the island's cafés. Ⓜ *Pont Marie*.

Le Loir dans la Théière, 3 Rue des Rosiers, 4ᵉ. Tranquil and popular old-fashioned tearoom in the Marais. Ⓜ *St-Paul*.

Ma Bourgogne, 19 Pl des Vosges, 4ᵉ. Vortex of café life in the Place des Vosges. Ⓜ *St-Paul*.

Mariage Frères, 30 Rue du Bourg-Tibourg, 4ᵉ. Paris' best-known purveyors of tea. Ⓜ *St-Paul*.

Ladurée, 16 Rue Royale, 8ᵉ. Exquisite and precious *salon de thé*, famous for its macaroons. Bring your laciest great aunt along for tea. Ⓜ *Madeleine*. Another branch at 75 Av des Champs-Elysées, 8ᵉ. Ⓜ *Franklin D. Roosevelt*.

Café de la Paix, 3 Place de l'Opéra, 9ᵉ. An historic landmark; if you can't afford a ticket to the Opéra, you might just be able to manage the price of a coffee here. Ⓜ *Opéra*.

Les Deux Magots, 6 Pl St-Germain-des-Prés, 6ᵉ. A hoot for all its pretensions, and usually full of tourists, but the chocolate and ice-cream are compensations. Ⓜ *St-Germain-des-Prés*.

Café de Flore, 172 Bd St-Germain, 6ᵉ. Fabled literary café, everything just so Parisian. Ⓜ *St-Germain-des-Prés*.

Le Procope, 13 Rue de l'Ancienne-Comédie, 6ᵉ. Paris' oldest, restored for the Revolution's Bicentennial. Ⓜ *Odéon*.

Le Sélect Montparnasse, 99 Bd du Montparnasse, 6ᵉ. The last place to get a feeling for what Montparnasse was all about between the wars. *Open until 2am.* Ⓜ *Vavin*.

Entertainment and Nightlife

Weekly entertainment guides come out on Wednesdays: *Pariscope* (including in summer an English language section written by *Time Out*, a nightlife hotline, **t** 08 36 68 88 55, and a website, *www.Pariscope.fr*), the similar *L'Officiel des Spectacles* , and *7 à Paris*. The Wednesday *Figaro* has weekly listings.

FNAC has ticket offices all over the city and a general number, **t** 01 44 09 18 00. **Virgin Megastore**, 52 Av des Champs-Elysées, **t** 01 49 53 50 00, *www.ticketnet.fr*, Ⓜ *George V*, is similar and open until midnight.

Film

The Parisians may well be the biggest film junkies in the world. Note that films dubbed in French are labelled v.f.; if shown in English, it will say *version anglaise*; if in the original language, with French subtitles, they'll say v.o. (*version originale*).

Opera and Classical Music

There are frequent lunchtime concerts in the churches, medieval music and choirs at Sainte-Chapelle and chamber music at the Orangerie at La Bagatelle. Apart from the Opéra and Opéra Bastille, try:

Cité de la Musique, 221 Av Jean Jaurès, 19e, **t** 01 44 84 44 84. Two high tech venues, one home to Pierre Boulez's Ensemble Inter-Contemporain. Ⓜ *Porte de Pantin*.

Théâtre des Champs-Elysées, 15 Av Montaigne, 16e, **t** 01 49 52 50 50. The Paris equivalent of Carnegie Hall, and a favourite of big-name classical performers; also some opera. Ⓜ *Franklin D. Roosevelt*.

Théâtre du Châtelet, Pl du Châtelet, 1er, **t** 01 40 28 28 40. Better opera than the Bastille. Ⓜ *Châtelet*.

Dance

There's a good range of dance to see in Paris, but little of it's home-grown. Many of the theatres and concert halls schedule dance performances, often by visiting companies.

Theatre and Performance Arts

Over the last 350 years, Paris has come full circle: the blockbusters in its theatres are multimedia extravaganzas. The only serious contemporary dramas are translations from the West End in London. Otherwise, French-speakers can still find plenty of Racine and Molière from the excellent Comédie-Française and frequent revivals of Ionesco, Anouilh, Genet and Co., not to mention Paris's perennial bland boulevard comedies, inevitably about extra marital hanky-panky.

Jazz, Blues, Rock, World Music, Clubs

Still considered the jazz capital of Europe, Paris since the early 1970s has been in the forefront of another phenomenon: world music, with its African, North African, Latin, Brazilian and Caribbean zouk clubs. Check out the smaller independent magazines for their day-by-day listings. Music bar **Cithea**, 112 Rue Oberkampf, 11e, **t** 01 40 21 70 95, has stacks of these, of which the most important is *Lylo*, a free rag. *Nova Mag*, available in any kiosk, is also very useful for all events.

Major bar hot spots are around the Carrefour de l'Odéon, the Marais, Rue du Trésor, the Butte aux Cailles (behind the Place d'Italie), Place Clichy and of course Place Pigalle. Clubs are concentrated in the same areas and tend to charge admission or an exorbitant price for a drink. Unfortunately, most discos in Paris take themselves seriously and are full of uncool people posing.

Chansons

Paris's own art form, first popularized by Aristide Bruant, revived in the 1950s and '60s by Jacques Brel, Georges Brassens and Juliette Greco and currently being revived again for both the Parisians and tourists.

Au Lapin Agile, 22 Rue des Saules, 18e, **t** 01 46 06 85 87 (*open 9pm–2am, closed Mon; adm €20*). A valiant attempt at bringing French traditional song back to life to busloads of Japanese tourists. Ⓜ *Lamarck-Caulaincourt*.

Cabarets, Drag and Ethnic Shows

Paris rivals Las Vegas for over the top kitsch-and-glitter-oozing, tit-and-feather spectaculars, invariably advertised as 'sophisticated', for fleecing tourists and businessmen; the **Moulin Rouge**, 82 Bd de Clichy, 11e, **t** 01 53 09 82 82, is the most famous.

Paris has been a wonder for nearly a thousand years, from the time when masons came to learn the magic numbers of Gothic architecture to the present day when we come to ponder the fearful symmetry of its latest geometric tricks – a pyramid of glass, a hollow cube, a sphere of a thousand mirrors. The Ville Lumière is France's collective dream, the vortex of all its vanity, its parasite and its showcase. But in many ways Paris has rarely been more delightful: *nouvelle cuisine* is out of fashion, the new museums are spectacular, the plonk in the cafés is better, the street markets are more seductive than ever; even rear-platform buses are back.

Ile de la Cité and Ile St-Louis

Paris made its début on the Ile de la Cité, and in their congenital chauvinism the Parisians regard their river islet to this day not only as the centre of the city, but the centre of all France. Baron von Haussmann's mid-19th-century rebuilding of Paris banished 25,000 people who lived on a hundred colourful tiny streets and, like the City of London and Wall Street, the area is deserted at night. But two of the most luminous Gothic churches ever built are reason alone for visiting, and there are other delights – shady squares and *quais*, panoramic bridges and the perfect symmetry of neighbouring Ile St-Louis, an island-village of the *haute bourgeoisie*. On a Sunday morning you can hear an echo of the old din in Place Louis-Lépine's bird market.

Ile de la Cité

Notre-Dame

www.catholique.paris.com; open daily 8–6.45; part or all of the cathedral is closed for services (Mon–Sat 8, 8,45, 10, 11.30, 12.45, 6.30, Sun 8, 9, 12, 6.15); guided tours of the cathedral in English Wed 12 noon; in French Mon–Sat 12 noon, Sun–Fri 2.30, also Thurs 6pm.

This site has been holy ever since Paris was *Lutetia*, when a temple to Jupiter stood here. In the 6th century a small church was erected; sacked by the Normans in 857, it was reconstructed but on the same scale, hardly large enough for the growing population. A proper cathedral had to wait for Maurice de Sully, bishop of Paris in 1160.

Cities all over France were beginning great cathedrals. Notre-Dame came along on the crest of the wave; its architecture was destined to become the consummate work of the early Gothic, the measuring stick by which all other cathedrals are judged. Because it was in Paris, the cosmopolitan centre of learning, Notre-Dame had a considerable influence in diffusing Gothic architecture throughout Europe; for over two centuries its construction site was a busy, permanent workshop. Henry VI of England was crowned here in 1430; seven years later Charles VII was present at a solemn *Te Deum* to celebrate the retaking of Paris from the English. French coronations commonly took place at Reims; the next one here would not come until 1804, the pompous apotheosis of Emperor Napoleon.

During the Revolution, the Parisians first trashed Notre-Dame, wrecking most of its sculptures; then they decided to demolish it. A few subtle voices stood up for its 'cultural and historical value' and the cathedral was saved to become the 'Temple of Reason'. Little upkeep took place for centuries; serious restoration work only began in the 1840s. Eugène Viollet-le-Duc, a man who spent his life trying to redeem centuries of his countrymen's ignorance and fecklessness, worked for the better part of two decades on the site. His approach to restoration was not scientifically perfect, but still far ahead of its time; his workshops produced original sculpture, attempting to capture the spirit of what had been destroyed or damaged.

To see the **façade** as it was intended, remember that, as with the temples of ancient Greece, originally all the statues and reliefs of a Gothic church were painted in bright colours. In the Middle Ages, when cathedrals were the great public living rooms of the cities and always open, there would have been no chairs **inside**, of course, just rushes strewn on the floor to soak up the mud from the hordes of people who passed through daily, gambling, making business deals, eating their lunch, waiting for the rain to stop or listening to the choir practice. The decorations of the altar and chapels were more colourful and artistic than anything there now. Today, we must be content with the architecture and the remnants of the stained glass, but it's more than enough. And it's big enough: 430ft long, with room for some 9,000 people. The plan set the pattern for the other cathedrals of the Ile-de-France: a wide nave with four side aisles, which curve and meet around the back of the altar. The side chapels were not original, but added in the 13th century to hold all the gifts pouring in from the confraternities and guilds. Today, sadly, there is not a single noteworthy painting or statue in any of them. Most of the chapels were remodelled to suit the tastes of the 17th and 18th centuries, or wrecked in the Revolution. But this is nothing compared with the vandalism committed in the age of the Big Louies. In the 18th century, nearly all of the stained glass was simply removed, to let in more light. To thank the Virgin for being born, the Sun King ordered the florid, carved-wood choir stalls, and a complete rebuilding of the choir, including a new altar, flanked by statues of His Majesty himself and his father. Thank God he spared the original choir enclosure. We can be even more thankful he didn't take out the three great **rose windows**.

Leaving the cathedral, turn right and right again, following the northern side of the cathedral along Rue du Cloître-Notre-Dame. Originally all of the island east of Rue d'Arcole was occupied by Notre-Dame's **cloister**. At the beginning of Rue du Cloître signs beckon you to ascend the **Tours de Notre-Dame** for the Quasimodo's-eye view over Paris and a chance to eyeball the gargoyles at close quarters (*open daily 9–8; adm*). No one has ever come up with a satisfactory explanation for the hordes of fanciful beasts that inhabit medieval churches. Plus there are the bells, the bells...

Rue du Cloître continues to the little **Musée de Notre-Dame** at No.10 (*open Wed, Sat and Sun 2.30–6; adm*), run by a society of friends of Notre-Dame, charming people who like to explain things to visitors and tell stories. The **Place du Parvis-Notre-Dame** extends in front of the cathedral. In the Middle Ages, the miracle plays and mystery plays put on by the confraternities were major public entertainments. Often they were held here, where the cathedral porch could serve as 'Paradise' ('Parvis').

Traced in the Parvis is the former route of Rue Neuve de Notre-Dame, laid out by Louis VII in the 12th century. When new, this was the widest street in Paris – all of 21ft across. To see what was underneath, go down to the **Crypte Archéologique du Parvis-Notre-Dame** (*open daily 10–6; closed Mon and hols; adm; combined ticket with Musée Carnavalet available; free Sun 10–1*). What was begun as an underground car park in 1965 had to become a museum when excavations revealed the 3rd-century wall of *Lutetia*, traces of Roman and medieval houses, 17th-century cellars, the Merovingian cathedral that preceded Notre-Dame, and foundations of the 1750 Enfants Trouvés, or foundlings hospital, where unwanted children were left on a revolving tray.

Around Ile de la Cité

The **Conciergerie** (*Quai de l'Horloge; open April–Sept 9.30–6.30, Oct–Mar 10–5; adm, free 1st Sun of month Oct–May; joint ticket with Ste-Chapelle; guided tours at 11 and 3*) was known as the 'Antechamber of Death'. But it wasn't always so grim. In its first, 4th-century incarnation it was the palace of *Lutetia*'s Roman governors. Clovis requisitioned the palace *c.* AD 500, and established the Frankish monarchy within its walls; in 987 Hugues Capet moved in, and it stayed in the family for the next 800 years. As the kings grew wealthy, their palace grew ever more splendid. In 1358 Etienne Marcel's partisans stormed the palace and assassinated the king's ministers as the Dauphin Charles V stood helplessly by. It was a lesson in the vulnerability of the royal person in Paris, and the result was the construction of the better fortified Louvre. Abandoned by the kings, the palace evolved into Paris' seat of justice and its prison. Architecturally, the highlight of the Conciergerie is Philippe le Bel's **Salle des Gens d'Armes** (1314), or guardroom, one of the largest Gothic halls ever built. A large percentage of the guillotine's fodder passed through the dreary **Galerie des Prisonniers**: Marie Antoinette, Danton, Desmoulins, Charlotte Corday and St-Just.

At the **Sainte-Chapelle** (*Cour du Mai, Palais de Justice, 4 Bd du Palais; same opening hours as Conciergerie*), as at Notre-Dame, you will lose any notion you might have had about the Middle Ages being quaint and backward. Every inch declares a perfect mastery of mathematics and statistics, materials and stresses. The spectacular **upper chapel** can only be entered from below; emerging from the narrow stair into it is a startling, unforgettable experience. The other cliché in the books is that the Sainte-Chapelle is a 'jewel box' for Saint Louis' treasured relics; this too is entirely apt: awash in colour and light from the tall windows, the chapel glitters like the cave of the Forty Thieves. The glass is the oldest in Paris (13th-century), though much was restored a century ago. The atmosphere of the chapel is heightened by the lavish use of gold paint and the deep-blue ceiling painted with golden stars.

A **flower market** in Place Louis-Lépine offers a haven of dewy green fragrances in the desert of offices. On Sunday mornings a **bird market** takes over, a tradition dating back to the birds sold in the Middle Ages on the Pont au Change.

At the tip of the Ile, the **Pont Neuf** is the longest and oldest bridge in Paris. By the late Middle Ages the ancient umbilical bridges tying the mother island to the banks of the Seine had become jammed with traffic, and on 31 May 1578 the cornerstone for a new bridge was laid by Henri III. Behind the equestrian statue of Henri IV, steps lead down to the **Square du Vert-Galant**, the leafy prow of the Ile de la Cité. The Vert-Galant, or 'gay old spark', was a fond nickname for Henri IV. You can embark for a tour of the Seine's other bridges on a *vedette du Pont Neuf* at the end of the square.

Ile St-Louis

Nearly all the houses on Ile St-Louis went up between 1627 and 1667, bestowing on the island an architectural homogeneity rare in Paris. Although it charmed the Parisians of the *Grand Siècle*, it fell out of fashion in the 18th century, and in the 19th enjoyed a Romantic revival among bohemians. Since the last war property prices have rocketed to the stars. The fine *hôtels particuliers* have nearly all been restored or divided into flats; bijou restaurants sprout at every corner, and during Paris's big tourist invasions its famous village atmosphere decays into the gaudy air of an ice-cream-spattered 17th-century funfair.

You can do a circuit of the outside ring of streets dappled with the shadows from plane trees, and then walk the length of the bustling central **Rue St-Louis-en-L'Ile** in half an hour, so long as you are not seduced into every charming little shop and café. There is one striking building as well, at No.51, the **Hôtel de Chenizot** (1730). A bearded faun's head and pot-bellied chimeras enliven its doorway, one of Paris's rare rococo works. The first tiny chapel on the island, dedicated to the Virgin, was quickly deemed too dinky and common by the new islanders, and in 1664 Le Vau designed a new parish **church** (No.19), which remained unfinished until 1725. Although the clock is the only distinguishing feature of the boxy exterior, inside this is the perfect Baroque society church. At No.2, on the corner of Quai d'Anjou, is the **Hôtel Lambert**. Designed in 1641 by Le Vau, today it belongs to the Rothschilds, and sometimes on weekdays they leave the gate open so you can sneak a peek at the *cour d'honneur*.

The Marais and Bastille

One of the less frantic corners of old Paris, the Marais is the aristocratic quarter par excellence. The main attractions are the grand *hôtels particuliers* of the 16th to 18th centuries and the museums they contain. In the area that has perhaps changed the least over the last 300 years, take time to look at details, like the 17th-century street signs carved into many old buildings or the subtle sculptural decoration.

When the Seine changed its present course, the old bed remained as low, marshy ground, especially at its eastern edge. Charles V enclosed the Marais within his new wall in the 1370s, and set the tone by moving in himself, and nobles and important clerics followed. What really made the Marais' fortune was Henri IV's construction of the striking Place des Vosges in 1605, today a favourite with tourists, Parisians and schoolchildren alike. During the Revolution most of the great *hôtels particuliers* were confiscated and divided up as homes for warehouses and clothing-makers. In the 1950s and '60s, Parisians finally rediscovered what had become a lost world. The old working population is long gone and the Marais has settled into a mixture of gay

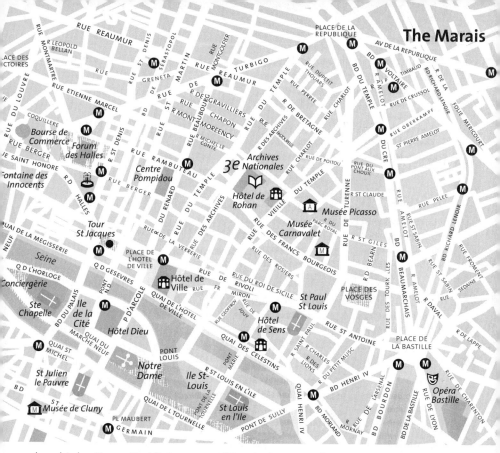

bars, hip boutiques, Hasidic Jews around Rue des Rosiers, and new immigrants from North Africa and the Middle East.

The **Place des Vosges**' association with royalty began long before the Place ever appeared. The Hôtel des Tournelles, a turreted mansion built here in the 1330s, was purhcased by Charles VI in 1407. Catherine de Médicis had the palace demolished when her husband Henri II was killed there in a joust, and she seems to have had the original inspiration to replace it with Paris's first proper square. In 1605, Henri IV finally began the building of what would be known as the 'Place Royale', a centrepiece the sprawling Marais badly needed. After the Revolution, when all the names of *ancien régime* streets were changed, Napoleon gave it its present name. Today the *place* is a favourite with tourists, Parisians, groups of schoolchildren and everyone else. It's utterly pleasant under the clipped linden trees, and the statue of Louis XIII looks fondly foolish with his pencil moustache and Roman toga. The architecture, refreshingly free of any Renaissance imitation, invites contemplation. You'll notice a lot of the 'brick' is really painted plaster; even aristocrats can cut corners.

It is only fitting that the **Musée Carnavalet**, 23 Rue de Sévigné (*open Tues–Sun 10–6; closed Mon and public hols; adm*), the city museum of Paris, should be housed in the grandest of all the *hôtels particuliers*. The museum explores ancient and medieval Paris, with shop signs, and reproductions of rooms including the bedchamber of

Marcel Proust, the ballroom of the Hôtel Wendel, the Fouquet jeweller's from Rue Royale, 1901, and a private room from the Café de Paris. Another section has paintings.

The **Hôtel de Rohan** (*87 Rue Vieille-du-Temple; open for special exhibitions only*) is one of the last and most ambitious of all the Marais mansions. In the courtyard, over the door to the Rohans' stables, is a masterpiece of rococo sculpture, Robert le Lorrain's theatrical **Horses of Apollo** (entrance at 87 Rue Vieille-du-Temple; once inside, go through the arch to the right). The interior is one of the best preserved in Paris.

The huge neoclassical bulk on the Rue des Archives is the **Archives Nationales** (*open Mon and Wed–Fri 10–5.45, Sat and Sun 1.45–5.45; closed Tues; adm*). The oldest part of the complex is a turreted gateway built in the 1370s. The truly grand horseshoe-shaped courtyard facing the Rue des Francs-Bourgeois belongs to the main part of the Archives, the Hôtel de Soubise. The part you can visit is called the **Musée de l'Histoire de France**, which isn't for everyone, but with a little knowledge of French this collection of documents can be utterly fascinating. The best thing in the museum is a painting on the far wall: a funny 16th-century allegory of the *Ship of Faith*, piloted by the Jesuits, and rowed by priests and nuns, smiling beatifically down.

The **Musée Picasso** (*5 Rue de Thorigny; open summer 9.30–6, winter 9.30–5.30; closed Tues; adm*) is in the Hôtel Salé, the 'Salted Palace', which takes its name from its original occupant, Jean Bouiller, a collector of the hated *gabelle* (salt tax) for Louis XIV. Picasso's heirs donated most of the works here to the state in the 1970s in lieu of inheritance taxes. There are few really famous pictures, but representational works can be seen from all Picasso's diverse styles. One room of the museum contains paintings from Picasso's personal collection, including works by Corot, Matisse and Cézanne. There is also a sculpture garden of Picasso's work from many periods.

Centre of a small Jewish community since the 1700s, a wave of immigration from Eastern Europe in the 1880s and '90s made the **Rue des Rosiers** what it is today – one of the liveliest, most picturesque little streets in Paris. Recently, a number of Sephardic Jews from North Africa have moved in, adding to a scene that includes bearded Hasidim, old-fashioned *casher* (kosher) grocery shops, and famous delicatessen restaurants. There are several **synagogues**, including one around the corner at 10 Rue Pavée, designed with a stunning curvilinear façade by Hector Guimard.

Strangely enough, Paris did not become an archiepiscopal see until 1623; for over a thousand years its bishops were subject to the archbishops of the little town of Sens. In the Middle Ages these influential clerics spent most of their time in the capital. One of them, *c.* 1475, built the **Hôtel de Sens**, a medieval confection overlooking the Seine (today the river is two streets away). Reconstructed, it is one of the loveliest buildings in Paris. The palace is now **Bibliothèque Forney** (*library open Tues–Fri 1.30–8, Sat 10–8.30; exhibitions Tues–Sat 1.30–8; view the gardens at the back, off Rue du Figuier*), a remarkable institution dedicated to the old crafts and industries of France.

Place de la Bastille

There's nothing to see of the famous fortress, of course – unless you arrive on the no.5 Métro, coming from the Gare d'Austerlitz, where some of the foundations survive around the platform. The square has been redesigned, with the outline of the fortress

The Storming of the Bastille

On the morning of the 14th July 1789, after a rousing speech by Camille Desmoulins in the Palais Royal (*see* p.114), some 600 people, including women and children, advanced across Paris to the grim fortress that had become a symbol of royal despotism. They battled all afternoon against a small garrison of Swiss Guards and retired veterans until, at about 5pm, the arrival of a detachment of revolutionary militia decided the issue. The gates were forced, the governor and many of the defenders massacred, and the last seven inmates of the Bastille were acclaimed as heroes among the crowd: the prisoners comprised four swindlers who were about to be transferred to another prison, an English idiot named Whyte, a gentleman whose family had petitioned the king to lock him up for incest and one genuine political prisoner – who had been in the Bastille since some obscure conspiracy in 1759 and didn't want to leave. The demolition commenced the following day.

set into the pavement. It is the only square in town created not by kings or planners but by the people of Paris. Since they cleared the space back in 1789, the Place has been the symbolic centre of leftist politics, the setting for monster celebrations. Today, the centrepiece of the Place de la Bastille is the 153ft **Colonne de Juillet**. The 'July column', restored for the bicentennial of the Revolution, was erected over the elephant's pedestal in honour of those who died in the 1830 revolt.

As part of Mitterrand's notions of 'bringing culture to the people', he conjured up the startling façade of the **Opéra Bastille** (*guided tours (French only) t 01 40 01 19 70 for times and buy a ticket from the office, www.opera-de-paris.fr. Box office open daily 11–6.30 (except Sun); tickets on sale 2 wks in advance, t 08 92 89 90 90*). There used to be a small railway station here, and the buildings included a Métro pavilion that was one of the finest works of Hector Guimard. The government planners typically levelled it without a second thought in 1985. Uruguayan-Canadian architect Carlos Ott was chosen by President Mitterrand in 1983 as the winner of the design competition for the new opera house. The architectural criticism has been harsh; Ott was up against popular ideas about what an opera house should look like. On the inside, Ott did everything you could ask of an architect – the sight lines and acoustics are excellent – but the auditorium is hardly intimate: this is a stage meant for spectacle.

Le Viaduc and the Promenade Plantée

A short walk from Place de la Bastille down Rue de Lyon, or bus no.20, takes you to Avenue Daumesnil and one of Paris' latest not-so-grand projects. The old railway viaduct high above the north side of the avenue has been planted up into a charming garden walk; as you follow the long-gone tracks, the garden narrows and opens out in a series of flowery vistas, cuts right through the middle of apartment blocks, and affords views into the second-floor windows of houses that used to rattle to the passing of trains. Below, along the length of Avenue Daumesnil, every single railway arch now houses an *atelier* of high-class specialized craft: furniture, glass, art paper, wood, aromatherapy oils, lampshades, and even Le Viaduc restaurant and bar at no.43, modishly making the most of its reclaimed setting.

Les Halles and Beaubourg

This is the site of the old Paris of merchants and markets, the only *quartier* on the Right Bank without either a royal palace or a royal square. It was – at least until recently – the Paris of the Parisians, the place you would go to buy your turnips, pick up a strumpet or start a revolution. The streets are medieval, or older, and their names betray the gritty workaday spirit of the place: Street of the Knifesmiths, of the Goldsmiths, Goose Street. Only 30 years ago, these streets were crowded with hand-carts and barrels night and day. No part of Paris has seen greater changes in those 30 years and certainly not for the better. Once Les Halles was a vast colourful wholesale distribution market for all Paris, an 800-year-old institution, the 'Belly of Paris' as Emile Zola called it, surrounded by slums. Bars and bistrots thrived on its fringes; they stayed up all night too, giving poets and prostitutes a place to refresh themselves. In the 1920s and through to the 1950s, Parisian toffs and English and American swells liked to end up here after a night of carousing. But markets make politicians nervous; it was sacrificed in 1969 and by 1977 the last of Baltard's pavilions had disappeared – the same year London demolished Covent Garden. Today its replacement, the Forum des Halles, is a subterranean labyrinthine 'new town' of failing shops, the park is as full of life as a cinder cemetery, and the streets are bleak un-spaces of plannerized compromise dominated by skateboarders and fast food outlets.

The planners did go to great lengths to make this something more than just another shopping mall. Besides the ice-cream and chain stores, there is plenty of modern art to study, as well as questionable cultural amenities, and at the **Forum des Images** (*open Wed–Sun 1–9, Tues 1–10, closed Mon*) you can while away an afternoon watching old French television shows, movies or newsreels.

About three-quarters of the new Forum is underground, and most of the old marketplace is now the **Jardin des Halles**. One curious fragment of Catherine's palace remains: the tall column called the **Colonne de Médicis**, now standing at the south-western corner of the building on Rue de Viarmes. Inside, a spiral staircase leads to a platform where Catherine and her astrologers (including, briefly, Nostradamus) would contemplate the destinies of the dynasty and of France.

The entrance to the market's own parish church, **St-Eustache**, is on Place du Jour. The façade, a pathetic neoclassical pudding, was added in the 1750s. St-Eustache, begun in 1532, soon became one of the most important churches in the city, second only to Notre-Dame. Richelieu, Molière and Madame de Pompadour were baptized here, and Louis XIV had his first communion. The interior shows the plan typical of great Parisian churches since Notre-Dame. The art inside, meticulously detailed at the entrance, is disappointing. Don't miss the forlorn chapel in the left aisle, near the entrance, entirely filled with Raymond Mason's 1969 work, *The Departure of the Fruits and Vegetables from the Heart of Paris*.

The crowds of young people who have made the **Square des Innocents** their main city-centre rendezvous can be seen literally dancing on the graves of their ancestors. At one time, the entire neighbourhood was perfumed by a ripe stench of decaying corpses from the Halles' neighbour, the Cimetière des Innocents. In 1786 the cemetery was demolished, and the cleared site was converted into a market. Later it was remodelled into the present square, and the **Fontaine des Innocents** was installed at its centre. The only surviving Renaissance fountain in Paris (1549) is the work of Pierre Lescot, though the decorative reliefs are by Jean Goujon.

Centre Pompidou

Place Georges-Pompidou and Rue St-Martin; www.centrepompidou.fr; open Mon and Wed–Sun 11am–9pm, last adm 8pm; adm; English audioguides extra; Atelier Brancusi open 2–6. Closed Tues.

The 'Beau Bourg' was a village, swallowed up by Paris in the Middle Ages, that has lent its name to the neighbourhood ever since. By the 1920s it had become a grey, unloved place; the government cleared a large section, meaning to relocate the flower market from the Halles. Nothing happened, leaving the void as a challenge to Paris planners until the end of the 1960s. It was Georges Pompidou who came up with the idea of a 'department store for culture' accessible to the widest possible public. The design finally chosen was the most radical of all those submitted. The architects, Richard Rogers and Renzo Piano, turned traditional ideas of building upside down – or rather, inside out; the technological guts of the building are on the outside, celebrating the essentials instead of hiding them, and painting them in colours keyed to help the observer understand how it all works: electrics in yellow, air-conditioning in blue, white for ventilation ducts, etc. After the Centre opened in 1977, Parisians and tourists voiced their opinion by making it overnight the most visited sight in the city.

Inside, you won't need a ticket for the **escalator**, by far the Centre's most popular attraction. Like everything else mechanical, it runs along the outside, providing a spectacular view over Paris that changes dramatically as you ascend; for a special treat, come back and do it at twilight, when the city is illuminated.

The major permanent feature of the Centre is the **Musée National d'Art Moderne**. This superlative collection of 20th-century art takes up where the Musée d'Orsay leaves off: at the turning point of modernity in 1904, when the Fauves (Derain, Vlaminck, Matisse, Marquet) liberated colour from its age-old function of representing nature. Van Gogh had blazed a trail by using colour to express emotions. The Fauves went a step beyond, applying colour and line on a two-dimensional surface as an intellectual expression, the way a poet uses words on a piece of paper. As Van Gogh was a prophet for the Fauves, Cézanne's experiments in rendering volume with nuances of colour inspired Cubism. The Cubist works of Picasso, Braque, Juan Gris and Duchamp analyse form by depicting it simultaneously from a hundred points of view on a flat surface, destabilizing our perception in order to broaden it. A prism of aftershocks fills the next rooms, especially the first abstract works, born of Wassily Kandinsky, imaginative Expressionism and the geometric fundamentals of Mondrian and his de Stijl followers. At every point the display explores the cross-pollination between pure and applied art, setting a Mondrian canvas of flat squares and defined boundaries with sculptures composed of squares and flat planes alongside 1920s architectural models by Paul Nelson and Le Corbusier, where the same principles have been used to transform the spaces we live in.

The excellent audioguide is especially helpful on the lower floor, 'Post 1960', where the familiar images of Pop Art and new realism and displays of space-age plastic furniture give way to the explorations of artists' cautionary responses to technology in the 1960s: Robert Rauschenberg's *Oracle* and Sigmar Polke's *Pasadena*, questioning the truth of the sudden flood of media images, information and advertising pouring over an unprepared public. The art on this floor is participatory, kinetic, interactive. Also on this floor are a Graphic Art Gallery and a New Media Centre.

On other floors of the Centre are a public library (the BPI) and musical research institute (IRCAM), a gift shop with goods inspired by the modern art collections, a café, a bookshop, a restaurant, halls for temporary exhibitions, two cinemas, two concert spaces and, on the sloping plateau in front of the centre, the **Atelier Brancusi**, a reconstruction of the Paris studio where the Romanian sculptor lived from 1925 to 1927.

Around the Centre Pompidou

Saint Merri, or Medericus, was an abbot of Autun buried here in the early 8th century. A chapel was built over his relics, on a site then on the outskirts of the city; in the Middle Ages, with all the bankers and cloth merchants in this area, **St-Merri** became one of the richest parish churches of Paris. The last part to be finished was the bell tower, which contains a 14th-century bell called the Merri, the oldest in the city. What you see on it today are replacements from the 1840s, including the statues of saints and the little winged **hermaphroditic demon** that leers over the main portal. There are concerts on Sunday afternoons; after these, you can have a free guided tour (*one Sunday of each month; call ahead to check times on* **t** *01 42 71 93 93*).

Behind the Centre Pompidou, the broad sheet of water of the **Stravinsky Fountain** serves as a play pool for a collection of monsters created by that delightful sculptress from Mars, Nikki de Saint-Phalle. Her colourful gadgets are each dedicated to one of Stravinsky's works; at any moment, they are likely to start spinning around and spraying you with water. The black metal mobiles between them are by Jean Tinguely.

The Louvre

Pyramide (Cour Napoléon); **t** *01 40 20 51 51, www.louvre.fr; open daily except Tues 9–6; Mon and Wed evenings until 9.45 (Wed eve everything is open; Mon eve Richelieu wing only). Adm lower on Sun and after 3pm; under 18, free adm; free for everyone on first Sun of every month. At weekends or on any day in summer, come early to avoid the queues. For details on which rooms are closed, call* **t** *01 40 20 51 51.*

Here it is, the delicious, often indigestible 99-course feast that all visitors must swallow. 'Biggest Museum in the World' they call it, certain they have surpassed the Vatican, the Smithsonian, the British Museum and the other monsters. It isn't even as big as it used to be, for all post-1848 art has been moved to the Musée d'Orsay.

'Louvre' was the name of the area long before any palaces were dreamt of. The original castle was built some time after 1190 by Philippe-Auguste. Charles V rebuilt and extended it in the 1360s. During the worst of the Hundred Years War, 1400–30, the kings abandoned the Louvre and Paris. The first to return was François Ier, in 1527; he demolished the old castle and began what is known today as the *Vieux Louvre*, the easternmost part of the complex, in 1546. Henri IV, Louis XIII and Louis XIV all contributed in turn to the palace. The next royal resident was a reluctant Louis XVI, brought here by force from Versailles in October 1789 and installed in the Tuileries.

Republican governments kept their offices in the Tuileries after 1795; they consolidated the art collections and made them into a public museum in 1793. Napoleon moved in in 1800, and started work on the northern wing. During the next 15 years his men looted the captive nations of Europe for their finest paintings and statues.

The Louvre was 350 years in the building, and the best parts are the oldest. Start at the eastern end, on Rue de l'Amiral de Coligny. The majestic **colonnade** (begun 1668) marks the beginning of the French classical style; its architect was Claude Perrault, brother of Charles, the famous writer of fairy tales. The outer façades of the **north wing**, facing Rue de Rivoli, are contributions of Napoleon (right half, viewed from the street) and Napoléon III (left half); both lend much to the imperial dreariness of that street. As for the **south wing**, facing the Seine, the left half is the beginning of Catherine de Médicis' long extension; its completion (right half) was done under Henri IV. The Napoleons, with their symmetrical brains, naturally had to make the Louvre symmetrical too; between them they more than doubled the size of the palace, expanding the south wing and building the northern one to mirror it.

Before a *carrousel* became a merry-go-round, the word meant a knightly tournament, involving races, jousts and even singing. The **Arc du Carrousel**, like the other monument Napoleon built to himself, the Vendôme column, is a mere copy, in this case of the Arch of Septimius Severus in the Roman Forum. A sculptural ensemble is a collection of separate works by **Aristide Maillol**, a wonderful turn-of-the-20th-century Catalan-French sculptor who started his career at age 40 and believed that any subject could be most effectively represented by female nudes of heroic proportions.

In 1981, his first year in office, President Mitterrand decided to shake it up a bit with the *Projet du Grand Louvre*, a total refurbishing of the palace, museum and the adjacent Tuileries gardens. The entire north wing, which had housed the Ministry of Finance, was cleared to expand the museum space, and a giant underground car park and plush shopping mall was burrowed under the Jardin du Carrousel. And then there's the **Pyramid** – for a simple geometric bagatelle, architect I. M. Pei's 1988 entrance to the Louvre has certainly generated a lot of ink.

Once through the door and down the long curving stairway, you are in the **Hall Napoléon**, where you buy your ticket. From here you have a choice of three entrances into the labyrinth, up escalators marked **Denon**, **Sully** and **Richelieu**, the three sections into which the Louvre has been divided: Sully is the old Louvre, Denon the south wing, Richelieu the north wing. A colour-coded **orientation guide** is available.

Highlights of the Collections

Egyptian Art: The finest and most complete collection outside Egypt itself. Keep an eye out for the surprises that make the subtle Egyptians come to life – like the dog with a bell around his neck, a sort of Alsatian, with a quizzical look. The **Mastaba of Akhetep**, a complete small funeral chapel (*c.* 2300 BC) from Saqqara. Exceptional exhibits of **Coptic Art** up to the Middle Ages.

Middle Eastern Art: The various civilizations of **Mesopotamia** (*Richelieu 3, 4, ground floor*) are well represented. You may have never heard of **Mani**, a great civilization centred on the Euphrates, now in Syria, that reached its height *c.* 1800 BC, but its people were some of the Middle East's most talented artists. From **Babylon**, which destroyed Mani: a black monument carved with the **Code of Hammurabi**, the oldest known body of laws. **Medieval Islamic** ceramics and metalwork (*Richelieu entresol*) including the *Font of St Louis*, used to baptize future kings of France.

Classical Antiquity: The ***Venus de Milo*** (*Sully 12*), for whom neither date nor provenance is known, only that the villagers of Milos sold her to the French in 1820 to keep the Turks from getting her. **Roman-era copies** of Greek works. **Etruscan art**. Rome: some penetrating, naturalistic portrait busts including *Caligula, Nero, Hadrian* and *Marcus Aurelius*. The **Cour du Sphinx**: a big room assembling some of the best antique works from all periods, including the *mosaic of the Four Seasons* and a huge anthropomorphized *River Tiber*. 5th to 7th-century **early Christian art**, mostly from Syria.

Sculpture: From the Middle Ages onwards, in the *entresol* and *ground floor* of *Denon* and *Richelieu*. See especially **French Renaissance sculpture**, not only for the quality of the work but also because there's hardly any of it in the rest of Paris. Guillaume Costou's *Marly Horses* (*c.* 1740, the originals of the ones in the Place de la Concorde).

French Painting: The earliest known French easel painting, a 1350 portrait of King Jean le Bon. Georges de la Tour, greatest of the French followers of Caravaggio, with his startling contrasts of light and shadow. Watteau's *Gilles*. Delightful landscapes by Corot and the Barbizon school, forerunners of Impressionism. David's unfinished *portrait of Madame Récamier*, the famous Paris beauty. Delacroix's *Liberty Leading the People*, the Revolutionary icon painted for the revolt of 1830, where the bourgeoisie and workers fight side by side. Géricault's dramatic *Radeau de la Méduse*.

Flemish, Dutch and German Painting: Fine 15th-century altarpieces by van Eyck, van der Weyden and Memling, Hieronymous Bosch's delightful *Ship of Fools*, Joachim Patinir's gloomy *St Jerome in the Desert*, and some beautiful, meticulous works of Quentin Metsys. From the height of the Renaissance, from Duke Federico's Palace at Urbino, 14 remarkable *Portraits of Philosophers*. Two masterpieces of light and depth by Jan Vermeer. Joyous scenes of peasant life by David Teniers and others, some odd allegories from Jan Brueghel and 15 Rembrandts. The *Life of Marie de' Medici*, over 1,000 square metres of unchained Peter Paul Rubens, recently installed in *Richelieu 2*.

Italian Painting: The Grande Galerie: (*Denon 8, first floor*). The third (and least well preserved) part of the three-piece *Battle of San Romano* by Paolo Uccello, greatest and strangest of the Early Renaissance's slaves of perspective. Some fine late altarpieces by Botticelli, an eerie *Crucifixion* by Mantegna, and good works by da Messina, Baldovinetti, Piero della Francesca, Carpaccio and Perugino. Raphael's dreamlike *St Michael and the Dragon* and his portrait of the perfect Renaissance courtier, *Baldassare Castiglione*. Leonardo da Vinci's haunting *Virgin of the Rocks* and *Virgin and Child with St Anne*. The star attraction is the room itself, flooded with light.

The Salle des Etats: The Louvre's undisputed superstar, *Mona Lisa*, 'the most famous artwork in the world', as a local guide trumpets her, smiling from behind the glass (installed after she was slashed a few years back), as the tourists with their flash machines close in like papparazzi. In the same room: Titian's smiling portrait of *François Ier* and works by Correggio, Pontormo, del Sarto and others, and Veronese's room-sized *Wedding at Cana*, which besides Jesus and Mary includes nearly all the celebrities of the day: Emperor Charles V, François Ier and Suleiman the Magnificent sit at the table, while Titian, Tintoretto and other artists play in the band.

Late Italian and Spanish Painting: Francesco Guardi's colourful series of 12 works on *Venetian Festivals* (1763), a sweet document of the Serenissima near the end of its career. On the grand staircase, next to the *Winged Victory of Samothrace*, a detached Botticelli fresco called **Venus and the Graces**: five perfect Botticelli maidens maintaining their poise and calm amid the crowds. One El Greco *Crucifixion*; from the golden age of Spanish painting in the 1600s, at least one of each of the masters: Velázquez (*Infanta Margarita*), Ribera, and two Zurbaráns. Several Goyas.

Objets d'Art: Blinding jewels and heavy gold gimcracks, tapestries, Renaissance bronzes, Merovingian treasure, sardonyx vases... In the extravagantly decorated **Salle d'Apollon** (*Denon 8, first floor*): Louis XIV's crown jewels, Henri II's rock crystal chess set, Napoleon's crown and Josephine's earrings, Charlemagne's dagger, St Louis' ring, Louis XV's crown, and a 107.88 carat ruby in the shape of a dragon called *La Côte de Bretagne*. The rest of the collection is separate, on the first floor in *Sully 4–5* and *Richelieu 1, 2* and *3*. Don't miss it.

Palais Royal

Welcome to the most unabashedly retro area of Paris. Dusty, dignified, and thoroughly obsolete in a number of unimportant ways, it hasn't been popular with Parisians or anybody else since the 1830s. But you may find it one of the most unexpected delights Paris has to offer. This *quartier* is about old books, pretty things and good architecture; in other words, the elements of civilization. Though not a well-defined quarter like the Marais, it has assumed and thrown off various identities over the centuries: it was an area of court servants, artists and hangers-on when kings lived at the Louvre or Tuileries, and briefly Paris' tenderloin when the Palais Royal was full of bordellos.

Originally Cardinal Richelieu built the **Palais Royal** for himself, beginning in 1629. Naturally he willed it to the king, whose money he was playing with, long before his death in 1642. Anne of Austria and four-year-old Louis XIV moved in soon after, but left for the more defensible Louvre when the uprising of the Fronde got hot, and gave it to his brother Philippe, Duc d'Orléans. Much rebuilt, the Palais Royal currently houses the *Conseil d'Etat*, which advises on proposed laws and serves as an appeal court. Next door is the **Théâtre Français**, attached to the Palais-Royal complex in 1786. Ever since, it has been the home of the Comédie Française, the company founded by Louis XIV out of Molière's old troupe. In the lobby, Houdon's famous statue of Voltaire is displayed along with the chair on which Molière died.

But the real attraction is not these mournful buildings, but the sweet surprise behind them. Pass under the arch between the theatre and the palace into the **Jardin du Palais Royal**. The last descendant of the Duke of Orléans had in 1781 hit on the idea of cutting down his enormous debts by selling off part of the gardens for building lots. His architects chopped the greenery down by a third, and enclosed it with an arcaded quadrangle of terraced houses, *à la* Place des Vosges. Under the arcades, several cafés soon opened; gambling houses and bordellos thrived. The latter were quite refined, fronting as hat, or even furniture, shops. The police couldn't do a thing about it. They could not, in fact, even enter the Palais grounds without the duke's permission – such were the privileges of princely families before 1789.

Ironically enough, this privilege helped make the Palais Royal gardens, and the cafés that proliferated around its arcades, one of the birthplaces of the Revolution. Like the Tuileries, this was one of the bastions of the *nouvellistes*, or news-mongers. You came here if you wanted to argue politics. Typically, the attack on the Bastille was spontaneously conceived here, when Camille Desmoulins jumped on to a café table and started talking, on the morning of 14 July.

Fashion and vice both moved to the Grands Boulevards after 1838, when Louis-Philippe closed the gambling houses. Later, because the Dukes of Orléans were pretenders to his throne, Louis-Napoléon confiscated both the gardens and the palace. Ever since, the garden has kept well out of the mainstream of popularity. The arcades that were once packed day and night now hold only a few quietly fascinating shops, selling antiques, military models, perfumes or recycled designer clothing from the 1950s. The gardens themselves are well clipped and neat.

One of the oldest and prettiest of Paris' *passages*, built in 1826, the **Galerie Véro-Dodat**, east of the Jardin, wowed the Paris crowds with its mahogany, marble and bronze decoration, as well as its use of a new technological marvel – gas lighting. Véro and Dodat were two butchers who made it big and went out of their way to impress. There are some interesting shops both new and old. The **Galeries Vivienne and Colbert**, just north of Place des Victoires, were built in the 1820s, and along with the Véro-Dodat they are the most luxurious and well-restored survivors of the genre, light and airy, with neoclassical reliefs and mosaic floors.

The second of Paris' 'royal' squares (after Place des Vosges), **Place des Victoires** was laid out by Hardouin-Mansart in 1685 to accommodate an equestrian statue of Louis XIV. Like its predecessor, the piazza was planned as an intimate, enclosed public space. Over the last century, the Parisians have done their best to spoil the effect. Façades were altered, and in 1883 Rue Etienne-Marcel was cut through, entirely wrecking the dignified atmosphere. By the 1950s it reached a nadir of tackiness, but lately there has been a clean-up and the place now attracts fashion shops.

The **Bibliothèque Nationale** (*58 Rue de Richelieu; entrance on Rue Vivienne; open Mon–Sat 9–6; adm*) was born in 1537 when a decree of 1537 inaugurated the *dépôt légal*, the requirement that anyone publishing a book must send a copy to the king – who was concerned with seeing anything that might be seditious. Louis XIV's minister, Colbert, put the library on a sound footing when he consolidated all the king's holdings in two adjacent *hôtels particuliers*. You can't use the facilities without a reader's card, but have a look inside at the old building. The main reading room has been transferred to the new site at Quai François-Mauriac; here you can see a museum of coins and medals. The exit on the opposite side of the Bibliothèque takes you to Rue de Richelieu, facing the **Square Louvois**, with a pretty fountain (1844) allegorizing the 'Four Rivers of France': the Seine, Loire, Garonne and Saône.

Opéra and Faubourg-St-Honoré

This area was to the Paris of the early 1800s what the Champs-Elysées would be later in the century: the city's showcase and playground of the élite. It's still the home of all luxury, the main source of what the French call *articles de Paris*; here you'll find the gilded fashion houses and the jewellers whose names are known around the galaxy and beyond. Close to the Louvre and the *Grand Axe*, this corner of town attracted monumental projects from three of France's most unpleasant despots: Louis XIV's Place Vendôme, Napoleon's self-memorial that became the Madeleine, and Little Napoléon's incomparable Opéra.

Construction of **La Madeleine** was begun in 1764, but this church was fated to see many changes before its completion. The death of the architect in 1777 occasioned a complete rethink; the new man opted for a neoclassical Greek cross plan. Only a quarter finished by 1792, the revolutionary government pondered over a new use for the project. But Napoleon knew what was best: a Temple of Glory, dedicated to himself. The previous plans were scrapped, and in 1806 architect Barthélemy Vignon came up with an imitation Greek temple. Napoleonic efficiency got the colonnades up in nine years, but once more, political change intervened; after 1815 the restored Bourbons decided to make it a church after all. After the chilly perfection of the Madeleine's exterior, the inside comes as a surprise: windowless and overdecorated, creamy and gloomy, more like a late-Baroque Italian church – or ballroom.

Place Vendôme, the second of Louis XIV's 'royal squares', after Place des Victoires, was laid out in 1699 by the same architect, Jules Hardouin-Mansart. The most satisfactory of all 17th-century French attempts at urban design, the square seems the utter antithesis of a building like the Opéra – but both were built to impress. Here, however, Hardouin-Mansart does it with absolute decorum. Balls were sometimes held in the square, but cafés or anything else that would encourage street life or spontaneity were strictly forbidden. Originally, the square was to house embassies and academies, but the final plan proposed the present octagon of eight mansions, with uniform façades, and an equestrian statue of – guess who – in the centre. Today the square still has a not-too-discreet aroma of money about it, home to the Ritz Hotel, Cartier, Van Cleef & Arpels and a fleet of other jewellers.

The **Opéra** (*tours of the interior daily 10–5; guided tours at 10.30 and 12 noon; museum open Mon–Sat 10–4.30 exc performance days; separate adm for both. Tours include the main hall on days when there is no performance; check beforehand, t 01 40 01 22 63, if you want to see Chagall's ceiling*) is the supreme monument of the Second Empire, conceived in 1858, after Napoléon III was leaving a slightly more intimate theatre and one of the rabble got close enough to try and assassinate him. A competition was organized for a new Opéra, and the plan chosen was the largest, submitted by a fashionable young architect named Charles Garnier. After winning the competition, Garnier still had to convince a sceptical Napoléon and Eugénie. Asked what style his work was supposed to be, the architect replied: 'It is no style. Not Greek or Roman; it is the style of Napoléon III.' That won the Emperor over immediately. Finally open in 1875, three years after Napoléon's death, the biggest and most sumptuous theatre in the world soon passed into legend, much of it due to Gaston Leroux's novel *Fantôme de l'Opéra*. Envied and copied throughout the world, this building contributed much to the transformation of opera into the grand spectacle and social ritual it became in the Belle Epoque. It may have seemed that way to François Mitterrand when, in the 1980s, he decided on the overtly political gesture of sentencing opera to the proletarian Bastille. Today the behemoth sits a bit forlorn, home mainly to its dance company.

The inside is impressive, awash with gold leaf, frescoes, mosaics and scores of different varieties of precious stone, from Swedish marble to Algerian onyx. The highlight of the tour may be the hall itself, with its **ceiling** (1964) painted by Marc Chagall; the nine scenes, lovely if perhaps incongruous in this setting, are inspired by some of the artist's favourite operas and ballets. The **Musée de l'Opéra** is in the Imperial Pavilion (enter from main entrance); it has a collection of memorabilia and art, including a portrait of Wagner by Renoir.

Outside, the **Place de l'Opéra** was one of the status addresses of late 19th-century Paris; it included the original Grand Hôtel, opened for the World Fair of 1867. To your left and right stretch the western **Grands Boulevards**. A century ago these were the brightest promenades of Paris, home of all the famous cafés and restaurants. Today the glamour is gone but the streets are popular and crowded just the same.

The **Musée Jacquemart-André** (*158 Bd Haussmann; closed for renovation; open by appointment only*), assembled by Edouard André and his wife Nélie Jacquemart in the early 1900s, is the place to go if you feel like looking at beautiful pictures, but don't care to tackle the terrible Louvre. Nélie was a painter herself, and had a sharp eye. Their country home is also a museum (*see p.564*). The works from the Italian Renaissance rival the Louvre's own collection. Don't miss Tiepolo's fresco on the stairway, the *Reception of King Henri III in Venice*.

The *Grand Axe*

This is a part of Paris that every first-time visitor feels obliged to see. From the Louvre to La Défense, the monuments line up like pearls on a string – some natural, some cultured and some fake.

Jardin des Tuileries

The first gardens on this site were built at the same time as the Tuileries palace, in the 1560s. It was Catherine de Médicis' idea. Her new pleasure park, designed by Philibert de l'Orme and others, was soon the wonder of Paris; symmetrical and neat, it became the model for Le Nôtre's work and all the classical French landscaping that followed. Accounts suggest it was much more beautiful, and more fun, than the present incarnation. Louis XIV opened the park to the public and the new Tuileries became Paris' most fashionable promenade; it continued as such through the 18th century, featuring such novelties as Paris' first public toilets and first newspaper kiosk.

The centre of the park is shaded by avenues of chestnut trees, the *Quinconces des Marroniers*. Further up the Grande Allée (heading for the Place de la Concorde) is the **octagonal basin**, surrounded by some statues that have survived from the days when the Tuileries was a royal park. The **Chevaux Ailés**, two winged horses at the gates facing Place de la Concorde, are by Louis XIV's chief sculptural propagandist, Coysevox: *Mercury* and *Fame* (both copies). Le Nôtre's plan included narrow raised terraces at the northern and southern ends, the *Terrasse des Feuillants* and the *Terrasse du Bord de l'Eau*, both favourite tracks for Parisian joggers. At the Concorde end, the terraces expand into broader plateaux supporting buildings from the time of Napoléon III. To the north is the **Galerie Nationale du Jeu de Paume** (*open Wed–Fri 12–7, Sat and Sun 10–7, Tues 12–9.30; adm*), built for real tennis, the crazy medieval game where the ball bounces off walls, roofs and turrets. The building was once the Impressionists' museum in Paris; the collection has since been consolidated at the Musée d'Orsay. It now sits a bit forlorn, hosting contemporary art exhibitions. But its counterpart in the southwest corner, the **Musée National de l'Orangerie** (*closed for renovation until autumn 2004*), offers a fine permanent collection, complementary to the Musée d'Orsay, with a large lower level devoted to Monet, including one of the *Nymphéas* (Water-lilies), and two wonderful pictures by the Douanier Rousseau.

Place de la Concorde

Without the cars the Place de la Concorde would be a treat, the most spacious square and the finest architectural ensemble in Paris. Jacques-Ange Gabriel won the competition for its design by coming up with something utterly, unaccountably original. Breaking completely with the enclosed, aristocratic ethos of the other royal squares, Gabriel laid out an enormous rectangle, built up on one side only (the north), with the Seine facing opposite and the two ends entirely open. Later generations perfected the Place. The Pont de la Concorde over the Seine opened in 1790; under Napoleon, the Madeleine and Palais Bourbon were added to close the views and complete the brilliant architectural ensemble. A new exclamation mark along the

The Obelisk

The obelisk in the Place de la Concorde comes from Luxor on the Nile, *c.* 1250 BC in the time of Ramses II. It was a gift from France's ally Muhammad Ali, semi-independent Ottoman viceroy of Egypt in the 1830s, and this spot was chosen for it because any political monument would have been a sure source of controversy in the future. Accepting an obelisk is one thing; floating the 221-tonne block to Paris and getting it upright again a different matter. Look at the inscriptions on the base: scenes of the erection carved in intricate detail, with thanks in big gold letters to M. LEBAS, INGENIEUR, for managing the trick, 'to the applause of an immense crowd'.

Grand Axe, the Egyptian obelisk, appeared in 1836. But in the meantime the Place had changed its name six times, and seen more trouble than any square deserves. In 1782 the spot where the obelisk stands today held a guillotine, the venue for all the most important executions under the Terror. On the western edge of the Place stands a pair of winged horses to complement those on the Tuileries side. These familiar landmarks are copies of the **Marly horses**, sculpted by Coysevox's nephew, Guillaume Coustou, in the 1740s. Like their counterparts across the Place, they originally came from Louis XIV's château at Marly, destroyed in the Revolution.

Champs-Elysées

Just off the beginning of the Champs-Elysées, the **Grand Palais** (*t 01 44 13 17 17; open for special exhibitions 10–8, Wed 10–10; adm*), built for the 1900 exhibition, is one of the biggest surprises in Paris, and beyond any doubt the capital's most neglected and unloved monument. The main entrance on Avenue Winston-Churchill has been barricaded for years and whatever renovations were under way have been stalled. But you can peek through the glass doors at the grandest interior space in Paris, if not all Europe: a single glass arcade 1,100ft long with a glass dome at the centre, flanked by several levels of balconies and a grand stair. The building itself was an allegory: 'A Monument Consecrated by the Republic to the Glory of French Art'. In 1900, for a novelty, 22 works of the major Impressionists – already a bit dated – were included in a separate room, something that would have been unthinkable in 1878 or 1889. The 1900 show in fact proved a turning point, where modern art made its first big breakthrough to a wider public. As much as the Eiffel Tower, the Grand Palais is a symbol of an age, of both France and Europe at the height of their power, empire and confidence. It reflects, more than any building except the lost Crystal Palace in London, the exuberance of an architecture that had just realized its technological capabilities.

World-touring art exhibitions are held in the northern end of the Grand Palais. The rear of the Grand Palais has been declared a palace in itself, the **Palais de la Découverte** (*open daily 9.30–6, Sun and hols 10–7; closed Mon; adm; separate charge for planetarium shows Tues–Fri 11.30, 2, 3.15 and 4.30, Sat and Sun also 5.45*), a science museum. Before you go in, take a minute to look at one of the glories of the Grand Palais' original decoration, a colourful frieze of Sèvres terracotta designed by Joseph Blanc. It represents *The Triumph of Art*. Neither you nor the children will be bored, even if you can't read much French; there are lasers to play with, ant colonies, and computers. Whatever your age, the best part may be the Eureka rooms: hands-on games and tricks to learn about colours, optics and elementary physics.

The **Musée du Petit Palais** (*closed for renovation*) has a 'permanent collection' inside, but not quite a 'museum' – restorations and rearrangements have been going on for years.It consists of a large collection of 18th-century art and furniture (busts of Voltaire and Franklin by Houdon), a selection of medieval art and a smattering of works from the Renaissance, including Italian majolica and Venetian glass. The main attraction is 19th-century French painting and sculpture.

The **Avenue des Champs-Elysées** was the second step in the creation of the Grand Axe, the long radian that stretches, perfectly straight, from central Paris west to

La Défense. Catherine de Médicis had fixed its eastern point with her Louvre extensions and the Tuileries gardens in the 1560s. In 1616 everything west of the Louvre was royal meadows and hunting preserves; in that year Marie de Médicis ordered the first improvement, a tree-lined drive along the Seine called the *Cours la Reine*. In 1667 Louis XIV had Le Nôtre lay out a long straight promenade through the area, continuing the perspective of the Tuileries' Grande Allée. For the next few decades, the Champs-Elysées was a less aristocratic promenade; all Paris came on Sundays for a bit of fresh air, and in 1709 the pleasure promenade took its present name, the 'Elysian Fields'. The upper part of the avenue, already partly built-up, saw a speculative boom in the reign of Napoléon III. The lower part, below the Rond-Point, was saved only because it served as a pleasure ground for all the late 19th-century exhibitions, a delightful bower of groves and avenues, Chinese lanterns, brightly painted pavilions, ice-cream and lemonade. There was a glassed-in Winter Garden with banana trees; dances were held there at night. Outside there were *café-concerts* under the trees. Parisians and visitors agreed that it was the pleasantest place in the world.

The upper Champs-Elysées, after decades of decline, has been the subject of a major renovation which included everything from pavement surfaces to a second row of *platanes* (plane trees) on each side. Even the car dealers, hamburger stands, banks and obscure airline offices that took over the once-fashionable street in the 1970s have cleaned themselves up, and the scheme is working well.

Arc de Triomphe

Place Charles-de-Gaulle; pedestrian tunnel at the right-hand side of the Champs-Elysées; t 01 55 37 73 77, www.monum.fr; open Oct–Mar daily 10–10.30; April–Sept daily 10am–11pm; adm.

The Arc de Triomphe is not a tribute to Napoleon, although it certainly would have been if the Emperor had been around to finish it. The arch commemorates the armies of the Revolution: the heroic, improvized citizen levy that protected their new freedoms against the *anciens régimes* of the rest of Europe, and liberated other peoples.

In the 18th century, the Etoile was a rustic *rond-point* on the boundaries of the city. Napoleon did have the idea for the arch, after his victories of 1805–6; originally he wanted it in Place de la Bastille, but his sycophants convinced him that this prominent spot in the fashionable west end would be much more fitting. A life-size model was erected in 1810, during the celebrations for Napoleon's marriage to Marie-Louise of Austria. Not surprisingly, work stopped cold in 1815. Eight years later, Louis XVIII had the really contemptible idea of finishing it as a monument to his own 'triumph' – sending an army to put down a democratic revolt in Spain. But by the reign of Louis-Philippe, the 'myth of Napoleon' had already begun its strange progress. Times were dull; Frenchmen had forgotten the huge numbers of their countrymen Napoleon had sent to die for his glory. A massive effort to complete the arch was mounted in 1832, and they had it finished four years later. And four years after that, Napoleon's remains rolled under the arch, on a grey November day where the silence of the crowds was broken only by a few old veterans croaking '*Vive l'Empereur!*' Napoléon III had Baron Haussmann make the Etoile into the showcase of Paris.

It isn't just the location and the historical connotations that make this such an important landmark. It's also a rather splendid arch. Any Frenchman would recognize the group on the right side, facing the Champs-Elysées: the dramatic *Departure of the Volunteers in 1792*, also known as the *Marseillaise*. Inside is a small **museum** of the arch; from there you can climb up to the roof for a remarkable view of the Grand Axe and the pie-slice blocks around the Etoile (especially recommended after dark).

Montmartre

From the Eiffel Tower or the Centre Pompidou, gleaming white Montmartre resembles an Italian hill town from Mars. A closer inspection reveals honky-tonk tourist Paris at its ripest, churning euros from the fantasy-nostalgia mill for the good old days of Toulouse-Lautrec, can-can girls, Renoir and Picasso. On the other hand, the area has some of Paris' last secret alleys and picturesque streets.

The Romans called this 423ft 'mountain' *Mons Mercurii*, after its hilltop shrine to the god of commerce, but he lost his billing in the 9th century when the abbot of St-Denis renamed it the Hill of Martyrs, Montmartre, the *Butte Sacrée*. Montmartre became a *commune* during the Revolution, renamed Mont Marat. The first artists, poets and composers had already moved into Montmartre with the workers, drawn by cheap rents and the quality of its air and light. Ther police knew the village rather as the resort of dangerous *apaches*; when Erik Satie began his career playing piano in a Montmartre cabaret, he came to work armed with a hammer. After the First World War the bohemians moved off to the lower rents of Montparnasse.

Sacré-Cœur

Open daily 6.45–11; free; dome and crypt open daily 9–6; adm.

The story goes that between 1673 and 1689 Jesus Christ appeared to a nun from the Royal Abbey of Montmartre, demanding a church to the glory of his Divine Heart 'to serve France and repair the bitterness and outrages that have wasted her'. The project was put to every regime that followed, but nothing happened until the Commune and the fall of Rome. Many Parisians regard the result with some embarrassment, with its preposterous Romano-Byzantine architecture. For a real descent into the abyss, visit the clammy **crypt**, with its neglected chapels, broken chairs, dingy cases of relics salvaged from the Royal Abbey of Montmartre, overgrown statues of praying cardinals, and a slide show on the building of Sacré-Cœur. The view from the **dome** isn't that much more spectacular than the view from the parvis.

The Streets of Montmartre

The **Place du Tertre** was once the main square of Montmartre village. It's hard to imagine a more blatant parody of the Butte's hallowed artistic traditions: unless you come bright and early, you can scarcely see this pretty square for the easels of a couple of hundred artists. At the east end of the Place is **St-Pierre de Montmartre**, the Butte's oldest church, disguised with a 19th-century façade.

Part of the delight of little **Place des Abbesses** is Guimard's métro entrance, one of just two (the other is Porte-Dauphine) to survive with its glass roof intact. The outlandish church decorated with turquoise mosaics is one of Paris' architectural milestones, the neo-Gothic **St-Jean l'Evangéliste**, the first important building in reinforced concrete, built between 1894 and 1904 by Anatole de Baudot, a pupil of Viollet-le-Duc; step inside to see Baudot's innovative play of interlaced arches.

Leafy, asymmetrical **Place Emile-Goudeau**, with its Wallace fountain, steps and benches, is the antithesis of the classic Parisian square down on the 'plain' below; note the curious perspective down **Rue Berthe**, which like many other streets up here seems to lead to the end of the world. This square was the site of the famous **Bateau Lavoir** (no.13), a leaky, creaking wooden warehouse that Max Jacob named after the floating laundry concessions on the Seine. Among the 'passengers' who rented studio space in the Bateau were Braque, Gris, Van Dongen, Apollinaire and Picasso; in winter the tea in the communal pot froze every night and had to be reheated for breakfast. In 1907 Picasso invented Cubism here with his *Demoiselles d'Avignon*, the girls with multiple profiles. In 1970, just as the Bateau Lavoir was to be converted into a museum, it burned down and has been replaced by 25 more comfortable if less picturesque studios; there's a small display on its predecessor in the window.

The last two of Montmartre's 30 windmills, **Moulin du Radet** (now an Italian restaurant) and to the left, **Moulin de la Galette**, are on Rue Lepic, built in 1640 and currently being restored. In the 1814 occupation (according to local legend) the miller of the Galette, his three brothers and eldest son defended their property against the Cossacks. Only the son survived, and converted the windmill into a *guinguette*,

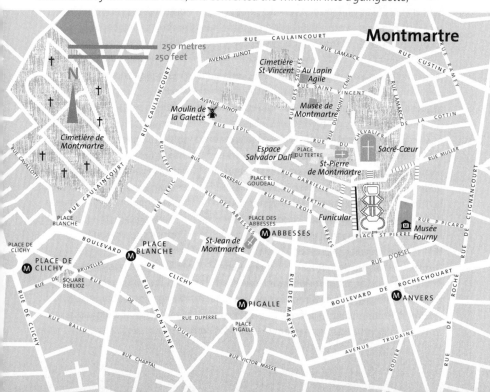

painted by Renoir (*The Ball at the Moulin de la Galette* (1876), Musée d'Orsay). **Avenue Junot**, the 'Champs-Elysées of Montmartre', was laid out in 1910, now a rare street of peaceful Art Deco houses with gardens.

The **Musée de Montmartre** (*12 Rue Cortot; open Tues–Sun 11–6; closed Mon; adm*) is a genuine neighbourhood museum, set up and run by the people of Montmartre. Behind a pretty courtyard full of giant fuchsias, you'll see prints, pictures and souvenirs that tell the real Montmartre story.

Le Lapin Agile on Rue des Saules opened in 1860 as the Cabaret des Assassins, but in 1880 a painter named Gil painted the mural of a nimble rabbit avoiding the pot, a play on his name: the *lapin à Gil*. In 1903 Aristide Bruant purchased the place to save it from demolition and it enjoyed a second period of success. Artists could pay for their meals with paintings – as Picasso did with one of his *Harlequins*, now worth millions. Now, every evening, *animateurs* attempt to recapture that first peerless rapture. Opposite, Montmartre's **vineyard** was planted by the Montmartrois in 1886 in memory of the vines that once covered the Butte.

The Latin Quarter

The Latin Quarter is one of Paris' great clichés. Its name was bestowed by a student named Rabelais, for Latin (with an excruciating nasal twang) was the only language permitted in the university precincts until Napoleon said *non*. Napoleon's 19th-century successors tended to regard the Latin Quarter itself as an anachronism, and rubbed most of its medieval abbeys, colleges and slums off the map. But once you too have dispersed any lingering romantic or operatic notions that the Latin Quarter evokes, it can be good fun, especially at night when it becomes the headquarters for an informal United Nations of goodwill.

This is one of the rare corners of Paris to preserve the pre-Haussmann higgledy-piggledy. To see it all, wander the streets bordered by the Seine to the north and Boulevard St-Germain to the south, with Boulevard St-Michel to the west and the tip of the Ile de la Cité to the east. **Rue du Fouarre**, a mere stump of a street, in the 12th century was the very embryo of the university. **Rue Galande** was once the start of the bustling Roman road to Lyon; its houses are medieval, but have been much restored. On **Rue de la Bûcherie** is what must be the most famous English-language second-hand bookshop on the continent, **Shakespeare and Company** (*open daily noon to midnight*). This is the namesake of Sylvia Beach's English bookshop that stood in Rue de l'Odéon between the wars. Beach's kindness and free lending library made her a den mother for many expat writers, but none owed her as much as James Joyce. After the *Ulysses* obscenity trial in 1921 precluded the publication of the book in Britain or the USA, Beach volunteered to publish it herself.

At the end of Rue de la Bûcherie, **Square René-Viviani** has Gothic odds and ends, melted by wind and rain, found near Notre-Dame; the tree on concrete crutches is the oldest in Paris. It's a false acacia, called a *robinier*, after Robin the botanist who planted it in 1602. Next to it is one of the oldest churches in Paris, the diminutive transitional Gothic **St-Julien le Pauvre** (*open daily 9–1 and 3–6; sung Mass Sun at 10, 11*

and 6), first built in 587. Enlarged in 1208, it became the university's assembly hall, an association that went sour when a student riot in 1524 left the church half-ruined. All members of the university were henceforth banned, and so they migrated up the hill to St-Etienne du Mont (*see* below), while poor St Julien was practically abandoned. In 1651 it was on the verge of collapse when the roof was lowered and the nave lopped off and it became a chapel for the Hôtel-Dieu.

On the other side of Rue St-Jacques, the church of **St-Séverin** (*open Mon–Sat 11–7, Sun 9–9*), with the menacing gargoyles, is named after a 6th-century hermit. The original Merovingian church here was rebuilt in 1031, though its replacement took 450 years to complete and gradually evolved into Flamboyant Gothic. The peaceful garden, enclosed by arcades, is actually the last charnel house in Paris. When the graveyard became too crowded, bones were dug up and embedded in the arches.

If 13th-century **Rue de la Huchette**, 'street of the little trough', seems a squeeze, take a look down the first right, **Rue du Chat-qui-Pêche** (named after a long-ago inn sign of a fishing cat). At 6ft wide it's the narrowest street in Paris, and the last really medieval one. Rue de la Huchette peters out in **Place St-Michel**, a traffic vortex laid out under Napoléon III and decorated with a striking fountain by Davioud of St Michel slaying the Dragon. It marks the beginning of the Latin Quarter's main drag, **Boulevard St-Michel**, or simply Boul' Mich, laid out in 1859. What you can't see any longer are its paving stones, which proved too convenient for slinging at the police in May 1968 and now lie under a thick coat of asphalt.

Musée National du Moyen Age (Musée de Cluny)

6 Place Paul-Painlevé; t 01 46 34 51 75, www.musee-moyenage.fr;
open daily 9.15–5.45; closed Tues; adm, reduced price Sun.

The baths, or Thermes, are the oldest surviving Roman monument in Paris, standing next to the Gothic Hôtel de Cluny, the Paris residence of the powerful abbots. They contain one of the world's greatest collections of medieval art, a continuous trove of the rare and the beautiful in exquisite detail to linger over all afternoon.

Among the highlights: in **Salle III**, a gorgeous English leopard embroidery believed to have been the saddlecloth of Edward III; in **Salle IV**, a delightful series of six tapestries called *La Vie Seigneuriale* on the good life 500 years ago, contemporary with the Hôtel de Cluny itself; in **Salle V**, 15th-century alabasters from Nottingham. Beyond, in the Roman section of the museum, **Salle VIII** contains the museum's newest exhibit: 21 sad, solemn, erosion-scarred heads of the kings of Judea from the façade of Notre-Dame. Revolutionaries, mistaking them for French kings, had beheaded the statues in 1793; a Catholic Royalist buried them face down in a courtyard. Lofty, vast **Salle XII** is the *frigidarium* of the Roman baths.

Upstairs, **Salle XIII** is a rotunda containing Cluny's greatest treasure: the six Aubusson tapestries of *La Dame à la Licorne*, dating from the late 15th century. Woven for Le Viste, a Lyonnese noble family, the tapestries were only rediscovered in the 19th century, rolled up and mouldering away in an obscure château in the middle of France. The lady, unicorn and lion appear in each scene, on a blue foreground and red background called *millefleurs*, strewn with a thousand flowers, birds and animals in the early Renaissance's fresh delight in nature. The first scenes appear to be allegories of the five senses, but the meaning of the sixth, where the legend on the tent reads *A mon seul désir*, will always remain a charming mystery.

Salle XIV, a long gallery of retables, painting and sculpture, contains two master-pieces: the *Pietà de Tarascon* (1450s), influenced by Italian and Flemish artists who painted in the papal entourage of Avignon, and a moving figure of *Marie Madeleine*, sculpted in Brussels *c.* 1500. Other rooms contain ivories, crowns, a rare golden rose, reliquaries, 4th-century lion heads in rock crystal, and exquisite works in gold and enamel. In **Salle XVIII**, where you can leaf through a 15th-century *Book of Hours*, the walls are hung with the first of 23 tapestries on the *Life of St Stephen* (1490). The chapel (**Salle XX**) is a flamboyant gem.

The Sorbonne

This area includes the ancient confines of Paris University, founded in spirit by Peter Abelard, one of the greatest thinkers of the Middle Ages. The high standards of inquiry and scholarship set by Abelard made the Left Bank a 'paradise of pleasure' for intellectuals and students from across Europe. Private citizens and religious orders built college-hostels to house the scholars and in 1180 Philippe Auguste enclosed the whole area in walls. Paris's first college, supplying room and board to poor students, was founded at the same time, and among those that followed was the Sorbonne, founded in 1257 by Robert de Sorbon, chaplain to St Louis. The heady freedom of

Calendar of Events

Dates for nearly all the events listed below change every year. The central tourist office provides precise dates.

1 Jan *La Grande Parade de Paris*: a New Year's Day parade from Porte St-Martin to the Madeleine via the Grands Boulevards.

March *Festival des Instruments Anciens*: medieval, Renaissance and Baroque music, mostly in the city's churches.

April *Foire du Trône*: ancient traditional funfair, Porte Dorée, Bois de Vincennes.

1 May Trade unions march and people buy sprigs of *muguet* (lily-of-the-valley) while the National Front rallies around the statue of Joan of Arc in Place des Pyramides.

Late May–June French Open Tennis Championships at Roland Garros.

Pentecost Dual pilgrimages by modern Catholics and traditionalist Lefèbvrites from Chartres to the Sacré-Cœur.

Mid-June International fireworks contest, in Chantilly; *Festival de Saint-Denis*, classical music concerts, through early July.

Late June St John's Eve: fireworks show at Sacré-Cœur; *Fête du Marais* – jazz and classical music and drama.

21 June *Fête de la Musique*, free concerts across town.

Late June Waiters' race – 8km circuit holding their trays, beginning and ending at the Hôtel de Ville; beginning of the *Foire de Paris* at the Porte de Versailles, the closest equivalent of the old St-Germain fair.

Early July *Festival de Saint-Denis*: classical music; *La Villette Jazz Festival*: two-week-long, big-name jazzfest at Parc de la Villette.

14 July Bastille Day: Military parade on the Champs-Elysées; fireworks at Trocadéro; *Bastille Ball*, rollicking all-night gay party.

Sept *Festival de l'Automne*: music dance and drama lasting until December.

Oct FIAC – *Foire Internationale de l'Art Contemporain*: choice selections from galleries around the world.

First Sat in Oct Wine harvest in Montmartre.

Mid-Oct *20km de Paris race*, open to all.

Nov *Salon d'Automne*: major art salon in the Grand Palais.

25 Nov *Les Catherinettes*: women in the fashion trade who are 26 that year and single don outrageous hats made by co-workers – *'coiffer la Sainte-Catherine'*.

Christmas Eve Midnight *Réveillon* feast – Parisians eat out and gorge like geese. Billions of oysters meet their maker.

New Year's Eve Saint-Sylvestre, occasion for another ultra-rich midnight feast – in a week, Paris downs 2,000 tons of *foie gras*.

---

thought that made Paris University great in the 13th century drew the greatest thinkers of the day. But when Philippe le Bel convinced the theological judges at the Sorbonne that they should condemn the Knights Templars in 1312, he cursed the university with a political role that compromises its independence to this day.

In 1470 three Germans were invited to the Sorbonne to start the first printing press in France, beginning a renaissance of intellectual life on the Left Bank. Unfortunately the Sorbonne was too reactionary to satisfy the new thirst for knowledge. Richelieu, appointed chancellor in 1622, tried to revive the Sorbonne's flagging status with extensive rebuilding. Nothing he could do, however, halted the Latin Quarter's decline into a volatile slum. The Revolution had no qualms about closing the whole university down. Napoleon resuscitated it, but there was no going back to the old ways – if the Sorbonne was political, so were the post-Revolutionary students, who played roles in the upheavals of the 19th century, battled the Nazis in Place St-Michel, protested against the war in Algeria and in 1968 shocked the government with their uprising. But the government has accomplished its agenda anyway: the rebellious Sorbonne has been blasted into a centreless prism of 13 campuses scattered through Paris.

Enter the *cour d'honneur* at 17 Rue de la Sorbonne to see what survives from Richelieu's day: the domed **Chapelle de Ste-Ursule de la Sorbonne** (1630), open only (and rarely) for temporary exhibitions. The interior decoration was destroyed when the *sans-culottes* converted it into a Temple of Reason, except for paintings in the spandrels by Philippe de Champaigne and the white marble tomb of Richelieu. If you come between lectures (or join one), take a look in the **Grand Amphithéâtre** to see the celebrated fresco of *Le Bois Sacré* by Puvis de Chavannes.

Panthéon

Place du Panthéon. Open daily 10–5.30; adm; under-18s free.

Old Ste-Geneviève was demolished because Louis XV, after a close call with the grim reaper in 1744, had vowed to construct a new basilica to hold the relics of Paris's patroness. Some French critics trumpet the result, by Jacques-Germain Soufflot, as 'the first example of perfect architecture', when in fact the Panthéon is a textbook case of how *not* to build, an impoverished bastard of design that has always had difficulties even standing up. It had just been completed in 1790 when the Revolution kicked off its muddled history by co-opting it as a Panthéon to honour its great and good. Napoleon reconverted the Panthéon to a church; Louis-Philippe thought the church was better as a pantheon, but in 1851 monks persuaded Napoléon III to reconvert the building to a church. In 1871 it became the Left-Bank HQ of the Commune; and it went back to a church again until 1885, when Victor Hugo died. Hugo was so inflated that no ordinary tomb would hold him, and his funeral inaugurated the building's current status as the pantheon of France's Great Men.

The Panthéon stands on the summit of the Gallo-Roman Mont Leucotitius (Mont Lutèce), which has been known since the Middle Ages as **Montagne Ste-Geneviève**. In 451, fresh from pillaging and deflowering 11,000 virgins in Cologne, Attila and the Huns marched towards Lutèce looking for more fun. Paris' Romans fled in terror to Orléans, but the native Celts, the Parisii, stuck around when Geneviève, a holy virgin, assured them that God would spare the city. She was right; at the last minute, the Huns veered off and sacked Orléans. When Clovis converted to Christianity, he built on Montagne Ste-Geneviève a basilica dedicated to SS Peter and Paul. In 512 he was buried there, next to his wife Clotilde, and Geneviève, but such a cult grew around the miracle-working tomb of Geneviève that the church was expanded and renamed. In 1220 Philippe Auguste's wall around the Latin Quarter was finished – at no.3 Rue Clovis you can see a stretch of it – and by the next year, so many students had moved into the quarter that a new chapel, St-Etienne, was built next to Ste-Geneviève to accommodate them. In 1802 old Ste-Geneviève was demolished to make way for Rue Clovis. Fortunately, **St-Etienne du Mont** (*open daily 7.45–12 and 2–7.30*) on Place Ste-Geneviève remains charming, asymmetrical and intact.

Mouffetard and Jussieu

This *quartier*, east of the medieval walls that cradled the Latin Quarter for most of its history, offers an unusual cocktail of sights and smells – gossipy village streets, a tropical garden and a Maghrebi mosque. Picturesque and piquant, the **Place de la**

Contrescarpe (behind St-Etienne) dates only from 1852. For the next hundred years Paris' tramps flocked here, and now, even though most of the houses have been restored, it still has a bohemian atmosphere, particularly at weekends. Leading off Place de la Contrescarpe is **Rue Rollin**, a treeless street of blonde houses. Place de la Contrescarpe also stands at the top of **Rue Mouffetard**, one of the most ancient streets in Paris, following the path of the Roman road to Lyon. Since Roman times it has been lined with inns and taverns for the wayfarer. While strolling down the 'Mouff' and poking about in its capillary lanes and courtyards you can pick out a number of old signs, such as the carved oak at no.69 for the Vieux Chêne, which began as a Revolutionary club. Rue du Pot-de-Fer owes its name to the Fontaine du Pot-de-Fer, one of 14 fountains donated by Marie de Médicis. In 1928, 25-year-old George Orwell moved into a seedy hotel at no.6 Rue du Pot-de-Fer to live off his savings while he wrote; when he was robbed he was reduced to washing dishes in a big hotel in the Rue de Rivoli – the source for his first published book, *Down and Out in Paris and London*. Further south, beyond Rue de l'Epée-de-Bois, begins Rue Mouffetard's **market** (*closed Mon*), where shops spill out to join pavement stalls, cascading with fruit and vegetables, cheeses, seafood, pâtés, sausages, bread and more, with an occasional exotic touch such as the African market in Rue de l'Arbalète.

The **Arènes de Lutèce**, on the other side of Rue Monge, are the slight remains of *Lutetia*'s Roman amphitheatre (now a garden, football pitch and *boules* court) dating from the 2nd century. It was discovered in 1869, restored in 1917 and, incredibly, almost demolished in 1980 for a housing project. Don't miss the knotty beech in the gardens, famous as the crookedest tree growing in Paris.

The **Grande Mosquée de Paris** (*Rue Georges Desplas; open for visits daily 9–12 and 2–6; closed Fri; adm*) was built between 1922 and 1926 in remembrance of the Muslim dead in the First World War and as a symbol of Franco-Moroccan friendship, and is nominally the central mosque for France's four million-plus faithful. A series of interior courtyards gives on to the sumptuous prayer room, where the domes were decorated by teams of Moroccan artisans competing in geometric ingenuity. Behind the mosque, at 41 Rue Geoffroy St-Hilaire, there's a Turkish **hammam** (*men Fri and Sun, women on other days 11–8; closed Tues*), with a quiet courtyard café serving mint tea.

The coolly elegant riverside **Institut du Monde Arabe**, 1 Rue des Fossés St-Bernard (*open Tues–Sun 10–6; closed Mon*), completed in 1987, is nearly everyone's favourite contemporary building in Paris. Its walls are covered with window panels inspired by ancient Islamic geometric patterns, but equipped with photo-electric cells that activate their dilation or contraction according to the amount of sunlight.

Further along the river is the pleasant **Jardin des Plantes**, containing a garden **labyrinth** (up on the little hill), topped by a bronze temple with a sundial; the tropical forest of the **Serres Tropicales** (Tropical Greenhouses) just south (*open 1–5, summer 1–6, closed Tues; adm*); the **Botanical School gardens** (*open summer Mon–Fri 7.30am–8pm; winter Mon–Fri 7.30–5.30; closed Sat, Sun and hols*); the **Muséum National d'Histoire Naturelle**, including the new interactive **Grande Galerie de l'Evolution** (*36 Rue Geoffroy-St Hilaire; open Fri–Mon and Wed 10–6, Thurs 10–10; closed Tues; adm*); and, in the long building beyond it, the **Galerie de Minéralogie** (*open Nov–Mar 10–5,*

April–Oct 10–6; closed Tues; adm). Allée de Jussieu leads to the **Ménagerie** (*open daily 10–5; adm*), with small animals, to be viewed up close, and the massive and eclectic brick **Galerie de Paléontologie** (*open daily 10–5; closed Tues; adm*).

St-Germain

France is one country where brainy philosophers get respect, and St-Germain is their citadel. Since the 1960s it has cooled considerably; and, in the inevitable urban cycles, the haunts of the avant-garde have now been gentrified. But despite the absurd rents and surplus posers St-Germain's essential conviviality remains intact. Its narrow streets, scarcely violated by the planners of the last two centuries, its art galleries, cafés and bookshops, and the Luxembourg Gardens cluttered with chairs, all invite you to gas the day away in the scholarly spirit of those first eggheads, Voltaire and Diderot, if not Camus, Sartre, Simone de Beauvoir and Foucault.

If urbanity is St-Germain's middle name, it owes much to its parent, the Benedictine abbey of St-Germain-des-Prés. The monks, specialists in ancient manuscripts, set the intellectual tone of the quarter; art, food and fashion from the rest of Europe and the East were introduced into Paris through the abbey's month-long fair. Theatres prospered; the first coffee houses opened here; and actors, Protestants and foreign artists could live in peace in the then independent town of St-Germain. Ideas circulated more freely as well. In its cafés Paris' intellectuals kept the spark alive in a circle around Jean-Paul Sartre and Simone de Beauvoir.

When Childebert Ier, son of Clovis, returned from the siege of Saragossa in 543, his booty included a piece of the True Cross and the tunic of St Vincent. Germanus, bishop of Paris, convinced Childebert to found an abbey to house the relics. When Germanus himself was canonized, the church became **St-Germain-des-Prés**. It was one of the most important Benedictine monasteries in France, and until Dagobert (d. 639) it was the burial place of the Merovingian kings. Of this early church little has survived: capitals, now in the Musée de Cluny, and the base of the massive tower on the west front. The rest was rebuilt in 1193; architect Peter de Montreuil added a **Lady Chapel**, as beautiful as his Sainte-Chapelle. In 1789 St-Germain's precious tombs and reliquaries were destroyed, and the famous library confiscated. In 1840 Victor Hugo led a campaign for St-Germain's restoration, and for the next 20 years much of what the Revolutionaries missed fell victim to the hacks hired to save it. The marble shafts in the columns above the arcade are the only Merovingian work *in situ* in Paris.

Serene **Place Furstemberg** with its delicate paulownia trees is a dainty gem of urban design that traces the ancient cloister of the abbots' palace. In the old abbey stable is the **Musée Delacroix** (*open 9.30–5; closed Tues; adm*), the last home of Eugène Delacroix, who moved here in 1857. Sketches, etchings and a dozen minor paintings hang in his lodgings and *atelier*, and there's a quiet garden.

Down Rue Bonaparte, the **Ecole des Beaux-Arts** (*courtyards open 8am–8pm; other adm only during exhibitions*) holds exhibitions in the oldest buildings on this site: Queen Marguerite de Valois' Chapelle des Louanges (1606; the first dome in Paris) and

A Literary Rendez-vous

Whether **Les Deux Magots** is '*le rendez-vous de l'élite intellectuelle*', according to its own menu, or the 'Two Maggots' of American teenagers, the café does offer grandstand views of St-Germain. Inside, the two statues of Chinese mandarins or *magots* date from the shop's original vocation – selling silks. The name was retained when it became a café in 1875; Mallarmé, Verlaine and Rimbaud gave it its literary seal of approval in the 1880s, and the café has distributed its own literary prize since 1933. A few doors down Boulevard St-Germain, its rival **Le Flore** opened in 1890. It too attracted a brainy clientele: Picasso and Apollinaire would edit art magazines in the back, Sartre and Camus were regulars, but stalwartly ignored each other's presence. On the south side of the boulevard, 'Le Drugstore', a groovy hangout in the 1960s, has recently succumbed to changing tastes, although its neighbour, **Brasserie Lipp**, still packs in Paris' *Who's Who* with a *choucroute* unchanged since 1920.

a chapel (1619; with elegant doors by Goujon) built for an Augustine monastery after Marguerite's death. In 1816 this convent became the school of fine arts. The main courtyard contains a collage of architectural fragments, most notably the central façade of Henri II's Château d'Anet (1548), with another fine door by Goujon. The **Rue des Beaux-Arts** is one of the main axes of the slowly churning St-Germain art world. The original galleries opened in the 1920s and shocked the public by being the first to show modern and abstract works. In 1900 Oscar Wilde, aged 46 but broken by his prison term, came to die 'beyond his means' in the former Hôtel d'Allemagne (no.13).

Off Rue St-André-des-Arts is the **Carrefour de Buci**, in the 18th century one of the most fashionable crossroads of the Left Bank, and now the city's most fashionable market, particularly at weekends. When you can pull yourself away from the meticulous displays of smoked salmon and *pâtés en croûte*, backtrack a few giant steps along Rue St-André-des-Arts for a look at the cobblestoned **Cour du Commerce St-André**, opened in 1776. This is Paris' oldest *passage*, built before new iron and glass engineering techniques were to make them the marvel of the Right Bank. Midway, to your left, extend three courtyards known as the **Cour de Rohan**. In the first courtyard, the gentle Dr Joseph-Ignace Guillotin and a carpenter named Schmidt used sheep to test their decapitation machine. There's a Renaissance house covered with vines in the second courtyard, part of the *hôtel particulier* of Diane de Poitiers.

The quartier's other big church, **St-Sulpice**, dates from 1646; by the time the builders reached the façade in 1732, the original Baroque plan seemed old-fashioned, resulting in a competition, won by an even more antique design by a Florentine named Servandoni. Inside the grey, cavernous nave, railway clocks tick down the minutes to the next TGV to heaven. The organ is one of the most seriously overwrought in Paris; the holy water stoups are two enormous clam shells, gifts from Venice to François Ier. In such a setting, the lush, romantic murals by Delacroix in the first chapel on the right radiate warmth. The last chapel before the right transept contains the Hallowe'en *tomb of Curé Languet de Gergy* (1750) by Michelangelo Slodtz. The copper strip across the transept traces the Paris meridian, and if you come at the winter solstice you'll see a sunray strike the centre of the obelisk.

Built by Louis XV in 1782, the neoclassical **Théâtre de l'Odéon** was the first public theatre in Paris designed exclusively for drama, its austere Doric temple façade attractively set in the semicircular Place de l'Odéon. After fires in 1807 and 1818, the theatre was reconstructed to the original design. For decades, however, the Odéon was a flop. During the Revolution its troupe split, the pro-Republican actors going off to the Comédie Française and the Royalists sticking it out here until they were carted off to the slammer. In the next century the theatre had a few successes (Bizet's *L'Arlésienne*, in 1872), but it only became popular after the Second World War when Jean-Louis Barrault and Madeleine Renaud quickened its pulse with contemporary drama.

Jardin du Luxembourg

The Jardin du Luxembourg is a welcome Left Bank oasis of greenery. Metal chairs are scattered under the trees and around a shady café and bandstand, although the scarce lawns are out of bounds. But the kids have all the fun, on an opulent carousel designed by Charles Garnier, riding pony carts and mini-cars, sailing boats in the Grand Bassin, or watching performances of *guignol* in the **Théâtre des Marionettes du Luxembourg** (*shows Wed–Mon from 11am; call t 01 43 26 46 47; adm*). Near the gate, the park remembers its foundress, Marie de Médicis, with the long pool of the **Fontaine de Médicis** (just east of the Palais du Luxembourg), a romantic rendezvous under the plane trees, dating from 1624 and adorned with 19th-century statuary.

Widowed Marie de Médicis, Regent of France, always dreamed of a replica of her girlhood home, Florence's enormous Pitti Palace. Architect Salomon de Brosse managed to dissuade her in favour of a more traditional French mansion, the **Palais du Luxembourg** (*Rue de Vaugirard; open one or two Sun per month for guided tours; contact t 01 44 61 20 84*) but decorated it with Florentine touches – the rusticated bands of stone that give it a corrugated look, and its 'ringed' Tuscan columns. At the west end of the big Palace, at Rue de Vaugirard, the delightful **Petit Luxembourg** was Paris' first public art gallery, and the **Musée de Luxembourg** (*open Tues–Thurs 10–7; Mon and Fri 10–11, Sat and Sun 10–8; adm*) still puts on temporary exhibitions.

Montparnasse

In the Middle Ages Montparnasse was where the flour was ground for the Left Bank's baguettes; in 1780 there were still 18 working windmills. The first houses date from the 17th century, when Louis XIV built the Observatoire. Land was still cheap enough in the early 1800s for Montparnasse to experience a first flash of fashion with its dance halls, *guingettes* and cabarets. After the Second World War the culture vultures retreated to St-Germain and the north side of Bd du Montparnasse, while the neighbourhood where Americans drank themselves silly was singled out for Paris' first experiment in American-style property development. Until the advent of London's Canary Wharf, the **Tour Montparnasse** (*viewing platforms open summer daily 9.30am–11pm; winter daily 9.30am–9.30pm; adm*) was the tallest skyscraper in Europe, 656ft high and visible for miles around, perched at the top of Rue de Rennes.

The 56th floor offers not only views but a bar, *Ciel de Paris*; the 59th floor is an open terrace. On a clear day you can see for 25 miles. The submerged shopping mall in front overlooks Place du 18 Juin 1940, and the streets around are filled with the everyday shops and bars of the real, non-touristy Paris of the Parisians.

Exhibition Paris

This isn't the cosy Paris of quaint *bistrots* and narrow streets; this is Paris, the national showcase of France. Here at the self-designated centre of civilization both the buildings and the spaces between are on an heroic scale, monuments baked through the centuries then iced and glazed by a succession of world fairs.

Musée d'Orsay

*1 Rue de la Légion d'Honneur, **t** 01 40 49 48 14, www.musee-orsay.fr;*
open Tues, Wed, Fri, Sat 10–6, Sun and 20 June–20 Sept 9–6, Thurs
10–9.45pm; closed Mon; adm, free first Sun of month and for under-18s.

The Gare d'Orsay is a monument born on the cusp of the 19th century: a daring work of iron weighing more than the Eiffel Tower, with a nave taller than Notre-Dame, thrown up in two years for the 1900 World Fair. Unfortunately, its platforms were too short for modern trains, and the station was abandoned in 1960. It opened as a museum in 1986, nine years after the design was approved. The core exhibits came from the former Jeu-de-Paume Museum and the 19th-century rooms of the Louvre. Here under one huge roof are gathered all its combative schools of painting and sculpture from 1848 to 1910, rounded out with a magnificent array of furniture, decorative arts, architectural exhibits and photography.

Highlights of the collections include: **sculptures**; the **Salle de l'Opéra**, dedicated to Garnier's extraordinary folly; the greatest works of **Gustave Courbet** (1819–77), the formulator of Realism and the first artist to completely buck the *salon* system; **Manet's** *Olympia* (1865), which made people spit venom when shown in the Salon des Refusés; **Impressionist paintings before 1870**, when Monet, Renoir and Bazille first took their easels out of doors; **Manet**'s *Déjeuner sur l'Herbe* and *Sur la Plage*; **Whistler's Mother**; **Monet**'s *Régates à Argenteuil*, his steam-filled *Gare Saint-Lazare* and his *Rue Montorgueil*; **Pissarro**'s *Les Toits Rouges*; *L'Inondation à Port-Marly*, considered the masterpiece of **Albert Sisley** (1839–99); **Renoir**'s irresistible evocation of Paris's *bal-dansants*, the *Moulin de la Galette* (1876); **Degas**'s *A la Bourse*, *L'Absinthe* and *Les Repasseuses*; **late Impressionists** (after 1880) including Monet's series that portray the same subject at different times of day – *Les Meules* (Haystacks), five of *Les Cathédrales de Rouen* and two versions of the *Nymphéas* (Water-lilies) painted at Giverny – plus Renoir's *Paysage Algérien*, *Fête Arabe à Alger*, and *Les Grandes Baigneuses*; **Van Gogh**'s *La Guinguette*, *L'Arlésienne*, *La Chambre de Van Gogh à Arles* and the merciless *Autoportrait*, painted during his first fit of madness in Arles; **Cézanne**'s *La Maison du Pendu* and *Une Moderne Olympia*, inspired by Manet; **postimpressionism** including **Georges Seurat**'s *La Cirque*; the **Salle Redon**: devoted to the works of the elusive

Odilon Redon (1840–1916), master colourist and pre-Freudian painter of dreams, who belonged to no school but inspired the Symbolists, Surrealists and Metaphysical painters who followed; the **Salle Toulouse-Lautrec**; **Gauguin**'s lush paintings from the South Seas; **Fauvism**, represented by **André Derain**'s *Le Pont de Charing Cross* (1902); **Symbolists** including *The Wheel of Fortune* by Burne-Jones, and the famous *Portrait of Proust* by Jacques-Emile Blanches. And there's more besides painting: dragonfly **Art Nouveau** jewellery by Lalique, furniture by Guimard, a desk by Henry Van de Velde and glass by Tiffany and Gallé, and the **Tour Guimard**, furniture designed by architects – beautiful chairs by Guimard, Gaudí, Bugatti, Mackintosh and Frank Lloyd Wright..

Musée Rodin

77 Rue de Varenne; t 01 44 18 61 10, www.musee-rodin.fr; open Tues–Sun 9.30–5.45, Oct–Mar 9.30–4.45, gardens an hour later in summer; adm.

The Hôtel Biron (1731), built by Jacques-Ange Gabriel, is one of the most charming and best-preserved mansions in Paris from that period. When Auguste Rodin moved here in 1908, he was 68. The house is now the Musée Rodin; as well as his works, one room is dedicated to sculptor Camille Claudel, Rodin's mistress. Upstairs are paintings that Rodin owned and left to the state. Outside, amid the roses of the *Cour d'Honneur*, are *The Thinker* and other masterpieces in a delightful garden setting.

Hôtel des Invalides

In 1670 Louis XIV's under-minister of war, Louvois, persuaded his warmongering king to provide a hospital for old soldiers, which could just incidentally double as a monument to the military glory of Louis himself. Set at the head of an enormous Esplanade stretching to the Seine, the **Invalides** has Siamese-twin churches, back to back, originally sharing the same altar and chancel: **St-Louis** (*open daily 10–6*) for the old soldiers and staff, and the Eglise-du-Dôme for royals. A large section of the **Musée de l'Armée** (*open daily 10–6; Oct–Mar daily 10–5; adm*) is devoted to Napoleon's life. Save your ticket for the **Eglise-du-Dôme**. The pointy dome is so impressive that the church is named after it, and so prominent on the skyline that it was freshly gilded with 27½ lbs of gold for the bicentennial of the Revolution. The big porphyry sarcophagus of **Napoleon's tomb** contains no fewer than six coffins fitted tightly together.

Eiffel Tower and Trocadéro

t 01 44 11 23 23, www.tour-eiffel.fr; open winter daily 9.30am–11pm; summer daily 9am–midnight; adm exp. If you arrive late, count on a good hour's wait for the lift to the first (€3.70), second (€7) and third (€10.20) platforms.

The incomparable souvenir of the 1889 Fair, the Eiffel Tower was built to celebrate the Revolution's centenary and the resurrection of France after her defeat by Prussia in 1870. It is 300m (1,000ft) of graceful iron filigree; belly-up between its four spidery paws, its 9,700 tons sit with extraordinary lightness on the soft clay, exerting as much pressure as that of a man sitting in a chair. It was erected in two years, for less than the estimated 8 million francs, welded together with 2,500,000 rivets. Gustave Eiffel was already famous for his daring bridges and viaducts; in 1886 he had designed the structural frame of the Statue of Liberty. Originally the tower was painted several tints, lightening to yellow-gold at the top, so its appearance dissolved and changed according to the time of day and weather; now, every five or six years, forty painters cover it with 7,700lb of a sombre maroon colour called *ferrubrou*. In 1986 sodium lamps were installed in the structure; it's usually lit up until midnight.

To reach the **Jardins du Trocadéro**, cross the Pont d'Iéna, commissioned after Napoleon Ier's victory at Jena in Prussia and decked out with proud imperial eagles. The gardens stretching to the Seine were laid out for the 1878 fair and restored in 1937; today they are home to a 1900s *carrousel*.

The main feature of the Place du Trocadéro is the superb view from the courtyard of the **Palais de Chaillot** across the river and south. This palace is one of the legacies of one of the very last World Fairs, the 1937 Paris Exposition Universelle. Today the palace, facing Place du Trocadéro, provides a home for four museums. The oldest, in the east wing, is the **Musée National des Monuments Français** (*open daily 10–6*), a collection of exact, lifesize copies of France's finest architectural features, sculptures and mural paintings from the early Romanesque period to the 19th century. The **Musée de l'Homme** (*open Wed–Mon 9.45–5.15; closed Tues; adm*) is an excellent anthropology museum. As you might expect, gloriously detailed ship models make up the bulk of the exhibits in the **Musée de la Marine** (*open Wed–Mon 10–6; closed Tues; adm*). France has its own tradition on the sea, and you'll get an extra helping of it here.

Another nearby relic of the 1937 Fair, the huge **Palais de Tokyo**, contains in its east wing a new **Musée d'Art Moderne** (*11 Av du Président Wilson; open Tues–Fri 10–5.30, Sat, Sun 10–6.30; adm*). There's a small collection of works from Matisse onwards, as well as changing exhibitions, usually on contemporary artists. In the west wing is the innovative **Site de Création Contemporaine** (*open Tues–Sun noon–midnight*), designed to break down many of the barriers of traditional museums, with guides replaced by '*médiateurs*' encouraging dialogue in a challenging multimedia setting.

Peripheral Attractions

Many of the sights of Paris are within walking distance of one another. However, this section includes a few attractions located just beyond the city centre, starting at La Villette in the northeast corner, and continuing clockwise around the city.

Parc de la Villette

Ⓜ *Porte de la Villette; 19ᵉ. Cité des Sciences et de l'Industrie open Tues–Sat 10–6, Sun 10–7; adm. Musée de la Musique (Ⓜ Porte de Pantin) open Tues–Sat 12–6, Sun 10–6; adm. You can take a boat from Canal St-Martin.*

When the slaughterhouse was metamorphosed into the **Cité des Sciences et de l'Industrie**, a rectangle of glass and exposed girders reminiscent of the Centre Pompidou, Mitterrand's critics had their fun. As a science museum it duplicates the Palais de la Découverte (*see* p.118), only it's a little flashier and more up to date. There are **Planétarium** shows and 3-D films in the **Louis Lumière cinema**. Across the Canal de l'Ourcq, the southern half of the Parc de La Villette is occupied by the two new white asymmetrical buildings of the **Cité de la Musique**, designed by Christian de Portzamparc: they contain concert halls, the Conservatoire of dance and music, and a **Musée de la Musique** with 4,500 instruments.

Parc des Buttes-Chaumont

Ⓜ *Buttes-Chaumont; 19ᵉ.*

A rocky haunt of outlaws in the Middle Ages, well known to François Villon, the park, now Paris' loveliest, was begun in 1867. In an age when the 'picturesque' was fully in vogue, the natural charms of the Buttes weren't quite good enough. Haussmann's designers brought in thousands of tons of rock and created the artificial cliffs that are its fame today. The centrepiece is a landmark, a steep island in a lake, crowned by a small classical temple, modelled after the Temple of the Sybil in Tivoli.

Canal St-Martin

Once home to Paris' less than affluent, the long banks of the old canal between Rue du Faubourg-du-Temple and Rue Louis-Blanc (Ⓜ *République/Goncourt/Louis Blanc; 10ᵉ*) are fast coming to life as hip Paris' new 'in' zone. Fathers and sons on in-line skates race between the raised gardens of new apartment blocks, and fishermen dangle their feet along the cobbled banks beneath the green iron bridges. At 95 Quai de Valmy, the pink, green and yellow façades of the assorted shops make a colourful splash. At 102 Quai de Jemmapes is the site of the **Hôtel du Nord**, famous for being the location of Marcel Carné's 1938 film; it now serves traditional French cuisine in its setting full of *atmosphère*; 167 Quai de Valmy hops after 10pm to the strains of jazz.

Père-Lachaise Cemetery

Ⓜ *Père-Lachaise; 20ᵉ. Open Mon–Fri 7.30–6, Sat 8.30–6, Sun 9–6; 6 Nov–15 Mar daily 8–5.30.*

The 'most famous cemetery in the world', and the largest in Paris, Père-Lachaise has always been a favourite place for a stroll; Balzac said he liked to come here to 'cheer himself up'. In design, it is a cross between the traditional, urban French cemetery, with ponderous family mausolea in straight rows, and the modern, suburban-style model. At the main entrance you can buy a good map to all the famous stiffs. There are few signs to help you find the graves of the great and good, such as Héloïse and Abélard, Chopin, Balzac, Molière, Simone Signoret, Sarah Bernhardt, Proust, Isadora Duncan and Oscar Wilde.

Bois de Vincennes

Ⓜ *Porte Dorée for the zoo,* Ⓜ *Château de Vincennes for the castle.*

Like the Bois de Boulogne, its matching bookend at the other end of Paris, Vincennes owes its existence to the French kings' love of hunting. They set it aside for that purpose in the 1100s, and Philippe Auguste even built a wall around it to keep out poachers. In the 14th century the Valois kings built its castle at the northern end of the park – a real fortified castle, not just a château, for this was the time of the Hundred Years War. As long as the nearby Marais was fashionable, so was Vincennes, but when Louis XIV left Paris in the opposite direction, for Versailles, the neglected hunting ground was turned into a public park. Besides the open spaces, the main attraction is the **zoo** (*open daily 9–5 or 5.30, until 6 or 6.30 in summer; adm*), one of the largest in Europe. Adjacent is one of the prettier parts of the park, the **Lac Daumesnil** with its islands, one blessed with a fake ruin like the one in Buttes-Chaumont. Further east (**Ⓜ** *Château de Vincennes, then bus no.112*) is the **Parc Floral** (*open daily 9.30–5, summer till 8; adm*): water lilies, orchids and dahlias, with rides and entertainments.

The **castle** (*open Oct–Mar daily 10–11.45 and 1.15–5; April–Sept daily 10–11.45 and 1.15–6; long and short guided tours; adm, free to under-18s*), the finest example of medieval secular architecture in Paris, shows what the French could build even in the sorrows of the 1300s. Begun under Philippe IV in 1337, it was completed in 1380. Louis was always short of prison cells and Vincennes made a convenient calaboose. Napoleon, another ruler who liked to keep his cells full, made it a prison again while rebuilding the fortifications just in case. During the First World War the trenches around it were used for shooting spies. The highlight of the tour is the **donjon**, the 14th-century keep, strong and taciturn outside but a beautiful residence within, containing stained glass and sculptural work. The **Salle des Gens d'Armes** is a lovely Gothic vaulted space. In the bedroom on the second floor England's King Henry V died in 1422. Besides these, the tour inside takes you through the **Résidence Royale**, built by Le Vau for Louis XIV, and the **Sainte-Chapelle**, almost a copy of the famous one.

The Catacombes

*1 Place Denfert-Rochereau; **Ⓜ** Denfert-Rochereau; **t** 01 43 22 47 63; open Tues 11–4, Wed–Sun 9–4; closed Mon and hols; adm; take a torch.*

Place Denfert-Rochereau is one of the Left Bank's busiest traffic fandangos, guarded by the sphinx-like Lion de Belfort. The two pavilions with carved friezes survive from the *Barrière d'Enfer*, or 'tollgate of hell', in the Farmers-General wall. An apt name, as one of the pavilions (no.1) serves as the entrance to the Catacombes. Down, down the 90 steps of a spiral stair. and a tramp through damp and dreary tunnels to a vicious blue puddle called the *source de Léthé*, inhabited by little pale-eyed creatures who dine on bone moss. Then the doorway inscribed: 'Halt! This is the empire of the dead.' But of course you don't halt at all, for beyond is the main attraction: the last earthly remains of Mirabeau, Rabelais, Madame de Pompadour and five to six million other Parisians removed here beginning in 1786 from the putrid, overflowing cemetery of the Innocents and nearly every other churchyard in Paris.

Bois de Boulogne

After the Eiffel Tower, the Bois de Boulogne was not so long ago the most visited place in Paris – the 'world capital of prostitution', no less. The Bois owes its current appearance to Napoléon III, who spent his early years in London and gave the Bois to the city as its own Hyde Park. Roads, riding and walking paths crisscross it, but for anyone with children in tow the biggest attraction is on the Neuilly side, to the north (Ⓜ *Les Sablons*) where the **Jardin d'Acclimatation** (*open 10–6, till 7 in summer; activities at weekends and during school hols; adm*) has nearly every possible activity for kids – camel and canal-boat rides, playgrounds, a small zoo, a doll's house with antique toys, a *guignol* (puppet show), children's theatre, bumper cars, crafts and games.

The most scenic spots in the Bois include the **Lac Inférieur**, with its islets and emperor's kiosk (near *RER Av Henri-Martin* or Ⓜ *Ranelagh*); the **Shakespeare garden** by the open-air theatre in the **Pré Catelan**; the **Grande Cascade**, an artificial Swiss Alps waterfall just east of Longchamp; and, for garden- and rose-lovers, the sumptuous **Parc de Bagatelle** (*a 15min walk or bus 43 from* Ⓜ *Pont de Neuilly or take bus 244 from* Ⓜ *Porte Maillot or RER Rueil-Malmaison; open spring/summer daily 8.30–8,*

The charming **Musée Marmottan** (*2 Rue Louis-Boilly,* Ⓜ *La Muette; open Tues–Sun 10–6.30; closed Mon; adm*) is on the edge of the Bois. The Marmottan family collected medieval miniatures, tapestries and Napoleonic art and furniture, but the Monets are the highlight: some of the *Nymphéas* ('Water-lilies'), one of the *Cathédrales de Rouen* and a view of the British Houses of Parliament.

La Défense

Ⓜ*/RER La Défense; t 01 49 07 27 57, www.grandearche.com; open summer daily 10–8; winter daily 10–7; ticket office closes ½ hour earlier; free.*

Forty years ago this was a dismal suburban industrial area, its only feature a *rond-point*, laid out by Madame de Pompadour's brother back in 1765 when the area was still a noble park and hunting preserve. After the siege of 1870, a statue commemorating the defence of Paris was set up here: 'La Défense' gradually gave its name to the whole area. In 1955 the national government (not the Ville de Paris) decided to make a modern, American-style business district out of the vacant land, and by 1960 glass towers were sprouting like toadstools, a surreal scene for older Parisians. French directors were not slow to seize on La Défense's cinematic potential. Jacques Tati's poor bewildered Monsieur Hulot was baffled by glass doors. In *The Little Theatre of Jean Renoir* there is a vignette of a modern woman who falls hopelessly in love with her electric floor polisher; the tidy corporate people of La Défense provide a sort of Greek chorus. Today, about 150,000 people work here and there are about 55,000 residents.

The **Parvis**, also called the Podium or the Dalle, is the long pedestrian mall aligned with the Grand Axe. Sorry monoliths dubbed with corporate acronyms are interspersed with a wealth of abstract sculptures and mosaics. At the eastern end, with a broad view over Paris, is the **Takis Fountain**, illuminated in the evenings with coloured lights. In the centre, near the Agam Fountain, is the original sculpture of the '**Défense**'. Since its opening in 1989, though, the star of the show has unquestionably been François Mitterrand's personal monument, the **Grande Arche**. There's a lift, running up a glass tube through the hole; take the ride through the air to the top for a panoramic view of the city.

Ile de France

This is the cradle of the Capet kings, of France and of *francilien*, the medieval dialect that evolved into modern French. But how did the Ile-de-France get its name? In the Middle Ages any place between rivers could be an island, while *Francia* was the name given to the Paris basin under the Merovingians, long before it encompassed the entire country. In later years it maintained a quintessential quality: its gentle hills produce Brie, the Frenchiest of French cheeses, while its architects produced Gothic, the ultimate French style, leaving great cathedrals at Beauvais (*see* p.566), Amiens (*see* p.553), Soissons (*see* p.561), Laon (*see* p.557) and Chartres (*see* pp.327–31), all day trips out of Paris. In the last 150 years it has become quintessential in another way. While the Impressionists found bucolic subjects to paint here in the 1870s, the Ile de France has since been covered with urban sprawl; over one out of every five people in France now live in the region, too many in the dire state housing estates of the *banlieue*.

St-Germain-en-Laye

West of La Défense, the old town of St-Germain-en-Laye (RER A) grew up around a priory founded by Robert the Pious in 1050. The priory became a château lavishly rebuilt in brick by François Ier, and it saw the dawn of the Sun King, who spent most of his first 40 pre-Versailles years here and hired Le Nôtre to lay out the long gardens.

There are regular tours of the **château**, and the excellent **Musée des Antiquités Nationales** (*open Wed–Mon 9–5.15; closed Tues; adm*), an archaeological collection of treasures ranging from Lower Paleolithic to Merovingian France.

St-Denis: the Original Gothic Church

Ⓜ *St-Denis-Université.*

St-Denis, with its great abbey that was the necropolis of the kings of France, is today one of the classic *banlieues défavorisées*. Communist-run, gritty and poor, it saw its transformation from rural idyll to industrial inferno in the 19th century, when some 60 factories making everything from cars to pianos moved in. Today the old village is only the centre of a suburban agglomeration of over 100,000 people. It's well run, and still has a noticeable sense of civic pride.

The Abbey Basilica

Open April–Sept Mon–Sat 10–6.30, Sun 12–6; Oct–Mar Mon–Sat 10–4.30, Sun 12–4.30; adm.

St Denis, who after being decapitated at Montmartre shambled up here with his head tucked under his arm to begin his career as patron of France, is a truly shadowy character. Like so many other French saints he may be a half-conscious fabrication, papering over survivals of paganism that early missionaries had assimilated.

There was a cemetery here from Roman times, and an abbey from perhaps the 5th century, favoured by Dagobert and other Merovingian kings, who began the tradition of making it the site for royal burials. St-Denis' present glory is entirely due to its rebuilding under the remarkable Abbot Suger (1081–1151). Diplomat, counsellor to Louis VI and Louis VII, and ruler of France while the latter was away on the Crusades, Suger also found time, according to his own accounts, to invent Gothic architecture single-handedly. Perhaps his architects had something to do with it too, but the good abbot, constantly cajoling, suggesting, kibitzing over the sculptor's shoulder and even helping hoist the stones, must get a fair share of the credit. After his death, St Denis monks cranked out false chronicles, charters and bequests dating from as early as Charlemagne's time to prove certain rights of the abbey and its royal patrons. Wealth, influence and royal cadavers accumulated, and not surprisingly St-Denis became one of the chief targets of the revolutionaries of 1793. Twelve hundred years' worth of anointed bones were tossed into a pit; the revolutionaries trashed the tombs and carted off France's richest church treasure. Under the restoration, Louis XVIII started fixing the place up, and Viollet-le-Duc came to finish the job in 1859.

The basilica's **façade** is one of the triumphs of Suger and his architects, a marvel of clarity and order that pointed the way to all the Gothic cathedrals that followed. Inside, notice that the nave and transepts are in a different style, a confident mature Gothic. The unassuming **choir** is the real Gothic revolution, with its ribbed vaulting. From the west portals you can see how the walls tilt backwards. The **rose window**, with seasons and signs of the zodiac, is one of the few remaining bits of medieval glass, as are the *Tree of Jesse* and *Life of the Virgin* in the apse behind the main altar.

From the right aisle, you begin the tour of the **royal tombs**. These too were heavily restored after the desecrations of 1793 and few are of interest, even though they go as far back as Dagobert, who died in 639. In the right ambulatory hangs the **oriflamme**, flame-covered battle standard of the French kings, a 15th-century copy of the medieval original, lost in the Hundred Years War.

Musée de l'Art et de l'Histoire de la Ville de St-Denis

Rue Gabriel-Péri; open Wed–Sat and Mon 10–5.30, Sun 2–6.30; closed Tues; adm.

St-Denis also has a delightful museum, housed in an old Carmelite convent. From nun memorabilia and an exhibit on medieval daily life, the scene changes to modern industrial St-Denis: paintings by local artists of the canals and gas works, old shop fronts and the *roulottes* (caravans) many workers lived in. The biggest exhibit is devoted to the 1871 Commune: a floor of paintings, posters, cartoons and newspapers relates the story more thoroughly than you'll ever see in Paris.

Disneyland® Resort Paris

32km east of Paris at Marne-la-Vallée; RER A4; www.disneylandparis.com;
t 08705 03 03 03 (UK), t (407) 934 7639 (US), t 01 60 30 60 30 (in France) for all
information and booking; open daily, hours change according to season and
school hols; high season one-day adm to either the park or the studios €39;
low season €29; to both park and studios €49; 3-day tickets available;
combined RER/Disneyland® ticket gives you a return from Paris and one-day
entry for €45 high season, €39 low season.

'A cultural Chernobyl at the heart of Europe,' snarled theatre director Ariane Mnouchkine although, as the French themselves admitted, culture in Europe must be pretty thin gruel if it can be threatened by a cartoon mouse. The French government helped bring the fox into the chicken coop – an RER line and TGV line linked up to Marseille, Lyon, Lille, Charles de Gaulle airport and eventually London, and land made available on very favourable terms. Disneyland® Paris opened on 12 April 1992 and the first three years were characterized by a brutal baptism in red ink and farcical Franco-American misunderstandings. However, it all appears to have settled down.

The park is a fifth the size of the city of Paris, protected from the outside world by 30ft sloped dykes. They employ 11,000 smiling 'cast members' every year. Large theme hotels are run with guaranteed 'Have a nice day' friendliness. Besides the rides, the fun includes infinite 'shopping opportunities', special shows, characters, food (American, Mexican, Italian and other European), discos and American nightlife at the Festival Disney complex. If you go in summer, bring a good book: Tinkerbell herself must have designed the enchanted queue routes for the rides, that curl in and out, up and down, all the better to keep you believing you're almost there when there's still half the population of Europe waiting in front of you. In 2002 the Walt Disney Studios® Park opened, and the original park with Main Street, USA and its four 'lands' (Fantasyland, Frontierland, Adventureland, Discoveryland) is now known as Disneyland® Park, the two together making up the 'resort'.

Versailles

*Get there by RER C or train from Gare Montparnasse or from Gare St-Lazare to Versailles-Rive Droite, followed by a 15min walk. Château open April–Oct Tues–Sun 9–6.30; Nov–Mar Tues–Sun 9–5.30; closed hols; guided tours in English from 10am. You can visit, for various separate fees, the **Grands Appartements** (entrance A); the **Apartments of Louis XIV** and the **Apartments of the Dauphin and Dauphine** (entrance C); the **Opéra Royal**, a gem designed by Gabriel for Louis XV in 1768, which is all wood, painted as marble, but designed 'to resonate like a violin'. From April–mid-Oct the garden's **musical fountains** are turned on. A 'Passport' gives access to the **Château**, **Grand Trianon**, **Petit Trianon**, **Coach Museum** and the **Groves**.*

Versailles' name comes from the clods that the farmer turns over with his plough, referring to the clearing made for a royal hunting lodge. And so Versailles remained until the young Louis XIV saw Vaux-le-Vicomte and turned sour with envy. He would have something perhaps not better but certainly bigger, and he created for himself one of the world's masterpieces of megalomania. Versailles' 123 acres of rooms are strikingly devoid of art; the enormous façade of the château is as monotonous as it is tasteful, so as not to upstage the principal inhabitant. The object is not to think of the building, but of Louis XIV, and with that thought be awed; Versailles contributed greatly to the bankruptcy of France.

If there's no art in Versailles, there is certainly an extraordinary amount of skilful craftsmanship. Besides its main purpose as a stage for the Sun King (Versailles was open to anyone who was decently dressed, as long as they promised not to beg; anyone could watch the king attend Mass, or dine), the palace served as a giant public showroom for French products, especially luxury ones. As such it was a spectacular success, contributing greatly to the spread of French tastes and fashions throughout Europe. Today, Versailles' curators haunt the auction houses of the world, looking to replace as much of the original gear as possible – a bust here, a chair there. Even the gardens have been replanted with Baroque bowers.

The **Grands Appartements** are the public rooms open to all in Louis XIV's day. Then there are the **gardens**, last replanted by Napoléon III, with their 13 miles of box hedges to clip, and the 1,100 potted palms and oranges of the Orangerie. Not by accident, the sun sets straight into it on Saint Louis' day, 25 August, in a perfect alignment with the Hall of Mirrors. Louis kept a flotilla of gondolas on his Grand Canal, to take his courtiers for rides; today the gondoliers of Venice come to visit every September for the *Fêtes Vénitiennes*. The rest of the year you can hire a boat to paddle yourself about or a bike to pedal through the gardens, or even catch a little zoo train to a building far more interesting than the main palace, the **Grand Trianon** (*adm*). An elegant, airy Italianate palace of pink marble and porphyry with two wings linked by a peristyle, it was designed in 1687 for Louis XIV ('I built Versailles for the court, Marly for my friends, and Trianon for myself,' he said). After his divorce, Napoleon brought his new Empress Marie-Louise here.

The gardens in this area were laid out by Louis XV's architect, Jacques-Ange Gabriel, who also built the rococo **Pavillon du Jardin des Français** and the refined **Petit Trianon** nearby (*adm*), intended for Louis XV's meetings with Mme de Pompadour. Louis XVI gave the Petit Trianon to Marie-Antoinette, who spent much of her time here. Beyond the Petit Trianon is the **Hameau de la Reine,** the delightful operetta farmhouse built for Marie-Antoinette, where she could play shepherdess. Nothing escaped Louis XIV's attention, and even his carrots and cabbages were planted in geometric rigidity in his immaculate vegetable garden, **Le Potager du Roi** (*entrance at 10 Rue Maréchal Joffre, on the left side of Place des Armes, the square in front of the château; open April–Oct daily, guided tours Sat and Sun every hour 10–6; adm; book on **t** 01 39 24 62 62*).

Vaux-le-Vicomte

*Get there by train from the Gare de Lyon to Melun (61km), then take a taxi or shuttle bus 6km to the château. Open April–Oct daily 10–6; Mar and 1–11 Nov 11–5; other times by appt, call, **t** 01 64 14 41 90. Fountains play the 2nd and last Sat of month 3–6; romantic candlelight tours May–Oct 8pm–midnight; adm.*

Vaux was the prototype for Versailles but is much prettier: designed by Louis Le Vau and decorated by Charles Lebrun, set in the original *jardin à la française* by André Le Nôtre – who for the first time had a scale vast enough to play with vanishing points and perspectives to his heart's content. The whole shebang was master-minded by Nicolas Fouquet, Louis XIV's minister of finances, who adopted Hercules as his patron, just as Louis saw himself as Apollo.

Even if Fouquet aped a decorative mythology on the level of Disney's *Fantasia*, the concept of Vaux was undeniably Herculean. Not only did Fouquet unite the greatest talents of his time, but he created this country palace and gardens in only five years, employing 20,000 masons, decorators and gardeners, all with one aim in mind: to form a suitable stage for a grand fête to impress one single person, the king, on 17 August 1661. It was, by all accounts, the most splendid party in the history of France. The 23-year-old Louis was certainly impressed – and so miffed that he refused to sleep in the *chambre du roi* built just for him.

Vaux was used as lavish proof of Fouquet's graft, and cited in his embezzlement trial three years later, but it wasn't the expense that got Louis' goat that famous night. What niggled Apollo was that Hercules, a mere mortal, had upstaged him not only in extravagance but as an arbiter of taste. And like Apollo, who was often cruel, Louis punished Fouquet's hubris, personally intervening in his trial to insist on a sentence of solitary confinement for life. The king confiscated all Fouquet's property. Then he confiscated Fouquet's ideas to create Versailles, hiring Le Vau, Lebrun and Le Nôtre to repeat their work at Vaux, but on an appalling scale; Fouquet's tapestry weavers and furniture makers were employed to form the nucleus of the Gobelins factories; Louis hired Fouquet's fireworks makers to light his own fêtes; he even carted off Fouquet's 1,200 orange trees for his Orangerie at Versailles.

In the 19th century Le Nôtre's gardens, with their clipped hedges, statues and elaborate waterworks, were restored. Period furnishings and tapestries from the Gobelins and Savonnerie complement the surviving decorations, which include Lebrun's portraits of Fouquet in the **Salon d'Hercule** and his poignantly unfinished ceiling in the **Grand Salon**. Vaux's stables contain the **Musée des Equipages** full of beautiful antique carriages. Lastly, look for the carved squirrels – Fouquet's family symbol (because they hoard all their goodies).

Fontainebleau

*The train to Melun continues to **Fontainebleau**, 65km from Paris; get off at Fontainbleau-Avon, and take bus A or B from the station. The **tourist office**, 4 Rue Royale, **t** 01 60 74 99 99, hires out bikes and sells a detailed map). **Château**, t 01 60 71 50 70, open June–Sept Wed–Mon 9.30–6; Oct–May Wed–Mon 9.30–5; closed Tues; adm.*

At weekends half of Paris seems to be here; the **forest**, with its wonderful variety of flora – including 2,700 species of mushrooms and fungi – oak and pine woods, rocky escarpments and dramatic gorges, is the wildest place near the metropolis. It was always exceptionally rich in game and by 1150 had already been set aside as the royal hunting reserve of Louis the Fat. The medieval kings managed with a fortified castle-hunting lodge, but along came François Ier, who chose Fontainebleau to be his artistic showcase; down went most of the old castle and up went an elegant **château**, fit to be decorated by the artists the king had imported from Italy, especially the great Rosso Fiorentino, a student of Michelangelo. Work on the château continued under Henri II and the exquisite architect Philibert de l'Orme. Henri IV added two courts decorated by Flemish artists. Every subsequent ruler to Napoleon added their bit; the Revolution destroyed most of its furnishings, while Louis-Philippe hired ham-handed restorers, who left much of the art a shadow of itself.

With contributions from so many monarchs, the Château de Fontainebleau makes an interesting style book. Enter through the **Cour des Adieux**, where Napoleon bid farewell to his Imperial Guard after his abdication on 20 April 1814, and Louis XIII built the magnificent horseshoe staircase. The tour of the **Grands Appartements** includes the famous **Galerie François Ier** (1533–7), with Rosso's repainted frescoes framed in the original stuccoes; the Michelangelo-influenced **Chapelle de la Trinité** and the extraordinary, sumptuous **Salle de Bal**, both built under Henri II; the **Chambre de l'Impératrice**, with Marie-Antoinette's elaborate bed; and the **Salle du Trône**, designed for Napoleon. Other rooms were used by Pius VII during his stay in Paris. The **Petits Appartements** are less grand, but just as interesting (*tours only, June–Aug, 10, 11, 2.15 and 3*); the **Musée Napoléon Ier** concentrates on the daily life of a self-made emperor.

Fontainebleau's gardens, notably the Parterre, were first laid out by François; Henri IV added the water, dubbed the Tibre, and Le Nôtre rearranged the whole into geometric gardens. In 1812 Napoleon ordered English gardens to be planted around the Fontaine Belle-Eau.

Normandy

08

Normandy

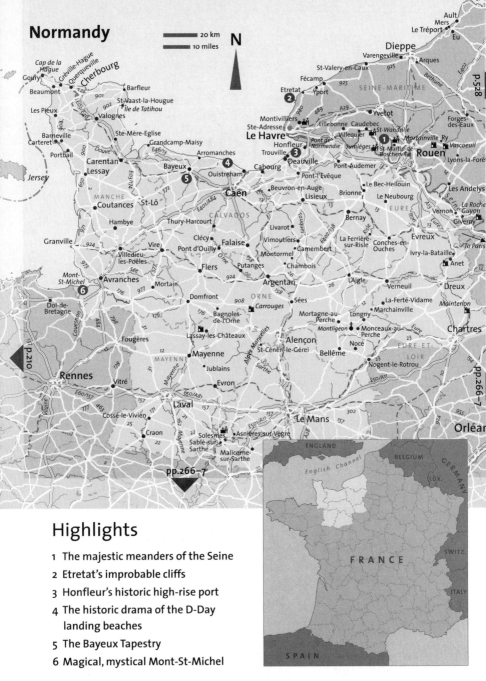

Highlights

1 The majestic meanders of the Seine
2 Etretat's improbable cliffs
3 Honfleur's historic high-rise port
4 The historic drama of the D-Day
   landing beaches
5 The Bayeux Tapestry
6 Magical, mystical Mont-St-Michel

Normandy is a land of heroes and conquerors. But the Norsemen who came from
Scandinavia, and gave Normandy its name, were the terrors of the Dark Ages. In 911
one Viking, Wrolf, or Rollo, was granted lands around the Seine by the Carolingian
king of France; he converted to Christianity and the precocious duchy was born. In

1066, with a rather famous conquest, Norman Duke William gained the English crown. King Philippe Auguste of France won Normandy from King John in 1204, leaving the English to cling on to the Channel Islands off the western Norman coast.

The Church enjoyed two periods of exceptional importance in the region, during the Dark Ages, and under the Norman dukes, but Normandy lays claim to two later French religious heroines. Defiant Joan of Arc was burnt at the stake in the region's historic capital of Rouen in 1431, when the English were briefly back in possession of these lands during the Hundred Years War. Thérèse de Lisieux, Normandy's answer to Bernadette of Lourdes, pushed piety to the limits in the 19th century.

Normandy has more than its fair share of art heroes – with Monet leading the charge, taught by Boudin, Honfleur's master of cows and clouds – plus major literary heroes. Corneille, playwright of the heroic par excellence, came from Rouen. André Gide mounted a brilliant challenge to Catholic morality and hypocrisy in a series of shattering Norman novels for which he won the Nobel Prize. Maupassant wrote the sharpest, bitterest short stories in the French language, as redolent of Normandy as the finest calvados. Then there's Flaubert, whose Madame Bovary wastes away so despondently in the Norman countryside, desperate for passion – the region's native *literati* have hardly given the province a good name. But Normandy's most stinking heroes are its cheeses, fêted below.

In more recent times, North American and British soldiers proved their heroism from the moment they landed on Normandy's beaches on D-Day, 6 June 1944, the greatest sea invasion the world has ever known. But the citizens and towns of the region had to pay a heavy price for becoming the chosen land by which Europe was liberated from the evil of Nazism.

Food and Drink

Anathema to the cholesterol-conscious, Normandy cuisine is often enriched by a rich dollop of cream and a dash of cider or calvados (apple brandy). The region is renowned for its **cheeses**, even if Camembert in particular has suffered from cheap imitations. Normandy's soft and creamy *fromages* start off smelly and get more pungent and tastier with age. Many of the classics, such as Livarot and Pont-l'Evêque, come from the Pays d'Auge, while the Pays de Bray has produced Neufchâtel since William the Conqueror's time. Fine butter is also made; *beurre d'Isigny* even has its own *appellation d'origine contrôlée*. Normandy has excellent **seafood**, of course: try mussels (with cream), oysters and scallops, and sole – *à la Normande*, cooked with cider, butter and mussels, or *dieppoise*, with wine and cream. Certain special regional meat dishes might turn your stomach, but locals love *tripes à la mode de Caen*, black puddings from Mortagne-au-Perche, or *canetons* (ducklings) from Rouen, stuffed with liver and served up in a blood and cream sauce. Normandy produces a considerable quantity of **cider**, and apples feature large in Normandy cooking. **Calvados** (nicknamed *calva*) can be added to just about anything, and is renowned as one of France's most densely flavoured brandies. The *Trou Normand*, traditionally a pause in a meal when diners drink a drop of *calva* to help the digestion, consists more often these days of a light apple sorbet.

Normandy, lush with cidery orchards and creamy meadows overseen by charming timberframe and brick farms, is best-known today for its superlative sights. In Haute Normandie (Eastern Normandy), Monet's garden at Giverny, Rouen's churches, the stunning abbeys and bridges on the Seine and Honfleur, smartest of all historic French ports, hog the limelight. Still more celebrated sights stand out in Basse Normandie (Western Normandy): the Bayeux tapestry, the D-Day beaches and Mont-St-Michel, eclipsing the region's most glamorous resorts, Trouville and Deauville. For beautiful, tranquil spots, head inland via the river valleys, in particular to the Orne, southern Normandy, or push further south still into the half-forgotten historic region of Maine, sandwiched between Normandy and the Loire Valley, but included here.

The Coast from Somme to Seine

The white cliffs of Haute Normandie stretch almost unbroken from the Bay of the Somme to the estuary of the Seine. This coast has been dubbed the Côte d'Albâtre: the churning waters often have a milky alabaster quality, with subtle tinges of beiges and turquoises, like the chalk cliffs above. Settled in the breaks, the resorts resemble one another. They sprawl slightly messily behind pebble beaches provided with a few beach huts. A modest casino often takes pride of place along the beach front, below slopes occupied by neo-Gothic Norman timberframe mansions. Neither of the war-scarred ferry ports of Dieppe or Le Havre provides the most obviously charming of French welcomes, but each conceals surprising attractions. Another historic spot along this coast, Fécamp's claim to fame these days is a fake Benedictine monastery, dedicated to liqueur rather than religion. The real star of this piece of French coast, though, is Etretat, its fabulous cliffs made doubly famous by a groundbreaking group of 19th-century artists, although it was Monet's impression of a sunrise over the cranes of Le Havre harbour which would give its name to this most celebrated of all art movements – Impressionism, which might be said to have been born here.

Dieppe

Behind its broad shingle beach, Dieppe may look a bit shabby nowadays, having suffered not just in the Second World War but also from poor property development since. However, this port, France's first ever seaside resort, still has a certain scruffy appeal. An intimidatingly grim medieval castle glowers down from its clifftop, a stern reminder that Dieppe has a long and very spicy history. It had the great advantage of its excellent natural harbour tucked in behind the cliffs, its waters helpfully deep – the place's name derives from the old Viking word.

Local sailors were often involved in bloody battles with the English in medieval times, although English pilgrims also stepped ashore here. Dieppe's heyday came with the 16th-century exploration of the New World. A native sailor, Jean Cousin, is claimed as one of the discoverers of Brazil. The renowned Florentine explorer Verrazano, the first European to discover the bay in which New York now stands,

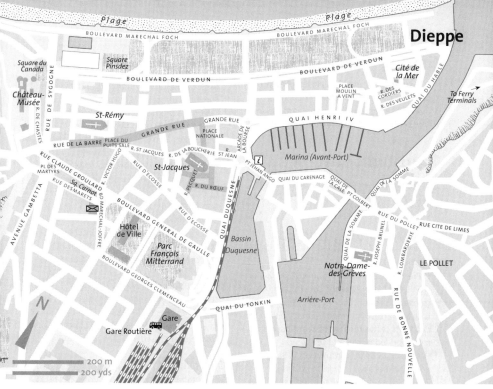

worked for the most famous of all Dieppe's merchants, Jean Ango. Ango had many other irons in the fire – he made a killing when one of his captains grabbed the Spaniard Cortés' treasure-filled fleet in 1522, and has been portrayed as a local hero ever since. Other Dieppois were among the first to settle in Canada. Louis XIV's anti-Protestant 1685 Revocation of the Edict of Nantes would cause many important local Huguenot merchants and craftsmen to emigrate to England, but ironically one powerful Dieppe Protestant, Abraham Duquesne, played a crucial role in reviving the Sun King's navy. That didn't stop disaster for Dieppe in 1694, when an Anglo-Dutch fleet under Admiral Berkeley reduced much of the port to rubble.

Eventually peace did come, and Dieppe embarked on its new, happier career as a tourist resort; the first, steam-operated ferry landed in 1825. Artists appreciated the setting: one of half a dozen **Itinéraires Impressionnistes** created by the Normandy tourist authorities and featuring outdoor reproductions of Impressionist canvases along with informative explanations focuses on Dieppe and neighbouring Pourville. Britons fleeing the rigid morality of the Victorian era escaped here to enjoy a taste of more open French living; they included Aubrey Beardsley and Walter Sickert, the latter inviting Wilde over after his imprisonment for homosexuality. A great deal of this much-loved Dieppe was destroyed in the Second World War. Particularly tragically, on 19 August 1942, the Allies sent an ill-fated force into the port on the disastrous Dieppe Raid to test the Nazis' coastal defences.

By Dieppe's lively **harbour**, restaurants with conservatory fronts line up behind the **Quai Henri IV** like a row of aquaria. Sailors moor their yachts in the Bassin Jehan Ango below this quay. The other grand harbourside row, arcaded **Quai Duquesne**, stands in

Getting There

Transmanche Ferries and Hoverspeed run services to Dieppe (*see* Travel). The ferries arrive on the eastern side of the harbour, close to the centre, but a shuttle bus is available.

Tourist Information

Dieppe: Pont Jehan Ango, Quai du Carénage, t 02 32 14 40 60, *www.DIEPPETOURISME.com*.

Where to Stay and Eat

Dieppe ✉ 76200

***Présidence**, 1 Bd de Verdun, t 02 35 84 31 31, *www.hotel-la-presidence. com* (*moderate*). Of the handful of hotels looking out to sea, this is the smartest, in a modern block below the castle. Its restaurant Le Panoramic specializes in grilled meats and sea views.

Windsor, 18 Bd de Verdun, t 02 35 84 15 23, *windsor@hotelwindsor.fr* (*moderate*). Reasonable option, well run, with sea views and a restaurant (*expensive–moderate*).

Le Grand Duquesne, 15 Place St-Jacques, t 02 32 14 61 10, *www.augrandduquesne.fr* (*inexpensive*). By the fine church, a recently renovated hotel with a good restaurant (*moderate*).

Restaurant du Port, 99 Quai Henri IV, t 02 35 84 36 64 (*moderate*). Of the countless restaurants vying for attention on the quays, this is the most tempting. *Closed Thurs*.

La Marmite Dieppoise, 8 Rue St-Jean, t 02 35 84 24 26 (*expensive–moderate*). Behind Quai Duquesne, an old-established favourite, reputed for fish stew. *Closed Sun pm and Mon*.

Bellevue, 70 Bd de Verdun, t 02 35 84 39 37 (*cheap*). On the eastern end of the seafront, one of the rare restaurants looking out to sea. *Closed Sun pm and Mon*.

Les Tourelles, 43 Rue du Commandant Fayolle, t 02 35 84 15 88 (*cheap*). Bargain, characterful, old-fashioned restaurant close to St-Remy church. *Closed Sun pm and Mon*.

Varengeville-sur-Mer ✉ 76119

**La Terrasse, Route de Vasterival, t 02 35 85 12 54 (*inexpensive*). Peaceful hotel by the beach, offering refined Norman fare (*moderate*). *Closed mid-Oct–mid-March*.

Offranville ✉ 76550

Le Colombier, Parc du Colombier, t 02 35 85 48 50 (*expensive–moderate*). Exciting modern French cuisine served in an archetypal Norman timber house in this attractive village southwest of Dieppe, marked out by its twisted spire. *Closed Sun pm and Mon*.

front of the Bassin Duquesne, reserved for the fishing fleet. High on the cliff opposite, **Notre-Dame du Bon Secours**, a 19th-century sailors' chapel, watches anxiously over the sea. Heading into town from Quai Henri IV, the buildings look jaded, though the main shopping **Grande Rue** contains good shops. On triangular **Place du Puits Salé**, the substantial form of the **Café des Tribunaux** stands out, haunt of many of the 19th-century artist visitors.

The behatted statue of St James on the fiery Flamboyant Gothic façade of the church of **St-Jacques** recalls the pilgrimage route to Santiago in Spain, although most of the building's statues were hacked off in the 16th century by fanatical Protestants. Many interesting Gothic features remain, though, including splendid rose windows. Packed with ornate side chapels inside, the strangest decoration adorns the sacristy, a bizarre little frieze among the riot of Renaissance detail, seemingly depicting South American ritual scenes, probably commissioned by Ango. To one side of St-Jacques, a swashbuckling Duquesne presides over **Place Nationale**, the main market square.

Dieppe's other major church, **St-Remy**, stands west off the Grande Rue, a colossal, bold Renaissance structure with grand Renaissance rose window, but touches of late Gothic in the choir windows and howling gargoyles. The great organ inside has been restored, held up on huge tubular columns. Nearby, Dieppe's **Petit Théâtre** houses the

Mémorial du 19 Août 1942 (*open daily 2–6.30; adm*), paying homage to the soldiers sent on the catastrophic Dieppe Raid. Of around 6,000 Allied troops, 1,380 were killed, 1,600 wounded and more than 2,000 captured. The Germans only lost 345 men, and shot down 107 RAF planes supporting the naval campaign.

From beside the ugly but popular **casino**, head out to the **beach** from the turreted **Porte des Tourelles**, sole remnant of Dieppe's 14th-century fortifications, built in typical layered patterns of brick and flint. Most of the 19th-century seafront villas have been kicked out by dull post-war apartment blocks. A wide, treeless expanse of grass separates the front from the brown shingle beach, although you'll find an excellent outdoor heated **pool** (*open June–early Sept daily; adm*), tennis courts and mini-golf; and on the eastern end stands the **Estran-Cité de la Mer** (*open daily 10–12 and 2–6; adm*), its aquaria and exhibits focusing on sea life from marine biology to shipbuilding.

Dieppe's **Château-musée** (*open June–Sept daily 10–12 and 2–6; rest of year Wed–Mon 10–12 and 2–5, closed Tues; adm*) peers down from on high about as invitingly as a coastal Norman Colditz, but it proves well worth a visit. The first reward for the climb is splendid views down on to the Channel's turquoise waters. Within, the regionally inspired paintings include harrowing scenes at sea, as well as more comforting Impressionist works. Elaborately carved ivories, for centuries a prized local craft, form the other major collection, items ranging from religious pieces and figurines of great Frenchmen to men's tobacco-graters showing women baring their breasts.

Around Dieppe

Surrounded by a dry moat of staggering proportions, the once mighty medieval **Château d'Arques** (*free*) southeast of Dieppe may be crumbling, but still looks daunting on its hill. An uncle of William the Conqueror, Count William d'Arques, foolish enough to take on his nephew, had the formidable trench dug. Needless to say his upstart of a relative won, sending him into exile. This became the last Anglo-Norman stronghold to fall to Philippe Auguste and France's troops in 1204. A stone frieze, the last detail of decoration left in the ruins, recalls with gusto the future King Henri IV of France's vital victory here over the Catholic Duc de Mayenne in the 16th-century French Wars of Religion.

Short-story writer Guy de Maupassant came into the world in 1850 at the elegant Henri IV-style brick and stone **Château de Miromesnil** (*open May–Sept Wed–Mon 2–6; closed Tues; adm*), set in lush gardens just west of Arques. But Maupassant's father was living above his means, and the family had to move on. An earlier resident, the enlightened Marquis de Miromesnil, served as a minister under Louis XVI, trying ineffectually to bring in reforms; the marquis' study and bedroom are highlights on the quirky visit. The Seine Maritime's main **cider-producing area** stretches south of here, home to firms such as Duché de Longueville at Anneville-sur-Scie, offering tours and tastings; or simply follow the picturesque **Route de la Pomme et du Cidre**.

West of Dieppe, the swish village houses of **Varengeville** sprawl wonderfully along wooded, winding lanes behind the cliffs. The **Bois des Moutiers** (*open 15 Mar–15 Nov daily 10–12 and 2–6; adm*) offers the charms of an English-style country garden created by Gertrude Jekyll around a house designed by Edwin Lutyens. Lutyens included Norman features, but managed to combine historical respect with his own especially elegant brand of modernity. Varengeville's **church** stands in near-suicidal isolation on the edge of the cliffs. From the churchyard you get splendid views down towards Dieppe. Enter the church via the side door and you're greeted by an aptly vomiting voyager carved on one alarmingly decorated column. Striking stained glass gives colour to the church's cheeks, including a piece by Georges Braque, who spent the last 20 years of his life here. Turning its back on the village, the grand Renaissance **Manoir d'Ango** (*open mid-Mar–mid-Nov daily 10–12.30 and 2–6.30; adm*) looks determinedly inland. By the time Jean d'Ango commissioned this summer residence in the 1530s and 1540s he could afford the finest craftsmen. Although parts were badly damaged during the Revolution, sumptuous elements remain, notably a Florentine loggia with busts of French royals and of Ango and his wife. Outside, the patterned brick dovecote is claimed to be the largest in France – a sign of massive wealth.

The Coast from Eu to Etretat

East from Dieppe: Eu and La Tréport

A trip east up the coast from Dieppe takes you to Normandy's border with Picardy and the town of **Eu**, a modest *ville royale* set back from the sea around the Bresle river.

Getting Around

Branch lines off the main **rail** track between Rouen and Le Havre serve Le Tréport, St-Valéry-en-Caux, Fécamp and Etretat.

Local **bus** services are infrequent. Cars Denis operates between Dieppe, Eu and Le Tréport. Bus services from Le Havre (*gare routière*) to Etretat and Fécamp are quite frequent, if slow.

Tourist Information

Eu: 41 Rue P. Bignon, **t** 02 35 86 04 68, *www.ville-eu.fr*.
Le Tréport: Quai Sadi Carnot, **t** 02 35 86 05 69, *www.ville-le-treport.fr*.
Fécamp: 113 Rue Alexandre Le Grand, **t** 02 35 28 51 01, *www.fecamp-tourisme.com*.
Etretat: Place Maurice Guillard, **t** 02 35 27 05 21, *www.etretat.net*.

Where to Stay and Eat

Eu ✉ **76260**
***Le Domaine de Joinville**, Route du Tréport, **t** 02 35 50 52 52, *joinville@chateauxhotels.*

com (*very expensive–moderate*). Stylish, wildly gabled former part of King Louis-Philippe's estates, out in its own little valley towards Le Tréport. Smart restaurant (*expensive*). Pool. *Restaurant closed Sun pm, Mon, Tues lunch and Wed lunch.*
****Hôtel Maine**, 20 Place de la Gare, **t** 02 35 86 16 64, *www.hotel-maine.com* (*inexpensive*). A real surprise behind the unassuming brick façade at the old railway station, the rooms colourful, the restaurant ornate, serving excellent Norman fish and meats (*moderate*). *Restaurant closed Sun pm.*

Le Tréport ✉ **76490**
Le Homard Bleu, **t** 02 35 86 15 89 (*expensive–moderate*). Finest reputation for seafood among the many quayside restaurants.

Sassetot-Le-Mauconduit ✉ **76540**
*****Château de Sassetot**, **t** 02 35 28 00 11, *www.chateau-de-sassetot.com* (*luxury–moderate*). Wonderfully grand, with its long 18th-century façade; in the 19th century Austrian Empress 'Sissi' made it her Normandy holiday home. Very comfortable

As early as the 10th century, Duke Rollo had a fort built here, marking the northern-most point of his territory. William the Conqueror's controversial marriage to Matilda of Flanders took place here. The dubious story goes that he dragged his somewhat reluctant bride round screaming by the hair before the event. Eu is also the place where William most courteously first received Harold, having rescued him from his captivity under Guy de Ponthieu, across in Picardy.

Eu still has a château, a 16th-century one. But it was never completed and is almost eclipsed by the enormous medieval church to **Notre-Dame et St-Laurent**. Its second dedication isn't to the well-known early Christian martyr grilled alive, but to a 12th-century Irishman, Laurence O'Toole, archbishop of Dublin. Aged and ailing, he pursued Henry II to France, wanting to plead the cause of Irish lords following the first Anglo-Norman invasion of the Emerald Isle, but he died at Eu before seeing the king, and was promptly canonized by a pope at odds with Henry. The church in his honour was begun as early as 1186, although the choir end was reconstructed in Flamboyant Gothic style after a destructive lightning strike in the 15th century. Inside, the grandiose 17th-century organ distracts from the medieval forms. Down in the crypt, a 13th-century effigy of Laurence survived the Revolution.

The **Château d'Eu** (*open April–Nov Wed–Mon 10–12 and 2–6; closed Tues; free while being restored*) represents little more than one wing of a vast castle planned in the 1570s for the notorious, only half-pious man-eater Catherine de Clèves, Countess of

rooms. Fine restaurant (*expensive–moderate*). Tennis court.

Fécamp ✉ 76400

★★★La Ferme de la Chapelle, t 02 35 10 12 12, *www.fermedelachapelle.fr* (*moderate*). The best hotel in Fécamp stands up on the cliffs, developed from a 16th-century farm. Fish features large in the restaurant (*moderate*). Pool. *Closed part of Jan; restaurant closed Mon lunch.*

★★Auberge de la Rouge, Route du Havre, t 02 35 28 07 59, *www.auberge-rouge.com*, at St-Léonard, 2km south of town (*moderate*). Pleasant small hotel with leafy garden and elegant restaurant serving complex cuisine (*expensive–moderate*). *Closed either Jan or Feb; restaurant closed Sun pm and Mon.*

Le Maritime, 2 Place Nicolas Selles, t 02 35 28 21 71 (*moderate*). Vibrant quayside setting for seafood.

Etretat ✉ 76790

★★★Domaine St-Clair Le Donjon, Chemin de St-Clair, t 02 35 27 08 23, *www.ledonjon-etretat.fr* (*luxury–moderate*). Set back on its height, with some sea views, a splendidly characterful, comfortable little neo-Gothic castle. A special setting for a meal (*expensive*). Pool.

★★★Dormy House, Route du Havre, t 02 35 27 07 88, *www.dormy-house.com* (*expensive*). Large, smart modern hotel with sea views, up west by the golf course. The luxurious restaurant has sea views too.

La Résidence, 4 Bd du Président Coty, t 02 35 27 02 87 (*inexpensive*). Fabulously carved beamed façade in the centre, but with reasonably priced old rooms. Sharing the sensational building, **La Salamandre**, t 02 35 27 17 07, offers organic produce as well as seafood (*moderate*).

★★L'Escale, Place Foch, t 02 35 27 03 69 (*inexpensive*). The rooms are sweet, cosy little varnished-wood cabins; brashly lit pizza parlour attached.

Le Galion, Bd René Coty, t 02 35 29 48 74 (*expensive–moderate*). Very appealing Norman ingredients with its beams and fireplace, a fine setting for refined cuisine.

L'Huîtrière, t 02 35 27 02 82 (*moderate*). Smart seafront seafood restaurant that makes the most of the sea views through its round windows.

Eu, and her second husband, the fanatical Catholic Henri de Guise. The assassination of this Balafré (Scarface) on the instructions of the cowardly King Henri III of France at the Château de Blois in 1588 didn't help with the completion of the ambitious project. In the 17th century, Louis XIV's awkward cousin, Mlle de Montpensier, 'La Grande Mademoiselle', spent part of her exile here, ordering the elegant terraced gardens.

Louis-Philippe, Duc d'Orléans, was yet to be elected king by the people to replace the much-loathed Charles X when he inherited the place in the 1820s and began restoring it. He loved this spot, and, once crowned, lodged his ministers during visits in separately built outhouses rather resembling stabling. In 1843, he invited a young Queen Victoria to the château – a significant moment in relations between the French and English monarchies. Louis-Philippe and Victoria enjoyed parades, concerts and picnics together, much merrier than making war. But France's so-called 'Citizen King' rapidly lost his popularity as his regime became increasingly intolerant. In 1848, he fled to England under the pseudonym of 'Mr Smith'. A frisky equestrian statue outside the château shows his eldest son, Ferdinand d'Orléans, never to become king, as his father was France's last monarch. Louis-Philippe's descendant, the Comte de Paris, did receive his French estates back in the 1870s, and Viollet-le-Duc partly restored the interiors, but the castle was then left to languish, even after the town bought it in 1964. Now, however, its regal demeanour is being restored.

Eu's main shopping street, **Rue Paul Bignon**, has some charming half-timbered buildings among the brick façades. Seek out the **Chapelle des Jésuites**, one of the rare religious institutions founded under the widowed Catherine de Clèves to have survived the Revolution. The Anguier brothers, local sculptors, did an elaborate job decorating the façade. Inside, Catherine's tomb remains in place. The Bresle valley is well known for its glass-making traditions, and the **Musée Traditions Verrières** (*open Easter–Oct Tues and weekends 1.30–6; adm*) across the river keeps the craft alive.

Le Tréport, at the Bresle estuary, Normandy's most northerly resort, faces Picardy's most southerly resort of Mers-les-Bains, backed by the vast, hideous St-Gobain glass-making factory. Avoid looking inland and these resorts retain some of their old charm. Le Tréport was briefly fashionable while Louis-Philippe stayed and sailed close by. The railway line then brought mass tourism from Paris. Today it has a pretty strip of a fishing and yachting harbour, and all the typical old-fashioned seaside attractions and stalls. Behind the seafront, the church of **St-Jacques** dominates on the hillside. **Mers-les-Bains** has preserved its seafront better than Le Tréport, its colourful array of villas sporting steep slate roofs and brightly painted balconies.

West from Dieppe to Etretat via Fécamp

The mainly drab and scruffy resorts between Varengeville and St-Valéry-en-Caux look much of a muchness, although **Sotteville** offers the challenge of a dizzyingly steep stairway down to its tiny beach, while **Veules-les-Roses** makes the curious boast of having the shortest river in the country, and appeals with its quaint cottages. A snake of yachts in the meandering river estuary at **St-Valéry-en-Caux** gives this small port its charm, although not much survived the Second World War beyond the wildly carved beams of the Maison Henri IV.

Somewhat upstaged by the Mont-St-Michel for the last 1,000 years, before the end of the first Christian millennium **Fécamp** had established itself as the premier pilgrimage centre in Normandy, claiming a phial of the Precious Blood of Christ. One St Waninge certainly founded a convent at Fécamp in 660. In the early 10th century, after the raiding Norsemen had settled and converted, Duke William Longsword refounded the **Benedictine abbey**, and had a hall-fort built by the monastery. His successors appreciated this spot; the abbey church even became the burial place for a couple of the Normandy dukes. In 1035, Duke Robert gathered his nobles in Fécamp to tell them that he was going off on pilgrimage to the Holy Land and that his seven-year-old illegitimate son William was to be his heir should he not return. He didn't, and William inherited Normandy. After 30 bitter years fighting the region's lords and then the English to assert his rights, he came back here in 1067 to celebrate his conquest of England, his triumphant Norman nobles now united. While the dukes then abandoned Fécamp, the abbey continued to flourish, establishing strong links with Italy. One Venetian monk brought over a whole selection of herbs with him in the 16th century and began the making of Benedictine liqueur, the town's speciality.

With such an extravagant history, today's Fécamp may appear a tad ordinary at first sight, a mainly workaday town spreading from a gap in the cliffs down a flat-bottomed valley. Although given a jarring new façade in the 18th century, most of the **abbey church** provides a fine example of sober Gothic architecture. Beautiful late-Gothic pieces inside include screens and statuary, and a remarkable Entombment of the Virgin. The fabulous phial is displayed on an Italian marble altar. Also observe the 12th-century relief panels of Christ's life on the sarcophagus beneath the gilded Louis XV high altar, teeming with action. The Lady Chapel contains medieval stained glass.

Alexandre Le Grand was leafing through old documents his ancestor had rescued from the abbey when it was closed at the Revolution when he came across the heady, not to say sickly-sweet Benedictine liqueur recipe cooked up by the Venetian monk Bernardo Vincelli with its supposed medicinal benefits. Cannily marketing the drink, he commissioned his mock-historic palace-cum-factory, the **Palais Bénédictine** (*open April–Sept daily 10–12 and 2–5; Feb–Mar and Oct–Dec daily 10.30–11.45 and 2–5; adm*) on the proceeds. Like an elaborate mix of Loire château, grand abbey and posh town hall, the building was the fruit of local architect Camille Albert's imagination. Its museum contains a vast mixed bag of historic religious objects, which Le Grand collected avidly. You're also treated to a tour of the distillery and a small tasting.

In the shopping area of town, the **Musée des Arts et de l'Enfance** (*open July–Aug daily 10–12 and 2–6; Sept–June Wed–Mon 10–12 and 2–5.30; adm*), the municipal museum in its grand 18th-century house, is really geared to grown-up children despite the title, the collections concentrating on regional painting, arts and crafts, as well as childhood objects from Roman times on. The separate area of the seafront retains odd reminders of the 19th-century period when Fécamp became a popular resort with Parisians. In one of the uninspiring modern blocks, the **Musée des Terre-Neuvas** (*open July–Aug daily 10–7; Sept–June Wed–Mon 10–12 and 2–5.30, closed Tues*) effectively recalls the gruelling Newfoundland fishing expeditions from which much of the local community had to scrape a living for centuries.

In a break in the cliffs west of Fécamp, packed with hotels and restaurants, **Etretat** looks as though it has sold its soul to tourism. When you see the spectacular **beach**, you'll understand why. East along the shingle, the two arches in the rock mimic, at low tide, the entrances to a mighty castle. The silhouette of a church perched high on the eastern cliffs adds to the drama. From this end of the beach you get the best view of the buttressed arch in the cliff to the west of Etretat. Beyond that, the place's most famous symbol, the **Aiguille** points skywards; this 'Needle' actually looks more like a space shuttle in stone awaiting lift-off. Etretat's lively centre has a distinctive covered market that served as a British and American military hospital in the last war. To the French, the town also provides the setting for a much-loved children's detective series featuring Arsène Lupin, the creation of Maurice Leblanc. Fans try solving the crimes of this gentleman burglar at the **Clos Lupin** (*open April–Sept daily 10–7; rest of year weekends and school hols 11–5; adm*), his old house. Head out of town for a sensational cliff walk, or to visit the decaying old village church, abandoned like a sickly leper.

Le Havre

A voracious ogre forced to vomit out another fleet of ships each time it gets too full – thus Maupassant described 19th-century Le Havre in his masterpiece set in the town, *Pierre et Jean*. Rather unwarrantedly vilified as an ugly, vacuous brute of a port, this giant at the mouth of the Seine, today France's second harbour after Marseille, was planned for King François Ier as a replacement for silting-up Honfleur and Harfleur further up the Seine. Even back then it was designed on a grid plan. It grew from strength to strength, trading with the Americas in particular: nearly 350 slaving vessels set out in the 18th century. Before the Second World War, Le Havre greeted the *beau monde* off the ocean liners. But such an important industrial base inevitably became one of the most bombed targets in France. For architectural historians at least, Le Havre's post-war reconstruction by Auguste Perret, with its wide, airy boulevards, has become a concrete classic.

Getting There

P&O Portsmouth **ferries**, *see* p.64.

Tourist Information

Le Havre: 186 Bd Clemenceau, t 02 32 74 04 04, *www.lehavretourisme.com*.

Where to Stay and Eat

Le Havre ✉ **76600**

***Vent d'Ouest, 4 Rue Caligny, t 02 35 42 50 69, *www.ventdouest.fr* (*expensive–moderate*). In the heart of Le Havre's shopping quarter, stylish themed rooms, including nautical ones, making up for dull post-war architecture.

***Hôtel de Bordeaux, 147 Rue L. Brindeau, t 02 35 22 69 44, *www.bestwestern.com/fr/debordeaux* (*moderate*). Comfortable hotel giving on to the dramatic Volcano Centre.

**Celtic, 106 Rue Voltaire, t 02 35 42 39 77, *www.hotel-celtic.com* (*inexpensive*). Good choice with its views of the Volcano Centre.

*Le Séjour Fleuri, 71 Rue Emile Zola, t 02 35 41 33 81 (*inexpensive*). For bargain-hunters, well kept and central, if dull architecture.

La Villa, 66 Bd Albert Ier, t 02 35 54 78 80 (*very expensive–moderate*). With its extravagant grotto of an entrance above the beach, the most luxurious restaurant in town, set in a grand brick Belle Epoque villa. Excellent French seasonal cooking. *Closed Sun pm, Mon, and Wed pm.*

Ste-Adresse ✉ **76310**

***Hôtel des Bains, 3 Place Clemenceau, t 02 35 54 68 90, *www.lapetiterade.com* (*moderate*). The best-located hotel, looking down over the Seine estuary, and the dramatic, swanky restaurant, **La Petite Rade** (*moderate*), also with sea views.

Le Roi Léopold, 11 Place Clemenceau, t 02 35 46 16 25 (*moderate*). Magnificent sea views and modern décor accompany excellent fish dishes.

Les Trois Pics, Sentier Alphonse Kerr, t 02 35 48 20 60 (*moderate*). Scruffier, but popular for fish, with its terrace above the beach. *Closed Sun pm and Mon.*

In the straight-lined centre, an elegant arch of a footbridge, one of the few curves in town, crosses the rectangular **Bassin du Commerce**, but it's the colossal **Espace Niemeyer** cultural centre that steals the show here, with its much greater swooping lines. One of Brazilian Oscar Niemeyer's fabulous constructions, opened in 1982, takes the form of a ship's funnel, the other of a volcano top. Between the Espace Niemeyer and the Bassin, a hefty monument records Le Havre's civilian war dead. Small pockets of grand pre-war houses have survived south of the Bassin, but the **Musée du Ancien Havre** contains only meagre flotsam and jetsam in melancholy surrounds. The Baroque **cathedral** puts on a better show, its well-turned yellow stone contrasting strongly with the concrete arcades of the Rue de Paris, a main shopping street leading up to the town hall with a massive public garden in front.

South of the centre, by the shore, in the slick glass block of the ground-breaking, brilliantly renovated 1960s **Musée Malraux** (*open Mon and Wed–Fri 11–6, Sat and Sun 11–7; adm*), you can admire vibrant paintings of boats by Normandy's greatest artists as a plethora of real vessels – tankers, tugs, ferries, yachts – slips silently by outside. You'll realize how many great French modern artists were born, brought up in or inspired by Le Havre. Boudin taught Monet around here; the master is represented by some fine seascapes, and by a huge wall of studies of cows and clouds, the subjects in which he remained unchallenged, but the Monet classics can't fail to win your heart. Native Raoul Dufy's joyous, vibrant canvases so run with colour, it's as though he had poured seawater on them. Othon Friesz is another forceful contemporary. By the

Capitainerie opposite the museum, a **plaque** commemorates the 800 passengers and crew of the *Niobé* who died when the ship was sunk by the Germans on 11 June 1940, but a more recent panel explains how the view from here gave rise to Monet's groundbreaking, once infamous painting, *Impression: Soleil levant*, the one of a blood-orange sun rising through a chaos of cranes and industrialization, the one from which Impressionism got its name.

Head north between the marina and the big seafront blocks to reach the long stretch of **beach**, with its elephant-sized shingle, tight-packed white beach huts and a neat array of beach restaurants. The latest Le Havre watersports craze is for kite surfing, but there are also more conventional swimming baths and boat trips on offer. Behind the wide car parks, a soaring tower marks Le Havre's skyline like a building escaped from New York, but the cross on top indicates that it's a church. Designed by Perret in his beloved (and cheap) concrete, the square-plan **St-Joseph** looks grim on the outside, but enter on a bright day and you'll feel you've been caught in a giant kaleidoscope. Take the invigorating promenade west to **Ste-Adresse**, Le Havre's wealthy suburb, the odd panel along the way illuminating an Impressionist canvas or the silhouettes of different types of cargo ship out in the bay. Across the water, the glamorous resorts of Trouville and Deauville twinkle seductively.

The Seine Valley from Le Havre to Rouen

Following the Seine's shapely meanders from Le Havre to Rouen provides one of the greatest yet least-known of quintessential Norman experiences. Once past the vast smelly industrial areas of Le Havre and Lillebonne, the scene turns surprisingly rustic, with apple farms tucked below the low white cliffs, and little ferries transporting local traffic across the wide river. The Seine looks magnificent, tracing its confident curves through the land. Not just barges glide along this trade route, but also huge tankers, like multi-storey apartment blocks on the move through the countryside. The evocative remnants of a whole string of major abbeys bear spectacular witness to the power of the Norman Church through medieval times.

Medieval Monasteries and Modern Bridges

Two major campaigns of monastery-building stamped the authority of the Church so exceptionally powerfully on Normandy, and on the Seine valley in particular. A series of monasteries was built along the river in the 7th century. These grew wealthy, an all too tempting and obvious target for the plundering Vikings in the 9th century, who destroyed the foundations. After the marauding Norsemen had eventually settled, their leaders ordered the second extraordinary wave of monastery- building. These establishments operated up to the Revolution. Then abandoned, ransacked or transformed into prisons and factories, many have been revived as cultural centres since the war, while a few have reverted to their original purpose.

The story of the Seine-side monasteries is introduced at the newly restored **Abbaye Notre-Dame Cœur d'Abbayes** (*open April–Sept daily 10–6; Oct–Mar Tues–Fri 10–5,*

Getting Around

A good **train** service links the two main Norman towns along the Seine, Le Havre and Rouen, but to explore the riverbanks in between, you need your own transport.

Tourist Information

Caudebec-en-Caux: Quai Guilbaud, **t** 02 32 70 46 32, *www.caudebec-en-caux.com*.
Parc Naturel Régional des Boucles de la Seine Normande: Maison du Parc, ✉ 76940 Notre-Dame-de-Bliquetuit, **t** 02 35 37 23 16.

Eating Out

Jumièges
Auberge des Ruines, 17 Place de la Mairie, **t** 02 35 37 24 05 (*expensive–moderate*). Timberframe inn on the pretty village square, serving local produce. *Closed Sun pm, Mon pm, Tues pm and Wed.*
Auberge du Bac, t 02 35 37 24 16 (*moderate*). Down by the Seine ferry, a tranquil, popular restaurant with terrace for outside dining. *Closed Mon and Tues.*

---

weekends 2–6; adm) in **Montivilliers**, now something of an historic suburb east of Le Havre, although it clearly has a much older heart. Philibert, abbot of nearby Jumièges, ordered the building of a convent for women here in 684, later destroyed by the Vikings. At the start of the 11th century, a new monastery was erected, for men. But when Duke Robert granted the institution a special charter of independence even from the bishops of Rouen in 1035, it was as a women's convent once again. Soon, under Abbess Elisabeth, the church of **St-Sauveur** went up, the beacon of the monastery. The town grew around the church and prospered until Le Havre's creation. The abbey, however, continued to thrive for a time. Come the Revolution, the abbey buildings were typically abused and transformed. The white stone buildings, decorated with flint bands, had to undergo major restoration work in the last few decades. Some parts, such as the wood-pillared cloister, were invented from scratch, but the original, atmospheric low-vaulted Gothic refectory makes a fine setting for exhibitions.

A splendid trio of modern toll bridges spans the Seine between Le Havre and Caudebec. The **Pont de Normandie** (1995) is one of the longest bridges in the world, held in place by two towering sets of tweezers, a contemporary engineer's sensational answer to the Gothic arch. It takes you over the sulphurous marshes of the Seine estuary to Honfleur (*see* p.173). Upstream, the **Pont de Tancarville** (1959), itself a feat of technology for its time, rises above the river on only slightly more modest tweezers. The **Pont de Brotonne** (1977), held up by cables in the form of sails, links Caudebec to the Brotonne forest. Further upstream, you can take one of the old ferries across the Seine, a major divide between the communities to north and south in centuries past; people on either bank refer to those '*de l'autre côté de l'eau* (the other side of the water)', rather as though they were separated by a sea. Today, the communities are linked by the **Parc Naturel des Boucles de la Seine**. The Maison du Parc, south of Brotonne bridge, set in particularly picturesque buildings at Notre-Dame-de-Bliquetuit, presents the area and its traditions, while special routes are marked out from here to help you discover its traditional orchards and cottages.

Caudebec was almost wholly destroyed in the last war, but at its heart stands one of the greatest Flamboyant Gothic churches in France, built between 1426 and 1515, and miraculously spared. Don't be put off by its blackened appearance; the intricacy of the Gothic canopies on the west front is as close as stone gets to lace. Look out for the little figures in period costume, the size of porcelain pieces. An ornate balustrade running around the roof spells out in stone tracery words from hymns to the Virgin, the *Magnificat* and *Salve Regina*. Inside, the stained glass windows survived too, some attributed to the great Flemish master Arnoult de Nimègue and his successor in Normandy, Engrand le Prince: one scene shows Moses leading the Israelites across the Red Sea, the Egyptian soldiers drowning in the brightest red waters, while others depict Norman saints. In addition, one chapel contains monumental statues saved from Jumièges abbey, and a remarkable Entombment scene. By the river, the interesting **Musée de la Marine de Seine** (*open daily 1.30–6.30; adm*) presents a broad picture of navigation on its waters.

The **Musée Victor Hugo** (*open Mon and Wed–Sat 10–12.30 and 2–6, Sun 2–5.30; closed Tues; adm*) occupies a delightful yet tragic riverside villa at **Villequier**. Hugo never lived in this fine brick house overlooking the Seine: it was his daughter Léopoldine who married a local. One afternoon she and her husband disappeared while boating on the river. Extracts from *Les Contemplations*, the series of poems Victor Hugo wrote to remember his drowned daughter, feature alongside letters, sketches and photos.

The **abbey of St-Wandrille** (*guided tours Easter–Oct daily 3.30, rest of year weekends and hols 3.30; adm; free visit to church, daily services 9.45 and 5*) was founded in the mid-7th century by a man who studied in Italy before serving at the Merovingian French court of King Dagobert. Supported by Bishop Ouen of Rouen, his abbey became a great centre of learning, and controlled priories as far afield as Provence. Seventeen abbots of St-Wandrille were canonized. Today the abbey has reverted to serving its original purpose, but behind its Baroque gate you can wander freely around the ruins of the vast 13th-century abbey church or go to the big barn of a modern church where the monks sing plainchant.

Among the ruins of the enormous **abbey of Jumièges** (*open mid-April–mid-Sept daily 9.30–7; rest of year daily 9.30–1 and 2.30–5.30; adm*), much more survives from the Gothic period than at St-Wandrille. It too was originally founded in the 7th century, by Philibert, again at the instigation of Ouen. A gruesome royal tale associated with the early abbey has come down to us from this late-Merovingian period. King Clovis II went abroad, leaving his two sons in charge of the kingdom. On his return, they didn't wish to relinquish power. Having beaten them, by way of punishment, Clovis had the nerves removed from their legs, placing them in a boat to float down the Seine to their fate; the then abbot of Jumièges rescued them. As at St-Wandrille, in the mid-9th century the Vikings laid waste to the abbey but, when their descendants settled, a great new Jumièges rose from the ashes. It was one of the first major Romanesque buildings in northern France, begun in 1040 under Abbot Robert Champart, who became a short-lived archbishop of Canterbury under King Edward the Confessor, a reminder of the ties that existed between the English crown and Normandy before William's conquest – Edward's mother was the daughter of Duke Richard of Normandy. William the Conqueror attended the consecration ceremony of Jumièges' abbey church in 1067; its soaring ruins stand like a huge disused medieval factory for God. Adjoining them are the remnants of the church of St-Pierre.

The most absorbing of the Seineside abbeys is the least known, **St-Georges** (*open April–Oct daily 9–6.30, Nov–Mar 2–5; adm*), at St-Martin-de-Boscherville. St-Georges remains fascinating both in outline and in detail, with much of the giant white medieval abbey church left standing. Building commenced in 1114; the massive edifice is one of the few great Romanesque buildings in Normandy to have survived the Revolution fairly unscathed. The awesome interior combines simplicity with complexity. Look out for details like the stone rope that goes round the walls, the bestiary on the capitals and the crinkly geometrical patterns on the arches. The local lord Raoul de Tancarville, a major contributor to the building, had participated in the Norman taking of Sicily, and some of these decorative ideas may have come back with him. Beside the church, the chapterhouse has preserved sculpted capitals so fine they look as though they've been executed in ivory. The breathtaking pieces illustrate violent biblical scenes. The museum in a separate building in the extensive walled garden relates the life of the Benedictine monks and the history of St-Georges.

Enjoy the last, especially picturesque meander in the Seine before the industrial quarters of Rouen come into view. Alfred Sisley, that master of river scenes, particularly appreciated this corner, as two panels (part of the Itinéraires Impressionnistes, *see* p.159) show on opposite sides of the Seine, encouraging you to take the enjoyable ferry linking the sweet villages of **Sahurs** and **La Bouille**.

Rouen

You may not wish to copy the most famous tour of Rouen: Emma Bovary committing adultery with her lover Léon as the horse-drawn cab bumps them round the cobbled streets in Flaubert's infamous novel. You certainly won't want to follow in the footsteps of Joan of Arc, whose visit to Rouen ended on the pyre. Close to the spot where La Pucelle was burnt stands a delicatessen called the Charcuterie Jeanne d'Arc, which certainly deserves a prize for bad taste. Otherwise the city fairly ignores her, as well as its other famous figures. It even turns its back on the Seine to which it owes its existence and its success.

When the Viking leader Wrolf (or Rollo) was accepted as duke of Normandy in 911, Rouen became his capital. Under him, the Seine quays were developed for trade. William the Conqueror died in the great city, but two of his successors as kings of England, Richard and John, were crowned dukes of Normandy in the cathedral; Richard's lion's heart was buried there. When King Philippe Auguste took Normandy from John early in the 13th century, he had a massive new castle built in Rouen. In 1418 at the start of the second half of the Hundred Years War the English king Henry V captured Normandy's capital after a long siege. It was during the ensuing decades of English occupation that Joan of Arc would be tried here and burnt at the stake. When peace came at last, commerce changed the face of the city. The archbishop Georges d'Amboise, a powerful figure in the late 15th century, was close to the French kings and Rouen benefited from the links. Textiles and pottery flourished. Then over the course of the 19th century Rouen grew into a large industrial city. As such it would

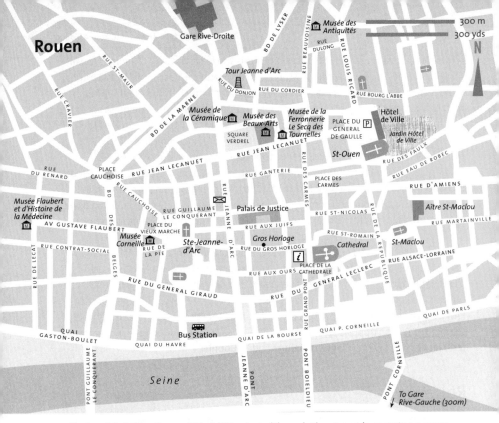

suffer terribly in the Second World War, but although the riverside remains a mess, the historic city has been so well restored that it's hard to realize the scale of the damage it suffered. The one time everyone really turns their attention to the Seine is for the spectacular biennial tall ships gathering at Rouen; the next of these armadas are scheduled for 2005 and 2007.

Place du Vieux Marché to the Cathedral, St-Maclou and St-Ouen

Joan of Arc was brought as a prisoner to Rouen in time for Christmas 1430. Her trial for witchcraft and heresy was conducted by Pierre Cauchon, Bishop of Beauvais. Found guilty, she recanted her claim once at the scaffold, but failed to do so when tested to the limits a second time. Her agonizing burning at the stake took place on 30 May 1431 on **Place du Vieux Marché**. Joan's ashes were chucked in the river; her heart, they say, would not burn. The combative, fish-tailed, scaly-slated church of **Ste-Jeanne-d'Arc** twists round the spot, like a giant hooded stingray putting up a final fight for life. The spectacular design by the Basque architect Arretche was executed in 1979 to include space for magnificent 16th-century stained glass saved from the church of St-Vincent. The **Musée Jeanne d'Arc** (*open mid-April–Sept daily 9.30–7; Oct–mid-April daily 10–12 and 2–6.30; adm*), on the south side of the square, proves a measly, disappointing thing hidden in the dismal basement of a touristy shop. Sadder still is the very meagre display of the **Musée Corneille** (*open Wed and weekends 2–6; adm*) in the classical playwright's stylish house west along the Rue de la Pie.

Flaubert too gets scant attention from his home town. The **Musée Flaubert et d'Histoire de la Médecine** (*open Tues–Sat 10–12 and 2–6; adm*) lies a long walk further west, attached to a grandiose hospital just outside the centre – Gustave's father and brother held important positions there. It's more a medical museum than a literary one – read *Flaubert's Parrot*, Julian Barnes' hilarious and moving homage to the writer, before hazarding a detour yourself.

Back in the heart of town, **Rue du Gros Horloge**, a major shopping street, links Place du Vieux Marché with the cathedral, but is divided at one point by the elaborate **Gros Horloge** gateway, with a clock dating back to the late 14th century. You can admire its mechanisms by climbing into the tower. North of Rue du Gros Horloge, the **Palais de Justice** stands apart from the shopping streets around, an island of intricate Flamboyant Gothic stone. The building was begun in 1499 as a merchants' hall, but when King François Ier created a Parlement de Normandie in 1514, the place became home to this important regional court. The exuberant architecture, despite the grime, counts among the greatest late Gothic inventions in France.

Getting There and Around

Rouen is just 1hr 10mins from Paris St-Lazare by **train**. For **taxis**, contact Radio-Taxis, **t** 02 35 88 50 50.

Tourist Information

Rouen: 25 Place de la Cathédrale, **t** 02 32 08 32 40, *www.mairie.rouen.fr*.

Where to Stay and Eat

Rouen ✉ **76000**
***Le Dandy**, 93 Rue Cauchoise, **t** 02 35 07 32 00, *www.hotels-rouen.net* (*moderate*). Warm, stylish, well-furnished rooms on a pedestrian street close to Pl du Vieux Marché.
***Vieux-Marché**, 15 Rue de la Pie, **t** 02 35 71 00 88, *www.hotelduvieuxmarche.com* (*expensive*). Excellent central location just off Place du Vieux Marché, and stylish, recently renovated rooms.
La Cathédrale, 12 Rue St-Romain, **t** 02 35 71 57 95, *www.hotel-de-la-cathedrale.fr* (*moderate–inexpensive*). Another of the best options in the very centre of town, set around a very pretty timberframe courtyard right by the cathedral, its good-value rooms recently renovated.
Le Vieux Carré, 34 Rue Ganterie, **t** 02 35 71 67 70, *vieux-carre@mcom.fr* (*inexpensive*).

Just north of the splendid Palais de Justice, with charming rooms set around a colourful timberframe courtyard. Simple food is possible (*cheap*).
Les Carmes, 33 Place des Carmes, **t** 02 35 71 92 31, *www.hcarm@mcom.fr* (*inexpensive*). Well-maintained, central little hotel with bright rooms, on a pleasant square presided over by Flaubert's statue.
Les Nymphéas, 7 Rue de la Pie, **t** 02 35 89 26 69 (*expensive*). Particularly beautiful restaurant, tucked away in a timberframe courtyard, serving superlative cuisine, but you have to pay more for specialities such as the duck. *Closed Sun pm, Mon and Tues lunch, and from mid-Aug for 3 weeks.*
La Couronne, 31 Place du Vieux Marché, **t** 02 35 71 40 90 (*expensive–moderate*). Claims to be the oldest *auberge* still going in France, dating back to 1345. Luxurious interior, relatively light Norman cuisine.
Dufour, 67 Rue St-Nicolas, **t** 02 35 71 90 62 (*moderate*). Coloured glass panes stop hoi polloi peering inside this magnificent timberframe house. The food is as Norman as the décor, the fish extremely good. *Closed Sun pm and Mon.*
Brasserie Paul, 1 Place de la Cathédrale, **t** 02 35 71 86 07 (*moderate*). For the terrace with the Monet view of the cathedral.
You'll find more posh restaurants around Place du Vieux Marché, and cheap ethnic options between St-Maclou and St-Ouen.

Rouen **cathedral**'s present-day fame stems in good part from Monet's gorgeous studies of the façade in changing lights. The Impressionist-celebrated, cleaned-up west front lords it over a square which was largely wrecked by bombing during the war and turns out to be something of a mess, architecturally, without Monet's beautifying brush. The sober north tower, the **Tour St-Romain**, is (along with the crypt) a rare survivor from the earlier Romanesque cathedral. The vast bulk of the edifice is 13th-century Gothic, from the great period of northern French cathedral-building. The north portal depicts scenes from the life of John the Baptist, a Tree of Jesse decorates the central doorway, while the south portal is dedicated to St Stephen. The late 16th-century southern tower, the **Tour de Beurre**, was apparently paid for by wealthy townspeople to avoid having to give up such little luxuries as butter during Lent. The statues here, their heads bent in different directions, are beautiful. Wandering right round the outside of the cathedral, the rows of triangular Gothic gables down the side create a fine effect. The north transept is a superb piece of Flamboyant Gothic, but the south transept portal proves even finer, with delicate Gothic panels telling the stories of Jacob and Joseph and local saints Ouen and Romain. The crossing is topped by a late-19th-century cast-iron tower that rockets into the sky like Rouen's answer to the Eiffel Tower. Antiques shops and art galleries fill the cathedral quarter.

Comparing a cathedral interior to a boudoir counts among Flaubert's more outrageous descriptions in *Madame Bovary*, but you might derive a certain sensuous pleasure from the shapely Gothic arches, and the wonderful bejewelled 13th-century stained glass in the choir. Art historians remain intrigued by one window depicting the life of Joseph which was actually signed, by one Clément de Chartres. Another famous window tells the Greek-like tragedy of St Julian the Hospitaller, who tried to avoid the prediction that he would murder his parents, a powerful story retold by Flaubert in his *Trois Contes*. Surprisingly little attention is paid to Joan of Arc in the cathedral, but one modern piece of stained glass does portray her: 'From the English in homage,' it reads. The d'Amboise family made sure they were remembered: Georges II d'Amboise, relative of the great archbishop Georges, ordered the exquisite Renaissance tomb for the two of them in the Lady Chapel, by Roulland Le Roux. The heavier Renaissance tomb was made for Louis de Brézé, seneschal of Normandy and husband of Diane de Poitiers (mistress of King Henri II – *see* 'Anet', p.167), who may have ordered it from Jean Goujon.

Two churches nearby challenge the cathedral in beauty. **St-Maclou's** porch is a masterpiece of Flamboyant Gothic seduction, built between 1500 and 1514. The doors, their relief work perhaps also by Goujon, represent Christ's circumcision and baptism and Old Testament figures. St-Maclou's square is very cute, with timberframe houses and a fountain of peeing figures. Close by, off Rue Martainville, the startling courtyard or **Aître St-Maclou** in the Ecole des Beaux-Arts served as a charnel house. Look at the carved beams and you'll get the sinister message: each upright sports a skull and cross-bones, while the crossbeams are decorated with the tools of the gravedigger.

Handsome streets fill the space between here and the former great Benedictine abbey church of **St-Ouen** (*open mid-Mar–Oct Wed–Mon 10–12.30 and 2–6, closed Tues; mid-Jan–mid-Mar and Nov–mid-Jan Wed and weekends 10–12.30 and 2–4.30*), a stunning Gothic building to rival any cathedral. The front has been heavily restored, but the interior combines Gothic power with simple Gothic elegance from the 14th and 15th centuries. Enter through the Porte des Marmousets, named after the figures monkeying around on the portal. Inside, the nave is sober, dignified and airy, its multi-columned piers punctuated with Gothic statue niches. The most impressive stained glass fills the strips of the choir chapels. Major art exhibitions are held in the church.

In a spectacular timberframe house on nearby, picturesque Rue Eau de Robec, with a stream running down it, the **Musée National de l'Education** (*open Mon and Wed–Fri 10–12.30 and 1.30–6, weekends 2–6; closed Tues; adm*) gives an evocative picture of French teaching from the 16th century on.

Rouen's Main Museums

Monet and Sisley, Boudin and Jongkind star in the rich **Musée des Beaux-Arts** (*open Wed–Mon 10–6; closed Tues; adm*) with its new, brilliantly displayed Impressionist galleries, but several of the Flemish works are also outstanding. Among the Italians, Caravaggio's *Flagellation of Christ* stands out. The smaller Spanish collections include ravishing still lives and a chirpy Velázquez fool. The substantial French sections feature a rare 16th-century Clouet of the goddess Diana. Portraits include a Poussin self-portrait and superb works by Largillère, de Troy, Vigée-le-Brun, David and Delacroix, plus busts and statues by Drouais. Views of historic Rouen prove illuminating, especially one by Paul Huet showing the pre-industrial city lying in shadow, dwarfed by the Seine valley. The short-lived prodigy Théodore Géricault, born in Rouen in 1791, is devoted a whole room.

Housed in a former Gothic church behind the museum, the **Musée de la Ferronnerie Le Secq des Tournelles** (*open Wed–Mon 10–1 and 2–6; closed Tues; adm*) displays an eccentric, amusing collection of wrought-iron objects from gateways and inn signs to keys going back to Gallo-Roman times. Rouen is better known for its pottery, and the much smarter **Musée de la Céramique** (*open Wed–Mon 10–1 and 2–6; closed Tues; adm*) tells the story of its making in Rouen, France and Western Europe. Masseot Abaquesne brought southern European techniques to Rouen in the mid-16th century, and production began on a major scale. All sorts of ceramic follies feature in the museum, including pottery busts, shoes, clocks, lions and even a ceramic violin.

At the **Musée des Antiquités** (*open Mon and Wed–Sat 10–12.30 and 1.30–5.30, Sun 2–6; closed Tues; adm*), the pointed helmet of Bernières d'Ailly (*c.* 900 BC) stands out among the pre-Roman exhibits, while the Gallo-Roman collections include two impressive mosaics showing Orpheus serenading wild animals and a nymph pursued by Poseidon. Some of the fine medieval tapestries may have been made to celebrate French victory in the Hundred Years War, and there are other medieval treasures including an exquisite enamel-covered book. You can learn more about Rouen's history at the **Tour Jeanne d'Arc** (*open Mon and Wed–Sat 10–12.30 and 2–5, Sun 2–5.30; closed Tues; adm*), but little about Joan, a short-term inmate here. The tower is a solid but solitary remnant of the enormous castle Philippe Auguste built on Rouen's hillside.

Moving to the river, in a former warehouse to the west, the **Musée Maritime** (*open Mon and Wed–Fri 10–12.30 and 2–6, weekends 2–6; closed Tues; adm*) has made some effort to bring Rouen's links with its river back to the fore, with models, and even a whale skeleton. You can also look round a traditional Seine barge, now at rest out of the water. One good reason to cross to the dull-looking south bank is to view challenging contemporary art exhibitions at the **FRAC** by the extensive **Jardin des Plantes**.

The Seine from Rouen to Paris

Richard the Lionheart's Château-Gaillard and Monet's Giverny hog the limelight along this stretch of the Seine, but do be tempted east from the river by Emma Bovary country, Lyons-la-Forêt, and the châteaux d'Anet and Maintenon. A visit to dramatic Seine-side La Roche-Guyon takes you into the surprisingly rural Vexin Français.

A Detour into Emma Bovary Country East of Rouen

The very handsome brick **Château de Martainville** stands out in flat countryside due east of Rouen, built in the late 15th century for Jacques Le Pelletier, intriguing emblems in darker brick adding an air of mystery to the exterior. The fashionable Renaissance transformations were commissioned by Le Pelletier's nephew. The rooms now serve as lovely settings for the **Musée Départemental des Traditions et Arts Normands** (*open Wed–Sat and Mon 10–12.30 and 2–5, Sun 2–5; closed Tues; adm*), with splendid examples of furniture from different corners of Normandy.

Twee little **Ry** is reckoned to have been the model for Yonville-l'Abbaye, the provincial Yawnville which drives Emma Bovary crazy for passion. Her story is given the most inappropriate treatment at the **Galerie Bovary Musée d'Automates** (*open Easter–Oct Sat–Mon and public hols 11–12 and 2–7; July and Aug also Tues–Fri 3–7; adm*), with scenes from the novel re-enacted by automata. The eerie village church behind its wood-carved porch has a far more appropriate, desolate character, although plaques here have created an unfortunate confusion between the fictional Emma and the real-life Delphine Couturier, whose tragic suicide after her marriage to a village doctor was clearly exploited by Flaubert. An Emma Bovary trail takes you into the countryside.

The very jolly, strikingly patterned **Château de Vascœuil** (*open July–Aug daily 11–7; May–June and Sept–Oct 2.30–6.30; April and early Nov 2.30–5.30; Mar weekends pm only; adm*) lies a hop and a skip east of Ry. It became the home to that monumental figure among 19th-century French historians, Jules Michelet, whose vast *Histoire de France* counts among the most famous books in the French language. The **Musée Michelet** inside is modest given the man's phenomenal output and cultural significance, and some may find the modern art by the likes of Calder, Vasarely and Dalí scattered around the garden more amusing.

Packed with the most gorgeous of timberframe houses, **Lyons-la-Forêt** presents the perfect picture of a Norman village. The covered market dates from the 17th century, as do many of the grandest dwellings. At the edge of Lyons, the church with its stone and flint chequerboard patterning goes back to the 12th century. The magnificent beech woods of the **Forêt de Lyons** were planted by the monks of the **abbey of Mortemer**; you can visit the ruins.

Getting Around

For Giverny, take a **train** from Rouen to Vernon, then a **bus**, **taxi** or **bicycle**.

Tourist Information

Ry: Les Trois Vallées, Maison de l'Abreuvoir, **t** 02 35 23 19 90.

Lyons-la-Forêt: 20 Rue de l'Hôtel de Ville, **t** 02 32 49 31 65.

Les Andelys: Rue Philippe Auguste, **t** 02 32 54 41 93, *otsi.andelys@wanadoo.fr*.

Evreux: Place Général de Gaulle, **t** 02 32 24 04 43, *information@ot-pays-evreux.fr*.

Dreux: 6 Rue des Embûches, **t** 02 37 46 01 73, *www.ot-dreux.fr*.

Where to Stay and Eat

Lyons-la-Forêt ✉ 27480

★★★La Licorne, Place Benserade, **t** 02 32 49 62 02, *licorne-hotel-restaurant@wanadoo.fr* (*expensive–moderate*). A timberframe delight in the heart of Lyons, the rooms lovely, the cooking classic Norman. *Closed mid-Dec–mid-Jan; restaurant closed Nov–Mar, Mon, and Tues lunch.*

★★Hostellerie du Domaine de St-Paul, Route de Forges-les-Eaux (D321), **t** 02 32 49 60 57, *www.domaine-saint-paul.fr* (*expensive, half-board compulsory*). Exceptionally pretty, extremely popular address behind its white-fenced entrance just outside town. The restaurant (*expensive–moderate*) offers stylish Normandy cuisine. *Closed Nov–Mar.*

Connelles ✉ 27430

★★★★Le Moulin de Connelles, 40 Route d'Amfreville, **t** 02 32 59 53 33, *www.moulinde-connelles.com* (*very expensive–expensive*). An extravagant 19th-century pastiche of Normandy timberframe architecture – a glorious château of a 'mill' by the Seine with all manner of luxuries: pool, tennis court and boats. Very fine restaurant too. *Restaurant closed Sun pm and Mon Oct–April.*

Les Andelys ✉ 27700

★★★La Chaîne d'Or, 27 Rue Grande, Le Petit-Andely, **t** 02 32 54 00 31, *chaineor@wanadoo.fr* (*expensive–moderate*). Charming Seine-side 18th-century inn with a lovely courtyard behind the church. Very decent restaurant (*expensive*). *Closed Jan; restaurant closed Sun pm Mon and Tues lunch.*

Giverny ✉ 27620

★★La Musardière, 123 Rue Claude Monet, **t** 02 32 21 03 18, *iraymonde@aol.com* (*moderate*). By the Fondation Monet, a large property with its own big garden. Traditional restaurant-cum-crêperie (*expensive–moderate*). *Restaurant closed Mon lunch.*

Les Jardins de Giverny, **t** 02 32 21 60 80 (*expensive–moderate*). A rose garden surrounds this Belle Epoque house 400m from the Fondation Monet; the refined cooking includes home-smoked fish. *Closed Mon.*

Along the Seine to Château-Gaillard, Giverny and the Vexin Français

After the industrial loops in the Seine south of Rouen, a dramatic chalk cliff road shadows the river from Pitres on the east bank as far as **Les Andelys**. Le Petit-Andely was built next to the river to provide supplies for the medieval **Château-Gaillard** (*open mid-Mar–mid-Nov Thurs–Mon 10–1 and 2–6, Wed 2–6; closed Tues; adm to keep, free outside*). When Richard the Lionheart returned from imprisonment in Austria after the Third Crusade, his former childhood friend, fellow crusader and, it has been rumoured, gay lover King Philippe Auguste of France was planning to take Normandy from him. To thwart him, Richard ordered the most advanced fortifications yet seen in Europe, incorporating lessons taken from the Arab and crusader castles. In a prodigious effort, Château-Gaillard was built in just one year, from 1196 to 1197. Philippe Auguste was duly deterred, but after the Lionheart's death his hapless brother King John seemed an easier adversary. In 1203 a French army besieged Château-Gaillard, which fell in March 1204, and Normandy was soon in the hands of the French monarch. King Henri IV and Cardinal Richelieu, aided by centuries of pilfering, helped see to its gradual demolition, but the ruins remain awesome. **Le Petit-Andely** below has narrow streets with half-timbered buildings and an open-air swimming pool.

Le Grand-Andely, founded by Romans and set back from the Seine, boasts an ample market square and the collegiate church of Notre-Dame. Inside, note the 16th-century stained glass and two fine altar paintings by Quentin Varin, the first teacher of Les Andelys' most famous son, Nicolas Poussin, born in 1594. Although he scarcely ever returned after leaving to study in Paris in his twenties, his birthplace pays its respects with the small **Musée Nicolas Poussin** (*open Wed–Mon 2–6; closed Tues; adm*), which displays one of his major classical paintings, *Coriolanus Answering His Mother's Tears*.

Giverny is all too famous because Monet settled here. His house and gardens are now presented under the name of the **Fondation Claude Monet** (*open April–Oct Tues–Sun 9.30–5.30; adm*). It's only a small place, generally infested with coachloads of tourists. Also, don't expect to see any original Monet canvases. Instead, wandering round the pretty pink-fronted house with its brightly coloured rooms you'll get a lesson in Japanese art, as virtually every inch of wall space is hung with Japanese prints by Japanese masters, as arranged by the great French Impressionist himself. Monet lived here until his death in 1926, and the property was only sold by one of his sons in 1966. By then it had fallen into a state of disrepair, and a large amount of the money needed to restore it was donated by wealthy Americans. Outside are the re-creations of Monet's two separate gardens. The first consists of the most densely planted rows of flowers imaginable, the colours and forms merging into a wonderful, unfocused blur – a bit like an Impressionist experience, in real life. The second, a Japanese water garden, looks immaculate, the big weeping willows dipping their fronds so contentedly into the lake, the oriental bridge crossing it so elegantly, and the waterlilies sitting so prettily on its surface. Nothing of course can equal Monet's mystical transformations of this spot in his *Nymphéas* series, arguably the crowning glory of modern art. Sadly, even his big, light-bathed studio has been turned into a mere souvenir shop selling poor reproductions of his works.

Along the main village street, the slick contemporary design of the **Musée d'Art Américain** (*open Mar–mid-Aug and Sept–Nov Tues–Sun 10–6; adm*) calls for visitors' attention with its cool yet welcoming formal front garden, pool and café. It displays works by American artists who came to France in the days when Monet was such an inspiration. The works are a mixed bag, but pieces by Mary Cassat, for example, stand out. Theodore Butler, one American artist who came to worship at the master's feet, ended up marrying his stepdaughter. He and his fellow Americans started out by staying at the Hôtel Baudy, which is still thriving (as a restaurant), as is a whole art industry in the village. Claude Monet and family are buried at the unfussy church.

Around another meander in the Seine, the **Vexin Français** makes for a delightful introduction to the Ile de France. To preserve it from rampant suburbia, the area has been made a Parc Naturel Régional. Paris' great patron saint Denis came to the area in the 3rd century, and converted the noble lady at La Roche Guyon. She is said to have built a grotto of an oratory in the cliffside, under the sensationally located **Château** de la Roche-Guyon (*open mid-Mar–mid-Nov daily 10–6; rest of year daily 10–4; adm*). One of the most vertiginous stairways in France, cut into the blindingly white Seine chalk in early Capetian times, climbs to its towering tubular keep. In the early 12th century, so the murky story goes, a Norman murdered the lord Guy de la Roche while he was at Mass and took over this keep, until the king wrought his revenge and sent the Norman's body on a raft down the Seine as a warning to his countrymen. A later medieval castle was built at the foot of the keep, remnants of it flanking the main 16th-century block. The mighty de la Rochefoucaulds, ancestors of the owners, are recalled in curiously tacky displays in the dilapidated apartments. Down in the cellar, the focus switches alarmingly to Rommel – when Hitler appointed him to review the Nazi coastal defences from Denmark to the Spanish frontier in 1944, La Roche-Guyon became his headquarters.

Evreux and the Eure Valley with its Royal Connections

The Eure joins the Seine below Rouen; its valley offers a quiet route through eastern Normandy to Chartres. **Evreux**, actually on the Iton river just west of the Eure, is encased in postwar architecture, but has a trio of attractions: an excellent museum with exceptional Gallo-Roman finds; a cathedral with splendid Flamboyant Gothic features and stained glass that the war bombs missed; and the abbey of St-Taurin, concealing a memorably excessive reliquary shaped like a miniature Gothic building.

Along the Eure, antiques dealers enliven **Ivry-la-Bataille**. **Anet** across the river is devoted to the great 16th-century court figure, Diane de Poitiers. A star of her time, after the death of her powerful husband Louis de Brézé (some 30 years her senior), she became the mistress of King Henri II, many years her junior, and married to Catherine de Médicis. The king lavished extraordinary gifts on Diane, including some of the finest châteaux ever built in France. He may have given her Chenonceau, but he actually had the **Château d'Anet** (*open April–Oct Wed–Mon 2–6.30, closed Tues; Nov–Mar weekends and hols 2–5*) specially made for her. The sumptuous scraps look incoherent now, but when it was completed in the 1550s, this castle was a ground-breaking piece of Italianate architecture, the design by Philibert de l'Orme, the most accomplished of French Renaissance architects. Excessive statues pay homage to Diana, goddess of the hunt, notably on the entrance gate, with a copy of Cellini's original, now in the Louvre. The group of deer and hounds alarmingly scrapping atop the gateway were originally mechanized and moved! Anet's surviving architectural masterpiece is de l'Orme's extraordinarily bold chapel, the patterned floor and ceiling filling the space with dizzying movement. Of the château proper, only one wing out of three survived the 19th century, but the half-dozen rooms you see are splendidly furnished, grand courtly portraits peering across the chambers. One cabinet contains some of Diane's personal possessions. Her tomb stands on bulging-breasted grotesques in the funerary chapel nearby, almost stripped bare at the Revolution.

Continue down the Eure valley to Dreux and Maintenon, with their own strong French royal connections. **Dreux**'s extravagantly crowned 19th-century **Chapelle Royale** (*open April–Sept daily 9–11.30 and 2–6.20*) stands out on the hillside above town, where a medieval fort once stood. It was built for the Duchess of Orléans in

1816, soon after the restoration of the French monarchy; by 1830, her son Louis-Philippe would become king, and the chapel the burial place of the new French royal family. But Louis-Philippe's remains would have to be brought back here from Weybridge, his Surrey refuge, as he died in exile, the last, failed king of France. He lies surrounded by countless other tomb effigies of further members of the family.

Feet bathing in the Eure river, the delightful brick and stone **Château de Maintenon** (*open April–Oct Wed–Mon 2–6, closed Tues; Nov–Mar weekends and hols 2–5*) looks as if it's been transported here from the Loire Valley, while the utterly romantic ruins of an aqueduct passing through the grounds give the place an enchanting Italianate back-drop. One lord of Maintenon had a powerful square keep built here in the 12th century. Then in the early 16th century, a royal finance minister under King François Ier had wings added in French Renaissance style. But the figure whose character still really marks the place is Françoise d'Aubigné, famously made Marquise de Maintenon by her illustrious lover, none other than the Sun King himself. Louis XIV gave her this castle in 1674, and Le Nôtre designed formal gardens for it, having the Eure specially canalized. Various wings were added for the marquise, including the one to house her private apartments, plus a gallery to connect the castle with the church, devout widow that she also remained. In 1684, however, she and the king would be secretly married, and he came here frequently to see the two last children he had, and to hunt. The illustrious de Noailles family which inherited the castle made many modifi-cations in the 19th century, but some exceptional decorations have survived, including one chamber covered with embossed Cordoba leather and two rooms decorated with the most cheerful Chinese hand-painted wallpaper. The gorgeous grounds have been converted into a golf course, but you can admire the ruins of the aqueduct from a distance, part of a massively overambitious plan to transport water a mere 80km from these parts to Louis XIV's palace at Versailles. Between the two, you can visit a string of further fine royal châteaux associated with the Sun King, on the **Route Historique du Roy Soleil** – Rambouillet, Dampierre and Breteuil. Chartres (*see* p.327) lies a short way south of Maintenon along the Eure.

Along the Risle Valley to the Perche

The Risle flows peacefully up from southern Normandy to join the Seine east of the great Pont de Normandie and historic Honfleur. Here we follow it back to its source. Normandy's typical architecture goes out of the window in the Perche, where manors and farms with ochre walls and earth-brown tiles embellish the countryside.

Down the Risle Valley

Pont-Audemer, a busy crossroads on the Risle, has preserved a core of picturesque timberframe houses, but is surrounded by postwar quarters. By contrast, **Le Bec-Hellouin** has remained untouched by the modern world. Beyond the picture-book timberframe village, the **abbey** (*open 8am–9pm; free; guided tours Wed–Mon at 10.30, 3 and 4*) exudes majestic calm. Its buildings are dominated by a 15th-century Gothic

Getting Around

Bernay, L'Aigle and Nogent-le-Rotrou have **train** stations. For the Perche use **buses** from the last two.

Tourist Information

Pont-Audemer: Place Maubert, **t** 02 32 41 08 21, *tourisme@ville-pont-audemer.fr.*
Bernay: 29 Rue Thiers, **t** 02 32 43 32 08, *www.bernay27.fr.*
La Ferté-Vidame: Mairie, **t** 02 37 37 68 59, *www.cc-la-ferte-vidame.*
Mortagne-au-Perche: Pl du Général de Gaulle, **t** 02 33 85 11 18, *office-mortagne@wanadoo.fr.*
Nogent-le-Rotrou: 44 Rue Villette Gâté, **t** 02 37 29 68 86, *www.ville-nogent-le-rotrou.fr.*

Where to Stay and Eat

Le Bec-Hellouin ✉ 27800
***L'Auberge de l'Abbaye, t** 02 32 44 86 02 (*expensive; half-board compulsory*). Delightful timberframe inn on the village green. The restaurant (*moderate*) serves many Norman apple specialities. *Restaurant closed Mon.*

La Ferrière-sur-Risle ✉ 27760
Roselion, 7 Route de Pont-Audemer, **t** 02 32 30 10 85 (*inexpensive*). B&B in just about the smartest house in town on the splendid main square, with big garden.

La Ferté-Vidame ✉ 28340
Manoir de la Motte B&B, t 02 37 37 51 69 (*moderate*), *www.lemanoirdelamotte.com.* Very smart 19th-century home on the outskirts, with neo-Gothic touches and château-sized elegant rooms and salons run by a charming couple. Madame Jallot will direct you to nearby **La Trigalle** restaurant, serving inventive to eccentric cuisine.

Mortagne-au-Perche ✉ 61400
****Hôtel du Tribunal**, 4 Place du Palais, **t** 02 33 25 04 77 (*moderate–inexpensive*). Characterful old hotel on the corner of a charming square. Restaurant (*moderate*) specializing in black pudding, of which Mortagne is the self-styled capital, as well as fish.

Bellême ✉ 61130
*****Hôtel du Golf**, Route du Mans, **t** 02 33 85 13 13, *www.belleme.com* (*moderate*). Out of town, with pretty views, a smart hotel like the golf course next to it. Restaurant.

Condeau 61110
******Moulin de Villeray and Château de Villeray t** 02 33 73 30 22, *villeray@chateaux-hotels.com.* Two luxurious sister establishments north of Nogent-le-Rotrou, the highly elegant château (*luxury–expensive*) up on the hill, the substantial, superbly converted mill (*very expensive–expensive*) down by the river. The refined cuisine (*expensive*) is served at the mill, or in its garden. Pool, tennis court, horseriding and canoeing possible.

tower soaring high above mighty beech trees, the sole, impressive surviving relic of the briefly powerful medieval Norman abbey, the statues perched high up helpfully named in large Gothic script. The monastery was founded by a local lord, Herluin, around 1032. Under the Italian theologians Lanfranc and then Anselm, it became a powerhouse of Norman Church education, many clerics trained here before heading to England. Lanfranc and Anselm were in fact appointed the first archbishops of Canterbury under William the Conqueror. A vast Gothic church was built at Le Bec-Hellouin in the 14th century, but all that remains today is its outline – its stone was sold off after the Revolution. However, the 17th- and 18th-century wings of the later Maurist abbey have survived, and you can visit the ex-refectory, now the abbey church, an enormous barrel-vaulted room with superb acoustics.

Between Brionne and Le Neubourg, two contrasting gardens compete for attention. The better established surrounds the medieval **Château d'Harcourt** (*open mid-June–mid-Sept daily 10.30–6.30; Mar–mid-June and mid-Sept–mid-Nov Wed–Mon 2–6,* *closed Tues; adm*), hidden on the edge of a timberframe and thatched Normandy village. The castle grounds contain the well-marked mature trees of an arboretum established at the start of the 19th century. Elegant paths lead to the crescent of a castle above the battered ruins of the outer bailey, protected by ancient defensive ditches. Banners in the mostly empty chambers tell how Harcourt descendants owned the place from the 11th century, down via the Lorraine family, to the 18th. Briefly revived and totally transformed for one Princess of Harcourt in 1694, the castle was soon once more abandoned. At the Revolution, much of its stone was sold, but a Paris solicitor with a passion for forestry then lavished money on creating the arboretum.

The extravagant gardens at the **Château du Champ de Bataille** (*open May–Sept daily 2–6; Mar–April and Oct–Nov weekends 2–6; adm*) are almost brand new, and have the outrageous flamboyance of brash, spoilt youth. They have been designed by the eternally youthful, *richissime* Paris decorator, Jacques Garcia. Born into a modest family in the capital's suburbs, he has risen to the grandest heights of interior decoration. His élite clientele has included the likes of the Sultan of Brunei, and it shows, with gilding sparkling everywhere, in the fountains and follies, and on the castle itself. This dates from the 17th century, built for Alex Le Créquy, who was exiled here after the mid-century anti-royalist Fronde in which he took part. The aristocratic wing bearing the family arms is matched by an identical brick wing opposite, built to hold splendid stables. The walled chess garden in box is followed by an alley of tall palms. Garcia found a plan of a Le Nôtre garden, which he has had recreated, but the extensive, excessive water gardens beyond are all his own contemporary design.

Back with traditional Normandy, **Bernay** (west on the Charentonne river) was one of the few lucky towns in Normandy to escape the Second World War bombs. It arose around a monastery founded by Judith of Brittany, wife of Duke Richard II of Normandy, in the early 11th century. The powerful Romanesque **abbey church of Notre-Dame** (*only open July–Aug Wed–Mon 10–12 and 2–6, plus Sept Fri–Mon 2–6*) has survived, stripped bare inside, but held up on staggeringly tall arches. Bernay's best art, saved from Le Bec-Hellouin abbey at the Revolution, stands proudly in the **church of Ste-Croix** opposite the covered market: remarkable Gothic statues and tombstones of abbots, together with a melodramatic Baroque crucifixion scene set in a semi-circular colonnade in the choir. The wide array of art in the town's **Musée des Beaux-Arts** (*open July–Aug Wed–Mon 10–12 and 2–7, closed Tues; Sept–June Mon–Sat 3–5.30, closed Sun; adm*) is of more varied quality.

Shapely slate roofs and patterned strips of brick give the **Château de Beaumesnil** (*open July–Aug Wed–Mon 10–12 and 2–6, closed Tues; April–June and Sept Fri–Mon 2–6; adm*) its exceptionally elegant 17th-century look. Surrounded by moats and charming gardens, it looks a bit lost by a flat little village southeast of Bernay. Inside, the central tower is taken up by a grand staircase. The château contains 18th-century furniture and a museum on bookbinding, with fine covers from Renaissance times on.

In its wooded valley, attractive, part-timberframe **La Ferrière-sur-Risle** stretches out around its long, rectangular square with a fine covered market. The dark nave of **St-Georges** contains an array of statues, including a naïve St George on a mule. A wildly decorated retable holds an Entombment painting that some have attributed to a follower of Leonardo; but it's dark, difficult to see, and was speckled with bird drop-pings when last visited. The medieval castle of **Conches-en-Ouches**, east of La Ferrière, looks like an outsized sandcastle, the crumbling ruins too dangerous to set foot on. The site overlooks the little valley of the Rouloir, with a train line running through it and seemingly under **Ste-Foy**, a jewel box of a late Gothic church containing stunning 16th-century Renaissance glass. In the north aisle you can follow episodes in the life of the Virgin, in the south aisle the Eucharistic story. In the choir, the cycle telling the Passion of Christ, attributed to the Normandy artist Romain Buron, was inspired by Dürer. Further scenes relate the life of the child saint Foy.

Le Perche

Céline Dion and Madonna count among the most famous North Americans descended from Percherons, the people of the pretty provincial backwater of the Perche, as well as a renowned breed of stocky horses. A separate little county from the 12th century to the Revolution, the Perche extended across largely forested lands between Chartres and Alençon, part of the medieval frontier territories between Normandy and the Ile de France. Its main lords ruled from Nogent-le-Rotrou, although Mortagne-au-Perche has retained more of its historic character. The Perche's best-known religious foundation is the Abbaye de la Trappe, the original Trappist monastery. The Perche was devastated in the Hundred Years War, but after-wards a whole flowering of little château-like manors occurred, built in delectable yellow ochre colour. Of some 300 constructed, around half have survived. But life wasn't a piece of cake for many locals, and from the 17th century a fair number joined the early French expeditions to go to North America in search of a better life. Important Percheron links with North America continued into the 19th century, when the tough Percheron horses became much prized by the pioneers pressing into the Far West. However, the Perche being split between four *départements* at the Revolution, the county became a neglected area back home. The creation in 1998 of its Parc Régional Naturel aims to protect its markedly separate character.

Entering the Perche via the northern gateway of **La Ferté-Vidame**, this place has a ghostly grandeur. A huge, ruined brick shell of a château stands out to one side of town, built in the 18th century by Antoine Le Carpentier for the hugely wealthy Marquis de Laborde, who made a fortune through tax-collecting and court banking. He had to relinquish the property to the king's cousin, the Duc de Penthièvre, before the Revolution, but that didn't stop him losing his head. The duke's daughter regained the dilapidated pile, and her son Louis-Philippe planned for its reconstruction, but work only got as far as the extremely grand stabling. Rebaptized Le Petit Château, this now contains an interesting museum on the famous owners of the aristocratic estate before Laborde, the powerful Catholic dukes of St-Simon. The earlier castle had been bought in 1632 by Claude (first duke of St-Simon and close to King Louis XIII), who had the previous, Protestant owners disinterred for his first wife's grand new Baroque church of St-Nicolas, which still stands. Louis, Claude's celebrated son by his second marriage, recorded the characters and events at Louis XIV's court in flamboyant style in his *Memoirs*. He frequently visited La Ferté-Vidame not just to find peace and write, but also to keep his links with the exceptional abbot who restored the reputation of the abbey of La Trappe to the west.

Founded in 1122 by Rotrou III, the nobleman for whom the Perche was first made into a county, the **abbey of La Trappe** functioned as a typical Cistercian community until the 16th century, after which it was neglected by absent abbots. Bizarrely, it took a reformed Ancien Régime libertine, Armand Jean Le Bouthillier de Rancé, to restore its fortunes and reinstate a particularly rigorous observance of the Cistercian rule. Claude de St-Simon and Rancé had been good friends in the abbot's wilder days and kept in touch afterwards, which is how Louis was introduced to this extraordinary figure. The statuary on the gateway looks surprisingly showy given the ascetic reputation of the Trappist order (the Cistercians of the Strict Observance). You can hear the famously silent white-robed monks speak eloquently and movingly on the explanatory video at the Accueil (the rest of the abbey is out of bounds).

As you wander from one delightful square to another in **Mortagne-au-Perche**, numbered panels explain the history of each historic spot, starting in the public garden with its weird statue of a baby riding a full-sized horse, a 19th-century work by Frémiet, best known for his militant St Michael atop Mont-St-Michel. This bizarre one represents a tale from Ovid. One little museum treats local traditions, another pays homage to the philosopher Alain, who was born here, and whose attacks on the French establishment in the First World War were a rare voice of sanity.

Southeast of Monceaux-au-Perche, the spires of the huge **basilica of La Chapelle-Montligeon** stand out against a wooded hillside. Dubbed 'the cathedral in the field', the enormous edifice was built as a place of pilgrimage at the end of the 19th century for the troubled Abbot Buguet, with the blessing of the bishop of Sées. The abbot's particular anxiety, apparently prompted by personal worries, concerned the suffering of souls in purgatory awaiting purification to enter paradise. The neo-Gothic excesses of the architecture climax with the garish transept stained glass. The road down from Monceaux-au-Perche to Marchainville via Longny-au-Perche is dotted with a gorgeous selection of Percheron manor houses.

Head south for the headquarters of the Perche regional park at the **Manoir et Domaine de Courboyer** (*open April–Oct daily 10.30–7; free grounds but adm for manor guided tour*), north of Nocé. Only the gorgeous towers and roofs of this castle of a manor stick their heads tentatively out of their little valley as you arrive. Down below, you'll see how the building counts among the most imposing and charming of the typical major Percheron properties built after the Hundred Years War. But until 2000 it was still serving as a rustic farm. The big sober interiors have preserved their man-sized fireplaces and the odd bit of wood panelling, and are now used for permanent and temporary exhibitions about the Perche. One rare historical object on display is a worn blue and white Protestant flag dating back to the 16th-century Wars of Religion. You can take a tour of the grounds in a horse-drawn carriage.

South of Nocé, the **Prieuré de Ste-Gauburge** contains the **Ecomusée du Perche** (*open daily 2–6; adm*), but the enchanting architecture is the prize display. On one fireplace,

Adam and Eve are shown being cast out of paradise; the religious have long been banished from this priory, signs all too clear of how it was converted into a farm. The buildings have kept a number of their original features, though, with a gorgeous church choir and a stairtower showing legends of the local saint. The chapterhouse was turned into a practical kitchen. The more substantial sections devoted to traditional crafts from clog- to cider-making are housed in a converted barn.

As you approach the town of **Nogent-le-Rotrou** to the east, dull modern blocks fight it out for your attention with the impressive remnants of the medieval castle. This **Château St-Jean** (*open Wed–Mon 10–12 and 2–6, closed Tues; adm*) contains another attractive museum on local traditions within its mighty walls.

The Côte Fleurie

The Côte Fleurie, which stretches west from the mouth of the Seine, became the seaside of Paris in the 19th century. Deauville took on the role of self-styled 21st *arrondissement* of the capital when it supplanted its rival Trouville and, with its famous horse-racing track, still comes in several furlongs ahead of the other seaside resorts. Tackiness now rivals glamour in these resorts, but all boast spacious, soft sandy beaches. The main cultural attraction, the exquisite historic port of Honfleur, has museums aplenty, and quays lined with amazing ancient high-rise houses.

Honfleur

Why would explorers ever have wished to leave for new worlds from as beautiful a place as Honfleur? But they did, most famously Samuel de Champlain in the early 17th century, whose voyages led to the founding of Quebec. Less trumpeted by the port is its slave-trading link with Africa; in the 18th century, local shipping magnates mounted well over 100 expeditions. They built splendid homes on the proceeds – the fantastic quayside houses of Honfleur's **Vieux Bassin** date from this time. **Quai Ste-Catherine** has the most spectacular display of multi-storeyed slate- and timber-sided-houses. They must have seemed the skyscrapers of their day. Touristy shops and restaurants do a roaring trade at ground level. At the end of Quai Ste-Catherine the painterly **Lieutenance** served as the well-located home of the governors of Honfleur. On one side stands a bust of Champlain. Behind Quai Ste-Catherine lies a delightful timberframe neighbourhood. A quirky belfry guards 15th-century **Ste-Catherine**, one of the finest French timberframe churches – the hull of a roof was made by local shipbuilders. The carvings below show definite touches of sailors' earthiness; the musicians in the organ gallery display an excess of shapely leg and unseemly bottom.

A number of 19th-century artists from Honfleur appreciated the exceptional beauty of their home town and tried to render it in art, as you can see in the varied collections in the substantial **Musée Boudin** (*open mid-Mar–Sept Wed–Mon 10–12 and 2–6; Oct–mid-Mar Wed–Mon 2.30–5 plus weekends also 10–12; closed Tues; adm*). This fine arts museum is named after Eugène Boudin, born in Honfleur in 1824, the son of a sailor. The poet Baudelaire came here in 1859 and was deeply moved by seeing his

Getting There and Around

Lisieux inland has good **rail** connections with Paris (*c.* 1hr 30mins). A regular train service links Lisieux with the Trouville-Deauville station (c.20 mins). Otherwise, to go along the coast, you'll have to rely on slower local **buses**.

Tourist Information

Honfleur: Quai Lepaulmier, **t** 02 31 89 23 30, *office-du-tourisme-honfleur@wanadoo.fr*.
Deauville: Place de la Mairie, **t** 02 31 14 40 00, *www.deauville.org*.
Trouville: 32 Quai F. Moureaux, **t** 02 31 14 60 70, *www.trouvillesurmer.org*.
Cabourg: Jardins du Casino, **t** 02 31 91 20 00, *www.cabourg.net*.

Where to Stay and Eat

Honfleur ✉ 14600

****La Ferme St-Siméon, Rue Adolphe Marais, **t** 02 31 81 78 00, *www.fermesaintsimeon.fr* (*luxury–very expensive*). Luxurious, on the Seine estuary slopes west of Honfleur,

rooms set in the large central manor or various thatched buildings around. The most refined cuisine (*very expensive*); a decadent swimming pool complex together with beauty treatments; and memories of Monet, Boudin, Sisley, Courbet and Jongkind, who used to meet here. *Restaurant closed Mon and Tues lunch.*
***L'Absinthe, 10 Quai de la Quarantaine, **t** 02 31 89 23 23, *www.absinthe.fr* (*expensive*). Slate-covered and flint-patterned 16th-century priest's house with jacuzzis in the stylish rooms. Appealing restaurant, **t** 02 31 89 39 00. *Closed 15 Nov–15 Dec.*
***L'Ecrin, 19 Rue Boudin, **t** 02 31 14 43 45, *www.honfleur.com/lecrin* (*very expensive–moderate*). Central, packed full of character.
Le Dauphin, 10 Place Pierre Berthelot, **t 02 31 89 15 53, *hotel.dudauphin@wanadoo.fr* (*expensive–moderate*). Timberframe hotel by the timberframe church of Ste-Catherine, with a mix of rooms.
Les Cascades, 17 Place Thiers, **t** 02 31 89 05 83 (*inexpensive*). Cheap, basic, well-located.
La Terrasse de l'Assiette, 8 Place Ste-Catherine, **t** 02 31 89 31 33 (*expensive*). Honfleur's most exclusive restaurant, with luxurious specialities like lobster. *Closed Mon.*

works with 'those horizons in mourning or streaming with molten metal, all those depths, all those splendours...'. Another highlight is Jongkind's silvery *Entrée du port d'Honfleur*. Dubourg's paintings, disparaged by many critics, actually give a good notion of the 19th-century Normandy seaside, ladies wandering along the beach hemmed in by elaborate dresses and protected by parasols, vessels with great sails colouring the background. The museum also has views by 20th-century artists. Dufy proves as irrepressible as ever, while Henri de St-Delis' naïve style is fun. Herbo stands apart in tackling the grittier, industrial side of the Seine estuary; from the top of the museum you get a great view of the Pont de Normandie crossing it.

Honfleur was also the birthplace in 1886 of maverick musician Erik Satie, and an experimental museum, the **Maisons Satie** (*open May–Sept Wed–Mon 10–7; mid-Feb–April and Oct–Dec Wed–Mon 11–6; closed Tues and Jan; adm*), does him proud. Your senses are bombarded in this deliberately eccentric place, quite in keeping with the enchanting quirkiness of Satie's music. On the way round you'll hear extracts as well as learning about his life. Finish the tour riding on a basketball on the musical merry-go-round playing a Satie piece, for adults and children alike!

Back at the Vieux Bassin, cross to **Quai St-Etienne** to wander round the oldest part of the port, known as the Enclos. The adorable church of St-Etienne, turned **Musée du Vieux Honfleur** (*open July and Aug daily 10–1 and 2–6.30; April–June and Sept Tues–Sun 10–12 and 2–6, closed Mon; mid-Feb–Mar and end Sept–mid-Nov Tues–Sun 2–5.30,*

La Table du Cuisinier, 2 Quai des Passagers, t 02 31 89 24 88 (*moderate*). Sister establishment of the above, with simpler and more reasonably priced but still delicious dishes such as the *croustillant de Pont-l'Evêque. Closed Tues.*

La Lieutenance, 12 Place Ste-Catherine, t 02 31 89 07 52 (*moderate*). Smart dining room and nice terrace, great for fresh fish.

Trouville ✉ 14360

**Les Sablettes, 15 Rue Paul Besson, t 02 31 88 10 66 (*inexpensive*). Charming and relatively cheap for this coast. *Closed Dec and Jan.*

Les Vapeurs, 160 Quai Fernand Moureaux, t 02 31 88 15 24 (*expensive*). Top dog on the restaurant-lined quay, renowned for both atmosphere and cuisine. The sister establishment **Les Voiles** next door (*moderate*) has a well-priced menu.

Deauville ✉ 14800

****Normandy Barrière, 38 Rue Jean Mermoz, t 02 31 98 66 22, *www.lucienbarriere.com* (*luxury*). Palatial Deauville timberframe extravaganza, by the casino, with almost 300 rooms. There is plenty of entertainment

laid on. The sumptuous restaurant is **La Potinière** (*expensive*).

**Le Trophée, 81 Rue du Général Leclerc, t 02 31 88 45 86, *information@letrophee.com* (*expensive–moderate*). Stylish, bright bedrooms behind a Norman façade. Good food.

**Le Patio, 180 Av de la République, t 02 31 88 25 07 (*moderate–inexpensive*). Still quite stylish but reasonably priced two-star. *Closed Jan.*

Cabourg ✉ 14390

****Grand Hôtel, Promenade Marcel Proust, t 02 31 91 01 79, *www.grandhotelcabourg. com* (*luxury–expensive*). An enormous wedding cake hotel with 70 rooms on the Cabourg seafront, where Proust stayed so faithfully. **Le Balbec**, the swanky restaurant with snooty service (*expensive*) looks out to sea. *Restaurant closed Jan, and Mon and Tues out of season.*

**Le Cottage, 24 Av du Général Leclerc, t 02 31 91 65 61 (*moderate*). A pleasing central seaside hotel.

**Beaurivage, Allée du Château/Route du Home, t 02 31 24 08 08 (*inexpensive*). More modest seafront option.

weekends also 10–12; adm), is hugged tightly by old houses. Inside, what with the clutter of large-scale models of boats, wood carvings and pictures, it's hard to focus on anything. But fragments of Honfleur's history emerge: French expeditions to Canada, 18th-century naval battles between the French and the British, the seafaring adventures of slave-trader General Hamelin of Honfleur... Tucked away to one side of the church, the **Musée d'Ethnographie** (*open same times as the Musée du Vieux Honfleur*) presents a fragrant picture of Normandy interiors, a very pretty, cleaned-up picture, except for the prison room. In the same quarter, the 17th-century salt lofts or **Greniers à Sel**, built to supply the Atlantic shipping fleets with the precious commodity needed to preserve cod, now house seasonal exhibitions. The tradition of painting, good and bad, flourishes around Honfleur to this day.

Trouville, Deauville and Cabourg

'The greatest events of my life have been a few thoughts, reading, certain sunsets at Trouville...,' Flaubert once stated. **Trouville** may have been beaten by Dieppe to become France's first seaside resort but, thanks to a better beach and good connections with Paris, it quickly became more popular, with Napoleon III bringing his court here in the 1850s. The view along Trouville's boardwalk, or *planches*, above the soft sweep of sands, with flags fluttering in the wind, must be one of the most familiar images of 19th-century French painting. Even after the élite had transferred their allegiance to Deauville, Trouville continued to draw crowds. It now has a relaxing, old-style seafront, with bars, ice-cream stands, grand old villas, a brash casino and aquaria. The long quay where fishing boats moor is a lively focus. On Rue Général Leclerc, the main street, the small **Musée Montebello** (*open April–Sept Wed–Mon 2–6.30; closed Tues*) shelters some charming works by Boudin and Trouville painters.

Fleeting glimpses of French actresses, sharply preserved matrons promenading with little dogs, poseurs with flawless skin lolling in unbelievably comfortable café chairs, *roués* staggering ruined from the casino – such are the images conjured up by **Deauville**, another product of the decadent Second Empire. In 1860, Napoléon III's half-brother, the Duc de Morny, strayed across the Touques from Trouville and decided to develop the empty dunes and marshes as a more exclusive resort. Another major contributor to Deauville's development was a property speculator called Eugène Cornuché, who rebuilt the seafront and the casino. Since it was a totally artificial town, its promoters played around with different styles, the most common one known locally as Anglo-Norman, using lashings of mock half-timbering to build up giant mansions that look like traditional Norman manor houses on steroids. Yet Deauville's architecture has a rather sterile feel, and it's all separated from the beach by a no-man's-land of gardens, though the beach is luxuriously fine and broad. Two large marinas have been fitted into the Touques estuary to cater to all the luxury yachts. Deauville also has two lavish tracks, **La Touques** for flat racing and the more casual **Clairefontaine** (*free guided tours every day in season 10.30am*) for steeplechases and trotting. In August the polo tournament at La Touques and the Grand Prix de Deauville, the traditional end to the racing season, are major social events. Deauville's Festival du Cinéma Américain follows in early September, and gets in a US film star to preside – Harrison Ford and Liz Taylor count among the best-known fans of the resort. Deauville unsurprisingly boasts one of the most luxurious thalassotherapy centres in France, and one of the country's finest golf courses.

Deauville may have played around with its seafront blocks, but at **Cabourg** the feel of the Belle Epoque has been slightly better preserved. A Proust family favourite, the resort served as a model for Balbec in Marcel's masterpiece. Much of the attention centres around the Grand Hôtel where Proust stayed with his beloved chauffeur Agostinelli, an unrequited love, but an immense inspiration. The hotel trades shamelessly on its associations by offering wildly expensive teas, but no refund is promised should the madeleines fail to unlock the floodgates of memory. However, Cabourg also has the free attraction of one of the finest beachfronts in Normandy, the odd grand old villa still playing its role among the big modern seafront apartment blocks.

The Cheesy Pays d'Auge

The Pays d'Auge lays on thick the classic clichés of Normandy countryside: half-timbered farms and rose-covered manors set among apple orchards in green valleys where horses and dappled cows graze.

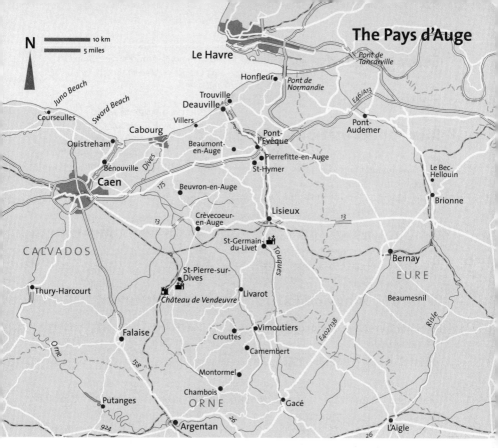

N 10 km
5 miles

Le Havre

Honfleur
Pont de
Normandie

Juno Beach

Sword Beach

Trouville
Deauville

Villers

Pont de
Tancarville

E46/A13

Pont-
Audemer

Courseulles

Cabourg

Pont-
l'Evêque

Ouistreham

Beaumont-
en-Auge

Pierrefitte-en-Auge

Le Bec-
Hellouin

Bénouville

Dives

St-Hymer

Caen

N13

Beuvron-en-Auge

Brionne

Crèvecoeur-
en-Auge

Lisieux

13

CALVADOS

St-Germain-
du-Livet

Touques

Bernay

St-Pierre-sur-
Dives

EURE

Thury-Harcourt

Château de Vendeuvre

Livarot

Beaumesnil

Orne

D58

Vimoutiers

E402/N138

Risle

Falaise

Croutte

Camembert

Montormel

Chambois

Putanges

ORNE

Gacé

924

Argentan

D26

L'Aigle

26

From the Coast to Lisieux

The northern Pays d'Auge (roughly above the N13 Lisieux to Caen road on the map) is perhaps the prettiest part of this, undoubtedly one of the prettiest areas in Normandy, where the valleys are at their most verdant, the half-timbered houses at their finest. Horse-breeding, cheese, cider and calvados-making are major concerns.

With its many smart stud farms marked off by white fencing, the D118 from Villers-sur-Mer to Pont-l'Evêque leads you up to the best-located village in the area, **Beaumont-en-Auge**, full of character, overseen by a pensive statue of the great astronomer Laplace, born here in 1749. A short distance east, **Pont-l'Evêque** of very fine and smelly cheese fame lost much of its soul in Second World War bombing. The higgledy-piggledy collection of old houses at **Pierrefitte-en-Auge** (towards Lisieux) has plenty of traditional character. **St-Hymer** hides sweetly in its little valley nearby. The **Cambremer Route du Cidre** offers a well-signposted circuit round the heart of the Auge cider *appellation* area where you can visit traditional cider-making farms, while the prettiness of **Beuvron-en-Auge**, with its exceptional variety of timberframe and brick façades, is no secret. As to the **Château de Crèvecœur** (*open July–Aug daily 11–7; April–June and Sept Wed–Mon 11–6, closed Tues; adm*) to the south, it could serve as a copybook illustration of a Norman motte-and-bailey castle. Its oldest ramparts went up before its lord joined William in his conquest of England, while later half-timbered

Getting Around

Lisieux inland has good **rail** connections with Paris (*c.* 1hr 30mins).

Tourist Information

Pont-l'Evêque: 16 bis Rue St-Michel, **t** 02 31 64 12 77, *www.pontleveque.com.*
Lisieux: 11 Rue d'Alençon, **t** 02 31 48 18 10, *www.ville-lisieux.fr/decouvrirfr.htm.*
Livarot: 1 Place Georges Bisson, **t** 02 31 63 47 39, *www.perso.wanadoo.fr/o.t.s.i.livarot.*
St-Pierre-sur-Dives: 23 Rue St Benoist, **t** 02 31 20 97 90, *www.mairie-saint-pierre-sur-dives.fr.*

Where to Stay and Eat

Beaumont-en-Auge ✉ 14950
Auberge de l'Abbaye, 2 Rue de la Libération, **t** 02 31 64 82 31 (*moderate*). Posh picture of a Normandy village restaurant. *Closed 1st half Oct, 1st half Feb and Tues, Wed exc July and Aug.*

Pierrefitte-en-Auge ✉ 14130
Auberge des Deux Tonneaux, **t** 02 31 64 09 31 (*moderate*). Characterful, bulging inn in delightful timberframe village tumbling down its hill. *Closed 15 Nov–15 Feb and Sun eves exc school hols.*

Crouttes 61120
Le Prieuré St-Michel B&B, **t** 02 33 39 15 15 (*moderate*). Luxurious rooms, more fit for a château than a priory! *Table d'hôte* by reservation.
Ferme Auberge du Haut de Crouttes, **t** 02 33 35 25 27 (*moderate*). In a delightfully rustic hamlet where hens run wild, a thin slice of a country restaurant serving copious farm produce, from Camembert galette, via duck in apples to *teurgoule*, Normandy rice pudding. Basic B&B rooms (*inexpensive*).

buildings cluster round the courtyard. Crèvecœur has been lovingly restored by a foundation created by the Alsatian Schlumberger engineering family, which explains why it now houses a museum on oil exploration as well as temporary exhibitions.

Lisieux attracts crowds of pilgrims, thanks to that 19th-century model of Catholic piety, Ste Thérèse de Lisieux. An outrageously large breast of a dome sticks out quite inappropriately from Lisieux's hillside, crowning the neo-Byzantine basilica built in her honour, and to dazzle the masses. The other main place of pilgrimage here is the bourgeois house where Thérèse Martin was brought up, the **Maison des Buissonnets** (*open Palm Sun–Sept 9–12 and 2–6; Oct, Feb and March 10–12 and 2–5; Nov and Dec 10–12 and 2–4*), after the family had moved from Alençon. Thérèse's religious fervour was provoked by several factors: the death of her mother when the little girl was just four; a terrible childhood illness which she thought she survived thanks to a miracle; and a crisis over Christmas presents. In 1888, aged just 15, Thérèse was allowed, given her exceptional ardour, to follow two of her sisters and join the Carmelite order. In under ten years she was dead from tuberculosis, having followed the rule with terrifying rigour – fervent Catholics may admire her example; non-believers may be appalled by such a seemingly self-destructive path. There's also a waxworks museum retracing the steps in Thérèse's life, the **Musée Thérèse Martin** (*open April–Oct daily exc Sun am 9.30–12 and 1.30–6; adm*), in a former Benedictine abbey.

In the town centre you'll see all too clearly how the heart was ripped out of Lisieux during the war. The mainly 13th-century **cathedral** has survived, skulking in a corner of a postwar square. Its rough interior exudes a rather purer spirituality than the kitsch places devoted to Ste Thérèse. The **Musée d'Art et d'Histoire** (*open Wed–Mon 2–6; closed Tues; adm*), in a timberframe building, covers traditional arts and crafts.

Just south of Lisieux, rural **St-Germain-du-Livet** boasts one of the most eccentrically picturesque châteaux in Normandy (*open Feb–Sept Wed–Mon 11–6; closed Tues*), one remarkable moated wing patterned with glazed green tiles. The rooms show temporary exhibitions. Fragments of original wall paintings survive.

The Augean Cheese Stables South of Lisieux

Livarot, Vimoutiers, Camembert and St-Pierre-sur-Dives fight it out for cheese-lovers' attention in this corner of the Auge. **Livarot** produces perhaps the most characterful of all the potent Normandy cheeses, but its **Musée des Ateliers de l'Art du Fer** (*open June–Sept Wed–Mon 10–12 and 2–7; April–May Wed–Mon 2–7; closed Tues; adm*) pays scant attention to the pongy produce, focusing instead on traditional metal-working. Camembert cheese, so far ahead in the cheese marketing stakes, has several museums and houses devoted to it, one at somewhat dismal **Vimoutiers**, a place torn to bits in the Battle of Normandy. To add insult to injury, the town's statue of the 'inventor' of the cheese, Marie Harel, was decapitated. In the makeshift **Musée du Camembert** (*open April–Oct Tues–Sun 9–12 and 2–6, Mon 2–6; Oct–Mar Tues–Sat 10–12 and 2–5.30, Mon 2–5.30, closed Sun*) you can learn how the goddess of gooey *fromage* was taught her techniques by a priest on the run from Brie (excuse the pun), and the important procedure whereby the curds are added in five separate ladlefuls.

However, the meltingly gorgeous village of **Camembert** running (apologies, we can't help ourselves) down its lush valley of meadows and orchards remains unique, its church speckled brown and white like the local cows. Harel perfected her cheese-making techniques up at the **Manoir de Beaumoncel** (*open 29 July–9 Aug 2.30–6.30*), and the place has retained its period atmosphere. She not only had the help of her priest; she also had a nose for business. The families of her three daughters continued the marketing success, while at the close of the 19th century a Le Havre merchant struck upon the idea of the round poplar box to help export the cheese in good condition to North America. Still more significantly, in 1916 the Camembert producers agreed to send one day's production a week to the war front, thus making Camembert something of a national symbol. Mass industrialization has followed and nowadays Le Président has by far the largest slice of the market. Set up in 1968, by 1992 it had sold its billionth Camembert. In 2000 it opened the **Ferme Président** (*open May–mid-Sept daily 10–12.30 and 2–7; Mar–April and mid-Sept–Oct Tues–Sun 10–12.30 and 2–5.30; adm*), a museum which relates clearly the Camembert story, even if it's a bit artificial and wooden. Afterwards, walk up to the Maison du Camembert, its entrance in the shape of an open poplar box, for a miserly free àtasting.

Head into the delectable hills around to buy *produits à la ferme*, with both milk and apple specialities available direct from the farmers – signs abound. You'll come across timberframe and brick villages and hamlets tumbling down steep slopes with their orchards and herds, like **Crouttes**, with its fine views, plus the secretive gardens of the former **priory of St-Michel** (*gardens open May–Sept daily 2–6; adm*) below.

West of Livarot, William the Conqueror was present at picturesque **St-Pierre-sur-Dives** for the consecration of its abbey. Mutilated pieces from down the centuries remain scattered surprisingly around the town centre. The exceptional market hall, also dating back in part as far the 11th century, has remained in a good state of repair, a great dark barn protected by stone walls and steep slopes of tiles. Well-known for its splendid Monday market, the place has a permanent display on cheesemaking at the **Musée des Techniques Fromagères** (*open mid-April–mid-Oct Mon–Sat 9.30–12.30 and 1.30–6; rest of year Mon–Fri 9.30–12.30 and 1.30–5.30*).

South of St-Pierre-sur-Dives, seek out a bonbon of a stately Louis XVI-style home, the **Château de Vendeuvre** (*open May–Sept daily 10–6; Mar–April and Oct–Nov Sun and hols only; adm*). Gutted in 1944, it has been lavishly restored with its original sugary pastel decor. It also contains a remarkable collection of furniture, bric-a-brac and life-size automata. In the orangery the countess shows off the world's largest collection of miniature furniture. Much of the present count's attention is devoted to his fanciful water garden with concealed fountains.

D-Day Beaches Along the Côte de Nacre

This is surely the most famous stretch of coastline in the Western World. The successful campaign by allied American, British, Canadian and other troops to defeat Nazi Germany began with the massive military landings here in early June 1944.

From Caen's Mémorial de la Paix to Omaha Beach

Caen's huge **Mémorial** (*open 9–6, summer 9–7; closed 2 weeks Jan; adm*), standing in a trendy new quarter off the northern ring road (*exit 7; bus 17 from the centre*), not only offers an extensive introduction to the Second World War, but also tries to tackle peace initiatives since. The flags of countless nations wave outside the vast block. The presentations inside are slick, but there's such a mass of information that it's some-times hard to know which way to turn. The separate section on the Nobel Peace Prize proves vacuous compared with the earlier clutter. New sections are being prepared on the Cold War, and man-made threats to the planet, and you can tour the rose gardens.

Head north through Caen's industrial sprawl via the Orne river. It's along here that the liberation of France began in June 1944 with the securing of crossings over the Orne, most famously Pegasus Bridge. At **Bénouville**, the **Café Gondrée** is almost as

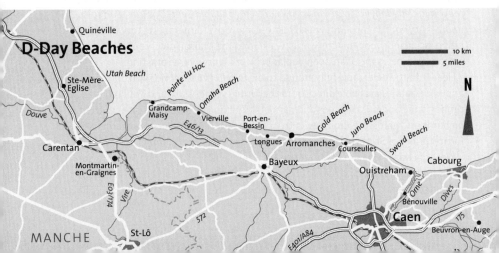

Getting Around

Buses from Caen will take you to Sword Beach, Juno Beach and the eastern side of Gold Beach, and to the villages of Ouistreham, Riva-Bella, Colleville, Lion-sur-Mer, Luc-sur-Mer, Langrune, St-Aubin-sur-Mer, Bernières-sur-Mer, Courseulles-sur-Mer, and Ver-sur-Mer. Buses from Bayeux serve the villages behind Omaha Beach, including Port-en-Bessin, Vierville-sur-Mer and Grandcamp.

Tourist Information

Ouistreham-Riva Bella: Jardins du Casino, t 02 31 97 18 63, *www.ot-ouistreham.fr*.
Courseulles: 54 Rue de la Mer, t 02 31 37 46 80, *tourisme.courseulles@wanadoo.fr*.
Arromanches: 2 Rue du Maréchal Joffre, t 02 31 22 36 45, *www.arromanches.com*.
Port-en-Bessin: 2 Rue du Croiseur-Montcalm, t 02 31 21 92 33.
Vierville-sur-Mer and **Omaha Beach**: Place de la Poste, t 02 31 22 51 85 07/t 02 31 92 44 24.
Grandcamp-Maisy: 118 Rue Aristide Briand, t 02 31 22 62 44.
Ste-Mère-Eglise: 6 Rue Eisenhower, t 02 33 21 00 33, *www.sainte-mere-eglise.info*.

Where to Stay and Eat

Crépon ✉ 14480

★★Ferme de la Rançonnière, Rte d'Arromanches, t 02 31 22 21 73, *hotel@ranconniere.com* (*expensive–inexpensive*). Full of medieval atmosphere. Try superlative local poultry in the barn-like restaurant (*expensive–moderate*). *Restaurant closed most of Jan.*

Arromanches ✉ 14117

★★Hôtel de la Marine, Quai du Canada, t 02 31 22 34 19, *hotel.de.la.marine@wanadoo.fr* (*moderate*). Extremely evocative views on to the Mulberry Harbour ruins from slightly dull but comfortable rooms. Large, reasonable seafront restaurant. *Closed mid-Nov–mid-Feb.*
★★Hôtel d'Arromanches, Rue du Colonel Michel, t 02 31 22 36 26, *hoteldarromanche@ ifrance.com* (*inexpensive*). On the pedestrian street just behind the seafront, has a couple of rooms with sea views, plus a bright restaurant, **Papagall** (*moderate*), serving Normandy cuisine. *Closed Jan–mid-Feb.*

Tracy-sur-Mer ✉ 14117

★★Hôtel Victoria, 24 Chemin de l'Eglise, t 02 31 22 35 37, *hotel-victoria@wanadoo.fr* (*moderate*). Smart 19th-century manor near Arromanches. *Closed Oct–Mar.*

Port-en-Bessin ✉ 14520

★★★★Château La Chenevière , t 02 31 51 25 25, *lachenevière.fr* (*luxury–very expensive*). A very smart hotel in this grand 19th-century château just south of the port, with pool, tennis and squash courts and gym as well as a highly regarded restaurant (*expensive*). *Closed Jan–mid-Feb; restaurant closed Mon, and Tues lunch.*

Ste-Marie-du-Mont 50480

Le Grand Hard, La Rivière, t 02 33 71 25 74, *www.domaine-le-grand-hard.com* (*moderate*) Lovingly restored farm set around a large courtyard with fountain, off the road to Utah Beach. High-standard hotel rooms and elaborate dishes. Riding centre attached; bike hire possible. *Closed 8 Jan–Feb, restaurant closed from mid-Oct.*

Quinéville-Plage ✉ 50310

★★★Château de Quinéville, 18 Rue de l'Eglise, t 02 33 21 42 67, *www.chateau-de-quineville.com* (*expensive–moderate*). Elegant, comfortable 18th-century château on the heights, with stylish restaurant. Pool. *Closed early Jan–mid-Mar; restaurant closed Mon–Fri lunch.*

much a museum as a bar. According to the plaque, it was the first house to be liberated in France, on the night of 5 to 6 June. The daring operations in this area were carried out by the Oxfordshire and Buckinghamshire light infantry. In summer 2000 the **Mémorial Pegasus** (*open May–Sept 9.30–6.30; Feb–April and Oct–mid-Dec 10–1 and 2–5; adm*) was opened by Prince Charles. The major exhibit is the original Pegasus

D-Day Heroics

The daring and scale of the Allies' D-Day landings and the greater Operation Overlord, the largest armada the world has ever seen, still seem staggering today. Planning began in January 1943, with General Sir Frederick Morgan in charge. He opted for Normandy as the place to land, considering the Pas de Calais too obvious. The Allied commanders Montgomery and Eisenhower agreed to the plan, only insisting on increasing its breadth. The Nazi leaders realized as 1943 advanced that an Allied attack was becoming more and more likely. However, through clever misinformation and vastly superior airpower, the Allies kept the Germans guessing.

A vast number of landing craft were assembled in Britain in the first months of 1944, although a contretemps with the uncooperative US Admiral King caused the planners to delay Overlord from May to June. That gave the Germans a few extra weeks to strengthen their coastal defences. At the end of 1943, Hitler had called on Rommel to organize the defence of Nazi-occupied France with Rundstedt, the latter settled rather too comfortably in Paris. Rommel had large sections of the coast mined much more intensively. He also insisted on the presence of Panzer tank divisions.

Leading up to the landings, Allied planes carried out extensive bombings on the rail network across northern France. But not all went according to plan. D-Day had been chosen to fall on 4 June, when the tides would be manageable. However, the weather let the Allies down for two days, and it was only on the evening of 5 June that Operation Overlord could swing into action. First, gliders carried British and American paratroopers across the Channel to secure the bridgehead's flanks. To the east, British paratroopers came down by the Orne above Caen and famously took the crossing now named after their insignia, Pegasus Bridge. American landings further west proved harrowing, with men landing in the sea or flooded fields, and some drowning.

But the Germans had been caught napping. They had only begun to pick up the advance of the Allied fleet at 2am. Blumentritt asked for permission at 4am to move a Panzer division to the beaches, but was told to wait until dawn. By then, the armada had reached Normandy, hundreds of ships covering the horizon as Allied naval bombers pounded the coast. The British and Canadian forces landed north of Caen and Bayeux, on beaches codenamed Sword, Juno and Gold. Because the Germans were so ill-prepared, some of these landings were relatively troublefree. However, Gold proved difficult to take: the bombardments hadn't managed to destroy a German-fortified village above the beach, so many soldiers were mown down as they came ashore. But by nightfall the 50th Division that landed on Gold had made the most progress inland. As to the crack American troops that arrived furthest west, on Utah Beach, they suffered the fewest casualties of all.

In terrible contrast, the Americans landing at Omaha beach northwest of Bayeux would encounter the worst from the start. Not only did they come face to face with the only formidable German formation on this coast, but on top of that their amphibious Shermans were launched too far from the sands and failed to provide adequate cover. The vast majority of over 4,500 American casualties on D-Day fell at Omaha. The Rangers given the impossible task of taking the Pointe du Hoc west of

Omaha were almost completely wiped out. Despite these tragedies, by the close of 6 June the Allies had established footholds along 60 miles of Normandy coast.

The hinterland would prove much more difficult to take. That said, such was the vast superiority of the Allied airforce that the Germans found it painfully hard to get reinforcements through the French countryside. Meanwhile troops and supplies would cross the Channel unimpeded. Most remarkably, two whole prefabricated ports, known as Mulberries, were floated across from England. Unfortunately storms from 19 to 21 June badly damaged these harbours, although the one established at Arromanches survived. By 26 June, 25 Allied divisions had landed in Normandy, with a further 15 to come. The German Western Army had 14 at their disposal. Rundstedt suggested to Hitler that he sue for peace, and was immediately replaced by Kluge.

Astonishingly, some two million Allied soldiers in all landed on the D-Day beaches, along with around 500,000 vehicles and 3 million tonnes of supplies. But after the initial success in the east, Caen proved devilishly difficult to take. On the western side, the hedgerows of the Cotentin peninsula would slow the American advance northwards. However, Cherbourg then fell surprisingly fast and this was followed by a vital breakthrough in the south of the Cotentin. On 25 and 26 July 'Lightning Joe' Collins led a crucial attack on just about the finest tank division the Germans had, the Panzer Lehr division. The Americans were ready to break through into Brittany, but Hitler, in a state of rage after the assassination attempt made against him on 20 July, ordered a great defence of Normandy. This would lead to the most terrible tank battle the Western Front ever witnessed, the Battle of the Falaise Gap.

Hitler wanted to catch the US divisions in the gap between Mortain and the sea. Mortain was the place where the Battle of the Falaise Gap would begin on 7 August 1944. Four of the best Nazi tank divisions were sent to surprise the Americans in the Sée valley. Unfortunately for them, the Allied decoding service had already informed Allied command of this plan and the Nazi divisions met with a shattering defeat. The same day, Montgomery had launched Operation Totalise from the eastern end of the Allied bridgehead. Canadian troops, backed by an émigré Polish division, were to storm south from the Caen area to Falaise. Although not entirely successful, these forces advanced far enough to present a major threat to the rear of the German divisions. The bulk of the German army in Normandy was trapped. The Allies encircled the Germans in the beautiful bowl of land west of Montormel – the dreaded Cauldron. Just a small corridor between Falaise and Argentan remained open, by which 300,000 soldiers and 25,000 vehicles retreated under cover of night. The remaining Germans were caught in the Allied encirclement: around 50,000 died, while 200,000 were taken prisoner. More than 1,300 German tanks were lost. Meanwhile on 19 August a US section under Patton had raced as far east as Mantes on the Seine just beyond the Normandy frontier, closing in on Paris. The liberation of the capital, and the rest of France, now looked possible.

The two war museums either end of the D-Day beaches, at Caen and at Quinéville, describe the whole context of the Second World War. The many other war museums in between concentrate on specific D-Day actions or themes.

Bridge, replaced by a modern replica in 1993. Across the river stand memorials to Major Howard, the operation commander, and to the 180 men who landed here.

Since the war, the string of seaside resorts from Ouistreham to Courseulles have practically linked up to make the most of the sands between Sword Beach and Juno Beach, so this isn't the easiest stretch along which to recall the actions of 1944, despite the occasional monument or recovered tank, for seaside pleasures dominate. **Courseulles**, a lively estuary port tucked away behind Juno Beach, has a sweet maritime museum, the **Maison de la Mer** (*open July–Aug daily 9.30–7; Feb–June and Sept daily 10–12.30 and 2–6; Oct–Jan Wed, weekends and hols 2–6; adm*), but has also recently seen the opening of the **Centre Juno Beach** (*open early June–Sept daily 9–7; Oct–Dec and Feb–June 10–1 and 2–6*), dedicated to the Canadians who landed here on D-Day. A big silver cross of Lorraine rises out of the dunes at **Graye-sur-Mer**, recalling that General de Gaulle finally made it back to France here, on 14 June 1944, having led the French Resistance from London.

The coast above Gold Beach looks wilder. Many stop on the heights east of **Arromanches** to look down on the remains of its Mulberry Harbour. A modern cinema up here, **Arromanches 360 degrees** (*open Feb–Dec daily 9.10–6.40, showings ten past and forty past each hour; adm*), presents a dramatic film about the D-Day landings on a 360° screen, but the crude hype promising '18 minutes of total emotion' could have been avoided. More soberly, the plain memorial by the white Virgin pays homage to the Sappers of the Royal Engineers who played a key role in preparations for the D-Day landings. Some came across in midget submarines, canoeing to the beaches on their reconnaissance missions. Their specialist skills proved crucial, but well over 6,000 would die in action between D-Day and VE Day. Arromanches didn't see any landing craft on D-Day itself – it was important that the sea here shouldn't have any wrecks in the way to hamper the construction of the Mulberry Harbours, whose elements arrived from D-Day +1. The main parts were five-storey-high concrete blocks, towed from England, then sunk on the rocks. By D-Day +9 the harbour was in operation. It survived the terrible storms of mid-June 1944, and by the end of that year, 220,000 men and around 39,000 vehicles had landed here. The harbour stopped operating in mid-November. The **Musée du Débarquement** (*open May–Aug daily 9–7; Sept 9–6; Mar–April and Oct 9.30–12.30 and 1.30–5.30; Nov–Dec and Feb 10–12.30 and 1.30–5; adm*) tells the story.

West of Arromanches at **Longues** is a row of concrete Nazi defence batteries, several with rusting guns still in place. These guns weren't hit by the naval shelling early on 6 June and so caused difficulties for the Allies that day. **Port-en-Bessin**, unlike most of the coastal villages and towns along the Côte de Nacre, has remained a working fishing harbour. It is also home to one of the most curious Normandy war museums, the **Musée des Epaves Sous-marines** (*open June–Sept and May weekends 10–12 and 2–6; adm*). Since 1968, owner Jacques Lemonchois has had the sole concession from the French government to salvage D-Day wrecks off the coast. The finds dredged up with stupendous determination are presented here, including whole tanks, ships' turbines, guns, plates and even the smallest items such as coat hooks, razors and old pennies, all rusted to a uniform brown, but as moving as old black and white film.

*This embattled shore, portal of freedom, is forever hallowed by the ideals, the valor
and sacrifices of our fellow countrymen.*

So reads one of the memorial sentences up at the **American cemetery** overlooking
Omaha Beach. With its temple of a memorial, its long, long rows of pure white crosses
on immaculately kept lawns and its evocative setting by the sea, this is a famed war
cemetery that powerfully recalls the price paid for freedom in Western Europe. The
large-scale maps at the memorial show the staggering size of the Reich in 1943. In the
weeks leading up to D-Day, the German 352nd Panzer tank division was moved to
guard Omaha Beach and inflicted terrible casualties on the American 1st Division as it
landed. But only a minority of the 10,000 buried here died on the beaches; most were
brought here from other areas where the Americans fought in France and in Belgium.
The **Musée Omaha** (*open mid-Mar–mid-Nov daily 9.30–6.30; mid-Feb–mid-Mar
10–12.30 and 2.30–6; adm*) outside displays the everyday objects given to the US
soldiers, such as toothbrushes and army-issue condoms, plus larger objects like vehicles. Down on the beach, it still seems odd for people to be sand-yachting on such
symbolic terrain. The steep slope at the back of the beach at **Vierville**, on the western
end of Omaha beach, recalls the scenery used in Spielberg's *Saving Private Ryan*,
although the D-Day beach scenes in that film were in fact shot in Ireland.

Its mix of natural beauty and horrifying war memories makes the **Pointe du Hoc**
one of the most moving war locations along the D-Day coast. Big chunks of Nazi
cement bunkers still lie on their sides on the clifftop, the ground around them puckered with the big holes of heavy shelling. Either side stretch the beautiful pincers of
the vicious cliffs in which the Rangers were fatally caught. A small **Musée des Rangers**
(*open April–Oct Tues–Sun 10–1 and 3–6, Mon 3–6; adm*) at the low-key, pretty fishing
port of **Grandcamp-Maisy** recalls the tragedy.

Across the Cotentin Marshes to Utah Beach

You have to cross the war-notorious Marais du Cotentin to reach the deeply moving
war sights of Utah Beach, Ste-Marie-du-Mont and Ste-Mère Eglise. The main road
takes you past Isigny, known for its exceptional butter. South of Carentan, little-
known **Graignes** has a devastated church, a reminder that this peaceful spot became
the scene of one of the parachuting tragedies of June 1944. Some US soldiers dropped
over the nearby Cotentin marshes drowned, but others gathered here, aided by their
metal clickers, nicknamed crickets. The soldiers were taken in by the villagers.
Unfortunately the Germans spotted them. On Sunday 11 June, while the villagers
were at Mass, the Nazis began their attack. Many of the Americans were killed; any
taken prisoner were executed. The priest was murdered, the houses pillaged.

Above **Carentan**, just west of St-Côme-du-Mont, the new centre at **Les Ponts d'Ouve**
(*open Easter–Sept daily 9.30–7; rest of year Tues–Sun 9.30–1 and 2–5.30; adm*) offers an
introduction to the **Parc Régional des Marais du Cotentin et du Bessin** and observatories for birdwatchers around a recently created lake, with typical Norman horses, cows
and sheep grazing beyond. The museum and its helpful English video explain how in
winter each year the marshes 'whiten with water', as the locals put it, forming a huge

natural lake and barrier, practically cutting off the Cotentin from the mainland. Take the country roads east for the atmospheric peace of **Le Grand Vey**, in fact a tiny hamlet, its old cobbled quay sloping gently down to the extensive mudflats of the Baie du Grand Vey, a secretive area beloved of keen ornithologists.

Encircled by two rows of chestnut trees, then by a circle of old stone houses, the church of **Ste-Marie-du-Mont**, rising from its hillock, stands at the heart of the village, as it stood at the heart of the action the night of D-Day. Panels dotted around the atmospheric village recall (in French only) how fighting broke out immediately between the American parachutists falling from the sky and the Germans on guard. Now you can take your time to enjoy the church's architecture, the Romanesque carvings down below, the Gothic additions above, all topped by an overdone Renaissance dome. Utah Beach, which the locals were forced to help the Germans place stakes in, lies down past lanes named after American soldiers who died in the landings.

But first, for a fuller picture of the difficult American parachute operation the night of 5 to 6 June 1944, visit **Ste-Mère-Eglise** and its war museum, one of the most interesting in Normandy. In one of the most famous images of the D-Day landings, American parachutist John Steele was left stranded in mid-air as his parachute got stuck on the church tower; Red Buttons memorably played his part in the film *The Longest Day*. As Steele dangled, Ste-Mère-Eglise became the first village to be liberated in France. While the war movie classic made rather light of the crucial events, the **Musée Airborne** (*open Feb–Nov, check times on www.airborne-museum.org; adm*) respectfully remembers the thousands of soldiers less fortunate than Steele (who survived his ordeal), as well as explaining the D-Day airborne operations in detail. The two large rooms centre around spectacular exhibits, in one a US WACO glider, in the other a C47 Douglas. Ste-Mère-Eglise's historic **church** interior has Gothic vaults in the Angevin style which look, appropriately enough, like parachutes in stone. A modern stained-glass window pays homage to the paratroopers, who are also honoured in the town's street names. Rural local traditions are recalled at the **Ferme-Musée du Cotentin** (*open July and Aug daily 11–7; June and Sept 11–6; April–May 2–6; adm*).

Cows chew the grass contentedly by the Nazi bunkers behind immensely long **Utah Beach**, the only landing beach on the Cotentin peninsula. The **Musée du Débarquement** (*open June–Sept daily 9.30–7; May 10–6; April and Oct 10–12.30 and 2–6; Mar 10–12.30 and 2–5.30; Nov–Feb weekends and hols 10–12.30 and 2–5.30; adm*) lies at its southern end, surrounded by a cluster of tanks, guns and monuments, housed in a building whose fragmented architecture reflects the upheaval of the war. Above, the views stretch from the St-Marcoul islands to Pointe du Hoc.

North by the beach at **Quinéville**, the rambling **Musée de la Liberté** (*open June–Sept daily 9.30–7.30; Mar–May and Oct–Nov daily 10–6; adm*) first takes visitors back to the time before France was occupied by the Nazis. There's a mass of information, on the build-up to the Second World War, on the invasion of France and the shortlived flight of civilians, on daily life under the Nazis, on German policies and propaganda in France, on collaboration and the Resistance. You need to read French to appreciate this museum to the full, but the basic outlines are given in English.

Caen

Caen shot to greatness under William the Conqueror and his wife Matilda of Flanders. From a meagre village by the Orne, it grew into one of the main centres of the extraordinarily powerful Norman dukedom. As well as getting ramparts and a castle, it received as a gift from William and his wife two enormous Romanesque abbeys. The couple were apparently forced into their acts of benevolence. William had married Matilda, a cousin, in the early 1050s, but she proved not to be a distant enough relation to avoid the wrath of the papacy, and they were excommunicated. William's powerful friend in the Church, Lanfranc, is said to have had the punishment lifted in exchange for an expiatory abbey from each of the spouses. The abbeys have survived, but much of Caen was devastated in some of the fiercest bombardments after the D-Day landings. The fighting continued around the city until 20 August.

From afar, the town looks at first like a mass of postwar blocks dominated by a towering modern hospital, the city's most popular tourist sight, the Mémorial de la Paix, standing nearby (*see* p.180). In fact a great many historic buildings have survived or been rebuilt in the centre. The mighty castle walls date from the time of Henry I, William's successor as duke of Normandy and king of England. The bailey walls conceal a couple of fine museums. The **Musée de Normandie** (*open Wed–Mon 9.30–6; closed Tues; adm*) contains beautiful Gallo-Roman and Merovingian artefacts from across the region, but sadly little seems to have survived from the Viking period.

The **Musée des Beaux-Arts** (*open Wed–Mon 10–6; adm*), in a sunken modern bunker within the bailey, displays a colourful collection, surprisingly rich in Italian art, with two Veroneses and Perugino's *Marriage of the Virgin*. Among the Flemish highlights count a serene Van der Weyden *Virgin and Child*, a typically detailed Breughel the Younger tax-collecting scene, and Rubens' bold ruddy-faced *Abraham and Melchior*. The 17th-century French school features a disappointingly dark Poussin. More interestingly, Robert Tournières, born in Caen in 1668, painted some particularly piercing

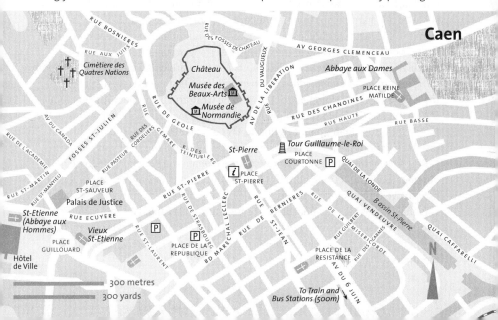

Getting There and Around

Brittany Ferries sails from Portsmouth to Caen-Ouistreham, north of town; a **bus** service links the Gare Maritime to central Caen. There are good train services from Caen inland, but only bus services to the coast. The Bus Verts de Calvados, **t** 0810 214 214, *www.busverts14.fr*, run a special D-Day beaches service.

Tourist Information

Caen: Place St-Pierre, **t** 02 31 27 14 14, *www.ville-caen.fr*, *tourisminfo@ville-caen.fr*.

Where to Stay and Eat

Caen ✉ 14300

★★★Le Dauphin, 29 Rue Gemare, **t** 02 31 86 22 26, *dauphin.caen@wanadoo.fr* (*expensive–moderate*). In a former priory, central stylish, comfortable. Gym. Excellent Normandy cuisine. *Restaurant closed lunchtime in summer, and late-July–early Aug.*

★★Les Cordeliers, 4 Rue des Cordeliers, **t** 02 31 86 37 15 (*inexpensive*). Plenty of character, in an old town house.

★St-Etienne, 2 Rue de l'Académie, **t** 02 31 86 35 82, *contact@hotel-saint-etienne.com* (*inexpensive*). Simple hotel in another old town house; an attractive option.

La Bourride, 15 Rue du Vaugueux, **t** 02 31 93 50 76 (*very expensive*). Exclusive little restaurant of the highest order, bringing Normandy classics up to date in an historic building. *Closed Sun and Mon.*

Café Mancel, Le Château, **t** 02 31 86 63 64 (*moderate*). Within the castle walls, a lively place to sample modern cuisine, plus jazz every 2nd and 4th Sat in the month. *Closed Sun pm and Mon.*

L'Embroche, 17 Rue Porte au Berger, **t** 02 31 93 71 31 (*moderate*). Family cooking, well-known because Edith Piaf's grandparents ran this place. *Closed Sat lunch, Sun, and Mon lunch.*

portraits, notably that of the glistening-eyed engraver Andran. The museum also has an extensive collection of Old Master drawings and a Monet *Nymphéas*.

At the foot of the castle, the **church of St-Pierre** and its elaborate Gothic spire were rebuilt after the war. Inside, the stonework becomes lace-like. East beyond the lively café-surrounded **Place Courtonne**, overseen by the old Tour Guillaume-le-Roi, you come to the **Bassin St-Pierre**, the broad, rather bare marina in the centre of Caen.

Coyly distant from its twin, the **Abbaye aux Dames** was built for William's wife Matilda, east of the castle, in what is now a quiet administrative quarter. More subdued and harmonious than the Abbaye aux Hommes, its church mostly dates from the early 12th century. Inside, the decoration is limited to little heads and animals on the capitals and to the crinkly patterning around the arches. The false ambulatory gives the interior added depth. A black marble slab marks Matilda's tomb.

The most famous and forceful church in Caen is **St-Etienne**, attached to the massive **Abbaye aux Hommes** dominating the western side of town. Architecturally, St-Etienne was a ground-breaking building. The sheer vertical wall of masonry of the façade looks formidably daunting. Inside, try not to let the greyness of the stone distract you from the power of the architecture. Although the choir was redone in Gothic style in the 13th century, the rest is the Romanesque original, the three different levels prefiguring northern Gothic. An extraordinary lantern tower lets in light above the crossing. Lanfranc was the first abbot of St-Etienne, and the church was chosen as William's burial place. His funeral in 1087 turned into a fiasco, though, with various factions causing mayhem during the ceremony. Then his putrefying body broke up as it was being lowered into the tomb and the stench caused the mourners to flee. The tomb was desecrated in the Wars of Religion.

The enormous 18th-century wing of the abbey has been turned into Caen's town hall. Traffic races madly around the **Place Guillouard** in front of it. The other major buildings overlooking the square include the skeleton of the Gothic church of Vieux St-Etienne and the pompous Ancien Régime Palais de Justice. Not far away to the north, the triangular **Place St-Sauveur** towards the main shopping area has retained its grandeur too, with elegant houses looking on to a statue of Louis XIV in one of his favourite fancy-dress guises, as a Roman emperor.

Avoid the busy N13 to Bayeux by taking the enchanting D22. Beside **Thaon**, seek out an exceptionally beautiful medieval church, lost in its meadow, forgotten by time. Continue via **Fontaine-Henry**, **Creully**, **St-Gabriel-Brécy** and **Vienne-en-Bessin**.

Bayeux to St-Lô

Capital of a small rich territory known as the Bessin, Bayeux was one of the very few cities in Normandy to be spared large-scale destruction in the war. So close to the D-Day landing beaches, it was the first town in France to be liberated, on D-Day +1. Thanks to this good fortune, many fine streets and houses survive, although restorers

Getting There and Around

There are direct **trains** from Caen to Bayeux. Change at Lison after Bayeux to reach St-Lô.

Tourist Information

Bayeux: Pont St-Jean, **t** 02 31 51 28 28, *bayeux-tourisme@mail.cpod.fr*.

St-Lô: Place du Général de Gaulle, **t** 02 33 77 60 35, *sce.tourisme@mairie-saint-lo.fr*.

Where to Stay and Eat

Bayeux ✉ **14400**

★★★**Château de Bellefontaine**, 49 Rue de Bellefontaine, **t** 02 31 22 00 10, *www.hotel-bellefontaine.com* (*expensive*). On the outskirts, spacious rooms in an 18th-century manor set in delightful gardens with tennis court and waterways. *Closed Jan.*

★★**Hôtel d'Argouges**, 21 Rue St-Patrice, **t** 02 31 92 88 86, *dargouges@aol.com* (*moderate–inexpensive*). Elegant cheaper 18th-century retreat right in the centre.

Le Pommier, 40 Rue des Cuisiniers, **t** 02 31 21 52 10 (*moderate*). Popular with tourists, but maintaining local traditions of fish and tripe. *Closed Wed.*

Le Petit Bistrot, 2 Rue Bienvenu, **t** 02 31 51 85 40 (*moderate*). Great place for fish, a chic little address opposite the cathedral.

La Table du Terroir, 42 Rue St-Jean, **t** 02 31 92 05 53 (*moderate*). For meat-lovers, a local favourite, run by a devoted butcher. *Closed Sun and Mon.*

Around Bayeux

★★★★**Château d'Audrieu**, ✉ 14250 Audrieu, **t** 02 31 80 21 52, *www.chateauaudrieu.com* (*luxury–expensive*). Luxurious 18th-century elegance southwest of Bayeux, with pool and restaurant. *Closed Dec–mid-Feb; restaurant closed Mon–Fri lunch, Sun eve, Mon eve.*

★★★**Château de Goville**, ✉ 14330 Le Breuil-en-Bessin, **t** 02 31 22 19 28, *chateaugoville@wanadoo.fr* (*expensive*). More a romantic little manor than a château, southwest of Bayeux, with sweetly furnished rooms and a fine collection of dolls' houses. *Restaurant closed Tues and Wed in winter.*

★★**Château de Sully**, Route de Port-en-Bessin, ✉ 14400 Sully, **t** 02 31 22 29 48, *chsully@club-internet.fr* (*very expensive–expensive*). Northwest of Bayeux, with a smart 18th-century exterior, simpler modern rooms in château and annexe. Pool and tennis court. Restaurant. *Closed 25 Nov–10 Mar; restaurant closed Mon–Wed lunch and Sat lunch.*

have sometimes been heavy-handed with the plaster. In appalling contrast, St-Lô became known as Capital of Ruins, just about the most devastated town in the Battle of Normandy, but one which has received a fair deal of cultural nursing since.

Bayeux

Displayed at the **Musée de la Tapisserie de Bayeux** (*open May–Aug daily 9–7; mid-Mar–April and Sept–Oct daily 9–6.30; rest of year 9.30–12.30 and 2–6; adm*), the most famous tapestry in the Western World is not in fact a tapestry but an embroidery, and it probably wasn't made in Normandy, let alone Bayeux. The conventional story of its creation, now much disputed, runs something like this. Odo de Conteville, William the Conqueror's powerful half-brother and bishop of Bayeux, seemingly commissioned the work, no doubt before 1082, when he was imprisoned by William. Odo, a military bishop, took part in the conquest of England and features a couple of times in the embroidery. After the victory, he acquired estates in southern England and it may have been made across the Channel, possibly in a Canterbury or Winchester nunnery. In France, it was long believed that William's wife Matilda had commissioned the piece, and it is still commonly referred to in French as the *Tapisserie de la Reine Matilde*. Certainly many places in Normandy and neighbouring Brittany feature.

Visiting the embroidery begins with an in-depth introduction, although this hasn't kept up with recent scholarship. However, the copy of the work and the explanatory commentaries running below it prove very helpful. Best of all are the accounts quoted from the contemporary chroniclers Guillaume de Poitiers and Guillaume de Jumièges. The embroidery has 55 'panels' in all, over half of which are devoted to the period before William's invasion, explaining his motives: to stop Harold usurping his right to the kingdom of England as promised by King Edward the Confessor and accepted by Harold on holy relics. The chaotic Battle of Hasting is where the embroidery ends. Artistically, the blue, green, beige and red horses steal the show, while the Viking-prowed ships in stripy beach colours come a delightful second. The men, with their vague features and bonnets for hats, look rather comical; the spies could not look more inept. The violent combat appears acrobatic rather than distressing, although the frieze of the dead below the scenes reminds us that this was no circus.

Bayeux's second trump card is its **cathedral**. Construction began under Odo's predecessor, but Odo's wealth no doubt helped it advance rapidly, and the place was consecrated in 1077, with all the major figures of William's court in attendance. It is often said that the embroidery was originally made to hang in the cathedral, though this is now hotly disputed. A fire in 1105 destroyed sections of the Romanesque structure, which explains the daunting Gothic of the exterior, although the soaring spires are Romanesque originals. Inside, the Gothic nave looks superb, but the upper levels are supported on distinctive rounded Romanesque arches. The carved panels between the arches are embellished with ornamental details influenced by Middle Eastern art.

The **Musée Baron Gérard** (*open daily 10–12.30 and 2–6; adm*), in the former bishops' palace, displays the collections of the eponymous 19th-century noble: ceramics, archaeological artefacts and paintings. Fine lace is displayed here and in the **Conservatoire de la Dentelle** (*open Mon–Sat 10–12.30 and 2–6; closed Sun*).

Bayeux has the largest British war cemetery in Normandy; opposite stands the big **Musée Mémorial de la Bataille de Normandie** (*open May–mid-Sept daily 9.30–6.30; rest of year daily 10–12.30 and 2–6; adm*), where the overwhelming mass of military memorabilia is in danger of making the war itself fade into a blur. In amongst the plethora of objects are personal items such as the papers informing the family of Canadian airman James Lanfranchi that he wouldn't be coming home. The separate **Mémorial Général de Gaulle** (*open mid-Mar–mid-Nov daily 9.30–12.30 and 2–6.30*) recalls this most forceful of Frenchmen's role in the war.

To St-Lô, Capital of Ruins

Between Bayeux and St-Lô, the exquisite **Château de Balleroy** (*open July and Aug daily 9–5; mid-Mar–June and Sept–mid-Oct Wed–Mon 9–5, closed Tues; adm*) was designed by the celebrated architect François Mansart in the 1630s for the Balleroy family. Bought from them by the American billionaire Malcolm Forbes, its outhouses contain a hot-air ballooning museum. The nearby **Abbaye de Cerisy-la-Forêt** (*church open Easter–Oct daily 9–6.30; museum open 10.30–12.30 and 2.30–6.30*) is an awesome piece of medieval religious architecture, the Romanesque foundation established by William the Conqueror's father, Duke Robert, but given many Gothic additions.

The hill town of **St-Lô** lay at an important road junction, and the terrible fighting for it between Americans and Germans in 1944 officially left 95 per cent of it destroyed. Yet the place retains vestiges of its past, including parts of its medieval ramparts, while the remnants of the prison gate have been turned into a war memorial. The town has been given a splendid curving contemporary building to house its **Musée des Beaux-Arts** (*open Wed–Mon 10–12 and 2–6; closed Tues; adm*), one round room devoted to a delightfully saucy series of Bruges tapestries. Other curiosities include Old Master drawings and portraits of the local Matignon-Grimaldi family, related to the present royal family of Monaco. The collection of 19th-century landscapes is particularly strong and modern art is represented by the likes of Picasso, Léger and Miró. Photographs and models give a picture of pre-war St-Lô, and paintings of the devastation. Just the front of St-Lô's Gothic **Notre-Dame** was savagely amputated in the conflict. Its most peculiar feature, the south choir, fans out eccentrically from the side aisle. Some pieces of Gothic stained glass have survived, while a postwar creation retells the story of Thomas à Becket. Horse enthusiasts head for the **Haras National** (*tours June–Sept daily 2.30, 3.30, 4.30, plus July–Aug 11am; adm*), a smart stud farm.

The Suisse Normande and Falaise

The pallid stone of the Calvados coast gives way to darker and darker rock as you head south from Caen. The Suisse Normande is the name given to a small, charming stretch of the Orne valley from around Thury-Harcourt to Putanges. The crests of the hills don't reach very high here, but the banks of the Orne do become dramatically rocky as you climb up from the Caen plain. Around the hairpin meander of the Boucle du Hom is **Thury-Harcourt**, from where the roads west lead to some of the highest

Getting Around

Public transport is limited in these parts. There are no trains, but there is a fairly regular **bus** service from Caen to Falaise, Thury-Harcourt and Clécy.

Tourist Information

Thury-Harcourt: Place St-Sauveur, **t** 02 31 79 70 45, *otsi.thury@libertysurf.fr*.
Pont d'Ouilly: Rue de la 5e République, **t** 02 31 69 39 54.
Falaise: Forum, **t** 02 31 90 17 26, *www.otsi-falaise.com*.

Where to Stay and Eat

Clécy ✉ 14570
★★★**Le Moulin du Vey**, **t** 02 31 69 71 08, *reservations@moulinduvey.com* (*moderate*). Most charming place to stay or eat, in a converted mill, with terraces by the Orne river (*expensive*). Closed most Dec and Jan; restaurant closed Sun pm and Mon lunch.

Pont-d'Ouilly ✉ 14690
★★**Auberge St-Christophe**, **t** 02 31 69 81 23 (*inexpensive*). Appealing, unpretentious little address with classic restaurant (*expensive–moderate*). Closed Feb–early Mar.

'peaks', the Mont Pinçon winning the prize at 365m. Continue south along the Orne to the prettiest and liveliest stop in the Suisse Normande, **Clécy**, beyond the striking **Pain de Sucre**, or Sugarloaf rock. Narrow roads clamber up to the old village on the hill, but the riverbank sees most of the action with its tightly packed shoal of restaurants and its boats and pedalo-hire. Further riverside meanders bring you out at **Pont-d'Ouilly**. Follow the west bank up past St-Philbert-sur-Orne to appreciate the craggy scenery around the Roche d'Oëtre and the Gorges de St-Aubert. You soon come into riverside **Putanges**, southern gateway of the Suisse Normande; here too it's easy to hire boats.

Named after the dramatic cliff on which its medieval castle stands, the town of **Falaise** is intimately linked with William the Conqueror, and with the seduction story that led to his birth. Duke Robert of Normandy was wandering down from his mighty fort to the river one day when his eye fell on Arlette, a young woman doing her washing. They became lovers, and soon their bastard son William was born here in 1027. On one of the main squares, a stirring 19th-century statue of the Conqueror on rearing horse calls his troops to action. The six Norman dukes before William feature below.

Falaise became an important seat of ducal power, and although much of the historic town had all too obviously to be reconstructed, albeit in pleasing stone, after the war, a steep path above the equestrian statue of William leads to the massive medieval **castle** (*open daily 10–6; July and Aug 10–7; Oct–Mar closed Tues; adm*) which miraculously survived 1944. It counts among the best examples of medieval military architecture in northern France. The impressive keeps were built for William's successors, English kings Henry I and Henry II, while the big barrel of the Tour Talbot was added for French king Philippe Auguste. It's a shame the town saw fit to add an Eastern European-style block of flats one side of the fort, but the castle interiors have been restored in stylish modern fashion.

Back on William's square, the church of **La Trinité** stands out with its triangular entrance porch. Inside, don't miss the scenes of martyrdoms and medieval life on the nave capitals, the Flamboyant Gothic window with its wild petal tracery, and the ambulatory raised on tubular columns. At the opposite end of town, the grand **church** of **St-Gervais**, by a busy road junction, had to be much restored after the war, but preserves some Gothic angels and gargoyles on the outside and some mischievous medieval carving inside. A Falaise-born artist deeply influenced by Cézanne in his *cloisonné* country scenes and still lifes is celebrated at the **Musée André Lemaître** (*open April–Sept daily 10–12.30 and 1.30–6; adm*). The **Musée Août 44 La Bataille de la Poche de Falaise** (*open early April–11 Nov Wed–Mon 10–12 and 2–6; closed Tues; adm*), recalling Second World War action in these parts, lies a short way out of town.

Montormel, southeast of Falaise, with its splendid wide views down over typical *bocage*, is a more moving place to learn about the crucial Allied actions around here that led to Hitler's fall. The vital campaign has gone down in history as the Battle of the Falaise Gap or Falaise Pocket. The **Mémorial de Montormel** (*open May–Sept daily 9–6; Oct–mid-Dec and mid-Jan–April Wed and weekends 10–5; adm*), located in a bunker of a modern building, looks down on to the now tranquil depression in the countryside which the Germans came to know as the Cauldron. Extracts from soldiers' writings speak of rivers obstructed by the corpses of men and horses, of the most appalling stench of death, of the Normandy lanes turned into yawning graves. Down on the flat, the village of **Chambois** still feels drained by war. A memorial recalls the final hours of the Battle of Normandy here, for it was at Chambois that the Allied forces came together after 77 days of fighting. An impressive but empty medieval keep towers over the rather vacant main square. As an antidote to the battle sites, take a guided tour round the exquisite Ancien Régime **Haras National du Pin** (*open April–mid-Oct daily 9.30–6; rest of year 2.30–5; adm*), a regal stud farm set in delightful countryside.

To the Parc Régional Normandie-Maine

This seductive slice of territory stretches from lacy Alençon in the east to the wonderfully dishevelled pear orchards around Mortain in the west. It straddles southern Normandy and northern Maine.

In the northeastern corner of the regional park, the little city of **Sées** comes as a bit of a surprise, with a big but little-known cathedral which seems to have got lost wandering off into the Normandy countryside and quietly settled itself down here. The building has a pale grey look due to the local stone more than the heavy 19th-century operation to restore it. The local **Musée d'Art Religieux** (*open July–Sept Wed–Mon 10–6; closed Tues*) is dedicated to religious paraphernalia.

The grubby little local stones give a grey tinge to some of the buildings of historic **Alençon**, the first French town to be liberated by French forces at the end of the war. Although bombed in the action, several grand buildings stand out. The very cultured sister of King François Ier, Marguerite d'Angoulême, married Duke René of Alençon in the late 15th century, and patronized the splendid Flamboyant finishings of **Notre-Dame**. Inside, small Gothic dogs and dragons scamper comically along the ribs of the elaborate vaults. The Renaissance puts in an appearance in some extremely refined stained glass from the early 16th century.

Getting Around

A **train** line between Caen and Le Mans serves Argentan, Sées and Alençon.
You can get to Bagnoles by **bus** via Argentan.

Tourist Information

Alençon: Place de la Magdeleine, **t** 02 33 80 66 33, *www.paysdalencontourisme.com.*
Carrouges: 24 Place du Général Leveneur, **t** 02 33 27 40 62, *si.carrouges@wanadoo.fr.*
Bagnoles-de-l'Orne: Place du Marché, **t** 02 33 37 85 66, *www.bagnoles-de-lorne.com.*
Domfront: 12 Place de la Roirie, **t** 02 33 38 53 97, *ot.bocagedomfrontais@wanadoo.fr.*

Where to Stay and Eat

Bagnoles-de-l'Orne ✉ 61140
★★★**Le Manoir du Lys**, Route de Juvigny, **t** 02 33 37 80 69, *www.manoir-du-lys.fr* (*luxury–moderate*). Brightly converted manor house next to a forest and golf course, with tennis court and covered pool. *Closed Jan–mid-Feb.*
★★**La Potinière du Lac**, 2 Rue des Casinos, **t** 02 33 30 65 00, *lapotinieredu-lac2@wanadoo.fr* (*inexpensive*). Central, eccentric cheap hotel with chequered pepperpot tower overlooking the lake. Restaurant (*moderate*). *Closed mid-Nov–mid-Mar.*

Mortain ✉ 50140
★★**Hôtel de la Poste**, 1 Place des Arcades, **t** 02 33 59 00 05 (*inexpensive*). Thirty rooms within large granite walls.

Alençon has long been known in France for its lace, a tradition which was started by Colbert in the late 17th century. Until then Venice had a virtual monopoly, but the *point d'Alençon* began to satisfy the huge French demand. Alençon's **Musée des Beaux-Arts et de la Dentelle** (*open Sept–June Tues–Sun 10–12 and 2–6; July and Aug Mon also; adm*) has taken over a former Jesuit college to display its attractive collections of first-class lace and second-rate paintings. Next door is the shapely curve of the former Jesuit seminary, now the public library, with a splendid reading room. The **Halle au Blé**, a striking 19th-century domed corn exchange close to the museum, hosts temporary exhibitions. By the river Sarthe, the small **Musée de la Dentelle et du Général Leclerc** (*open April–Sept Mon–Sat 10–12 and 2–6; Jan–Mar and Oct–Dec Mon–Sat 10.30–12 and 2–5.30; adm*) also focuses on the story of local craft. At one time 8,000 people in the area made lace for the aristocracy and clergy; in fact, before the Revolution no one else was allowed to wear it. There is a lace-making school in town now, with some 10 pupils. You can buy pieces at phenomenal prices – once you hear the number of hours required to make them you'll understand why. Above, a second museum recalls Alençon in the war.

West of Alençon, the hilly area is known as the **Alpes Mancelles**. The absurd story to explain the name goes that a couple of confusingly named evangelizing brothers from Italy, Cénéri and Cénéré, settled here in the 6th or 7th century as the area supposedly reminded them of the Alps. Utterly picturesque **St-Cénéri-le-Gérei**, perched above a hairpin bend in the Sarthe river, lost its castle to English soldiers in the Hundred Years War, but its 11th- to 12th-century chapel has just about survived a lot of surgery. Some of the cutest devils imaginable feature among the medieval wall paintings heavy-handedly restored in the 19th century. Other striking images include a Virgin, cross-eyed with anxiety, protecting her praying flock under her cape. By contrast the Christ in majesty exudes serenity. Down in its meadow set in a meander in the river, the **Chapelle du Petit-Saint-Célerin** makes an enchanting sight.

Northwest of Alençon the mammoth, moated **Château de Carrouges** (*open mid-June–Aug daily 9.30–12 and 2–6.30; April–mid-June and Sept 10–12 and 2–6; Oct–Mar 10–12 and 2–4.30; adm*) shows medieval brick architecture at its most playfully rugged. The tour starts in the courtyard decorated with waves and lozenges of black brick. It then takes you through rooms with big fireplaces, fine tapestries and painted beams, while stories are told about the château's families.

Set in its glade surrounded by beautiful forests, the surprising little spa town of **Bagnoles-de-l'Orne** has a touch of the fairytale about it. Swans glide around the lake, willows weep beside it, streams cascade away among shaded rocks...and people with circulatory problems come to take the radioactive waters. Local legends spur them on, like the tale of the Franciscan who managed, after taking a gulp, to jump across the highest rocks above town, nicknamed the Saut du Capucin. The town boasts a small domed casino, an Art Deco church, a few showy hotels, and far too many pâtisseries to be good for the health.

Historic **Domfront** stands aloof on its rocky spine beyond the beech woods of the Forêt des Andaines. The ruins of the haughty medieval castle date as far back as King Henry I of England, while Henry II and Eleanor of Aquitaine were frequent visitors as they travelled up and down their little empire. Domfront is in fact associated with a couple of reconciliation attempts between Henry II and his friend turned over-zealous archbishop of Canterbury, Thomas à Becket. A dozen or more towers still stand guard over the upper town. Far down below, lorries trundle noisily past the Romanesque **Notre-Dame-sur-l'Eau**, which has lost a large part of its nave, although the choir end has retained some remarkable Romanesque frescoed faces, and a splendid medieval effigy of a knight with pinched waist, sporting natty garb. West of Domfront you enter pear-growing territory, with splendid orchards of tall, unkempt trees. Follow the **Route de la Poire**, visiting one or two of the little fruit museums along the way.

From **Mortain**, you get gorgeous views down on to the patchwork of fields and hedges leading west to Mont-St-Michel (*see* p.206). The town's Romanesque to Gothic church of **St-Evroult** has held on to several impressive reliquaries, most prized of which is the Chrismale, a 7th-century Celtic casket probably made at the Scottish monastery of Iona (*only on display July and Aug Tues and Thurs at 3pm*). Others are permanently displayed around the altar.

Maine

Somewhat ignored these days, the historic province of Maine, between Normandy and the Loire Valley, has become a very peaceful provincial backwater...except in mid-June when the world-famous car race hits the historic Plantagenet city of Le Mans.

Eastern Maine

Le Mans is undoubtedly the highlight of Eastern Maine – alias the *département* of the Sarthe. A tour down the Sarthe river offers a taste of some quieter attractions.

Getting There and Around

Le Mans has excellent high-speed **train** links with Paris-Montparnasse (under 1 hour). Local **bus** services radiate out from Le Mans.

Tourist Information

Le Mans: Hôtel des Ursulines, Rue de l'Etoile, **t** 02 43 28 17 22.

Where to Stay and Eat

Le Mans ✉ 72000
****Concorde**, 16 Av du Général Leclerc, **t** 02 43 24 12 30, *www.concordelemans.com*

(*very expensive–moderate*). Large, modern, stylish and not bad value, with restaurant.
La Chamade, 9 Rue Dorée, **t** 02 43 28 22 96 (*moderate*). Refined regional cuisine. *Closed Wed, and Sat lunch.*

Asnières-sur-Vègre ✉ 72430
Manoir des Claies, **t** 02 43 92 40 50 (*moderate*). Delightful B&B in a gorgeous, lovingly done-up 15th-century house. *Table d'hôte* is possible by reservation only. *Closed Nov–Easter.*

Solesmes ✉ 72300
****Grand Hôtel de Solesmes**, **t** 02 43 95 45 10 (*moderate*). Large, comfortable hotel opposite the abbey, with a terrace for sunny days, and delicate cuisine (*expensive*).

Le Mans

Le Mans' superbly restored historic centre occupies a thin spur of rock, a colossal many-buttressed cathedral lording it over one side, while on the other side fine houses overlook the Sarthe river. They rest on Gallo-Roman walls, among the best-preserved in France. Moving to medieval times, as William the Conqueror expanded his duchy, his troops took hold of Le Mans. It went on to become an important centre of the Angevin kings who succeeded the Normans on the English throne. Geoffrey Plantagenet, founder of the dynasty, hailed from Le Mans. Henry II Plantagenet of England was born here in 1135. Even one French king, Jean II le Bon, came into the world just outside town in 1319, but would end his days in London, captured in the Hundred Years War. The brilliant array of 16th-century houses in the upper town proves that some in Le Mans prospered after that conflict. At the end of the 19th century the local Bollée family started making motor vehicles. The first major car race took place in 1906; the internationally famed 24-hour competition took off in 1923.

The exterior of the **cathedral** looks an incoherent mess, although the flying buttresses around the choir give it a spectacular spidery appearance. The narrow, dark Romanesque nave is held up on pillars with beefy primitive-leaved capitals. The Ascension stained glass window, from around 1140, counts among the very oldest in France, even if it has been heavily restored and Christ has gone missing altogether. From the crossing and transepts, the style suddenly changes, with a viciously sharp opening arch and the light of Gothic flooding in.

The pride of the collection at the fine arts **Musée de Tessé** (*open Tues–Sun 9–12 and 2–6; closed Mon; adm*), just outside the historic centre, is the so-called **Plantagenet Enamel**, made for Geoffrey Plantagenet's tomb in the cathedral, its style reflecting the influence of Byzantine art. More gorgeous Limoges enamelwork features in the museum, which also contains Italian paintings. The most cherished local pieces are the triptych panels by the so-called Master of Vivoin; the Virgin's radically combed-back hair recalls Loire courtly fashions in the mid-15th century. The Gothic church of

La Couture in the lower town has domed vaulting, and a Virgin attributed to the great 16th-century sculptor Germain Pilon. Up in the handsome old town (used as a setting in the film *Cyrano de Bergerac* starring Gérard Depardieu), some of the houses are covered with beams carved with Gothic figures. One fine mansion contains the **Musée de la Reine Bérengère** (*open Tues–Sun 9–12.30 and 2–6.30; closed Mon; adm*), recalling Le Mans' history through painting, pottery and pewterware.

The son of Henry II, Richard the Lionheart, married one Berengaria of Navarre, much ignored by her adventuring bisexual husband and by history, but well remembered in Le Mans for founding the **Abbaye de la Piété Dieu de l'Epau** (*open daily 9.30–12 and 2–6*) after Richard's death. The abbey stands in a walled park east of town. Largely destroyed in the Hundred Years War, then rebuilt in the 14th century, it offers a fine example of a beautifully sober Cistercian monastery. The pleasing golden-brown architecture with its magnificent Gothic window tracery survived the Revolution almost intact. Now used for conferences as well as exhibitions, the abbey presents an interesting permanent display on Cistercian life, peppered with good quotes. 'Build as you believe... Rigour in prayer makes for rigour in construction,' run just a couple. The effigy of big-nosed Berengaria reading her book lies in the chapter house.

To find the excellent **Musée de l'Automobile** (*open Mon–Fri 10–7, Sat and Sun 10–6; adm*) and racetrack follow signs south of town for the 'Circuit des 24 Heures'. The local heroes, the Bollées, are well represented by early models of their automobiles and some hilarious archive film. There's also a gleaming collection of cars from the late 19th century to the present day. The celebrated 24hr race takes place in mid-June.

Down the Sarthe from Le Mans

Malicorne-sur-Sarthe, the first obvious stop along the Sarthe below Le Mans, has the friendly remnants of a château on its outskirts. The main attraction in the scrappy centre is the pottery shops, the potters here best known for copying the styles of the major schools of French ceramics, as the **Espace Faïence** (*open daily in high season 10–7; rest of year Wed–Mon 10–12.30 and 2.30–6.30, closed Tues; adm*) demonstates.

Asnières-sur-Vègre, north of Solesmes, has a delightful, cleaned-up medieval character with its 12th-century bridge and lovingly restored yellow-stone houses. The church contains remarkable 13th-century frescoes, the scene of hell showing demons stirring a soup of human heads. The **abbey of Solesmes** (*open 9.15–6.15, services at 10, 1, 1.50, 5, plus compline at 8.30*) looms large and menacing over the Sarthe river. Celebrated for its development of plainchant singing, it served as a priory for nearly a thousand years, but then acquired greater significance when it was transformed into a Benedictine abbey in 1837, by order of Pope Gregory XVI. However, in the early part of the 20th century, as French Church and state clashed, the monks of Solesmes went into exile on the Isle of Wight for over 20 years. Nowadays, you can hear the monks sing plainchant mass in the abbey church. Made up of a wide mix of styles, some dating back to the 11th century, this edifice contains some truly extravagant sculpture. The two great set pieces represent the Entombments of Christ and the Virgin. The first (end 15th century) demonstrates the finesse of late-Gothic sculpting, although the figures show a stony, static grief. The group round the Virgin (mid-16th century) teems with Renaissance movement and texts – it has been described as a fine early example of Counter-Reformation propaganda art. It's even said that the Jewish doctors whom the boy Jesus is shown lecturing represent leading Protestants, including Luther and Calvin. **Sablé-sur-Sarthe**, a lively, delightfully white-stoned river town and boat stop, lies close to the border with Anjou (*see* **Loire Valley**).

Western Maine

Western Maine – or the *département* of Mayenne – is divided down the middle by the Mayenne river. A handful of historic villages and unspoilt countryside are the main attractions. Unlike eastern Maine, taken over by large, monotonous fields, western Maine has preserved its *bocage* – the old fields divided up by hedgerows, where cows and horses graze. Mayenne is horse-mad, with a strong tradition of trotting races, although many of the beasts that don't make the grade end up being eaten. Roadside crucifixes show how Catholic traditions have lasted in this area.

The enormous rounded towers of the 15th-century castle of **Lassay-les-Châteaux** (*open Easter weekend, May weekends, public hols and June–Sept 2.30–6.30*) make an impressive introduction to northern Mayenne, while the short tour affords a good lesson in late medieval fortification. The historic village is built in gritty granite with ruddy tinges like the castle. The town of **Mayenne** may have lost much of its appeal as a river port, but you can hire river boats here. A short way southeast, the sophisticated Gallo-Roman settlement of *Noviodunum* has been unearthed at the quiet village of **Jublains**; an **archaeological museum** (*open May–Sept daily 9–6; Oct–April Tues–Sun 9.30–12.30 and 1.30–5.30; adm*) tells the story. The centre of **Evron** is dominated by a great abbey church in golden stone, built to house a supposed Holy Thorn. In the 14th-century stained glass of the choir you can follow its story. Delightful hilltop **Ste-Suzanne** has a ruined Romanesque keep above its modest **château** (*open May–Sept daily 10–6; Oct–April Tues–Sun 9.30–12.30 and 1.30–5.30*).

Back by the Mayenne, at **Laval**, capital of the *département*, the remaining wing of a medieval **castle** surveys the river. Its interiors have been turned into a **museum** (*open*

Tourist Information

Laval: Allée du Vieux St–Louis, t 02 43 49 46 46, *www.mairie-laval.fr*.
Lassay-les-Châteaux: 8 Rue du Château, t 02 43 04 74 33, *otsi.lassay-les-chateaux@ wanadoo.fr*.
Mayenne: Quai Waiblingen, t 02 43 04 19 37, *www.mairie-mayenne.fr*.
Evron: Place de la Basilique, t 02 43 01 63 75, *tourisme.evron@wanadoo.fr*.
Craon: 4 Rue du Murier, t 04 43 06 10 14.
Château-Gontier: Péniche l'Elan, Quai d'Alsace, t 02 43 70 42 74, *www.ville-chateau-gontier.fr*.

Where to Stay and Eat

Laval ☒ 53000
Le Bas du Gast, 6 Rue de la Halle aux Toiles, t 02 43 49 22 79, *www.chateaubasdugast@ wanadoo.fr* (*very expensive–expensive*). Luxurious B&B in spectacular central historic house with garden. *Closed Dec and Jan.*
**Grand Hôtel de Paris, 22 Rue de la Paix, t 02 43 53 76 20 (*moderate–inexpensive*). Central, with some spacious, stylish rooms.
Bistro de Paris, 67 Rue du Val de Mayenne, t 02 43 56 98 29 (*expensive–moderate*). Swanky décor for refined cuisine. *Closed Sat lunch, Sun pm and Mon..*

Tues–Sun 10–12 and 2–6; adm) largely devoted to Art Naïf, inspired by the great Henri 'Le Douanier' Rousseau, a native of Laval, although only one of his paintings features here. For yet more artistic exuberance, head southwest for **Cossé-le-Vivien** and the **Musée Robert Tatin** (*open April–Sept daily 10–7; Oct and Mar 2–6; Nov–Dec and Feb weekends and public hols 2–6; adm*). Tatin's exuberant, colourful, rustic creations include large outdoor sculptures, the design of the building and the decoration of the interiors. South again, the racecourse and the splendid, slightly worn Ancien Régime **Château de Craon** together form an elegant ensemble, while back east by the Mayenne the historic town of **Château-Gontier** makes a stylish, cultured last riverside halt before Anjou, even if it has lost its château.

The Cotentin or Cherbourg Peninsula

With its tough granite character and its coast dotted with pretty ports, this area presages Brittany. Cherbourg has a fine war museum and the vast new Cité de la Mer. After the romantic cliffs and villages of the Cap de la Hague, just marred by its nuclear installations, the flat western side of the Cotentin ends with the magical Mont-St-Michel. (For Utah Beach and the Cotentin marshes, *see* pp.185–6.)

St-Vaast-la-Hougue, the Ile Tatihou and Barfleur

St-Vaast-la-Hougue and Barfleur compete for the prize of prettiest port in the Cotentin. **St-Vaast-la-Hougue** has a more eccentric character, with a confusion of low spits stretching into the sea. Forts to the south and on the island of Tatihou add a military twist to the horizon. They went up in 1694, to guard against any repeat of the recent Battle of La Hougue, when much of the French fleet was set alight by the Anglo-Dutch enemy. Today St-Vaast's pretty port has developed into a very popular marina. The island of **Tatihou** makes an exhilarating excursion via amphibious craft (*book on t 02 33 23 19 92*). Explore the sea fort as well as the former *lazare*, the quarantine hospital for crews struck by infectious diseases. Today, it houses a ship repair yard, a **maritime museum** (*open April–Sept daily 10–6; Feb and Easter hols 2–5.30; adm*) and a maritime garden.

Barfleur was once a great Channel port, favoured by the royal Plantagenets when they were to-ing and fro-ing between Normandy and England in the Middle Ages. Its lovely port, the quays often lined with nets, is protected by a somewhat English-looking square-towered church. To the west, beyond the lichen-stained villages and natural harbours, tall lighthouses guard the scenic rocky coast to Cherbourg.

Cherbourg

Badly damaged by the war, Cherbourg may not look immediately appealing, but it has a dramatic natural setting and, beyond the chaotic jumble of its ports and modern apartment blocks, some gripping tales to tell. A crazy attempt to build a huge sea wall to protect the harbour began under Louis XVI. Huge sea defences eventually

Getting There and Around

By **ferry** to Cherbourg; *see* **Travel**. For **trains** to and from Cherbourg, you need to change at Lison to go east to Bayeux and Caen, or south to Coutances and Granville. The last lies at the end of a separate line from Paris through southern Normandy.

Tourist Information

St-Vaast-la-Hougue: 1 Place Général de Gaulle, **t** 02 33 23 19 32, *www.saint-vaast-reville.com.*
Barfleur: Rond-Point Guillaume Le Conquérant, **t** 02 33 54 02 48, *www.ville-barfleur.fr.*
Cherbourg: 2 Quai Alexandre III, **t** 02 33 93 52 02, *www.ot-cherbourg-cotentin.fr.*

Where to Stay and Eat

St-Vaast-la-Hougue ✉ 50550

***La Granitière, 74 Rue Maréchal Foch, **t** 02 33 54 58 99, *www.hotel-la-granitiere.com* (*moderate*). Central manor, with garden.
Hôtel de France, 20 Rue Maréchal Foch, **t 02 33 54 42 26, *www.france-fuchsias.com* (*moderate–inexpensive*). Charming central hotel with excellent seafood restaurant

Les Fuchsias (*moderate*) and a lovely garden. *Closed Jan–Feb; restaurant closed Mon and Tues out of high season.*

Barfleur ✉ 50760

Le Conquérant, 18 Rue Thomas Becket, **t 02 33 54 00 82 (*inexpensive*). Appealing hotel in the port, in a 17th-century house.
Le Moderne, 1 Place Charles de Gaulle, **t** 02 33 23 12 44. For a seafood feast (*very expensive–moderate*), plus a few bargain rooms (*inexpensive*). *Closed Jan–mid-Mar.*

Cherbourg ✉ 50100

La Régence, 42 Quai Caligny, **t 02 33 43 05 16, *www.logis-de-france.fr* (*inexpensive*). Rooms with sea views, and a traditional seafood restaurant (*moderate*).
Ambassadeur, 22 Quai Caligny, **t 02 33 43 10 00, *www.ambassadeur hotel.com* (*inexpensive*). View of the port too.
Le Vauban, 22 Quai Caligny, **t** 02 33 43 10 11 (*expensive–moderate*). Most refined restaurant, boats passing by as you enjoy the seafood. *Closed Sun pm and Mon.*
Café de Paris, 40 Quai Caligny, **t** 02 33 43 12 36 (*moderate*). 19th-century rival to the above.
Le Laurent, 59 Rue au Blé, **t** 02 33 93 07 07 (*moderate*). In the shopping heart, quite refined cooking in a rustic dining room. *Closed Sun and Mon lunch.*

went up successfully, their fortified arms stretching some 12km around to protect the port. Cherbourg, long a major naval centre, boasts of its record for the longest tradition of submarine-building in the world, going back over 100 years. France's nuclear submarines are built in Cherbourg these days. In the first half of the 20th century, transatlantic liners plying their way between Europe and America often stopped in port. These ships were taking many emigrants across the Big Pond, of course, not just glamorous tourists. Now, impressive cruise liners sometimes make a halt here.

The grand remnants of the former transatlantic **railway station** on the seafront, dating from the inter-war period, has recently been restored to house part of the **Cité de la Mer** (*open June–mid-Sept daily 9.30–7; late-Jan–May and mid-Sept–Dec 10–6; adm*), bringing a derelict part of the harbour back to life. The principal building rivals London's Tate Modern in staggering scale, but it contains just a ticket office, shops and restaurants at one end. The main attractions are housed in a brand new temple of glass and wood beyond, where you can weave round all manner of panels, exhibits and interactive booths covering the history of undersea exploration. Competition became intense between the French and the Americans in the 20th century. Jacques Cousteau's name lives on for the passion he transmitted for undersea archaeology and exploration. But US researchers hold the record for sending a vessel into a trench over 10km under the earth's surface, back in 1960. The exhibition spaces centre round the Aquarium Abyssal, the deepest aquarium in Europe. However, the Cité's main exhibit lies outside, *Le Redoutable*, the largest submarine in the world open to visitors. English texts mean English-speaking visitors are well catered-for.

From the large **marina** across the other side of the Avant-Port, you get an excellent view of the Cherbourg coastline. There are plenty of opportunities for practising water sports here. Behind the marina, the much-restored Gothic church of **La Trinité** stands by a square with an equestrian statue of Napoleon, bearing one of the emperor's more dubious quotes: 'I resolved to renew the marvels of Egypyt in Cherbourg.' Around the theatre and the glass- and steel-covered market on the bustling **Place Centrale**, a number of characterful stone pedestrian streets packed with shops, pubs and restaurants have managed to survive among the modern blocks. The **Musée Thomas Henry** (*open May–Sept Tues–Sat 10–12 and 2–6, Sun and Mon 2–6 only; Oct–April Wed–Sat 2–6; adm*) contains a few good Old Masters. David Tenier's well-known mocking *Monkey's Ball* features among the Flemish pieces. The collection of French portraits displays more decorum. Some are by the most famous of all Cotentin artists, Jean-François Millet, better known for his landscapes. A plaque on the museum outside notes how L'Hoste and Mangot made the first-ever Channel crossing by hot-air balloon in July 1886.

High up above Cherbourg, reached by hairpin bends worthy of the Alps, stands the mid-19th-century **Fort du Roule**, which still bears the scars of shells from the vicious but remarkably short battle for the town in June 1944. The views down on the port are spectacular. Inside, the **Musée de la Libération** (*open same as Musée Henry; adm*) is just about the clearest Second World War museum in Normandy, the build-up to the D-Day landings and the taking of Cherbourg presented with a rare, striking simplicity.

Cap de la Hague and the Western Cotentin

With its towering cliffs and hedgerows, the La Hague peninsula west of Cherbourg was a major area of Viking settlement in Normandy; most of the place-names ending in -*ville* indicate villages founded by Norsemen. **Querqueville**, with a great view back over Cherbourg, has preserved the rare, tiny Chapelle de St-Germain, which dates in part to before the Viking invasions. Up on the heights at **Ludiver**, between Tonneville and Flottemanville, the huge COGEMA nuclear reprocessing plant is visible, along with much of the north Cotentin coast. The concentration of nuclear sights around Cherbourg has made the area rich, hence the money lavished on the **planetarium** (*open July–Aug daily 10–7; Sept–June Mon–Fri 9–1 and 2–5.30, Sat and Sun 2–6; adm*).

Back by the coast, the copper-green statue of Jean-François Millet at **Gréville-Hague** indicates this was his place of birth. Millet painted the squat Norman church several times before moving on to his more familiar themes of peasant life in the Seine valley. The **Maison Natale du Peintre Jean-François Millet** (*open daily June and Sept 11–6; July and Aug 11–7; April–May 2–6; closed Oct–Mar; adm*) recalls his works, as well as displaying 19th-century rural artefacts. At **Omonville-la-Rogue** on the coast, the typical wealthy, well-defended farmstead of **Le Tourp** (*for opening times call t 02 33 01*

85 89) has been converted into a cultural centre on the La Hague area, comparing it with other coastal communities. **Omonville-la-Petite** was the last home of the popular poet Jacques Prévert, author of *Paroles*. Prévert also wrote the scripts for several French cinema classics. The **Maison Jacques Prévert** (*open same times as Millet museum; adm*) hosts an annual exhibition on his work.

The sensational western side of the Cap de la Hague looks out to the distant Channel Islands. Watch the sun set at **Goury** on the very tip of the peninsula, with the Gros du Raz lighthouse in the foreground. At the southern end of the magnificent arc of sand and surf of the **Baie d'Ecalgrain**, some of the tallest cliffs in Europe rise out of the sea at the **Nez de Jobourg**. As you turn the corner, the views remain breathtaking, but the vast nuclear reprocessing plant is a huge, unavoidable blight on the landscape. Environmentalists are concerned about the abnormally high levels of radioactivity in the waters around here and at Flamanville, where there's a nuclear power station. Unsurprisingly, the beaches, backed by precipitous dunes, look remarkably unspoilt.

Heading swiftly south, the popular resorts of **Carteret** and **Barneville-Plage** face each other across a wide inlet, Carteret with its port backed by green cliffs, Barneville with a good stretch of even beach some way down from the traditional squares of its old hillside Norman village. Boats leave for Jersey from here. The coast flattens out right down to the bay of Mont-St-Michel, the sea receding an awfully long way at low tide, leaving vast expanses of sands. **Portbail**, an enchanting little historic port tucked away out of sight from the sea, has the church of Notre-Dame to defend it down by its inlet; its defensive tower even comes with crenellations. The remains of a 6th-century baptistry have been unearthed nearby.

The name of **Lindbergh-Plage** reminds visitors that the pioneering aviator Charles Lindbergh flew over this spot to complete the first-ever transatlantic flight, back in 1927, but even that thrilling thought can't impart excitement to the dull dunes and long expanses of sand stretching south. The small town of **Lessay** is dominated by its Romanesque abbey, which suffered in the Second World War, but has been lovingly restored. Amusing Romanesque figures run along the outside, while the interior is sober, held up on plain pillars and capitals. The sands continue unrelentingly southwards. The medieval **Château du Pirou** so skulks behind the coast perhaps because its builders were trying to avoid the fate of its predecessor, destroyed by Vikings. Legend has it that the people within managed to escape the Norsemen by a spell turning them into geese; unfortunately the recipe to turn them back into human beings went up in flames. The moated castle is lovely, and ducking and diving along the empty ramparts takes your imagination back to warring medieval times. The castle chapel lies in an outbuilding, along with the *Tapisserie du Pirou*, a modern work following the style of the Bayeux embroidery, but illustrating the story of the Norman conquest of Sicily in the 11th century.

Inland, the miniature hilltop city of **Coutances** was badly damaged in the liberation of Normandy, but preserved its dramatic Gothic cathedral. The massive octagonal crossing tower stands out, a triumph of Norman Gothic architecture. The interior is more showy still, although heavily restored. The transepts and very light ambulatory chapels contain fine stained-glass windows. Take a casual stroll through the pleasant

Tourist Information

Barneville-Carteret: 10 Rue des Ecoles, t 02 33 04 90 58, *www.barneville-carteret.net*.
Coutances: Place Leclerc, t 02 33 19 08 10, *www.bons-plans-tourisme.com*.
Granville: 4 Cours Jonville, t 02 33 91 30 03, *www.ville-granville.fr*.

Where to Stay and Eat

Omonville-la-Petite, Goury, St-Germain-des-Vaux ✉ 50440

**La Fossardière, Hameau de la Fosse, t 02 33 52 19 83 (*inexpensive*). Charming, in an old-stone, well-flowered hamlet by a stream, breakfasts served in a former bread oven!
Auberge de Goury, Port de Goury, t 02 33 52 77 01 (*expensive–moderate*). Superlative grilled fish and views from the tip of the Cap de la Hague. *Closed Mon.*
Le Moulin à Vent, St-Germain-des-Vaux, t 02 33 52 75 20 (*moderate*). Decent restaurant beside a former windmill, with splendid sea views. *Closed winter evenings.*

Bricquebec ✉ 50260

***L'Hostellerie du Château, t 02 33 52 24 49, *lhostellerie.chateau@wanadoo.fr* (*moderate*). The original owner took part in the Battle of Hastings, and Queen Victoria visited. The place is atmospheric, the rooms relatively simple. Restaurant. *Closed late-Dec–Jan.*

Barneville-Carteret ✉ 50270

***La Marine, 11 Rue de Paris, Carteret, t 02 33 53 83 31 (*moderate*). Some pleasing rooms looking over the water, and a chic restaurant with seafood specialities (*very expensive–expensive*). *Closed mid-Nov–Feb; restaurant closed Sun pm and Mon out of season.*
L'Hermitage, 4 Promenade Abbé Leouteiller, Carteret, t 02 33 04 46 39 (*inexpensive*). A few delightful rooms above a good seafood restaurant with terrace on the port.
**Les Isles, 9 Bd Maritime, Barneville-Plage, t 02 33 04 90 76 (*inexpensive*). Just across the road from the beach, smart hotel by the mock castle. Restaurant (*moderate*).

Bréville 50290

***La Beaumonderie, 20 Rte de Coutances, t 02 33 50 36 36, *www.la-beaumonderie.com* (*expensive–moderate*). Elegant Belle Epoque villa with garden, sea views, pool, tennis and squash. Order rooms with views rather than road-side. Smart restaurant. *Restaurant closed Sun pm and Mon lunch out of season.*

Granville ✉ 50400

***Le Grand Large, 5 Rue de la Falaise, t 02 33 91 19 19, *www.hotel-le-grand-large.com* (*moderate*). Grand, modern hotel above luxury beauty institute, with well-equipped rooms looking out to sea. *Closed 2 wks Dec.*
**Le Michelet, 5 bis Rue Jules Michelet, t 02 33 50 06 55 (*inexpensive–cheap*). Bright, tastefully decorated little rooms.

Musée Morinière (*open Mon and Wed–Sat 10–12 and 2–5, Sun 2–5; closed Tues*) by the small terraced botanical garden, even if it only contains modest pieces. South of Coutances, the quirky 17th-century **Manoir de Saussey** (*open April–Sept daily 2–6.30; Oct, Nov and Mar weekends 2.30–5*), topped by pottery finials and surrounded by neat themed gardens, contains further curious collections: amazingly sophisticated glass; more rustic pottery; and some very naff cribs.

Towards Villedieu-les-Poêles, the ruined Benedictine church at **Hambye** (*open April–Oct daily 10–12 and 2–6; adm*), although battered and roofless, and plundered by locals for its stone at the Revolution, remains one of the finest examples of Norman Gothic architecture. A ragged tower rises 100ft above the narrow arches on which it remains improbably perched. Some of the monastic buildings have fared better than the church. The guided tour (*not Tues*) takes you to the monks' parlour with its 13th-century flower-decorated ceiling, while the kitchen has a magnificent fireplace.

Copper-crazy **Villedieu-les-Poêles**, the 'City-of-God-the-Cooking-Pots', got its funny name from specializing in metal-working. An excessive number of minor museums and workshops showcase this pretty town's trades, notably the **Fonderie des Cloches** (*open mid-July–Aug daily 9–6; June–mid-July daily 10–12 and 1.30–5.30; Feb hols–May and Sept–mid-Nov Wed–Mon 10–12 and 1.30–5.30, closed Tues; adm*), one of the last completely traditional bell foundries in Europe, and the **Maison de la Dentellerie et Musée de la Poeslerie** (*open Easter–11 Nov daily 10–12.30 and 2–6.30; adm*), combining lacemaking traditions with copper working ones in a fine courtyard. As if these weren't enough, the **Maison de l'Etain** (*open daily 9–12 and 1.30–5.30; adm*) has a large pewter collection; **Le Royaume de l'Horloge** (*open July and Aug daily 9–12.30 and 2–6.30; Sept–June closed Sun am; adm*) is devoted to clockmaking; and the **Musée du Meuble Normand** (*open same times as Maison de la Dentellerie; adm*) presents Normandy furniture.

Granville

Back on the coast, gay old Granville, proudly located on a natural fortification of a rock sticking dramatically out into the sea, its port tucked away below, might have been a rival to St-Malo in the tourist stakes had its architecture remained more homogenous. It still has plenty of appeal. The rock was first fortified by the English in the late 1430s, during the Hundred Years War, frustrated at not being able to wrest nearby Mont-St-Michel from the French. English soldiers returned in the late 17th century to smoke out irritating corsairs, bombarding the place; the granite fortifications and houses were rebuilt in style. Granville has had a reputation for being a bit stick-in-the-mud bourgeois, but in recent years has come out of its shell or perhaps more accurately its closet, thanks to two brilliant gay men born and recalled here.

The Villa Les Rhumbs, a delightful pink house in the posh residential area on the cliffs, was turned into the **Musée Christian Dior** (*open April–25 Oct Tues–Sun 10–12.30 and 2.30–7; closed Mon; adm*) in 1997, and puts on an annual fashion exhibition. Dior's parents bought the villa around 1905, the year of Christian's birth. He started his career by making costumes for himself and his friends for the Granville carnival. The family moved to Paris, but Dior would often return for the summer, until his father went bankrupt in the early 1930s, just as Dior began his meteoric rise in the fashion world. By 1947 he had opened his own fashion house. Inspired by the Belle Epoque traditions, he clothed the likes of Marlene Dietrich and Olivia de Havilland. He died in 1957, not long after the young Yves St-Laurent became his assistant.

The bookshop owner and art collector Richard Anacréon is not widely known like Dior, but left Granville a greater legacy. Born in the port in 1907, through A l'Originale, the shop he opened in Paris during the war, he fostered close relations with many significant writers and artists. Anacréon died in his home town in 1992, leaving it his books and paintings. A well-located former school became the **Musée d'Art Moderne Richard Anacréon** (*open summer Wed–Mon 11–6; winter Wed–Sun 2–6; adm*). A controversial figure among Granville's inhabitants in his lifetime, they can now thank him for Fauvist canvases by the likes of Vlaminck, Derain, Friesz and Chabaud, Pointillist works, and pieces by Picabia, Van Dongen and Utrillo. Acrobatic ballet dancers by Rodin also feature. One of Anacréon's closest literary friends was Colette, and one corner of the museum contains rare mementoes.

The quirky rooms of the **Musée du Vieux Granville** (*open April–Sept Wed–Mon 10–12 and 2–6, closed Tues; rest of year Wed, Sat and Sun 2–6; adm*) occupy an historic house just above the main gate into the old town. The days of pirate raids between England and France are recalled, and the issue of bathing is seriously treated. A poster from 1837 advertises the rules of the bathing police: men and women were segregated, women bathing on the north side of the rock, men on the south side.

The ruined medieval **Abbaye de la Lucerne**, southeast of Granville (*open early Feb–Dec daily 10–12 and 2–6.30; Nov–Easter closes 1hr earlier; adm*), gained its subtitle 'd'Outremer' (from across the sea) by showing persistent loyalty to England. In 1204, when Philippe Auguste seized Normandy, the monks of La Lucerne remained stubbornly faithful to their previous master, King John. When the English reappeared during the Hundred Years War, the abbey provided a chaplain for King Edward III. This didn't prevent the abbey becoming one of the largest religious houses in France, which it remained until 1791. The church (1164–78) was built in a strong, unadorned Norman Romanesque. Its crossing tower set the model for many churches in the region. A good deal of restoration has been undertaken, especially of the choir, with its superb 1780 organ now regularly used for concerts and services.

To Mont-St-Michel via Avranches

Mont-St-Michel is one of the very greatest sights in the Western world – a mirage of a rock topped by a vertiginous abbey, isolated in its vast bay. It makes a mesmerizing sight viewed from any angle, or from up in the old town of Avranches.

South of Granville to Avranches

The coast road south from Granville offers distant, fascinating glimpses of Mont-St-Michel, the Tombelaine rock in the middle distance adding an additional surprising natural feature not seen in the normal clichés of the mount. At **Les Genêts** or at **Vains**, visit the **Maisons de la Baie**, containing a mine of information on local wildlife; from Vains there are organized walks across to the mount at low tide from May to October. Do not attempt this journey without a guide: real tragedies unfortunately occur.

The city of **Avranches** sits atop a clutch of granite hills that fall precipitously to the great flat plain of the bay. Its history has been inextricably bound up with that of the mount since St Michael's apparitions to its Bishop Aubert in the 8th century. Visit Avranches' 19th-century church of **St-Gervais** and its treasury (*open June–Sept daily 9.30–12 and 2–6; adm*) to gawp at St Aubert's supposed skull, the hole said to have been made by the archangel's over-insistent finger. Avranches' *mairie* contains a matchless treasure in the form of the **Manuscrits du Mont-St-Michel** (*open June–Sept daily 10–12 and 2–6; adm*), saved at the Revolution from the abbey library. They count among the finest illuminated books in the world, and a selection is put on show each summer. The **Musée Municipal** (*open June–Sept daily 9.30–12 and 2–6; adm*) has a more prosaic re-creation of an illuminator's workshop, plus displays of religious sculpture, ethnographic bits and pieces, and an art collection, inevitably featuring many

Getting There and Around

By **train**, reach Avranches from Caen changing at Lison (west of Bayeux), but for Mont-St-Michel, go on to Pontorson-St-Michel and catch a **bus**.

Tourist Information

Avranches: 2 Rue Général de Gaulle, t 02 33 58 00 22, www.ville-avranches.fr.

Le Mont-St-Michel: 4 Rue Général Leclerc, t 02 33 60 14 30, OT.Mont.Saint.Michel@ wanadoo.fr.

Pontorson: Place de l'Hôtel de Ville, t 02 33 60 20 65, www.ville-pontorson.fr.

Where to Stay and Eat

Avranches ✉ 50300

★★La Croix d'Or, 83 Rue de la Constitution, t 02 33 58 04 88 (moderate–inexpensive). Former coaching inn, with comfortable rooms and decent restaurant (expensive––moderate). Closed Jan.

Ducey ✉ 50220

★★★Moulin de Ducey, 1 Grande Rue, t 02 33 60 25 25, www.moulindeducey.com (moderate). Comfortable modern rooms in a converted mill. Closed mid-Jan–mid-Feb.

★★Auberge de la Sélune, 2 Rue St-Germain, t 02 33 48 53 62, www.selune.com (inexpensive). Appealing riverside address with good solid rooms, tennis court, and inventive cuisine (moderate). Closed mid-Nov–mid-Dec; restaurant closed Mon in winter.

Mont-St-Michel ✉ 50116

★★★La Mère Poulard, t 02 33 89 68 68, www.mere.poulard.com (expensive). The most famous name here, with pretty rooms in a warren of historic buildings. The image-plastered restaurant is famed for its omelettes, but also serves other local fare .

★★★Auberge St-Pierre, t 02 33 60 14 03, www.auberge-saint-pierre.fr (moderate). Atmospheric timberframe building dating back to the 15th century, some rooms with views. Popular restaurant. Closed Jan.

★★Le Mouton Blanc, t 02 33 60 14 08 (moderate). Cheaper and nice, but no views.

views of Mont-St-Michel. You can enjoy spectacular views of the real thing from the **Plate-forme**, where King Henry II of England is said to have knelt for a day dressed only in a hair shirt, doing penance in front of Avranches' now-vanished cathedral for his part in the murder of Thomas à Becket. The king performed this act at the instigation of one of the greatest abbots of Mont-St-Michel, also bishop of Avranches, Robert de Torigni. The terraces of the **Jardin des Plantes** may tempt you down the hillside.

Mont-St-Michel

The most alluring of all French religious buildings, a mirage of a monastery rising so magically out of its bay – what a glorious piece of Christian symbolism the abbey of Mont-St-Michel is. From afar, its triangular shape evokes the Holy Trinity; the narrow spit joining mainland to island seems to represent clearly the straight and narrow path to God; and the church steeple pointing fixedly to the skies acts as a sharp reminder for pilgrims to turn their thoughts heavenwards. The needle is topped by a gilded statue of St Michael, the weigher of souls at the Last Judgement.

Some kind of a Christian building existed on the rock before St Aubert founded the first shrine to St Michael, but this bishop counts as the first significant figure in the mount's history. A medieval manuscript relates the story: in the year 708, the Archangel Michael swooped down into Aubert's dreams and commanded the bishop to build a shrine to him on the rock in the middle of the bay. Aubert dismissed the message twice, but the third time the archangel supposedly gave Aubert a vicious prod in the side of the head, prompting him into action. Aubert first had a small oratory built, a grotto modelled on that at Mount Gargano in Italy, where St Michael was said to have put in an earlier appearance. Monks were then sent across the Alps to fetch relics of St Michael.

In 966 the mount became the site of the first Benedictine foundation in Western Normandy. Later it was decided to replace the buildings with a more substantial Romanesque abbey. Donations of land from nobles and of money from visiting pilgrims brought the place considerable wealth; it became a celebrated school of learning, and renowned for its illuminated manuscripts. Robert de Tombelaine and Anastase the Venetian were among the most revered scholars of the 11th century who ruled the abbey. However, it was under Abbot Robert de Torigni (1154–86) that the place knew its greatest period. The number of monks reached its peak of 60, and such was the prolific production of manuscripts in this period, and so great the size of the abbey library, that Mont-St-Michel became known as the 'City of Books'.

This holy mount also became a strategic and symbolic military stronghold in the Middle Ages. Early in the 13th century Breton soldiers fighting for King Philippe Auguste of France set fire to part of the abbey, destroying much of it. The repentant royal, after his victory, donated an enormous sum to build a magnificent new monastic wing, the Merveille, or Marvel, a great architectural achievement. The ramparts around the bottom of the mount date mainly from the 15th century, built to defend the rock from the English stationed nearby in the Hundred Years War. The war over, French pilgrims came to thank St Michael for delivering them from the English.

French kings followed the Mont-St-Michel pilgrimage religiously, but abbey life was radically altered in the 16th century when the crown took control of the appointment of abbots across France under the system of *commende*. Some of the *abbés commendataires* scarcely visited the place, only interested in its revenue; inevitably monastic life and scholarship suffered dramatically. With the installation of the Maurist Benedictine order in 1622, religious life somewhat revived, but the place stood in a precarious state. Only some 10 monks inhabited the abbey before the Revolution, replaced by prisoners until 1863. Then 19th-century restorers moved in in force. The neo-Gothic spire of 1897 was the work of Victor Petigrand, a pupil of Viollet-le-Duc.

Recently, a few monks have returned to the abbey, keeping a little spiritual flame alive on the holy mount, while the place has been declared a UNESCO World Heritage Site. Environmentally, however, the bay itself has been silting up fast, and a massive project is now under way to reestablish Mont-St-Michel as a proper island.

Touring Mont-St-Michel's Abbeys and Museums

This heavenly-looking sight, sometimes described as the 8th wonder of the world, can be hellish to visit in high season. The highly picturesque **Grande Rue** snaking up to the abbey, crammed with shops selling tat, becomes a terrible crush, it's so narrow. And it's extremely steep. Such a gem from a distance, the **abbey** (*open May–Aug daily 9–7; Sept–April daily 9.30–6; adm*) turns out to be austere and forbidding close up, designed to incite reflection and awe. The buildings were made from granite quarried locally and on the Iles Chausey, out beyond the bay – heaving the great stones up such steep rock was an incredible achievement. Reaching the square in front of the church, you'll see how, following storm damage, a classical façade was tacked on to one of the earliest Romanesque buildings in Normandy, built in plain style. Inside, even the luminous late-Gothic choir has little decorative detail. But construction of the church was an extraordinary feat of engineering: its crossing was placed on the very top of the rock, and most of the rest of the edifice rests on four supporting lower chapels or crypts, all of which you can visit if you opt for the detailed *tour-conférence*, which also takes you right up among the church's flying buttresses.

The brilliant **Merveille** forms the main focus of the ordinary visit. Daringly built on the north side of the mount, this towering medieval block basically consists of two rooms on each of its three floors. On the top level the cloister garden's galleries are held up on delicate double columns. Originally a peaceful retreat, nowadays it tends to feel about as calm as Paris in the rush hour. The refectory next to it is beautifully lit, but the diagonal windows block out any views , to stop the monks being distracted from God by the stupendous vistas. On the Merveille's middle level, the vast Salle des Hôtes was where prestigious pilgrims were received. The room next door is thought to have served as both the abbey's chapterhouse and its scriptorium, where manuscripts were prepared. A copy of Frémiet's statue of St Michael (in fact a 19th-century addition) is displayed in the massive cellar on the lowest level of the Merveille, where mountains of provisions for the abbey and its pilgrims were stored. Close up, God's *generalissimo* looks mean and militant in armour, sword raised for action above his spiky headgear, only the wings adding a slightly softer touch. At night the abbey is gloriously lit. In high season, look out for special night-time tours, when these buildings are filled with an amazing eerie Gothic grandeur.

Smaller attractions lie along the Grande Rue. Tucked into the rock, the other serious religious stop besides the abbey is **St-Pierre**, a charming building from the 15th and 16th centuries, where gaudy homage is paid to Joan of Arc. The **Archéoscope** (*open early Feb–mid-Nov daily 9–7; adm*), almost opposite, offers a lively, contemporary introduction to the abbey. Smoke, lights and videos bombard the senses and although the commentary is in French the splendid film footage and the special effects are easy to appreciate. By contrast, the **Musée Historique** (*open Feb– 14 Nov daily 9–6; adm*), up close to the entrance to the abbey, is amusingly archaic. Various torture instruments here remind you of the abbey's secondary use as a prison. The **Logis Tiphaine** (*open June–15 Sept daily 9–7; Feb–May and 16 Sept–mid-Nov daily 9–6; adm*), close by, was built for the wife of the most famed Breton and French warrior of the Hundred Years War, Bertrand du Guesclin. Down at the bottom of the street, the simple **Musée Maritime** (*open Feb–Dec daily 9–6; adm*) climbs four floors filled with model ships and boats. Videos explain aspects of the bay and its natural habitat in sensible manner.

To escape the crowds, follow the old *chemin de ronde*, enjoying spectacular views of the monastic buildings. The path winds down to the **Tour Gabriel**, from where you can walk out to the old quay. Clamber along the rocks to see the little **chapel of St-Aubert**, hidden out of sight from the seething tourist hordes.

Brittany

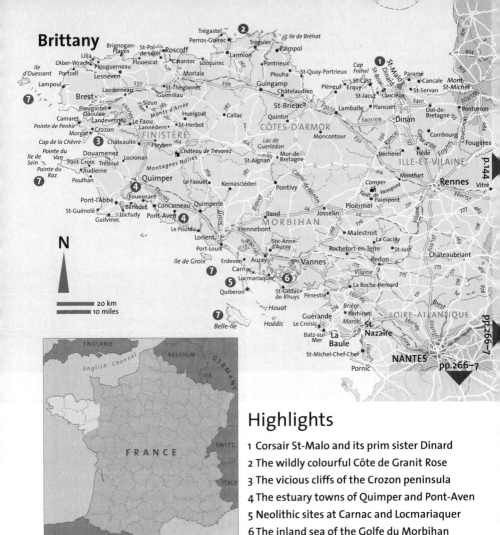

Brittany

Highlights

1 Corsair St-Malo and its prim sister Dinard
2 The wildly colourful Côte de Granit Rose
3 The vicious cliffs of the Crozon peninsula
4 The estuary towns of Quimper and Pont-Aven
5 Neolithic sites at Carnac and Locmariaquer
6 The inland sea of the Golfe du Morbihan
7 Boulder-strewn islands

Along Brittany's ceaselessly dramatic coastline, Neolithic monuments and ruined
fortifications mingle with spectacular beaches, bays and ports, as well as with Nazi
blockhouses left from the Second World War. The region's northern side is rockier, the
south gentler, with uninterrupted sweeps of sand, while the cliffs of the west create
the most savage Breton scenery of all. A garland of islands encircles the Breton coast,
each with its own personality; one in the sheltered Golfe du Morbihan conceals the
finest Neolithic tomb in France. Morbihan was a happening place 5,000 years ago;
Carnac counts as its greatest Neolithic sight. The region's place names, though, from
St-Malo to the Pointe de St-Gildas, most often recall the holy men who crossed the
Channel in the Dark Ages to set up communities, creating Brittany, little Britain.
Arthurian legend also crossed the sea, now most evident in the Forest of Brocéliande
near the region's capital, Rennes.

Food and Wine

A thin black buckwheat pancake is the national meal –
only the Bretons can comprehend its miserable culinary attractions.

Balzac, *Les Chouans*

How wrong Balzac was. The Breton crêpe (or the savoury *galette*) is now considered the aristocrat of the pancake world. Delicate and thin, it comes with all sorts of fancy fillings and, in Brittany, crêperies are reliable and cheap places to eat. Brittany is also known for its seafood. Don't be surprised if shellfish is served in its shell, or if oysters and clams come *cru* (raw). If you order a *plateau de fruits de mer* you will be faced with a sumptuous spread including crab, *langoustines* (Dublin Bay prawns), *crevettes* (shrimps), *palourdes* (clams), *coques* (cockles), *bigorneaux* (winkles) and *bulots* (whelks). Wash it down with a white Muscadet from the south of Brittany. *Cotriade* is the traditional Breton sailors' soup, made with a combination of whiting, cod, hake, haddock, mackerel, eel, and even mussels. Certain fish are particularly prized, such as St-Pierre (John Dory), *bar* (sea bass), *dorade* (sea bream), *rouget* (red mullet), turbot and sole. The marshes of Guérande in southern Brittany produce highly regarded salt, the *fleur de sel*. Crunchy little sprigs of *salicornes* (samphire) are another speciality from the salt-pans, increasingly experimented with in Breton cuisine, as is algae. Brittany is known for its pork, for *saucissons* (salamis), *andouilles* (chitterlings) and *boudins* (black pudding). The town of Châteaubriant is renowned for the thick grilled fillet steak named after it. *Kig-ar-farz* (meat-and-pudding in Breton), a traditional dish back in fashion, mixes meat and vegetables cooked together in a broth.

Butter always features large in Breton cuisine, including its puddings. Gâteau Breton may be a dense, dry Breton butter cake, but *kouign aman* positively drips with the stuff. Various Breton towns, notably Pleyben and Pont-Aven, produce crisp buttery biscuits known as *galettes*. *Far,* a solid eggy pudding, often comes with dried fruit. Brittany, like neighbouring Normandy, is apple country, and makes good cider and delicious but relatively rare lambig, the Breton equivalent to calvados. Cervoise, the traditional beer, was supposedly drunk by the most famous Breton of all, Astérix.

To find tranquil corners of Brittany in high summer, travel up the river estuaries or *avens*; the most renowned of these, Pont-Aven, was where Paul Gauguin and Emile Bernard transformed European painting in the late 19th century. Up other estuaries stand highly picturesque historic towns such as Dinan, Lamballe, Morlaix, Quimper and Vannes, tucked well out of sight from would-be invaders. The celebrated Breton calvaries (outdoor crosses carved with the story of Christ's Passion) are mainly a feature of the Finistère in the west, the most traditional part of Brittany, where Breton (closely related to Welsh) was spoken as the first language by many children right up to the first half of the 20th century. A small hard core keeps it alive, while a tiny minority fights for an independent Breton nation. But most Bretons are content merely to assert good-naturedly their cultural identity; Breton dance, music and the *pardons* – when local saints are taken out of their humid churches for an airing – are still going strong.

In recent decades, stretches of the Breton shore have fallen victim to appalling oil slicks caused by careless tankers. The beaches recover fast, the wildlife not so swiftly. Other portions of the coast have been polluted by farm fertilizers, but environmental issues are now being taken more seriously. Most of Brittany's beaches are of a high standard, while practically the whole coast is a paradise for watersports enthusiasts and sailors – some of the tallest lighthouses in the world warn you off the rocks.

Around the Bay of Mont-St-Michel

The daytime mirages and evening sunsets across the **Bay of Mont-St-Michel** make for some of the most mesmerizing images in Brittany. Although the holy mount itself stands in Normandy (*see* p.206), much of the spectacular bay out of which it rises lies within the Breton border. A semi-submerged forest of wooden posts emerges at low tide, an amazing sight, where mussels really do grow on trees; tractor tours are available from **Le Train Marin** at Cherrueix, **t** 02 99 48 84 88, or a greater variety of tours and information via the **Maison de la Baie** at Le Vivier-sur-Mer, **t** 02 99 48 84 38. **Mont-Dol** is another granite mount rising dramatically from the flats, this one surrounded by bucolic countryside. The tale goes that St Michael fought Satan in this gorgeous spot, and the marks of their legendary struggle have supposedly been left in the rocks.

Dol-de-Bretagne became the seat of one of the seven founding bishoprics of the Breton Church in the Dark Ages. Tradition has it that Samson of South Wales brought Christianity here, and that, centuries later, Nomenoë, one of the most important independence-minded figures in Brittany's history, had himself crowned the first Breton king in 850. The besieging of Dol by William the Conqueror is depicted on the Bayeux tapestry. The troops of his descendant King John burned down its Romanesque **cathedral** in 1204. It was almost completely rebuilt in the 13th century in deeply

Getting Around

Use the **bus** services from St-Malo.

Tourist Information

Dol-de-Bretagne: 3 Grande Rue des Stuarts, **t** 02 99 48 15 37, *www.pays-de-dol.com*.
Cancale: 44 Rue du Port, **t** 02 99 89 63 72, *www.ville-cancale.fr*.

Where to Stay and Eat

Cancale and Around ✉ 35260
****Maisons de Bricourt, **t** 02 99 89 64 76, *bricourt@relaischateaux.com* (*luxury–expensive*). One of the best hotels in northern Brittany, in three delightful locations. Owned by one of the finest chefs in the region, Olivier Roellinger, who runs two restaurants, **Le Relais Gourmand** (*expensive*) and **Le Coquillage** (*moderate*). *Restaurants closed Tues and Wed.*

**La Pointe du Grouin, t 02 99 89 60 55, *www.lapointedugrouin.com* (*moderate*). Headland location to die for, splendid views from rooms and smart restaurant (*expensive–moderate*). *Closed Oct–Mar; rest-aurant closed Tues, and Thurs out of season.*
Le Châtelier, t 02 99 89 81 84, *www.hotelechatelier.com* (*inexpensive*). Modern, converted farm on the D355 to St-Malo – like staying with a charming French family.
Le St-Cast, t 02 99 89 66 08 (*expensive–moderate*). Among the many restaurants looking on to the quays, serving particularly delicious seafood specialities in its conservatory dining room. *Closed Wed, also Tues and Sun eve out of season.*

defensive, sober style. The main façade has virtually no decoration, but one ugly male gargoyle does stand out – said to be a likeness of King John! Inside, dramatic 13th-century stained glass, some of the oldest in Brittany, gives colour to the distant apse – the building is 330ft long. Dol was an important halt on the Tro Breizh, the major pilgrimage route around the cathedrals of Brittany's seven founding saints, but the **Cathédralescope** (open April–Oct 10–7; adm) offers a more general introduction to cathedrals around Europe. Rare Romanesque houses have survived along Dol's main street. South of town the **Menhir de Champ-Dolent** counts among Brittany's most impressive standing stones; legend says it fell from the skies to separate two feuding brothers. A cross was placed on top to Christianize it. The menhir is slowly sinking into the ground; it is said that when the stone disappears altogether, the world will end.

Tourists packed tight as oysters in their bags occupy the quayside below the steep slope of the delightful oyster port of **Cancale**, looking across the vast bay to Mont-St-Michel. Learn about an oyster's life at the **Ferme Marine** (open mid-June–mid-Sept, visits 11, 2 (in English), 3, 5; mid-Feb–mid-June and mid-Sept–Oct, visits Mon–Fri 1pm; adm). The spectacular rocky **Pointe du Grouin** closes off the western end of the bay, l'Ile des Landes with its scaly dragon's back a bird reserve just out to sea. Colette particularly loved the coast west to St-Malo, seductively described in her scandalous novel of adolescent sexual awakening by the sea, Le Blé en herbe (The Ripening Seed).

St-Malo

St-Malo has one of the most spectacular, fiery and controversial histories of any French city. A Celtic and then a Gallo-Roman settlement grew up west of the present town, at Alet, and the first cathedral was possibly built there around 380. With the arrival of immigrants from across the Channel it thrived, and in the 6th century a man called Malo – or Maclou, or perhaps even Mac Low – came from Britain to work miracles. At the start of the Middle Ages, the city shifted to St Malo's rock, and bishop Jean de Chatillon saw to it that the new town was defended by solid ramparts as well as ordering a grand cathedral. St-Malo's fleet became active in both trade and war. But the city cultivated its independent streak down the centuries: 'Ni Français, ni Breton: Malouin suis (Neither French nor Breton, but Malouin)' ran a popular motto.

Countless French explorers set out from St-Malo, most famously Jacques Cartier, who claimed Canada for France in the 1530s. The Iles Malouines (the Falklands) were discovered by its adventurers. St-Malo grew glorious, and notorious. Merchants made fortunes from far-flung trade, including the slave trade. Malouin corsairs made a killing from British and Dutch merchants. In return, fleets were sent to try and destroy St-Malo, but the series of spectacular island forts built around it made attacks diffi-cult. Swashbucklers like Duguay-Trouin and Surcouf became the scourge of the English, but the city's most famous son is France's greatest, most miserable Romantic writer, François-René de Chateaubriand. In the 19th century, time was up for the corsairs and slave-traders: cod-fishing took centre stage, and a radical change in Anglo-French relations brought a very different breed of invaders – tourists. Bombed almost to rubble by the Allies at the end of the war, St-Malo was brilliantly restored.

To appreciate the location of the *ville intra-muros* (the historic walled city), take a bracing walk along the glorious **ramparts**, with their many gates and bastions, their watch-towers and statues of St-Malo's hot-headed heroes. Down below, the streets are dark with tall, tightly packed granite-clad mansions. The **Maison de Corsaire** or **Demeure des Magon de la Lande** (*open Feb–Nov Tues–Sun 10.30–12 and 2.30–6; adm*) is one of the few great 18th-century merchant houses to have survived the Second World War intact. You'll get a good picture of the life of the wealthy traders of the Ancien Régime from the wonderfully enthusiastic guide, even if the place has been split into many flats. Deals were struck, voyages planned, exotic products stored while family life went on, though the Magons only spent around three months of the year in their town house; such wealthy families built estates known as *malouinières* just out of town. Dark and dismal by contrast, the **Musée d'Histoire** (*open Tues–Sun 10–12 and 2–6; adm*), locked away in a grim part of the city's château, tells the story of St-Malo's past in rambling, chaotic fashion.

Getting There and Around

Brittany Ferries and **Condor Ferries** (*see Travel*) operate services from Portsmouth and Poole respectively. **Ryanair** flies to Dinard airport from London-Stansted; a **shuttle bus** then takes you to central St-Malo.

The town has reasonable rail connections across Brittany and Normandy, but the railway **station** is a fair walk from the old centre. For **bus** information around St-Malo, call **t** 02 99 56 06 06; for the wider area, **t** 02 96 68 31 20.

For local **taxis**, Allô Taxis Malouins, **t** 02 99 81 30 30, offers a 24hr service.

Tourist Information

St-Malo: Esplanade St-Vincent, **t** 02 99 56 64 48, *www.saint-malo-tourisme.com*.

Where to Stay and Eat

St-Malo ✉ 35400

★★★★**Grand Hôtel des Thermes**, 100 Bd Hébert, Courtoisville, **t** 02 99 40 75 75, *www.thalas-sosaintmalo.fr* (*luxury–expensive*). The grandest hotel along the long beach east of the historic centre, with a thalassotherapy centre, covered pool and gym. Very elaborate dishes served in the Art Deco dining room of **Le Cap Horn** (*expensive*). *Closed 2 weeks Jan.*

★★★**La Villefromoy**, 7 Bd Hébert, **t** 02 99 40 92 20, *www.villefromoy.fr* (*expensive–moderate*).

On the eastern beach, rooms in a refined 19th-century villa, or in its very comfortable annexe by the garden. *Closed Jan–Feb.*

★★**France Chateaubriand**, Pl Chateaubriand, **t** 02 99 56 66 52, *www.hotel-fr.chateaubriand.com* (*moderate*). Crowds spill out around this characterful hotel at the heart of historic St-Malo.

★★**Univers**, Place Chateaubriand, **t** 02 99 40 89 52, *www.hotel-univers-saintmalo.com* (*moderate*). Also on the square, cheaper, with character and good seafood restaurant.

★★**Le Nautilus**, 9 Rue de la Corne de Cerf, **t** 02 99 40 42 27, *www.lenautilus.com* (*inexpensive*). Central, cheerful little rooms above a loud, young bar.

★**Les Charmettes**, 64 Bd Hébert, Courtoisville, **t** 02 99 56 07 31, *www.hotel-les-charmettes.com* (*inexpensive*). Bargain-hunters' address with just a few rooms looking out to the eastern beach. *Closed mid-Dec–mid-Feb.*

A La Duchesse Anne, Place Guy La Chambre, **t** 02 99 40 85 33 (*expensive*). Classic Malouin seafood restaurant set within the thick town ramparts. *Closed Dec–Jan, Mon lunch and Wed, plus Sun eve out of season.*

Delaunay, 6 Rue Ste-Barbe, **t** 02 99 40 92 46 (*expensive*). Fairly formal, with a good reputation for very fresh dishes. *Closed Sun.*

Le Chasse-Marée, 4 Rue du Grout St-Georges, **t** 02 99 40 85 10 (*moderate*). A real find, a little restaurant away from the crowds where you can taste refined seafood dishes. *Closed Sat lunch and Sun.*

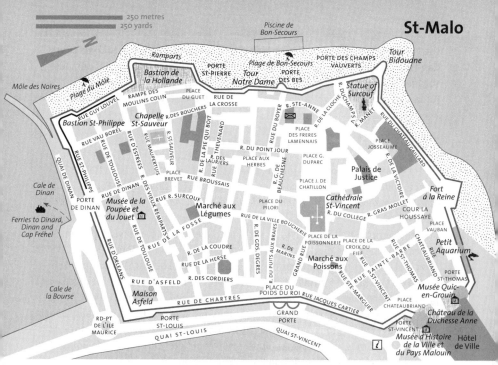

250 metres
250 yards

Piscine de
Bon-Secours

Ramparts

Bastion de
la Hollande

PORTE
ST-PIERRE

Plage de Bon-Secours

Tour
Notre Dame

PORTE
DES BÉS

PORTE DES CHAMPS
VAUVERTS

Tour
Bidouane

Môle des Noires

Plage du Môle

Plage du Môle

RAMPE DES
MOULINS COLIN

PLACE
DU GUET

RUE DE
LA CROSSE

R. STE-ANNE

Statue of
Surcouf

Bastion St-Philippe

Chapelle
St-Sauveur

R. DES BOUCHERS

RUE DU BOYER

R. DE LA CLOCHE

R. DES CHAMPS

R. MANET

RUE DE CHATEAUGAILLARD

RUE GUY LOUVEL

RUE VAU BOREL

R. ST-SAUVEUR

R. DE LA PIE QUI BOIT

R. THEVENARD

PLACE
DES FRERES
LAMENNAIS

PLACE
JOSSEAUME

Bastion St-Philippe

RUE DE TOULOUSE

RUE D'ESTREES

R. DES
LAURIERS

R. DU POINT JOUR

PLACE AUX
HERBES

PLACE G.
DUPARC

R. DE LA VICTOIRE

QUAI DE DINAN

RUE ST-PHILIPPE

RUE DE DINAN

R. MAUPERTUIS

PLACE
BREVET

RUE BROUSSAIS

R. DE
BEAUCHESNE

PLACE J. DE
CHATILLON

Palais de
Justice

Cale de
Dinan

PORTE
DE DINAN

Musée de la
Poupée et
du Jouet

R. DES VIEUX REMPARTS

RUE R. SURCOUF

Marché aux
Légumes

PLACE DU
PILORI

Cathédrale
St-Vincent

R. DU COLLEGE

R. GRAS MOLLET

COUR LA
HOUSSAYE

Fort
á la Reine

Ferries to Dinard,
Dinan and
Cap Fréhel

RUE DE LA FOSSE

RUE DE LA VILLE BOUCHERIE

PLACE
VAUBAN

RUE DE TOULOUSE

RUE D'ORLEANS

R. DE LA COUDRE

RUE DE LA HERSE

R. DES GDS. DEGRES

R. DU PUITS AUX BRAIES

R. DE
MARINS

PLACE DE LA
POISSONNERIE

GRAND RUE

PLACE DE LA
CROIX DU
FIEF

R. SAINTE-BARBE

RUE S.ST-VINCENT

RUE STE-MARGUER.

RUE CHATEAUBRIAND

Petit
Aquarium

PORTE
ST-THOMAS

Cale de
la Bourse

Maison
Asfeld

RUE D'ASFELD

R. DES CORDIERS

RUE DE CHARTRES

PLACE DU
POIDS DU ROI

Marché aux
Poissons

RUE JACQUES CARTIER

PLACE
CHATEAUBRIAND

Musée Quic-
en-Groin

RD-PT
DE L'ILE
MAURICE

PORTE
ST-LOUIS

QUAI ST-LOUIS

GRAND
PORTE

QUAI ST-VINCENT

PORTE
ST-VINCENT

Château de la
Duchesse Anne

Musée d'Histoire
de la Ville et
du Pays Malouin

Hôtel
de Ville

The cathedral's sharp spire acts as a landmark in town as well as out to sea. Black and white photos in the side entrance show the extent of its devastation in the Second World War, although the nave, its vaulting and most of the 13th-century Gothic choir survived the bombs, and you can still make out Romanesque carvings high up on the columns' capitals. God and the saints share the honours with Jacques Cartier, who features in stained glass and is buried in a chapel off the choir. Down below the cathedral you'll find the main shopping quarters; the favourite square is **Place Chateaubriand**, with its wonderful concentration of cafés below the castle.

When the tide recedes, the **beaches** spread generously; ant trails of tourists head by foot for the **islands**. Languishing Romantics visit **Le Grand Bé** to see Chateaubriand's tomb. The two forts you can visit, the **Fort National** (*open June–Sept at low tide during the day; adm*) and the **Fort du Petit Bé** (*open Easter–mid-Nov; adm*), have stunning views back on to the city, as well as interesting stories. You can only reach the atmospheric if barren rocky island of **Cézembre** by boat, from Porte de Dinan.

St-Malo's seaside resort, **Paramé**, stretches east of town behind a glorious arc of beach which unfolds with the tide. The **Musée Jacques Cartier** (*open Mon–Sat 10–12 and 2.30–6; adm*), further east in a small farm-cum-manor house, pays its respects to France's best-known explorer. Nearby, the **Rochers Sculptés de Rothéneuf** (*open daily exc in bad weather: Easter–Sept 9–9; rest of year 10–12 and 2–5.30; adm*) feature cartoonish, legendary corsair figures hewn out of the rock as therapy for a sickly priest, the abbé Fouré, in the late 19th century.

South of St-Malo, beyond the ferry port, **Alet-cum-St-Servan**, the city's older sibling, has plenty of character. The **Mémorial 39/45** (*open April–mid-Nov Tues–Sun*) in Alet's fort recalls St-Malo in the Second World War. The 14th-century **Tour Solidor** guarding the Rance estuary contains the old-fashioned **Musée International du Long-Cours Cap-Hornier** (*open Tues–Sun 10–12 and 2–6; adm*) which tells the story of perilous voyages around Cape Horn. The swish, highly commercial eight-room **Grand Aquarium** (*open daily, July 9–8; Aug 9–10; Sept–June 10–6.30; adm*), lies south of town.

The North Breton Marches

Brittany's eastern frontier is guarded by two of the mightiest medieval forts in France, built in the dark mottled stone of the region. The **Château de Fougères** (*open mid-June–mid-Sept daily 9–7; April–mid-June 9.30–12 and 2–6; mid-Sept–Dec and Feb–Mar 10–12 and 2–5; closed Jan; adm*) brooding down in its valley turns out to be an immense empty shell, with virtually nothing to see behind the surviving thirteen towers. But the great lengths of walls, the machicolations and loopholes, and the conical slate roofs make for a perfect picture of medieval defence. Although often described as a Breton frontier castle, for much of the medieval period the place was a pawn in local power games. Fougères and its castle saw all too much action in the Chouannerie too, the violent anti-Revolutionary, pro-Catholic and pro-royalist uprising in which so many Bretons fought against the new French Republic in the 1790s. Visitors sometimes miss Fougères' upper town completely. Known as the **Bourg Neuf**, it is in fact packed with historic buildings, including one of the oldest belfries in the province, a sign of early mercantile independence, and the church of St-Léonard, whose vertigo-inducing tower you can climb. Among the elegant 18th-century façades, the **Musée Emmanuel de La Villéon** (*open 15 June–15 Sept daily 10–12.30 and 2.30–6; rest of year Wed–Sun 10–12 and 2–5; adm*) presents the works of a local artist who painted sensitive Impressionistic scenes of Brittany and the Breton poor.

Getting Around

TGV high-speed **trains** from Paris to Rennes occasionally stop at Vitré.
For Fougères area **bus** services, call **t** 02 99 99 02 37, for Vitré, **t** 02 99 26 16 00.

Tourist Information

Fougères: 2 Rue Nationale, **t** 02 99 94 12 20, *www.ot-fougeres.fr.*
Vitré: Place Général de Gaulle, **t** 02 99 75 04 46, *www.ot-vitre.fr.*

Where to Stay and Eat

Fougères ✉ 35300
****Le Balzac**, 15 Rue Nationale, **t** 02 99 99 42 46 (*inexpensive*). Well positioned in a grand house in the upper town, with decent rooms.

Les Vins et une Fourchette, 1 Rue de la Fourchette (*moderate*). By the castle, serving interesting dishes in the amusingly converted little rooms of a former butcher's shop. *Closed Sun and Mon.*

Vitré ✉ 35500

****Le Minotel**, 47 Rue Poterie, **t** 02 99 75 11 11 (*inexpensive*). Well located in the historic town; the rooms have been renovated but are unimaginative.
Auberge St-Louis, 31 Rue Notre-Dame, **t** 02 99 75 28 28 (*moderate*). A façade covered with *fleurs de lys*, a refined wood interior and an appealing terrace, with fine seafood and local produce. *Closed Sun eve and Mon.*
Taverne de l'Ecu, 12 Rue de la Baudrairie, **t** 02 99 75 11 09 (*moderate*). Going since the 15th century apparently, the cuisine now combining Mediterranean and Breton touches. *Closed Tues and Wed.*

Press on into the towering beech woods northwest of Fougères to visit the **Parc Floral de Haute Bretagne** (*open Mar–mid-Nov*) at the **Château de la Foltière**, beautifully landscaped gardens created from nothing by an impassioned engineer.

South of Fougères, **Vitré** boasts a picturesque turreted triangular castle built in the same speckled stone as the town's array of 15th- and 16th-century houses. The **château** (*open July–Sept daily 10–6; April–June daily 10–12 and 2–5.30; Oct–Mar Mon and Wed–Fri 2–5.30; adm*) has been much tampered with, but while visiting the mixed bag of a museum within you get to clamber up and down parts of the ramparts.

Rennes

Rennes, the capital of Brittany, is full of vitality – not surprisingly, with up to 50,000 students and researchers milling around its fine old streets and squares packed with bars, *bistrots* and bookshops. Historically, the early Celtic settlement here lay at an obvious crossing of trade routes, where the Ille and Vilaine rivers meet (although the Vilaine has long been covered by a road). Armorica (ancient Brittany) was divided between five main tribes by the time the Romans arrived, the Riedones settled

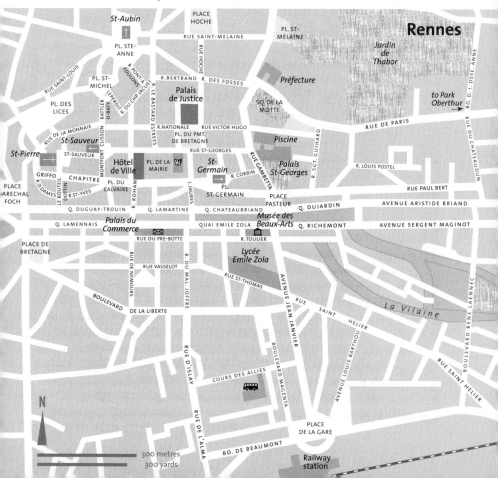

Getting Around

The city has good **rail** links in all directions, and with Paris (also reachable by **air**).

Tourist Information

Rennes: 11 Rue St-Yves, **t** 02 99 67 11 11, *www.ville-rennes.fr*.

Where to Stay and Eat

Rennes ✉ 35000

****Le Coq-Gadby**, 156 Rue d'Antrain, **t** 02 99 38 05 55, *www.lecoq-gadby.com* (*expensive*). North of the centre, with garden and pool. Fine restaurant. *Restaurant closed Sun*.

***Mercure Pré Botté**, Rue Paul Louis Courier, **t** 02 99 78 82 20, *H1056@accor-hotels.com* (*expensive*). Chain hotel, but in a great building in the centre.

****Hotel des Lices**, 7 Place des Lices, **t** 02 99 79 14 81, *www.hotel-des-lices.com* (*moderate–inexpensive*). A few of the rooms overlook Rennes' most spectacular square.

****Le Victor Hugo**, 14 Rue Victor Hugo, **t** 02 99 38 85 33 (*inexpensive*). Intimate little hotel along a fine street full of antiques shops.

***Hotel de Léon**, 15 Rue de Léon, **t** 02 99 30 55 28 (*inexpensive*). Characterful bargain.

L'Escu de Runfao, 11 Rue du Chapitre, **t** 02 99 79 13 10 (*expensive*). In a beautiful traditional 16th-century house; cuisine with daring touches. *Closed Sat lunch and Sun eve*.

Café Breton, 14 Rue Nantaise, **t** 02 99 30 74 95 (*cheap*). Stylish. *Closed Sun*.

Le Bocal Pty Resto, 6 Rue d'Argentré, **t** 02 99 78 34 10 (*cheap*). Beautiful, bohemian café for a good meal. *Closed Sat lunch, Sun and Mon*.

around Rennes. In the Dark Ages, when the Franks pressed west, the area became part of their buffer zone guarding against the fearsome Bretons. Rushing on to the Hundred Years War, the most feared of all Breton warriors, Bertrand du Guesclin, won his spurs here in a legendary jousting competition; he went on to smash English armies around France. Among the major religious figures associated with Rennes, St Melaine stands out, spreading the Benedictine rule across Brittany.

From the 16th century, Rennes became the seat of the Parlement de Bretagne, the aristocratically run regional law court. But at various times the city and its leaders were at the centre of major protests, notably in the 1675 Révolte du Papier Timbré, against a crippling tax on all official documents. The Parlement was moved to Vannes for 15 years by way of punishment. Major misfortune followed in the terrible fire of 1720, when much of the centre went up in flames. Carefully planned new quarters arose. The Breton Parlement challenged royal authority just before the Revolution; the Crown tried to dissolve the Parlement in 1788, and an anti-royalist riot ensued, the melodramatic writer Chateaubriand claiming that the first blood of the Revolution was shed here. However, with the advent of Republicanism, the anti-Revolutionary Chouan became active in town. Rennes had gained a university in the 18th century, but it was at the Lycée Zola that Jewish scapegoat Alfred Dreyfus underwent his second trial in 1899, condemned again by the military, although President Loubet saw to his pardoning a few days later. The Breton capital today is highly regarded for its high-tech research centres and also hosts a couple of major modern music festivals.

The name and shape of **Place des Lices** recall medieval jousts, and this spectacular, bustling square is overseen by a precarious-looking collection of lofty timberframe houses, dating from the mid-17th century. Stylish 19th-century covered markets occupy the centre of the square. South, atmospheric old streets surround the **Cathédrale St-Pierre**, built on the site of a Gallo-Roman temple, but only dating back to 1560; behind the front, it's all glistening 18th- and 19th-century decoration. Paintings of Breton saints line the walls. The ornately gilded earlier Flemish altarpiece in one chapel fits in well. The nearby church of **St-Sauveur** looks soberly classical on the outside, but inside an absurdly overdone baldaquin dominates, set off by vulgar modern stained glass. Closer to the covered Vilaine, the **Chapelle St-Yves** (*open summer Mon–Sat 9–7; winter 9–6; Sun and public hols 11–6*) and its surrounding buildings contain the tourist office and a permanent exhibition on Rennes.

North of Place des Lices, atmospheric old squares provide popular meeting places. Lively, pretty **Place St-Michel** is packed with bars and cafés. Tucked away nearby, the timberframe houses of **Place du Champ Jacquet** look down on a statue of Leperdit, heroic mayor of Rennes during the Revolution, who managed to curb the violent excesses with rhetoric. Just north, **Place Ste-Anne** counts among the busiest social hubs in town, overseen by the church of St-Aubin. Trendy **Rue St-Malo** leads off it.

In contrast to the quirky old squares to the west, controlled French classicism rules in the squares to the east. On **Place de la Mairie**, the town hall's concave curve contrasts dramatically with the bulging front of the theatre. Much more sober and serious, **Place du Parlement de Bretagne** was the address of the former home of the law courts of Brittany, built and sumptuously decorated in the Ancien Régime. In a terrible accident in 1984, when a fishemen's demonstration got out of hand, much of the Parlement burnt down, but it has slowly been restored.

Overblown 19th-century buildings line the south bank where the Vilaine once ran openly. One houses the splendid **Musée des Beaux-Arts** (*open Wed–Mon 10–12 and 2–6; closed Tues and public hols*), a major fine arts collection which Rennes acquired thanks to the plunderings of private and foreign collections during the Revolution and the Napoleonic Empire. Violence proves an alarmingly frequent theme on many of the canvases, but the place's most famous painting is Georges de la Tour's most peaceful and touching *Le Nouveau-né*, depicting a glowing new-born baby. The 19th-century collections are the first to include Breton subjects, the works by Bernard and Sérusier eclipsing those by Gauguin and Picasso.

The renovated **Musée de Bretagne** (*open as Beaux-Arts; adm*) has recently moved to a cutting-edge new building by leading contemporary architect Christian de Porzamparc. Its collections cover the history of Brittany from prehistoric times to the present with a large array of artefacts. To find a restful, shaded spot near the centre, head north up the hillside to the genteel **Jardin du Thabor** public gardens, reached from the western side by the smart buildings of the former monastery of St-Melaine.

Around Rennes and North to Dinan

The Forest of Paimpont, or Brocéliande

Arthurian legend has triumphed over history in the purple Forest of Paimpont (30km west of Rennes – follow signs for Plélan-le-Grand). Arthurian aficionados call it Brocéliande, for its legends focus on Merlin and Viviane, with whom the magician falls passionately and fatefully in love. He conjures up a beautiful castle for Viviane,

Getting Around

Limited **bus** services run between Rennes and these parts – **t** 02 99 30 87 80, or **t** 02 97 01 22 10. Dinard airport lies not far to the north. Dinan is on a **railway** line between Dol and St-Brieuc. For Dinan local bus services, contact CAT, **t** 02 96 68 31 20. Hire a **boat** on the Rance at Dinan.

Tourist Information

Paimpont: 5 Esplanade Brocéliande, **t** 02 99 07 84 23, *syndicat-dinitiativepaimpont@ wanadoo.fr*.
Tréhorenteuc: Place Abbé Gillard, **t** 02 97 93 05 12, *valsansretour@club.internet.fr*.
Bécherel: **t** 02 99 66 75 23, *www.becherel.com*.
Combourg: **t** 02 99 73 13 93, *www.combourg.org*.
Bazouges-la-Pérouse: **t** 02 99 97 40 94, *tourisme.baz@voila.fr*.
Dinan: 6 Rue de l'Horloge, **t** 02 96 87 69 76, *www.dinan-tourisme.com*.

Where to Stay and Eat

Paimpont ✉ 35380

★★**Relais de Brocéliande**, 5 Rue des Forges, **t** 02 99 07 81 07, *www.le-relais-de-broceliande.fr* (*inexpensive*). Pretty, traditional provincial hotel with fine restaurant (*expensive–moderate*) for seafood and wild boar.

Combourg ✉ 35270

★★**Hôtel du Château**, 1 Place Chateaubriand, **t** 02 99 73 00 38, *hotelduchateau@chateaux-hotels.com* (*expensive–moderate*). Grand house with pleasing rooms, good restaurant and terrace overlooking the main square and the lake. *Closed most of Jan; restaurant closed Sat lunch, Sun eve and Mon lunch.*
★★**Hôtel du Lac**, 2 Place Chateaubriand, **t** 02 99 73 05 65, *www.Hotel-Restaurantdulac.com* (*inexpensive*). Practical modern rooms overlooking the water, plus reliable restaurant (*moderate*). *Closed Feb, and Oct–Mar; restaurant closed Fri lunch.*

Dinan ✉ 22100

★★★**Hôtel d'Avaugour**, 1 Place du Champ Clos, **t** 02 96 39 07 49, *www.avaugourhotel.com* (*luxury–moderate*). Stylishly redecorated, historic hotel on the largest of Dinan's squares, the best rooms giving on to the charming garden in the former ramparts. *Closed mid-Nov–mid-Dec and Jan–Feb.*
★★**Hôtel d'Arvor**, 5 Rue Pavie, **t** 02 96 39 21 22 (*inexpensive*). On the site of a former Jacobin monastery, although the rooms are comfortably modern. *Closed Jan.*
Au Vieux St-Sauveur, 21 Place St-Sauveur, **t** 02 96 85 30 20 (*inexpensive*). Nice rooms above a pub in a splendid medieval house overlooking a wonderful square.
Chez la Mère Pourcel, 3 Place des Merciers, **t** 02 96 39 03 80 (*expensive–moderate*). Smart dining in a timberframe house, with the most impressive 16th-century wooden staircase . *Closed Feb, Sun eve and Mon.*
Relais des Corsaires, 3 Rue du Quai, **t** 02 96 39 40 17 (*moderate*). A merry seafood restaurant down at the portside, in one of the prettiest old houses of lower Dinan. *Closed Mon eve and Tues.*

hidden underwater, making her the Lady of the Lake. She takes in a baby boy she finds on the banks, heroic Lancelot du Lac. Arthur's bitter and twisted half-sister Morgane le Fay also features large: she turns evil after her lover Guyomart is unfaithful to her, and in her secret valley in Brocéliande traps knights who have been disloyal to their ladies. They are showered with all the pleasures they could wish for, but are deprived of their freedom and, if they try to escape, terrifying visions stop them in their tracks. Lancelot eventually comes to their rescue. To get your bearings in the forest head first for **Paimpont**, a purple village with a substantial abbey standing by a mirror-like lake. Around Brocéliande's much-reduced woodlands, **Comper** has been 'identified' as the place where Merlin built Viviane her invisible underwater palace, while the real château there has become the jumbled **Centre de l'Imaginaire Arthurien** (*open*

July–Sept Thurs–Tues 10–7; April–June and Oct Thurs–Mon 10–5.30; adm), with exhibitions on the legends. The remnants of a Neolithic burial site have been turned into 'Merlin's tomb'. Morgane le Fay's secret valley, the **Val Sans Retour** (Valley of No Return), lies just south of Arthur-obsessed **Tréhorenteuc**, reached by a purple track.

Romantic Châteaux between Rennes and Dinan

West of Hédé up the N137, at the rickety medieval **Château de Montmuran** (*open June–Sept Sun–Fri 2–6; adm*) with its connections with the warrior Du Guesclin, you're presented with the Romantic version of history. In the village of **Les Iffs** next door, admire the monkeying Gothic sculptures and refined Renaissance windows. Hilltop **Bécherel** to the west may only have fragments of its fortifications left, but the grand old linen merchants' houses below have survived. Second-hand books provide the main trade today, and Bécherel champions Breton culture. West of town, the grounds of the Ancien Régime **Château de Caradeuc** (*open July–Aug daily 12–6; April–June and Sept–Oct weekends and public hols 2–6; adm*) contain some preposterous garden ornaments, including, ironically, a rare statue of ill-fated Louis XVI, since one Marquis de Caradeuc famously defied the royal-appointed governor of Brittany in the 1760s.

The park of the **Château de la Bourbansais** (*open April–Sept daily 10–7; rest of year 2–6; adm*) up the N137 looks elegant, but the château proves more beautiful still in its speckled schist, built with a careful 16th-century regard for symmetry. You can visit a series of exquisitely panelled Louis XVI-style rooms inside, the masterpiece of the carpenter Mancelle whose son saved them from Revolutionary violence by plying the Republican troops who came to the château with wine. There is a little zoo too.

The medieval towers of the sinister **Château de Combourg** (*open Easter–Oct Sun–Fri 2–5.30; July and Aug also open Sat; park open daily 10–12; adm*) rise above the lake beside the modest town of Combourg. Chateaubriand (*see* 'St-Malo'), who spent some of his unhappy childhood here, described it vividly in his memoirs. His father, who made his fortune from corsair and slave-trading expeditions from St-Malo, dominated this house with his terrifying moods. Their stories are retold on the tour round the chambers fancifully restored in neo-Gothic style. East, avant-garde artists invade the sleepy hilltop village of **Bazouges-la-Pérouse** in summer, while the nearby **Château de la Ballue** also displays contemporary art in playful Baroque gardens.

Dinan

The views from Dinan's **Tour du Gouverneur** take in much of the staggering three kilometres of fortified walls and towers which still encircle the historic upper town. The **Château de Dinan** (*open June–Sept daily 9–7; Feb–May and Oct–Dec Wed–Mon 9–7; closed Jan; adm*) is a slightly misleading name for a soaring keep along the ramparts, built for Duke Jean IV of Brittany late in the 14th century. Exhibits on Dinan's history fill the different levels, while the dank basement of neighbouring **Tour de Coëtquen** contains evocative medieval tomb effigies. The **Tour de l'Horloge**, Dinan's central belfry, dates from the 15th century. Almost kissing dromedaries count among the decorations in Gothic **St-Sauveur** on its lovely square. The story goes that in the 12th century the crusader Riwallon le Roux made a vow that he would build a church if he returned alive from Arab imprisonment, which he evidently did, with vivid memories. The heart of the medieval warlord Bertrand du Guesclin lies in a chest in the north transept. He won a famous joust with one Thomas of Canterbury here in the Hundred Years War, as recalled on the square named after him. Other major religious buildings stand out in the upper town. A winding street of timberframe houses descends to lower Dinan, where you can take a delightful walk or boat trip along the Rance.

In a peaceful village a short way south, a palm tree grows in the middle of patterned hydrangeas in the cloister of the enchanting **abbey of Léhon**.

The Côte d'Emeraude and the Bay of St-Brieuc

Delightful resorts with glorious sandy beaches tucked under the cliffs line the first half of the stretch of Breton shore known as the Emerald Coast. To the west, this coast becomes much more rugged and unspoilt. Coming to the immense Bay of St-Brieuc, the views almost match those across the Bay of Mont-St-Michel.

West from Dinard

We have one Mrs Faber to thank for the still seductive if slightly jaded **Dinard**. She settled on this almost virgin coast in the 1850s, and helped create St-Malo's spouse across the Rance estuary. By the turn of the century royalty swanned around town and the wealthy built palatial villas. In the first half of the 20th century the place attracted artists too, including Picasso. Sadly, several of the swanky buildings on the promenade behind the central Plage de l'Ecluse have been destroyed, but there is still action aplenty, with a casino, pools and the beach. However, the most exhilarating parts of Dinard are its coastal paths. Head round the **Pointe du Moulinet** for a stunning view of St-Malo. Beyond the landing stage for the ferry you come to the romantic **Promenade du Clair de Lune**. Steps lead steeply up to a diminutive **aquarium** (*open mid-May–mid-Sept Mon–Sat 10.30–12.30 and 3.30–7.30, Sun 2.30–7.30; adm*), in a circular 1930s building. Heading west, the coastal path past the **Pointe de la Malouinet** to **St-Enogat** provides one of the most unforgettable walks in northern Brittany.

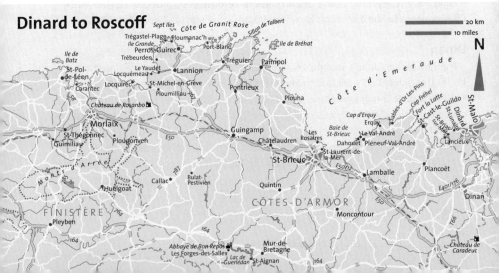

Dinard to Roscoff

Getting There and Around

Ryanair offers cheap **flights** from London-Stansted to Dinard-Pleurtuit. Plancoët, Yffiniac and St-Brieuc have **railway** stations, but public transport along the coast is limited; for details, contact CAT, **t** 02 96 68 31 20.

Tourist Information

Dinard: 2 Bd Féart, **t** 02 99 46 94 12, *www.ville-dinard.fr.*
St-Lunaire: Bd du Général de Gaulle, **t** 02 99 46 31 09, *otsi.stlunaire@worldonline.fr.*
St-Cast-le-Guildo: Place Charles de Gaulle, **t** 02 96 41 81 52, *www.ot-st-cast-le-guildo.fr.*
Erquy: Bd de la Mer, **t** 02 96 72 30 12, *tourisme.erquy@wanadoo.fr.*
Pléneuf-Le Val-André: Cours W.- Churchill, **t** 02 96 72 20 55, *www.val-andre.org.*

Where to Stay and Eat

Dinard ✉ 35800

★★★★Grand Hôtel Barrière, 46 Av George V, **t** 02 99 88 26 26, *www.lucienbarriere.com* (*luxury–expensive*). Distinguished address in town, aloof above the Rance promenade, with elegant rooms. Pool and cocktail bar as well as the **George V** restaurant (*expensive*). *Closed Nov–late Mar.*
★★★Villa Reine Hortense, 19 Rue de la Malouine, **t** 02 99 46 54 31, *www.villa-reine-hortense.com* (*luxury–very expensive*). Another grand old Dinard establishment.

Richly furnished within, many rooms looking out to sea. *Closed Oct–Nov.*
★★★Novotel Thalassa, Av Château Hébert, **t** 02 99 16 78 10, *www.H1114@accor-hotels.com* (*expensive*). A monster of a new luxury health hotel with seawater treatments, above St-Enogat's rocks. Rooms have splendid sea views; the restaurant provides both diet and gastronomic meals. Pool.
★★Printania, 5 Av George V, **t** 02 99 46 13 07, *www.printaniahotel.com* (*moderate*). Looking over to St-Malo from above the Rance, the rooms have fine views. The restaurant is slightly kitsch, with Breton furniture and waiters in Breton dress. *Closed late-Nov–mid-Mar.*
★Hôtel du Prieuré, 1 Place du Général de Gaulle, **t** 02 99 46 13 74 (*inexpensive*). Its seven rooms and its seafood restaurant (*moderate*) have superb views on to Dinard's eastern beach. *Closed Jan; restaurant closed Sun eve and Mon out of season.*
La Salle à Manger, 25 Bd Féart, **t** 02 99 16 07 95 (*expensive*). Gastronomic restaurant; lobster from its own tank is a speciality.

Lancieux ✉ 22770

★★★Hôtel des Bains, 20 Rue du Poncel, **t** 02 96 86 31 33, *Bertrand.Mehouas@wanadoo.fr* (*moderate*). Neat small hotel with comfortable modern rooms, just 200m from beach. Garden. Restaurant de la Mer opposite.

Plancoët ✉ 22130

★★★★Hôtel l'Ecrin, 20 Les Quais, Plancoët, **t** 02 96 84 10 24, *ecrin@chateauxhotels.com*

Debussy was apparently inspired to write *La Mer* at **St-Lunaire**. The Belle Epoque Grand Hotel still dominates the main beach but, as the name of the resort indicates, a Celtic saint got here well before the property developers. The legend goes that dense fog greeted Lunaire and his companions in the 6th century. Impatient to find land, Lunaire took out his sword and cut through the fog – with God's help, the horizon suddenly opened up before him. The coast all around **St-Briac** is cluttered with posh villas. Many late 19th-century artists paid homage to the place, among them Renoir, Signac and Emile Bernard. The village itself looks out on to the Frémur estuary.

The first part of the *département* of the Côtes d'Armor's shoreline across the Frémur estuary is littered with lovely holiday homes around the resort of **Lancieux**. Ruddy streaks of colour stain some of Lancieux's rocks – according to legend a Dark Ages saint arrived here to be battered by the pagans he tried to convert to Christianity, and the blood he shed reddened the rocks. The 19th century is well preserved in corners of

(*expensive*). A luxury establishment with just a few rooms, best-known for its excellent but not overfussy restaurant, **Chez Crouzil** (*very expensive*). *Closed early Jan–Feb; restaurant closed Mon, and Sun eve and Tues lunch out of season.*

St-Cast-le-Guildo ✉ 22380

★★★Les Arcades, 15 Rue du Duc d'Aiguillon, t 02 96 41 80 50 (*moderate*). Comfortable quiet rooms, some with sea views. *Closed Oct–Mar; restaurant closed Sun eve and Mon out of season.*

★★Hôtel Les Mielles, 3 Rue du Duc d'Aiguillon, t 02 96 41 80 95 (*inexpensive*). Cheaper sister of the above.

Sables-d'Or-les-Pins/Fréhel ✉ 22240

★★★La Voile d'Or, Allée des Acacias, t 02 96 41 42 49, *la-voile-dor@wanadoo.fr* (*expensive–moderate*). Contemporary architecture by the water, with slick rooms. Reputed, creative restaurant (*very expensive–expensive*). *Closed late Nov–late Feb.*

★★Manoir St-Michel, Le Carquois, t 02 96 41 48 87 (*expensive–moderate*). North of the resort, appealing hotel with a fine Breton exterior and spacious, well-furnished rooms. *Closed Nov–Mar.*

★★Hôtel de Diane, t 02 96 41 42 07, *www.hotel-diane.fr* (*moderate–inexpensive*). Period charm in the resort itself.

Erquy ✉ 22430

★★Le Relais, 60 Rue du Port, t 02 96 72 32 60 (*inexpensive*). Near the port, with lovely views across the bay and a popular seafood restaurant (*moderate*).

★★Beauséjour, 21 Rue de la Corniche, t 02 96 72 30 39, *hotel.beausejour@wanadoo.fr* (*inexpensive*). A quiet, well-kept hotel a bit above the port, with sea views. *Closed early Jan and late Feb.*

L'Escurial, t 02 96 72 31 56 (*expensive*). Imaginative dishes served on the seafront. *Closed Mon, and out of season Sun eve.*

Le Relais St-Aubin, Route de la Bouillie, St-Aubin, t 02 96 72 13 22. A refined restaurant (*moderate*) 3km inland, with a blissfully calm setting, in a converted 17th-century priory, some dishes cooked in the fireplace. Leafy garden. *Restaurant closed Mon.*

Pléneuf/Le Val-André ✉ 22370

Domaine du Val, 22400 Planguenoual, t 02 96 32 75 40, *www.chateau-du-val.com* (*expensive–moderate*). Large, pleasant hotel in a restored castle and outbuildings just above the coast, with all mod cons including covered pool and tennis court. Good, pricey restaurant (*expensive*) with huge wine list.

★★Grand Hôtel, 80 Rue Amiral Charner, t 02 96 72 20 56, *www.grand-hotel-val-andre.fr* (*moderate*). In the resort itself, its comfortable rooms separated from the beach by a few pines. Seafood dominates on the menus. *Closed Jan; restaurant closed Mon lunch.*

Au Biniou, 121 Rue Clemenceau, t 02 96 72 24 35 (*moderate*). Exotic touches added to Breton produce. *Closed Feb, and Tues eve and Wed out of season.*

St-Jacut, a resort with many fine beaches on its thin finger of a promontory, although it has much older roots. The now-ruined but still impressive **Château du Guildo** once guarded the entrance to the Arguenon river. **St-Cast** beyond boasts seven beaches, while its old fishermen's quarter is now a picturesque shopping area.

The wild heathery heaths of Cap Fréhel come as a surprise. Isolated on its promontory, stung by winter storms, **Fort La Latte** (*open April–Sept daily 10–12.30 and 2.30–6.30; rest of year weekends and public hols only 2.30–5.30; adm*), the most sensational of Brittany's coastal castles, went up largely in the 14th century, but significant parts date from the 17th. The colours of the rocks are almost as sensational as the views as you approach. **Sables-d'Or-les-Pins**, dreamed up by developers in the 1920s, was never finished, but retains some of its character by a glorious stretch of golden beach.

Whereas the coast along the Baie du Mont-St-Michel is flat as a pancake, cliffs line the shores of the equally spectacular **Baie de St-Brieuc**, where every fishing port-cum-beach resort has its own marina. The magnetic triangular **Ile Verdelet** is this bay's answer to Mont-St-Michel, drawing your attention, although it's reserved for birds.

The Celts once guarded this coastline from the splendid vantage point of **Cap d'Erquy** above the port of **Erquy**. The local pink rocks have long been quarried – the stone went into the building of the Arc de Triomphe. With the dramatic Ile Verdelet at one end of its long, broad sandy beach, **Le Val-André** was chosen as the site for a big new resort in the 1880s, and its promenade stretches some 2½ kilometres. **Dahouët**, a secretive port with a glitzy new marina hides away behind Pointe de la Guette. The Vikings hid here too during their 9th-century raids on the Breton coast, while later Dahouët became one of the first French ports from which boats left for the gruelling cod-fishing expeditions off Newfoundland, at the start of the 16th century. The coast down from Dahouët, with St-Brieuc coming into view at the bottom of the bay, is little known by Breton standards. Steep roads and paths lead down to sandy coves between the cliffs. The **Dunes de Bon Abri** count among some of the most gorgeous in Brittany. At low tide, the mussel-farming tractors go in and out from these dunes; dogs race joyfully up and down; and trotting horses train on the sands, pulling their comical chariots.

Inland from St-Brieuc

A trio of historic towns, Lamballe, Moncontour and Quintin, lie within easy enough reach of the coast, and make good bases for exploring inland, rural Côtes d'Armor.

Once capital of the quarrelsome county of Penthièvre, **Lamballe** is one of Brittany's most attractive, but also most overlooked, market towns. Its **Musée Mathurin Méheut** (*open June–Sept Mon–Sat 10–12 and 2.30–6.30; rest of year Tues, Fri and Sat 2–5; adm*) shows the obsessive love Méheut (1882–1958) had for Brittany. The museum occupies part of the timberframe Maison du Bourreau, tucked in a corner off the sloping Place du Martray. Admire Breton horses in the magnificent, central 19th-century **Lamballe Haras** or Stud Farm (*open mid-June–mid-Sept daily 10.30–12.30 and 2–6; Feb–mid-June and mid-Sept–mid-Nov Wed and weekends 2–5; adm*). Developed for strength, they served in the First World War pulling artillery. Ironically, it's thanks to the French predilection for horse meat that the stocky breeds of *postiers* have survived.

Picture-postcard **Moncontour** looks like an escapee from the Dordogne. It was long a stronghold of the lords of Penthièvre, and the prosperity of its linen merchants explains the fine 17th- and 18th-century houses by the outsized Baroque façade of St-Mathurin. Its pinnacled belfry was a quirky 20th-century addition; some of the splendid old stained-glass windows date back to the 1500s.

As at Moncontour, the hill at **Quintin** provided an excellent site for the lords of Penthièvre to fortify in medieval times. A first castle went up at the start of the 13th century, guarding what was a major inland route through northern Brittany, and subsequent buildings followed down the centuries, each either devastated by war or left incomplete through lack of resources. The scrappy bits and pieces dominate one side of town. The displays inside are a bit scrappy too, but at least the Bagneux family that owns the **Château de Quintin** (*open mid-June–mid-Sept daily 10.30–12.30 and 2–6; Easter–mid-June and mid-Sept–Oct Wed–Mon 2–6; closed Nov–Easter; adm*)

Getting Around

St-Brieuc has an **airport** for internal flights. Lamballe is on the high-speed TGV **rail** line between Paris and Brest.

For **bus** services from St-Brieuc to the three towns, contact CAT, **t** 02 96 68 31 20.

Tourist Information

Lamballe: Maison du Bourreau, Place du Martray, **t** 02 96 31 05 38, *otsi.lamballe@netcourrier.com*.
Moncontour: 4 Place de la Carrière, **t** 02 96 73 49 57, *www.pays-moncontour.com*.
Quintin: Place 1830, **t** 02 96 74 01 51, *www.quintin.fr*.
Mûr-de-Bretagne: Place de l'Eglise, **t** 02 96 28 51 41, *otsi.guerledan@wanadoo.fr*.

Where to Stay and Eat

Lamballe ⊠ 22400

Le Tenos, 14 Rue Notre-Dame, **t** 02 96 31 00 41 (*inexpensive*). Birthplace of the artist Mathurin Méheut, now a B&B.

Quintin ⊠ 22800

Le Clos du Prince, 10 Rue Croix-Jarrots, **t** 02 96 74 93 03 (*moderate*). Unforgettable B&B, beautifully decorated with antiques.

Mûr-de-Bretagne and Caurel ⊠ 22530

★★★Auberge Grand'Maison, 1 Rue Léon le Cerf, **t** 02 96 28 51 10 (*moderate*). The best in the area, with superlative food (*expensive*). *Closed Sun eve and Mon, Oct and early Mar.*
★★Le Relais du Lac, **t** 02 96 67 11 09 (*inexpensive*). In a converted posting inn nearby, in the lakeside village of Caurel. Restaurant.

runs it with bounding enthusiasm. Quintin has fine old streets of linen merchants' mansions, while the vast 19th-century church with its soaring spire claims a truly exceptional piece of cloth: a fragment of the Virgin's girdle. Among Quintin's lovely squares, **Place 1830** has all the timberframe charm you could wish for. The **Grand'Rue**, the principal shopping street, leads to elegant cobbled **Place du Martray**.

Inland, the splendid serpentine **Lac de Guerlédan**, in the geographical heart of Brittany, only dates from the 1920s, but some picturesque historic sites stand around it. In the pretty town of **Mûr-de-Bretagne** the main attraction is Chapelle Ste-Suzanne, its ceiling covered with quirky 18th-century paintings. The lake's main resort, **Beaurivage**, offers boating and an artificial beach. The medieval church of **St-Aignan**, to the east, contains several treasures. West, the ruins of the **Abbey of Bon Repos** are eclipsed in beauty by **Les Forges-des-Salles** (*open July–Aug daily 2–6.30; Easter–June and Sept–Oct weekends 2–6.30; adm*), an Ancien Régime iron-making village.

The Goëlo Coast

The Goëlo coast stretches up the western side of the Bay of St-Brieuc. **St-Brieuc** was founded by a Welshman, one of the seven saints credited with establishing the first Celtic bishoprics of Brittany. It may be the capital of the Côtes d'Armor but only the odd trace of its history survives, notably its defensive medieval cathedral. From the west of town, set off on a glorious roller-coaster ride up and down the cliffs of the Côte du Goëlo via the swanky villas and rough shacks of **St-Laurent-de-la-Mer**, and **Les Rosaires**, where the élite do their dog-jog along the promenade. Head inland via Trégomeur with its valley zoo to arrive at **Châtelaudren**, where the **Chapelle Notre-Dame-du-Tertre** (*open July and Aug only, Mon–Sat 10–12 and 4–7; adm*) is decorated with an astonishing array of late-Gothic paintings, biblical scenes featuring across the ceiling, the harrowing stories of St Marguerite and St Fiacre in the side chapel.

Back on the Goëlo coast, **Binic** had one of the most important cod-fishing fleets in 19th-century Brittany. A few old houses and streets recall those days, but the place has long been converted to tourism – its port has been turned in good part into a yacht harbour. **St-Quay-Portrieux** is a still larger port-cum-resort. Out to sea, the smattering of islets known as the Rochers de St-Quay add character to the seascape.

The Breton-speaking frontier lies around **Plouha**, which at once feels more archetypally Breton. Some of the tallest cliffs in the region, 330ft (100m) high, plunge down to flat stretches of sand or tiny makeshift harbours: at **Gwin Zégal** the little boats are simply tied up to posts planted in the waters. The chapel of **Kermaria-in-Isquit** (west of Plouha village) is decorated with a striking *Danse macabre* from *c.* 1490, the boogying skeletons trapping people from all walks of life in a wild disco dance.

The rocky chaos makes it look as if a hailstorm of meteorites has just rained down on the coast at **Paimpol**. This port is known across France for its tough maritime past, its name synonymous with the demeaning life of the Breton fishermen exploited by

Getting Around

A **bus** service runs from St-Brieuc to Paimpol via Binic, St-Quay-Portrieux and Plouha, **t** 02 96 68 31 20. Book **ferry** tickets to the Ile de Bréhat in advance via Les Vedettes de Bréhat, **t** 02 96 55 79 50, *www.vedettesdebrehat.com.*

Tourist Information

St-Brieuc: 7 Rue St-Guéno, **t** 02 96 33 32 50, *www.baiedesaintbrieuc.com.*
Châtelaudren: 2 Rue des Sapeurs Pompiers, **t** 02 96 74 12 02.
Binic: Av du Gén-de-Gaulle, **t** 02 96 73 60 12, *officedetourismedebinic@wanadoo.fr.*
St-Quay-Portrieux: 17 bis Rue Jeanne-d'Arc, **t** 02 96 70 40 64, *www.saintquayportrieux.com.*
Paimpol: Place de la République, **t** 02 96 20 83 16, *tourisme@paimpol-goelo.com.*

Where to Stay and Eat

Plélo ✉ 22170
Ferme-Auberge Au Char à Bancs, t 02 96 74 13 63 *(moderate).* Beautiful inn in its own picturesque valley 3km north of Châtelaudren. Traditional Breton fare *(expensive–moderate)* and luxurious B&B.

St-Quay-Portrieux ✉ 22410
***Ker Moor, 13 Rue du Président Le Sénécal, **t** 02 96 70 52 22, *www.ker-moor.com*

(moderate). Neo-Arabic, delightful folly of a villa on its own headland. Restaurant *(expensive). Closed Oct–Mar; restaurant closed Sun in winter.*

Paimpol ✉ 22500
***Le Repaire de Kerroc'h, 29 Quai Morand, **t** 02 96 20 50 13, *kerroch@chateauxhotels. com (expensive–moderate).* Proud old building on the quays, with plush Empire style within. Refined cuisine. *Restaurant closed Mon lunch, Tues and Wed lunch.*
Hotel de la Marne, 30 Rue de la Marne, **t 02 96 20 82 16 *(moderate).* Reasonable rooms and excellent food *(expensive). Restaurant closed Sun eve and Mon.*
La Vieille Tour, 13 Rue de l'Eglise, **t** 02 96 20 83 18 *(expensive).* Inventive Breton cuisine. *Closed Mon lunch.*

Pointe de l'Arcouest ✉ 22620
***Le Barbu, t 02 96 55 86 98, *www.lebarbu.fr (moderate).* In poll position for the ferry to Bréhat, with great sea views and pool. Restaurant. *Closed mid-Nov–Feb.*

Ile de Bréhat ✉ 22870
Bellevue, Port Clos, **t 02 96 20 00 05, *www. hotel-bellevue-brehat.com (moderate).* In a lovely location overlooking the port. Restaurant. *Closed much of Dec and Jan.*
**La Vieille Auberge, t 02 96 20 00 24 *(moderate).* A small hotel in the main village in the middle of the island. Restaurant. *Closed Nov–mid-April.*

the shipowners during centuries of long-distance cod fishing, emotionally evoked in Pierre Loti's tearjerking 19th-century novels. However, despite expectations, Paimpol hides away at the back of a bay; the shipowners' mansions on the quays have been replaced by a modern development with all the character of a shopping arcade; and swanky yachts rather than fishing boats fill the harbour. Just a whiff of atmosphere lingers in the air: behind the quay you can find old squares and winding, cobbled streets, especially around the Place du Martray and the Place de l'Eglise. The **Musée de la Mer** (*open mid-June–Aug daily 10–12 and 3–7; Easter–mid-June and Sept 3–6; adm*) pays its respects to Paimpol's maritime past in a former cod-drying building. South of town, look round the impressive remnants of the medieval **Abbaye de Beauport**.

With their gradations of pinks and oranges, the shattered rocks of the **archipelago of Bréhat** are of a rare beauty. Bréhat, the main island, consists of just two large pieces of rock joined together by a diminutive bridge. The south island is more densely populated and much lusher than the north, bright with exotic flowers in season. The north island is more barren and exposed, the slashed rocks facing each other at the end said by legend to be two dreadful siblings, turned to stone where they killed their father.

The Trégor and Côte de Granit Rose

The Trégor straddles the *départements* of the Côtes d'Armor and the Finistère, stretching from the Trieux estuary to the Morlaix river. Its capital, Tréguier, is a delightful religious town. South of Tréguier, you enter traditional, restful Brittany. By contrast, the Côte de Granit Rose to the west, with its outrageous display of pink boulders, teems with tourists as one of the most famous stretches of shore in France.

Inland Trégor

Pontrieux, stretching over both banks of the Trieux, grew up to serve as a port for inland Guingamp. Its squares and streets almost mirror each other either side of the river. A large number of craftspeople have recently set up shop here, while a dramatic tourist train follows the Trieux to Paimpol. Perched above the river, the **Château de la Roche-Jagu** (*open July–Aug daily 10–7; Sept–June 10.30–12.30 and 2–6; adm; gardens free*) is the only survivor of some ten forts built along the Trieux in medieval times. The place hosts temproary exhibitions and the gardens have been carefully restored.

Guingamp, a traditional small market town, has a big main church dedicated to its Black Virgin, Notre-Dame du Bon Secours. Her *pardon* on the first Saturday in July is a major event for Catholics in this part of Brittany. Down from the church, triangular **Place du Centre** is bordered by grand houses, its charm enhanced by the Renaissance Fontaine de la Plomée, distinctly uncharacteristic of Brittany in its finesse.

West towards Callac, the Chapelle St-Blaise at **Pestivien** has an exceptional calvary covered with grey lichen, the elongated figures looking down on the dead Christ conveying a rare sense of emotion for Breton sculpture. Notre-Dame de Bulat in **Bulat-Pestivien** became a particularly revered spot in Brittany because the saintly

Getting Around

Lannion has a **train** station, as well as a little **airport** with regular flights to and from Paris. Guingamp is the main transport hub for inland Trégor, with a railway station served by TGVs. For local **bus** services, **t** 02 96 68 31 20.

Tourist Information

Pontrieux: Maison Eiffel, **t** 02 96 95 14 03, *www.ulys.com/pontrieux*.
Guingamp: Place du Champ au Roy, **t** 02 96 43 73 89, *otguingamp@wanadoo.fr*.
Tréguier: Hôtel de Ville, **t** 02 96 92 22 33, *ot-pays-de-treguier@wanadoo.fr*.

Where to Stay and Eat

Brélidy ✉ **22140**
★★★**Château de Brélidy, t** 02 96 95 69 38, *www.chateau-brelidy.com* (*expensive*). Small 16th-century country château, in its own grounds south of Pontrieux, with comfortable rooms and salons. *Closed Jan–Mar.*

Guingamp ✉ **22200**
★★★**Le Relais du Roy**, 42 Place du Centre, **t** 02 96 43 76 62 (*expensive*). Exclusive little 16th-century hotel on the smart central square. Elegant restaurant (*moderate*). *Closed mid-Dec–early Jan; restaurant closed Sun eve.*
La Boissière, 90 Rue de l'Yser, **t** 02 96 21 06 35 (*expensive–moderate*). The most characterful restaurant in town in its own picturesque grounds. *Closed Sat lunch and Mon.*

Tréguier ✉ **22220**
★★★**Kastell Dinec'h**, Route de Lannion, **t** 02 96 92 49 39 (*moderate*). Breton manor hidden in the countryside west of Tréguier. Charming restaurant for hotel guests. Pool.
★★★**Aigue Marine**, Port de Plaisance, **t** 02 96 92 97 00, *www.aiguemarine.fr* (*moderate*). Large hotel down by the yacht harbour, with comfortable rooms, pool and restaurant (*expensive*). *Closed early Jan–late Feb; restaurant closed lunchtimes exc Sun.*

13th-century Breton lawyer and defender of the poor, St Yves, often came to pray to the Virgin here. The richly decorated church dates mainly from the 14th and 15th centuries. A mocking series of lively stone skeletons greets you, one preaching vehemently, brandishing bones. Christ has lost his arms at the top of the **calvary of Kergrist-Moëlou**. Inside the church, the painted ceiling by a local artist clumsily records the Vatican council of 1871.

Tréguier and the Jaudy Estuary

Tréguier stands well back from the frivolous rocks of the Côte de Granit Rose, down the Jaudy estuary. The soaring cathedral steeple makes it very clear who was boss in centuries past – Tréguier was one of the original seats of Christian power in Brittany. Tugdual or Tugwall, a Welsh monk, is reckoned to have been the first bishop in 540, but his renown was eclipsed by local boy Yves Helory de Kermartin. A highly educated churchman and lawyer, he died on 19 May in 1303 after a life dedicated to bringing justice to the poor, and was buried here. A cult grew up around his relics, and official recognition came from the pope in Avignon in 1347; since that time Yves' relics and his *pardon* have counted among the holiest in Brittany. His reputation for incorruptibility, some may find it ironic to learn that it had him declared patron saint of lawyers.

Tréguier is still renowned for its Gothic **cathedral**, the most quirky and charming in Brittany. From 1347 the tomb of St Yves was installed inside. The eccentric interior has been described as a 'laboratory of medieval architecture', where each mason followed his own whim rather than aiming for a coherent plan. Lawyers from around the world attend the annual Pardon de St-Yves: one of the stained-glass windows in St Yves' chapel was even donated by the US bar. The cloister, done in lacy Gothic tracery, serves as a museum of tomb effigies collected from churches and abbeys destroyed at the Revolution. In the treasury you can still pay your respects to the skull of St Yves. Below the streets of the old town with their numerous monastic and timberframe buildings, fleets of yachts now moor.

Two extraordinary peninsulas stretch seawards either side of the beautiful Jaudy estuary. To the east, the **Presqu'île Sauvage** ends with the **Sillon de Talbert**, a fragile strip of sand and pebbles extending against the odds into the sea. On the other peninsula, visit the **Chapelle St-Gonéry** (*open 15 June–15 Sept daily 10–12 and 2–5; April–mid-June and mid-Sept–mid-Oct Fri pm and weekends; adm*) at **Plougrescant**, as crooked as a building from a fairytale and decorated with naïve biblical scenes.

The Côte de Granit Rose

The Côte de Granit Rose covers roughly 20km of gorgeously granite coast from the Pointe du Château west to Trégastel-Plage. It is not just that the rocks are deep pink here; they have also been whipped by the elements into bizarre shapes: the Die, the Bottle, Napoleon's Hat and even the Upturned Foot.

At **Pors-Hir** the houses sit among vast boulders. The **Pointe du Château**, or Castel Meur, has trapped one of the most photographed houses in Brittany, sensationally caught between two lumps of rock. A Maison d'Accueil presents information on the extraordinary geology. The magical rockscapes continue around **Pors Scarff**, sonorous pebble banks sloping down to the water. Around **Pors Burguélès** houses mingle in greater number among the boulders, some built between piles of rock, some seemingly perched on them. **Port-Blanc** looks absolutely stunning; the tower sticking up out of one of the tallest boulders may once have formed part of some fortifications, but it now houses an oratory. A glorious high road leads to **Trévou-Tréguignec**, while two spectacular rock-protected beaches lie below it. The waters around **Port Royau** are so strewn with rocks that it seems an act of folly to have placed a port here.

It is a relief for **Perros-Guirec** that in the 17th century the royal engineer Vauban opted for Cherbourg instead of here as the site for a new military port. Perros-Guirec is now a beautiful, sprawling Breton resort with a modern marina. Grand villas and hotels climb its slopes, with a spectacular corniche road at the top. **St-Jacques** in the upper part of town amazes with its colour; the dome looks like a sunburned breast. Below, Trestraou beach boasts a thalassotherapy centre and a casino. Boats leave for trips to the ornithological reserve of the **Sept Iles**, where rare sea birds call, including puffins and gannets spring and summer.

The coastal path from Perros-Guirec to Ploumanach becomes increasingly cluttered with the craziest rocks in Brittany. The **Plage St-Guirec** is one of the most dramatic beaches in the region, the little oratory perched on a rock dedicated to a saint who landed here in the 6th century. A wooden statue of him has stood here since the 12th century. Traditionally, young women anxious to get married would come to stick a pin

Tourist Information

Perros-Guirec: 21 Place de l'Hôtel de Ville,
t 02 96 23 21 15, *www.perros-guirec.com*.
Trégastel: Place Ste-Anne, t 02 96 15 38 38,
www.ville-tregastel.fr.

Where to Stay and Eat

Port-Blanc ✉ 22710

**Grand Hôtel, Bd de la Mer, t 02 96 92 66 52,
www.hotel-port-blanc.com (inexpensive).
Classic to retro, overlooking the gorgeous
rocky bay. Restaurant *(moderate)*. *Closed
Nov–mid-Mar*.

Perros-Guirec ✉ 22700

***Le Manoir du Sphinx, 67 Chemin de la
Messe, t 02 96 23 25 42, *lemanoirdusphinx@
wanadoo.fr (expensive)*. A villa lording it over
the Plage de Trestingnel, with fabulous
views, and a garden going down to the
rocks. *Closed early Jan–mid-Feb; restaurant
closed Sun eve, Mon lunch and Tues lunch*.
**Au Bon Accueil, 11 Rue de Landerval, t 02 96
23 25 77, *au-bon-accueil@wanadoo.fr (inexpensive)*. Most of the comfortable modern

rooms have port views. Restaurant *(moderate)*. *Restaurant closed Fri and Sun eve*.
Le Gulf Stream, 26 Rue des Sept Iles, t 02 96 23
21 86 *(moderate)*. Wonderful set-up on the
Perros-Guirec hillside, facing the seal. Warm,
welcoming and not too expensive.
*Les Violettes, 19 Rue du Calvaire, t 02 96 23
21 33 *(inexpensive)*. Bargain, with restaurant.

Ploumanach ✉ 22700

**Les Rochers, Chemin de la Pointe, t 02 96 91
44 49, *hoteldesrochers@wanadoo.fr (inexpensive)*. By the beach, rooms of a high
standard. Restaurant for simple meals.
Closed Nov–Mar; restaurant closed Mon.
**Hotel du Parc, t 02 96 91 40 80 *(inexpensive)*. Popular choice 200m from the beach;
restaurant *(moderate)*. *Closed Oct–Mar*.

Trégastel-Plage ✉ 22730

***Armoric, Plage du Coz Pors, t 02 96 23
88 16, *www.hotels-bretagne.com/armoric/
(expensive–moderate)*. Good old solid
seaside hotel by this stretch of coast.
**Beau Séjour, Plage du Coz Pors, t 02 96 23
88 02 *(moderate)*. A slightly cheaper alternative with sea views and restaurant. *Closed
mid-Nov–mid-Feb; restaurant closed Wed*.

in the statue's nose: his proboscis was pierced so many times that it eventually came off. The walk around **Ploumanach**'s Parc Municipal takes you past absurd pink granite formations which turn a fiery colour in the setting sun. Behind Ploumanach's light-house (pink too, of course), the **Maison du Littoral** goes into detail about how all this pinkness comes from a vein of magma which remained open and active for an excep-tionally long time. Postcards here show that not so long ago this coast was nowhere near as desirable as it is now; the poor used to live in makeshift caves under the rocks.

Trégastel-Plage has the most melodramatic pink rocks of the lot. Its **aquarium** *(open July–Aug daily 9–8; May, June and Sept daily 10–12 and 2–6; adm)* lies under a pile of enormous rosy boulders, resembling a daring feat of wacky modern architecture. The sea deserts the resort at low tide, when you can tramp past the rocky piles and isles. The walk takes you to some spectacularly silly rock formations, including the Skull, the Great Chasm and, naturally enough for Brittany, the Pile of Crêpes.

To the Trégor Finistérien and Morlaix

After Trégastel, the pinkness goes out of the rocks and the crowds thin. Around Trébeurden and the Léguer estuary it is still resort territory, but then the coast becomes much wilder as it enters the Finistère, the most Breton of Brittany's

Getting Around

Morlaix is well-served by TGV **rail** services. For local **buses, t** 02 96 68 31 20, or **t** 02 98 44 46 73. The **ferry** port of Roscoff lies nearby.

Tourist Information

Pleumeur-Bodou: t 02 96 23 91 47, *www.pleumeur-bodou.com.*
Trébeurden: Place de Crech-Héry, **t** 02 96 23 51 64, *www.ville-trebeurden.fr.st.*
Lannion: Quai d'Aiguillon, **t** 02 96 46 41 00, *www.ot-lannion.fr.*
St-Michel-en-Grève: t 02 96 35 74 87.
Locquirec: Place du Port, **t** 02 98 67 40 83, *www.locquirec.com.*
Morlaix: Place des Otages, **t** 02 98 62 14 94, *officedetourisme.morlaix@wanadoo.fr.*

Where to Stay and Eat

Trébeurden ✉ 22560

★★★Ti Al-Lannec, 14 Allée de Mezo Guen, **t** 02 96 15 01 01, *www.tiallannec.com* *(very expensive–expensive)*. Tasteful rooms and terraced garden overlooking the sea, plus good restaurant. *Closed Nov–Mar.*
★★Ker An Nod, 2 Rue de Pors Termen, **t** 02 96 23 50 21, *www.kerannod.com (inexpensive).* Down by the port, the place to enjoy perfect sunsets from the small, neat rooms or the restaurant *(moderate). Closed Jan–Mar.*

Le Yaudet ✉ 22300

★★Ar Vro, t 02 96 46 48 80, *arvro@wanadoo.fr (inexpensive).* A simple, rural hotel in a wonderful, peaceful location. Restaurant *(moderate).*

St-Michel-en-Grève ✉ 22300

★★Hôtel de la Plage, Place de l'Eglise, **t** 02 96 35 74 43 *(inexpensive).* Great views across the bay; some rooms have terraces, and you can eat out *(moderate)* for the views.

Locquirec ✉ 29241

★★★Le Grand Hôtel des Bains, 15 Rue de l'Eglise, **t** 02 98 67 41 02, *www.grand-hotel-des-bains.com (very expensive–expensive).* A joy of a seaside hotel, with charming rooms, terraces, pool and follies. Stylish restaurant. *Closed Feb; restaurant closed lunchtimes.*
L'Hôtel du Port, 5 Place du Port, **t** 02 98 67 42 10 *(inexpensive).* A simple choice overlooking the port, with simple restaurant.

Morlaix ✉ 29600

★★Hotel de l'Europe, 1 Rue d'Aiguillon, **t** 02 98 62 11 99, *www.hotel-europe-com.fr (moderate).* Some style and central. For the brasserie, call **t** 02 98 88 81 15 *(cheap). Restaurant closed Sun.*
Les Bains Douches, 45 Allée du Poan Ben, **t** 02 98 63 83 83 *(cheap).* Eccentric restaurant in a former public baths. The food is typical French *bistrot* fare. *Closed Sun and Mon eve.*

départements, covering the whole western tip of the province. The town of Morlaix dramatically straddles the old medieval counties of the Trégor and the Léon.

From the Ile Grande to the Lieue de Grève

The **Ile Grande**, although no longer an island, protects an important bird sanctuary. The wooded island to the east puts in a claim to being the Avalon of Arthurian legend. Inland, by **Pleumeur-Bodou**, a vast satellite centre dominates the landscape. The first-ever satellite broadcast between the USA and Europe was made possible thanks to this giant golf-ball of a building, now home to a **telecommunications museum** *(open April–Sept daily 10–12 and 2–5; adm)*. There's also a planetarium and fake Gaulish village on the site. **Lannion**, up the Léguer, has become bloated on high-tech industries generated by Pleumeur-Bodou, although the historic centre retains refined town houses. Two beautiful churches stand out in outlying quarters, the **church of Brélévenez** on its hilltop, fortified by the Knights Templar, and the **chapel of Loguivy-lès-Lannion** with its delightful fountains down by the river. Inland along the

Léguer, the **Chapelle de Kerfons** conceals a wealth of decorative delights, while the **Château de Tonquédec**, also hidden in woods, offers a spectacularly sturdy image of a ruined medieval castle.

Back by the coast, **Trébeurden**, with its port, rocks and numerous beaches, presents many different facets, making it a popular resort. At peaceful **Le Yaudet**, on a magical height above the southern bank of the Léguer estuary, there is talk of a pre-Celtic sacred site on the hill, although the theory that Astérix and Obélix had their village here is clearly preposterous – the cartoon evidence proves they lived on the flat by the sea. Le Yaudet's chapel contains some admirable kitsch. The **Domaine du Dourven**, a deliciously pine-scented estate on its own headland, holds contemporary art exhibitions. Down at the **Pointe de Séhar**, the flat, rounded peninsula made almost entirely of pebbles and boulders has a messy charm. The unspoilt coastal path heads due south from here along the cliffs of Trédrez, ending with the glorious **Beg ar Forn**.

Extremely steep country roads lead down to **St-Michel-en-Grève**, one end of the legend-filled bay of the **Lieue de Grève**. The sea waters withdraw some two kilometres at low tide. For centuries the Croix de Mi-Lieue, a cross planted in the middle of the bay, served as a sign to travellers and pilgrims to take the short cut across the sands whenever it was fully out of the water. Inland, **Ploumilliau**'s church contains a well-known statue of the once much-feared Breton Grim Reaper, l'Ankou, while the **Château de Rosanbo** (*open May–June daily 2–5; July–Aug daily 11–6; Sept–Oct Sun 2–5; closed Nov–April; adm*), a grand Ancien Régime building in landscaped gardens, is owned by a family who trace their aristocratic line here back 1,000 years.

The Trégor Finistérien from Locquirec to Morlaix

Delightful **Locquirec**, just in the Finistère, takes up a whole little spit of land, giving you nine beaches to choose from. The **Beg an Fry** headland has a more savage beauty. Coming round to the island-strewn Bay of Morlaix, it's clear that Neolithic builders had an aesthetic eye when it came to positioning their burial sites. The **Cairn of Barnenez** (*open daily for guided visits at 10.15 and 11.15 and 2.15–5.45; adm*), the largest Neolithic barrow built in Europe is a vast, step-layered, dry-stone structure constructed with infinite care. It overlooks the bay, including the sensationally located 16th-century **Château du Taureau**, untouchable on its rocky island.

Tucked out of sight in its deep river estuary, **Morlaix** unsurprisingly became a haven for Breton corsairs in centuries past. English entanglements mark its history, but for many centuries the place also prospered thanks to the cloth trade. Nature has provided a fine enough setting, but the extraordinary theatricality of the town comes from the massive arches of the 19th-century viaduct which cross the centre. The **Eglise et Musée des Jacobins** (*open Easter–Oct daily 10–12 and 2–6; Nov–Easter Wed–Mon 10–12 and 2–5, closed Tues; adm*) presents Morlaix's history and culture among wide Gothic arches. The grimy **Maison de la Duchesse Anne** (*open April–Sept Mon–Sat; t 02 98 88 23 26 to check times; adm*) is the best-known of the so-called 'lantern houses' in town, thought to have been inspired by the lucrative cloth-trading links with Spain, hence the patio. Surprises await you at the **Eglise St-Mathieu**, with its detailed Renaissance façade and its opening Virgin. Seawards, Morlaix's marina is overseen by the elegant 18th-century Manufacture de Tabac factory. Southeast of Morlaix, at **Plougonven**, the calvary offers an excellent introduction to this special Breton outdoor art, Christ's story crisply sculpted. Characterful **Guerlesquin**'s centre really consists of one elongated square divided up by historic buildings. The most elegant, the Présidial, might be judged one of the prettiest prisons in France.

The North Finistère Coast: Roscoff to Brest

Roscoff and the Ile de Batz

Cross-Channel visitors may find that old **Roscoff** makes rather too much play of its pirating past, when shipowners, corsairs and smugglers were engaged in a centuries-long struggle with the English. Sailing vessels were so important that they were even carved on the outside of the **Notre-Dame de Kroaz Batz**, whose merry steeple looks as if it has been built out of stone bells. Around the church, the grand granite houses

Getting There and Around

Roscoff's **ferry** port, served by Brittany Ferries from Plymouth and Irish Ferries from Rosslare (*see* **Travel**), lies east of town. Armein Excursions run the ferry to the Ile de Batz, t 02 98 61 77 75.

Roscoff and St-Pol-de-Léon have **railway** stations and frequent connections with Morlaix for the TGV service between Paris and Brest. Brest is a Ryanair cheap **flight** destination from London-Stansted.

Buses from Brest serve the coast in all directions, t 02 98 44 46 73. Book ferry tickets to Ouessant in advance from Penn ar Bed, t 02 98 89 02 12, *penn-ar-bed.fr*, or Finist'Mer, t 02 98 89 16 61, f 02 98 89 16 78; or you can fly from Brest-Guipavas with Finist'Air, t 02 98 84 64 87.

Tourist Information

Roscoff: 46 Rue Gambetta, t 02 98 61 12 13, *www.sb-roscoff.fr/Roscoff*.
Ile de Batz: t 02 98 61 75 70, *Mairie.iledebatz@libertysurf.fr*.
St-Pol-de-Léon: Place de l'Evêché, t 02 98 69 05 69, *www.saintpoldeleon.fr*.
Carantec: 4 Rue Pasteur, t 02 98 67 00 43, *carantec.tourisme@wanadoo.fr*.
Le Conquet: Parc de Beauséjour, t 02 98 89 11 31, *www.leconquet.fr*.
Ouessant: Place de l'Eglise, Lampaul, t 02 98 48 85 83, *OTOuessant@aol.com*.

Brest: Place de la Liberté, t 02 98 44 24 96, *Office.de.tourisme.brest@wanadoo.fr*.

Where to Stay and Eat

Roscoff ✉ 29680
★★★Le Brittany, 22 Bd Ste-Barbe, t 02 98 69 70 78, *www.hotel-brittany.com* (*expensive*). Great if you stay in the old part of the hotel, wonderfully located by the old port. The rooms in the annexe are less interesting. The cuisine at the Yachtman restaurant is adventurous. Pool. *Closed mid-Nov–late Mar; restaurant closed Tues–Sun lunch, and Mon.*
★★★Le Gulf Stream, 7 Rue Marquise de Kergariou, t 02 98 69 73 19, *www.hotel-roscoff.com* (*expensive–moderate*). A modern hotel with many attractions, including sea views, heated swimming pool in the well-flowered garden extending down to the beach, and excellent seafood. The *institut marin* for seawater treatments is just 100m away. *Closed mid-Oct–mid-Mar; restaurant closed Sun eve and Mon lunch.*
★★Les Chardons Bleus, 4 Rue Réveillière, t 02 98 69 72 03 (*inexpensive*). Well-kept hotel in a central Renaissance house, with tastefully decorated rooms and a restaurant (*moderate*). *Restaurant closed Thurs, and Sun eve out of season.*
★★Hôtel des Arcades, 15 Rue Réveillière, t 02 98 69 70 45, *www.acdev.com* (*inexpensive*).

reflect Roscoff's 16th- and 17th-century prosperity. Onion-selling to Britain began early in the 19th century. The **Musée des Johnnies** (*open June–15 Sept Wed–Mon 10–12 and 3–6; closed Tues; adm*) tells the story of the Breton salesmen who got on their bikes. Other attractions include a slightly wilting aquarium and a flourishing semi-tropical garden. From the old port you can take the short boat trip out to the unspoilt **Ile de Batz** with its palm oasis.

St-Pol-de-Léon

St-Pol-de-Léon is named after Welsh Pol, one of the seven founding saints of Brittany. According to legend he served King Marc'h at his Cornish court in Tintagel before setting sail to evangelize Armorica around 512. Landing first on Ushant, he met with strong resistance from the locals and quickly left to found a monastery on Batz, where he triumphed over an evil dragon. At the invitation of the local lord Withur, he crossed to the mainland and was proclaimed bishop at Withur's castle, which had just been devastated by raiders. Pol gave the community the impetus to rebuild and

Good-value option, rooms recently redone, some with sea views. The dining room (*moderate*) looks out on to the Channel. *Closed Oct–Mar.*

Le Temps de Vivre, Place de l'Eglise, **t** 02 98 61 27 28 (*expensive*). Excellent inventive restaurant in an old corsair's house. *Closed Mon and Tues.*

L'Ecume des Jours, Quai d'Auxerre, **t** 02 98 61 22 83 (*expensive–moderate*). Delightful, set in a 16th-century house looking out to sea. Good value for fine cooking. *Closed Wed.*

Le Surcouf, 14 Rue Réveillière, **t** 02 98 69 71 89 (*cheap*). Pretty good-value seafood menus. *Closed Tues and Wed.*

Ile de Batz ✉ 29253

Roch Armor, **t** 02 98 61 78 28, *www.rocharmor. net* (*inexpensive*). At the port, with restaurant (*moderate*). *Closed mid-Oct– mid-Mar.*

Grand Hôtel, **t** 02 98 61 78 06 (*inexpensive*). Very similar to the above. *Closed mid-Nov–mid-Mar.*

St-Pol-de-Léon ✉ 29250

★★France, 29 Rue des Minimes, **t** 02 98 29 14 14, *www.hoteldefrancebretagne.com* (*inexpensive*). Enjoyable hotel in a swish building. Although the rooms are basic, some have sea views.

La Pomme d'Api, 49 Rue Verderel, **t** 02 98 69 04 36 (*expensive*). Restaurant in an old

Breton house, with refined décor and excellent food. *Closed Mon.*

Le Conquet and the Pointe St-Mathieu ✉ 29217

★★★Hostellerie de la Pointe St-Mathieu, **t** 02 98 89 00 19, *www.pointe-saint-mathieu. com* (*moderate*). Fine hotel and restaurant (*expensive–moderate*). *Closed Feb; restaurant closed Sun eve.*

★★La Pointe Ste-Barbe, **t** 02 98 89 00 26, *www.hotelpointesaintebarbe.com* (*moderate–inexpensive*). Modern block just above the ferry jetty. Rooms and restaurant (*very expensive–moderate*) with tremendous sea views. *Closed mid-Nov–mid-Dec; restaurant closed Mon out of season.*

★★Le Relais du Vieux Port, 1 Quai du Drellac'h, **t** 02 98 89 15 91 (*inexpensive*). Lovely rooms at a good price; crêperie downstairs (*cheap*).

Ouessant/Ushant ✉ 29242

★★Roch Ar Mor, Lampaul, **t** 02 98 48 80 19, *www.perso.wanadoo.fr/rocharmor* (*moderate– inexpensive*). The most attractive of the hotels in the main town. Restaurant with wide array of choices *expensive–cheap*). *Closed Feb–early Mar; restaurant closed Sun eve and Mon.*

Ti Jan ar C'hafé, Kernigou, **t** 02 98 48 82 64 (*moderate–inexpensive*). Charmingly redone little hotel away from the crowds. *Closed mid-Nov–mid-Dec and Jan.*

the place soon flourished. In the Middle Ages the city became a major stop on the Tro Breizh pilgrimage route. The little town's religious architecture still dramatically dominates the flat plain for miles, but the cathedral towers are well and truly beaten by the staggering spike of **Notre-Dame du Kreisker**, the tallest spire in Brittany, 'of worrying lightness' according to one Breton art historian, commissioned by proud local merchants, not the Church. The Gothic **cathedral** contains many fine tombs made for the bishops of the Léon (northern Finistère), plus St Pol's supposed skull and bell from Tintagel. **Carentec**, the pretty resort down from St-Pol 'discovered' at the start of the 20th century, is one of the area's most exclusive holiday spots.

West Along the Coast

Along the artichoke-covered coast between Roscoff and Plouescat, vegetables grow almost to the edge of the sea. Inland, superb towering beeches, a big bulging dove-cote and a gibbet mark the grounds of the **Château de Kerjean** (*open July–Aug daily 10–7; June and Sept Wed–Mon 10–12 and 2–6; adm*), the grandest castle of the Léon, although the Renaissance style was adopted in wonky manner here, and the place suffered badly at the Revolution. The château now houses a permanent collection of Léonard furniture from local farms. To the west, the incongruous **Basilique du Folgoët** lords it over a modest village close to Lesneven. This Flamboyant Gothic pilgrimage church was constructed in the 15th century in honour of the Virgin Mary and the piety of a village idiot obsessed by her ('Folgoët' means 'Madman of the Wood' in Breton). Some of the sculpture is impressive and deeply moving, from the *Mater dolorosa* outside –her grief shown in thick stone tears – to the rood screen within.

Back on the coast, after Plouescat, wild sandy dunes stretch to the **Grève de Goulven**, strewn with huge dollops of granite. At the bay's western end, sandyachts come out to play at low tide. Further west, granite blocks have been worn down by the elements into the Toad, the Sphinx, the Camel, and the Elephant, among many weird and wonderful shapes. The resort of **Brignogan-Plages** curves round a great horseshoe bay full of more wild rocks which make up for the characterless buildings. Seek out the boulder-strewn beaches at Les Chardons Bleus and **Ménéham**, the latter a hamlet of thatched cottages.

On your way to the built-up **St-Michel peninsula** and its popular beaches, stop to see the engraved tombstones of the **Iliz-Koz** and the **buried church of Tremenac'h** (*open 15 June–15 Sept Tues–Sun 2–6; rest of the year Sun only 2.30–5; adm*). Legend claims that the church was drowned by the sand as punishment for an evil band of youths who accidentally captured the devil's cat. The engulfed church was only uncovered by accident by a bulldozer in the 1960s.

Continuing west, views open up on to the towering spectacle of the **Ile Vierge light-house**, the tallest in Europe (263ft), built at the end of the 19th century; the previous lighthouse by its side looks childlike. Round a further bay you come to the **Pays des Abers**, with the three deeply indented estuaries of the Wrac'h, Benoît and Ildut. **Lilia** typifies the area's little ports, with its rockscapes from which mountains of seaweed are gathered. **Plouguerneau** pays its respects to the *goémoniers*, or seaweed-collectors, with its museum. Seaweed is now used not just as a fertilizer, but in cuisine, cosmetics and pharmaceuticals. **Portsall** had the misfortune of being all too closely linked with the environmental disaster of the *Amoco Cadiz*. It has kept the tanker's massive anchor, an ironic memorial. Seaweed-gathering ports tucked away behind rocks signalled by huge lighthouses characterize the coast of the **Pays d'Iroise** down to Le Conquet; the Mer d'Iroise is the name for the stretch of sea linking the Channel with the Atlantic. The **Corsen headland** claims to be the closest point on the mainland to North America, New York just 5,080km away. **Trézien lighthouse**, which can be climbed, appears to have strayed inland. There are also wild beaches to appreciate in this area. Most visitors go to **Le Conquet** to take the ferry to Ushant, but the harbour and its beaches also have their own charm.

The terrifyingly beautiful rocks of **Ouessant** or **Ushant** have proved lethal in all too many a notorious shipwreck. Tragedy has stalked the islanders too. Until recently, it was the lot of many a Ouessant woman to become a widow before her time. While the men were away fishing or in the navy, the women were left to tend their allotments. These have been abandoned, but the other mainstay, sheep, survive, although the tiny blackish brown breed peculiar to the island is now rare. Ferries arrive in the **Baie du Stiff**, where the enormous Phare du Stiff marks the highest point on Ushant. Along the island's north coast you'll find the most fearsome rock formations, assaulted by angry waves. Bustling **Lampaul** (named after Welsh saint Pol) in the west opens out on to a surprisingly friendly bay with small beaches around it. Two museums stand nearby: the **Maison du Niou Uhella Ecomusée** (*open June–Sept daily 10.30–6.30; April–May Tues–Sun 2–6.30; Oct–Mar Tues–Sun 2–6; adm*) crams information on the island's history and life into two charmingly claustrophobic cottages. The unusual **Phare de Créac'h Lighthouses Museum** (*open June–Sept daily 10.30–6.30; April–May Tues–Sat 1–6.30, Sun 10.30–6.30; Oct–Mar Tues–Sun 2–5; adm*) explains the history and technology of lighthouses and sea marks. Beyond rise the bristling mounds of rocks of the **Pointe de Pern**, Ouessant's most westerly point, classified a national monument.

Brest

Bombs tragically rained down on **Brest** in the Second World War, destroying what had become one of the Nazis' major U-Boot or submarine ports. For centuries the country's main naval harbour in the north, the place was rapidly rebuilt in an American-looking grid-plan of streets sloping down to a string of docks. But the new Brest has presence, plus the advantage of overlooking one of the most beautiful bays in France. The main tourist attraction, **Océanopolis** (*open 9–6; adm*), on the bay east of town, with massive contemporary bridges framing the background, is a centre for the study of the world's oceans, and also one of the best aquaria in France, clarifying Brittany's sometimes murky waters. From the port by Océanopolis you can take a boat tour of the Rade de Brest, or then visit the chain of ponds and lakes in the botanical gardens in the Vallon du Stang Alar. In the centre of Brest, the name of the main shopping street, **Rue de Siam** (now lined with slick black fountains), recalls the exotic arrival of ambassadors from the King of Thailand in 1688. The **maritime museum** occupies part of the much-transformed **Château de Brest**, built to guard the Penfeld estuary which divides the town in two. Some of its walls date back to Gallo-Roman times. The museum is devoted to shipbuilding traditions, but major events in the history of castle and town also emerge. The **Museum of Fine Arts** (*open Wed–Sat and Mon 10–11.45 and 2–6, Sun 2–6, closed Tues*) displays some detailed old school paintings of Brest, giving you a notion of how the port looked in its heyday, although the place is best known for its works by the Pont-Aven School (*see* p.250).

Inland Northern Finistère

From the late 15th century, elaborate outdoor calvary platforms covered with sculptures in granite telling the story of Christ's life and Passion became the rage in western Brittany. Occasionally, a local story or saint might creep in too. These calvaries were just one element in the distinctive stone-fenced *enclos paroissiaux* (parish church enclosures) which flourished up to the 17th century.

Parish Enclosures and Calvaries around the Elorn

In war-damaged **Plougastel-Daoulas**, the church's elaborate calvary survived, covered with over 150 sculpted figures completed between 1602 and 1604, after the parish had suffered terribly from the plague in 1598. Some say that the bulbous protrusions on the crosses are symbols of the bubonic plague. The beautiful, many-fingered peninsula west of Plougastel-Daoulas, stretching into the Rade de Brest is well-known for producing fine strawberries, but relatively untouristy. The significant medieval **abbey of Daoulas** is set slightly south, in a village packed with religious edifices. The church retains some lovely Romanesque features. The abbey itself now hosts a major annual ethnography exhibition. Outside, the Romanesque cloister and its washbasin with extraterrestrial-looking faces are remarkable. A medicinal garden has also been recreated.

Landerneau was a prosperous river port in centuries past. The highlight of the historic town is the Rohan bridge; the chaos of houses built upon it are still inhabited. Nearby, on a height close to the Elorn river, the **church of Pencran** is set in an *enclos paroissial* mostly dating from the 16th century and whose calvary has a particularly moving image of the grieving Mary Magdalene. Skulls feature across the ossuary entrance, while elaborate carvings decorate the church. East at **La Roche-Maurice**, the 16th-century **church of St-Yves** is best known for its rood screen on which twelve red-cheeked apostles line up underneath the figure of the crucified Christ. Brutal reminders of death are stamped on its ossuary. The *enclos* south at **La Martyre** reserves a memorable welcome for you along a lovely old village street.

The well-known parish enclosures to the northeast of the Elorn valley around Landivisiau and St-Thégonnec don't stand in such picturesque locations, but the churches are richly decorated. The interior at **Lampaul-Guimiliau** shows off an extravagant series of 17th-century painted altarpieces. The organ perched on stilts and the main crossbeam with a polychrome crucifixion scene stand out. While the wild baldaquin-covered baptismal font looks entertaining, the Entombment is more sober. The ossuary, converted into a shop, contains a retable covered with plague saints.

Getting Around

Local **trains** between Brest and Morlaix stop at Landerneau, La Roche-Maurice, Landivisiau, Guimiliau and St-Thégonnec. **Bus** services are extremely limited, **t** 02 98 44 46 73.

Tourist Information

Plougastel-Daoulas: Place du Calvaire, **t** 02 98 40 34 98.
Landerneau: Pont de Rohan, **t** 02 98 85 13 09.

Where to Stay and Eat

Ty-Dreux ✉ 29410
B&B (*inexpensive*) in a former weaver's village, south of Guimiliau along the D111. Contact Jean or Annie Martin, **t** 02 98 78 08 21.

St-Thégonnec ✉ 29410
***Auberge St-Thégonnec**, 6 Place de la Mairie, **t** 02 98 79 61 18 (*moderate*). Old stone façade, comfortable rooms and a restaurant.

Ar Prospital Coz, 18 Rue Lividic, **t** 02 98 79 45 62 (*inexpensive*). This former church presbytery is now a spacious B&B.

Commana ✉ 29450
Kerfornedic, close to the Lac du Drennec, **t** 02 98 78 06 26 (*inexpensive*). Gorgeous 17th-century B&B, 2km outside Commana.

Brennilis ✉ 29690
Auberge du Youdig, **t** 02 98 99 62 36, *www.youdig.fr*. Eccentric B&B (*inexpensive*) and typical Breton meals (*moderate*).

Brasparts ✉ 29190
Domaine de Rugornon Vras, **t** 02 98 81 46 27 (*inexpensive*). Detached B&B accommodation in a stone house well placed for walks.

Huelgoat ✉ 29690
Hôtel du Lac, 9 Rue du Général de Gaulle, **t** 02 98 99 71 14 (*inexpensive*). Small hotel and restaurant. *Closed Jan; restaurant closed Mon.*

Two naive riders greet you at the arch into **Guimiliau**'s *enclos paroissial*. The figures are so blotched with lichen that it looks as if they're afflicted by disease. However, their expressions show more vitality than the statues on any other Breton calvary. In the Last Supper, several apostles peer from behind Christ's shoulder. One woman on the calvary is shown naked, her big breasts indicating the nature of her 'crime': she represents Kat Golled, Lost Catherine, a local woman whose lover turned out to be the devil. The interior of the church writhes with sculptural detail. One retable tells the story of St Miliau, the 6th-century Breton chieftain after whom the village is named.

St-Thégonnec boasts arguably the grandest of all *enclos paroissiaux*, from the second half of the 16th and early 17th centuries. The church itself was terribly damaged by a fire in the late 1990s, ruining its wildly elaborate interior. However, St-Thégonnec is also well-known for its calvary dating from 1610, which includes a statue of Thégonnec, who sailed to Ireland to become bishop of Armagh later in life.

The Monts d'Arrée

Other Bretons were long suspicious of the people of the Monts d'Arrée, an isolated ridge of hills which in centuries past acted as a kind of no-man's-land between the county of Léon to the north and of Cornouaille to the south.

On the north side, **Sizun** continues the theme of the *enclos paroissiaux*, with substantial gateway and splendid ossuary, but no proper calvary. The nearby **Maison de la Rivière** to the northwest is devoted to the rivers, fish and environment of the Monts, while the **Maison du Lac** explains how the Elorn river was dammed to form the Drennec Reservoir to the southeast. Rural traditions are the theme at the charmingly restored **Moulins de Kerouat** between Sizun and **Commana**, the latter with elaborate *enclos paroissial* and riotous altarpiece to St Anne.

Head up to the dinosaur's back of the **Roc Trévézel**. The Chemin des Crêtes, a 40km track along the heather- and myrtle-covered ridge, passes here. To the south, the **Montagne St-Michel-de-Brasparts** looks rotund but barren, just a small chapel placed on top. The disused nuclear power station below may not tempt you, but a group of mainly avant-garde craftspeople run the appealing **Maison des Artisans**. To the west, the **Domaine de Menez Meur**, the Monts d'Arrée's animal park, is set among mossy walled old tracks; Breton horses are the main attraction.

On the southern slopes of the Monts d'Arrée, the church and village of **Lannédern** lie on one of the most open, joyous of slopes. The *enclos paroissial* is photogenic in the extreme, with carved deer featuring several times along with their protector, St Edern. **Loqueffret** too has a deeply appealing church and calvary, with acrobatic carved figures, while the **Maison du Recteur** recalls the life of an old-styled Breton village priest. Hidden in a wooded valley a bit east, **St-Herbot** has a gem of a Breton church. The decoration includes a small calvary outside, where the crucified Christ has been given a caricature of a large Jewish nose and his ribs stick out painfully from his emaciated body. The porches are wonderfully embellished; over one stands a statue of St Herbot , protector of cattle and horses. Even in quite recent times, local farmers would cut locks off the tails of their beasts and present them to him on the altar.

One legend says that the intriguingly shaped giant granite boulders at **Huelgoat** were brought together in a show of strength by the Celtic giant god Gawr; another tale blames a grumpy Gargantua for throwing down the rocks in a fit of pique at being served bad Breton gruel. The town itself stands by a lake created in the 18th century to help exploit a silver-bearing mine in the valley. Out of town, the **Camp d'Artus** contains a few rare vestiges of a pre-Roman Armorican tribe; later legend claimed that this was one of King Arthur's Breton camps, hence the name.

West and South Finistère

The Crozon Peninsula and the Aulne Valley

Picture Brittany as a dragon's head biting into the Atlantic, and the Crozon peninsula is its savagely barbed tongue. It is truly sensational. Find tranquillity along the beautiful Aulne valley, shadowed by the Montagnes Noires.

Le Faou, northern gateway to the Crozon peninsula, has a heart of attractive old slate-covered houses. An exceptionally pretty corniche road leads to the **abbey of Landévennec** (*open May–Sept Mon–Sat 10–7, Sun 12–7; other school hols daily 2–6; rest of the year weekends 2–6; adm*), which celebrated its 1,500th anniversary in 1985 and has a funky modern museum. Along with St-Sauveur in Redon, this place was the main centre for spiritual and literary endeavour in Dark Ages Brittany. Archaeological digs have uncovered layer upon layer of abbeys, and for just about the first time in France it has been possible to draw up a picture of a Carolingian abbey.

Getting Around

There are no **trains** serving the peninsula, but there are **buses** from Brest or Quimper as far as Camaret, t 02 98 44 46 73. Châteaulin along the Aulne has a limited train service.

Tourist Information

Châteaulin: Quai Cosmao, t 02 98 86 02 11.
Pleyben: Pl Charles de Gaulle, t 02 98 26 71 05.
Le Faou: 10 Rue Gén-de-Gaulle, t 02 98 81 06 85.
Camaret-sur-Mer: Quai Kléber, t 02 98 27 93 60, *ot.camaret@wanadoo.fr.*
Crozon/Morgat: Bd de Pralognan-la-Vanoise, t 02 98 27 07 92.

Where to Stay and Eat

Le Faou ✉ 29580

★★★Hôtel de Beauvoir, 11 Place de la Mairie, t 02 98 81 90 31, *www.hotel-beauvoir.com* (*moderate*). Hotel with a solid reputation both for its rooms and its gastronomic restaurant, **La Vieille Renommée** (*expensive–moderate*). *Closed some of Nov and Dec; restaurant closed Mon lunch and Tues lunch.*

Camaret-sur-Mer ✉ 29570

★★★Thalassa, Quai du Styvel, t 02 98 27 86 44, *www.hotel-thalassa.com* (*moderate–inexpensive*). Modern and comfortable bayside hotel. *Closed Oct–Mar; resturant open eves.*
★★Le Styvel, Quai du Styvel, t 02 98 27 92 74 (*inexpensive*). A small family establishment, with restaurant (*moderate*). *Closed Jan.*
La Voilerie, 7 Quai Toudouze, t 02 98 27 99 55 (*moderate*). A consistently good restaurant.

Morgat ✉ 29160

★★★Grand Hôtel de la Mer, 17 Rue d'Ys, t 02 98 27 02 09 (*moderate*). Large Belle Epoque hotel, redone in the 1990s. Panoramic restaurant. *Closed Nov–Mar; restaurant closed Mon lunch, Tues lunch and Sat lunch.*
★★Hôtel Julia, 43 Rue de Tréflez, t 02 98 27 05 89 (*inexpensive*). White hotel with pretty rooms, garden and restaurant (*moderate*). *Closed Nov–Feb; restaurant closed Mon.*

A large portion of the Crozon peninsula's north shore is reserved for the French army, but the views over to Brest are dramatic. You emerge from the military landscape near the **Plage de Trez Rouz**, named after the blood from dead English and Dutch sailors that stained its rocks after the naval battle of Camaret in 1694. **Camaret**'s striking *sillon*, or pebbly jetty, curves out into a protected bay. The Tour Vauban, the thick-set, reddy-orange tower at the end of the spit, was built for the great French military engineer after whom it's named, recalled in the museum inside. Then comes the Chapelle Notre-Dame de Rocamadour, a squat, well-scrubbed Breton church. The wooden skeletons of several large abandoned fishing boats add a melancholic note.

A string of spectacular headlands lines the western side of the Crozon peninsula. After the sensational **Pointe du Toulinguet** and the inconsequential Neolithic **Alignements de Lagatjar**, you come across messy former Nazi fortifications, one turned into a shell and bird museum, another into the **Musée Mémorial International de la Bataille de l'Atlantique**. Between 1939 and 1945 some 45,000 Allied merchant navy sailors lost their lives keeping supply convoys going between Britain and North America. Around 30,000 German submarine sailors also died in this atrocious Atlantic conflict, at an average age of just 20.

The **Pointe de Penhir**, the most breathtaking of all the Crozon's headlands, is also the most tourist-infested. A huge cross of Lorraine commemorates Breton fighters in the Second World War. The outstanding natural feature here, the **Tas de Pois**, consists of a series of rocks ricocheting out to sea. The path from the Pointe de Penhir to the Cap de la Chèvre leads along a gloriously rugged coast. At the **Anse de Dinan** the bay changes with the tides; at low tide you can take a geology lesson just by walking below the cliffs. Looking south, the **Pointe de Dinan** rocks form what looks like a fort with a draw-bridge, hence the nickname of the Château de Dinan. At **Cap de la Chèvre**, the most southerly of the Crozon headlands, the views open up on to the enormous Bay of Douarnenez. The alarming war memorial with the tail of an aeroplane sticking out of a hole in the ground commemorates French naval pilots killed in action. **Morgat** boasts a long stretch of sand around its protected bay. To see the coastal caves, take a boat trip to the **Grotte de l'Autel**, a natural 'cathedral' with its natural 'altarpiece'. The only way to appreciate the coastline to **Telgruc-sur-Mer** and **Trez Bellec Plage** is to walk.

Heading inland, east of the Aulne estuary, at **Trégarvan**, the church is set on a lovely slope above the river. Inside its Gothic interior, an old clock ticks like a slow heartbeat. Locals love to fish in the boulder-strewn river as it flows through **Châteaulin**, a pretty town often bypassed by tourists. Cross the water for the rural **chapel of St-Sébastien-en-St-Ségal**, in a quiet spot, but teeming with sickly-sweet decoration inside.

Pleyben rivals St-Thégonnec as grandest of all the Breton *enclos paroissiaux*. The calvary, its most famous feature, resembles a massive triumphal arch. The ossuary, dating from the mid-16th century, has been converted into a tiny museum.

The grand **Château de Trévarez** (*open July–Aug daily 11–6.30; April–June and Sept daily 1–6; Oct–Mar Wed, weekends and school and public hols 2–6; adm*), below Châteauneuf-du-Faou, may be nicknamed the Château Rose, but actually looks more orange than pink, a rare brick building in Brittany. It was built in the 19th century for a Breton politician, the Marquis de Kerjégu, copying the style of the 16th-century Loire châteaux. **Spézet** is a bastion of Breton culture, its church containing stanied glass of rare finesse for the region.

The Bay of Douarnenez and Locronan

The Bay of Douarnenez can put in a claim to being one of the most beautiful in the country, and is one of the most immersed in legend – the ruins of the city of Ys are

The Legend of Wicked Ys

King Gradlon built Ys to satisfy the desires of his wild daughter Dahut, whose Norse mother had died at sea giving birth to her. The grieving Gradlon indulged his decadent girl's every whim. No one except Bishop Corentin of Quimper stood up to her. He tried to show Gradlon that his blind paternal love could lead to disaster, warning him of Dahut's immodest clothing and her refusal to go to church. However, to fulfil his daughter's wishes, Gradlon built her a new city on the sea – without any boring churches – designed to be so splendid that even the ocean would be dazzled. Dahut went to reign in Ys, where the people became increasingly wicked and the devil himself seduced the fallen princess, tempting her into giving him the keys to the gates holding back the ocean's waters. In the terrible finale, Gradlon's stallion Morvark proves powerful and nimble enough to run over the waves and escape from the drowning city, but the king tries to save his daughter too – such is the weight of her sins that they drag the horse down. At the last moment Guénolé, a saintly monk from Landévennec abbey, arrives to save Gradlon from the engulfing waves, but only by persuading him to let go of his daughter, dashed to pieces on the rocks.

Getting Around

Buses from Quimper, **t** 02 98 90 88 89, serve Locronan and Douarnenez.

Tourist Information

Douarnenez: 2 Rue du Docteur Mével, **t** 02 98 92 13 35, *www.douarnenez-tourisme.com*.
Locronan: Place de la Mairie, **t** 02 98 91 70 14, *www.locronan.org*.

Where to Stay and Eat

Ste-Anne-la-Palud ✉ 29550

****Hôtel de la Plage, **t** 02 98 92 50 12, *www.relaischateaux.com/laplage* (*luxury–expensive*). Plush hotel, sole building right by the beach. Fine seafood restaurant. Pool and tennis court. *Closed Nov–Mar; restaurant closed Tues lunch*.

Plonévez-Porzay ✉ 29550

Manoir de Moëllien, **t 02 98 92 50 40, *www.moellien.com* (*moderate*). Characterful hotel with rooms in the outbuildings of a sturdy little 17th-century manor; also has a well-regarded restaurant. *Closed Nov–Mar; restaurant closed Tues, Wed and Thurs lunch*.

Locronan ✉ 29180

Le Prieuré, 11 Rue du Prieuré, **t 02 98 91 70 89, *www.hotel-le-prieure.com* (*inexpensive*). On the tourist trail during the day, but staying here allows you to tour Locronan earlier in peace. Restaurant (*moderate*). *Closed mid-Nov–mid-Mar*.

Au Fer à Cheval, Pl de l'Eglise, **t** 02 98 91 70 74 (*moderate*). Good restaurant in the heart of the village. *Closed Sun, and Mon and Fri eves*.

The handful of crêperies in Locronan are all exceptionally beautiful.

Douarnenez and Tréboul ✉ 29100

Ty Mad, **t 02 98 74 00 53 (*inexpensive*). Delightful hotel in the quiet lanes up from the Plage St-Jean at Tréboul. *Closed Oct–Mar*.

Hôtel de France, 4 Rue Jean Jaurès, **t 02 98 92 00 02, *hotel-de-francedz@wanadoo.fr* (*inexpensive*). In Douarnenez centre, simple but comfortable rooms and pleasant restaurant (*moderate*). *Restaurant closed Sun eve and Mon out of season*.

Chez Fanch, 49 Rue Anatole France, **t** 02 98 92 31 77 (*moderate*). Good seafood restaurant.

supposed to lie under its waters. **Douarnenez** has guts to match its beauty – it's a practical, political, but also poetic fishing town. The fishing industry has been the mainstay since Gallo-Roman times, but it rarely made the locals' fortunes. In the early 20th century the workers exploited in the town's canning factories rose up against the squalid conditions of their existence; they also voted for France's first ever Communist mayor in 1921. After the war, things looked up, although the fishing industry has of course suffered in recent times. Colourful houses look down the **Port de Rosmeur**, still among the dozen largest fishing ports in France. West at **Port-Rhu**, the riverbank has been turned into an excellent boat museum, the **Musée du Bateau** (*open 15 June–15 Sept daily 10–7; 5 June–14 June and 16 Sept–Oct Tues–Sun 10–12.30 and 2–6; adm*), where you can admire real, not model boats, and even board some. Picturesque **Tréboul**, further west, has a cute marina.

You only have to take one look at **Locronan**'s central Place de l'Eglise to see how upmarket this town was in centuries past. The substantial granite homes of cloth and sail merchants mostly date from the 18th century, their ornate dormer windows sticking out of tall silvery-slate roofs. There is still one weaver's shop, although the trade which made the place rich has long died out. Described by Chateaubriand as 'a masterpiece of humidity', **Ronan**'s church is the slightly unstable focal point of the town, named after a fervent Christian who came from Ireland in the early Dark Ages.

The 15th-century building was funded by Breton dukes. Lovely Flamboyant Gothic tracery rails, some cut with the shapes of hearts, run around the outer sides. The legend of how Ronan was wrongly accused by an evil woman of killing her daughter features on an elaborate pulpit. The Locronan *pardons* count among the most celebrated pilgrimages in Brittany. But Locronan has become something of a victim of its own tourist success: virtually all the houses have been turned into restaurants, crêperies, or boutiques. The **Conservatoire de l'Affiche en Bretagne**, set apart, with stunning views up the hill from the village, houses collections of Breton posters.

The Bay of Audierne and the Pays Bigouden

The Cap Sizun and Pays Bigouden form the most southwesterly corner of the Finistère, one of the wildest parts of the Breton coast. The Pointe du Raz, Brittany's Land's End, sticks out above the huge long curve of the bay of Audierne. Inland, Pont-l'Abbé is capital of the Pays Bigouden, where a uniquely tall coiffe used to be worn.

Two famous headlands reach out into the ocean beyond the southern side of the Bay of Douarnenez, in the area known as the Cap Sizun. The more northerly **Pointe du Van** has been less spoilt by mass tourism, the chapel of St-They observing the coast. The **Baie des Trépassés**, or Bay of the Dead, separates this headland from that of the Pointe du Raz. Legends of death have piled up here like bits of wreckage: the place has

Getting Around

No trains, but reasonable **bus** services radiate out from Quimper and Pont-l'Abbé, t 02 98 90 88 89.

Boats to the Island of Sein leave from Ste-Evette, west of Audierne; book tickets in advance from Penn Ar Bed, t 02 98 70 70 70, *penn-ar-bed.fr*, or Vedettes Biniou, t 02 98 70 10 70.

For cruises from Bénodet to Quimper or the Iles de Glénan, contact Les Vedettes de l'Odet, t 02 98 57 00 58.

Tourist Information

Audierne: t 02 98 70 12 20, *www.audierne-tourisme.com*.
St-Guénolé/Penmarc'h: Place du Maréchal Davout, St-Pierre, t 02 98 58 81 44, *www.penmarch.fr*.
Loctudy: Place de la Mairie, t 02 98 87 53 78, *www.loctudy.fr*.
Pont-l'Abbé: Place de la République, t 02 98 82 37 99, *www.ot-pontlabbe29.fr*.
L'Ile-Tudy: 1 Rue des Roitelets, t 02 98 56 30 14.
Bénodet: 51 Av de la Plage, t 02 98 57 00 14, *www.benodet.fr*.

Where to Stay and Eat

Plogoff ✉ 29770
★★Ker-Moor, Plage du Loch, Route de la Pointe du Raz, t 02 98 70 62 06, *www.hotel-kermoor.com* (*moderate–inexpensive*). Probably the best of the hotels near the Pointe du Raz. The owner is also the chef here and can cook up a storm.
★★La Baie des Trépassés, t 02 98 70 61 34, *hoteldelabaie@aol.com* (*inexpensive*). Large, modern, and outrageously well-placed by the beach of this famous bay. *Closed mid-Nov–mid-Feb.*.

Audierne ✉ 29770
★★★Le Goyen, Place Jean Simon, t 02 98 70 08 88, *www.le-goyen.com* (*expensive–moderate*). Almost incongruously posh hotel with fine seafood restaurant. *Closed mid-Oct–Mar; restaurant closed Mon and Tues.*
★★Hôtel du Roi Gradlon, 3 Bd Manu Brusq, t 02 98 70 04 51, *www.auroigradlon.com* (*inexpensive*). Nothing olde worlde, but a modern white block plonked right above a fine beach with a restaurant (*expensive–moderate*). *Closed mid-Dec–mid-Jan; restaurant closed Wed eve.*

been claimed as a point of departure for the afterlife, while the souls of drowned sailors are said to return here annually in search of the loved ones they left behind. The **Pointe du Raz** is the most famous of Breton headlands, and the most overrun by tourists (you even have to pay to park). At the shopping-mall-style visitor centre you can find out about local history and legend. Towards the end of the wild promontory, the Phare de la Vieille and Phare de la Plate come into view.

Audierne still feels like a busy fishing port, with plenty of Breton atmosphere. Safely anchored up the Goyen estuary, the town's west bank is lined with shipping merchants' houses. Audierne boasts the largest lobster tanks in Europe, which you can visit. **Ste-Evette**, a very pretty spot just outside town, has a long string of beaches. Boats leave from here for the **island of Sein**. It seems a miracle that the place has not been swallowed up by the ocean: its highest point doesn't reach 32ft above sea level, and the island is almost ceaselessly windswept. There are bars you can take refuge in if the weather turns nasty, but there's little to visit apart from the village with its dull church, two menhirs chatting to one another outside, and a little museum commemorating the local heroes of the Second World War – while France capitulated in 1940, the men of this gritty island immediately took up General de Gaulle's call to join him across the Channel and fight for a free France, forming a huge percentage of the first wave of volunteers.

Plonéour-Lanvern ✉ 29720

**Manoir de Kerhuel, t 02 98 82 60 57, *manoirkerhuel@wanadoo.fr* (*moderate*). Splendid Breton manor in grounds with pool and tennis court. Restaurant (*expensive–moderate*). *Closed mid-Nov–mid-Dec and Jan–late Mar; restaurant closed Mon–Sat lunch.*

St-Guénolé ✉ 29760

***Le Sterenn, Rue de la Joie, t 02 98 58 60 36, *www.lesterenn.com* (*moderate–inexpensive*). Modern hotel right on the coast, with fine views of the rocks and reefs, and a spacious seafood restaurant (*expensive–moderate*). *Closed Nov–Mar.*
**Hôtel de la Mer, t 02 98 58 62 22 (*inexpensive*). Rustic hotel in a port house. Restaurant (*expensive–moderate*). *Closed late Nov, and mid-Jan–mid-Feb; restaurant closed Mon.*

Loctudy ✉ 29750

**Hôtel de Bretagne, 19 Rue du Port, t 02 98 87 40 21, *hoteldebretagne@msn.com* (*inexpensive*). Charmingly done up. *Closed late Nov–early Dec and Jan.*

Pont-l'Abbé ✉ 29120

**Hôtel de Bretagne, 24 Place de la République, t 02 98 87 17 22 (*inexpensive*).

Well-kept central 18th-century hotel, with an old Breton feel and a restaurant (*expensive–moderate*). *Closed mid-Jan–mid-Feb; restaurant closed Mon lunch.*

L'Ile-Tudy ✉ 29980

Hôtel Moderne, 9 Place de la Cale, t 02 98 56 43 34 (*inexpensive*). Actually a very basic old hotel, but it's in a great atmospheric location. Restaurant (*moderate*).
**Résidence Euromer, 6 Av du Téven, t 02 98 51 97 00, *www.EUROMER.fr* (*inexpensive*). Right by the beach, large, well-run modern hotel centred round its own pool. *Closed Oct–Mar.*

Ste-Marine ✉ 29120

**Hôtel de Ste-Marine, 19 Rue du Bac, t 02 98 56 34 79, *www.hotelsaintemarine.com* (*moderate*). Close to the old village chapel, with rooms and the restaurant (*expensive*) overlooking the harbour. *Closed Dec–Feb.*

Bénodet ✉ 29950

***Gwell-Kaër, 3 Av de la Plage, t 02 98 57 04 38 (*moderate*). Close to the beach; many rooms have terraces. Restaurant.
***Kastel, Corniche de la Plage, t 02 98 57 05 01, *www.hotel-kastel.com* (*moderate*). Right by the beach, stylish choice, with restaurant.

Back on the mainland, at **Pont-Croix** up the Goyen river, cobbled streets as treacherous as Alpine slopes lead from the river to the historic centre of town. Capital of the Cap Sizun, its centrepiece is the church of Notre-Dame de Roscudon, with a rocket of a Gothic spire and an extravagant Flamboyant Gothic porch. East, at **Confort-Meilars**, the church has preserved many of its 16th-century decorative features.

Heading down the bay of Audierne, at the doll-like port of **Pors-Poulhan** a statue of a girl blushing orange with lichen under her tall coiffe marks the entrance to the Pays Bigouden, an area of Brittany lovingly remembered in Pierre Jakez Hélias' *Le Cheval d'Orgueil* (*The Horse of Pride*). From **Penhors**, with its chapel exposed to the ocean winds, one of the longest beaches in Brittany curves round the Bay of Audierne down to St-Guénolé, backed by a curious bank of ancient pebbles.

The steeple of the **Chapelle de Tronoën** stands out of the melancholy countryside inland like a lichen-rusted trident. It possesses the most famous calvary in Brittany, and one of the oldest, dating from around 1450. The stone figures may have been eaten away by the winds, but you can pick out some 20 scenes from Christ's life on the friezes. The three crosses rise up above them like bent masts. On the coast, the rocks of the dramatic spit of the **Pointe de la Torche** are lashed by crashing waves.

Just north of **St-Guénolé**, one of a cluster of pungent fishing ports along the south side of the Pays Bigouden, you'll find a small museum of prehistory, then, further down the coast, Notre-Dame de la Joie, where sailors who made a lucky escape from storm or shipwreck came to thank the Virgin, and further south still, on the very southwestern corner of Brittany, three lighthouses in a row. Dwarfing the older ones, the **Phare d'Eckmühl** (*open daily 10–12 and 2–6; adm*) has a beam that can reach over 40 miles out to sea. Climb up to enjoy the overview of the Pays Bigouden and the local rocks, but be warned that the smell of rotting algae can be overpowering.

The screech of greedy gulls fills the streets of the gritty twin fishing ports of **Le Guilvinec** and **Lechiagat**, while **Lesconil** has a more genteel air. Potatoes brought the port of **Loctudy** to life in the 19th century, then sea-bathing became fashionable, and rich families from Quimper and Pont-l'Abbé started building along its coast and river estuary. Loctudy has remained a chic resort ever since, as well as continuing to thrive as a fishing port. Its beaches with rock pools and slowly sloping sands are popular with young families. The **church of St-Tudy**, somewhat notorious for its little carving of a male erection, lies just up from the port, surrounded by its sandy cemetery.

Pont-l'Abbé was once a thriving river port. Its castle houses the town hall, the tourist office and the **Musée Bigouden** on local history and traditions. Even in the late 1990s you could still see the occasional old Bigoudène wandering around town in her towering coiffe, but most of those who stuck to this extraordinarily formal daily dress have now sadly passed away. The Bigoudène coiffe edged gradually skywards from the middle of the 19th century and reached its dizzying height around 1935.

L'Ile Tudy isn't in fact an island, but a delightful, thin spit of land connected to the mainland by a sandy causeway, with an exceptionally picturesque huddled old village on the end. A great stretch of beach heads east to irresistible **Ste-Marine**, where the crescent of Breton houses around the port have mostly been converted into restaurants and cafés. **Bénodet**, Ste-Marine's big cheerful brother, lies on the opposite side of the piney Odet river, its central beach well protected within the estuary. Many regattas start out from the harbour, and tourist cruise boats leave from the quays in front of the church, either taking you up the twisting wooded meanders of the Odet to Quimper or out to the tiny stepping-stone Iles de Glénan. Both trips are wonderful.

Quimper

The joyous twin spires of Quimper cathedral soar above the centre of this delightful historic city on the banks of the Odet river. Legend claims that Quimper became the seat of power of King Gradlon of Cornouaille (*see p.242*) some time in the Dark Ages, and that he appointed Corentin, a holy hermit he encountered while out hunting one day, as his bishop. Corentin is thought to have been one of the major figures in the founding of Brittany after the fall of the Roman Empire. The **Cathédrale St-Corentin** is mainly Gothic, the wonderful spires only added in the 19th century. Look between them and you will see the tragic figure of Gradlon on his horse. Much of the cathedral's interior decoration vanished with the Revolution, but murals and stained glass have been added since, telling of Breton religious figures. The **Musée Départemental Breton** (*open June–Sept daily 9–6; rest of year Tues–Sat 9–12 and 2–5, Sun 2–5; adm*) has taken over the bishops' palace and follows a chronological path through Armorican and Breton civilization. Upstairs, discover fine collections of Breton costume, furniture and pottery.

The **Musée des Beaux-Arts** (*open July–Aug daily 10–7; rest of year Wed–Mon 10–12 and 2–6; Oct–Mar also closed Sun am; adm*), housed on Place Laennec north of the

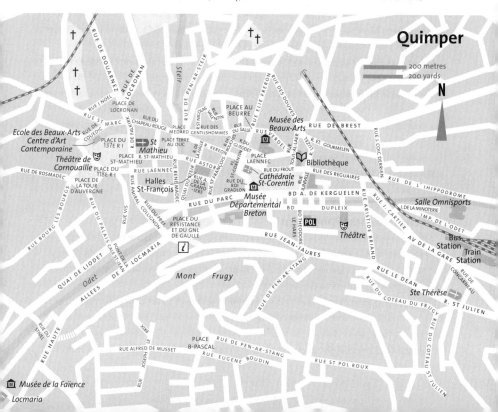

cathedral, was purpose-built to display the collection of Jean-Marie de Silguy, who was particularly interested in fine Flemish and French art from the 18th and 19th centuries. Since then, the museum has acquired an impressive array of Breton-inspired works. The Pont-Aven School is represented by striking pieces by Emile Bernard, Charles Filiger and Paul Sérusier. Alfred Guillou depicts costumed women arriving by boat for a *pardon*. Charles Cottet's blacker paintings convey how tough Breton life used to be. Evariste Luminais interprets the end of the city of Ys. One room is devoted to Max Jacob of Quimper, a gay Jew who converted to Catholicism. Better known as a writer, he lived with Picasso in their early years in Paris.

Quimper's best shopping streets lead off from the cathedral squares. **Rue Kéréon** has the poshest boutiques and finest carved-beamed old houses. A row of mini pedestrian bridges spans the Odet river. The pottery quarters lie across the water, in the shadow of the big Romanesque church of Locmaria. The **Musée de la Faïence** (*open mid-April–Oct Mon–Sat 10–6; adm*) tells the story of Quimper pottery; the 'Petit Breton', a caricature peasant in baggy pants, bright breeches and waistcoat, sporting a black Breton hat, first featured in the mid-19th century, and caught on quickly. Visit **HB Henriot Faïenceries** (*open Mon–Fri exc public hols; call **t** 02 98 90 09 36, to check times; adm*) to see how traditional Quimper pottery is made.

Concarneau and Pont-Aven

After the wild shores and fishing ports of the Pays Bigouden, the extremely pictur-esque stretch of Finistère coast east of Bénodet is better protected, with its deeply wooded, cosy estuaries known as *avens*. Pont-Aven and Concarneau became places of pilgrimage for painters in the late 19th century.

Proust, Sarah Bernhardt and a king of Egypt also counted among the more illus-trious early visitors to the resort of **Beg-Meil**, with its sandy coves looking out on to the beautiful Baie de la Forêt. A double row of pines forms the backdrop to the beach at **Le Cap Coz**, an unlikely strip of land that crosses the bay. Cherry and apple orchards flourish inland; **Fouesnant**, with its cheerful centre, is synonymous with good Breton cider. Its neighbour **La Forêt-Fouesnant** has a delightful church and beach, plus the well-hidden wood-surrounded modern marina of **Port-La-Forêt**.

    Concarneau's Ville Close, a long-fortified island, crams an awful lot into its small space. The ramparts were largely built for Duke Pierre II of Brittany in the mid-15th century, much added to in the mid-16th century, then altered by Vauban in the late 17th century. Through the first triangular fortifications, the **Musée de la Pêche** (*open 15 June–15 Sept daily 9–8; rest of year daily 9.30–12.30 and 2–6; adm*) tells the history of canned fish, which explains the rusty mid-19th-century tin reverentially included among the models of fishing boats and even some whole boats. The separate **Vidéo-Mer** (*open summer hols daily 10–6 and some evenings; rest of period April–Nov daily*

Getting Around

Very limited **bus** services, **t** 02 98 90 88 89.

Tourist Information

Fouesnant/Les Glénan: **t** 02 98 56 00 93, *www.ot-fouesnant.fr.*
Concarneau: Quai d'Aiguillon, **t** 02 98 97 01 44, *www.ville-concarneau.fr.*
Pont-Aven: 5 Place de l'Hôtel de Ville, **t** 02 98 06 04 70, *www.pontaven.com.*

Where to Stay and Eat

La Forêt-Fouesnant ✉ 29940
***Manoir du Stang, t/f 02 98 56 97 37, *stang@chateauxhotels.com* (*expensive–moderate*). A restored Breton manor turned smart hotel, hidden in its own wooded valley. *Closed mid-Sept–Mar.*

Concarneau ✉ 29900
***Hôtel de l'Océan, Plage des Sables Blancs, **t** 02 98 50 53 50, *www.hotel-ocean.com* (*expensive–moderate*). The only three-star hotel in town, by the beach, with pool as well as restaurant. *Restaurant closed winter.*
Ker Moor, Plage des Sables Blancs, **t 02 98 97 02 96 (*expensive–moderate*). Nicely done rooms and direct access to the beach.

Pont-Aven and Around ✉ 29930
***Roz Aven, 11 Quai Théodore Botrel, **t** 02 98 06 13 06, *www.hotelpontaven.online.fr* (*moderate*). An especially charming hotel,

divided between three different characterful buildings by the port. *Closed mid-Nov–Feb.*
Le Moulin de Rosmadec, Venelle de Rosmadec, **t 02 98 06 00 22 (*moderate*). Delightful little hotel in a converted 15th-century mill right in the centre of Pont-Aven. Fine restaurant (*expensive*). *Closed Feb.*
Hôtel Les Mimosas, 22 Square Botrel, **t 02 98 06 00 30 (*inexpensive*). At the southern end of the quays, with less immediate charm but a peaceful location. Restaurant (*moderate*) with terrace. *Closed mid-Nov–mid-Dec.*
La Taupinière, *c.*4 km west of Pont-Aven, Route de Concarneau, St-André, **t** 02 98 06 03 12 (*very expensive–expensive*). The high prices reflect the reputation of this refined restaurant. *Closed Mon and Tues.*

Riec-sur-Bélon ✉ 29340
***Domaine de Kerstinec, at the Pont-du-Guilly towards Moëlan, 3km south, **t** 02 98 06 42 98 (*moderate*). Some of the smartest rooms in the area, in 19th-century farm buildings. The dining room (*very expensive–moderate*) overlooks the Bélon river.

Moëlan-sur-Mer ✉ 29350
***Les Moulins du Duc, **t** 02 98 96 52 52, *www.hotel-moulins-du-duc.com* (*expensive–moderate*). Lakes, the river and a pool add their charms to the characterful rooms set out in various little buildings along the river. Lovely restaurant in the mill (*expensive*). *Restaurant closed Mon and Tues lunch.*
Hotel Kerfany, Blorimond-en-Moëlan, **t 02 98 71 00 46 (*inexpensive*). More affordable, with peaceful rooms in a big new Breton house. Restaurant (*moderate*).

The Pont-Aven School Returns to the Primitive

This innovative circle of artists, led by Gauguin and Emile Bernard, painted shockingly bold blocks of bright colour, separated by thick black cloisonné lines. Horizons were flattened and forms greatly simplified. People turned into statues. The style of these brave artists' images harked back to more primitive forms and to a different conception of visual arts still familiar in Asia and Africa. It had a moving simplicity that may have alarmed many contemporaries, but today these canvases have an immediate emotional and aesthetic appeal. Many of the Pont-Aven painters stayed at the Pension Gloanec, run by Marie-Jeanne Gloanec.

2–6; adm), shown on a large screen, gives a vivid impression of working conditions on board a fishing boat. Concarneau's fishing harbour is still going reasonably strong. Between 1870 and 1950 its quays were crammed with painters' easels. When in 1905 the sardine shoals which had fuelled the local economy suddenly moved on, the artists played a large part in organizing charitable assistance for the community.

Between Concarneau and Pont-Aven a slightly wilder stretch of coast leads down to the Pointe de Trévignon; there then follows a delightful string of narrow little *avens*. Gorgeous sandy creeks replace the great stretches of beach. The beautiful village of **Pont-Aven** becomes a tourist black spot in high summer. Blame one Paul Gauguin, who has taken on the role of a local deity. Thanks to him and a handful of other painters, European art took a great leap forward in this little Breton village in the 1880s and 1890s. If today's tourist hordes come to worship Gauguin, they often find him rather absent, although you can always see his work on the tins of Pont-Aven butter biscuits, and a few minor representative pieces in the **Musée de Pont-Aven** (*open July–Aug daily 10–7; Feb–June and Sept–Dec daily 10–12.30 and 2–6; closed Jan; adm*), which also puts on a superb programme of temporary exhibitions. Visit the **Chapelle de Trémalo** (walkable above Pont-Aven) and the **church of Nizon** (3km northwest) for an encounter with the statues of the crucified Jesus that inspired Gauguin's *Yellow Christ* and *Green Christ*.

It can take a surprising amount of patience to seek out the *aven* ports east of Pont-Aven, such as **Rosbras**, **Bélon** (of oyster fame), **Port-Bélon**, **Kerfany**, **Brigneau**, **Merrien** and **Doëlan**, but make the effort. At **Le Pouldu**, you arrive at a larger resort also favoured by the ground-breaking artists of the late-19th century, recalled in the fake murals at **La Maison de Marie Henri**. Inland, **Quimperlé** typifies the historic Breton ports built well upstream, protected from the ocean. The town's main monument, the extraordinary church of Ste-Croix, was built on the round model of the Holy Sepulchre in Jerusalem. Northwest, the splendid restored **Manoir de Kernault** (*open high season 11–7; rest of year school hols and Sun 2–6; adm*) presents exhibitions on Breton culture within splendid Breton architecture.

Morbihan

The Morbihan ('Little Sea' in Breton) is the *département* which covers most of southern Brittany, named after the island-strewn, amazingly indented Golfe du Morbihan in the east.

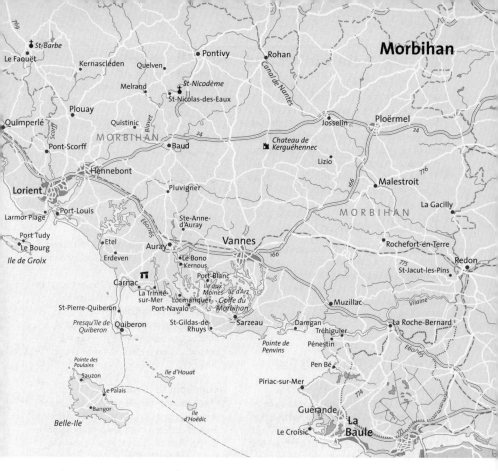

Western Morbihan

Along the western coast of the Morbihan, massive lengths of wild beaches stretch out in front of you, but the marks of the Second World War and of the military past remain provocatively visible.

Lorient and the Ile de Groix

Lorient (The Orient) was built from scratch in the 17th century to serve the French colonies. When this trade dried up, the harbour became a major naval and fishing port. After the Nazis established a submarine base here in the Second World War, the Allies bombed it to bits. Despite an initially grim grid-pattern look Lorient has a gritty appeal. The swanky Bassin à Flots, the marina, lies at the centre of town, while on board *La Thalassa* (*open July–Aug daily 9–7; rest of year Mon–Fri 9–12.30 and 2–6, Sat and Sun 2–6; adm*), moored nearby on Quai de Rohan, you can learn about life at sea for a marine biologist as well as for fishermen. Opposite, on **Quai des Indes**, pop into the Chambre de Commerce to view the vast Art Deco murals giving a visual notion of Lorient's colonial past. Beyond, the town's central church spire sticks out like a stylized fish bone. **Rue de Liège**, lined by palms, has some style. Out of the centre, you can visit

Getting There and Around

Lorient is easily reached by TGV **train** from Paris. It also has a small **airport**, Lorient-Lann-Bihoué. From Lorient, buses, t 02 97 21 28 29, serve the towns close to the coast. For **ferries** to Groix from central Lorient, contact **SMNN**, t 02 97 64 77 64, *www.mn-les-iles.com*. Inland, Hennebont has a railway station.

A **bus** service from Lorient to St-Brieuc stops at Hennebont, Baud and Pontivy.

Tourist Information

Lorient: Maison de la Mer, Quai de Rohan, t 02 97 21 07 84, *www.tourisme-lorient.com*.
Port-Louis: 47 Grande Rue, t 02 97 82 52 93.
Groix: Quai de Port-Tudy, t 02 97 86 53 08, *tourisme.groix@free.fr*.
Pontivy: 61 Rue du Général de Gaulle, t 02 97 25 04 10.

Where to Stay and Eat

Lorient ✉ 56100
★★★**Hôtel Mercure**, 31 Pl Jules Ferry, t 02 97 21 35 73 (*moderate*). Comfortable but dull postwar architecture.
★★**Victor Hugo**, 36 Rue Carnot, t 02 97 21 16 24, *hotelvictorhugo.lorient@wanadoo.fr* (*inexpensive*). A short walk from the landing stage for boats to Groix.
Le Vent d'Ouest, 1 Rue Maître Esvelin, beneath the Mercure, t 02 97 21 57 06 (*moderate*). Modern restaurant with startlingly bright dining room, and equally colourful dishes.
Le Bistrot du Yachtman, 14 Rue Poissonnière, t 02 97 21 31 91 (*moderate–cheap*). Close to the Bassin à Flot; good-value classic dishes.

Port-Louis ✉ 56290
★★**Du Commerce**, 1 Place du Marché, t 02 97 82 46 05 (*inexpensive*). Well-kept hotel on a shaded square. Restaurant (*moderate–cheap*). Closed Jan–Feb.
Avel Vor, 25 Rue de Locmalo, t 02 97 82 47 59 (*expensive*). Elaborate seafood dishes. *Closed Sun eve and Mon.*

Groix ✉ 56590
★★**La Marine**, 7 Rue du Général de Gaulle, t 02 97 86 80 05, *www.hoteldelamarine.com* (*moderate–inexpensive*). Charming, with its yew-shaded courtyard up in the main village, and its shell-decorated restaurant. *Closed Jan; restaurant closed Sun eve and Mon out of season.*
★★**Hôtel Escale**, on Port-Tudy's quay, t 02 97 86 80 04 (*inexpensive*). Cheerful, with lovely views on to the harbour.
★★**La Jetée**, 1 Quai de Port-Tudy, t 02 97 86 80 82, *laurence.tonnerre@freesbee.fr* (*inexpensive*). Nicely presented rooms at the busy port.

Hennebont ✉ 56700
★★★★**Château de Locguénolé**, Route de Port-Louis, Kervignac, t 02 97 76 76 76 (*luxury–expensive*). Luxurious 19th-century manor in 120 hectares of grounds sloping down to the Blavet, south of town. Pool and tennis court. Posh restaurant (*very expensive–expensive*). *Closed Jan; restaurant closed Mon–Thurs lunch.*

Pontivy ✉ 56300
★★**Hôtel de l'Europe**, 12 Rue F. Mitterrand, t 02 97 25 11 14, *www.hotelleerieeurope.com* (*inexpensive*). Some rooms have kept a quite startling 19th-century ambience.

the hideous concrete **U-Boat buildings** (*open July–Aug daily 1.30–6.30; rest of year only Sun 2–6; adm*), ironically among the few buildings to survive the Allied bombings. Nearby, former fishermen also show you round the *Victor Pleven*. As regards cultural events, Lorient is known above all for its great annual gathering of Celtic groups from across Europe at the **Festival Interceltique** in the first half of August.

The spiky citadel of **Port-Louis**, across the waters from Lorient, guards memories of France's 17th- and 18th-century colonial companies in the **Musée de la Compagnie des Indes** (*open April–Sept daily 10–6.30; Oct–mid-Dec and Feb–Mar Wed–Mon 2–6; adm*). Grand models of ships, maps and documents, plus fine objects in glass cabinets, give a notion of how colonial trade developed, and of the bitter battles with the Dutch and

British companies. But the tale told is only a partial one: references to the huge French slave trade only emerge if you keep your eyes peeled.

Gulls and rabbits rule on **Groix**, an island scented with honeysuckle in summer. The geology of the island sets it apart from the mainland, with a diversity of rocks that makes it a geologist's dream. Some 2,500 people live on Groix; you can learn about their history and traditions at the **Ecomusée** (*open July–Aug daily 9.30–12.30 and 3–7; May–June and Sept daily 10–12.30 and 2–5; rest of year Wed–Sun 10–12 and 2–5; adm*) at pretty **Port Tudy**, which used to be crammed with fishing boats; Lorient usurped its role in the 20th century. The main settlement is known as **Le Bourg**, a place with a quiet charm. Secretive covered fountains and Neolithic stones lie scattered inland. Powdered garnet tints the eastern beaches red.

Inland from Lorient up the Scorff and Blavet Rivers

Some way north of **Pont-Scorff**, with its thriving craft community, the chapel at **Kernascléden** contains a splendid display of 15th-century wall paintings. The depiction of hell shows devils come to pluck the damned from a tree, to be cooked in cauldrons. Just before Le Faouët, the church of **St-Fiacre** offers a fine example of Breton architecture, awkward and appealing at the same time. The rood screen is a fantastic multicoloured piece, the wood carved as delicately as lace. The great sloping roofs of the covered market dominate the central square of **Le Faouët**, its scale recalling important fairs, although now it tends to be a drowsy place. The fine arts museum (*open April–Oct daily 10–12 and 2–6; adm*) in the former Ursuline convent holds a small permanent collection with works by the 19th- and 20th-century artists who came to paint here. The Flamboyant Gothic **chapel of Ste-Barbe** a little north was one of their favourite spots, with French Renaissance stained-glass windows.

Heading northeast from Lorient up the Blavet river, **Hennebont**, as well as having an industrial past recalled in small musuems in the outskirts, has a major Gothic church in the centre, and the popular **Haras National** (*open July–Aug daily 9–7; Sept–June Mon–Fri 9–12.30 and 2–6; Sat and Sun 2–6; adm*), a grand stud farm. Reaching deeply rural, chestnut-wooded parts, the absurdly picturesque restored thatched village of **Poul-Fétan** stands high above the valley near Quistinic. At plain little **Baud**, the town's former public baths have been turned into the **Conservatoire Régional de la Carte Postale**, a surprisingly intriguing museum where you can explore traditional Breton culture via old postcards, but using modern techniques. The statue of the **Vénus de Quinipily**, an ancient curiosity, hides in these parts. As the name of **Melrand**'s **Village de l'An Mil** (*open May–Aug daily 10–7; Sept–April 11–5; adm*) indicates, this evocative ruined settlement dates back to around the year 1000, although the thatched farm buildings are modern interpretations. The country churches of **St-Nicodème** near **St-Nicolas-des-Eaux** and **Notre-Dame** in **Quelven** both prove surprisingly substantial and finely finished. **Pontivy** comprises a sober, imposing, straight-lined Napoleonic town tacked on to an eccentric, winding medieval one. Its château has two of the fattest, squattest towers in France. Once one of the mighty Rohan family's castles, it now hosts temporary exhibitions. The churches around Pontivy put on temporary exhibitions in the Art dans les Chapelles programme (held annually in high season).

To the Quiberon Peninsula

The **Etel estuary** is the least known of the Morbihan's enormous river mouths, but extraordinarily beautiful in parts, with very few modern additions beyond the oyster farms. By contrast, the nearby **Quiberon peninsula** counts among the most touristy parts of Brittany, although in the Second World War the place was one of the last Nazi strongholds to fall in France, on 8 May 1945. A precariously narrow strip of sand known as a *tombolo* connects the peninsula to the mainland. The western side, battered by the sea, has a rocky shoreline unreassuringly known as the **Côte Sauvage**.

Getting Around

A summer **train** service runs to Quiberon from Auray. There are **bus** services to Locmariaquer, Carnac and Quiberon. Book **boat** trips from Quiberon to the islands from SMNN, **t** 08 20 05 60 00, *www.mn-les-iles.com*.

Tourist Information

Quiberon: 14 Rue de Verdun, **t** 02 97 50 07 84, *www.quiberon.com*.
Belle-Ile: Quai Bonnelle, Le Palais, **t** 02 97 31 81 93, *www.belle-ile.com*.

Where to Stay and Eat

Quiberon ✉ 56170

★★★★**Sofitel Thalassa**, Pointe du Goulvars, **t** 02 97 50 20 00, *sofitel.com-ho557@accor-hotels.com* (*luxury–moderate*). Very large, rather uninspiring-looking luxury hotel, but right by the sea and renowned for its sea-water treatments. Pool and tennis court. Restaurant (*expensive*). *Closed Jan.*
★★★**Bellevue**, Rue de Tiviec, **t** 02 97 50 16 28 (*moderate*). Comfortable, modern and quite peaceful, set back just behind the beach, with pool. Restaurant. *Closed Oct–Mar; restaurant closed lunchtimes.*
★★**La Petite Sirène**, 15 Bd René Cassin, **t** 02 97 50 17 34 (*moderate*). Well located next to the sea-water treatment centre, with restaurant (*expensive*). *Closed mid-Oct–late Mar; restaurant closed Mon–Wed lunch and Sat lunch.*
Le Bon Accueil, Port Maria, **t** 02 97 50 07 92 (*inexpensive*). Basic friendly hotel handily close to the ferry terminal.
La Chaumine, 36 Place du Manémeur, **t** 02 97 50 17 67 (*expensive–moderate*). A good restaurant with a rustic dining room in a fisherman's cottage. *Closed Mon.*
Le Verger de la Mer, Boulevard du Goulvars, **t** 02 97 50 29 12 (*moderate*). Another good restaurant with lots of charm. *Closed Tues eve and Wed.*
Le Vivier, **t** 02 97 50 12 60 (*moderate*). On the most spectacular of the Côte Sauvage headlands, with a great view to accompany platters of mussels or *langoustines*.

Belle-Ile-en-Mer ✉ 56360

★★★★**Castel Clara**, Goulphar, **t** 02 97 31 84 21, *castelclara@relaischateaux.com* (*luxury–expensive*). Isolated above the southern cliffs, a large, luxury modern hotel with restful rooms and its own thalassotherapy and beauty centre. Excellent seafood cuisine (*expensive*). *Closed mid-Nov–mid-Feb.*
★★★**Le Clos Fleuri**, Route de Sauzon, Le Palais, **t** 02 97 31 45 45 (*moderate*). Spacious and comfortable peace and quiet outside town.
★★**Le Vauban**, 1 Rue des Ramparts, Le Palais, **t** 02 97 31 45 42, *www.hotelvauban.com* (*moderate*). Neat little hotel away from the quayside crowds, with some lovely views out to sea. Meals possible for those staying at the hotel. *Closed mid-Nov–mid-Feb.*
★★**L'Atlantique**, Quai de l'Acadie, Le Palais, **t** 02 97 31 80 11 (*moderate–inexpensive*). Right by the port, very nice rooms with sea views.
La Saline, **t** 02 97 31 84 70. Restaurant (*moderate*) worth seeking out, just inland along the quays.
Le Contre Quai, Rue St-Nicolas, **t** 02 97 31 60 60 (*moderate*). A simple rustic décor, but its cuisine is highly reputed. *Closed Oct–Mar.*
Le Roz Avel, Rue du Lieutenant Riou, **t** 02 97 31 61 48 (*moderate*). Tasty dishes, including Belle-Ile lamb. *Closed middle Nov, Jan and Feb, and Wed.*

The most spectacular views are from the **Beg er Goalennec** headland, where the waves spit angry foam against the small cliffs; the eastern side proves much gentler.

Quiberon itself is a popular resort looking out to Belle-Ile. In the course of the 19th century it became the largest sardine-fishing port in Brittany, but now, apart from the odd row of fishermen's cottages, it doesn't look particularly Breton. The Grande Plage turns into a very busy family beach during the summer holidays; part of the area is dominated by a thalassotherapy centre, created in 1963 by the dynamic Breton cycling hero Louison Bobet, setting the trend for such establishments around Brittany.

Boats head out from Quiberon to a splendid trio of islands: Belle-Ile, Houat and Hoëdic. It was Monet and Sarah Bernhardt who made a name for **Belle-Ile** at the turn of the 20th century. Although the mainland remains within view, the Bellilois are proud of their independence. The largest Breton island – around 20km long and almost 10km across in parts – Belle-Ile has a magnificent weaving coastal path. For centuries monks effectively ruled the place, but, as it acquired strategic importance in the 17th-century wars, the military authorities called upon Vauban to put up serious defences. During the 19th century the citadel served as a prison of note; then Napoléon III decided to fortify the island on a grand scale. Many of these forts survive in a good state of repair. The island's capital and main port, **Le Palais**, is dominated by the spectacular star-shaped structures of Vauban's citadel, slowly being restored. The **museum** (*open July–Aug daily 9–7; April–June and Sept–Oct 9.30–6; rest of year 9.30–12 and 2–5; adm*) inside is crammed with bits and bobs on the island's history. Even the beaches on the protected northeastern side of the island (the '*dedans*', or 'inside') are fortified. The villages dotted around the island each have character.

'Duck' and 'duckling' are the translations of the Breton names of the two gorgeous little sandy and rocky islands close to Belle-Ile, although **Houat** is shaped like a *langoustine*, **Hoëdic** like a whelk; on both, the sound of strident seagulls fills the air.

Mega Megalith Country

The most famous concentration of Neolithic monuments in France is crammed into the short stretch of Morbihan coast between Erdeven and Gavrinis. Such is the density of stone alignments and tumuli here that the authorities seem at a loss as to what to do with them all. Often ignored by tourists, extraordinary lines of megaliths run out of the little town of **Erdeven**, the main road cuts right through a section of them. **Carnac** has a daunting density of Neolithic monuments. The local map shows four tumuli, at least 16 dolmens and half a dozen isolated menhirs beyond those gathered in the four famous great alignments of **Le Ménec**, **Kermario**, **Kerlescan** and **Le Petit Ménec**. When you visit these ten thousand or so standing stones, consider the some half-million to one million days of work that one researcher has estimated it would have taken to erect them. These alignments, probably erected *c.* 3000 BC, stretch across four kilometres. Most of the stones are lined up in roughly parallel rows, but circular or four-sided enclosures end some of the rows. The reasons for the alignments remain a mystery, but they may well have been places of worship, concentrating on important changes in the seasons. Because their complete structures

Tourist Information

Erdeven: 7 Rue de l'Abbé Le Barth, B.P.27,
t 02 97 55 64 60, *www.ot-erdeven.fr*.
Carnac: 74 Av des Druides, t 02 97 52 13 52,
www.ot-carnac.fr.
Locmariaquer: Place de la Mairie, t 02 97 57 33
05, *www.perso.wanadoo.fr/ot.locmariaquer*.

Where to Stay and Eat

Carnac ✉ 56340

★★★★Le Diana, 21 Bd de la Plage, t 02 97 52
05 38, *www.lediana.com* (*luxury–expensive*).
Modern beachside luxury, with pool.
Restaurant (*expensive*). *Closed Nov–Easter*.
★★★Le Bateau Ivre, 70 Bd de la Plage, t 02 97 52
19 55 (*expensive–moderate*). On the eastern
edge of the beach, comfortable, with pool.
★★Les Rochers, 6 Bd de la Base Nautique,
t 02 97 52 10 09 (*moderate*). Cheaper option

along Carnac beach, larger rooms with
balconies. Restaurant. *Closed Nov–Easter*.
★★Les Ajoncs d'Or, Kerbachique, between
Carnac and Plouharnel, t 02 97 52 32 02,
www.lesajoncsdor.com (*moderate*). A joy of a
characterful old stone family house turned
hotel, set in a beautifully tended walled and
shaded garden. *Restaurant closed lunch*.
La Calypso, t 02 97 52 06 14 (*expensive*). Set
apart by the Pô, characterful place serving
refined cuisine. *Closed Mon*.

St-Philibert ✉ 56470

★★Les Algues Brunes, Route des Plages, t 02 97
55 08 78 (*inexpensive*). A calm retreat well-
shaded by pine trees. *Closed mid-Sept–May*.

Locmariaquer ✉ 56740

★★L'Escale, 2 Place Dariorigum, t 02 97 57 32 51
(*inexpensive*). Unpretentious modern hotel,
beautifully situated on the waterfront.
Simple restaurant-crêperie. *Closed Oct–Mar*.

aren't known, it is hard to prove definitively any astronomical use. The alignments mighmayt also have been connected with funeral rites and ideas of an afterworld, especially given the density of major tombs scattered in the vicinity. These standing stone rows have inspired some very entertaining, fanciful notions, from the legend of St Cornély, which claims that Roman legionnaires who tried to persecute Christians here were turned to stone, to the joke that American GIs who arrived to liberate this area thought the menhirs had been planted by the Nazis as anti-tank defences. The **visitor centre** (*open May–Aug daily 9–7; Sept– April daily 10–5; adm for guided tours*) offers a partial introduction to the Neolithic subject, but, as the major alignments are fenced off, book a guided tour to see them close up.

If you get hooked by the subject, visit the **Musée de la Préhistoire Miln-Le Rouzic** (*open June–Sept Mon–Fri 10–6.30, weekends 10–12 and 2–6.30; Oct–April Wed–Mon 10–12 and 2–5; adm*) in the centre of Carnac's old town, named after two of the most passionate archaeologists to have researched here: James Miln, a Scotsman who started his work on the area in 1874, and his assistant Zacharie Le Rouzic. As well as admiring the tombs and jewellery, you can learn about the theories on Neolithic life, not just death, in these parts. The nearby church of **St-Cornély** tempts visitors with its decoration, including an outdoor baldaquin with a top in granite tied like a bow on a present.

Carnac also has a staggeringly beautiful stretch of coastline. On the western side, at low tide the flat sands of the Pô estuary can blind you in the sunshine; flat-bottomed oyster boats lie like beached whales on the firm bed. Past the picturesque village of **St-Colomban** you come to Carnac's marina, and then its pine-backed beaches, red life-guards' ladders planted in the sands. **La Trinité-sur-Mer** means yachting to the French; this port down its river attracts the finest yachtsmen in the country.

At the western entrance to the Golfe du Morbihan, **Locmariaquer**'s peninsula has another major concentration of megalithic sights. Like Carnac, it is also a sprawling, highly popular summer resort. Three vast Neolithic monuments, the **Grand Menhir Brisé**, the **Tumulus Er-Grah** and the **Table des Marchands** (*open May–Sept daily 10–7; Oct–April 10–12.30 and 2–5; adm*) are presented together at the Centre d'Informations Archéologiques. The connection between the great menhir and the two tumuli actually remains unclear, but their massive scale indicates the site's importance. This spot may have stood at a central or symbolic point in a whole network of megaliths along the Morbihan coast. Weighing in at some 350 tonnes, the Grand Menhir Brisé (dating from between 5000 and 4000 BC) must have been awe-inspiring when it stood upright, some 60ft high, rather than prostrate and broken. You wonder how Neolithic people could possibly have erected such a mammoth piece of stone. In the Table des Marchands, part of an engraved bull was discovered on one of the roof's slabs, while a matching piece of the engraving was later discovered in the tomb on the island of Gavrinis. The most remarkable carving visible inside features rows of crooks, possibly symbols of authority. From the village of Locmariaquer, the views on to the flat, calm inland gulf of Morbihan are enchanting. The dolmen of **Les Pierres Plates** lies neglected on the beach, several of its stones bearing mysterious carvings.

The Golfe du Morbihan

Auray and the Northern Golfe du Morbihan

The magical Golfe du Morbihan, with just the narrowest of openings to the ocean, is an inland sea peppered with islands, some 40 in all. The two largest – Ile aux Moines and Ile d'Arz – make for wonderful days out. Major Neolithic sites lie scattered around the sides of the gulf, and close by stand the historic towns of Auray, Ste-Anne-d'Auray and Vannes, the last the capital of the *département* of Morbihan.

Auray has an attractive enough upper town above its river, with its fair share of grand houses and churches, but down by the water the port of **St-Goustan** proves irresistible. A few may find it too perfect, almost like a film set, with restaurants established in virtually every building. You can climb on board the Musée *La Goélette*, the polished schooner moored here. The nearby port of **Le Bono** may be more secretive, but competes in sheer quaintness, and beside it the Neolithic site of **Kernous** counts among the most beautiful in Brittany, the trees surrounding the main tomb seeming almost to bow inwards to pay homage.

Ste-Anne-d'Auray draws large numbers of Catholic faithful away from the seductive coast. Breton legend has it that Anne, mother of the Virgin Mary, was born here, a story that may have derived from a muddle with Ana, mother goddess of the Celtic pantheon. A local peasant, Yves Nicolazic, witnessed a recurring apparition of St Anne in 1623, telling him to build a chapel to her. After he had also 'unearthed' a miraculous statue of the saint, the Church responded. The 17th-century building was replaced in the 19th century by an enormous neo-Renaissance church. Inside, everything serves as a lesson in 19th-century religious propaganda. The *pardon* of Ste-Anne-d'Auray

Getting Around

Vannes and Auray lie on the high-speed TGV rail line between Paris and Quimper. Ste-Anne-d'Auray also has a railway station. **Bus** services, **t** 02 97 21 28 29, serve smaller places around the gulf.

Tourist Information

Auray: 20 Rue du Lait, **t** 02 97 24 09 75, *www.auray-tourisme.com*.

Ste-Anne-d'Auray: 12 Place Nicolazic, **t** 02 97 57 69 16, *tourismesteanne@wanadoo.fr*.

Vannes: 1 Rue Thiers, **t** 02 97 47 24 34, *www.pays-de-vannes.com/tourisme*.

La Roche-Bernard: 14 Rue du Dr Cornudet, **t** 02 99 90 67 98.

Where to Stay and Eat

Auray ✉ 56400

L'Eglantine, Place St-Sauveur, **t** 02 97 56 46 55 (*moderate*). Among several beautiful crêperies at St-Goustan port, this is a smarter restaurant, with *bouillabaisse* and the like. *Closed Wed lunch*.

Le Bono ✉ 56400

★★★Hostellerie Abbatiale, Manoir de Kerdréan, **t** 02 97 57 84 00, *www.abbatiales.com* (*moderate*). Stylish, with pool, tennis court and golf course. Restaurant (*expensive*).

L'Ile aux Moines ✉ 56780

Le San Francisco, Le Port, B.P.7, **t** 02 97 26 31 52, *www.ileauxmoines.com* (*moderate*). Former Franciscan convent, with some sought-after cosy rooms and two dining rooms with views. Simple restaurant (*cheap*). *Closed Nov–Jan; restaurant closed Mon*.

Vannes ✉ 56000

★★★Le Roof, Presqu'île de Conleau, **t** 02 97 63 47 47 (*expensive–moderate*). The most exclusive hotel in Vannes, out of the centre, with wonderful views. Restaurant (*expensive*).

★★Marina, 4 Place Gambetta, **t** 02 97 47 22 81 (*inexpensive*). Overlooking the port, which comes to life in the evenings.

De Roscanvec, 17 Rue des Halles, **t** 02 97 47 15 96 (*moderate*). A charming little restaurant in an old Vannes house. *Closed Mon*.

La Table des Gourmets, 6 Rue Alexandre Le Pontois, **t** 02 97 47 52 44 (*moderate*). Looking on to the ramparts from outside Vannes' walls, specializing in gastronomic Breton cuisine. *Closed Sat lunch and Mon*.

Billiers ✉ 56190

★★★★Domaine de Rochevilaine, Pointe de Pen-Lan, **t** 02 97 41 61 61, *www.domainerochevilaine.com* (*luxury–expensive*). Exclusive hotel with a splendid headland to itself. Rooms in various lovely stone buildings. Pool and seawater treatments as well as an excellent restaurant.

La Roche-Bernard ✉ 56130

★★★L'Auberge Bretonne, 2 Place Duguesclin, **t** 02 99 90 60 28, *www.auberge-bretonne.com* (*very expensive–expensive*). Chic little address with one of the most revered restaurants in Brittany. *Closed early Nov–early Dec and most Jan; restaurant closed Mon lunch, Tues lunch, Fri lunch and Thurs*.

★★Auberge des Deux Magots, 1 Place du Bouffay, **t** 02 99 90 60 75, *aubergelesdeux-magots.roche-bernard@wanadoo.fr* (*inexpensive*). On a lovely square, in an old house with two carved monkeys, old-fashioned French rooms and traditional French restaurant (*expensive–moderate*). *Restaurant closed Sun eve, Mon and Tues lunch*.

draws tens of thousands of people every year on 25 and 26 July, and Pope John Paul II visited the place on his 1996 tour. The biggest memorial in Brittany to the vast number of Bretons who died in the First World War also stands here.

Back at the Golfe du Morbihan, a gorgeous confusion of spits reaches into its waters. Book places well in advance (**t/f** 02 97 57 19 38, *sagemor@wanadoo.fr*) for the small boat from Larmor-Baden to the **cairn of Gavrinis** (*open April and June–Sept daily 9.30–12.30 and 1.30–6.30; May Mon–Fri 1.30–6.30 only; adm*). Set apart on its own island, this is the most mysterious Neolithic site in France, roughly reckoned to date from the 4th millennium BC. Many of the engraved patterns in the tomb look like magnified fingerprints, semi-abstract forms that perhaps represent a goddess mother linking the world of the living with the world of the dead – you'll need to use your imagination. Other intriguing patterns include spirals and a stylized human figure with an axe and a crook; serpentine shapes writhe below.

A cruise around the Golfe du Morbihan counts among the greatest experiences in Brittany. Take a boat from Vannes' modern harbour a short way from the centre.

Apart from the crowds, **l'Ile aux Moines** is a little Breton paradise, with creeks and beaches, fishermen's cottages, walled gardens, the odd Neolithic sight, and heavenly views. **L'Ile d'Arz** is flatter, less wooded and less popular, but still delightful, with thin strips of beach. However, you don't even need to go out on to the gulf to be mesmerized by its beauty; just follow the stunning coastal path below **Arradon**.

Vannes

Hidden away at the back of the Golfe du Morbihan, **Vannes** may have been the site of the sea-faring Celtic tribe of the Venetes, wiped out by Caesar. The shadowy figure of St Patern, one of the seven founding fathers of the Breton Church in the Dark Ages, appears to have made this spot his spiritual centre. It was fought over by Bretons and Franks, and the independence leader Nomenoë briefly made the place his capital. After the bitter Breton War of Succession, the Breton dukes established Vannes as one of the main centres of the duchy. But with Anne de Bretagne's marriage to King Charles VIII Brittany was joined to the French crown's territories, the act of union signed at Vannes. Grand town houses from the Ancien Régime show that merchants thrived here. Now the city is a vibrant place, with a lively cultural scene.

A croissant of cafés curves out from the gateway separating Vannes' central harbour from its old town. Up posh **Rue St-Vincent** you come to a series of characterful, sloping squares. Château-Gaillard, a smart 15th-century mansion, houses the **Musée d'Histoire et d'Archéologie** (*open June–Sept daily 10–6; Oct–May school hols 1.30–6; adm*), with many of the finest finds from the Morbihan's Neolithic sites on display. The **Cathédrale St-Pierre** sits slightly awkwardly atop Vannes' hill, hemmed in on all sides by pretty streets. Mainly built in sober Gothic style, it has some Renaissance additions, including a round side chapel dedicated to the evangelizing saint Vincent Ferrier, and a wildly carved chapel on the east end. The Act of Union between Brittany and France was signed behind the thick walls of **La Cohue**, opposite the cathedral, which now contains a collection of museums (*open 15 June–Sept daily 10–6; rest of the year daily 1.30–6; adm*). The most famous work in the **Musée des Beaux-Arts** is Delacroix's *Crucifixion*, although it's not one of his best. Otherwise the museum is mostly devoted to Breton subjects. The **Musée du Golfe et de la Mer** covers the history and ethnography of the Golfe du Morbihan. Beyond the choir end of the cathedral, Place Brûlée leads down to the imposing **Porte Prison**.

The Southern Golfe du Morbihan

The **Presqu'île de Rhuys**, the long spit of land that forms the protective southern barrier to the Golfe du Morbihan, has become rather crowded with its two popular ports on the western tip beyond Arzon, **Port-Navalo** more traditional, **Port Crouesty** brasher, more artificial. For an overview of the Presqu'île, climb either of the Neolithic tombs east of **Arzon**. The **Petit Mont** (*open July–Aug Sun, Mon and Wed–Fri for tours at 10, 11.30, 3 and 5; April–June and Sept Wed and Fri tours 10 and 11.30; adm*) is one of the most surprising Neolithic sites in Brittany. The Nazis turned it into a bunker, the savage alteration actually making it even more interesting to visit. The name of the **Butte de César** derives from the now disputed theory that Caesar watched his Roman fleet smash the becalmed ships of the Venetes from here.

Heading east past wild beaches, the abbey church of **St-Gildas-de-Rhuys** is dedicated to one of the most influential Celtic religious figures in southern Brittany's conversion to Christianity. The medieval architecture has been rather messed up, but the Romanesque apse must have filled pilgrims with awe. The **Château de Suscinio** (*open July–Aug daily 10–7; April–June and Sept daily 10–12 and 2–7; Oct–Mar Thurs, Sat and Sun 10–12 and 2–5, Mon, Wed and Fri 2–5; adm*), a huge ruin of a medieval castle plonked surprisingly close to the beach, was built for the Breton dukes to enjoy the hunting, when the peninsula was covered with forests. Massive walls and towers aplenty survive, although the castle fell into decline in the 16th century. In part restored, it contains an historical museum with odd startling exhibits – don't miss the caricature faces on the medieval flooring.

Around the Vilaine Estuary

The **Pointe de Pen-Lan** marks the entrance to the beautiful **Vilaine estuary**, or Vilaine Maritime, visitable by boat from the marina by the dam. On the south side of the Vilaine, the comical lighthouse at **Tréhiguier** has been turned into the cute little **Maison de la Mytiliculture** (*open July and Aug daily 11–1 and 3.30–6.30; adm*), explaining the mysteries of mussel cultivation. At **Pénestin**, the arc of a beach is backed by high cliffs of hardened sand which turn a lustrous golden colour at sunset, hence the place's nickname of La Mine d'Or, the Gold Mine.

Up the Vilaine, at historic **La Roche-Bernard**, narrow streets tumble down the steep hillside from the pretty squares above. The **Musée de la Vilaine Maritime** (*open mid-June–mid-Sept daily 10.30–12.30 and 2.30–6.30; early June and late Sept daily 2.30–6.30; April–May and Oct weekends 2.30–6.30; adm*) occupies the 16th-century **Maison des Basses-Fosses**, which looks unassuming from the upper town, but plunges dramatically downhill. Inside, the struggles to build *La Couronne*, the first French ship to be built with three decks, and to span the Vilaine with a bridge are detailed.

Inland Eastern Morbihan

Several very picturesque, prettified little towns lie scattered around the Oust river, which flows across the eastern Morbihan to join the Vilaine at Redon. But first, head due north of Vannes for some shocking contemporary art.

The wonderfully wacky art of the **Domaine de Kerguéhennec** (*open mid-Jan–mid-Dec Tues–Sun 10–6; adm*) lurks around the grounds of this beautiful estate and even infiltrates the staid Ancien Régime château. The combination of well-ordered classical architecture and exuberant-to-irreverent contemporary works is thought-provoking; mull over these matters in the cool café-cum-library in the former stables.

One of Brittany's sturdiest medieval castles dominates the river Oust at **Josselin**. This is one of the very rare Breton châteaux still owned by descendants of a great feudal family, the Rohans. Their ownership was interrupted in the 14th century by Olivier de Clisson, one of the most feared knights in Breton history, who also became leader of the French army. He had the **Château de Josselin** (*open mid-July–Aug daily 10–6; June–mid-July and Sept daily 2–6; April, May and Oct weekends and school hols 2–6; adm*) fortified with 17 towers, three of which survive, surveying the Oust. From the river the place looks distinctly unwelcoming with its sheer walls. By contrast, approaching from the town side there is scarcely a hint of military architecture, and a fabulous riot of Gothic motifs and symbols covers the inner façade. The tour takes you round five extravagant neo-Gothic rooms. The town virtually knocking at the door of the castle is dominated by the church of Our Lady of the Bramble Patch.

After the solid granite mansions of **Lizio**, an overgrown historic village south of Josselin with a couple of eccentric little local museums, **Malestroit**, right on the Oust, has a popular port. The centrepiece in town, the church of St-Gilles, was built in curious red-tinged stone, and contains charming decoration. To the west, the substantial **Musée de la Résistance Bretonne** (*open mid-June–mid-Sept daily 10–7; rest of year Wed–Mon 10–12 and 2–6; adm*) by **St-Marcel** is a moving war museum, with a wealth of information on the important local parachute expeditions.

East again, **La Gacilly** slopes up from the Aff rather than the Oust. The Breton cosmetics magnate Yves Rocher began building up his empire here, starting with haemorrhoid cream, the recipe handed down to him by his grandmother. His glamorous company has grown into a global name, and has pumped money and life into what was a moribund old village. **Le Végétarium** (*open mid-June–mid-Sept daily; April–mid-June, weekends and public hols; adm*), dedicated to botanical research, lies on the Rocher site, along with a botanical garden. Up in the village, a thriving community of craftspeople has been encouraged to settle. East of La Gacilly, explore the atmospheric Neolithic monuments of **St-Just**, abandoned over miles of heathland.

Recently re-cobbled streets have added further to the beauty of **Rochefort-en-Terre**, one of the prettiest villages in Brittany. At the end of the 19th century a colony of artists fell in love with the place. Although not nearly as talented or innovative as the painters in Pont-Aven, they are remembered in the **museum** by the beautiful fake **château** (*both open July–Aug daily 10–7; June and Sept daily 2–7; April and May weekends and public hols 2–7; adm*), the latter assembled here at the beginning of the 20th

Tourist Information

Josselin: Place de la Congrégation, t 02 97 22 36 43, *ot.josselin@wanadoo.fr*.
Rochefort-en-Terre: Place des Halles, t 02 97 43 33 57, *www.rochefortenterre.com*.
Redon: Place de la République, t 02 99 71 06 04.

Where to Stay and Eat

Josselin ✉ **56120**
★★Hôtel de France, Place Notre-Dame, t 02 97 22 23 06 (*expensive*). In the centre of town.
La Carrière, 8 Rue de la Carrière, t 02 97 22 22 62 (*expensive*). Refined town house not far from the château, with a pretty garden.

century by an American artist, Alfred Klots. The few rooms on show are decorated in a unique Americano-Hispanic-Italiano-Breton style. In fact, virtually every house in Rochefort-en-Terre has interesting details, while Place du Puits is the most absurdly picturesque square. The church may seem a little neglected, left to one side of the village, but it holds its own, the decorative details including multicoloured sheep.

Redon was long an important crossroads, or crosswaterways, with the Vilaine, Oust and Canal de Nantes à Brest meeting here. A sweet little museum down by the water recalls the thriving days of river transport. The stocky abbey church of St-Sauveur now vies for attention with a neo-Renaissance town hall in upper Redon, but through the Middle Ages was among the most influential religious centres in Brittany.

La Baule to St-Nazaire via Le Croisic

Guérande, La Baule and the Le Croisic Peninsula

Guérande overlooks the vast salt marshes on which its wealth was built in medieval times. Solid protective granite ramparts still surround the streets with their fine granite houses packed with craftshops and crêperies. The most impressive entrance into town, the **Porte St-Michel**, once served as home to the town governors; it has been converted into the **Musée du Château** (*open April–Sept daily 10–12.30 and 2.30–7; Oct Tues–Sun 10–12 and 2–6, Mon 2–6; adm*), displays devoted to local history. Explore the **Pays Blanc** (White Country), the desolate landscape of the salt marshes below Guérande, mounds of crystals piled high in the grid of saltpans in summer. Information and guided tours are offered at **Terre de Sel** (*open July–Aug daily 9.30–12.30 and 2.30–7; April–June and Sept daily 10.30–12.30 and 2.30–6; adm*) at **Pradel** and **La Maison des Paludiers** (*open Feb–Nov daily 10–12.30 and 2–5*) at **Saillé**.

Chic kitsch, the best of yachting facilities and 9km of the finest unbroken sand well protected from the Atlantic count among the attractions of **La Baule**, southern Brittany's poshest, busiest resort. A curve of condominiums has pushed out the villas that once lined the waterfront, but inland, fantasy flourishes: Normandy beamed homes, Basque chalets, modern thatched villas, even the odd Arabic folly vie for your attention. **Pornichet** offers more of the same, **Le Pouliguen** more traditional charm.

The rocky **Le Croisic peninsula** is exposed to the ocean. Traffic is more of a blight in summer than bad weather. **Batz-sur-Mer**, straddling the peninsula, looks a traditional Breton village with its cluster of whitewashed houses; visit the **Musée des Marais Salants** (*open June–Sept and school hols daily 10–12 and 3–7; rest of the year weekends 10–12 and 3–7; adm*). At the historic **port of Le Croisic**, only a narrow channel of water allows the boats into the harbour. In the suburbs, the starfish-shaped **Océarium** (*open June–Aug daily 10–7; Feb–May and Oct–mid-Nov daily 10–12 and 2–6; mid-Nov–mid-Dec 2–6; adm*) is the major tourist attraction with its aquaria.

The Brière Natural Park

The secretive marshes of the Brière stretch between the Vilaine and St-Nazaire. Reeds proliferate, providing materials for what is the most densely thatched area in

Getting Around

There's a TGV **train** from Paris to La Baule and Le Croisic (3hrs). Nantes **airport** is also convenient. **Bus** services, t 02 40 11 53 02.

Tourist Information

Guérande: 1 Place du Marché aux Bois, t 02 40 24 96 71, *www.ot-guerande.fr*.
La Baule: 8 Place de la Victoire, t 02 40 24 34 44, *www.labaule.fr*.
Le Croisic: Place du 18 Juin 1940, t 02 40 23 00 70, *www.ot-lecroisic.com*.
Brière: t 02 40 66 85 01, *www.parc-naturel-briere.fr*.
St-Nazaire: Base Sous-Marine, t 0820 014 015, *www.saint-nazaire-tourisme.com*.
Pornic: Place de la Gare, t 02 40 82 04 40, *www.ot-pornic.fr*.

Where to Stay and Eat

Guérande ✉ 44350

⋆⋆Les Remparts, 14–15 Bd du Nord, t 02 40 24 90 69 (*inexpensive*). Pleasant, comfortable rooms and good food (*moderate*). *Closed late Nov–Jan.*
⋆⋆Roc Maria, 1 Rue du Vieux Marché aux Grains, t 02 40 24 90 51 (*inexpensive*). Hotel in a charming house, with crêperie.

La Baule ✉ 44500

⋆⋆⋆⋆Hermitage Barrière, 5 Esplanade Lucien Barrière, t 02 40 11 46 46, and **⋆⋆⋆⋆Royal Thalasso** , 6 Av Pierre Loti, t 02 40 11 48 48, *www.lucienbarriere.com* (*luxury–very expensive*). Huge sister luxury hotels offering sea-water treatments, pools, etc. Buffet July and Aug (*moderate*). *Closed Jan.*
⋆⋆⋆⋆Castel Marie-Louise, 1 Av Andrieu, t 02 40 11 48 38, *www.relaischateaux.com/marielouise* (*luxury–expensive*). More manageable scale neo-Gothic mansion with plushest of rooms and a large garden with pool in the heart of La Baule, plus high-class, imaginative restaurant. *Closed mid-Nov–mid-Dec; restaurant closed Mon–Sat lunch.*
⋆⋆⋆Le St-Christophe, Place Notre-Dame, t 02 40 62 40 00, *info@st-christophe.com* (*expensive–inexpensive*). Good example of

La Baule's early 20th-century architecture, a smart option made up of three villas at the heart of the resort, with garden.
⋆⋆La Palmeraie, 7 Av des Cormorans, t 02 40 60 24 41, *www.hotel-lapalmeraie-labaule.com* (*moderate*). Lovely flower garden shaded by pines. *Closed Oct–Mar.*

Le Croisic ✉ 44490

⋆⋆⋆⋆Le Fort de L'Océan, t 02 40 15 77 77, *www.chateaushotels.com/ocean* (*expensive*). Superbly located above the ocean, a converted fort with immaculate rooms and a remarkable seafood restaurant. Pool. *Closed mid-Nov–mid-Dec and early Jan–early Feb; restaurant closed most weekday lunches.*
⋆⋆Castel Moor, Av du Castouillet, t 02 40 23 24 18, *www.castel-moor.com* (*inexpensive*). A good cheaper option. *Closed Jan.*
Bouillabaisse Bretonne, t 02 40 23 06 74 (*moderate*). Good for seafood. *Closed Jan–Mar, and Mon.*

Around the Brière

⋆⋆⋆⋆Hôtel de la Bretesche, ✉ 44780 Missillac, t 02 51 76 86 96, *www.bretesche.com* (*luxury–expensive*). In a dreamy location by a Gothic castle reflected in its lake, and right by a stunning golf course; the extremely comfortable rooms, restaurant (*moderate*) and salons are in the castle's outbuildings. Pool. *Closed mid-Jan–early Mar.*
⋆⋆Auberge de Kerhinet, ✉ 44410 Kerhinet, t 02 40 61 91 46, *www.pays-blanc.com/aubergedekerhinet* (*inexpensive*). Set in a perfect picture of restored thatched houses in the most touristy spot in the Brière. The restaurant (*expensive*) specializes in local produce. *Closed mid-Dec–mid-Jan; restaurant closed Tues and Wed outside July and Aug.*
Auberge de Kerbourg, ✉ 44410 Kerbourg, t 02 40 61 95 15 (*expensive*). Memorable Briéron house serving delicious cuisine, some seasonal produce coming from the immaculate garden. *Closed mid-Dec–mid-Feb, and Sun eve, Mon, and Tues lunch.*

Pornic 44210

⋆⋆Beau Soleil, 70 Quai Leray, t 02 40 82 34 58, *www.annedebretagne.com* (*moderate–inexpensive*). Modern wedge of a building with neat rooms at the heart of the action.

France. The best way to explore this peaty **Pays Noir** (Black Country) – the second-largest marsh in France – is in a punt, with a local guide. **Port des Fossés Blancs** and **Bréca** are good places from which to take a boat out on the waterways. The park authorities have taken the prettiest Briéron hamlet of **Kerhinet** under their wing and made it into their main showcase, and it looks gorgeous, if slightly twee; the **Musée du Chaume** (*open April hols and June–Sept daily 10.30–1 and 2.30–6.30; adm*) explains the principal features of the traditional Briéron home. The real heart of the Brière marsh is the posse of semi-islands around **St-Joachim** north of St-Nazaire. **L'Ile de Fédrun** is where the tourist action is concentrated. **Rozé** was once an important Briéron port; the region's creation and history is covered at the **Maison de l'Eclusier** (*open as Musée du Chaume*), while bird lovers head for the adjoining **Réserve Ornithologique Pierre Constant** (*open June–Sept daily 9–6; adm*).

St-Nazaire

Hard hit by war bombs, hard hit by the recent decline of shipbuilding in Europe, and hard hit by guidebooks, St-Nazaire at the Loire's estuary still has bags of character. It was one of the major European ports to operate transatlantic services from the 1860s, and many sailed off from here to seek a new life in the Americas. During the First World War, thousands of North American soldiers arrived at St-Nazaire before being sent out to the front in northeastern France. The port's most glorious period came between the two wars, when the most famous of France's ocean liners were built here, the *Paris*, the *Ile-de-France*, the *Champlain* and, most impressive of the lot, the *Normandie*, which was requisitioned by the US government during the Second World War, then spectacularly burned and sank in New York harbour in 1942. Discover an interactive ocean-liner universe at **Escal'Atlantic** (*open July–Aug daily 9.30–7.30; April–June and Sept–Oct daily 9.30–12.30 and 1.30–6; Nov–Dec and Feb–Mar Wed–Sun 10–12.30 and 2–6; adm*), a fantastically sleek, high-tech exhibition. St-Nazaire also has an excellent **Ecomusée** (*open same times; adm*) which includes a tour of the *Espadon*, the first French submarine to cross the North Pole under the ice, in 1964. Although St-Nazaire town centre was terribly smashed up by bombing, it has attractions, such as its shopping centre in the shape of a liner, and Place du Dolmen with a Neolithic monument in the centre. And to the west a series of sandy beaches line up. Most memorably of all, St-Nazaire boasts a giant serpent of a bridge arching over the mouth of the Loire. When it was opened in 1975, this was the longest bridge in France.

South of St-Nazaire

South of the Loire estuary along the Côte de Jade, **St-Michel-Chef-Chef** and **St-Brévin-les-Pins** are very lively, but in style they fit in more with the long, flat Vendée beach resorts further south. However, **Pornic** can claim to be the most southerly of truly Breton resorts. Take the stunning coastal path out from its fishing harbour, passing below the (private) castle and the poshest villas to reach the new marina. Follow the coastal path north or south and you'll come across secretive sandy creeks, the odd Neolithic chamber, Nazi blockhouses and *carrelets*, big square fishing nets suspended in mid-air, awaiting action.

The Loire Valley

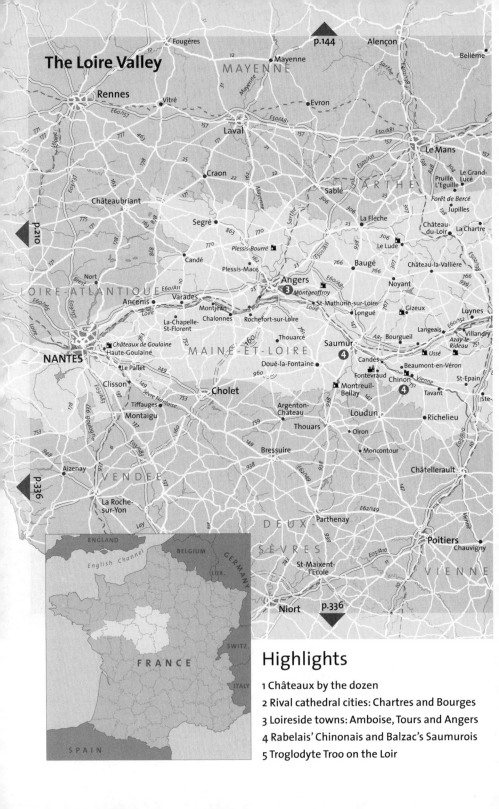

The Loire Valley

p.144
p.210
p.336
p.336

MAYENNE

Fougères
Mayenne
Alençon
Bellême
Rennes
Vitré
Evron
Laval
Le Mans
Pruillé
L'Eguille
Le Grand-
Lucé
Craon
Sablé
SARTHE
Forêt de Bercé
Jupilles
Châteaubriant
La Flèche
Château-
du-Loir
La Chartre
Segré
Le Lude
Candé
Baugé
Château-la-Vallière
Plessis-Bourré
Plessis-Macé
Noyant
Nort
Angers
Montgeoffroy
LOIRE-ATLANTIQUE
Varades
St-Mathurin-sur-Loire
Gizeux
Luynes
Ancenis
Montjean
Longué
Langeais
Villandry
La-Chapelle-
St-Florent
Chalonnes
Rochefort-sur-Loire
Bourgueil
Azay-le-
Rideau
Thouarcé
Saumur
Château de Goulaine
Haute-Goulaine
MAINE-ET-LOIRE
Candes
Beaumont-en-Véron
St-Epain
NANTES
Le Pallet
Doué-la-Fontaine
Fontevraud
Chinon
Clisson
Montreuil-
Bellay
Ussé
Tavant
Tiffauges
Cholet
Argenton-
Château
Loudun
Richelieu
Montaigu
Thouars
Ste-
Aizenay
Oiron
Moncontour
VENDÉE
Bressuire
Châtellerault
La Roche-
sur-Yon
DEUX-
Parthenay
Poitiers
ENGLAND
SÈVRES
Chauvigny
BELGIUM
GERMANY
English Channel
LUX.
St-Maixent-
l'Ecole
VIENNE
SWITZ.
FRANCE
ITALY
Niort
SPAIN

Highlights

1 Châteaux by the dozen
2 Rival cathedral cities: Chartres and Bourges
3 Loireside towns: Amboise, Tours and Angers
4 Rabelais' Chinonais and Balzac's Saumurois
5 Troglodyte Troo on the Loir

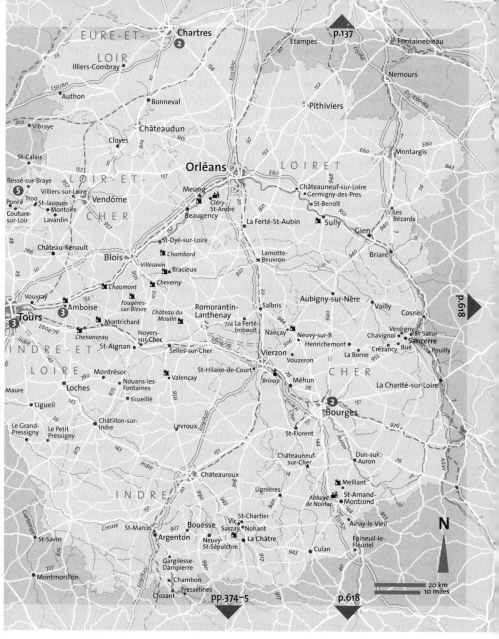

p.137
p.618
PP.374–5
p.618

EURE-ET-
LOIR
Chartres
2
Illiers-Combray
Etampes
Fontainebleau
Nemours
Authon
Bonneval
Pithiviers
Vibraye
Châteaudun
Cloyes
Montargis
St-Calais
Bessé-sur-Braye
LOIR-ET-
Orléans
LOIRET
Villiers-sur-Loire
Vendôme
Meung
Châteauneuf-sur-Loire
Germigny-des-Pres
Ponce Troo
St-Jacques
Montoire
CHER
Cléry-
St-André
St-Benoît
Couture-
sur-Loir
Lavardin
Beaugency
La Ferté-St-Aubin
Sully
Les
Bézards
Château-Renault
St-Dyé-sur-Loire
Gien
Blois
Chambord
Lamotte-
Beuvron
Briare
Villesavin
Bracieux
Vouvray
Chaumont
Cheverny
Amboise
Fougères-
sur-Bièvre
Château du
Moulin
Romorantin-
Lanthenay
Salbris
Aubigny-sur-Nère
Vailly
Cosne
Tours
Montrichard
La Ferté-
Imbault
Nançay
Verdigny
St Satur
Sancerre
Chenonceau
Noyers-
sur-Cher
Neuvy-sur-B
Chavignol
Pouilly
St-Aignan
Selles-sur-Cher
Henrichemont
Crézancy
Bué
INDRE-ET-
Vierzon
La Borne
LOIRE
Montrésor
St-Hilaire-de-Court
Vouzeron
CHER
La Charité-sur-Loire
Maure
Nouans-les-
Fontaines
Valençay
Brinay
Méhun
Loches
Ecueillé
Bourges
2
Ligueil
Châtillon-sur-
Indre
Levroux
St-Florent
Dun-sur-
Auron
Le Grand-
Pressigny
Le Petit
Pressigny
Châteauneuf-
sur-Cher
Meillant
Châteauroux
Lignières
Abbaye
de Noirlac
St-Amand-
Montrond
INDRE
St-Chartier
Ainay-le-Vieil
St-Savin
St-Marcel
Bouesse
Vic
Sarzay
Nohant
Epineuil-le-
Fleuriel
Argenton
Neuvy-
St-Sépulchre
La Châtre
Culan
N
Montmorillon
Gargilesse-
Dampierre
Chambon
Fresselines
Crozant

20 km
10 miles

In a roundabout way, you could consider the English responsible for the enchanting
castles strewn along France's greatest river and its tributaries. In 1418, near the start
of the second half of the Hundred Years War, they forced the future Valois king
Charles VII to flee from Paris to the Loire Valley. His successors, Louis XI, Charles VIII
and Louis XII, stayed, these kings and their courtiers building a plethora of white-
stoned pleasure palaces. François Ier, brought up at the Château d'Amboise right by
the Loire, would move the monarchy back to Paris but hedged his bets by also

ordering the building of Chambord, the biggest of all the Loire châteaux. Then, during sticky moments in the Wars of Religion later in the 16th century, Catherine de Médicis and sons sought royal refuge along the Loire Valley one final time.

However, the truth is, the Loire's credentials as France's Valley of the Kings predate Charles VII hotfooting it out of Paris. The Orléanais, in the east, was a stomping ground of the Capetians, while Anjou, to the west, was the cradle of the Plantagenets before the Blésois and Touraine in between became the haunts of the Valois kings. All these royals helped embellish the splendid Loire-side towns of Orléans, Amboise, Blois, Tours, Saumur, Angers and Nantes, as well as giving rise to so many châteaux.

Food and Wine

Were you to go by Gargantua's diet described by Rabelais in his brazen, bawdy giants' tales set in the region, you'd expect to be served cartloads of tripe at every meal along the Loire, washed down with at least a barrel or two of wine. And you wouldn't be entirely surprised to eat the odd stray pilgrim in a salad. There is one special Rabelaisian food you can still seek out – *fouaces*, dough balls that puff up when cooked in the oven, stuffed with various fillings. Today, however, the common features of Loire Valley cuisine are freshwater fish, fine vegetables grown in the river valley sands, goats' cheeses in a variety of building block shapes, and orchard fruits.

The most common fish on Loire menus is *sandre* (pike-perch), although it rarely comes from these parts nowadays. Other fleshy fishy favourites include *brochet* (pike), *brème* (bream) and *alose* (shad). *Anguilles* (eels) count as another river speciality, perhaps served in a *matelote* (stew). Meat dishes are often accompanied by regional wine sauces, or sometimes by fruit – pork served with apples or prunes. Gélines de Touraine chickens, who strut around in sleek black feathers at home, have an exceptional taste in the pot. Game from the region's many forests features large in autumn, mushrooms a favourite accompaniment. In addition, the majority of French *champignons de Paris* are actually produced, along with more exotic mushrooms, in the Loire Valley's vast underground caves and former stone quarries.

Locally grown pears and apples make it into a number of delicious desserts, most famously *tarte Tatin*, an apple tart with a caramelized top, invented by accident by an absent-minded woman from the Sologne. Good strawberries, raspberries, blackberries and even kiwis are produced in the region. Bitter oranges have to be imported from Haiti to Angers, though, to create its exceptionally famous liqueur, Cointreau.

The Loire Valley boasts almost as many wine *appellations* as châteaux. Sancerre and Pouilly-Fumé (made from sauvignon blanc grapes), and Vouvray and Montlouis (the tingling result of chenin blanc) count among the best whites, while the highly popular if more hit-and-miss Muscadet wine region spreads out from Nantes, its main grape the confusingly named Melon de Bourgogne. The areas around Chinon, Bourgueil and Saumur produce the fruitiest reds, predominantly made from cabernet franc grapes, while Saumur also conjures up a creditable sparkling white. Anjou, for so long wrongly associated simply with rosés, turns out to have an amazing diversity of *appellations*, including deliciously dry Savennières and splendidly sweet Bonnezeaux and Quarts-de-Chaume.

This chapter starts among the rounded wine hills of Sancerre along the Loire east of Orléans, and, after a detour into the peaceful, half-forgotten old province of the Berry, takes you down the greater Loire Valley as far west as Nantes. With fifty or more châteaux to visit on the way, you will be spoiled for choice. The archetypal Loire Valley château fuses the exuberance of late Gothic with the controlled delicacy of the Renaissance, creating some of the most dreamy homes on this planet – the Château d'Ussé is even claimed to have directly inspired Charles Perrault's *Sleeping Beauty*. Some have violent stories quite in contrast to their looks, and the parties were legendary; Leonardo da Vinci arranged some humdingers for François Ier at Amboise.

In the spaces between the castles and cities, charming villages lie scattered in famous vineyards, from Sancerre in the east to Muscadet in the west; others are built dramatically into the cliffs, notably around Saumur and in the Loir (without an 'e') valley. The latter, north of the Loire and a miniature mirror of it, is covered in the final section of the chapter, with the famed cathedral city of Chartres, near its source.

The Berry

The Loire river east of Orléans acts as the frontier between Burgundy and the ancient province of the Berry. Divided between the *départements* of the Cher and the Indre, the Berry experienced its greatest days in medieval times. Compared with the bustling corridor of the Loire from Orléans to the Atlantic, it now feels extremely tranquil, and on a typical Berrichon day you're likely to encounter more Romanesque churches than young people. Bourges, utterly splendid old capital of the province, has an exceptionally sturdy old heart, though, given a big jolt each spring with the very raucous and youthful Printemps de Bourges rock festival. To the east, by the Loire, the vine-covered hills around Sancerre attract a just slightly more sober crowd.

The Sancerrois and the Pays Fort

The attention lavished on Sancerre wine has often diverted attention away from the beauty of **Sancerre** town. Set atop a sensuous hill, with dreamy views down on the river, the place can't be said to rule the Berry bank of the Loire these days. Vines really do. Since the war, they have taken over virtually every inch of territory, and the townhouses look shoved unceremoniously together on their hilltop. During the Hundred Years War, though, Sancerre *ville* acted as an important frontier post of the shrivelled French kingdom. On the town's pinnacle, a formidable if tottering flint tower remains standing, the last major vestige of the medieval castle, largely destroyed as punishment for Sancerre becoming a Protestant stronghold in the Wars of Religion. Below, the main square has kept its charm, despite the modern additions. The houses along the steep streets leading away from it boast barn-door-size entrances, made to receive the grape harvest.

Sauvignon blanc is the variety that dominates Sancerre white wines today. A small amount of delicate, fruity red wine is made from pinot noir. The two big names in

Getting Around

From Cosne-Cours-sur-Loire **train** station at the bottom of Sancerre's hill, a bus takes you up to the town. **Bus** services from Bourges serve Sancerre and Henrichemont.

Tourist Information

Sancerre: Rue de la Croix de Bois, **t** 02 48 78 03 58, *www.sancerre.net/otsi*.
Henrichemont: 3 Place de l'Hôtel de Ville, **t** 02 48 26 74 13.

Where to Stay and Eat

Sancerre ✉ 18300

Le Panoramic, 18 Rempart des Augustins, **t 02 48 54 22 44, *panoramicotel@wanadoo.fr* (*inexpensive*). The spectacular views surpass the dullish modern architecture of this well located, comfortable hotel, with its smart restaurant, **La Tasse d'Argent**, **t** 02 48 54 01 44 (*moderate*). *Restaurant closed Wed out of season, and Jan.*

La Tour, Nouvelle Place, **t** 02 48 54 00 81 (*expensive*). Swishest restaurant on the main square, a good place to try regional specialities such as goat's cheese and Berry lentils.

Auberge La Pomme d'Or, Place de la Mairie, **t** 02 48 54 13 30 (*expensive–moderate*). In an interesting corner of gabled houses by the classical town hall, a reputed restaurant with small but well-chosen menus. *Closed Tues eve and Wed.*

St-Satur ✉ 18300

***Hôtel de la Loire, 2 Quai de la Loire, **t** 02 48 78 22 22, *www.hotel-de-la-loire.com* (*moderate*). Lovingly restored, characterful rooms down by the Loire.

Sancerre itself are Mellot and Vacheron, with some of the most highly visible shops. Head into the hills to explore the vinous villages of the Sancerrois. **Verdigny** is one of the most reputed, the Dezat family based here largely responsible for bringing Sancerre its postwar success. Goat's cheese shops also vie for attention, for instance at **Chavignol**, renowned for its *crottins*, 'droppings'! Other appealing wine villages include **Amigny**, **Venoize**, **Bué**, **Reigny** and **Crézancy**. Across the Loire, the vineyards of rival **Pouilly-Fumé** also call for a visit. Or at **St-Satur**, enjoy the rare opportunity of **canoeing** on the river by booking with Loire.Nature.Découverte (**t** 02 48 78 00 34).

The area's cheeses may be celebrated, but since the 1950s, far more profitable vines have pushed the goats west into the **Pays Fort**. In its pretty hills, the heavily restored **Château de Maupas** (*open mid-April–Sept daily 2–7; adm*) piles high its huge collection of plates, while at **La Borne** a whole array of contemporary potters stand almost as tightly packed as pieces in a kiln. **Henrichemont**, by contrast, was a model of order when it was built as a new town in the early 17th century. The **Château de Menetou-Salon** (*open July–Aug daily 10–6.30; adm*) may be an ugly neo-Gothic pile and flaunt vulgar decorations within, but Menetou-Salon white wine has a quiet distinction.

Bourges

'The huge, rugged vessel of the church overhung me in very much the same way as the black hull of a ship at sea would overhang a solitary swimmer,' wrote Henry James of Bourges cathedral. 'It seemed colossal, stupendous, a dark leviathan.' UNESCO was just as impressed and made the cathedral a World Heritage Site in 1992.

Avaricum, capital of the Bituriges tribe, was one of the glories of pre-Roman Gaul. Caesar destroyed it in 52 BC, following a Celtic revolt. The town regained its importance through the Gallo-Roman centuries, and had a bishop as early as the 3rd century, St Ursin, who held relics of one of the great early Christian martyrs, St Etienne (Stephen). The French crown took possession of the viscounty of Bourges in 1101, when Philippe Ier bought it, making eastern Berry one of the earliest possessions of the Capetian kings outside the Ile de France. Louis VII was in fact crowned in the cathedral. In 1360 Jean, one of the extravagant sons of King Jean le Bon who competed with each other in commissioning lavish works, was made Duc de Berry. The ruthless man fleeced his subjects to support his taste in the arts. In 1412 he tried negotiating with the English, causing French troops to besiege Bourges; he submitted to them.

After the duke's death in 1416, the future King Charles VII inherited his territories and Bourges became one of the bases of his peripatetic court pushed out of Paris. Charles has generally been portrayed as a weak, indecisive figure, often mockingly referred to as '*le petit roi de Bourges*'. Two extraordinarily powerful figures came to his rescue. One was Joan of Arc. The other was Jacques Cœur, one of the most successful merchants in French history, who had one of his main bases in Bourges, supplying the French court with exotic luxuries. Appointed Charles VII's finance minister, Cœur began working the miracles economically which Joan of Arc had previously inspired militarily. However, his influence earned him many enemies and in 1451 he was arrested on false charges of poisoning the king's mistress, Agnès Sorel. Just as Charles had done nothing to aid Joan, so he did nothing for Cœur, who escaped to work for the pope while his confiscated money helped to finance the expulsion of the English from France. Charles became known as '*le bien servi*' (the well-served).

Charles VII's son, the future King Louis XI, was born in Bourges and saw to the founding of Bourges University in 1463. German students would bring with them the seeds of Luther's preaching and planted them in the brain of Jean Calvin, a student here in 1530. By the 17th century Catholicism was ascendant again, although more friction was inevitable with the rebellious aristocratic Condé family based at Bourges taking on the monarchy. When Louis XIV came, he destroyed the Grosse Tour – a

Getting Around

Bourges has reasonable **rail** links with Tours.

Tourist Information

Bourges: 21 Rue Victor Hugo, **t** 02 48 23 02 60, *ville-bourges.fr*.

Where to Stay and Eat

Bourges ✉ 18000
***Le Bourbon, Bd de la République, **t** 02 48 70 70 00, *www.alpha-hotellerie.com* (*expensive–moderate*). Smart hotel, in a converted 16th-century abbey, with swanky restaurant, **L'Abbaye St-Ambroix**, in a former chapel.

***Hôtel d'Angleterre, 1 Place des Quatre Piliers, **t** 02 48 24 68 51, *hotel.angleterre@wanadoo.fr* (*moderate*). Excellent central location and elegant exterior; unimaginative, if comfortable, rooms.

Le Jacques Cœur, 3 Place Jacques Cœur, **t** 02 48 70 12 72 (*expensive*). Grand neo-Gothic dining room in which to enjoy traditional fare. *Closed Sun eve and Mon*.

Le Bourbonnoux, 44 Rue Bourbonnoux, **t** 02 48 24 14 76 (*moderate*). On an atmospheric street for restaurants and food shops, serving inventive regional cuisine. *Closed Fri, Sat lunch, and Sun eve in winter*.

D'Antan Sancerrois, 50 Rue Bourbonnoux, **t** 02 48 65 96 26 (*moderate*). Stylish white-stoned dining room, strong Berry tastes. *Closed Sun eve and Mon*.

symbol of Condé power – and authority passed directly to the monarchy. Bourges declined, only really to pick up again with the explosion in its arms industry during the Second Empire. Booming Bourges employed more than 20,000 by the First World War. It has remained one of the major centres of the French arms industry, yet its population has traditionally been strongly left-wing.

The almond-shaped old town boasts the first French Gothic **cathedral**, built south of the Loire, begun in 1195 under Archbishop Henri de Sully. His brother commissioned Notre-Dame in Paris, but Bourges' St-Etienne looks just as magnificent. Its five-portalled façade is unique, a staggering achievement in Gothic architecture, although suffering from the ravages of time. Below the arches stands a wealth of 13th-century sculpture featuring saints, the Virgin and the Last Judgement. The north and south side portals have retained arresting Romanesque sculptures from the earlier cathedral. Unfortunately the ground wasn't strong enough to support the weight of completed towers and the bell-less Tour Sourde (or Mute Tower) had to be propped up by a vast pillar. However, like Chartres (dating from the same period), St-Etienne spectacularly demonstrates the engineering possibilities of the flying buttress, which allow for so much glass inside. Within, the rows of Gothic lancet arches reach much higher than those of Notre-Dame. The massive 17th-century organ pipes obscure sections of the façade's rose window, but look out for the complex 15th-century astronomical clock below. The side chapels contain a wealth of art. Amazing 13th-century stained-glass windows remain in the ambulatory, their stories teeming with little figures set in a whole array of geometrical frames. Visit the crypt (*open Mon–Sat 9.30–12.15 and 2–5.15, Sun 2–5.15; adm*) to admire vestiges of the 13th-century rood screen, the Duc de Berry's magnificent tomb and several tall statues saved from the towers. Grotesque carvings accompany you up the Tour de Beurre with its views over Bourges.

The **Palais Jacques Cœur** (*open daily 9.30–12.15 and 2–5.15, or 6.30 in summer; adm*), the great merchant's château of a house, was built on Gallo-Roman walls, but this is another Gothic masterpiece. The most delightful sculpture adorns the building, providing the joy on the tour, as the rooms prove disappointingly empty beyond their entertainingly carved fireplaces. Even above the entrance, stone people look out from false windows; as Henry James wrote, they 'appear to be watching for the return of their master, who left his beautiful house one morning and never came back'. The Hôtel Cujas housing the **Musée du Berry** (*open Mon and Wed–Sat 10–12 and 2–6, Sun 2–6; closed Tues*) was built around 1515 for Durand Salvi, a Florentine trader. It contains two exceptional exhibits: a Gallo-Roman necropolis and some extremely moving marble mourners from the Duc de Berry's tomb. A rich merchant family of German origin had the fine Hôtel Lallemant built (1490–1518), now housing the elegant **Musée des Arts Décoratifs** (*open Tues–Sat 10–12 and 2–6, Sun 2–6*). Its Renaissance features include a loggia, frescoes and an oratory with an engrossing coffered stone ceiling. Another joyous late-Gothic house, the **Hôtel des Echevins**, built as a new town hall in 1487, contains the riot of 20th-century colour of the **Musée Estève** (*open Mon and Wed–Sat 10–12 and 2–6, Sun 2–6*), with abstract works by this native of the Berry. The **Musée des Meilleurs Ouvriers de France** (*open Easter–Dec Tues–Sat 10–12 and 2–6, Sun 2–6*), in the 17th-century classical archbishops' palace, encourages modern crafts.

Along the Cher, Indre and Creuse Valleys through the Berry

The Cher Valley

West of Bourges, the unassuming town of **Mehun-sur-Yèvre** conceals an atmospheric fragment of one of the Duc de Berry's magnificent châteaux. **Brinay**'s church of **St-Aignan**, north by the Cher, contains some of the most moving Romanesque wall paintings in France, the Magi riding to visit the baby Jesus, while the women's faces show the agonies of grief in Herod's horrific Massacre of the Innocents.

South along the Cher, the 12th-century **Abbaye de Noirlac** (*open Feb–Dec daily 9.45–12.30 and 2–5, or 6.30 in summer; adm*) offers one of the finest examples of a Cistercian abbey left in France. Most of the architecture was completed within one hundred years of the original monks' arrival in the mid-12th century. The denuded buildings suggest states of uncluttered meditation and daunting austerity, although

Getting Around

The **train** lines from Bourges to Montluçon serve St-Amand-Montrond; the one to Poitiers stops at Argenton-sur-Creuse. **Bus** services between the towns are limited.

Tourist Information

St-Amand-Montrond: Place de la République, t 02 48 96 16 86, *www.perso.wanadoo.fr/ot.stamand.orval*.

La Châtre: 134 Rue Nationale, t 02 54 48 22 64, *ot.la-chatre@wanadoo.fr*.

Gargilesse: Le Pigeonnier, t 02 54 47 85 06.

Argenton-sur-Creuse: 13 Place de la République, t 02 54 24 05 30, *accueil@ot-argenton-sur-creuse.fr*.

Le Blanc: Place de la Libération, t 02 54 37 05 13, *tourisme.leblanc@wanadoo.fr*.

Mézières-en-Brenne: Le Moulin, 1 Rue du Nord, t 02 54 38 12 24, *tourisme.mezieresenbrenne @wanadoo.fr*.

Where to Stay and Eat

St-Hilaire-de-Court ✉ 18100

**Château de la Beuvrière, t 02 48 75 14 63, *hotellabeuvriere@aol.com* (*expensive–moderate*). Bargain, pleasing rooms in a simple little château on the south bank of the Cher from Vierzon. Pool and tennis court. *Closed mid-Nov–Easter*.

Bruère-Allichamps ✉ 18200

Auberge de l'Abbaye de Noirlac, t 02 48 96 22 58 (*moderate*). Reliable restaurant opposite the abbey, serving Berry specialities in a Cistercian dining room. *Closed Wed, and mid-Nov–mid-Feb*.

Nohant-Vic ✉ 36400

***La Petite Fadette, Place du Château, t 02 54 31 01 48, *www.auberge.petitefadette.com* (*expensive–moderate*). Delectable stop for Sand pilgrims, with a delightful restaurant.

St-Chartier ✉ 36400

***La Vallée Bleue, Route de Verneuil, t 02 54 31 01 91, *www.chateauvalleebleue.com* (*expensive–moderate*). Period charm at George Sand's doctor's house, a manor on the verge of being a château. Pool. *Closed Nov–Mar; restaurant closed lunch*.

Bouesse ✉ 36570

Château de Bouesse, t 02 54 25 12 20, *www.chateau-bouesse.de* (*moderate*). Unmissable along the pretty D927 west of Neuvy-St-Sépulchre, a spectacular castle with good restaurant. *Closed Jan–Mar*.

Argenton-sur-Creuse 36200

***Manoir de Boisvillers, 11 Rue du Moulin de Bord, t 02 54 24 13 88, *manoir.de.boisvilliers@ wanadoo.fr* (*moderate–inexpensive*). In the centre of town, rooms with views either on to the river or the garden.

the original asceticism of the Cistercian life was gradually abandoned here. The monks' dormitory, converted in the 18th century into charming individual rooms with stylish fireplaces, might set a modern hotelier dreaming. By the Revolution, there were only six religious men to get rid of. Today, panels recall the once-ordered ways of the community that brought so much life to this place. The Eté Musical de Noirlac consists of an excellent series of summer concerts held at the abbey.

East, the curving form of the **Château de Meillant** (*open April–Oct daily 9–11.45 and 2–6.45; Feb–Mar and Nov 10–11.45 and 2–5.30; adm*) is mirrored in its crescent of a moat on which swans glide by. The first part of this major Gothic castle went up for Etienne de Sancerre, but it was the mighty Charles Ier d'Amboise whose money most left its mark. Charles held the highest posts in France and also became governor of Milan in the early 16th century – hence the saying that 'Milan made Meillant'. While the outer row of towers and walls looks stern, enter the courtyard and the place appears more welcoming, the Tour du Lion plastered with entertaining sculptures. The separate chapel boasts more fantastical carvings, and beautiful stained glass. The interiors were heavily transformed for 19th-century good living.

Continuing along the Cher, the modestly charming craft and jewellery town of **St-Amand-Montrond**, overseen by the remnants of spikey fortifications, has acquired a flash modern pyramid, **La Cité de l'Or** (*open winter Wed–Mon 9.45–5.30; summer Wed–Mon 9.45–6.30; closed Tues exc July and Aug; adm*), focusing on local gold production. Just south, the pink circular ramparts of the **Château d'Ainay-le-Vieil** (*open Mar and Oct–Nov Wed–Mon 10–12 and 2–6; April–Sept Wed–Mon 10–12 and 2–7; adm*) stand out above a romantic moat. The courtyard within has suffered from heavy-handed plastering, but the decorated octagonal tower boasts a hilarious array of sculptures, including a couple in local costume, and a woman bathing. Inside, the oratory has murals with possible portraits of the original owners. Mementoes abound of the Colberts too, proprietors from 1467. Three brothers served as Napoleonic generals, hence the imperial souvenirs. Outside the walls, a rose garden scents the air.

One of the best-loved books in French literature takes literary pilgrims south to flat **Epineul-le-Fleuriel** and its rather dull former **schoolhouse** (*open April–mid-Nov Wed–Mon 10–12 and 2–6; closed Tues; adm*); to appreciate the visit, you need to know and love the classic romantic tearjerker *Le Grand Meaulnes*, by Alain-Fournier, in part inspired by this place. The book was published in 1913, just before the First World War, in which the author died. A few villages to the west of Epineul, such as Saulzais-le-Potier and Vesdun, battle it out for which sits closest to the exact central spot of France, not an easy point to calculate. The brown-freckled **Château de Culan** (*open Easter– Oct daily 10–7; adm*), its towers like the thickest of brown crayons sticking straight up out of a rocky outcrop, provides a more substantial objective. One lord supported Joan of Arc, as recalled in the eccentric interiors. The great Condé family became its owners in the Ancien Régime, and, when they defied the king, some of it was destroyed by royal order. A medieval-style garden winds its way down the steep slope, while falconry displays are put on in season. The countryside undulates prettily around hilltop **Châteaumeillant** with its medieval churches, its castle now housing the police station! North towards Lignières, the **Prieuré d'Orsan** (*open Easter–Oct daily*

10–7; adm) has been lovingly restored, given the most beautiful of gardens, designed with the medieval spirit in mind.

The Indre Valley

Head west for the Indre and its Vallée Noire, an 'eminently rustic' area championed by local heroine George Sand. The Pays de George Sand centres around hillside **La Châtre**, with its series of charming squares and winding streets. The cobbled-together **Musée George Sand et de la Vallée Noire** (*open Feb–Dec daily 9–12 and 2–5 or 7 in summer; adm*) is divided between a collection of stuffed birds, memorabilia of *la bonne dame de Nohant*, and displays on local traditions. Since 1992 the town has gained a reputation for its July music festival, '*Chopin chez George Sand*'.

Sand spent much of her childhood and adult life at the **Nohant-Vic.**. The manor now known as the **Maison de George Sand** (*open July–Aug daily 9.30–7; May–June 9.30–12 and 2–7; April and Sept 10–12.30 and 2–6; Oct–Mar 10–12.30 and 1.30–5; adm*) stands by an adorable church. Sand moved from room to room as family (she had two children, Solange and Maurice), work and romantic whim dictated. The tour guides bring Sand and her entourage wonderfully to life.

The nearby Romanesque church of **Vic** may look inconsequential, but within contains wonderful early 12th-century paintings, the Christian stories enacted by figures with highly arched eyebrows, startled eyes and prominent red circles on the cheekbones. The **Château de Sarzay** (*open daily 10–12 and 2–6; adm*), its conical towers packed tightly together, is a superb remnant of a bigger medieval château built to keep the English at bay. The dusty interiors are filled with cobwebby bric-a-brac. The mill featured in Sand's novel *Le Meunier d'Angibault*, the **Moulin d'Angibault** (*open June–Aug Tues–Sun 11–7; mid-April–May and Sept–Oct Tues–Sun 2–5*) now turns once again, in grounds ambitiously described as the **Parc Romantique George Sand**.

George Sand Dons the Berry's Trousers

The remarkable eccentric George Sand was born Amantine-Aurore-Lucille Dupin in 1804. Her father was a descendant of the Polish king Augustus II, her mother the daughter of a Parisian bird-seller. Early and disastrously married, she had the courage to press for formal separation and would then conduct a string of relationships with some of the most famous men of her day, notably the composer Chopin and the poet Musset. Unfortunately her novels have none of the brilliant insight and finesse of that other literary woman she so admired, George Eliot. Sand was often writing desperately to stave off financial disaster. *La Mare au Diable*, the first of a series of novels set in the Berry, proves a banal work. Her life as an early advocate of socialism and precursor of feminism turns out to be much more interesting than her writings, but she has come to be caricatured all too simply as a trouser-wearing, cigar-smoking aristocrat with an insatiable appetite for socializing and brilliant lovers. Many of the leading artistic lights of the 19th century visited her at her Berrichon home. Sand certainly stirred the passions. Baudelaire once described her as a latrine, but Flaubert greatly loved her and cried like a calf for its mother when she died.

Off the Sand pilgrimage trail, the unassuming town of **Neuvy-St-Sépulchre** boasts a rare, round medieval church, built to house a relic containing three drops of Christ's blood, and modelled on Jerusalem's church of the Holy Sepulchre.

The Creuse Valley

'*Creuser*' means 'to dig' in French, and the Creuse valley crossing through the south-western corner of the *département* of the Indre has certainly carved itself quite a gorge. Claude Monet was attracted to **Fresselines** and Crozant in 1889, completing 23 paintings. Unfortunately, none of his canvases stayed on, but Fresselines has turned one of its big barns into a gallery displaying paintings by the 1850–1930 Crozant school. The ruins of a great fortress mingle with the natural walls of rock at **Crozant**, on the southern end of the manmade **Lac de Chambon**. In 1356, the Black Prince failed to take the place. A Protestant fief in the Wars of Religion, it was partially destroyed by an earthquake in 1610. Taking the slippery, steep rocky paths around its remnants makes an exhilarating walk; for a more tranquil time, go for a little cruise on the lake.

At picture-book **Gargilesse** above the Creuse, the Romanesque church contains a striking array of capitals, including the 24 harp-playing elders of the Apocalypse. Beneath their sober gazes, a reputed international harp festival takes place every August. The effigy of an elderly medieval lord is now protected behind bars, but in past times barren women would come to take chippings from his groin, hence his humiliating mutilation. The lower church's caricature wall paintings include Galopin, supposedly one of the Magi's horses, and a Berrichon donkey taking Mary into exile in Egypt. The homely little **château** (*open July and Aug daily 2.30–7; May–June and early Sept closed Tues; adm*) next door has been lovingly restored, while a cluttered cottage in the village, nicknamed the **Villa Algira**, is dedicated to George Sand and her most stable lover Manceau, as well as to her artistic son Maurice, a pupil of Delacroix.

The old houses on **Argenton**'s riverbanks, with their carelessly stacked levels of tumbling balconies, look like a hangover from the Middle Ages. However, the **shirt museum** (*open mid-Feb–Dec Tues–Sun 9.30–12 and 2–6; adm*), with contributions from stars such as Frank Sinatra and Richard Burton, shows how Argenton made it into the industrial age. In neighbouring **St-Marcel**, you can see fashions going back to prehistory and Gallo-Roman times at the excellent modern **Musée Archéologique d'Argentomagus** (*open Wed–Mon 9.30–12 and 2–6; closed Tues exc July and Aug; adm*). **Le Blanc**, another pleasant riverside town, advertises itself as a main gateway into the **Brenne** of 'a thousand lakes', designated a Regional Nature Park in 1989, a place that appeals to keen ornithologists.

The Sologne

The silvery, heathery woods and secretive lakes of the Sologne fill the big hunched back of the Loire from the Cher up to Orléans. This is a mysterious, in places melancholic land. The magical party in Alain-Fournier's *Le Grand Meaulnes* takes place here, as does the shooting party in Jean Renoir's cinema classic *La Règle du Jeu*. The Sologne, teeming with wildlife, is still regarded as something of a hunter's paradise.

Getting Around

The **train** from Orléans to Bourges serves La Ferté-St-Aubin and Salbris. A branch line from Salbris serves Selles-St-Denis and Villeherviers.

Tourist Information

Romorantin-Lanthenay: 32 Place de la Paix, t 02 54 76 43 89, *romorantin-lanthenay@ fnotsi.net.*
Aubigny-sur-Nère: 1 Rue de l'Eglise, t 02 48 58 40 20, *www.aubigny.org.*

Where to Stay and Eat

Romorantin-Lanthenay ✉ 41200

★★★★Grand Hôtel du Lion d'Or, 69 Rue Georges Clemenceau, t 02 54 94 15 15, *hotel-liondor.fr (luxury–expensive).* Outrageously luxurious hotel in the centre. Sublime cuisine. *Closed mid-Feb–Mar and late-Nov–early Dec; restaurant closed Tues lunch.*
★★Le Colombier, 18 Place du Vieux Marché, t 02 54 76 12 76 *(inexpensive).* More down-to-earth, a former coaching inn with traditional restaurant *(moderate). Closed Feb; restaurant closed Sun eve and Mon.*

La Ferté-Imbault ✉ 41300

★★A La Tête de Lard, 13 Place des Tilleuls, t 02 54 96 22 32, *www.aubergealatetedelard. com (moderate–inexpensive).* Really friendly

hotel, despite its name (which means 'pig-headed'). Serves tasty Sologne cuisine *(expensive–moderate). Closed late-Jan–mid-Feb and mid-Sept; restaurant closed Sun eve, Mon and Tues lunch.*

Vouzeron ✉ 18330

★★★Le Relais de Vouzeron, Place de l'Eglise, t 02 48 51 61 38 *(moderate–inexpensive).* Charming former posting inn in the midst of the Sologne forests, with pleasing restaurant *(moderate). Closed mid-Dec–mid-Jan; restaurant closed Mon.*

Aubigny-sur-Nère ✉ 18700

La Chaumière, 2 Rue Paul Lasnier, t 02 48 58 04 01, *www.hotel-restaurant-la-chaumiere. com (moderate).* Variety of decent rooms at different prices close to the centre. Reasonable restaurant. *Restaurant closed Sun eve and Mon.*

Around La Ferté-St-Aubin ✉ 45240

★★★Château les Muids, t 02 38 64 65 14, *muids@chateauxhotels.com (expensive–moderate).* Elegant 18th-century château south of town, in delightful grounds with pool and tennis court. Fine restaurant, including home-smoked specialities.
La Ferme de La Lande, just northeast of town, t 02 38 76 64 37 *(inexpensive).* Very tempting little country restaurant in immaculate 18th-century timberframe farm. *Restaurant closed Sun eve, Mon, and Wed eve.*

Had Leonardo da Vinci's plans gone ahead for a château for King François Ier, **Romorantin-Lanthenay** would no doubt be more famous. As it was, a bout of the plague in 1518 devastated the town and the monarch decided to have his fabulous new hunting lodge built at Chambord (*see* p.286). Romorantin-Lanthenay was left to become a symbol of *la France profonde*, backward, provincial France. Lately, the town has prospered through the location of a ground-breaking car plant. The smart **Musée de Sologne** (*open Mon and Wed–Sat 10–12 and 2–6, Sun 2–6; closed Tues; adm*) celebrates the area in its restored mill buildings on branches of the river flowing through town. Visit the **Espace Matra** devoted to automobiles (*same ticket, open same times*).

The **Château du Moulin** (*open April–Sept Mon and Wed–Sat 10–12.30 and 2–6.30, Sun 2–6.30; closed Tues; adm*), star of the brick châteaux of the Sologne, is a dreamy castle hidden west of Romorantin. Swans glide along in the moat below its patterned orange and purple walls. The château is named after Philippe du Moulin, loyal servant of Charles VIII, who rescued the king from his first disastrous foray into Italy in 1495. A

Sologne lake-stopper made out of oak and said to be a staggering 800 years old counts as the most curious object at **Aliotis** (*open April–Sept 10–6.30; Mar 1.30–6.30; Feb 11–6; Jan and Dec Wed, Sun and hols 1.30–6; adm*), the Sologne aquarium by Villeherviers, east of Romorantin. The development of the region's lakes for fishing dates back to early medieval times. **St-Viâtre** to the north sits amid the densest concentration of *étangs*.

Little **Nançay**, some way east by Neuvy-sur-Barangeon, appears thinly disguised as Vieux-Nançay in *Le Grand Meaulnes*. It looks like the typical Sologne village, its low brick workers' cottages contrasting with the big brick château lording it to one side, only the houses here have now been converted into a posse of chic boutiques. The château's superbly restored outbuildings house an art gallery-cum-museum, the **Galerie Capazza** (*open mid-Mar–mid-Dec weekends and public hols 9.30–12.30 and 2.30–7.30; adm*), one section paying homage to Alain-Fournier.

Aubigny-sur-Nère is particularly proud of its links with Scotland; its attractive carved-beamed houses were built under Robert Stuart, after a fire in 1512. This Stuart had inherited the town from a celebrated ancestor, John Stuart of Darnley, whose Scottish troops greatly helped the French armies fight the English in the Hundred Years War – from then on the trusted *gendarmes écossais* became the French royal guard until the Revolution. The Stuart family remained in charge of Aubigny until 1672. Louis XIV then donated it to Louise de Kéroualle, sent as ambassador to England. Charles II of England was seduced and Louise became a favourite. Aubigny's cross-Channel connections are charted in the **Château des Stuarts** (*open July–mid-Sept daily 2.30–7; Easter–June and mid-Sept–Oct weekends 2.30–6; Nov–Easter Sun 2.30–6; adm*). Continue southeast along the Nère to the grand **Château de la Verrerie** (*open Mar–11 Nov Wed–Mon 10–6; July and Aug also open Tues; adm; restaurant and expensive B&B, t 02 48 81 51 60*), a muscular castle built for the French Stuarts, set by a romantic lake.

Explore the typical brick and timberframe Sologne villages between Aubigny-sur-Nère and **La Ferté-St-Aubin**, which acts as the northern gateway into the Sologne below Orléans. Its pale brick **château** (*open mid-Feb–mid-Nov daily 10–6; adm*), a little dilapidated but among the most beautiful in the region, starred in the shooting party of Jean Renoir's *La Règle du Jeu*.

The Loire Valley

From the Berry Border to Orléans

Briare's claim to fame was created by one Gustave Eiffel. While his great Parisian erection sticks so vulgarly into the air, Briare's extraordinarily long bridge, which carries canal boats over the Loire, extends extremely elegantly over the river. The diminutive huddle of riverside houses behind the cobbled quays nearby offers a good picture of a traditional little Loire-side community. Look into hiring a canal boat at the marina. Briare's other attraction is mosaics, best seen at **St-Etienne** church, commissioned by the heirs of Jean-Felix Bapterosses, the industrialist who changed the face of Briare, his commercial tricks and triumphs retold at the **Musée de la Mosaïque et des Emaux** (*open June–Sept daily 10–6.30; Feb–May and Oct–Dec 2–6; adm*).

Getting Around

Bus services from Orléans serve Sully-sur-Loire and Châteauneuf-sur-Loire.

Tourist Information

Briare-le-Canal: 1 Place Charles de Gaulle, t 02 38 31 24 51, *Tourisme.Briare@wanadoo.fr*.
Gien: Place Jean Jaurès, t 02 38 67 25 28, *ot-gien@wanadoo.fr*.
Sully-sur-Loire: Place de Gaulle, t 02 38 36 23 70, *ot.sully.sur.loire@wanadoo.fr*.
St-Benoît-sur-Loire: 44 Rue Orléanaise, t 02 38 35 79 00.
Châteauneuf-sur-Loire: 3 Place Aristide Briand, t 02 38 58 44 79.

Where to Stay and Eat

Gien ✉ 45500

**La Poularde, 13 Quai de Nice, t 02 38 67 36 05 (*inexpensive*). Discreetly down by the Loire, with simple rooms but fancy cooking (*expensive–moderate*). *Closed early Jan; restaurant closed Sun eve and Mon lunch*.

**Sanotel, 21 Quai de Sully, t 02 38 67 61 46, *www.perso.wanadoo.fr/sanotel* (*inexpensive*). Modern hotel with the best views in town from the south bank.

Les Bézards ✉ 45290 (Boismorand)

****Auberge des Templiers, t 02 38 31 80 01, *templiers@relaischateaux.com* (*expensive*). The height of luxury in the area, rooms and facilities including pool dotted around the extensive grounds beyond the entrance on the busy N7. The cuisine (*very expensive*) has an extremely high reputation. *Closed Feb*.

St-Benoît-sur-Loire ✉ 45730

**Hôtel du Labrador, 7 Place de l'Abbaye, t 02 38 35 74 38 (*inexpensive*). Beside the abbey, unexciting on the outside, but with reasonable rooms. *Closed late-Dec–late Jan*.

Châteauneuf-sur-Loire ✉ 45110

Hôtel du Parc/Restaurant de la Capitainerie, 1 Square du Général de Gaulle, t 02 38 58 42 16, *lacapitainerie@libertysurf.fr* (*inexpensive*). By the gates of the former *château*. Simple rooms and traditional cuisine (*moderate*). *Restaurant closed Sun eve and Mon lunch*.

Gien, site of an ancient crossing over the Loire, was bombed to smithereens in the Second World War, but was then harmoniously restored using typical regional patterned brick and stone. The **Château de Gien**, built in the 1480s for Anne de Beaujeu, daughter of King Louis XI, and covered in intriguing brick tattoos, somehow survived most of the destruction. The interiors are now devoted to that royal pastime par excellence, hunting; the fascinating **Musée International de la Chasse** (*open June–Sept daily 9–6; rest of year 9–12 and 2–6; adm*) offers a heady-to-nauseating insight into the outrageously refined art of its aristocratic practitioners. Beside the château stands the modern church of **Ste-Jeanne d'Arc**; the war bombs left only the soaring 15th-century entrance tower, a typical feature of the medieval churches of the Orléanais. Gien has a well-established tradition of producing pottery, and local artists created the elongated religious statues inside. On the western side of town, the **Musée de la Faïencerie and factory shop** (*museum open Mon–Sat 9–12 and 2–6, Sun 10–12 and 2–6; adm; factory shop open Mon–Sat 9–12 and 2–6*) reveals Gien's pottery styles as rather derivative. The factory produces an appealing modern range.

The **Château de Sully** (*open April–Sept 10–6; Feb–Mar and Oct–Dec 10–12 and 2–5; adm*) makes one of the most beautiful pictures along the Loire. Its sturdy pepperpot towers, sometimes reflected in the river waters, look a model of their medieval kind, although rebuilt in 1908. Three great families owned the château. From the 10th to the 14th centuries, it was the barons of Sully. Then the dukes of La Trémoille transformed the place, notably with the building of the rectangular Vieux Château; Joan of Arc was halted here in her lightning campaign of 1429 by the powerful courtier Georges de la Trémoille – not all the French proved to be fans of the Maid. In 1602, the place became the property of Maximilien de Béthune, one of France's greatest ministers; he worked loyally for King Henri IV and was rewarded with estates and the title of Duc de Sully. The interiors have been considerably embellished in recent times.

The abbey church of **St-Benoît-sur-Loire** or **Fleury** dominates the flat but atmospheric sweep of the Loire known as the Val d'Or. A massive structure in light stone topped by black slate, it dates from the 11th to 13th centuries, although the origins of this, one of the most significant Benedictine monasteries in Europe, go back far further. Around 672, a band of monks was sent off from Fleury to pilfer the bones of their founder, the great Italian St Benedict, from Monte Cassino near Naples. A terrible wrangle ensued, but a papal decree accepted that the remains should stay at Fleury. Théodulfe, a close adviser to Charlemagne, was made abbot, and thus the monastery became a major centre of learning in the Carolingian empire. The Capetian kings of France then became generous patrons in the 11th and 12th centuries. The abbey church is considered one of the most important Romanesque churches in France. The impressive narthex, or entrance tower, is decorated with powerful period sculpture, while the Byzantine-style choir is decorated with a mosaic floor. Pilgrims tour the dark crypt and stay to listen to the monks' plainchant mass (*at 12 normal weekdays, at 11 weekends and special days*). The little oratory at nearby **Germigny-des-Près**, built for Théodulfe, retains a rare, glittering 9th-century mosaic.

Unfortunately for the town of **Châteauneuf-sur-Loire**, it lost most of its château with the Revolution and, in the course of the 19th century, virtually all of the Loire river trade on which it had thrived for centuries. Yet the sumptuous castle stables which survived the Revolution give off a distinct whiff of Ancien Régime grandeur and have been converted into the **Musée de la Marine de Loire** (*open April–Oct Wed–Mon 10–6; rest of year Wed–Mon 2–6; closed Tues; adm*), celebrating the life of the Loire mariners. In the war-damaged church of **St-Martial**, turn your nose up at the deliberately repellent tomb of Louis Phélypeaux de la Vrillère, who commissioned the château.

The Loire Valley around Orléans has been dubbed Cosmetics Valley after the many French perfume houses to have located there. Some 20 km northeast of Orléans, once through the dark Forest of Orléans, you emerge at the **Château de Chamerolles** (*open July–Aug daily 10–6; April–June and Sept Wed–Mon 10–6, closed Tues; Feb–Mar and Oct–Dec Wed-Mon 10–12 and 2–5; adm*), east of Chilleurs-aux-Bois. Recently given a major facelift, it now contains a slick museum dedicated to the history of perfume.

Orléans

At the crowning point of the Loire, Orléans could have been king of French cities. Under the Capetian royals it challenged its rival on the Seine until Paris seduced the sovereigns away. However, they periodically returned, at one point led by Orléans' uncrowned queen, Joan of Arc.

Getting Around

Orléans has two main **railway** stations, Orléans-Centre (for the historic centre) and Orléans-Les Aubrais. The city has good rail connections with Paris-Austerlitz, Blois and Tours, plus a few trains a day to Chartres and other towns round and about.

Tourist Information

Orléans: Place Albert Ier, **t** 02 38 24 05 05, *info@tourisme-orleans.com*.

Where to Stay and Eat

Orléans ✉ 45000

***Hôtel d'Arc, 37ter Rue de la République, **t** 02 38 53 10 94, *www.hoteldarc.fr* (*moderate*). Well-kitted-out rooms in an elaborate Belle Epoque building on the main pedestrian shopping street.

Jackotel, 18 Cloître St-Aignan, **t 02 38 54 48 48 (*inexpensive*). Modern, but tucked into a tranquil courtyard out by the church of St-Aignan's delightful square.

L'Abeille, 64 Rue Alsace Lorraine, **t 02 38 53 54 87, *hotel-de-labeille@wanadoo.fr* (*inexpensive*). On central pedestrianized shopping street, with some good-sized rooms.

Olivet ✉ 45160

***Le Rivage, 635 Rue de la Reine Blanche, Olivet, **t** 02 38 66 02 93, *www.monsite. wanadoo.fr/le.rivage.olivet* (*moderate*). South, on the banks of the Loiret, swanky-to-chichi rooms and restaurant (*expensive*). Closed late-Dec–late-Jan.

Eating Out

Les Antiquaires, 2–4 Rue du Lin, **t** 02 38 53 52 35 (*expensive*). Upmarket central choice, with beamed, atmospheric dining room. *Closed Sun eve and Mon.*

La Chancellerie, 27 Place du Martroi, **t** 02 38 53 57 54 (*moderate*). Well-located in an historic building on Orléans' main square, the food in uncomplicated brasserie style.

La Promenade/Le Martroi, Place du Martroi, **t** 02 38 42 15 00 (*moderate*). Sister establishments in prime position, the Promenade serving more refined cuisine (*closed Sun and Mon*) upstairs, the Martroi with outdoor seating below and cheaper brasserie food.

Le Brin de Zinc, 62 Rue Ste-Catherine, **t** 02 38 53 38 77 (*moderate–inexpensive*). Amusing place full of bric-a-brac, run with verve, offering a vegetarian menu.

Touristy restaurants as well as bars proliferate in the streets around Place du Martroi.

Orléans was an important Celtic settlement that grew into a major Gallo-Roman town, *Cenabum*. In 451 it became the target of the Hunnish invaders under Attila, until Aignan sent them packing from the city's doorstep (with a great deal of help from Roman soldiers) and became Orléans' saintly hero for almost a millennium before Joan outdid him. In 498 Clovis took the city. Converted to Christianity by his wife and a fortuitous victory, he assembled a council in Orléans in 511 that cemented the all-too-close relationship between French Crown and Church. Hugues Capet, founder of the Capetian dynasty, made the French monarchy hereditary and indivisible at the crowning of his son Robert II le Pieux in Orléans cathedral in 987. Robert left his mark on the city in the infamous *Jour des Saints Innocents* in 1022, when he had a number of Church intellectuals burnt as heretics. Thereafter, the royal retinue alternated between Paris and Orléans until Louis VI chose the Seine over the Loire. As Pope Honorius III banned the teaching of law in Paris in 1219, however, the majority of 13th-century royal lawyers were trained in Orléans. One student became Pope Clement V, and showed his gratitude by granting the city a university in 1306.

In the Hundred Years War, during the infamous English siege of Orléans from 1428 to 1429, the townspeople endured months of starvation. On 29 April 1429 Joan of Arc

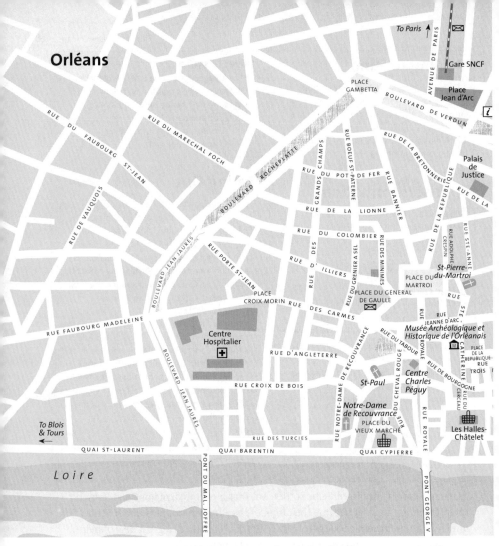

Orléans

To Paris

Gare SNCF

PLACE GAMBETTA

Place Jean d'Arc

BOULEVARD DE VERDUN

RUE DU MARECHAL FOCH

RUE DU FAUBOURG ST-JEAN

RUE DE VAUQUOIS

BOULEVARD ROCHEPLATTE

RUE DU POT-DE-FER

RUE BOEUF ST-PATENE

RUE DES GRANDS CHAMPS

RUE DE LA BRETONNERIE

Palais de Justice

RUE DE LA

RUE BANNIER

RUE DE LA LIONNE

RUE DU COLOMBIER

RUE ADOLPHE CRESPIN

RUE STE-ANNE

BOULEVARD JEAN JAURÈS

RUE PORTE ST-JEAN

RUE D'ILLIERS

RUE DES MINIMES

RUE DU GRENIER A SEL

RUE DES MINIMES

St-Pierre-du-Martroi

PLACE DU MARTROI

RUE

PLACE CROIX MORIN

RUE DES CARMES

RUE DU GENERAL DE GAULLE

PLACE DU GENERAL DE GAULLE

RUE FAUBOURG MADELEINE

Centre Hospitalier

RUE D'ANGLETERRE

RUE JEANNE D'ARC

Musée Archéologique et Historique de l'Orléanais

PLACE DE LA RÉPUBLIQUE

RUE TROIS

RUE STE-CATHERINE

BOULEVARD JEAN JAURÈS

RUE CROIX DE BOIS

RUE NOTRE-DAME DE RECOUVRANCE

St-Paul

RUE DU TABOUR

RUE DU CHEVAL ROUGE

RUE ROYALE

Centre Charles Péguy

RUE DE BOURGOGNE

RUE DU CERCEAU

To Blois & Tours

Notre-Dame de Recouvrance

PLACE DU VIEUX MARCHE

RUE DES TURCIES

RUE ROYALE

Les Halles-Châtelet

QUAI ST-LAURENT

QUAI BARENTIN

QUAI CYPIERRE

PONT DU MAL JOFFRE

PONT GEORGE V

Loire

broke through the English defences to enter the city briefly. The major French offensive began a week later. The French troops were actually under the command of Dunois, a royal bastard, but Joan spurred them on to victory when Dunois seemed prepared to give up. Orléans' liberation, celebrated on 8 May, came to be seen as pivotal in securing the unity of the French nation, although historically it was one in a string of victories through which the French forces slowly ousted the English.

In 1560 a meeting of the Estates General was assembled in the city in a desperate effort to avoid civil war between the increasingly antagonistic Catholics and Protestants. To add to the woes, the sickly young King François II died at the Hôtel Groslot, leaving as his widow Mary, Queen of Scots. Orléans went on to serve as short-lived headquarters for the radical Protestants, who attacked Orléans' churches, blowing up the cathedral. The St Bartholomew's Day massacres of August 1572 effectively silenced them. After the civil war, King Henri IV had Orléans cathedral rebuilt.

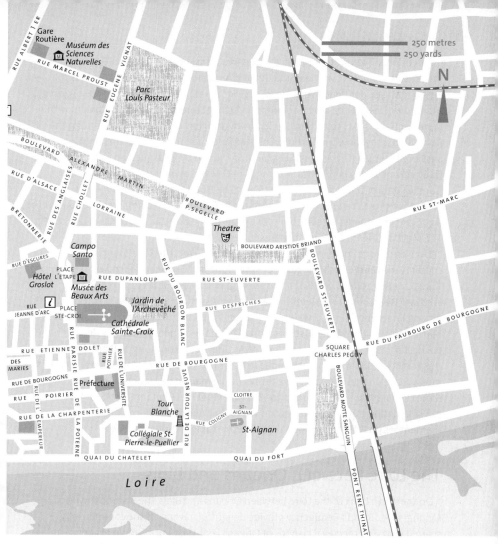

Orléans then thrived on New World trade, especially the refining of sugar cane carried up the Loire through the Ancien Régime, until the loss of French Caribbean territories.

Nazi attacks in June 1940 and American bombings in May 1943 devastated much of historic Orléans; the town was liberated on 16 August 1944 by US General Patton. A steady stream of business from Paris has been flowing Orléans' way since. Although Joan of Arc has unfortunately been adopted as a symbolic figure by the extreme right-wing French National Front, the Maid of Orléans still brings out practically everyone in town (and their dog) for the city's good-natured May celebrations.

The **Cathédrale Ste-Croix** rises majestically out of the centre of town. Oversensitive Proust called it the ugliest church in France, complaining that the tops of its towers resembled strawberry gâteaux. Only the radiating chapels around the choir and a couple of nave bays survived the Protestant destruction. The choir and transepts are 17th century, the rest largely 18th. Louis XIV's notably large nose forms the unintentionally comical centrepiece of the two transept rose windows. Triumphalist 19t-century windows commemorate Joan of Arc inside. By the cathedral stands the postwar **Musée des Beaux-Arts** (*open Tues–Sat 10–12.15 and 1.30–6, Sun 1.30–6; closed Mon; adm*). Despite the severe totalitarian architecture, a riot of excess awaits within. Sumptuous-to-sickly collections, culled from churches and monasteries during the Revolution, show how the Catholic Counter-Reformation led the Church into an over-passionate fling with Baroque. Seek out a *St Thomas* by Velásquez, an excellent Gauguin and the experimental scuptures of Orléans' own ground-breaking Henri Gaudier-Breska. Opposite, the brick fancy of the **Hôtel Groslot** (*open July–Sept Mon–Fri 9–7, Sat 5–9; Oct–June Tues–Sat 10–12 and 2–6, Sun 4.30–6; adm*) preserves parts of its original Mannerist façades, built for a high-ranking official under King François Ier. The Maid of Orléans features in many guises in the 19th-century interiors.

In a picturesque corner off grandiose Rue Jeanne d'Arc, the Renaissance Hôtel Cabu contains the **Musée Archéologique et Historique de l'Orléanais** (*open July and Aug Tues–Sat 10–12.15 and 1.30–6, Sun 1.30–6; May, June and Sept Tues–Sun 1.30–6; Oct–April Wed and weekends 1.30–6; adm*), presenting a breathtaking display of Gaulish bronzes among lesser collections. The Celtic horse dedicated to the Celtic god Rudiobus poses particularly magnificently. Just west, stroll along the arcades of **Rue Royale**, the poshest shopping street in town. Joan of Arc inevitably triumphs on **Place du Martroi**, the grandest square in town, the equestrian statue of 1855 by Foyatier. Close by, on messy Place Charles de Gaulle, the timberframe **Maison de Jeanne d'Arc** (*open May–Oct Tues–Sun 10–12.30 and 1.30–6; 2 Nov–April Tues–Sun 1.30–6; closed Mon; adm*) is a fake, dating from after the Second World War, and its mediocre models and mementoes do little to bring Joan's truly remarkable spirit back to life.

The Loire between Orléans and Blois

On the north bank of the Loire between Orléans and Blois, the historic towns of Meung-sur-Loire and Beaugency provide delightful havens off the commercially scarred N152. The medieval bishops of Orléans kept their out-of-town residence at **Meung** and clearly weren't ones to deprive themselves. Their **Château de Meung** (*open mid-Feb–Nov daily 10–12 and 2–7; rest of year Sat and Sun 2–6; adm*), although left to fall into disrepair, is a substantial building with plenty of dilapidated charm as well as dark dungeons where gory tales are told. Meung also boasts a huge **abbey church**, which looks like a cathedral in a village. Ornate reliquary boxes stand perched up high in several side chapels, while one window pays homage to Joan of Arc. Go down to the Loire to admire a splendid avenue of plane trees and to chuckle at the prim statue of Jean de Meun, principal author of the 13th-century bestseller *Le Roman de la Rose*. A second French poet has his place in Meung's history or, more precisely, in the prison of the bishops' palace. A notorious 15th-century wastrel, François Villon was admired for the puns and pathos of his poetry.

South of the Loire, the land is flat as a pancake, making the huge **Basilique de Cléry-St-André** rise all the more dramatically out of the fertile soils. In 1280 a local farmer

Getting Around

Meung and Beaugency have **rail** stations.

Tourist Information

St-Dyé-sur-Loire: 73 Rue Nationale, t 02 54 81 65 45.

Meung-sur-Loire: 42 Rue Jehan de Meung, t 02 38 44 32 28, *www.visitez-meung.com*.

Beaugency: 3 Place du Dr Hyvernaud, t 02 38 44 54 42, *tourisme.beaugency@wanadoo.fr*.

Where to Stay and Eat

Beaugency ✉ **45190**

★★★**Hôtel de l'Abbaye**, 2 Quai de l'Abbaye, t 02 38 44 67 35, *abbaye@chateauxhotels. com* (*moderate*). In a 17th-century monastery by the Loire. Smart restaurant (*expensive*) serving traditional food.

★★**Hôtel de la Sologne**, 6 Place St-Firmin, t 02 38 44 50 27, *hoteldelasologne.com* (*inexpensive*). Charming little hotel up the slope, surrounded by the main monuments. *Closed late-Mar–mid-April*.

Tavers ✉ **45190**

★★★★**La Tonnellerie**, 12 Rue des Eaux-Bleues, t 02 38 44 68 15, *tonnellerie@chateauxhotels. com* (*luxury–expensive*). Luxurious address, hidden behind an unassuming village façade. Pleasures include a pool and smart restaurant. *Closed Christmas–Feb; restaurant closed Mon lunch and Sat lunch*.

St-Dyé-sur-Loire ✉ **41500**

★★**Manoir de Bel Air**, 1 Route d'Orléans, t 02 54 81 60 10, *www.manoirdebelair.com* (*moderate*). Renovated manor, spectacularly located looking down on the Loire. Enjoy views of the river from the big dining room. *Closed late-Jan–late Feb*.

Chambord ✉ **41250**

★★**St-Michel**, Place St-Michel, t 02 54 20 31 31 (*moderate*). Exclusive location close to the entrance to the château, although the tourist hordes pass by. The restaurant offers a range of traditional French cuisine and has a big terrace. *Closed mid-Nov–mid-Dec*.

Restaurant du Château de Chambord, t 02 54 33 34 71 (*moderate*). Interesting new restaurant in the castle itself, with terrace.

supposedly ploughed up a statue of the Virgin and Child, and miracles began to happen. The original church, sponsored by King Philippe IV le Bel, was destroyed by English soldiers in the Hundred Years War. Superstitious King Louis XI attributed a difficult victory over the English at Dieppe to an act of intervention by the Virgin of Cléry. He saw to the church's magnificent reconstruction, and was buried here.

Beaugency counts among the most beautiful towns along the Loire, with its patched-up Gothic bridge, its cobbled quays, and its soaring medieval monuments set around a series of triangular squares. The most imposing is the skyscraping yet dangerously decaying 11th-century **Tour de César**. A competing tower nearby is a remnant of the church of **St-Firmin**. Romanesque **Notre-Dame** below is associated with a council of major significance for the medieval histories of France and England that took place in 1152 and announced the annulment of the French king Louis VII's marriage to Eleanor of Aquitaine. Eleanor took back her vast inheritance and promptly married Henri Plantagenet of Anjou, who became King Henry II of England in 1154, triggering centuries of conflict. The church retains a strong Romanesque feel, and massive columns with bold capital designs, one representing a preposterously large nose. The small, mangled remnants of the **Château Dunois** have been disappointingly restored and contain a confusing clutter of items, the **Musée Régional de l'Orléanais** (*open Wed–Mon 10–12 and 2–5, or 6 in summer; closed Tues; adm*). On a higher square, the fleurs-de-lys scattered over one façade signal Beaugency's **town**

hall (*open May–Sept Mon–Fri 11, 3, 4 and 4.30, Sat 11; rest of year Tues–Fri 3, 4 and 4.30; adm*). Inside, the exact significance of the exquisite embroideries remains a mystery.

Château de Chambord

Open April–Oct daily 9–5.45; rest of year 9–4.45; adm.

Set in its enormous glade south of the Loire, below the picturesque river port of **St-Dyé-sur-Loire**, which served greatly in its construction, the Château de Chambord, King François Ier's outrageously outsized 'hunting lodge', is a truly glorious and absurd monster of architecture. Work began in 1519 but the original architect remains a mystery. Leonardo da Vinci is tantalizingly linked to the place, although a name more concretely associated with it is that of Domenico da Cortona, an Italian Renaissance architect who came to France before Leonardo, in Charles VIII's train, and made models of various constructions for François as early as 1517. One was of a version of Chambord. The king possibly had a large say in keeping many traditional French features in the design, for Chambord's general forms are actually medieval. The solid round towers at the corners, with their roofs like great upturned funnels, resemble copybook pictures of a chivalric castle. But Chambord is also obsessively ordered in Renaissance fashion, sometimes described as the first apartment block in Europe, hundreds of rooms repeating the same pattern, reached by a staggering 14 major staircases and 70 lesser ones, the double central one considered a work of genius. Even the medieval riot of a roofscape, highlight of the tour, has a logic behind its wild visual fireworks.

Chambord was not just a hunting lodge but also a blatant statement of royal power during a blazing clash between megalomaniac European leaders, François Ier's main rivals the superior Holy Roman Emperor Charles V and jealous King Henry VIII of England. A building site through François's reign, Chambord was largely completed by his death in 1547. It would scarcely ever be lived in, however. Louis XV, in an act of dubious generosity, gave the palace to his father-in-law, the exiled king of Poland, Stanislas Leszcinski. After Leszcinski's death, this poisoned chalice of a castle was passed on to the Maréchal de Saxe, an eccentric military man with delusions of grandeur. The Revolution saw most of the interiors stripped of their contents. In 1809 Napoleon donated Chambord to Marshal Berthier, for whom the title of Prince of Wagram was created. One of his petty ambitions was to replace the innumerable F motifs (for François) with Ws. Later, Chambord was bought by public subscription for King Charles X's heir, Henri, Duc de Bordeaux, given the title of Comte de Chambord. With the 1830 revolution, the royal Orléans family fled and the count stayed in Austria for 41 years, returning to spend his one and only night here in July 1871. Now a national monument, as well as housing a museum of hunting it hosts exhibitions and events.

Blois

King Charles VIII of France bumped his head on a door at the Château d'Amboise (*see* pp.296–7) and died. Thus, in 1498 his cousin, Louis, count of Blois, became King Louis XII and the town of Blois briefly the centre of French politics.

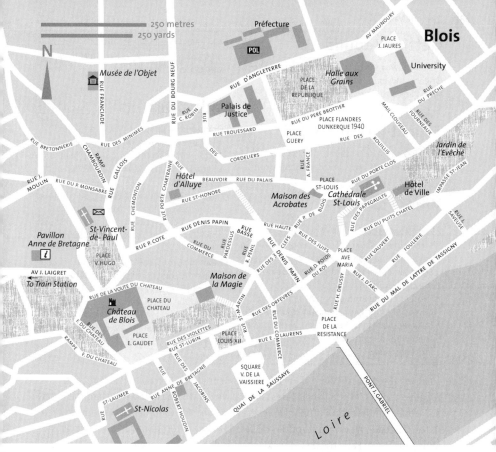

During the early Middle Ages, the powerful counts of Blois had their headquarters here until they also became counts of Champagne and were distracted by that region's riches. In the 12th century Etienne de Blois, a grandson of William the Conqueror, became the disastrous English king Stephen. At the end of the 14th century the county of Blois was sold to Louis d'Orléans, brother of King Charles VI of France. For several centuries it then became the seat of a string of royal relatives all confusingly carrying the title of Duc d'Orléans. Louis d'Orléans was assassinated in 1407 and his wife, Valentine Visconti, from Milan, took refuge here. One of her sons was the celebrated chivalric poet-duke Charles d'Orléans, held prisoner in England for ages after Agincourt in 1415. But on his return he settled back at Blois and his court brought prosperity and culture to the town. Charles' wife bore him a son, Louis, the one who became king when Charles VIII met his destiny with a door at Amboise. The new sovereign divorced his crippled wife to marry Charles VIII's widow, Anne de Bretagne, as stipulated in the royal marriage contract, and Blois became the seat of the court. Louis XII wished to claim his inheritance in Milan, via his Visconti grandmother, and followed the example of Charles VIII's forays into Italy, encouraging the French Renaissance. His daughter, Claude, would marry François d'Angoulême, who as François Ier became France's most notable Renaissance royal.

Getting Around

Blois **railway** station has regular services to Orléans and Tours. **Bus** services radiate out from Blois around the whole *département*.

Tourist Information

Blois: Pav. Anne de Bretagne, 3 Av Jean Laigret, t 02 54 90 41 41, *www.loiredeschateaux.com*.

Where to Stay

Blois ✉ **41000**
★★★**Mercure**, 28 Quai St-Jean, t 02 54 56 66 66, *www.mercure-blois.fr* (*expensive–moderate*). Big chain hotel, but by the Loire and close to the château, with restaurant.
★★**Hôtel Anne de Bretagne**, 31 Av Jean Laigret, t 02 54 78 05 38, *www.annedebretagne.free.fr* (*inexpensive*). Near the château, with nice if somewhat noisy rooms. *Closed early Jan–early Feb.*

★**A la Ville de Tours**, 2 Place de la Grève, t 02 54 78 07 86 (*inexpensive*). Characterful, central and close to the river.

Eating Out

L'Orangerie du Château, 1 Av Jean Laigret, t 02 54 78 05 36 (*expensive*). Upmarket restaurant, in an historic building behind the château. *Closed Wed and Sun eve, and mid-Feb–mid-Mar.*
Au Rendez-Vous des Pêcheurs, 27 Rue du Foix, t 02 54 74 67 48 (*expensive–moderate*). Refined food, especially fish, served in a cosy town house close to river. *Closed Sun and Mon lunch, plus 3 weeks Aug, 2 weeks Jan.*
L'Espérance, 189 Quai Ulysse Besnard (west along the Loire north bank out of town), t 02 54 78 09 01 (*expensive–moderate*). Behind the quirky architecture, inventive cuisine in a bright dining room overlooking the Loire. *Closed Sun eve and Mon, and mid-Aug and 1 week Feb.*

During the dreadful Wars of Religion, King Henri III was forced to flee Paris, and repaired to Blois. At the 1588 Estates General then gathered in town, he had the fanatical leaders of the ultra-Catholic Ligue, the Duke and the Cardinal de Guise, murdered in the château; the royal authorities declared that an attempt had been made on the king's life. But in Paris the de Guises were accorded an almost saintly status. Henri III got his come-uppance when he was assassinated in the capital the following year. With him, the Valois dynasty, which had ruled France since 1328, came to a bloody end.

As to Blois, it lost its pre-eminence, but retained a certain importance as a place of exile for irritating royals who fell out of favour, notably Louis XIII's difficult brother, Gaston d'Orléans. A tradition for producing luxury crafts flourished down the centuries. The Second World War wrought terrible destruction, however, and along with some dull postwar reconstruction came large amounts of social housing. But Jack Lang, high-profile socialist mayor and minister, has brought great energy to many projects in town in the last couple of decades, even if his mayoral reign has now ended.

The **Château de Blois** (*open July–Aug daily 9–7; April–June and Sept–Oct 9–6; Nov–Mar 9–12 and 2–5; adm*) has wings like an architectural game of Misfits, but the clashing styles are not unattractive. Each in fact provides a magnificent example of its own period. The exuberant late Gothic brick façade built for Louis XII, with his symbol of the porcupine, leads you into the grand inner courtyard. Here, the stone façade of the François Ier wing presents a fusion of Gothic and Renaissance styles. The steep roof and dormers are traditionally French (although the outer façade of arcaded storeys looks utterly Italian). The Gaston d'Orléans wing designed by Mansart stands in stark neoclassical contrast to the eccentricities of the other wings. An unfortunately ugly vast head of Gaston gloats like a slimy Caesar above his coat of arms. On the ground floor of the François Ier wing, in the **Musée Lapidaire**, admire the detail of the château's stonemasons' work close up. There's also a broader regional **archaeological museum** in the former kitchens. The restored **apartments** above are reached via François Ier's stageset of a staircase. Catherine de Médicis, Henri III's powerful mother, is recalled in several of the finest chambers, which include a little oratory and a study smothered in Renaissance motifs. The **Salle des Etats Généraux** is the vast early 13th-century medieval hall squashed between the Louis XII and François Ier wings, its cavernous space supported on a row of alarmingly slender columns. Blois' **fine arts museum**, with items from the French Renaissance and the courtly crafts of Blois, plus extravagant 19th-century paintings, occupies the first floor of the Louis XII wing. Enter the lobby of the Gaston d'Orléans wing to stare up at the sensational Baroque oval dome. To one side of this section stands the brightly redecorated stump of the château's church.

Outside, at the eastern end of the château's esplanade looking down on the Loire, a magnificent brick-patterned house has been transformed into the modern **Maison de la Magie** (*open July–Aug daily 10–6.30; April–June and Sept Tues–Sun 10–12 and 2–6; adm*), inspired by a highly respected Blois-born magician, Jean-Eugène Robert-Houdin. Live magic shows take place inside, while other spaces are devoted to the history of magic, techniques and elaborate demonstrations. The **Maison du Vin**, also on the esplanade, offers a useful introduction to the region's wines. A grand stairway takes you down to the main shopping quarters. Several major churches rise dramatically above the town houses. Behind the castle, the grandiose but isolated 17th-century church of **St Vincent-de-Paul** has been undergoing restoration. The **Musée de l'Objet** (*open mid-May–mid-Sept Tues–Sun 1.30–6.30; rest of year Sat and Sun 1.30–6.30; adm*) nearby is almost more bewildering than the Musée de la Magie. Set in the school of fine arts, it concentrates on everyday objects transformed into art, offering ironic, absurdist, or conceptual comments on contemporary life. Closer to the river, the massive spiky towers of **St-Nicolas** puncture the Blois skyline in front of the castle. Though intimidating from the outside, capitals within provide bawdy entertainment.

The principal shopping street, the Haussmann-like **Rue Denis Papin**, divides the historic town in two, and leads to the main crossing over the Loire, the refined **Pont Jacques V Gabriel**, marked by an Egyptian-style needle. The steep streets east of Rue Papin take you past many of Blois' most atmospheric former courtly residences, embellished with courtyards, wells, stairtowers, galleries and Gothic sculptures. The **Maison des Acrobates** at the top of Rue Pierre de Blois is the most appealing of all Loire town houses, covered with carved figures of jesters. The **cathedral** was largely rebuilt after a freak storm in 1678, following the old Gothic style.

The town's surprisingly central stud farm, the **Haras National de Blois**, lies not far away (*open mid-June–mid-Sept Mon–Sat for visits 10.30, 3.30 and 4.30; plus July and Aug Sun 10.30 and 3; rest of year daily exc Sun, visit 2.30; adm*).

South of Blois to Chenonceaux

Châteaux South of Blois

A whole clutch of châteaux hide out in the woods south of Blois. The immaculate Cheverny may be the best-known, but the others are worth seeking out if you want to discover smaller delights away from the crowds.

The **Château de Beauregard** (*open July and Aug daily 9.30–6.30; April–June and Sept daily 9.30–12 and 2–6.30; Feb–Mar, Oct–Nov and 20 Dec–4 Jan Thurs–Tues 9.30–12 and 2–5, closed Wed; adm*) looks sober on the outside, in the restrained style of the second French Renaissance of the later 16th century. The interiors, however, include the gilded Cabinet des Grelots and the 17th-century Galerie des Illustres, the latter offering a lesson in history and fashion, with 327 major French and European figures from the first Valois king to Louis XIII all represented like enlarged postage stamps along the walls. The Renaissance-style Jardin des Portraits is a further attraction.

The 17th-century **Château de Cheverny** (*open April–Sept daily 9.15–6.15, or 6.45 July and Aug; Oct–Mar 9.30–12 and 2.15–5; adm*), the most refined Loire château of all, was designed by Jacques Bougier for a governor of Blois, Henri Hurault – for whom all vestiges of the previous château on the site were wiped out, with its memories of his first wife and her lover, whom Henri is said to have murdered. The immaculate front looks so white and seamless that its stone might almost be mistaken for whitewashed

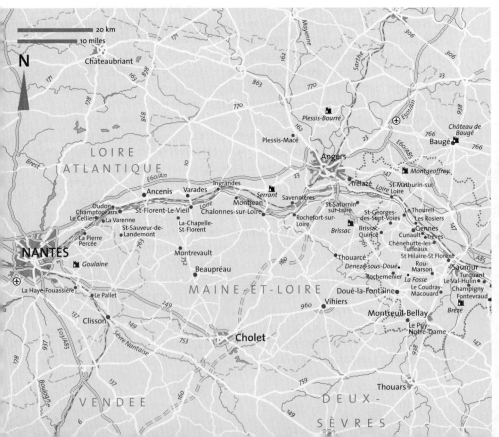

clapboard. The building is pleasingly symmetrical, each front window topped by a pediment like a stylized eyebrow. On the first floor, busts of 12 Roman emperors cross the façade. Cheverny boasts the finest collection of art of any Loire château, with its allegorical wall paintings by Jean Mosnier, three portraits of Hurault family members by the great court painter Clouet, a portrait of Jeanne d'Aragon attributed to Raphael, a Titian depicting the young Cosimo de' Medici and a tapestry cycle illustrating the Labours of Hercules. Cheverny's park is renowned for its pack of hunting dogs.

Troussay (*open Easter–Oct, call* **t** *02 54 44 29 07 for times; adm*), just west of Cheverny, is a *gentilhommière*, or manor house, rather than a château, providing a good example of the architecture and living arrangements of the minor nobility. However, its comparatively modest frame contains grand pieces of decorative art rescued from much larger Loire châteaux and houses that have disappeared off the map. The other, more amateurish collections deal with peasants and witchcraft in the Sologne.

A chip off the old block of Chambord is how the little **Château de Villesavin** (*open June–Sept daily 10–7; mid-Feb–May 10–12 and 2–7; Oct–Nov, plus Dec weekends 10–12 and 2–6; adm*) is frequently described. It was built for Jean Le Breton, trusted friend of King François Ier, who oversaw some of Chambord's construction and made use of its workmen. The pyramidal-topped pavilions, the Renaissance fountain, and the exquisite dormer windows are its highlights. The tour inside is short but sweet and takes in some worn but evocative Italianate wall paintings in the tiny chapel.

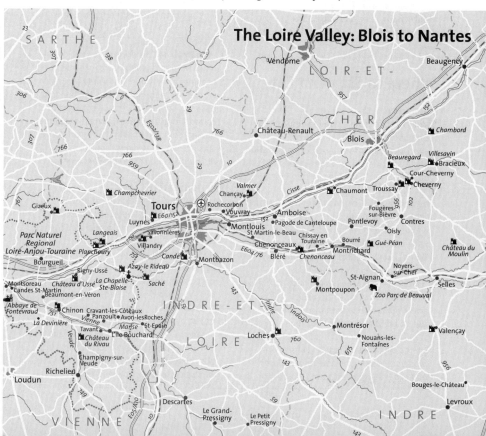

The **Château de Fougères-sur-Bièvre** (*open early May–mid-Sept daily 10–12 and 2–6.30; mid-Sept–early May daily exc Tues 10–12 and 2–4.30; adm*), southwest of Cour-

Getting Around

Check in Blois for **bus excursions** to the châteaux south of Blois. A **railway** line runs along the Cher Valley, with stations at Selles-sur-Cher, St-Aignan, Montrichard and Chenonceaux. A **bus** service from Amboise also serves Chenonceaux. For Valençay you need to change at Gièvres.

Tourist Information

Cour-Cheverny: 12 Rue du Chêne des Dames, t 02 54 79 95 63.
Selles-sur-Cher: 26 Rue de Sion, t 02 54 95 25 44.
Valençay: 2 Av de la Résistance, t 02 54 00 04 42, *www.pays-de-valencay.com*.
St-Aignan-sur-Cher: 60 Rue Constant Ragot, t 02 54 75 22 85, *www.perso.wanadoo.fr/ ot.st-aignan-sur-cher*.
Montrichard: 1 Rue du Pont, t 02 54 32 05 10.
Chenonceaux: 1 Rue Dr Bretonneau, t 02 47 23 94 45.

Where to Stay and Eat

Bracieux ✉ 41250
Bernard Robin/Le Relais de Bracieux, 1 Av de Chambord, t 02 54 46 41 22 (*very expensive–expensive*). Luxurious adaptations of classic Loire produce. *Closed Tues and Wed outside July and Aug, and 20 Dec–end Jan.*

Cheverny and Cour-Cheverny ✉ 41700
★★★**Château du Breuil**, Route de Fougères-sur-Bièvre, outside Cheverny, t 02 54 44 20 20, *www.chateauxhotels.com/breuil* (*expensive*). Wonderful dreamlike refuge hidden in a glade. *Closed mid-Nov–mid-Mar.*
★★**Hôtel des Trois Marchand**s, Place de l'Eglise, Cour-Cheverny, t 02 54 79 96 44, *www.hoteldes3marchands.com* (*inexpensive*). A bit of a tourist institution, with standard rooms and naff paintings, but also a large, plush restaurant (*expensive–moderate*) serving reliable meals. *Closed mid-Feb–late-Mar; restaurant closed Mon.*

Contres ✉ 41700
★★★**Hôtel de France**, 37 Rue Mauger, t 02 54 79 50 14, *www.hotels-france.com/hotel-de-france* (*moderate–inexpensive*). Practical rooms with modern comforts in a typical local building. With smart restaurant, **Les Rois de France** (*expensive–moderate*). *Closed late-Jan–Feb.*

Noyers-sur-Cher ✉ 41140
★★★**Le Clos du Cher**, 2 Rue Paul Boncour, t 02 54 75 00 03, *www.closducher.com* (*moderate*). On the Cher's north bank outside St-Aignan, hiding in its private park, with pleasant rooms furnished in style. Stylish cuisine.

St-Aignan ✉ 41110
★★**Grand Hôtel St-Aignan**, 7-9 Quai J-J Delorme, t 02 54 75 18 04, *grand.hotel. st.aignan@wanadoo.fr* (*inexpensive*). Old-fashioned French hotel, with large windows looking on to the Cher. *Closed late Nov.*

Chissay ✉ 41400
★★★**Château de Chissay**, t 02 54 32 32 01, *www.chateaudechissay.com* (*expensive*). Looking proudly pure and white among the woods above the valley road, the building has been somewhat mutilated for visitors' comfort, but it has many attractions. Superb dining room and imaginative avant-garde cuisine. Pool. *Closed mid-Nov–mid-Mar; restaurant closed Mon, and Tues lunch.*

Chenonceaux ✉ 37150
★★★**Bon Laboureur**, 6 Rue du Dr Bretonneau, t 02 47 23 90 02, *laboureur@chateauxho-tels.com* (*very expensive–moderate*). The closest hotel to the château, a bulging, ivy-clad village inn with pleasant rooms decked out with modern furniture, and pool. Posh gastronomic restaurant (*expensive*). *Closed mid-Nov–mid-Dec and early Jan–early Feb.*
★★**Hostel du Roy**, 9 Rue du Dr Bretonneau, t 02 47 23 90 17, *www.hostelduroy.com* (*inexpensive*). A little turret marks the façade, and the rustic touches have been laid on a bit, but the food is country-copious (*moderate–cheap*). *Closed mid-Nov–mid-Feb.*

Cheverny, is uncharacteristic of this region where châteaux are usually constructed of clean-cut white stone. Fougères looks much more medieval, with its massed towers, small irregular stones and inner courtyard enclosed on all four sides. Despite the stern exterior, little touches show Renaissance influences. Many rooms stand empty but the attics have fine rafters and displays recalling the skill of the Loire craftsmen.

The Cher Valley from Selles to Chenonceaux

The broad, fertile Cher valley flowing from the Berry border to join the Loire near Tours offers a peaceful tourist route until you hit upon the village of Chenonceaux, and its château (without the x). Arguably the most beautiful bridge in the world, this most famous of Loire castles was built over the Cher in the brightest limestone.

Selles-sur-Cher, a quietly pretty, white riverside town, is better known for its goat's cheese than for its waterside château or its battered Romanesque church. South at the splendid **Château de Valençay** (*open late-Mar–Oct 9.30–6, or 7.30 in July and Aug; adm*), the façades may be 16th-century, and typical of the region, mixing late-Gothic and French Renaissance styles, but the corner towers were given eccentric tops all of their own. 'Shit in a silk stocking' is the not entirely flattering way Napoleon once described his brilliant foreign minister Talleyrand, whom he allowed to abide here. The highly entertaining guided tour focuses on the wiley politician, who married the stunning Catherine Worlée, said to have 'no more intellect than a rose'. She was supplanted in her husband's affections by his nephew's wife, a driven, intelligent woman. The grounds are populated with a menagerie of animals and vintage cars.

The **Château de Bouges** (*open July and Aug daily 10–1 and 2–7; June Wed–Mon 10–12 and 2–7; April, May, June and Sept Wed–Mon 10–12 and 2–6; Mar and Nov weekends 10–12 and 2–5; adm*), off the D956 between Valençay and Levroux, is a jewel box of a little castle, sometimes compared to Versailles' Petit Trianon. It was built in 1762 for Count Charles Le Blanc de Marnaval, an owner of ironworks, and is immaculately furnished with the accoutrements of 18th- and 19th-century noble living.

In the enchanting Cher-side town of **St-Aignan**, the soaring tower of the church turns out to be a 19th-century addition to the large Romanesque church below. Inside, the restorers have operated to give it an almost hospital-like whiteness. The dark lower church contains intriguing Romanesque wall paintings, the most original showing St Gilles praying powerfully enough to save a ship from being wrecked. Climb the Jacob's ladder of a staircase beside the church to reach the terraces of the château (*not open*), with delightful views on to the town's array of old roofs, and down onto the river with its island. You can go boating from there. South of town, the **Zooparc de Beauval** (*open April–Nov 9–nightfall, Nov–Mar 10–nightfall; adm*) is a well-run establishment with remarkable wild cats, substantial aviary, and a new seal pool.

Vineyards run down the slopes west of St-Aignan. Head up the north bank to peek at the **Château du Gué-Péan**, a Sleeping Beauty of a castle lost among the woods. On the open plain beyond, **Oisly** has a well-regarded wine cooperative, while the **Abbaye de Pontlevoy** rises quite spectacularly out of its little town. Back down by the Cher, **Bourré** is renowned for its enormous former stone quarries, a few of which you can visit. One contains a mushroom farm, the **Caves Champignonnières des Roches** (*open*

Easter–Oct daily, visits 10 and 11, and on the hour 2–5; adm); another has recently been transformed by a sculptor into a curious little village of stone, the **Ville Souterraine** (*open April–Nov daily 10–6, tours on the hour; adm*); a third, **La Magnanerie** (*open Easter–Aug Wed–Mon, visits 11, 3, 4 and 5; Sept–Oct Thurs–Mon, visits 3, 4 and 5; adm*), serves as the setting for a silk-worm farm.

Riverside **Montrichard** has caves aplenty too, occupied by wine makers, none more extensive than the **Caves Monmousseau**. The town boasts a fine legacy of medieval buildings below the dramatic if crumbling remnants of its keep. The place played a cameo role in Steven Spielberg's film *Catch Me if You Can*, when the daring young fraudster, whose mother hailed from nearby, was caught here. You can escape by boat.

Get away from the madding crowds by visiting the **Château de Montpoupon** (*open July–Aug 10–6; April–June and Sept 10–12 and 2–6; Oct–Dec 10–12 and 2–4; adm*), a much-restored but charming Gothic to Renaissance castle to the south. The place thrived on hunting, and the smart museum in the outhouses is devoted to the theme.

Château de Chenonceau

Open mid-Mar–mid-Sept daily 9–7; late Sept daily 9–6.30; early Mar and first half of Oct daily 9–6; rest of Oct and mid–end Feb daily 9–5.30; first half Feb and Nov daily 9–5; mid-Nov–Jan daily 9–4.30; adm.

The most glamorous of all the Loire Valley's castles, the Château de Chenonceau is also the most visited, so be prepared for vast crowds. There turn out to be two distinct parts to the castle: the first, square block with its splendid windows and corner turrets was built between 1515 and 1521 for Thomas Bohier, an inspector of finances for kings Louis XII and François Ier. While Bohier accompanied François on his expeditions, his wife Katherine oversaw the building, and the initials TB and TK show up in numerous locations. Two prows of stone protrude over the river, the first containing the chapel, the second a delightful library. The pillars of the arch under the Bohier building were ingeniously fitted with kitchens, with a little stairway leading down to a platform where boats could dock and unload provisions. Several of François Ier's financiers, builders of some of the Loire's best châteaux, were implicated in financial scandals or used as scapegoats. After Bohier's death, he was found guilty of embezzlement and his son forced to give the château to the crown in 1535. So the profligate François gained yet another beautiful building and Chenonceau was reduced to serving the occasional royal hunt. François' successor King Henri II gave away Chenonceau as a love token to his mistress Diane de Poitiers. Queen Catherine de Médicis had her revenge on the death of her cheating husband in 1559, forcing Diane to part with Chenonceau in exchange for the Château de Chaumont (*see* opposite). Catherine ordered the second wing to be built over the Cher. Dating from the 1570s, it looks soberly classical despite a wonderful rhythm to its galleries. The light in the main chamber may be magical, but it would take a ball to really bring it to life.

In the 1560s, Catherine held her spectacular '*triomphes de Chenonceau*', with lavish provisions including a fountain spouting wine. The seductive powers of her *escadron volant*, a 'flying squadron' of beautiful, bright aristocratic young women, entrapped leading nobles of the realm, the better to spy on them. Catherine's flamboyant son, Henri III, had a devoted wife, Louise de Lorraine, and it was to her that Chenonceau was left. Altered at various periods by restoration work, but spared revolutionary destruction, the château has been owned by the Menier chocolate family since 1913. During the Second World War, the Cher lay on the frontier between German-occupied France and Vichy France and the château was used as a bridge by Resistance members. The outbuildings now contain a waxworks museum and a tea-house. Chenonceau stages a *son-et-lumière* (**t** 02 47 23 90 97), while a boat trip or gourmet cruise on the Bélandre (**t** 02 47 23 98 64) takes you under the château's arches.

The Loire from Blois to Tours via Amboise

Roads stick tightly to both banks of the Loire between Blois and Tours, giving wonderful views of its sandbanks and islands. From the north side, admire the dramatic **Château de Chaumont-sur-Loire** (*open early May–mid-Sept daily 9.30–6.30; April–early May 10.30–5.30; rest of year 10–5; adm*), up in one of the best locations along the Loire. It still has a strongly chivalric air, even though construction began late in the Gothic period at the start of the 1470s, after the previous castle had been razed on King Louis XI's orders, as punishment for Pierre d'Amboise's part in a rebellion. Subsequently pardoned, Pierre had the north and west wings built before his death in 1473. His powerful grandson Charles II d'Amboise had the place completed by the end of the century. On the imposing entrance towers, the Cs apparently refer to him, the Ds to Diane de Poitiers, forced to exchange Chenonceau for Chaumont by Catherine de Médicis. Catherine had acquired this lucrative property in 1550, but rarely stayed, although legend has it that it was at Chaumont that one of the famous astrologers of the day, either Ruggieri or Nostradamus, predicted the deaths of her husband and sons and the ultimate downfall of the Valois dynasty. Before the Revolution, it was turned into a lively centre of artistic production before being abandoned. In the 19th century wealthy new owners rescued it, so inside, you're treated as much to an extravaganza of neo-Gothic as Gothic, plus a collection of fine art pillaged from a pot-pourri of places. Visit, too, the extravagant 19th-century stables. The **Festival International des Jardins** (*open June–mid-Oct daily 9.30–nightfall; adm*) is held annually in the noble grounds, featuring cutting-edge landscape designers.

Amboise

French towns don't come more royal than Amboise. The **Château d'Amboise** (*open July–Aug daily 9–7; April–June 9–6.30; Sept–Oct 9–6; second half Mar and first half Nov 9–5.30; Feb–mid-Mar 9–12 and 2–5.30; mid-Nov–Jan 9-12 and 2–4.45; adm*) played its part as an important residence for a string of monarchs. The castle was forfeited to the crown in 1431 because of Louis d'Amboise's disloyal behaviour. King Charles VII – the first royal proprietor – showed little interest in the place, but his son Louis XI and his family spent much time here. At Amboise, Louis established the knightly order of St-Michel to encourage support for the French crown through flattery and favour.

Getting Around

Amboise has regular **rail** connections with Tours, while Noizay and Montlouis also have train stations. Regular **buses** between Tours and Amboise make occasional stops at Montlouis, Noizay, Vouvray and Rochecorbon.

Tourist Information

Chaumont-sur-Loire: 24 Rue du Maréchal Leclerc, **t** 02 54 20 91 73.
Amboise: B.P. 233, Quai du Gén de Gaulle, **t** 02 47 57 09 28, *tourisme.amboise@wanadoo.fr.*
Vouvray: RN 152 or Mairie, **t** 02 47 52 68 73/ **t** 02 47 52 70 88.
Montlouis-sur-Loire: Place de la Mairie, **t** 02 47 45 00 16, *tourisme-montlouis@wanadoo.fr.*

Where to Stay and Eat

Chaumont-sur-Loire ✉ 41150

La Chancelière, 1 Rue de Bellevue, **t** 02 54 20 96 95 (*moderate*). Restaurant tucked under the Loire cliffside, serving refined cuisine in two cosy dining rooms. *Closed Wed and Thurs.*

Amboise ✉ 37400

★★★★**Le Choiseul,** 36 Quai Charles Guinot, **t** 02 47 30 45 45, *le-choiseul.com* (*luxury–very expensive*). Exclusive hotel packed with interesting features, including superb former grain stores dug into the limestone rock, the so-called **Greniers de César**. The restaurant looking over the Loire is very highly regarded. *Closed mid-Nov–early Feb.*
★★★**Belle Vue,** 12 Quai Charles Guinot, **t** 02 47 57 02 26 (*inexpensive*). Above the busy riverside road by Amboise castle, a traditional, simpler, well-placed option. *Closed mid-Nov–mid-Mar.*
★★**Lion d'Or,** 17 Quai Charles Guinot, **t** 02 47 57 00 23 (*inexpensive*). Similar to the above, just slightly cheaper and with restaurant (*moderate*). *Closed Dec–Jan; restaurant closed Mon lunch.*

L'Epicerie, 18 Rue Victor Hugo, **t** 02 47 57 08 94 (*moderate*). In a lovely timberframe house close to the ramp up to the castle, serves classic, reliably good dishes.

Noizay ✉ 37210

★★★★**Château de Noizay, t** 02 47 52 11 01, *noizay@relaischateaux.fr* (*expensive*). This splendid little castle has all the ingredients to help you relax in style, including gardens, pool and tennis court, plus a fascinating history. Memorable restaurant too. *Closed mid-Jan–mid-Mar.*

Vernou-sur-Brenne 37210

★★**Les Perce-Neige,** 13 Rue Anatole France, *www.perceneige.com* (*inexpensive*). Charming village house with characterful pretensions, pleasing simple rooms, shaded garden, and good local cuisine (*moderate*).

Vouvray ✉ 37210

Domaine des Bidaudières B&B, Rue du Peu Morier, **t** 02 47 52 66 85, *www.bandb-loire-valley.com* (*expensive–moderate*). Italianate dream built on terraces a little east of town, with smart, sophisticated rooms. More like a discreet hotel than a B&B. Pool and lake.
La Cave Martin, t 02 47 52 62 18 (*moderate*). Wonderful Vouvray vineyard setting in which to enjoy simple menus on a summer evening. *Closed Sun eve and Mon.*

Rochecorbon ✉ 37210

★★★★**Les Hautes Roches,** 86 Quai de la Loire, **t** 02 47 52 88 88, *hautes.roches@wanadoo.fr* (*very expensive–expensive*). Fabulous hotel with the most extraordinary rooms along the Loire, luxuriously appointed in hillside caves. The excellent dining room features fish, and the salons are in the smart house alongside. Pool. *Closed end Jan–mid-Mar.*
L'Oubliette, 34 Rue des Clouets, **t** 02 47 52 50 49 (*expensive–moderate*). Set in a cave, serving good, standard regional food. *Closed Sun eve, Mon and Wed out of season, plus late Aug, late Oct and late Feb–mid-Mar.*

The château was a place of safety for Louis' wife to bring up the future King Charles VIII, born here in 1470. When Charles acceded to the throne, the castle became *the* favoured royal residence and he ordered most of the building work, financed by raising a special levy on the salt tax. Work began in 1492. Although a large proportion of his vast Gothic complex has disappeared, what remains still makes a fine impression. The two enormous towers above the riverside provided extraordinary entrances, with wide spiralling ramps. The jewel box Chapelle St-Hubert is a glorious work of late Gothic sticking prominently out from the ramparts, but Charles VIII's main remaining legacy is the wing over the Loire. Unfortunately, the magnificent objects he amassed, among them Joan of Arc's suit of armour and Lancelot's supposed sword, have long vanished. After his foolhardy forays into Italy, through which Renaissance artists and architects were introduced into France, Charles bumped his head in a dirty passageway in the castle where *'tout le monde pissait'*, collapsed and died. Louis d'Orléans took the crown and Charles VIII's widow, and moved to Blois.

However, the Château d'Amboise wasn't neglected. The so-called Louis XII-François Iᵉʳ wing was really built for Louise de Savoie, widow of Charles d'Angoulême of the Orléans royal branch. As Louis XII had no male heir, Louise's eldest son François d'Angoulême, brought up and extraordinarily well-educated with his sister at Amboise, became king in 1515. He tempted the ageing Leonardo da Vinci across the Alps, and the Italian genius helped organize memorable events for the royal court. In October 1534 François Iᵉʳ was not amused, however, to wake up at the château to find a pamphlet stuck to his door containing a stinging attack on the Catholic Mass. This Affaire des Placards led to the persecution of Protestants. With vast new châteaux going up for him at Fontainebleau and Chambord, François Iᵉʳ neglected Amboise more and more. But the children of his successors, King Henri II and Catherine de Médicis, were brought up here. In 1548 the six-year-old Mary Stuart arrived from Scotland to join them, her hand promised to the future King François II of France. The beautiful royal governess Diane de Poitiers, who had so set Henri II alight, produced a son, Henri d'Angoulême, who also joined the brood.

But the troubles between Catholics and Protestants were growing; France was ready to slide into civil war. One bloody precursor occurred in and around Amboise. In 1558 the dauphin François had married Mary, Queen of Scots and a year later became king. There were many Protestant sympathizers in high places outraged at the power Mary's Catholic uncles, the de Guises, were acquiring at court. A plot was hatched by the leading Protestant, Louis Prince de Condé, to capture the de Guises from the king's court at Amboise. But a defector revealed the plans. Many of the conspirators were captured at the nearby Château de Noizay, before the remaining rebels launched a disastrous attack on Amboise. The conspirators were terribly punished, and the Château d'Amboise was more or less abandoned by royalty. In Napoleonic times, most of it was dismantled. But following the restoration of the French monarchy, in 1821 the future King Louis-Philippe regained possession and work was carried out to turn it into a royal summer residence. His descendant, the Comte de Paris, still owns the place under the Fondation St-Louis.

The interiors have been immaculately restored. While most of the rooms in the Charles VIII wing stand rather empty, some contain interesting pieces of furniture and entertaining sculpture, notably the grand council chamber held up on columns flecked with fleurs de lys and ermine tails. Excellent furniture features in the lower rooms of the Louise de Savoie wing, but the style changes completely in the Louis-

Philippe rooms above, where the rich red walls and drapery serve as the backdrop to elegant Restoration furniture and royal family portraits.

The **town of Amboise** grew fat and happy at the château's feet. It supplied the court with its vast needs and picked up the crumbs from its table. Now it makes a good living from tourists, with wine and tapestry shops at the very feet of the castle. Walk beneath the impressive 14th-century **Porte de l'Horloge** gateway on to the main shopping street, **Rue Nationale**, and across town up to the **Collégiale St-Denis**, an interesting church containing a shocking statue of a drowned women, said to be Marie Babou, a mistress of François Ier. By the river, on Quai du Général de Gaulle, the fountain by the surrealist Max Ernst adds a lighter note. More unintentionally amusing is the green statue of a reclining Leonardo on the island opposite the castle.

Leonardo da Vinci's last home, the **Château du Clos Lucé** (*open Aug daily 9–8; late Mar–July and Sept–Oct 9–7; Feb–late-Mar and Nov–Dec 9–6; Jan 10–5; adm*), lies a good walk south of the centre. This fine 15th-century brick manor was embellished for Queen Anne de Bretagne as a peaceful retreat; her decorated oratory can still be seen. The owners have tried to recreate the atmosphere Leonardo might have known in certain rooms; others have an 18th-century feel, with some magnificent furniture rescued from the vast, vanished Château de Chanteloup nearby. While you do not get much of Leonardo the Artist beyond cheap copies inside, you are introduced to Leonardo the Arms Maker in the basement, where some of his most forward-looking drawings have been turned into models – the embarrassing problem with his engineering plans is that most of the machines he dreamt up lacked one vital element: a source of power. The delightful gardens have been transformed to display inventive exhibits relating to Leonardo's work.

Amboise to Tours

South of Amboise, the charming, slightly comic and melancholic **Pagode de Chanteloup** (*open July–Aug daily 9.30–7.30; June 10–7; May and Sept 10–6.30; second half April and Oct–Nov weekends 10–12 and 2–5; adm*) is the sole remnant of the great 18th-century Château de Chanteloup. The pagoda's seven decreasing circles end with a clownish hat of lead topped by a golden ball, reflected in a half-moon pool. Nearby, the **Parc des Mini-Châteaux** (*open Mar–11 Nov; adm*) looks a very artificial little outdoor theme park, but the models of dozens of the Loire Valley's most famous châteaux may appeal to children. The large-scale modern **Aquarium du Val de Loire** (*open year-round, exc second half Nov; adm*) displays fish swimming around which you normally find on your plate along the Loire, plus exotic creatures.

The Loire slopes between Amboise and Tours produce distinctive, often tingling white wines. The **Montlouis** vineyards cluster on the south side of the river, while the more extensive Vouvray vines stretch along the north bank. Both *appellations* produce the whole range of whites, from dry to sweet, all made with Chenin Blanc grapes, while many properties have cellars set in dramatic former stone quarries. To start trying Montlouis wines, tour the village of that name, the attractive **St-Martin-le-Beau**, or the **Château de la Bourdaisière** (*open May–Sept daily 10–7; April and Oct–mid-Nov 10–12 and 2–6; adm; also with luxury rooms, t 02 47 45 16 31*), a 19th-century reinvention of a grand 16th-century castle, the original built for Philibert Babou, who had to share his wife Marie with François Ier. The place has lovely grounds, and an exhibition devoted to *la pomme d'amour*, tomatoes to English-speakers.

In the lower town of **Vouvray**, signs signal *dégustations* at every turn, while the reputed Charcuterie Hardouin adds a drop of wine to many of its highly regarded products. The elegant upper village is just one of a whole string of enchanting ones strung along the Cisse valley, which steals a ribbon of land from the greater Loire valley to meander through meadows towards Tours. Magnificently seated on its terrace above the Loire, the **Château de Moncontour** (*open Easter–mid-Oct daily 10–7; rest of year Mon–Fri 10–6, Sat 3–6; adm*) includes a wine museum. Head up to Chançay for the **Château de Valmer** (*open July–Aug Tues–Sun 2–7; May–June and Sept weekends and public hols 2–7; adm*), where you can combine wine tasting with a look at the splendid terraced gardens. Approaching Tours, the Loire-side village of **Rochecorbon** conceals several small troglodyte attractions, plus you can go on a rare **mini-cruise** on the river aboard *Le St-Martin-de-Tours* (*Mar–Oct, t 02 47 52 68 88; adm*).

Tours

Tours, a luminous, very lively university town, offers a tempting break from all the castles. The city was not just a major Gallo-Roman settlement, but also a very significant early-Christian one, Gatien its first recorded bishop, at work before the Roman Emperor Constantine came to power. Martin, the most important bishop of Tours, was a Hungarian who started his career as a Roman legionnaire. Coming across a ragged beggar in Amiens, in northern France, he was so moved by pity that he took out his sword and cut his cloak in half to help the suffering man. The night after, Martin had a vision of Christ dressed in the other half of his garment. Duly converted, with Hilary, bishop of Poitiers, he would create the first monastery in France, at Ligugé near Poitiers, in 360. He then travelled to Tours to found a second monastery, Marmoutier. Made bishop of the city around 371, he is considered one of the great evangelizers of France. On his death, St Martin's cult spread across Europe, and would later inspire a man who proved more generous by half a cloak, St Francis of Assisi.

Well before then, among the pilgrims to St Martin's shrine in Tours was Gregory, a noble from the Auvergne, who stayed and became bishop himself in 573. His great work, the *Historia Francorum*, is one of the most important texts of the Dark Ages, a roller-coaster read, crammed with the events and superstitions of the period. The great Carolingian scholar Alcuin of York was named abbot in Tours in 796. He founded a brilliant school here and the city became one of the intellectual centres of Western Europe. After the Carolingian decline, the counts of Anjou overran Touraine, controlling it by 1044. Part of the Anglo-Angevin Plantagenet empire, it fell to the French early in the 13th century. The paranoid King Louis XI choose Tours as his capital after the Hundred Years War ended in 1453, and trade and culture flourished.

The novelist Balzac was born along Rue Royale, now Rue Nationale, in 1799. Several of his works expose the petty-minded shenanigans of his home town. Tours briefly

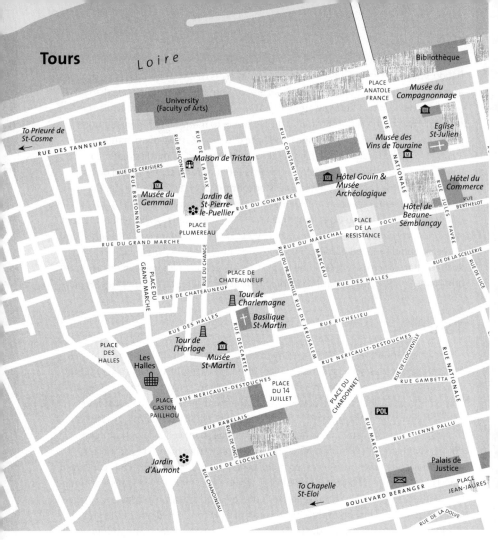

Tours

Loire

Bibliothèque

PLACE ANATOLE FRANCE

Musée du Compagnonnage

University (Faculty of Arts)

Eglise St-Julien

RUE NATIONALE

To Prieuré de St-Cosme

RUE DES TANNEURS

RUE DE LA PAIX

RUE CONSTANTINE

Musée des Vins de Touraine

Maison de Tristan

RUE DES CERISIERS

RUE BRICONNET

Hôtel Gouin & Musée Archéologique

Hôtel du Commerce

RUE BRETONNEAU

Musée du Gemmail

Jardin de St-Pierre-le-Puellier

RUE DU COMMERCE

Hôtel de Beaune-Semblançay

RUE JULES FAVRE

RUE BERTHELOT

PLACE PLUMEREAU

PLACE DE LA RESISTANCE

RUE DU MARECHAL FOCH

RUE DU GRAND MARCHE

RUE DE LA SCELLERIE

PLACE DU GRAND MARCHE

RUE DU CHANGE

PLACE DE CHATEAUNEUF

RUE DU PRÉ MERVILLE

RUE MARCEAU

RUE DES HALLES

RUE DE LUCE

RUE DE CHATEAUNEUF

Tour de Charlemagne

RUE DE JERUSALEM

RUE DES HALLES

Basilique St-Martin

RUE RICHELIEU

PLACE DES HALLES

Les Halles

Tour de l'Horloge

RUE DESCARTES

Musée St-Martin

RUE NERICAULT-DESTOUCHES

RUE DE CLOCHEVILLE

RUE NATIONALE

RUE GAMBETTA

PLACE GASTON PAILLHOU

RUE NERICAULT-DESTOUCHES

PLACE DU 14 JUILLET

PLACE DU CHARDONNET

RUE RABELAIS

RUE DE VINCI

POL

RUE MARCEAU

RUE ETIENNE PALLU

Jardin d'Aumont

RUE DE CLOCHEVILLE

RUE CHANOINEAU

Palais de Justice

PLACE JEAN-JAURES

To Chapelle St-Eloi

BOULEVARD BERANGER

RUE DE LA DOLVE

received the French government fleeing the Prussians who had advanced on Paris in 1870. With Gallic pluck, its leader Léon Gambetta evaded the capital's blockade by taking to a hot-air balloon to join his ministers in Tours. Rather surprisingly, the bourgeois city became the birthplace of the French Communist party in 1920. The Second World War brought terrible devastation, particularly to the riverside quarters, but Tours counted among the first towns in France to benefit from renovation promoted by the Loi Malraux of 1962. The university is massive, while numerous language schools attract a large number of foreign students to the city where the purest French in France is supposedly spoken.

The towers of the **Cathédrale St-Gatien** dominate the city from afar. Close up, the façade reveals a mass of Flamboyant Gothic detail topped by Renaissance domes. Inside, the choir contains superb 13th-century stained glass and the moving tomb of the two short-lived sons of the ill-fated Anne de Bretagne and Charles VIII. Look out

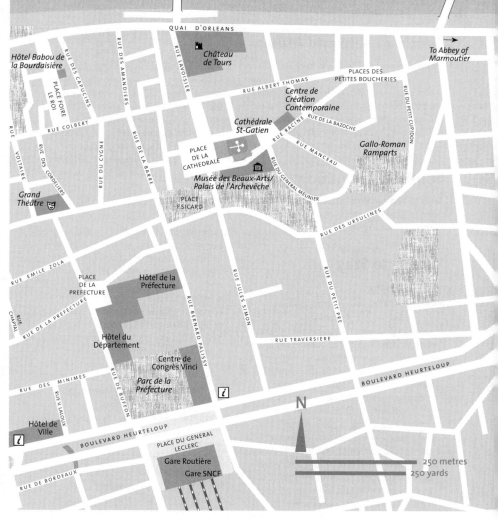

for all manner of representations of St Martin cutting his cloak in half. A triumphal arch next door leads to the aristocratic former archbishops' palace, now the setting for the **Musée des Beaux-Arts** (*open Wed–Mon 9–12.45 and 2–6; closed Tues; adm*), with an impressive collection of paintings. The most fascinating Tourangeau artist represented is Abraham Bosse, a 17th-century engraver who depicted all walks of life under Louis XIII. Balzac stands in several thoughtful poses in famous statues.

Behind the cathedral, old walled religious foundations line the hushed streets. This area provided the oppressive setting for Balzac's tale of vicious religious rivalry, *Le Curé de Tours*. The curve of **Rue Meusnier** exudes the air of an earlier age, its shape recalling the Roman theatre that once stood here. Up from the broken vestiges of the **Château de Tours**, used for temporary exhibitions, a lovely pedestrian bridge crosses the river islands to the traffic-busy north bank of the Loire, but the south bank offers a good starting point for a wonderful walk along the broad cobbled quays.

Getting There and Around

Ryanair flies direct from London-Stansted. The airport is 6km northeast of town, a cheap bus linking it with the central **bus** station by the main train station. Tours has excellent **rail** connections, including with Paris, and two big train stations – don't confuse the central one with that of St-Pierre-des-Corps.

Tourist Information

Tours: 78–82 Rue Bernard Palissy, B.P.4201, 37042 Tours Cedex, **t** 02 47 70 37 37, *www.ligeris.com, info@ligeris.com.*

Where to Stay

Tours ✉ **37000**

★★★★**Hôtel de l'Univers**, 5 Bd Heurteloup, **t** 02 47 05 37 12, *hotel-univers-sa@ wanadoo.fr (luxury–very expensive)*. Grand central hotel, *trompe-l'œil* portraits in the main reception room paying homage to the famous who have stayed in its serious, comfortable rooms, including Churchill. The restaurant has great style.

★★★★**Jean Bardet Château Belmont**, 57 Rue Groison, **t** 02 47 41 41 11, *sophie@jeanbardet. com (luxury–expensive)*. In a substantial town house north of the Loire (off Av de la Tranchée, beyond Pont Wilson), a very chic-to-chichi hotel with a restaurant (*very expensive*) renowned across France for the highest standards of cuisine, although recently rocked by a scandal over misleading

customers about wines. Garden with pool. *Restaurant closed lunchtime Mon and Tues.*

★★**Hôtel du Cygne**, 6 Rue du Cygne, **t** 02 47 66 66 41, *hotelcygne.tours@wanadoo.fr (inexpensive)*. Lovely old-fashioned character to this centrally located, good-value little hotel.

★★**Balzac**, 47 Rue de la Scellerie, **t** 02 47 05 40 87, *hotel.balzac@9online.fr (inexpensive)*. Another central small hotel with some charm, including a little inner courtyard where you can have breakfast in summer.

Eating Out

Charles Barrier, 101 Av de la Tranchée, **t** 02 47 54 20 39 (*very expensive–expensive*). Exceptional smart restaurant north of the Loire across Pont Wilson. *Closed Sat lunch, and Sun.*

Les Tuffeaux, 21 Rue Lavoisier, **t** 02 47 47 19 89 (*expensive–moderate*). Opposite Tours' meagre château, this place offers beams, tufa walls, and traditional Touraine cooking. *Closed Sun, Mon lunch and Wed lunch.*

La Rôtisserie Tourangelle, 23 Rue du Commerce, **t** 02 47 05 71 21 (*expensive–moderate*). Well-established, with impeccable manners. *Closed Sat lunch, Sun eve, and Mon.*

Le Petit Patrimoine, 58 Rue Colbert, **t** 02 47 66 05 81 (*moderate*). Lively narrow little restaurant, serving traditional Tourangeau dishes. *Closed Sun lunch.*

Place Plumereau has been colonized by cafés with superb terraces, but best enjoy these for a drink rather than a meal, as the restaurants are for the tourist hordes.

South and parallel to these, **Rue Colbert** is one of Tours' finest timberframe streets, while the antiques quarter follows down to **Rue de la Scellerie**, which boasts particularly grand mansions. Coming out on **Rue Nationale**, with its big stores, to the south you arrive at the major civic set piece of the **Place Jean Jaurès**, the colossal atlantes by Touraine sculptor François Sicard shouldering the weight of the town hall. At the other end of Rue Nationale, **Pont Wilson** is the grandest of all Tours' bridges. Hidden to one side behind a postwar precinct nearby, the church of **St-Julien** looks grubby and neglected, yet for centuries it was one of Tours' great monasteries; the interior retains pure Gothic dignity. The eccentric **Musée du Compagnonnage** (*open mid-June–mid-Sept daily 9–12 and 2–6; rest of year closed Tues; adm*) above is crammed with craftsmen's chef-d'œuvres, including magnificent old cakes preserved for posterity.

West of Rue Nationale, modern cafés line the way to the **Hôtel Gouin**. A riot of Renaissance detail has proliferated like brambles over its façade. The place houses the extensive **Musée Archéologique** (*open April–Sept daily 9.30–12.30 and 1.30–6.30; Feb–Mar and Oct–Dec daily 9.30–12.30 and 2–5.30; adm*), with items from around Touraine. **Rue du Commerce** leads into the student quarter, the bars and restaurants heralding the superbly restored timberframe façades of Place Plumereau. The surrounding network of streets is filled with noble houses. The **Musée du Gemmail** (*open April–mid-Nov Tues–Sun 10–12 and 2–6.30; adm*) nearby celebrates a 20th-century stained-glass art form. The term *gemmail* was coined by Jean Cocteau for this layering of coloured glass to such vibrant effect, invented by Jean Crotti.

The old religious **Quartier St-Martin** lies south of Place Plumereau. Two enormous towers standing in this prime shopping area offer a clue to the vastness of the Romanesque church that once stood here. The **Musée Martinien** (*open mid-Mar–mid-Nov Wed–Sun 9.30–12.30 and 2–5.30; closed Tues; adm*) occupies the former Chapelle St-Jean on Rue Rapin; off it lie the beautiful remains of the **cloister of St-Martin**. St Martin's tomb was rediscovered during an archaeological dig in 1860 and gave rise to the **Nouvelle Basilique St-Martin**, a self-important white whale of a building. The crypt contains St Martin's tomb and his cult remains alive and well.

West along the Loire (direction La Riche) many of the picturesque remains of the **Prieuré de St-Cosme** (*open April–Sept daily 9–7; Jan–Mar and Nov–Dec daily 9–12.30 and 2–5; adm*) date from the late 11th and 12th centuries. The Logis houses a museum in memory of abbot Pierre de Ronsard, more celebrated as a Renaissance poet who penned some of the most lyrical lines in the French canon. Wilting roses recur time and again in Ronsard's verse; his tomb lies appropriately amid delightful **rose gardens**.

South from Tours to Loches

Following the **Indre** river from Tours to medieval Loches avoids the dull N143 and allows you to potter along this delightful Vallée Verte with its shimmering poplars. Many villages along the gorgeous way are prettified by a watermill and a château.

Loches is named after the little fish which swim in its river's waters. A picturesque historic town, it is overseen by one of the most important medieval strongholds left in France. The counts of Anjou won Loches through marriage in the 10th century, when it became an outpost in their conflict with the counts of Blois controlling Touraine. The earliest remaining fortifications date from the 1030s. Royal connections start with Henri Plantagenet of Anjou (King Henry II of England) who added ramparts. King Philippe Auguste of France wrested Loches back from the English in 1205. Further fortifications and royal lodgings were added during the 14th, 15th and 16th centuries.

Start the tour at the **Château et Donjon de Loches** (*open April–Sept daily 9–7; Nov–Mar daily 9.30–5; adm*). The stunning medieval keep is reached by an arrow-head barbican and a drawbridge. Black jackdaws circle the sheer walls, while inside, the place has become something of a museum of torture and imprisonment. The separate Martelet tower held as its most famous prisoner Ludovico Sforza, duke of Milan, a notoriously ruthless politician of the end of the 15th century. He defended Naples against Charles VIII of France, but in 1500, during Louis XII's Italian campaign, was captured. At Loches, he decorated his cells with insignia and inscriptions which can still be deciphered. The regime for such a high-ranking prisoner wasn't harsh, although legend has it that, after years without daylight, when he was finally taken outside he died from the shock of seeing the sun.

King Charles VII is the French royal most closely associated with Loches. He spent some time in the **Logis Royal**, built with greater comfort in mind. Play is made inside of Agnès Sorel, his infamous mistress, immortalized in a memorable portrait by the 15th-century French court painter, Jean Fouquet, shown baring one breast. Agnès entered the royal court as a lady-in-waiting to Charles VII's queen, Marie d'Anjou, in 1444. Rapidly winning the king's affections, Agnès exercised political as well as emotional control over him. She bore him three daughters, but shocked many with her extravagant fashions and ways. The future King Louis XI detested her, as did the French Church, although when she died she was buried in a beautiful tomb in Loches' church of St-Ours; the effigy now rests in the royal lodgings. Joan of Arc, too, came to Loches and spurred on Charles VII to brave English-occupied territory to be crowned in Reims. Anne de Bretagne, the pious wife of two later French kings, Charles VIII and Louis XII, had an oratory made in the lodgings. The one masterpiece among the paintings in the château is a superb late 15th-century triptych by Bourdichon.

Still up in Loches' citadel, the church of **St-Ours** features some remarkable architecture and decoration, the picturesque **Maison Lansyer** (*open July–Aug daily 10–7; June*

Getting Around

The **rail** service between Tours and Châteauroux stops at Loches and other smaller stations along the Indre valley. From Loches there are **bus** services into southern Touraine, **t** 02 47 47 17 18.

Tourist Information

Loches: Place de la Marne, **t** 02 47 91 82 82, *loches.en.touraine@wanadoo.fr*.
Montrésor: 43 Grande-Rue, **t** 02 47 92 70 71, *otsi.montresor@wanadoo.fr*.
Le Grand-Pressigny: Mairie, **t** 02 47 94 96 82.

Where to Stay and Eat

Montbazon ✉ 37250
****Château d'Artigny, Route de Monts, along the D17, **t** 02 47 34 30 30, *www.grandesetapes.fr* (*luxury–very expensive*). Sumptuous early-20th-century pastiche of an Ancien Régime château above the Indre valley, the lavishly decorated rooms divided between castle and outbuildings.

Extravagant restaurant. Pool, tennis court, and spa. *Closed part of Dec and Jan..*
La Chancelière, 1 Place des Marronniers, **t** 02 47 26 00 67 (*expensive*). Elegant reputed restaurant. *Closed Sun and Mon.*

Loches ✉ 37600
***Hôtel George Sand, 37 Rue Quintefol, **t** 02 47 59 39 74, *www.hotelrestaurant-georgesand.com* (*moderate*). Author George Sand used to keep stables here. It's now a smart hotel on the Indre river, with fine local cuisine (*expensive–moderate*).
Hôtel de France, 6 Rue Picois, **t 02 47 59 00 32, *hdefranceloches@aol.com* (*inexpensive*). In a smart old town house, with a flowery inner garden, some rooms with views on to the medieval city and good food too.

Le Petit Pressigny ✉ 37350
La Promenade, **t** 02 47 94 93 52 (*expensive*). Reason in itself to discover southern Touraine, as visitors can taste gourmet cuisine at a reasonable price in this former inn given a modern make-over. *Closed Sun eve, Mon and Tues, and most Jan and late Sept–early Oct.*

and Sept 10–1 and 2–7; Nov–May Mon–Sat 10–1 and 2–6; adm) more traditional paint-ings by the accomplished 19th-century landscape artist after whom the house is named. Plunge down into the spectacular stone quarries below the citadel at the **Carrière Troglodytique de Vignemont** (*open Easter–Oct daily, tours on the hour at 10, 11, 2,3,4, and 5, with extra tours at 12 and 6 July and Aug; adm*).

A stunning road, strewn with exceptionally picturesque religious buildings (several of which you can visit), leads from Loches to the village of **Montrésor**, a place which exudes charm from every stone. The **Château de Montrésor** (*open April–Oct 10–12 and 2–6; adm*) overlooks a jumble of village houses. Behind its early medieval walls, most of the buildings date from the 15th century, ordered for the de Bastarnay family. Imbert de Basternay, who served several French kings, was grandfather to Diane de Poitiers (*see* 'Anet', p.167). At the Revolution much of the castle was burnt down, but in the mid-19th century the Polish count Xavier Branicki began its restoration, hence the large number of Polish pieces inside. Montrésor's church of **St-Jean-Baptiste**, commis-sioned by Imbert de Bastarnay, is disproportionately splendid for such a small village. The tomb effigies look like a family tucked up in bed. Other riches include a 17th-century *Annunciation* by Philippe de Champaigne. Head on to the sleepy village of **Nouans-les-Fontaines** for the surprise of one of the finest 15th-century canvases in France. The mysterious depiction of Christ's deposition in the church of St-Martin is attributed to the court painter Jean Fouquet. Christ's body spreads a ghostly white across the huge canvas, but the identity of the donors remains uncertain.

In the relatively unexplored southern tip of Touraine, the quietly pretty villages with their Romanesque churches, little châteaux and local museums lie along steep little valleys. The major sight on the River Claise, the **Château du Grand-Pressigny** (*open April–Sept daily 9.30–7; Oct–Mar 9.30–12.30 and 2–7; adm*) provides an almost comical example of impure Loire architecture, with a particularly striking fossil of a keep. Most here dates from the Middle Ages, although a confident Renaissance block divides the medieval parts. Its gallery contains a **Musée de la Préhistoire**; Le Grand-Pressigny lay at the centre of a European-wide export industry of top-quality flints in Neolithic times. René Descartes hailed from these parts, although he didn't spend much of his life here. Nevertheless, the dopey town near which that sparkling, highly readable genius of philosophy was born has renamed itself **Descartes** and put together a small museum dedicated to him.

The Loire from Tours to the Anjou Border

North of this stretch of the Loire, the handful of châteaux open to visitors may not look so inviting, but they all prove charming. South of the Loire stand a clutch of the most famous châteaux in France, in fact gracing the banks of the Cher and the Indre.

North of the Loire River

Traffic thunders along the main riverside road below the medieval **Château de Luynes** (*open April–Sept daily 10–6; adm*), looking down severely from its height, its towers spotted with large stone pimples. Inside the courtyard it's much more engaging. Charles d'Albret, later Duc de Luynes, bought the château in 1619. Brought up with the future King Louis XIII, the two had only a couple of years previously conspired to assasinate Concini, the Queen Mother Marie de Médicis' tyrannical Italian adviser-cum-lover. Charles went on to be the most important minister in the land, succeeded by one Cardinal Richelieu. Descendants of de Luynes still live here. The rooms are finely furnished, notably the vast sunken Salle des Jeux and the Grand Salon.

From **Cinq-Mars-la-Pile**, with its ruined medieval castle and its curious brick tower rising high above the Loire (a 2nd-century mausoleum for a Gallo-Roman merchant), the D34 leads north through forests to the **Château de Champchevrier** (*open mid-June–mid-Sept daily 10–6; adm*), a castle devoted to hunting. The stocky grey buildings, surrounded by alleys of towering plane trees lined up like ranks of giant guardsmen, looks forbidding. The howling of hounds underlines how important the hunt still is to Champchevrier. Much of the castle was built for the de Daillons, associated with the mighty Château du Lude (*see* p.334). Rooms reveal old hunting trophies, old carriages, family portraits, and splendid tapestries, including a superbly preserved series from cartoons by 17th-century Simon Vouet illustrating the classical Loves of the Gods.

A kitsch 1950s neo-Gothic bridge spans the Loire at Langeais, but the **Château de Langeais** (*open mid-July–mid Aug daily 9.30–8; April–mid-July and late-Aug–mid-Oct 9.30–6.30; mid-Oct–Mar 10–5.30; adm*) is the real thing – a villain of a Gothic Loire château, although it has been very heavy-handedly restored. King Louis XI ordered its building after the end of the Hundred Years War. There's none of the normal exuberance of so much late Gothic architecture here. The fate of Brittany's independence was effectively sealed when Anne de Bretagne went through with her enforced marriage to Charles VIII at the castle. Inside, the colourful warmth of the tapestries and furniture counters the coldness of the exterior. In the back garden, spot the crumbling remnants of one of the oldest stone keeps along the Loire, from the end of the 10th century.

Vines surround **Bourgueil**, a pretty market town with vestiges of an historic abbey. The area produces two *appellations*, both made from cabernet franc. **Chevrette** is a good village at which to start tasting. A trip into the woods to the north takes you to the enormous **Château de Gizeux** (*open May–Sept Mon–Sat 10–6.30, Sun 2–6; adm*), commissioned by the powerful Du Bellay family. The castle is almost eclipsed by the extent and beauty of the staggering stables, added in the 18th century. Two long galleries stand out inside, decorated with scenes of courtly life and famous French châteaux. The village church has splendid kneeling effigies of the Du Bellays.

South of the Loire River

The most beautiful clutch of fairytale castles in France overlooks the Cher and the Indre just before these tributaries reach the Loire west of Tours. Cross the Cher at the gorgeous riverside village of **Savonnières**, entering the **Parc Naturel Régional Loire-Anjou-Touraine**, to reach the **Château de Villandry** (*gardens open April–mid-Oct daily 9–7; Mar 9–6; mid-Oct–Feb 9–5.30; château open April–mid-Oct 9–6; mid-Oct–11 Nov and Feb–Mar 9–5; adm*). Here, the complex geometrical and symbolic gardens are a wonder to behold. They follow the spirit of Renaissance design, but were conceived by

Tourist Information

Luynes: 9 Rue A Baugé, **t** 02 47 55 77 14, *otsi@luynes.fr.*

Langeais: Place du 14 Juillet, **t** 02 47 96 58 22, *tourismelangeais@ifrance.com.*

Bourgueil: 16 Place de l'Eglise, **t** 02 47 97 91 39, *otsi-bourgueil@wanadoo.fr.*

Villandry: Le Potager, **t** 02 47 50 12 66, *office-tourismevillandry@wanandoo.fr.*

Azay-le-Rideau: Place de l'Europe, **t** 02 47 45 44 40, *otsi.azay.le.rideau@wanadoo.fr.*

Where to Stay and Eat

Azay-le-Rideau/La Chapelle-Ste-Blaise ✉ 37190

★★★**Le Grand Monarque**, 3 Place de la République, **t** 02 47 45 40 08, *www.legrand-monarque.com (expensive–moderate).* A former posting inn, offering good accommodation with a solid restaurant. *Closed*

Dec–mid-Feb; restaurant closed Sun eve, Mon, Wed lunch and Fri lunch out of season.

★★**Le Biencourt**, 7 Rue Balzac, **t** 02 47 45 20 75, *biencourt@infonie.fr (inexpensive).* Charming accommodation, divided between an 18th-century town house and a 19th-century school. *Closed 15 Nov–Feb.*

★★**Hôtel des Trois Lys/★Hotel Balzac**, **t** 02 47 45 42 08, *www.traiteur-touraine.com (inexpensive).* Simpler twin establishments, also in atmospheric old town houses. Restaurant.

Troglodyte Les Grottes, Rue Pineau, **t** 02 47 45 21 04 *(moderate).* Refined cuisine served in cosy caves a little east of the centre, a terrace outside available for warm days. *Closed Thurs, and late-Dec–late Jan.*

Saché ✉ 37190

Auberge du XIIe Siècle, Place de l'Eglise, **t** 02 47 26 88 77 *(expensive).* Old, beamed restaurant, a very inviting place to eat. *Closed Sun eve, Mon, and Tues lunch, and most Jan.*

a Spanish-American couple, Dr Joachim Carvallo and Anne Coleman, who bought Villandry in 1906. In this, the most enviable kitchen garden in France, flowers and fruit trees have to bow to the beauty of the beet, the charm of the cabbages, the perfection of the peppers. Further up, swans glide over the elegant 18th-century pools which provide irrigation. Climb the hill to read clearly the symbols drawn in the hedges of the ornamental gardens by the castle. Four boxes illustrate fickle love, love letters, tender love and mad, passionate love.

It was at medieval Villandry, on 4 July 1189, that Henry II of England signed a peace treaty with Philippe Auguste of France, two days before he died. The remains of the medieval castle were used by Jean Le Breton, a minister of François Ier, as foundations for his Renaissance castle. Certain French tastes remain, though, such as the splendid array of Loire windows in the slate roofs. The interiors were remodelled during the 18th century for the Castellane family. They are now hung with the Spanish art that the Carvallos brought over, including disturbing works from the school of Goya.

The beautiful moated **Château d'Azay-le-Rideau** *(open July–Aug daily 9–7; April–June and Sept 9.30–6; Oct–Mar Tues–Sun 9.30–12.30 and 2–5.30; adm)* was likened by Balzac to 'a diamond with its multiple facets set in the Indre'. The château went up from 1518 for Gilles Berthelot, a treasurer of France. The pepperpot towers, the steepness of the roof and the finial tips give a Gothic twist to the whole, but Italian influences can be seen in the château's symmetry and in the decorative medallions and candelabra. Building work was still incomplete when Berthelot fled to avoid financial scandal in 1527, leaving François Ier to pick up yet another Loire château. The visit takes in the low kitchen, which has some hilarious Gothic touches. After that, you're treated to a hackneyed round of tapestries, chests, bad copies of paintings and the odd good portrait. The gardens are used for an idiosyncratic *son-et-lumière*, **Les Imaginaires d'Azay-le-Rideau** (*for details, call* **t** *02 47 45 42 04*).

Azay-le-Rideau town is a lively tourist centre. The **Indre** valley either side of it, which featured so prominently in Balzac's hot-headed romance, *Le Lys dans la vallée*, looks exquisite. East from Azay, seek out **Les Goupillères** (*open July–Aug daily 2–7; Easter–June and Sept–Oct weekends and public hols 2–7; adm*), a farming hamlet quite out of the ordinary, its buildings actually hidden underground. Further east, the **Château de Saché**, lurking behind its long wall, turns out to be a rugged manor rather than a castle. It contains the **Musée Balzac** (*open April–Sept 9–7; Oct–Mar 9.30–12.30 and 2–5.30; adm*). The great author was always very well received by de Margonne, his mother's lover, seeking refuge to write and to avoid his creditors. Press on east for the **Château de Candé** (*open May–Oct daily 10–12 and 2–6; adm*) on the Indre's north bank near Monts, the secretive location where the Duke and Duchess of Windsor were married in 1937. The château is a 19th-century pastiche of a Loire Valley castle and the visit concentrates as much on the wooded grounds as the building.

West from Azay, the irresistible Indre flows past **Rigny-Ussé**, where another famous château nestles. The **Château d'Ussé** (*open April–Sept daily 9.30–6.30; mid-Feb–Mar 10–12 and 2–5.3;, Oct–11 Nov 10–12 and 2–5; adm*) supposedly inspired the tale of *Sleeping Beauty* when its author Charles Perrault was an overnight guest. If you can't remember the story, you may have a job piecing it together from the waxwork scenes at the top of the greatest tower. Do visit the gem of a chapel, the interlaced initials C and L referring to the couple for whom it was built, Charles d'Espinay and Lucrèce de Pons, before the guided tour around the heavily furnished apartments.

Chinon and the Chinonais

With medieval houses close-knit as chain mail fighting for space between the hill-side and the Vienne river, **Chinon** is dominated by the ruins of its great Plantagenet castle. This small town may appear distinctly provincial today, but it retains more than a spark of former glory. Chinon's protective white riverside cliff gave the location appeal in early Christian times, Brice and Mexme establishing early churches, while in the Dark Ages Queen Radegonde came to consult a hermit named Jean over her abusive husband Clotaire. Chinon's first great courtly age came with Angevin King Henry II of England, after he had seized it from his brother Geoffroy. It was excellently situated to administer his territories, that stretched between Scotland and Spain. He enlarged the castle to become the greatest fortress of its time in Europe. He died at Chinon in 1189 and his son, Richard Cœur de Lion, may have died here too after being wounded at the Battle of Châlus (*see p.384*). As for Henry's son John, he was married to Isabelle d'Angoulême in Chinon, but Philippe Auguste of France's forces triumphed over his in a one-year siege here. When French royalty returned in the Hundred Years War, it was in dire circumstances, the future King Charles VII chased out of Paris by the English. Joan of Arc first came here to help rescue him. Their meeting has been portrayed as a great event in French history. Just as fêted in town is writer François

Rabelais, born in the Chinonais in the late 15th century; the bawdy humour of his *Gargantua* cycle with its rowdy giants and immoral monks conceals profound Renaissance intellectual curiosity as well as satire.

From below, the **Château de Chinon** (*open April–Sept daily 9–7; Oct–Mar daily 9.30–5; adm*) seems an impressive string of battered towers. They mark the boundaries of three adjoining sections of castle that once stood here. The ruins of Charles VII's royal logis – where most of the exhibits are housed – was where Joan of Arc met the 'gentle dauphin' to convince him that she could rescue France. Her influential life is recalled in the little museum in the Tour de l'Horloge.

Charles VII kept discreetly in touch with his mistress, Agnes Sorel, by giving her a house down in town. If Chinon's castle is ruined and quiet now, the streets below are often bustling and still crowded with splendid houses embellished with showy stairtowers, symbols of courtly and mercantile pride. However, starting on the western end of the quays, the **Maison de la Rivière** (*open July–Aug Tues–Fri 10–12.30 and 2–6.30, Sat and Sun 3–6.30; April–June and Sept–Oct Tues–Fri 10–12.30 and 2–5.30, Sat and Sun 2–5.30*) focuses on the lives of the Vienne mariners, ferrymen and fishermen. The church of **St-Maurice** may be tightly squeezed in on Rue Haute St-Maurice, but its spire soars into the sky. The **Musée du Vieux Chinon** (*open April–Sept 10.30–12.30 and 2–7; adm*) occupies one of the most significant houses in town, the Maison des Etats Généraux, where Richard Cœur de Lion may have died and where Charles VII called the Estates General of France to meet in 1428, after the English had laid siege to Orléans. The most moving exhibit within is a copy of an 11th-century Crucifixion from the Chinon church of St-Mexme. The museum also displays St Mexme's cope, which turns out to be a piece of Arabian silk from the 11th century, decorated with a pattern of stylized wild cats, that was probably intended for a horse. Along Rue Voltaire, the **Musée Animé du Vin et de la Tonnellerie** (*open April–Sept daily 10.30–12.30 and 2–7;*

Getting Around

An exclusive **rail** connection from Tours serves Chinon. **Bus** services from Chinon serve L'Ile Bouchard and Richelieu, **t** 02 47 47 17 18.

Tourist Information

Chinon: Place d'Hofheim, **t** 02 47 93 17 85, *tourisme@chinon.com*.
St-Epain: 33 Grand'rue, **t** 02 47 65 84 63.
Richelieu: 6 Grande-Rue, **t** 02 47 58 13 62.

Where to Stay and Eat

Chinon ✉ 37500
Hostellerie Gargantua, 73 Rue Voltaire, **t** 02 47 93 04 71, *www.hostelleriegargantua.com* (*moderate–inexpensive*). In one of Chinon's most famous historic houses, with some comfortable rooms and a medievalstyle dining room (*moderate*) serving quite modern cuisine. *Closed Dec–Mar; restaurant closed Thurs.*
La Boule d'Or, 66 Quai Jeanne d'Arc, **t** 02 47 93 03 13 (*moderate–inexpensive*). Some pleasant rooms overlooking the river, and an interior courtyard for the restaurant (*moderate*). *Closed late-Dec–Jan; restaurant closed Mon lunch.*
Hôtel Diderot, 4 Rue Buffon, **t** 02 47 93 18 87, *www.hoteldiderot.com* (*inexpensive*). A delightful 18th-century town house set back in its own courtyard.
Au Plaisir Gourmand, 2 Rue Parmentier, **t** 02 47 93 20 48 (*expensive*). Chinon's outstanding restaurant, traditional cuisine cooked to perfection. *Closed Sun eve, Mon, and Tues lunch, and mid-Feb–mid-Mar.*

adm), devoted to Chinon wines and barrels, occupies a cave once quarried for stone. A statue of Rabelais presides over the crowd of cafés on **Place du Général de Gaulle**.

Rue Jean-Jacques Rousseau takes you on to several important religious buildings, the church of **St-Etienne**'s façade carrying the arms of Chinon, the church of St-Mexme appallingly scarred after the Revolution. South of St-Mexme, Joan of Arc appears in bellicose action on the big square named after her, although the maid is supposed not to have killed a single soul in battle. The path up the hillside beyond leads to the curious **Chapelle Ste-Radegonde** (*contact tourist office about tours*), built partly into the cliff, the small fragments of murals possibly showing the Plantagenets out hunting. The set of caves behind contain an atmospherically neglected museum of local traditions, and a magical underground well associated with the hermit Jean.

Southwest from Chinon, **La Devinière and the Musée Rabelais** (*open April–Sept daily 9.30–7; Oct–Mar 9.30–12.30 and 2–7; adm*) commemorate the wonderfully rude and erudite author, probably born on the farm. The museum proves sober, however.

Wine experts often find violets and rubies hidden in Chinon wines, made from cabernet franc grapes grown along the final stretch of the Vienne valley as it reaches the Loire. The low gravels by the river give lighter, fruity wines; the vines on the slopes and plateaux above yield more powerful wines with ageing potential in good years. In the exquisite vineyards east of Chinon, **Cravant-les-Coteaux** and **Panzoult** are highly regarded Chinon wine-making parishes with *domaines* to visit. Among other particularly spectacular vineyards to seek out for a tasting are the **Château de la Grille**, a little north of Chinon, and the **Château de Goulaine**, towards Beaumont-en-Véron.

The Vienne banks east from Chinon are littered with so many Romanesque churches, you get the impression the area must have been much more populated in medieval times than it is now. Close to L'Ile-Bouchard, at **Tavant**, the cramped crypt of the church of **St-Nicolas** (*open by appointment, t 02 47 58 58 06; adm*) conceals an extraordinary Romanesque fresco cycle, among the most refined in France. It's as though characters in a passion play had been caught in their energetic poses. At riverside **L'Ile Bouchard**, the apse of the Prieuré de St-Léonard has superb Romanesque carvings in its little semi-circular theatre of a church ruin. The wave-like long-haired and finger-pointing characters typify the best of mid-12th-century sculpting.

The **Manse valley**, a well-kept secret, offers a delightful alternative route north of the Vienne valley, picturesque villages, churches and ruins strung along the way. The name of the pleasant market town of **Ste-Maure** further east is synonymous to the French with white cylinders of goat's cheese.

Another enchanting excursion from Chinon leads south to Richelieu, past the **Château du Rivau** (*open July–Aug daily 1–7; June and Sept closed Tues; May–Oct weekends and hols 2–7; adm*), a fantastic walled white castle rising out of the wide, rolling Touraine fields, described rather overmodestly by one guide as 'in effect, a big farm'. The place was built in the mid-15th century for the Beauvaus, a warrior family who served successive French kings; in Le Rivau's sumptuous Italianate stables, horses were reared for François Ier's military campaigns. Inside, a mural depicts the biblical feast of Balthazar, and hunting trophies stare from the walls, but best are the playful new landscaped gardens, where homage is paid to Rabelais.

All that remains of the 16th-century **Château de Champigny-sur-Veude** is its outbuildings, but you'd be forgiven for mistaking their dazzling wings for a castle proper. These buildings are off limits, but you can visit the **St-Louis chapel** (*open July–Sept Wed-Mon 10–12 and 2–6; closed Tues; adm*). Its stained glass, given as a wedding gift to the proprietors by a wealthy cardinal, is one of the great Renaissance works of the Loire and concentrates on pious crusading King Louis XI.

King Louis XIII's great political fixer, Cardinal Richelieu, was a vandal of major proportions when it came to the French regions, having many provincial castles pulled down to stamp royal authority on the country. But he commissioned two outrageously ambitious architectural projects to his own greater glory at **Richelieu**, site of an ancestral home. With rough justice, the staggering château, designed by Jacques Lemercier to be one of the most ostentatious ever built in France, has been almost entirely demolished save a still-impressive solitary tower set in a lovely park, whereas the new town survives as a pretty unspoilt 17th-century vision of ordered urban planning. Although the courtiers the model town was planned for never came, the place has been preserved in aspic. Two major buildings face each other on **Place du Marché**, the covered market on one side, the church on the other.

The Loire from the Anjou Border to the Saumurois

Eastern Anjou begins after the Vienne joins the mighty Loire, beyond the chivalric plumes of steam rising from the Avoine-Chinon nuclear power station. Two spectacular villages on the south bank may be stuck together like Siamese twins, but they actually lie in different regions. **Candes-St-Martin** is steeped in Martin's memory (*see* 'Tours'). He had a church built here, dedicated to St Maurice, a martyred Roman soldier. In November 397 he came to sort out a religious quarrel but fell ill and died. Gregory of Tours, in his *History of the Franks*, tells of the unseemly argument over his body between a group from Tours and a group from Poitiers. The men of Tours settled it by stealing the body as the Poitevins slept. As the remains were carried up the Loire, the trees and shrubs on the banks are said to have flowered, and to this day an Indian summer is known in French as an *été de la St-Martin*. Enter the fortified medieval pilgrimage church dedicated to St Martin via the magnificent statue-filled side porch, held up by an improbably thin finger of a central column. Inside, the edifice appears unstable, with sloping floor and irregular bays. Painted sculptures perch on the columns. The medieval lords of **Montsoreau** once made a good living exacting river tolls. Their bright **Château de Montsoreau** (*open May–mid-Sept daily 9.30–7; Feb–April and Oct–Nov 2–6; adm*), virtually bathing in the Loire, has recently been restored to offer visitors a journey down the Loire through the seasons and the centuries using modern exhibitions set to music. The **Maison du Parc** next door to the castle presents an overview of the actvities of the **Parc Naturel Régional Loire-Anjou-Touraine**.

The **Abbaye de Fontevraud** (*open June–3rd Sun in Sept 9–6.30; rest of year 10–5.30; adm*) is truly exceptional, perhaps the best-preserved abbey in France. It was the first in a monastic order founded in the early 12th century by the charismatic Robert

Getting Around

The occasional TGV stops at Saumur's **railway** station, plus local services.

Tourist Information

Montsoreau: Av de la Loire, t 02 41 51 70 22, *otsi@ville-montsoreau.fr.*
Fontevraud-l'Abbaye: Allée Ste-Catherine, t 02 41 51 79 45, *officetourisme-fontevraud@ libertysurf.fr.*
Saumur: Place de la Bilange, t 02 41 40 20 60, *www.saumur-tourisme.com.*

Where to Stay and Eat

Candes-St-Martin ✉ 37500

La Route d'Or, Place de l'Eglise, t 02 47 95 81 10 (*moderate*). It's worth making a pilgrimage to this tiny, simple but stylish restaurant tucked into the square by the great church to St Martin. *Closed Wed.*

Montsoreau ✉ 49730

✶✶Hostellerie Le Bussy, 4 Rue Jeanne d'Arc, t 02 41 38 11 11, *hotel.lebussy@wanadoo.fr* (*inexpensive*). Warm historic house in which to stay just above the château.
Le Saut aux Loups, Route de Saumur, t 02 41 51 70 30 (*moderate*). In a sensational rock setting, this restaurant specializes in *galipettes*, monster mushrooms which come with various fillings. *Closed Mon, and mid-Nov–Feb.*

Fontevraud ✉ 49590

✶✶La Croix Blanche, t 02 41 51 71 11, *www. fontevraud.net* (*moderate–inexpensive*). Rooms round a courtyard at this traditional hotel, almost at the entrance to the abbey. Smart restaurant (*moderate*).
La Licorne, Allée Ste-Catherine, t 02 41 51 72 49 (*expensive*). A highly reputed restaurant set in an 18th-century house close to the church. *Closed Sun eve and Mon, and mid-Dec–mid-Jan.*

Saumur ✉ 49400

✶✶✶Anne d'Anjou, 32 Quai Mayaud, t 02 41 67 30 30, *www.hotel-anneanjou.com* (*expensive–moderate*). Exceptionally comfortable rooms in a superb historic house sandwiched between the Loire and the château, with smart restaurant **Les Ménestrels**, t 02 41 67 71 10 (*expensive*), in the garden. *Restaurant closed Sun.*
✶✶✶St-Pierre, Rue Haute-St-Pierre, t 02 41 50 33 00, *www.saintpierresaumur.com* (*moderate*). Very stylish, in the historic heart of town.
✶✶Le Volney, 1 Rue Volney, t 02 41 51 25 41, *le-volney.com* (*inexpensive*). Smaller centrally located family-run hotel. *Closed mid-Dec.*
Les Délices du Château, t 02 41 67 65 60 (*expensive*), and **L'Orangeraie**, t 02 41 67 12 88 (*moderate–inexpensive*). Stylish sister restaurants in the outhouses of the castle. *In winter, both closed Sun eve, Mon, and Tues eve, and mid-Dec–mid-Jan.*
Le Relais, 31 Quai Mayaud, t 02 41 67 75 20 (*moderate*). Pretty, serving refined cuisine down by the Loire. *Closed Sat, Sun and Feb.*

d'Arbrissel, a 'sower of the divine word' according to Pope Urban II. Women in particular were encouraged to join. After d'Arbrissel left Fontevraud, it was ruled by a long line of forceful abbesses; the monks would periodically protest at their treatment under their rule. One abbess, Mathilde d'Anjou, was the aunt of Henri Plantagenet, who stayed at Fontevraud before he set off for England to be crowned Henry II in 1154. The abbey became the burial place of the dynasty when Henry was buried at Fontevraud, although against his wishes – legend has it that the king's corpse bled to show his displeasure. Four Plantagenet tomb effigies remain in the vast void of the church, including that of Eleanor of Aquitaine, Henry II's formidable wife. Four separate communities developed at Fontevraud, one for noble women, one for lay and 'fallen' women, the third for monks, the fourth for lepers. In all, 149 Fontevrist monasteries were created, four in England.

During the Revolution, the nuns and monks were expelled from Fontevraud, and Napoleon had the place transformed into a vast penitentiary. The groundbreaking criminal and homosexual author Jean Genet revealed its chilling side in *Le Miracle de la Rose*. The last inmates only left in 1985. Beyond the church, the most impressive buildings you can visit include one of the largest cloisters in France (the chapter house decorated with scenes from the Virgin's life that feature several abbesses), the refectory and the kitchen, the last a strange octagonal structure filled with fireplaces.

A line of amazing **troglodyte villages** built into the Loire's cliff runs from Montsoreau to Saumur. There are no finer examples in the Loire Valley region. Look out for the particularly elegant troglodyte houses at **La Vignole** and **Turquant**, among which you can visit the exquisite **La Grande Vignolle** (*open April–Sept daily 10–6*) and **Le Troglo des Pommes Tapées** (*open July–Aug Tues–Sun 10–12 and 2.30–6; Easter–June and Sept–mid-Nov Sat and Sun 10–12 and 2.30–6; adm*), the latter continuing an old tradition of smoking apples. **Gratien et Meyer** nearer Saumur is one of the handful of wine houses with spectacular cliffside cellars producing Saumur's sparkling wines.

Saumur

Two famous works depict the stunning Loire-side town of Saumur, nicknamed 'the pearly of Anjou': the first is a page from the early 15th-century *Très Riches Heures du Duc de Berry*, showing a fantastic fairytale château bristling with towers and pinnacles. The other is Balzac's biting novel, *Eugénie Grandet*. The fictional inhabitants are a whole lot less appealing than the medieval manuscript's depiction of the castle.

The **Château de Saumur** (*open June–Aug daily 9.30–6; April–May 10–1 and 2–5.30; rest of the year Wed–Mon 10–1 and 2–5.30, closed Tues; adm*) looks more severely impressive in reality. Most of it was built for Louis Duc d'Anjou in the 14th century, its four towers stretching into the sky like thick upturned pencils. The outer fortifications were added in the 1590s for Huguenot Duplessis-Mornay, who founded an Académie Protestante which caused Saumur to be referred to as a Second Geneva. After the Protestant governor's enforced departure by order of Louis XIII in 1621, the castle went on to serve as a barracks, then as a prison, even housing the Marquis de Sade. The town bought the place in 1906 to house its museums. The **Musée des Arts Décoratifs** (*guided tour; adm*) consists of one of the most substantial collections of ceramics in the country. The **Musée du Cheval** contains a mass of saddles, stirrups, bits and boots, a sign of how horse-mad Saumur is. The town has long been home to France's most famous cavalry regiment – and to the associated showmanship of the Cadre Noir.

Below the castle a couple of grand churches stand out in town, topped by vicious steeples. On its delightful shaded, sloping square, **St-Pierre** has a misleading classical façade tacked on to a medieval form. Highlights inside include the mighty organ, tapestries and decorative choir stalls. Many houses around here hide behind grand gateways, recalling the days of the carriage. Hearty walks take you further out to two churches dedicated to the Virgin. **Notre-Dame de Nantilly** on its hillside is a basic Romanesque block with a Gothic aisle tacked on, but it holds a remarkable tapestry collection from the 16th and 17th centuries, while pilgrims pay homage to the 12th-century Virgin and Child. The spectacularly domed **Notre-Dame-des-Ardilliers**, wedged out west between the Loire and its cliffside, was built in seductive, head-spinning Baroque to combat the deep-rooted Protestantism of the town. Back in the centre, the historic quarters stretch out either side of bustling **Place de la Bilange**. Cross the bridge from here to appreciate the views of Saumur's substantial quays; in summer, take a river trip from them in an old-fashioned Loire boat. West of Place de la Bilange, the array of sumptuous Ancien Régime buildings were made for the cavalry school.

With changes in warfare, Saumur switched from horses to tanks, hence the **Musée des Blindés** (*open May–Sept daily 9.30–6.30; Oct–April 10–5; adm*) outside the centre, a specialist museum that turns out to offer a history of the major conflicts of the 20th century. A cluster of appealing Saumur **sparkling wine houses** are gathered together in **St-Hilaire-St-Florent** west of town: Veuve-Amiot, Langlois-Château, Ackerman and Bouvet-Ladubay, each with additional attractions, the last including an excellent contemporary art centre. The prestigious **Ecole Nationale d'Equitation and its Cadre Noir** (*open April–Sept Tues–Sat 9.30–11 and 2–4; adm*) up the hill presents the most glamorous side of French horsemanship left over from the cavalry days. Manure is plentiful in these parts, as are cool, dark quarries, perfect for growing mushrooms. Saumurois production is on a vast scale, to be seen at the **Musée du Champignon** towards Gennes (*open Feb–15 Nov daily 10–7; adm*). A cave or two west, a contemporary sculptor in stone has carved out exquisitely detailed miniatures of Loire Valley sights from Amboise to Angers in the underground galleries at the **Parc Miniature Pierre et Lumière de Loire** (*open Feb–Dec daily 10–7; adm*).

Troglodyte Territories South of Saumur

A truly amazing secretive land where people once lived in caves, and where a hardy handful still do, lies south of Saumur. Pass through the vineyards on the plateau above the Loire valley which produce one of the Loire's best reds, Saumur-Champigny. You come to the enormous **Château de Brézé** (*open Mar–mid-Nov daily 10–6.30; adm*), standing out on a wood-topped hillock above the vines south of Champigny itself. The place is immense underground as well as overground, provided with the deepest dry moat in Europe, leading to a labyrinth of caves. The tour focuses on this sophisticated subterranean maze, developed from as early as the 10th and 11th centuries. Narrow corridors with defensive chicanes lead to a virtual underground village, with large silos, a bakery, and what may have been a forge. Such 'Roches' weren't uncommon in medieval Anjou; this is just a very grand one. Three of the largest underground galleries have been transformed to present a slide show of subterranean sights around the world. The castle above ground is a major Renaissance pile from the 16th century, much restored in the 19th. You will only see a few rooms on the visit, but wine tastings take place in the 17th-century outbuildings.

In **Le Coudray-Macouard** the fine houses and troglodyte caves hide behind stone walls, but you can glimpse a typical underground house by visiting **La Magnanerie** (*open 15 May–15 Sept Mon–Fri for visits 11, 2.30, 4 and 5.30, Sun 3 and 4.30; adm*) and also learn about silk-making, a thriving local industry from Ancien Régime times until an epidemic in 1855 killed the silkworms.

Getting Around

There's a regular **bus** service from Angers to Doué-la-Fontaine, but buses are rarer to Montreuil-Bellay and Le Puy-Notre-Dame. There is also an occasional bus service from Saumur.

Tourist Information

Doué-la-Fontaine: 30 Place des Fontaines, t 02 41 59 20 49, *tourisme.doue.la.fontaine@ wanadoo.fr*.
Montreuil-Bellay: Place du Concorde, t 02 41 52 32 39, *off.tourisme-montreuil-bellay@ wanadoo.fr*.
Le Puy-Notre-Dame: 16 Rue des Hôtels, t 02 41 38 87 30, *le.puy.notre.dame@wanadoo.fr*.

Where to Stay and Eat

Rou-Marson ✉ **49400**
Les Caves de Marson, Rue Henri Fricotelle, t 02 41 50 50 05 (*moderate*). Great troglodyte setting, where you can taste *fouaces*: dough balls stuffed with various fillings. *Must book*.

Rochemenier ✉ **49700**
Les Caves de la Genevraie, 13 Rue du Musée, t 02 41 59 34 22 (*moderate*). Another good troglodyte address serving *fouaces*. *Closed Christmas–mid-Jan; booking essential*.

Montreuil-Bellay ✉ **49260**
★★Splendid Hôtel/Relais du Bellay, 96 Rue Nationale, t 02 41 53 10 00, *www.splendid-hotel.fr* (*moderate–inexpensive*). Two elegant hotels joined together, by the château.

The sleepy town of **Doué-la-Fontaine** has a couple of truly spectacular troglodyte sights to startle you. The first, in town, is **Les Caves-Cathédrales des Perrières** (*open mid-April–mid-Oct Tues–Sun 10–12.30 and 1.30–7; adm*), consisting of a series of inter-connecting bottle-shaped chambers left over from 18th-century quarrying. The second, the surreal **Zoo de Doué** (*open Feb–mid-Nov daily 10–6; adm*), lies out towards Cholet; the visitors' trail leads through interconnecting craters that act as large cages for birds, big cats,and even giraffes. Back in central Doué, further smaller troglodyte sights include **La Cave aux Sarcophages** (*open April–mid-Sept 10–12 and 2–7; adm*), used for extracting stone tombs in the Dark Ages, **La Rose Bleue**, a craft pottery in a lovely cave setting, and **La Sablière**, with its rose-water distillery, which brings us to Doué's other claim to fame – the soil around town is ideal for cultivating roses, in their millions. One rosery has taken over the garden of Doué's vanished château, while a rosewater distillery occupies part of the surviving stables, which mostly occupied though by the **Musée des Commerces Anciens** (*open July–Aug daily 9–7; May and June daily 9.30–12 and 2–7; mid-Mar–April and Oct–mid-Nov Tues–Sun 9.30–12 and 2–6; adm*). Here, rows of old-fashioned shops have been recreated by a passionate collector, although the guided tour is rather prepackaged. A large medieval crater in town known as **Les Arènes** (once thought to have been a Roman theatre) plays host to an annual rose festival. Out on the Cholet road again, **Les Chemins de la Rose** (*open mid-May–mid-Sept daily 9.30–7; adm*) is a substantial garden specializing in rare roses.

Further subterranean sights near Doué include **La Fosse de Forges Maisons Troglodytes** (*open June–Sept daily 9.30–7; Mar–May and Oct 9.30–12.30 and 2–6.30; adm*), with underground farm buildings purpose-built in the 17th century, and the older **Rochemenier** (*open April–Oct daily 9.30–7; adm*), a whole village hiding under-ground, while the **Caverne Sculptée of Dénezé-sous-Doué** (*open June–Aug daily 10–7; Sept 10–6; April–May Tues–Sun 2–6; adm*) conceals an array of crude, mysterious carv-ings, possibly executed by a secret society during the troubled Wars of Religion.

Leaving major troglodyte territory, the pimply-walled town of Montreuil-Bellay is dominated by the dreamy silhouette of the **Château de Montreuil-Bellay** (*open April–Oct Wed–Mon 10–12 and 2–5.30; closed Tues; adm*). The Château-Vieux, begun in 1420, has two octagonal towers and typical big Loire-style roof windows. The small freestanding building with the curious roof is a 15th-century kitchen. Behind it, the Petit-Château probably served for the religious community based at the castle's church. Inside this intriguing château, delightful painted angels sing on the ceiling, in the Gothic oratory. West, **Le Puy-Notre-Dame**'s church owes its grandeur to a venerated piece of the Virgin's girdle brought back from the crusades and long believed to promote fertility. Certainly beautiful vineyards have flourished around here.

The Loire from Saumur to Angers

Two heavenly stretches of Loire-side road run between Saumur and Angers – try not to miss either the south or north route. In places, the great width of the meandering waters and the sandy shore create a coastal illusion. To the west, the dazzling light limestone gives way to dark stone, strikingly affecting the architecture.

Along the north bank, the bare road rides on top of the Plantagenet **Grande Levée**, a protective wall built in the early Middle Ages to prevent flooding. Fully exposed to the wide skies, the splendid riverside villages, such as **St-Clément-des-Levées** and **Les Rosiers**, have substantial abandoned cobbled quays, testifying to the once-great rivertrade carried out here. Set a little back, the symmetrical **Château de Montgeoffroy** (*open mid-June–mid-Sept daily 9.30–6.30; last week Mar–mid-June and mid-Sept–mid-Nov 9.30–12 and 2.30–6.30; adm*) provides a rare example of pure 18th-century architecture along the Loire, built for the Maréchal de Contade between 1773 and 1775 and still an immaculate family home. On entering, you're greeted by the man himself, beaming from a painting. The household inventory drawn up before the end of the 18th century confirms it has retained the furniture of that time.

Head north for the **Château de Baugé** (*open May–mid-Sept 10–6, mid-Sept–mid-Nov 2–6*), an ochre Gothic castle overseeing its small town's big market square. The interiors have recently been refashioned to introduce you to medieval Anjou and its main characters using imaginative modern museum techniques. The protagonist, Duke René d'Anjou, who used the château for hunting parties, was a fascinating 15th-century figure, but not the paragon of chivalric culture presented here (*see* 'Angers', p.320). At the **Chapelle de la Girouardière** (*open Wed–Mon 2.30–4.15*) in town, pay homage to a fragment of Christ's True Cross on an exquisite piece of medieval gold work. With its two horizontal bars, rather than the usual one, this Croix d'Anjou, through marriage, became the Croix de Lorraine, and then, much later, symbol of the French Resistance.

Back at the Loire, on the south bank, some exceptionally picturesque former ports dip their toes happily into the river. At **Trèves**, the single remaining castle tower stands out next to the medieval church. **Cunault**'s church of **Notre-Dame** offers another example beyond Fontevraud of just how ambitious early medieval Angevin architecture could be. Entering the vast black tomb of the nave, crane your neck to peer up at the action

Getting Around

Bus services run between Saumur and Angers. To reach the villages of the Aubance and Layon valleys, take buses from Angers.

Tourist Information

St-Mathurin-sur-Loire: Place Charles Sigogne, t 02 41 57 01 82, *ot.stmathurinsurloire@wanadoo.fr*.
Baugé: Place de l'Europe, t 02 41 89 18 07, *www.tourisme-bauge.fr.st*.
Cunault/Gennois: Place Victor Dialland, t 02 41 67 92 55 or t 02 41 67 92 70.
Brissac-Quincé: 8 Place de la République, t 02 41 91 21 50, *www.brissac-tourisme.asso.fr*.

Where to Stay and Eat

Chênehutte-les-Tuffeaux ✉ 49350
★★★★**Le Prieuré**, t 02 41 67 90 14, *prieure@grandesetapes.fr* (*luxury–moderate*). Some spectacular rooms in a Renaissance building

with luxurious dining room (*expensive*) and terrace. Avoid the comfortable but ugly maisonettes in the grounds, which have a pool, tennis and mini-golf. *Closed Jan–Feb.*

Les Rosiers ✉ 49350
★★★**Auberge Jeanne de Laval/Les Ducs d'Anjou**, 54 Rue Nationale, t 02 41 51 80 17 (*moderate*). Charming, reputed for its cuisine (*expensive*). Most of the rooms are a modestly slimming walk away from the restaurant, in a grandiose house. *Closed Dec exc Christmas; restaurant closed Mon lunch.*
★★**Au Val de Loire**, Place de l'Eglise, t 02 41 51 80 30 (*inexpensive*). Neat, smart little rooms and carefully prepared local food (*moderate*). *Closed mid-Feb–mid-Mar; restaurant closed Sun eve and Mon.*

Thouarcé ✉ 49380
Relais de Bonnezeaux, Route d'Angers, t 02 41 54 08 33 (*expensive–moderate*). Much appreciated restaurant which took over the railway station, with vineyard views. *Closed Sun eve, Mon, and Tues eve.*

carved on the capitals. Off the ambulatory, a side-chapel contains the polychrome reliquary chest of 5th-century St Maxenceul. His memory was upstaged by the arrival of St Philibert's relics in the 9th century, rushed east by monks fleeing the Vikings. Later, the community claimed to hold some real Christian whoppers: a ring belonging to the Virgin Mary and a phial of her milk. At **Gennes**, two medieval churches stand opposite each other, while tucked away in the hillside the remnants of an amphitheatre reveal Gallo-Roman roots. **Le Thoureil**, fully exposed to the Loire, has fine 17th-century houses built for Dutch merchants trading along the great river.

Neolithic folk liked these parts too, judging by the concentration of menhirs and dolmens in the hinterland. Also seek out the delightful Romanesque church at **St-Georges-des-Sept-Voies**. The nearby **Orbière** or **Hélice Terrestre** (*open May–Sept daily 11–8; rest of year Wed–Sun 2.30–6.30; adm*) is a wacky contemporary troglodyte dwelling transformed into a work of art by the larger than life late Jacques Warminski. A surprise awaits in the 'musical sphere': stamp around inside to hear it.

Reaching the villages of **Gohier** and **St-Saturnin-sur-Loire**, a major shift in geology is reflected in the dark stone that suddenly dominates the architecture. South from here lie two quietly beautiful wine-producing valleys, the Aubance and the Layon. The big tourist attraction of the **Aubance**, the muscular **Château de Brissac** (*open July–mid-Sept 10–5.45; April–June and mid-Sept–Oct Wed–Mon 10–12 and 2.15–5.15; adm*), has a classical body trying to squeeze out of a medieval one. The original was built for Pierre de Brézé, who served kings Charles VII and Louis XI. In 1502 Pierre's nephew sold the Gothic pile to René de Cossé (a minister under Charles VIII), whose family still owns it. At the end of the Wars of Religion Charles II de Cossé, then governor of Paris, opened the gates of the capital to the reconciling Henri IV. His reward was to be made a Maréchal de France and a duke. Charles marked his elevated rank on his extravagant château, for which he and his master mason, Jacques Corbineau, are to be blamed or congratulated. The guided tour takes you through just a few of the 200 or so rooms.

The steep slopes of the **Layon valley** are carpeted with vines. Although the sights along the way are small, the route is gorgeous, marked by windmills. A whole range of wines is produced in the calm villages, while two tiny areas produce exceptional sweet whites, Bonnezeaux and Quarts-de-Chaume, Anjou's answer to Sauternes.

Angers

Apocalyptic Angers, black Angers...the titles for the historic capital of Anjou aren't reassuring. But this turns out to be an intensely welcoming, cultured city built either side of the chunky Maine river just north of the Loire. The title 'Black Angers' comes from the town's slate mines rather than a grim character; that of the apocalypse from two fabulous tapestry cycles.

Angers was the centre of a Celtic tribe, the Andes or Andecaves, before becoming Gallo-Roman *Juliomagus*. As the regional counts under the Carolingian kings became increasingly independent, the Ingelgérien family took power in Angers under Foulques le Roux in 898 – the first of a line of Angevin counts to go by the name of

Getting Around

Angers has excellent **train** links along the Loire and with Paris (*1hr 30mins*).

Tourist Information

Angers: Place Kennedy, t 02 41 23 50 00, *www.angers-tourisme.com*.

Where to Stay and Eat

Angers ✉ 49000

★★★★**Château de Noirieux**, 26 Route du Moulin, 49125 Briollay, t 02 41 42 50 05, *noirieux@relaischateaux.com* (*luxury–expensive*). North of town, in the countryside and overlooking the Loir river, this is the height of luxury. The stylish rooms are set in a 15th-century manor house. Gourmet restaurant (*very expensive–expensive*). *Closed early Feb–early Mar and late Oct–mid-Nov; restaurant closed Mon and Tues.*

★★★**Hôtel d'Anjou/La Salamandre**, 1 Bd Foch, t 02 41 88 24 82, *www.hoteldanjou.fr* (*expensive–moderate*). Restored to a high standard.

The restaurant t 02 41 88 99 55 (*expensive*) serves accomplished cuisine in a neo-Gothic setting. *Restaurant closed Sun.*

★★**Hôtel du Mail**, 8 Rue des Ursules, t 02 41 25 05 25 (*inexpensive*). Characterful rooms set in a grand 17th-century town house in a quiet street.

★★**Le Cavier**, t 02 41 42 30 45, *www.lacroix cadeau.fr* (*inexpensive*). Amusing and atmospheric hotel in a traditional Anjou windmill, but in a commercial belt north of town, on the road to Laval. Pool. Characterful restaurant (*moderate*), plus simpler food.

L'Entracte, 9 Rue Louis de Romain, t 02 41 87 71 82 (*moderate*). Warm interior, including stained glass, in which to enjoy good food. *Closed Sat lunch, Sun, and most Aug.*

Les Trois Rivières, 62 Promenade de Reculée, t 02 41 73 31 88 (*moderate*). A view on to the Maine as well as good cuisine, on the Doutre side of the river. Fish a speciality.

La Ferme, 2 Place Freppel, t 02 41 87 09 90 (*moderate–cheap*). Popular restaurant with a terrace in the shadow of the cathedral where you can try dishes made with Anjou wines. *Closed Sun eve, Wed, late-July–mid-Aug, and Christmas.*

the Falcon. The most famous, the formidable Foulques Nerra (Black Falcon), greatly expanded the family territories. Foulques V had a son called Geoffroy – nicknamed Plantagenêt because he habitually wore a piece of broom (*genêt*) in his helmet – who married Mathilda, daughter of King Henry I of England, in 1128. Their son, Henri Plantagenet, famously became King Henry II of England in 1154. Angers no longer stood at the centre of Plantagenet territories; Chinon was Henry's main headquarters in these parts, but he didn't neglect the ancestral family town.

After the French crown wrested control of Anjou from the Plantagenets (don't rely on Shakespeare's propagandist *King John* for the facts), Angers remained in an important strategic position, close to the border with Brittany. Blanche de Castille, regent for her young son King Louis IX, commissioned a new castle in the 1230s and had the city protected by a great wall. In the next century King Jean le Bon offered Anjou as a dukedom to his son Louis, who vied with his royal brothers to see who could lead a life of most extravagance. However, Louis' energetic administration also encouraged civic schemes, including the development of a university. Later, Joan of Arc was supported by Yolande d'Aragon, wife of Duke Louis II d'Anjou. These two produced a son who came to be nicknamed *le bon roi René* (Good King René) – he claimed the kingdom of Sicily – but who was actually duke of Anjou and count of Provence and Piedmont. René, a deeply cultured man, may have spoken a handful of languages, composed poetry and music, encouraged other artists and shown enough sensitivity to introduce new flowers to northern France. But he also bled his subjects dry. King Louis XI forced him to return Anjou to the monarchy in 1474 and René left for Provence.

Granted a new royal charter and acquiring the first printing press on the Loire in 1476, Angers continued to grow commercially and academically. Trade was particularly prosperous through the 17th century, Anjou wines and fruit very successfully exported to England and Holland. The anti-Revolutionary tide reached Angers in 1793, before a couple of thousand pro-royalist, pro-Catholic Vendéens were shot on what is now known as the Champs des Martyrs. Catholicism then reasserted itself in a big way and a Catholic university was even set up in 1875. During the Second World War, Angers was damaged by bombs, but in contrast to the other big cities along the Loire the historic centre was much less affected. Culture has bloomed here since, including one of the most important theatre festivals in France.

The rough medieval pentagon of the **Château d'Angers** (*open May–Aug daily 9.30–6.30; Sept–April 10–5.30; adm*) is the most imposing military fortification in the Loire Valley. Seventeen towers rise from walls made of local black schist – repellent to invaders and not as pleasing as white limestone on the eye, although once through the fortified gateway you will find a château within a château where lightness prevails. The main attraction within is the fabulous **tapestry of the Apocalypse** commissioned by Louis Ier d'Anjou, and one of the greatest artistic enterprises undertaken in medieval France, even if housed in an ugly postwar bunker. It tells the biblical story of St John's revelation in 76 scenes (eight panels didn't survive mistreatment during the Revolution). The evil beast with its seven heads and ten horns features prominently in this epic fantasy of the violent, bestial clash between Good and Evil before Christ comes to mete out muscular justice. In one or two scenes the evil knights appear to bear English helmets, while Saracens crop up elsewhere, indicating how period politics infiltrated the art.

North of the castle promenade, grand late-medieval and Renaissance houses line up along the cobbled streets leading to the **Cathédrale St-Maurice**, its three towers soaring up beyond a long stairway leading from the Maine. The building mostly dates from the 12th century, the single west portal filled with sculpture reminiscent of that at Chartres, but the eight formidable saints in battle gear above are copies of 16th-century works. The graceful and much-vaunted Angevin vaulting inside influenced church-building in the west of France through the 13th century. Stained glass from the 12th to the 15th centuries embellishes the sombre interior. The vast 18th-century organ is held up by colossal atlantes so heavily loaded they look as though collapse might be imminent. Behind the cathedral on **Place Ste-Croix**, half-men, half-beasts, a mermaid and a three-balled man count among the weird cast who clamber over the beams of the remarkable half-timbered house known as the **Maison d'Adam**.

The ruined **Eglise de Toussaint** was restored in the early 1980s and turned into the **Galerie David d'Angers** (*open mid-June–mid-Sept daily 9–6.30; rest of year Tues–Sun 10–12 and 2–6; adm*) cluttered with sculptures, all the work of a remarkable local 19th-century artist from these parts. Given financial support by the town authorities from an early age, he even took his city's name by way of gratitude, and sent home plaster-casts of his works when he headed off to Paris. For Angers, the sculptor made a statue of Good King René which stands by the castle. Nearby, the splendid 15th-century house known as the Logis Barrault contains the **Musée des Beaux-Arts d'Angers**, just emerging from a major renovation. The **Tour St-Aubin** stands out in this neighbour-hood, a massive, lone 12th-century tower, a remnant of Angers' main Benedictine abbey, with some very fine Romanesque carvings. **Place du Ralliement**, the square at the heart of Angers' shopping quarter, is dominated by its ornate theatre.

In medieval times chains were placed across the Maine to stop boats slipping by without paying taxes, hence the names of the bridges, Pont de la Haute Chaîne and Pont de la Basse Chaîne. These lead across to the quarter known as **La Doutre** (a contraction of *de l'autre côté*). Behind the great line of tall plane trees, the 1175 **Hôpital St-Jean** (*open mid-June–mid-Sept daily 9–6.30; rest of year Tues–Sun 10–12 and 2–6; adm*) claims to be the oldest hospital building in France, and is certainly among the most beautiful. In the sublime Salle des Malades, two rows of slender sandstone columns hold up the parachute-like Angevin vaults, but could the aesthetics act as any kind of anaesthetic for the dreadfully sick crammed together in beds here in the past? Now, the walls are hung with the second overwhelming cycle of **Apocalypse tapestries** in Angers, conceived by 20th-century artist Jean Lurçat. Rather than being inspired by the Bible, he was profoundly affected by manmade realities like the Hiroshima bomb. Woven at Aubusson (*see* p.379), the tapestries were begun in 1957. They burst with colour, light and energy, good as well as well as evil. Further modern tapestries and displays of tapestry-making are to be seen in the adjoining **Musée de la Tapisserie Contemporaine** (*same ticket as the Hôpital St-Jean*).

Attractions on the outskirts of Angers include the **Cointreau factory and museum**, the **slate museum of Trélazé**, and the **air museum** by Angers' small country airport at Marcé (*details from the tourist office*). Two contrasting châteaux north of Angers confusingly carry the name of Plessis. The elegant moated **Château du Plessis-Bourré** (*open July–Aug daily 10–6; April–June and Sept Fri–Tues 10–12 and 2–6, Thurs 2–6, closed Wed; Feb–Mar and Oct–Nov Thurs–Tues 2–6, closed Wed; adm*), near Ecuillé, between the Sarthe and Mayenne rivers, looks invitingly formal and white. It was built from 1468 to 1473 for Jean Bourré, finance minister and general factotum to Louis XI. Inside, the vaulting, wood carving, floor tiling and a monumental fireplace all take you back to Bourré's period. But most shocking is the painted ceiling of the Salle des Gardes, covered with the weirdest paintings along the Loire, including such mysterious images as a woman sewing up a magpie's anus and Venus standing up peeing into a bowl. Some have ventured alchemical explanations, others merely see bawdy illustra-tions of common sayings. The dark, forbidding schist fortifications at the **Château du Plessis-Macé** (*open July–Aug daily 10.30–6.30; April–June and Sept–Oct Wed-Sun 1.30–5.30; adm*) stand west of the Mayenne river, closer to Anjou's historic frontier

with Brittany. Once through the imposing walls, an appealing shambles of a courtyard opens up, mixing smooth tufa with rugged schist in almost comical fashion. The
interiors were much altered by the 19th-century owners.

The Loire from Angers to Nantes

Although the villages perched along the Corniche Angevine on the south bank of this
stretch of the Loire get more attention, there are charming sights and wonderful views
along the north bank too. At the **Pointe de Bouchemaine** where the Maine and Loire
merge, the expanse of water can seem Amazonian in winter and spring, but in
summer it dwindles as riverbank flowers and dykes emerge. The narrow, winding road
along the north bank enters the prosperous walled vineyards of **Savennières**,
producing a highly prized mature dry white wine. Down in the midst of the river, the
houses on the adorable **Ile Béhuard** regularly find themselves with their feet in the
water, but the church is perched on a protective rock.

The busy N23 takes you right past the gates of the autocratic **Château de Serrant**
(*open July–Aug daily 10–5.15; April–June and Sept–Oct daily 10–12 and 2.15–5.15; adm*).
Its outer sides may be of dark schist, but within the courtyard the walls are of blinding
limestone. Begun in the middle of the 16th century, this castle's design has been linked
to the great architect Philibert de l'Orme. The extravaganza of a **chapel**, though, is
attributed to the later Hardouin Mansart, of Versailles fame, and serves as a
mausoleum to the Marquis de Vaubrun, who died in battle in 1675. An Irish family, the
Walshes, important Jacobite supporters after King James II of England's overthrow in

Getting Around

Local **buses** serve both the north and south
banks of the river.

Tourist Information

Savennières: 1 Rue de la Mairie, t 02 41 72 84
46, or t 02 41 72 85 00, *www.savennieres.com*.
Chalonnes-sur-Loire: Place de l'Hôtel de Ville,
t 02 41 78 26 21.
Montjean-sur-Loire: R. d'Anjou, t 02 41 39 07 10.
St-Florent-le-Vieil: Rue de Rénéville, t 02 41 72
62 32, *off.tour.florentlevieil49@wanadoo.fr*.

Where to Stay and Eat

L'Ile Béhuard ✉ 49170
Les Tonnelles, 12 Rue du Chevalier, t 02 41 72 21
50 (*very expensive–expensive*). Enchanting
place with shady terrace on secretive island.
Closed Sun eve, Mon, and mid-Dec–Jan.

Rochefort-sur-Loire ✉ 49190
★★Le Grand Hôtel, 30 Rue René Gasnier, t 02 41
78 80 46, *www.le-grand-hotel.net* (*inexpensive*). Signposted by palm trees along the
village street, the rooms are basic, but the
food (*moderate*) is lovingly prepared. *Closed
late-Oct–early Nov, plus a week in Jan; restaurant closed Sun eve and Wed.*

La Chapelle-St-Florent ✉ 49410
Moulin de l'Epinay, t 02 41 72 70 70 (*cheap*).
Crêperie in a windmill, enjoying spectacular
views over southern Anjou.

St-Sauveur-de-Landemont ✉ 49270
★★★★Château de la Colaissière, t 02 40 98
75 04, *colaissiere@chateauxhotels.com*
(*luxury–expensive*). Dreamy walled castle
with superb Loire windows, extravagant
rooms set round the courtyard, and excellent restaurant (*expensive*). Pool. *Closed
most Jan; restaurant closed Sun and Mon
out of season.*

1688, became the next proprietors. The castle entrance carries the family coat of arms, the three swans, one pierced by an arrow, recalling a fairytale story of an ancestor wounded in battle and left to die in the water until rescued by the birds. The sumptuous rooms reflect refined Ancien Régime living. Napoleon visited in 1808; he only stayed a few hours but his room has remained, shrine-like, intact to this day.

Ingrandes marks the end of present-day Anjou on the north bank. It has a typical Angevin silhouette, plus a spire that resembles an obelisk. The Hôtel de la Gabelle is a reminder of the much-resented salt tax of the Ancien Régime. Brittany was tax-free, but in Anjou the tax was often extortionate. To stop contraband activities, a special police force made up of *gabelous* patrolled the border to catch salt-smugglers.

Close to the pretty village of Varades, the **Palais Briau** (*open Aug daily 2–6; April–July and Sept–Oct Sat and Sun 2–6; adm*) is a sumptuous brick and stone château, built for François Briau, a model of a 19th-century engineer, who installed all the mod cons of his day in his rooms with a view. **Ancenis** long served as a Breton frontier port. Although its château by the river now stands in ruins, the town above has a bright air. The sloping vineyards around here produce Coteaux d'Ancenis wines. A many-sided keep rises high above the village of **Oudon**, a landmark along this stretch of the Loire, one you can sometimes climb to enjoy superb views. From up around **Le Cellier**, you can enjoy further dreamy views of a stretch whose beauty inspired Turner.

Head from Angers to the Corniche Angevine on the Loire's south bank via **Rochefort-sur-Loire**, in gorgeous Angevin wine country. Down at **Chalonnes'** old quays, river boats rest under the trees. Loire navigation provides the main theme for **Montjean** even today, with its great quays and a traditional boat, a *gabare*, that sails in the summer; book a trip from the quayside or the scruffy **Ecomusée**, which gives a broad picture of river-trading down the centuries. You get plunging views down onto the Loire next to the grand neoclassical church at clifftop **St-Florent-le-Vieil**. Go inside to admire a dramatic statue of a local hero of the Guerre de Vendée, the Marquis de Bonchamp. As over 150,000 Vendéens fled across the Loire from the Republican forces, Bonchamp, in a rare act of mercy, spared his Revolutionary prisoners, despite the bloody tactics of the Republican army. In the memorial by David d'Angers, he looks like a combination of classical virtue and a Christ of the Resurrection. **Champtoceaux** occupies another promontory high above the Loire, although the Coulée de la Luce, a natural amphitheatre turned public garden, allows you to descend elegantly to the riverside. The freckled church tower at **La Varenne**, which you can climb for great views, indicates the most westerly point in Anjou. Vines slope gracefully down into the Loire Atlantique and Muscadet-producing country. Following the Loire's bank to Nantes, look out for the adorable tiny Romanesque chapel at **St-Simon**, while **La Pierre Percée** beyond presents a big cobbled slope running down to the old river port.

Nantes and Muscadet Country

Cosmopolitan Nantes feels oceanic, even though the Atlantic still lies some 50km away, and the shipping trade that once made this city such an important colonial port has long moved seaward. Nantes' greatest legacy, its splendid 18th-century buildings, were paid for in large part by the slave trade, although ironically Nantes is best known in French history for an edict of tolerance, signed here by King Henri IV in 1598 at the end of the Wars of Religion. The best Muscadet wine territories extend southeast from the Nantes suburbs down to the surprisingly Italianate town of Clisson.

Nantes

Back in Gaulish times, the Loire around Nantes acted as a divide between the territories of the Namnetes and Pictones tribes to north and south. A few remnants of a Gallo-Roman settlement have been found on the south bank. Christianity came early, and the new religion soon got the upper hand, the bishops of Nantes becoming powerful figures. The city grew up north of the Loire. During the Dark Ages the county of Nantes lay in the Frankish Marches, fought over by Franks and Bretons. Nomenoë, Breton leader in the mid-9th century, conquered Nantes. But soon the Vikings sailed up the Loire to wreak havoc; one bishop of Nantes, Gohard, had his throat cut at the altar.

In the mid-14th-century Breton War of Succession, a subplot in the first half of the Hundred Years War, the city switched hands between the rival Penthièvre and de Montfort factions, respectively supported by French and English royalty. Under the victorious de Montforts, Nantes won out over Rennes to become ducal capital. In the second half of the Hundred Years War, a major aristocrat from the region, Gilles de Rais (or Retz), having helped Joan of Arc in her triumphs along the Loire, ended up accused of raping and murdering scores of young boys in his castles. He may have been framed, but was certainly hanged in Nantes in 1440. At the end of the medieval period, under François II, the last duke of Brittany, Nantes thrived as the region's capital and a university was inaugurated. The duke's only child Anne was born at the Château de Nantes in 1477, and the city would remain close to her heart. She was forced to marry two French kings, and her second royal wedding, to Louis XII, took place in the chapel of Nantes castle. Anne would die at another château along the Loire, Blois, in 1514, but her heart was returned to the city of her birth. Her daughter by Louis XII, Claude de France, was married to the next king of France, François Ier, who organized Brittany's official union with France in 1532, an act sealed at the Château de Nantes.

During the brutal Wars of Religion, Nantes fell for a time to the Duc de Mercœur, ultra-Catholic governor of Brittany, before King Henri IV signed the famous Edict of Nantes granting freedom of worship to Protestants. A century later, Louis XIV revoked it, rekindling the persecution of the Huguenots. By then Nantes had become a major colonial port with France's acquisition of her Caribbean territories in the 17th century, and by the 18th it was one of the most significant European slaving centres. The Montaudoin family alone equipped 357 ships for the sickening triangular trade between 1694 and 1791. New industries grew up in Nantes, and its population rapidly doubled. Sugar was refined and cotton turned into printed calico, or *indiennes*, which went back to Africa to be bartered for more slaves. The Revolution banned the slave trade for a time and the terrifying Carrier was sent to Nantes to make the stubborn

Getting There and Around

Nantes has an international airport, with direct **flights** from the UK on BA/Air France. There are also fantastic **train** links to Paris by TGV (*2hrs*). The rail connections are also good along the Loire Valley. A railway line runs down through the main Muscadet area to Clisson.

Tourist Information

Nantes: 7 Rue de Valmy, t 02 40 20 60 00, *www.nantes-tourisme.com*.
Clisson: 6 Place de la Trinité, t 02 40 54 02 95, *www.clisson.com*.

Where to Stay and Eat

Nantes ✉ 44000

★★★La Pérouse, 3 Allée Duquesne, t 02 40 89 75 00, *www.hotel-laperouse.fr* (*moderate*). The most exciting hotel in central Nantes, in ultra-modern style and well located.
★★Cholet, 10 Rue Gresset, t 02 40 73 31 04, *hotelcholet@wanadoo.fr* (*inexpensive*). Close to the theatre, with good-value, pleasantly renovated rooms.

★★Hôtel des Colonies, 5 Rue du Chapeau Rouge, t 02 40 48 79 76, *hoteldescolonies.fr* (*inexpensive*). Quiet rooms close to the central pedestrian area.
★St-Daniel, 4 Rue du Bouffay, t 02 40 47 41 25 (*inexpensive*). Good value and central.
Auberge du Château, 5 Place de la Duchesse Anne, t 02 40 74 31 85 (*moderate*). Intimate restaurant opposite the castle, serving classic fine Nantes cuisine. *Closed Sun and Mon, and most Aug.*
Le Carnivore, 7 Allée des Tanneurs, t 02 40 47 87 00 (*expensive–cheap*). Traditional meat lovers might be surprised to see bison and ostrich on the menu.
La Cigale, 4 Place Graslin, t 02 51 84 94 94, (*moderate–cheap*). Art Nouveau décor, a tourist sight in itself, for a classic brasserie.
Le Chiwawa, 17 Rue Voltaire, t 02 40 69 01 65 (*moderate–cheap*). Inventive cuisine. *Closed Sat lunch, Sun, and Mon lunch.*

Clisson ✉ 44190

La Bonne Auberge, 1 Rue Olivier de Clisson, t 02 40 54 01 90 (*expensive–moderate*). Excellent gastronomic restaurant. *Closed Sun eve, Mon, Tues lunch and Wed lunch, and mid-Aug–early Sept and mid-Feb.*

royalists in town wed the cause of the Revolution; his 'Republican marriages' were enforced couplings, offenders tied in pairs, bundled on to a boat with a hole in the bottom, and drowned in the Loire. In the 1830s modern techniques of canning fish were developed; this big industry replaced the slave trade.

After the First World War, as part of the German reparations, the channels of the Loire flowing through the city centre were filled in by German workers. Allied bombing raids in the Second World War left scars, while the large modern road through the centre known as the Cours des 50 Otages commemorates the execution of fifty French hostages in 1942. High-tech industries have replaced shipbuilding since the war, but sugar from the Caribbean apparently still arrives, much heading for Nantes' many biscuit factories, a last benign relic of its darker slaving past.

The massive **Château de Nantes** or Château des Ducs de Bretagne (*open Sept–June Wed–Mon 10–6; July and Aug Wed–Mon 10–7; closed Tues; adm*) could count as just about the most westerly of the castles of the Loire. Originally the river lapped at its walls; now the Nantais like to take their dogs for a walk in the dry moat. It may be an architectural mess, but the dark outer walls enclose some more graceful wings. Work is under way to create a grand new museum for 2008 which should acknowledge the city's slave-trading past among other things – meanwhile, look out for temporary exhibitions. Rue Rodier leads straight from castle to cathedral. To take a slightly more circuitous but more regal route, opt instead for the wide mid-18th-century boulevard,

Cours St-Pierre, Place Foch at the end graced by a rare statue of King Louis XVI atop his column. Beyond, Cours St-André leads you up to the Erdre riverboat station, where you can book for a cruise. Back with the **Cathédrale St-Pierre** (begun in 1434), while the exterior of this bulky, squat building may look grey, inside this is the cleanest cathedral you are ever likely to see. It is also just about the emptiest – the interior had to be restored and cleaned after a fire in 1972. The major interest is the exquisite tomb of François II Duc de Bretagne and his two wives, commissioned by Anne de Bretagne.

The splendid, whiter-than-white 1900 **Musée des Beaux-Arts** (*open Wed–Mon 10–6; closed Tues and public hols; adm*) on the other side of Cours St-Pierre offers a good crash course in the history of Western art from the 13th century to the present day. French highlights include a couple of candlelit De la Tours, a Watteau, several Greuzes, and portraits by Tournières. Lecomte du Nouys' vision of white women enslaved in an Islamic harem presents a surprisingly different take on slavery, while Monet transports you to Venice and the otherworldly visions of his *Nymphéas* (Waterlilies). Raymond Hains, a conceptual artist, pays homage to the Nantes biscuit industry via a barcode.

Rue du Roi Albert leads up from the cathedral square to the administrative quarter and the **Préfecture**, the masterpiece of Ceineray, one of two architects who transformed central Nantes around the Revolution. The façade of this building, begun in 1763, carries the arms of France and Brittany. The more lively shopping area of the **Bouffay quarter** spreads west from the castle, with plenty of historic houses on the way to the quirky church of Ste-Croix. Across the broad Cours des 50 Otages tram route, aim f**or Place Royale,** a sober square planned by the architect Crucy, the other main architect to transform Nantes. A wonderful array of cafés spreads out just south opposite the colonnaded, temple-like **Bourse**, the former Exchange on Place du Commerce, another work by Crucy. Cross the dauntingly wide boulevard where the Loire once flowed to reach the former island of **Feydeau**, now sadly isolated by busy roads. This is where some of the very grandest Ancien Régime families had their town houses, carved with grotesque Baroque masks, somehow quite fitting given the ugly slave-trading connections. Back north of Place du Commerce, the mid-19th-century sweeps of stairs of the elegant shopping arcade, **Passage Pommeraye**, look romantically kitsch today. They lead to Rue Crébillon and on to Crucy's more serious **Place Graslin**, dominated by its theatre. Utterly elegant **Cours Cambronne** nearby could hardly be more perfect for promenading your poodle.

The **Musée Thomas Dobrée** (*open Tues–Fri 9.45–5.30, Sat and Sun 2.30–5; closed Mon and public hols; adm*) stands west on Rue Voltaire. Anne of Brittany's shining golden reliquary heart is the finest piece of craftsmanship in a museum crammed with the stuff collected by Thomas Dobrée, who commissioned the grand neo-Romanesque house to contain it. He also restored the 15th-century Manoir de la Touche next door, its ground floor now devoted to Nantes at the time of the Revolution, upstairs to Bronze Age, Celtic, Gallo-Roman and Merovingian finds. Further west, in the **Ste-Anne quarter**, the little **Musée Jules Verne** (*open Mon and Wed–Sat 10–12 and 2–6, Sun 2–6; adm*) pays its respects to the 19th-century visionary author from Nantes. Along Quai de la Fosse you can tour the **Maillé Brézé** (*open June–Sept daily 2–6; Oct–May Wed, Sat, Sun and school hols 2–5; adm*), a decommissioned naval escort vessel.

Muscadet Country to Clisson

The Loire Atlantique makes one extremely well-known wine, Muscadet. The **Château de Goulaine** (*open mid-June–mid-Sept Wed–Mon 2–6, closed Tues; late Mar–mid-June and mid-Sept–Oct Sat, Sun and public hols 2–6; adm*) just southeast of Nantes makes a good first impression, both as a reputed Muscadet-producing estate and a significant historic castle with many a tale to tell, run today by an 11th-generation marquis who doubles as a crime- and wine-writer. A good place for a general introduction to Muscadet wines is the **Maison des Vins de Nantes** at **La Haye-Fouassière** (*open Mon–Fri 8.30–12.30 and 2–5.45; July–Aug also Sat and Sun 10.30–12.30 and 2.20–6; adm*), overlooking hectare upon hectare of vines. At **Le Pallet**, the **Musée du Vignoble Nantais** (*open May–Sept Tues–Sun 10–12.30 and 2–6; Oct–April Tues-Sun 2.30–6; adm*) is a startlingly slick wine museum, which also recalls the great scholar, theologian and tragic lover of Heloïse, Pierre Abélard, born into a noble family here in 1079. The major Muscadet estate of the **Château de la Galissonnière** nearby is well used to receiving foreign visitors. But be bold and try smaller estates too.

Clisson is the town where Brittany and Italy meet, although the covered market and the feudal **Château de Clisson** (*open April–Sept Wed–Mon 9.30–12 and 2–6; Oct–Mar Wed–Sun 9.30–12 and 2–6; adm*) look French enough. The castle's massive ruins dominate the valley where the Maine joins the Sèvre Nantaise. Clisson was devastated in the Vendée uprising (*see* p.342). The new town that arose looks shipped straight from Italy, thanks to the passion and pennies of Pierre and François Cacault of Nantes and their friend, the sculptor Frédéric Lemot (known for his statue of King Henri IV on Paris' Pont-Neuf). Lemot's distinguished villa, **La Garenne Lemot** (*open Mar–Oct Tues–Sun 10–12 and 2–6; Nov–Feb Tues–Sun 10–12; adm*), with its exhibitions on the French love affair with Italy, and its grounds full of follies, lures visitors across the river.

Chartres and the Loir Valley

Chartres

With the gift of the *Sancta Camisia*, the supposed blouse of the Virgin Mary, in the late Dark Ages Chartres became one of the greatest pilgrimage cities of Western Europe, which it remains today. What a mesmerizing sight its medieval cathedral must have made for pilgrims through the Middle Ages, rising so startlingly from afar above the flat surrounding landscape. Even today, this stupendous Christian symbol appears almost isolated on the immense horizon of the Beauce cereal plain. It's as though the city around it didn't exist. In fact, a major medieval town grew up at the cathedral's feet, and round the now-vanished castle of the counts of Chartres, jealous rivals of the bishops of the city from the 10th century. Down by the Eure river, a multitude of trades established themselves, competing in smelliness.

Explore this lower town, and you'll discover that Chartres has a much older history, the curving streets in one quarter following the lines of a major Gallo-Roman theatre. The Romans found this part of Gaul inhabited by the Carnutii, after whom Chartres is named. Their settlement, built around a sacred well, already had religious significance and was a key target for the Christians. Typically, they substituted the worship of the Virgin Mary for that of the ancient mother goddess. The first Christian basilica went up in the 4th century, this place of worship to be rebuilt several times after fires. One early bishop, 6th-century Lubin, is traditionally credited with fixing the boundaries of the vast diocese of Chartres stretching between the Seine and Loire valleys.

The first Holy Roman Emperor, Charlemagne, was given the relic containing the Virgin's blouse by Empress Irene of Constantinople. She mistakenly hoped that a daughter of hers might wed the mighty figure, reuniting Europe's Eastern and Western empires. For his grandson King Charles the Bald to have donated such a precious object to the cathedral of Chartres in the mid-9th century shows the importance of the city's religious community by that time. The official reason for the gift was in compensation for a portion of land closer to Paris which Charles' ancestor Pépin had taken by force from the bishopric. It may have been donated for the consecration of a new cathedral rebuilt during the times of the destructive Norse raids. The story goes that when the Viking Rollo came to lay siege to the town in 911, Bishop Gantelme exposed the Virgin's tunic on the ramparts; the Norseman supposedly fled, made peace with the Frankish king, and settled down as first duke of Normandy.

Towards the end of the 10th century, a brilliant religious student by the name of Fulbert came to Chartres from Reims. Fulbert made the Chartres cathedral school into one of the greatest centres of Christian learning and became bishop of the city in 1006. For two centuries, during a period sometimes described as the First Renaissance, the Chartres cathedral school's reputation radiated far and wide; only with the founding of the University of Paris would its importance decline. Fulbert promoted the cult of the Virgin. Unfortunately, the Carolingian cathedral burned down during his time. The influential man managed to persuade many of the leading figures across France, as well as the likes of King Canute in England, to donate generously towards the building of a more magnificent Romanesque edifice, carried out under the architect Béranger, roughly on the scale of the current cathedral; the crypt holding the Virgin's relic was greatly enlarged for pilgrims to parade past it easily.

Great men succeeded Fulbert, and promoted the teaching of classical authors. Bernard de Chartres famously compared the scholars of his day to dwarves perched on the shoulders of giants – the philosophers of Antiquity – allowing them to see further. The scholars of the time strove to unite the ideas of the great pagan thinkers with Christian thought, and honoured them by having them carved on the west front of the cathedral when it was extended in the mid-12th century.

Medieval Chartres meanwhile was growing into a city about the same size as the present version. But a terrible fire in 1194 destroyed much of the town and severely damaged the cathedral; it was to the great relief of the people when, three days after the conflagration, a procession appeared carrying the precious relic, rescued from the crypt by attentive priests. A huge wave of enthusiasm swept across the city, and the whole populace set about helping in the construction of a new, more brilliant Gothic cathedral. Everyone who could pitched in with labour, helping extract stone from the Berchères quarries, or giving funds for the inspired new 'Palace of the Virgin' – even

Getting Around

Chartres has good **train** links with Paris-Montparnasse (1hr) and the odd train to Orléans. Vendôme has high-speed train services to Paris. Slower trains serve Châteaudun.

Tourist Information

Chartres: Place de la Cathédrale, t 02 37 18 26 26, *info@otchartres.fr*.

Bonneval: 2 Square Westerham, t 02 37 47 55 89, *www.bonnevaltourisme.com*.

Châteaudun: 1 Rue de Luynes, t 02 37 45 22 46, *tourisme.chateaudun@wanadoo.fr*.

Vendôme: Hôtel du Saillant, 47 Rue Poterie, t 02 54 77 05 07, *ot.vendome@wanadoo.fr*.

Montoire-sur-le-Loir: 16 Place Clemenceau, t 02 54 85 23 30, *montoire@tourisme.cc*.

La Flèche: Bd de Montréal, t 02 43 94 02 53, *otsi-lafleche@libertysurf.fr*.

Where to Stay and Eat

Chartres ✉ 28000

★★★Le Grand Monarque, 22 Place des Epars, t 02 37 18 15 15, *www.bw-grand-monarque. com* (*expensive*). The best hotel in Chartres, quite distinguished and comfortable, close to the cathedral, if on a very busy square for traffic. Posh restaurant (*closed Sun eve and Mon*) and cheaper but stylish, busy brasserie (*open daily to late*).

★★Hôtel de la Poste, 3 Rue du Général Koenig, t 02 37 21 04 27, *www.hotelposte-chartres. com* (*inexpensive*). Reasonable if lacking character, again on a busy road, but close to the cathedral. Big restaurant (*moderate*). *Restaurant closed Fri eve and Sun eve*.

Le Buisson Ardent, 10 Rue au Lait, t 02 37 34 04 66 (*moderate*). Perhaps the best option up by the cathedral, in an historic building, offering good regional cuisine at a much more reasonable price than the more renowned Vieille Maison opposite.

Le St-Hilaire, 11 Rue du Pont St-Hilaire, t 02 37 30 97 57 (*expensive–moderate*). One of several enchanting restaurants in old houses down in the Basse Ville by the Eure. The chef goes to the greatest efforts to make fine regional dishes using finest local ingredients. *Closed Sat lunch, Mon lunch, and late July–early Aug and Christmas.*

Moulin de Ponceau, 21 Rue Tannerie, t 02 37 35 30 05 (*expensive–moderate*). Converted 16th-century tanning mill with pretty dining rooms and terrace over the Eure, excellent settings for an enjoyable meal. *Closed Sat lunch and Sun eve, and mid-Feb–early Mar.*

St-Prest ✉ 28300

Manoir des Prés du Roy, t 02 37 22 27 27, *www. manoirdespresduroy.com* (*moderate*). Just 7km north of Chartres, by the Eure river, a delightfully restored manor house in spacious grounds, with beamed restaurant.

La Ville-aux-Clercs ✉ 41100

★★Manoir de la Forêt, Fort-Girard, t 02 54 80 62 83 , *www.manoirdelaforet.fr* (*moderate*). Big block of a hunting lodge in lovely grounds, with traditional rooms and a delightful restaurant (*expensive–moderate*).

Troo ✉ 41800

Château de la Voûte, t 02 54 72 52 52 (*moderate*). A gem of a B&B on Troo's slope.

Le Petit Relais, Place du Château, t 02 54 72 57 92 (*moderate*). Adorable one-woman restaurant in the upper village.

Luché-Pringé ✉ 72800

★★Auberge du Port-des-Roches, t 02 43 45 44 48 (*inexpensive*). Sweet little roadside inn west of Le Lude. Lovely terrace by the river for summer dining (*moderate*). *Closed Feb; restaurant closed Sun eve and Mon.*

Philippe Auguste and Richard Cœur de Lion, who were then fighting over the area. Over the next decades, donations poured in from nobles in France and abroad, but the city corporations made wealthy by mass pilgrimage also gave generously.

By 1260 the building was nearly complete. The relative rapidity of the work gave Chartres a stylistic unity seen in few other medieval cathedrals. It perfected the concepts of roof vaulting and the flying buttress, enabling it to carry large expanses of glass-filled sides. Inside, carving the thick pillars into apparent bundles of slender columns accentuated the verticality and lightness. The façade's south tower is a Romanesque survivor; the northern one was struck by lightning in 1506 and rebuilt, more ornately, to the plans of Jehan Texier de Beauce in the early 16th century; he followed the Flamboyant Gothic style, but also added a little Renaissance building below. In medieval times, the cathedral roof would have been covered with lead, but this was stolen at the Revolution. A fire in 1936 destroyed the forest of timbers holding up the roof, and a new, bold metallic structure replaced them, topped by copper tiles.

Joyously, most of the cathedral's medieval decoration has survived down the centuries. In the words of the eminent French art historian Emile Mâle, 'Chartres is medieval thought in visible form'. More than 10,000 figures in stone or glass make this cathedral a period encyclopedia; it would take a thorough knowledge of the Scriptures and of medieval philosophy, and a lifetime's work, to decipher all the scenes. The mid-12th-century west porches escaped the 1194 fire relatively unscathed. It is generally said that various schools of French sculptors, from St-Denis, Etampes and Chartres, carved the serene tall Romanesque statues which flank the doors, although an Australian scholar has recently proposed that Italian masons may have executed these works. The statues are supposed to represent Old and New Testament figures, although certain researchers have speculated as to whether some might also bear a likeness to medieval royals, such as Eleanor of Aquitaine and her sons. The central tympanum shows the Christ of the Apocalypse being crowned by two angels, hence the nickname of the Portail Royal. Mary sits enthroned in the right-hand portal, holding out the baby Jesus; above them, note the depiction of classical scholars, together with the instruments most associated with their areas of learning. In the left-hand portal, as well as the Ascension scene in the tympanum, the signs of the zodiac and associated labours of the month prove engrossing.

Down the cathedral's sides, the substantial protruding north and south porches contain just as great a concentration of sculpted figures, but from the Gothic period, with more of a sense of movement and drama than in the west front Romanesque pieces. On the south portal, the central tympanum represents Christ and the Last Judgement, that to the left, St Stephen's stoning, set above other Christian martyrs, that to the right, the generosity of St Martin (*see* 'Tours') and St Nicholas in particular. The big statues below feature the apostles. The recent cleaning of the north portal has really brought the Old and New Testament figures here to life. The three tympanums present a delightful Nativity, the Virgin's Assumption and seating beside Christ, plus the more alarming tale of Job on his pile of manure – among the many Old Testament prefigurings of Christ brought to the fore across the whole portal. The big statues represent a wide variety of biblical characters. Traces of the original colouring given to these statues have reemerged with the cleaning, particularly noticeably with the black figures. The Queen of Sheeba is even shown standing on a black lad. Blacks were, unfortunately, generally reserved evil roles in medieval Christian iconography.

Inside blaze the finest **stained-glass windows** in the world, 173 of them, mostly original. As was the custom, different trade guilds as well as wealthy individuals supported the making of the stained glass. Look at the bottoms of the windows and you'll see goldsmiths, bakers, weavers, tavern-keepers, furriers and blacksmiths at work below the biblical stories and saintly tales. Particularly outstanding are the tall windows in the west front picturing the life of Christ, the rose windows, and the distinctive Notre-Dame de la Belle Verrière. The northern rose window and lancets were donated by Queen Blanche of Castille, the southern rose window and lancets by Pierre Mauclerc, the latter Duke of Brittany, but also count of nearer Dreux. Thibault VI of Chartres gave some of the brilliant windows around the choir. On the floor of the nave, look out for the labyrinth (fully revealed on Friday mornings). Many other Gothic cathedrals once had a similar one, but this is a rare survivor, its much-disputed significance encouraging all sorts of flaky interpretations. You can also visit the vast Romanesque crypt, sanctuary of the Virgin's blouse spared by the fire of 1194.

Beyond the cathedral's south portal stand the main shopping streets and squares of the **upper town**, filled with grand houses, some with elaborately carved creatures on their beams. The prettiest corners are around Place de l'Etape du Vin and Place de la Poissonnerie. Beyond the north portal the **Centre International du Vitrail** (*open Mon–Fri 9.30–12.30 and 1.30–6, weekends and public hols 10–12.30 and 2.30–6; adm*) occupies a medieval timberframe building, built to stock produce brought in as tax in kind from the cathedral's lucrative territories. The upper floor received grain, the lower floor, with columns and carved capitals fit for a church, wine. Now the place is devoted to stained-glass making up to the present day, studios thriving all around.

Behind the cathedral, the **Musée des Beaux-Arts** (*open Wed–Mon 10–12 and 2–5; adm*) occupies the former bishops' palace. The brick and stone Ancien Régime façade may look rather plain, but Baroque puts on quite a show as you enter, with a dramatic main staircase and chapel. Certain notable religious objects have been brought here from the Chartres church of St Peter, including the exquisite 16th-century enamels of the apostles, originally given by King Henri II to his mistress Diane de Poitiers, but much of the fine religious statuary comes from further afield, while the so-called Charlemagne glass is reckoned to be 12th-century Syrian enamel work. Among the collection of paintings, Zurbaran's *St Lucy* is the most highly regarded religious work. Remarkable portraits include Molière by Mignard, the Duc de St-Simon by Largillère, and Erasmus, attributed to Holbein. The modern art sections range from a Courbet nude bather to dramatic pieces by Soutine and Vlaminck. Henri Navarre's heady sculptures also feature prominently. Alarming depictions of Chartres include a bird's eye view of the city besieged in 1568, and the cathedral on fire in 1836. Local crafts are also represented, along with collections of arms, and ethnography from Oceania.

From around the terraced gardens at the back of the cathedral, steep paths plunge down to the river. One even carried the nickname of Rue Glisse Putain – Slipping Tart Street – as prostitutes going down to serve the barracks tended to slide down in the mud on rainy nights. Explore the **Basse Ville** by the Eure, often completely missed by visitors, but exceptionally picturesque, packed with old churches and converted mills, and medieval bridges spanning the river, on which you can go boating in season.

For a really different, wacky view of Chartres cathedral, head into the suburbs for the **Maison Picassiette** (*open April–Oct Wed–Sat 10–12 and 2–6, Sun 2–6; adm*), so called after the nickname given to Raymond Isidore, describing someone who steals things from other people's plates. Born in 1900, Isidore became a cemetery sweeper who developed an obsession with shards of broken porcelain and glass, which he used from 1930 until 1962 to plaster every inch of his house with naïve, colourful mosaics.

The Loir Valley

The Loir (without an e) meanders down through four French *départements* from below Chartres almost to Angers, its wide, flat valley often seeming to be cut too big for its slender size. The names Loir and Loire suggest there might be a connection between the two, and similarities do exist: limestone in lovely whites and beiges; troglodyte villages; Romanesque churches; and characteristic châteaux.

The source of the Loir lies southwest of Chartres, close to the dilapidated, melancholic small town of **Illiers-Combray**, with its museum and public garden dedicated to Proust, whose aunt and uncle had a house here. The place served as an inspiration for the magically detailed descriptions of the narrator's childhood in the early parts of the greatest French masterpiece of the 20th century, *A La Recherche du temps perdu*, and the **Maison de la Tante Léonie** (*open mid-Jan–mid-Dec Tues–Sun, guided tours 2.30 and 4, plus 11am July–Aug; adm*) has kept a good deal of period atmosphere, thanks in part to the legacy of Proust's servant and her family, who donated lots of the objects.

Past **Bonneval** behind its ramparts, and the secretive **Conie river**, an enjoyable place to go boating, **Châteaudun** imposes a halt. Its vast grey-stoned fortress soaring way above the Loir stops you in your tracks. While the locals love to mess about in boats on the waters below, the historic upper town has a more hushed air, its bright-stoned, big central square and well-ordered grid of streets recently scrubbed clean.

The entrance to the **château** (*open July–Aug daily 9.30–7; April–June and Sept 9.30–6.15; Jan–Mar and Oct–Dec 10–12.30 and 2–5; adm*) stands discreetly tucked away in an extremely picturesque corner of the upper town. With its magnificent mix of Gothic and Renaissance wings, it can lay claim to being the most northerly of the typical greater Loire Valley castles. The word *dun* comes from a Celtic word for a rocky promontory, and the natural site was an obvious spot for Thibault le Tricheur and subsequent counts of Blois to fortify through the Middle Ages. The huge round Grosse Tour or keep, over 100 feet high, went up for Thibaud V at the end of the 12th century. In 1391, Louis d'Orléans, son of King Charles V of France, acquired the castle. His illegitimate child Jean d'Orléans was the bastard Dunois who led the French troops to end the English siege of Orléans, aided by Joan of Arc. He would receive many estates and titles in recognition of his military services. He and his wife had the Sainte Chapelle built from the 1450s. The relic it held of a supposed piece of wood from Christ's cross may have vanished, but fifteen dignified Gothic statues still stand proudly inside. Splendidly ornate stairtowers protrude from the two main wings of the castle. The Dunois one has been given over to a contemporary exhibition on the importance of food and feasting in medieval times. The presentations are a bit hit and miss, but there's entertaining material to eke out. Among the most unusual dishes featured are pustulent whores served in a green sauce, or buggers in a grand Parisian concoction, part of a banquet given by the King of Hell, as imagined by 13th-century poet Robert de Houdereau. Regular cookery demonstrations take place, but not of these particular dishes.

The attractive historic heart of **Vendôme** is tightly embraced by the arms of the Loir and overseen by the remnants of a ruined castle, where, in the 11th century, Geoffrey Martel of Anjou and his wife Agnès de Bourgogne witnessed three stars falling in a fountain, which they took as a sign to order the building of the massive Abbaye de la Trinité which dominates the centre. The most precious relic it held was a tear of Christ, donated by the papacy for Geoffrey's military services to the Church. Much of the abbey church may be Romanesque, but its splendid façade is a last blaze of Gothic, the great window alight with fiery tongues of stone licking their way skywards. The choir and side chapels contain some of the oldest stained glass in France (one piece dating from c. 1140). The other remaining abbey buildings dating from the 17th and 18th centuries contains the local **Musée du Cloître** (open Wed–Mon 10–12 and 2–6; adm), one floor with works by Louis Leygue, a 20th-century sculptor from the town. Nearby spacious, lively, café-lined **Place St-Martin** is overseen by a soaring tower to rival that of the abbey, all that remains of another church, and by a statue of the Marquis de Rochambeau, the man to whom the USA in large part owes its independence, thanks to his crucial role in the Battle of Yorktown. He died back at his château close to Vendôme in 1807. In the height of summer, take a boat tour round the centre of town.

West of Vendôme you enter **Coteaux du Vendômois** wine territory, granted appella-tion status in 2000. At **Thorée-la-Rochette**, head straight for the railway station, either to look at the wine museum and shop, or for a return trip to Troo on board an old train (open June–mid-Sept, Sat, Sun and public hols at 2.25; July–Aug additional Sun trips 9.30 and 5.30; adm; t 02 54 72 80 82). Seek out the extraordinary wall paintings in the 15th-century church of St-Hilaire at **Villiers-sur-Loir**, but the prudish should avert their eyes from the choir stalls with their bawdy scenes. At **Montoire**, a pact with the devil was sealed with a handshake in the **railway station** (exhibition open mid-April–mid-Sept Mon–Fri 11–12 and 3–6; adm) – here, Pétain met with Hitler in October 1940 to accept officially the German occupation of France. On a happier note, the town holds a vibrant annual world folklore festival and has opened a museum on unusual instruments. By the charming south bank of the river, the tiny truncated 11th-century **Chapelle St-Gilles** (open April–Sept Tues–Sat 10–12 and 3–7, Sun 11–3; adm) conceals three overwhelming depictions of Christ. Nearby, **Lavardin**'s ruined hillside castle looks like a Romantic painting. The church below is plastered with further wall paintings, including a queue of naked people waiting to enter paradise.

The secretive village of **Troo** climbs the steep bank of the Loir west of Montoire, its cliff punctured with troglodyte caves turned into houses, a couple open to visitors in summer and certain weekends. The upper village conceals several attractive elements: semi-ruined ramparts, a large church, a 'speaking well', and an earth fort with a path snailing up to the top. In the valley, the enchanting box-like **St-Jacques-des-Guérets** is decorated with fine Romanesque art. On the outskirts of Bessé-sur-Braye, the **Château de Courtanvaux** offers a storybook vision of a late-Gothic silhouette above lovingly tended gardens. The lyrical French Renaissance poet Pierre de Ronsard (see 'Tours') was born near Couture-sur-Loir, at the **Manoir de la Possonnière** (*open July–Aug Wed–Sun 3–7; April–June and Sept–15 Nov Sat, Sun and hols 3–6; adm*). Learning is literally written all over the house here, the windows graced with Latin inscriptions. Many of these were ordered by Ronsard's father in celebration of his marriage. In the hillside opposite, seven cave entrances penetrate the rock, further inscriptions engraved over each, recalling their various uses for the medieval pilgrims who stopped here. The Loir passes by **Poncé**, partly colonized by craftspeople. At the **Château de Poncé** (*open April–Sept daily 10–12.30 and 2–6; adm*), the great Renaissance staircase is the highlight, its coffered stone ceiling filled with a plethora of sculptures, while a bust of Ronsard stands at the top of the stairs, accompanied by a delicious poem he wrote to the Loir, as though to a rumbustious friend.

Just west, the valley vineyards produce intriguingly rare white Jasnières *appellation* wine. The more ordinary but pleasant Coteaux du Loir whites, reds and rosés come from around the little market town of **La Chartre-sur-le-Loir**. Bending up northwards from here around the village of Jupilles, the **forest of Bercé** conceals mighty oaks, some 300 years old. **Jupilles' Maison du Sabot et de l'Artisanat du Bois** (*open Easter– mid-Nov Mon–Sat 10–12 and 2.30–6.30, Sun 2.30–6.30; adm*) is devoted to wood, espe- cially clog- and toy-making. A little further north, two gardens call for a visit, that at **Pruillé L'Eguillé** (*open mid-Mar–mid-Nov Fri–Wed 2–6; closed Thurs; adm*) specializing in conifers, that at the **Château du Grand Lucé** (*open May–Sept Tues–Sun 10–7; adm*) in the formal French style, beside a fine 18th-century castle.

Back close to the Loir, beyond the orchards of Vaas, the **Château du Lude** (*open April–Sept gardens Thurs–Tues 10–12 and 2–6; château Thurs–Tues 2.30–6; also open Wed mid-June–Aug; adm*) competes in scale with some of the grandest Loire châteaux, each corner marked by a massive round tower covered with Renaissance decoration. The place was modified in the 18th century for the finance minister the Marquis de Talhouët, given a grand classical façade, plus inner courtyard and interiors which have something of the air of a great Parisian townhouse. From the spectacular ballroom, with its floral marquetry floor, you trip through a series of spacious salons.

Take the prettier Loir north bank from Le Lude to reach **La Flèche**, lying in a pleas- ingly open spot on the river. Here, the first Bourbon king, Henri IV, founded an exceptionally grand Jesuit school, the Collège Royal, now the **Prytanée National Militaire** (*open July–late-Aug daily 10–12 and 2–6; adm*). Philosopher René Descartes (*see pp.30 and 305*) was its star pupil. Henri IV requested that his heart and that of his tempestuous wife Marie de Médicis be buried in the school's stunning Chapelle St-Louis; they were ceremonially burnt in 1793. Napoleon turned the college into the élite military training school it remains to this day.

Two last memorable châteaux open to visitors lie by the banks of the Loir before Angers: the rustic **Château de Bazouges** (*open mid-June–mid-Sept Thurs–Sun 3–6; adm*), its concentration of towers just appearing out of the trees on the riverbank beside a village full of fishermen and river boats; and the **Château de Durtal** (*open July–Aug daily 10–12 and 2–7; April–June and Sept Sat, Sun and public hols 2–6; adm*), a self-important edifice with fat towers lording it over the little town grovelling below.

Atlantic Coast
Vendée, Poitou, Charentes

The Atlantic Coast

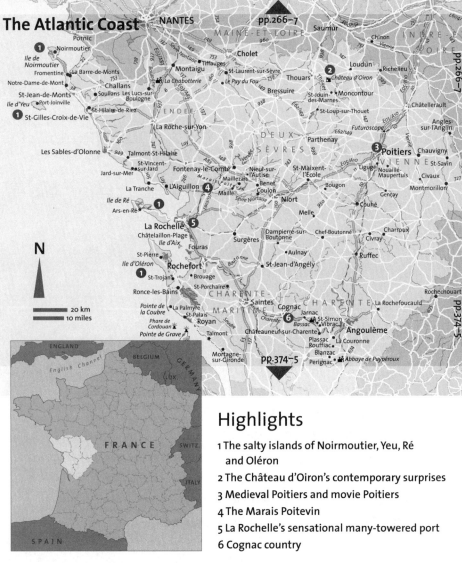

NANTES pp.266–7

MAINE-ET-LOIRE

Pornic
Noirmoutier
Ile de Noirmoutier
Fromentine • La Barre-de-Monts
Notre-Dame-de-Mont
St-Jean-de-Monts
Ile d'Yeu • Port-Joinville
St-Gilles-Croix-de-Vie

Challans
Soullans Les Lucs-sur-Boulogne
St-Hilaire-de-Riez

VENDÉE

La Roche-sur-Yon

Montaigu
La Chabotterie
Le Puy du Fou

Cholet
Tiffauges
St-Laurent-sur-Sèvre
Bressuire

Saumur

Chinon

Loudun • Richelieu
Thouars Château d'Oiron
St-Jouin-des-Marnes • Moncontour
St-Loup-sur-Thouet

Châtellerault

Angles-sur-l'Anglin

DEUX-SÈVRES

Parthenay
Futuroscope

Poitiers Chauvigny
VIENNE St-Savin

Les Sables-d'Olonne
Talmont-St-Hilaire
St-Vincent-sur-Jard
Jard-sur-Mer

Fontenay-le-Comte
Maillezais
Maillé
Benet
Coulon

Nieul-sur-l'Autise
St-Maixent-l'École
Bougon

Liguge • Nouaillé-Maupertuis
Civaux
Gençay Montmorillon

L'Aiguillon
La Tranche
Ile de Ré
Ars-en-Ré

Niort
Melle
Couhé

Charroux
Civray

La Rochelle
Châtelaillon-Plage
Ile d'Aix
Fouras
St-Pierre
Ile d'Oléron Rochefort
St-Trojan • Brouage
Ronce-les-Bains

Surgères

Dampierre-sur-Boutonne Chef-Boutonne

Aulnay

St-Jean-d'Angély

Ruffec

Rochechouart

N

20 km
10 miles

Pointe de la Coubre
Phare de Cordouan
Pointe de Grave

La Palmyre
St-Palais
Royan
Talmont

CHARENTE-MARITIME
Saintes
Cognac
Jarnac
St-Simon
Châteauneuf-sur-Charente
Plassac
Rouffiac
Blanzac
Pérignac

Brouage

CHARENTE
La Rochefoucauld

St-Simon
Bassac Vibrac
Angoulême
La Couronne

Abbaye de Puypéroux

Mortagne-sur-Gironde
PP.374–5

pp.266–7

pp.374–5

ENGLAND
English Channel
BELGIUM
LUX.
GERMANY
FRANCE SWITZ.
ITALY
SPAIN

Highlights

1 The salty islands of Noirmoutier, Yeu, Ré and Oléron
2 The Château d'Oiron's contemporary surprises
3 Medieval Poitiers and movie Poitiers
4 The Marais Poitevin
5 La Rochelle's sensational many-towered port
6 Cognac country

A hot Holland with hints of the Spanish *costas*, France's flat Atlantic coast from the Loire to the Gironde has sandy beaches stretching to the horizon. Here sunbaked terracotta roof tiles replace the slate to the north. Whitewashed houses and white stones shine blindingly in the sun. The stretch of resorts includes a few old-world charmers, such as St-Vincent-sur-Jard or Fouras, as well as bigger, brasher seaside spots like Les Sables-d'Olonne. Blissful island resorts and oyster ports float just out to sea. The coast's two great ports, La Rochelle and Rochefort, are now as busy with yachts and tourists as they once were with freighters and men-of-war.

Just inland, the marshlands turn out to be surprisingly beautiful, especially the dreamy Marais Poitevin. While the coastal flatness can be very painterly and picturesque, it becomes more monotonous further from the sea, though relieved

Food and Drink

Along large stretches of this coastline, enormous oyster and mussel parks emerge in the shallow waters as the tide goes out. The coast's other great culinary asset used to be salt. Although production has declined radically, some is still produced, the Fleur de Sel being the best quality. On the islands, the patterning of the salt pans still marks the landscape. Duck and other fowl are traditionally hunted in the marshlands behind the coast, while the sheep reared on these salty lands yield a succulent meat. White Charolais cows graze in vast numbers here too. Eels, frogs and snails thrive in the region. Eels turn up in *matelote* (stew); snails often feature on menus under the aliases of *lumas* and *cagouilles*. Further inland, pork and geese are more popular, while goats give tasty *chabichou* cheese. *Farci poitevin*, another regional speciality, combines pork with sorrel, garlic and lettuce, wrapped in cabbage leaves. Cabbage also features in regional soups, which may incorporate ham, potato and *mojettes*, big white beans which are a particular speciality of the Vendée. For the sweet-toothed, *brioche vendéenne*, a wonderfully light bread once prepared for special occasions, now makes for a wonderful breakfast. *Tourteau fromagé* is another sweet, bread-like speciality, made with *fromage blanc*.

The small amount of wine produced in this region proves of mixed quality, but that of Les Fiefs Vendéens is palatable, if a little pricey, and you can find pleasant surprises among the vineyards of the Haut-Poitou. The region's alcoholic highlight, however, is cognac, a dash of which is often added to a sauce to add depth and flavour, or mixed with grape juice to make a mouthwatering sweet apéritif, Pineau des Charente. Taste cognac by itself and you'll be hit by an extraordinarily rich array of flavours from caramels to violets. Though it seems sacrilegious, concerns about alcohol consumption have led to cognac being served as a long drink, with tonic and so on.

by gentle river valleys, most importantly the Charente, the land of cognac. One intriguing way of visiting the interior, apart from following the river valleys, is to take the Route d'Or, the medieval pilgrims' Golden Way to Santiago de Compostela, stopping at the region's wildly decorated Romanesque churches – such as those at Aulnay, Saintes or St-Savin, the last a UNESCO World Heritage Site – dating from around the time of Eleanor of Aquitaine. Poitiers, the city where she held her outrageous 12th-century troubadour court, boasts a superlative church for each day of the week. Yet while the association between Poitou-Charentes and the Middle Ages has given it an image of being stuck in the past, it is no stick-in-the-mud; this is also the land of Futuroscope, said to be the largest high-tech cinema centre in the world.

The Vendée

Noirmoutier, Yeu and the North Vendée Coast

The lovely islands of Noirmoutier and Yeu beat the resorts of the northern Vendée mainland coast hands down.

Shaped like a sperm trying to break away into the Atlantic, the seductive island of **Noirmoutier** has now been chained to the mainland by a road bridge. This salty place proves extremely fertile, and is renowned for the best spring potatoes in France. The eastern side of Noirmoutier's tail is oyster-farming territory; the western side has long beaches of soft sand and modest seaside villages. Barren salt marshes separate the northern head of the island from the rest. **Noirmoutier-en-l'Ile**, little more than a village, but the cultural capital, is overseen by a sturdy medieval **castle** (*open mid-June–early Sept daily 10–7; early Feb–mid-June and early Sept–Oct Wed–Mon 10–12.30 and 2.30–6, closed Tues; adm*) containing a small historical museum with exotica and scrimshaw brought back by sailors. The village church, concealing a crypt of stunted columns, is dedicated to St Philibert, credited with making the island fertile in the 7th century. He was a much-venerated figure in the later Dark Ages, his precious relics rushed further and further east as the Vikings pressed inland. On the opposite side of the canal from Noirmoutier's castle, creosote-boarded buildings house an aquarium, a salt house and a museum on small-scale shipbuilding, the **Musée de la Construction Navale** (*open mid-June–early Sept daily 10–7; early April–mid-June and early Sept–early Oct Tues–Sun 10–12.30 and 2.30–6, closed Mon; adm*). Superlative beaches lie to the northeast, with beach huts framed by gnarled woods.

In old documents, the **Ile d'Yeu** was in fact referred to as God's Island, l'Ile Dieu. Its mix of Breton coastline and white Vendéen houses certainly gives it a very special charm, so although it is harder to reach than the neighbouring islands, don't expect to arrive at a haven of peace. **Port Joinville**, the harbour, is busy and workaday. After the Second World War, Vichy's Marshal Pétain was imprisoned here after his death sentence was commuted, in a curious sunken citadel hidden below the water tower. The house that Pétain's wife lived in has been converted into a little historical museum. If you're on a day excursion, head for the sandy beaches east of Port Joinville. The beaches get better as you lose sight of the harbour. They end around the **Pointe des Corbeaux**, with a lighthouse and a pile of rocks that looks like a giant's pebble collection. If you have more time, hire a bike and cycle around the island, heading west from Port Joinville to the other lighthouse and along the picturesque rocky coasts. **Port des Vieilles** has the only sizeable and safe beach on the south coast.

Back on the mainland, just behind the coast, the odd modest white house or traditional thatched *bourrine* stands out like an egret in the **Marais Breton** and **Marais de Challans**, peculiarly atmospheric strips of marshlands. Grazing Charolais cows add their touches of whiteness among flat pastures divided up by little canals. The **Ecomusée du Marais Breton Vendéen-Le Daviaud** (*open May–mid-Sept Mon–Sat 2–7; Feb–April and mid-Sept–Oct Tues–Sun 2–7; adm*), behind La Barre-des-Monts, focuses on the natural life of the Marais. At **Soullans**, the modern **Musée Milcendeau-Yole** (*open July–Aug Mon–Sat 10–7, Sun 2–7; May–June and Sept Tues–Sat 10–12 and 2–6, Sun 2–6; Feb–April, Oct and Nov and Christmas Tues–Sun 2–6; adm*) presents the works of lifelong local artistic friends Charles Milcendeau and Jean Yole, the former's perceptive paintings speaking louder than the latter's words. At the **Ecomusée de la Bourrine du Bois Juquaud** (*open July–Aug Mon–Sat 10–7, Sun 2–7; May–June Mon–Sat 10–12 and 2–6, Sun 2–6; Feb–April Tues–Sun 2–6; adm*), behind St-Hilaire-de-Riez, the displays in

Getting Around

For the Ile d'Yeu, take a **boat** with Cie Yeu Continent, **t** 02 51 49 59 69, *www.compagnie-yeu-continent.fr* (*year-round*) from Fromentine; or with VIIV, **t** 02 51 39 00 00, *www.ile-yeu.com* (*late-Mar–Sept*) from Fromentine or St-Gilles-Croix-de-Vie; or **fly** with Oya Hélicoptères, **t** 02 51 59 22 22, *www.atlantique-aviation.fr* (*year-round*) from La Barre-de-Monts, south of Fromentine.

St-Gilles-Croix-de-Vie and Les Sables-d'Olonne have **railway** stations.

Tourist Information

Ile de Noirmoutier: Noirmoutier-en-l'Ile, **t** 02 51 39 80 71, *www.ile-noirmoutier.com*.
Ile d'Yeu: Place du Marché, Port-Joinville, **t** 02 51 58 32 58, *www.tourisme@ile-yeu.fr*.
St-Gilles-Croix-de-Vie: t 02 51 55 03 66, *www.stgillescroixdevie.com*.
Les Sables-d'Olonne: 1 Promenade Joffre, **t** 02 51 96 85 85, *info@ot-lessablesdolonne.fr*.

Where to Stay and Eat

Noirmoutier ✉ 85330

***Le Général d'Elbée, Place du Château, **t** 02 51 39 10 29, *www.generaldelbee.com* (*luxury–moderate*). Smart 18th-century house in the centre of the main town, with modern rooms by the pool. *Closed Oct–Mar.*
***Fleur de Sel, Rue des Saulniers, **t** 02 51 39 09 07, *www.fleurdesel.fr* (*expensive–moderate*). Bright modern hotel on the edge of town, with pool and creative cuisine. *Closed early-Nov–late-Mar; restaurant closed Sun pm and Mon.*
Les Douves, 11 Rue des Douves, **t 02 51 39 02 72, *hotel-les-douves@wanadoo.fr* (*moderate*). Stylish, modern, with pool. *Closed Jan.*
*Beau Rivage, Plage des Dames, **t** 02 51 39 06 66 (*inexpensive*). Simple rooms that overlook a splendid beach in just about the best location on the island.

L'Ile d'Yeu ✉ 85350

***Atlantic Hôtel, 3 Quai Carnot, Port-Joinville, **t** 02 51 58 38 80, *www.hotel-yeu.com* (*inexpensive*). Small, comfortable rooms, many overlooking the port. *Closed most Jan.*
L'Escale, 14 Rue de la Croix du Port, **t 02 51 58 50 28, *yeu.escale@voila.fr* (*inexpensive*). Welcoming hotel, one house with quite stylish rooms, another with simple ones.

Challans ✉ 85300

***Château de la Vérie, Route de St-Gilles-Croix-de-Vie, **t** 02 51 35 33 44, *www.chateau-verie.com* (*expensive–moderate*). Modest 16th-century château with very elegant rooms and refined cuisine. Pool and tennis court. *Restaurant closed Sun pm and Mon outside July–Aug.*

Les Sables-d'Olonne ✉ 85100

***Atlantic' Hôtel, 5 Promenade Godet, **t** 02 51 95 37 71, *atlantic@chateauxhotels.com* (*expensive–moderate*). Modern seafront hotel with many comforts, including air-conditioned rooms and indoor pool. Good seafood restaurant.
Antoine, 60 Rue Napoléon, **t 02 51 95 08 36, *www.antoinehotel.com* (*inexpensive; half-board compulsory July–Aug*). A peaceful, pleasant option in an 18th-century town house in the centre. Evening restaurant for residents only.
Beau Rivage, 40 Promenade Georges Clemenceau, **t** 02 51 32 03 01. Very special upmarket seafood restaurant (*very expensive–expensive*). *Closed Sun pm and Mon out of season and much of Jan and Oct.*
Le Galion, 18 Place Navarin, **t** 02 51 21 11 61 (*moderate*). Amusing ships' décor and large terrace with sea views. *Out of season closed Sun pm and eves Mon–Thurs, and late Nov and Jan.*

the charming little cottages reveal the traditional, quiet ways of these parts, in such contrast to the frenetic activity along the coastal strip in summer nowadays.

Long strips of pine-backed beaches alternate with long strips of modern resorts and campsites down the north Vendée coast from Noirmoutier to Les Sables-d'Olonne, sand-yachting one of the biggest crazes along these wide strands, although you can practise all manner of watersports along this stretch. **Fromentine** bustles in summer with yachtsmen. **St-Jean-des-Monts** has some pleasant enough seafront apartments, and a few that look distinctly wacky, facing the generous beach. A rash of campsites stretches to **St-Gilles-Croix-de-Vie**, an older, popular resort which trumpets its **Corniche Vendéenne**, whose rocks bring to mind outsized dollops of elephant dung. The coast seems wilder and less friendly south of St-Gilles. Just inland, go to the **church of La Chaize-Giraud** to take in the memorable worn carvings of the Annunciation and the three kings kneeling in front of a stonily indifferent Mary.

The huge beach in front of the salt marshes north of **Les Sables-d'Olonne** may be battered by waves, but the town's pride and joy is the lovely broad, protected curve of flat, safe sands backed by the Remblai promenade. To the French, Les Sables is synonymous with popular seaside holidays. The place appears a bit confusing at first sight, with commercial port, marina, conference centre, casino and several strands of water converging here. Along the seafront, modern apartment blocks have shouldered out most of the grand old bourgeois buildings, although some of the streets inland have kept their character. When the beach begins to pall, choose between a boat trip out to sea, the shorter boat tour to **Les Salines** (the commentary explaining the life of the saltworkers), the **seashells museum** by the fishing port, the **zoo**, or the **Musée de l'Abbaye Ste-Croix**, its challenging contemporary art set in a transformed historic building. Or, a car ride away, the large **automobile museum** (towards Talmont-St-Hilaire) attracts enthusiasts with models from the ancient to the more modern.

The Vendée Hills and the Guerre de Vendée

The bitter civil war known as the **Guerre de Vendée** (*see* over) takes you into the territory of Baroness Orczy's novel, *The Scarlet Pimpernel*. Her swashbuckling hero may have cocked a snook at the French Revolutionary powers of the early 1790s, but the reality in the Vendée was far different, and the people suffered appallingly for their uprising against the Revolution. Even today, when locals mention the 'Grande Guerre' they may be referring to the Guerre de Vendée, not to the First World War.

East of Challans several modern museums recall the Guerre de Vendée. **Les Lucs-sur-Boulogne** has a contemporary block of a **memorial** (*open July–Aug daily 10–7; Feb–June and Sept–Dec 9.30–6*) dedicated to its memory with an exhibition of works by contemporary artists interpreting the wars. A major Vendéen shrine is the nearby **Logis de la Chabotterie** (*open July–Aug daily 10–7; rest of year Mon–Sat 9.30–6, Sun 10–7; adm*). Effectively the anti-Revolutionary uprising came to an end in 1796 at this freckled manor, when the wounded Vendéen hero Charette was arrested. The interiors have been over-restored, but inside you can learn a lot about Charette and the war. The most moving and evocative homage to the Vendéens is the **Refuge de Grasla** (*open June–mid-Sept daily 11–1 and 2–6; May Sat and Sun 2–6; mid-Sept–mid-Oct Sun 2–6; adm*), a refugee camp of makeshift huts reconstituted in the woods a little way east of La Chabotterie.

Tiffauges, a village southwest of Cholet, may look fairly unexciting, but the main figure associated with its burly ruined **Château de Barbe Bleue** (*open July–Aug daily*

Getting Around

There are **bus** services from Angers.

Tourist Information

Le Puy du Fou: To book, contact Vendée Résa, **t** 02 51 64 11 11, *www.puydufou.com*.
Cholet: Place Rougé, **t** 02 41 62 22 35.

Where to Stay and Eat

Tiffauges ✉ **85130**
La Barbacane, 2 Place de l'Eglise, **t 02 51 65 75 59, *www.hotel-barbacane.com* (*moderate*). Welcoming, homely village hotel with lush garden and pool.

St-Laurent-sur-Sèvre ✉ **85290**
***La Chaumière, at La Trique, 1km north via N149, **t** 02 51 67 88 12 (*moderate*). Midway

between Le Puy du Fou and Cholet, comfortable old-fashioned inn with restaurant decorated with Vendéen heroes (*expensive*). *Closed late Sept and late Dec; restaurant closed Sun pm and Mon out of season.*

Cholet ✉ **49300**
***Château de la Tremblaye, **t** 02 41 58 40 17, *chateau.de.la.tremblaye@wanadoo.fr* (*very expensive–moderate*). Stylish 19th-century pastiche of a Loire château outside Cholet, with characterful rooms and restaurant (*moderate*). *Closed mid-Jan and early Feb; restaurant closed Sun pm and Mon lunch.*

Maulévrier ✉ **49360**
Château Colbert, **t 02 41 55 51 33, *colbert@ chateauxhotels.com* (*moderate*). A big, jolly, slightly tackily decorated but very good-value 18th-century castle above a wonderful oriental garden in the centre of town, with big restaurant (*expensive*). *Closed most Feb.*

11–7; rest of period May–June and Sept Mon–Fri 10–12.30 and 2–6, Sat and Sun 2–7; adm) is anything but dull. His story isn't a pretty one, yet the guides don't shy away from telling it. Gilles de Rais lived in the same period as Joan of Arc, in the early 15th century. Unlike Joan, he suffered a cruel childhood, but like her became a war hero fighting the English. However, he squandered his fortune, and had to sell his family châteaux in the Pays de Retz on the Breton border. Taken in by an alchemist, he is supposed to have descended into the vilest depravity in an attempt to restore his fortune, through all manner of appalling superstitious practices, and confessed to the violation and murder of around 150 children. How his confession was extracted isn't certain, but what is sure is that he was hanged and then burnt in Nantes for child murder on a vast scale. Bizarrely, it's said that the crowd at the execution pardoned him after he'd spoken on the virtues of a proper education. Even more strangely, after his death he apparently came to be regarded as a protector of children. The château now puts on lots of jolly entertainments for children.

The extremely well-known but more artificial **Le Puy du Fou** offers shows on a much vaster scale, a fake Gallo-Roman amphitheatre being the latest addition. A castle has stood here since 1540, with sober brick and granite galleries. In 1794 it was set on fire by the Revolutionary *colonnes infernales* and partially destroyed. The main event at Le Puy du Fou, the **Cinéscénie** (*mid-June–1st weekend in Sept Fri and Sat only, c. 10.30pm; adm*) brings together a large cast of enthusiastic locals and professional actors to recount the history of the Vendée and the Guerre de Vendée in dramatic style. During the day, the **Grand Parcours** (*open June–mid-Sept daily 10–7; adm*) in the fake villages built around the grounds also offers falconry, equestrian displays, craftspeople at work, and a show on the saintly 7th-century Philibert (*see* 'Noirmoutier', p.338).

The Guerre de Vendée

The Guerre de Vendée came about through local determination to defend the Catholic faith against radical Revolutionary policies. From 1792, uprisings multiplied as the Vendéens saw how harshly their priests were being treated. The Revolutionary national guard, referred to as *les Bleus* because of the colour of their uniforms, crushed these uprisings, at the same time destroying statues of saints and shutting churches. Resistance leaders, notably Cathelineau and Stofflet, rose from the ranks of the people. Independently, certain aristocrats led actions against the Revolutionary guards. The execution of Louis XVI early in 1793 led to protests just as the allied European powers were threatening French borders. Republican authorities, desperate for new troops, attempted to enforce conscription by lottery of 300,000 bachelors across France aged 18–40. Riots broke out around the country, but were quickly stamped out, except, through incompetence, in the Vendée. A few important army officers, notably d'Elbée and Bonchamp, even joined the Vendéen side.

The conflict escalated through June 1793, and the Vendéens experienced early victories, taking control of Cholet, and of Saumur and Angers along the Loire. Towards the end of June they even attacked Nantes. By then Cathelineau had become virtual leader of the chaotically organized Vendéens, but with his death on 29 June fortunes were reversed. Kléber and Marceau headed the violent Republican troops sent to stifle the uprising, and at the battle of Cholet in October 1793 the Vendéens suffered a bruising defeat. They retreated, well over 50,000 in number, and crossed the Loire at St-Florent-le-Vieil. Their leader Bonchamp had been mortally wounded in action, but before he died, in a memorably rare act of mercy, he asked for the lives of 5,000 captive Republican soldiers to be spared.

The action then moved north of the Loire. In a campaign known as the Virée de Galerne, the Vendéens, under the hothead Henri de La Rochejacquelin, a general at the tender age of 21, swept into the province of Maine. Some 15,000 men may have been killed in the Vendéens' terrible defeat at Le Mans in December 1793. The Vendéens suffered a further massive loss at Savenay near Nantes. Early 1794 saw the thorough devastation of the Vendéens' territories by the *colonnes infernales*, vicious troops led by the Republican Turreau, who tortured, pillaged and burned as they went along. In Nantes, Carrier organized ritual drownings of Vendéens in the Loire.

The mass fighting at last died down, to be replaced by the actions of smaller anti-revolutionary bands such as the Chouans, particularly in Brittany. In 1795 peace was negotiated between the Vendéen leaders and the Republic, but guerrilla action continued. Eventually, in 1801, the Concordat passed laws guaranteeing Catholic free-doms, but the brutal repression by the *colonnes infernales* left a deep scar across the Vendée and southwestern Anjou. Some estimates put the numbers who died between 200,000 and 300,000. The 1989 bicentennial of the Revolution wasn't seen as cause for celebration in these parts.

Cholet in southwestern Anjou is an unassuming town, but the Guerre de Vendée is presented seriously in its swanky modern museum, the **Musée d'Art et d'Histoire** (*open Wed–Mon 10–12 and 2–6; closed Tues; adm*). The most striking room contains noble portraits of the main Vendéen leaders, commissioned by Louis XVIII after the restoration of the French monarchy. The **Musée du Textile** (*open Wed–Sun 2–6; adm*) noisily recalls the textile trade responsible for Cholet's prosperity (it was renowned for chequered handkerchiefs). East of town, the **Chapelle des Martyrs** in the Forest of Nuaillé-Vezins was originally built for a local lordly family, but has been converted into a memorial to the Vendéens massacred here in March 1794.

The Southern Vendée and the Marais Poitevin

With their relative tranquillity, the resorts between Les Sables-d'Olonne and La Rochelle offer a relaxing holiday. Head east up the Sèvre Niortaise river from the Bay of Aiguillon for the magical green, watery maze of the Marais Poitevin.

The sea once lapped at the castle of **Talmont-St-Hilaire** (*open mid-June–mid-Sept daily 11–7; April–mid-June 10.30–12.30 and 2–6.30; mid-Sept–Oct 2–6; adm*), although it now lies 3kms away. The late 12th-century castle belonged to Richard Cœur de Lion. Some impressive if scrappy remnants of the ramparts and the keep survive just above the summer-busy town, and the tour round the cramped spaces is quite amusing. In July and August visitors can dress up in medieval costume.

A striped pelt on the bed at **Belesbat**, or the **Maison Clemenceau** (*open July–Aug daily 9.30–6.30; mid-May–June and Sept 10–12.30 and 2–6.30; rest of year Tues–Sun 10–12.30 and 2–5; adm*) at **St-Vincent-sur-Jard**, recalls the nickname of 'The Tiger' given to Georges Clemenceau, the famously forceful early-20th-century French socialist prime minister. Born in inland Vendée, he studied and practised medicine, partly in the US – he married an American – before becoming a politician. A man of passionately held beliefs, Clemenceau is perhaps best known for presiding over the Versailles Peace Conference at the end of the First World War. During his last years Clemenceau spent much of his time at this rented house on the beach, writing his memoirs at a plank of a desk looking out to sea. The place may look modest, but the gifts from world leaders give it an atmospheric colonial air. Peacefully old-fashioned and relatively unspoilt by modern developments, St-Vincent-sur-Jard and the little resort of **Jard-sur-Mer** look across a wide wood-fringed bay. Further down the coast **La Tranche-sur-Mer** has been colonized by campers while **L'Aiguillon-sur-Mer** is divided in two by a large estuary. The sea recedes a long way from L'Aiguillon's sensational strand at low tide, turning it into a vast muddy plain. Oysters and mussels are cultivated nearby.

The Marais Poitevin

Frogs-a-croaking, blue-velvet dragonflies flitting past, white Charolais cows munching in meadows neatly divided by countless canals...all in the shade of the most gorgeous giant poplars. The Marais Poitevin is the loveliest waterland in France, even at the height of the season when the waterways clog up with a peasoup layer of duckweed, and with tourist boats. Take to the water in a *plate* or *batai*, the local names for a punt (it is probably a good idea to get a guide for your first trip).

The Marais Poitevin's canalized marshes are of course a man-made phenomenon, the drainage work probably started by monks in the Dark Ages, continued by five local

Getting Around

This is not an easy area to reach by public transport. Look for excursion possibilities from the major towns nearby: Les Sables-d'Olonne, Fontenay-le-Comte, Niort and La Rochelle.

Tourist Information

St-Vincent-sur-Jard: Place de l'Eglise, **t** 02 51 33 62 06, officedetourisme.stvincentsurjard@ wanadoo.fr.

La Tranche-sur-Mer: Place de la Liberté, **t** 02 51 30 33 96, www.ot-latranchesurmer.fr.

L'Aiguillon-sur-Mer: t 02 51 56 43 87, www. laiguillonsurmer.com.

Fontenay-le-Comte: Tour de l'Octroi, **t** 02 51 69 44 99, www.cc-pays-fontenay-le-comte.fr.

Coulon: Place de l'Eglise, **t** 05 19 35 99 29, ot@ville-coulon.fr.

Niort and the Marais Poitevin: 16 Rue du Petit St-Jean, **t** 05 49 24 18 79.

Where to Stay and Eat

St-Vincent-sur-Jard ✉ 85520

★★L'Océan, Rue Georges Clemenceau, **t** 02 51 33 30 09, www.hotel-restaurant-ocean.com (*moderate; half-board compulsory in high*

season). A charming, relaxed hotel just inland from the Clemenceau museum. Big restaurant with lots of seafood. *Closed mid-Nov–mid-Feb.*

Velluire ✉ 85770

★★Auberge de la Rivière, t 02 51 52 32 15 (*moderate*). Hogs an exceptional spot on the edge of the marshes near Fontenay, and serves good local cuisine. *Closed Jan–Feb.*

Maillezais ✉ 85420

Le Collibert, Rue Principale, **t** 02 51 87 25 07 (*moderate*). In this restaurant they go out of their way to tempt you with local specialities, including dark eels in wine and cabbage leaves, snails, and surprising local Mareuil wines. *Closed Mon, and mid-Nov–mid-Dec and mid-Jan–Feb.*

Coulon ✉ 79510

★★★Au Marais, 46 Quai Louis Tardy, **t** 05 49 35 90 43, www.hotel-aumarais.com (*moderate*). In poll position by the punting quay, in typical buildings. *Closed mid-Dec–Jan.*

Le Central, 4 Rue d'Autremont, **t** 05 49 35 90 20 (*moderate*). Restaurant opposite the church serving regional specialities, plus a handful of basic rooms (*inexpensive*). *Closed Sun pm and Mon, and early Oct, late Jan and late Feb.*

abbeys co-operating in the Middle Ages to dig the Canal des Cinq-Abbés, and further continued by Dutch Protestants in the 17th century, hence the Ceinture des Hollandais. A major achievement in the 19th century was the drying of the western marshes, hence the division today between the Marais Désséché, which stretches from as far west as La Tranche-sur-Mer and the Bay of Aiguillon, and the Marais Mouillé in the east, which is where to go boating.

Northern gateway to the Marais Poitevin and once capital of the Bas Poitou, old **Fontenay-le-Comte** has a few old streets lined with 16th-century houses recalling a time when Fontenay flourished, although the church of Notre-Dame, its steeple soaring above them, dates mostly from the Middle Ages. Its entrance is decorated with wise and foolish virgins. Beside it, the earnest **Musée Vendéen** (*open mid-June–mid-Sept Tues–Fri 10–12 and 2–6, Sat and Sun 2–6; rest of year Wed–Sun 2–6; adm*) tells the town's history and mentions that the brilliant scholar Rabelais came here to learn Greek in 1520 before retreating to the more discreet abbey of Maillezais. The 16th-century poet Nicolas Rapin left a much more concrete mark on Fontenay with his **Château de Terre-Neuve** (*open May–Sept daily 9–12 and 3–6; adm*), built on the outskirts of town. In the Wars of Religion, when Fontenay was a Protestant stronghold, Rapin helped pen the *Satire Ménipée*, a highly influential political attack on fanatical Catholics. His château, although much restored, shows the influence of Italian style on French architecture in his time. The interior is filled with decorations such as a ceiling covered with alchemical symbols and with elaborate fireplaces.

Heading into the heart of the Marais Poitevin, it now seems improbable that rural **Maillezais** was once the seat of a bishopric. But go to one end of the village and you can visit the ruins of a vast medieval **abbey** (*open July–Aug daily 10–7; Feb–June and Sept–Dec daily 9.30–6; adm*). Founded in the 10th century by a count of Poitou, it became such an important religious centre that three dukes of Aquitaine, including Eleanor of Aquitaine's great-grandfather, were buried here. From the mid-14th century to the mid-17th, the abbey church was turned into a cathedral. A sweet little **punting port** lies just down from the abbey.

The bright village of **Coulon**, radiating from its clean-scrubbed church, is the major spot for hiring a boat. The **Maison des Marais Mouillés** (*open July–Aug daily 10–8; Feb–June, Sept–Oct, and Christmas hols daily 10–12 and 2–7; Nov 2–7; closed Mon in Mar and Oct; adm*) covers the history and ecology of the marshes. Many village houses have been turned into restaurants and shops; local specialities include angelica, derived from a plant that thrives in these parts, and *myocastor* (i.e. coypu) pâté.

Three Romanesque churches in the vicinity are particularly remarkable: **Maillé** with its entertainingly eccentric portal; **Benet**, with its delightful floating angels; and **Nieul-sur-l'Autise** (*open July–Aug daily 10–7; Feb–June and Sept–Dec 9.30–6; adm*), the most substantial, located in the supposed birthplace of Eleanor of Aquitaine, and offering interesting historical tours. **Niort** is the bustling main town on the eastern edge of the Marais Poitevin. Two enormous medieval keeps have been joined into one to oversee its vibrant centre and contain the main historical museum.

Down the Thouet

A little-sung but delightful tributary of the Loire, the Thouet flows up through the *département* of Deux-Sèvres. Our route takes you in the opposite direction, down from Thouars to Parthenay, where pilgrims once padded their way to Santiago de Compostela, and well away from the motorways rushing through western France.

Below Montreuil-Bellay (in the Loire Valley, *see* p.316), follow the Thouet to **Thouars**, a slightly scrappy town where several grand buildings stand out, including a church with an intriguing Romanesque façade full of carved figures. **Loudun** has a much better preserved historic character. A sleepy place now, in the 17th century it was shaken by scandal when a local priest was accused of bringing demons into the Ursuline convent, a story famously taken up by Aldous Huxley in *The Devils of Loudun*.

The **Château d'Oiron** (*open April–Sept daily 10.30–5.30; rest of year 10.30–4.30; adm*) rises out of the flat cereal plains like a mirage. Its French Renaissance parts were built for the Gouffier family, then it was greatly added to in the 17th century when it briefly became the property of Mme de Montespan, Louis XIV's powerful mistress. The beautiful collegiate chapel, a mix of late-Gothic architecture and Renaissance embellishments, contains a couple of finely executed 16th-century family tomb effigies as well

Tourist Information

Thouars: 3 bis Bd Pierre-Curie, **t** 05 49 66 17 65, *thouarstourisme@wanadoo.fr*.
Loudun: 2 Rue des Marchands, **t** 05 49 98 15 96.
Parthenay: 8 Rue de la Vau St-Jacques, **t** 05 49 64 24 24, *OFFICE-TOURISM@district-parthenay.fr*.

Where to Stay and Eat

Oiron ✉ 79100

★★Le Relais du Château, Place des Marronniers, **t** 05 49 96 54 96 (*inexpensive*). A rustic inn with simple rooms and hearty regional cuisine (*moderate*). *Restaurant closed Sun pm and Mon.*

Loudun ✉ 86200

★★Hostellerie de la Roue d'Or, **t** 05 49 98 01 23 (*inexpensive*). Old-style rooms in former posting inn, plus good country fare (*moderate*). *Restaurant closed Sat and Sun pm out of season.*

St-Loup-Lamairé ✉ 79600

Château de St-Loup, **t** 05 49 64 81 73, *www.chateaudesaint-loup.com* (*very expensive*). In splendid grounds, with B&B rooms in the medieval keep where the French king Jean le Bon was apparently briefly kept as a prisoner of the English after the medieval Battle of Poitiers. Meals possible for B&B guests.

Amailloux ✉ 79350

Château de Tennessus, **t** 05 49 95 50 60, *www.tennessus.com* (*expensive*). Surrounded by a moat, reached by a drawbridge, this splendid 14th-century fortress, *c.* 7km north of Parthenay off the N149 towards Bressuire, is owned by a British couple, and makes another exceptional B&B stop.

as a couple of much more gruesome ones. Claude Gouffier, a powerful figure under King Henri II, was caught in the excitement at the discovery of the New World, and followed the trend among the wealthy to gather objects from around the globe in cabinets of curiosities. Hence the crocodile, and the inspiration for the works you can see in the château. The interiors include some remarkable period rooms. Don't miss the Chambre du Roi, with its garlands and mottoes, some alluding to the bitterness of Louis Gouffier, exiled from court after being accused of plotting against Richelieu. The Cabinet des Muses drips with gold, but best of all is the breathtaking gallery with its murals of the Trojan War. However, many rooms contain wacky contemporary curiosities. In the 1990s the decision was taken not to refurnish the then neglected château according to Ancien Régime tastes but to commission modern artists and locals to create challenging pieces, playing on the theme of the cabinet of curiosities.

South from Oiron, **St-Jouin**'s fort of a church and **Moncontour's** dilapidated hilltop keep peer suspiciously at each other across the shallow Dive valley. St Jouin himself, an influential 4th-century abbot, is said to figure among the statues ranged on the Poitevin-style façade, but a wild Eve entwined by a snake steals the show. The church's long nave descends in levels to a mesmerizing choir and ambulatory bathed in a greeny-white light. Look up to see the action-packed capitals and keystones. Back on the banks of the Thouet, **Airvault** boasts the impressive Romanesque abbey church of St-Pierre, where the Poitevin style once again comes to the fore. As well as a ring of elders carved round the door, you can see the remains of one of those mysterious equestrian statues found on so many Poitou churches – thought possibly to represent the first Christian Roman emperor, Constantine. The interior details are good, too.

A medieval keep stands guard at the gates to the pure 17th-century **Château de St-Loup** (*open May–Sept daily 2–7; rest of year Sat, Sun and public hols daily 2–7; adm*), a delightfully airy building in brick and stone, with so many windows that the walls of its salons seem almost transparent. The much older keep briefly served as a prison to King Jean le Bon of France after he was captured by the Black Prince. You only see a few rooms on the ground floor, but can also wander round the elegant gardens.

Pretty bridges and a riverbank bordered by a curve of weeping willows make the Thouet particularly attractive at **Parthenay**. One bridge leads to a medieval gateway into the old town where you'll find the little local museum and tiny theatre. Climb the slope of the Rue de la Vaux St Jacques, lined with picturesque timberframe and thin brick façades, to reach the towering historic buildings of the upper town. Pass by the remnants of a church façade with another fragment of a Poitou equestrian figure, just the horse's rump protruding bizarrely, to reach the ruined medieval castle on its rocky outcrop, overlooking a bucolic bend in the Thouet.

Poitiers and Futuroscope

The capital of Poitou has known successive periods of greatnesss, even if it has very much declined in size and importance since medieval times when it was the third largest city in France, a golden period reflected in its superb Romanesque churches. The hill town still retains its historic atmosphere, though, and as a university town is fairly lively most of the time. With the creation of showy Futuroscope north of town in the 1980s, Poitiers was put firmly back on the modern map.

Poitiers lies on one of those French hilltop sites (here almost encircled by the Clain and Boivre rivers) that must have seemed an obvious base for the local Celtic tribe, in this case the Pictones or Pictavi. The Romans called the town which they developed here *Limonum*. The city became one of the most important early-Christian centres in Gaul, thanks to St Hilaire and his great protégé, St Martin, who in the 4th century founded the first monastery in France, Ligugé, just to the south. Several major historic battles were fought around the city. In 507 at the battle of Vouillé (to the northwest) the Frankish king Clovis succeeded in driving the Visigoth king Alaric II out of Poitiers, briefly one of his seats of power. Radegonde, wife of Frankish king Clothaire Ier, sought refuge from her husband's violence and taunts at her childlessness by founding a convent in Poitiers where she encouraged learning. She was considered a saint for her charitable works even before she died here in 587. When the Moors swept up from Spain in the 8th century, they reached as far north as Poitiers, and burnt down the church of St-Hilaire, but were so decisively defeated by Charles Martel, grandfather of Charlemagne, in 732 that they retreated back to Iberia.

Poitiers was the ancestral seat of Eleanor of Aquitaine's formidable family, who brought it something of a golden age with their celebrated, even notorious chivalric courts, drawing the greatest love troubadours of the day. Trade boomed and the population soared. Pilgrims poured into its splendid churches. The city first became part of the Anglo-French Angevin empire when Eleanor married Henry II Plantagenet here in 1152. The major battle of Poitiers of the Hundred Years War (in fact fought beside Nouaillé-Maupertuis to the southeast) saw the French nobility crushed and the French king himself captured by the Black Prince. Du Guesclin won Poitiers and

Poitou for the French monarchy in the early 1370s and the province then became an apparage of the feared, extravagant Jean Duc de Berry (*see* 'Bourges', p.271). When the future king Charles VII of France was chased out of Paris, he took refuge with his court in the Berry and the Loire, but also briefly in Poitou. It was in Poitiers that he was declared king in 1422. Joan of Arc, when she arrived on the scene to help him, was sent here to have her credentials and her virginity tested by the French Church before her wild claims were accepted. Poitiers' glory days were cut short with the Wars of Religion in the second half of the 16th century. The city's stagnation was to last for centuries. Since the Second World War, the university, the motorway, the TGV and Futuroscope have at last made the Poitevins look forwards.

The heart and soul of historic Poitiers despite so many competing churches, **Notre-Dame-la-Grande** boasts one of the most captivating Romanesque façades in France. At the top, Christ sits in majesty although, as with most of the other human figures,

Getting There

Ryanair flies from London Stansted to Poitiers-Biard airport. Compagnie des Radio-Taxis, **t** 05 49 88 12 34, runs 24hrs a day. Poitiers has excellent **rail** links with Paris thanks to the TGV service. Futuroscope has its own TGV station; or there's a **bus shuttle** service to it from Poitiers railway station, plus some direct services from the airport.

Tourist Information

Poitiers: 45 Place Charles de Gaulle, **t** 05 49 41 21 24, *www.ot-poitiers.fr*.

Where to Stay and Eat

Poitiers ✉ 86000

★★★**Le Grand Hôtel**, 28 Rue Carnot, **t** 05 49 60 90 60, *grandhotelpoitiers@wanadoo.fr* (*moderate*). Slightly impersonal but swish modern number set back in a small central modern precinct off this main street.

★★**Hôtel de l'Europe**, 39 Rue Carnot, **t** 05 49 88 12 00, *hoteldeleurope@wanadoo.fr* (*inexpensive*). Makes a grand impression set back in its courtyard, with traditional French rooms.

★★**Hôtel du Plat d'Etain**, 7 Rue du Plat d'Etain, **t** 05 49 41 04 80, *hotelduplatdetain@wanadoo.fr* (*inexpensive*). Pleasing, a former posting inn tucked away in a great central position behind Place du Maréchal Leclerc. *Closed mid-Dec–early Jan.*

Le Maxime, 4 Rue St-Nicolas, **t** 05 49 41 09 55 (*expensive*). Very fine restaurant where the chef performs magic with regional produce. *Closed Sat, Sun and mid-July–mid-Aug.*

Le St-Hilaire, 65 Rue Renaudot, **t** 05 49 41 15 45 (*expensive–moderate*). Don't be put off by the entrance, in a modern building: the restaurant itself is hidden in 12th-century cellars. The chef uses spices to good effect. The waiters dress in medieval style. *Closed Sun, Mon and early Jan.*

Le Pavé de la Villette, 21 Rue Carnot, **t** 05 49 60 49 49 (*moderate*). Meats are the speciality, including garlicky local kid. *Closed Sun.*

Les Bons Enfants, 11 Bis Rue Cloche Perse, **t** 05 49 41 49 82 (*moderate–cheap*). Sweet tiny restaurant. *Closed Mon and mid-Feb.*

Also look at the appealing terraces around Notre-Dame-la-Grande.

Inside Futuroscope, **Kadélicescope** offers traditional French gastronomic cuisine or a buffet of specialties from around the world. There's also a crêperie, a brasserie, a pizzeria and fast food outlets.

Chasseneuil-du-Poitou ✉ 86360

★★★**Le Clos de la Ribaudière**, 10 Place du Champ de Foire, **t** 05 49 52 86 66, *www.ribaudiere.com* (*expensive–moderate*). The best hotel near Futuroscope, away from the mayhem and modern chain hotels, in delightful grounds by the Clain river. Some of the more glamorous rooms are in a grandiose little 19th-century château, others in a modern block close to the pool.

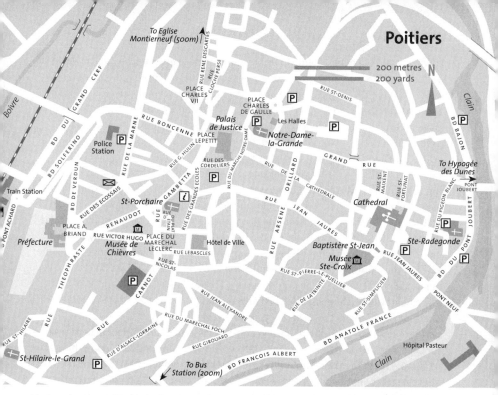

his face has been hacked off. Below his mandorla stand statues of the apostles and St Hilaire (in the top left arch) and St Martin (with his shield in front of him in the right). The best carving runs along the band above the ground floor arches, from Adam, trying to hide his private parts, via Nebuchadnezzar, to prophets holding scrolls as if the were advertisements. Then come New Testament scenes. A wealth of Romanesque creatures adds to the medieval excitement. The interior has fared less well; according to a grouchy Henry James, the geometrical patterns added inside in the 19th century were 'the most hideous decorative painting that was ever inflicted upon passive pillars and indifferent vaults'. Cafés spill out over the large pedestrian square surrounding the church, and to one side stands the busy covered market.

The **Palais de Justice** (*open Mon–Fri daily 8.45–12 and 1.15–5.30*), or law courts, now a confusing amalgam of buildings, has a core that dates back to the Plantagenets when this was the palace of Poitiers. Gothic alterations were made for Jean Duc de Berry, and much later, after the buildings had been converted into courts, a grand classical façade was added. Enter via the majestic staircase to gasp at the enormous 13th-century Grande Salle or Salle des Pas Perdus, measuring almost 160ft in length, and lacking any central columns to hold up the ceiling. Jean Duc de Berry had the splendid Gothic end done in grand style: angels hold coats of arms above the massive triple fireplace, while, much higher up, four idealized lords stand aloof. These days, when the courts are in session, lawyers in black and white garb flit in and out of the doorways of the massive room as though engaged in a theatrical farce.

Nearby, **St-Porchaire**, with its Romanesque heads on the outside, has a refined Gothic interior in which to take refuge from the busy shops of Rue Gambetta. The town hall and big department stores preside over **Place du Maréchal Leclerc**. Wide Rue Victor Hugo leads off the square to the **Musée de Chièvres** (*open June–Sept Tues–Fri 10–12 and 1.15–6, Mon 1.15–6, Sat and Sun 10–12 and 2–6; Oct–May Tues–Fri 10–12 and 1.15–5, Mon 1.15–5, Sat and Sun 2–6; adm*). Rupert de Chièvres, a wealthy 19th-century traveller, art collector and bachelor, left the splendid and varied art objects in his grand home to the town. Some of the furniture is outstanding.

Take the **Grand Rue**, with its old-style shops, down to Poitiers' still older historic quarter towards the Clain river. You come to a chaotic but fascinating array of buildings. The modern **Musée Ste-Croix** (*open same hours as Musée de Chièvres; adm*) offers a chronological introduction to Poitiers and Poitou culture, including Gallo-Roman statues and funerary stelae, exquisite and weird Romanesque carvings, and vestiges of the vanished 12th-century church of Ste-Croix – Poitiers once had many, many more churches than it does today. There are beautiful pieces of medieval Limoges work too. Most of the paintings date from the 19th and 20th centuries, a mixed bag, with the small sculptural works by the likes of Rodin, Camille Claudel, Maillol and Max Ernst.

The nearby **Baptistère St-Jean** (*open July–Aug daily 10–12.30 and 2.30–6; April–June and Sept Wed–Mon 10.30–12.30 and 3–6, closed Tues; Oct–Mar Wed–Mon 2.30–4.30; adm*) contains a rare remnant of Gallo-Roman Christianity, an octagonal baptismal font, reckoned to date from the 4th or 5th century. It is surrounded by something akin to a junk yard of Merovingian tombs covered with intriguing patterns, while the walls above bear fascinating fragments of medieval wall paintings. Compare the Christ of the Ascension, surrounded by the apostles showing their wonder in exaggerated hand gestures, angels floating along almost waving the good news, with the Christ of the Last Judgement, standing out against a dramatic black background. The faded cavaliers bring to mind the horsemen of the Apocalypse, but one rider is clearly labelled as the Emperor Constantine.

Although the city now somewhat ignores its **cathedral**, this massive, stern-faced building reflects the might of Poitiers in medieval times. On the main façade, the carved Day of Judgement stands out. Inside, the vast edifice held up on Plantagenet-style vaults contains many delightful decorative details. Kings holding a crown in each hand are a recurring motif. Don't miss the atmosphere-charged **Ste-Radegonde**, tucked out of sight below the cathedral. Radegonde founded the original church here as a funerary chapel for the nuns of the abbey of Ste-Croix, and was herself buried here. Much of the subsequent medieval edifice very much resembles the cathedral, only on a more human scale, but the Flamboyant Gothic portal is quite distinctive, with statues of Poitiers' saints. Inside, the wall paintings were added in the 13th century, but much restored in the 19th. The superb rounded Romanesque apse is held up on chunky columns with chunky decoration. In the crypt, the sarcophagus of Ste Radegonde dates from the 8th or 9th century. Then there's the monument to a footstep; legend has it that Christ appeared to Radegonde to announce her death and to tell her of the special place that awaited her in heaven – as he went off, he supposedly left an imprint of his right foot in the stone. The pretty banks of the Clain lie below this church, while from high up on the other bank, standing beside the vast gilded Virgin and Child, you get excellent views over the roofs of Poitiers.

Back in the historic centre, two major churches call for attention either end of the old heart of town. **St-Hilaire-le-Grand** to the south is by far the more spectacular, another great early-medieval pilgrimage church on the route to Santiago de Compostela. Outside, the 19th-century restorers got carried away, in particular ruining the façade, but the series of Romanesque apses decorated with animal panels and other figures is truly beautiful. Enter the church for a splendid view down to the raised choir with its thin Romanesque arcade. The nave is more striking still, and extraordinarily wide with its six side aisles. Three curious octagonal cupolas hold up the main nave bays. In the choir, one capital shows St Hilaire being placed in his tomb, while some of the faded ochre wall paintings depict dignified bishops of Poitiers and the lives of saints. Beyond St-Hilaire, the picturesque public garden, the **Parc de Blossac**, has views down on to the Clain from its shaded walks behind the remaining portions of the city's ramparts. The severe **Mortierneuf** church stands in a neglected area north of the centre, the most sidelined of the city's plethora of fascinating churches, although it was consecrated by Pope Urban II, no less, in 1096.

Futuroscope

*Entrance is expensive, but you are unlikely to regret it. For English-speaking visitors, dubbing earphones are provided at the Maison de la Vienne by the main entrance. For information and bookings in the UK, call **t** (020) 7499 8049; in France, **t** 05 49 49 30 00, www.futuroscope.com.*

Springing up in the midst of the flat Poitou farmland north of Poitiers, Futuroscope film park is at the cutting edge of world cinema. The buildings, although all created by the same Belgian group, aren't in the least harmonious: the Pavillon du Futuroscope looks as if a ball has got caught in its glass sides; organ barrels hold the Tapis Magique (Flying Carpet); the Kinémax is the dark crystal-like structure. Futuroscope claims to offer the best large-scale screens anywhere in the world, and they deliver some unforgettable visuals, even if the contents of the films themselves are of varied quality. To do the place justice takes two days. The film park was conceived and built by the Poitou-Charente regional council, Jean-Pierre Raffarin providing much of the impetus, long before he became French Prime Minister in 2002. Three of the films are devoted to the region. **Le Pavillon de la Vienne** presents two: after you have sat quietly through the bureaucratic one, you are treated to a wild ride across Poitou-Charentes, shaken around so violently in your seat that anyone with a wobbly heart should give it a miss. The **Atlantis** building, with its hemispheric screen showing 3-D presentations, also has alarmingly unstable seats. The vast Imax films are stunning, the **Kinémax** screen, the size of two tennis courts, stupendous. Other screens have their good and bad points: the circular screen is liable to cause neck ache; the **Tapis Magique** underfloor screen is a bit awkward. There are a few simpler spaces with quieter interactive presentations, computer games sections and games for younger children. Evenings end with a vulgar but vibrant fireworks show around the artificial central lake with its shooting fountains.

Around Poitiers

South of Poitiers by the Clain, **Ligugé** claims to have been the site of the first monastery in France, founded by Hilaire and Martin in 361; Martin (*see* 'Tours', p.299) spent almost ten years here. The badly cemented crypt contains tombs from the Dark Ages. The messy buildings contain a scrappy museum on monasticism and a display of enamel works produced by the monks here.

Much more charming **Nouaillé-Maupertuis**, a short way east, has medieval fortifications around its towering abbey church. The edifice encloses a large stone tomb said to be that of St Junien, painted with striking birds from the 8th or 9th century. The site of the battle of Poitiers that so marked the course of the Hundred Years War is just a modest little field nearby, with an explanatory panel and memorial.

Eastern Poitou

East of Poitiers, the Vienne and Gartempe valleys run up through quiet eastern Poitou. However, three stunning little towns stand out. For such a small place **Chauvigny** has a mighty medieval centre, with the remnants of five forts crammed into its upper village, all topped by Romanesque St-Pierre. Inside the church, the columns are sculpted with memorable, bold figures, some representing biblical characters, others monsters, including winged sphinxes wearing jesters' hats. Very rarely, one is signed: '*Gofridus me fecit*'. Chauvigny's main keep, the **Donjon de Gouzon** (*open 15 June–Aug Mon–Fri 10–12.30 and 2.30–6.30, Sat and Sun 2.30–6.30; April– 14 June and Sept–Oct daily 2–6; adm*), has been turned into a slick little museum. A funky lift takes you up to the terrace with views over the roofs and vegetable gardens in town and as far as the nuclear power station on the Vienne. On the floors below, the beautiful spaces prove more impressive than the exhibits, one level dedicated to local pottery, from Neolithic times on. Chauvigny still produces dinner services (available from La Boutique du Planty on Route de Montmorillon down in town), and several are featured here, one made for the Ritz, another starring Astérix and Obélix.

Chauvigny's biggest tourist draw takes place in the massively walled **Château Baronnial**, which holds regular displays of falconry. This château was built for the bishops of Poitiers in the early Middle Ages when they were lords of the land. The few remaining rooms in the neighbouring **Château d'Harcourt**, built a little later in the Middle Ages for the viscounts of Châtellerault, are devoted to seasonal displays by contemporary artists. Lower Chauvigny has its own attractions, including a Romanesque church, and a bathhouse turned centre for contemporary art.

Just south of Chauvigny, big lime trees shade the beautifully located **St-Pierre-les-Eglises** and its cemetery. The waters of the Vienne shimmer close by. The superb faded frescoes in the apse reflect a rare sense of movement for such early paintings, from the three kings travelling to offer their gifts to Mary and Jesus, to St Michael battling it out with a dragon. Despite the menacing towers of two nuclear power plants, **Civaux**, south along the Vienne, merits a brief halt for the most curious cemetery walls in France, constructed from Merovingian sarcophagi, carved with bold, multi-

Tourist Information

Chauvigny: 5 Rue St-Pierre, **t** 05 49 46 39 01, *www.chauvigny.cg86.fr.*

St-Savin: 20 Place de la Libération, **t** 05 49 48 11 00, *otsi-st-savin@worldonline.fr.*

Angles-sur-l'Anglin: La Place, **t** 05 49 48 86 87, *www.AnglesSurAnglin.com.*

Where to Stay and Eat

Chauvigny ✉ 86300

★★Le Lion d'Or, 8 Rue du Marché, **t** 05 49 46 30 28 *(inexpensive)*. Traditional provincial hotel in the lower village. Restaurant *(moderate)*.

St-Savin-sur-Gartempe ✉ 86310

Hôtel de France, Place de la République, **t** 05 49 48 19 03, *www.hoteldefrance86.fr* *(inexpensive)*. Nice old house on the pleasant square, with decent rooms and traditional restaurant *(moderate)*. *Restaurant closed Sun pm and Mon outside July and Aug.*

Angles-sur-l'Anglin ✉ 86260

Relais du Lyon d'Or, **t** 05 49 48 32 53, *www.lyondor.com (moderate)*. A perfect fit in the adorable upper village, a charming posting inn set back in its own courtyard, with tasty cuisine. *Closed Jan–Feb; restaurant closed Mon and Tues lunch.*

barred crosses. A little museum gives more details. **Montmorillon**, on the Gartempe river further east, has a number of impressive historic monuments on its hilltop, including a rare Romanesque octagonal building. Down below, the medieval streets have been given a new lease of life by a whole range of people setting up boutiques associated with bookmaking, including illuminated work and Arab calligraphy.

Due east of Chauvigny, the vast abbey church of **St-Savin** (*open July–Aug daily 9.30–7; April–June and Sept Mon–Sat 9.30–12.30 and 2–6, Sun 2–6; Feb–Mar and Oct–Nov daily 2–5.30; adm*) contains nothing less than the finest cycle of early medieval wall paintings in France, nicknamed the Sistine Chapel of Romanesque art, and declared a World Heritage Site by UNESCO. Four bands along the nave ceiling depict Old Testament scenes from Genesis and Exodus. God's greatness is subtly indicated by presenting him as much taller and nimbler than the mere mortals. Fallen Eve dances memorably with a snake. Noah's ark carries a comical dog's head of a prow. Noah is later shown drunk in bed, cape open to reveal his inebriated erection. Not much survives of Abraham's story, but Joseph's tribulations in Egypt remain visible. The last series, telling the story of Moses, includes memorable scenes of the horses of the Egyptian chariots jumping up as the Red Sea closes in. On the guided tour you can see further murals in the entrance porch. Unfortunately, the most interesting paintings of all, those in the crypt depicting the legend of the persecuted Christian doctors Savin and Cyprien, said by legend to have been hounded down to these parts, have been so badly attacked by fungi that they are no longer shown. Instead, a reasonable photographic copy is displayed in the chapterhouse.

Angles-sur-l'Anglin, north of St-Savin, is an utterly gorgeous village set above meanders in the Anglin river, in a corner where the Poitou meets the Touraine and Berry. Its name is supposed to derive from 5th-century Angles who settled here. The medieval **château** (*open July–Aug Wed–Mon 10–12.30 and 2.30–6.30; closed Tues; adm*) has romantically crumbling towers and lodges rising out of the limestone cliff above the river. Above the ruins, steps hewn into the rock lead up to a Romanesque chapel converted into a showroom for the local cutlery and embroidery.

Pilgrimage Churches Southwest of Poitiers

The millions of visitors rushing down the A10 between Poitiers and Bordeaux each year may think the countryside rather dull and flat. But off the motorway, or more precisely off the D950 between Poitiers and St-Jean-d'Angély, seek out some of the most exuberant pilgrimage churches in France, and the cutest donkeys in the world.

First, though, the startling stepped tumuli grouped together near **Bougon** (south of St-Maixent-l'Ecole) form one of the finest Neolithic burial sites in France, dating back to the 5th millennium BC. The slick contemporary **museum** (*open July–Aug Wed–Mon 10–7, Tues 2–7; rest of year Thurs–Tues 10–6, Wed 2–6; adm*) provides explanations. In summer, people practise supposed Neolithic revolutionary crafts in the grounds.

Melle (a good way southeast of Niort) boasts the finest equestrian statue in Poitou, thought to represent the emperor Constantine, on the church of **St-Hilaire** down in the valley. With his straight back, long flowing hair, slim figure and stern face, he looks not only dignified, but close to divine. Knights holding shields stand in the portal below. Inside, the capitals with their curvaceous monsters are superb. Two other Romanesque churches are worth seeking out in Melle: **St-Pierre**, on the edge of the hill, with further remarkable and sometimes earthy carvings; and up in the centre, recently restored **St-Savinien**. Melle's name derives from the word *metallum*, and the place produced silver coins from local mines during the Dark Ages. Learn more at the **Mines d'Argent des Rois Francs** (*open June–Sept daily 10–12 and 2.30–7.30; Mar–May and Oct–Nov weekends and public hols only 2.30–7; adm*) outside town.

Enclosed in its cypress-bound cemetery, **St-Pierre** at **Aulnay** is one of the most famous Romanesque churches in France. On the façade the equestrian statue has disappeared, but, lower down, St Peter is hanged upside down, while Christ sits in majesty. Four layers of figures, angels, knights, virgins and seasonal labourers embellish the central arch. Even better is the virtuoso display of carving on the south transept, where the most fabulous medieval creatures fight it out for space in the

Getting Around

You'd do as well to hire your own Poitou donkey to get around as to rely on public transport.

Tourist Information

Melle: 3 Rue Emilien Traver, t 05 49 29 15 10, *tourisme.pays.mellois@wanadoo.fr.*

Where to Stay and Eat

St-Maixent-l'Ecole ✉ 79400
***Le Logis St-Martin**, Chemin de Pissot, t 05 49 05 58 68, *www.logis-saint-martin.com* (*expensive–moderate*). Cosy

rooms in a prettily renovated 17th-century stone house above the Sèvre Niortaise south of town, with a delightful garden and very refined restaurant (*expensive*). *Closed Jan.*

Melle ✉ 79500
***Les Glycines**, 5 Place René Groussard, t 05 49 27 01 11 (*inexpensive*). Little hotel in a characterful medieval house, with pleasing restaurant (*moderate*). *Restaurant closed Sun pm and Mon out of season.*

Aulnay-de-Saintonge ✉ 17470
***Hôtel du Donjon**, t 05 46 33 67 67, *http://hoteldudonjon.multimania.com* (*inexpensive*). Beams, old stone and regional furniture greet you in this lovingly restored village house with smart rooms.

outer ring of the arch. They're followed by an extraordinary row of seated elders of the Apocalypse, curious kneeling men squeezed in below them. An inner semicircle of mythical creatures stands caught in an embroidery of stone. In the upper window, don't miss the amazing row of folded knights. Inside, around the capitals and the apse, more carved details cry out for attention. Just nearby, in a prettier setting, the church of **St-Mandé** has its own intriguing portal, serpents clearly an obsession.

Dampierre-sur-Boutonne has an intriguing if scruffy 16th-century **château** (*open July–Aug daily 10.30–6.30; late June and early Sept 2–6; adm*), the highlight of which is a ceiling plastered with mysterious and perhaps alchemical symbols. Follow the signs from the village to the **Asinerie du Baudet du Poitou** (*open June–Sept daily for tours 10.45, 11.30, 2.30, 3.15, 4, 4.45 and 5.30; for times Feb–May and Oct–Nov, t 05 46 24 68 94*). These utterly adorable donkeys with their heavy, tatty coats and muddy dreadlocks look like a cross between a yak and a grunge victim knocked out by a week of spliffs at Woodstock. For a greater variety of animals, visit the **Zoorama Européen** (*open May–Aug daily 9–7; April Wed–Mon 9–7, closed Tues; Feb–Mar and Oct–Nov Wed–Mon 9–12 and 2–6; closed Tues*) to the north.

La Rochelle and the Ile de Ré

La Rochelle is a wonderfully cheerful town, so when you are sipping an apéritif by its historic quays it is hard to think of the terrible squalor suffered by the British sailors once locked up in one of the sturdy medieval towers at the entrance to the port. And if you are eating at a quayside table it is hard to empathize with the besieged Protestants of La Rochelle who in 1628, in the most infamous time in La Rochelle's history, were reduced to such desperation that they ate not just rats, but leather too. The island of Ré just off the coast has become desperately chic these days.

La Rochelle

A little fishing village before the 12th century, La Rochelle, with its well-protected harbour, developed rapidly under Duke Guillaume d'Aquitaine. In 1199 his daughter Eleanor granted La Rochelle special status as a *commune*, with its first mayor, Robert de Montmirail, the first of a long line of powerful leaders of which La Rochelle is proud. The town grew rich, in particular through the export of salt and wine.

The seeds of La Rochelle's terrible entanglement with the French monarchy were sown in the 16th century, when the city became the major centre of French Protestantism. Its merchants had grown still richer by then, some of them counting among the first French to benefit from trade with Africa and the New World. As Protestants were so well protected within La Rochelle's walls, many powerful Huguenots found refuge here, including the young Henri de Navarre (much later to become King Henri IV), brought here by his formidable mother, Jeanne d'Albret. Protestantism grew more militant, and in 1568 one mayor of La Rochelle had the Catholic churches razed to the ground. Regional royal authority being ignored, in 1573 the crown decided to intervene, sending troops led by the Duc d'Anjou, the future

King Henri III, but La Rochelle successfully resisted the siege, which lasted about six months. The city became a quasi-independent Protestant state in a Catholic nation, and when Richelieu and Louis XIII, Henri IV's firmly Catholic son, decided to extract the thorn from France' side, La Rochelle called on England for protection. The Duke of Buckingham landed on Ré with his fleet in 1627, but was easily defeated by the French navy. More dramatically still, Richelieu had an elaborate mile-long sea barrage built across the entrance to the port to stop supplies reaching La Rochelle by sea. The Rochelais didn't believe it would withstand the power of the ocean, and the mayor at the time, Jean Guiton, called on the citizens never to give in. But the barrage held and the royal stranglehold proved too strong. In October 1628, the town surrendered after 13 months of terrible isolation. Only 5,000 out of a population of 28,000 survived.

However, La Rochelle revived, and although much is made of the town's sufferings for its Protestantism, not quite so much mention is made of its merchants' eager participation in the slave trade. In the 18th century La Rochelle was one of the top slaving ports in France, with 400 ships recorded heading out on expeditions; much of the glorious period architecture arose through slave-trading profits. Canadian fur was also important to La Rochelle's merchants until 1763 and the French colonial losses in North America. Slave trading was banned in the 19th century, and La Rochelle took on a much lower profile. The creation of a deep-water port north of town at La Pallice at the end of the 19th century helped revive commerce. Many prisoners, including Dreyfus, left from La Rochelle to serve a life sentence on Devil's Island in the French colony of Guyana, right up to the outbreak of the Second World War.

Like the other major French Atlantic ports, La Rochelle was turned into a Nazi submarine base in the Second World War. At the end of the conflict the Nazis clung on desperately to these vital positions, and La Rochelle was only given up to the Allies on 7 May 1945. Luckily the city avoided heavy bombardment. The strong Resistance movement which had been active around La Rochelle was honoured afterwards; one mayor, Vieljeux, was among those deported and killed by the Nazis. In recent decades, La Rochelle's fortunes have been closely associated with its long-serving socialist mayor, the dynamic Michel Crépeau, who died in 1999. An early environmentalist, he made the preservation of the old town a model of urban conservation in France.

All three spectacular medieval towers on La Rochelle's **Vieux Port** are open to the public (*open July–Aug daily 10–7; mid-May–June and early Sept 10–12.45 and 2–6.30; Jan–mid-May and mid-Sept–Dec Tues–Sun 10–12.30 and 2–5.30; adm*). The **Tour de la Lanterne**, by far the tallest with its crocketed Gothic spire, served not just as a seamark for centuries but also as a prison, and inside is covered with centuries-old graffiti of British and Dutch sailors. From the top of the tower, a cordon of trees marks where the ramparts once ran; these elegant gardens, much appreciated by the Rochelais, end with the **Plage de la Concurrence**, although the estuary outside La Rochelle is hardly an ideal spot for a swim. At the narrow neck of the entrance to the inner port, the **Tour de la Chaîne** and the **Tour St-Nicolas** stand guard opposite each other, divided only by a thin channel. A chain used to be strung between them in centuries past to regulate trade and to stop illicit traffic passing through at night. The interior of the **Tour de la Chaîne** proves a bit of a disappointment, with its panels in

French recalling the town's history. Behind, restaurants line the historic quay, the **Cour des Dames**, which leads to the chubby statue of Victor-Guy Duperré, twenty-second child of a Rochelais family, who grew up to become a scourge to the British on the seas in the early 1800s. He wasn't popular with the Algerians either, after commanding the fleet which captured Algiers in 1830, leading to the founding of France's North African colonies. Beyond Duperré's statue the gateway through the mighty **Grosse Horloge tower** beckons. This tower is another landmark of the Vieux Port. The original building dates from the 14th century, part of the city's formidable

Getting There and Around

Ryanair and Flybe **fly** from the UK. The **shuttle bus** from the airport to central Place de Verdun takes *c.* 15–30mins. **For taxis:** Abeilles, **t** 05 46 41 22 22/**t** 05 46 51 55 55 or Auto Plus, **t** 05 46 34 02 22. For local **bus** information contact RTCR, **t** 05 46 34 02 22. Régie d'Aunis-Saintonge, **t** 05 46 09 20 15, runs **bus** services all year from La Rochelle's Place de Verdun to the island of Ré.

Boat Trips

Companies by the **Vieux Port** (Cours des Dames) offering mini-cruises round the nearby islands of a couple of hours, half-day or day include:

Croisières Océanes, t 05 46 50 68 44.
Croisières Inter-Iles, t 05 46 50 51 88.
Ré-Croisières, t 05 46 41 50 40.
Navipromer, Tour de la Châine, **t** 05 46 01 52 96.

For sea journeys from **Les Minimes,** try:
Kapalouest, 32 Av des Amériques, **t** 05 46 29 26 55. A mini-catamaran.
Notre-Dame des Flots, t 05 45 32 17 63, *notredamedesflots@yahoo.fr.* To tour on an old-fashioned sailing boat.
Association Loisirs de la Mer, at Les Minimes, **t** 05 49 52 97 80. Sea-fishing trips.
Cap' Mousse, t 06 61 50 42 25, **Yacapartir, t** 06 87 04 02 71, and **Destination Océan, t** 05 46 45 17 29. Yachting trips with skippers.
Rivages, t 05 46 44 70 93. To hire a yacht.

Aunis Motonautic, t 05 46 44 23 66. To hire a motorboat.

Tourist Information

La Rochelle: Place de la Petite Sirène, Le Gabut, **t** 05 46 41 14 68, *www.larochelle-tourisme.com.*
Ile de Ré: 5 Rue de la Blanche, Le Bois-Plage-en-Ré, **t** 05 46 09 00 55, *www.iledere.fr.*

Where to Stay and Eat

La Rochelle ✉ 17000

****Résidence de France,** 43 Rue du Minage, **t** 05 46 28 06 00, *www.hotel-la-rochelle.com* (*very expensive–moderate*). The loveliest central hotel, a 16th-century inn embellished by a new tower set around an interior courtyard, with stylish décor. **Le Patio** restaurant (*moderate*) has a crisp white dining terrace.
***St-Jean-d'Acre,** 4 Place de la Châine, **t** 05 46 41 73 33, *www.hotel-la-rochelle.com* (*moderate*). In great location overlooking the old port, in characterful old buildings. Several restaurant possibilities.
***France-Angleterre et Champlain,** 20 Rue Rambaud, **t** 05 46 41 23 99, *www.bw-fa-champlain.com* (*moderate*). Former convent from the 17th century, with plenty of charm, hidden behind its walls, with garden. Mix of traditional and contemporary rooms.

medieval ramparts, but in the 18th century the tower was embellished with its elaborate top, including its terrestrial and celestial globes. On the other side of the Vieux Port, the **Tour St-Nicolas** was constructed as a residence for the port governors in the 14th century. Worn Gothic figures and devices look over the intriguing labyrinth of little rooms and stairways, where it's easy to become disoriented.

A short walk into town from the Quai Duperré at the back of the Vieux Port takes you to the grand **Place de l'Hôtel de Ville**. The statue in the centre represents a defiant Jean Guiton, mayor at the time of Richelieu's siege. Although he failed to withstand the siege, although he failed to follow his promise to kill himself rather than surrender, and although he even went on to join the French navy afterwards, he has gone down in La Rochelle as a hero, a symbol of the city's proud defiance. Behind the crenellated Gothic walls of the town hall courtyard, a colourful, almost comical ceramic statue of Henri IV pops up under a canopy, sporting caramel leggings and a purple top. The more restrained Baroque caryatids in the exquisite courtyard below represent Prudence, Justice, Fortitude and Temperance.

Trianon, 6 Rue de la Monnaie, **t 05 46 41 21 35, *www.hoteltrianon.com* (*moderate*). Charming old-style hotel closer to the little beach and gardens, with traditional restaurant. *Closed Christmas–Jan; restaurant closed Sat lunch and Sun out of season.*

Henri IV, 31 Rue des Gentilshommes, **t 05 46 41 25 79, *HENRI-IV@ wanadoo.fr* (*moderate– inexpensive*). In a 16th-century building right in the historic centre, by the Grosse Horloge.

Richard Coutanceau, Plage de la Concurrence, **t** 05 46 41 48 19 (*very expensive–expensive*). Very stylish, renowned for inventive seafood dishes, looking out to sea. *Closed Sun.*

Les Flots, 1 Rue Chaîne, **t** 05 46 41 32 51 (*expensive–moderate*). More creative dishes from the same family as the above, looking out on to the towers of the Vieux Port.

André, 5 Rue St-Jean du Pérot, **t** 05 46 41 28 24 (*moderate*). A seafood institution in the centre of historic La Rochelle, with its long front resembling a ship.

A Côté de Chez Fred, 30 Rue St-Nicolas, **t** 05 46 41 65 76 (*moderate*). Surprising little fish restaurant attached to the adjoining fishmonger's. *Closed Sun and Mon.*

Café du Nord (*cheap*). A good bet among the touristy restaurants on the Vieux Port.

La Flotte-en-Ré ✉ 17630

****Le Richelieu, 44 Av de la Plage, **t** 05 46 09 60 70, *www.hotel-le-richelieu.com* (*luxury– expensive*). The most exclusive address on

Ré: a beautiful, luxurious hotel in this wonderful village, with a thalassotherapy centre, pool and tennis, and fantastic restaurant (*expensive*). *Closed early Jan–early Feb.*

St-Martin-de-Ré ✉ 17410

***La Jetée, 23 Quai Georges Clemenceau, **t** 05 46 09 36 36, *www.multi-micro.com/ lajetee* (*expensive–moderate*). Stylish modern hotel by the port, with rooms around a patio.

Les Colonnes, 19 Quai Job Foran, **t 05 46 09 21 58 (*moderate*). More typical building at the heart of the action by the port, with a bar spilling out below. Has one of the most popular of the restaurants by the waterside. *Closed mid-Dec–Jan; restaurant closed Wed.*

*Le Sully, 19 Rue Jean Jaurès, **t** 05 46 09 26 94 (*inexpensive*). For a pleasant cheaper option, in the shopping streets up from the port.

La Baleine Bleue, Quai Launay Razilly, **t** 05 46 09 03 30 (*moderate*). Irresistible restaurant on the port's central island, attracting the smart set.

Le Bois-Plage-en-Ré ✉ 17580

L'Océan, 172 Rue St-Martin, **t 05 46 09 23 07, *www.re-hotel-ocean.com* (*expensive– moderate*). Delightful relaxing hotel in a relatively unspoilt part of the island, with a typical regional design and a maritime feel, plus stylish restaurant (*moderate*). *Closed early Jan–early Feb; restaurant closed Wed.*

Many of La Rochelle's arcaded streets lie around the town hall and behind the Grosse Horloge. **Rue du Palais** and **Rue Chaudrier** form the main, grand shopping drag. Here two great civic buildings, the **Bourse** and the **Palais de Justice**, stand side by side. Stone prows of vessels and naval trophies stick out of the ornate exchange (now the chamber of commerce), while the decorations of the law courts are more discreet. One curiosity among the tempting shops around here is the **Musée du Flacon à Parfum** (*open Tues–Sat 10–12 and 2–7, Mon 2–7; adm*), along the Rue du Temple, with its extensive collection of scent bottles.

The town's best museum, the **Musée du Nouveau Monde** (*open Mon and Wed–Sat 10.30–12.30 and 1.30–6, Sun 1.30–6; closed Tues; adm*), is one of the few in France to confront the subject of slavery seriously. The story is told in good part by displaying the luxuries purchased on the proceeds of the trade, including the sumptuous mansions which house the museum. One of the two, the Hôtel Fleuriau, was named after a shipowning family who had a flourishing plantation on Santo Domingo; it is estimated that in the 18th century La Rochelle ships alone transported some 140,000 slaves from West Africa to the West Indies, principally to Santo Domingo. The paintings and engravings offer an insight into the often disturbing mentality of the period. The revolutionary mementoes of the anti-slavery movement are much more heartwarming. Napoleon then reinstated slavery, but the trade declined after him. The museum also has an exceptional series of photos of Indian chiefs by Edward S. Curtis.

Although the **Musée des Beaux-Arts** (*open Wed–Mon 2–7; closed Tues; adm*) is housed in another grand mansion nearby, the Hôtel de Crussol d'Uzès, the collections have been shoved unceremoniously to the top of the building, reached by a shoddy staircase. At the entrance, the black and white representations of Christ's story by Rouault are striking, but they're followed by a chaotic display of mainly cloying, overblown canvases. Bouguereau, born in La Rochelle and a great Salon favourite for his purer than pure nudes, comes out comparatively well here with a touching portrait of Mme Deseilligny. Also compare some classic maritime scenes with a vibrant Signac pointilliste view of La Rochelle.

Across on one corner of the massive, barren **Place de Verdun**, the **cathedral** proves rather vacuous behind its wide classical façade, and contains some truly sickly 19th-century decoration, both in the stained glass and the paintings. Blame Bouguereau for the worst excesses in the choir end. The sailors' ex-votos are more moving.

The **Musée d'Orbigny-Bernon** (*open Mon and Wed–Sat 10–12 and 2–6, Sun 2–6; closed Tues; adm*) has more charm than the fine arts museum. Ceramics from around France are the forte. Some striking engravings illustrate the siege of La Rochelle and the persecution of Protestants. Further sections are devoted to Oriental miscellany and to the Second World War. Around the corner, stone heads pop out startlingly from the **Maison Vennette**, an elaborate mansion built for a doctor who decorated his home with busts of famous medical figures from down the ages. The highlight of the **Muséum d'Histoire Naturelle** (*undergoing restoration; check times with tourist office*) is an 18th-century cabinet of curiosities. Those particularly interested in the history of Protestantism might visit the little **Musée Protestant** (*open July–15 Sept Mon–Sat 2.30–6; adm*) back near the Vieux Port behind Quai Duperré, next to the large Protestant church, the wonkily arcaded **Cloître des Dames Blanches** an oasis of peace on the other side.

On the south side of the Vieux Port, quayside cafés and restaurants front the attractive modern village of the **Gabut quarter**. La Rochelle's modern museums lie beyond its new, ultra-modern **aquarium** (*open July–Aug daily 9am–11pm; April–June and Sept 9–8; Oct–Mar 10–8; adm*), one of the best in France, with sensational lighting effects and a shark pool where you almost feel you're plunging in with the creatures. The main exhibits at the **Musée Maritime Neptunéa** (*open April–Sept daily 10–6.30, or 7.30 July–Aug; Feb–Mar and Oct 2–6.30; adm*) are real ships, several of which you can board. The rest of this major educational museum occupies the former fish market. Further south, the **Musée des Automates** and **Musée des Modèles Réduits** (*open 15 June–Aug daily 9.30–7; Feb–May and Sept–Oct 10–12 and 2–6; Nov–Jan 2–6; adm*) might amuse youngsters, the first with its animated figures, the second with some quite splendid model boats. South again, you arrive at **Les Minimes**, La Rochelle's massive modern marina, full of fabulous real boats (*see* p.358 for trips).

Ile de Ré

The Ile de Ré's similarity in name to the Egyptian sun god Ra acts as a reminder of the fact that this island is a highly prized destination for French sun-worshippers, who enjoy its special microclimate. The opening in 1988 of a road bridge (*expensive toll*) connecting it with the mainland has made the island somewhat less exclusive, and more clogged up with traffic. **Rivedoux**, closest to the bridge, is too close to the industrial quarters of La Rochelle for comfort, but its sandy beach is popular. Heading along the southern side of the island, **Ste-Marie-de-la-Mer**, with old fish farms among its rocks, has old streets full of charm, with shutters painted various shades of green. **Le Bois-Plage**, close to long stretches of sand, is the island's wine centre. The southern road continues to purpose-built **La Couarde**, popular for its beaches.

The road north from the toll bridge leads past the roofless Cistercian **Abbaye des Châteliers** and round **La Flotte**, a stylish village, home to Ré's new thalassotherapy centre. Its delightful strip of beach backed by pines dwindles to nothing at high tide, but the **Maison du Platin** (*open April–Oct Mon–Fri 10.30–12.30 and 2.30–6, plus summer Sun 2.30–5.30; adm*), from the name given to the stretch of sand revealed at low tide, gives a taste of traditional Ré life. **St-Martin-en-Ré** is Poitou-Charente's answer to St-Tropez. Even if the yachts are smaller here, they congregate in impressive number around the gorgeous circular harbour, a perfect stage for Côte d'Azur-style posing, restaurants and boutiques all around. Climb the church tower for a wider view of the port and the island. The **Musée Ernest Cognacq** (*open July–Aug Wed–Fri 10–7, Sun 2–7; rest of year Wed–Fri 10–12 and 2–6, Sun 2–6; adm*), named after the celebrated founder of Paris' Seine-side Samaritaine department store, who was born in the town, uses the medieval and Renaissance wings of a fine town house to present diverse historical and art collections. Even the St-Martin penitentiary, set among the pointed Ancien Régime fortifications just inland, looks quite picturesque.

Heading towards the western part of the island, a road branches off north to **Loix**, past the isolated whitewashed building of the **Ecomusée du Marais Salant** (*open June–Sept daily 10–12.30 and 2–7; April–May daily 2–6; mid-Feb–Mar and Oct–mid-Nov daily 2–5; adm*), which recalls the strong salt-making tradition of Ré and offers daily guided walking tours. The spiky Gothic spire of the church of **Ars-en-Ré** serves a second purpose, as a seamarker, hence the striking black and white paint. Beyond **St-Clément-des-Baleines**, with its centre on Ré flora and fauna, the **Phare des Baleines** lighthouse stands out, open to visitors for its great views. The **Arche de Noé zoo** (*open June–Aug daily 10.30–7; April–May daily 2–7; Sept–Oct daily 2–6.30; adm*) close by particularly honours a huge turtle that landed on Ré in 1978. **Les Portes-en-Ré** lies tucked away in the least accessible corner of the island, and close to some of the best beaches, suffering less from the far receding tides. The **Maison du Fier** (*open summer Sun–Fri 10–12.30 and 3–7, Sat 3–7, closed Mon; rest of year exc Dec and Jan weekends and school hols 3–6; adm*) presents the natural world on Ré, to be discovered more closely on foot in the Réserve Naturelle de Lilleau des Niges.

The Coast South from La Rochelle

Châtelaillon-Plage was once the medieval capital of the little region of Aunis below Poitou, but now has the cheerful look of a small, modern seaside resort, with lots of hotels lined up behind the mimosas of the promenade. **Fouras**, by contrast, has kept a strong historical atmosphere. A splendid solid medieval **keep** (*open June–15 Sept Tues–Sun 10–12 and 3–6.30; rest of year Sun and public hols 2.30–5.30; adm*) sticks out from a high prow of land above the beaches. Fortifications here have long guarded the northern entrance to the Charente river. The main building dates from the 15th century, while Vauban had further layers of defence added in the 17th. The museum inside contains a miscellany of sea shells, maps and models – navies often fought off the waters of Fouras, most notably in 1809, when much of the French fleet was destroyed by the British in the *Journée des Brûlots*, the Day of the Fire Ships. A spit of land, the **Pointe de la Fumée**, tapers off north of Fouras. From its tip packed with oyster farms take a ferry out to the **Ile d'Aix**, a tiny crescent of an island that produces exotica in mother-of-pearl and conceals a concentration of Napoleonic memorabilia

Getting Around

There is a local **rail** link between La Rochelle and Rochefort, and **bus** services to the resorts.

Tourist Information

Châtelaillon-Plage: 5 Av de Strasbourg, t 05 46 56 26 97, *www.chatelaillon-plage.fr*.
Fouras: Av du Bois Vert, t 05 46 84 60 69, *www.fouras.net*.
Rochefort: Av Sadi Carnot, t 05 46 99 08 60, *www.tourisme.fr/rochefort*.

Where to Stay and Eat

Châtelaillon-Plage ✉ 17340

**Les Flots, 52 Bd de la Mer, t 05 46 56 23 42 (*moderate–inexpensive*). A bright seafront address, plus really appealing seafood restaurant (*moderate*) with terrace. *Closed mid-Dec–Jan; restaurant closed Tues*.
**Majestic, Place St-Marsault, t 05 46 56 20 53, *www.majestic-chatelaillon.com* (*moderate–inexpensive*). Grand 1920s building by a lovely plane-lined avenue, not far from the beach. Restaurant. *Closed Jan*.

Fouras ✉ 17450

**Grand Hôtel des Bains, 15 Rue du Général Brüncher, t 05 46 84 03 44, *www.perso.* *wanadoo.fr/grand.hotel.des.bains* (*moderate–inexpensive*). Set around a large, summery courtyard, this well-run, clean and charming hotel was once a lovely inn. Restaurant for residents only (*dinner only; moderate*). *Closed Nov–Easter*.
**La Roseraie, 2 Rue du Port Nord, t 05 46 84 64 89 (*inexpensive*). Equally delightful hotel at the base of the Pointe de la Fumée. It looks like a large friendly family villa.
La Jetée, Pointe de la Fumée, t 05 46 84 60 43 (*moderate*). The best place for fresh seafood.

Rochefort ✉ 17300

***La Corderie Royale, Rue Audebert, t 05 46 99 35 35, *www.corderieroyale-hotel.com* (*luxury–moderate*). Excellent central location in a wonderful 17th-century building offering peace away from the crowds by the Charente. Rooms are very comfortable, the cuisine of a high standard. Swimming pool in a lovely courtyard.
**Roca Fortis, 14 Rue de la République, t 05 46 99 26 32 (*inexpensive*). In a bright old-stone town house with courtyard, the rooms may be a bit worn, but are spacious and full of character, and the place is well run.
L'Escale de Bougainville, Quai de la Louisiane, t 05 46 99 54 99 (*expensive–moderate*). The most reputed cuisine in town, with stylish dining rooms opposite the marina. *Closed Sun pm and Mon, and mid-Jan*.

in its **Musée Napoléon** (*open June–Sept daily 9.30–6.30; rest of year Wed–Mon 9.30–12.30 and 2–5, closed Tues; adm*). The house was built for the megalomaniac himself in 1808 and it was here that he spent his last days on French soil in July 1815, before being shipped off to St Helena. The television game-show star **Fort Boyard** (*not open for visits*) lurks out to sea, its massive oval defence started under Napoleon Ier, completed under Napoleon III. In 1871 it was turned into the Alcatraz of the Atlantic, receiving Communards from the failed uprising in Paris.

Rochefort

Rochefort, an extremely handsome, muscular town, was born a child of war. In the 1660s it grew rapidly into a square-shouldered worker to construct a fleet for the Sun King capable of taking on the great sea powers of the time, England and Holland. Rochefort seemed ideally located: it lay up the Charente estuary, 15km from the sea, protected from the weather and easy to defend. Vast war vessels were put together here. A grand grid of streets up from the river was constructed under Michel Bégon, the royal naval *intendant* at the end of the 17th century, now best known for giving his name to the begonia plant. Shortly before the Revolution, in 1780, Lafayette sailed from here on his second expedition to America, on board the *Hermione*. But orders dried up at the start of the 20th century, and in 1944 the Nazis torched some of the great old riverside buildings before leaving. Depressed, bruised and blackened, Rochefort waned. Things began to look up when Jacques Demy shot a successful musical here in the 1960s: *Les Demoiselles de Rochefort*, starring Catherine Deneuve. The grid of streets, now scrubbed clean, is lined with palms.

Down by the Charente, the **Corderie Royale**, one of the historic buildings to have survived, looks stunningly long, supported on one side by scrolled buttresses. Ships' ropes were laid out, twisted and treated here. The **Centre International de la Mer** (*open April–Sept daily 9–7; rest of year 9–6; adm*) inside offers a permanent exhibition on ropemaking, plus temporary exhibitions. Beyond one end of the Corderie Royale and the provisions building which could churn out 20,000 kilos of bread a day, the dock has been transformed into Rochefort's yacht marina. Beyond the other end, a fascinating copy of Lafayette's *Hermione* (*guided tour only; open July–Aug daily 10–7; rest of year 10–1 and 2–6; adm*) is being put together using old-fashioned techniques. The name is a bit of a cheat, as the new ship is actually modelled on the old frigate *Concorde*, whose plans ended up in Greenwich when the vessel was seized by the British. In the olden days, some 1,500 workers might have taken a year to complete such a vessel; the new *Hermione* was started in 1997 and should be completed by 2007. On weekday tours you can often see specialist craftsmen at work. Further splendid vessels are the glory of the **Musée de la Marine** (*open April–Sept daily 10–6.30; Oct–mid-Nov and mid-Dec–Mar Wed–Mon 10–12 and 2–5, closed Tues; adm*), set in an elegant building just up from the *Hermione*, only this time they are scale models. You can also examine elaborately engraved pieces, including coconuts, carved by the prisoners who did much of the shipbuilding work. Beyond the **Porte du Soleil**, once the imposing main entrance to the arsenal, you enter the upper town, an elegant building converted into a covered market standing opposite the gateway.

Grandiose **Place Colbert** is the centre of city life in the grid plan town, the intimidating classical church of **St-Louis** rising over one corner, away from all the cafés. Not far off, the **Maison Pierre Loti** (*guided tour only; open July–15 Sept daily 10–6, tours every half-hour; rest of year Wed–Mon, tours at 11, 12, 2, 3 and 4; closed Jan; adm*) may not look much on the outside, but a riot of decoration awaits within, created by a man whose 'life was one long carnival,' according to one 19th-century admirer. Loti, born here in 1850, was in fact baptized Julien Viaud. He gained his pen name on Tahiti, once he had become a sailor; he also began writing exquisite romantic fiction. The entertaining if over-reverent tour takes you past the bourgeois rooms with family portraits to a richly decorated Renaissance hall and a grand medieval room. Much play is made of Loti falling in love with a young Turkish woman on his first journey to Istanbul, but no mention is made of the fact that he also had quite an appetite for sex with men. On his trips around the world he picked up a lot of exotica and half-digested ideas: hence the Arab room, the Turkish salon and the travesty of a mosque. But Loti was also a dedicated defender of the foreign peoples he visited. His novels are today somewhat neglected, but in 1891 he was elected to the Académie Française, beating one Emile Zola for the honour. The **Musée d'Art et d'Histoire** (*open July–Aug daily 1.30–7; rest of year Tues–Sat 1.30–5.30; adm*) close by contains a splendidly detailed scale model of Rochefort from 1835, and the town's art collections, while the **Musée des Commerces d'Autrefois** (*open 15 Mar– 15 Nov daily 10–12 and 2–7; rest of year daily 10–12 and 2–6; adm*) pays homage to the shops of yesteryear.

On the busy boulevard encircling Rochefort's centre, the grand 18th-century **Ancienne Ecole de Médecine Navale** (*open Feb–15 Nov Tues–Sun; closed Mon; adm*) housed the first naval hospital in the world, and still contains a cabinet of curiosities. Plant-lovers head half a mile out of the centre for the **Conservatoire du Bégonia** (*guided visits only; book via tourist office: tours Tues–Sat at 2, 3, 4 and 5; adm*). A further half-mile out takes you to the unmissable **Pont Transbordeur de Martrou**, built in 1900, marking the flat landscape south of Rochefort almost as sensationally as the modern toll bridge over the Charente river.

Fantastically preserved in a time warp, the silting old harbour of **Brouage** south of the Charente was going out of use as Rochefort was going up. Founded in 1555 for trading in lucrative salt, it produced one of France's most famous explorers, Samuel de Champlain, Protestant founder of Quebec. During the siege of La Rochelle, Richelieu had the place turned into a heavily defended arsenal. But by the end of the 17th century, silting and the decline in the salt trade led to its abandonment. It's a pleasure now walking round the top of the town's splendid graffiti-covered ramparts, isolated in the midst of wide green marshland and saltpans.

The Ile d'Oléron

Oystery Ile d'Oléron, a large, laid-back island extremely popular with campers, is linked to the mainland by one of the longest bridges in France. At high tide the channel between mainland and island fills with seawater, but at low tide extensive mudflats and oyster beds lie exposed. **St-Trojan**, at the southern end of the island, is the best place to stay. To find the nearest beach, head a good walk south for the

Getting Around

You can get to Royan by **train** via Saintes.

Tourist Information

St-Trojan-les-Bains: Carrefour du Port, t 05 46 76 00 86, *OT-ST-TROJAN-LES-BAINS@ wanadoo.fr*.
Le Château d'Oléron: Place de la République, t 05 46 47 60 51, *www.ot-chateau-oleron.fr*.
St-Pierre-d'Oléron: Place Gambetta, t 05 46 47 11 39, *www.oleron.org/saint-pierre/*.
St-Palais-sur-Mer: 1 Av de la République, t 05 46 23 22 58, *www.saint-palais-sur-mer.com*.
Royan: Palais des Congrès, t 05 46 23 00 00, *www.royan-tourisme.com*.

Where to Stay and Eat

L'Ile d'Oléron/St-Trojan ⊠ 17370
**L'Albatros, 11 Bd du Dr Pineau, t 05 46 76 00 08 (*inexpensive*). In a delightful location right by the southern coastal path, unspoilt by roads, with a terrace right by the sea – a special little place even if the rooms aren't that exciting. *Closed early Nov–early Feb.*
**La Forêt, 16 Bd Pierre Wiehn, t 05 46 76 00 15, *hotellaforetoleron.com* (*moderate–inexpensive*). Big modern block set among shady trees, with pool. *Closed Oct–Mar.*

La Belle Cordière, 76 Rue de la République, t 05 46 76 12 87 (*moderate*). Attractive restaurant serving inventive cuisine.

Le Gua ⊠ 17680
***Moulin de Châlons, 2 Rue du Bassin, t 05 46 22 82 72, *chalons@chateauxhotels. com* (*expensive–moderate*). Big old block of a tidal mill giving you an excellent flavour of the watery landscapes typical of this coastal strip. Well-renovated rooms and good restaurant. *Closed early Jan–early Feb; restaurant closed Sun and Mon out of season.*

St-Palais-sur-Mer ⊠ 17640
***Résidence de Rohan, Route de St-Palais, Vaux-sur-Mer, t 05 46 39 00 75, *www.residence-rohan.com* (*expensive–moderate*). Appealing rooms split between a charming 19th-century villa and a modern block set in shaded grounds with a pool and tennis court. *Closed mid-Nov–mid-Mar.*
**Téthys, 60 Av de la Corniche, Nauzan, t 05 46 23 33 61 (*inexpensive*). Very well located. Some rooms have sea views, as does the dining room. *Closed Oct–April.*

Meschers-sur-Gironde ⊠ 17132
**Les Grottes de Matata, Bd de la Falaise, t 05 46 02 70 02 (*inexpensive*). Modern building with majestic views over the Gironde estuary, plus crêperie in a cave.

glorious wide **Plage de Gatseau**, a couple of beach bars sinking into its powdery sands backed by woods. There's also a beachside Novotel thalassotherapy centre (*www. thalassa.com*). Unfortunately, it's not the best place for bathing due to the tidal squeeze between island and mainland; for safer swimming, try the **Grande Plage** on the southwestern tip of Oléron, with a black mussel-clad wreck stranded in its sands.

Le **Château d'Oléron** is the most important historic village on the island, although it in fact has a substantial **citadel** rather than a castle, commissioned by Richelieu. The very modest port below is strung along the channel coming in from the sea. From Le Château, meandering lanes lead up through the attractively shabby territory of the eastern oyster farms to **St-Pierre-d'Oléron**, the island's bright little capital. In the small **Musée de l'Ile d'Oléron Aliénor d'Aquitaine**, Pierre Loti (*see* 'Rochefort', above), whose family had a holiday home in this village, is better remembered than the great Eleanor of Aquitaine.

Back by the coast, **Boyardville** served as the base for the builders of Fort Boyard and has now become a popular tourist port for ferries around the islands. Continue north for a truly splendid curve of pale sandy beach, the **Plage de la Gautrelle**. The island becomes drabber as you reach the northern tip with its big black and white striped lighthouse. Much of the west coast is marred for beach-lovers by rocks sandwiched between the sand and the sea, and the plastic rubbish brought in by the tides.

Ronce to Royan, and the Gironde

Moving back to the mainland, by Marennes, above the extensive oyster parks in the Seudre estuary, the impressive 18th-century **Château de la Gataudière** (*open June–Sept daily 10–12 and 2–6; April–May and Oct–Nov daily 10–12 and 2–5; adm*) has retained period furniture, and the memories of semi-illustrious owners. **Ronce-les-Bains** south of the Seudre estuary, is a cheerful, simple, shaded resort protected by Oléron's tail. The piny hillocks of the **Forêt de la Coubre** bobble up and down south to the tall thin phallus of the lighthouse of La Coubre. The exposed Atlantic coast beyond is highly dangerous, with strong undercurrents and shifting sandbanks. The deafening roar of the waves should put you off taking a dip, but the vast stretches of untouched dunes are impressive. Things calm down beyond the Pointe de la Coubre, where a row of popular resorts looks across the vast mouth of the Gironde estuary. In the midst of the estuary, the **Phare de Cordouan** (*see* p.421) sticks up like a bizarre little tongue. Modern **La Palmyre** has purpose-built, Spanish-style villas under the pines, a marina, and an absurdly packed zoo in summer. Beaches lead on down to St-Palais, the nudist one wildly popular with gay men. **St-Palais-sur-Mer** has a genteel charm. By far the most stylish resort along this stretch, it offers a string of little rocky creeks, large fishing nets suspended picturesquely above.

Much of central **Royan** was destroyed by bombing in the Second World War, hence the mishmash of modern architecture, but it is hugely popular as a summer resort, thanks to its large, well-protected curve of sand which appeals to those who don't pay too much attention to the architecture. The enormous cement silo of a church is hard to avoid. Step into it and you feel as if you have been swallowed by Jonah's whale. Once it has spat you out, wander to the covered market, in the shape of a clam. However, the landmark which stands out most on the horizon is the watertower, like a giant cement ice-cream cone.

You'll find more traditional architecture south down the Gironde estuary. **Talmont** could scarcely have a better-located church, standing out over the water. The village too is charming; in summer the hollyhocks grow as high as the cottages. Things quieten towards **Mortagne-sur-Gironde**. In the Middle Ages the local hermits helped pilgrims to cross the Gironde on their journey to Santiago de Compostela. In the low cliff face you can visit a hermitage and chapel dug into the rock.

Up the Charente

The gentle vine-clad banks of the Charente offer a peaceful alternative to the busy beaches and roads of the Atlantic coast. Heading upriver from splendid naval Rochefort (*see* p.363), you pass through a series of historic towns pickled in the past – Saintes, Cognac, Jarnac and Angoulême – quietly pretty villages and the odd vast castle.

Introduced by balustraded gardens, the lovely **Château de la Roche-Courbon** (*gardens open daily 9–12 and 2–6.30, winter till 5.30; château mid–Feb–mid-Jan Mon–Sat 10–12 and 2–5.30, Sun 2–5.30; closed Thurs in winter; adm*) hides in woodland close to St-Pourchaire between Rochefort and Saintes. Most of the castle dates from the 15th century, but it was considerably embellished in the 17th century. In the early 20th century Pierre Loti campaigned to save it from ruin, describing it as a true Sleeping Beauty, and Rochefort's prince of camp did manage to give it the kiss of life. On the short guided tour, enjoy the rustic 17th- and 18th-century panel paintings; in the Cabinet de Peintures, doubling as a bathroom, the labours of Hercules compete with the life of Christ. But the highlight is the spectacular terraced garden.

Saintes

The intense architectural legacy of Saintes on the Charente is now introduced to visitors at the **Centre d'Interprétation de l'Architecture et du Patrimoine** (*check with tourist office for times*) in the centre of town. it makes chronological sense to go and look at the Roman sights first. Named after the Celtic Santon tribe, the place grew into an extremely important Gallo-Roman city: with 30,000 inhabitants it was the capital for a time of the Roman province of Aquitaine. The early 1st-century AD **Arch of Germanicus**, moved to a picturesque location by the Charente, pays tribute to Emperor Tiberius and family. The **Musée Archéologique** (*open June–Sept Mon–Sat 10–6, Sun 2–6; rest of year till 5; adm*) nearby is a confusing little thing divided between two buildings, and a bit disappointing given the scale of the Gallo-Roman city. Some of the glass and pottery stands out, along with fragments of a chariot from a 1st-century tomb. The second building, a former abattoir, holds the more interesting offcuts from Gallo-Roman buildings; the explanatory sheet in English helps a lot.

The still spectacular ruined Roman amphitheatre, or **Arènes** (*open June–Sept daily 10–6; rest of year Mon–Sat 10–5, Sun 2–5; adm*), lies outside the historic centre. Built around 40 AD under the reign of Claudius, it could seat 15,000. The ribs of its stairways plunge down the grassy slopes through which some rows of stone seats poke out. The place serves for major cultural events. While in the neighbourhood, visit the medieval church of **St-Eutrope**, marked by its soaring steeple, named after the first bishop of Saintes. The main façade may look dull, but the interior contains entertaining carving. In the choir, the apostles are grouped two by two under elegant Gothic canopies. Below, visit the surprising semi-subterranean church, with a tomb said to be that of St Eutrope.

Back on the east bank of the Charente, beyond the Roman arch, the major **Abbaye aux Dames** (*open mid-April–Sept daily 10–12.30 and 2–7; rest of year Sun–Tues and Thurs 2–6, Wed and Sat 10–12.30 and 2–6; adm*) was consecrated in 1047 and later became something of a finishing school for noble ladies. The badly damaged church façade is notable for its exuberant and disturbing sculpture, especially in the central portal, including brutal martyrdoms, the horrid image of little figures pierced by swords repeated over and over. Inside, the extra-wide nave was topped by cupolas, a dramatic feature in Saintonge architecture, and has wonderful acoustics, perfect for concerts. You can explore many other parts of the abbey, right up to the belltower.

Getting Around

A **railway** line links Saintes, Cognac and Angoulême along the Charente river.

Tourist Information

Saintes: Villa Musso, 62 Cours National, t 05 46 74 23 82, *www.ot-saintes.fr.*
Cognac: 16 Rue du 14 Juillet, t 05 45 82 10 71, *www.tourism-cognac.com.*
Jarnac: Place du Château, t 05 45 81 09 30, *www.mairie-jarnac.com.*
Angoulême: Place des Halles, t 05 45 95 16 84, *www.mairie-angouleme.fr.*
La Rochefoucauld: 1 Rue des Tanneurs, t 05 45 63 07 45, *office-de-tourisme-la-rochefoucauld@wanadoo.fr.*

Where to Stay and Eat

Saintes ✉ 17100

★★★★Le Relais du Bois St-Georges, Rue de Royan, t 05 46 93 50 99, *www.relaisdubois.com* (*expensive*). A big, vibrant establishment on the edge of town, with air-conditioned rooms, indoor pool, tennis courts, croquet lawn, lake and piano bar, as well as a first-class restaurant.
★★Hôtel des Messageries, Rue des Messageries, t 05 46 93 64 99, *hotel-des-messageries.com* (*inexpensive*). Central, calm and simple.

Cognac ✉ 16100

Les Pigeons Blancs, 110 Rue Jules Brisson, t 05 45 82 16 36 (*moderate*). Family-run 17th-century posting inn, close to the centre , with elegant rooms. *Closed early Jan; restaurant closed Sun pm and Mon lunch.*
★★Domaine du Breuil, 104 Rue Robert Daugas, t 05 45 35 32 06 (*moderate*). Set apart in elegant grounds on the outskirts of town. Bright comfortable rooms reached through dull institutional doors. Superb terrace at the back, even if the food is only average.
★★La Résidence 25 Av Victor Hugo, t 05 45 32 16 09 (*inexpensive*). Right in the centre, this is a good cheaper option with character.

Jarnac ✉ 16200

Restaurant du Château, 15 Place du Château, t 05 45 81 07 17 (*moderate*). An extremely

A pedestrian bridge leads across the Charente to the main centre of town. A lead skullcap of a roof covers the cathedral tower, resembling a rocket in stone. Inside, this mainly 15th-century edifice, overseen by several bishops from the mighty de la Rochefoucauld family (*see* p.372), proves sober. By contrast, the **Musée Dupuy-Mestreau** (*open June–Sept Tues–Sat 11–6, Sun 2–6; rest of year Tues–Sat 10–12.30 and 1.30–5, Sun 1.30–5; adm*), in an historic mansion nearby, contains a massive clutter of objects, including curiosities such as painted panelling from Madame de Montespan's family château and a pair of Louis XVI's slippers. In the 16th century the ground-breaking potter Bernard Palissy set up his workshop in Saintes where he developed his wild glazed enamel designs; there are seemingly no originals left in town, but you can see copies here. A certain Joseph Guillotin, a surgeon from Saintes, is also recalled. He did *not* invent the Revolution's killing machine named after him. What he did say at the National Assembly in 1789 was that capital punishment should be the same for all strata of society, and he recommended the least painful machine he knew.

The **Musée du Présidial** and the **Musée de l'Echevinage** (*both open same times as Musée Dupuy-Mestreau; adm*) are really sister fine arts museums set in the thick of the bright main shopping streets. The first presents collections from the 15th to the 18th centuries; a couple of surprisingly good Flemish works stand out, along with a portrait of a magistrate by Rigaud. The Musée de l'Echevinage, set back from the shops in its posh courtyard, displays run-of-the-mill 19th- and 20th-century works.

cheerful and appealing address on Jarnac's main square, serving excellent fresh seasonal dishes. *Closed 1–15 Mar; Aug; Sun eve, Wed eve and Mon.*

Bassac ✉ 16120
★★L'Essille, t 05 45 81 94 13, *l.essille@wanadoo. fr (inexpensive).* Quietly charming little hotel on the Charente, with restaurant *(expensive–moderate). Closed Jan–Feb; restaurant closed Wed lunch, Sat lunch and Sun pm.*

Asnières-sur-Nouère ✉ 16290
★★★ Moulin du Maine Brun, off D939 12km northwest of Angoulême, **t** 05 45 90 83 00, *mainebrun@chateauxhotels.com (expensive–moderate).* Seductive renovated riverside mill, well-furnished rooms, a fine restaurant and pool plus large grounds. *Closed Nov–Jan; restaurant closed some Mons and Tues.*

Angoulême ✉ 16000
★★Hôtel du Palais, 4 Place Francis Louvel, **t** 05 45 92 54 113 *(inexpensive).* Appealing old-style address on an attractive small square. *Closed late Dec.*

La Ruelle, 6 Rue des Trois Notre Dame, **t** 05 45 95 15 19 *(expensive).* This restaurant's setting is almost as impressive as the cuisine, the first boldly historical, the second delicately subtle. *Closed Sat lunch and Sun.*

Verteuil-sur-Charente ✉ 18510
★★La Paloma, Rue de la Fontaine, **t** 05 45 29 04 49 *(inexpensive).* A basic, cheap rustic inn with a pretty terrace for dining *(moderate). Closed early Mar and mid-Oct–early Nov; restaurant closed Sun pm and Mon outside July and Aug.*

Nieuil ✉ 16270
★★★★Château de Nieuil, Route de Fontafie, **t** 05 45 71 36 38, *www.chateaunieuilhotel. com (luxury–expensive).* Historic style in an enchanting little castle with all modern comforts in the 11 splendid rooms. Superb regional cuisine served in the stables restaurant *(expensive)*, and pool and tennis court in the grounds. *Closed Nov–mid-April; restaurant closed Sun pm and Mon outside July and Aug.*

Horse-lovers might head out to the sober **Haras National** (*open July–Aug Tues–Sun for tours at 2.30, 4 and 5.30; rest of year Mon–Fri 2–5; adm*), a major national stud farm.

Cognac and Jarnac

Cognac is a town as well as a spirit, but of course the spirit dominates the town. The buildings of massive individual cognac houses loom over the Charente. Behind them, the slick if rather misleadingly named new **Musée des Arts du Cognac** (*open June–Sept Wed–Mon 10–12 and 2–6; rest of year Wed–Mon 2–5.30; closed Tues; adm*) has taken over an historic cognac-merchant's home built beside the 17th-century ramparts. It covers the history of cognac-making and all its associated trades, from vine-tending to packaging, using modern museum techniques, and not neglecting visitors' sense of smell. The future King François Ier was born in the riverside château in 1494, taken over by the **Otard** cognac house at the Revolution. Its guided tour plays on the royal history, although the historic parts of the château are a bit of a mess, encased in later commercial structures. **Hennessy** makes its presence most felt in Cognac through sheer size. As well as visiting its glamorous shop, you can go on a guided tour of its cellars, crossing the river in a little boat. The house was founded by an Irishman who fought for Louis XV but after 12 years changed from warring to spirit-making. **Martell** claims to be the oldest cognac house, set up by Jean Martell from the Channel Islands. Among other attractions on its tour, you can see a copy of a

Cognac-making

To many in the English-speaking world, Cognac is synonymous with brandy (a word derived from the Dutch *brandwijn* or burnt wine). Cognac is distilled from the grape of the ugni blanc vines planted in a wide radius around the town of Cognac on the Charente, divided into six areas: the most famous, the Grande Champagne and the Petite Champagne, stretch south from the Charente valley below Cognac and Jarnac. The cognac-makers produce a light white wine which is 'burned', or distilled, twice. The resulting *eau de vie* or spirit is then aged for many years in oak barrels. A surprising percentage evaporates in time, 'the angels' share'. Unlike the *bouilleurs de cru*, the colourful term for home distillers, the bigger cognac houses blend *eaux de vie* from different areas of the region, the *maître de chai* creating a distinctive flavour.

The major cognac houses, like Hennessy, Martell, Courvoisier, Rémy Martin, or Hine, have become household names. Most of these big companies are based in the riverside towns of Cognac and Jarnac, many with their cellars on the quays, as in centuries past the barrels would be transported by water. Six (five in Cognac, one in Jarnac) are well set up for visitors, with slick tours in which the making of cognac and the history of the individual house are well explained. But there are in fact some 250 cognac houses in all, as well as many smaller local producers from whom you can buy direct. If you buy from them, then the cognac will be much more marked by local characteristics. The labelling of cognac is complex. Three-star cognac is actually ordinary cognac which has been aged for five to nine years. V.O. (Very Old) and V.S.O.P. (Very Superior Old Pale) are considered a level up, aged between 12 and 20 years (the use of English hints at who used to buy the most brandy). Then come the special blends which will have been left to mature 20 to 40 years, or sometimes longer, such as X.O., Vieille Réserve, Grande Réserve, Royal and Napoléon. The term Fine Champagne means that the cognac is made from blends only from the Petite and Grande Champagne areas. The age of some of the cognacs is staggering.

gabare, a traditional river boat. The other two major cognac houses you can easily visit are **Camus**, still family-run, and **Rémy Martin**. A visit to the latter actually takes you out to see some of the vines; they also claim to have the largest barrel-making plant in Europe. At the entrance to the town's public gardens, the **Musée de Cognac** (*open June–Sept Wed–Mon 10–12 and 2–6; Oct–May Wed–Mon 2–5.30; closed Tues; adm*) mixes displays on the art of cognac-making with 'art' art – Flemish and Mannerist works, and local Impressionists.

The centre of **Jarnac** is marred by brutish buildings which have muscled in along its quays. The brick **Courvoisier château**, with its fussy windows and Napoleon hat logo, dominates the main square. On a **river cruise** you can see the elegant façades of some of the other cognac houses, as well as the prettier side of town. Along the quays, the bizarre **Donation Mitterrand** (*open July–Aug daily 10–12 and 2–6; Jan–June and Sept–Oct Wed–Sun 2–6; adm*) was the gift of François Mitterrand, born at Jarnac, the son of a station master, grandson of a vinegar-maker. Although Mitterrand remained sour about his home town, he did make sure it benefited from his fame, donating these extravagant presents given to him when he was president of France.

Cognac to Angoulême

The most delightful stretch of the Charente lies between Cognac and Angoulême. 'We live at the speed that Cognac ages,' locals like to say. Along the north bank, penetrate the walls of **Bassac**'s quiet abbey to admire the Gothic church with its tall Romanesque tower. Be aware, however, that monks still live here. Inside the church, the 18th-century embellishments turn out to be surprisingly excessive, even erotic, as in the exquisite carved torsos of the atlantes. The boatmen's village of **St-Simon** has recently been given a new lease of life by the revival of its boating past. At **Vibrac**, delightful bridges cross the confusing number of arms of water. To the south a big cross of Lorraine pays tribute to heroes of the Resistance.

On the south bank of the river, the façade of the church of St Pierre at **Châteauneuf-sur-Charente** is enlivened by acrobats, men kicking monsters, and what looks like a cow flying up towards a Paschal lamb (which looks a bit like a cow itself). It also has a near-complete equestrian statue of Constantine, an evocative figure with robes flying, albeit minus head and arms. For a detour into particularly delightful Charente countryside, head down from Châteauneuf-sur-Charente towards **Plassac-Rouffiac**, the pine-cone dome of its church giving this village a special character. Entwined naked men holding each other by the foot count among the more bizarre carvings inside. **Le Maine Giraud** (*open daily 9–12 and 2–6; English audioguide; adm*), a pretty 15th-century manor house, is still a working farm where cognac is produced. It was also the ivory tower of the much-loved 19th-century French Romantic writer, Alfred de Vigny, an Anglophile who married a well-connected Englishwoman and made Shakespeare popular in France, as well as having liberal political ambitions. **Blanzac** church boasts Gothic figures and wall paintings, but to see the wonderful 12th-century crusading frescoes hidden in the **Chapelle des Templiers de Cressac** nearby, call t 05 45 64 08 74, after 6pm, to arrange a tour. **Pérignac** church, though roughly restored, boasts some delightful Romanesque carvings, including little men sprouting from various parts. The hilltop church of **Puypéroux** looks plain and badly restored, but this edifice contains one of the most disturbing little collections of Romanesque sculpture in France. Rarely does medieval art show man and beast more alarmingly combined and, symbolically, the bestiality within mankind.

Historic **Angoulême** stands proud on its hill high above the Charente, surrounded by ancient ramparts, a sprawling industrial town down below. The city may lie a bit off the beaten track these days, but it has known more important times. In 1200 King John of England came here to marry Isabelle d'Angoulême. Much fought over in the Hundred Years War, it later became the birthplace of King François Ier's brilliant sister, Marguerite d'Angoulême (better known as Marguerite de Navarre), who penned the Boccaccio-like tales of the *Heptaméron*. Angoulême witnessed the first motorless flight in France, in 1806, when General Resnier, a native of the city, launched himself from the ramparts on a machine he had invented – to help in a possible Napoleonic invasion of Britain. He survived the landing with just a broken leg.

Angoulême's early 12th-century **cathedral**, with its tall Italianate north tower, its enormous cupola and its façade covered with a Last Judgement, looks extremely impressive at first sight, but close up you can see how it suffered from a heavy-handed restoration by Paul Abadie in the 19th century. The bishops' palace has been turned into the town's **Musée des Beaux-Arts** (*closed for works until 2005*), highlights including an amazing elaborate Celtic helmet from the 4th century BC, made of gold and discovered in 1981 in a cave north of Angoulême; a 6th-century sarcophagus; Romanesque capitals; and a splendid collection of African carvings.

Against the hillside, the bold form of a funkily converted paper mill holds the **Musée de la Bande Dessinée** (*open July–Aug Mon–Fri 10–7, Sat and Sun 2–7; rest of year Tues–Fri 10–6, Sat and Sun 2–6; adm*). One of the few Grands Projets built outside Paris under Mitterrand, this comic book centre itself looks unreal, with the sides of its vertiginous glass curve joined together by a perilous red bridge. If you are interested in French cartoons, you will love the place. At the **Musée du Papier d'Angoumois** (*open April–Oct Mon and Wed–Fri 10–12 and 2–7, Sat and Sun 11–12 and 3–7; rest of year Mon and Wed–Fri 2–6, Sat and Sun 3–6; adm*), in the restored Moulin de Fleurac west of Angoulême, specialist paper is still made by hand.

The spectacular **Château de la Rochefoucauld** (*open Easter–Nov daily 10–7; rest of year Sun and public hols 2–7; adm*) dominates its little town. One de La Rochefoucauld, godfather to François Ier, introduced the French king to Leonardo da Vinci – which is how Leonardo came to draw the castle. However, the most celebrated family member was the razor-sharp wit François de la Rochefoucauld, who, while leading a colourful political and love life, exposed the shallow values of 17th-century courtiers in his viciously revealing *Maximes*. Inside the splendid courtyard, one gallery conceals saucy sculptures to make you chuckle; otherwise the decoration is decorously Renaissance. The main staircase, built around an amazing twisting cord of stone, leads up to grand chambers. You can also descend to the kitchens, and even further down into the grottoes under the castle. Disaster struck in 1960 when the medieval keep collapsed because of these fragile foundations. Much money has gone into its restoration.

Verteuil-sur-Charente, straddling the Charente river some way north, is dominated by another grand family château (*not open*), where François de la Rochefoucauld wrote many of his maxims. The church conceals a life-size Entombment scene attributed to the masterly 16th-century sculptor Germain Pilon. Unassuming **Civray** boasts one of the most startling of all Poitevin Romanesque churches, **St-Nicolas**, its façade covered with richly carved arcades. Inside, late-medieval frescoes illustrate the 8th-century hermit St Gilles absolving a king of his sins. A piece of Christ's foreskin, coyly termed the 'Sainte Vertu', helped give the **abbey of St-Sauveur** at **Charroux** its preeminence. Charlemagne donated the precious relic, later presented to Charles VII at his sacred crowning at Reims as good juju against the English, after which it vanished from sight. Following the Revolution, much of the abbey's stone was cannibalized, but some fine vestiges remain, including the skeleton of an octagonal tower, the Tour Charlemagne, giving an indication of its scale at its apogee.

The Southwest

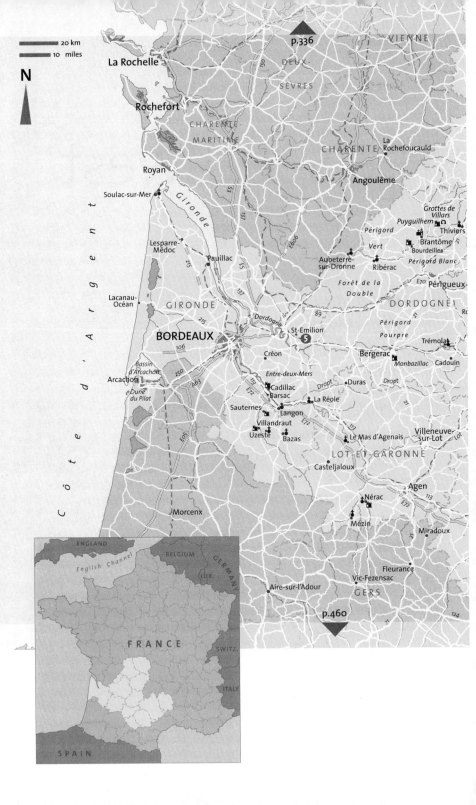

p.336

VIENNE

La Rochelle

Rochefort

CHARENTE-
MARITIME

CHARENTE

La
Rochefoucauld

Royan

Angoulême

Soulac-sur-Mer

Grottes de
Villars

Puyguilhem

Thiviers

Périgord

Brantôme

Lesparre-
Médoc

Vert

Bourdeilles

Pauillac

Aubeterre-
sur-Dronne

Ribérac

Périgord Blanc

Lacanau-
Océan

GIRONDE

Forêt de la
Double

Périgueux

DORDOGNE

Dordogne

Périgord
Pourpre

BORDEAUX

St-Emilion

Trémola

Créon

Bergerac

Monbazillac

Cadouin

Bassin
d'Arcachon

Entre-deux-Mers

Dropt

Duras

Dropt

Arcachon

Cadillac

Dune
du Pilat

Barsac

La Réole

Sauternes

Langon

Villandraut

Le Mas d'Agenais

Villeneuve-
sur-Lot

Uzeste

Bazas

LOT ET GARONNE

Morcenx

Casteljaloux

Agen

Nérac

Mézin

Miradoux

Fleurance

Vic-Fezensac

Aire-sur-l'Adour

GERS

p.460

Côte d'Argent

Gironde

20 km

10 miles

N

ENGLAND

BELGIUM

GERMANY

English Channel

LUX.

FRANCE

SWITZ.

ITALY

SPAIN

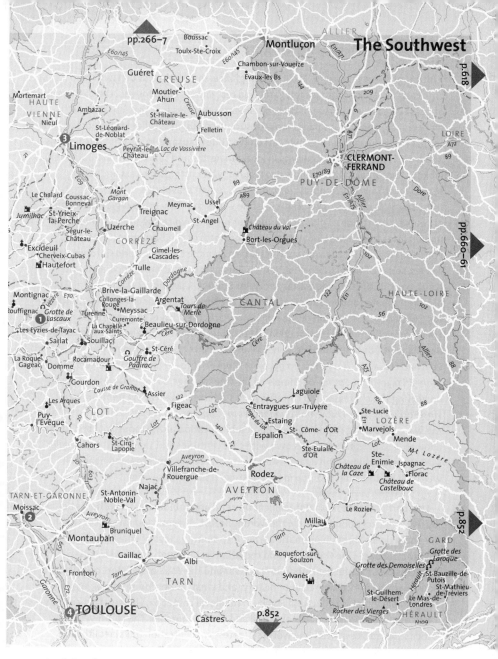

pp.266-7

Boussac
Toulx-Ste-Croix

Montluçon

ALLIER

The Southwest

p.618

Chambon-sur-Voueize
Évaux-les-Bs

Guéret
CREUSE

Mortemart
HAUTE
VIENNE
Nieul
Ambazac
Moutier-
Ahun
St-Hilaire-le-
Château
Aubusson
Felletin

St-Léonard-
de-Noblat

③ Limoges
Peyrat-le-
Château
Lac de Vassivière

CLERMONT-
FERRAND

LOIRE

PUY-DE-DÔME

Le Chalard
Coussac-
Bonneval
Mont
Gargan
Meymac
Ussel
Jumilhac
St-Yrieix-
la-Perche
Treignac
St-Angel
Château du Val
Uzerche
Chaumeil
Bort-les-Orgues
Séqur-le-
Château
CORRÈZE
Excideuil
Cherveix-Cubas
Gimel-les-
Cascades
Hautefort
Tulle

HAUTE-LOIRE

CANTAL

Montignac
Brive-la-Gaillarde
Rouffignac
Grotte de
Lascaux ①
Collonges-la-
Rouge
Meyssac
Argentat
Tours de
Merle
Turenne
Curemonte
Les Eyzies-de-Tayac
La Chapelle-
aux-Saints
Beaulieu-sur-Dordogne
Sarlat
Souillac
St-Céré
La Roque
Gageac
Rocamadour
Gouffre de
Padirac
Domme
Gourdon
Causse de Gramat
Assier
Laguiole
Les Arques
Figeac
Entraygues-sur-Truyère
Ste-Lucie
LOZÈRE
Puy-
l'Évêque
LOT
Estaing
St- Côme- d'Olt
Espalion
Marvejols
Mende
Cahors
St-Cirq-
Lapopie
Ste-Eulalie-
d'Olt
Mt Lozère
Aveyron
Ste-
Enimie
Ispagnac
Villefranche-de-
Rouergue
Rodez
Château de
la Caze
Florac
Najac
AVEYRON
Château de
Castelbouc
TARN-ET-GARONNE
St-Antonin-
Noble-Val
Moissac ②
Aveyron
Le Rozier
GARD
Bruniquel
Millau
Grotte des
Laroque
Montauban
Grotte des Demoiselles
Gaillac
Albi
Roquefort-sur-
Soulzon
St-Bauzille-de-
Putois
Fronton
Tarn
Sylvanès
St-Mathieu-
de-Tréviers
TARN
St-Guilhem-
le-Désert
Le Mas-de-
Londres
Garonne
④ TOULOUSE
Rocher des Vierges
HÉRAULT
Castres
p.852

pp.660-61

p.852

Highlights

1 Lascaux, 'Sistine Chapel of prehistoric art'
2 Moissac's Abbaye de St-Pierre, crown jewel of French sculpture
3 The luxuries of Limoges
4 The million red bricks of Toulouse, the *Ville Rose*
5 Wine and subterranean mysteries of St-Emilion

Food and Wine

Although it may not seem like it at first glance, the southwest diet, with an emphasis on duck and goose fat, garlic and red wine, is good for you; the native rate of heart disease is half that of the United States. Besides *foie gras* (studded with a black truffle) and various pâtés, look for succulent *maigrets* (fillet of duck breast) and *confits* (duck preserved in its own fat) or even duck sausage. In autumn mushrooms and truffles are prized ingredients in local omelettes and sauces. Around Bordeaux, look for beef steaks with shallots cooked over vine cuttings, oysters and other seafood, with stewed lamprey (*lamproie*) the region's favourite.

The sunny southwest produces more fine wines than any other region. Bordeaux, of course, holds pride of place, covering four regions, which together produce 500 million litres a year: the Libournais along the north of the Dordogne (St-Émilion, Pomerol, Fronsac); the Entre-Deux-Mers, between the Dordogne and Garonne; the Graves, south of the Garonne (Sauternes, Barsac, etc.); and the Médoc, along the south bank of the Gironde estuary north of Bordeaux (Margaux, Pauillac). The English acquired a taste for Bordeaux and claret in the time of Eleanor of Aquitaine, and after 1853, with the construction of the railway to Paris, the market began to expand in France as well. An ideal introduction to Bordeaux wines is offered at the **Maison des Bordeaux et Bordeaux Supérieur**, between Bordeaux and Libourne on the N89, near Beychac-et-Caillau (*t 05 56 72 90 99, open Mon–Fri 8.30–12 and 2–5; June–Sept Mon–Fri 9.30–5.30, Sat 10–6*); there's a film, free tastings, commentaries and advice on visiting the châteaux. You can study the subject before leaving home at *www. vins-Bordeaux.fr*, or *www. maisondebordeaux.com*. The Haut Pays is the term for all of the wine-producing region upriver. Bordeaux's location at the mouth of the Garonne allowed it to give priority to its own wines for centuries, but many of these smaller AOC areas are riding high again. Estates here are family concerns, and nearly all welcome visitors who just pop in for a taste or a tub of loose wine.

This part of France, with Bordeaux at one end and Toulouse at the other, is defined by rivers of exceptional beauty: the Dordogne, Lot, Aveyron and Tarn, all of which meander down through dramatic gorges into sunny valleys of vines and orchards to join the big one – the Garonne – and the Atlantic. Although battered by the Albigensian Crusade, the Hundred Years War and the Wars of Religion, much of the southwest has since kept clear of history (and what passes for progress), leaving it a remarkably intact architectural legacy of medieval châteaux, villages, 13th-century new towns (*bastides*) and Romanesque and Gothic churches. The southwest has other superlatives as well: the world's greatest concentration of Palaeolithic art, beginning with Lascaux; the spectacular wines of Bordeaux; the biggest sand dune in Europe; the immense subterranean fantasies of the Gouffre de Padirac and the Aven Armand; the breathtaking Gorges du Tarn; and effervescent pink Toulouse.

The Limousin might be considered a missing link in southwest France, a quieter version of Périgord, only in granite rather than honey-coloured stone; the Parc Naturel Régional Périgord-Limousin has recently been created on their frontier. Beyond the capital of Limoges, however, most of the Limousin feels lost in the past.

The Limousin

Even the French have trouble telling you much about what lies in the three shy, retiring and rural *départements* of the Limousin. Limoges, famous for pottery, springs first to mind, while many can name Oradour-sur-Glane, a town martyred by the Nazis. Aubusson may ring a bell for its tapestries, while the Corrèze has a cluster of gorgeous villages south of its main town, the cheerfully named Brive-la-Gaillarde.

Into the Eastern Limousin or the Creuse

The Creuse river cuts diagonally through the eastern Limousin, passing Guéret, a town which could put in a strong claim to being the least-known *départemental* capital in France, and the historic tapestry towns of Aubusson and Felletin.

A Detour into the Northeastern Creuse

If you're desperately seeking out-of-the-way corners in France, try the northeastern Creuse. Aim for pretty **Boussac**, which shares the same gorgeous brown roofs with its freckled Gothic **château**. One lord, Jean Ier de Brosse, fought alongside Joan of Arc. Tapestries are the theme of the visit inside: the château long held France's most beautiful cycle of tapestries, those of the Lady with the Unicorn, now in the Musée de Cluny in Paris. Contemporary tapestries are exhibited today. South of Boussac, bizarre

Getting Around

The main **train** station is Guéret, on the Bordeaux–Lyon line. Public transport to towns such as Boussac, Aubusson and Felletin is much more limited.

For details on **bus** services from Guéret, **t** 05 55 51 96 60.

Tourist Information

Boussac: Place de l'Hôtel de Ville, **t** 05 55 65 05 95.
Guéret: 1 Av Charles de Gaulle, **t** 05 55 52 14 29.
Aubusson: 67 Rue Vieille, **t** 05 55 66 32 12.
Felletin: 2 Petite Rue du Clocher, **t** 05 55 66 54 60.

Where to Stay and Eat

Boussac ✉ 23600
Relais Creusois, t 05 55 65 02 20 (*expensive*). One of the main gastronomic stops in the Creuse, which also has pretty views on to the Petite Creuse valley.

Guéret ✉ 23000
★★Hôtel Auclair, 19 Av de la Sénatorerie, **t** 05 55 41 22 00 (*inexpensive*). A clean hotel in the centre of Guéret, with pool and garden. Restaurant (*moderate*).

St-Hilaire-le-Château ✉ 23250
Château de la Chassagne, t 05 55 64 50 12/ **t** 05 55 64 55 75 (*moderate*). Superlative luxury, spacious B&B rooms in this adorable little château just south of St-Hilaire, with pastures in front and woods behind. No restaurant.
★★Hôtel du Thaurion, t 05 55 64 50 12 (*moderate–inexpensive*). A renovated roadside inn run with the same cheerful enthusiasm by the same family as the château above. The rooms are comfortable and the regional cuisine (*expensive–moderate*), reputed to be the best in the Creuse, is served in a plush dining room.

Aubusson ✉ 23200
★★Hôtel de France, 6 Rue des Déportés, **t** 05 55 66 10 22 (*moderate–inexpensive*). A pleasant central hotel.

twisted granite boulders, the **Pierres Jaunâtres**, have great views over the Auvergne, but nearby **Toulx-Ste-Croix** has even better: on clear days, the views over the Puys de Dôme are staggering. The main street splits its Romanesque church in two; a couple of worn lions guard the entrance to the nave and a curious round porch tower is roofed with the chestnut tiles typical of the region. A lighthouse of a tower at the north end of Toulx-Ste-Croix has the best views of all.

Two soporifically charming places lie tucked away in Les Combrailles, an undulating plateau spanning the Limousin and Auvergne. When Vikings were threatening, monks from Limoges carried the relics of St Valérie to well-hidden **Chambon-sur-Voueize**. But the massive Romanesque church **Ste-Valérie** can scarcely be called discreet, and boasts a remarkable array of apse chapels that cluster round the choir like pups feeding greedily off their mother. **Evaux-les-Bains**, Chambon's rival, is proud of its decorative and naturally colourful church of St Peter and St Paul.

The Creuse Valley South from Guéret

Backed by wooded hills, **Guéret** was the capital of the mini province of La Marche before it became capital of the Creuse. Steeped in provincial atmosphere, Guéret also has a museum devoted to fine arts, with brutish, naked Roman gods, medieval enamel works and reliquary arms, and Impressionist views by Armand Guillaumin.

Back down the Creuse, **Moutier-Ahun** lies prettily by the river, its landmark a stub of a church, entered by way of a Flamboyant Gothic gateway teeming with tonsured monks. Inside (*adm*) are virtuoso Baroque late 17th-century wooden stalls by Simon Bauer, where sphinxes, dogs and grotesques with Carmen Miranda headgear keep company with saints. Linden trees trace the nave, destroyed in the Wars of Religion.

At **Masgot** south of Ahun, houses are decorated with late 19th-century naive carvings by François Michaud, one of many stone carvers who found work in the restoration of medieval buildings. A Neolithic trail leads through the delightful **Gorges du Péry** from Masgot to St-Hilaire-le-Château.

Aubusson, with its granite houses, would look Breton were it not for its brown roof tiles. The remains of a medieval castle stand on the rocks above town, and the attractive main street has several shops selling tapestries. The **Musée Départemental de la Tapisserie** (*open July–Aug Wed–Mon 10–6, Tues 2–6; rest of year Wed–Mon 9.30–12 and 2–6; adm*) explains the techniques and displays tapestries from down the centuries. To see old looms, go to the **Maison du Vieux Tapissier** in the old town.

Felletin, down the Creuse, is more attractive than its competitor. Of its two old churches, the Eglise du Moutier contains charming old frescoes and naive statues and retables, while the other one, the Eglise du Château, is often used for temporary tapestry exhibitions. Tapestry-making continues here at the **Manufacture Pinton**; ask at the tourist office about visits. Dead quiet and dead pretty, the village of **Crocq**, east of Felletin, is dominated by the twin towers of a ruined castle. The sweet granite **Chapelle de la Visitation** has a stepped gable front and contains a delightful 16th-century altarpiece on the life of the Limousin saint Eloi. A dramatic grisaille Last Supper has figures in rich costumes with severe Flemish faces in an elaborate architectural setting, although the artist's control of perspective was clearly shaky.

The Tapestry Tradition: Aubusson and Felletin

It may have been Flemish weavers who first established tapestry-weaving in Aubusson and Felletin in the 14th century, creating Gothic scenes of warriors and verdant landscapes, then moving on to complex historical and mythological subjects. In 1665 Aubusson was declared a *Manufacture royale*, a privilege Felletin received in 1689, a time when cartoons were by court artists such as Charles Le Brun. But with the Revocation of the Edict of Nantes, many of the Aubusson Protestant manufacturers went into exile. Fortunes revived under Louis XV, and although the Gobelins and Beauvais by then produced more refined tapestries, the fashion spread to these parts for pastoral scenes *à la* Watteau. The lack of demand for luxury goods after the Revolution spelled a sharp decline for tapestry-making, but the need for copies and replacements for older works preserved the art. Aubusson owes much of its 20th-century revival to Jean Lurçat, who introduced more striking colours and bolder textures, and encouraged artists such as Picasso and Rouault to draw cartoons.

The Central Limousin

Eight villages in the centre of the Limousin vanished with the creation of beautiful Lac de Vassivière. The red-tinged Limousin race of cows hail from the surrounding hills, while the Monts d'Ambazac northeast of Limoges form a tough granite barrier between the northern Marches and the rest of the region.

Woods surround the many arms of the **Lac de Vassivière**. Lost in the heart of one of the quietest regions in France, it comes surprisingly to life in summer, teeming with bathers, boaters and windsurfers. One island, reached via the south side, is the site of the **Centre d'Art Contemporain** (*open June–mid-Oct daily 11–1 and 2–7; rest of year Tues–Sun 11–1 and 2–6; adm*), a 1.5km walk from the car park, but well worth the hike. Conceptual pieces dot the island's woods, many of which are integrated into the natural setting. Exhibitions are held in the clean granite and brick building designed by Aldo Rossi, matched by a large chimney of a tower with a snailing staircase inside.

St-Léonard-de-Noblat surrounds a quirky pilgrimage church. Born into an aristocratic Frankish family in the 6th century, Léonard became a hermit and one day saved the life of a queen who went into labour while hunting with her husband. To thank Léonard, the king offered him a *noble lieu* – as much land as his donkey could walk round in 24 hours – on which Léonard founded a religious community to reform former captives and criminals through Christian labour. An eccentric tower rises from his church, and there are some entertaining stone sculptures down below; an extraordinary crowd of Gothic and Romanesque columns cluster in the choir. The statue on the next square is of Gay-Lussac, the great physicist and chemist born here, and a little museum is devoted to his discoveries. The town is also proud of its marzipan.

The **Monts d'Ambazac** reach as high as 2,296ft and the climate can be harsh. Etienne Muret, a hermit from Auvergne, settled here in 1076 and led an exemplary life of spirituality and poverty. His followers, the order of Bons Hommes, founded Grandmont and acquired massive riches. The order was closed down before the Revolution and its treasures dispersed, although one fabulous reliquary chest (1190)

Getting Around

St-Léonard-de-Noblat has a **railway** station, but this area isn't well-served by public transport.

Tourist Information

Ile de Vassivière: Beaumont-du-Lac, t 05 55 69 76 70.
St-Léonard-de-Noblat: Place du Champ de Mars, t 05 55 56 25 06.
Ambazac: 3 Av Gen de Gaulle, t 05 55 56 70 70, *www.ot-vassiviere.fr*.

Where to Stay and Eat

Pallier ✉ 23340
Commanderie de Pallier, Gentioux, t 05 55 67 91 73 (*inexpensive*). The past centuries seem to have been cleaned up, pickled and beautifully preserved at this superbly characterful B&B, which is excellent value for such high standards. Restaurant (*moderate*).

Lac de Vassivière and Peyrat-le-Château ✉ 87470
★★★La Caravelle, t 05 55 69 40 97 (*inexpensive*). A comfortable modern hotel, right by the water, the beach and a major campsite on

the western side of the lake, a lively corner in summer. Rooms have lake views.
★★Le Bellerive, 29 Av de la Tour, t 05 55 69 40 67, *www.lebellerive.fr* (*inexpensive*). Attractive option near the lake, with charming rooms.

St-Léonard-de-Noblat ✉ 87400
★★Le Grand St-Léonard, 23 Av du Champ de Mars, t 05 55 56 18 18 (*inexpensive*). Wide-fronted, updated posting inn, which seems an appropriate enough place to stay in this venerable old town. The food (*expensive–moderate*) is worth stopping for too.

Monts d'Ambazac
A few really interesting B&Bs with excellent hosts add to the gentle attractions of the Monts d'Ambazac.
Château de Chambon, Bersac-sur-Rivalier, 87370, t 05 55 71 52 91 (*inexpensive*). A little taste of rustic château life, in this 16th-century manor house with very spacious rooms. Amazing value.
Les Chênes, Les Sauvages, 87240 St-Sylvestre, t 05 55 71 33 12 (*inexpensive*). Experience an environmentally friendly night with the Rappellis, who have built their green-conscious retreat in a peaceful corner of the local hills. M. Rappelli's paintings hang on the walls. Restaurant (*moderate*).

remains in the church of **Ambazac**. This is one of the most ostentatious pieces of Limoges enamel work ever made, a true little treasure house topped by a curious statue of a bird. A bit further north, the church of **St-Sylvestre** contains a late-Gothic silver reliquary bust of Etienne Muret. In the neighbouring hamlet of **Grandmont**, a few sad vestiges of the mighty monastery have been incorporated into the houses.

Limoges

Limoges is a lively university city synonymous with luxury; even one of its 6th-century saints, Eloi, was a goldsmith. Later, the city was renowned for its exquisite *émaillerie champlevée*, first made in the abbey of St-Martial around 1185 and exported across Western Europe. Porcelain took off after the discovery of all-important kaolin in the 1760s at St-Yrieix; Auguste Renoir, born in Limoges, started off as a porcelain painter. To produce such luxuries meant exploiting local labour, which responded by founding France's powerful trade union, the Confédération Générale du Travail, or CGT, and Limoges remains a militant and progressive force in a sleepy rural region.

High above the Vienne river, the **Musée Municipal de l'Evêché** (*open July–Sept daily 10–11.45 and 2–6; rest of year Wed–Mon 10–11.45 and 2–5, June till 6*) has taken over the 18th-century bishops' palace. It throws up some surprises: fragments of Gallo-Roman frescoes, a figure of a decapitated Gaulish god and two plates with childlike graffiti that turn out to be rare examples of Celtic writing. There are fine Romanesque capitals and tombs, and two heads with curled hair. The best early medieval enamels were stolen in the 1980s, but there are still a few good pieces and a large collection of painted enamels inspired by German and Italian engravings. The paintings aren't up to much, beyond Renoir's *Portrait de Jean*. A separate building by the gardens is devoted to the Resistance; although Limoges of course honours its Resistance fighters, it is embarrassed that it celebrated Pétain's visit in 1941 so enthusiastically.

You can enter the **cathedral** via an enormous telescoping porch tower that resembles an industrial chimney, or through the fine Flamboyant portal of St-Jean on the north side. The interior is splendid and simple, influenced by the Gothic of the north. An elaborate Renaissance rood screen is at the back of the church. In the choir, monumental tombs stand out, as does the 19th-century imitation medieval stained glass. The **Haute Cité** quarter around the cathedral has grand houses but not a lot of life.

The nearby **Boulevard Louis Blanc**, by contrast, is far too busy – a major artery for cars, and porcelain and enamel shops. Head into the historic butchers' quarter, **La Boucherie**, where one shop on the Rue de la Boucherie has been turned into an Ecomusée (*open summer only*) showing how the butchers' families lived. Nowadays people come to shop and eat. The Gothic **Chapelle St-Aurélien** was saved from Revolutionary vandals by the butchers' fraternity which still owns it. It has a belltower and a collection of statues, furniture, and the relics of the second bishop of Limoges.

Getting There and Around

Limoges-Bellegarde **airport** lies 10km west of the city; Ryanair and Flybe fly from the UK. The **railway** station, the Gare des Bénédictins, is a neo-Byzantine and Art Deco building, covered in proud symbols. The main **bus** station on Rue Charles Gide is slightly closer to the centre, a short walk from Place Jourdan.

Tourist Information

Limoges: 12 Bd de Fleurus, **t** 05 55 34 46 87, *www.ville-limoges.fr*.

Where to Stay and Eat

Limoges ✉ 87000

***Le Richelieu, 40 Av Baudin, **t** 05 55 34 22 82, *www.hotel-richelieu.com* (*moderate*). Opposite the town hall just outside the main ring of boulevards, with good rooms and service.

***Royal Limousin, Place de la République, **t** 05 55 34 65 30, *www.royal-limousin.com* (*moderate*). Comfortable central, modern.

Le Marceau, 2 Av de Turenne (on Place Marceau), **t 05 55 77 23 43 (*inexpensive*). Quite basic but comfortable hotel kept for 22 years by the same owner. The restaurant (*moderate*) specialises in fish.

Philippe Redon, 3 Rue d'Aguesseau, **t** 05 55 34 66 22 (*expensive*). Near the main covered market. Interesting dishes combining Limousin meats with seafood.

Brasserie de Vanteaux, 122 Rue d'Isle, **t** 05 55 49 01 26 (*moderate*). Tasty classics at reasonable prices. *Closed most of Aug, Sun eve and Mon*.

L'Amphitryon, 26 Rue de la Boucherie, **t** 05 55 33 36 39 (*moderate*). An attractive timber-frame front in the old butchers' quarter, with fine porcelain on the tables and refined cuisine, the best-known in Limoges.

Most visitors ignore all this and head straight for the porcelain. You're unlikely to find more beautiful vases, pots and plates in one place than at the **Musée National de la Porcelaine** (*open July–Aug Wed–Mon 10–5.45; rest of year Wed–Mon 10–12.30 and 2–5.45; adm*). The building alone, a mishmash of Italianate, neo-Gothic and arts and craft, is an arresting sight. A video explains the stages in making porcelain, using a mixture that includes kaolin. Meissen in Saxony was the first to produce European porcelain in 1710; Limoges followed in the 1770s. The first European manufacturers obsessively made fake Chinese pieces; funnier still are the pieces made in China during the Ancien Régime showing Europeans with long noses. Limoges is best known for its refined, bordered dinner services, but here too are modern creations.

You can see the different stages of production and decoration in making Limoges porcelain at the **Bernardaud** (*call t 05 55 10 55 91 for times*). A more unusual but engrossing visit is to the very old-fashioned **Four des Casseaux** in the labyrinthine GDA factory (*call t 05 55 33 28 74 for details*).

The Western Limousin

West of Limoges, a slice of charming country has been incorporated into the Parc Naturel Régional Périgord-Limousin, where a Richard Cœur de Lion tourist trail is dedicated to that overromanticized Anglo-French king. On a different plane, the atrocities committed by the Nazis are kept painfully alive at Oradour-sur-Glane.

Oradour-sur-Glane and the Monts de Blond

Oradour-sur-Glane is perhaps *the* most painful symbol to the French of the German atrocities of the Second World War. The Nazi division descended on the old village on 10 June 1944, just a few days after D-Day. They rounded up everyone they could find, divided the men into groups and shot them, before pillaging the buildings and setting them alight. Just five men hiding in a barn managed to get away. The women and children were herded into the church, where they thought they would be safe. Instead the Nazis gassed them, threw grenades into the church, then set it alight. Only one woman escaped the hellish turmoil, managing to smash her way out through a stained-glass window. In all, there were 642 victims that day at Oradour-sur-Glane, 205 of whom were children. Most were beyond recognition and laid unidentified in mass graves. Why Oradour? Not special in any way, nor a centre of the Resistance, it was a random scapegoat which happened to lie on the division's route.

The burnt-out ruins of the 328 buildings of Oradour are heartrending to visit. Old sewing machines and coffee grinders lie among the rubble. There are still pots in the fireplaces. There's a bike here, a car there. The metal rings are all that remain of the barrels in the wine shop. The memorial in the **cemetery** has family photos of the victims. In 1999 a new **memorial museum** was opened to offer a wider historical context. Bad feelings remain towards the people of Alsace who fought with the Nazis; 14 members of Das Reich division came from there. To the horror of the people of Oradour, they were amnestied after their trial in 1953; Oradour responded by cutting

Getting Around

Limoges is the hub of the **train** service through this area.

Tourist Information

Oradour-sur-Glane: Place du Champ de Foire, t 05 55 03 13 73, *www.oradour-sur-glane.fr.st*.
Mortemart: Place Château des Ducs, t 05 55 68 98 98, or t 05 55 68 12 09.
Rochechouart: 6 Rue Victor Hugo, t 05 55 03 72 73, *www.ville-rochechouart.fr*.
Châlus: 28 Av F.-Mitterrand, t 05 55 78 51 13.

Where to Stay and Eat

Nieul ✉ 87510

★★★★La Chapelle St-Martin, St-Martin-Fault, c. 10km northwest of Limoges towards Oradour-sur-Glane, t 05 55 75 80 17, *www.relaischateaux.fr, chapelle@relais-chateaux.fr* (*expensive*). A really luxurious, exclusive little hotel in a 19th-century bourgeois house; excellent restaurant.

Cieux ✉ 87520

★★Auberge de la Source, 1 Av du Lac, t 05 55 03 33 23 (*moderate*) A traditional, renovated, former coaching inn, just 8 rooms, which is near to Cieux's lake. Part of Logis de France. Restaurant (*expensive–moderate*). *Closed mid-Jan–mid-Feb.*

Mortemart ✉ 87330

★Le Relais, t 05 55 68 12 09 (*inexpensive*). By the quaint covered market, this is a delightful stop both for a good meal and a simple room.

Champagnac-la-Rivière ✉ 87150

Château de Brie, closer to Châlus than Rochechouart, t 05 55 78 17 52 (*moderate*). With so many châteaux tantalizingly set along the local tourist route it seems only fair that one should offer B&B rooms for the night. A stay doesn't come cheap, but the rooms in this stocky little 15th-century castle are memorably decorated in various styles.

La Roche-l'Abeille ✉ 87800

★★★Au Moulin de la Gorce, t 05 55 00 70 66, *www.relaischateaux-fr/moulingorce* (*expensive–moderate*). An oasis of luxury off the beaten track (off the D704 some 12km north of St-Yrieix), this has grown charmingly from its origins as a 16th-century watermill into a waterside inn with extremely refined rooms and restaurant (*expensive*).

its links with the French state. In 1983 one of the Germans responsible for the massacre, Lieutenant Barth, was tracked down. Sentenced to life imprisonment, he was released in the late 1990s on grounds of ill health. General Lammerding, who was in charge of the division, escaped justice altogether, and died of natural causes in 1971. On a more positive note, in 1999 some Alsatians, including the mayor of Strasbourg, were invited to attend the inaugural ceremony for the new museum.

The tranquil **Monts de Blond** to the north offer some relief after Oradour-sur-Glane. This thin strip of granite heights once separated the *langue d'oïl*-speakers of northern France from the *langue d'oc* speakers of the south. But the look here is more Breton or Scottish, or even Arthurian. A local map pinpoints the dolmens; other 'Arthurian' features, the black lakes and thick forests, date from recent times.

Two delightful villages wait on the northern side of the Monts de Blond. **Montrol-Sénart** has huge views and rustic art – a crucifixion by the Romanesque church, and the stoup and the statuary within. **Mortemart** has remnants of two monasteries and a château; don't miss the carved choir stalls in the big airy church. As well as the monkeying around under the seats, there is a hilarious end piece showing a lord and a monk, one of them mooning.

Parc Naturel Régional Périgord-Limousin

Although hit by a massive meteorite 200 million years ago, **Rochechouart** doesn't look different from its neighbours, except perhaps that things are a bit twisted – the slate spire of its church and the remarkable columns in its speckled late-Gothic château. This now serves as the Haute-Vienne's newly enlarged **Musée d'Art Contemporain** (*open daily 10–12.30 and 1.30–6, but check in winter, **t** 05 55 03 77 77; adm*), strong on modern British and Italian artists. The **Espace Météorite** (*open summer and school hols Mon–Fri 10–12.30 and 1.30–6, Sat and Sun 2–6; spring Sun–Fri 2–6; winter Mon–Fri 2–6; adm*) tells the story of the rock from space that hit with a force 14 million times stronger than the Hiroshima bomb.

The gruesome martyrdoms at **Les Salles-Lavauguyon** were only found under the whitewash in 1986. These extraordinarily rich Romanesque frescoes of proud dogged saints patiently enduring their various grisly fates are painted against sumptuous bands of colour, the costly blue particularly surprising.

The cemetery by the time-battered church in **Le Chalard** contains a rare collection of carved and curiously uplifting Romanesque tombs. **St-Yrieix-la-Perche** is worth a halt just to see the 15th-century reliquary bust of St Yrieix in the Gothic church. The beaten silver head is rendered down to the beard stubble, added as gold points.

The **Château de Coussac** (*open mid-Mar–Nov daily 2.30–6; July–Sept till 7*), aloof on the edge of the village of Coussac, has been the home of the Bonneval family for over ten centuries. The square multi-towered castle derives mainly from the 14th century; the tour takes in family portraits and objects, and splendid tapestries from Aubusson. One Bonneval died heroically defending François Ier at the Italian battle of Marignan. The most eccentric was Claude-Alexandre, born in 1675: exiled from France, he converted to Islam, reorganized the Turkish army and was honoured with the title of a three-tailed pasha. The present Brazilian marquise has added an exotic touch.

The meanders of the Auvézère river shaded by sycamores create the enchanting setting for **Ségur-le-Château**, where the ruined schist castle was besieged by Richard the Lionheart in 1177. **Arnac-Pompadour** is home to a national stud farm, created for Louis XV, who bought the castle (*brief tour of the exteriors possible, **t** 05 55 98 55 47*) for his mistress Jeanne Poisson (Joan Fish), who understandably preferred to be known as the Marquise de Pompadour.

The Entrails of Richard Cœur de Lion

Duke of Aquitaine in 1169, Richard Cœur de Lion was crowned king of England in 1189. Ten years later he was mortally wounded while besieging the **Château de Châlus**, intent on punishing the treacherous Aimar V, Viscount of Limoges. One day, as Richard was overseeing the siege, Pierre Basile, a dextrous soldier defending the castle, stood at the top of the keep using a pan to deflect the arrows of the enemy. Richard, impressed, got up and applauded. The sharp-eyed Basile spotted him, drew his crossbow and shot him, and Richard died 10 days later in Chinon on the Loire. It serves as a reminder of how extensive the Plantagenet possessions were that Richard's entrails ended up in the Limousin, his body in the abbey of Fontevraud by the Loire, and his heart in Rouen. As for Pierre Basile, he was flayed alive.

Southern Limousin and Upper Vézère, Corrèze and Dordogne Valleys

Dark stone and slate dominate the little-explored upper valleys of the Vézère and the Corrèze. Five dams have effectively tamed the mighty Dordogne into a series of well-regulated lakes. Further downstream, a swathe of the southern Limousin and northern Périgord and Quercy once formed the territory of the Viscounty of Turenne, one of the most stubbornly independent of fiefdoms in France, embellished with a clutch of gorgeous red villages.

The Upper Vézère and Corrèze Valleys

Treignac on the Vézère doesn't really make the grade in the beauty stakes, but it is often lively, and from the Gothic bridge you get a good view of the ruined castle walls. Old houses with sculpted entrances lie between Place de la République and Place du Collège. From Treignac, a magnificent alley of beeches takes you up to panoramic **Mont Gargan**. In the midst of the pudding-shaped **Monédières hills** between the Vézère and the Corrèze, the easily reached Suc-au-May offers more great views. Here **Chaumeil** has a tough but likable huddle of stone houses.

Northeast of Chaumeil, the Corrèze river starts off on its path to join the Vézère. **Gimel-les-Cascades**, with its waterfalls (*adm*), is tucked down a valley with dramatic wooded views. As for **Tulle**, the capital of the Corrèze, beyond the cathedral and Musée du Cloître most of its charm has been destroyed. The museum, in a Benedictine monastery, has 13th-century chapterhouse frescoes, a collection of tulle – the net fabric named after the town – arms and accordions, a local passion.

Back north along the Vézère, **Uzerche** is much more appealing than Tulle, its towers rising on a narrow promontory above a hairpin bend in the river. A prehistoric precious metals route from Britain and Brittany to the Mediterranean may have passed this way, and the relics of two Breton saints, Léon and Coronat, ended up in the former abbey church of **St-Pierre**, decorated with Moorish-Gothic arches and archaic carvings. But much earlier traces of civilization have been found here; find out more at the **Centre Régional de Documentation sur l'Archéologie du Paysage en Limousin** (*open daily 10.30–12.30 and 2.30–6.30; July and Aug closed Mon am; adm*).

Down the Dordogne River in the Limousin

Bort, the Limousin town furthest up the Dordogne, may be ugly, but it is overseen by the extraordinary **Orgues de Bort**, massive tubes of rock, some over 300ft high. The plateau above affords spectacular views of the Dordogne valley and Cantal mountains. Just north of Bort rises the picture perfect mid-15th-century **Château du Val**, with superb pepperpot roofs that narrowly escaped disappearing under the waters with the first plan for the Bort dam.

Art-lovers might make a detour west through sleepy **Ussel** and **St-Angel** to **Meymac**, which has been given a shot in the arm with the establishment of a contemporary art centre in the former abbey. Continuing down the Dordogne from Bort, beyond the

Getting Around

Brive-la-Gaillarde is the main transport hub, with the Corrèze's **airport** and main **train** station. For reservations for Brive-Laroche airport, **t** 05 55 86 88 36. A fair number of trains using the Paris-Toulouse line stop at Brive. Local railway lines run from here along the Vézère and Dordogne valleys.

Tourist Information

Uzerche: Place de la Libération, **t** 05 55 73 15 71.
Meymac: Place de l'Hôtel de Ville, **t** 05 55 95 18 43, *www.meymac.fr*.
Beaulieu-sur-Dordogne: Place Marbot, **t** 05 55 91 09 94.
Collonges-la-Rouge: Place de l'Ancienne Gare, **t** 05 55 25 47 57.
Turenne: Place du Foirail, **t** 05 55 85 94 38.
Brive-la-Gaillarde: Place du 14 Juillet, **t** 05 55 24 08 80.

Where to Stay and Eat

Uzerche ✉ 19140

★★Hôtel Teyssier, Rue du Pont Turgot, **t** 05 55 73 10 05, *www.hotelteyssier.free.fr* (*inexpensive*). A recently renovated old-fashioned provincial hotel, and one of the few places to stay in the upper Vézère. The food is copious.

Beaulieu-sur-Dordogne ✉ 19120

★★Le Turenne, 1 Bd St-Rodolphe-de-Turenne, **t** 05 55 91 10 16 (*inexpensive*). Turreted old hotel in a medieval house with bags of atmosphere, and a charming restaurant to match, with duck specialities.

Collonges-la-Rouge ✉ 19500

★★Relais St-Jacques, La Porte Plate, **t** 05 55 25 41 02 (*inexpensive*). An utterly delightful simple hotel in an adorable house; the only drawback is the tourist crowds outside.
Le Prieuré, Place de l'Eglise, **t** 05 55 25 41 00 (*moderate*). A very cosy restaurant in a central location by the church.

Turenne ✉ 19500

La Maison des Chanoines, Route de l'Eglise, **t** 05 55 85 93 43 (*moderate*). With its lovely stone front covered with ivy, this used to be the home of church canons, but is now an extremely attractive stop for tourists. The food's good, served in a vaulted cellar.

Brive-la-Gaillarde ✉ 19100

★★★La Truffe Noire, 22 Bd Anatole France, **t** 05 55 92 45 00, *www.la-truffe-noire.com* (*moderate*). On the outer layer of the historic onion, by the big central avenues encircling the old town. A terrace separates the rooms from the road, and it's soberly comfortable and friendly with a restaurant (*expensive*).
Chez Francis, 61 Av de Paris, **t** 05 55 74 41 72. Lively *bistrot* with the odd eccentric touch of regional cuisine.

Varetz ✉ 19240

★★★★Château de Castel-Novel, 5km northwest of Brive, **t** 05 55 85 00 01, *www.castelnovel.com*, *novel@relaischateaux.com* (*expensive; half board obligatory*). Arguably the grandest hotel in the Limousin, and once home to Colette. The towers date back to the 15th century; rooms are sumptuously furnished. Restaurant (*very expensive–expensive*).

grim dams at L'Aigle and Le Chastang, **Argentat** originally marked the high point of the Dordogne's navigability. For centuries Argentat's boatmen would load timber, cheese, leather, pelts and wine on to their flat-bottomed *gabares* and sail down to Bordeaux, where the boats themselves would be sold for firewood. The town, under its *lauze* roofs, has the air of a cheerful, prosperous pensioner.

The **Tours de Merle** may be lost up the Maronne river from Argentat, but ruined castles don't come much more romantic than this massive complex. But what was it doing in a meander in a minor river, like an armoured knight hiding in the woods? Why, collecting tolls. As as alternative to the busy roads to Beaulieu, seek out the country roads south to the Cère valley.

Lovely riverside **Beaulieu-sur-Dordogne** still looks credibly medieval, built around the 12th-century abbey of St-Pierre, with its magnificent tympanum of the Last Judgement. Christ has his arms outstretched in triumph while a carnival of monsters rolls across the lintel, supported by a figure Freda White described as 'flowing upward like a flame of prayer' (to continue down the Dordogne, *see* p.397).

The Old Viscounty of Turenne Between Beaulieu and Brive

Just four families succeeded each other across ten centuries as the Viscounts of Turenne, who commanded a remarkable degree of autonomy from other overlords. Established by the Comborns, who obtained privileges from the kings for their part in the crusades, they were followed by Comminges from the Pyrenees in the 14th century and the Rogers, who gave Rome two popes, Clement VI and Gregory XI. But the best known viscounts were the La Tour d'Auvergnes (1444–1738). The Protestant Henri Ier de La Tour d'Auvergne supported the future Henri IV of France, while his son, another Henri, became known as Le Grand Turenne for his battle prowess.

Three castles are crammed on the narrow ridge of **Curemonte**. None is open to visitors, but one holds memories of Colette, who spent the early days of the Second World War here. Just south, tiny **La Chapelle-aux-Saints** caused a stir in the early 1900s when the Homme de La Chapelle-aux-Saints was found in a cave; the excitement was caused by evidence that this Neanderthal had been given a ritual burial back in 45,000 BC. Although he was moved to the Musée de l'Homme in Paris, a **museum** here explains his importance.

The extraordinary measled stones of **Meyssac** affect, or rather infect, its whole appearance, from its Gothic church and the pillars of its covered market to the turrets of its picturesque old houses. Whereas Meyssac looks slightly alarming, **Collonges-la-Rouge** is utterly irresistible. And knows it. It was here that the Association des Plus Beaux Villages de France was born in 1982, preserving lovely villages while inevitably turning them into tourist traps. It owes its wealth of fine houses with turrets sticking out left, right and centre to the administrators of the Viscounty of Turenne, who based themselves here in the 16th century. The Romanesque Gothic **church** has the fanciest towers in town; remarkably, during the bitter Wars of Religion, Protestants and Catholics reached some kind of agreement to share it. The entrance has curious lobed arches, and figures of the Christ of the Ascension above the Virgin and two posses of apostles, strikingly carved in white limestone against the red sandstone. Inside, the church is full of quirky corners and statues.

After Collonges' vivid tints, most of the blood seems drained out of **Turenne**, which looks a much tougher nut, although it too is a Beau Village. Once the tiny capital of the viscounty, its streets strain to make it up to the dramatic castle ruin. On the way up you might stop for a breather at the grand but cold classical church, with a defensive tower topped by a spiked slate roof. Begun in the late 16th century when Turenne was a Protestant stronghold, its gilded retable with its cluster of putti adds a note of Catholic excess. Further up, remnants of three rings of walls surround the ruined castle, marooned like an ark on its hilltop; its watch tower sticking up like a figurehead. Fantastic views open out from a formal garden to a network of high castles.

Old **Brive-la-Gaillarde** is an attractive onion of a town, its layers encased in the outer skin of the busy boulevard. Built on the Corrèze just before it joins the Vézère, Brive stands in contrast to ugly Tulle. A row of protruding busts marks the Renaissance façade of the **Musée Labenche** (*open April–Oct Wed–Mon 10–6.30; rest of year Wed–Mon 1.30–6; closed Tues; adm*) where, among relics and portraits of leading lights, the surprise is a series of fine classical tapestries made at Mortlake, south London.

Northern Dordogne and Périgueux

Cross into the *département* of the Dordogne (or Périgord, as it is still known in France), and a warm sun gilds the limestone and a distinct twang flavours the local accent. Ironically, what so delights visitors today – idyllic landscapes, a thousand castles, fortified churches, and medieval villages with *lauze* roofs – were born of long centuries of war, poverty and neglect. This, of course, has changed dramatically in the past thirty years as the English, after ruling the roost before the Hundred Years War,

Getting There and Around

Périgueux's **train** station, in Rue Denis-Papin, is 4hrs from Paris (change in Limoges), 75mins from Bordeaux, 3hrs from Agen or Toulouse. Buses from the station also link Périgueux to the Paris–Bordeaux TGV in Angoulême, by way of Brantôme. **Buses** depart from Place Francheville and the station to Sarlat, Montignac, Ribérac, Bergerac, and Brantôme. The biggest car park in the city is up at Place Montaigne, near the Musée du Périgord.

CFTA **bus** lines link Brantôme to Périgueux and Angoulême, three times a week. CFTA also runs between Ribérac, Mareuil and Angoulême and between Ribérac and Périgueux via Tocane St Apre, at least three times a day, **t** 05 53 08 43 12.

Tourist Information

Brantôme: Pav. Renaissance, **t** 05 53 05 80 52.
Périgueux: 26 Place Francheville, **t** 05 53 53 10 63, *www.ville-perigueux.fr*.
Ribérac: Pl Charles de Gaulle, **t** 05 53 90 03 10.

Where to Stay and Eat

Brantôme ✉ 24310
★★★**Hôtel Chabrol**, 57 Rue Gambetta, **t** 05 53 05 70 15 (*very expensive–expensive*). Excellent, elegant restaurant in handsome old white building on the river Dronne, serving generous portions of favourites such as *millefeuille de ris de veau au foie de canard et truffe*, and wonderful hot desserts. *Closed mid-Nov–mid-Dec, Jan and Feb. Oct–June closed Sun and Mon eves.*
★★★**Moulin de l'Abbaye**, 1 Rte de Bourdeilles, **t** 05 53 05 80 227, *www.relaischateaux.fr/moulin.com* (*expensive*). Dreamy, ivy-covered hotel-restaurant in a delightful garden, just outside the centre on the Dronne. Exquisite dishes, based on local ingredients (*expensive*). *Closed Nov–late April.*
★★**Périgord Vert**, 6 Av de Thiviers, **t** 05 53 05 70 58 (*inexpensive*). Reliable Logis de France hotel in ivy-swathed building. Restaurant (*cheap*). *Closed mid-Dec–mid-Jan.*
Chez Mérillou, Rue A-Maurois, **t** 05 53 05 74 04 (*inexpensive*). Very pleasant B&B.
Au Fil de l'Eau, 21 Quai Bertin, **t** 05 53 05 73 65 (*moderate*). Beside the Dronne, and you can eat outside. *Closed Tues and Wed eves out of season and Oct–Mar.*

Bourdeilles ✉ 24310
★★★**Château de la Côte**, at Biras, southwest of the centre on the D106, **t** 05 53 03 70 11, *www.chateaudelacote.com* (*expensive–moderate*). 15th-century château lost in an immense park; 14 beautiful rooms furnished with antiques, pool, tennis and helipad, golf, riding, and canoeing nearby. Restaurant (*expensive*). *Closed mid-Nov–mid-Mar.*

have moved back in a big way to their 'Dordogne-shire.' The *département*, one of the largest in France, divides itself into four quarters, each with its own colour. Jules Verne dubbed northernmost Périgord 'Green' for its forests and rivers that remain lush even in midsummer. 'White Périgord' of the pale stone is the home of the Dordogne's capital Périgueux. 'Black Périgord' is named for the dense forests around Sarlat, while 'Purple' has been stuck on the wine area around Bergerac.

Northern Périgord

Brantôme is a charming town of medieval and Renaissance houses built on an island in the Dronne. A 16th-century dogleg bridge crosses to its white **abbey** built against a steep bank (*open Oct–June Wed–Mon 10–12.30 and 2–5, closed Tues; July and Aug daily 10–7; Sept Wed–Mon 10–12.30 and 2–6, closed Tues; adm*), founded by Charlemagne in 769, sacked by the Normans in the 11th century, when the bell tower (the oldest in France) was rebuilt on its Merovingian base. A bas-relief of the *Massacre of the Innocents* under the porch and a carved capital, used as a font, survive from the

Périgueux ✉ 24000

****L'Univers, 18 Cours Montaigne, t 05 53 53 34 79 (*inexpensive*). Near the museum, with dining under the arbour in summer (*moderate*). *Closed 3 weeks in Mar.*

*** Bristol, 37–39 Rue Antoine Gadaud, t 05 53 08 75 90, *www.bristolfrance.com* (*inexpensive*). Modern hotel near the centre of town, with spacious rooms and the usual facilities. Parking, but unfortunately no restaurant.

Le Roi Bleu, 2 Rue Montaigne, t 05 53 09 43 77 (*expensive*). Smart restaurant with chic selections such as *tartare de saumon fumé aux chips de légumes et langoustines rôties.* *Closed Sat lunch and Sun and one week in summer.*

Le Rocher de l'Arsault, 15 Rue de l'Arsault, t 05 53 53 54 06 (*expensive*). Tasty *tatin de foie gras* and other regional delicacies in a Louis XIII dining room. *Closed several weeks in summer.*

Le 8, 8 Rue de la Clarté, t 05 53 35 15 15, near the cathedral (*moderate*). Very good reputation for imaginative regional dishes in small and lively dining room. *Closed Sun and Mon.*

Aux Berges de l'Isle, 2 Rue Pierre-Magne, t 05 53 09 51 50 (*moderate*). Terrace overlooking the river and St-Front. Try the refined *pavé de bœuf au foie gras* and one of the luscious desserts. *Closed Sat lunch, Sun eve and Mon.*

Chancelade ✉ 24650

****Château des Reynats, just to the west of Périgueux, t 05 53 03 53 59 (*very expensive–expensive*). A 19th-century, turreted château, with attractive rooms. Close to a golf course, with a park, pool and tennis courts. The restaurant (*expensive*) serves exquisite specialities based on regional cuisine, but with an imaginative touch. *Restaurant closed Sat lunch, Sun and Mon lunch.*

Ribérac ✉ 24600

**Hôtel de France, 3 Rue Marc-Dufraisse, t 05 53 90 00 61 (*inexpensive*). Family-run hotel in a 16th-century post house – the best and biggest hotel in town, with an old-fashioned dining room and a garden courtyard. A wide choice of fish and duck dishes and a vegetarian menu (*moderate*). *Restaurant closed Mon, and Tues and Sat lunch out of season.*

Le Chevillard, 2 km from the centre at Gaynet, on the Bordeaux road, t 05 53 91 20 88 (*moderate*). An old farm with a large garden and abundant good food at kind prices. *Closed Mon and Tues exc summer and Jan.*

La Bergerie, 4km north of Ribérac on the D708, t 05 53 90 26 97 (*moderate*). A restaurant among the corn fields in an old *bergerie* with a pretty patio. The menus are delicious and good value: *joue de porc braise au Bergerac. Closed Tues and Wed exc summer and Jan.*

original church. The best bits are the curious *grottes et fontaines sacrées* in the cliff behind the abbey. It survived the Wars of Religion thanks to Abbé Pierre de Bourdeilles (1540–1614), known in French literature simply as Brantôme. Brantôme used the abbey's revenues to finance his escapades as a soldier of fortune and lover of court ladies. Injured in battle, he settled here and wrote spicy accounts of his time, all so true that he left instructions for his heirs to wait 50 years before publishing them.

Of the 1,001 châteaux of Périgord, the most splendid is the **Château de Puyguilhem** (*open early Feb–Mar and 12 Nov–end Dec Tues–Thurs and Sun 10–12.30 and 2–5.30; April–June, Sept–11 Nov and Christmas daily 10–12.30 and 2–6; July and Aug daily 10–7; adm*), northeast of Brantôme near Villars. Built in 1524, its rooftop forest of richly carved dormers and chimneys is just as impressive within – it resembles the hull of a ship. Saved from collapse in the 1930s, Puyguilhem has been refurnished with period pieces and Renaissance tapestries. The nearby **Grotte de Villars** (*open July and Aug daily 10–7; May, June and Sept daily 10–12 and 2–7; April and Oct daily 2–6.30; adm*) combines natural art – brilliant white, translucent stalactites and draperies – with prehistoric drawings in magnesium oxide from the Aurignacian era (30,000 BC).

From Brantôme, follow the Dronne 7km southwest to **Bourdeilles**, seat of the oldest of Périgord's four baronies. High over the river, their **château** (*open Feb, Mar and 12 Nov–end Dec Mon, Wed, Thurs and Sun 10–12.30 and 2–5.30; April–June, Sept–11 Nov and Christmas–New Year Wed–Mon 10–12.30 and 2–6, closed Tues; July and Aug daily 10–7; adm*) guarded the frontier between English Guyenne and France. Naughty writer Brantôme was born here, in 1540, and the adjacent Renaissance château was built by his sister-in-law, Jacquette de Montbron, to impress Catherine de Médicis (who in fact never visited). She even designed it herself – a rare and perhaps unique feat for a woman in the 16th century.

Peaceful and full of happy cows, this corner of Périgord manages to stay relatively aloof from the tourist madness. It does have a picture-postcard village, **St-Jean-de-Côle**, with a Gothic humpback bridge and steep tile roofs on the houses, and a church tower with delightful carvings, especially one of God modelling Adam out of clay. In summer you can get inside the 15th-century **Château de la Marthonie** (*open July and Aug daily 10–12 and 2–6.30; adm*).

More Romanesque awaits 7km west in the 12th-century church of **Thiviers**, built over Merovingian foundations, with a Renaissance porch and sculpted capitals. A plaque opposite the Maison de la Presse commemorates the town's link with Jean-Paul Sartre, who spent much of his (predictably) miserable childhood here.

Northeast of Thiviers, lost on the ferny forested frontier of the Limousin like Sleeping Beauty's castle, is the enchanting **Château de Jumilhac** (*tours June–Sept daily 10–7, night visits June and Sept Tues and July and Aug Tues and Thurs; Mar–May open Sat, Sun and public hols 2–6.30; visits at other times with a minimum of 4 people and by appt; adm*). Antoine Chapelle, the brain behind it, converted a former Templar strong-hold into a fantasia of towers, turrets and chimneys coiffed with blue slate pepperpots, topped in turn by an equally fantastic array of forged-iron froufrous.

West of Jumilhac, the river Isle loops down to pick up the waters of the Auvézère just before Périgueux. The busiest market town in the area, **Excideuil** once belonged to the

Viscounts of Limoges, who built a vertiginous fortress on a butte of Jurassic limestone. The best scenery in the area is along the Auvézère, beginning at **Cherveix-Cubas**, from where you can drive, ride, or trek along the delicious **Gorges de l'Auvézère**.

South of Cherveix stand the striking domed towers of the **Château de Hautefort**, the 12th-century fortress of the battling troubadour, Bertran de Born, which was rebuilt in 1640 by a famous miser, Jacques-François de Hautefort (the model for Harpagon in Molière's *L'Avare*). You can visit the immaculate French **gardens** (*open early Feb–early Mar and early Oct–early Nov daily 2–6; end Nov Sun 2–5; mid-Mar–early Oct daily 10–12 and 2–6; most of July and Aug daily 9.30–7, last adm 6.15; adm*).

Périgueux

Set in a fertile valley on the river Isle, the capital of the Dordogne is a cheerful city of 35,000 people who produce and market truffles, *foie gras* and fat strawberries, and print all the postage stamps in France. The old streets around the famous five-domed cathedral of St-Front have been intelligently restored over the past decades to give the city a lively and lovely heart; another plus is its exceptional museum.

Set back from the river, the **Cité**, the oldest part of Périgueux, has a handful of Gallo-Roman and medieval souvenirs tucked between the modern buildings, including the 65ft **Tour de Vésone**, the central *cella* of a circular 1st-century AD Gallo-Roman temple. Just west in Rue des Bouquets are the ruins of the **Villa de Pompeïus**. Pompeïus, whoever he was, wallowed in a de luxe set of heated Roman baths; frescoes and mosaics survive as well. From 2004 the site will form part of a new museum dedicated to Gallo-Roman Périgueux and Gallo-Roman life in general. The impressive if now mutilated church of **St-Etienne-de-la-Cité** stands on the site of a Temple of Mars. In the 11th century it was rebuilt by a Crusader who took notes, becoming the prototype of the Périgourdin domed Romanesque church, with wide Byzantine domes not only over the crossing but cupping the length of the nave.

The compact medieval quarter of **Puy-St-Front** has been beautifully restored; you can peep inside some of the courtyards, and around the last remnant of Puy's walls, the **Tour Mataguerre**. If St-Etienne was the prototype, the **Cathédrale St-Front** was the ultimate expression of medieval Périgord's particular romance with domes. It's especially breathtaking from a distance, and especially so at night when it is illuminated. Close up, it is much harder to overlook the fact that most of what you see was rebuilt at the end of the 19th century, when additions were added to the 11th-century original, including the pinnacles on the domes. Inside the most lingering impression is one of vastness (it's one and a half times as long as a football pitch); in its minimal decoration it looks more like a mosque. **Place Daumesnil**, next to St-Front, is the centre of a fascinating web of 15th- and 16th-century pedestrian lanes. Steep, stepped streets descend to the river; houses in Rue du Plantier have terraced gardens, while medieval Rue du Port-de-Graule is lined with tiny boutiques. The pedestrian **Rue Limogeanne** has been Périgueux's busiest shopping street since the Middle Ages; most of the houses here, and on Rue de la Sagesse, date from the 16th century.

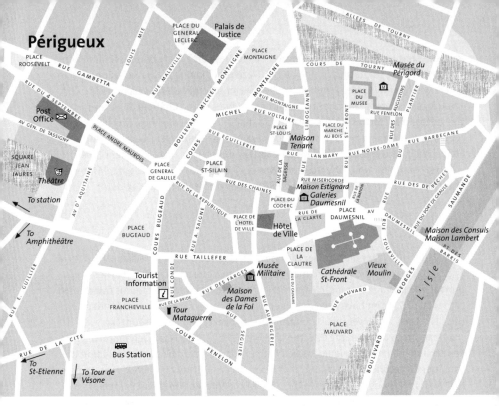

The **Musée du Périgord** (*22 Cours Tourny; open April–Sept Mon–Fri 10–6, Sat and Sun 1–6; Oct–Mar Mon–Fri 10–5, Sat and Sun 1–6; closed Tues and hols; adm*) is a cut above the average provincial museum. Ethnographic collections, devoted to stone-age cultures, form a comparative introduction to the prehistoric section, which includes three of the oldest complete skeletons ever found. The Gallo-Roman rooms are filled with jewellery, frescoes, mosaics, and a 2nd-century BC altar dedicated to the Eastern cult of Cybele and Attis, although from 2004 many of these will move to the new museum at the Roman villa. The Beaux-Arts section has ceramics and enamels from Limoges, followed by paintings and sculptures.

West of Périgueux: the Dronne and Forêt de la Double

The Dronne is a charmingly bucolic river by the gentle rolling hills of the **Double Forest**, crisscrossed by streams that feed moody marshes, created by medieval monks to farm fish for Lent. The big town here, with nearly 5,000 souls, **Ribérac** has the Romanesque Notre-Dame, with a handsome apse and dome; in fact this entire area bubbles with multi-domed Romanesque churches: to see them all, pick up the tourist office's map of *églises romanes à coupoles*.

The most fascinating churches in the area, however, have no domes and lie 2km into the Charente at the ivory-tinted hill town of **Aubeterre-sur-Dronne**. The uncanny **Eglise Monolithique** (*open daily 9.30–12 and 2–6; adm*) was founded in a cave in the 5th century. In the 11th century Benedictines enlarged the holy precinct, quarrying into the limestone to create the tallest rock-cut church in the world, rising 65ft from the ground and supported by two blackened columns as thick as sequoias. A stairway cut in the rock leads to the upper galleries with windows peering down into the shadowy depths. The floor is pitted with the graves of medieval monks, and below these an ancient mithraeum was found, where adherents of Mithras would be baptized in a rain of hot blood from a bull sacrificed above. Rampaging Protestants smashed up Aubeterre's other gem, the 11th-century **St-Jacques**, although they spared the magnificent three-arched Romano-Hispano-Moorish façade.

The Vézère Valley

Some 400,000 years ago, people settled on the fair banks of the Vézère. It was a Palaeolithic paradise: bulging cliffs pocked with caves, fresh water, river pebbles, abundant flint, and herds of bison and reindeer to hunt. Long forgotten, the existence

Getting Around

Public transport is thin on the ground in the Vézère valley. There are **bus** connections to Montignac (Lascaux) from Périgueux and Sarlat run by CFTA (**t** 05 53 08 43 13). Les Eyzies station has regular **trains** linking it to Périgueux and Agen. Parking in Les Eyzies in season is notoriously frustrating.

Tourist Information

Montignac: Place Bertran-de-Born, **t** 05 53 51 82 60, *www.bienvenue-montignac.com*.
Les Eyzies-de-Tayac: in the centre, **t** 05 53 06 97 05. The hours for the caves are prone to change: pick up the latest schedules here.

Where to Stay and Eat

Montignac ✉ **24290**
★★★★**Château de Puy Robert**, 2km from Lascaux on the D65, **t** 05 53 51 92 13 *www.relaischateaux.com/puyrobert* (*very expensive–expensive*). Bijou turreted 19th-century château in a 20-acre park with a pool; luxurious rooms in the Relais et Châteaux tradition. The restaurant (*very expensive*) uses local ingredients to concoct innovative, exquisite dishes. *Closed mid-Oct–early May.*
★★★**Relais du Soleil d'Or**, 16 Rue du Quatre-Septembre, **t** 05 53 51 80 22, *www.le-soleil-dor.com*, (*moderate*). Old inn surrounded by a

shady park, with a heated pool, tennis and canoeing on site. In the restaurant (*expensive*) traditional southwestern cuisine is given a modern, lighter touch. *Closed mid-Jan–mid-Feb; restaurant closed Mon lunch and Nov–Mar Sun eve.*

Les Eyzies-de-Tayac ✉ **24620**
★★★**Hôtel du Centenaire**, **t** 05 53 06 68 68, *www.hotelducentenaire.fr* (*expensive*). Plush Relais et Châteaux in the centre yet far from the brouhaha. Outdoor heated pool, sauna and gym. Its crowd-puller is the rather pompous dining room (*very expensive*), where chef Roland Mazère concocts the most exquisite meals in the entire region, based on the freshest local ingredients, accompanied with wines from one of the best wine cellars in the Dordogne. *Closed Mon, Tues, Wed and Fri lunches.*
★★**Hôtel du Centre**, **t** 05 53 06 97 13 (*moderate*). Family-run hotel with comfortable rooms bang in the middle of town, but maintains a modicum of seclusion. The restaurant (*expensive–moderate*) serves regional specialities, indoors or out under the parasols. *Closed Nov–mid-Feb.*
★★★**Les Glycines**, by the river, **t** 05 53 06 97 07, *www.les-glycines-dordogne.com* (*moderate*). Pretty rooms in a garden setting, with a pool. The restaurant (*moderate*) has its own kitchen garden and serves fine regional lamb and beef dishes, as well as other Périgordin faves. *Closed Sat lunch and Wed out of summer and Nov–Feb.*

708

Forêt de la Double

709

DORDOGNE

Périgueux
E70

6

89

38

Lussac

21

Dordogne

Libourne

St-Emilion

St-Michel-de-
Montaigne

Périgord

Pourpre

BORDEAUX

Castillon-
la-Bataille

Ste-Foy-la-
Grande

Bergerac

Créon

Château de
Monbazillac

Abbaye de la
Sauve-Majeure

Pellegrue

Ribagnac

Beaumont-du-
Périgord

Château de
la Brède

Entre-Deux-Mers

Sauveterre-de-
Guyenne

25

of these early settlers was first hinted at in 1862 when a deposit of carved flints and bones was uncovered at La Madeleine. This set off a quest for signs of 'antediluvian man', leading to a torrent of discoveries. In 1895 the first Magdalenian paintings in France were noted at Les Eyzies' Grotte de la Mouthe, but it was the finding of Lascaux in 1940 that really put it on the map. To date, 200 Palaeolithic sites have been discovered along the Vézère, now designated a World Heritage site by Unesco.

Montignac

Once a busy river port, Montignac sits pretty on the Vézère, its wooden balconies reflected peacefully in the waters, belying a violent past when the ruined **Château de Montignac** was the chief citadel of the Taillefer, the Counts of Périgord, who of all the vassals of the king of France stood apart for having no redeeming virtues whatsoever.

Lascaux I and II

*Guided tours (**t** 05 53 51 96 03 for schedule of English tours); open July and Aug daily 9–7; otherwise daily 10–12 and 2–5.30; closed Jan and Mon Nov–Mar; tickets (which include Le Thot Centre de Préhistoire) available from the booth near the Montignac tourist office May–Sept; other times tickets purchased at Lascaux II.*

Montignac remained pensioned off from history until one morning in September 1940, when two local lads and two young war refugees from Paris went in search of treasure in a pit above Montignac used as a dead donkey dump and stumbled across the **Grotte de Lascaux**, which had been virtually vacuum-sealed when the original entrance was blocked by an ancient landslide. Within 15 years of its discovery, however, the fabulous 'Sistine Chapel of Prehistoric Art' was fading under a film of white calcite deposits caused by carbonic acid from the breath of a million visitors, and on 20 April 1963 Lascaux was closed forever to the public.

Disappointment at the closure was so universal that the *département* financed the 15-year-long construction of **Lascaux II**, 650ft below the original. This painstaking reproduction of the Hall of the Bulls and the long narrow *Diverticule axiale* was painted

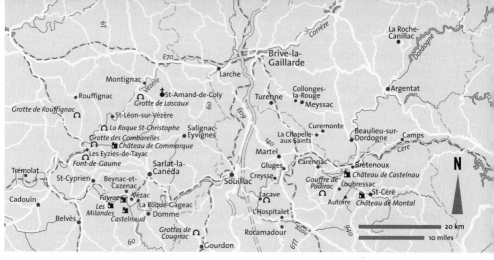

with the same colours and techniques used 17,000 years ago. Far better than any photograph ever could, it reproduces the ravishing exuberant life, movement and the clever use of natural protuberances, faults and shadows of the original paintings, although it hardly explains how an artist limited to a lamp of animal fat and juniper twigs could get the proportions of a 16ft bull so perfectly. Scattered among the animals is a vocabulary of mysterious symbols and a Dr Seuss-ish beast dubbed the 'unicorn', the only known 'imaginary' creature yet discovered in prehistoric art.

Around Montignac

Six km southeast of Montignac, the golden *lauze*-topped **Château de La Grande Filolie** (14th–15th century) (*not open to the public*) is one of the Dordogne's dreamiest châteaux. Just as striking, the fortified church of **St-Amand-de-Coly** (6km east) (*open early July–mid-Aug daily 10.45–12.15; mid-Aug–end Aug daily 3.30–7; adm*) has a massive *clocher-mur* and a superb roof of *lauzes*, looming like a skyscraper over its narrow valley and hamlet. It is stirring, wholesome Romanesque, unusually built on a slope. The dome hovers 66ft over the nave; stand under it and sing, and like all true Romanesque churches it rings like a bell.

Down the Vézère from Montignac to Les Eyzies

Le Thot Centre de Préhistoire (*same hours, same ticket as Lascaux II*) features audio-visuals on Palaeolithic art and on the creation of Lascaux II; there's a replica of the tiny chamber at the back of Lascaux with its stick man 'sorcerer'; and living (or mechanical) examples of the animals that once roamed the Vézère valley.

In 1944, in reprisal for Resistance activity, the retreating Nazis burned the village of **Rouffignac**. Only the church of St-Germain remained; under the bell tower a doorway of 1530 survives, its lintel carved with mermaids. If it's open, don't miss the Flamboyant Gothic interior, with elaborate vaulting and twisted columns. Five km south is the **Grotte de Rouffignac**, 'the Cave of a Hundred Mammoths' (*open mid–Mar–June and Sept–Oct daily 10–11.30 and 2–5; July and Aug daily 9–11.30 and 2–6; adm*). A little electric train takes you 4km down into the bowels of the earth as the guide illuminates the vivid etchings, drawings of mammoths and woolly rhinoceroses, and niches in the clay floor formed by generations of hibernating bears. The ceiling of the innermost chamber is an excellent pastiche of horses, mammoths, bison, and an ibex.

Down the river from the idyllic hamlet of **St-Léon-sur-Vézère** is the curved prow of **La Roque St-Christophe**, a cliff more than half a mile long, sliced into five shelves, one of which is the largest natural terrace in Europe (*open Nov–Feb daily 11–5; Mar, April and Oct daily 10–6; May, June and Sept daily 10–6.30; July and Aug daily 10–7; adm*). Inhabited from Mousterian times until the Middle Ages and beyond, the caves along the tiers sheltered about 1,000 people, who in later times had their own church and cemetery. After the 900s the cave system was fortified against the Vikings.

Les Eyzies-de-Tayac, the 'World Capital of Prehistory'

The Vézère and Beune rivers meet at Les Eyzies, where the first known bones of *Homo sapiens sapiens* were discovered in 1888 at a place called Cro-Magnon. As the valley's chief crossroads, with major prehistoric sites in every direction, Les Eyzies is swamped with summer visitors. A good place to start is the **Musée National de la Préhistoire** (*open mid-Nov–mid-Mar daily 9.30–12 and 2–5; Sept–mid-Nov and mid-Mar– June daily 9.30–12 and 2–6; July and Aug daily 9.30–7; closed Tues; adm*), tucked under the overhanging cliffs that dominate Les Eyzies, in a 16th-century castle. Some rooms are a Louvre of prehistory, with the largest collection anywhere of Palaeolithic reliefs and sculpture in stone, bone and ivory, while others star the very first prehistoric sculptures – buxom, balloon-bottomed beauties known as the 'Venuses'.

Close by, a second overhang protects the **Abri Pataud** (*open early Feb–Mar and early Nov–mid-Dec Tues–Thurs 10–12.30 and 2–5; April–June, Sept–early Nov, Christmas and New Year also Sun; July and Aug daily 10–7; adm*) where Upper Palaeolithic hunters lived over a span of nearly 20,000 years. A museum in the nearby shelter contains the finds, including one of the oldest known reliefs, an ibex dated 18,000 BC.

Grotte de Font-de-Gaume

Tours Sun–Fri Oct–mid-May 9.30–12.30 and 2–5.30; mid-May–Sept 9.30–5.30; closed Sat and public hols; adm. Reservations essential in summer and can be made days in advance: **t** *05 53 06 86 00.*

The Grotte de Font-de-Gaume, a 10-minute walk east of Les Eyzies, has nothing less than the finest prehistoric art open to the public in France. The paintings and engravings in remarkable flowing lines from *c.* 12,000 BC were created with the same drawing and colour-blowing techniques used at Lascaux, and similarly employ natural relief to lend volume to the figures. Some of the paintings are damaged, others look as if they were made yesterday, as in the magnificent friezes of bison, reindeer and horses. The partially painted, partially engraved black stag and red doe are unique in the canon of Upper Palaeolithic art, only visible after the guide traces the lines with a light.

More Sites around Les Eyzies

The Beune valley is especially rich in cave art. Some 800 engravings dated 12,000–10,000 BC have been distinguished in the last 400ft of the **Grotte des**

Combarelles (*reserve, t 05 53 06 86 00; same hours as Font-de-Gaume; buy tickets at Font-de-Gaume; adm*), including 140 horses and 48 rare human representations – hands, masks, women and a seated person. Many are incomplete, most are superimposed in wild abandon, and others only appear when lit from various angles. Most beautiful of all is the reindeer leaning forward to drink from a black cavity suggesting water. Three km down the road, 100 paintings and engravings decorate the **Grotte de Bernifal** in Meyrals (*t 05 53 29 66 39; open July and Aug daily 9.30–6.30; Sept daily 9.30–12.30 and 2.30–6.30; adm*). The dominant animal is the mammoth, similar to the ones in Rouffignac, but the star of the show is a rare ancestor of the ass.

The **Abri du Cap Blanc** (*open April–June and Sept–early Nov daily 10–12 and 2–6; July and Aug daily 10–7; adm*) has a vigorous, 42ft frieze of nearly life-size horses in high relief, following the natural contours of the limestone cliff; the shelter also yielded a Cro-Magnon tomb and tools. Just beyond rise the romantic ruins of the 13th-century **Château de Commarque**, ruined by the English in the Hundred Years War.

The Dordogne Quercynois

Before gracing the *département* that bears its name, the Dordogne flows through the Lot, or Quercy – rugged country, shot with green valleys, dramatic cliffs and caves.

St-Céré and Around

The Dordogne bristles with castles, but the oldest, the burnished red **Château de Castelnau** (*guided tours Oct–Mar Wed–Mon 10–12.15 and 2–5.15, closed Tues; April–June and Sept daily 8.30–12.15 and 2–6.15; July and Aug daily 9.30–6.45; closed public hols; adm*) is still the most redoubtable, set on a conical 750ft outcropping where the river flows into the *département* of the Lot. Begun in the year 1000 and rated the second military castle in France after Pierrefonds in the Oise, it was restored by Jean Mouliéret, tenor at the Opéra Comique, who refurnished one wing with *objets d'art.*

The main base for the area is **St-Céré**, on the banks of the Bave, which tumbles down into the Dordogne. The town reached its peak in the 15th century and has barely changed since, especially Place du Mercadial, the market square, surrounded by half-timbered buildings. St-Céré has been an art colony since 1945, when Jean Lurçat, the tapestry master of Aubusson (*see* p.379) based himself here: his symbol, the Coq Arlequin, was designed to restore Gallic pluck after the war. His work in the **Galerie du Casino** (*open daily 9–12 and 2–6.30; closed Tues out of season*) is worth a look.

Only 2km west of St-Céré, the golden **Château de Montal** (*open Palm Sun–Oct daily 9.30–12 and 2.30–6; closed Sat; adm*) was built by Jeanne de Balzac, who was enraptured by the Italian Renaissance and decided to replant some of it in this corner of *la France profonde*. At the end of the 19th century the château was stripped of all its finery, but in 1908, oil tycoon Maurice Fénaille stepped in, repurchased as many of its original works as he could, and donated the château and all its fittings to the state. From the exterior, Montal looks like a typical medieval castle, but step inside the rough walls and a magical courtyard opens up, decorated with ornate dormers and an

Getting Around

The main SNCF **rail** line between Paris and Toulouse stops at Brive and usually at Souillac. **Buses** link St-Céré with Bretenoux, Puybrun, Lacapelle and Figeac.

The **Train Touristique du Haute Quercy**, 'Le Truffadou', runs from Martel to St-Denis. The steam train leaves Martel at 2.30 and 4pm Sun and public hols April–Sept, and Wed mid-July–mid-Aug. A diesel train runs more regularly, t 05 65 37 35 81.

Rocamadour's station is 4km from town and connected by taxi. Only the cars of visitors with bookings in Rocamadour's hotels are allowed in the village. In summer, when the car parks outside the gates fill up fast, park on top at the château or a 600m walk away at L'Hospitalet and walk or take the lifts. A train runs from the car park in the valley.

There are frequent trains to **Souillac** from Paris, Brive, Cahors and Toulouse, and bus services to Sarlat (t 05 65 33 16 73) and Martel (t 05 65 37 81 15). Direct trains from **Sarlat** go to Bordeaux, Les Eyzies, Bergerac, and Souillac; July and Aug there are daily links to Bergerac known as *Autorail Espérance* – a guided tour, with tastings of local products along the way (tickets and info from the train station). There are bus connections to Souillac and Brive (t 05 65 37 81 15), and to Périgueux (t 05 53 89 01 48).

Tourist Information

St-Céré: Place de la République, t 05 65 38 11 85, *www.quercy.net/quercy/saint-cere*.
Rocamadour: L'Hospitalet, t 05 65 33 22 00, *www.rocamadour.com*.
Souillac: Bd Louis Jean Malvy, t 05 65 37 81 56, *www.souillac.net/fr*.
Sarlat: Rue Tourny, t 05 53 31 45 45, *www.sarlat.com*.
Domme: Place de la Halle, t 05 53 31 71 00, *www.domme-tourisme.com. Closed Sun early-Nov–Jan*.

Sports and Activities

Quercyland at Les Ondines near Souillac, t 05 65 37 33 51, offers bouncy castles, water slides and mini-golf (*open May–Sept daily 11–8*); plus canoe and kayak descents down the Dordogne from an hour to several days in length; also try Safraraid, t 05 65 37 44 87, for canoes/kayaks, from St-Sozy and Souillac.

Where to Stay and Eat

St-Céré ✉ 46400
★★★Ric, 2km south in St-Vincent-du-Pendit, t 05 65 38 04 08 (*moderate*). Five rooms with marvellous views over St-Céré, and a

imaginative frieze over 100ft long. The interior is just as beautiful. Further west, a belvedere overlooks the 100ft-high falls of the river Autoire; across the bridge and up the path is a tremendous view stretching from the natural amphitheatre of the **Cirque d'Autoire** to the little village of **Autoire** and all the way to the Dordogne valley. Autoire's steep brown-tiled roofs form an exquisite ensemble; even back in the 1700s, Parisians chose it to build summer homes. Another exceptionally lovely village, 15th-century **Loubressac**, has sloping brown-tiled roofs overlooking the confluence of the Bave, the Cère and the Dordogne.

The Gouffre de Padirac

Open April–early July and Sept daily 9–12 and 2–6; rest of July daily 9–6.30; Aug daily 8.30–6.30; first half of Oct daily 9–12 and 2–5; adm exp.

The chasm at Padirac plunges down 296ft through the limestone of the Causse de Gramat before forming 13 miles of galleries. It is spectacularly beautiful, and spectacularly popular: be prepared to queue (and bring a sweater). The 90-minute **guided tour** takes you along an underground canyon to the river Plane, where gondoliers wait to row you past the Grande Pendeloque, an enormous stalactite. On foot once more, the

beautiful pool. The pretty restaurant (*expensive*) serves classic southwest cuisine with a creative touch (*dinner only*).

Victor Hugo, 7 Av Victor Hugo, **t 05 65 38 16 15, *www.hotel-victor-hugo.fr* (*inexpensive*). Nine pretty rooms in a 16th-century inn in the centre of town, run by a transplanted Irishman, Monsieur Tom. Lovely *cuisine recherchée* (*moderate*). *Closed Mon, also Sun in summer.*

Rocamadour ✉ 46500

One advantage of staying in Rocamadour is seeing it without the coaches, but book.

****Château de Roumégouse, Rignac, **t** 05 65 33 63 81, *www.integra.fr/relaischateaux/ roumegouse* (*expensive*). Six km east in Rignac, romantic Relais et Chateaux in a pretty park with a terrace and a well-known restaurant (*expensive–moderate*) featuring traditional Quercy *foie gras*, truffles and seasonal dishes. *Hotel closed early Nov–Mar; restaurant closed Mon lunch, Tues and Wed.*

***Beau Site, Rue R.-le-Preux, **t** 05 65 33 63 08, *www.bw-beausite.com* (*moderate*). The fanciest place in town (a Best Western), in the same family for five generations, in a medieval house. Its dining room, Jehan de Valon (*expensive–moderate*), serves exquisite food. *Closed early Nov–early Feb.*

Ste-Marie, Place des Senhals, **t 05 65 33 63 07, *www.hotel-sainte-marie.fr* (*inexpensive*). A simple family place in the heart of things; the restaurant (*moderate*) is one of the best in town – leave room for dessert. *Closed mid-Nov–Easter.*

Souillac ✉ 46200

***Les Granges Vieilles, **t** 05 65 37 80 92, (*moderate*). Large country house in a shaded park just outside town, on the D703 from Sarlat. Some of the rooms are elegant and spacious; all have views on to the park and there is a pool. Menus (*moderate*) tending towards the regional, and you can eat on the patio.

***La Vieille Auberge, 1 Rue de la Recège, **t** 05 65 32 79 43, *www.la-vieille-auberge.com* (*inexpensive*). A whiff of Louis XV by the river; and a pool, sauna, hammam and jacuzzi. The excellent restaurant (*moderate*) serves dishes based on the recipes of a century ago, including mountains of *foie gras* but with a lighter touch. *Closed mid-Nov–mid-Dec.*

Sarlat ✉ 24200

***Relais de Moussidière, **t** 05 53 28 28 74 (*expensive–moderate*). Traditional stone manor house set on a cliff with simple, modern rooms, 40-acre landscaped park, a

---

tour contines into the Salle des Grands Gours, a fascinating series of basins, flowing one into the other, with a 20ft waterfall and a green lake at the bottom. And then, after all that, comes the breathtaking grand finale: the Salle du Grand Dôme, a vaulted space soaring up to 305ft, capable of containing two Notre-Dames.

West of Padirac

From the river, **Carennac** presents an enchanting cluster of roofs, walls and turrets around its famous honey-coloured **Prieuré St-Pierre**. Founded in 932 and fortified in the 16th century, it managed to repulse Protestant attacks to preserve some of the finest Romanesque art in the area: the beautiful 12th-century tympanum, sculpted by the school of Toulouse. The frieze below is decorated with an unusual zigzag pattern of animals; in the shadowy interior, capitals carved with primitive birds, animals and monsters add to its atmosphere of archaic mystery. The **cloister** (*open Jan–Mar and early Nov–Dec Mon–Fri 10–12 and 2–5, Sat 2–5; April–mid-June Wed–Mon 10–12 and 2–6.30, closed Tues; mid-June–mid-Sept daily 10–7; mid-Sept–early Nov Mon and Wed– Sat 10–12 and 2–6, Sun 2–6, closed Tues;* **t** *05 65 10 97 01; adm*) houses a 15th-century *Mise en Tombeau*, a poignant composition of eight intricately detailed figures.

pool and lake. Riding, golf and tennis nearby. Restaurant (*expensive*). *Closed Nov–Easter*.

***La Madeleine**, 1 Place de la Petite Rigaudie, t 05 53 59 10 41, *www.hoteldelamadeleine-sarlat.com* (*moderate*). Near the medieval centre, converted from a 19th-century town house; rooms are air-conditioned and soundproof and there's a private garage. Owned by a chef, the restaurant (*expensive*) serves regional specialities – *civet d'oie* in *vin de Cahors* – and lighter, more modern dishes. *Closed Jan–mid-Feb; restaurant closed mid-Nov–mid-Mar*.

****La Couleuvrine**, 1 Place de la Bouquerie, t 05 53 59 27 80 (*inexpensive*). Unusual antique-furnished rooms in the 14th–18th-century ramparts. The restaurant (*moderate*) prides itself on its market-fresh produce. *Restaurant closed early Jan–early Feb*.

Chez Pierre Henri Toulemon, 4 Rue Magnanat, t 05 53 31 26 60, *www.toulemon.com* (*inexpensive*). Up the steps through big oak doors, this *chambres d'hôte* bang in the middle of the old town is classified an historical monument. Very atmospheric.

Le Présidial, near the Place de la Liberté, t 05 53 28 92 47 (*moderate*). Elegant dining room and large patio. Extravagant regional dishes such as *suprême de pigeonneau en croûte sauce aux truffes*, with a choice of French wines.

Criquettamu's, 5 Rue des Armes, t 05 53 59 48 10 (*moderate*). They do tasty things with *foie gras*, magrets and morel mushrooms. *Closed Mon and end Oct–end Mar*.

Domme ✉ 24250

***L'Esplanade**, t 05 53 28 31 41 (*moderate*). Tranquil hotel with cosy rooms, some over-looking the Dordogne. Half-board is mandatory in season – but the restaurant (*expensive*), with a terrace, serves some of the richest food in Périgord, especially when asparagus is in season. *Closed Mon, and Nov–Feb*.

****Le Nouvel Hotel**, Grande Rue, t 05 53 28 38 67 (*inexpensive*). The rooms are comfortable, many with exposed stone walls and one with a wide balcony looking out over Domme's roof tops. The restaurant (*moderate*) was originally stables. There is a roadside terrace for summer. Menus are varied, from cassoulet to *gambas flambées à la vielle prune*. The hotel has just earned its second star. Owner and chef, Jacques Allegre, is welcoming (he also has houses to let if you are interested). *Closed early Nov–Easter*.

La Porte del Bos, t 05 53 28 58 55 (*inexpensive*). B&B in the medieval centre, with en suite rooms, garden, pool and view. *Closed early Nov–Easter*.

Proud medieval **Martel**, the 'City of Seven Towers', resolves under the microscope to a rustic village of 1,400 souls. Severely depopulated over the last century, despite its beauty it wears a melancholy air. In Place des Consuls you'll find the covered market and the huge Palais de la Raymondie (*c.* 1300), now the **Musée d'Uxellodunum** (*open July–Aug Mon–Fri 10–12 and 2–6*), with prehistoric and Gallo-Roman finds. Its *beffroi* is the first of the 'seven towers'. Another is the bell tower of **St-Maur**, a fortified but exquisite Gothic church built into the walls with excellent 16th-century stained glass.

The Dordogne is at its scenic best between Martel and Souillac, meandering cheer-fully through dramatic countryside. The riverside village of **Gluges** fairly cowers beneath a steep riverside cliff, with a church half cut into the rock, and a cave, converted to a fortress in the Middle Ages. Continue along the river to **Creysse**, an exquisite village built around a Romanesque church. Further down, **Lacave** is named after a spectacular subterranean wonder (*open April–June daily 9.30–12 and 2–6; July daily 9.30–12.30 and 1.30–6.30; Aug daily 9.30–6.30; Sept daily 9.30–12 and 2–5.30; end Mar and Oct–early Nov daily 10–12 and 2–5; adm*) – a mile of caverns where the reflec-tions of stalactites in the water give the illusion of an underwater city.

Rocamadour

From neighbouring **L'Hospitalet**, you can get the picture-postcard view of Rocamadour, wedged tight under its overhanging cliff. You can also meet, probably more intimately than you might wish, the 150 Barbary apes and macaques at liberty in the **Forêt des Singes** (*open April–June and Sept daily 10–12 and 1–6; July and Aug 10–7; Oct–early Nov 1–5, Sat, Sun and public hols also 10–12; adm*), only one of a dozen roadside attractions cashing in on the fame of Rocamadour. There's no place quite like it, a vertical cliff-dwellers' town where golden stone houses and chapels are piled on top of one another, while far, far below the little Alzou continues its work of aeons, cutting ever deeper into the gorge. Thanks to its cult of the Black Virgin, Rocamadour has been one of France's top pilgrimage shrines since the 12th century. After falling into decay, it was given a Disney-style restoration, and the pilgrims have been replaced by tourists.

The holy road from L'Hospitalet enters Rocamadour by way of the 13th-century **Porte du Figuier**, one of four gates that defended the village's one real road; you'll find a lift near the second gate, **Porte Salmon**. Beyond, the 15th-century Palais de la Couronnerie is now the **Hôtel de Ville** and tourist office. The street continues through another gate into the **Quartier du Coustalou**, the least restored part of the village, with jumbly houses and a fortified mill. The Grand Escalier leads up via Place des Senhals and Rocamadour's oldest street, Rue de la Mercerie, to a small square, the **Parvis de St-Amadour**, the centre of the holy city, where the pilgrim could visit seven churches just as in Rome, but in a much abbreviated space. These days only two are open all year; for the others you need to take a guided tour (*ask at the tourist office*). Rocamadour's holy of holies, the Flamboyant Gothic **Chapelle Notre-Dame**, dates only from 1479, after a rock crashed off the cliff through the original sanctuary. Inside, darkened by candle smoke, the miraculous Black Virgin still holds court, the proof of her mystic power in the *ex-votos* and chains from petitioners which fill the chapel. Above, the rusty sword in the stone cliff is the legendary Durandel, entrusted by Roland as he died at Roncevalles to the Archangel Michael, who flung it here from the Pyrenees. A hairpin walk (or lift from the Parvis de St-Amadour) takes you up to the 15th-century **château** (*open daily 8–8; adm*), offering a vertiginous view over Rocamadour.

Souillac: Dancing Isaiah and Banjo-strumming Automats

Back on the Dordogne, Souillac doesn't look like much, but its church of **Ste-Marie** makes it a mandatory stop to see one of the true jewels of the Midi. Ste-Marie is Romanesque at its most Roman, striving above all for monumental presence – best seen outside in the majestic apse. The interior is even better: a single, domed nave,

Creamy Cabécou

When it comes to dining, Rocamadour is famous throughout the southwest for its creamy, flat cylinders of goat cheese, so special that they've been classified like wine: AOC *cabécou de Rocamadour*. Connoisseurs like them ripe, pungent, and coated with a tawny crust – the perfect accompaniment to a well-aged Cahors, at their very best between June and November.

graceful and strong. The surviving fragments of the portal have been reconstructed inside the main door. Flanking the relief are the two figures without which no French portal would be complete: St Peter (with the keys) and St Paul (with the book). Outstanding as these reliefs are, the eye is inevitably drawn below to the **'dancing' Isaiah**. Poised on one foot, with stone draperies flowing, the composition is unlike anything else produced in the Middle Ages; a virtuoso display of careful precision and extreme stylization: studied and consistent, a vision of form that is the work of a true artist – one of the greatest between the Greeks and Donatello.

Souillac has acquired another attraction, the ambitious **Musée de l'Automate**, run in collaboration with the robotic experts of the Cité des Sciences de La Villette in Paris (*open Nov–Mar Wed–Sun 2–5; April and May Tues–Sun 10–12 and 3–6; June, Sept and Oct daily 10–12 and 3–6; July and Aug daily 10–7; adm*). Scores of mechanical dolls haunt the premises, and they have some modern robots to keep them company.

Sarlat-la-Canéda

Cocooned inside a clinking ring of 20th-century sprawl, this noble and golden Renaissance town is architecturally the *foie gras* of southwest France and a favourite location for filming swashbucklers. One architectural gem, the 16th-century **Hôtel de Maleville** (now the tourist office) has two distinct Renaissance façades, one French, one Italian. The French one overlooks elongated **Place de la Liberté**, Sarlat's favoured café stop. The narrow **Rue des Consuls** contains many magnificent hôtels; the **Hôtel Selve de Plamon** (Nos. 8–10) stands out – it's early Gothic on the ground floor, Flamboyant Gothic on the first and Renaissance on the second.

Sarlat's great oddity is the **Lanterne des Morts**, a stubby stone rocket built at the end of the 12th century; its original use has been forgotten. Below stretch the flying buttresses and bulb-topped steeple of the **Cathédrale St-Sacerdos**, completed in the dull 17th century; there's nothing particularly to recommend it apart from its spaciousness. Opposite the cathedral stands the most ornate town house in Sarlat, the **Hôtel de la Boétie** (1525), built by the father of the precocious Etienne de la Boétie, who was born here in 1530. La Boétie is mainly remembered as Montaigne's perfect pal in the latter's beautiful *Essay on Friendship*. A 19th-century street, the **Traverse**, cuts the wealthy Sarlat of aristocratic town houses from the steeper, popular neighbourhood to the west, where some alleys are scarcely wide enough to walk arm-in-arm.

Les Mai

One last thing that may or may not be in Domme when you visit is a tall pine pole in Place de la Halle, decorated with hoops and tricolors and a sign reading *Honneur à Notre Maire*; you may well spot similar poles in other villages or towns, or even next to private homes, honouring a boss, a newly married couple, or a newborn baby. They are called *Les Mai*, or maypoles, and are erected at boozy confabs known as *Plantations de Mai*. They are meant to rot away rather than ever be taken down. The Périgourdins have been planting *les Mai* ever since Gallo-Roman times, when a newly elected official would be honoured with a similar pole crowned with a garland. Since the Liberty Trees of the Revolution, they have taken on an added republican virtue.

Domme: the 'Acropolis of Périgord'

Founded by Philippe the Bold in 1281, lovely, honey-hued Domme is a typical *bastide* – but one whose grid plan was remarkably transported on to a steep cliff over the Dordogne. The **Porte des Tours** is the best preserved of its three gates, framed by two fat guard towers, but as with any *bastide*, the focal point is its market square, **Place de la Halle**. One side gives on to the **Belvédère de la Barre**, with panoramic views from Monfort to Beynac. The turreted, asymmetrical Governor's House (from the 1500s) is now the tourist office, where you can buy tickets for the **Grottes de Domme** (*open Mar–Oct daily 2–6; April–June and Sept daily 10–12 and 2–6; July and Aug daily 10–7; adm*) entered through the market in the middle of the square.

The Central Dordogne

This pretty region has always been a major crossroads, once for merchants and armies, now for tourists; few of its fairytale castles were built for decoration.

La Roque-Gageac and a Flurry of Châteaux

Often called *the* most beautiful village in France, the warm stone houses and brown roofs of **La Roque-Gageac** are piled against the overhanging cliff so harmoniously that they hardly seem real. Facing the sunny south (the colours are especially intense at sunset), the village is sheltered enough to grow an exotic garden of cacti by the little church, set on a throne of rock. A few minutes away in **Vézac**, you can wander through some of the prettiest French gardens in the region, by the 17th-century riverside **Château Marqueyssac**, with over 150,000 ancient box trees in hedges on panoramic terraces (*park open mid-Nov–Jan daily 2–5; Feb–April and Oct–mid-Nov daily 10–6; May, June, and Sept daily 10–7; July and Aug daily 9–8*).

The overpowering **Château de Beynac** at Beynac-et-Cazenac soars high over the Dordogne (*open Mar–Nov 10–6.30; Dec–Feb 10–dusk; adm*). Partially wrecked when it was taken by Simon de Montfort in 1214, a monumental 17th-century stairway, a Grand Siècle salon and late 15th-century frescoes survive inside. Opposite Beynac, the powerful hulk of its longtime English nemesis, the **Château de Castelnaud**, stands arrogantly on the cliffs. Its **Musée de la Guerre au Moyen Age** (*guided tours in French and English; open Mar–June and Sept–mid-Nov daily 10–6; July and Aug daily 9–8; mid-Nov–Feb 2–5; adm*) fills the castle once again with catapults and crossbows.

A wooded lane north of Castelnaud follows the river past the privately owned **Château de Fayrac**, built between the 14th and 17th centuries and romantically restored in the 19th. Further on, in its own hamlet, is Castelnaud's third château, **Les Milandes** (*open April–June and Sept Mon–Sat 10–6, Sun 10–7; July and Aug daily 9.30–7; Oct daily 10–5; adm*), a Renaissance beauty which captured the imagination of the cabaret star Josephine Baker in the 1930s. At the time the highest paid performer in Europe, she purchased Les Milandes and 600 acres, and used it to hide people wanted by the Nazis. After the war she spent millions on its restoration, filled it with 13 adopted children, and hosted anti-racism conferences until she fell so deeply into

Getting Around

Trains on the Sarlat–Bordeaux line stop at Le Buisson, Bergerac and St-Emilion; Le Buisson is also on the main Périgueux–Agen line.

Activities

Flat-bottomed *gabares* in La Roque-Gageac offer hour-long **tours**, **t** 05 53 29 40 44 (*Easter–early Nov daily 10–6, www.norbert.fr*); others depart from Beynac, **t** 05 53 28 51 15 (*Easter–early Nov daily 10–6; reserve out of season*). You can also float down the river in a **canoe** and get a bus lift back: contact Canoë-Dordogne, **t** 05 53 29 58 50. Or rise above it all in a **balloon** from La Roque-Gageac, with Mongolfière du Périgord, **t** 05 53 28 18 58.

Where to Stay and Eat

La Roque-Gageac ✉ 24250

★★La Belle Etoile, t 05 53 29 51 44 (*inexpensive*). Modest but welcoming family hotel with a terrace and views of the river and village. Great food (*moderate*): *tatin de foie gras au jus d'agrumes. Closed Mon and Wed lunch.*

★★ Périgord, t 05 53 28 36 55 (*inexpensive*). Huge house in large peaceful grounds outside the village with a pool, tennis and restaurant (*moderate*). *Closed Jan–mid-Mar.*

La Ferme Fleurie, t 05 53 28 33 39 (*inexpensive*). Good B&B near the village. *Open Easter–Oct.*

La Plume d'Oie, t 05 53 29 57 05 (*expensive*). Modern, attractive restaurant overlooking the Dordogne, serving excellent, light renditions of Périgourdin specialities. There are also four pretty rooms to rent (*moderate*). *Closed Sat lunch, Sun eve, Mon eve and Tues lunch. Always book.*

Le Pres Gaillardou, t 05 53 59 67 89 (*moderate*). Highly recommended, with a superb five-course menu, in a charming stone building, partially furnished with antiques. *Closed Mon lunch and Jan and Feb.*

Trémolat ✉ 24510

★★★★Le Vieux Logis, by the church, **t** 05 53 22 80 06, *www.relaischateaux.com* (*very expensive–expensive*). Utterly sybaritic 17th-century manor with a stunning garden and pool. The restaurant serves the best meals for miles around: heavenly *salade du terroir* and *langoustes*, with an excellent wine list. *Closed Tues and Wed lunch.*

debt that she had to sell Les Milandes in 1964. Today it is a shrine to her memory; if you're lucky, the Flamboyant Gothic Chapel where Josephine married may be open.

Cadouin and Christ's Turban

In the 12th century, the **abbey** at Cadouin got hold of a precious relic that put it square on the pilgrimage map of France – the St Suaire, the cloth used to wrap the head of Christ, a lesser Shroud of Turin. In 1100 Hugues, brother of King Louis the Fat of France, purchased the cloth, and when he died he gave it to his confessor, who passed it on to a priest from Périgord, who returned home with it hidden in a vat of Communion wine. He could not help blabbing his secret, however, and it wasn't long before the monks at Cadouin got it off him. Pilgrims to Compostela poured in until the Hundred Years War, when the monks deposited the holy relic in Toulouse's Eglise du Taur for safekeeping; it didn't return to Cadouin until 1456. In 1935 a scientific examination of the cloth showed it to be an 11th-century Egyptian weaving.

The **abbey church** (*open Sept–Dec and mid-Feb–June Wed–Mon 10–12.30 and 2–5.30, closed Tues; July and Aug daily 10–7*) was consecrated in 1154. The interior, with its three naves and domes, has been stripped naked to reveal the vigorous architecture in all its purity. The reliquary holding the St Suaire originally hung behind the altar; only the dangling chains remain. The Flamboyant Gothic **cloister** took so long to build that the west gallery is entirely Renaissance, with a hearty mix of sacred and profane sculpture.

Bergerac to Bordeaux

Bergerac

Bergerac is a fine little city where swans swim in the Dordogne and a cluster of medieval, half-timbered houses basks by the old river port. In the 12th century it became a majoar crossroads, thanks to a bridge – at that time the only one on the river – and naturally evolved into a commercial city. The Bergeracois converted to Protestantism with gusto, and by the end of the 17th century an estimated 40,000 inhabitants had emigrated to England and Holland. The city only revived at the end of the 19th century thanks to wine and the national gunpowder works.

And tobacco. Bergerac is the home of the national Institut du Tabac and celebrates the much-maligned weed, first popularized in France by Catherine de Médicis who used it to cure her migraines, in the **National Tobacco Museum** (*open Tues–Fri 10–12 and 2–6, Sat 10–12 and 2–5, Sun 2.30–6.30; adm – but no smoking!*), in the handsome, turreted Maison Peyrarède in Place du Feu. It's full of curiosities that trace the evolution of snuff, pipes, cigars and cigarettes in Europe. The picturesque 16th-century Cloître des Récollets serves as the **Maison des Vins** (*open Feb–mid-June and Sept–Dec Tues–Sat 10.30–12.30 and 2–6; mid-June–Aug daily 10–7*), headquarters of the regional

Getting There and Around

Bergerac's **airport**, Roumanières, lies 10km to the south; Ryanair and Flybe fly from the UK. The **station** is on the Bordeaux–Sarlat line; for the Périgueux–Agen line change at Le Buisson.

Tourist Information

Bergerac: 97 Rue Neuve d'Argenson, t 05 53 57 03 11, *www.bergerac-tourisme.com*.

Where to Stay

Bergerac ✉ 24100

***Le Bordeaux, 38 Place Gambetta, t 05 53 57 12 83, *www.hotel-bordeaux-bergerac.com* (*moderate*). Modern hotel in the centre, with a garden and pool; its restaurant (*expensive–moderate*) serves unusual delicacies – the most upriver version of *lamproie à la bordelaise*, and *aiguillettes de canard au miel*.

***La Flambée, 153 Av Pasteur, t 05 53 57 52 33, *www.laflambee.com* (*moderate*). Welcoming family-run hotel outside the centre on the Périgueux road, with pool and tennis in a panoramic park. Kitchen (*moderate*) noted for its delicious southwest specialities.

**Le Family, 3 Rue du Dragon, near Place du Marché Couvert, t 05 53 57 80 90 (*inexpensive*). Central and friendly; parking available, and restaurant.

Eating Out

L'Imparfait, 8 Rue des Fontaines, t 05 53 57 47 92 (*expensive–moderate*). In the historic centre, serving fresh cuisine. *Closed Sun in winter, and mid-Nov–mid-Jan*.

Le Poivre et Sel, 11 Rue de l'Ancien Port, t 05 53 27 02 30 (*moderate*). Old, timbered and elegant restaurant with a pretty patio. Culinary delights include *gambas flambés au pastis* and a good choice of salads.

Château de Monbazillac, t 05 53 58 38 93 (*moderate*). Outside the centre, a restaurant in the former *chais* of this château – a favourite for its fine classic cuisine, with a long wine list and summer dining on the terrace. *Closed Nov–start of April*.

Ferme-Auberge Le Montell, at Lamonzie-St-Martin, 8km along the road to Bordeaux, t 05 53 24 07 59 (*moderate*). Well-prepared farm dishes with *tourain à l'ail*, duck and chicken and home-made desserts. *Closed Sept. Always book*.

wine council, stocking a wide selection of Bergerac vintages and other regional products. Tree-filled **Place de la Myrpe** contains the town's photo opportunity: a suitably nosed statue of swashbuckling **Cyrano de Bergerac**, although Rostand's poet cavalier never set foot in the town, and nor did his real-life inspiration, Savinien Cyrano.

Around Bergerac

High on a ridge, 6km south of Bergerac, the **Château de Monbazillac** (*open June–Sept daily 10–7; May and Oct daily 10–12.30 and 2–7; Nov–April daily 10–12 and 2–5; closed Jan; adm*) was erected in 1550 and essentially remains the same as the day it was built, undamaged and unimproved: a nice compromise between the necessities of defence and beauty. The grounds and two lower floors are open to the public, with displays on the château's golden wine and the noble rot that makes it so good.

Further down the Dordogne, swathed in vineyards next to the hamlet of St-Michel-de-Montaigne, stands the **Château de Montaigne**, where Michel Eyquem de Montaigne was born in 1533. The eldest of eight children of a Catholic father and Jewish mother, Montaigne learnt Latin as his first language and Greek as a child's game. He followed a legal career as a court counsellor in Périgueux and Bordeaux until 1572, when he despaired over the hypocrisy of the law and the horror of the St Bartholomew's Day Massacre, and retreated from the world (helped by a sizeable dowry from his wife) to his château above the Dordogne. He was 39 at the time, and vowed to spend the rest of his life doing nothing at all; instead, he wrote three volumes of Essays. The freest French thinker of the 16th century, Montaigne was also the most sceptical. The only sane response to the world, he reasoned, was to accept constant mutability and chaos with a smile. *'Que sais-je?'* ('What do I know?') was his motto. In 1885 the château went up in flames, but the **round tower** where Montaigne wrote his celebrated *Essays* survived (*guided tours Wed–Sun Nov–April 10–12 and 2–5.30; May, June, Sept and Oct 10–12 and 2–6.30; July and Aug 10–6.30; closed Jan and early Feb; adm*). On the top floor is the philosopher's famous inner sanctum, a library, where he could sit at his desk surrounded by bookshelves and windows; the beams still bear the Greek and Latin maxims Montaigne liked to ponder.

St-Emilion

Set in a natural amphitheatre surrounded by vines, St-Emilion is a gem, a lovely town mellowed to the colour of old piano keys. Its lanes, called *tertres*, are so steep that handrails have been installed down their centres. The town's greatest secrets are kept underground – not only the ruby nectar in its cellars, but Europe's largest subterreanean church. Four of these secrets can only be seen on the tourist office's guided tour (*see* box, right). If you're staying the night, save the tour of the town walls for dusk, when the views are at their most romantic.

The ruined Romanesque **Cloître des Cordeliers** (*open daily 10–12 and 2–6.30*) was built in 1383 by the Franciscans. Note the carving of two snakes entering a jar in the adjacent chapel – a symbol that goes back to the ancient Greeks and which the

Getting Around

There are two **railway** stations near St-Émilion, 2km away in the countryside, on the Bordeaux–Bergerac–Sarlat line, and Libourne, 7km away, on the Bordeaux–Paris TGV line. Several Citram **buses** link it daily to Bordeaux and Libourne, **t** 05 56 43 68 43.

Tourist Information

St-Emilion: Place des Créneaux, **t** 05 57 55 28 28, *www.saint-emilion-tourisme.com*. The place to book a tour of the Eglise Monolithe, the Chapelle de la Trinité, the catacombs and the Grotte de l'Ermitage.

Where to Stay

St-Emilion ✉ **33330**
Don't expect to find any bargains.
★★★★Château Grand-Barrail, Route de Libourne, **t** 05 57 55 37 00, *www.grand-barrail.com* (*luxury*). Very exclusive, with attitudes to match. Good restaurant (*expensive*). *Closed end of Nov–mid-Dec and Feb.*
★★★★Hostellerie de Plaisance, Place du Clocher, **t** 05 57 55 07 55, *www.hostellerie-plaisance.com* (*expensive*). Handsome stone building housing the most luxurious hotel in town (with facilities for the disabled); it has a gourmet restaurant. *Closed Jan.*
★★★Palais Cardinal, Place du 11 Novembre 1918, **t** 05 57 24 72 39 (*expensive–moderate*).

Stately family-run hotel with small but handsome rooms, and a heated pool; ask for a room overlooking the lovely garden terrace. *Closed Dec–Feb.*

Lussac ✉ **33330**
Château de Roques, **t** 05 57 74 55 69 (*moderate*). On the D21 on the road to St-Médard. B&B amid the vineyards with copious country cooking and free wine-tasting. *Closed mid-Dec–early Feb.*

Eating Out

Francis Goullée, 27 Rue Guadet, **t** 05 57 24 70 49 (*expensive–moderate*). Taste-packed Rabelaisian cuisine. *Closed Sun eve and Mon and early Dec–after Christmas.*
Le Tertre, on Tertre de la Tente, **t** 05 57 74 46 33 (*expensive–moderate*). Gastronomic cuisine and good wine list. *Closed Tues in summer, Mon and Tues out of season, and mid-Nov–mid-Dec.*
L'Envers du Décor, Rue du Clocher, **t** 05 57 74 48 31 (*moderate*). Excellent value wine bar with a terrace, where you can try a wide variety of local labels by the glass, with a snack or light meal. *Closed weekends out of season.*
Ferme Auberge du Cros Figeac, **t** 05 57 24 76 32 (*moderate*). In a lovely vineyard setting on the road to Libourne: exquisite meats grilled over vines, and a memorable warm *foie gras* with apple. Book. *Closed Sun eve, Mon and Tues eve.*

friars must have copied from the Eglise Monolithe, where it appears twice. Further up, **Place du Marché** is a magnificent urbane stage set, where cafés are shaded by a Liberty Tree planted in 1848.

Built into the flank of the cliff here is the strange **Eglise Monolithe**, started by the Benedictines in the 8th century; when they had excavated a cavity measuring 124 by 66ft in the 11th century, they gave it up to construct the Collégiale. It is a primitive, sombre and uncanny place, its nave supported by ten rough, ill-aligned pillars. The only decoration that remains are bas-reliefs: four winged angels, signs of the zodiac, and a dedicatory inscription. Bell ropes from the original bell tower hung through the hole in the ceiling. Next door is the round **Chapelle de la Trinité**, built in the 13th century by Augustinian monks and converted into a coopery during the Revolution. In the adjacent 8th-century **catacombs** you can make out the engraved figures of three corpses with upraised arms, weird zombies symbolic of the Resurrection. Bones were deposited through the funnel-like cupola connecting the catacombs with the cemetery. The **Grotte de l'Ermitage**, the cave of the hermit Emilion, was reshaped over the centuries into a chapel. The cave's spring has been worshipped since pagan times.

St-Emilion's landmark 11th–15th-century **bell tower** rises up 173ft from Place des Créneaux; you can climb up for a superb view of the town. Here, too, is the entrance to the **Collégiale**, a hotchpotch begun in 1110; in the choir are 15th-century stalls and the treasure, and Emilion's saintly relics. From the tourist office you can enter the pretty twin-columned Gothic **Cloître de la Collégiale**. There are more grand views from the top of the austere Norman **Tour du Roi** (*open July and Aug daily 10.30–12.45 and 2.15–8; Sept–June 2–6.30; adm*), all that remains of the castle built by Henry III (*c.* 1237).

Then there's the wine. No one can really explain why St-Emilion is so good, except that it has been subject to the strictest quality control in France for centuries. The **Maison du Vin**, Place Pierre-Meyrat (**t** 05 57 55 50 55), and the tourist office have booklets on the *chais* open for visits – and how much you'll pay for a tasting. Another alternative is to take one of the tourist office's tours (*May–Sept Mon–Sat; English available*).

Bordeaux

Bordeaux is both terribly grand and terribly shabby and monotonous, a mercantile city that has lost its port, a city of long flat vistas tinted in a thousand nuances of white. Most of the city as you see it today was begun in the 18th century, when Bordeaux's *intendants* started demolishing its poky, crowded medieval streets to replace them with the Place Royale (now Place de la Bourse) and other new squares, wide *cours* or *allées* planted with trees to link them, and the first public gardens; to adorn them, 5,000 new buildings went up, including the riverfront Grande Façade. By the beginning of the Revolution, Bordeaux was the third city in France, and one of the most cosmopolitan, with a population of over 100,000 and close trading contacts with the new United States.

During and immediately after Napoleon, Bordeaux hit one of its low ebbs and – although its first-ever bridge over the Garonne was built in 1822, its quays were modernized and it had one of the first railways in France (1841) – little new industry came its way. However, Bordeaux still managed to spread; these days the 220,000 Bordelais have the dubious honour of taking up more room per capita than any other city-dwellers in France. Even the vineyards fell victim – today you'll find some of the most august wine châteaux totally immersed in sprawl.

The South Side of Town: Ste-Croix and St-Michel

The first monuments that beckon in this genteelly dilapidated neighbourhood are in the vicinity of the former monastery church of **Ste-Croix**. Built in the 12th century, this once had an exuberant Old Curiosity Shop of a façade that was entrusted in 1860 to Paul Abadie who, full of the destructive self-confidence of his time, completely dismantled it and put it back together all wrong. The south tower, portal, figures of Avarice and Luxury, and some carved capitals in the transept survived the Abadie touch.

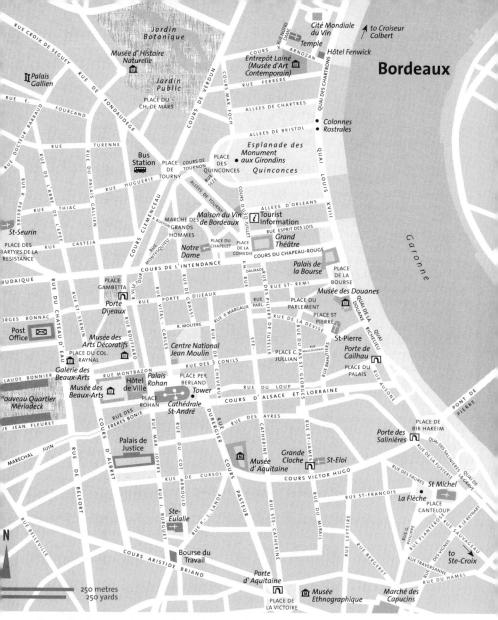

Since Charlemagne's day, a church has stood at the site of **St-Michel**, in what is now a lively Portuguese–North African neighbourhood. A morning flea market takes place under its 15th-century detached bell tower, the 'arrow' or **Flêche**, at 377ft the highest monument in southwest France. Grimy, Flamboyant Gothic St-Michel was a product of Bordeaux's medieval prosperity, largely built by the city's guilds. It is missing one of its best features – the stained glass, blasted away by Allied bombers in the last war. The chapels furnished by the guilds contain the best art. On the river near St-Michel, the **Porte des Salinières**, the 'salt' gate (1755), overlooks the **Pont de Pierre**, the oldest of Bordeaux's bridges, built in 1842 and prettily lit at night by a necklace of street lamps.

Getting There

Bordeaux International **airport** (Flybe, Bmibaby, BA, Air France) is 12km west of the centre at Mérignac, **t** 05 56 34 50 50, *www.bordeaux-aeroport.fr*. A shuttle bus links the airport to the railway station, the tourist office and the Barrière Judaïque.

All **trains** use Bordeaux St-Jean station in Rue Charles-Domerq, **t** 08 36 35 35 35. TGVs from Paris-Montparnasse take 3hrs; regular trains from Paris-Austerlitz take 4½hrs. Other connections are Périgueux; Sarlat by way of St-Emilion and Bergerac; Tarbes by way of Orthez, Pau and Lourdes; TGVs or regular trains to Hendaye by way of Dax, Bayonne, Biarritz and St-Jean-de-Luz, or to Toulouse (2hrs) by way of Agen and Montauban, or 3hrs by way of Moissac. Local lines run to Mont-de-Marsan, Pointe de Grave and Arcachon.

The station for Citram **buses** serving most towns and villages in the Gironde is at Allée des Chartres, just off Place des Quinconces, **t** 05 56 43 68 43.

Bordeaux has a ring road called the *rocade*, making it sometimes easier to circumvent it than to penetrate to its centre. There are a number of car parks in the centre.

Getting Around

The city's CGFTE **buses** (**t** 05 57 57 88 88 for information) are frequent, convenient and huge; from the station, bus no.7 will take you to Place Gambetta and the Chartrons; bus no.1 follows the river.

You can hire **bikes** at Bordeaux Vélo, Quai Louis XVIII, **t** 05 56 44 77 31.

Cabbies are not allowed to cruise in Bordeaux, but there are **taxi** ranks in key locations, and 24-hour ranks at the railway station and Place Gambetta.

Tourist Information

Bordeaux: 12 Cours du 30 Juillet, **t** 05 56 00 66 00; also Gare St-Jean (June–Sept), **t** 05 56 91 64 70; *www.bordeaux-tourisme.com*.

There is also an introduction to wine tasting at the Maison du Vin de Bordeaux, 3 Cours du 30 Juillet/Place de la Comédie; they also run regular excursions to some of the most famous vineyards with tastings.

To save money on tours, visits, transport and accommodation you can take up the package 'Bordeaux Découverte' which includes two nights in a two–four star hotel, a tour of the city and a vineyard, as well as free access to main sites and museums. Book at least ten days in advance. Contact the tourist office.

Shopping

Bordeaux is a great town for antiques, with a bric-a-brac **antiques market** in Place St-Michel (*Tues–Sun*) and shops on Rue Bouffard, by the Musée des Arts Décoratifs, and Rue Notre-Dame in the Chartrons.

English **books** are available at Bradley's Bookshop, 8 Cours Albret. One of the last remaining shops of its kind in France, founded in 1814, Au Sanglier de Russie, 67 Cours d'Alsace et Lorraine, sells a huge range of **exotic brushes**.

Where to Stay

Bordeaux ✉ 33000

★★★★**Burdigala**, 115 Rue Georges-Bonnac, **t** 05 56 90 16 16, *www.burdigala.com* (*luxury–expensive*). Luxury and personality in the heart of town, with elegant, air-conditioned rooms individually styled with wood, stone and marble.

★★★**Ste Catherine**, 27 Rue du Parlement, **t** 05 56 81 95 12, *www.bordeaux-hotelquality.com* (*expensive*). In a handsomely restored 18th-century *hôtel particulier* near the Grand Théâtre, the most comfortable hotel in its class, with exceptionally nice rooms.

★★**Le Continental**, 10 Rue Montesquieu, **t** 05 56 52 66 00, *www.hotel-le-continental.com* (*expensive–moderate*). Elegant hotel on a central pedestrianized street.

★★★**Le Majestic**, between the Grand Théâtre and Place des Quinconces, **t** 05 56 52 60 44, (*moderate*). Dead central with comfortable air-conditioned rooms, an inner garden and garage, but no restaurant.

★★**Les Quatre Sœurs**, 6 Cours 30-Juillet (near the Quinconces), **t** 05 57 81 19 20 (*moderate–inexpensive*). Where Richard Wagner slept, before he was run out of town for dallying with the wife of a local politician; the rooms are cosy, overlooking either the street or a courtyard.

★★Notre-Dame, 36 Rue Notre-Dame, t 05 56 52 88 24 (*inexpensive*). Pretty little hotel in a 19th-century building in the Chartrons.

★★La Tour Intendance, 16 Rue Vieille-Tour, t 05 56 81 46 27 (*inexpensive*). Centrally located, on a pedestrian-only lane off Cours de l'Intendance; simple and sweet.

Amboise, 22 Rue Vieille-Tour (near Place Gambetta), t 05 56 81 62 67 (*inexpensive*). One of the best of the cheaper options.

Eating Out

Unlike most folks, who pick a bottle to go with their meal, the Bordelais tend to choose a vintage first, then create a menu that will enhance the wine. The wide choice of Bordeaux specialities range from the famous *entrecôte à la bordelaise* to the more rarefied pleasures of lamprey, which is 'in season' in April and May. Prices here have remained reasonable;. Note that you could starve in August or on Sundays, when the city's beaneries shut down as tight as a clam.

Le Chapon Fin, 5 Rue Montesquieu, t 05 56 79 10 10, *www.chapon-fin.com* (*very expensive–expensive*). The oldest restaurant in Bordeaux (since 1825) and one of the best. Sarah Bernhardt and Edward VII stopped in whenever they were in town. Its sumptuous rococo décor and inner garden are a perfect match for the lovely regional food; long lists of *grands crus*. *Closed Sun and Mon.*

Jean Ramet, 7 Place Jean-Jaurès, t 05 56 44 12 51 (*expensive*). One of Bordeaux's classiest restaurants where chef Ramet prepares both old-fashioned and original dishes to the delight of his fashionable customers. *Closed Sun and Mon.*

Le Vieux Bordeaux, 27 Rue Buhan, t 05 56 52 94 36 (*expensive–moderate*). Dine in their delightful closed courtyard. Famous for the high quality of every dish. *Closed Sat lunch, Mon lunch and Sun.*

La Tupina, 6 Rue Porte-de-la-Monnaie, near St-Michel, t 05 56 91 56 37, *www.latupina. com* (*expensive–moderate*). Bailiwick of Jean-Pierre Xiradakis, master of bringing out the true tastes of ingredients, and a good place to fill up on hearty delights.

Didier Gelineau, 26 Rue du Pas St-Georges, t 05 56 52 84 25 (*expensive–moderate*). Charming restaurant offering haute cuisine at affordable prices: try the breaded lamb chops with truffles. *Closed Sat lunch, Mon lunch and Sun.*

L'Alhambra, 111 bis Rue Judaïque, t 05 56 96 06 91 (*moderate*). For a delicious beef fillet with a creamy mustard sauce or poached pineapple with kirsch sorbet. *Closed Sat lunch, Mon lunch and Sun.*

Chez Philippe, 1 Place du Parlement, t 05 56 81 83 15 (*moderate*). Fish-lovers come to worship here. *Closed Sun and Mon.*

Restaurant de Fromages Baud et Millet, 19 Rue Huguerie, t 05 56 79 05 77, *www.baudetmillet.com* (*moderate*). Offers hundreds of wines from around the world to go with its 200 types of farm cheese, *raclettes* and other dishes. *Closed Sun.*

Bistro du Sommelier, 163 Rue Georges-Bonnac, t 05 56 96 71 78 (*moderate*). Simple meals and a wide array of bottles. *Closed Sat lunch and Sun.*

Entertainment and Nightlife

The premier **stage** remains Victor Louis' Grand Théâtre, Place de la Comédie, box office t 05 56 00 85 95 (*open 11–6; closed Sun and Mon*), followed by the Théâtre Femina, 8 Rue de Grassi, box office t 05 56 48 26 26. The Orchestre National Bordeaux Aquitaine frequently performs in the Palais des Sports, Place de la Ferme Richemont, t 05 56 79 39 61. The ultramodern Espace Culturel du Pin Galant, out at Mérignac due west of Bordeaux, t 05 56 97 82 82, puts on a full calendar of performances. Of Bordeaux's **cinemas**, the Trianon Jean Vigo, Rue Franklin, t 05 56 44 35 17, is the most likely to show something good in VO; also try UGC, 13–15 Rue Georges Bonnac, t 08 92 70 00 00.

To top off a late night in Bordeaux, finish up at the Marché des Capucins near St-Michel for a bowl of onion soup with the workers unloading the produce. **Bars** here open from 1 to 5am; try **Le P'tit Déj**, 8 Place des Capucins.

From here busy Cours Victor Hugo will take you to the bustling heart of Bordeaux, past the 14th-century belled gate built under the reign of the Black Prince, the **Grosse Cloche**, to pedestrian-only **Rue Ste-Catherine**, the city's main shopping street since Roman times, and often swarming with bargain-hunters.

Musée d'Aquitaine

20 Cours Pasteur; open Tues–Sun 11–6; closed Mon and public hols; adm.

Continue along Cours Victor Hugo for one of the most compelling museums in southwest France, its subject is the history of Aquitaine, and one of its first works is the mysterious 25,000-year-old bas-relief of the *Venus with a Horn* from Laussel in the Dordogne. The excellent Gallo-Roman section has coins, mosaics, sculptures and a fascinating set of reliefs from everyday life in ancient *Burdigala*. Further on is a legless but still impressive bronze Hercules, and a room dedicated to finds from a mithraeum discovered in 1982 during the construction of a car park: in the 2nd and 3rd century, Mithraism, an all-male, monotheistic religion from the east, posed serious competition to Christianity. A statue shows the birth of Mithras, rising from earth with the cosmic globe in one hand and a knife to slay bulls in the other; there are statues of Cautes and Cautopatès, his two companions, and a rare *Léontocéphale*, a lion-headed man holding keys, his legs entwined with chicken-headed snakes.

Cathédrale St-André

Bordeaux's great Gothic cathedral was built under English rule between the 13th and 15th centuries. Like St-Michel, it has a lofty detached bell tower, the **Tour Pey-Berland** (*open June–Sept daily 10–6.30, otherwise daily 10–12.30 and 2–5.30; closed Mon and public hols; adm*), which was used as a lead ball factory from 1793 until 1850, when it was repurchased by the archbishop, truncated and crowned with a shiny Notre-Dame-d'Aquitaine. The views over Bordeaux are superb. The cathedral itself is supported by an intricate web of buttresses; its west front, originally part of the city wall, is bare. A fine 14th-century tympanum with the *Last Supper* crowns the north transept door; the nearby Porte Royale (used by visiting kings and dignitaries) has another, with a rhythmic *Last Judgement*. The south portal, dedicated to the Virgin, lost its tympanum to make room for carts when the church was converted into a feed store during the Revolution. As in the Middle Ages, the doors are usually left wide open, as a pedestrian shortcut; the single nave is nearly as long and wide as Notre-Dame (410 by 145ft).

Just north of the cathedral, the **Centre National Jean Moulin** (*open Tues–Fri 11–6, Sat and Sun 2–6*) contains a collection devoted to the Occupation, Resistance and Deportation, from posters to an ingenious folding motorcycle. Upstairs, the office of the courageous Resistance leader Jean Moulin has been reconstructed.

Musée des Beaux-Arts and Musée des Arts Décoratifs

20 Cours d'Albret; open Wed–Mon and hols 11–6; adm.

Most of the large, luxurious **Palais Rohan** (1770s) holds Bordeaux' city hall (*guided tours Wed 2.30; adm*), but one wing contains paintings by artists rarely seen in French provincial museums – Titian, Perugino, Van Dyck, Rubens, Reynolds, Ruysdael, Chardin, Delacroix, Boudin, Magnasco, and Bordeaux native Odilon Redon (1840–1916), introspective precursor of the Surrealists. There is also a selection of minor paintings by major 20th-century artists – Matisse, Bonnard, Renoir and Seurat.

Behind the museum is the **Nouveau Quartier Mériadeck**, the largest single urban renovation scheme in France. Seven hectares were set aside for greenery and fountains, and the buildings facing this central mall were designed in cruciforms to spare pedestrians the sight of the plain-jane skyscraper. Most of Mériadeck is occupied by government bureaucracies, and it shrivels to a desert after dark. It was, however, the first major project in Europe to make large-scale use of geothermal heating (1981).

Nearby the excellent **Musée des Arts Décoratifs** (*39 Rue Bouffard; during temporary exhibitions open Wed–Mon 11–6, otherwise 2–6; closed Tues and hols; adm, free the first Sun of each month*) has a perfect home in a neoclassical *hôtel particulier* (1779), with fine furniture, wallpaper, ceramics, paintings, gold and silverwork, glass, jewellery, and costumes. In summer, brunch and lunch are served in the elegant courtyard.

St-Seurin

Open daily 8–12 and 2–6.30.

Bordeaux's oldest church, founded by the city's 5th-century bishop Severinus, still stands, although in an often remodelled state (). The 14th-century porch with lavish sculptures survives, as does, rather unusually, an 11th-century porch, hidden behind the undistinguished façade of 1828. Inside, a 7th-century sarcophagus does duty as an altar in the **Chapelle St-Etienne**, and there is a beautiful 15th-century alabaster retable in the **Chapelle Notre-Dame-de-la Rose** and 14 alabaster panels in the choir. Note, too, the magnificent 15th-century episcopal throne, curiously made of stone imitating wood, and the sculpted choir stalls. The **crypt** (you may have to ask the sacristan to open it) holds a collection of 6th- and 7th-century treasures; excavations have revealed the 4th-century **Palaeo-Christian crypt** underneath, with sarcophogi and frescoes (*guided tours June–Sept daily 3–7; adm*).

Quartier St-Pierre

From the 3rd to the 12th century, St-Pierre was a separate walled quarter outside Bordeaux, built around the Palais de l'Ombrière, home of the dukes of Aquitaine and kings of England, of which only the **Porte Cailhau** (*guided tours June–Sept daily 3–7; adm*) survives, overlooking the river with its asymmetrical turrets and tower. From here, you can see the 18th-century **Grande Façade** project that created a kilometre of homogenous architecture from Cours du Chapeau Rouge to Porte de la Monnaie, a row of pale stone houses, with arcades and *mascarons*, topped by two floors of large windows and mansard roofs with dormers.

The presence of the Parlement from the 15th century on led to the construction of stately 18th-century *hôtels particuliers*. You can see the best of them by walking straight through Porte Cailhau to Rue du Loup, crossing Rue Ste-Catherine, and turning right into Rue de Cheverus. From here turn left up Rue Poquelin-Molière, right into Rue Grassi, and right again into Rue St-Rémi, which leads into Bordeaux's neoclassical showcase, the **Place de la Bourse**. In the centre a fountain of the Three Graces (1864) holds court between the Palais de la Bourse and the Hôtel des Douanes, which must be the most grandiose customs house in the world, now home to the **Musée des Douanes** (*open daily 10–6, closed Mon; adm*).

The Golden Triangle

Bordeaux's Golden Triangle of good taste and luxury shops is formed by Cours de l'Intendance, Cours Georges-Clemenceau and Allées de Tourny. Setting the tone is the lavishly Baroque **Notre-Dame** (1684–1707), in Place du Chapelet, modelled after the Gesù in Rome. Behind it, in the centre of the Golden Triangle, is the shopping mall, the **Marché des Grands-Hommes**.

Bordeaux's **Grand Théâtre,** designed by Victor Louis (1773), is its proudest showcase, resembling a Greek temple fronted by a row of mighty Corinthian columns and crowned with statues of goddesses and muses. If it looks fairly restrained from the outside, all sumptuous hell breaks loose within. The vestibule has more columns; the bold grand stair was copied by Garnier for the Paris Opéra; the auditorium has golden columns and a domed ceiling hung with a crystal chandelier weighing 2,860 lbs.

The Esplanade des Quinconces and Around

Just down the Cours 30 Juillet rises the overblown 19th-century **Monument aux Girondins**, a lofty column crowned by Liberty over a fountain mobbed by Happiness, Eloquence, Security, a crowing cockerel and a host of other allegories. The Nazis stripped the fountain of its bronzes in 1943; to everyone's surprise they weren't melted down, but later found squirrelled away in Angoulême. Stretching out endlessly from here is Europe's largest squares-cum-car parks, the **Place des Quinconces**.

In contrast, the **Jardin Public**, Bordeaux's first patch of greenery (1756), redesigned a century later in the romantic *style anglais*, makes for a delightful wander; it contains the **Jardin Botanique** (*open daily 8–6*) and the **Musée d'Histoire Naturelle** (*open Wed–Mon 11–6, Sat and Sun 2–6; adm, free the first Sun of each month*). Behind the museum, a monumental entrance and a few arches known as the **Palais Gallien** are all that remains of the 15,000-seat Roman amphitheatre of *Burdigala* (3rd century AD).

The Chartrons

The Chartrons quarter prospered in the 17th century when Flemish wine merchants set up shop here, followed by the Germans, Irish and English, who founded fabulously wealthy wine dynasties. The area declined during the Revolution when many Chartrons merchants were guillotined and most of the others moved abroad. Its commerce revived into the 20th century, but since the 1960s Bordeaux has sought a new role for the quarter while maintaining as much of its original wine trade as possible. There's the new (and utterly sterile) **Cité Mondiale du Vin** on the Quai des Chartrons, as well as hotels and a conference centre, with exhibitions and shops open to the general public. The vast neoclassical Entrepôt Lainé, where spices and other goods imported from France's colonies were unloaded, now hosts the giant installations of the **capc Musée d'Art Contemporain** (*open daily 11–6, Wed until 8; closed Mon and hols; adm, free the first Sun of each month*), as well as a charming café.

The old wine trade is remembered in the **Musée des Chartrons**, 41 Rue Borie (*open Mon–Fri 2–6; adm*), with a collection of lithographed wine labels and bottles going back to the 1600s. Then there's **Vinorama**, 12 Cours Médoc (*open June–Sept Mon–Sat 10.30–12.30 and 2.30–6.30, Sun 2–6.30; otherwise Tues–Fri 2–6.30, Sat 10.30–12.30 and 2.30–6.30; adm*), a cheesy museum of talking wax figures who explain the history of Bordeaux wine, complete with tastings of wines.

The Gironde

Bordeaux's *département*, the Gironde, is full of superlatives. It is the largest in France, contains 2,170 miles of rivers and 72 miles of Atlantic coast. In the Gironde you'll find France's largest two lakes, Europe's largest estuary, its oldest lighthouse, its highest sand dune and the northern fringes of Les Landes, its largest forest. Not to mention the largest and, by most criteria, the best wine region in the world.

Southeast of Bordeaux

Entre-Deux-Mers

This is one of France's best-kept secrets: a lovely undulating plateau of soft limestone (the name comes from *inter duo maria*, 'between two estuaries': the Dordogne and the Garonne), occasionally reaching over 320ft in altitude, pocked with natural cavities. Its fine, blond stone was quarried to build Bordeaux, leaving behind tunnels converted into mushroom farms.

Créon, a *bastide* of 1316, is one of the chief towns in the region. Three kilometres to the east stand the remarkable ruins of the Benedictine **Abbaye de la Sauve-Majeure** (*open June–Sept Tues–Sun 10–6.30; Oct–May Tues–Sun 10–1 and 2.30–5.30; closed Mon; adm*), founded in 1079. The great Romanesque church dates from the golden age of the 1200s, although only the skeleton survives. Few skeletons, however, command such presence: three of the twelve massive pillars that supported the triple nave still stand, culminating in a row of five 'bread oven' apses, while the lofty hexagonal bell tower still rises with panache from the fourth bay, fitted with a viewing platform on top. The most spectacular capitals are in the choir and apses: there are scenes of drinking griffons, fighting centaurs, scenes from Genesis, Daniel in the Lion's Den and Samson; more relics are in the **museum** in the former monastery.

Along the Garonne

The most dramatic scenery in the Entre-Deux-Mers overlooks the Garonne, where the vineyards produce AOC Premières Côtes de Bordeaux instead of white wine. Here you'll find **Cadillac**, a riverside *bastide* of 1280, which gave birth to a local boy named Antoine Laumet, who went off to seek his fortune in America, where he adopted the

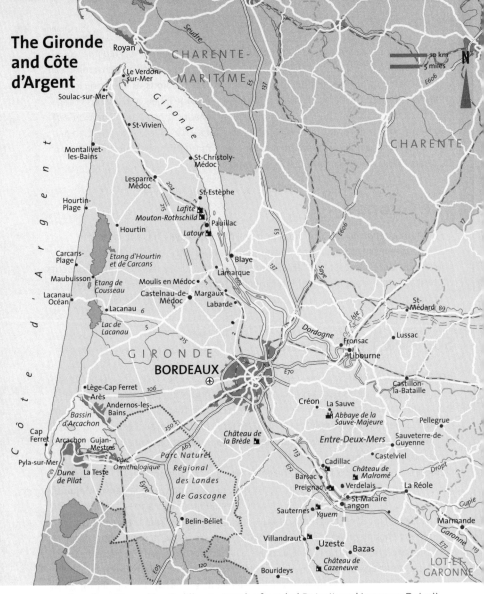

The Gironde and Côte d'Argent

Royan

Le Verdon-sur-Mer

Soulac-sur-Mer

Gironde

St-Vivien

CHARENTE

Montalivet-les-Bains

St-Christoly-Médoc

Lesparre-Médoc

St-Estèphe

Hourtin-Plage

Lafite

Mouton-Rothschild

Pauillac

Hourtin

Latour

Carcans-Plage

Étang d'Hourtin et de Carcans

Blaye

Lamarque

Maubuisson

Étang de Cousseau

Moulis en Médoc

Lacanau-Océan

Castelnau-de-Médoc

Margaux

Labarde

St-Médard

Lacanau

Lac de Lacanau

Dordogne

Fronsac

Lussac

GIRONDE

Libourne

BORDEAUX

Castillon-la-Bataille

Lège-Cap Ferret

Arès

Créon

La Sauve

Andernos-les-Bains

Abbaye de la Sauve-Majeure

Pellegrue

Bassin d'Arcachon

Sauveterre-de-Guyenne

Cap Ferret

Arcachon

Gujan-Mestras

Château de la Brède

Entre-Deux-Mers

Castelviel

Pyla-sur-Mer

Parc Ornithologique

Cadillac

Dropt

Dune de Pilat

La Teste

Parc Naturel Régional des Landes de Gascogne

Château de Malromé

La Réole

Barsac

Preignac

Verdelais

St-Macaire

Gupie

Belin-Béliet

Sauternes

Yquem

Langon

Marmande

Garonne

Villandraut

Uzeste

Bazas

LOT-ET-GARONNE

Bourideys

Château de Cazeneuve

grander alias of Lamothe-Cadillac. In 1702 he founded Detroit, and in 1902 a Detroit car-maker in turn adopted his name, and the rest is history. The village also boasts something even bigger than its eponymous car: the **Château de Cadillac** (1620), built by Henri III's favourite *mignon*, the fabulously wealthy Nogaret de La Valette, Duc d'Epernon (*open April–June and Sept–mid-Oct Tues–Sun 10.30–12.30 and 2–6; July and Aug daily 10–7; mid-Oct–Mar Tues–Sun 10–12 and 2–5.30; adm*). After serving duty as a women's prison, the château has lost some of its original sparkle, but is still worth a visit: with great vaulted guard rooms below and painted ceilings above, tapestries from the 13th and 17th centuries and, best of all, eight monumental chimneypieces, beautifully sculpted in part by Jean Langlois and decorated with rare marbles.

Perched on its rock over the Garonne, **St-Macaire** is one of the Gironde's medieval gems. In the 18th century, when the Garonne slightly altered its course, the Macariens woke up one morning to find their quays left high and dry – in effect taking away any economic impulse to modernize. Three fortified gates still defend the town. Best of all is the irresistible Place du Mercadiou, or 'God's marketplace', lined with Gothic arcades and houses in a picturesque variety of styles from the 13th to the 16th centuries. Sitting atop the village ramparts, **St-Sauveur**, part of a 12th-century Benedictine

Getting Around

Trains from Bordeaux on the Soulac line stop in many of the Médoc villages, including Pauillac; the area is also served by Citram **buses** from Bordeaux.

If you're driving from the north, there's a **ferry** across the Gironde between Blaye and Lamarque near Fort Médoc, sailing roughly every 1½ hours in July and Aug, much less other times; call **t** 05 57 42 04 49.

Tourist Information

Villandraut: Place du Général de Gaulle, **t** 05 56 25 31 39.
Bazas: 1 Place de la Cathédrale, **t** 05 56 25 25 84, *www.ville-bazas.fr.*
Pauillac: the Maison du Tourisme et du Vin du Médoc, La Verrerie, **t** 05 56 59 03 08, *www.pauillac-medoc.com*, hires out bikes, offers a guide to the châteaux and tasting courses, and sells over 300 wines from all the Médoc *appellations*, at châteaux prices.

Where to Stay and Eat

Cadillac ✉ 33410
★★★Château de la Tour, D10, **t** 05 65 76 92 00 (*expensive*). Plush place to stay, overlooking the château, with a pool and tennis, and a good restaurant (*expensive–moderate*) – lobster ravioli and elegant desserts. *Restaurant closed Christmas.*
L'Entrée Jardin, 22 Rue de l'Oeuille, opposite the castle, **t** 05 56 76 96 96 (*moderate*). Old stone building with a patio. Refined, local cuisine. *Closed Sun eve, Mon eve, and Thurs eve Nov–April.*
Au Fin Gourmet, 6 Place de la République, **t** 05 56 62 90 80 (*cheap*). Platefuls of standard regional fare. Buzzing with locals at lunchtime. *Open Tues–Sun lunch only.*

Sauternes ✉ 33210
Le Saprien, in the village centre, **t** 05 56 76 60 87 (*moderate*). Well-prepared fish and other dishes according to the market, topped off with Sauternes by the glass. *Closed Sun eve, Mon, and Wed eve.*
Les Vignes, Place de l'Eglise, **t** 05 56 76 60 06 (*moderate*). Charming little country inn for lamb in Sauternes, *magret* grilled over the chimney, and *bordelais* treats. *Closed Tues.*
Broquet *chambres d'hôtes*, in the centre, **t** 05 56 76 60 17 (*inexpensive*). One of the few places to stay, with four rooms and a pool.

Bazas ✉ 33430
Château d'Arbieu, just east of Bazas on the D655, **t** 05 56 25 11 18 (*expensive*). Five comfortable B&B rooms, plus a pool and billiards.
★★★Domaine de Fompeyre, Route de Pau, **t** 05 56 25 98 00 (*expensive–moderate*). Modern hotel with 35 rooms in a delightful four-acre park overlooking Bazas, with a tropical garden, pools, tennis and billiards; the lovely restaurant (*expensive*) serves lovely food. *Closed Sun eve in winter.*
Les Remparts, Place de la Cathédrale, overlooking the Jardin de Sultan in the Espace Mauvezin, **t** 05 56 25 95 24 (*moderate*). For the most succulent *entrecôte* in town, game or fish specialities. *Closed Sun eve and Mon out of season, Mon lunch in summer.*

Pauillac ✉ 33250
★★★★Château de Cordeillan-Bages, Rte des Châteaux, **t** 05 56 59 24 24, *www.cordeillanbages.com* (*expensive*). Lovely little hotel in a sea of vineyards, with 25 charming rooms in the Relais et Châteaux tradition and the best restaurant (*very expensive–expensive*) in Médoc, using the best local ingredients. Astounding wine selection. *Closed Mon, Tues lunch, Sat lunch, and mid-Dec–Jan.*

priory, has an interesting carved portal and tympanum, and a curious plan, ending in a choir shaped like a cloverleaf.

The 14th-century **Château de Malromé**, 6km northeast of St-Macaire in St-André-du-Bois (*open April–June and Sept–early Nov Thurs–Sat visits at 3, 4 and 5, Sun and public hols open 2–6; July and Aug visits daily 10.30, 11.30 and 2–6.30; adm*), was completed in the 18th and 19th centuries by the Counts of Toulouse-Lautrec. The famous artist often spent summers here with his mother, and died here in 1901 aged 37. Reproductions of his works are displayed in a plush Second Empire setting. Toulouse-Lautrec is buried nearby in the Basilique Notre-Dame at **Verdelais**, a pilgrimage church (*open July and Aug daily 3–7; April–June and Sept–Nov Wed–Sun 3–7; otherwise by appt*) with a medieval miracle-working statue of the Virgin.

La Réole presents a stately river façade, especially with the mass of the 18th-century Prieuré des Bénédictins on its riverside terrace. In nearby Place Rigoulet, the old priory church of **St-Pierre** has a pair of pretty Gothic chapels, a painting of the *Marriage of the Virgin* (1666), and mermaids carved on the capitals in the nave. Among the old boutiques and houses in medieval La Réole is the oldest **Hôtel de Ville** still standing in France, built in the early 1200s by order of Richard the Lionheart, pierced with irregularly placed mullioned windows. Rue Peysseguin is a charming street, with La Réole's synagogue and medieval houses.

South of the Garonne: the Graves and the Bazadais

Graves isn't so sombre when you remember that it has more to do with gravel than boneyards; the greatest vineyards in the *appellation* look as if they're growing out of gravel pits. The most famous Graves vintner was the great Enlightenment philosopher Montesquieu, whose *De l'Espirit des Lois* (1748) was the basis of the United States Constitution. His delightful ivory tower (and still flourishing vineyard) was the moated **Château de la Brède**, off the N113 (*open April–June Sat, Sun and public hols 2–6; July–Sept Wed–Mon 2–6, closed Tues; Oct daily 2–5.30; early Nov Sat, Sun and public hols 2–5.30; adm*); it has a lovely park of ancient cedars, and his library and bedroom, preserved as it was when he died.

The world's finest dessert wines are grown here in a microclimate of special autumnal mists that promotes the essential *Botrytis cinerea*, or noble rot. **Barsac**'s two *premiers grands crus classés* come from Château Coutet, a *gentilhommière* built around a medieval tower; and a former charterhouse, the Château Climens, which many oenophiles rate as second after Yquem (*visits by appointment*). The neighbouring village of **Sauternes** snoozes away without a care in the world, with its disdainful Maison de Vin and a couple of friendly wine shops in the centre. The spectacular 17th-century **Château de Lafaurie-Peyraguey** has a *premier cru classé* vineyard set in 13th-century walls; equally exalted are the adjacent **Château Rabaut-Promis** and the 19th-century Italianate **Château Filhot**, in a stunning park (*visits daily 8.30–12.30 and 2–7*).

The famous and magnificently positioned **Château d'Yquem** (*open for visits if you apply three weeks beforehand; www.chateau-yquem.com*) is just north of Sauternes. The château dates from the 15th to the 17th centuries. The pale gold wines produced on its 250 acres have been the quintessence of Sauternes since the 18th century, a position confirmed since the 1855 classification that put it in a class all of its own. You can also visit the elegant 17th-century **Château de Malle** in nearby Preignac (*open April–Oct daily 10–12 and 2–7; visits to the chais by appointment, t 05 56 62 36 86, www.chateau-de-malle.fr; adm*), with its distinctive breast-shaped towers; it is one of the few châteaux in France never to have fallen into ruin.

The port at **Langon**, the capital of the southern Graves, is the highest on the Garonne to feel the tide. Its Gothic church of **St-Gervais** contains a surprise: a Zurbarán (the *Immaculate Conception*), long forgotten and discovered by the local *curé* by accident in 1966. The most beautiful capitals of the 12th-century church of **Notre Dame de Bourg** are now in the Cloisters Museum in New York.

South of Sauternes: A Detour into the Landes

Landes in French means moors, sand and maritime pines, and once they begin south of the Garonne they don't stop until the foothills of the Pyrenees, constituting the largest single forest in Europe. There is already a definite Landaise air about **Villandraut**, the birthplace of Pope Clement V, who built the strong, moat-belted **Château de Villandraut** on a plain instead of on a hill, and without a keep; it became a model for other 'clementine' castles in the area (*open June–late Sept daily 10–12.30 and 2.30–6.30; July and Aug daily 10–7; otherwise Sat and Sun only 2–5; adm*).

Southwest of Villandraut, **Bourideys** is a perfect and utterly tranquil example of a Landes village. Further east, overlooking the gorge of the river Ciron, sits the irregular polygonal **Château de Cazeneuve** (*open June–Sept daily 2–6, park opens at 11m; adm*). Built in the 11th century by the d'Albrets, the family of Henri IV, the castle was turned into a pleasure palace in the 17th century. Their descendant, the Duke of Sabran-Pontevès, owns it to this day. Of special note are the *salles troglodytes* cut into the central court, a Greek nymphaeum, furnished royal apartments, and sculpted chimneypieces, as well as a mill, lake, bamboo garden and lovely park along the river.

The little town of **Uzeste** has a small but dignified collegiate church, paid for by Clement V, who was buried here when he died from indigestion after eating a plate of ground emeralds, prescribed by his doctor. His once bejewelled tomb (1315–59) took some mighty whacks from the local protestants, but what survives shows a great attention to detail. These days Uzeste is especially zesty in August or September, when a five-day music festival fills its streets.

Bazas and its Cathedral

For the past 2,500 years, Bazas has been the capital of a little cattle-rearing region south of the Garonne, and home to a unique relic – the blood spilled at the beheading of St John the Baptist, supposedly wiped up in a cloth by a local woman. To shelter the precious relic, a triple church was built on the town's most prominent site; in 1233 when this threatened to fall over, the present **cathedral** was begun in its magnificent setting, atop the vast, gently sloping Place de la Cathédrale. A flamboyant rose window, pinnacles, buttresses and a gallery were added around 1500 to set off the three great 13th-century Gothic doorways. The central portal is devoted entirely to the

Last Judgement; the north portal is dedicated to the Mission of the Apostles; the south portal belongs to the Virgin. All survived the Huguenots in 1578 when the bishop ransomed the façade for 10,000 écus; the interior was completely wrecked.

The Gironde Estuary and Médoc

North of Bordeaux, freighters and tankers promenade along Europe's largest estuary, along with dainty fishing smacks. From March to September the prize catch is elvers (*pibales*), only two inches long, a delicacy that can demand as much as €150 a kilo on the market and must be eaten with wooden forks. **Pauillac** started off an important port here, and was home to one of the oldest sailing clubs in France, long pre-dating the views over the estuary to the Braud nuclear power plant. But Pauillac is best known for the purest gravelly ridges which produce the mightiest Médocs of all. Here you'll find the legendary **Château Latour** (*visits by appointment only, t 05 56 73 19 80*), which introduced stainless-steel vats to Bordeaux in the 1960s, and the **Château Mouton-Rothschild**, which owes much of its current fame to Baron Philippe de Rothschild. One of his first moves, in the 1920s, was to bottle all the wine at the château, an idea that seemed eccentric at the time. The tour (*open Mon–Thurs 9.30–11 and 2–4, Fri till 3; April–Oct also Sat and Sun; ring ahead, t 05 56 73 21 29; adm*) takes in the *grand chai*, with its immaculate blond wood barrels, a collection of wine labels by famous artists (Dalí, Picasso, Warhol, etc), a museum of art devoted to wine, and finishes with a descent into the cellar. Mouton's eternal rival, the **Château Lafite-Rothschild** (owned by the Baron's cousins), broods over the Pauillac-Lesparre road (*visits by appointment only, t 01 53 89 78 00; Mon–Fri 9–10.30 and 2–3.30; closed late Mar–early April and Aug–Oct; www.lafite.com*). Lafite's cellars, designed by Ricardo Bofill, have bottles as old as 1797.

To the north lies **St-Estèphe**, an *appellation* that produces vigorous, deeply coloured wines that differ from other Médocs in their need for extra-long periods of bottle-ageing. The leading producer is **Château Cos d'Estournel** (*open Mon–Fri 10–12 and 2–4, ring ahead, t 05 56 73 15 50; tastings for a fee; closed Aug and picking season*), which is also the most striking landmark along the *route des châteaux*, with its *chais* designed as a replica of the palace of the Sultan of Zanzibar.

The Côte d'Argent

From Médoc's Pointe de Grave to the Basque lands in the south runs a nearly straight, wide 228km ribbon of silver sand, 'the Silver Coast', with the giant rolling waves of the Atlantic on one side and deep green pine forests on the other. .

Soulac-sur-Mer and the Phare de Cordouan

The current resort, **Soulac-sur-Mer**, 'the Pearl of the Côte d'Argent', replaced an older Soulac that was methodically swallowed up by sand in the 18th century. All that remains of the medieval port where English pilgrims to Compostela disembarked is

Getting Around

Frequent **trains** link Bordeaux to Soulac-sur-Mer, Le Verdon-sur-Mer and Pointe de Grave; there are bus links from Lesparre station direct to Vendays-Montalivet. Some trains are replaced by bus from Pauillac (t 05 58 59 00 63).

In summer, the little PGVS train runs along the ocean from Pointe de Grave to Verdon and Soulac (*April–June and Sept Sat and Sun, July and Aug daily*).

There are trains nearly every hour from Bordeaux to Arcachon, and in the summer, TGVs direct from Paris Montparnasse. Several Citram **buses** a day run from Bordeaux (8 Rue Corneille, t 05 56 43 68 43) or from the station coinciding with the TGVs serving Pyla, Andernos, Arès and Cap Ferret. There are frequent half-hour boat crossings from Arcachon to Cap Ferret and to Andernos (t 05 57 72 28 28).

Tourist Information

Soulac-sur-Mer: 68 Rue de la Plage, t 05 56 09 86 61, *www.soulac.com*.
Lacanau-Océan: Place de l'Europe, t 05 56 03 21 01, *www.lacanau.com*.
Arcachon: Esplanade Georges-Pompidou, t 05 57 52 97 97, *www.arcachon.com*.

Sports and Activities

Soulac's tourist office can tell you where to parachute, land yacht (*char à voile*), surf, kayak surf, body board, speed sail, canoe, gallop, play Paintball, or tennis; at night, you can leave what money you have left at the **Casino de la Plage**, t 05 56 09 82 74.

In **Lacanau** you can rent surfboards and learn how to use them, even in the off season: try **Lacanau Surf Club**, t 05 56 26 38 84, or **Surf Sans Frontières**, t 05 56 03 27 60. Sail, windsurf or kayak at **Voile Lacanau Guyenne**, t 05 56 03 05 11.

In **Arcachon**, Les Bateliers Arcachonnais (t 05 57 72 28 28) and **Arcachon Croisière Océan** (t 05 57 52 24 77) make excursions every afternoon to the Ile aux Oiseaux, which is given over to sea birds, oyster farms and sailing boats. The Ile's landmarks are its picturesque *cabanes tchanquées*, huts perched on stilts. In July and August both companies also offer days on the sandy Banc d'Arguin, a wildfowl refuge at the entrance of the Bassin. Les Bateliers Arcachonnais also offer tours of the oyster beds, and 4-hour trips up the cool, forested river Leyre; both companies also offer cruises up the coast, the evening one with Arcachon Croisière includes a seafood platter.

Where to Stay and Eat

Soulac-sur-Mer ✉ 33780
**Hôtel des Pins, t 05 56 73 27 27, *www.hotel-des-pins.com* (*moderate*). Simple Logis de France: nothing fancy, but pines and sea views and a beach 100m away; one of the best restaurants in the area (*moderate*), for good reliable food. *Closed mid-Jan–mid-Mar*.

the **Basilique Notre-Dame de la Fin des Terres**, always the first shrine that pilgrims visited in France. Even this was buried twice by the voracious dunes, but now sits tidily in a sand-lined hollow. It has a remarkable 13th-century apse: the statue of the Virgin worshipped by the pilgrims is still in place, and there are good carved capitals.

From June to September, *La Bohème II* sails out from Le Verdon-sur-Mer to an islet in the Gironde's shipping lanes and Europe's oldest surviving lighthouse, the **Phare de Cordouan** (*for times and bookings in English, call t 05 56 09 62 93 , April–Sept*). Inside, the first floor houses royal apartments just in case the king came to call; and the second has a chapel. Another 250 steps lead to the lantern for a bird's-eye view of the estuary.

The Lakes

More pines, more sand, more water...one of the selling points of the Côte d'Argent is the proximity of its calm lakes to the Atlantic breakers, popular with windsurfers and sailors who don't want to get too wet. **Etang d'Hourtin** and its contiguous twin **Etang**

★★Michelet, 1 Rue Bernard Baguenard, **t** 05 56 09 84 18 (*inexpensive*). Popular seaside villa near the beach, with 20 pleasant rooms and a warm welcome. *Closed Jan and early Nov–early Dec.*

Lacanau-Océan ✉ 33680

★★★Hôtel du Golf, **t** 05 56 03 92 92 (*moderate*). Perfect for golfers, with a 30% discount on green fees and a heated pool.

★★L'Oyat, Front de Mer, **t** 05 56 03 11 11 (*moderate*). On the seashore; half-board – the restaurant (*moderate*) has some of the best food in town. *Closed Nov–Mar.*

Arcachon ✉ 33120

Fashionable Arcachon is usually more expensive than the rest of the region. Book months in advance for July or August.

★★★★Arc-Hôtel sur Mer, 89 Bd de la Plage, **t** 05 56 83 06 85, *www.arc-hotel-sur-mer.com* (*expensive*). Medium-sized, modern but stylish hotel where the rooms all have balconies and overlook the water or the garden; heated pool, sauna and Jacuzzi.

★★★Semiramis, 4 Allées Rebsomen, **t** 05 56 83 25 87 (*expensive*). Charming 19th-century villa in the Ville d'Hiver. No two of the 18 rooms are alike. The pool is set in a garden of palms, mimosas and acanthus.

★★Marinette, 15 Allée José-Maria de Hérédia, **t** 05 56 83 06 67 (*inexpensive*). Large white house in the Ville d'Hiver, with comfortable rooms. Breakfast on a flowered terrace, but no restaurant. *Closed Nov–mid-Mar.*

Le Patio, 10 Bd de la Plage, **t** 05 56 83 02 72 (*moderate*). Surrounded by bright clutter, a waterfall and delicious aromas, try the lobster salad, oysters in flaky pastry, hot stuffed crab and *bouillabaisse océane*. *Closed Tues in winter, and Mon lunch.*

Pyla-sur-Mer ✉ 33115

★★★Haitza, Place Louis-Gaume, **t** 05 57 52 79 27 (*moderate*). Simple quiet rooms set in the pine woods, a stone's throw from the beach. *Open April–Sept.*

★★La Guitoune, 95 Bd de l'Océan, **t** 05 56 22 70 10 (*moderate*). A favourite weekend retreat of the Bordelais, with comfortable rooms and an excellent seafood restaurant.

★★Côte Sud, 4 Av Figuier, **t** 05 56 83 25 00 (*moderate*). Delightful, intimate 1940s villa in the pines, a 5min walk from the beach, with an excellent little restaurant; for something unusual try the *civet d'esturgeon aux huîtres pochées*. *Closed early Nov–Jan.*

Lège-Cap-Ferret ✉ 33970

The trendiest spot on the Bassin these days.

★Hôtel de la Plage Chez Magne, in the Port de l'Herbe, **t** 05 56 60 50 15 (*inexpensive*). Simple eight-room wooden hotel by the beach, with a good fish restaurant (*moderate*).

★★Sporting Les Dunes, 119 Avenue de Bordeaux, **t** 05 56 60 61 81 (*inexpensive*). Down at Cap-Ferret, a little duneside and seaside place. *Open April–Nov.*

de Carcans stretch 16km from north to south, making the longest lake in France. A cycle track runs between the Atlantic and the lake, between **Hourtin-Plage**, a small family resort in the north, and **Carcans-Maubuisson**, a sports-orientated resort to the south, with a 15km sandy beach. Otters, rare in France, are occasionally sighted here. South of the big lake, dunes and trees encompass the lovely **Etang de Cousseau**, with 13km of paths for cyclists and walkers, who may sight a wide variety of migratory waterfowl along the way, along with boar, deer, aquatic tortoises, genets, European mink and otters. Further south, **Lac de Lacanau** has been a favourite escape of the Bordelais since the early 1900s. They built summer villas at **Lacanau-Océan**, now a big resort famous for Europe's surfing championships in mid-August.

Arcachon and its Bassin

The straight line of the Côte d'Argent is broken by the Bassin d'Arcachon, which in the mid-19th century discovered its double destiny as a nursery for oysters and a resort for the Bordelais; the Dune du Pilat alone attracts a million visitors a year. Yet mass tourism has left corners untouched: if you squint, the little villages in the back Bassin could be part of a 17th-century Dutch landscape painting, sheltering their distinctive shallow-keeled sailboats called *pinasses*, painted green, pink or yellow.

Arcachon was similarly a fishing village, until 1852 when two brothers, Emile and Isaac Pereire, extended the railway from Bordeaux and laid out a new resort with winding lanes and four residential sections, each named after a season. The sheltered **Ville d'Hiver**, always 3°C warmer than the rest of Arcachon, attained full fashion status by the 1860s – Gounod, Debussy, Alexandre Dumas and Napoléon III were all habitués of its gingerbread villas, some 200 of which survive. The **Ville d'Eté**, facing the Bassin and cooler in the summer, has most of Arcachon's tourist facilities, seaside promenades and sheltered beaches. Its most notorious resident was Toulouse-Lautrec, who had a house by the ocean and liked to swim in the nude.

The Dune du Pilat

Eight km south of Arcachon, the white Dune du Pilat rises between the sea and trees like Moby Dick: at 347ft it's the highest pile of sand in Europe, at a mile and a half, the longest, and at 550yds the widest. It began to form 8,000 years ago with the merging of two sets of dunes, and more or less grew to its present dimensions in the 18th century, when a huge sandbank offshore was destroyed and all the sand was blown here. Like all dunes, it's in a constant state of flux, and every year it inches inland at the rate of 17ft a year. A wooden stair helps you get to the top of the behemoth for an unforgettable view – especially at sunset.

Around the Bassin d'Arcachon

East of Arcachon, pines line the Bassin at **La Teste de Buch**, which has houses dating back to the 18th century, and includes in its boundaries the **Lac de Cazaux**, the second largest lake in France. The Bassin d'Arcachon is the fourth-largest oyster producer in France, and the first in Europe in trapping microscopic oyster embryos and larvae swishing about the sea in search of a home – they simply can't resist stacks of canal roof tiles, bleached in a mix of lime and sand. The Bassin's oyster capital is **Gujan-Mestras**, where *oustaous* (oyster huts) provide the perfect backdrop for ordering a plate of oysters or attending the oyster fair in early–mid-August (you can eat them in non-R months now); there's even a **Maison de l'Huître**, at the Port de Larros, where you can learn their secrets (*open daily 10–12.30 and 2.30–6; Oct–Mar closed Sun*).

The **Parc Ornithologique du Teich** (*open daily 10–6; July and Aug daily 10–8; adm; bring binoculars, or rent them on the site*) is the kind of marshy delta beloved of migratory waterfowl, who stop off en route between Africa and Scandinavia. It is also a nesting ground for grey herons, black cormorants, white storks, black and white oystercatchers, egrets, kingfishers, dabbling garganeys and spoon-billed shovelers. There's an information centre, the **Maison de la Nature du Bassin d'Arcachon**, and a fine viewpoint over the delta from the **Point d'Observation du Delta de Leyre**.

The northwestern curve of the Bassin is sprinkled with little oyster port-resorts set between the calm waters and rough Atlantic, all part of **Lège-Cap Ferret**. The prettiest port is **L'Herbe**, an intimate hamlet of wooden houses on tiny lanes, founded in the 17th century. The miles of ocean beaches culminate in the sandy tail of **Cap Ferret**, which in the past 200 years has grown 4km and gobbled up several fashionable villas in its wake. A path leads around to the tip of the cape, with splendid views of the Dune du Pilat, most breathlessly from the top of the 258 steps of the lighthouse (*open July and Aug daily; otherwise closed Mon and Tues, and mid-Nov–mid-Dec*). The cute **Tramway du Cap Ferret** (*t 05 56 60 60 20; early June–Sept daily frequent journeys*) covers the several kilometres from the jetée Bélisaire at the Bassin to the Plage de l'Horizon, one of the ocean beaches.

Down the Lot

Outsiders often lump it together with the Dordogne to the north, but in fact the noodling Lot's heartstrings have always pulled it in the other direction – to the south. Its landscapes are more rugged, tossed up in wild limestone plateaux called *causses*, and what soil it has, especially in Quercy, is said to be the worst in France (the vines that produce black *vin de Cahors* don't seem to mind).

The Lozère

The Lot (and the Tarn) both have their sources on either side of big bald **Mont Lozère** (5,574ft), the tallest non-volcanic peak of the Massif Central. It lent its name to the Lozère, the altogether loftiest and least populated *département* in France. In the 1960s and '70s the Lozère was a favourite spot for setting up hippy communes. Of the two rivers, the Lot takes the easier, northerly route, passing by the Lozère's midget capital, **Mende**, an overgrown village gathered around the skirts of its cathedral. This was built in 1369 by Urban V, who was born in nearby Pont-de-Montvert, but in 1579 the cruel but efficient Protestant Captain Merle blew up most of it and wrecked along the way the town's pride and joy, *la Non-Pareille*, the biggest bell in all Christendom; all that remains is the 7ft clapper, stashed under the pretty organ. Its crypt of St-Privat, dating from the 3rd century, is one of the oldest in France

The north bank of the Lot is closed off by a lonely basalt and granite plateau called the **Aubrac**, dotted here and there with stone huts or *burons* where shepherds slept and made their cheese. The chief town is **Marvejols**, a medieval *ville royale* which supported Henri de Navarre in the Wars of Religion, attracting the attentions of the Duc de Joyeuse, who massacred three-quarters of the population. When Henri became king, he made amends by rebuilding the lofty fortified gates.

The climate here is rough and ready, but it's one that wolves from Mongolia, Canada and Europe find amenable enough; over 100 are bred and kept in semi-liberty in the **Parc du Gévaudan**, 9km north of Marvejols at **Ste-Lucie** (*open Nov–Mar daily 10–5; April–May and Sept–Oct daily 10–6; June–Aug daily 10–7; www.loupsdugevaudan.com; adm*). A museum compares lupine folklore to reality; wolves, for instance, are good family beasts, who regurgitate to feed their mate and cubs, and rarely, if ever, attack man. This point is emphasized, as the Lozère is famous for the Bête du Gévaudan, who

Getting Around

Mende and Marvejols are linked by **train** to Paris, Marseille and Béziers. At least one bus a day links Mende and the upper Lot to Rodez. From Rodez (on the rail line from Toulouse) there are one or two **buses** weekdays to Espalion, Laguiole and Conques.

Tourist Information

Mende: 2 Rue Henri Rivière, t 04 66 94 00 28, *www.ot-mende.fr.*

Where to Stay and Eat

Mende ✉ 48000

Note that Mende is also a convenient base for visiting the Gorges du Tarn (*see* pp.446–7).
★★★Lion d'Or, 12 Bd Britexte, t 04 66 49 16 46, *www.liondor-mende.com* (*moderate–inexpensive*). A Best Western hotel, the fanciest in town, with comfortable modernized rooms, a pool, garden and riding stables. Good *cuisine de terroir* in the restaurant.
★★★Pont Roupt, 2 Av du 11 Novembre, t 04 66 65 01 43 (*moderate–inexpensive*). Modern, unfussy, agreeable hotel, just outside of town on the Lot, with an indoor pool and brasserie (*expensive–moderate*).
Auberge La Boulène, outside of town at Aspres, t 04 66 49 23 37, *www.laboulene.com* (*inexpensive*). A *ferme-auberge* attached to a riding stable with rooms overlooking the *causse* and fine restaurant (*moderate*). Book.

Laguiole ✉ 12210

★★★★Michel Bras, 6km from Laguiole on the Rte de l'Aubrac, t 05 65 51 18 20 (*luxury–expensive*). Chic, formal rooms in a small hotel attached to one of the most famous restaurants in southwest France (*expensive*). Michel Bras is an individualist and a perfectionist. *Book. Closed Nov–Mar.*
★★★Régis, 3 Place de la Patte-d'Oie, t 05 65 44 30 05 (*inexpensive*). Long-standing family hotel with a pool and renovated rooms. *Closed mid-Nov–mid-Dec.*

over a three-year period in the 1760s killed 99 people (mostly children and women). Louis XV sent his best hunters to shoot the beast, and although wolves were bagged the killings continued, then suddenly stopped (also *see* 'Saugues', p.702).

The Uplands of the Rouergue and the Gorges du Lot

West of the Lozère, the Lot cuts into the uplands of the Rouergue, or *département* of the Aveyron. A series of quaint villages decorate its upper stretches; **Ste-Eulalie-d'Olt**, with an 11th-century church, and fortified **St-Côme-d'Olt** are both members of the Beaux Villages club; *Olt* was the river's Celtic name. Further down at **Espalion**, a 13th-century bridge, medieval houses and Renaissance château are reflected in the river's waters. Espalion has two museums: the **Musée de Rouergue**, with exhibits on music, costume, and folkways housed in the cells of a prison of 1838 (*at time of writing only open July and Aug; phone tourist office for details, t 05 65 44 10 63*) and the **Musée Joseph Vaylet** (*open July–Aug daily 10–12 and 2–7; May, June, Sept and Oct Wed–Sun 10–12 and 2–6; Dec–April Sat and Sun only 2–6; closed Nov*) on local arts and, rather surprisingly, diving, in honour of the two locals who invented the diving suit. Best of all are two churches: Romanesque **St-Hilarion de Perse** with an unusual *Last Judgement* on the tympanum and carved capitals within, and, 4km south of Espalion, 16th-century **St-Pierre de Bessuéjouls**, where the tower hides an 11th-century chapel, its capitals inspired by Conques, its altar covered with interlacing.

Cheese-, knife- and food-fanciers in general may be tempted by a detour to **Laguiole**, 24km north of Espalion, the capital of the lofty Aubrac. Laguiole cheese

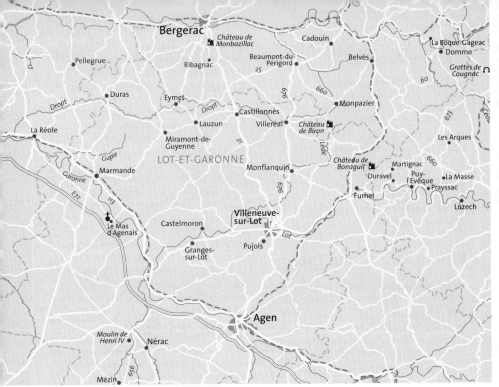

comes from cows grazed above 2,600ft, while the knife-making tradition originated with a local who in 1829 came up with the idea of a folding blade so shepherds could carry knives in their pockets. Napoléon III granted the firm the permission to mark each knife handle with a bee, but by the 1950s the local industry had died out completely. But in 1981, Laguiole was revived with panache – with a new range of knives designed by Philippe Starck, who is also behind the avant-garde factory, topped by a 60ft knife. You can visit the forge and watch them in action (*Call to find out when: t 05 65 48 43 34, www.forge-de-laguiole.com*).

Below Espalion, the **Gorges du Lot** offers ravishing scenery between the picture-postcard village of Estaing and Entraygues-sur-Truyère. **Estaing** was the cradle of the counts of the same name, one of whom saved the life of Philippe Auguste, and another, Charles-Hector, a great admiral and Republican, who tried out to do the same for Louis XVI and Marie Antoinette and was guillotined for his trouble. At the end of the gorge, **Entraygues-sur-Truyère** stands at the confluence of the Lot and Truyère.

Conques and the Abbey

Further down the Lot, but tucked away in a steep wooded valley of the Dourdou, hides one of the blazing stars of French Romanesque. Conques Abbey was set up by the hermit Dadon in the late 8th century and financed by Charlemagne, but it soon became apparent that the abbey's only resources were water and birdsong. Conques needed a miracle to prosper, and its abbot decided that if none was in the offing, he'd steal one in the form of relics, the cash cows of the medieval church economy. He sent his most trusted monk to Agen, where the abbey had grown sleek from the miracle-

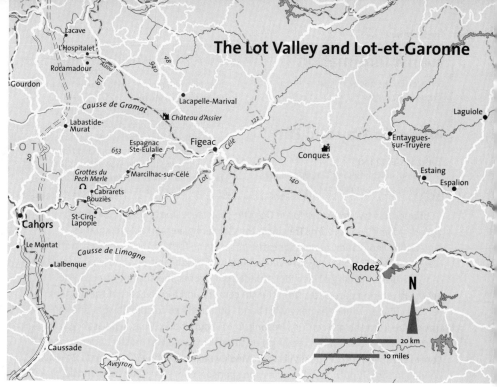

working bones of a 3rd-century girl martyr, St Foy. The monk from Conques, disguised as a layman, enrolled as a novice, and spent ten years gaining the trust of the brothers until they left him alone guarding the relics. He tossed them in a bag and ran for it. No sooner were the relics installed than the miracles began; the donations rolled in and Conques became a stop on the pilgrimage route to Compostela.

Many of the pilgrims' gifts went into a fabulous golden reliquary for St Foy's bones. The fact that you can still see this and the rest of Conques' medieval treasure is due to the prescience of the mayor during the Revolution. He called a town meeting, announced the Revolution, and distributed the treasure among the people, adding: 'I shall remember which family has which gem.' When the government officials arrived, the mayor confessed that Conques in its Revolutionary enthusiasm had already redistributed the abbey's wealth. There wasn't much the officials could do. When the Terror was over, every single bit of the treasure was returned.

The **Abbatiale Ste-Foy** (*open daily 9am–8pm*) was salvaged in the 19th century by the tireless Prosper Mérimée and the Beaux Arts, and now shelters 24 monks who once again make it their business to take care of pilgrims. The basilica was completed *c.* 1140 and served as a model for St-Sernin in Toulouse; its tympanum is sculpted with an extraordinary *Last Judgement* of 124 figures, with most of their original paint. The interior is lofty, majestic, pure and harmonious, designed to 'process' large crowds of pilgrims in a processional path around the central altar. The master of the tympanum sculpted the bas relief of the *Annunciation* in the north transept. The Romanesque cloister, with a lovely serpentine basin in the centre, was long used as a quarry.

Tourist Information

Conques: By the abbey, **t** 05 65 72 85 00, *www.conques.fr.*

Where to Stay and Eat

Conques ✉ 12320
***Moulin de Cambelong, t 05 65 72 84 22, *www.moulindecambelong.com*

(*expensive–moderate*). Delightful watermill on the Dourdou, converted into a hotel with nine charming rooms and a fine restaurant to match (*expensive*).
**L'Auberge Saint-Jacques, t 05 65 72 86 36, *www.aubergestjacques.fr* (*inexpensive*). In the medieval centre facing the basilica, with comfy quiet rooms, restaurant and free morning wake-up calls provided by the good fathers and their bells. *Closed Jan.*

Conques has two **treasures** (*open Oct–Mar daily 10–12 and 2–6; April–Sept daily 9.30–12.30 and 2–6.30; adm*). **Trésor I** in the cloister has remarkable reliquaries donated by Pepin and Charlemagne (the latter in the form of the letter A), and the **Majesté de Ste Foy**, the only surviving reliquary of its kind in the world – a magnificent, awful, compelling golden idol, studded with gems and ancient cameos. The head with staring gaze dates from the 5th century, and formed part of the original heist from Agen, while the body, with hands outstretched to hold flowers, and the throne are from the 9th century. **Trésor II**, in the tourist office, has Renaissance and later works. On top of the exceedingly picturesque village, the mostly underground **Centre Européen d'Art et de Civilisation Médiévale** (*open Mon–Fri 8–12 and 1.45–6.45*) opened in 1993; it puts on exhibitions and sponsors concerts of medieval music.

Figeac

Figeac, just north of the Lot on its tributary, the Célé, gave the world Champollion, who cracked Egyptian hieroglyphics, and Charles Boyer, the archetypal French lover of the silver screen (and the inspiration for the cartoon skunk, Pepe le Pew). But for the unsuspecting visitor it's Figeac's medieval heart of golden sandstone that comes as the most charming surprise of all, its curving lanes packed with tall houses crowned with covered terraces, which came in handy for drying textiles for sale. A dozen small piazzas form focal points; on one, **Place Vival**, is the 13th-century Hôtel de la Monnaie, one of the most beautiful medieval secular buildings in France, now home to the tourist office and the little eclectic **Musée du Vieux Figeac** (*open July and Aug daily 10–7.30; Sept–April Mon–Sat 10–12 and 2.30–6; May and June Mon–Sat 10–12 and 2.30–6, Sun 10–1; adm*). Just west of Place Vival, **Rue Caviale** is one of Figeac's prettiest streets, leading into Place Carnot, the ancient market square. In Rue Séguier, the **Musée Champollion** (*open July and Aug daily 10–12 and 2.30–6.30, other times closed Mon; Nov–Feb daily 2.30–6.30; adm*) is in the 14th-century house where Jean-François Champollion was born in 1790. A precocious linguist, he was fascinated with hieroglyphics as a teenager and suspected they might be a form of writing. The discovery in 1799 by French soldiers of the Rosetta Stone, with inscriptions in hieroglyphics, Greek and a demotic script, proved the key. A copy of the Rosetta Stone is engraved in the pavement outside; inside are audio-visuals on how he cracked the code.

The much-tampered-with 12th-century **Notre-Dame du Puy**, at the top of the hill, retains a carved 14th-century portal and capitals inside, and affords wonderful views

Getting Around

Figeac's **railway** station is on the Brive–Toulouse branch line, with direct connections to Gramat, Rocamadour and Capdenac. The SNCF runs regular **buses** from Figeac to St-Cirq-Lapopie, St-Géry and Cahors; private companies also link Figeac to Toulouse, St-Céré, and Lacapelle-Marival.

Tourist Information

Figeac: Hôtel de la Monnaie, Place Vival, **t** 05 65 34 06 25.

Where to Stay and Eat

Figeac ✉ 46100

★★★★Château du Viguier du Roy, Rue Droite, **t** 05 65 50 05 05, *www.chateau-viguier-figeac.com* (*luxury–expensive*). Renovated 14th-century building with cloister, plus 18th-century houses, enclosed courtyard and terrace with a pool. 17 rooms and 3 suites, individually furnished with appropriate antiques. Its restaurant, La Dinée du Viguier (*expensive*), is Figeac's gourmet shrine. *Closed end Oct–early April; restaurant closed Mon lunch and Sat lunch all year; also Sun eve and Mon eve in winter.*

★★Hostellerie de l'Europe, 51 Allées Victor-Hugo, **t** 05 65 34 10 16 (*inexpensive*). Stylish hotel with garden, pool, garage. Its restaurant, Chez Marinette (*moderate*), does wonderful things with mushrooms and other traditional Quercy ingredients.

★★Le Terminus St-Jacques, 27 Av Georges-Clémenceau, by the station, **t** 05 65 34 00 43 (*inexpensive*). Nicest of the cheaper options, with a bit of garden; the restaurant (*moderate*) serves a tender slice of beef with Roquefort sauce.

La Puce à l'Oreille, 5–7 Rue St-Thomas, **t** 05 65 34 33 08 (*moderate*). Restaurant in a 15th-century mansion; traditional menus – duck confits – and unusual dishes. Book. *Closed Sun eve and Mon, exc July and Aug.*

over Figeac's medieval roofscape. From here descend by way of picturesque Rue Delzhens, past the **Hôtel du Viguier** to Rue Roquefort and **St-Sauveur**, once Figeac's greatest medieval church. The chapterhouse was given its remarkable ogival vaulting in the 15th century, and in the 17th century, to cover up some of the damage caused in the Wars of Religion, a local sculptor added the naïve painted reliefs of the Passion.

The classic Figeac excursion is to its mysterious 26ft obelisk-needles or *Aiguilles*, erected in the 12th century on the summit of two nearby hills – the **Aiguille de Lissac** to the west and the **Aiguille du Pressoir** to the south. Their original purpose has long been forgotten, but they may well have been set up by the abbey of St-Sauveur either to lift the spirits of pilgrims, or perhaps to set the limits within which fugitives were guaranteed the abbey's asylum.

The Limargue and the Château d'Assier

Northwest of Figeac runs a long broad swathe of land known as the Limargue – a lush micro-region of chestnut forests and meadows of wildflowers. It has some charming villages on either side of the N140 around **Lacapelle-Marival**, and one of the most blustering castles ever built by man, the once enormous **Château d'Assier** (*open May and June Thurs–Mon 10–12.30 and 2–6.45; July and Aug daily 10–12.30 and 2–6.45; Sept–April Thurs–Mon 10–12.30 and 2–5.30; adm*), straddling the divide between the Limargue and the **Causse de Gramat**. Built in the 16th century by Galiot de Genouillac, François Ier's Captain General of Artillery, only the simple west wing of the quadrangle remains intact after centuries of cannibalizing by the locals. The interior façade is a handsome Renaissance work: stone windows and walls bear medallions of Roman emperors, while a frieze shows swords and cannons relating to Galiot's deeds or those of Hercules, to whom Galiot fancied a resemblance. The interior, once the best furnished in France, now contains only one of its grand stairways. A pendant in the vault is inscribed with Galiot's motto: *J'aime fort une* ('I love fortune' or 'I love one very much') – the declaration of a lifelong affair with himself. Galiot also built the **church** in Assier (1540s) as a personal shrine to himself and his weapons. Although Gothic in form, the decoration is Renaissance: devoted to cannons, battles, and artillery, with nary a Christian symbol in sight. Inside, under the star vaulting, is Galiot's tomb.

The Célé Valley and Grotte du Pech Merle

Once past Figeac, the Célé splashes through valleys and steep gorges protected by cliff forts, the *châteaux des Anglais* left over from the Hundred Years War. **Espagnac-Ste-Eulalie** is the beauty spot: a tiny hamlet watched over by a striking *clocher* belonging to a 12th-century convent fittingly named Notre-Dame-du-Val-Paradis. With a population of 240, **Marcilhac-sur-Célé** is one of the valley's larger villages, with more ducks than people. The ruins of the abbey's Romanesque church form a court-yard around what is now the parish church, decorated with 15th-century frescoes; the original Romanesque church's south portal has a rare Carolingian tympanum.

Four km above the Célé village of **Cabrerets**, the **Grotte du Pech Merle** is one of the finest prehistoric caves open to the public (*open mid-April–1 Nov; guided tours 9.30–12 and 1.30–5: buy a time-stamped ticket when you arrive; adm*). Its entrance was redis-covered in 1922 by two teenage boys, who were inspired by the cave finds in the Dordogne. They wormed their way through a narrow 400ft passage and found just what they were looking for: a magnificent decorated cave. The 80 drawings and hundreds of symbols date from three distinct periods, from the Solutrean to the Magdalenian (20,000–15,000 BC). The tour begins with the **Chapel of the Mammoths**, a gallery carved by an underground river, with a great spiral frieze of mammoths, horses and bison outlined in black. The **Ceiling of Hieroglyphs** is covered with finger drawings of female and animal figures and circular signs. Beyond is the **Hall of Discs**, where water dripping slowly through hairline fissures in rock left rare concentrations in concentric circles. Even more extraordinary are the footprints left by a woman and her 12-year-old child in the clay at least 12,000 years ago. The **Bear's Gallery**, with claw marks and a bear's head carved faintly in the wall, leads to the two beautiful **spotted horses**. Six feminine 'negative hands' (made by blowing paint over hands) seem to be yearning to stroke or hold the horses. Over the horses is a rare picture of a large pike.

St-Cirq-Lapopie

St-Cirq appeared to me, embraced by Bengal fires –
like an impossible rose in the night...
I no longer have any desire to be anywhere else.
André Breton

Back on the Lot, close to Pech Merle, waits Breton's Surrealist dream village, St-Cirq-Lapopie. Built of harmonious golden stone and topped by high-pitched brown tile

Tourist Information

St-Cirq-Lapopie: Pl du Sombral, t 05 65 31 29 06.

Where to Stay and Eat

St-Cirq-Lapopie ✉ 46330

***La Pélissaria, t 05 65 31 25 14 (*moderate*).
Intimate hotel run by charming couple in a
13th-century house, with ten lovely rooms.

**Auberge du Sombral, t 05 65 31 26 08 (*inexpensive*). Medieval house in the centre, with
eight charming rooms under its steep-
pitched roof. *Closed mid-Nov–Mar.* The
restaurant (*moderate*) serves delicious
regional food.

Lou Bolat, on the side of the road as you start
to climb out of the village, **t** 05 65 30 29 04
(*moderate*). Pretty café-bar-restaurant-
crêperie with a terrace.

roofs, St-Cirq hovers in its spectacular setting 330ft above the river Lot just before it
meets the Célé. In season parking is difficult (there's a car park just west of St-Cirq,
next to the belvedere), but in winter you may well have it all to yourself. Only a few
crumbling but panoramic walls survive above the **church** (1522–40), now the most
prominent building, its buttressed apse high on the bluff, its turreted watchtower
running up the side of the stout bell tower. Many of the cut Gothic stones from the
walls were reused in the houses.

South of St-Cirq rises the dry, sparsely populated **Causse de Limogne**. More woodsy
than the Causse de Gramat, its rocky emptiness is dotted with dolmens, magnificent
pigeonniers, abandoned walls and stone huts. Lavender is grown commercially here,
and most of the Lot's truffles hide out near the roots of its twisted dwarf oaks. What is
modestly claimed to be 'the world's biggest truffle market' is held at **Lalbenque**
(*Dec–Mar Tues at 2pm sharp*).

Cahors

The anomic clutter of the newer parts of Cahors matches its immediate surroundings – some of the most discouraging landscapes in France – but in the heart of the
town you'll find a medieval city of surprising subtlety and character. Its star attraction
is the Pont Valentré which, as any Frenchman will tell you, is the most beautiful
bridge on this planet. Cahors' golden age, funded by merchant finance and money-
lending, lasted from the 13th century until the Hundred Years War, giving it impressive
palaces, a new set of fortifications, a university and the completion of the cathedral.
The disruption of trade meant a strangling of its business affairs, but the refined little
city made a modest living off its rents and wine trade and, during the Renaissance,
had a reputation as a cultured place, full of academies and libraries.

Cahors' charms are discreet, but a careful eye can make this well-preserved and
genteel medieval town come alive. The broad, leafy **Boulevard Gambetta** follows the
course of the old walls, but old Cahors' high street was **Rue du Château-du-Roi**, north
of the cathedral, and **Rue Nationale**, south of it. Along this are most of the merchants'
palaces; to each side, the ranks of alleys crowded with tall houses give an idea of how
dense the medieval town was.

Inspired by St-Etienne in Périgueux, the domed **Cathédrale St-Etienne** was begun in
the 10th century, but not completed until the 1400s. The original entrance, moved

Getting Around

Cahors has frequent **rail** connections north to Gourdon, Souillac and Paris, and south to Montauban and Toulouse; from here SNCF **buses** go towards Fumel and Figeac.

Tourist Information

Cahors: Place François Mitterrand, t 05 65 53 20 65, *www.mairie-cahors.fr*.

Sports and Activities

Summer **Quercyrail** excursions in a 1950s omnibus, Micheline, chug along the river Lot to Cajac, Château de Cénevières and St Cirq-Lapopie; information and tickets from the Cahors tourist office.

Safaraid, t 05 65 35 98 88. River excursions from Bouziès and Cahors as far as St-Cirq-Lapopie and Vers (*April–Nov*). Also hire of canoes, kayaks and *gabares*.

Babou Marine, in Cahors, t 05 65 30 08 99, hires houseboats for up to 12 people.

Where to Stay and Eat

Cahors ✉ 46000

★★★Le Terminus, 5 Charles de Freycinet, t 05 65 53 32 00 (*expensive–moderate*). Charming, resolutely retro, ivy-covered hotel. Garage, disabled access, TV and Cahors' best restaurant, **Le Balandre** (*expensive*). *Closed Sun and Mon exc July, Aug and end of Nov.*

★★L'Escargot, 5 Bd Gambetta, t 05 65 35 07 66 (*inexpensive*). Simple comfortable rooms in the big stone walls of the old palais Duèze, including two family rooms. The restaurant (*moderate*) is popular with locals and serves regional favourites. *Closed Sun out of season.*

Au Fil des Douceurs, anchored off Quai Verrerie, t 05 65 22 13 04 (*expensive–moderate*). For a romantic evening on the Lot (literally), try the regional and fish dishes. *Closed Sun eve and Mon in winter.*

Le Rendez-Vous, 49 Rue Clément Marot, t 05 65 22 65 10 (*moderate*). Popular place in the heart of old Cahors; for a splurge try the ravioli filled with *foie gras* in truffle juice. *Closed Sun and Mon.*

Mercuès ✉ 46090

★★★★Château de Mercuès, t 05 65 20 00 01, *www.relaischateaux.fr/mercues* (*expensive*). Sumptuously renovated Relais et Châteaux on a spur high above the valley – the last word in luxury with hanging gardens, a pool and tennis. *Closed Nov–Easter.* The restaurant (*very expensive–expensive*) is equally classy, and the vast cellars feature owner Georges Vigouroux's famous wines. *Closed Mon and Tues lunch out of season, and Nov–Easter.*

Le Montat ✉ 46090

Les Templiers, 5km south of Cahors, t 05 65 21 01 23, *www.templiers.fr* (*expensive–moderate*). A 12th-century Templar priory, serving delicious regional specialities, with an *haute cuisine* touch. *Closed Sun eve, Tues, end of Jan–early Feb and early July.*

around to become the **north portal** in the 14th century, is one of the finest in southern France. Inside, fine frescoes from Genesis (*c*. 1320) are high above the west door, and others are under the first of the two domes in the nave. The Gothic **apse** (1330) is an odd pentagonal structure; its chapels contain fine sculptural work (1484–91). More of the same is in the **cloister** (1509), spread with flowing Flamboyant decoration, which leads you to the Renaissance **Archidiaconé**. Through here, in Rue de la Chantrerie, Cahors' wine-growers have restored **La Chantrerie** (13th-century) and made it into a wine museum (*open July and Aug Wed–Mon 10–12.30 and 3–6.30; closed Tues*).

North of the cathedral extends the **Quartier des Soubirous**, the wealthy merchants' quarter in medieval times; *soubirous* means superior, for the way the area climbs uphill towards the citadel. Neglected for centuries, the Cadurciens have recently begun to restore some of its old mansions. **Rue du Château-du-Roi** is an elegant street reminiscent of Siena or Perugia. Its most impressive façade is at No.102, the 13th-century **Hôpital de Grossia**. The alley to the right of it will bring you to a tiny courtyard decorated with modern murals and a musical fountain that works about half the time. Now Rue des Soubirous, the street continues to the austere church of **St-Barthélemy** and the adjacent **Palais Duèze**. The best surviving parts of it can be seen from Boulevard Gambetta, including the graceful **Tour de Jean XXII**, and, further north, the *barbacane* with its massive **Tour des Pendus**.

The **Pont Valentré**, the only remaining of Cahors' three bridges, survived because it was out of the way and carried little traffic. Begun in 1308, and financed with the help of Pope John XXII (a native of Cahors), the bridge took nearly a century to complete. With the Hundred Years War in full swing, it isn't surprising that defence became the major consideration: the three towers that look so picturesque are three rings of defences; each had its portcullis, and slits for archers and boiling oil.

The Lot West of Cahors

Abruptly leaving the cliffs and *causse* behind, after Cahors the Lot winds around in big lazy loops through the heart of the Cahors wine region. **Luzech** enjoys the most striking setting of the river villages, on a narrow isthmus where two loops of the Lot nearly meet. Some remains of a Gallo-Roman citadel survive on the steep hill above the town at the Oppidum d'Impernal. Below, what remains of medieval Luzech gathers itself under the stout *donjon épiscopal* (or Tour Impernal) and around the 13th-century Maison des Consuls, now the small **Musée Municipal** (*open Mon–Sat 9.30–12.30 and 3–5.30; July and Aug Mon–Sat till 6, Sun 10–12 and 2–4*) with finds from the oppidum. Luzech's Flamboyant Gothic church, **Notre-Dame-de-l'Isle**, was begun in 1505, in the same style as the Cahors cathedral cloister, with a flamboyant portal.

Prayssac started out as a round *bastide*, a mere circle of houses around a market-place. Now the biggest producer of *vin de Cahors*, Prayssac is also worth a mention for its addiction to marble statuary, starting with the unforgettable nude Venus on Venus Square. Signs point the way up the ridge to the *circuit des dolmens*: there are two, along with *garriotes* (corbelled stone huts) and three huge menhirs amid the rocks known as Chaos. The oldest of the Cahors wine dynasties is headquartered here at the **Clos de Gamot**; the family also owns the elegant, 17th-century **Château de Cayrou**, by the river in Puy-l'Evêque. The hills close in on the river again at **Puy-l'Evêque**, giving the village its exceptional setting, best seen from the bridge. A 13th-century *donjon*, similar to Luzech's, sits at the highest point of the town. Not long after, many of the local nobles added their houses in its shadow, creating a lovely ensemble. Take a look around its medieval streets, the battered Flamboyant Gothic portal of **St-Sauveur** (near the top of the town), and views over the valley. Two hamlets nearby have churches frescoed with the *Seven Deadly Sins* – **La Masse** and **Martignac**; while **Duravel**, on the main road, has a good 11th-century church.

North of the Lot: La Bouriane

In this most Périgordian corner of Quercy, *borie* means a 'farmhouse', especially a fortified medieval retreat of Cahors's merchant élite; scattered farmhouses amid lush

Getting Around

There are **trains** from Gourdon to Cahors.

Tourist Information

Gourdon: Rue du Majou, t 05 65 27 52 50.

Where to Stay and Eat

Gourdon ✉ 46300
***Hostellerie de la Bouriane**, Place du Foirail, t 05 65 41 16 37, *www.hostellabouriane.fr*

(*moderate*). Large country inn that has long been the place to stay in Gourdon; lovely rooms and delicious food (*expensive–moderate*)– including some fish. *Restaurant closed for lunch exc Sun, also Mon eve and Sun eve in winter.*

Bissonnier La Bonne Auberge, 51 Bd Martyrs, t 05 65 41 02 48 (*moderate–inexpensive*). Nicest of the slightly cheaper places, in the medieval town and run by the same family since the early 18th century. Rooms can be noisy. Restaurant (*moderate*). *Closed Dec and Jan, Mon lunch and Sun eve out of season.*

landscapes of chestnuts, pines and meadows are the order of the day. The star attraction is **Les Arques**, a sleepy village that's always had an artist or two ever since the Cubist sculptor Ossip Zadkine of Smolensk bought a home here in 1934; a little **Musée Zadkine** (*open June–Sept school hols and Sat and Sun 10–1 and 2–7; otherwise 2–5; adm*) has a collection of his work. Next to the museum is the superb 11th-century church of **St-Laurent**; Zadkine loved it and initiated its restoration.

Harmoniously piled on a bluff, rose-coloured **Gourdon**, the capital of the Bouriane, is easily spotted from miles around. In the 18th century the city walls went down to form a circular boulevard. The massive church of St-Pierre, begun in 1302, is flanked by two 100ft towers, linked by a gallery over the rose window. For a view *from* Gourdon equal to the view *of* Gourdon, climb the stairs here to the site of the old castle. Below, the famous **Rue Zigzag** is lined with medieval houses. Near the church, the 13th-century consulate was converted in the 1700s into the **Hôtel de Ville**, with graceful arcades on the ground floor. Main **Rue du Majou** is lined with more medieval relics: handsome houses, a fortified gate and chapel.

North of Gourdon are the **Grottes de Cougnac** (*open Palm Sun–Sept daily 9.30–11 and 2–5; July and Aug daily 9.30–6; Oct daily 10–11 and 2–4; adm*). One is full of stalactites. The second, 300yds away, preserves the *département*'s second most important collection of prehistoric paintings: black and red outlines of goats, deer, mammoths, symbols and humans, some pierced by lances. Amongst them, palaeontological detectives have found fingerprints believed to be 20,000 years old.

Lot-et-Garonne

The Lot next flows into the rolling and fertile Lot-et-Garonne, famous for high-class prunes, *pruneaux d'Agen*, although it produces masses of other fruit as well, notably grapes; as Bordeaux's neighbour it has excellent wine regions that get better all the time. The east is dotted with castles and *bastides* similar to the Dordogne; the southern *département* is part of Gascony. Throughout, rugby is taken as seriously as prunes, especially in Villeneuve and Agen.

Château de Bonaguil

It's so perfect that it seems ridiculous to call it a ruin.
Lawrence of Arabia, 1908

At the east end of the Lot-et-Garonne, tucked in the wooded hills where no one can ever find it, is one of the most useless but photogenic castles in France, as stunning as a Hollywood set, espeically on summer nights when it's illuminated until midnight. Begun in the 13th century by the knights of nearby Fumel, in the 1460s it passed to the hunchback baddie Brengon de Rocquefeuil. Brengon surrounded it with a moat and a surging prow of walls and towers – just as all the other French nobles were abandoning their medieval castles. By the 18th century Brengon's lair was such a white elephant that it changed hands for 100 francs and a bag of walnuts and was partially demolished in the Revolution. The **interior** (*open Feb–end of Nov daily 10.30–12 and 2–4.30; June daily 10–12 and 2–5; July and Aug daily 10–5.45; closed Jan and Dec, exc school hols; www.bonaguil.org*), however, can't begin to match the exterior: there are fireplaces in the void, graffiti and views from the walls.

Bastide Country

Bonaguil stands on the edge of the rolling hills and woodlands that Stendhal called the 'Tuscany of France', planted with a superb collection of castles and *bastides* – planned towns from the Hundred Years War, when this peaceful region was on the front lines. One of the most strategic, set on a high hill with views for miles around, is **Monflanquin**, founded in 1256. It has preserved most of its original *bastide* elements: the central square bordered with wide arcades, or *cornières*, a fortified church, its grid plan and blocks of medieval houses; the exhibitions in the new Espace Bastides will tell you all about them. Others include **Villeréal**, 13km north, founded in 1269 on the Dropt; the shop-filled arcades of the main square overlook the 14th-century *halle*, and the façade of the church is framed by two towers and retains the loopholes in the apse from where the citizens shot at the rampaging English. Another, **Monpazier**, 'the most perfect *bastide*', is 15km further up the river Dropt. Founded by Edward I in 1284, its 16th-century *halle* still has its original grain measures. Note that the regulation arcades, or *cornières*, around the square are irregular, and that narrow spaces were left between the houses – not to give the residents air or light as much as a place to throw their rubbish.

The vast **Château de Biron** (*open Oct–Mar Tues–Sun 10–12.30 and 2–5.30; April daily 10–12.30 and 2–5.30; May, June and Sept daily 10–12.30 and 2–6.30; July and Aug daily 10–7; adm*) was founded in the 11th century to command the northern approaches to the Agenais. In 1189 Gaston de Gontaut (an ancestor of Lord Byron) got his hands on it, and the family remained in charge for 24 generations, creating along the way one of the more eclectic castles in France, beginning with a 12th-century Tour Anglaise, 13th-century Romanesque walls and the Tour du Concierge. In the 15th century Pons de Gontaut-Biron added the delicate Pavillon de la Recette and a two-storey chapel – the ground floor for the villagers, and the upstairs for the nabobs. The moat was filled in under Richelieu, who didn't like the great lords of France feeling safe or secure.

Getting Around

Monsempron-Libos (nearest station to Bonaguil) has a few **trains** to Les Eyzies and Périgueux, and Agen. More frequent **buses** run up the Lot valley as far as Cahors.

Agen's **airport** La Garenne is to the southwest, t 05 53 77 00 88, and is served by three flights a day to Paris on Air Littoral, t 08 25 83 48 34. There are several trains a day to Monsempron-Libos, Penne, Périgueux, Les Eyzies, and TGVs to Bordeaux, Toulouse and Paris.

Rent a houseboat in summer to sail along the Canal Latéral from the Crown Blue Line, t 05 53 89 50 80, by the canal lock at Le Mas d'Agenais, or from Aquitaine Navigation, t 05 53 84 72 50, at Le Coustet in Buzet. You can take a trip on a *gabare* with Croisière du Prince Henry at Nérac, t 05 53 65 66 66. Boat trips lasting 1½ hours leave from the Port de Plaisance in Agen, t 05 53 87 51 95.

Parc Walibi, at Roquefort near Agen, is one of the biggest amusement/water parks in southwest France (*open late April–late Sept; July–Aug daily 10–6*; t 05 53 96 58 32).

Tourist Information

Monflanquin: Place des Arcades, t 05 53 36 40 19.
Villeneuve-sur-Lot: 47 Rue de Paris, t 05 53 36 17 30.
Agen: 107 Bd Carnot, t 05 53 47 36 09, *www.ot-agen.org*.
Nérac: 7 Av Mondenard, t 05 53 65 27 75, *www.ville-nerac.fr*.

Activities

You can hire an **electric boat** or **canoe** from Lot Elec Avenue in Villeneuve, t 05 53 95 69 77.

Where to Stay and Eat

Pujols ✉ **47300**
La Toque Blanche, t 05 53 49 00 30, *www.la-toque-blanche.com* (*expensive*). Classic, intimate and elegant restaurant which attracts gastronomes from across France. Panoramic views are accompanied by some of the most delicious duck dishes you've ever had; extensive wine list. *Closed Sun night, Mon and Tues lunch.*
Auberge Lou Calel, t 05 53 70 46 14 (*moderate*). Annexe to La Toque Blanche, in a handsome medieval house with a big fireplace and

Villeneuve-sur-Lot and Pujols

The bustling market city of Villeneuve-sur-Lot likes its rugby *à treize* so much that it needs three stadia to contain all the action. Although now spread every which way, it grew out of yet another *bastide*, founded in 1264 by Alphonse de Poitiers, St Louis' brother and Count of Toulouse. The central market square, **Place Lafayette**, is still framed in its *cornières*, rebuilt in the 17th century after the riots of the Fronde. Near by, the brick **Ste-Catherine** was completed in the 1930s, replacing a Gothic church in danger of collapse. The magnificent Gothic and Renaissance stained glass of the latter was incorporated in the new church. St James the Greater appears three times, recalling the Compostela pilgrims who passed through Villeneuve; it was one of the few places on the Lot with a bridge, the **Pont Vieux**.

Walled, medieval antique-dealing **Pujols**, 2km from the Pont Vieux, was originally a Celtic oppidum. To enter its ancient square, pass under the arch of the tower of the Flamboyant Gothic St-Nicolas. Inside, the church has star vaulting and curious tribunes with little fireplaces so the local barons could attend Mass more snugly. A second church in Pujols, Ste-Foy la Jeune, dates from the 1400s and contains some excellent frescoes, one showing St Foy of Agen (and now of Conques).

terraces overlooking the valley and Villeneuve; delicious food. *Closed Tues eve, Wed and Thurs lunch.*

Agen ✉ 47000

****Hôtel-Château des Jacobins**, Place des Jacobins, t 05 53 47 03 31 (*moderate*). Very comfortable, beautifully restored, ivy-covered *hôtel particulier* in the centre, with parking and a pretty garden.

***Le Provence**, 22 Cours du 14-Juillet, t 05 53 47 39 11 (*moderate*). A pleasant little hotel in the centre, with spruce, soundproofed rooms.

*Les Ambans**, 59 Rue des Ambans, t 05 53 66 28 60 (*inexpensive*). One of the nicest cheap hotels (showers in every room).

Mariottat, 25 Rue Louis Vivent, t 05 53 77 89 77, f 05 53 77 99 79, *www.restaurant-mariottat. com* (*expensive–moderate*). Handsome town house in the centre; the chef-owner works wonders with the best the daily market provides. *Closed Sat lunch, Sun eve and Mon.*

Fleur de Sel, 66 Rue C Desmoulins, t 05 53 66 63 70 (*moderate*). Charming restaurant with expert menus with regional fare. *Closed Sat lunch, Sun, Mon lunch and mid-Aug.*

La Bohême, 14 Rue Emile Sentini, t 05 53 68 31 00, *www.laboheme-france.com*

(*inexpensive*). The chef will give you excellent southwest cooking with a personal slant; try the *foie gras* with blueberries.

Boé ✉ 47550

****Château St-Marcel**, 3km south of Agen on the N113 towards Toulouse, t 05 53 96 61 30 (*expensive*). 17th-century castle which belonged to Montesquieu. Sumptuous suites furnished with antiques, or more modern (and far less pricey) rooms in the annexe; a pool and tennis. The restaurant (*expensive– moderate*) serves imaginative, delicate combinations of local ingredients. *Closed Sun eve and Mon.*

Nérac ✉ 47600

***Hôtel d'Albret**, 40 Allées d'Albret, t 05 53 97 41 10 (*inexpensive*). Simple family-run hotel, with a much-loved restaurant (*moderate*) with an outside terrace. *Closed Sun eve.*

Relais de la Hire, 11 Rue Porte-Neuve, t 05 53 65 41 59 (*moderate*). One of the best places to dine in the area, south of Nérac in Francescas, in an 18th-century house, where the freshest ingredients appear in creations such as *artichaut de l'Albret soufflé au foie gras. Closed Sun eve and Mon.*

Agen

Agen owes much of its current prosperity to its location between Bordeaux and Toulouse; transport depots, fruit-packing and bureaucracy are the things that keep the money coming in. Admittedly these aren't big tourist magnets, but this shapeless, rather staid departmental capital does have an ace up its sleeve: one of the finest provincial art museums in France. Or come when the Agenais show their wild and crazy side, when their beloved rugby squad is thumping some hapless opponent.

The **Musée Municipal des Beaux Arts** (*open Wed–Mon 10–6; closed Tues; adm*) occupies four beautifully restored 16th- and 17th-century *hôtels particuliers* in Place du Dr-Esquirol. The star of the Gallo-Roman section is the *Vénus du Mas*, a 1st-century Greek marble. The medieval collection includes tombstones and effigies, goldwork, and Romanesque and Gothic capitals. A beautiful spiral stair leads up to the 16th- and 17th-century paintings and ceramics. Beyond minor works by Tiepolo and Greuze are five Goyas, including a powerful *Self Portrait*. The last rooms move on to the 19th century – Corot, Sisley and Boudin.

Agen's cathedral, **St-Caprais** (north of the museum in Rue Raspail), is named after a local boy who was beheaded for declaring his faith. There isn't much to see inside, but

Pruneaux d'Agen

The first plums in the area were brought from Damascus by the Crusaders in 1148, and took so well that today some 65 per cent of all French plums come from the Lot-et-Garonne. Most are dried as *pruneaux d'Agen* which, as every French gourmet knows, are the finest in the universe. Most of them don't come from Agen at all, but from the rich Lot valley between Villeneuve and Aiguillon, a businesslike agricultural paradise. In **Granges-sur-Lot**, one plum farm has created the **Prune Museum** (*open Mon–Sat 9–12 and 2–7, Sun and hols 3–7; Nov–Mar till 6.30; closed last two weeks Jan; adm*) for the curious and the constipated.

the Romanesque tri-lobe apse has good *modillons* sculpted with heads of humans and animals. In the northwest corner of Agen an impressive 23-arch aqueduct, the **Pont Canal** (1839) carries the Canal Latéral over the Garonne, not far from the favourite promenade, the **Esplanade du Gravier**.

The Néracais

This pleasant *pays* is often called the 'Pays d'Albret'; its long history as the feudal domain of the d'Albrets has given it an identity that endures to this day. Its capital, fat **Nérac**, counts scarcely more than 7,000 inhabitants, but its association with the family in the 1500s has given it some fine monuments and the air of a little capital, if you see it from the right angle. The d'Albret family came into prominence in the 15th and 16th centuries: the French kings showered every sort of prize on the family, and with their help Henri d'Albret became king of Navarre, at which point François Ier found him a fitting match for his sister, Marguerite d'Angoulême, or Marguerite de Navarre. Already a widow at 35, she was the most eligible lady of France – not just for being the king's sister, but for a wit, charm and intelligence that stood out even in Renaissance courts. Marguerite turned their favoured residence of Nérac into a brilliant court where poetry and humanistic learning were the order of the day.

South of Nérac, around **Mézin**, the countryside is lush and delightful. On the D656, along the valley of the Gélise, you'll pass *pigeonniers* on stilts, and farmers hanging signs out to sell you asparagus and *cèpes, foie gras*, armagnac and *Floc de Gascogne*, the 'Flower of Gascony' – the apéritif wine, made since the 1500s and revived, uniquely for France, almost exclusively by women.

The **Moulin de Henri IV** (*open Feb Wed–Sun 2–6; Mar and early Oct–Dec Sun 2–6; April–early Oct Wed–Sun 10.30–12 and 1–7.30;*), north of Nérac, is one of the famous sites of the southwest. If it looks more like a castle, it is that too; fortified mills are not uncommon, built in feudal times when grain was precious. The story has it that the nobleman who built it had four daughters of different ages, and made the mill's four towers different heights in their honour. In later times the mill belonged to the d'Albrets, and it passed from them to Henri IV.

Western Lot-et-Garonne: Down the Garonne

In fact, it isn't just the Garonne; you have a choice of following the river or the **Canal Latéral Garonne**, the 19th-century waterway that parallels the river, providing a complement to the Canal du Midi, and providing boats with a passage from the Mediterranean to the Atlantic.

An elegant modern suspension bridge crosses both the Garonne and the canal, and although the customary sign announces the village of **Le Mas d'Agenais**, not a house is to be seen. Mas is up in the clouds, closed into itself; it is special, and it knows it. It isn't large, just a few lovely streets and squares, a brick medieval gateway, a wooden market *halle* from the 1600s, and a beautiful view over the Garonne from its park. It also has one of the region's best churches, **St-Vincent**, begun in 1085, replacing a church of *c.* 440 built on the site of a Roman temple. The interior contains a wealth of sculptural decoration and two relics: an early Christian sarcophagus, said to be that of the obscure martyr Vincent, and a Roman *cippus* with a confusing inscription, maybe the base for the statue of a pagan god. Mas' claim to fame, a Rembrandt, was donated to the church in 1873. Originally, *The Face of Christ on the Cross* was part of a series of seven on the Passion; all the rest are now in Munich.

Down the Aveyron

South of the Lot, the next major river is the Aveyron, flowing down the *département* of the same name. This area, known as the Rouergue after the Rutène Celts, is famous for its wide open spaces pierced by deep ravines, its clear skies and environmental purity – the award-winning insect film, *Microcosmos,* was filmed here. The Aveyron twists down to the Tarn north of Montauban, capital of the Tarn-et-Garonne, a *département* that contains enough fruit to have kept Carmen Miranda in hats forever.

Rodez and Villefranche-de-Rouergue

Rodez was a major Gallo-Roman city on a breast-shaped hill that thrived in the Middle Ages, when the locals felt flush enough to build a cathedral on top of town. It was the 13th century, and what is surprising about **Notre-Dame** is that they chose northern Gothic for their model, and stuck with it over the next three centuries. Was it an aftershock of the Albigensian crusade that made Rodez march in step with the conquerors, or did they just prefer the style? No one knows. The west front, part of the city wall, resembles a red cliff pierced by a large rose window. The 16th-century **bell**

Getting There and Around

Rodez's **airport** has flights from Paris and is also served by Ryanair from the UK. There are **trains** to Paris, Toulouse, and Montpellier; **buses** from Place du Foirail, t 05 65 68 11 13, go to Millau, Villefranche-de-Rouergue, Cahors, Albi, and Montauban. Cordes is a 6km **taxi** ride (t 05 63 56 14 80) from the train station at Vindrac, coming from Villefranche or Toulouse.

Tourist Information

Rodez: Pl du Maréchal-Foch, t 05 65 75 76 77.
Villefranche-de-Rouergue: Promenade du Guiraudet, t 05 65 45 13 18, *www.villefranche.com*.
Cordes: Maison Fontperyrouse, on top of town, t 05 63 56 00 52.
St-Antonin-Noble-Val: Place de la Mairie, t 05 63 30 63 47.
Bruniquel: Promenade du Ravellin, t 05 63 67 29 84, *www.bruniquel.fr.fm*.

Where to Stay and Eat

Rodez ✉ 12000

★★★**Hostellerie de Fontanges**, 2km north of Rodez at Onet-le-Château, t 05 65 77 76 00 (*inexpensive*). A handsome 16th-century château with stylish rooms, pool, tennis and golf nearby, and imaginative cooking.
Goûts et Couleurs, 38 Rue de Bonald, t 05 65 42 75 10 (*moderate*). The best restaurant in Rodez: a pretty, cosy place, where chef Jean-Luc Fau adds a light, exotic sparkle to his delicious specialities, such as salmon marinated in a soy mousse, with asparagus and grilled sesame seeds. *Book*.

Belcastel ✉ 12390

★★★**Le Vieux Pont**, t 05 65 64 52 29 (*moderate*). Two sisters have converted their family

home by the 15th-century bridge into a hotel restaurant, with seven well-equipped rooms and rich, flavourful cuisine (*expensive*) based on local ingredients, served on a riverside terrace in summer. *Closed Sun eve, Mon eve, Jan and Feb.*

Najac ✉ 12270

★★**L'Oustal del Barry**, Place du Bourg, t 05 65 29 74 32 (*moderate*). Century-old family hotel in the centre with trendy-rustic rooms and an excellent restaurant (*expensive–moderate*), serving seasonal dishes; try the *astet najacois*, roast pork with *filet mignon* inside. *Closed early Nov–mid-Dec; restaurant closed Tues lunch and Mon to non-residents.*

Cordes-sur-Ciel ✉ 81170

★★★★**Le Grand Ecuyer**, Rue Raymond VII, t 05 63 53 79 50 (*expensive–moderate*). On top of Cordes, 15 elegant rooms in a medieval setting, and Yves Thuriès' cuisine – famed for delicacy, finesse and *savoir-faire*, with seafood specialities; save room for the classy desserts. *Closed Nov–Feb.*
★★★**Le Vieux Cordes**, Rue St-Michel, t 05 63 53 79 20 (*inexpensive*). In a 13th-century building with charm and mod cons, including modems. Parking nearby. Run by the tireless Yves Thuriès (twice honoured as the Best Worker in France), with fine dining (*moderate*) on salmon or duck under a massive wisteria.

St-Antonin-Noble-Val ✉ 82140

★★**Le Lys Bleu de Payrols**, 29 Place de la Halle, t 05 63 68 21 00 (*moderate*). Several medieval houses in the heart of town, the rooms furnished with antiques and minibars. The little restaurant serves good pizza for dinner.
Bès de Quercy, on the D926 towards Caylus, t 05 63 31 97 61 (*inexpensive*). *Ferme-auberge* with four comfortable B&B rooms; meals (*cheap*) with chicken, duck or guinea fowl.

tower, however, steals the show, a Flamboyant Gothic masterpiece of pinnacles and stone lace standing 288ft tall and crowned by a statue of the Virgin. Inside, the tall pillars have no capitals, as if emphasizing the height. The lively 15th-century choir stalls are by the local sculptor André Sulpice, and there are other things to seek out – the rococo organ cabinet, the remarkable tomb of Bishop Jean-François Croizier, the Flamboyant choir screen, and a painted stone *Deposition*.

Following the Aveyron west, **Belcastel** is one of those medieval towns hanging over the river, so picturesque that they resemble a stage set, complete with a medieval bridge and 15th-century château. It lies midway between Rodez and the *bastide* of **Villefranche-de-Rouergue**, founded in 1252 by Alphonse de Poitiers at the confluence of the Aveyron and the Alzou. One of the larger towns in the area, Villefranche has preserved its medieval essence, with a dense grid of pale limestone houses built by merchants. The central arcaded *place* is perfect, with the church of **Notre Dame** in one corner, a Gothic arch yawning under a massive tower. Inside, take time to examine the ravishing choir stalls by André Sulpice, who spent 15 years on the project.

Villefranche was still a going concern in 1642, the date of the octagonal Baroque **Chapelle des Pénitents-Noirs** (*open July–mid-Sept daily 10–12 and 2–6*) on Boulevard de la Haute-Guyenne (the very next year, however, 10,000 starving peasants, squeezed to the limit by the town, revolted; many were executed in Place Notre-Dame for their presumption). The Counter-Reformation decoration reaches its apogee in the wooden retable on the *Adoration of the Cross*. Just outside of town, the **Chartreuse St-Sauveur** (*same hours*) is a rare charterhouse of 1450 that survived the Revolution intact.

Najac, Cordes, St-Antonin-Noble-Val and Bruniquel

Beyond Villefranche, the Aveyron retreats into a wooded gorge, its twists and turns lassoing along the way the promontory of **Najac** and one of the most theatrical castles in France (*open July and Aug daily 10–1 and 3–7; June 3–6; April, May and Sept 3–5; adm*), hovering on the tip of an old volcanic cone. Built in 1269 by Alphonse de Poitiers, it gave its master control over the entire valley, although by the time of the Revolution it was so damaged it was sold for 12 francs. Najac's Gothic church was built in the same century; the Inquisition ordered the locals to pay for it as punishment for supporting the Cathars.

At Laguépie the Aveyron makes a sharp turn to the west: at this point it's only 13km to one of the loftiest and most famous of all *bastides*, **Cordes-sur-Ciel** ('in the sky'), founded and heavily fortified in 1222 by Count Raymond VII of Toulouse. Although friendly to the Cathars, it was never captured in the Albigensian crusade (hence its fine state of preservation), although the Inquisitors were certainly on hand to mop up the heretics after the fact. In later years its most famous resident was Albert Camus. The huge *halle* in the main square dates from the 14th century; the medieval wells here go down 370ft through the rock. The 13th-century Maison Prunet is now the **Féerie de l'Art du Sucre** (*open July and Aug daily 5–7; April–June daily 10–12.30 and 2–7; Sept–Mar daily 10–12 and 2.30–6.30; adm*), packed full of sugary sculptures by Cordes' renowned chef, Yves Thuriès. The **Musée d'Art et d'Histoire** at the Portail Peint (*open July and Aug Sun–Fri 11–12.30 and 3.30–6.30; Easter–June and Sept–early Nov Sun and public hols 3.30–6.30; adm*) keeps the charter of 1222 and the illuminated city code, as well as other odds and ends. The terraces of the lower town have been converted into an updated oriental dream garden, the **Jardin des Paradis** (*open July and Aug daily; otherwise contact tourist office for details; adm*).

To the west, the Aveyron then snakes below **St-Antonin-Noble-Val**. The Romans named it *Nobilis Vallis*; the St Antonin was tacked on when the saint's body floated downstream and a monastery was founded. St-Antonin has an exceptional assortment of medieval houses. Foremost is the lovely Gothic **Place des Halles** and its **Maison des Consuls** (1120) – unfortunately 'improved' by Viollet-le-Duc. Along the Promenade des Moines are the remains of the tanneries which once made St-Antonin's fortune. The paths around St-Antonin make for fine walking, especially up to the 660ft **Rocher des Anglars** with its belvedere over the gorge; for more big scenery, take the narrow corniche road, the D173 past medieval **Penne**, with its astonishing castle hanging over the cliffs.

Next down the river is picturesque **Bruniquel**, former Protestant stronghold and current artists' colony, overlooking the cliffs at the confluence of the Aveyron and Vère. Rising 300ft over the rivers, the **château** (*open July and Aug daily 10–7; June and Sept Sun and hols 2–6; May Sun and hols 10–12.30 and 2–6*) dates back to the 12th century – the tour includes the keep, the knights' room and chapel, and an elegant Renaissance gallery. The nearby **Maison des Comtes Payrol** (*open April–Sept daily 10–6; adm*) is a fine example of 13th-century civic architecture.

Montauban

Originally covered with silvery willows, hence *Mons Albanus* ('white hill'), Montauban prefers to be known as 'the pinkest of the three pink cities' (ie pinker than Toulouse and Albi). Founded by the Counts of Toulouse in 1144, Montauban was such a successful experiment in city planning that it spawned dozens of baby Montaubans, known as the *bastides*, in the 13th and 14th centuries.

The finest gift bestowed on Montauban was its central square, the **Place Nationale**. Although the prototype for the *bastide* market square, none can match its urbane sophistication; first, it isn't even a square at all, but a subtle, irregular trapezoid with covered chamfered corners. Its unique 'double cloister' arcades date from 1144 and were originally built in wood; after a fire in 1614 they were rebuilt exactly as they were in warm brick. On this stage the Montaubanais bought their food, hanged their thieves and issued their proclamations.

In Place Victor-Hugo, **St-Jacques** is a church and assembly hall built by the city's consuls in the 13th century. During the repairs following the Hundred Years War, it was given an octagonal bell tower; the neo-Roman portal with its tile decoration dates from the 19th century; the interior is typically southern Gothic, with a large single nave. Down from St-Jacques, **Place Bourdelle** is named after Bourdelle's dramatic 1895 *Monument to the War Dead of 1870*, an early major work, showing the influence of his master Rodin. The Tarn here is spanned by the **Pont Vieux**, a 677ft structure begun in 1311 – a technological *tour de force*, with seven uneven arches and, originally, three towers, demolished in the early 1900s to let more traffic through.

The **Musée Ingres** (*13 Rue de l'Hôtel de Ville; open Sept–June Tues–Sun 10–12 and 2–6; mid-Oct–Easter also closed Sun am; July and Aug daily 9.30–12 and 1.30–6; adm*), housed in the bishops' palace at the eastern end of the bridge, is a monument to the city's favourite son, Jean-Auguste-Dominique Ingres (1780–1867). The painter's dona-

Getting Around

Montauban's **train** station on Rue Solengro is well served by trains between Paris and Toulouse via Angoulême, and Toulouse and Bordeaux via Moissac and Agen. Transport Jardel (t 05 63 22 55 00) and Autocars Barrière (t 05 63 93 34 34) run **buses**.

Tourist Information

Montauban: L'Ancien Collège, Pl Praux–Paris, t 05 63 63 60 60, *www.ville-montauban.fr*.

Where to Stay and Eat

Montauban ✉ 82000
★★★Hostellerie Les Coulandrières, on the D958 at Montbeton, t 05 63 67 47 47 (*moderate*).

The prettiest place to stay, 3km west of the city. A modern inn under a superb cedar tree, with a pool and park and bright rooms; the restaurant (*moderate*) is one of the best, featuring delicious seafood. *Closed Sun eve.*

★★★Mercure Montauban, 12 Rue Notre Dame, t 05 63 63 17 23 (*moderate*). Usual attributes of a chain hotel, worth considering for its central location. Restaurant.

★★Hôtel d'Orsay, Rue Salengro, t 05 63 66 06 66 (*inexpensive*). Opposite the station, with very comfortable rooms, and the best food in town at the welcoming **La Cuisine d'Alain** (*expensive–moderate*), which takes local traditions and gives them an original slant; the *à la carte* includes Montalbanais *cassoulet*. Fabulous desserts. *Closed Sun, Mon lunch and Christmas–New Year.*

tions make up the core of the collection, including thousands of drawings, portraits, and mythologies such as the *Dream of Ossian*. He also gave the museum a Masolino predella panel, a *Nativity* by Carpaccio, and a striking *St Jerome* attributed to Ribera. Montalbanais sculptor Antoine Bourdelle (1861–1929) gets a room to himself; his most acclaimed work, the *Last Centaur Dying*, stands out in front of the museum.

The **Cathédrale Notre-Dame** was rebuilt between 1692 and 1739 by Louis XIV's own architects. Its white stone and frostily perfect classicism in a city of warm brick betrays its Parisian origins. The vast interior is full of equally frigid furnishings, and one of Ingres' major works, the enormous *Vow of Louis XIII*, commissioned for the cathedral (1820–1824).

In 1679 Montauban's *intendant* Foucault initiated the greening of the pink city by planting thousands of elms on the banks of the Tarn, along the broad street that now bears his name, **Cours Foucault**. Popular ever since, its focal point, closing the view between the long alleys of trees, is Bourdelle's *La France veillant sur ses morts*, a First World War monument inspired by the temples and sculpture of ancient Greece.

Moissac

There's only one reason to visit Moissac, but it's hard to beat: the **Abbaye de St-Pierre**, founded by Clovis in 506 and one of the crown jewels of French sculpture. Sheltered by a 12th-century tower, the sublime **porch** is one of the most powerful and beautiful works of the Middle Ages. The **tympanum** rests on a lintel recycled from a Gallo-Roman building, decorated with eight large thistle flowers and enclosed in a cable or vine, spat out by a monster at one end and swallowed by another monster at the other. In the centre, Christ sits in the *Judgement of Nations*. You might notice that

Getting Around

Moissac is on the **railway** line between Bordeaux, Agen, Montauban and Toulouse.

For **bus** information, ring the tourist office.

An old barge, *Le Grain d'Or*, offers **cruises** on the Canal Latéral and the river Tarn, call **t** 05 63 04 48 28 for information.

Tourist Information

Moissac: 6 Place Durand-de-Bredons, **t** 05 63 04 01 85.

Where to Stay and Eat

Moissac ✉ 82200

★★Le Pont Napoléon, 2 Allées Montebello, **t** 05 63 04 01 55 (*inexpensive*). Delightful old-fashioned hotel overlooking the Tarn. Purchased by master chef Michel Dussau, its reputation of serving the best food in Moissac (*expensive*) on its lovely terrace will only increase. *Closed Wed, Sun eve and Mon lunch*.

he has three arms, one on the Book of Life, one raised in blessing, and another on his heart; no one knows why. The four symbols of the Evangelists twist to surround him, and two seraphim carrying scrolls are squeezed under the rainbow. The rest of the tympanum is occupied by the 24 Elders, each gazing up from their thrones at Christ. The whole wonderfully rhythmic composition could just as easily be an old-timers' band raising their glasses in an intermission toast to a stern, but respected and beloved bandleader.

But that's not all. The door's central pillar, the **trumeau**, is sculpted with pairs of lions in the form of Xs symbolically guarding the church. On either side are *Peter*, *Isaiah*, *Paul* and *Jeremiah*, elongated, supple figures that sway and almost dance. To the right are scenes from the life of the Virgin; to the left, poor Lazarus' soul is taken into the bosom of Abraham, while below the soul of the feasting Dives is carried off to hell. Look for the miser with demons on his shoulder, refusing alms to a beggar, and Lust, serpents sucking at her breasts.

The **interior** of the church had to be rebuilt in 1430 and can't compete with the fireworks on the portal. Only one chapel retains its 15th-century geometrical murals, which inspired the restoration on the other walls; some excellent polychrome sculpture survives as well.

Behind the church is the abbey's famous **cloister** (*open Jan–Mar and Oct–Dec daily 10–12 and 2–5; April and May daily 9–12.30 and 2–6; June and Sept daily 9–6; July and Aug daily 9–7; adm*), whose 76 magnificent capitals, set on alternating paired and single slender columns of various coloured marbles, come from the end of the 11th century; they are the oldest *in situ* in France. They also mark an artistic turning point, towards more fluid, stylized poses with a sense of movement, exquisite modelling, and a play of light and shadow hitherto unknown in Romanesque sculpture. The capitals are carved with foliage inspired by Corinthian capitals, but with luxuriant virtuosity; others have birds and animals intertwined. Some 46 capitals tell the lives of the saints – don't miss the dynamic martyrdoms: St Lawrence on the grill, while two Romans blow on the flames; St Martin dividing his cloak with the beggar; St John the Baptist and the feast of Herod; St Peter on his cross next to St Paul's beheading. Other scenes are rare – the city of Jerusalem vs. unholy Babylon, the story of Nebuchadnezzar, and Shadrach, Meshach and Abednego in the furnace.

Down the Tarn

Dordogne, Lot, Aveyron – heading south, the next of the Garonne's great tributaries is the Tarn. Like the Lot, it has its origins at Mont Lozère, but the scenic drama begins when it meets the soft limestone plateaux of the Grands Causses, where it cuts through a spectacular canyon on its way to Millau and Roquefort country, past Albi of the great red cathedral, sweeping down to Toulouse only to change its mind and head up to Montauban and Moissac (see pp.442–3) and join the Garonne there.

Getting Around

Millau is served by **trains** from Paris, Rodez, Toulouse, Montpellier, Perpignan and Béziers. **Buses, t** 05 65 59 89 33, from the train station make a circuit to Meyrueis, Aven Armand, Ste-Enimie, and down the Gorges du Tarn back to Millau; others travel to Albi and Rodez.

Tourist Information

Ste-Enimie: at the Mairie, **t** 04 66 48 53 44.
Millau:1 Av Alfred-Merle, **t** 05 65 60 02 42.

Sports and Activities

Canoes and kayaks can be hired at most ports in the Gorges du Tarn, especially at Ste-Énimie.
Bateliers de la Malène, t 04 66 48 51 10. Boat rides for four or five people at a time down the most scenic sections of the Gorges du Tarn and minibus rides back to La Malène (*several times daily end Mar–start Nov*).

Where to Stay and Eat

For all hotels in the Gorges du Tarn, book well in advance. Mende (see p.424) is also close by.

Ste-Enimie/La Malène ✉ 48210
****Château de la Caze, towards La Malène, **t** 04 66 48 51 01, *www.ila-chateau.com/caze* (*luxury–expensive*). The prettiest castle along the Tarn is also the most fashionable place to stay, with elegant rooms and apartments individually styled with charm and antiques, a pool, terrace and lovely restaurant (*expensive*) with a Gothic fireplace, serving the likes

of saddle of lamb with baby artichokes. *Closed mid-Nov–mid-Mar.*
***Manoir de Montesquiou, La Malène, **t** 04 66 48 51 12 (*expensive–moderate*). Ivy-covered
15th-century manor house, with romantic rooms furnished with antiques, and a restaurant (*expensive–moderate*) where the chef does delicious things with morels and free range chickens. *Closed Nov–Mar.*
Auberge du Moulin, Ste-Énimie, **t 04 66 48 53 08 (*inexpensive*). Rooms in a restored stone mill. Restaurant (*moderate*). *Closed 15 Nov–mid-Mar.*

Millau ✉ 12100
***International, 1 Place de la Tiné, **t** 05 65 59 29 00 (*moderate–inexpensive*). A large modern family-run hotel disguised as a chain, with comfortable air-conditioned rooms; restaurant (*moderate*) has a view and dishes such as monkfish peppered with spices. *Closed Dec.*
***Château de Creissels, 2km southwest of Millau, **t** 05 65 60 16 59, *www.chateau-de-creissels.com* (*inexpensive*). Big rooms furnished in an antique style in a 12th-century château and a modern addition. Restaurant (*moderate*). *Closed Jan and Feb.*
Cevenol Hotel, 115 Rue du Rajol, **t 05 65 60 74 44, *www.cevenol-hotel.fr.* (*inexpensive*). Views over the *causse*, a pool and terrace for sitting outside in the summer. Roquefort specialities in the restaurant. *Closed mid-Nov–early Mar.*
Capion, 3 Rue J-F Alméras, **t** 05 65 60 00 91 (*moderate*). A local culinary institution off Rue Jean-Jaurès, featuring a surprising array of dishes from the most traditional to exotic. Excellent value. *Closed Tues eve, Wed out of season, and most of July.*

The Grands Causses and the Gorges du Tarn

Some of France's emptiest and most monotonous spaces are the four grey lime-stone plateaux of the **Grands Causses** south of the Massif Central. Although it certainly rains here, the *causses* are arid – they soak up water like a sponge, and are fit only for grazing sheep, who find enough to drink in water holes called *lavognes*. For all the emptiness, however, the region is extraordinarily rich in flora and fauna; the Grands Causses, Mont Lozère and much of the southern half of the Lozère and western Gard fall into the confines of the **Parc National des Cévennes** (*see* p.859).

For most visitors, the fascination with the Grands Causses has everything to do with what water has wrought here: the great subterranean cavities, the peculiar forma-tions, the cliffs and magnificent gorges.The most famous of these, the spectacular 53km **Gorges du Tarn**, runs through a fault between the **Causse de Sauveterre** and **Causse Méjean**. Time your visit carefully, if possible – the canyon is too crowded (and hot) in July and August, but if it's cloudy, you'll miss the beautiful colours of the gorge's stone. May and September are ideal. November to March are deserted.

The Tarn's bed changes from granite to limestone in **Florac**. Beyond here, the 40 or so streams that feed the crystal-clear river are subterranean resurgences that spill down the cliffs. The canyon begins in earnest at **Ispagnac**. **Quézac** has a Gothic bridge built by Pope Urban V to permit pilgrims to visit the church he built here, to house a statue of the Virgin discovered in 1050. The next village, **Castelbouc**, built into the cliff under a ruined castle, is just as famous for its impiety: while the local men were off at the Crusades, the local lord, as the only male, took it upon himself to solace their women. His exertions eventually killed him in the arms of a lover, and his soul flew out of the castle in the form of a giant billy goat (or *bouc*). Further down, you can visit the (intact) **Château de Prades** on its rocky perch, built in the 13th–15th centuries by the priors at Ste-Enimie to defend the gorge.

Ste-Enimie itself is set under steep cliffs; the descent by the D986 from Mende is wonderfully scenic and offers a splendid view over the village and its site. It owes its lushness to generations of peasants who brought the soil in, basket by basket. It owes its name to a beautiful Merovingian princess (d. 628) who came down with leprosy when her father, Clotaire II, engaged her to be married against her will. An angel advised her to come here to be cured in a local spring, and it worked, but whenever she tried to leave the area the leprosy returned. So she stayed with her followers and built a convent, which the devil kept knocking down until she gave chase (*see* below). From the D986 it's a 30-minute walk to her Grotte-Ermitage, with fine views. There are even better ones from a belvedere 6km south, on the same D986.

The main river road, the D907, carries on to **St-Chély** and **Pougandoires**, both villages set in striking *cirques* or curls in the river. The most beautiful of the gorge's castles, the 15th-century fairytale **Château de la Caze** (*see* p.445) was built by Soubeyrane Alamand, who was famous for his eight lovely daughters, the Nymphs of the Tarn.

At **La Malène**, the 'Bad hole' boatman waits to take you through the **Détroits**, the narrowest part of the gorge, where rock walls (at their best in the morning) rise over 1,300ft above the river and into the magnificent burnished red **Cirque des Baumes**. By road, the best view of the narrows is from the **Roc des Hourtous** on the south bank of the river, reached by way of the D43 from La Malène. At the lower part of the Cirque des Baumes is a jumble of massive rocks called the **Pas du Souci**. While chasing Satan, St Enimie realized that she could never catch him up and asked the Roque Sourde to help her. The cliff dutifully gave way and fell on top of him and only a small hole in the pile allowed him to slip out and return to hell. Geologists prefer to date the rock slide to an earthquake in 580. The valley then widens at **Les Vignes**, from where a road winds up to the **Point Sublime,** a viewpoint over the gorge that lives up to its name. From Les Vignes the river funnels down its canyon with a few rapids to **Le Rozier**, built at the junction of the Gorges du Tarn and the steep **Gorges de la Jonte**. There are magnificent excursions possible by car or foot in all directions; the day-long walk along the **Corniches du Causse Méjean** is one of the most breathtaking, but bring plenty of water (and avoid the by-ways with iron ladders, if you're subject to vertigo).

A drive up the Gorges de la Jonte will take you to the remarkable pit of the **Aven Armand** north of **Meyrueis**, discovered in 1887 and now reached by way of a subterranean funicular (*open end Mar–May and Sept daily 10–12 and 1.30–6; June–Aug daily 9.30–7; Oct–early Nov daily 9.30–12 and 1.30–5; adm*): this consists of a massive chamber, with a wonderland of 400 stalagmites known as the Virgin Forest – its discoverers, not inaccurately, compared it to something out of the *Arabian Nights*.

Millau and Roquefort-sur-Soulzon

After squeezing through its gorge, the Tarn flows past **Millau**, a bustling city in the valley between the Causse Noir and the Causse du Larzac. By the 12th century Millau discovered its vocation, making fine gloves from the skins of young lambs slaughtered so that the maximum amount of their dam's milk is available for cheese. After booming in the 19th century, the glove business nearly died in the 1930s: the old tanning techniques couldn't compete with faster modern methods. In recent times, however, the fashion houses in Paris realized that the old ways are still best.

The city has erected plaques in the historic centre that explain what's what; the atmosphere already hints of the Mediterranean. Handsome arcaded **Place du Foch**, the heart of town, is the address of the **Musée de Millau** (*open April–June and Sept daily 10–12 and 2–6; July and Aug daily 10–6; closed Sun out of season*), with artefacts of the Rutènes Celts and Millau's predecessor, the large Gallo-Roman city of *Contatomagos*, which was famous for red stamped or *sigillum* vases, which were mass produced, so to speak, by 500 potters. Examples have been discovered as far away as Scotland and India. The museum's great pride and joy, however, is the skeleton of a plesiosaurus, a marine dinosaur who swam around here 180 million years ago. Another section tells the story of glove-making.

You can visit the **excavations of Contatomagos** at La Grafesenque, 1km south of Millau (*open daily 9–12 and 2–6.30*) or take the scenic D110 16km east to **Montpellier-le-Vieux** – not an earlier version of Montpellier, but a fantastic chaos of boulders and rocks that hauntingly resembles a ruined city (*open late Mar–Aug daily 9.30–7; Sept–early Nov daily 9.30–6; adm*). The largest of the Grands Causses, the **Causse du Larzac**, begins at Millau and continues all the way to Lodève in Languedoc. A route to Compostela passed through here, and the pilgrims, prone to attack in the empty wilderness, were given succour by the Knights Templar, whose greatest survival is **La Couvertoirade**, a walled commandary similar to Middle Eastern *caravanserai*.

Another *causse*, du Combalou, stands above **Roquefort-sur-Soulzon**. In prehistoric times part of it collapsed, forming a maze of caverns. The story goes that one day in the early Middle Ages a young shepherd left his bread and cheese in one of them and lost track of it; when he found it, it was mouldy but surprisingly delicious. Originally known as *ruppefortis*, Roquefort cheese owes its unique qualities to the high rate of cool natural humidity in the caves, and the *penicillium roqueforti* that grows on bread. You can learn all about it, in French and in great detail at the cellars of **Roquefort Société** (*open July and Aug daily 9.30–6.30; Feb–June and Sept–Oct daily 9.30–12 and 1.30–6.30; Nov–Jan daily 10–12 and 1.30–4.30; adm; bring a pullover*) complete with *son et lumière* and tastings, or a bit more modestly at family-run **Roquefort Papillon** (*open April–June and Sept daily 9.30–11.30 and 1.30–4.30; July and Aug daily 9.30–6*).

South of Roquefort, the 12th-century Cistercian **Abbaye de Sylvanès** was founded by a brigand who got religion. The typically severe church is exceptionally wide, and after falling into near total ruin was restored over a 15-year period. It has a national reputation for its July/August festival of religious music and summer courses on illumination, Byzantine painting, and bookbinding (*t 05 65 98 20 20*).

Albi

'Red Albi', the brick capital of the Tarn, has often been compared to a Tuscan hilltown piled under its church, in this case the extraordinary **Cathédrale Ste-Cécile**, a huge red fortress. This show of ecclesiastical force psychologically goes beyond the fact that the cathedral was part of the city's defences; it was to remind Albi who was boss. After all, in the early 12th century when the austere St Bernard came to tell the Albigeois to repent, they laughed him out of town. They sympathized with the Cathars and gave them refuge, and the Cathars in turn made Albi the seat of a bishop – hence, the word 'Albigensians'. Albi itself was never taken in the Crusade that took its name, but was made to pay afterwards by the Inquisition. Horrified by its cruelties, in 1234 the people rescued several heretics condemned to the stake and chased the bishop into the cathedral, from where he excommunicated the entire town. Subsequent bishop-inquisitors, determined to protect the episcopal person, used their position to accuse anyone with money of lapsing in the faith, in order to expropriate their wealth. This they used to build themselves a castle, the Palais de la Berbie, and then in 1280 began a new cathedral in the purest southern Gothic style. It was no sooner consecrated in 1480 when an arty string of bishops began embellishing it. Biggest of these decorations is the exotic 256ft bell tower that wouldn't look too out of place in Central Asia. Another is the finely carved stone porch at the top of the stairs, a preview of the richness of the **interior** (*open daily 9–12 and 2.30–6.30; June–Sept daily 8.30–7*). This positively glows with colour, the vaults completely covered with 16th-century frescoes by painters from Bologna. On the west wall, an enormous, harrowing 15th-century fresco of the *Last Judgement,* by an unknown

Getting Around

Albi's **train** station is a 10-minute walk from the centre in Place Stalingrad and is linked by the Occitan night train with Paris, and frequently by train with Toulouse.

The **bus** station is in Place Jean-Jaurès, t 05 63 54 58 61.

Tourist Information

Albi: Place Ste-Cécile, t 05 63 49 48 86, www.mairie-albi.fr.

Where to Stay and Eat

Albi ☑ 81000

★★★★**La Réserve**, Rte de Cordes, t 05 63 60 80 80 (*expensive*). An elegant Relais et Châteaux on the banks of the Tarn in a French colonial style mansion, with 20 rooms, a pool, tennis and top-notch restaurant (*expensive*). Closed Nov–April.

★★★★**Chiffre**, 50 Rue Séré-de-Rivières, t 05 63 48 58 48 (*moderate*). In the heart of town, air-conditioned rooms in a traditional hotel full of mod cons, with a garden terrace.

★★**Georges V**, 29 Av Maréchal Joffre, t 05 63 54 24 16, www.hotelgeorgesv.com (*inexpensive*). Opposite the train station, formerly the house of an apothecary, with delightful rooms and a very warm welcome. *Book.*

Moulin de la Mothe, Rue de Lamothe, t 05 63 60 38 15 (*expensive*). Wonderful, refined regional cusine by chef Michel Pellaprat on the banks of the Tarn in a charming brick-walled garden or indoors by the fire. *Closed Sun eve, Tues eve and Wed.*

Auberge Rabelaisienne, 22 Av du Colonel-Teyssier, t 05 63 47 97 19 (*moderate*). Cosy bourgeoise house specializing in classics like *foie gras*, free range pigeon, and *gigot de lotte*. *Closed Sun eve, Mon lunch.*

French or Flemish painter, was mutilated to provide an entrance to the tower chapel; now a magnificent 18th-century organ replaces the central figure of Christ the Judge. The Flamboyant *jubé* or choir screen, carved by Burgundians, is a masterpiece of delicate tracery in stone, in spite of being deprived of its many figures in the Revolution. Behind, the choir itself (*adm*) is decorated with a full quorum of biblical figures.

The **Musée Toulouse-Lautrec** (*open July and Aug daily 9–6; Sept–June daily 10–12 and 2–5; adm*) is next door in the Palais de la Berbie, or bishop's palace. This castle was stripped of most of its towers and walls after the Edict of Nantes, and in 1922 found a new role as an art museum, housing the world's largest collection of works by Henri de Toulouse-Lautrec (born in Albi in 1864), donated by his mother and relatives. One of the rare paintings is the famous *Au Salon de la rue des Moulins* (1894). Most of the other works are drawings, including remarkable portraits and caricatures, as well as the famous posters. His famous hollow walking stick is here too, the one he filled with cognac when supposedly detoxing. There are other paintings, including fine ones by Matisse and the Fauves.

You can easily spend a day poking around the rest of Albi; the tourist office has set up three different walks. The old quarter below the Cathedral, **Vieil Alby**, has handsome *hôtel particuliers*, including the artist's birthplace (at 14 Rue de Toulouse-Lautrec) where he had the two accidents that stunted the growth in his legs; also look for the charming, decrepit 11th–13th-century **Collégiale St-Salvy** and its cloister.

The centre of life in modern Albi is **Place du Vigan**; from here the Lices Pompidou (named after the president, who as a young man taught in Albi) leads to the river and its two bridges; from the Pont du 22-Août there are fine views of the city, its mills and the 13th-century **Pont-Vieux**.

Gaillac

Down the Tarn from Albi, Gaillac is a merry town under its red tile roofs, in the midst of one of France's oldest wine regions. Grapes were first grown here under the aegis of the **Abbaye St-Michel**, founded in the 10th century; rebuilt after the Wars of Religion, it preserves a 13th-century polychrome Virgin among its treasures, some of which have been moved into the adjacent museum.

The oldest part of Gaillac is behind the abbey, and there are 17th-century gardens to visit, as well as a wonderfully old-fashioned **Musée d'Histoire Naturelle**, in 2 Place Philadelphe-Thomas (*open summer Wed–Mon 10–12 and 2–6; winter Fri–Sun same hours*). Gaillac's vineyards stretch as far north as Cordes, and produce fine red, rosé and white wines in three distinct areas; for something different, try Gaillac AOC Fraîcheur Perlée, lightly sparkling with 'pearls', drunk as an apéritif or with seafood.

Castres

South of Albi, Castres is famous for its colourful old houses of tanners, weavers and dyers overhanging the Agout, and the historic centre on either side of the river, chock-a-block with buildings from every period. The grandest of these is the 17th-century episcopal palace designed by Mansart, a building now shared by the Hôtel de Ville and the **Musée Goya** (*open daily 9–12 and 2–6; Oct–Mar till 5; Sun opens at 10; closed Mon exc in July and Aug; adm*). Castres has nothing less than the second most important collection of Spanish painting in France after the Louvre, thanks to the art-loving native, who moved to Barcelona and donated his three Goyas to the town, including a *Self-portrait with glasses* and the *Assembly of the Philipines Company*. The museum has nearly all Goya's engraved works, including the famous anti-war *Los Caprichos*. Other paintings, spanning the 15th to 20th century, are by Macip, Pacheco, Velázquez (*Portrait of Philip IV*), Ribera, Valdés Real, and Cano. Other nationalities are represented as well, the English with George II's fancy-dress ivory helmet, topped by a winged dragon. Next to the palace along the river bank stretches a beautifully kept **garden** *à la française* by Le Nôtre.

Tourist Information

Castres: Rue Milhau-Ducommun, t 05 63 62 63 62.

Where to Stay and Eat

Castres ✉ 81199

★★★**Renaissance**, 17 Rue Victor-Hugo, t 05 63 59 30 42 (*inexpensive*). Pretty 17th-century half-timbered building in the historic centre with antiques and mod cons.

★★★**Europe**, 5 Rue Victor-Hugo, t 05 63 59 00 33 (*inexpensive*). A charmingly restored 18th-century house, with delightful rooms and modern baths.

Le Périgord, 22 Rue Émile-Zola, t 05 63 59 04 74 (*inexpensive*). Little old-fashioned hotel in the centre, offering simple en suite rooms.

Le Victoria, 24 Place du 8 Mai 45, t 05 63 59 14 68 (*expensive–moderate*). In a vaulted cellar, delicious classic southwest food: *foie gras*, *canard* and fish. *Closed Sat lunch, Sun, and part of Aug.*

La Mandragore, 1 Rue Malpas, t 05 63 59 51 27 (*moderate*). Tasty southwest favourites, and other things besides, with a choice of regional wines. *Closed Sun and Mon lunch.*

Castres is also famous for the great progressive politician Jean Jaurès (b. 1859), whose life is the subject of the **Musée Jaurès** in Place Pélisson (*same hours as Goya*). A brilliant journalist as well as France's youngest deputy (elected aged 26) Jaurès fought successfully for the re-trial of Dreyfus and co-founded the French Socialist party with Aristide Briand; his arguments against colonialism, nationalism and the death penalty were so convincing that he had scores of enemies, one of whom, appropriately named Villain, assassinated him in 1914.

Toulouse

One thing that keeps southwest France from nodding off in its goose fat and wine is this big pink dynamo, the *Ville Rose*, built of millions of pink bricks. Toulouse has 650,000 lively inhabitants, counting 110,000 university students, and 70 per cent of the industry in the Midi-Pyrénées region. It should have been the rosy capital of a nation called Languedoc, but it was knocked out of the big leagues in the 1220s by the popes and kings of France and their henchman Simon de Montfort. Nearly eight centuries later, it is finally getting its rhythm back. The city's air and space industries have attracted research centres, 600 related high-tech firms and élite schools of engineering and aviation. Since 1964 Toulouse, the fourth city in France, has been capital of its largest region, the Midi-Pyrénées.

Place du Capitole

Big Place du Capitole is the heart of Toulouse, emblazoned with the Cross of Languedoc, the arms devised in 1095 by the city's greatest Count, Raymond IV, when he led the first Crusade. Rimmed with neoclassical brick façades, the square is dominated by the city hall, or **Capitole**, named after the *capitouls*, who were first appointed by the Counts to run the city in the 12th century. Pedestrians cut through its **Cour Henri IV** to Square Charles de Gaulle, defended by the **Donjon** of 1525, where the *capitouls* kept the city archives; it's now the city tourist office. Running north from Place du Capitole, narrow **Rue de Taur** commemorates the bull which dragged the body of Toulouse's first saint, Sernin, through the city streets to his death in *c*. 240. An oratory was built over Sernin's tomb, replaced in the 14th century with **Notre-Dame-du-Taur**, with a *clocher-mur* that looks like a false front in a Wild West town.

Basilique St-Sernin

Sernin's tomb had attracted so many pilgrims that in 403 he was moved 300 yards to the north, and when earlier churches failed to hold the crowds, this basilica was begun in 1075. Completed in 1220, it's the largest surviving Romanesque church in the world (only the abbey church of Cluny, destroyed in the Revolution, was bigger). Modelled after Conques, its plan is identical to the basilica of St James at Compostela, begun at the same time. Seen from Rue St-Bernard, this apse is a fascinating play of white stone and red brick, a crescendo culminating in the octagonal **bell tower** that is Toulouse's landmark; St-Sernin's original three storeys of arcades were increased to

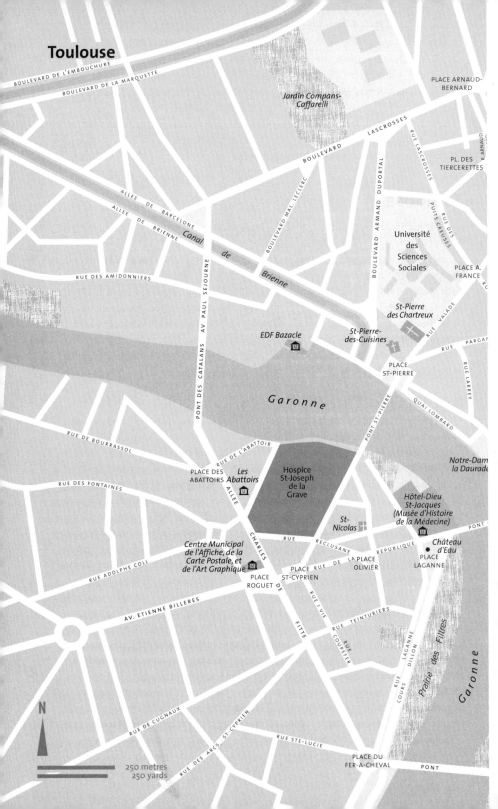

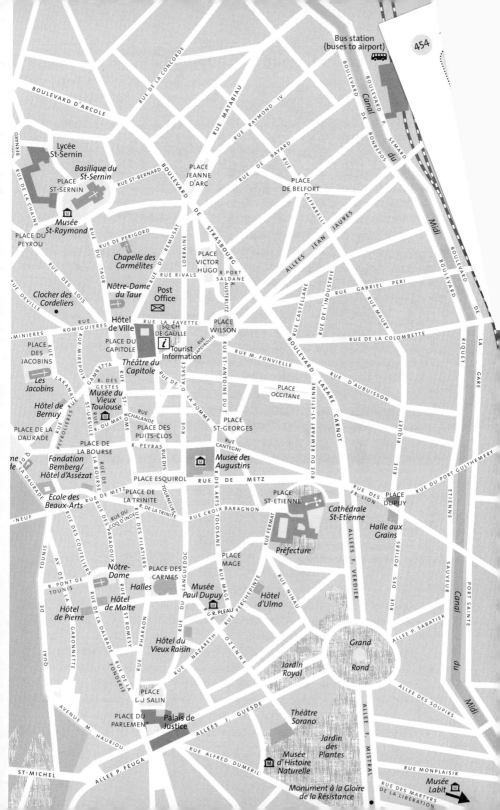

Bus station
(buses to airport)

BOULEVARD D'ARCOLE

RUE DE LA CONCORDE

RUE MATABIAU

BOULEVARD DE BONREPOS

Canal

P. SEMARD

du

Midi

BOULEVARD DE

RUE RAYMOND IV

RUE DE BAYARD

PLACE
JEANNE
D'ARC

PLACE
DE BELFORT

RUE

Lycée
St-Sernin

Basilique du
St-Sernin

PLACE
ST-SERNIN

RUE ST-BERNARD

BOULEVARD

CAFFARELLI

RUE DE LA CHAINE

RUE DE LA CHAINE

RUE DU TAUR

Musée
St-Raymond

DE

STRASBOURG

ALLEES JEAN JAURES

BOULEVARD

RUE DE PERIGORD

PLACE DU
PEYROU

Chapelle des
Carmélites

PLACE
VICTOR
HUGO

RUE RIVALS

R. PORT
SALDANE

RUE GABRIEL PERI

BOULEVARD DE LA GARE

RUE DE LORRAINE

RUE DE REMUSAT

AUSTERLITZ

RUE DE L'INDUSTRIE

RUE MAURY

RIQUET

RUE DES LOIS

RUE DEVILLE

Clocher des
Cordeliers

Nôtre-Dame
du Taur

Post
Office

RUE LA FAYETTE

SQ CH
DE GAULLE

PLACE
WILSON

RUE DE LA COLOMBETTE

RUE
ROMIGUIERES

Hôtel
de Ville

PLACE DU
CAPITOLE

Tourist
Information

RUE LAPEROUSE

RUE M. FONVIELLE

LAMINIERES

PLACE
DES
JACOBINS

RUE MIREPOIX

Théâtre du
Capitole

RUE ST-ANTOINE DU T

PLACE
OCCITANE

BOULEVARD LAZARE CARNOT

RUE D'AUBUISSON

Les
Jacobins

GAMBETTA

R. DES
GESTES

Musée du
Vieux
Toulouse

LAKANAL

RUE
CHALANDE

RUE DE D'ALSACE

PLACE
ST-GEORGES

RUE DU REMPART ST-ETIENNE

RIQUET

Hôtel de
Bernuy

RUE
ST-URSULE

R. DU MAY

PLACE DES
PUITS-CLOS

LA POMME

RUE

RUE CANTEGNI

PEYROLIERES

PLACE DE LA
DAURADE

PLACE DE
LA BOURSE

R. PEYRAS

PLACE
ST-GEORGES

RUE DES FR. LION

PLACE
DUPUY

Fondation
Bemberg/
Hôtel d'Assézat

RUE DE LA BOURSE

RUE DES ARTS

Musée des
Augustins

RUE DES

RUE DU PORT GUILHEMERY

DE LA DAURADE

Ecole des
Beaux-Arts

RUE DE METZ

PLACE DE
LA TRINITE

PLACE ESQUIROL

PLACE DE METZ

PLACE
ST-ETIENNE

Cathédrale
St-Etienne

RUE DES POTIERS

RUE DES COUTELIERS

R. DE LA TRINITE

RUE CROIX BARAGNON

RUE FERMAT

ALLEES F. VERDIER

PORT SAINTE

Canal

ST-NEUF

RUE DU
COQ D'INDE

RUE DES PARADOUX

RUE DES FILATIERS

RUE TOULOUSE

Préfecture

Halle aux
Grains

AV. DE TOUNIS

R. PONT DE TOUNIS

Nôtre-
Dame

PLACE DES
CARMES

Halles

RUE DU LANGUEDOC

Musée
Paul Dupuy

PLACE
MAGE

Hôtel
d'Ulmo

RUE NINAU

du

Midi

QUAI

GARONNETTE

Hôtel
de Malte

RUE ST ROMESY

R. PLEAU

RUE PERCHEPINTE

ALLEE P. SABATIER

Hôtel
de Pierre

RUE DE LA DALBADE

RUE PHARAON

RUE NAZARETH

RUE MAGE

RUE OZENNE

Grand
Rond

DE

RUE DE LA FONDERIE

Hôtel du
Vieux Raisin

Jardin
Royal

ALLEE DES SOUPIRS

PLACE
DU SALIN

PLACE DU
PARLEMENT

Palais de
Justice

ALLEES J. GUESDE

Théâtre
Sorano

ALLEE F. MISTRAL

AVENUE M. HAURIOU

Jardin
des
Plantes

RUE MONPLAISIR

ST-MICHEL

ALLEE P. FEUGA

RUE ALFRED DUMERIL

Musée
d'Histoire
Naturelle

Monument à la Gloire
de la Résistance

RUE DES MARTYRS
DE LA LIBERATION

Musée
Labit

Getting There and Around

By plane: Toulouse's airport is at Blagnac, 10km from the centre, t 05 61 42 44 00 (Bmibaby, easyJet, Flybe, Air France, BA from the UK). The airport bus, t 05 34 60 64 00, journeys to and from Toulouse's SNCF station daily every 20mins.

By train: Trains run from Paris–Austerlitz through Gourdon, Souillac, Cahors and Montauban to Toulouse in 6½hrs; TGVs from Paris-Montparnasse do the same in around 5hrs – by way of Bordeaux.

The slow trains to Bordeaux take 2½hrs and stop in Montauban, Moissac and Agen. Other connections include Albi (1hr) and Castres (1½hrs), Auch, Carcassonne and Marseille.

By coach: The coach station is next to the railway station at 68 Bd Pierre Semard, t 05 61 61 67 67; there are buses to Foix, Albi, Gaillac, Auch and Montauban.

By métro: The métro runs northeast to southwest from Joliment, the railway station and the Capitole to the Mirail.

The metro and city buses are run by SEMVAT, which has an information office at 7 Place Esquirol, t 05 61 41 70 70, but you'll hardly ever need either: all the sites are within walking distance in the compact centre.

By car: The most convenient pay car parks are at Place du Capitole, Allée Jean Jaurès, Place Victor Hugo and Place St-Etienne; closest free parking is at Place St-Sernin and Allées Jules Guesde.

Tourist Information

Donjon du Capitole, Rue Lafayette, t 05 61 11 02 22, *www.mairie-toulouse.fr/* or *www. ot-toulouse.fr*.

Shopping

On Wednesday mornings **Place du Capitole** has a lively food and flea market. Sunday morning sees a huge flea market around St-Sernin and along the length of the boulevards. There is a good fruit and veg market along Bd de Strasbourg (*daily exc Mon*).

The Pink City is the shopping mecca of the southwest, although specifically local products, besides Airbuses, are mostly violet – soaps, eau-de-cologne or sweets – and rubbery aniseed or mint-flavoured *cachou* pellets, invented here a century ago.

The Bookshop, 17 Rue Lakanal, t 05 61 22 99 92, has books in English.

Where to Stay

★★★★**Grand Hôtel de l'Opéra**, 1 Place du Capitole, t 05 61 21 82 66, *www.grand-hotel-opera.com* (*luxury–expensive*). The most beautiful hotel in Toulouse, with 50 sumptuous Italianate rooms and three suites in a former convent, with indoor pool, fitness room and a magnificent restaurant (*see below*).

★★★★**Hôtel des Capitouls**, 22 Descente de la Halle aux Poissons, t 05 34 31 94 80 (*expensive–moderate*). Stylish boutique hotel with 14 rooms, located in former fish warehouse in now-trendy historic Toulouse. Sumptuous meals offered in proprietors' **Restaurant Le 19**, opposite.

★★★**Hôtel des Beaux Arts**, 1 Place Pont-Neuf, t 05 34 45 42 42 (*expensive–moderate*). Charming, welcoming hotel in an 18th-century hôtel with pleasant, soundproofed rooms overlooking the Garonne.

five for the sole purpose of upstaging the campanile of the Jacobins across town. The odd, asymmetrical **Porte Miège-ville** on the south side, has a tympanum carved by the 11th-century master Bernard Gilduin, showing the *Ascension of Christ*, a rare scene in medieval art. On the brackets are figures of David and others riding on lions; the magnificent capitals tell the story of the Redemption. The eight capitals on the south transept door, the **Porte des Comtes**, also by Gilduin, show the torments of hell.

Begun in 1969, the 'de-restoration' of the **interior** stripped the majestic brick and stone of Viollet-le-Duc's ham-handed murals and fiddly neo-Gothic bits. In the process some 12th-century frescoes have been found; note the serene angel in the third bay of the north transept, which also has the best capitals. For a small fee you

★★★**Mermoz**, 50 Rue Matabiau, **t** 05 61 63 04 04, *www.hotel-mermoz.com* (*expensive–moderate*). Near the station, with delightful air-conditioned rooms overlooking inner courtyards and perhaps the best breakfast in Toulouse.

★★★**Hôtel de Diane**, 3 Route de St-Simon, **t** 05 61 07 59 52 (*moderate*). In a country setting, yet close to the centre, with a pool and an excellent restaurant serving southwest favourites).

★★**Hotel Ours Blanc**, 25 Place Victor Hugo, **t** 05 61 23 14 55, and 2 Rue Victor Hugo, **t** 05 61 21 62 40, *www.hotel-oursblanc.com* (*moderate–inexpensive*). On two sites on opposite sides of Victor Hugo car park. Rooms are quite small but neat with TVs, telephones and sound proofing.

★★**Park Hôtel**, 2 Rue Porte-Sardane, **t** 05 61 21 25 97, *www.au-park-hotel.com* (*inexpensive*). Modern rooms with most creature comforts, including a sauna and Jacuzzi.

★**Anatole France**, 46 Place Anatole France, **t** 05 61 23 19 96 (*inexpensive*). Some of the nicest cheap rooms in Toulouse, near the Capitole, all with showers and phones.

★**Hôtel des Arts**, 1 bis Rue Cantegril, **t** 05 61 23 36 21 (*inexpensive*). Friendly place near Place St-Georges in a lively part of town.

Eating Out

Toulouse claims to make a *cassoulet* that walks all over the cassoulets of rivals Carcassonne and Castelnaudry.

Les Jardins de l'Opéra, in the Grand Hôtel de l'Opéra, **t** 05 61 23 07 76 (*see above; very expensive–expensive*). Toulouse's finest gastronomic experience, and one of the most beautiful restaurants in the south-west: a glass-covered oasis overlooking a garden pool. The food matches the setting: aromatic mushroom dishes (morels stuffed with *foie gras*, when available), seafood cooked to perfection, a classic *cassoulet*, topped off by delicate desserts. *Closed Sun, Mon, end of July and most of Aug.*

Michel Sarran, 21 Bd Armand-Duportal, **t** 05 61 12 32 32, *www.michel-sarran.com* (*very expensive–expensive*). For a wonderful synthesis of sun-soaked southwest and Provençal cusines: superb food in an elegant town house, and charming service too. *Closed Sat, Sun, Aug and Christmas.*

Le Pastel, 237 Rue de St-Simon, in a villa at Mirail, **t** 05 62 87 84 30 (*expensive*). Make the extra effort to book for some of the finest, most imaginative gourmet food in Toulouse at some of the kindest prices. *Closed Sun and some of Aug.*

Le Cantou, 98 Rue Vélasquez, **t** 05 61 49 20 21 (*expensive*). A lovely ivy-covered house in a beautiful garden, in the suburb of St-Martin-du-Touch, for some of the very best regional cuisine in Toulouse, with an enormous southwest wine list. *Closed Sat and Sun.*

Grand Café de l'Opéra, 1 Place du Capitole, **t** 05 61 21 37 03 (*expensive*). Excellent versions of the classics, with an emphasis on seafood, in a cosy brasserie atmosphere. *Closed most of Aug.*

Chez Emile, 13 Place St-Georges, **t** 05 61 21 05 56 (*expensive–moderate*). An institution serving some of the finest seafood in Toulouse or a *confit de canard. Closed Sun and Mon, just Sun and Mon lunch in summer.*

Sept Place St-Sernin, address as the name, **t** 05 62 30 05 30 (*expensive–moderate*).

can enter the **ambulatory** (*open daily 10–11.30 and 2.30–5.30; July and Sept daily 10–6; closed Sun am*) to see the 17th-century bas-reliefs and panels on the lives of the saints whose relics are housed here. Opposite the central chapel are seven marble bas-reliefs (1096) by Bernard Gilduin.

On the south side of Place St-Sernin, the rich archaeological collections of the **Musée St-Raymond** (*open daily 10–6; June–Aug daily 10–7*) include gold torques from the legendary swamp treasure of the Tectosages, the remarkable Celtic tribe who founded Toulouse, a superb set of busts of Roman emperors and fine marbles depicting the *Labours of Hercules*. The surrounding neighbourhood has been the city's Latin Quarter ever since 1229 when the **University of Toulouse** was founded in Rue des Lois.

Large ivy-covered house in a perfect spot opposite the cathedral, just as pretty inside. The menus are delightful and varied: try *canard aux figues et salade d'herbes. Closed Sat and Sun.*

Le Bibent, 5 Place du Capitole, **t** 05 61 23 89 03 (*moderate*). One of the most beautiful brasseries in Toulouse, with a grand dining room last remodelled in the Roaring '20s, and a terrace; excellent shellfish selection.

Le Colombier, 14 Rue Bayard, **t** 05 61 62 40 05 (*moderate*). A contestant in the best *cassoulet* in Toulouse contest, with all the other southwest treats as well. *Closed Sat lunch, Sun, Aug and Christmas.*

Benjamin, 7 Rue des Gestes (off Rue St-Rome), **t** 05 61 22 92 66 (*moderate–cheap*). In the centre of old Toulouse, serving up the likes of fennel and courgette terrine, or steak with *cèpes*, for some of the friendliest prices in town.

La Daurade, anchored at the Quai de la Daurade, **t** 05 61 22 10 33 (*moderate–cheap*). Dine on a barge (*péniche*) in a magnificent setting; the food is just as lovely. Book. *Closed Sat lunch and Sun.*

A la Truffe du Quercy, 17 Rue Croix-Baragnon, **t** 05 61 53 34 24 (*cheap*). The same family for three generations has been dishing out delicious southwestern home-cooking and Spanish options too. *Closed Sun and hols.*

Cafés, Bars and Wine Bars

Le Père Louis, 45 Place des Tourneurs, between Rue Peyras and Rue de Metz, **t** 05 61 21 33 45. The most resolutely traditional bar in Toulouse which has drawn Toulouse's quinquina-drinkers for over a century; in fact, it's so traditional it's been declared an historical landmark. *Open daily 9.30am–10pm; closed Sun and Aug.*

Le Mangevins, 46 Rue Pharaon, **t** 05 61 52 79 16. Has a wide variety of wines accompanied by fancy snacks or local menus. *Open Mon–Fri 12noon–2am.*

Entertainment and Nightlife

The weekly *Flash* , avaialble at any newsstand, will tell you what's on in Toulouse. The Orchestre National du Capitole is now one of the top symphony orchestras in France. They often play in the acoustically excellent Halle aux Grains, Place Dupuy, just east of Cathédrale St-Etienne (**t** 05 61 62 02 70).

In July and August, the city puts on a music festival; in September the cloister of the Jacobins is the site of the Festival International Piano aux Jacobins (book early, **t** 05 61 22 44 05). From October to June, the prestigious Théâtre du Capitole, Place du Capitole, **t** 05 61 22 31 31, presents a series of opera and dance.

Toulouse stays up later than any other city in the southwest, but places open and close like flowers in the night – check posters. Favourite music bars include:

Puerto Habana, 12 Port St-Etienne, **t** 05 61 54 45 61. For a lively night out *à la cubana*, with live salsa and great dance floor. *Closed Sun.*

El Barrio Latino, 144 Av de Muret, **t** 05 61 59 00 58. Another good Latin music venue. Also a restaurant. *Closed Sun–Wed.*

Le Maximo, 3 Rue Gabriel Péri, **t** 05 61 62 08 07. The current place to be seen. Young and hip music bar, loud and packed.

Les Jacobins

The Spanish priest Domingo de Guzmán tried hard to re-convert Languedoc's heretical Cathars before the Albigensian Crusade, and in 1215 founded a preaching order in Toulouse, just west of Place du Capitole. The Dominicans soon became so popular that in 1230 they built a great mother church, **Les Jacobins** (*open daily 9–7; adm for the cloister*), a masterpiece of southern French Gothic that so impressed the popes that they sent it the relics of the greatest Dominican of them all, St Thomas Aquinas (d. 1274). One aspect of the Order's appeal was their reaction to Rome's love of luxury, which they expressed so successfully here that Les Jacobins became the prototype for all Dominican churches. Gargoyles are the only exterior sculpture in the harmonious pile of buttresses, alternating with flamboyant windows; its octagonal bell tower of brick and stone crowned with baby towers is a landmark on the city skyline. The interior is breathtakingly light and spacious, consisting of twin naves, crisscrossed by a fantastic interweaving of ribs in the vault, reaching an epiphany in the flamboyant *palmier* in the apse. A small door leads out into the lovely **cloister** (1309), with brick arcades and twinned marble columns.

Pastel Palaces

Just south of Les Jacobins, at the end of Rue Gambetta, is one of the city's most splendid residences, the **Hôtel de Bernuy**, built in 1504 by Don Juan de Bernuy, a Spanish Jew who fled the Inquisition and became a citizen – and *capitoul* – of Toulouse. The Gothic exterior hides an eclectic fantasy courtyard, a mix of Gothic, Plateresque and Loire château, topped by a lofty tower, now enjoyed by students; the *hôtel particulier* is now the prestigious **Lycée Pierre de Fermat**, named after the famous mathemetician.

The elaborate **Hôtel d'Assézat** (1555) is just west, off Rue de Metz, a wide street rammed through medieval Toulouse in the 19th century. Built by a magnate of the pastel trade (dyer's woad – the source of Toulouse's wealth in the Renaissance), its rhythmic decoration of columns is similar to the old Louvre. Inside, the **Fondation Bemberg** (*open daily 10–12.30 and 1.30–6; closed Mon; night visits Thurs at 9pm; themed visits Thurs at 7pm; adm*) has a fine collection of Renaissance and modern French paintings, including over 30 by Bonnard. Rue de Metz continues to Toulouse's oldest bridge, the **Pont Neuf** (1544–1632), with its seven unequal arches. One of the finest views of the Pont Neuf and riverfront is to the south along the **Quai de Tounis**. Rue du Pont de Tounis leads back to Rue de la Dalbade, the favourite address for the nobility; the sooty **Hôtel de Pierre** at No.25 is, extravagantly for the *ville rose*, made of stone, with a grandiose Baroque façade.

The Quartier du Jardin

South of the Place du Parlement, Allées Jules-Guesde replaces the walls torn down in 1752. Here, by the **Théâtre Sorano**, a plaque marks the exact spot where the hated Simon de Montfort was brained (by a woman with a home-made catapult). The Grand Rond at the end of Allée Jules-Guesde was planned as a garden in the midst of six wide radiating promenades, or *allées*, of which only four were laid out: the old **Jardin Royal** and the 19th-century **Jardin des Plantes** are delightful refuges from the big city. If you're fond of Egyptian, Indian and Far Eastern art, don't miss the **Musée Georges Labit** (*43 Rue des Martyrs-de-la-Libération, off Allée Frédéric-Mistral; open daily 10–5; summer daily 10–6; closed Tues and hols*) – considered the best oriental museum in France after the Musée Guimet in Paris.

Around the Cathédrale St-Etienne

In the mesh of quiet lanes between the old *parlement* and the cathedral are distinguished houses, all pink brick, with grey shutters and wrought-iron balconies, such as the ornate **Hôtel du Vieux Raisin** (1515), 36 Rue du Languedoc. The **Musée Paul-Dupuy**

(*13 Rue de la Pleau; open daily 10–5; summer daily 10–6; closed Tues and hols*) is named after the collector who left Toulouse his watches, automata, fans, faïence and ivories.

The **Cathédrale St-Etienne** was begun in the 11th century and only completed in the 17th, resulting in a church that seems a bit drunk. In the centre of the façade rises a massive brick bell tower with a clock, over the Romanesque base. To the right is a worn, asymmetrical stone Gothic façade, where the portal and rose window are off-centre; to the left extends the bulge of the chapel of Notre-Dame.

It's even tipsier inside, but many of its best decorations are stowed away in the **Musée des Augustins** (*open daily 10–6; closed Tues and hols; Wed night until 9pm*) at the corner of Rue de Metz and Rue d'Alsace. The museum, one of the oldest in France, is housed in a 14th-century Augustinian convent. Gothic sculptures occupy the flamboyant chapterhouse, and the church holds religious paintings by Van Dyck, Rubens and Murillo. Best of all are the Romanesque works from St-Etienne – the delicate, fluid scene of the dancing Salome and the beheading of the Baptist. The first floor has paintings by Guido Reni, Simon Vouet, Guardi, Delacroix, Ingres, Manet, Morisot, Vuillard, Maurice Denis and Toulouse-Lautrec.

Toulouse's Left Bank

Just over the Pont Neuf, the round brick tower of a pumping station, built in 1817 to provide drinking water to the city, has found a new use as the **Galerie Municipale du Château-d'Eau** (*open daily 1–7; closed Tues and hols; adm*). The hydraulic machinery is still intact, while upstairs you can visit one of Europe's top photographic galleries; an annexe has been installed in an arch of the Pont Neuf. Opposite, a medieval pilgrimage hospital houses a **Musée d'Histoire de la Médecine** (*open Wed–Sun 2–6*).

Gascony, the Basque Lands and the Pyrenees

13

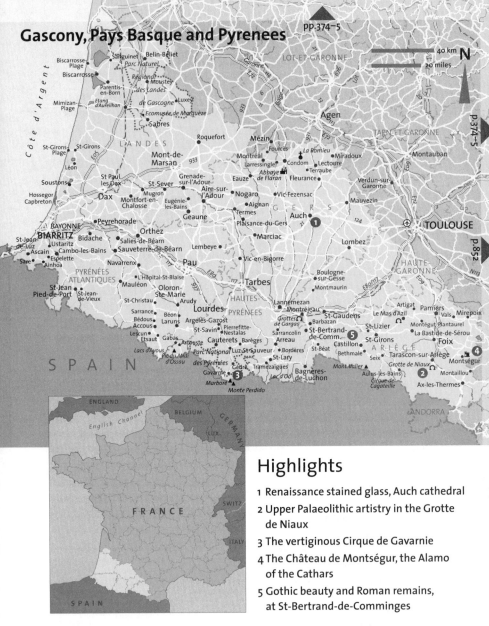

Gascony, Pays Basque and Pyrenees

PP.374–5

40 km
20 miles
N

Highlights

1 Renaissance stained glass, Auch cathedral
2 Upper Palaeolithic artistry in the Grotte de Niaux
3 The vertiginous Cirque de Gavarnie
4 The Château de Montségur, the Alamo of the Cathars
5 Gothic beauty and Roman remains, at St-Bertrand-de-Comminges

This far southwest corner of France is a land of strong character and panache, of garlicky, twanging, Armagnac-swigging Gascons like Henri IV and D'Artagnan, *pelote*-players and old Basque whaling ports, the majestic *cirques* and peaks of the Pyrenees, the endless pine forest of the Landes and the endless ocean beaches of the Côte d'Argent. This is not one of France's wealthy, arty areas; besides a few Palaeolithic painted caves and some great medieval churches (especially St-Bertrand-de-Comminges), the one five-star man-made attraction, Auch cathedral, was something

Food and Wine

A good part of the finer things in life appear on the table. Gascony is France's top producer of *foie gras*, *confits*, and other ducky delights, as well as the home of the classic *poule au pot*, the favourite of Henri IV (stuffed with ham and breadcrumbs, then boiled with vegetables), and *garbure*, a hearty soup based on goose, salt pork, sausage and cabbage. Game, especially pigeon, is very popular.

Marseille has its *bouillabaisse*, but the Basques maintain that their version, *ttoro* (pronounced tioro), is the king of them all; the cooks of St-Jean-de-Luz make the best ones. Another icon is the red pepper, the *piment d'Espelette*; Basque housewives still hang them on the walls of their houses for drying (and for decoration). Some go into *piperade*, the relish that can accompany almost any Basque dish. Other treats include the sheep cheese from the Pyrenees, the best in France, and the famous Bayonne ham, which is hung for over a year.

The region is famous for golden Jurançon, the Gascon version of Sauternes, which is often served with *foie gras* (there's also a dry version); Pacherenc, the wines of Tursan and Chalosse, and the inimitable Madiran, the most tannic wine in France, perfect with rich duck dishes, red meat and cheese. The Basques use mountain herbs to make Izarra liqueur. Then there's armagnac (*see* p.474) – older than cognac and somehow quintessential to the Gascon soul.

of a fluke. Pau and Biarritz were favourite if now forgotten Victorian retreats; today people are mainly drawn to the region's natural beauty, its open space, its serenity, and the Gascon and Basque flair for the finer, simpler things of life.

Parc Naturel des Landes de Gascogne

'Landes' means moors, but the moors that take up most of this second-largest *département* in France have never had a Thomas Hardy to evoke their strangeness. Rather they were a territory outside the pale, swept by storms off the Bay of Biscay, winds powerful enough to lift hay wagons off the ground and stop up the rivers with sand, creating insalubrious marshlands. The only inhabitants were 'Tartars', who walked about on yard-high stilts (*tchanques*), raising sheep for their manure to grow their miserable crops of rye, as the land was too poor for wheat.

Then one day in 1856, as Napoléon III changed trains at Labouheyre, he had a flash of inspiration; he would promote business in the Landes, through drainage, followed by 'scientific exploitation' – not of timber, but of resin. Maritime pines were planted over an area a third the size of Belgium, and although the invention of new solvents has since cut into the resin trade, the pines still supply much of France's lumber, paper and the '*pâte fluff*' for disposable nappies. The dunes have been converted into a playground, the Côte d'Argent. The farmhouses, made of beams and white plaster, with a large sloping roof on the west, are being converted into *gîtes*.

The **Parc Naturel des Landes de Gascogne** stretches from the Bassin d'Arcachon in the north (*see* p.422) to Brocas in the south. The park encompasses the Grand and

Tourist Information

Belin-Béliet: for Parc Régional, 33 Route de Bayonne, **t** 05 57 71 99 99, *www.parc-landes-de-gascogne.fr*.

Activities

Few rivers are as ideal for rowing gently down the stream as the Grande Leyre. The season runs from May to September. The seven bases along the river hire canoes and can arrange to pick you up downstream: details from the park information office.

Where to Stay and Eat

Moustey ✉ 40410

La Haut Landaise, Place du Bourg, 'Place de Platanes', **t** 05 58 07 77 85 (*moderate*).

A 17th-century *auberge* in the middle of Moustey. The name is a play on words: the owners are from Holland but they serve up fine southwestern family fare, some of the best in the area. *Closed Mon, and school hols in winter.*

Sabres ✉ 40630

★★Auberge des Pins, Route de la Piscine, **t** 05 58 08 30 00, *www.auberge-des-pins.com* (*moderate*). Offers the complete Landais experience: renovated rooms in a typical country house, set in a pretty park, with an excellent restaurant (*expensive–moderate*) serving delicious dishes involving *cèpes, langoustines*, roast pigeon, *magrets* (try the salad of *foie gras* and asparagus tips) and a chance to try a variety of southwest wines, as well as a superb *tourtière*; English spoken. *Closed Jan; restaurant closed Sun eve and Mon out of season.*

Petite Leyre rivers, immersed in greenery. Paths and rural roads will get you into the pines, passing by villages and churches from the days when most visitors were pilgrims en route to Compostela.

Located on the Leyre and the N10 from Bordeaux, modest **Belin-Béliet** was, until the 11th century, a fierce rival of Bordeaux; it was the birthplace of Eleanor of Aquitaine in 1122, and (some say) of her favourite son, Richard Cœur de Lion. The castle she was born in is now a low mound, marked by a stele. The church of **St-Pierre-de-Mons** was built during Eleanor's reign, although its bell tower was only fortified during the Hundred Years War – that time bomb she left behind by her marriages.

Moustey stands at the confluence of the Grande Leyre and the Petite Leyre. Unusually, its square has two churches from the 1200s, side by side: one, Notre-Dame, the chapel of a pilgrims' hospital, houses the Parc Régional's **Musée du Patrimoine Religieux et des Croyances Populaires** (*open June, July and Aug daily 10–12 and 2–7; Sept 2–6; April, May and Oct weekends and hols only, 2–6; adm*), with exhibits on popular beliefs and superstitions.

From Moustey the D120 follows the valley of the Petite Leyre, a favourite with otters. **Luxey**, a sweet little village, is the site of the **Atelier de Produits Résineux** (*open end Mar–end May and Sept–Nov daily 2–6; June–mid-Sept daily 10–12 and 2–7; adm*), in an old resin distillery, where you can learn all about the sticky stuff. In the early 1900s, 30,000 *gemmeurs*, or tappers, worked the forest; today there are a mere 50. Since 1960, new techniques using sulphuric acid have doubled the yield; now, instead of 1,000, the *gemmeur* only has to visit 500 trees in five days to fill a 200-litre barrel.

The lush Grande Leyre is kept clear for canoes. **Sabres**, on its banks, attracts plenty of tourists on their way to the Eco-musée, but don't neglect its 11th-century church, with a triangular *clocher-mur* and carved portal. Sabres was so cut off from the rest of the world that, when the first German soldiers in their long black coats marched through the village in 1940, some old women believed that the Huguenots were back in town.

Marquèze and the Eco-musée de la Grande Lande

The only access to Marquèze is by a steam train that chugs 5km from Sabres. June–Sept departures at 10.10, 10.50, 11.30, 12.10, 2, 2.50, 3.20, 4, 4.40 and 5.20, last return from Marquèze 7pm; April, May and Nov five departures Mon–Sat 2–6.40, Sun and hols nine departures 10.10–4.40; adm. Brochure in English. To book, call t 05 58 07 50 47.

Until the 1940s, the Landes were divided into *quartiers*. Each *commune* had between six and twelve *quartiers*; the most important had the church, school, *mairie* and shops. The other *quartiers* were all more or less alike: in the centre, a *maison du maître*, or landowner's house, along with the servants' house, the shepherds' houses, the miller's house, and the *maisons des métayers*, or farm labourers' houses. Other houses belonged to the *brassiers*, who lived only from the strength of their *bras*, or arms. Around the houses were barns, pigsties, mills, ovens, sheepfolds, hives and chicken coops (on stilts, because of the foxes). Marquèze was an abandoned *quartier* of Sabres, rescued in 1978 by the Parc Naturel to become the first *éco-musée* in France. Its surroundings have been meticulously maintained, including the orchard and stream, the fields and Landais sheep; one goal of all *éco-musées* is to conserve old varieties of seeds, trees and domestic animals in danger of being lost forever.

Down the Côte d'Argent

Three million visitors a year descend on the 'Silver Coast,' as it was dubbed by a Bordeaux newspaperman in 1905. There's room: this is the biggest beach in Europe, 228km of pale sand between the forest and the bracing Bay of Biscay, which sends big rollers ideal for surfing. Just on the other side of the dunes are lakes formed by the streams that crisscross the Landes, ideal for calmer sports and for birdwatching.

Biscarrosse to Mimizan

Biscarrosse is a big town but a dull one, and owes what panache it has to its land-of-lakes setting. In the early days of aviation it was an important seaplane port, a past remembered at the **Musée Historique de l'Hydraviation** at 332 Av Louis Bréguet (*open July and Aug daily 10–7; Sept–June Wed–Mon 2–6, closed Tues and hols; adm*), with models, mementoes of great aviators, photos and a video. Rockets occasionally blast off from the Centre d'Essai des Landes, which keeps the coast between Biscarrosse-Plage and Mimizan-Plage strictly off limits. **Biscarrosse-Plage** is a rather characterless resort that sprouted up in the 1970s; one of the best things to do is take the coastal road north towards Arcachon for the magnificent dunes (see p.423).

If the Atlantic is too rough, the lakes, especially the Etangs de Cazaux et de Sanguinet, have sandy beaches as well. **Sanguinet** itself stands over a Gallo-Roman village; its submerged stone temple can be seen under the surface of the lake.

Getting Around

Public transport is thin on the ground. **Buses** link Arcachon to Biscarrosse in the summer; contact Autobus d'Arcachon, t 05 56 83 07 60; others go down to Mimizan, ring t 05 58 09 10 89. For the southern Côte d'Argent, the nearest **stations** are in Dax and Bayonne, and from there buses travel to the main points.

Tourist Information

Biscarrosse-Plage: t 05 58 78 20 96, *www. biscarrosse.com*.
Mimizan-Plage: 38 Av Maurice-Martin, t 05 58 09 11 20, *www.mimizan-tourisme.com*.
Léon: Place Jean-Baptiste Courtiau, t 05 58 48 76 03, *www.ot-leon.fr*.
Hossegor: Place des Halles, t 05 58 41 79 00, *www.hossegor.fr*.
Capbreton: Av Georges Pompidou, t 05 58 72 12 11, *www.tourisme.fr/capbreton*.

Where to Stay and Eat

Biscarrosse ✉ 40600
★★★**La Forestière**, Av du Pyla, t 05 58 78 24 14, *www.hotellaforestiere.com* (*expensive– inexpensive*). At Bicarrosse-Plage, this is the nicest place on the sea, and also has a pool. *Open April–mid-Oct*.
★★**La Caravelle**, at Ispe (5314 Route des Lacs), t 05 58 09 82 67, *www.lacaravelle.fr* (*moderate; half board only in summer*). Near

the golf course, this is a lovely, quiet place, right on the Etang de Cazaux et de Sanguinet; but the food is so good that many non-guests drop in for a meal. *Closed Nov–mid-Feb*.

Mimizan ✉ 40200
★★★**Au Bon Coin du Lac**, 34 Av du Lac, t 05 58 09 01 55, *www.jp-caule.com* (*moderate*). This wonderful hotel right on the lake is hands down the most delightful place to sleep and eat in Mimizan. There are only 4 luminous, elegant rooms and 4 apartments; tables from the equally attractive restaurant (*expensive*) spill out along the lakeside terrace, where the house specialities are small crabs stuffed with tiny vegetables and shrimp. The desserts are out of this world, and the cellar offers a magnificent array of wines and armagnacs. *Closed Feb; restaurant closed Sun eve and Mon*.
★★★**Côte d'Argent**, 6 Av M-Martin, t 05 58 09 15 22, *www.hotelcotedargent.com* (*moderate*). Best of the options by the beach, this hotel is only 5 minutes from the sea. *Open May 15–Sep 30*.
★★**L'Emeraude des Bois**, 68 Av du Courant, t 05 58 09 05 28, *emeraudedesbois@ wanadoo.fr* (*inexpensive*). Set among lofty old trees a few minutes from the centre of Mimizan, this is an attractive old house; the restaurant (*moderate*) is excellent and serves many old French favourites. *Open April–Sept; restaurant only open for dinner*.

If Biscarrosse feels put out by the adjacent rocket-testing area, **Parentis-en-Born** and its lake have been undermined, since 1955, by petroleum derricks – the first lake platforms in Europe, sucking up the contents of France's biggest oil field. And with all these pine trees there has to be a paper mill somewhere, and **Mimizan** won the prize. But don't let it put you off: Mimizan, the 'Pearl of the Côte d'Argent', has character. Once a Roman port, it had a 12th-century abbey, of which only the *clocher-mur* and Gothic portal have survived the usual vicissitudes, not the least of which was being buried in sand along with the rest of the town, in 1342. In the old days the abbey and town enjoyed salvage rights that made them the dread of sailors; whenever a ship foundered, the abbey bell would toll, and Mimizan would pounce.

North of Mimizan, the lovely **Etang d'Aureilhan** planted with flowers and shrubs enchanted the Duke of Westminster, who in 1910 built himself a Tudor-style manor; today only the façade and two wings are intact along the D87. South of Mimizan the coast is empty; small villages sometimes have road access to the beaches.

Soustons ✉ 40140

***Relais de la Poste**, t 05 58 47 70 25, *www.relaischateaux.fr/poste* (*expensive*). The very best place to eat and stay is 10km east of Soustons, at Magescq, with comfortable rooms set in a park with huge pines, a heated pool and tennis court. But it's the exquisite Landais cuisine (*very expensive–expensive*), prepared by Bernard and Jean Coussau, that has made it renowned: the pigeon with *girolle* mushrooms, the *foie gras*, duck fillets, and potatoes sautéed in goose fat that melt in your mouth, accompanied by warm, crisp bread made in the Relais' special oven, a superb list of wines from Bordeaux and Burgundy as well as the finest armagnacs. *Closed Nov and Dec; restaurant closed Oct–May Mon and Tues, and Mon eve and Tues eve in season; book.*

Hossegor ✉ 40150

Of the two towns, Hossegor has the nicer places to stay, many set back in the trees.
Le Relais du Lac, 1675 Av du Touring Club, t 05 58 43 69 03 (*expensive–inexpensive*). New hotel on lakeside with modern, comfortable rooms and a good restaurant (*moderate*). *Closed Dec–Feb.*
****Les Huîtrières du Lac**, 1187 Av du Touring Club, t 05 58 43 51 48 (*moderate*). Owned by a family of oystermen, this lovely place is on the main lake road. Rooms are pleasant and immaculate; be sure to reserve one with a view. The restaurant naturally features oysters and other seafood is also good.

****Hôtel Barbary Lane**, Av de la Côte d'Argent, t 05 58 43 52 19, *www.barbary-lane.com* (*moderate–inexpensive*). A welcoming, family-run Logis de France hotel with a pool, 1km from the beach. *Closed Dec–mid-Mar.*
Dégustation du Lac, 1830 Av du Touring Club, t 05 58 43 54 95 (*moderate*). Besides the hotel restaurants, try Marianne Lamoliate's fine establishment for exquisite seafood platters and fish soup at very reasonable prices, served on a charming terrace. *Closed Oct–Mar, and Tues exc July and Aug.*

Capbreton ✉ 40130

***L'Océan**, a big white hotel near the port at 85 Av G-Pompidou, t 05 58 72 10 22, *www.hotel-capbreton.com* (*moderate*). The nicest place here, with large, comfortable, soundproofed rooms and a restaurant (*moderate*). *Restaurant closed Tues and Wed exc July and Aug.*
****Bellevue**, Av G-Pompidou, t 05 58 72 10 30 (*inexpensive*). Eleven rooms and a delightful restaurant (*moderate*) serving good seafood but lots of other dishes as well if you hate fish. *Closed Dec and Jan.*
Pêcheries Ducamp, 4 Rue du Port d'Albret, t 05 58 72 11 33 (*expensive–moderate*). This delightful place is a fishmonger's converted into a restaurant, where waitresses in plastic boots and aprons serve nothing but the freshest of fish and shellfish, beautifully prepared. *Closed Tues, and Fri lunch out of season; also end Sept and 3 weeks in Jan.*

The Southern Côte d'Argent

Things pick up again around **Léon**. Traditional houses give the town its tone, while the most beautiful river in the Landes, the **Courant d'Huchet**, brings visitors from far and wide. The Huchet flows 12km down to the sea, in a lush *African Queen* setting, passing under a canopy of trees hung with garlands of ivy and creeper, through majestic ferns, hibiscus and water lilies. Throughout April to the end of October, the flat-bottomed boats of Les Bateliers du Courant d'Huchet make the trip, lasting up to four hours (*2hr trips daily at 8am; 3–4hr trips daily at 2.30pm; book ahead – up to two weeks ahead in August – on* t 05 58 48 75 39, *www.batelier.com*).

The biggest holiday centre between Arcachon and Biarritz is **Capbreton-Hossegor**, two *communes* with a warm, sandy tidal lake, two rivers and a canal and the Pyrenees hovering on the horizon. In the early 1900s, artists and writers from Biarritz set up a colony around the Lac d'Hossegor, and in the 1930s the property developers followed. Capbreton too has been filled with much new building; its marina – the only one between Arcachon and Bayonne – named Mille Sabords (translated as 'Blistering Barnacles!' whenever Capt. Haddock says it in *Tintin*). Along the ocean beach, only swim in the designated areas with lifeguards; the big rollers that bring champion surfers to Capbreton hit the coast just to the north.

Inland Southern Landes

Mont-de-Marsan

Mont-de-Marsan isn't exactly cosmopolitan – except for six days in July when it explodes in honour of the Magdalene, with *corridas*, *courses landaises*, and a megaton of fireworks. Made departmental capital, what character it has is in its neoclassical administrative buildings. To create a harmonious neoclassical ensemble, even the Gothic church of the Magdalene was destroyed in the early 19th century and replaced with the current bland model. What Mont-de-Marsan is proudest of is the only museum in France solely devoted to modern figurative sculpture, the **Musée Despiau-Wlérick** (*open Wed–Mon 10–12 and 2–6; closed Tues and hols; adm*), in a medieval keep at 6 Place Marguerite-de-Navarre. Two native sons dominate here: Charles Despiau (1874–1946), Rodin's assistant, and Robert Wlérick (1882–1944) who sculpted half of the Monuments aux Morts in the Landes. In May some of the museum's inhabitants are taken out for a breath of air, standing around the streets.

During the Féria de Ste-Madeleine, the action takes place down by the train station at the venerable **Arènes du Plumaçon**, built in 1889. Children love the **Parc de Nahuque** (*open Mon–Fri 9–12 and 2–7, Sat, Sun and hols 3–7, till 6 in the winter; adm*)**s**; part of it is home to free-range swans, donkeys, Tibetan goats and small animals.

Getting There

A few **trains** on the Bordeaux–Tarbes line stop. For information on the *département's* bus network contact **RDTL**, 99 Rue Pierre Benoit, **t** 05 58 05 66 00.

Tourist Information

Mont-de-Marsan: 6 Place du Général-Leclerc, **t** 05 58 05 87 37, *www.mont-de-marsan.org*.

Where to Stay and Eat

Mont-de-Marsan ✉ 40000
★★★Abor, on the Grenade road, **t** 05 58 51 58 00, *www.aborhotel.com* (*moderate–inexpensive*). Set in the forest, this air-conditioned, modern hotel has a pool and a good restaurant (*moderate*) with a garden terrace.
★★★Le Renaissance, 225 Av de Villeneuve, **t** 05 58 51 51 51, *www.le-renaissance.com* (*moderate–inexpensive*). Actually neoclassical in spite of its name, a handsome manor house set amid verdant lawns, with a pool; rooms are large and comfortable and the bathrooms luxurious. The restaurant (*very expensive–moderate*) draws in hungry clients from all over the area. *Restaurant closed Nov–May weekends, summer Sat lunch and Sun eve, and last week in July*.
★★Richelieu, Rue Wlérick, **t** 05 58 06 10 20 (*inexpensive*). A typical old-fashioned hotel in the medieval centre, quiet, and comfortable; the restaurant (*moderate*) serves good, hearty Landais dishes at reasonable prices. *Restaurant closed Sat*.

Down the Adour

South of Mont-de-Marsan the very first toes of the Pyrenees embrace the green-blue Adour, an important river and one so prone to flooding that it has made itself an extra-wide bed to lie in, a swampy muddy prairie of islets and canals known as the *barthes*. The *barthes* are a special environment, host to 130 species of bird, terrapins, and 50 or so little *poneys barthais*, the last members of a native species living in semi-liberty. The fertile hills south of the Adour offer a striking contrast to the dream-like infinity of flat pine forests to the north; here the main tree is oak, standing amid rolling fields of grain, vineyards, and pastures.

Aire-sur-l'Adour and the Tursan

Aire-sur-l'Adour is a hoary old town that went on to become the occasional capital of the Visigothic kings of Aquitaine in the 5th century, who were Arian Christians. Their most memorable deed in Aire involved a young Catholic princess named Quitterie who refused to marry a local Visigoth lord, who took it badly and cut off her head. She picked it up and walked up the hill; a miraculous fountain at once gushed forth. In the tortuous associative logic of religion, Quitterie and her fountain were soon performing miraculous cures of headaches and mental illness. She is the patron saint of Gascony, and her cult is widespread on both sides of the Pyrenees. The church of **Ste-Quitterie** still presides over upper Aire. In the old days, a constant stream of pilgrims assured that it was always open; nowadays you have to arrange for a tour (*call* **t** *06 77 02 43 44, or the mairie,* **t** *05 58 71 47 00*). The façade was much chewed by Huguenots, Revolutionaries and the weather. However, the portal under the bell tower is still intact and decorated with an impressive Gothic Last Judgement. The interior was reworked in reheated Baroque, but the sculpted Romanesque capitals are good. The crypt was originally part of a temple to Mars and the miraculous spring flowed where the baptistry is now. In the old days, the mentally ill were locked in cells here in hope of a cure. The magnificent 3rd- or 4th-century marble sarcophagus shows a great scene of God, dressed in a Roman toga, creating man. A sacrificial altar, probably from the Roman temple, is opposite; test its bizarre acoustics.

The first town of importance down river, **Grenade-sur-l'Adour** is a *bastide* town founded in 1322; its *cornières* are still intact, and the church conserves a pretty Flamboyant Gothic retable. Better known, however, is the chapel just across the river, **Notre-Dame-du-Rugby**, hung with rugger jerseys. But the stained glass and other art is what stays with you, especially the statue made by an old captain of a young Jesus handing off the ball to his Mother.

A region of broken valleys south of Aire and Grenade, the **Tursan** is the source of most of the Landes' geese and ducks, as well as good wine. It also has a spa, **Eugénie-les-Bains**, named after its godmother, the Empress Eugénie, although by rights it should be renamed Michel-Guérard-les-Bains after the chef who put it on the map when he transformed it into a healthy *nouvelle cuisine* pleasure dome (*see* box). Eugénie's waters are used for treating obesity and digestive troubles.

Tourist Information

Aire-sur-l'Adour: Place Charles-de-Gaulle,
t 05 58 71 64 70, *otsi.aire@wanadoo.fr*.
Grenade-sur-l'Adour: 1 Pl des Déportés, t 05 58
45 45 98, *www.tourismegrenadois.com*.
Eugénie-les-Bains: Rue René Vielle, t 05 58 51 13
16, *www.ville-eugenie-les-bains.fr*.

Where to Stay and Eat

Aire-sur-l'Adour ✉ 40800

Chez l'Ahumat, 2 Rue Pierre-Mendès-France,
t 05 58 71 82 61 (*inexpensive*). Set on a quiet
lane near the centre of Aire, has some of the
nicest low-price rooms around. The restaurant (*moderate–cheap*) features delicious
Landaise cuisine at exceptional prices as
well, served with local wines. *Closed 1st two
weeks May, 1st two weeks Sept; restaurant
closed Wed.*

Segos ✉ 32400

★★★Domaine de Bassibé, 8km south of Aire on
the N134, and then east on the road to
Madiran, t 05 62 09 46 71, *www.bassibe.fr*
(*expensive*). Considerably more opulent and
highly recommended, this is a lovely place, a
venerable farm set in a park with century-
old trees and a pool, and cosy, comfortable
rooms; member of the prestigious Relais et
Châteaux chain. The restaurant (*expensive*),
in a renovated *chais*, is excellent as well.
*Closed Jan–Easter; restaurant closed Tues and
Wed exc July and Aug.*

Grenade-sur-l'Adour ✉ 40270

★★★Pain Adour et Fantaisie, Place des Tilleuls,
t 05 58 45 18 80, *www.chateauxhotels.com/
fantaisie* (*expensive–moderate*). Set in a
handsome old house in the arcaded heart of
the *bastide*, has comfortable rooms overlooking the river and a celebrated restaurant
(*very expensive–expensive*), where Philippe
Garret prepares excellent, aromatic dishes
prepared from a wide variety of ingredients,
many local (home-smoked salmon from the
Adour, asparagus from the Landes), followed
by luscious desserts. *Restaurant closed Sun
eve, Mon and Wed, exc in July and Aug; it's a
good idea to reserve.*

Eugénie-les-Bains ✉ 40320

Eugénie-les-Bains is the little paradise
created by Christine and Michel Guérard.
★★★Les Prés d'Eugénie, t 05 58 05 06 07, *www.
michelguerard.com* (*luxury*). Set in a beautiful 30-acre wooded park full of rare trees
and flower gardens, one of the dreamiest
small hotels in all France; romantic rooms
with wrought-iron balconies occupy the
main neoclassical wing, while others,
exquisitely furnished with antiques, are in a
19th-century convent near the herb garden.
A gymnasium, billiards hall, sauna, beauty
centre, tennis courts, heated pool and
thermal slimming centre are on the
grounds, and guests can join in courses on
nouvelle cuisine. Closed Jan and Feb.
★★La Maison Rose, t 05 58 05 06 07
(*expensive*). This charming country inn was
also refurbished and redecorated by
Christine Guérard. Most rooms come with
kitchenettes. The **restaurant** (*very expensive*),
the one which attracts visitors from around
the world to this remote corner of the
Landes, is best known by the name of the
legendary sorcerer of saucepans, Michel
Guérard. After installing himself in Eugénie-
les-Bains in the early 1970s, Guérard hit the
world of *haute cuisine* like a comet, earning
a constellation of stars and toques from the
guides. He has remained firmly at the
summit ever since, adding new imaginative
dishes to his repertoire, based on the finest
natural ingredients and especially products
from the Landes. The Baroque dining room
provides an exquisite stage setting for each
exquisite dish. The wine list covers most of
the great vineyards of the southwest, and
includes the excellent white Baron de
Bachen vin de Tursan that Guérard produces
in his own vineyard. *For a table, book as far in
advance as possible, t 05 58 05 06 07). Closed
Thurs lunch and Wed, except in high season;
also closed Dec–Feb.*
Les Charmilles, t 05 58 05 06 07 (*expensive*). La
Ferme aux Grives, a recent Guérard acquisition, is an old Landais farm and specializes in
the kind of food the original owners may
have dined on – wonderful country hams,
melt-in-your-mouth roast suckling pig, and
big desserts.

Hilltop **Samadet** is synonymous with the 1732–1840 Manufacture Royale de Fayence de Samadet, remembered in the **Musée de la Faïencerie** (*open April–Oct daily 10–12 and 2–6.30; Nov–Mar Tues–Sun 2–6, closed Mon and hols; adm*). After Louis XIV bought his first faïence (having melted his gold and silver plates to pay for his wars), it became fashionable on the tables of aristocrats. Samadet is characterized by stylized animal and floral motives, painted in rich pure colours. Pieces sell for small fortunes.

The Chalosse and St-Sever

The Chalosse is the 'Secret Garden of the Landes'. One of the best views of it is from **St-Sever**, which enjoys a superb setting on a balcony between the Chalosse and the endless sea of pine forests to the north. The lofty plateau of Morlanne was the site of the Roman *castrum*, where St Severus converted the 5th-century Roman governor. Not a stone remains of this, but you can drive up for the view. Below stretches the town, the goose-feather capital of France, stuffing the by-product of the *foie gras* industry into duvets, sleeping bags and jackets.

The town grew up around the **abbey of St Sever** founded in 988 by the Count of Gascony. It reached its golden age under Abbot Grégoire de Montaner of Cluny (1028–72) who rebuilt the church with seven staggered apses. The nave, damaged in the Hundred Years War, was rebuilt in the 1300s. Worse was yet to come: Protestants, Revolutionaries, and 19th-century restorers whose leaden neo-Romanesque touch destroyed much of the abbey's charm. Fortunately, they left the capitals alone. Those from the 11th century have simple designs. Later sculptors added figures. The finest capitals of all, in the north tribune, are attributed to the vigorous School of Toulouse.

In 1280 Eleanor of Castile, wife of Edward I, founded another monastery in St-Sever, the **Couvent des Jacobins**. The cloister now houses the **Musée des Jacobins**

Tourist Information

Saint-Sever: Place du Tour-du-Sol, t 05 58 76 34 64, *www.saint-sever.fr*.

Where to Stay and Eat

St-Sever ✉ 40500
**Le Relais du Pavillon, Rte de Grenade, Quartier Péré (at the crossroads of the D924 and D933), t 05 58 76 20 22, *www.hotel-landes.com* (*inexpensive*). A peaceful modern haven in a garden with pool and restaurant (*expensive–moderate*). *Closed 1st two weeks in Jan; restaurant closed Sun eve and Mon.*
Hôtel Alios, 40 500 Bas-Marco, t 05 58 76 44 00 (*inexpensive*). Basic hotel with reasonable restaurant (*moderate*). *Closed 2 weeks in Aug; restaurant closed Fri eve and Sun exc May–July.*

Montfort-en-Chalosse ✉ 40380
**Aux Tauzins, on the D2 towards Hagetmau, t 05 58 98 60 22 (*inexpensive*). This family-run place has been open for decades, a cosy old country inn with comfortable rooms, set in a garden with a pool. The restaurant (*moderate*) makes excellent use of the good things from the Chalosse. *Closed Jan,1st 2 weeks in Feb and 1st 2 weeks in Oct; restaurant closed Sun eve and Mon out of season.*
Domaine de Testilin, t 05 58 98 61 21, *www.domaine-de-testilin.fr* (*inexpensive*). At Baights, this warm and friendly hotel offers 12 lovely rooms in a magnificent *maison de maître*, set in a park; the food (*moderate*) is equally lovely, featuring succulent *magrets* and other regional specialities, washed down with *vin du Tursan*. *Closed 1st 2 weeks in Oct; restaurant closed Sun and Tues eves, and Mon.*

(*to visit, call* **t** *05 58 76 34 64*), with Gallo-Roman artefacts, items relating to the pilgrimage route and the celebrated illuminated 11th-century *Apocalypse of St-Sever* (now in the Bibliothèque National in Paris).

The Adour is at its most scenic between St-Sever and **Mugron**, the 'Belvedere of the Chalosse'. West of Mugron, the pretty 13th-century *bastide* of **Montfort-en-Chalosse** was founded by the king of England. The **Musée de la Chalosse** (*open April–Oct Tues–Fri 10–12 and 2–6.30, weekends and hols 2–6.30; winter Tues–Fri 2–6; closed mid-Dec–mid-Jan; adm*) is contained in a well preserved master's house from the 1890s, and concentrates on wine. The church of Montfort is equally worth a look, a charming combination of Romanesque and Gothic; but, as with many villages in the Chalosse, many people come to Montfort just to eat.

Dax

With five wells pouring out over 7 million litres of hot mineral water every day, Dax easily makes its living as France's top thermal spa, full of flowers, mimosas and mini-vans transferring patients to and fro. The story goes that an old Roman soldier stationed here had a dog so stiff with rheumatism that he left it behind when his legion went to Spain. When he returned, he was amazed to see Fido frisking about like a pup. Curious, he followed the dog to a pool of hot mud on the Adour. The soldier joined his dog in the mud and quickly spread word of a cure. Word reached Julia, the daughter of Augustus, who was afflicted with rheumatism. She became the first celebrity to take the cure, and renamed the place *Aqua Augustus* after her dad, a name that contracted on Gascon tongues to Dax. Its current career as a full-time spa took off after the construction of the railway from Bordeaux in 1854.

From the 4th century to the mid-1800s, Dax was corseted in its walls on the left bank of the Adour; eight of the original 49 towers have survived near the river. It has the perfect centrepiece for a spa, the arcaded **Fontaine Chaude**, built in 1818 around the most generous of hot springs in France. In Gascon it's called *Lou Bagn Bourren*, the Boiling Bath; housewives found it handy for cooking hardboiled eggs, dipping chickens for plucking and washing the sheets.

Mud Baths

Dax calls itself 'La Première Station de Pélothérapie' or 'First in Hot Mud Pie Cures'. Originally pits were dug along the river, oozing with the mud from the *barthes* where everyone could wallow to their heart's content. These days, the mud is scientifically gathered, mixed with hot water from the fountain and ripened in large solar basins. Here algae and bacteria incubate in the mud mix which contribute in some mysterious way to the anti-inflammatory, soothing effect when the plasticky grey mud is heated and applied to aching joints and bad backs. The spas apply 1,000 cubic metres of the stuff every year, by prescription only; if you'd like to try a bath, however, the **Thermes Borda**, 30 Rue des Lazaristes, **t** 05 58 74 86 13, is *open daily Mon–Sat from 2 to 6.*

Getting Around

A special bus service links Dax to Biarritz and Bordeaux **airports**; ring the Dax tourist office to reserve a place. The **train** station is on the TGV Atlantique route from Paris. For regional bus information, call **t** 05 58 56 80 80. For a **taxi**, call **t** 05 58 74 71 53, or **t** 05 58 91 25 25.

Tourist Information

Dax: Place Thiers, **t** 05 58 56 86 86, *www.dax.fr.*

Where to Stay

Dax ✉ 40100

In Dax 16 out of 58 hotels are connected to thermal establishments. High season is September and October, when it can be hard to find a place that will take you for just one or two nights. Note that at least half-board is obligatory in nearly every hotel.

***Hôtel Splendid, 2 Cours Verdun, **t** 05 58 56 70 70 (*expensive–moderate*). Built in 1928, with an enormous lobby, Art Deco furnishings and grand old bathrooms intact; along with a spa cure there's a health centre on the premises, and lounging about in white bathrobes is *de rigueur. Closed Jan and Feb.*

Beausoleil, 38 Rue du Tuc-d'Eauze, **t 05 58 74 18 32, *www.hotel-beausoleil-dax.fr* (*moderate*). This white, old-fashioned hotel oozes charm and comfort, peace and quiet and offers lots of personal attention. Restaurant (*moderate*). *Closed Christmas–mid-Feb; restaurant closed Mon eve.*

Auberge des Pins, 86 Av Francis-Planté, **t 05 57 74 22 46 (*inexpensive*). A charming little inn with a large garden just outside the centre, country family-style meals (*moderate–cheap*), which they will adapt to any diet. Free minibus service to the baths. *Closed mid-Dec–mid-Jan.*

Le Richelieu, 13 Av Victor-Hugo, **t 05 58 90 49 49, *www.le-richelieu.fr* (*inexpensive*). Centrally located, with a pleasant patio for

sunny days and a restaurant (*moderate*) that tries harder than most; the owners have also opened a '**Club Rétro**' on Rue St-Eutrope where for a small cover charge you can dance and sing to French golden oldies.

★Au Fin Gourmet, 3 Rue des Pénitents, **t** 05 58 74 04 26 (*moderate–inexpensive*). Right in the centre by the Fontaine Chaude, with rooms ranging from the very basic to others with private bathrooms and TVs as well as studios. Half- or full-*pension* is mandatory, but the food (*moderate*) is very good with many Landais recipes on the menu (try the delicate *cèpe* omelette) served in a choice of pretty little rooms. *Closed Dec and Jan.*

Hôtel Loustalot, 60 Place Joffre, **t** 05 58 74 04 13 (*cheap*). Just over the bridge; the décor inside is more modern than the exterior suggests, and there's a chance of finding a room for only one or two nights.

Eating Out

As most guests dine in their hotels, Dax has relatively few restaurants.

L'Amphitryon, 38 Cours Gallieni, **t** 05 58 74 58 05 (*expensive–moderate*). Friendly place with constantly changing menus that feature plenty of delights from Amphitryon's watery realm. *Closed Sat lunch, Sun dinner, Mon, Jan, and last fortnight in Aug.*

Restaurant du Bois de Boulogne, Allée du Bois-de-Boulogne, **t** 05 58 74 23 32 (*moderate–cheap*). With a shady summer terrace, overlooking the Adour, this is another good bet for seafood lovers, but the chef also does good regional meat dishes. *Closed Sun eve.*

Le Moulin de Poustagnacq, Saint-Paul-lès-Dax, **t** 05 58 91 31 03 (*expensive–moderate*). When the Dacquois do dine out, they usually get in their cars and head out of the centre. This popular place overlooks a forest and pond; the kitchen uses local ingredients to create imaginative dishes such as crayfish tempura seldom seen in the Landes, served with a wide choice of wines. *Closed Sun eve, Mon, and Tues lunch.*

From the Fontaine Chaude, Rue Cazade leads to the **Musée de Borda** (*open Tues–Sat 2–6; closed Sun, Mon and hols*). This houses a bit of this and that: Upper Palaeolithic ivories, Roman bronzes, mosaics, coins and a statue of Sleeping Eros. In the medieval section are a pair of Merovingian sarcophagi, and a stone where debtors who couldn't pay were made to sit in Rue du Mirailh; every time someone passed by they had to receive three smacks on the bottom.

The ponderous **Cathédrale Notre-Dame** is the third church on the site. Its mongrel Baroque-classical interior is morose, but has two features from the Gothic cathedral: 80 choir stalls from the mid-1500s, carved with a lunatic asylum of figures twisting about the seats, and the early 13th-century Portal of the Apostles installed in the left transept to protect it from the elements. Its tympanum depicts the Weighing of Souls.

Behind the cathedral, pedestrian-only Rue Neuve leads to Cours de Verdun with the handsome Atrium Casino, built in 1929 and scarcely touched since. Up the Adour, in the riverside **Parc Théodore Denis**, the elegant white Arènes is the busiest arena in the Landes, with both *courses landaises* and Spanish *corridas* from June to October.

The Gers

You've seen the Eiffel Tower and Mont Blanc, but have you been to the *département* that produces more garlic than any in France? No doubt everyone knows the Gers as home of the World Championship Snail Races (in Lagardère) and the World Championship Melon Eating Contest (in Lectoure), but, beyond these, *département* 32 may seem a bit obscure. Most of the Gers, in fact, is serious farmland, a stronghold of Coordination Rurale, the group that is always dumping tons of manure on some poor *préfecture* and capable of sticking a sharp Gascon rapier into anybody's political career; it will come as no surprise that the Gers is very well taken care of. It's probably the only *département* with more geese than people, not to mention the ducks, and a few million free-range chickens. It's the perfect place to dip into *la France profonde* at its best, and home to one great unmissable sight: the cathedral of Auch.

The Armagnac

'Armagnac' can mean the old territories of the counts of Armagnac, the big bosses in Gascony before the French rubbed them out in 1473. But to people today it is more likely to mean the area that produces the finest French brandy. (Cognac? They've never heard of it.) This roughly includes everything west and north of Auch.

Condom and La Romieu

With a name like **Condom**, what's a town to do? The natural instinct of the Gascon, of course, would be to flaunt it: they have opened a **Musée des Préservatifs** (*open June–Sept daily 9–12 and 3–7*) and they stage an exhibition of prophylactics in the summer. Nobody knows where the name came from. Condom's one sight is its **Cathédrale St-Pierre**, begun in 1507, a magnificent building, but one that has taken its bumps over the centuries, from the Wars of Religion to the mobs of the Revolution, and the 19th-century restorers. The interior is an excellent example of the southern approach to Flamboyant Gothic, featuring complex vaulting and big gallery windows.

Getting Around

You aren't going to get very far here without a car. From Auch, there are **bus** connections (ring **t** 05 62 05 76 37) to Condom and some of the larger villages.

Tourist Information

Condom: Place Bossuet, **t** 05 62 28 00 80, *www.condom.org.*

Eauze: Place d'Armagnac, next to the church, **t** 05 62 09 85 62, *www.eauze.net.*

Marciac: Place du Chevalier, **t** 05 62 08 26 60. The main website for the area is *www.gers-gascogne.com.*

Where to Stay and Eat

Condom ✉ 32100

★★★**Hôtel des Trois Lys**, right in the centre on Rue Gambetta, **t** 05 62 28 33 33, *www.les-trois-lys.com* (*expensive–moderate*). Occupying an 18th-century mansion, this hotel is welcoming and well kept. It has just enough room at the back for a small swimming pool. Restaurant (*moderate*). *Closed Feb; restaurant closed Sun and Mon lunch.*

★★**Logis des Cordeliers**, Rue de la Paix, **t** 05 62 28 03 68, *www.logisdescordeliers.com* (*moderate*). With pool but no restaurant. *Closed Jan.*

Moulin du Petit Gascon, on the road to Eauze, by Ecluse de Grange, **t** 05 62 28 28 42 (*moderate*). Simple *auberge* that offers generous and good traditional southwest cuisine. *Closed Sun eve and Mon exc mid-June–mid-Sept and most of Nov.*

Montréal ✉ 32250

Chez Simone (opposite the church), **t** 05 62 29 44 40 (*moderate*). This old building decorated with frescoes shelters a superb restaurant known for its duck and *foie gras*, truffle omelettes and old armagnacs. *Closed Sun eve, Mon and Tues.*

Fourcès ✉ 32250

Château de Fourcès, **t** 05 62 29 49 53, *www.chateau-fources.com* (*expensive*). A superbly restored château on the edge of this *bastide* village, with fine spacious rooms, a ravishing garden and a swimming pool. The food (*expensive–moderate*) is also a treat, professional and inventive, and service is friendly. *Closed Nov–Mar.*

L'Auberge, **t** 05 62 29 40 10 (*moderate*). This restaurant on Fourcès' circular square offers simple, good-value local food. There's a terrace in summer and roaring fire in winter. *Closed Wed in winter.*

Eauze ✉ 32800

Henri IV, 1 Place St Taurin, round the corner from the church, **t** 05 62 09 75 90 (*inexpensive*). This place will provide a quiet night's sleep. Restaurant (*moderate*). *Restaurant closed Fri lunch in summer.*

Auberge du Moulin de Pouy, Moulin de Pouy, **t** 05 62 09 82 58 (moderate). Home cooking., and a pretty terrace. *Closed Sun eve, Mon and 1st half Sept.*

Marciac ✉ 32230

La Petite Auberge, on the arcaded square, **t** 05 62 09 31 33 (*moderate–cheap*). A popular spot for lunch, with simple and filling meals. *Closed Wed eve and Thurs exc July and Aug.*

The nearby abbey of Flaran (*see* below) gets most of the tour buses, but **La Romieu**, east of Condom, is more rewarding if you only have time for one. Its monastery was founded in 1082, but it hit the jackpot in the 14th century, when a local, Arnaud d'Aux, had a cousin who became pope – Clement V, the Gascon elected with the connivance of the king of France. Arnaud became a cardinal, and presided over the trial of the Templars in 1307, and must have picked up considerable loot from them. In 1312, he began spending on the **abbey** (*open Oct–May daily 10–12 and 2–6; July and Aug 10–12.30 and 2–7.30; June and Sept 10–12 and 2–7; closed Jan and Sun am*). The church's interior is a delight, but the real treasure is the so-called sacristy, an octagonal hall intended as a tomb for Arnaud d'Aux. Frescoes of beautiful angel musicians look

All For One and One For The Road: Armagnac and Floc

The vines in the Gers date back at least 1,000 years, but until the Middle Ages the 10° white wine they produced could barely travel across the table; the main variety of grape, folle blanche, was nicknamed *picquepoul*, 'tingle-lips'. Turning tingle-lips into a fine amber brandy was an idea introduced in 1285 by Arnaud de Villeneuve, a medical student at the University of Salerno, who joined the University of Montpellier and went on to become the personal doctor of Clement V. In Salerno, the Arab-Italian faculty had perfected the ancient Egyptian art of distilling essences, and the first record of the Gascons applying this fine art to grapes dates from 1411.

What all armagnac has in common is the use of acidic, low-alcohol white wine. The essential technique for making armagnac hasn't changed since 1818, when the Marquis de Bonas patented an armagnac still that permitted a single-pass distillation process as opposed to the two-step process formerly used, and still used to make cognac. Fresh from the still, armagnac is rough 58–63° brandy; it is then put in a oak cask in a darkened store room. In the first ten years of ageing some 6 per cent of the brandy is lost every year through evaporation ('the angels' share') and is carefully replaced by distilled water; meanwhile the brandy receives its distinctive burnished hues by dissolving the tannins of the wood. After ten years it is transferred into old casks with no tannin. The finest brandies are aged for up to 40 years. When the *maître de chai* decides that the armagnac has at last reached its apogee of finesse, further evolution is stopped by transferring it to glass vats or bottles.

Everywhere that armagnac is produced, you'll also find floc de Gascogne, the 'Flower of Gascony', an aperitif that has been made here since the 1500s. Essentially, floc is grape juice mixed with armagnac, but don't sniff – it has been strictly AOC since 1989. Fresh and fruity, it goes down quite well chilled in summer. Uniquely in France, floc owes its revival and success almost exclusively to women, who in 1980 formed the only French female wine confraternity (perhaps consorority is the proper word), the Dames du Floc de Gascogne. Their symbol is a bouquet of violets, roses and plum flowers – the traditional perfumes of armagnac.

down from the ceiling, and portraits of family members and biblical personalities line the walls – along with a set of completely mysterious painted designs. If someone is around with the keys, ask to see the unusual double-spiral staircase.

Abbaye de Flaran

Open July–Aug daily 9.30–7; Feb–June and Sept–first week in Jan daily 10–12.30 and 2–6; closed last 3 weeks Jan and hols; guided tours; adm.

Just south of Condom on the outskirts of Valence, the Abbaye de Flaran was founded by the Cistercians in 1151. Although the Cistercians did not care to dress up their buildings, they were hardly otherworldly mystics. Following the lead of Bernard, one of the most mean-spirited ayatollahs in history, they did have two little weaknesses: money and power. In the order's golden age, the 12th century, they acquired vast lands, and used the most up-to-date agricultural methods to exploit them, while their leaders meddled in politics. Bernard was the great enemy of Abelard and the universities, and Cistercians dedicated themselves to stamping out free-thinking wherever they could find it. As such, they weren't warmly welcomed in the south; this is one of their very few colonies here. The church, begun in 1180, shows the restrained elegance common in the best Cistercian buildings; there's an equally austere cloister, a lovely chapter house, built with Roman columns, the refectory and library.

West of Condom: the Bas-Armagnac

The countryside is green and delicious, and signs for armagnac pop up at every crossroads. The main route west, the D15, passes **Larressingle**, the 'Carcassonne of the Gers' – a wonderful specimen of Gersian hyperbole, but just the same this medieval fortified village (the smallest in France) makes a striking sight. East of here, **Montréal** is an English *bastide* of 1289, snoozing on its balcony, while its Roman ancestor lies down on the plain at **Séviac**. One of the mega-villas of Roman Gaul, it was built on the usual peristyle plan; highlighs are the baths and pool, and the well-preserved mosaics. More finds can be seen in the **museum** on the site (*open July and Aug daily 10–7; Mar–June and Sept–Nov 10–12 and 2–6; adm*).

North of Montréal, **Fourcès** was one of the few medieval *bastides* laid out in the form of a circle. **Mézin**, beyond, was the home of Armand Fallières, president of France from 1906 to 1913. His presidency caused no embarrassment, so the villagers named their main square after him. There is a **museum** (*open July and Aug daily 10–12 and 2.30–6.30; April–June and Sept–Oct Tues–Sun 2.30–5.30*) with exhibits on Fallières' life, and on corks, too. Mézin grew up around a Cluniac abbey, and it retains the church – Romanesque in the apse while the rest is graceful Gothic. Over the altar, note the carving of a grimacing giant and a pot of flowers.

Everyone in the Bas-Armagnac comes to the Thursday morning market at **Eauze**, the centre of the armagnac trade. The Vikings trashed it in the 840s, and nothing but *eau-de-vie* has come out of it since. The market takes place on the edge of the old town, in a delightful open place where the branches of the plane trees have been tied together to make a roof. The **Musée Archéologique** (*open June–Sept Wed–Mon 10–12.30 and 2–6; Feb–May and Oct–Dec Wed–Mon 2–5; closed Tues, hols, 1st weekend in July and Jan*) now exhibits 'Le Trésor d'Eauze', Roman treasure dating from the 3rd century AD, discovered nearby in 1985. The treasure includes 28,003 coins and about 50 precious objects. The museum also houses discoveries from a nearby site of a rich Roman colony dating from the 1st–4th century AD. The convivial **Café Commercial**, centre of all Eauze's comings and goings, has a rugby mural on the wall. The only other noteworthy thing about Eauze is its **war memorial**.

Nogaro to Marciac: the Pays d'Artagnan

The biggest village in the eastern Armagnac, **Nogaro** has plenty of brandy and *foie gras*, but likes better to dress up in racing colours and expound on the joys of speed at its race track – heady stuff, for a place where every day seems like Sunday and dogs sleep in the middle of the street. The town's sedentary church, begun in the 11th century, it has some lively capitals, and a window of the Coronation of the Virgin, claimed to be a work of Arnaut de Moles.

Termes-d'Armagnac takes its name from the Latin *terminus*; this village was the boundary between the Dukes of Armagnac and Viscounts of Béarn. What remains of its strong castle, built by Thibaut de Termes, who fought with Joan of Arc, is now the **Musée du Panache Gascon** (*open June–Sept Wed–Mon 10–7.30, Tues 2–7.30; Oct–May Wed–Mon 2–6*), with dioramas of historical scenes. **Aignan**, in the middle of delicious country east of Termes, is one of the most attractive villages in the Gers. The original seat of the counts of Armagnac, it was wrecked by the Black Prince in 1355, but retains its arcaded square and 12th-century church. Charles de Batz – D'Artagnan – was born at the Château de Castelmaure north of nearby **Lupiac**.

Plaisance-du-Gers, little capital of the 'Pays d'Artagnan', hasn't done much for itself since the Black Prince burned it down on his 1355 tour. Just south of Plaisance, the beautiful D946 branches east for Auch, with views of the Pyrenees; further south is the busy village of **Marciac**, a late 13th-century *bastide* that now stands the Gers on its ear each August with one of France's biggest jazz festivals (*ring the tourist office for details*). Marciac is also known for furniture-making, and for the tallest tower in the Gers, the 293ft steeple of its church, a glorious 14th-century building.

Auch

Auch with its 23,000 people could be a lovely little town, if it wanted to. It has all the ingredients: a pretty setting over the River Gers, and a core of monuments inherited from the days when its archbishops were in control. But Auch seems to have no ambitions to be anything more than an overgrown farmers' market. The centre is dowdy, and every open space has been pressed into service as a car park. Visitors will just have to settle for two of the greatest artistic achievements France has ever produced: Arnaut de Moles' stained-glass windows, and a set of choir stalls that have to be seen to be believed. Both are in the cathedral.

Cathédrale Ste-Marie

At first sight this building is a bit disconcerting, with its strange façade looming over Place de la République. This is one of the last cathedrals in France to be completed and the west front was not added until the 1600s. The French would call it *classique*, which means lots of bits and pieces from Italian Renaissance style books pasted together. Walking around the sides, you can see the Flamboyant Gothic intent of the first architects. Work, however, didn't really get rolling until 1463, when France was awakening to the Renaissance. In the early 1500s, Auch had an archbishop who had travelled in Italy and had access to serious money; Cardinal Clement-Lodève was the brother of Georges d'Amboise, sometime chief minister to Louis XII. It was under him that the stained glass and the choir were begun.

Nobody knows much about Arnaut de Moles, except that he came from St-Sever in the Landes, and that he started work here in 1507. If he hadn't chosen the obscure medium of **stained glass**, and to leave his life's work in the middle of the Gers, he might have gained the renown he deserves; his brilliant High Renaissance draughts-

Getting Around

Auch has **rail** connections to Agen (via Fleurance and Lectoure), and to Toulouse. Auch is also the centre of what **bus** service there is (**t** 05 62 05 76 37): to Tarbes, Bordeaux, Toulouse and Mont-de-Marsan; slightly more frequently to Condom, Vic-Fézensac, Fleurance, Lectoure and nearby villages.

Tourist Information

Auch: 1 Rue Dessoles, **t** 05 62 05 22 89, *ot.auch@wanadoo.fr*.

Where to Stay

Auch ✉ 32000

★★★★Hôtel de France, Place de la Libération, **t** 05 62 61 71 71, *auchgarreau@intelcom.fr* (*expensive–moderate*). Few hotels in all of France have as many stories to tell as this place. As the Armes de France it was a noted establishment 200 years ago. The Auscitains claim that no less a personage than the son of Louis XVI, the poor Dauphin Louis, was smuggled out of Paris during the terror and ended up here, working as a stable boy (until recently, his descendants still lived in the area, though no one took their claim to the throne very seriously outside the Gers). For all that, it is a thoroughly modern hotel, with luxurious rooms and amenities including a sauna. No pool, but they will arrange sports such as riding and golf in the countryside. **★★★Le Robinson**, just south of Auch, **t** 05 62 05 02 83, *www.hotelrobinson.net* (*inexpensive*).

In a beautiful forest setting, this hotel has cleanly stylish modern rooms with balconies and television.

★Hôtel de Paris, Av de la Marne near the train station, **t** 05 62 63 26 22 (*inexpensive*). This is a family-run, well-cared-for hotel and restaurant (*moderate–cheap*). *Closed Nov; restaurant closed Sun eve*.

Eating Out

Jardin des Saveurs, in the Hôtel de France (*see above*), **t** 05 62 61 71 71 (*very expensive–moderate*). This famous hotel also claims the highest-rated *département* restaurant, with new chef Roland Garreau as accomplished as his legendary predecessor, André Daguin: the very best *foie gras* (four different 'flavours'), perhaps with a hint of truffles, along with all the other natural delights of the southwest. Some of the dishes on offer are traditional favourites (it's a surprise to find *cassoulet* on the menu in such a place), others inspired flights of fancy. For accompaniment, they have probably the best cellar in the southwest. *Closed Sun eve*.

Claude Lafitte, Rue Desoules, **t** 05 62 05 04 18 (*expensive–moderate*). Here is a champion of regional cooking and fresh local ingredients: charcuterie and Gascon favourites such as Henri IV's *poule au pot*. *Closed Sun eve, Mon, and Tues eve*.

★★Relais de Gascogne, 5 Av de la Marne, **t** 05 62 05 26 81 (*inexpensive*). This restaurant-with-rooms (*moderate*) delivers good local cuisine such as *daube à l'armagnac*, *cassoulet*, duck and fish. *Closed end Dec–mid-Jan*.

---

manship has much in common with his contemporary, Albrecht Dürer. New advances in technique helped him achieve incredible colour effects. In all, Arnaut's work, in which he engraved details on the glass with acid, is an art that seems much closer to painting, born of an age obsessed with tricks of light, colour and composition.

The eighteen windows in the ambulatory chapels make a complete account of the Christian story. Old and New Testament figures are mixed together according to the medieval idea of typology, in which everything in the Old prefigures something in the New. Their complex symbolism makes a progression from Genesis, through the Crucifixion, to the Resurrection. At the end, the artist signs off: 'On the 25 June 1513 these present works were completed for the honour of God and Our Lady. *Noli me tangere*. Arnaut de Moles.'

The **choir** is completely enclosed as in a Spanish cathedral, and it's usually locked, but someone is sure to be around with the key (*take a torch: it is badly lit*). The entire space is filled with a set of 113 **stalls**, made of heart of oak, soaked in water for fifty years to harden and permit the carving of the tiniest of details. Two centuries ago, a monk of Auch tried to count all the figures on the stalls, and came up with over 1,500. At first glance, expending so much time and talent on a locked-up place for monks to plant their bottoms might seem a mad obsession. But take this rather as a glorious example of that Renaissance innovation, art for art's sake, the first great work executed for the Church in France where religious symbolism takes a back seat to pure artistic expression. These stalls took over fifty years to make and many hands assisted, but unlike Arnaut's windows there is no grand scheme; rather, within limits each artist seems to have done as he pleased. Some mirror the figures in the glass, which was under way at the same time; others represent other biblical personages or vignettes. Hercules makes an appearance, slaying Antaeus; others are pure flights of fancy, concealed among the Gothic traceries, on the arms or under the seats. It's great fun and takes two hours to look over: see if you can find the camel, the winged bulldog, the skeleton, the baby snake, the saw, the two-headed monk, the unicorn...

The Rest of Auch

Auch turns its back towards the River Gers; just the same, this is its best face, with a quiet riverfront boulevard and the **monumental stair**, built in the 1860s, leading down from the apse of the cathedral. There are 370 steps if you're going that way, and landings with a statue of D'Artagnan and a modern work that consists of the story of Noah, in Latin, engraved in the pavement. Also behind the cathedral is the striking 14th-century **Tour d'Armagnac**, a proud monument for all Gascons. Unfortunately, the tower and its building never belonged to the Armagnacs, but they served as the offices of the archbishops and their prisons. South of the stair and the cathedral is the old **Quartier du Caillou**, a forbidding tangle of narrow alleys that often turn into stairways. The locals call these old streets the '*pousteries*', a fittingly strange setting for a place that briefly was the home of Nostradamus. The wizard spent some time in Auch in the 1540s, and taught at the old Jesuit College on Rue de la Convention.

There's more life north of the cathedral. Just off Place de la République stands the lovely **Maison Fedel** from the 15th century, which now houses the tourist office; it leans in so many directions at once it seems to be made of pastry. Rue Dessoles is the main street; at its opposite end are relics of the **Priory of St-Orens**, once one of the most powerful monasteries in Gascony.

From here, find your way to Rue Daumesnil and the **Musée des Jacobins** (*open Tues–Sun 10–12 and 2–6, till 5 Oct–April; closed Mon and hols exc July and Aug; adm*), housed in a 17th-century monastery. Founded in the middle of the French Revolution, in 1793, this is one of the best-run little provincial museums in France. There are 1st-century frescoes from a Roman villa near Auch, a big statue of Emperor Trajan with a big Roman nose, a fine Renaissance *gisant* of Cardinal Jean d'Armagnac, and some beautifully made musical instruments. Holding pride of place among the paintings are the works of a local boy named Jean-Marie Roumeguère, who specialized in sunrises, sunsets, and burning houses. The upstairs is devoted to Gascon crafts, an exhibit on D'Artagnan, and a room of lovely 18th-century faïence from Auch and Samadet. Best and last is a collection of pre-Colombian and colonial Latin-American art. Some of the best of these works are 19th-century fakes, proudly given a display case of their own.

The Valley of the Gers

This *pays*, called the Lomagne, is a country of knobby hills known for wheat and garlic (a third of all the garlic in France!) and not much else.

Lectoure

High on its hill, Lectoure was the military key to Gascony from Celtic times to the Middle Ages, when it became the capital of the counts of Armagnac. In 1473, as France was beginning to recover from the Hundred Years War, Louis XI decided to assert greater control over the south. His army attacked Lectoure, which was defended by Count Jean V in person; after a long siege, the two sides agreed on a peace. But the French were just joking. When Jean V opened the gates they sacked and burned the town, and murdered the count and most of the population. That put an end to the Armagnacs once and for all, and to the independence of Gascony.

Louis XI rebuilt the city, and in the Wars of Religion Lectoure had the good sense to side with the future Henri IV. Henri and his son Louis XIII favoured Lectoure, but with the dividing of France into *départements* Lectoure lost out to Auch, and now has an aristocratic and somewhat forlorn air about it, sitting up on its cliff with its memories. Some of these are kept in the excellent **Musée Lapidaire** (*open Mar–Sept daily 10–12 and 2–6; rest of year closed Tues and hols; adm*). From under its cathedral came a score of Gallo-Roman tauroboles, funeral monuments decorated with bulls' heads

Tourist Information

Lectoure: Pl de la Cathédrale, t 05 62 68 76 98.
Fleurance: 112 bis Rue de la République, t 05 62 64 00 00, *www.gascogne.com/fleurance*.

Where to Stay and Eat

Lectoure ✉ 32700

**Hôtel de Bastard, Rue Lagrange in the centre, t 05 62 68 82 44, *www.hotel-de-bastard.com* (*moderate*). The nobleman who built this stately town mansion in the 1700s may have been a real bastard, but the current owners are actually quite amiable. The atmosphere is conservative French provincial, the rooms airy and tasteful;

there's a terrace with a pool looking out over the rooftops and a small garden. In the restaurant (*expensive–moderate*), along with traditional Gascon fare, the cooking takes some detours, usually in the direction of Italy. *Closed Sun eve and Mon Oct–May.*

Auberge des Bouviers, Rue Montebello, t 05 62 68 95 13 (*moderate*). Happy place where the windows are full of flowers and the cooking first class.

Fleurance

Le Fleurance, Route d'Agen, *www.occitania.com/ lefleurance/index.html* (*moderate*). In town in its own shady park, with 23 simple rooms, some with balcony or private garden. Reasonable restaurant with terrace overlooking park. *Closed 1–15 Jan.*

dedicated to Cybele, the Great Goddess of Asia Minor whose cult became widespread in the western Empire. Translations of the inscriptions (into French) give a fascinating insight into life in ancient *Lectora*. Along with them is an early Christian marble sarcophagus, jewellery from Roman and Merovingian times, and bits of mosaics found around the town, including Ocianus, a very strange face, full of foreboding.

Lectoure **cathedral**'s present incarnation was begun in 1488, as part of Louis XI's rebuilding programme. There is little of note inside, but, if the sacristan is around, ask if you can go up the bell tower, for a view that takes in half the Gers. Failing that, the view from the Bastion on the east edge of the town is almost as good.

Into the Lomagne

There are quite a few châteaux that can be visited in this out-of-the-way region (*ask at the Lectoure tourist office*). One of them, at **Terraube**, once belonged to a renowned warrior of the Hundred Years War, Hector de Galard, who lives on as the Jack of Diamonds in the French pack of cards (in France, all the face cards are historical personages). Terraube also has a famous well, into which Blaise de Montluc's men stuffed all the local Protestants. Here too is another *bastide* (1272), **Fleurance**, one of the few in Gascony to grow into a real town, with an elegant ensemble of 18th-century buildings around the central Place de la Halle. The real reason for stopping is Notre-Dame, with three stained-glass windows by Arnaut de Moles, as good as the ones in Auch and perhaps even more colourful.

The Pays Basque

You'll know you've crossed into the Pays Basque or Euzkadi when you find a village with a *fronton* (*pelote* court), where the shop signs are full of z's and x's, and every-thing except the dogs is painted red, white and green. Those are the colours of the Basque flag, which waves proudly over the autonomous Basque provinces in Spain, but is discouraged by the authorities in the three of the seven provinces of Euzkadi that are in France. Sights, frankly, are few and far between. The real attraction is the Basques themselves, a taciturn though likeable lot, and their distinctive culture, language and way of life. The setting also helps: tidy emerald landscapes that have been well tended by the oldest people in Europe for millennia.

Basques love to play outlandish games. Many are based on pure brute strength, the celebrated *force basque*. One can imagine them, in the mists of time, impressing each other by carrying around boulders – because that's what they do today, in the *harri*

Getting Around

Ryanair, **t** 05 59 43 83 93, **flies** daily from London-Stansted. The no.6 bus from Biarritz goes to the airport, the Aérogare de Parme, **t** 05 59 43 83 83. There are flights from Paris Orly with Air France, **t** (0) 820 820 820, and three a day from Charles de Gaulle.

Bayonne and Biarritz are on the main **rail** line from Paris and Bordeaux to Spain, with daily TGVs. Other lines from Bayonne go to Orthez and Pau, and to St-Jean-Pied-de-Port. There is a parallel **bus** service down the coast run by **ATCRB, t** 05 5926 0699 – about a dozen a day from Bayonne and Biarritz to St-Jean-de-Luz and Hendaye.

altxatzea. Related to this is the *untziketariak*, in which we see how fast a Basque can run with 100lb weights in each hand. They probably invented tug-of-war. At the same time they developed *pelote*, the fastest ball game in the world. Every Basque village has a *fronton*, usually right in the centre. *Pelote* may be played with another wall on the left side, *a jaï-alaï*, the fastest and most furious form.

Modern Basque nationalism started in the 18th century in Bilbao. The development of Basque culture proceeded apace in Spain, while at least on the political side it ran into a stone wall in France. Franco's rule was a catastrophe for the Basques; ETA (*Euzkadi ta Askatasuna*, or Basque Homeland and Liberty) was founded in 1959. Its bombing campaign near the end of Franco's reign was singularly effective – notably when they blew up his successor, Carrero Blanco. In the new Spain the Basques got full autonomy and the right to their language and culture; this left ETA out in the cold as a band of die-hards demanding total independence. It does not keep them from continuing their terror tactics in Spain. Although most French Basques decided long ago that being French wasn't so bad, there are plenty of nationalists, who are sure to grow more vocal with the recent autonomy gains of the Corsicans.

Biarritz

For their 1959 season, the designers at Cadillac came up with something special: a convertible, nearly 25ft long, with the highest tailfins in history (22 inches). They called it the Biarritz, a tribute to the Basque village that was chosen by fortune at the end of the 19th century to become the most glittering resort in Europe. Now freed

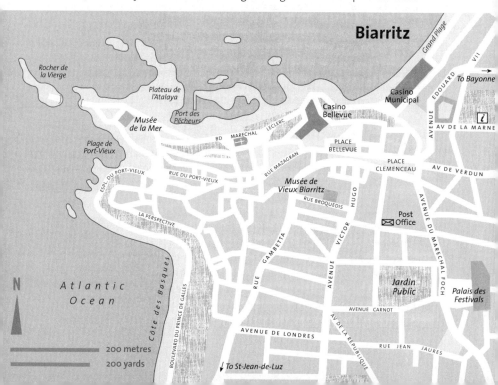

Getting There and Around

Ryanair **flies** to Biarritz from the UK.
Public transportation in the Bayonne-
Biarritz area is run by STAB; Infobus provides
information on all services, t 05 59 59 04 61.
Regular **buses** connect the two cities, from the
Hôtel de Ville in Bayonne to the Hôtel de Ville
in Biarritz – line 1 or 2, or faster, the Express
BAB. Biarritz's **rail** station is far from the city
centre; the no.2 bus terminates here.

Tourist Information

Biarritz: 'Javalquinto', t 05 59 22 37 10,
www.biarritz.fr.
Bayonne: Place des Basques, t 05 59 46 01 46,
www.bayonne-tourisme.com.

Sports and Activities

If you should feel a sudden desire to take up
surfing, there are five schools in Biarritz.
Thalassotherapy – the use of sea water for
aiding stress, fitness or recovery from diseases
– is also big business; Biarritz has two of the
most up-to-date establishments, the **Institut
Thalassa**, 11 Rue Louison Bobet, t 05 59 41 30 01,
and **Les Thermes Marine**, 80 Rue de Madrid,
t 05 59 23 01 22. Golf thrives in Biarritz, with 10
courses and several more in St-Jean-de-Luz. Or
else, you can fritter away francs on the *tiercé*,
quarté and *quinté* at the **Hippodrome de la
Cité des Fleurs** on Avenue du Lac Marion, still
one of France's premier racing venues.

Where to Stay

Biarritz ✉ **64200**
****Hôtel du Palais**, Villa Eugénie, 1 Av de
l'Impératrice, t 05 59 41 64 00, *www.hotel-
du-palais.com* (*luxury*). Probably the most
prestigious address on France's west coast.
Built in Biarritz's glory days on the site of
Napoléon and Eugénie's villa, this beach
compound, where the amenities even
include a private putting green, has a circuit
of old wrought-iron fences to separate you
from the rest of the world. Some of the
rooms are palatial, many with period
furnishings. Restaurant (*very expensive–
expensive*). *Closed Feb; restaurant closed
lunch July and Aug.*
****Café de Paris**, 5 Place Bellevue, t 05 59 24
19 53, *www.cafedeparis-biarritz.com* (*expensive*). A chic alternative close to the sea. It is
one of Biarritz's best restaurants (*very
expensive–expensive*) but also has rooms
above, all with magnificent sea views, some
with huge terraces (the rooms are overpriced and a bit scruffy). *Closed lunch
Mon–Sat, and Tues.*
***Plaza**, Av Edward VII, t 05 59 24 74 00
(*expensive–moderate*). Built in 1928, has a
touch of restrained Art Deco elegance. It has
retained much of its original decoration,
with a quiet sense of decorum to match.
***Château de Clair de Lune**, 48 Av Alan
Seeger, t 05 59 41 53 20, *www.chateaude-
clairdelune.com* (*expensive–moderate*). An
alternative far from the centre. It's in a Belle
Epoque villa in a delicious park, with tranquillity assured, and lovely rooms, though
it's a bit expensive.
***Maison Garnier**, 29 Rue Gambetta, t 05 59
01 60 70, *www.hotel-biarritz.com* (*moderate–
inexpensive*). This place is currently fashionable, set in a 19th-century Basque house.
There are seven exquisitely restored rooms,
all with antique furniture.
Hostellerie Victoria, 11 Av Reine Victoria,
t 05 59 24 08 21 (*moderate*). In a delightful
villa from the old days, close to Grande
Plage. *Closed 20 Oct–1 April.*

from the burden of being the cynosure of fashion, the resort has become a pleasantly
laid-back place. Come in the off season, and you'll notice the other Biarritz – the
retirement capital of France. After September, it declines into an overgrown village.

In the 1860s, Biarritz was a simple fishing village, with memories of a great whaling
past, when it began to make part of its living from a new phenomenon, the desire of
northerners to spend a holiday beside the sea. It owes its present status to Empress
Eugénie. As a girl, she and her mother had summered at Biarritz. As empress, she

Bayonne ✉ 64100

If you're not too concerned about proximity to a beach, the animated streets of Bayonne might make a nice, cheaper alternative.

Hôtel Ibis, 44–50 Bd Alsace-Lorraine, Quartier St-Esprit, **t 05 59 50 38 38 (*moderate*). A functional chain hotel with a small garden and a restaurant, in the station quarter of the town.

Hôtel Loustau, 1 Place de la République, **t** 05 59 55 08 08, *www.hotel-loustau.com* (*moderate*). Modern, clean and functional.

*Hôtel des Arceaux, 26 Rue Port-Neuf, **t** 05 59 59 15 53 (*inexpensive*). One of the best options, near the cathedral.

*Monbar, 24 Rue Pannecau, **t** 05 59 59 26 80 (*inexpensive*). On a lively street in Petit Bayonne, across the Nive, and well kept.

Eating Out

Biarritz ✉ 64200

La Rotonde, Hôtel du Palais, **t** 05 59 41 64 00 (*very expensive–expensive*). This may be the southwest's ultimate trip in luxurious dining: a magnificent domed room with its original decoration, and views over the beach and sea. They've just changed chefs and the personality of the cuisine is yet unclear – only expect it to remain first-rate. There is a formidable wine list. *Closed lunch in July and Aug, exc Sun, and Feb.*

Les Jardins de l'Océan, Hôtel Régina et Golf, 52 Av de l'Impératrice, **t** 05 59 41 33 00 (*expensive*). Good for a slightly more modest seafood extravaganza. You may be tempted to splurge on the grand *plateau de fruits de mer*, including lobster. *Closed most of Jan.*

Le Clos Basque, 12 Rue Louis Barthou, **t** 05 59 24 24 96 (*moderate*). An authentic little bistro with stone walls and Spanish tiles inside, and a charming terrace outside. Local

specialities such as squid with peppers. *Closed Sun eve exc July and Aug, and Mon.*

Café de la Grand Plage, 1 Av Edouard VII, **t** 05 59 22 77 88. Part of the casino, facing the ocean and overlooking the Grand Plage. It's a 1930s-style brasserie-café, with a wide range of drinks, snacks and meals.

Bar Jean, 5 Rue des Halles, **t** 05 59 24 80 38. A Biarritz classic. It's *the* place to go for superb fresh *tapas*, oysters and a good choice of wines in a traditional Spanish tiled *bodega*. *Closed Jan and Feb, and Tues and Wed Oct–April.*

Bistrot des Halles, Rue du Centre, **t** 05 59 24 21 22 (*moderate*). Usually crowded for both lunch and dinner. As in any French town, you won't go wrong looking around the market, and you won't do better than the daily special (usually a grilled fish or steak) here. *Closed Sun exc school hols, and end Oct.*

Bayonne ✉ 64100

Le Cheval Blanc, Rue Bourg Neuf, just round the corner from the Musée Bonnat, **t** 05 59 59 01 33 (*expensive–moderate*). At the top of the heap, by popular acclaim. Even though the Tellechea family has been running this place for a long time, they never get tired of finding innovative twists to traditional Basque cooking: from stuffed squid crab dishes to a *poulet basquaise* with *cèpes*. *Closed Sun eve and Mon exc Aug, and 1st week July and 3 weeks in Feb.*

Francois Miura, 24 Rue Marengo, **t** 05 59 59 49 89 (*moderate*). A stylish small restaurant with modern furniture and contemporary paintings, specializing in fish dishes. *Closed Sun eve and Wed.*

The Bayonnais, 38 Quai Corsaires, **t** 05 59 59 01 33 (*moderate–cheap*). A traditional Basque restaurant in the old town, with décor dedicated to local sporting heroes. *Closed Sun in winter and Mon in July and Aug.*

dragged Napoléon III down with her and established the summer court, in a palace built on the most prominent spot along the beach in 1854. Everybody who was anybody in Paris soon followed, along with dukes and factory-owners with marriageable daughters. Queen Victoria came; the Prince of Wales left so much money in the casino they named two streets after him. The Belle Epoque brought grand hotels, the casino, a salt-water spa and acres of villas. The First World War started Biarritz's fall from fashion; in the 1920s everybody started shifting to Nice and Cannes.

Biarritz has begun to shake off the dust with the dramatic refurbishment of its hotels and the splendid Municipal Casino on the Grand Plage, with its entertainment centres and grand café. France Telecom has made it the experimental city for the communications of the future. Plenty of young people come, for surfing; stuck in its odd angle of coast, Biarritz provides what many claim are the Atlantic's only perfect waves, making it the modest Malibu of Europe.

The **Atalaya**, on the tip of Biarritz's little peninsula, is the height where the watch would send up smoke signals when whales were sighted. To the right, the **Port des Pêcheurs** now holds only pleasure craft; to the left is the old port, now the beach of **Port-Vieux**, and the best place in Biarritz for a stroll. Napoléon III and Eugénie built the causeways and tunnels, connecting crags and tiny islands into a memorable walk above the surf. Up on top of the Atalaya, the **Musée de la Mer** (*open July and Aug daily 9.30–midnight; May, June and Sept 9.30–7; rest of year 9.30–12.30 and 2–6; closed Feb and Christmas; adm; seals are fed at 10.30 and 5*), in an Art Deco building, contains an imaginatively decorated old aquarium.

Descending eastwards from the Atalaya, Bd Maréchal Leclerc takes you to the church of **Ste-Eugénie**; the organ inside won a prize at the 1900 Paris World's Fair. It faces the beautiful **Casino Bellevue**, now used for exhibitions.

Below this, the shore straightens out into the long, luscious **Grande Plage**, which before Eugénie was called (for reasons not entirely clear) the Plage des Fous. Further up the beach, behind the wrought-iron fences, is Biarritz's landmark, the sumptuous **Hôtel du Palais**. This is the spot where Eugénie built her palace, which was destroyed by fire in 1881. The present hotel, begun in 1905, is the successor to an even grander one that also burned down. Across the street, the Russian aristocrats built their onion-domed church of **St-Alexandre-Nevsky** (1908). **Avenue Edward VII**, which becomes Avenue de l'Impératrice further on, was the status address of Belle Epoque Biarritz, lined with ornate hotels and residences now largely converted to other uses. In the shady streets behind them, scores of villas still survive, in a crazy quilt of styles.

There is a wide choice of other **beaches**. At Biarritz' southern limits is the broad expanse of the Plage de la Milady, Plage Marbella and the Côte des Basques, a favourite of the surfing set. Under the old town is the tiny Plage du Port Vieux. The Grande Plage and Plage Miramar, the centre of the action, are lovely if often cramped, but further out, stretching along the northern coast in Anglet, there are plenty more.

Bayonne

Arthur Young, in the 1780s, called it the prettiest town he'd seen in France. Young had a good eye; even today, Bayonne is as attractive and lively an urban setting as you'll find. From the beginning, it was predominantly a Gascon town rather than Basque, but the two peoples have always got along. English from 1151 to 1452, Bayonne gave the Plantagenets a strong base in the south, and in return enjoyed considerable privileges, not to mention a busy trade with Britain. All that ended when Charles VII marched in at the end of the Hundred Years War. Not long after, an even bigger disaster hit – the River Adour suddenly moved, leaving the port high and dry. But Bayonne, close to Spain, was important to Paris; in 1578 they sent down engineers to dig a canal and redirect the Adour, and the port was back in business. A century later, Louis XIV dispatched Vauban to make Bayonne impregnable (it took Wellington two goes to capture it). An armaments industry gave us the word 'bayonet'. The city's other passion was chocolate. Jewish refugees from Spain introduced it to Bayonne in the 1600s, and Louis XIV and his courtiers spread it across France; some of Bayonne's *chocolatiers*, like Daranatz and Cazeneuve, are still in business.

Grand Bayonne and the Cathedral

Bayonne's main street is a river, the little Nive, and it is one of the most delightful centrepieces a city could ask for, lined on both sides with busy quays and tall houses trim-painted in bright colours. The Nive also marks the division between the two old quarters, Grand Bayonne and Petit Bayonne. The former is the business end, jammed with shopping streets. One of these, narrow Rue Argenterie, will take you to the Northern Gothic **Cathédrale Ste-Marie** (*open Mon–Sat 7.30–12 and 3–7, Sun and hols 3.30–6.30; no visits during services*), a work largely financed by Bayonne's whalers. The bishops exacted a tenth of their profits and the most prized parts of each whale for themselves – the tongue and the fat. Despite all the loot from cetaceans, the cathedral still wasn't finished until the 1800s. So far from the Ile-de-France, and so long in building – what is surprising is how well it all fits together. Best of all, it still enjoys the setting a Gothic cathedral should have – among tightly packed tall buildings, where its verticality makes the impression its designers intended. No church in the southwest save the Jacobins in Toulouse can match its lofty interior. The sacristy shelters the only sculptures that survived the Revolution: one tympanum of the Last Judgement, and another of the Virgin Mary, surrounded by angel musicians.

Just behind the cathedral, the **Château-Vieux** was the seat of Bayonne's English and then French governors; tours run by the tourist office will take you here, and also through the amazing expanses of subterranean chambers under Bayonne. In medieval times they were used for storing wine.

Petit Bayonne

Petit Bayonne, the livelier side of the Nive, is an old, unspoiled city neighbourhood crowded with popular bars and restaurants. Right in the middle is the **Musée Basque** (*open May–Oct Tues–Sun 10–6.30; Nov–April Tues–Sun 10–12.30 and 2–6; closed hols; adm*), the largest collection of Basque artefacts anywhere. Then there's the **Musée Bonnat** at 5 Rue Jacques Laffite (*open as Musée Basque; adm*), bequeathed by Bayonne's Léon Bonnat, a famous salon painter of the late 19th century: there's his philistine fluff, but also works by quattrocento masters Domenico Veneziano and Maso di Banco, and highly stylized Catalan-Aragonese paintings from the same age. There is a late *Madonna* by Botticelli; plus two El Grecos, plenty by Rubens, and works by Murillo, Ribera, and Goya. Ingres was a favourite of Bonnat's; among his works here is an unspeakable portrait of the unspeakable last Bourbon, Charles X. The **Château-Neuf** (*open Tues–Fri 2–6, Sat 9–1, closed Sun–Mon*), begun in 1460 by the French, looms

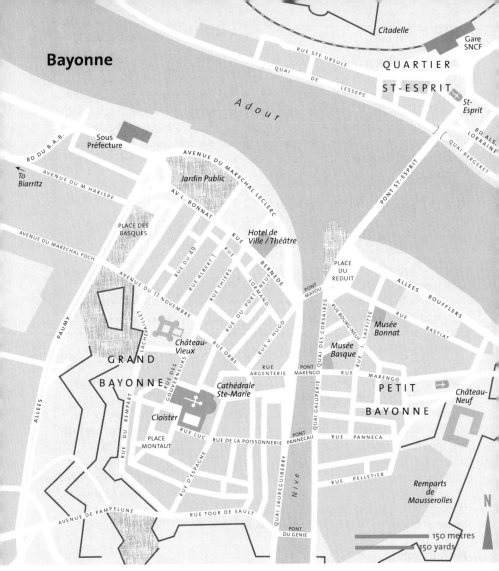

Bayonne

Adour

QUARTIER
ST-ESPRIT

Citadelle

Gare
SNCF

St-
Esprit

RUE STE URSULE

QUAI   DE   LESSEPS

PONT ST-ESPRIT

BD ALS.
LORRAINE

QUAI BERGERET

BD DU B.A.B.

To
Biarritz

AVENUE DU M HARISPE

Sous
Préfecture

AVENUE DU MARECHAL LECLERC

Jardin Public

AV L. BONNAT

PLACE DES
BASQUES

AVENUE DU MARECHAL FOCH

AVENUE DU 11 NOVEMBRE

RUE DU 49

RUE ALBERT I

RUE THIERS

RUE

Hotel de
Ville / Théâtre

RUE DU PORT NEUF

RUE ORBE

BERNEDE

LORMAND

RUE V. HUGO

PONT
MAYOU

PLACE
DU
REDUIT

ALLEES   BOUFFLERS

QUAI DES CORSAIRES

RUE BOURG-NEUF

RUE J. LAFFITTE

RUE
BASTIAT

Musée
Bonnat

Musée
Basque

PAUMY

LACHEPAILLET

Château-
Vieux

GRAND

BAYONNE

RUE DES GOUVERNEURS

RUE DU REMPART

RUE LUC

PLACE
MONTAUT

ALLEES

Cloister

Cathédrale
Ste-Marie

RUE
ARGENTERIE

RUE DE LA POISSONNERIE

RUE D'ESPAGNE

PONT
MARENGO

RUE   MARENGO

PETIT

BAYONNE

RUE   PANNECA

PONT
PANNECAU

QUAI GALUPERIE

QUAI JAUREGUIBERRY

Nive

RUE   PELLETIER

Château-
Neuf

Remparts
de
Mousserolles

N

AVENUE DE PAMPELUNE

RUE TOUR DE SAULT

PONT
DU GENIE

150 metres
150 yards

over the town with the Remparts de Mousserolles. Baroque fortifications are notable
for the space they take up; to defend a city, it was often necessary to destroy at least
half of it, as Vauban did here; today the ramparts are a city park.

The Côte Basque

St-Jean-de-Luz

For those who do not naturally gravitate towards the beach, a seaside resort needs
a certain intangible quality. In all of southern France, there are very few places that
can do this: one is St-Jean-de-Luz. The name is perfect. Light and colour can be
extraordinary here, illuminating an immaculately white Basque town and the acres

of glistening rose-silver seafood its restaurants roll out to lure in customers. Best of all, the fishermen on the quay still strut around as if they own the place.

Unfortunately, the name really has nothing to do with light (*luz* in Spanish); etymologists have traced it back to a Celtic or Latin word meaning mud. St-Jean grew up in a swampy nowhere that had a good harbour. It started thriving when the Adour started silting up the harbour of Bayonne in the Middle Ages.

A casual visitor could walk around St-Jean and never notice it had a beach, but it's a good one, tucked away on the northern side of town, protected by a jetty, and very safe for swimming. At its centre is the lavish **casino**, built in 1924. St-Jean naturally turns its face to the port and France's largest tuna fleet. Behind the port is the town hall and the adjacent **Maison de Louis XIV**, where the Roi-Soleil stayed for his wedding to the Spanish Infanta.

From the port, Rue Gambetta takes you to **St-Jean Baptiste**, largest of all Basque churches in France, where Louis XIV and Maria Teresa were married. It is a lesson in

Tourist Information

St-Jean-de-Luz: Place Maréchal Foch, **t** 05 59 26 03 16, *www.saint-jean-de-luz.com*.
Hendaye: 12 Rue des Aubépines, **t** 05 59 20 00 34, *www.hendaye.com*.

Where to Stay and Eat

St-Jean-de-Luz ✉ 64500

****Chantaco, Route d'Ascain, **t** 05 59 26 14 76, *www.hotel-chantaco.com* (*luxury–expensive*). The emphasis is on golf, with the area's most famous course next door. The hotel, in a 1930s-style Andalucían villa, with a patio covered in vines, is set in a lovely park, and offers tennis courts and a pool in addition to golf. Here you'll find de luxe rooms and service, with prices to match. Some rooms have mountain views. No restaurant. *Closed Nov–April.*
****Parc Victoria, 5 Rue Cèpe, **t** 05 59 26 78 78, *www.parcvictoria.com* (*luxury–expensive*). Set in a gracious mansion on the outskirts of town. It's a beautifully decorated, intimate place (only eight rooms and four suites), in its own park with a pool. *Closed Nov–April; restaurant closed Tues in winter.*
Hôtel de la Plage, 33 Rue Garat, **t 05 59 51 03 44, *www.hoteldelaplage.com* (*expensive–moderate*). A comfortable hotel. *Closed 11 Nov–1 May.*
Bakea, 9 Place Camille Julian, across the harbour in Ciboure, **t** 05 59 47 34 40, *www.hotel-bakea.com* (*inexpensive*). Twelve inexpensive rooms. *Closed Dec and Jan.*
Auberge Kaiku, 17 Rue de la République, **t** 05 59 26 13 20 (*expensive*). The oldest house in St-Jean (1540), rolls out one of the most sumptuous tables; no fixed menus here, but you can negotiate your way to a fine marine repast. Service is slow when it's busy. *Closed Tues and Wed, and Mon–Fri lunch in summer.*
Pasaka, 9 Rue de la République, **t** 05 59 26 05 17 (*moderate*). Has a cosy interior and two terraces, where you can feast on local grilled sardines, or *ttoro* (a satisfying Basque fish soup with potatoes and saffron).
Chez Pantxua, Port de Soccoa, **t** 05 59 47 13 73. A long-established local favourite decorated with Basque paintings, serving *fruits de mer* and fish according to the catch of the day. *Closed Mon and Tues.*
Le Patio, Rue de l'Abbé-Onaïndia, **t** 05 59 26 99 11. A place with a Spanish accent that serves up a very gratifying *parillada* (seafood mixed grill) with just about everything you can imagine, including lobster.

Hendaye ✉ 64700

***Hôtel Serge Blanco, Bd Mer, **t** 05 59 51 35 35, *www.thalassoblanco.com* (*expensive*). Named after the famous Basque rugby star who is the proprietor and whose empire features a thalassotherapy centre and restaurant on the beach. *Closed Christmas.*
Santiago, 29 Rue Santiago, **t 05 59 20 00 94, *www.hotelsantiago.net* (*inexpensive*). One of the cheapest hotels. *Closed Nov–Feb.*

Basque subtlety, plain and bright outside, and plain and bright within. The aesthetic is in the detail, especially the wooden ceiling formed like the hull of a ship, and the three levels of wooden galleries. Another feature, also typical of Basque churches, is the altarpiece, dripping with Baroque detail. The main door of the church was sealed up after Louis and Maria Teresa passed through on their wedding day.

Urrugne and Hendaye

To get to Hendaye, you have a choice of the scenic Corniche Basque (the D912), or else the inland N10 or the motorway; these two pass through **Urrugne**, where the church of St-Vincent has a Renaissance portal with excellent reliefs, damaged by English artillery in 1814. Note the inscription on the sundial: *vulnerant omnes, ultima necat*, referring to the hours – each one wounds, the last one kills. Just outside Urrugne, garden-lovers won't want to miss the 30,000 trees and million flowers of **Parc Floral Florenia** (*open mid-Mar–mid-July and Sept Tues–Sun 10–7; mid-July–Aug daily 10–9; Oct Tues–Sun 2–6; closed Nov–mid-Mar; adm*). It will seem hard to believe, but it opened only in 1993. A local official, after visiting Vancouver's Butchert Gardens, was inspired to create something like it back home. Girard got everyone else in the area involved with the project and, young as the plantings are, they're already impressive.

Hendaye is divided into the old town and Hendaye-Plage with a long and broad beach where old villas are gradually replaced by concrete hotels. Hendaye's border location puts it in the news every century or so; an uninhabited island in the river belongs to neither country, and is under joint administration – Spanish from February to July, French the rest of the year. In 1659, the Treaty of the Pyrenees was signed here, and the following year representatives returned to plan the marriage of Louis XIV and Maria Teresa. A pavilion was erected for the occasion and decorated by Velázquez – who died from the bad cold he caught here. In October 1940, Hendaye's station was the scene of the famous meeting between Hitler and Franco.

Into the Pays Basque

In the green hills there's nothing as pretty, simple and functional as a traditional Basque cottage, with its long, low gable along the façade, and half-timbering and shutters, painted deep red or green. Older houses have carved lintels over the door.

La Rhune and Around

La Rhune, westernmost monument of the Pyrenean chain, is full of cows and sheep, crossed by tracks used by Basque smugglers for centuries. The summit had a reputation as an *akelarre*, a ritual ground for sorcery; up until the 18th century the villages always paid a monk to live on top as a hermit for four years, to keep the witches away and to pray for good winds. Also on its slopes is a reserve for the Basque pony, the *pottok*, drawings of which have been found in prehistoric caves of the Dordogne.

Coming in from Hendaye or St-Jean, the first of the villages below La Rhune is **Ascain**, with its landmark bridge over the Nivelle and a 16th-century church on its

Tourist Information

Sare: Mairie, t 05 59 54 20 14, *www.sare.fr.*
St-Pée-sur-Nivelle: Place de la Poste, t 05 59 54 11 69.
Ustaritz: Centre Lapurdi, t 05 59 93 20 81.
Cambo-les-Bains: Av de la Mairie, t 05 59 29 70 25.

Where to Stay and Eat

Ascain ✉ 64310

**Hôtel du Pont, Route de St-Jean-de-Luz, t 05 59 54 00 40 (*moderate–inexpensive*). Rooms overlooking the Nivelle and its bridge and a delightful restaurant with a garden terrace: *feuilleté de langoustines* and other delicate dishes.

Sare ✉ 64310

***Arraya, Place du Village, t 05 59 54 20 46, *www.arraya.com* (*moderate*). The fanciest in Sare. It's quite expensive for the area, but a memorable restaurant (*moderate*). Specialities such as *mesclange*, veal stuffed with *foie gras*, artichoke hearts and morels. *Closed Nov–Mar.*

Ainhoa ✉ 64250

Itthurria, Place du Fronton, t 05 59 29 92 11, *www.itthurria.com* (*expensive–moderate*). A large traditional Basque house with a celebrated restaurant (*expensive*), featuring dishes such as pigeon with garlic, and local *foie gras. Closed Nov–mid-April; restaurant closed Thurs lunch and Wed exc July–Sept.*
**Oppoca, Place du Fronton, t 05 59 29 90 72 (*inexpensive*). On the main street of this pretty village, in a restored 17th-century post house. Despite lovely rooms, some furnished with antiques, it still seems a bit dear. There is also a fine restaurant with a terrace, serving seafood and *confits. Closed mid-Nov–mid-Dec.*

Espelette ✉ 64250

**Euzkadi, Rue Principle, t 05 59 93 91 88, *www.hotel-restaurant-euzkadi.com* (*inexpensive*). Worth travelling out of your way for, even in an area rich in good restaurants. There are nice rooms with a small pool and tennis, and a remarkable restaurant (*moderate*) where the chef is passionate about traditional Basque country recipes and traditions. Some of the house specialities are things you won't see elsewhere, such as *axoa*, a stew of veal and peppers, and *tripoxa*, a black pudding in a pepper and tomato sauce. *Closed Nov and Dec; restaurant closed Mon and Tues exc July–Sept.*

Cambo-les-Bains ✉ 64250

Domaine de Xixtaberri, t 05 59 29 85 36, restaurant, t 05 59 29 22 66, *www.xixtaberri.com* (*moderate*), up in the hills at Quartier Hegala. A *ferme-auberge* that is simple but special. There is a restaurant (*moderate*) with menus full of duck and *foie gras. Restaurant closed June–Sept.*
**Bellevue, Rue des Terrasses, t 05 59 93 75 75 (*inexpensive*). An old, pleasant establishment with a view, near the top of town. Restaurant (*moderate*). *Closed Sun eve and Mon in winter.*
***Hostellerie du Parc, Place de la Mairie, t 05 59 93 54 54, *www.hotels-basque.com* (*inexpensive*). In the lower part of town, with 10 pretty rooms, a little garden, and a restaurant (*moderate*) that turns out some truly refined dishes: roast pigeon with *cèpes* and salmon *roulés* with *foie gras* inside. There is outside dining in summer. *Closed Tues.*
**Chez Tante Ursule, Bas Cambo, t 05 59 29 78 23 (*inexpensive*). A small rustic hotel with a modern annexe. There is also an excellent restaurant (*expensive–moderate*). Try the pimentoes stuffed with *morue* or salads with *foie gras* or *boudin noir. Closed mid-Feb–mid-Mar; restaurant closed Tues.*

lovely square. From here you can take the D4 up to the Col de St-Ignace and take an old, open tramway to the top, the **Petit Train de la Rhune** (*mid-Mar–mid-Nov daily every half-hour from 9am, 8.30am in summer, plus night runs in July and Aug*). In Neolithic times, La Rhune was a holy mountain, as evidenced by the wealth of stone circles, dolmens and circular tumuli on its slopes.

Just beyond the pass lies **Sare**, one of the capitals of the Basque soul. For its independent ways, people jokingly call it the 'Republic of Sare'. Since the 1400s, it was a centre for 'night work' – smuggling. Folks on both sides of the border never saw the logic of paying duty to French and Spanish foreigners. In 1938 and '39, Sare's night workers helped their countrymen escape Franco's troops; a few years later, they smuggled Allied pilots and spies back the other way.

East of Sare, the D4 gives you a choice of destinations: east to **Ainhoa** or north to **St-Pée-sur-Nivelle**, where there is another attractive church, with a spectacular Baroque altarpiece, and a ruined feudal castle, burned by the villagers in 1793. They weren't just angry with the local baron; this castle had long been known as the 'Château des Sorciers'. The trouble with 'witches' began in 1609. A lawyer named de Lancre was sent from Bordeaux and like most witch-hunters revealed himself as a murderous psychotic. On the testimony of children and tortured women, he had several hundred people condemned to the stake over the next three years. When he started barbecuing priests, the Bishop of Bayonne put an end to it.

Ainhoa, one of the southernmost of all *bastides*, was founded in the 13th-century. A Navarrese baron started it, not only to keep the English out, but with the intention of charging tolls and making money off pilgrims to Compostela. Ainhoa is a lovely village with many old houses – note the lintel over the door of the Maison Gorritia on the main street, telling how a mother built it in 1662 with money sent home by her son in the West Indies. From either St-Pée or Ainhoa, the next step is **Espelette**, the charming village of old houses famous for red peppers; in the late summer you'll see them hanging everywhere.

Cambo-les-Bains

From Bayonne, one road into the heart of the Basque country is the D22, the beautiful **Route Impériale des Cimes**, built in the time of Napoleon over the hilltops. Otherwise, the main D932 up the Nivelle valley leads to Cambo-les-Bains, a genteel spa that became briefly fashionable when Napoléon III, Eugénie and the Prince of Wales visited from Biarritz, the latter to see a legendary *pelote* star named Chiquito de Cambo play. Cambo's attraction is the **Villa Arnaga** (*open April–Sept daily 10–7*), the home of dramatist Edmond Rostand, who came here to treat his pleurisy. The house contains mementoes from his life and the Paris of the turn of the last century; the real attraction is the splendid 18th-century-style French gardens.

St-Jean-Pied-de-Port

This town's real name in Basque is *Donihane Garazi*. The French name is even more curious, but port is an old mountain word for a pass, and St-Jean stands at the foot of the pass of Roncevaux, the 'Gate of Spain' of medieval legend. From the 8th century, Arab armies passed this way to raid France; Charlemagne and Roland came back the other way to raid Spain, and passed into legend along the way. Pilgrims from all over Europe came through on their way to Compostela, and another visitor, Richard Cœur

Roland the Rotter

All over the south of France, the very mountains and rocks carry the memory of Roland. His fame spread across Europe, remembered in everything from Ariosto's epic *Orlando Furioso* to the mysterious statue of 'Roland the Giant' in front of Bremen city hall. But who is this Roland really? Outside the *Chanson de Roland*, information is scarce. The chronicler Eginhardt, writing *c.* 830, mentions a Roland, Duke of the Marches of Brittany, who perished in the famous ambush in the Pyrenees in the year 778. Two hundred years later, this obscure incident had blossomed into one of the great epics of medieval Europe. Here is the mighty hero, with his wise companion in arms Oliver. He is the most *puissant* knight in the army of his uncle Charlemagne, come down from the north to crusade against the heathen Muslims of Spain. Charlemagne swept all before him, burning Pamplona to the ground before coming to grief at an unsuccessful siege of Zaragoza. On their return, Roland and Oliver, with the rearguard, are trapped at the pass of Roncevaux, thanks to a tip from Roland's jealous stepfather Ganelon. Though outnumbered, the French cut down Saracens like General Custer or John Wayne against the savage Injuns. Finally Roland, cut with a hundred wounds, sounds his horn Oliphant to warn Charlemagne and the main army, alas too far away to rescue them.

History says it wasn't a Muslim horde at all, but rather the Basques who did Roland in. And why shouldn't they get their revenge on these uncouth Franks who were devastating their lands, trying to force this democratic nation to kneel before some crowned foreign thug? We might excuse a people who did not even have a word for 'king' if they were not impressed with Charlemagne or his duke. How this affair metamorphosed into an epic will never be known, but tales and songs must have spread and refined themselves, until the caterpillar Roland of history re-emerged into the written word as the mythological butterfly of the *Chanson*. As in many epics from Virgil to El Cid, a modicum of propaganda is involved. For the French, up in Paris, glorification of Carolingian imperialism provided poetic justification for the expansionist dreams of the medieval Capetian kings. And replacing the embattled Basque farmers with bejewelled infidel knights makes perfect sense: the time of the *Chanson* also witnessed the beginning of the Crusades.

de Lion, put the original town – now nearby St-Jean-le-Vieux – to siege in 1177. When he took it, that most pitiless of warriors razed it to the ground; the kings of Navarre refounded St-Jean on its present site soon after.

St-Jean today makes more of its living from visitors; it's the main centre for mountain tourism in the Basque lands. Old houses with wooden balconies hang over the little river, and facing the bridge stands the church of **Notre-Dame**, founded by Sancho the Strong of Navarre in commemoration of the battle of Navas de Tolosa (1212), where the Christian Spaniards finally put an end to Muslim dominance of the peninsula. The streets climb up from here to the so-called **Prison des Evêques** (*open April–Nov daily 10–7*). The house in fact seems to have belonged to a merchant. The bishops who lived in the mansion above it *c.* 1400 weren't exactly kosher – supporters of the Antipope at Avignon during the great Schism – and the chains and

Tourist Information

St-Jean-Pied-de-Port: Place Charles-de-Gaulle,
t 05 59 37 03 57.

Where to Stay and Eat

St-Jean-Pied-de-Port ✉ 64220
Hôtel Central, Place Charles de Gaulle, t 05 59
37 00 22 (*inexpensive*). An old family hotel
and restaurant (*expensive–moderate*) with
views over the River Nive, which yields such
delights as salmon and eels for the table.
Closed Dec–Feb.
★★Ramuntcho, 1 Rue France, t 05 59 37 03 91
(*inexpensive*). One of the nicest places to
stay in the old town, just inside the Porte de
France. Rooms have balconies and a view.
The restaurant (*moderate*) serves good
simple dishes. *Closed 15 Nov–26 Dec; restaurant closed Tues and Wed in Jan and Feb;* .
Les Pyrénées, Place Général de Gaulle, t 05 59
37 01 01 (*very expensive–expensive*). A hotel
restaurant that is one of the most esteemed
culinary temples in all the Basque country.
People come from miles around for cooking
that, while not notably innovative, brings
the typical Basque-Gascon repertoire of
duck, *foie gras* and game dishes to perfection; they're especially noted for their
desserts. *Closed Mon eve Nov–Mar and Tues
exc July–Sept. plus 20 Nov–22 Dec.*

shackles in the cellar wall were probably used by local authorities in the 18th century
to lock up poor peasants who didn't pay their salt tax.

Just east stands St-Jean's original, **St-Jean-le-Vieux**. The town destroyed by the
Lionheart has only the Romanesque tympanum of its church to remind it of its
former importance. North of St-Jean-le-Vieux on a height above the D933, a venerable
stone pillar with a cross is known as the **Croix de Ganelon**, supposedly the spot where
Roland's treacherous stepfather was pulled apart by wild horses on Charlemagne's
command. South of St-Jean, the D933 leads down to the Spanish border and, 16km
beyond that, the cold, misty **pass of Roncevaux** itself.

Béarn

The Béarn, once an independent state, is a stalwart Ruritania, an isolated region
known for its grazing land. The scenery is terrific, not only in the Pyrenees, but looking
at them from the intensely green rolling foothills. Most of Béarn is contained in the
valleys of two impetuous rivers, the Gave d'Oloron and the Gave de Pau. Pau, the
resort of the Victorian British, has grown into one of the liveliest cities of the southwest. From Pau's famous balcony, you can see Béarn's choice stretch of mountains.

Along the Gaves de Pau and d'Oloron

Peyrehorade and Around

For centuries, this river town was Béarn's window on the world. Now it's a time
capsule, with a pretty riverfront boulevard, and the ruined 13th-century Château
d'Aspromonte on a hill. To the south is **Bidache**, which by some quirk owed no allegiance to the viscount nor the king of France, and remained practically independent
up to the Revolution. Today, it offers the visitor the romantically ruined **Château de
Gramont** (*open June–Sept daily 2.30–6.30, exc Mon in Sept; the birds fly at 3.30 and*

5pm; adm), home of trained eagles, vultures, falcons and kites. For a surprise, take the D29 east to **Sorde**, where a Roman villa metamorphosed into a Benedictine **abbey** (*open April–mid-Nov Tues–Sun 10.30–12 and 2.30–6.30; mid-Nov–Mar Mon–Fri 9–12 and 1.30–4.30*) during the Dark Ages: the abbot's residence occupies the central part of the ancient Roman villa. Its mosaics are excellently preserved, with fresh colours.

Salies-de-Béarn

Salies may be the loveliest town in Béarn, a vision of steep-gabled houses overlooking the River Saleys. 'Salt City', they call it, and ever since Roman times an endless supply of the ever-popular NaCl has made its fortune. A mighty underground source, seven times saltier than the sea, once poured out enough water to make the area a saline swamp. Nearly everyone lived from salt, collecting the water, boiling it down, and carting the precious mineral off to the warehouse. Undercut by competition in the 19th century, Salies found new life by becoming a spa.

A walk through the old town is a delight. By Place du Bayaa, with the bronze boar's head fountain, are two small museums: a **Musée des Arts et Traditions Locales** (*open mid-May–mid-Oct Tues–Sat 3–6*), and, on Rue des Puits-Salants, a **Musée du Sel** (*open as above*), where you can learn everything you wanted to know about salt in the old

Tourist Information

Peyrehorade: *mairie*, 147 Quai du Sablot, **t** 05 58 73 00 52.
Salies-de-Béarn: Rue des Bains, **t** 05 59 38 00 33, *www.bearn-gaves.com*.
Sauveterre-de-Béarn: Place Royale, **t** 05 59 38 58 65, *www.bearn-gaves.com*.
Orthez: Rue du Bourg Vieux, **t** 05 59 69 02 75/ **t** 05 59 69 37 50, *www.mairie-orthez.fr*.

Where to Stay and Eat

Salies ✉ 64270

**Hôtel du Golf, t 05 59 65 02 10 (*inexpensive*). A posh-looking place with reasonable rates, a golf course and a good restaurant.
*Hélios, Domaine d'Hélios, **t** 05 59 38 37 59 (*inexpensive*). In the same complex as the Hôtel du Golf, but less expensive, with a garden setting and use of the golf course.
La Terrasse, Rue Saley, across from the church on Rue l'Oumé, **t** 05 59 38 09 83 (*moderate–cheap*). For *confits* and suchlike. *Closed Feb, Mon, and Tues eve.*

Sauveterre-de-Béarn ✉ 64390

*Hostellerie du Château, Rue Bérard, **t** 05 59 38 52 10 (*cheap*). An excellent-value hotel; the

pretty rooms have a view over the valley and it has an equally good restaurant.

Orthez ✉ 64300

La Reine Jeanne, behind the tourist office on Rue du Bourg-Vieux, **t 05 59 67 00 76, *www.reine-jeanne.fr* (*inexpensive*). Pleasant, simple rooms; the same can be said of the restaurant (*moderate*), where you can have *truite saumonée* and braised duck. *Closed 2 weeks Feb–Mar.*
Auberge du Relais, just west of Orthez, on the D933 at Berenxin, **t 05 59 65 30 56, *www.auberge-du-relais.com* (*inexpensive*). In a rustic setting with a park and swimming pool; the restaurant (*moderate–cheap*) has an outdoor terrace. *Closed Sat exc July and Aug.*
Auberge St-Loup, 20 Rue du Pont Vieux, **t** 05 59 69 15 40 (*expensive–moderate*). Orthez's longtime favourite restaurant has had its cuisine revitalized by a new young chef; duck is the star of the menu – as *confits*, *aiguillettes*, in pies and everything else you could do to a quacker; also lots of interesting seafood dishes. Summer dining is in a pretty garden courtyard; it's just across the river near the medieval bridge. *Closed Sun eve, Mon, and Nov.*

days. Many of the old half-timber houses still have the outdoor basins called *coulédés*, where they kept their salt. The **spa area** is set in a park on the north edge of town. Besides the parfait-striped Moorish bathhouse, there is the old casino, now a library, a Victorian bandstand, and the Hôtel du Parc, worth a look for its spectacular lobby.

Sauveterre-de-Béarn

A *sauveterre* was supposed to be a place of peace, exempt from all the terrors of feudal warfare; all the local barons, counts and dukes would promise to leave it alone. To show just how successfully this worked in practice, here is Sauveterre-de-Béarn, with the most imposing fortifications of any town in the region. Viscount Centulle IV gave this *sauveterre* its charter in 1080, and for the next two centuries it prospered, as evidenced by the ambitious Romanesque church of **St-André**. But the real attraction of Sauveterre is its lovely setting on the wooded banks of the Gave d'Oloron, where you can see the town's landmark, a fortified, half-demolished medieval bridge called the **Pont de la Légende**.

L'Hôpital-St-Blaise and its Moorish Church

L'Hôpital-St-Blaise may be little more than a few houses in a clearing south of Gurs, but do stop for the unusual and beautiful 12th-century church of **St-Blaise**. Its Greek plan with its central dome is enough of a surprise, but so is the delicate stone lattice-work that fills some of the windows, an art that was popular in Islamic Spain. Doubtless the architects came from Spain, and they skilfully wove Andalucian elements into the Byzantine plan: lobed arches in the apse, and a dome made of four pairs of round arches, interlaced to form an eight-pointed star. Among the few carved decorations, note one very un-Christian symbol, the Pythagorean pentagram on the left transept. The village has cobbled together an endearingly screwy home-made *son et lumière* to entertain you; just drop a coin in the box by the door.

Orthez

After seeing half a medieval bridge in Sauveterre, you might like to have a look at a whole one. Gaston Fébus spent much of his time here; Froissart, the chronicler of the Hundred Years War, wrote of Fébus's sophisticated court, with 'knights and squires coming and going, talking of arms and love', and where all the news from Scotland to Spain passed over the dinner table. Orthez was wakened from its dream with a start in 1569, when Protestant soldiers burned the place to the ground.

Orthez's centre having moved away from the river, this beautiful fortified bridge is now hard to find – go to the end of Rue du Bourg-Vieux, and take a right into Rue des Aiguilletiers. Fébus built it, c. 1370, but it was heavily restored after damage by Wellington's army in 1814. Note the little window in the central tower; this was medieval Orthez's garbage disposal – everything was simply tossed out into the Gave de Pau. The Protestants of 1569 expanded on the concept, using the window to dispose of all the town's priests and nuns.

In the centre, the tourist office is in the **Maison de Jeanne d'Albret**, a restored 15th–18th-century mansion. Beyond this, in Rue Moncade is the charming **Hôtel de la**

Lune, where Froissart stayed when he visited Gaston Fébus's court in 1388. Further out, Rue Moncade becomes the spine of a medieval bourg that grew up around the castle of the Béarn viscounts. Only the tall, five-sided keep, the **Tour Moncade**, survives, and the great hall of Gaston Fébus, who unintentionally killed his only son and heir here, in one of Froissart's more chilling stories from the Hundred Years War.

Pau

Pau has the air of a Ruritanian capital, from the 14th century when Gaston Fébus made it his chief seat in Béarn. Henri IV was born there, but after Louis XIII seized Béarn in 1640 Pau dwindled into a medieval relic. In the hotels and shops, however, you may see old Victorian hunting prints, a reminder of Pau's days as the Gascon outpost of the British Empire. The trend started with some of Wellington's veterans, who retired here, but the real impetus came with a Scottish doctor named Taylor, who

Getting Around

You can **fly** to Pau from the UK with Ryanair. The **rail** station, with connections to Bordeaux, Tarbes and Lourdes, is by the river, underneath the Boulevard des Pyrénées on Av Jean Biray. For the coast and the mountain villages, **buses** leave from Place Clemenceau. The **TPR** line (t 05 59 82 95 85) has frequent services to Salies-de-Béarn-Bayonne-Biarritz, Nay-Lourdes, Mauléon, Monein, Mourenx and Orthez (via Lescar). There are also services to Tarbes, Mont-de-Marsan, Oloron and up the Gave d'Ossau to Laruns and Gourette.

Tourist Information

Pau: Place Royale, t 05 59 27 27 08, *www.pau.fr*

Where to Stay

Pau ✉ 64000

★★★**Roncevaux**, 25 Rue Louis-Barthou, just off Place Royale, t 05 59 27 08 44, *www.hotel-roncevaux.com* (*moderate*). Comfortable, quiet and reasonably priced.

★★★**Bristol**, 3 Rue Gambetta, t 05 59 27 72 98 (*inexpensive*). On the posher end of the scale, the Bristol is as old-fashioned as its name, and similar to the Roncevaux, above.

★★★**Hôtel Montpensier**, 36 Rue Montpensier, t 05 59 27 42 42, *www.hotelmontpensier.fr*

(*inexpensive*). A charming, old-fashioned place; although there is no restaurant, meals are available to order.

★★**Grand Hôtel du Commerce**, 9 Rue Maréchal Joffre, t 05 59 27 24 40 (*inexpensive*). A traditional hotel close to the castle with a decent restaurant (*moderate*).

Eating Out

Le Viking, 33 Bd Tourasse, t 05 59 84 02 91 (*expensive–moderate*). A rustic and intimate little restaurant, treating local produce with style; try their stuffed courgette flowers with *cèpes* or *poires williams* with Jurançon wine for dessert. *Closed Sat and Sun lunch, and Mon.*

Au Fin Gourmet, 24 Av. Gaston-Lacoste, down below the Boulevard des Pyrénées, t 05 59 27 47 71 (*expensive–moderate*). For more ambitious dining. Fried crayfish tails with orange come specially recommended.

Restaurant La Brochetterie, 16 Rue Henri-IV, t 05 59 27 40 33 (*moderate*). Very popular for its grilled duck and spit roasted pig and lamb. *Closed Mon.*

Chez Pierre, 16 Rue Louis-Barthou, t 05 59 27 76 86 (*moderate*). A firm favourite, considered 'très British' with its golf clubs over the bar, but serving firmly southwest French cuisine, notably *foie gras* and Béarnais *cassoulet*. *Closed Sun, and Mon and Tues lunch.*

in 1869 wrote a book called *The Climate of Pau*. Pau became one of the star resorts of Europe. The British built the first golf course on the continent, along with a race track and a casino; they established cricket and hunt clubs, fancy milliners' shops and tea rooms. Then fashion moved to Biarritz. For a while, Pau struggled on, as Parisians replaced the Anglo-Saxons; a few even learned to play cricket and drink tea.

Pau's old centre is a delightful place, a lively pedestrian zone of restaurants and cafés around **Nouste Henric's castle** (*open for guided tours only Jan–Mar daily 9.30–11.45 and 2–4.15; April–mid-June and mid-Sept–Oct daily till 5; mid-June–mid-Sept daily 9.30–12.15 and 1.30–5.45; closed hols; adm*), a vision of Renaissance turrets and gables, like a château on the Loire. It is entered through a carved marble triple arch; beyond this is the courtyard, the heart of the residential palace. In 1620, after the conquest of Béarn, Louis XIII took its contents to Paris and made the castle a prison. Restored by Viollet-le-Duc in the 1830s, enough of the original furnishings have been reassembled to make the tour worth the trouble. The highlight is **King Henri's Cradle**: in 1553, Jeanne d'Albret had rushed back home from the north so the heir to Gascony could be born in Pau, and the affair was so hurried that no one could find a proper cradle – so Jeanne used a big tortoise's shell, now displayed here in a charming shrine.

The cliffs above the Gave de Pau give the city its most memorable embellishment, the **Boulevard des Pyrénées**, providing a dreamy panorama over a 50-mile stretch of mountains and the wooded foothills. But beware: its charms can be dangerous. Charles Maurras, the writer and politician, had a kind of mystic experience here in the 1880s, when he first realized 'the natural necessity of submission for the order and beauty of the world'. He went on to found the fascist Action Française, and he ended his life in prison as a Vichy collaborator.

The **Musée des Beaux Arts**, 10 Rue Mathieu Lalanne (*open Wed–Mon 10–12 and 2–6; closed Tues; adm*), is a surprisingly good collection. The majority of the paintings are 18th- and 19th-century French, with Pyrenean landscapes well represented, but there is also an odd night scene by Luca Giordano, an equally unexpected *Last Judgement* from Rubens, even an El Greco, the *Ecstasy of St Francis*. Perhaps the best-known work is a classic of Degas, the *Cotton Brokers' Office in New Orleans*.

There isn't much else in Pau. The city's churches were wrecked by Protestant fanatic Jeanne d'Albret, but there is another museum, dedicated to Jean-Baptiste Bernadotte. A soldier who worked himself up through the ranks to become a confidant of Napoleon, Bernadotte fell out with the emperor over his warmongering. The heirless king of Sweden made him an adopted son, and Bernadotte wound up leading troops against Napoleon in the Russian campaign. In 1826 he assumed the Swedish throne, and ruled for 26 years as Charles XIV, ancestor of the kings who rule today. The **Musée Bernadotte** (*open 10–12 and 2–6 pm, closed Mon*) contains personal relics and period furniture. In the same neighbourhood, some of the villas of the English survive on the streets off Rue Montpensier.

North of Pau: the Vic-Bilh

Looking at a relief map, you'll see how the tremendous run-off from the Pyrenees creates wild landscapes of narrow, closely packed parallel valleys. Nowhere is this more pronounced than in the area between Pau and Aire-sur-l'Adour, the tract of deepest Gascony people call the Vic-Bilh, the 'old country'. There are no trains, few buses, and no main routes through it.

Oloron-Ste-Marie, the Vallée d'Aspe and the Vallée d'Ossau

Oloron-Ste-Marie

Oloron, gateway to the Béarnais Pyrenees, was burnt by the Normans, then reappeared as twin towns, Oloron on its high hill and Ste-Marie, a medieval bourg across the river. This has a typically bastard French **cathedral**: Romanesque in front, Gothic behind and a little of everything else mixed in. But the portal is a remarkable flight of medieval fantasy in the style of Moissac. It has two remarkable *voussures*. One is

Tourist Information

Oloron-Ste-Marie: Allées du Comte de Tréville, t 05 59 39 98 00, *www.ot-oloron-ste-marie.fr*.

Accous: Moulin Bladé, on the N 134, t 05 59 34 71 48.

Laruns: Maison de la Vallée d'Ossau, t 05 59 05 31 41/t 05 59 05 35 49.

Where to Stay and Eat

Oloron-Ste-Marie ✉ 64400

Hôtel du Commerce, Place des Casernes, 64910 Navarrenx, t 05 59 66 50 16, *www.hotel-commerce.fr* (*inexpensive*). Beautiful, traditional Béarnais house – rustic with exposed beams throughout – yet modern and comfortable. Restaurant (*moderate*) offers a good mix of regional and *nouvelle cuisine: cabillaud à l'andouille de Navarrenx* or *magret de canard* in honey. *Closed Oct.*

Hôtel des Voyageurs, Urdos, t 05 59 34 88 05 (*inexpensive*). The last place before the border. Traditional, regional menus (*moderate–cheap*). *Closed end Oct–early Dec.*

Château de Boués, about 6km out of town on the D155 off the D918, t 05 59 39 95 49 (*inexpensive*). Lovely château with a few rooms.

St-Christau ✉ 64660

***Au Bon Coin, on the D 918 (Route des Thermes), t 05 59 34 40 12 (*moderate–*

inexpensive). Modern hotel in a lovely forest setting. In this perfect isolation, there are pretty rooms at reasonable rates, a pool, gardens and an excellent restaurant (*expensive–moderate*) serving both simple Béarnais favourites and some surprising seafood dishes – from peppers with crabmeat to lobster lasagne. *Closed Sun eve and Mon.*

The Upper Aspe Valley

Maison de l'Ours, Etsaut, t 05 59 34 86 38 (*inexpensive*). Rooms and meals are offered, along with nature walks and other activities.

Laruns and Environs ✉ 64440

**Hôtel de la Poste, Eaux-Bonnes, t 05 59 05 33 06, *www.hotel-de-la-poste.com* (*inexpensive*). Ten nice rooms and a restaurant (*moderate–cheap*) with dishes such as salmon terrine and grilled lamb *persillade*. *Closed mid-Oct–8 May.*

*Le Glacier, t 05 59 05 10 18, *www.leglacier.fr.st* (*inexpensive*). The ski station at Gourette, high up at the Col d'Aubisque, can be a pain to reach but it promises some memorable scenery. The hotels up there are modern and all of a piece; Le Glacier is the cheapest.

Auberge Bellevue, Rue de Bourguet, Laruns, t 05 59 05 31 58 (*moderate*). One of the best places in the mountains, where you can have a fine Béarnais *garbure* or a *confit* at very reasonable prices. *Closed Jan and June, and Tues eve and Wed in winter.*

carved with the 24 Elders of the Apocalypse; the other recalls the parable from Matthew:22 about the preparations for a wedding feast. The joys of heaven are described in Gascon terms: they're hunting boar, fishing for salmon, bringing in wine and cheeses. At the top of the arch, a demon underlines the point that 'many are called but few are chosen'. On the tympanum, by a different artist, is the Descent from the Cross. On the right, the statue on horseback is Constantine, representing the true faith (some say he's really Gaston IV of Béarn). The trumeau between the doors shows two Saracen captives, perhaps an allusion to Gaston IV's successes in the Crusades. Inside, the choir and apses are impressive Flamboyant Gothic work. If it's near Christmas, you can see the cathedral's elaborate crèche, carved in about 1700.

Modern Oloron spreads along three valleys, where the Gave d'Aspe and Gave d'Ossau come together to make the **Gave d'Oloron**. The Gave d'Ossau bridge is a 13th-century original, while the Pont de Ste-Claire over the Gave d'Aspe was an early iron work of Gustave Eiffel. Between the two bridges, you can take the formidably steep Rue Dalmais up to the **Quartier Ste-Croix**, the acropolis of medieval Oloron. The square around the church was the site of the important fair in the Middle Ages; parts of the market hall survive. Restorations disfigured Ste-Croix's exterior, but there is some good Romanesque carving on the apses. The interior rises to a splendid Moorish dome in the form of an eight-pointed star, like the one in l'Hôpital-St-Blaise. Carvings on the capitals are a full illustrated Bible, including Salome's Dance.

The Vallée d'Aspe

From here the N134 follows the Gave d'Aspe to the pass, the Col du Somport, from the Latin *summus portus*, the 'highest gate'. The first place of interest is **St-Christau**, its waters a sure cure for skin diseases; it was one of the first spas of France, and the first to be forgotten. What's left of it stands in a quiet clearing around a stately building called the Rotonde built over the source in the 1630s. From here the serious mountains begin; the N134 continues south through a dramatic gorge, the **Défilé d'Escot**, and then skirts the charming village of **Sarrance** with its chapel, a place of pilgrimage since the 1400s. Kings have visited, and Marguerite d'Angoulême set the frame story here for her collection of tales, the *Heptaméron*.

Around **Bedous**, the green hills give way to stark grey cliffs, and there may be a chill in the air even in summer; Bedous isn't much, but it's proud to be the birthplace of the explorer Pierre Laclede, founder of St Louis, Missouri. **Lescun**, high above the valley, offers the greatest natural attraction of the area, the spectacular **Cirque de Lescun**. Back on the N134, at the tiny village of **Etsaut** is the **Maison du Parc** (*t 05 59 05 41 59*), information centre for this part of the Parc National des Pyrénées. Etsaut also has another nature centre, the **Museum of the Bear** (*open mid-June–mid-Oct 9.30–12.30 and 2–6.30*). Just across the road from Etsaut, **Borce** is the one hamlet in this part of the Pyrenees that never suffered from fires or wars. It is also the home of a celebrity: Jojo, a bear found by local children in 1985, when he was a lost cub.

The most curious stretch of the GR10, the **Chemin de la Mâture**, meets the highway a little further south. Pyrenean pines made the longest and straightest masts France could get. The Chemin, built at tremendous expense in the 1860s, was nothing more

This Valley is Doomed

While you're here, take a minute to think the unthinkable. Imagine a four-lane highway, lined with heavy trucks, running up the middle of the Vallée d'Aspe, and then through a 5-mile tunnel under the Col de Somport into Spain. Imagine also that your EU tax money is going to help pay for it. This plan has been in the works for a long time, and has proved hard to stop – the road on the Spanish side is already finished. The plan has become the one of the biggest environmental issues in France. The Aspois themselves are divided; many businessmen and landowners just can't wait, while most people are bitterly opposed to what they see as the total destruction of their home and their way of life.

The anti-road campaign found an unexpected ally – the Pyrenean brown bear. Only two decades ago, villages paid bounties for bears; now the government has banned all hunting, and reimburses herdsmen for any sheep the bears nab at double their value. It is probably too late. The handful of surviving bears (a dozen or so) may not be enough to breed successfully. They are the last in France. As a symbol of something wild and free in a Europe that is becoming increasingly flattened into suburbia, the bears have caught the public's fancy. There is still hope; the roadworks have been on the government's schedule for five years now, but it hasn't happened yet.

than a long steep slide, down which the trunks would go to the valley on rollers. Following the GR10 this way will bring you to the striking mountain lakes, the Lacs d'Ayous, all under the pyramidal 9,573ft **Pic du Midi d'Ossau**.

The Vallée d'Ossau

Closer to the heart of the Pyrenees, this valley is a little wilder than the Aspe. The people who live here, a self-governing community of shepherds, claim to be a race apart, and some have speculated that they are direct descendants of the Celtiberians. Coming from the direction of either Oloron or Pau, you'll first pass **Arudy**, centre of the Pyrenean marble trade. Here the **Maison d'Ossau** (*open July and Aug daily 10–12 and 3–6; Jan–June and Sept Tues–Fri 2–5; Oct–Dec Sun only 3–6; adm*) provides an introduction to the valley, including exhibits on nature and traditions of the area

At **Béon** and **Aste**, steep winding roads lead up to the marble quarries; here you can also visit **La Falaise aux Vautours** (*open June–Aug daily 10.30–12.30 and 2–6.30; May and Sept daily 2.30–6.30; adm*), an observation centre (with cameras hidden on the cliffs and interactive computers) for the many birds of prey that live around the mountaintops: kites, eagles, buzzard, and the rarer lammergeyer, and since 1998, Egyptian vultures. **Laruns**, the little capital of the Ossau, won't detain you, unless you come on 15 August when everyone's in traditional costume for the valley's big festival.

Seven km south of Laruns, a narrow dead-end road to the right leads into the Gorges du Bitet, a narrow defile full of waterfalls. **Gabas** is the usual base for ascending the Pic du Midi. The Little Train of Artouste begins at **Artouste**, a ski resort south of Gabas; built for dam-workers, the train with its open carriages has become a tourist attraction, and makes its scenic 11km run year-round (*book, t 05 59 05 34 00*). To reach it, take the *téléphérique* near the Lac de Fabrèges up to the rail terminal.

Lourdes

Even a century ago, honest souls like Emile Zola were disgusted by the holy circus of Lourdes. But in our times, when vulgarity and commercialism crasser than Lourdes are on the television any night of the week, being shocked isn't so easy. And it's hard to be dismissive about a place that means so much to so many sincere people. The pilgrims in fact upstage Lourdes itself: coachloads of chattering Italian housewives, youngsters with guitars who have walked or hitched from Ireland; youth groups from Missouri. It's not uncommon to hear them singing in the streets.

Apparitions of the Virgin are common in the Pyrenees, and Bernadette's visions in 1858 would probably not have made much of a stir but for two factors. First, the spring soon developed a reputation for curing hopeless cases. Second, anti-clericalism

Getting There and Around

Come on a religious holiday and your introduction to Lourdes will be the sight of cars parked along the main roads for miles. At other times, it will always be hard to park around the central hotels (try around the market and *mairie*). The no. 1 **city bus** shuttles between the rail station and the Grotte. Lourdes also has good **bus** connections to the Pyrenean valleys: there are at least eight buses a day up the valley to Argelès and Cauterets, slightly fewer to Luz and Barèges.

Tourist Information

Lourdes: Place Peyramale, **t** 05 62 42 77 40, *www.lourdes-france.com*.

Where to Stay

Lourdes ✉ 65100

In France, only Paris has more rooms. Nearly all close in winter and require half-board.

★★★★**Grand Hôtel de la Grotte**, 66 Rue de la Grotte, **t** 05 62 94 58 87, *www.hotel-grotte. com* (*expensive–moderate*). Traditional grand hotel just below the château, with rooms overlooking the basilica. *Closed Nov–Mar.*

★★★**Moderne**, Av Bernadette Soubirous, **t** 05 62 94 12 32, *www.hotelmodernelourdes. com* (*expensive–moderate*). Another real palace of the Belle Epoque. *Closed Dec–Mar.*

Hôtel Beauséjour, 16 Av de la Gare, **t** 05 62 94 38 18, *www.hotel-beausejour.com* (*moderate*). Fine old hotel opposite the

station. Totally renovated with classy, modern and comfortable interior. Rooms at the front are large but can be noisy. There is a brasserie (*moderate–cheap*) with garden and terrace. *Open all year.*

★★**Hôtel Majestic**, 9 Av Maransin, **t** 05 62 94 27 23 (*inexpensive*). A good option not far from the shrines, with comfortable rooms, a terrace and simple restaurant. *Closed Nov–mid-April.*

St-Savin, Rue des Pyrénées, **t** 05 62 94 06 07 (*inexpensive*). Neat rooms on a street where you might even find parking. *Open all year.*

★★**Le Virginia**, Adé, 5km north of Lourdes on the N 21, **t** 05 62 94 66 18 (*inexpensive*). A motel outside the centre with separate cottages and a restaurant (*moderate*). *Restaurant open all year.*

Eating Out

Le Magret, 10 Rue des 4 Frères-Soulas, **t** 05 62 94 20 55 (*expensive–moderate*). Worth a visit for good unpretentious local cuisine and southwest wines. *Closed Mon and Jan.*

Pizzeria da Marco, Rue de la Grotte (*cheap*). An inexpensive oasis for Italian pilgrims (most of whom are convinced that French food is inedible, though they say the wine isn't bad), with Italian pasta and wines. *Closed Mon, and Sat lunch.*

A La Petite Bergère, Bartrès, **t** 05 62 94 04 28 (*moderate–cheap*). It's worth travelling out to Bartrès for the food at La Petite Bergère. On the garden terrace, you can try lamb and chicken dishes, shad and salmon, prepared in often surprising ways. *Closed Wed.*

Bernadette

Bernadette Soubirous was 14 years old, a sickly, asthmatic girl in a religious family that had come down in the world, reduced to living in a hovel that had once been a prison cell. On 11 February 1858, Bernadette, her sister and a friend went out to the 'old cave', Massabielle, to gather scraps of wood. To reach the spot, a shallow canal had to be crossed. Bernadette, worried about her asthma, stayed behind. There, at about 1pm, she felt a warm breeze that seemed to caress her face. Then the vision manifested itself. A 'girl', as Bernadette first described her, spoke kindly in Gascon, telling her 'three secrets', and directing her to dig in the cave, where the miraculous spring came forth.

Bernadette's talkative sister soon spread the word around. Crowds began gathering around the spring. The Virgin appeared three more times to Bernadette, and to many others as well. By April a kind of hysteria had taken over Lourdes, and miracles could not be far behind. The first was bestowed on Louis Bouriette; blind in one eye, he procured some mud from around the spring and made a compress of it, and regained his sight. Newspapers picked up on the story, and Lourdes became a very busy place. Throughout the carnival that followed, Bernadette seemed to be the only one to keep her head. She continued to have her visions, and described them politely to anyone who troubled to ask; that was all.

Bernadette entered a convent up north in Nevers in 1866, where she led a secluded life. Always subject to ill health, she died there in 1879, at the age of only 35. A movement for canonization sprang up immediately, and in 1933 Bernadette was made a saint. As for her role in history and religion, her own wishes sum it up best: 'The less people say about me,' she once said, 'the better.'

and free thinking were in the ascendant everywhere, and such a simple country miracle proved a tonic for the faith. Massive promotion of the pilgrimage began in the 1870s, after the Paris Commune and the end of papal rule in Rome. The Church saw itself and society in crisis, and Lourdes was the response. Within a few years, Lourdes had become what it is now: the biggest (if not the most dignified) Christian pilgrimage site in the world, drawing over five million visitors a year.

The Cité Religieuse

When the pilgrims are in town, the Boulevard de la Grotte is the closest thing the Pyrenees can offer to a North African souk – jam packed with people chatting in every imaginable tongue, and vast heaps of sea-shell shrines, medallions, Virgin Mary toaster covers, gargantuan rhinestone rosaries, and gilt plastic-framed magic pictures that show Bernadette in the grotto when you look one way, and a smirking pope when you look the other.

After running the gauntlet, you'll cross the little bridge over the Gave de Pau and enter the '**Domaine de la Grotte**' – no shorts or beach clothes, no dogs, no smoking. Everything is impeccably organized, as it has to be, and there are guides, maps and signposts everywhere, along with visitors' centres that speak every language known to Catholicism. The Domaine begins with the pretty **Esplanade des Processions**, with room for 40,000 people – and it's often full in the evening. At the end of this stands the **Basilique du Rosaire**, built in 1883. Unlike the souvenirs, this bit of kitsch fails to amuse. The 'Romanesque-Byzantine' style, invented in 19th-century France, undoubtedly marks the low point of Christian sacred architecture, a degenerate parody of the medieval Age of Faith; Emile Zola found it 'ugly enough to make one cry'. The frescoes and mosaics within match the architecture perfectly.

Even when it was new the Basilica often proved too small to accommodate the crowds, but not until the 1950s was a larger facility built. The chilly **Underground Basilica Pius X**, to the left of the Esplanade, seats 20,000. Walk around the back of the Basilique du Rosaire to see where it all started, the little **Grotte de Massabielle**, and the adjoining spring, where the water that doesn't get packed into little bottles is channelled into pools to bathe the sick. Up above on the hillside, pilgrims trek a **Calvaire** made of giant bronze statues.

Roadside Attractions and More Mysteries

Beyond the *cité religieuse* Lourdes has a formidable array of holy sites and dubious 'museums' to entertains its pilgrims. Among many others, there's the **Musée de Lourdes**, at the car park L'Egalité (*open April–Oct daily 9–11.45 (Sun from 10) and 1.30–6.15; adm*), with dioramas of little Bernadette's vision and village life in the 1850s. Of course there's also a branch of the **Musée Grévin** (*87 Rue de la Grotte; open April–Oct daily 9–11.30 and 1.30–6.30; also July and Aug evenings 8.30–10pm; adm*), with more of the same, along with Jesus and 12 pasty-faced Apostles reproducing Leonardo's *Last Supper*. And if you can stand any more, there's the **Musée de la Nativité** (*21 Quai St-Jean; open Easter–Nov daily 9–12 and 1.30–7; July and Aug also 8.30pm–10pm; adm*), and the **Musée du Petit Lourdes** (*67 Av Peyramale; open April–Oct daily 9am–7pm; April–June and mid-Sept–Oct closed lunch; adm*), with the village of Bernadette's time in miniature and some toy trains. On Rue des Petits-Fossés, a building that was once a prison and later the home of Bernadette's family can be visited: **Le Cachot**, 'the cell' (*open May–Sept daily 9–12 and 2–7; Oct–April daily 3–5*).

Visitors also like to take trips up the mountains that fringe the town; you can ride to the top of the 3,081ft Pic du Jer on a **funicular railway**; there is a grand view, and **caves** to explore near the summit (*open daily 10–6; adm includes fare and cave visit; www.picdujer.info*).

The High Pyrenees

Tarbes

Almost half the 220,000 people of the Hautes-Pyrénées live in or around this grey, unfathomable toadstool of a departmental capital. Among all the cities of southern France Tarbes is the one most sadly wanting in personality (Salon-de-Provence comes in a close second). For all its industry and bureaucrats, Tarbes is really just a big market town, and its liveliest corner is **Place Marcadieu**, with metal *halles* built in 1880. The

Getting There and Around

Tarbes-Lourdes **airport**, halfway between the two cities, has a daily flight from Paris on Air France; **t** 05 62 32 92 22.

Another easy way to get into the region is the **TGV** from Paris. Tarbes is also the hub for **buses**; most start from Place du Forail near the market (**t** 05 62 34 76 69). There are at least a dozen a day to Lourdes, and many to Argelès, Arrens and Pierrefitte; others go to Bagnères and a few to Pau.

Tourist Information

Tarbes: 3 Cours Gambetta, **t** 05 62 51 30 31, *www.tarbes.com*.

Where to Stay and Eat

Tarbes ✉ **65000**

★★★Hôtel l'Aragon, Juillan, on the D921 towards Lourdes, **t** 05 62 32 07 07, *www. hotel-aragon.com* (*moderate*). A modern but gracious establishment set in spacious gardens. Even if you don't stay you should try to drop in for dinner. The restaurant, **t** 05 62 32 07 07 (*expensive*), is run by the Cazaux brothers; it's quite popular, with a reputation for the best food around; garden terrace. *Closed Christmas, 9–25 Feb and 4–20 Aug.*

★★★Henri IV, 7 Av Bertrand Barère, between the rail station and Place de Verdun, **t** 05 62 34 01 68 (*moderate*). A good bargain, with helpful staff and very comfortable rooms.

★★Hôtel de l'Avenue, Av Bertrand Barère, **t** 05 62 93 06 36 (*inexpensive*). Basic, with the cheapest rooms in town.

L'Isard, Av Maréchal-Joffre, near the rail station, **t** 05 62 93 06 69 (*inexpensive*). Restaurant (*moderate*) with rooms: usually crowded at lunchtime. *Closed Sun eve.*

L'Ambroisie, 48 Rue Abbé, **t** 05 62 93 09 34 (*expensive*). A popular local restaurant in an old presbytery, with a terrace and garden. Tuna steak and beef roasted with Madiran wine are especially recommended. *Closed Sun and Mon.*

Place got its centrepiece at the same time: the **Fontaine Duvignau**, with an allegory representing the four valleys that stretch up to the mountains from here, dripping with cute allegorical maidens, bears, and izards.

Besides the market, Tarbes is also an army town. On Cours de Reffye is the Haras Nationaux, a cavalry stud farm founded by Napoleon, a compound of Empire-style buildings with a **Maison du Cheval** (*open July–Feb Mon–Fri 10–12 and 2–5*) to explain what it's all about. Just north of the Haras is the heart of the old town, with the **cathedral**, an ungainly thing full of Baroque fripperies. Nearby, on Rue de la Victoire, you might visit the **Birthplace of Marshal Foch** (*open Thurs–Sat 9–12 and 2–5, till 6.30 May–Sept*), the Hero of the Marne.

The real reason for stopping at Tarbes is the **Jardin Massey**, a remarkable, wrought-iron-fenced island of civility, with trees and plants from around the world, including palms in the beautiful Orangerie. The entire 14th-century **cloister** from St-Sever-de-Rustan is here as well; the carving is first-rate, and strange: birds pull a woman's toes, swans kill a bear, and a fellow chases a lady with a long knife. A neo-Moorish villa houses the **Musée Massey** (*major restoration programme due to end summer 2004; currently open 1st week of month only Sun–Fri 10–12 and 2–5; adm*). There's a bronze mask of about the 3rd century BC, said to represent the Pyrenean god Ergé, possibly an equivalent of Mars. There's also a picture gallery, with a view of Tarbes by Utrillo, a work attributed to Pontormo, and some ripe Dutch paintings of the 1600s. Most of the space, however, is taken up with the **Musée International des Hussards**.

High Pyrenean Valleys: the Lavedan

It wasn't just after Franco's death that Spain wanted to become part of Europe. On the contrary, the island that is now Iberia began snuggling up to the continent a few million years ago, and, as it threw up the Pyrenees, the highest points naturally grew up near the northern edge, as if on the crest of a wave. A trio of the chain's giants, Balaïtous, Vignemale and Monte Perdido, look down on a host of smaller fry as well as the most astounding sight the mountains have to offer, the great natural wall of the Cirque de Gavarnie. The mountain views are never short of spectacular, a paradise for skiers and hikers, though beyond sports and activities there isn't a lot to do.

Argelès and St-Savin

Heading south from Lourdes on the N21, the big mountain on your left is the **Pic du Pibeste**. **Argelès-Gazost**, one of the centres of mountain tourism, is here: an attractive medieval centre of stone houses, and below that a spacious spa resort laid out in the 1890s. From here, there is a choice of roads: either down the D921 into the heart of the mountains, or a detour west into the **Val d'Azun**, passing through medieval villages with Romanesque churches such as Arras, Aucun, and Arrens to the glacier-covered face of **Balaïtous** on the Spanish border.

South of Argelès, the D921 passes through one of the most densely inhabited valleys of the Pyrenees. Beautifully sited on a shelf, **St-Savin** once had a Benedictine abbey. Of this only the church remains, but it's a good one. The austere exterior is punctuated by buttresses representing the twelve Apostles. Some odd Renaissance paintings can be seen around the altar: mythological figures and allegories of the liberal arts. The abbot who commissioned them in 1546, François de Foix-Candale, translated the mystic books of Hermes Trismegistus. Note the Crucifixion; Christ seen from one side seems to be dead, while alive from the other.

The forested slopes around St-Savin are one of the most delightful corners of the valley. Further south, **Pierrefitte** is the crossroads for Cauterets or Luz-St-Sauveur.

Cauterets

In the 18th century Cauterets became fashionable among French aristocrats, and with the rediscovery of the beauties of nature in the Romantic era, the élite poured in from all over Europe, drawing crowned heads and several presidents of France. Cauterets is still a major tourist centre, comfortably down at heel. Among the relics of the old days is the rail station, an 1890s wooden confection now used as a coach station. Another remarkable feature is the **Gave de Cauterets** and its rapids, flowing right through the centre with houses closely built up along both sides. Cauterets has also become a ski resort, with a *téléphérique* up to the slopes on the Cirque du Lys, tucked under 8,853ft **Moun Né**; it runs in summer too.

The Route to the Cirques

The other road from Pierrefitte, the D921, will be a little busier. This leads up to the cirques, the most obviously spectacular and most-visited sites in the Pyrenees. These

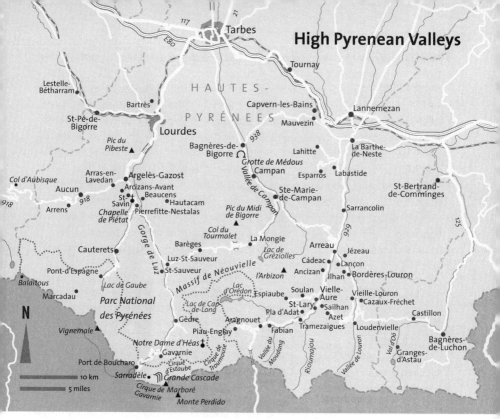

High Pyrenean Valleys

Tarbes
Tournay
Lestelle-Bétharram
Bartrès
Capvern-les-Bains
Lannemezan
St-Pé-de-Bigorre
Mauvezin
La Barthe-de-Neste
HAUTES-
PYRÉNÉES
Lourdes
Pic du Pibeste
Bagnères-de-Bigorre
Lahitte
Grotte de Médous
Campan
Esparros
Labastide
St-Bertrand-de-Comminges
Col d'Aubisque
Arras-en-Lavedan
Argelès-Gazost
Ste-Marie-de-Campan
Aucun
Arcizans-Avant
Beaucens
Sarrancolin
Savin
Hautacam
Arrens
Chapelle de Piétat
Pierrefitte-Nestalas
Pic du Midi de Bigorre
Col du Tourmalet
La Mongie
Arreau
Cauterets
Barèges
Lac de Gréziolles
Cádeac
Jézeau
Luz-St-Sauveur
Cádeac
Lançon
Pont-d'Espagne
St-Sauveur
l'Arbizon
Ancizan
Ilhan
Bordères-Louron
Balaïtous
Lac de Gaube
Massif de Néouvielle
Lac d'Orédon
Espiaube
Soulan
Vielle-Aure
Vieille-Louron
Marcadau
Parc National
Lac de Cap-de-Long
St-Lary
Sailhan
Cazaux-Fréchet
des Pyrénées
Pla d'Adat
Azet
Castillon
Vignemale
Gèdre
Aragnouet
Fabian
Tramezaigues
Loudenville
Piau-Engaly
Notre Dame d'Héas
Bagnères-de-Luchon
Port de Boucharo
Gavarnie
Cirque d'Estaube
Cirque de Troumouse
Granges-d'Astau
Sarradèle
Grande Cascade
Cirque de Gavarnie
Monte Perdido

N
10 km
5 miles

mountains may be good granite, but there are layers of mostly limestone to either side. In places like the Gavarnie, these strata were pushed up to form the highest peaks of the chain. In geological periods when the climate was much warmer, rainfall on the northern face started to erode the limestone, and the Ice Age glaciers finished the job, leaving landforms that seem to have been gouged out by an ice-cream scoop.

First, though, the road passes through the long Gorge de Luz, and arrives at **Luz**. This is a medieval-looking place of not much interest, except for its 14th-century church, **St-André**, built by the Knights Hospitallers. Across the Gave de Gavarnie from Luz stands another spa: **St-Sauveur**, with sulphurous waters to fix up your aches, and an impressive arched bridge embellished with imperial eagles, the gift of satisfied customer Napoléon III.

Continuing south, the D921 traverses more gorges, and then passes the hydro-electric plant, at **Pragnères**. From any high ground at **Gèdre**, the next village, you can glimpse the Cirque de Gavarnie. **Gavarnie**, the highest village in the Pyrenees , is the traditional base for the area.

Cirque de Gavarnie

There are two ways to see the Cirque de Gavarnie: either walking (about 4hrs) or on the back of a donkey. (The families with the donkeys usually only take you one way; if you want them to wait for the trip back, make arrangements in advance.) On the way, you will pass the lovely **Jardin Botanique**, part of the Parc National, with hundreds of

Pyrenean species. The spectacular panorama of the cirque takes in the 7,547ft **Pic des Tantes** on the right, then fragments of the tremendous glacier that once covered all of Gavarnie. Near the centre is the huge gash in the wall, the **Brèche de Roland**. In local legend, the hero (*see* p.491) smote at the mountain with his sword Durendal in futile rage when he was surrounded by the Saracens. One of the most spectacular sights (if you can get close enough to it) is the **Grande Cascade**, the highest waterfall in Europe; the water drains out of semi-frozen marshes, high above on the Spanish side. On the eastern edge loom two formidable mountains: **Marboré** ('marble' in Gascon) and behind it, visible from some angles, the second-tallest peak of the entire chain, 10,904ft **Monte Perdido**, entirely on the Spanish side of the border. For another view, there is a steep motor road (the D923) from Gavarnie village up to **Port de Boucharo**, where it peters out into a hiking trail; this is the only reliable path into Spain in a stretch of some 40km, and a long-favoured route of smugglers. Along the way, you can get out and climb to the top of Pic des Tantes.

Tourist Information

Argelès-Gazost: Grande Terrace, t 05 62 97 00 25, *www.argeles-gazost.com*.
Pierrefitte-Nestalas: Av Jean-Moulin, t 05 62 92 71 31, *www.pierrefitte-nestalas.net*.
Cauterets: Place du Maréchal Foch, t 05 62 92 50 27, *www.cauterets.com*.
Gavarnie: Route Nationale, t 05 62 92 49 10, *www.gavarnie.com*.
Barèges: t 05 62 92 16 00.
Luz-St-Sauveur: t 05 62 92 81 60/30 30, *www.luz.org*.

Activities

You can find out everything about the natural wonders, hiking and sport at the Maisons du Parc of the Parc National des Pyrénées. There is one at Cauterets, t 05 62 92 52 56, at Luz, t 05 62 92 38 38, and at Gavarnie, t 05 62 92 49 10.

Where to Stay and Eat

Argelès-Gazost ✉ 65400
**Bon Repos, Av des Stades, t 05 62 97 01 49, *www.bonrepos.com* (*inexpensive*). Sometimes we take France for granted, but it's gratifying to think that nearly always, when you find a hotel with a name like this, the establishment is likely to provide just that. There are 18 rooms, a pool, a welcoming

family and very reasonable rates. *Closed mid-Oct–end April, but open for Easter.*
Hôtel Victoria, 25 Rue de l'Yser, t 05 62 97 08 34, *www.victoria-argeles.com* (*inexpensive*). Simple, family-run hotel with pretty garden terrace for breakfast.

St-Savin ✉ 65400
**Le Viscos, t 05 62 97 02 28, *www.hotel-leviscos.com* (*moderate–inexpensive*). On the edge of the village, with beautiful views over this exceptional corner of the valley, this hotel has functional rooms, but a restaurant (*expensive–moderate*) you'll remember. M. Saint-Martin presents innovative dishes that are never over the top; everything seems just right, as in the *lotte* (monkfish) in a casserole with ham. Also wonderful are simple desserts such as tarts made with wild strawberries. *Closed Jan; restaurant closed Sun eve and Mon exc July and Aug.*
**Panoramic, a block from the church, t 05 62 97 08 22 (*inexpensive*). The hotel alternative is this venerable (but not very friendly) village inn with grand mountain views. *Closed Oct–Easter.*

Cauterets ✉ 65110
***Hôtel Club Aladin, t 05 62 92 60 00, *www.hotel-balneo-aladin.com* (*moderate*). Such luxury as the town can provide is limited to this modern hotel, with a pool, in-room TVs and gym. *Closed Oct–Dec and 1st week in June.*

Anywhere else, the **Cirque de Troumouse** would be a star attraction, but next to the awesome Gavarnie it gets stuck with the role of little sister. It's just as broad, but much lower, with neither a waterfall nor a *brèche* – but it may afford more peace and quiet in July and August when all the trails around Gavarnie are packed. To get there, take the D922 from Gèdre up the Gave de Héas. The last part of the route is a toll road, but it leads up to a 6,500ft peak for a grand view of the cirque. Even less visited is the **Cirque d'Estaubé**: a trail from the Lac des Gloriettes is the only way in.

On the way back, you can take a convenient short-cut into the next valley, the **Vallée d'Aure**, by means of the D918 from Luz. This is big skiing country, beginning with **Barèges**, an old thermal resort that has successfully made the transition to concentrating on winter sports. Barèges and **La Mongie**, just down the road, have between them the greatest number of pistes in the Pyrenees. A *téléphérique* from La Mongie (*June–Sept 9.30–4.30; reservations* **t** *05 62 56 71 11, www.picdumidi.com*) goes to the top of the **Pic du Midi de Bigorre** to a magnificent observatory, built by the University

Le Sacca, 11 Bd Latapie-Hurin, **t** 05 62 92 50 02 (*inexpensive*). Clean and modern with good restaurant. Owner/chef Jean-Marc Canton successfully refines traditional dishes with some imaginative *legumes*, which is pretty rare in this region.

Hôtel César, 3 Rue César, **t** 05 62 92 52 57, *www.cesarhotel.com* (*inexpensive*). Conveniently situated for the *thermes* and ski lift alike, this hotel has a good traditional restaurant (*moderate*). *Closed May and 1st 3 weeks Oct; restaurant closed Wed in winter.*

Gèdre ✉ 65120
★★Brèche de Roland, **t** 05 62 92 48 54, *www. gavarnie.com/hotel-la-breche* (*inexpensive*). One of the famous old hotels of the Pyrenees, this is an old mansion, all mountain austerity outside but retaining many of its original furnishings and walnut panelling within. There is a garden and a restaurant (*moderate*) with outdoor terrace, and the management helps arrange winter sports, and helicopter rides. *Closed mid-Oct–April exc hols and weekends.*

Gavarnie ✉ 65120
★★★Hôtel-Club Vignemale, **t** 05 62 92 40 00, *www.hotel-vignemale.com* (*expensive*). This hotel has little to justify its rates, but its restaurant (*for groups only*) is the best in the valley: mountain trout and *écrevisses*, and good desserts on a pretty outdoor terrace. *Closed mid-Oct–mid-May.*

★★Le Marboré, **t** 05 62 92 40 40, *www. lemarbore.com* (*inexpensive*). Set in a distinctive 19th-century building, this place has a sauna and gym. *Closed mid-Nov–mid-Dec.*

Compostelle Hôtel, Rue de l'Eglise, **t** 05 62 92 49 43, *www.compostellehotel.com* (*inexpensive*). Sylvie can arrange mountain guides, and all rooms are named after mountain flowers. *Closed end-Sept–end-Dec.*

Luz-St-Sauveur ✉ 65120
★★★Le Montaigu, on the D 172 to Vizos, **t** 05 62 92 81 71, *www.hotelmontaigu.com* (*moderate–inexpensive*). A beautiful hotel in a beautiful setting, this is a modern building in a traditional style. Rooms are spacious and comfortable, some with balconies and all with a great view.

Les Cimes, in the centre of Luz, **t** 05 62 92 82 03, *www.cimes.fr.st* (*inexpensive*). This is a good choice at the lower end of the scale.

Barèges ✉ 65120
★★Hôtel de l'Europe, **t** 05 62 92 68 04 (*inexpensive*). Traditional hotel and quite swish for the region. *Closed Oct–May.*

Hôtel Central, **t** 05 62 92 68 05 (*inexpensive*). Basic hotel/restaurant in centre of town, with garden and terrace with a view.

Auberge du Lienz, just east, near the cable car up the Pic de l'Ayre, **t** 05 62 92 67 17 (*moderate*). Home-cooking in a lovely setting. *Closed Nov and 1st week May.*

of Toulouse in 1881, with one of the biggest telescopes in Europe. It is now open to the public as a **Musée des Etoiles,** with splendid viewing platforms and observatories and a restaurant. Farther east, another cable car leads up to the **Lac de Greziolles**; beyond the hairpin turn there's a favourite postcard subject, the **Cascade de Garet**.

The Vallée d'Aure and Vallée de Louron

These sunny mountains are 'the Pyrenees of the Nestes of the Garonne' – the mighty Garonne, in fact, hatches out of *nestes*, the Gascon word for river. During the Spanish Civil War the population picked up a bit, and during the Second World War, the traffic went the other way, as local shepherds and woodcutters helped Jews, German dissidents and escapees from French political prisons flee over the mountains; in the Aure Valley alone, an estimated 1,500 of the 2,000 who made the attempt survived to make it to Spain.

The Vallée d'Aure

Moulded by ancient glaciers into a giant fishhook, the Vallée d'Aure receives more sunshine than most French valleys and is blessed by a warm Spanish wind which sweeps the surrounding peaks clear of clouds and mists. Perhaps because of its sunny disposition, the valley was one of the first, back in the 1950s, to reverse its decline by attracting tourists and skiers. Another feather in its cap is the recent opening of the Aragnouet-Bielsa tunnel, confirming the Aure's age-old links with Spain that began with a Neolithic track linking the Garonne valley and the Atlantic with those of the Ebro and the Mediterranean.

South of **Lannemezan** and the A64, the D929 follows this old trail through dismal scenery to **Sarrancolin**, famous for red marble with grey veins used in Versailles and for the grand stair of the Paris Opéra. The medieval town has picturesque lanes, especially Rue Noire, but the pride of Sarrancolin is the church of **St-Ebons**, begun in the 12th century. Inside, the relics of St Ebons (d. 1104) are preserved in a magnificent 13th-century gold and copper enamel casket made in Limoges. Carefully preserved through the centuries, the casket was stolen in 1911, and given up for lost – until one dry year, when the waters in the Neste d'Aure were exceptionally low and it was spotted in the middle of the river where the thief had dropped it.

The main valley road continues 7km south to **Arreau**, the pretty, slate-roofed capital of the Quatre Vallées, at the meeting of the Aure and Louron rivers and various roads. A popular base for walks, rafting, hang-gliding and skiing, Arreau has a 17th-century *halles* and 16th-century Maison des Lys; the diminutive Château des Nestes contains the tourist office and a **Musée des Cagots** (*open mid-Dec–Oct Mon–Fri 9–12 and 2–6.30, daily in July and Aug*), dedicated to the pariahs of the Pyrenees, a people whose origins were as mysterious as the elaborate ways in which they were segregated. The best church around is 3km east of Arreau at **Jézeau**, beautifully set on the mountain flank. Ask at the *mairie* for the key before setting out: when it was enlarged in the 16th century, the church was given a magnificent Renaissance retable, poly-

Getting Around

All **trains** between Pau, Tarbes and Toulouse stop at Lannemezan, and from there **buses** continue to Sarrancolin, Arreau, and St-Lary. Once a day there's a direct connection between Tarbes and St-Lary. For information, call **t** 05 62 98 00 49.

Tourist Information

Arreau: Place du Monument, **t** 05 62 98 63 15, *www.vallee-aure.com*.
St-Lary: 37 Rue Vincent Mir, **t** 05 62 39 50 81, *www.saintlary.com*.
Piau-Engaly: **t** 05 62 39 61 69.
Bordères-Louron: Maison du Tourism, **t** 05 62 99 92 00.

Where to Stay and Eat

Arreau ✉ 65240

Hôtel d'Angleterre, on the edge of town, **t 05 62 98 63 30, *www.angleterre-hotel.com* (*moderate–inexpensive*). A big comfortable country inn, with a heated pool and garden terrace to sit out on; the owners arrange rafting or hang-gliding excursions. The restaurant (*expensive–moderate*) serves good hearty food. *Closed Oct–May exc weekends and hols.*
*Hôtel de l'Arbizon, in the centre, **t** 05 62 98 64 35 (*inexpensive*). A tidy little place; some rooms have balconies over the river. *Closed 2 weeks June.*
Hostellerie du Val d'Aure, just south of Arreau in Cadéac, **t 05 62 98 60 63, *www.hotel-valdaure.com* (*inexpensive*). Quiet, well-furnished rooms on the banks of the Aure, with pool and tennis. Restaurant (*moderate*). *Closed Oct–Dec, April–mid-May and weekdays Jan–Mar; restaurant closed Tues and Thurs lunch.*

St-Lary-Soulan ✉ 65170

In the town that helped inaugurate package ski holidays in the Pyrenees, there are no bargains. The restaurants in St-Lary, such as they are, are notoriously mediocre: most people eat in their hotels.

Hôtel La Pergola, 25 Rue Vincent-Mir, **t** 05 62 39 40 46, *www.hotellapergola.fr* (*moderate–inexpensive*). Comfortable hotel in heart of village in its own park. Good restaurant. (*expensive–moderate*) with inventive regional cuisine. *Closed Nov; restaurant closed Mon and Tues lunch in winter.*
Hôtel de la Neste, 5 minutes north of Saint-Lary in Vigneac, **t 05 62 39 42 79, *www.hotel-delaneste.com* (*inexpensive*). By the river, the hotel enjoys a grand view of the mountains; all rooms have bath, TV and mini-bar, and there's a pool. The restaurant is only open to residents. *Closed Nov.*
La Terrasse Fleurie, 21 Rue Principale, **t 05 62 40 76 00, *www.la-terrasse-fleurie.com* (*inexpensive*). The nicest choice, with wooden balconies and comfortable rooms.
*Pons 'Le Dahu', Rue de Coudères, **t** 05 62 39 43 66, *www.hotelpons.com* (*inexpensive*). Inexpensive and sunny.
Le Barbajou, in Fabian, at the beginning of the Route des Lacs, **t** 05 62 39 61 34 (*inexpensive*). Five comfortable *chambres d'hôte*.
Chez Lulu, in Sailhan, **t** 05 62 39 40 89 (*moderate–cheap*). Here you can dine on the summer terrace. There are Gascon favourites. *Closed May, Nov-Dec and Mon.*

Vallée de Louron ✉ 65590

Le Peyresourde, Bordères-Louron, **t 05 62 98 62 87 (*inexpensive*). The fanciest hotel in the valley, with restaurant. *Closed Oct.*
Auberge des Isclots, overlooking the Lac de Loudenvielle at Aranvielle, **t** 05 62 99 66 21 (*inexpensive*). This *auberge* is utterly pleasant, with doubles, or cheaper *gîte d'étape* rooms in a dormitory. There are good-value menus (*moderate*), with *magret* or *confit de canard*.
Le Relais d'Avajan, Avajan, **t** 05 62 99 67 08 (*inexpensive*). A handful of reasonably priced rooms and stout food (*cheap*). *Closed weekends in winter.*
Accueil sans Frontière Pyrénées, Germ, **t** 05 62 99 65 27 (*inexpensive*). The favourite place to stay in the region is this complex of well-furnished *gîtes* and hostel accommodation, with a camp site, good food, swimming pool and loads of information and equipment for summer and winter sports in the area.

chrome statues, and, on the wooden ceiling, vigorous, imaginative paintings by an unknown hand, including a remarkable *Last Judgment* that has inspired Jézeau's enthusiasts to call it 'The Sistine Chapel of the Pyrenees'.

St-Lary and Around

St-Lary claims to be nothing less than the biggest sports resort in the Pyrenees. It certainly had a head start. By 1957 the town had built its first aerial cableway, at the time the largest in the world, to the ski slopes of Pla d'Adet (these days it looks quite puny); most recently it built a deluxe modern spa at Soulan, to treat rheumatism and nose-ear-throat troubles in the hopes of attracting tourists in spring and autumn. Another recent project has been the restoration of the old core of St-Lary, including the 16th-century Maison Fornier in Place de la Mairie, now home to the **Musée du Parc National** (*open mid-Dec–Oct Mon–Fri 9–12 and 2–6.30, daily in July and Aug*). But it's the great outdoors that brings people to St-Lary – in the winter, ice-skating and skiing; in the summer, paragliding, riding, rock-climbing, canyoning and walking.

Continuing up from St-Lary, the village, sheer rock and ruined **castle of Tramezaïgues** stands like an exclamation mark at the beginning of the arcadian 12km-long **Vallée du Rioumajou**. Daniel Defoe came this way in 1689, during one of the worst winters in history; he fictionalized the experience in *Robinson Crusoe*. The D929 continues to **Fabian**, the crossroads for the Réserve Naturelle de Néouvielle, and then to **Le Plan d'Aragnouet**, with a photogenic Templars' chapel. At Le Plan a road branches off for **Piau-Engaly**, the highest and snowiest ski resort in the Pyrenees, with illuminated night skiing to prolong the thrills.

In 1935, the great south-facing granite massif of **Néouvielle** became the first national reserve in France. Golden eagles soar high overhead, and the reserve has the highest growth of pines in Europe. Thank the power monopoly EDF for the road up from Fabian, which for a few months in the summer allows you (and half the population of St-Lary) to motor as far as the **Lac d'Orédon** and **Lac de Cap-de-Long**, both within easy striking distance of other lovely lakes.

The Vallée de Louron: the Valley of Romanesque Churches

Arreau stands at the foot of the 25km-long Vallée de Louron, green and tranquil compared to its neighbours. It has a pair of ski resorts, at **Val-Louron** (7,415ft) and **Peyresourde** (7,352ft), and is increasingly a popular base for hang-gliding and paragliding daredevils. By the 16th century, the wool and cloth business in the Vallée de Louron was good enough for the inhabitants of its villages to pool their money to hire painters to decorate their churches. Unfortunately they are often locked; the afternoon tours offered on Thursdays by the Maison du Tourisme at **Bordères** (t 05 62 99 92 00; *you must ring ahead and book*) are the easiest way to get into them. Heading up the valley, **Lançon** (take the D219 from Arreau) has a Romanesque church, not with murals but an unusual bell tower topped with a pepperpot roof; **Ilhan** just south has fine views of the valley. South of Bordères-Louron, **Vielle-Louron**'s church has both walls and ceilings covered with 16th-century paintings. **Loudenvielle**, south of its large man-made lake, and the power station at **Tramezaygues** 8km further south, are the bases for walks in the upper Vallée de Louron. Other good Romanesque churches are just to the east: one at **Cazaux-Fréchet** and another at **Armenteule**, isolated and decorated with a curious carved frieze. **Mont** has the finest frescoes in the whole valley, painted in 1573 by one Melchior Rodiguis of St-Bertrand-de-Comminges. Lastly, tucked off the main route, is a clean and pleasant little hamlet lost in nature called **Germ** (yes, really), named after a saint so obscure that he never made it out of the valley.

Into the Haute Garonne: The Comminges

East of the Vallée de Louron extends the southernmost bit of the *département* of the Haute Garonne, formerly known as the Gascon province of the Comminges. Located exactly midway between the Atlantic and Mediterranean, the Comminges encompasses the upper valley of one of France's four great rivers, the Garonne, and as its relics show, has been inhabited since the cows (and bison and woolly mammoths) came home in the last Ice Age.

Up the Garonne

Montréjeau and the Grotte de Gargas

At the confluence of the Neste and Garonne, **Montréjeau** stands on a natural terrace, where it was founded as a *bastide* in 1272. It has lovely views over to the Pyrenees from its two main squares, arcaded Place Valentin Abeille and Place Verdun, with the market and public garden; on Boulevard de Lassus, skirting the edge of the plateau, an orientation table has been set up.

There's always an ineffable quality to prehistoric caves, but the **Grotte de Gargas** (*open daily 10–12 and 2–6 but only by appointment,* **t** *05 62 39 72 39*) south of Montréjeau is more uncanny than most. Gargas is one of the oldest-known decorated caves known, from the Aurignacian era (*c.* 33,000 BC), and its oldest paintings and engravings of animals (and unusually, two birds) are still rather awkward, compared to the more graceful works of the Magdalenian era (*c.* 12,000 BC). But Gargas is set apart by its bizarre mutilated hands – 231 pictures, made by blowing paint through a tube around a hand. Nearly all are somehow deformed. Fingerprints suggest that both living and amputated hands were used for models, and guesses are that they were damaged either through frostbite, disease, accidents or ritual mutilation.

St-Bertrand-de-Comminges

Before Lourdes, the local religious centre was St-Bertrand-de-Comminges. Magnificently set on a promontory over the Garonne, the massive Gothic church of **Ste-Marie** makes an unforgettable sight, a kind of inland Mont-St-Michel, with its nearly windowless walls, tower and buttresses rising up like an ocean liner.

St-Bertrand was settled by Iberians, and their Celtic cousins gave it its name, *Lugdunum*, the 'Citadel of the Rising Sun'. By 76 BC, the region was empty except for guerrilla tribes holding out against the joys of Roman rule; they were known as the

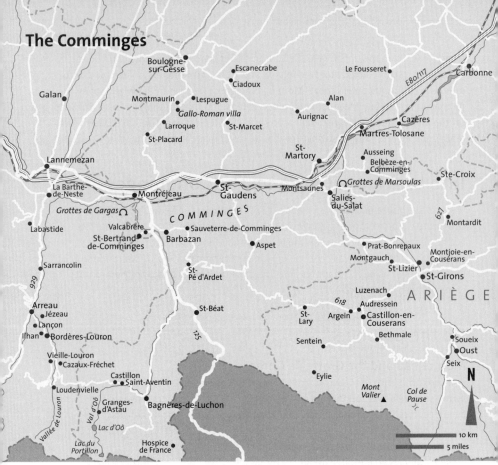

The Comminges

Convenii, the 'robbers of souls'. Even Pompey thought twice about going after them, and decided to win them over by kindness, declaring them to be Roman colonists. The ferocious Convenii turned out to be excellent citizens, and their *Lugdunum Convenarum* grew by leaps and bounds. When Caligula exiled the Tetrarch Herod, Salome and family in 39 AD from Palestine, this is where they came. After the Dark Ages, the town next appears in the 11th century, in the biography of Bertrand de l'Isle-Jourdain, a cousin of the remarkable Count of Toulouse Raymond IV, who fought with El Cid and led the First Crusade. Bertrand shared Raymond's energy; when appointed bishop of Comminges he rebuilt the church and the town, and performed enough miracles to be canonized by popular demand in 1175. In the late 13th century, another Bertrand, Bertrand de Got of Bordeaux, was named bishop and built a Gothic church.

Cathédrale Ste-Marie

Open Feb–April and Oct Mon–Sat 10–12 and 2–6; May–Sept Mon–Sat 9–7; Nov–Jan Mon–Sat 10–12 and 2–5.

When Bertrand de Got rebuilt St-Bertrand's cathedral, he left the 100ft bell tower and the rather severe façade intact. The richly decorated portal also dates from the

12th century, its tympanum carved with the Three Magi (and the future St Bertrand) paying their respects to the Virgin, an image known in the Pyrenees as 'the Seat of Wisdom'. As you enter, don't miss the embalmed crocodile; no one knows who left it here, but guesses tend towards a passing Crusader. On the left, columns support one of the most lavish **Renaissance organs** in France, known as 'the Third Wonder of Gascony', decorated with finely carved wooden panels representing the Labours of Hercules. Although its 3,000 pipes were purloined in the Revolution, the organ was restored in the 1970s and works a treat, as you can hear every Sunday at 10.30am.

The nave is closed off from the choir by an opulently carved Renaissance rood screen, but to continue any further down the nave you have to buy a ticket. It's worth it: the superb **choir stalls** were carved between 1523 and 1551 by sculptors from Toulouse. Inspired perhaps by the great choir stalls then under way at Auch, they expressed a large part of their humanistic view of the universe on the 66 stalls: wicked sins and somberly elegant religious and secular scenes intermingle with an imaginary bestiary. Behind the high altar, a chapel holds the **tomb of St Bertrand**, decorated with folksy 15th-century paintings, showing Bertrand de Got (Pope Clement V) as big as the Jolly Green Giant.

Tourist Information

Montréjeau: Place Valentin Abeille, **t** 05 61 95 80 22.

St-Bertrand-de-Comminges: by the cathedral, **t** 05 61 95 44 44.

St-Béat: t 05 61 79 45 98.

Where to Stay and Eat

St-Bertrand-de-Comminges ✉ 31510

L'Oppidum, up in the medieval town, **t 05 61 88 33 50 (*inexpensive*). This pretty place has 15 comfortable rooms, some sleeping as many as six. The restaurant serves local specialities: stuffed trout and veal (*moderate*). *Closed mid-Nov–mid-Dec; restaurant closed Sun eve and Mon.*

*Hôtel du Comminges, facing the cathedral, **t** 05 61 88 31 43 (*inexpensive*). An old ivy-covered building that was once a private house, with nicely furnished large rooms, and an interior garden to sit in as well as the terrace in front. *Closed Nov–Mar.*

Chez Simone, a street back from the cathedral, **t** 05 61 94 91 05 (*cheap*). If you crave a good old stuffed Gascon chicken, ring Simone and have her cook one up to go with the homemade desserts and pretty views from the terrace. *Closed eve exc July and Aug; also Christmas and Jan.*

Le Lugdunum, Valcabrère, **t** 05 61 94 52 05 (*moderate*). For something unique in France, book a table here and dine like Pompey himself. Here chef Renzo Pedrazzini (born locally of Italian parents) bases his dishes on the recipes compiled in the *Ten Books of Cooking* by the gastronome Apicius in the 1st century. No Caesar salads or hummingbirds' tongues, but dishes such as partridge in cold sauce and young boar, served with spiced wines; a local herbalist supplies authentic ingredients. The restaurant terrace has an equally delicious view of St-Bertrand. *Closed Sun eve–Wed eve in winter.*

Barbazan ✉ 31510

***Hostellerie des Sept Molles, on the D9 just east of Barbazan, in Sauveterre-de-Comminges, **t** 05 61 88 30 87 (*expensive–moderate*). The all-white Relais et Château hotel is perched on a high hill with luminous rooms, spread out in several buildings, with a heated pool, tennis, and bubbling stream in the grounds. The restaurant has a lovely terrace for summer dining, or a roaring fire in the winter, and specializes in baby lamb with *mounjetado*, the local version of *cassoulet*. *Closed mid-Feb–mid-Mar.*

The delightful **cloister** is another legacy of St Bertrand d'Isle-Jourdain. The west gallery is the oldest; in the centre you'll find one of the **Pillar of the Evangelists**, carved with four column-like figures, topped with the Labours of the Months and signs of the zodiac. Upstairs, the treasury has two exquisite medieval copes that belonged to Clement V, who also donated the alicorne, a horn from a unicorn (really a narwhal). Water that passed through the alicorne was considered a sure-fire antidote for poison. Catherine de Médicis tried all she could to get her son Charles IX to get it, without success; in 1594 a band of Huguenots under Corbeyran d'Aure stole it, but even Corbeyran feared the vengeance of St Bertrand, and he returned the alicorne in exchange for a complete amnesty. And it's still in the treasury.

Lugdunum Convenarum and Valcabrère

To visit the excavations of *Lugdunum Convenarum*, first check the opening hours with the tourist office, and then follow the road for Valcabrère. In the centre the Forum temple with its big podium is believed to have been dedicated to the cult of Rome and the Emperor. The baths, or **Thermes du Forum**, were built about the same period; you can make out the hot and cold rooms (*caldaria* and *frigidaria*) and much of the plumbing. Across the D26 stood the commercial heart of *Lugdunum*, the *macellum*, with 26 boutiques paved with black and white mosaics – a 1st-century AD covered shopping mall. Measuring over 500 square metres, it is among the largest and most opulent covered markets ever discovered in the western Roman empire. Towards the car park, a raised circular sanctuary of uncertain import has recently been unearthed. The large **Thermes du Nord** were run by the city; they included an early version of the sauna, as well as an open-air pool, a *palaestra* (an open-air exercise area), and a row of small shops. South of the *macellum*, *Lugdunum*'s palaeo-Christian **basilica** dates from the mid-5th century, has a pretty green, red and white mosaic floor and was used at least into the 8th century. The little **theatre** in the hillside was damaged when a road was run through in the 18th century. A **museum** near the site houses the numerous finds.

On the edge of *Lugdunum*, in the rural hamlet of **Valcabrère**, the 11th- or 12th-century **Basilique St-Just** (*open April and May daily 10–12 and 2–6; June daily 9–12 and 2–7; July–Sept daily 9–7; Oct–Mar weekends and school hols*) is one of the most beautiful churches in the Pyrenees, isolated in a field, with the cathedral at St-Bertrand looming behind its shoulder. The square apse with radiating polygonal chapels is a unique essay in medieval geometry, as well as a collage of Roman bits and bobs; note the theatre mask embedded in the wall, and a relief of a supper party. The portal was inspired by Roman models, crowned with a tympanum showing Christ in majesty while on the sides are marble column statues of saints; the capitals over their heads relish various forms of martyrdom. The interior, beautiful in its simplicity, has fine acoustics; note the re-use of antique columns and Roman and Merovingian capitals.

South of St-Bertrand: St-Béat

Further south, squeezed in between the Cap det Mount and the Cap d'Ayre mountains, **St-Béat** has long been known as the 'Key to France': any army from Spain would have to beat its way past its citadel, so naturally well defended that it could be held with only a handful of men. It was the home of the Garunni, the tribe who gave their name to the River Garonne; in 75 BC Pompey founded a fort here. While in the area, he might have noticed that the two mountains that enclose St-Béat were made of white marble. One massive vertical excavation is said to have been carried off to Rome to become Trajan's Column; an altar discovered nearby, dedicated by two quarrymen, thanked the gods for allowing them to extract such a chunk without accident. Not surprisingly, much of St-Béat is built of marble, including the **clock tower**, all that remains of its 11th-century castle. Elsewhere in St-Béat, the **Maison Consulaire** in Rue Galliéni dates from 1553; it inspired the balcony scene in Rostand's *Cyrano de Bergerac*. The street is named after Maréchal Joseph-Simon Galliéni, who was born here in 1849 and who, as his last great act for the *patrie* in 1914, rounded up Paris taxis to transport troops to the Battle of the Marne; his statue stands on the right bank.

The Upper Comminges: Bagnères-de-Luchon and its Valleys

Set in a sunny amphitheatre, surrounded by the highest peaks of the Pyrenees and a web of luscious valleys, the 'Queen of the Pyrenees', **Bagnères-de-Luchon**, or just Luchon as everyone calls it, wears two different hats: as France's fourth (some say fifth) largest spa and as a base for the mountains. It attracted rheumatic Romans: 'The Best After Naples' reads the old Latin slogan on the baths. In the mid-18th century it underwent a revival: an entire *Who's Who* descended upon Luchon, from Flaubert and Louis Napoléon to Bismarck and Mata Hari.

Modern Luchon is bustling, but the gilded days of its spa have left a burnished glow, especially along the elegant **Allée d'Etigny**. Lined with lime trees, grand old hotels, restaurants and cafés, it culminates in the lovely **Parc des Quinconces**, with its catalpas and tulip trees, and Luchon's **thermes** (1849). Since 1973, these have had a natural cave sauna and '*vaporarium*', good for respiratory ailments; singers, preachers and lawyers form a large part of the clientele. The **Musée du Vieux Luchon**, 18 Allée d'Etigny (*open daily 9–12 and 2–6; closed hols*), has displays on the early days of mountaineering and memorabilia of celebrity visitors, and tools used (and invented) by the legendary Norbert Casteret (1897–1987), father of French speleology.

Exploring the majestic high-altitude scenery around Luchon can take up an entire holiday. The classic excursion is to the **Port de Venasque**, at the top of the superb **Vallée de la Pique**, lined with silver firs and beeches – unfortunately, many ill from the worst acid rain in the Pyrenees. To make it to the 8,078ft Port de Venasque and back, start early in the morning and count on at least a 6hr march past forests, waterfalls and pastures. The reward: an unforgettable view of the Maladetta *massif*, the 'accursed mountains', a jagged, 6km-long, glacier-crowned spine, reaching 11,233ft at Aneto, the highest peak in the Pyrenees.

Other excursions include the D46 into the **Vallée du Lys**, carved by glaciers with a rare symmetry. Along the way you can peer down an abyss, the Gouffre Richard, then

Getting Around

Both **trains** and **buses** pull in at the *gare*. All come by way of Montréjeau, with connections to Lourdes, Tarbes and Toulouse. For information, t 05 61 79 03 36.

Tourist Information

Bagnères-de-Luchon: 18 Allée d'Etigny, t 05 61 79 21 21, *www.luchon.com*.

Where to Stay and Eat

Luchon ✉ 31110

★★Hôtel d'Etigny, 3 Av Paul Bonnemasion, t 05 61 79 01 42 (*expensive– moderate*). Opposite the baths, an atmospheric, old-fashioned place with a restaurant (*moderate*). *Closed Nov–April.*

★★★Corneille, 5 Av A. Dumas, t 05 61 79 36 22, *www.hotel-corneille.com* (*moderate*). Handsome 19th-century hotel set in a lovely garden on the edge of Luchon, with tranquil rooms and a restaurant (*moderate*). *Closed Nov–mid-Dec.*

Jardin des Cascades, near the church of Montauban-de-Luchon, east of Luchon, t 05 61 79 83 09 (*inexpensive*). A few double

rooms, enchanting views from the terrace of the restaurant (*expensive–moderate*) and excellent preparations of *pistache* and other traditional dishes. The restaurant's always packed, so book. *Closed Oct–end Mar.*

★Hôtel des Deux Nations, 5 Rue Victor-Hugo, t 05 61 79 01 71 (*inexpensive–cheap*). Quiet, yet central and an old favourite, this hotel-restaurant is run by a friendly family, who are also more than competent in the kitchen (*moderate*).

Around Luchon ✉ 31110

★★L'Esquerade, Castillon-de-Larboust, t 05 61 79 19 64, *www.esquarade.com* (*inexpensive*). A favourite of *les sportifs* and lazybones alike, this is a handsome old mountain inn, set in the lush green valley. Opt for the *demi-pension* scheme, or just stop by to eat (*expensive–moderate*) – the local dishes are superb and reasonably priced. *Closed early April and mid-Nov–mid-Dec; restaurant closed Mon lunch and Tues lunch.*

★★Le Sapin Fleuri, Bourg d'Ouell, t 05 61 79 21 90, *www.hotel-sapin-fleuri.com* (*inexpensive*). At 4,620ft, this comfortable little Logis de France chalet hotel is in a magnificent setting. Regional cuisine (*moderate*) is served on a summer terrace (booking essential). *Closed 10 Oct–26 Dec.*

take the road up to the ski resort, **Superbagnères**, with superb views. Best of all, continue up the main road to the Cirque de Lys and its **Cascade d'Enfer**, a waterfall splashing through a cleft in the rocks that could pass for the gate of hell. Another excursion is up the **Vallée d'Oô**, by way of **St-Aventin**, a 12th-century gem of a church 5km from Luchon. Perched high on its promontory, it has a tympanum carved with a Christ in Majesty and fine capitals, one with a bear; according to the story, bears would come to Aventin, a hermit, to have thorns removed from their paws. Inside, the stoup is a remarkable pre-Romanesque work. Around Aventin's tomb are more sculpted capitals; murals show him with St Sernin, patron of Toulouse. At Castillon, the road forks; take the left along the Neste d'Oô, which is driveable as far as the **Granges d'Astau**. There you can pick up the GR 10, passing the silvery waterfall known as the **Chevelure de Madeleine** to the stunningly azure **Lac d'Oô**, the loveliest of a pocket of glacier lakes, set in nearly lunar surroundings, near a 900ft waterfall.

West of Luchon, the **Vallée de Larboust** leads up to the **Col de Peyresourde**, one of the highest passes in the Pyrenees. Just after the turn-off for the Vallée d'Oô, on the D618, **Cazaux** has a church with a remarkable late medieval mural of the Last Judgement. The iconography is unique: the Christ is shown sitting atop a rainbow, not in majesty, but with the bleeding wounds of the Passion. On his right, the Virgin pleads for mercy, but intercedes in a most unusual way: she bares her breasts and squirts milk on her son's wounds. Unfortunately, the church is usually locked, but the Luchon tourist office may help locate the key.

St-Gaudens and the Petites Pyrénées

For 90 per cent of people travelling in the region, bedazzled by the beauty of the Pyrenees, the area north and west of the Garonne of the baby mountains, or 'Petites Pyrénées', is *terra incognita*. Yet these rolling hills of the Comminges were beloved in antiquity and have seemingly changed little since. The departmental roads are still lined on either side with ancient plane trees, rare in the rest of France, where one or both sides are sacrificed to road-widening schemes. Here there's not enough traffic.

St-Gaudens, with a population of 13,000, is the metropolis in these parts. It is named after a 12-year-old shepherd boy who met a band of Moorish cavalrymen who demanded that he convert to Islam. Gaudens asked his mother if it was all right, but she said no. The Moors then chopped off his head, but his body had the panache to pick it up, and with the Moors in hot pursuit, he ran with it to the nearest church. No wonder Gascons make such good rugbymen. The most important church, however, is the **Collégiale**, with a great square bell tower. Along the nave, 18th-century tapestries from Aubusson illustrate the martyrdom of St Gaudens. Best of all are the capitals by the choir, by sculptors from Aragon: bears fight, monkeys make faces, Adam seems to gag on the forbidden fruit. Just east of the Collégiale, the **Musée du Comminges** (*open summer Tues–Sat 9–12 and 2–6; winter Tues–Fri and last Sun in month 9–12 and 2–6*) has tools, costumes, and memorabilia related to the army heroes from the Pyrenees: Foch, Joffre and Galliéni.

Getting Around

St-Gaudens is the transport centre for the region, with **trains** to Toulouse and Luchon, and TER **buses** to Montréjeau, Lannemezan, Tarbes, Lourdes, and Luchon.

Tourist Information

St-Gaudens: 2 Rue Thiers, **t** 05 61 94 77 61, *tourisme@stgaudens.com*.

Where to Stay and Eat

St-Gaudens ⊠ 31800
★★★**Hostellerie des Cèdres**, just outside St-Gaudens in Villeneuve de Rivière, **t** 05 61 89 36 00, *www.hotel-descedres.com* (*moderate*). Set in a large park, the building formerly belonged to the Marquise de Montespan, Louis XIV's mistress. Rooms are elegantly furnished with antiques, and there is a pool, tennis courts, and a fitness room. The restaurant (*expensive–moderate*) specializes in various veal dishes the marquise would have approved of. *Restaurant closed Mon out of season.*
★★**Pedussaut**, 9 Av de Boulogne, **t** 05 61 89 15 70 (*inexpensive*). This hotel has an excellent restaurant (*moderate– cheap*), serving good-value menus full of regional ingredients. *Restaurant closed Sun eve in winter.*

Montmaurin ⊠ 31350
Caso Nuosto, in the woods not far from the Roman villa, **t** 05 61 88 25 50 (*inexpensive*). Very friendly place with three *chambre d'hôte* rooms in a restored old farmhouse, with a pool and garden.

North of St-Gaudens on the River Save, the **Gallo-Roman Villa** at **Montmaurin** (*open May–Aug daily 9.30–12 and 2–6; Sept–April Tues–Sun 9.30–12 and 2–5; adm*) stands in bucolic splendour. In the 1st century a certain Nepotianus, owner of the surrounding 7,000 hectares, built himself a country estate. The Save flooded and covered it in muck, but by the 4th century Nepotianus' heirs were ready to rebuild: nothing would do but a white marble palace with 200 rooms, the largest and most luxurious villa ever discovered in France. In the centre of Montmaurin, a **museum** (*same hours and tickets*) in the *mairie* contains a model of the villa and Roman and prehistoric finds.

The Ariège

Once the proud and independent Comté de Foix, the Ariège occupies several frontiers: obviously Spain and Andorra, but also the more subtle division between Gascony and Languedoc. The difference was most acute when the medieval Cathar heresy thrived on the Languedoc side of the Ariège, and Montségur became the Cathars' Alamo.

The Western Ariège: the Couserans

The Couserans, once a vassal of the Comminges, is the emptiest corner of the Ariège, but it also has the most beautiful: two rivers, the Lez and the Salat, and their tributaries literally cascading down from the tremendous frontier range form its heart. Its valleys are renowned among students of folklore for their costumes.

St-Lizier

Piled on its hill, St-Lizier is the age-old capital of the Couserans. Begun in the 11th century, its **cathedral** looks fairly normal, but step inside: the nave and choir are built on different axes, the left wall is tilted, the columns don't match up, the transepts are uneven. Rare 12th-century frescoes decorate the arches, while in the apse there's a 14th-century Christ Pantocrator with a stern but startled expression (a comment on the architecture). The pretty two-storey 12th-century cloister is to the right, and the treasure with a 14th-century reliquary bust of St Lizier. The tour includes a perfect 18th-century pharmacy, with its armillary sphere that doctors would consult for the most auspicious time for an operation.

The road from the cathedral leads to the massive **Palais des Evêques** (1660) (*open April–May and Oct daily 2–6; June and Sept daily 10–12 and 2–6; July–Aug daily 10–7; closed Mon exc school hols*), that incorporates three Roman towers and has excellent views over the Couserans. Housed in the palace is the **Musée Départemental**, with the ethnographic collections, particularly on the Vallée de Bethmale.

The Valleys of the Couserans

Francis Bacon's 'One triumphs over nature only by obeying its rules,' is the slogan of the **Biros valley**, one of the finest places for walks in the Pyrenees, with the majestic

Getting Around

Buses link St-Girons to Toulouse; others descend daily to Seix and Aulus-les-Bains (t 05 61 66 08 87).

Tourist Information

St-Lizier: Rue Neuve, t 05 61 96 77 77, www.ariege.com/st-lizier. They have daily tours in season, 10–12 and 2–6, the only way you can get in to see the cathedral treasure and hospital pharmacy.
Aulus-les-Bains: t 05 61 96 00 01.

Where to Stay and Eat

St-Girons (by St-Lizier) ✉ 09200
***Eychenne, 8 Av Paul-Laffont, t 05 61 04 04 50, www.ariege.com/hotel-eychenne (moderate). Built as St-Girons' posthouse and in the same family for six generations. Over the decades they have made it into a wonderfully comfortable inn with a heated pool and garden. The vast old-fashioned dining room (expensive–moderate) has a menu of classic French specialities, including home-made foie gras, and one of the Ariège's best wine lists. Closed Dec–Jan; restaurant closed Sun eve and Mon Nov–Mar.

**La Clairiere, Av de la Résistance, t 05 61 66 66 66, www.ariege.com/la-clairiere (inexpensive). Modern wood-shingled hotel and restaurant (moderate) just outside St-Girons, with a garden and swimming pool. Restaurant closed Sun eve, Mon, and Nov–April.
Le Relais d'Encausse, t 05 61 66 05 80, mornings t 05 61 96 21 03 (inexpensive). Just 1.5km outside St-Girons, at Saudech, in an old country house full of character. It has been beautifully restored by the owner, Lysette Cathala. There are four rooms, and a salon with a fireplace.

Aulus-les-Bains ✉ 09140
***Hostellerie La Terrasse, t 05 61 96 00 98, in the main street (inexpensive). The most delightful place to stay and eat (moderate) in Aulus, with a terrace over the Garbet and an interior furnished with antiques. Try one of the delicious specialities of the house, croustade de foie gras de canard aux coquilles Saint-Jacques. Closed Dec–mid-May; half board only July and Aug.
**Les Oussaillès, t 05 61 96 03 68, www.ariege.com/les-oussailles (inexpensive). Mock Gothic turrets and balconied rooms. In the restaurant (moderate) you can feast on delicious salads, trout or veal, or ask for a picnic basket to take away. Even vegetarians are catered for.

backdrop of **Mont Valier** (9,369ft), once thought to be the highest of the Pyrenees; its abrupt east flank, rising 5,577ft is the loftiest rock face in the range. The classic route up Valier is to drive up the Riberot valley (south of Bordes-sur-Lez) to the car park, then walk 4 hours to the Refuge des Estagnous (t 05 61 96 76 22), leaving the remaining ascent until morning.

Bordes-sur-Lez stands at the entrance of the **Vallée de Bethmale**, celebrated for both its beauty and its delightful traditional red and black costumes and scimitar-shaped clogs decorated with copper nails and hearts. The most traditional village, **Ayet-en-Bethmale**, is the starting point for the valley's prettiest walk, to the romantic Lac de Bethmale (about 2 hours, there and back). At the top of the valley, the D17 continues east over the beautiful Col de la Core to the **Vallée de Salat**. The main centre is **Seix**, a convivial old cheese-making village, with houses overlooking the Salat and places to hire canoes or kayaks for thrills and spills.

From the north, the equally beautiful **Vallée du Garbet** (take the D32 between Soueix and Seix) leads to **Aulus-les-Bains**, the spa of the Couserans, in a cirque of wild rocky walls and waterfalls – one of the most spectacular settings in the Pyrenees. A brand-new glass and wood *thermes* is worthy of its surroundings, with a pool open to the general public. The most popular walk from Aulus is to the gorgeous triple waterfall with an irresistible name, the **Cascade d'Arse**. Another beauty spot is the **Col d'Escot**, overlooking the **Cirque de Cagateille**.

The Lower Ariège

The northwest corner of the Ariège has for its centrepiece the Grotte du Mas-d'Azil, a cave with a record-breaking occupancy rate for more millennia than tongue can tell. It occupies the green hilly *piedmont* area where the mountains meet the plain, where far too often the traditional free spirit of the mountains collided head on with less tolerant central powers.

Le Mas-d'Azil

It sounds like something you'd expect in California: a drive-through prehistoric cave. But there it is – the D119 winds right into the 214ft mouth of the **Grotte du Mas d'Azil**. People were here by c. 30,000 BC and they stuck around until the end of the Ice Age (8000 BC), an epoch called Azilian after this cave. Even after that it was rarely empty. Christians were here in the 3rd century; in the 9th century there was an abbey; Moors, Cathars, and Protestants all took refuge here. Their traces can be seen in the **galleries** (*open April–Sept Tues–Sun; call* **t** *05 61 69 99 90 for hours and winter opening*). Tools from the Azilian technological revolution are in the **museum** (*same hours*) in **Le Mas-d'Azil**, a *bastide* and Protestant stronghold; they say Calvin himself preached here.

Tourist Information

Le Mas-d'Azil: opposite the church, **t** 05 61 69 99 90.
La Bastide-de-Sérou: **t** 05 61 64 53 53.

Where to Stay and Eat

Le Mas-d'Azil ✉ 09290

Hôtel Gardel, on the main square, **t 05 6169 90 05 (*inexpensive*). Pleasantly old-fashioned. The restaurant (*moderate–cheap*) features freshwater fish and Ariègeois cheeses. *Closed mid–Nov–mid-Mar; restaurant closed Sun eve Sept–May.*

Le Jardin de Cadettou, St-Ferréol, **t** 05 61 69 95 23, *www.cadettou.fr* (*inexpensive*), just outside the centre. This hotel serves the best food in Le Mas-d'Azil in its cosy dining room. The restaurant (*moderate*) specializes in an unusual variety of *confits. Closed Jan;* restaurant closed Mon, Sat lunch and Sun eve exc July and Aug.

Lanoux/Artigat ✉ 09130

Thibaut, 1km from Artigat, **t** 05 61 68 58 45 (*inexpensive*). Handy if you want to spend time in the *pays de Martin Guerre*, and extremely friendly and helpful to boot. There is a restaurant (*moderate*). *Closed Dec–Mar.*

La Bastide-de-Sérou 09240

Château de Rhodes, **t** 05 61 03 24 50, *www. chateaurhodes.com* (*expensive*). A truly lovely place set majestically in its own park just 3–4km from La Bastide-de-Sérou. Beautifully renovated throughout and crammed with antiques as well as all mod cons, including pool, jacuzzi, billiards and tennis. In the excellent restaurant (*expensive*), the Anglo-French chef offers Thai, Indian and Japanese flavours. *Closed Nov–mid-Mar; restaurant closed Sun eve–Wed lunch.*

The region around Le Mas-d'Azil is called the **Montagnes du Plantaurel** – mountains that are really gentle hills. At **Montégut-Plantaurel**, you can visit the **Sculpture Monumentale d'Amnesty International**, by Christian Lovis; northeast, **Artigat** was the scene of one of the most haunting stories to come out of the 16th century, when a man returning from war convinced most of the village and his 'wife' that he was who he said he was, even if he bore only a faint resemblance to Martin Guerre. When the real Guerre returned, there was trouble. The imposter's trial in Toulouse was the basis for *The Return of Martin Guerre* – the book by Natalie Zemon Davis and the film with Gérard Depardieu, filmed in the lushest Ariège.

Foix and Around

Foix may be among the tiniest departmental capitals in France, but it's one of the most striking, a wing of a town tucked between the Arget and Ariège rivers, crowned with a triple tiara of towers on its immense rock. This was once the base of the Counts of Foix, who, with the Counts of Toulouse and Carcassonne, protected the Cathars and fought for their independence in the Albigensian Crusade. Later their power spread over the Pyrenees, especially under Gaston Fébus (d. 1391). His grandson, another Gaston de Foix, made his reputation as the Renaissance's 'perfect knight', before he was killed in the Battle of Ravenna.

Getting Around

Foix is on the Toulouse–Barcelona **rail** line, with connections to Pamiers, Tarascon-sur-Ariège, Ax-les-Thermes and L'Hospitalet (with bus connections to Pas de la Casa and Andorra). The station is on Av Pierre Semard, **t** 08 92 35 35 35.

Several runs are taken by SNCF **buses**; all depart from the station at the north end of town off Cours I.-Cros. SALT buses, **t** 05 61 65 08 40, link Pas-de-la-Casa and Toulouse; and Sovitours, **t** 05 61 01 02 35, link Foix, Lavelanet, Mirepoix and Perpignan.

Tourist Information

Foix: 29 Rue Declassé, next to the *mairie*, **t** 05 61 65 12 12, *www.ot-foix.fr.*

Where to Stay and Eat

Foix ✉ 09000

Barbacane, Av de Lérida, **t 05 61 65 50 44 (*moderate–inexpensive*). One of the nicer places to stay in the centre of town, in a grand bourgeois mansion. *Closed Nov–Mar.*

***Audoye-Lons, Place Duthil, **t** 05 61 65 52 44 (*inexpensive*). In a former posthouse near the Ariège River, a comfortable place to stay, with a terrace restaurant (*moderate*). *Closed mid-Dec–mid-Jan; restaurant closed Fri eve and Sat lunch in winter.*

***Hôtel Pyrène, Rue Serge-Denis, Le Vignoble (2km north on the N20), **t** 05 61 65 48 66/05 61 65 51 12, *www.hotelpyrene.com* (*inexpensive*). Up-to-date furnishings, a pool and garden. *Closed mid-Dec–mid-Jan.*

Le Phoebus, 3 Cours I.-Cros, **t** 05 61 65 10 42, *www.ariege.com/le-phoebus* (*expensive–moderate*). Popular local restaurant with a balcony facing the château. They serve local produce with a rich twist; try duck liver with caramelized apples. There's a good wine list. *Closed Sat lunch and Mon.*

Le Sainte-Marthe, 21 Rue Noël Peyrévidal, **t** 05 61 02 87 87 (*expensive–moderate*). Restaurant serving classics such as *cassoulet*, but also inventive dishes such as a tart of *boudin noir* with *champignons*. *Closed Tues and Wed exc July and Aug.*

Ringed by 19th-century development, old Foix is still intact, closed in by its rivers and the mighty rock of the castle. Down at the bottom of Rue des Marchandes you'll find the market square and its church, **St-Volusien**, begun in the 11th century by the Counts, but mostly rebuilt; don't miss the 16th-century terracotta *Deposition*.

The **Château des Comtes de Foix** (*open May–June and Sept daily 9.45–12 and 2–6; July–Aug daily 9.45–6.30; Oct–April daily 10.30–12 and 2–5.30; closed Mon and Tues Nov–Mar, and Jan; adm*) has seen its share of action, especially under its Cathar Count Raymond Roger. His arch-enemy Simon de Montfort vowed to 'make the Rock of Foix melt like fat and grill its master in it'. When he failed after four tries, Montfort burned the rest of Foix to the ground, and Roger surrendered – but got his castle back a few years later when Montfort was killed. The château houses the Musée Départemental with a complete mammoth skeleton, pre-Roman and Roman altars, and Romanesque capitals from St-Volusien, one showing the siege of Toulouse in 507.

Six km northwest of Foix on the D1 you can take a fantastic 75-minute boat ride down the **Rivière Souterraine de Labouiche**, nothing less than 'Europe's Longest Subterranean River Open to the Public' (*open either 1 April or Easter to Pentecost, 2–6 and Sun and school holidays 10–12 and 2–6; Pentecost–Sept 10–12 and 2–6; July–Aug 9.30–6; Oct to 11 Nov Sun only 10–12 and 2–6; adm. In season early to avoid the crowds*).

Montségur

A steep road winds down to the small village of Montségur, a cute little place built in tiers on the hillside with more footpaths than streets. Here **L'Occitadelle** offers an

Getting Around

Public transport is pretty thin on the ground here, although there are bus connections from Toulouse to Lavelanet and Mirepoix (Pouplain t 05 61 01 54 00; SALT buses t 05 61 65 08 40) and from Foix to Lavelanet on Sovitour buses, t 05 61 01 02 35.

Tourist Information

Montségur: t 05 61 03 03 03, *www. montsegur.org*.
Mirepoix: t 05 61 68 83 76, *www.ot-mirepoix.fr*.

Where to Stay and Eat

Montségur and Environs ⊠ 09300
**Costes, t 05 61 01 10 24 (*inexpensive*). Pleasant creeper-covered old hotel with a garden in the middle of town. It has an excellent restaurant (*moderate*), serving omelettes with *cèpes* and other

southwestern delicacies. *Closed mid-Nov–Mar, and Mon Sept–June*.
Hôtel Couquet, 81 Rue Principale, t 05 61 01 10 28 (*inexpensive*). Ageing but well-kept, basic accommodation.
L'Occitadelle, t 05 61 01 21 77 (*moderate*). Well-prepared dishes, such as perch in sorrel sauce. *Closed Fri and Nov–end Jan*.

Mirepoix ⊠ 09500
***La Maison des Consuls, 6 Place du Maréchal Leclerc, t 05 61 68 81 81, *www.maisondesconsuls.com* (*moderate*). Stylishly decorated hotel in the Maison des Consuls, an arcaded building with wonderful carved beams. Antique-furnished rooms overlook the medieval streets.
**Commerce, Cours Docteur-Chabaud, t 05 61 68 10 29, *www.chez.com/lecommerce* (*inexpensive*). The nicest place in town, with a shady garden and good restaurant, with a menu based on seasonal ingredients. *Closed Jan and early Oct; restaurant closed 12–25 Nov, and Sat exc July and Aug*.

The Cathars, the Inquisition, and the Fall of Montségur

Few beliefs have had the staying power of dualism, a doctine first expounded by the Greek Gnostics. Good and Evil were explained as eternal opposing forces, Good residing somewhere beyond the stars, while Evil was here and now – in fact all of creation was Evil, the work of a fallen spirit, identifiable with Satan. Although condemned by the Church, dualism made an organized revival in the 9th century with the 'Bogomils' in the Balkans. By the 11th century it had spread through much of Europe. The Church burned as many as it could catch, but in southern France the faith attracted many merchants, craftsmen, poor people and members of the nobility.

These 'Cathars' believed that their faith was a return to the virtue and simplicity of the early Church. Their teaching encouraged separation from the Devil's world; feudal oaths were forbidden, and believers solved differences by arbitration in courts of law. They promoted vegetarianism and non-violence; marriages were by simple agreement and enhanced the freedom of women. They also had a more mature attitude towards capitalism than the Roman church, with no condemnation of loans as usury, and no church tithes, and no big church organization, making a favourable contrast with the corrupt machinery of the Church of Rome. There was also a very forgiving attitude towards sinners: if creation itself was the Devil's work, how could people not err? Cathars were divided into the mass of believers, upon whom the religion was a light yoke indeed, and the few *perfecti*, those who had received a sacrament called the *consolament*, and were required to lead a life devoted to faith and prayer. Most Cathars conveniently took the *consolament* on their deathbeds.

In 1203, a Spanish monk, Domingo Guzman, embarked on a mission to save the souls of the heretics, founding the Order that would become the Dominicans. But by 1209, the papacy saw enough of a threat to prefer a policy of genocide. When the terror, enforced by French arms and promises of southern land to good Catholic crusaders, failed to kill enough Cathars, the Church turned to specialists – the followers of Dominic. The first Inquisitors, based in Toulouse, torched so many people that the Toulousains rioted and expelled them in 1235. But they were back the next year, more murderous than ever. In May 1242, knights from Montségur killed the 12 top Inquisitors. The next year 6,000 men under Hugues des Arcis began their siege of Montségur, where some 350 Cathars lived, protected by a garrison of 150 men.

Montségur held out for ten months, into the difficult winter; impatiently, Hugues des Arcis hired mercenaries from the surrounding villages, who in the dead of night led the Crusaders up to the east end of the hill, where they killed the defenders and captured a tower within catapult range of the castle. The Cathars held out another two months in the snow, but on 2 March, as all chances of relief were eliminated, the commander, Pierre Roger de Mirepoix, opened talks. The Cathars were given two weeks' grace. If they became Catholics they would be free, if not, they would be burnt alive. Not a single one took up the offer; all 225 chose to jump into the fire.

audio-visual on the history of the Cathars and the Albigensian Crusade. Montségur's little **Musée Archéologique** (*t 05 61 01 06 94; open Feb–Dec; check times; closed Mon in Feb and Dec*) has finds from excavations and a model of the château.

The Castle of Montségur

Open Sept–June daily 9–6, July–Aug 9–7; guided visits July–Aug at 11am and 1, 3, 4.30 and 5.30pm; adm. It takes about 20mins to walk up to the château.

The castle of Montségur on its rocky outcrop is a magnet for anyone fascinated by the virtuous heretics (*see* box, p.523). But for many southerners, Montségur symbolizes the lost soul of an aborted nation, symbolized by the 'Occitania Indépendante!' scrawled under the castle (*see* p.46). At the beginning of the path to the fortress, a stone memorial marks the **Camp des Crémats**, where a stockade full of wood was set alight as the archbishop of Narbonne arrived to take possession of Montségur and the souls who converted to Catholicism. In the castle itself there's not much to see, but a curious feature are two lateral openings in its triangular walls, aligned to the rising of the sun on the summer solstice; celebrations are held every 21 June.

Mirepoix, and the Vertical Church of Vals

Mirepoix, a major Cathar stronghold, is one of the prettiest villages in the Ariège. It looks very much as it did in the 14th century, with its half-timber houses and arcaded square. In 1317, Pope John XXII elevated Mirepoix to a bishopric as part of a scheme to bring danger zones of heresy back into the fold. The Lévis, the rulers installed by Simon de Montfort, began to enlarge the church of St-Maurice into a cathedral. They went for broke: the bell tower stands 190ft high, and behind the handsome Gothic portal it measures 73ft across, making it the second widest single nave in Europe, only a tad smaller than the cathedral of Gerona in Spain.

Towards **Pamiers** are a pair of Romanesque churches well worth a detour. The one at **Teilhet** is fortified with a *clocher-mur*, sculpted with a knight; the portal has beautifully capitals and a frieze of grotesques. Two km further on, the unique church at **Vals** (if locked, the key is available from Mme Andrieu, who lives in the last house on the right, with brown shutters) stands on a huge rock that supported a temple to the Celtic god Rahus. An uncanny tunnel and stair follow a natural fault to the 8th-century church, excavated in the living rock. To this, a vaguely Mozarab apse was added in the 11th century; in the 1100s it was beautifully frescoed by Catalan artists. A second, upper nave was added, dedicated to the Virgin Mary; above that, orientated sideways is a 12th-century chapel of St-Michel, built into a *clocher-mur*.

Tarascon-sur-Ariège and the Upper Ariège Valley

Up the Ariège from Foix, Tarascon-sur-Ariège is one of the main crossroads of the *département*. It held a similar status in the dawn of time; today it's the capital of prehistory in the Pyrenees.

Tarascon-sur-Ariège and its Caves

Tarascon-sur-Ariège was settled by the Tarusques, a Ligurian tribe mentioned by Pliny. It has an isolated baby mountain for a landmark, crowned by a round clock-tower. But most of all Tarascon is famous for its caves; its new **Parc Pyrénéen de l'Art**

Getting Around

The **railway** between Tarascon-sur-Ariège, Ax-les-Thermes and L'Hospitalet is the highest in Europe and was a great engineering feat when it opened in 1888.

Tourist Information

Tarascon-sur-Ariège: Av des Pyrenées, t 05 61 05 94 94, *www.pays.de.tarascon.com*.
Ax-les-Thermes: 6 Av Théophile Declassé, t 05 61 64 60 60, *www.vallees-ax.com*.

Where to Stay and Eat

Tarascon-sur-Ariège ✉ 09400
★★**Hostellerie de la Poste**, 16 Av V. Pilhes, t 05 61 05 60 41, *www.hostellerieposte.com* (*inexpensive*). With a terrace over the river and a restaurant (*moderate*).
★★**Le Confort**, 3 Quai A. Sylvestre, t 05 61 05 61 90 (*inexpensive*). Small and nice, overlooking the Ariège. *Closed Jan.*

Hôtel-Restaurant Le Bellevue, 7 Place Jean-Jaurès, t 05 61 05 52 06 (*inexpensive*). Adequate small hotel with a decent restaurant (*moderate*), serving local dishes such as *azinat*, Ariège's famous cabbage soup.

Ax-les-Thermes ✉ 09110
★★**Le Grillon**, Rue St-Udaut, t 05 61 64 31 64, *www.hotel-le-grillon.com* (*inexpensive*). Lovely views, a garden and pretty panelled rooms, making it the nicest place to stay in Ax. The excellent restaurant (*moderate; hotel residents only*) serves Ariègeois specialities, such as *confit de canard* with apples. *Closed Tues and Wed exc school hols.*
★★**L'Orry Le Saquet**, t 05 61 64 31 30, *www.auberge-lorry.com* (*inexpensive*). Just south of Ax, with nice rooms, a garden, a terrace, and a fireplace in winter. They also have a refined kitchen (*very expensive–moderate*) that keeps travellers coming back year after year. Inventive cuisine combines, for example, fish with *cèpes* and *foie gras*. *Closed Jan and Toussaint; restaurant closed Tues eve and Wed exc July and Aug.*

Préhistorique (*open April, May, Sept and Oct Thurs–Sun and Tues 10–6, Wed 10–7; July–Aug daily 10–8; closed Mon; adm exp*) was opened to console the many hopefuls turned away from the Grotte de Niaux; it has perfect replicas of the art, 'the biggest facsimile in the world' and a 'sonar labyrinth', too.

From Tarascon it's 5km up to the **Grotte de Bédeilhac** and its huge porch (*open summer daily 10.30–5.30; winter by appointment, t 05 61 05 95 06; bring something warm*). A large stalactite cave, it was only in 1906 that the Abbé Breuil, the 'father of prehistory' discovered its Palaeolithic art: deer, horses, bison, goats, and symbols, and four bison modelled out of clay with a pubic triangle inscribed above them. A Neolithic skeleton of a man measuring only 4ft 6in tall was found near the entrance.

If you think Bédeilhac is a monster of a cave, a few kilometres south of Tarascon on the N20 is the **Grotte de Lombrives** (*departures July and Aug daily every 20mins 10–7; school hols and June and Sept at 10, 2, 3.30 and 5; May at 2, 3.30 and 5; rest of year at 2 and 3.30, or call for appointment, t 05 61 05 98 40; adm*), the biggest cave in Europe open to the public, so vast that even though visits are by a little train you'll still only see a fraction of the whole. Among the stalactite and stalagmite formations is the remarkable Mammoth, the throne of King Bébrix, and the sepulchre of Pyrène, his daughter, the lover of Hercules and namesake of the mountains that became her funerary monument. Lombrives goes on and on – it's said to have subterranean links to Niaux – and has upper galleries, 150ft up, accessible only by ladders. Numerous skeletons, nearly all women and children, were found up there; in his *Gallic Wars*, Caesar wrote how the Romans snuffed out many Pyrenean tribes by walling them up in their cave refuges, but in Lombrives all the legionnaires had to do was take away the ladders. Another cave nearby, the **Grotte de Bethléem**, was apparently used by the Cathars for initiation ceremonies of the *consolament*; no one knows what kind of mumbo-jumbo they got up to, but there's a very Pythagorean pentangle deeply engraved in the wall.

The Grotte de Niaux

Open July–Aug daily visits every 45mins 9.15–5.30 (9.15 and 1pm in English); Sept 10–5; Oct–June at 11, 2.30 and 4; only 20 people admitted at a time; reservations essential, t 05 61 05 88 37. Arrive 15mins before your departure time. The walk in the cave is nearly 2km and not advised for anyone who has difficulty walking. Bring something warm.

The most beautiful prehistoric art in the Pyrenees, and according to many, the best after Lascaux and Spain's Altamira, is in Niaux, discovered in 1906 in the cliffs. A winding road leads up to its gaping mouth, marked by a metal prow-like structure extending into space. Mysterious signs are painted in red and black near the entrance, reminiscent of the private symbols of Joan Miró, and appear to direct visitors to the superb **Salle Noir**, decorated with an immensely powerful and poetic composition of charcoal line drawings from *c.* 10,500 BC. Bison, horses and mountain goats are beautifully rendered, a few superimposed but all wonderfully clear, making expert use of the natural contours and formations of the walls.

Up the Ariège to Ax-les-Thermes and Montaillou

There are two ways to continue southeast of Tarascon to **Ax-les-Thermes**. The N20 or 'Route du Pastis' is often saturated with traffic trundling to Spain by way of the duty-free republic of **Andorra**. The alternative is the far more scenic D20/D2 or Route des Corniches. Ax has a long history, but a long record of fires to go with it. Its name may come from the Iberian word *ats*, meaning 'stinker', after its sulphurous waters. One of the first people to exploit Stinker-les-Thermes was St Louis, who built a hospital for Crusaders who caught leprosy. Besides the spa, Ax is also the best base for exploring the highest mountains of the Ariège.

Northeast of Ax, **Montaillou** is synonymous with Emmanuel LeRoy Ladurie's now classic study of a 14th-century village. Even after the fall of Montségur, Catharism continued to exist in pockets, especially in the mountains of the Ariège and Catalunya; in spite of the threat of the Inquisition, there was even a heresy revival in 1300 until 1326, when the last Cathars were all rounded up, burned at the stake, imprisoned, or made to wear a big yellow cross sewn on their backs. Ladurie owed the amazing detail in his *Montaillou: The Promised Land of Error* to the zeal of the head Inquisitor, Jacques Fournier, Bishop of Pamiers, who painstakingly had every word of his inquiries recorded. The incorruptable, ascetic Fournier so distinguished himself for his diligence in catching heretics that in 1334 he was elected Pope Benedict XII. Only a handful of souls live in Montaillou now, but in the 1970s Ladurie looked through the telephone directory and found the same surnames common 650 years ago.

The North

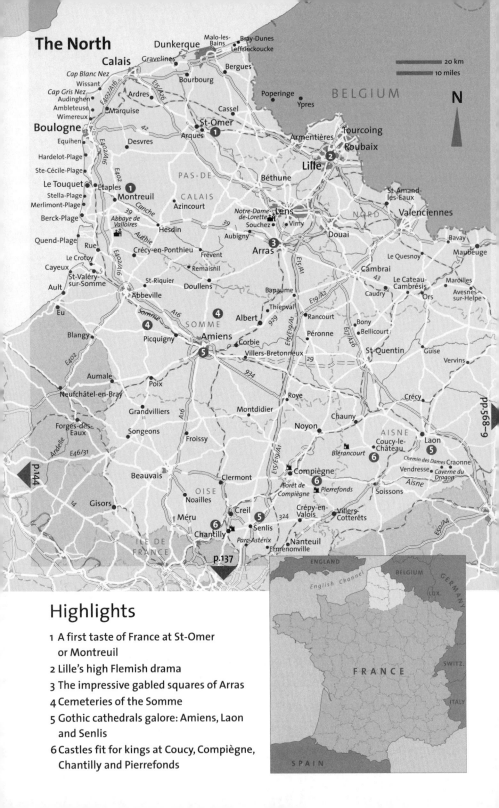

The North

Highlights

1 A first taste of France at St-Omer or Montreuil

2 Lille's high Flemish drama

3 The impressive gabled squares of Arras

4 Cemeteries of the Somme

5 Gothic cathedrals galore: Amiens, Laon and Senlis

6 Castles fit for kings at Coucy, Compiègne, Chantilly and Pierrefonds

Food and Drink

All sorts of special stews feature on northern French menus, particularly popular ones made with beer, rabbit, or mixed meats (the last known as *hochepot*) – this is a part of France where much of the traditional cooking is warming and copious. Soups are another favourite, from vegetable soups to broths into which tripe and even frogs may be popped. There are a lot of similarities with Flemish or Belgian cuisine, including a delight in sweet things and chocolate in particular. In the autumn, hillocks of white sugar beet are gathered by vast fields. The origins of pungent Maroilles, much the best-known cheese, date back to a 10th-century abbey. Beer, of course, is the popular local tipple – gin is also produced, as well as chicory coffee.

So much muscle and blood in the earth.
Sebastian Faulks, *Birdsong*

Killing fields, Gothic cathedrals, Flemish art and cross-Channel shopping count among the contrasting attractions of the North of France, which in this book means the modern regions of Nord Pas-de-Calais and Picardy. Nord Pas-de-Calais embraces historical French Flanders and Hainaut along the frontier with Belgium, plus Artois and the Côte d'Opale to the west. Picardy includes the tragic Somme valley and *département*. The name of the Somme inevitably brings to mind horrific images of the First World War. Bombs are still found every year by the thousand, and from time to time, the bodies of war victims are still unearthed. So much of northern France was smashed to bits in the two world wars that it may come as a surprise to find glorious cities in these parts. In Nord Pas-de-Calais head for St-Omer and Montreuil, Arras and Lille. In Picardy, the cathedral cities of Laon and Senlis stand out, as do the castle towns of Coucy, Compiègne and Chantilly.

To most, France's north conjures up the image of bleak industrial mining country, its name justifiably blackened by the likes of Zola, who in *Germinal* revealed the horrors of the miners' lives. Coal mining petered out here in the 1990s, but its reputation lives on, together with the transformed slag heaps. But in fact, most of the North of France consists of huge, gently undulating fields, while in southern Picardy large swathes of forests have been preserved, once the reserve of royal hunts. And then there's the quietly spectacular coast running down from Belgium to Normandy, soft sands and high dunes on offer practically the whole way.

Calais

Like Venice, Calais is best approached by sea. But the comparison ends there; it would take a drug-crazed advertising man to describe Calais as a Venice of the north. However, ugly though it may be, Calais remains close to many an Englishman's heart – mainly, it has to be admitted, for cheap booze and cigarettes. Its historic symbolism as an outpost of England may not have been entirely forgotten, but Calais has been so fought over down the centuries that very little of its history remains visible.

What is clear is that Calais' centre is now divided in two by a no man's land of bridges and roads. Starting in the northern half, if you're visiting in holiday season, consider climbing to the top of the **lighthouse** (*open July–Aug and French school hols daily 2–6*), one of the tallest in France. Not far off, another tower rising hopefully out of town is that of the brick church of **Notre-Dame**. Its crossing had to be rebuilt after the war, hence its different colour. Charles de Gaulle married his Calais bride here in 1921, between the wars which so devastated the place.

The big, shabby, post-war **Place d'Armes**, close to the port and busy with bars and shops, is overseen from one corner by a grim 13th-century **watch tower** – a rare vestige of the old town, and about as friendly as a guard dog. **Rue Royale** heads south,

Getting There and Around

P&O Stena Line, **SeaFrance** and **Hoverspeed** **Ferries** (*see* **Travel**) operate fast cross-Channel boat services from Dover to the port on the eastern side of Calais; the companies run cheap or complimentary buses into the centre for foot passengers. The Channel Tunnel terminal lies a little west of Calais, between Coquelles and Fréthun.

Calais has two **railway stations**, the central Calais-Ville and the station serving the Channel Tunnel, Calais-Fréthun. Calais-Fréthun is linked by regular high-speed services to Paris-Gare du Nord (*c. 1hr 30mins*). For **taxis** in Calais, call **t** 03 21 97 89 89/**t** 03 21 97 35 35/**t** 03 21 97 05 22/**t** 03 21 97 13 14.

Tourist Information

Calais: 12 Bd Clemenceau, **t** 03 21 96 62 40, *www.OT-calais.fr*.

Where to Stay and Eat

Calais ✉ 62100

★★★Holiday Inn, 6 Bd des Alliés, **t** 03 21 34 69 69, *www.holidayinn-calais.com* (*expensive*). In an unremarkable but usefully tall building with sea views between the port and the main shopping street. Restaurant (*moderate*) offering basic French fare. *Restaurant closed Sat and Sun lunch.*

★★★George V, 36 Rue Royale, **t** 03 21 97 68 00, *www.GEORGEV-CALAIS.com* (*moderate*). Comfortable, set in the thick of the action on the main shopping street. Restaurant (*expensive–moderate*) serving northern French classics as well as good fish. *Restaurant closed Sat lunch and Sun.*

★★Hôtel des Dunes, 48 Route Nationale, 62231 Blériot-Plage (west of town; if without a car, take bus line 3 from outside Calais' theatre), **t** 03 21 34 54 30, *www.les-dunes.com* (*moderate–inexpensive*). A bit more individuality, as well as being very close to the beach. The restaurant (*moderate*) serves delicious fish dishes. *Restaurant closed Sun eve, and Mon off season.*

★★Kyriad Calais Plage, Digue Gaston Berthe, **t** 03 21 34 64 64, *www.hotel-plage-calais.com* (*inexpensive*). Standard chain hotel, but in a good location very close to the western beach, and with simple restaurant (*moderate–cheap*).

★★Tudor-Bristol, 6 Rue Marie Tudor, **t** 03 21 34 53 24, *Hotel-Bristol-Tudor@wanadoo.fr* (*inexpensive*). Cheap and central.

L'Aquar'aile, Résidence Les Ridens, 255 Rue Jean Moulin, **t** 03 21 34 00 00 (*expensive–moderate*). One of the region's best seafood restaurants, with views, perched high up in a modern block behind the western beach. *Closed Sun eve and Mon.*

Le Channel, 3 Bd de la Résistance, **t** 03 21 34 42 30 (*expensive–moderate*). Popular for fish, with views over the marina. *Closed Sun eve and Tues, plus late-July–early Aug and Christmas–mid-Jan.*

La Sole Meunière, 1 Bd de la Résistance, **t** 03 21 34 43 01 (*moderate*). Next to Le Channel, with similar features. *Closed Sun eve and Mon.*

Au Côte d'Argent, 1 Digue Gaston Berthe, **t** 03 21 34 68 07 (*moderate*). Excellent seafood restaurant with marine décor, in prime location by the beach. *Closed Sun eve and Mon.*

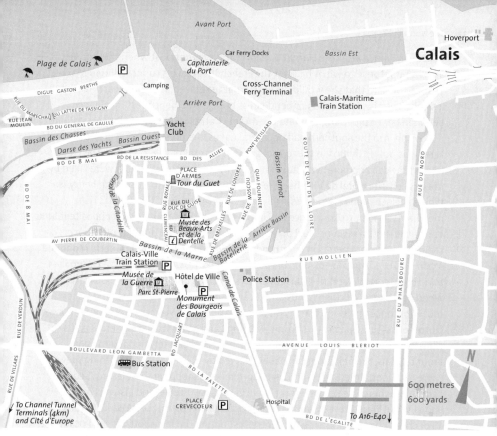

Avant Port

Hoverport

Car Ferry Docks

Bassin Est

Plage de Calais

Capitainerie
du Port

Cross-Channel
Ferry Terminal

Calais-Maritime
Train Station

DIGUE GASTON BERTHE

Camping

Arrière Port

RUE DU MARECHAL DU LATTRE DE TASSIGNY

RUE JEAN
MOULIN

BD DU GENERAL DE GAULLE

Bassin des Chasses

Yacht
Club

Darse des Yachts

Bassin Ouest

BD DE 8 MAI

BD DE LA RESISTANCE

BD DES

ALLIES

PONT VETILLARD

Bassin Carnot

ROUTE DE QUAI DE LA LOIRE

RUE DU NORD

BD DE 8 MAI

Canal de la Citadelle

PLACE
D'ARMES

Tour du Guet

RUE ROYALE

RUE DU
DUC DE GUISE

RUE DE LONDRES

RUE DE MOSON

QUAI FOURNIER

AV PIERRE DE COUBERTIN

CLEMENCEAU

Musée des
Beaux-Arts
et de la
Dentelle

RUE DE BRUXELLES

Arrière Bassin

Bassin de la Marne

Bassin de la
Batellerie

Arrière Bassin

RUE MOLLIEN

Calais-Ville
Train Station

Musée de
la Guerre

Hôtel de Ville

Police Station

RUE DU PHALSBOURG

Parc St-Pierre

Monument
des Bourgeois
de Calais

Canal de Calais

RUE DE VERDUN

BOULEVARD LEON GAMBETTA

BD JACQUART

AVENUE   LOUIS   BLERIOT

Bus Station

BD LA FAYETTE

N

RUE DE VILLARS

600 metres
600 yards

To Channel Tunnel
Terminals (4km)
and Cité d'Europe

PLACE
CREVECOEUR

Hospital

BD DE L'EGALITE

To A16-E40

the top part of the main shopping artery cutting through the two halves of town. At the end of Rue Royale, gardens stand either side; those of the **citadel**, the remnant of a fort built by Louis XIV's military genius Vauban, are the more interesting.

Beside the other garden, **Parc Richelieu**, stands the reasonably interesting if rather characterless 1960s brick and glass **Musée des Beaux-Arts et de la Dentelle** (*open Mon and Wed–Fri 10–12 and 2–5.30, Sat 10–12 and 2-6.30, Sun 2–6.30; closed Tues; adm*). It contains displays of the industrially produced but beautiful lace for which Calais was long renowned, plus an introduction to Flemish art. It also holds an interesting collection of sculptures, starting with a provocative little equestrian statue of Napoleon, but the main focus is Rodin's set of studies for his late 19th-century masterpiece, *The Burghers of Calais*, made to recall the terrible siege of Calais by King Edward III of England's troops from 1346 to 1347. After 11 months of appalling suffering, the townspeople surrendered. Keen to humiliate them still further, Edward insisted that six of the town's leading merchants should come out barefoot, noosed and begging, to present him with the keys to Calais. Some of Rodin's desperate, ragged figures still wear their dignity, if little else, while others look utterly lost in their individual agony. The English king's wife, Queen Philippa of Hainaut, is said to have been so distressed by the scene that she entreated her husband to show mercy to the six sacrificial burghers. They were spared, as was the town of Calais on that occasion. Calais remained the last piece of territory to which the English monarchy held on in France after the Hundred Years War. It was only lost when the Duc de Guise arrived by surprise to win it back for the French in 1558. This supposedly led Mary Tudor to declare that she would die with Calais engraved upon her heart – with its loss, she saw the destruction of her dearest hopes to cement a lasting alliance between her Catholic England and the mighty Catholic Spain of her husband Philip.

Crossing into the southern half of central Calais, the finished group of Rodin's sculptures was put up in 1895 in the formal gardens in front of the town hall. The French text on the commemorative plaque mistakenly implies that the men were killed by the English. The **Hôtel de Ville** itself, rebuilt after the war with its soaring belfry, is typical of such grand Flemish edifices, reflecting the pride of the region's rich merchants in their towns. Concealed in the unremarkable public park opposite it lurks one of the most awesome Nazi bunkers you'll ever have the dubious pleasure of seeing, almost 100 metres in length, now the **Musée de la Seconde Guerre Mondiale** (*open May–Aug daily 10–6; April and Sept daily 11–5.30; Oct–mid-Nov Wed–Mon 12–5; mid-Feb–Mar Wed–Mon 11–5*). Just one of its rooms is devoted to the First World War, when Calais was in British hands and received its first pasting from bombs. The museum concentrates on the German occupation from May 1940 to autumn 1944. A clutter of cuttings, posters, uniforms, weapons and other war paraphernalia fills the claustrophobic spaces. At one point the Germans deliberately flooded the plain around Calais; the fields were so badly affected by the sea salt that nothing grew there for a long time. Back with Calais' light relief – shopping – Boulevard Jacquart continues where Rue Royale left off. Boulevard La Fayette beyond also has major shops, while Place Crèvecœur, just off it, hosts a morning market Wed, Thurs and Sat.

For cheap shopping outside the centre, just before the ferry port, off the Rocade Est (eastern ringroad), the **Zone Marcel Doret** offers one choice. West of town, by the Channel Tunnel (exit 12 or 14 from the A16 motorway), rises the vast **Cité Europe** mall, with around 150 shops. The separate **Parc La Française** a bit to the north features other big stores. If you think (rightly) that Calais hypermarkets and cheap stores are not what French shopping and gastronomy are really about, save your euros for the beautiful historic town of St-Omer (*see* p.542), not far inland.

A more relaxing attraction close to Calais, long, sandy suburban **beaches** stretch west from the port, first backed by cheap apartment blocks and rows of sometimes graffiti-covered white shacks that watch the ferries ploughing in and out of port. Then just a small line of dunes divides the string of houses from the comfortable sands. The name of **Blériot-Plage** and a monument there honour Louis Blériot, the Frenchman who succeeded in making the first-ever cross-Channel flight, in July 1909. Let it not cross your mind that he might have been trying to escape from Calais.

From Calais into French Flanders

East of Calais, you can start polishing up your Flemish simply by turning on the car radio as you enter French Flanders. The canalized Aa estuary is guarded by **Gravelines** and its two coastal outposts, Grand-Fort-Philippe and Petit-Fort-Philippe. The Philippe

Getting Around

Norfolkline (*see* **Travel**) runs a good-value car-only **ferry** service to Loon-Plage west of Dunkerque, which has regular **train** connections with Paris-Gare du Nord and with Lille.

Tourist Information

Gravelines: 11 Rue de République, **t** 03 28 51 94 00, *www.tourisme.fr/gravelines*.
Dunkerque: Le Beffroi, **t** 03 28 66 79 21, *www.ot-dunkerque.fr*.
Bray-Dunes: Place J. Rubben, **t** 03 28 26 61 09, *otbraydunes@worldonline.fr*.
Bergues: Beffroi, **t** 03 28 68 71 06, *tourisme. bergues@wanadoo.fr*.
Cassel: Grand'Place, **t** 03 28 40 52 55, *www. ot-cassel.fr*.

Where to Stay and Eat

Gravelines ✉ 59820

***Hostellerie du Beffroi**, Pl Ch. Valentin, **t** 03 28 23 24 25, *www.hoteldubeffroi.com* (*moderate*). Smart central brick hotel in Flemish style, in the shadow of the towering belfry. Modern restaurant (*moderate*). *Restaurant closed Sat lunch and Sun eve.*

Bergues ✉ 59380

★★Au Tonnelier, 4 Rue du Mont de Piété, **t** 03 28 68 70 05 (*inexpensive*). Charming central hotel with pleasing restaurant (*moderate*). *Closed late Aug and Christmas; restaurant closed Mon lunch.*
★★Hôtel du Commerce, 2 Rue du Mont de Piété, **t** 03 28 68 60 37 (*inexpensive*). Surprisingly nice, spacious and unpretentious neighbour of the above.
Le Cornet d'Or, 26 Rue Espagnol, **t** 03 28 68 66 27 (*expensive*). The poshest restaurant, by the water, with rich décor to accompany grand-style cuisine. *Closed Sun eve and Mon, and early Sept.*
Taverne Bruegel, **t** 03 28 68 19 19 (*moderate*). The most picturesque restaurant, in an excellent spot by the water, mainly serving simple regional platters.

Cassel ✉ 59670

Estaminet T'Kasteel Hof, **t** 03 28 40 59 29 (*moderate*). With great views at the top of Mont Cassel, a chaotically charming restaurant serving local Flemish dishes and Flemish beers. *Closed Mon–Wed.*
La Taverne Flamande, **t** 03 28 42 42 59 (*cheap*). Flemish specialities down in the grandiose main square, with terrace. *Closed Tues eve and Wed.*

referred to is Philip II of Spain, whose soldiers took French Flanders for the Emperor in the late 1580s. After the failure of the Spanish Armada sent to destroy England in 1588, some of his fleet was scattered in disarray along this coast. Gravelines' moated ramparts date back in part to the late 17th century, when Vauban, Louis XIV's great military architect, was called upon to fortify strategic points along France's new frontiers. His arsenal now houses the **Musée du Dessin et de l'Estampe Originale** (*open Wed–Mon 2–5, plus July–Aug mornings 10–12; closed Tues; adm*), with exhibitions on the graphic arts. The lighthouse at the end of the canal stands out like a black and white stick of liquorice. At **Grand-Fort-Philippe**, the **Maison de l'Islandais** (*open early April–late-Sept Wed–Mon 2–6; closed Tues; adm*) recalls the fishermen of these parts, including those who went off on the gruelling cod-fishing expeditions around Iceland. The large beaches look immediately enticing, although the enormous casserole pots of a nuclear power station will deter you from going too far east.

Dunkerque

Dunkerque (or Dunkirk), France's third-largest port after Marseille and Le Havre, has industrial outskirts so large it can be hard to find the centre. Comparable to Calais, this war-torn port is hardly an obvious tourist destination. However, it has been able to restore more of its historic buildings, even though it was 80 per cent destroyed by bombs in the Second World War. The central harbour attracts plenty of yachts, but the tall ship, the *Duchesse Anne*, stands out, moored by the **Musée Portuaire** (*open Wed–Mon 10–12.45 and 1.30–6; closed Tues; adm*). Former dockers helped put together this appealing, substantial museum on the history of Dunkerque, set in former tobacco warehouses. You can also tour the *Duchesse Anne*, which turns out to have been built as a German naval training vessel. In July and August the museum organizes boat trips round the port, and weekend tours up one of France's tallest lighthouses.

The Flemish love their soaring towers, and Dunkerque boasts several more. The **Tour Leughenaer**, the town's oldest monument and a lone reminder of the massive fortifications built in the 14th century when the mighty dukes of Burgundy ruled over Flanders, stands at one end of the central harbour. Nearby, the brick belfry of the mock-historic town hall puts on a show. Most impressive of all, a huge **belfry** rises opposite the Gothic church of St-Eloi, plaques outside recalling Second World War bravery, while up high you can admire the bells and an industrial panorama. Down below, **St-Eloi** is Dunkerque's most graceful building, with stunning tracery on the rose window of its white façade. It is dedicated to a major French Merovingian bishop, influential in consolidating Christianity in northern France under 7th-century King Dagobert. In fact, the port derives its name from a church (Kerque in Flemish) in the dunes. Dunkerque has a long history, but one dashing figure dominates from the past – 17th-century corsair Jean Bart. The airy church interior with its gilded touches contains his tombstone, plus others written in Flemish and Spanish as well as in French, reminders of the different cultures that affected the area. A grandiose statue of Bart, once the scourge of the English navy, oversees the rather vacuous square nearby named after him, and from which the main shopping area extends.

A little way east, close to the canal, the **Musée des Beaux-Arts** (*open Wed–Mon 10–12.15 and 1.45–6; closed Tues; adm*) offers an interesting trawl through northern European art from the 16th century, and contains some fine still lives, portraits by Pourbus and Reyn, and a noble head of a young turbanned black man by Rigaud.

Head seawards along the canal to reach the **Musée de la Guerre** (*open May–Sept 10–12 and 2–5.30; adm*), tucked away behind an outdoor sculpture park in bastions erected to try to protect the port after the humiliating Franco-Prussian War of 1870. These defences proved utterly useless against the German onslaught of 1940. The Nazis struck Holland on 10 May. Franco-British forces moved into Belgium to defend it, but, ill-prepared for the full force of the German Blitzkrieg, they had to beat a very hasty retreat towards Dunkerque. In those demoralizing days, the British put together Operation Dynamo, a brave plan to rescue the soldiers caught in the Dunkerque pocket using not just naval ships, but also a very large fleet of private vessels, many tiny. Between 27 May and 4 June, some 225,000 British, 125,000 French and 16,000 Belgians were saved by the skin of their teeth. It is generally accepted that Operation Dynamo was crucial in stopping Britain being beaten by the Nazis, although a common view long held by many French people was that the French troops were largely abandoned. Dunkerque, in the meantime, had been reduced to rubble, and the townspeople suffered 8,000 deaths. Just south of Dunkerque centre is a British war cemetery and memorial. On the shore just above the museum, a monument recalls 250 boats lost in the evacuation as well as the airmen, seamen and soldiers who died.

Dunkerque's seaside resort of **Malo-les-Bains** stretches out from here. The place can't exactly turn its back on the industrial quarters, the horizon to the west marked by the black silhouettes of massive smoke-spewing factories. But the promenade is quite cheerful, a few Belle Epoque follies still standing among the dull modern blocks, while lovely flat sands extend unbroken to the Belgian border. At **Leffrinckoucke**, there is a French national war cemetery with panels describing the events in sober tone. The resort of **Bray-Dunes**, the last town before the frontier, has retained some of its old-fashioned villas, and has a basic memorial on its beach-front promenade. The former border post along the coast road is now a Belgian chocolate shop!

Bergues and Cassel

A short way inland, crossed by the waterways that typify the area, and surrounded by moated ramparts, **Bergues** makes a pleasant discovery so close to the massive industrial surrounds of Dunkerque. It developed around an abbey dedicated to St Winoc, a Breton who Christianized these parts in the Dark Ages. On the Groenberg, the town's highest point, a couple of striking towers stand out, one sharply pointed, the other looking like a caricature of a giant in stone. They are virtually all that remains of the abbey, brought down at the Revolution. Below, the atmosphere of an old fortified town has been quite well recreated after the war devastation. A proud Flemish **belfry** dominates proceedings, decorated with bartizan towers, copper-meringue ornaments and 50 bells. Several houses round and about boast high-scrolled Flemish gables. The grandiose classical building with its balustraded roof and small obelisks is the **town hall**. A couple of busts here pay homage to Alphonse de Lamartine, France's greatest Romantic poet but also an ambitious mid-19th-century liberal politician. The massive, severe, wholly restored church of St-Martin takes up most of another square nearby. Beside it, the elaborately scrolled building originally served as an almshouse, but has been turned into the **Musée du Mont de Piété** (*open Feb–Dec Wed–Mon 10–12 and 2–5; closed Tues; adm*), its main claim to fame a work by Georges de La Tour, *The Nightwatchman with a Dog*.

For the best views over French Flanders, head up one of the winding routes to **Cassel**, a hilltop town some 20km south of Bergues. Cassel's highest point may not even reach 600ft, but it commands vast panoramas over the flat countryside around. Local legend has it that the hill was formed by a clod of earth falling from the giant boots of Reuze Papa and Reuze Maman – Flanders is full of tales of such Gargantuan figures, effigies of whom are still brought out for local festivals. Real armies have fought over Cassel's strategic site for centuries, and it was even immortalized in a nursery rhyme: the Grand Old Duke of York led forces against the French Revolutionary army here. During the First World War, General Foch, leader of the French army, had his headquarters at Cassel, and is remembered with an equestrian statue by the **Moulin Kastel-Meulen** (*open Sat, Sun and French school hols 10–12 and 2–5; adm*) – French Flanders once had thousands of these windmills, but this is one of the few to survive and still grind flour. Down below, the small town stretches around a sloping cobbled main square. The grandest building, **La Chatellainie**, serves for temporary exhibitions. A brick church stands out one end of the square, a typical Flemish Hallekerque, in which the side aisles are as tall and wide as the central nave.

East of Cassel, the main road leads across the Belgian border to **Poperinge** and **Ypres** (Ieper in Flemish), an area which saw some of the most appalling fighting in the First World War, the infamous place where gas was first put to use by the Germans. Some 100,000 soldiers from the British Empire lost their lives here. On the Menin Gate, the number of dead soldiers listed is overwhelming. Every night two buglers still sound the *Last Post* here. 'A more sacred place for the British race does not exist in the whole world,' Winston Churchill said of Ypres in 1919. Immaculately maintained British and Commonwealth cemeteries mark the lands all the way down from Ypres, through the areas around Arras and Albert, and down across the Somme river.

Lille

Lille, capital of French Flanders and City of Culture in 2004, comes as a big surprise, a place where Parisian chic meets Belgian chocolate. Hidden in layers of heavy industry, the centre has outrageous Flemish Baroque buildings and elegant shopping streets that used to be something of a secret, until the arrival of the Eurostar.

A bone of contention for much of its history, Lille survived its frequent changes of overlord as a market town and textile centre. The successfully expansionist Capetian king Philippe Auguste may have pushed the Plantagenets out of northwest France, but he also won a famous battle against the count of Flanders and the Germanic emperor Otto IV at Bouvines east of Lille in 1214. However, down the centuries, Lille and what is now French Flanders were not a part of the French kingdom, but ruled instead by powerful figures on its edges. For a long time capital of the successfully independent counts of Flanders, in 1369 Lille became a part of the Flemish territories of the massively powerful dukes of Burgundy, dangerous cousins of the French kings. When the last duke of Burgundy, Charles the Bold, was killed in 1477, his heir, Marie de Bourgogne, was married to Habsburg Maximilian of Austria. Through Habsburg expansion, Lille and Flanders became part of the Spanish Netherlands, up to 1667, when Louis XIV's troops took the town for the greedy Sun King. Fortified to Vauban's plans, in 1708 the town suffered appalling conditions as the Duke of Marlborough's men besieged it. Many starved. Dutch forces controlled Lille for a few years after that.

By the time Charles de Gaulle was born here in 1890, Lille had developed into an industrial powerhouse. It was occupied by German forces in both world wars. Bombs rained down on the city in the Second World War, after which Lille's industrial base declined. Like its southern counterpart, Marseille, it has since suffered from a bad press, fuelled by images of gross industrialization and racism. Now a banking, administrative and university town, with some 100,000 students, central Lille in fact proves a deeply likeable place.

If you're walking in from Lille-Europe train station, don't get distracted by the vast **Euralille** shopping centre, which has about as much atmosphere as an airport

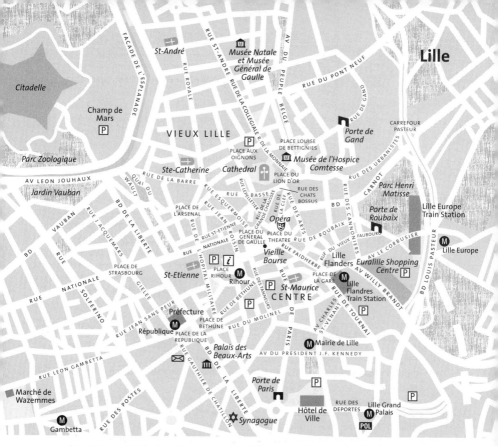

terminal; just ten minutes' walk away, many of the same shops are to be found along the enchanting streets of Vieux Lille. Rue Faidherbe leads from the more central Lille-Flandres station to the centre; off it, the **Eglise St-Maurice** is a rare vestige of the city's medieval prosperity. In the form of a Flemish Hallekerque, the church exterior has recently been scrubbed clean to reveal its white stone. In the more lugubrious interior, a seeming forest of columns holds up the spacious five aisles.

The very heart of Lille is split in two, Place du Théâtre to the right, Place du Général de Gaulle (also known as the Grand' Place) to the left, with the Vieille Bourse in between. Two outrageous buildings from the early 20th century flaunt themselves on **Place du Théâtre**. The sparklingly white **opera house** is crowned by the *Triumph of Apollo* by Hippolyte Lefebvre, a sculpture that's more than a match for the most ludicrous of opera plots. The architect was Louis-Marie Cordonnier, also responsible for the **Palais de la Bourse** with its rocketing Flemish belfry. The **Vieille Bourse**, although on a smaller scale, also smacks of excess, Baroque this time. Designed by Julien Destrée in the 1650s, the recently restored inner courtyard shelters market stalls. Plaques on the walls behind sing the praises of leading men of commerce and science. Above the colonnade, the stones have been squeezed and twisted like Plasticine to create grotesque animal faces.

In the centre of **Place du Général de Gaulle**, Lille's dominatrix of a **Déesse** (Goddess) holds court, a symbol of the city's success in repulsing the Austrian forces in 1792. The

Getting There and Around

Lille-Europe is just 2hrs from London-Waterloo by **Eurostar**. The station has fantastic links with other parts of France and is only 10–15mins' walk from the city centre. Coming from Paris-Gare du Nord, trains arrive at Lille-Flandres station. Lille-Lesquin **airport** is less than 10km from the centre, but for internal flights. Toll-free **motorways** from the Channel ports of Calais and Dunkerque bring you swiftly to Lille. For **taxis**, t 03 20 06 06 06/ t 03 20 06 64 00/t 03 20 55 20 56.

Tourist Information

Lille: Palais Rihour, Place Rihour, t 03 20 21 94 21, www.lilletourism.com.

Where to Stay and Eat

Lille ✉ 59800

★★★★**Carlton**, 3 Rue de Paris, t 03 20 13 33 13, www.carltonlille.com (luxury–very expensive). The plushest address in town, opposite the opulent opera building.

★★★★**Alliance**, 17 Quai du Wault, Lille 59027, t 03 20 30 62 62, alliancelille@wanadoo.fr (luxury–very expensive). Converted 17th-century convent with smart modern rooms and restaurant (moderate) in the cloister with sensational roof.

★★★**Grand Hôtel Bellevue**, 5 Rue Jean Roisin, t 03 20 57 45 64, www.grandhotelbellevue.com (very expensive–expensive). In the very heart of town. Ask for one of the well-furnished rooms over the Grand' Place.

★★**Brueghel**, 5 Parvis St-Maurice, t 03 20 06 06 69, www.hotel-brueghel.com (moderate).

Well located and well run, overlooking the St-Maurice church , deeply appealing old style with comfortable small rooms.

★★**Hôtel de la Paix**, 46 bis Rue de Paris, t 03 20 54 63 93, www.hotel-la-paix.com (moderate). Stylish, in grand building, well kept by a woman passionate about painting.

★★**Ibis Opéra**, 21 Rue Lepelletier, t 03 20 06 21 95, www.accorhotels.com (moderate–inexpensive). Very handily located in the midst of luxury shopping streets.

★**Mister Bed City**, 57 Rue de Béthune, t 03 20 12 96 96, www.misterbed.fr (inexpensive). Cheap chain hotel in excellent position in the most popular shopping street.

A l'Huîtrière, 3 Rue des Chats Bossus, t 03 20 55 43 41 (very expensive–expensive). Seafood heaven at the back of a sensational fish shop. Closed Sun eve and bank hols, and late July–late Aug.

Le Compostelle, 4 Rue St-Etienne, t 03 28 38 08 30 (expensive). The finest setting for a smart traditional Flanders dinner, in the only Renaissance mansion in Lille with a courtyard.

Les Compagnons de la Grappe, 26 Rue Lepelletier, t 03 20 21 02 79 (moderate). Set back in its own courtyard off a prime shopping street, striking arty décor and food and wine as interesting as the setting. Closed Sun.

Le Porthos, 53 Rue de la Monnaie, t 03 20 06 44 06 (moderate–cheap). Opposite the Hospice Comtesse, filled with lively lawyers during the week .

Bistrot de Pierrot, 6 Place de Béthune, t 03 20 57 14 09 (moderate–cheap). By the Palais des Beaux-Arts, this very well-known atmospheric bistrot is run by a bit of a TV star, Pierrot. Closed Sun and bank hols.

object in her hand, which looks like a whip from a distance, is described as a boutefeu, used to light cannons. This square has many grand façades, and looks predominantly Flemish, particularly the massive stepped gable of the La Voix du Nord building, headquarters of the largest newspaper in the region – the bronze figures on high stand for the historic provinces of Flanders, Hainaut and Artois.

A third grand square connects with Place du Général de Gaulle, although **Place Rihour** has none of the architectural swagger of the other two: it's a bit of a 20th-century mess. A mausoleum-like war memorial dominates one corner. Behind it hides the tourist office, in the sorry remnants of the **Palais Rihour**, the Lille home of the immensely powerful late-medieval dukes of Burgundy, who owned Flanders for a very prosperous time. The chapel above the tourist office is used for exhibitions. A little west, **St-Etienne**, on Rue de l'Hôpital Militaire, is one of several grand Baroque churches tucked into Lille's residential streets. **Rue Nationale** and **Rue de Béthune**, respectively north and south of Place Rihour, are major shopping arteries.

The immense **Place de la République** at the end of Rue de Béthune looks overblown and vacuous at the same time. Two stupendously pompous 19th-century buildings face each other across the huge space: the **Préfecture**, and the **Palais des Beaux-Arts** (*open Mon 2–6, Wed–Sun 10–6; closed Tues; adm*). Reopened by the French president in 1997, this is the most obvious cultural call in Lille. Don't miss the excellent medieval and Renaissance galleries of the first basement level, which include Donatello's bas-relief *Feast of Herod*. Still further down you will find the archaeological section and amazingly detailed large-scale 18th-century town models. In the ground-floor sculpture gallery, Rodin's caramelized figure of *L'Ombre*, the Shadow, and pieces by Camille Claudel, his put-upon lover, stand out. Rubens' powerful depiction of the deposition of Christ opens proceedings among the paintings, superbly displayed on the first floor. Interiors by De Witte and De Hooch and landscapes by Van Ruysdael and Sieberecht catch the attention, but Courbet's *Après dîner à Ornans*, described as a manifesto of Realism in painting, looks disappointingly dull. The most talked-about works in the foreign collections are typically disturbing fruits of Goya's imagination; *Le Temps, dit Les Vieilles* shows two caricatures of decrepit society women who look like coquettish grimacing cadavers dressed up for their walk. Boudin and Sisley provide prettier pictures from back home, but perhaps the highlight of the 19th-century French selection is Emile Bernard's cloisonné *Les Cueilleuses de pommes*. Born in Lille, Bernard was the man who, along with Gauguin, led the once-shocking School of Pont-Aven in Brittany (*see* p.250). There are also works by Picasso and Léger.

A short walk southeast from the Musée des Beaux-Arts brings you to the **Porte de Paris**, the most imposing of Lille's surviving gateways, now isolated by traffic. This homage to Louis XIV, designed by Simon Vollant, shows Victory crowning the Sun King. In a modern square to one side stands the **Hôtel de Ville**, completed in 1932. Another flabbergasting Flemish **belfry** (*open first Sun April–last Sun Sept Sun–Fri 10–5.30; closed Sat; adm*) blasts up from it over 300ft into the sky. The legendary giant founders of Lille, Phinaert and Lydéric, portrayed on its side, look quite dwarfed by it. Climb up for views over the whole of Lille. At night, the tower turns into a great lighthouse.

Back by the Grand' Place, go exploring the glamorous shopping streets of **Vieux Lille**, strung with delightful squares. Pretty Rue Esquermoise is followed by Rue de la Barre, off which lies the neglected old church of **Ste-Catherine**. Rue Lepelletier and Rue Basse are further elegant streets. Rue des Chats Bossus (the Hunchbacked Cats), the continuation of Rue Basse, ends in the charming triangular Place du Lion d'Or. The vast, incomplete and hideous 19th-century **cathedral** lurks in this quarter, thankfully, surprisingly well hidden from view. Along Rue de la Monnaie, another good shopping street, you arrive at the **Musée de l'Hospice Comtesse** (*open Wed–Sun 10–12.30 and 2–6, Mon 2–6; adm*), central Lille's second most important museum, set within a former hospital, founded way back in 1237, rebuilt in 1468 after a fire, and much altered again after another fire in the 17th century. Its collections concentrate on Flemish arts. The community building in the main courtyard contains fine Flemish paintings, ceramics and furniture, plus a couple of rooms covered with Delft tiles. Look out also for the paintings of Flemish interiors and urban scenes, including processions and the **Lille Braderie**, an annual market that still exists (*first week Sept*) as a massive antiques fair. The impressive main medieval ward is used for temporary exhibitions. The ceiling of the chapel beyond was adorned in the mid-19th century with 66 coats of arms representing the hospital's principal benefactors.

On Rue Princesse north of the centre, in a quiet, wealthy corner of town made up of broad, straight-lined streets, the **Maison Natale et Musée Général de Gaulle** (*open Wed–Sun 10–12 and 2–5; adm*) is signalled by the French flag waving above the door. This is where Charles de Gaulle was born on 22 November 1890, in his maternal grandmother's substantial house. Charles only lived here for the three months following his birth, but he visited his grandmother regularly afterwards. Inside, the overwhelming feeling is of bourgeois piety preserved in aspic. In the workshops, the general's life story is told in indigestible fashion, but a bullet-ridden Citroën highlights the great risks he took. Moving west, beyond the massive, free Champ de Mars car park, the Lille **citadel** (*tours arranged via the tourist office; adm*) hides behind woods within a loop of the river Deule. The French army still owns this startling star-shaped fortification, a well-preserved example of Vauban's defensive architecture.

Moving into Lille's outlying towns, **Roubaix**'s new **Musée d'Art et d'Industrie La Piscine** (*open Tues–Fri 11–6, Sat and Sun 2–6; closed Mon; adm; take the metro to Gare-Roubaix and it's a short walk*) is indeed set in a former public swimming baths. On top of that, this interwar extravaganza was built in the shape of a Cistercian abbey! The vast mosaic-bottomed pool has been turned into a sculpture garden where catwalk shows also take place. In fact fashion features large alongside the good collections of 19th and 20th century art, which is only appropriate, given that the area around Lille remains the most important for textile production in France.

Major roads speed round the **Musée d'Art Moderne** at **Villeneuve d'Ascq** (*open Wed–Mon 10–6; adm*), in the Lille suburbs (*metro to Pont de Bois, then bus 41 to Parc Urbain*). The architecture looks like something lifted from a 1960s university campus. The museum contains a good collection by great names of 20th-century art, including magnificent Modigliani figures, outshining the Braques and Picassos.

Reaching the countryside southeast of Lille, the modestly attractive village of **Bouvines** is dominated by a grandiose 19th-century church containing a panoply of stained glass telling of King Philippe Auguste's major victory here. God scarcely gets a look-in in all the violent, swashbuckling chivalric action.

Into Artois and Hainaut from Calais

As well as preserving terrible memories of the First World War, this area boasts two splendid small cities, St-Omer and Arras. Such Hainaut towns as Douai and Cambrai are for the more culturally adventurous traveller, hiding surprisingly good museums.

Getting There and Around

Arras is easy to reach by **train**, on the Paris-Gare du Nord–Dunkerque line. Change at Arras for St-Omer. Douai lies on the Paris-Gare du Nord–Valenciennes line. Change at Douai for Cambrai.

Tourist Information

St-Omer: 4 Rue du Lion d'Or, **t** 03 21 98 08 51, *www.tourisme.fr/saint-omer.*
Arras: Place des Héros, **t** 03 21 51 26 95, *www.ot-arras.fr.*
Douai: 70 Place d'Armes, **t** 03 27 88 26 79, *www.ville-douai.fr.*
Cambrai: 48 Rue de Noyon, **t** 03 27 78 36 15, *www.villedecambrai.fr.*

Where to Stay and Eat

Recques-sur-Hem ✉ **62890**
★★★★Château de Cocove, Av de Cocove, **t** 03 21 82 68 29, *chateaudecocove@hotmail.com* (*expensive–moderate*). A rural idyll in an 18th-century country house southeast of Ardres, with spacious rooms and fine menus served in the restaurant in former stables.

Tilques ✉ **62500**
★★★★Château de Tilques, **t** 03 21 88 99 99, *www.chateautilques.com* (*very expensive–moderate*). Luxurious brick castle in a punting marsh village northwest of St-Omer, with refined restaurant also in former stables. Tennis court.

St-Omer ✉ **62500**
★★St-Louis, 25 Rue d'Arras, **t** 03 21 38 35 21, *www.hotel-saintlouis.com* (*inexpensive*). Traditional provincial hotel just below the centre, with reasonable restaurant (*moderate*). 30 rooms. *Closed Christmas period; restaurant closed weekend lunch.*

★★Ibis, 2–4 Rue Henri Dupuis, **t** 03 21 93 11 11, *www.ibishotel.com* (*inexpensive*). Part of a chain, but in an exceptionally nice building, well-located at the top of the old town, with basic restaurant (*cheap*).
Le Cygne, 8 Rue Caventou, **t** 03 21 98 20 52 (*expensive–moderate*). Excellent smart restaurant on a fine little square. *Closed Sun eve and Mon.*
La Belle Epoque, Place Paul Painlevé, **t** 03 21 38 22 93 (*moderate*). Just off the major square, lively address for traditional dishes, with small terrace. *Closed Sun, Tues and bank hols.*

Arras ✉ **62000**
★★★L'Univers, 5 Place de Croix Rouge, **t** 03 21 71 34 01, *www.hotel-univers-arras.com* (*moderate*). In a former 16th-century monastery, characterful rooms around the plush courtyard. Lovely restaurant (*expensive–moderate*).
★★Les Trois Luppars, 49 Grand-Place, **t** 03 21 07 41 41 (*moderate–inexpensive*). Wonderful step-gabled Gothic building on Arras' most fabulous square, with neat modern rooms.
★★Diamant, 5 Place des Héros, **t** 03 21 71 23 23, *www.arras-hotel-diamant.com* (*inexpensive*). Bijou address on second-grandest square.
La Faisanderie, 45 Grand-Place, **t** 03 21 48 20 76 (*expensive*). Among the many restaurants on the main square, and one of several with spectacular cellar dining room, this one offers by far the best cuisine. *Closed Sun eve, Mon and Tues lunch, and most Aug, early Jan and late Feb.*

Cambrai ✉ **59403**
★★★Château de la Motte Fénelon, Square du Château, **t** 03 27 83 61 38, *www.chateaude-lamotte.com* (*expensive–moderate*). Separated from the town by its own gardens, smart rooms in a classical 19th-century house or simpler ones in outbuildings. Posh restaurant in the vaulted cellar. Tennis court.

The giant Nazi **Blockhaus d'Eperlecques** (*open July–Aug daily 10–7; May–June and Sept daily 10–12 and 2.15–7; Mar–April and Oct–Nov 2.15–5; adm*), hides on the edge of a forest a bit north of St-Omer, off the N43 road from Calais. The self-guided tour round this fascinatingly hideous concrete monstrosity reveals how it was planned in order to launch revolutionary V2 rockets on London. Fortunately, Allied pilots managed to bomb the bunker out of action before it was up and running. As a more peaceful alternative, hire a boat to explore the painterly marshes around these parts, for example from the charming village of **Tilques**.

St-Omer and Around

The very grandest buildings of St-Omer stand out from the rest in this historic, once ultra-religious little town, as they were made in fine pale stone rather than brick. An impressively solid square stone tower, almost English in appearance, rises from the **Basilique Notre-Dame**, the former cathedral, and the crowning glory of this now rather charmingly down-at-heel ex-city. The building was erected between the 13th and 15th centuries. Walk all the way round the cobbled squares surrounding it to enjoy the carvings and the flamboyant window tracery. Inside, a Catholic extravaganza awaits beyond the enormous organ on which figures play gilded instruments. The interior is crammed with statues, including the tomb of one Audomari, the 7th-century evangelizer of these parts, sent by King Dagobert to impose Christianity; the name of the town derives from that of this saintly figure.

Place Foch, a short walk away, is the archetypal French square, with masses of café terraces from which to watch the world go by, all in the presence of the pompous 19th-century **town hall**. An excellent array of shops lines the streets off this square. The delightful **public gardens** lie just a stone's throw away, across busy Boulevard Vauban; after Louis XIV's troops had seized control of St-Omer for France in 1677, the Sun King's beloved engineer had the town fortified with massive brick ramparts, some now balustraded, the dry moats below transformed into formal *parterres*.

Back in the historic centre, many spectacular buildings stand out in the neat grid of streets and squares sloping gently down the hill. Almost all have seen better days. The one exception is the restored **Hôtel Sandelin** (*check times with tourist office*), with all the elegance you'd expect of the finest Ancien Régime town house in central Paris, seemingly ready to receive gilded carriages. The fine arts museum inside has been undergoing major renovation. The other town museum, the **Musée Henri Dupuis** (*open Wed–Sun 10–12 and 2–6; adm*), between the cathedral and Place Foch, is a musty natural history museum containing a lot of stuffed birds, plus a fine Flemish kitchen. Place Victor Hugo nearby has plenty of life, though, in contrast to much quieter but almost equally stylish Place Sithieu. As to the **Chapelle Walloone** further down, it cries out for attention. A chapel built on the scale of a cathedral, its soaring scrolled façade is split into five levels like an extravagant Baroque brick cake. The inside is sadly neglected, but the buildings around the adjoining cloister have been converted into a fantastic high-tech library where you can inspect medieval manuscripts saved from the region's abbeys. Walk down Rue St-Bertin, past intimidating buildings that once housed St-Omer's many religious communities, including one reserved for English Jesuits in the times when Catholics were terribly persecuted in England. Some way further down are the meagre ruins of the **Abbaye St-Bertin**.

Huge lorries trundle east from St-Omer through industrial **Arques**, a major glass-producing town. You can visit a glass-making factory here and buy an enormous range of glassware and tableware at **Arc International**'s vast shop. South of St-Omer, by **Helfaut**, **La Coupole** (*open July–Aug daily 10–7; Sept–June daily 9–6; adm*) sounds an enticing name for what turns out to be another horrifically large but compelling Nazi V2 installation camouflaged in the countryside, covered by a vast dome. The subtitle to the place, the Centre d'Histoire de la Guerre et des Fusées, gives you more of a picture of the contents. With state-of-the-art displays, this subterranean museum not only tells the story of the terrifying long-range rockets designed by German scientists, in particular Von Braun, to bombard London in the Second World War. It also reveals how rocket technology then developed after the conflict in the American-Soviet race to be the first into space: America took on the Nazis' Von Braun!

War Memorials around Arras

A memorial to Indians who died in the Great War lies northeast of Béthune, close to Neuve-Chapelle. The subcontinent's contribution to the war effort is often forgotten, although books such as David Omissi's selection of soldiers' letters in *Indian Voices of the Great War* have brought more attention to the matter. Southwest of **Lens** stands one of the most emblematic of French First World War memorials, at the French national cemetery of **Notre-Dame de Lorette** along the so-called Crêtes du Sacrifice. The Battle of Lorette raged from October 1914 to October 1915. Losses were extremely heavy; the vast cemetery is dedicated to over 40,000 dead. At **Souchez** nearby, the **European Centre for Peace** in fact focuses in particular on trench warfare in Artois.

On 9 April 1917 the Canadians won the extremely important strategic heights at Vimy, so **Vimy Ridge** came to be chosen as the site for a **Canadian National Memorial and Park**. Some 3,600 Canadians lost their lives here; they are remembered along with the 11,285 Canadians who went missing in action in other parts during the First World War. The two wings of the noble monument symbolize the British and French origins of so many Canadians. Canadian students conduct the free guided tours (*open daily 10–6*). The park is well known for its trenches and underground tunnels.

Arras

A pageant of spectacular scrolled Flemish gables line up to be admired around Arras' **Grand-Place**, the greatest of several staggering squares at the centre of the most glamorous city in French Flanders. Arras became one of the richest towns in medieval Europe thanks to its dynamic merchants and its thriving international markets, held on its huge squares. Among the luxuries produced in town were fine tapestries, exported across Europe – one even features as a celebrated, fatal stage prop in Shakespeare's *Hamlet*. Central Arras looks so much the historic part, so well restored, that it's hard to imagine the war damage from which it suffered.

The misleadingly named **Petit-Place**, or **Place des Héros**, adjoining the Grand'Place proves extraordinarily grandiose too. Here, the **town hall** dominates, with an impressive array of dormer windows popping out of its steep acres of roofing. Most startling is the **belfry** (*open May–Sept daily 9–6.30; rest of year 9–12 and 2–6; adm*) rocketing some 250ft skywards. From inside the town hall, not only can you climb to the top of the belfry (the lift helps) for panoramic views, but you can also go on a tour of subterranean Arras and its **Boves**, or tunnels (*open same times as belfry; adm*). Stone was extracted down the centuries for Arras' building, creating elaborate galleries and caves. All these tunnels could be used for storage and for refuge. Catholics held secret masses in them in Revolutionary times. During the First World War, when Arras lay so close to the front line, British troops even set up an underground hospital.

Behind the town hall, the more down-to-earth **Place Vacquerie** leads through to the most significant religious buildings left in Arras, those of the **Abbaye St-Vaast**, named after the first bishop of the city. The abbey lives up to the unintentional pun – it is enormous, rebuilt on a palatial scale during the Ancien Régime for a certain Cardinal de Rohan, among the most ostentatious and corrupt bishops of 18th-century France. The place now contains the **Musée des Beaux-Arts** (*open Wed–Mon 9.30–12 and 2–5.30; closed Tues; adm*). The artefacts take you as far back as Gallo-Roman times. A number of rooms concentrate on Arras' history. You can also see how a regional tradition of pottery developed. Sadly, virtually no medieval Arras tapestries have survived beyond one piece showing St Vaast taming a bear, but some intense medieval carvings have found refuge here. Arras' original cathedral was brought down by Revolutionary fanatics, and the abbey's huge neoclassical church, completed in the 19th century, took over the role. Wall paintings inside tell the life of St Vaast, that bear popping up again, while more typical Christian images adorn other corners.

Ironically supported by one of Arras' late-Ancien Régime bishops, the town's most infamous citizen became the most terrifying exponent of French Revolutionary Terror – Maximilien Robespierre. Brought up in part in Arras (his father was a barrister in Artois), Maximilien followed in his father's footsteps, practising here before he moved to Paris to such devastating effect. **Robespierre's house** (*open April–Sept Tues–Sun 2–6.30, closed Mon; rest of year Tues and Thurs 2–5.30, weekends 3–6.30*) still stands, near the abbey. It contains a few sad mementos of the Incorruptible One, plus an unrelated display on cycling. Which has been the greater force for good in French culture, you might ask, the guillotine or the bicycle? Rue Robespierre leads off Place du Théâtre, a modest square by Arras' standards, but surrounded by delightful buildings, including the theatre itself. The shopping street Rue Gambetta passes to the side.

Arras is a place of harrowing First World War memories. Beyond the elegant if neglected Ancien Régime quarter around the striking octagonal Place Victor Hugo lies a huge **British cemetery** containing over 2,500 graves, and the names of some 40,000 British soldiers who disappeared without trace in the carnage. Vauban's 17th-century citadel nearby is a reminder of Louis XIV's wars to acquire Flanders; it still holds a regiment of the French army. The **Mur des Fusillés**, also in this neighbourhood, recalls the Second World War Resistance fighters shot here.

The Towns and Countryside of Hainaut

Historic **Douai** was once a major religious and intellectual centre. Philip II of Spain endowed it with a university in 1562. Its religious houses promoted the Counter-Reformation with zeal, and Douai became an important gathering place for English, Irish and Scottish Catholics hounded out of their home countries by Protestantism. The dynamic William, later Cardinal, Allen, here organized the translation of the Bible into English, the so-called Douay Bible, first published in town in 1610 – Kennedy, first

Catholic president of the United States, took his presidential oath on a Douay Bible. Hundreds of foreign priests were trained in town. Many went back to England to preach, often coming to a sticky end as Catholic martyrs. Through most of the 18th century the Parlement, or main law court, of French Flanders was also based here, taking over a former abbey on the River Scarpe. Its wide Gothic arches have survived.

Owing to extensive war damage, Douai no longer retains a cohesive historic core, but several other grand buildings stand out in the dull postwar reconstruction. Climb the big fat medieval Flemish **belfry** (*open daily 2–6*), part of the very Gothic-looking **Hôtel de Ville**, to get a bird's eye view over the town. The tower is armed with one of the largest collections of bells in Europe, 62 in all; on Saturday mornings you can hear them in full swing.

The main attraction over the river, the **Musée de la Chartreuse** (*open Wed–Sun 10–12 and 2–6; adm*), has inviting brick and stone façades from the 16th and 17th centuries. Some of the art within is outstanding. The *Polyptique d'Anchin* by the late 15th-century Douai artist Jean Bellegambe stands out as the most remarkable of his works on display, for the richly coloured main panels and the staggering grisaille work on the back. The foreign highlight is Veronese's *Portrait of a Venetian Woman*. The few 19th-century pieces include works by Boudin, Jongkind, Sisley, Renoir and Pissarro. Douai's post-Impressionist Henri Edmond Cross also puts on a good show.

A short way east, one of the region's many former coal mines has been converted into a large mining museum. The long guided tour round the **Centre Historique Minier de Lewarde** (*open daily 8–5; closed Jan; adm*) goes into the technical aspects of mining as well as the appalling conditions which the miners of northern France had to endure. Much grimmer still, try reading Zola's harrowing mining epic, *Germinal*.

For centuries an important fortified frontier post, **Cambrai** resembles Douai in that it still looks battered and bruised, suffering from dreary postwar reconstruction, but it has some likeable fragments surviving from the past. The Battle of Cambrai at the end of the First World War saw the first-ever, if very faltering, major use of tanks in warfare. The massive **cathedral** dates from the 18th century. At the end of its apse stands a splendid statue of the town's most illustrious archbishop, François de Salignac de la Mothe Fénelon, nicknamed the Swan of Cambrai, one of the most charismatic figures of Louis XIV's reign. David d'Angers' 19th-century Romantic rendition of the man makes him look like an heroic dandy of a salon intellectual. For a time he was a supremely successful establishment figure, until his veiled criticisms of the monarchy and his writings in support of mystical religion led to his fall from grace; he even saw one of his books condemned by the pope. The unmissable grisaille *trompe-l'œil* in the transepts were executed by Martin Geeraerts in the 1760s.

Beyond the excessive Baroque decoration of the late 17th-century **Chapelle du Grand Séminaire** opposite the cathedral, you come to the rich collections of the **Musée de Cambrai** (*open Wed–Sun 10–12 and 2–6; adm*), housed in a surprisingly bold mix of old and new architecture. French speakers might appreciate the half-hour film on the history of Cambrai, but anyone can marvel at the craftsmanship of the medieval masons and sculptors on display. The museum also boasts an exceptional collection of carved alabaster figures from the late 16th and early 17th centuries, most rescued from Cambrai's long-vanished Gothic cathedral. Some of the paintings offer further notions of historic Cambrai, while Flemish art fashions are charted. The outstanding work from the 19th century is Ingres' *Head of the Grand Odalisque*. As t the Baroque church of **St-Géri**, near Cambrai's ugly main square, contains a Rubens *Entombment*, infuriatingly hard to make out in any detail, although close-up photos show Christ's body like a carcass, and St John in a blood-red robe held by Mary.

Painting is the one good reason for pressing east. In **Valenciennes**, the feathery light Ancien Régime works of Antoine Watteau are celebrated in his home town. Henri Matisse was born in the very drab **Le Cateau-Cambrésis** in 1869, and spent his child-hood at nearby Bohain-en-Vermandois. Although he escaped just about as quickly as he could from what he considered a very bleak part of France, he later kindly donated a reasonable number of works to his birthplace, presented in the well revamped **Musée Matisse** (*open June–Sept Wed–Mon 10–7; Oct–May Wed–Mon 10–12.30 and 1–6; closed Tues; adm*). The many drawings prove more absorbing than the few slapdash paintings on display. Another local artist, Auguste Herbin, is also honoured, although his brash experiments in geometric designs become repetitive.

East of Le Cateau-Cambrésis, on the Canal de la Sambre à l'Oise, lies **Ors**, where Wilfred Owen, the most famous of all the British Great War poets, died. Around here the monotonously flat countryside of so much of French Flanders starts to change as you enter the **Parc Naturel Régional de l'Avesnois**. Cows begin to put in an appear-ance, and this is cheese country, the pungent local speciality, **Maroilles**, named after a quietly pretty waterside village. Beyond, **Avesnes-sur-Helpe**, which served as the head-quarters for the German commanders Hindenburg and Ludendorff in the First World War, has preserved mighty fortifications built during earlier conflicts.

So too have a string of towns on the northern edge of the regional park, Maubeuge, Bavay and **Le Quesnoy**, the latter's vertiginous brick walls heroically scaled by New Zealand troops who liberated the place at the end of the First World War. Arriving in the modest centre of **Bavay**, you might be forgiven for thinking that you have come upon a bomb site, but closer inspection reveals the groundplan of Gallo-Roman *Bagacum*. In the modern bunker of a **museum** (*open Wed–Mon 9–12 and 2–5; closed Tues; adm*), the Gallo-Roman treasures attest that the local Nervii tribe thrived in its corner of a region known to Caesar as *Belgica*; now, the Belgian frontier lies close by.

Artois' Côte d'Opale

Dramatic headlands followed by plump dunes and long beaches stretch down from Calais to Normandy. Nicknamed the Côte d'Opale because of the iridescent, milky-green colour of its waters, some of this coast resembles that of southeast England – not surprisingly, as they are both chips off the same geological block, although this northern French coast is pretty uncrowded compared with the southen English one.

Resorts West from Calais

To enjoy one of the most powdery-soft beaches in northern France, head for Wissant a short distance west of Calais, but hidden from its industry by **Cap Blanc-Nez** (Cape

White Nose). This headland has spectacular views of England and of rural Artois. The ugly grey obelisk is a First World War memorial dedicated to the Dover Patrol which guarded the British Expeditionary Forces sent across the Channel. Up on Mont d'Hubert behind it, the **Musée International du Transmanche** (*in the basement of the restaurant with a panoramic view – open April–Sept daily 10–6; adm*) catalogues great Channel crossings and all the attempts to dig a tunnel between France and England.

The modest little resort of **Wissant** sits tucked away behind an immense, 12km-long, curving beach, squeezed in by pillowy dunes. In summer, you can lie on the generous soft white sands after which the resort is named and contemplate the harshness of the white cliffs of Dover. Before the sands smothered it with their stifling embrace, Wissant served as a cross-Channel port. Caesar may have set off from here on his second invasion of Britain in 54 BC. Thomas à Becket left French shores for the final time from Wissant before he was murdered in Canterbury in 1170. The Nazis installed big bunkers on the dunes, some of which have toppled down on to the beach – nowadays sunbathers lean against them in summer.

Cap Gris-Nez is as close as France comes to rubbing noses with Britain, just under 30km away. This headland has been colonized by tourists and the village of Framzelle behind has turned into aggressive B&B territory. The remnants of concrete bunkers recall how the Nazis could fire rockets at England from such close quarters. The shipping-flow into and out of the Channel is regulated from the cape, while millions of migrating birds use the headland as a useful marker on their seasonal flights. Sinister Nazi war facilities are still to be seen at **Audinghen**, where the **Musée du Mur de l'Atlantique** displays a wide array of war-time weaponry around a massive concrete gun emplacement, while at **Ambleteuse** the **Historique de la Deuxième Guerre Mondiale** tells the war story through an extensive collection of uniforms.

Wimereux can claim one of the most attractive seafronts on the Côte d'Opale, with waves crashing in close to the promenade, and some older mansions with turrets and timbered gables holding their own among the modern blocks. The parish **cemetery** contains the grave of the Canadian doctor, Lieutenant-Colonel John McCrae, author of 'In Flanders Fields', one of the most famous of Great War poems.

On the north side of Boulogne, the **Colonne de la Grande Armée** (*open April–Sept Mon and Thurs–Sun 9–12 and 2–6; Oct–Mar Mon and Thurs–Sun 9–12 and 2–5; adm*) stands out, surely one of the greatest monuments ever raised to a non-event. In the early 1800s Napoleon kept an army of some 200,000 encamped at Boulogne while he and his commanders tried to work out a way of invading England, but eventually gave up on the idea. The cemetery of **Terlincthun** down the hillside from the column recalls the follies of war with soldiers' graves from both world wars.

Boulogne

A heady perfume of fish suffuses the Boulogne air. It probably has done ever since Roman times, when the town became the base for the Romans' British fleet. Caesar left from here on his first invasion of Britain in 55 BC. Boulogne today is the largest port in northern Europe for preparing fish. The harbours for industrial and craft fishing lie west of the Liane river, the shopping and tourist town east of it.

Getting There and Around

Boulogne hopes its Channel **ferry** services resume in coming years. **Trains** from Calais-Ville to Boulogne take 30–40mins. Le Touquet has a little **airport** still used by the jet-set.

Tourist Information

Wissant: Place de la Mairie, t 03 21 82 48 00, *www.ville-wissant.fr*.

Wimereux: Quai Alfred Girard, t 03 21 83 27 17, *www.ville-wimereux.fr*.

Boulogne-sur-Mer: 24 Quai Gambetta, t 03 21 10 88 10, *www.tourisme-boulognesurmer.com*.

Etaples-sur-Mer: Bd Bigot Descelers, t 03 21 09 56 94, *www.etaples-sur-mer.com*.

Le Touquet-Paris-Plage: Place de l'Hermitage, t 03 21 06 72 00, *www.letouquet.com*

Montreuil-sur-Mer: 21 Rue Carnot, t 03 21 06 04 27, *otmontreuilsurmer@nordnet.fr*.

Hesdin: Place d'Armes, t 03 21 86 19 19, *www.paysdes7vallees.com*.

Where to Stay and Eat

Wissant ✉ 62179

★★**Le Vivier**, t 03 21 35 93 61, *www.levivier.com* (*inexpensive*). The sweet old stone part lies on the church square in the village, with seafood restaurant (*moderate*). The modern part outside the village has rooms with terraces. *Restaurant closed Tues and Wed*.

Wimereux ✉ 62930

★★★**Atlantic**, Digue de Mer, t 03 21 32 41 01, *www.hotel-atlantic.fr* (*moderate*). Stylish, with good views out to sea shared by many rooms and the restaurant. *Restaurant closed Sun eve and Mon lunch*.

★★**Spéranza**, 43 Rue du Général de Gaulle, t 03 21 32 46 09 (*inexpensive*). Tucked in a street just behind the *Atlantic*. Its timber gables conceal some cheerfully painted, good-value rooms.

Boulogne ✉ 62203

★★★**Hôtel de la Matelote**, 70 Bd Ste-Beuve, t 03 21 30 33 33 (*expensive*). Smart new hotel by the beach and Nausicaà, with Boulogne's best seafood restaurant next door (*very expensive–expensive*). *Closed early Jan; restaurant closed Sun eve and Thurs lunch*.

★★**Hôtel de la Plage**, 170 Bd Ste-Beuve, t 03 21 32 15 15 (*inexpensive*). Some good, standard rooms in the same quarter.

★★**Ibis Vieille Ville**, Rue Porte Neuve, t 03 21 31 21 01, *www.accorhotels.com* (*moderate–inexpensive*). Well-located chain hotel just outside the upper city's ramparts.

Chez Jules, Place Dalton, t 03 21 31 54 12 (*moderate*). Welcoming, full of life, the best

---

Just behind the sieved white sands of Boulogne's pretty **beach**, but facing the grim black structures of an industrial plant the other side of the harbour, rises the major modern maritime centre of **Nausicaà** (*open Feb–June and Sept–Dec daily 9.30–6.30, July–Aug daily 9.30–8; closed Jan; adm*). The unappealing name refers not to seasickness but to a heroine in Homer's *Odyssey* who comes to Ulysses' rescue after he's been shipwrecked. Plunge into its darkened spaces for a mind-altering underwater adventure. Inside are big aquaria and exhibitions; although the place looks dreadfully commercial in parts, it tries hard to transmit a serious ecological message.

Surprisingly, the striking equestrian **statue** by the beach beyond Nausicaà isn't another provocative French homage to Napoleon or Joan of Arc, but represents the South American independence fighter General José de San Martin. Having liberated Argentina from Spain in 1816, he went on to free Chile and Peru, before retiring to Boulogne, where he ended his days.

Boulogne's main shopping area extends across the lively if dreary-looking grid of postwar streets that climb the slope to the Ville Haute, principally Rue Thiers. Rue Monsigny off it has a nice selection of café terraces. The best place to watch the

brasserie in the commercial centre, with people-watching terrace. *Closed Sun eve, much of Sept and Christmas.*

Le Doyen, 11 Rue du Doyen (nr Place Dalton), **t** 03 21 30 13 08 (*moderate*). Pretty, and a bargain. *Closed Sun and most Jan.*

Up in the ramparted Ville Haute there's a very wide choice of pleasant touristy restaurants along Rue de Lille.

Hesdin-l'Abbé ✉ 62360

***Cléry**, **t** 03 21 83 19 83, *www.hotelclery-hesdin-labbe.com* (*expensive–moderate*). Rooms in a gem of a miniature château and its outbuildings, in elegant grounds *c.* 10km southeast of Boulogne. Stylish restaurant. *Closed most Jan; restaurant closed Sat lunch.*

Le Touquet ✉ 62650

****Westminster**, 5 Av du Verger, **t** 03 21 05 48 48, *www.westminster.fr* (*luxury–expensive*). The image of a palatial 1930s hotel, with luxurious rooms and evening restaurant (*expensive–moderate*) near the centre. *Restaurant closed Tues outside July–Aug, and Jan–Mar.*

***Le Bristol**, 17 Rue Jean Monnet, **t** 03 21 05 49 95 (*expensive–moderate*). Swanky pink extravaganza just behind the seafront.

Le Nouveau Caddy, 130 Rue de Metz, **t 03 21 05 83 95, *www.letouquet.com* (*inexpensive*). A central cheerful place near the beach.

Flavio, 1–2 Av du Verger, **t** 03 21 05 10 22 (*very expensive–expensive*). The top restaurant in town, with ostentatious cuisine as well as décor. *Closed Mon outside July–Aug, and early Jan–early Feb.*

Montreuil-sur-Mer ✉ 62170

*****Château de Montreuil**, 4 Chaussée des Capucins, **t** 03 21 81 53 04, *www.chateaude-montreuil.com* (*luxury–very expensive*). Luxurious modern manor exclusively located in the citadel. Superlative restaurant (*very expensive–expensive*). *Closed mid-Dec–early Feb; restaurant closed Thurs lunch and Mon and Tues lunch in low season.*

***Les Hauts de Montreuil**, 21-23 Rue Pierre Ledent, **t** 03 21 81 95 92, *leshautsdemontreuil@wanadoo.fr* (*very expensive–moderate*). Comfortable hotel set around a charming old timberframe town house, with a modern annexe, restaurant and terrace.

Le Clos des Capucins, Place du Général de Gaulle, **t 03 21 06 08 65 (*moderate–inexpensive*). Cheerful, bright, central little stop with a good restaurant.

Auberge de la Grenouillère, **t** 03 21 06 07 22 (*expensive*). You'll find a whole selection of very tempting restaurants up in the walled town, but below Montreuil, at La Madeleine, this is a superb restaurant in a restored farmhouse by the river Canche. *Closed Tues, plus Wed outside July–Aug, and most Jan.*

Boulonnais go by is on **Place Dalton**, opposite the much-altered Gothic church of **St-Nicolas**. The steep **Grande Rue** leads up to the Ville Haute, passing the **Musée Libertador San Martin** at No.113 (*open Fri–Tues 10–12 and 2–6; closed Wed, Thurs and public hols*), which draws in many South American visitors.

Enter the **Ville Haute** by one of four impressive gateways. Stairways up from these take you on to the well-preserved **ramparts**, which you can walk all the way round, although you get views of sprawling modern Boulogne rather than of the sea. Up on the ramparts, you can make out the seated evangelists and the saints perched high up around the staggering, lanky dome of the **Basilique Notre-Dame**. The whole daunting church, built in honeyed stone, was erected in the first half of the 19th century, a powerful replacement for the cathedral destroyed by fanatics at the French Revolution. Inside, the tall classical columns hold up an array of peeling oval ceilings. The maze of **crypts** (*open Tues–Sun 2–5; adm*) below contain colourful religious statuary collected from the area, with several representations of Notre-Dame de Boulogne, this version of the Virgin always shown carrying her baby in a boat. The star exhibit is a reliquary piece donated to the town by King Philippe le Bel in the

14th century, the colourful box made to contain supposed drops of Christ's blood collected by Boulogne's crusading 'hero', Godefroi – he played a crucial part in the First Crusade and particularly in the triumphant, bloody taking of Jerusalem in 1099.

Separated by its dry moat from the rest of the Ville Haute, the **château** looks impressively complete with its many sturdy towers. It was built, like the ramparts, in the 13th century for Philippe Hurepel, second son of King Philippe Auguste, the French monarch who kicked King John of England out of France. The collections of the **town museum** (*open Wed–Mon 10–12.30 and 2–5; adm*) are superbly displayed inside. In the stunning circular walkway round the basement, you can see how the medieval masons built on Roman foundations. Also admire the stone sculptures rescued from Boulogne's Gothic cathedral. Further rooms contain exquisite carved heads. But the museum's most surprising collections come from far further afield; the place has an excellent array of Egyptian and ethnographic items thanks to the great 19th-century Egyptologist from Boulogne, Auguste Mariette, and to other Boulonnais explorers.

Rue de Lille, the main street cutting across the upper town, is packed with restaurants and gift shops. It leads to the grand square, overseen by a gathering of major buildings including the town hall, the law courts and the belfry.

The Coast South of Boulogne

A **war cemetery**, its pinnacled entrance tower designed by Sir Edwin Lutyens, greets you before the port of **Etaples**, a place with traumatic memories of the Great War. The town hosted the main war hospital, at one stage handling over 20,000 casualties. One nurse here was Vera Brittain, who lost her brothers and her fiancé in the fighting and wrote moving accounts of her war experience. Etaples' cemetery contains almost 11,000 graves, making it the largest British and Commonwealth cemetery in France. The town was also one of the main centres for training reinforcements. A few trainees rebelled, notably in the so-called case of the Monocled Mutineer of 1917. Historically, down-to-earth Etaples has been devoted to fishing, as you can see in its fishermen's quarter, its maritime museum, and at **Maréis** (*open July–Aug 9.30–8; Sept–Jun 9.30–1 and 2–6.30; adm*), a more interactive centre which includes a renovated trawler, a simulator screen to allow you to try your hand at navigating, plus fish touch-tanks.

Le Touquet-Paris-Plage was born with pretensions, created in the 1890s to rival the Belle Epoque delights of Deauville and Trouville in Normandy. It was long popular with British high society, some of whom got into the habit of hopping over the Channel by plane. However, the seafront looks rather downmarket these days, only the geometric shape of **Aqualud Water Park** (*open mid-Feb–early Nov 10.15–5.45; adm*) providing a distraction from the endless dull car parks and wall of apartment blocks. But a whiff of the grander Le Touquet still exists behind the seafront, with the surviving Art Deco architecture, casino and grand hotels. Plus there are seawater treatment centres right by the beach, a race course, and golf courses scattered beyond the rather naff, pine-shaded pastiches of Norman villas on the outskirts of town. Just north of the resort, the mouth of the Canche river remains relatively unspoilt.

South of Le Touquet, clone-like modern apartments blocks have been springing up behind the enormous beaches and dunes of the new resorts of **Stella-Plage** and

Merlimont-Plage. The **Bagatelle Parc d'Attractions** (*open April–Sept; for times and closing days, see www.bagatelle.fr or call t 03 21 89 09 91; adm*) theme park draws family crowds a short distance inland before the better established resort of **Berck-Plage**. Although surrounded by large medical clinics, the promenade becomes really jolly in summer, offering all the old-fashioned seaside pleasures. The **Musée Municipal** (*open July–Aug Wed–Mon 10–12 and 2–7; late Mar–June and Sept–Dec Wed–Sun 10–12 and 3–6, Mon 3–6; closed Tues; adm*) celebrates the sea, with one floor devoted to maritime paintings. **Quend-Plage**, surrounded by pine-covered dunes, has a more discreet charm than the other resorts, plus a comical little cinema in the centre.

Inland Artois

Set atop a rocky outcrop above the wooded valley of the Canche, picturesque **Montreuil** is still contained within its historic walls, and shows little inclination to outgrow them. During the 13th century the place had a thriving port, one of the wealthiest in the north, trading in grain, wine and wool, but the Canche began to silt up and by 1400 was virtually impassable. In 1537 the army of Habsburg Holy Roman Emperor Charles V besieged and virtually destroyed the town. Afterwards, François Iᵉʳ ordered its rebuilding in radically different manner, but as the sea receded west and the French frontier moved east, Montreuil became a backwater. It did continue to serve as a stop for the Paris-Calais mail coaches. Victor Hugo passed through, and would set part of *Les Misérables* here – this is where Jean Valjean briefly achieves peace and prosperity as mayor. Today the sea lies a full 15km away, although the town is still sometimes rather absurdly referred to as Montreuil-sur-Mer.

Spectacular **ramparts** form an almost impregnable ring around the upper town. In the northwest corner, a little bridge leads to the **Citadelle** (*open Mon and Wed–Sun 9–12 and 2–6; closed Tues and Oct; adm*), its various parts reflecting different building campaigns down the centuries. The Tour de la Reine Berthe is where one of France's least distinguished kings, Philippe Iᵉʳ, is supposed to have confined his Dutch queen in 1091 after he had repudiated her in order to marry another woman, Bertrade de Montfort. Two further massive towers were built for Philippe Auguste. The 17th-century additions include the citadel's entrance designed by Vauban.

During the First World War, Montreuil became the headquarters of the British Army in France, which explains why Field Marshal Haig surveys the **Grande-Place** or **Place Général de Gaulle** on horseback. Haig became a familiar figure in the countryside around Montreuil, riding out every morning preceded by another horseman carrying a Union Flag. North of the Grande-Place, the intertwining streets and squares packed with restaurants and gift shops have great charm; the little white cottages in the older streets look as if they have been washed up from a fishing village. Montreuil has a curious range of churches. **St-Saulve** on Place Gambetta is the largest, a fine Gothic pile, but it didn't survive the sack of 1537 intact. The mock Flamboyant **Chapelle de l'Hôtel-Dieu** across the square was built in the 1870s. Go down the street to the right of the Hôtel-Dieu and you come to a quiet little square with the whitewashed **Chapelle de Ste-Austreberthe**. From here, Rue Porte Becquerelle and Rue de Paon take you to the little cobbled alleys of **Clape-en-Bas** and **Clape-en-Haut**.

Hesdin lies up the lovely Canche from Montreuil. The main Place d'Armes seems almost too big for the town, with its grand, very Flemish-looking **town hall** fronted by a magnificent Baroque porch. The French fleur-de-lys at the top was added in the 18th century, but the coat of arms in the centre of the balcony is Habsburg. Nearby, the large church of **Notre-Dame** was built between 1565 and 1585 on the Flemish Hallekerque model. Its brick façade is mainly Gothic, but it has an impressive Renaissance-style stone porch. The river runs playfully through the middle of the town, under little hump-backed bridges, sometimes disappearing under buildings. In Rue Daniel Lereuil, you can locate the 1697 birthplace of that notoriously naughty priest, the Abbé Prévost, author of the scandalous morality tale *Manon Lescaut*.

A short way west of Hesdin along the delightful Authie valley, the walled gardens of the **Abbaye de Valloires** (*garden open early Mar–early Nov 10–5, or 6.30 in summer; abbey open same period, but closed Tues; adm*) hide a huge collection of rare roses and bushes. The little town of **Crécy-en-Ponthieu** tumbles down the hillside of the Maye valley, below the site of the battle of Crécy, one of the most significant encounters near the beginning of the Hundred Years War. The obelisk opposite the town hall is dedicated to Jean de Luxembourg and his '*vaillants compagnons d'armes morts pour la France à Crécy le 26 août 1346*'. That year, King Edward III of England and his army went on a successful rampage through northern France. Edward's men defeated the French army of King Philippe VI, reckoned to have been three times its size. Edward III's warrior son, who came to be known as the Black Prince, won his spurs here. Legend has it that he adopted his motto, the Germanic '*Ich dien* (I serve)', at Crécy as well as his insignia of the so-called Prince of Wales' feathers, taken from the badge of King John of Bohemia. Panels in French at the car park by the battlefield explain the action.

To the north of Hesdin lies the site of the **Battle of Agincourt** (Azincourt), where Henry V of England's troops famously defeated a French force five times larger in one rain-soaked day in 1415. Among the most important prisoners taken was Charles d'Orléans, father of a future king of France, Louis XII, and inspiration to Joan of Arc, whose part in French victories 15 years later would help reverse the English triumph. A new **Centre Historique** (*open July–Aug daily 9–7; April–June and Sept–Oct daily 10–6; Nov–Mar Wed–Mon 10–5; adm*) helps make sense of the battleground.

The Somme into Picardy

First World War battlefields still draw large numbers of visitors to the *département* of the Somme. Its capital, Amiens, a fascinating cathedral city, straddles the River Somme. East of it lies the major arena of the 1916 Battle of the Somme.

The Bay of the Somme

In the giant landscape of the Bay of the Somme, borders between earth, sea and sky often become hard to distinguish. The light has an opaque quality celebrated by such writers as Jules Verne and Colette and by painters like Degas and Seurat. At low tide the sea recedes for miles in an ever-changing mix of subtle colours fading into the horizon. Birds love the place. One of the bay's most beautiful parts has become the

Wildlife Reserve of Marquenterre (*open April–Sept 10–5; Oct–11 Nov and Christmas hols 10–4; adm*), a 2,300ha stretch of marsh, lake and dunes, all well-organized for visitors.

The little towns around the Bay of the Somme seem lost in the immensity of the landscape and left behind by history in the rarely broken stillness. **Le Crotoy** is one of the places where Joan of Arc was briefly held prisoner after her capture by the Burgundians in 1430. When Jules Verne stayed here, he spent a lot of time with the inventor and experimenter in submarine technology, Jacques-François Conseil, who provided the inspiration for *Twenty Thousand Leagues Under the Sea*. Atmospheric **St-Valéry-sur-Somme**, on the south side of the bay, is the port from which William, Duke of Normandy, sailed to conquer England in 1066.

Heading up the canalized Somme to Abbeville, a **Chinese war cemetery** lies north of the river by Noyelles-sur-Mer. **Abbeville**'s centre didn't entirely disappear in the Second World War bombing; surrounded by postwar squares linked by amusing high passageways, the mighty façade of **St-Vulfran** still puts on a fine Gothic show. On the edge of town, the little brick **Château de Bagatelle** has 18th-century charm. A bit further out, the church of **St-Riquier**, named after a Dark Ages evangelizer in these parts, boasts startling Flamboyant Gothic grandeur.

Amiens

Amiens' Gallo-Roman predecessor *Samarobriva* was, in the 2nd century AD, the most important city in northern Gaul, twice the size of Paris' predecessor *Lutetia*. At one of the town's gateways, on a bitter winter's day in the 4th century, one Martin, an officer in the Roman army, was so moved by the sight of a naked beggar that he drew his sword to cut his cloak in two to help the poor man (*see* 'Tours', p.299, for the rest of the story). The city on the Somme thrived in the Middle Ages, best demonstrated by its huge Gothic cathedral, described by John Ruskin as the most perfect creation of medieval Christianity in northern Europe. Amiens' merchants continued to prosper down the centuries. In the First World War Amiens served as a vital Allied communications centre, but in the Second World War much of the place was destroyed in only two days, 18 and 19 May 1940, when German bombs rained down on the city.

The **cathedral** fortunately survived. It was begun in 1220, after Amiens had acquired no less a prize of a Christian relic than the head of John the Baptist, brought here in dubious circumstances after the Fourth Crusade. Much of the cathedral was completed within 50 years, giving it an unusual unity of style. Also unusually for a medieval building, it has a known first architect, Robert de Luzarches. From the outside, the whole structure seems too tall for its length, while the strange slender spire was only added in 1529. But the exterior detail is totally absorbing. Ruskin called the staggering west façade 'the Bible in stone'. In the small roundels around the base of the portals vignettes of everyday 13th-century life feature. The central statue of Jesus, the *Beau Dieu*, was, legend has it, sculpted directly from a vision of Christ.

Inside, the cathedral soars like few others. Vaults and columns seem to reach for the sky and high windows give the nave a rare luminosity. If the façade is the Bible in stone, the stalls of the choir might well be described as the Bible in wood, carved by Amiens craftsmen between 1508 and 1522. In the ambulatory, two major series of

Getting Around

Amiens is the main hub for public transport in this area. Amiens **railway station** lies on the Paris–Gare du Nord–Calais line; trains also stop at Abbeville, Noyelles-sur-Mer and Rue. You can reach a few of the towns near the First World War battlefields on the Amiens–Arras and Amiens–St-Quentin/Laon lines, in particular Albert and Villers-Bretonneux.

Tourist Information

Le Crotoy: 1 Rue Carnot, **t** 03 22 27 05 25, *maison.du.tourisme@wanadoo.fr*.

St-Valéry-sur-Somme: 2 Place Guillaume le Conquérant, **t** 03 22 60 93 50, *www.saint-valery-sur-somme.com*.

Amiens: 6 bis Rue Dusevel, **t** 03 22 71 60 50, *www.amiens.com/tourisme*.

Péronne: 1 Rue Louis XI, **t** 03 22 84 42 38, *www.ot-peronne.fr*.

St-Quentin: 27 Rue V. Basch, **t** 03 23 67 05 00.

Where to Stay and Eat

Le Crotoy 80550

*Les Tourelles, 2 Rue Pierre Guerlain, **t** 03 22 27 16 33, *www.lestourelles.com* (*moderate–inexpensive*). Tempting waterside address once owned by perfumer Guerlain, many rooms with wonderful views of the Somme estuary. Good local dishes served in the restaurant (*moderate*). *Closed most Jan*.

Amiens ✉ 80000

***Grand Hôtel de l'Univers, 2 Rue de Noyon, **t** 03 22 91 52 51, *hotelunivers.amiens@wanadoo.fr* (*moderate*). Near the cathedral.

Le Victor Hugo, 2 Rue de l'Oratoire, **t 03 22 91 57 91 (*inexpensive*). Also near the cathedral.

Les Marissons, 68 Rue des Marissons, Pont de la Dodane, **t** 03 22 92 96 66 (*expensive–moderate*). Serves really refined cooking. *Closed Sat lunch and Sun*.

Remaisnil ✉ 80600

Château de Remaisnil, Doullens, **t** 03 22 77 07 47, *www.remaisnil.com* (*very expensive–expensive*). Grand, beautifully decorated 18th-century country château 35km north of Amiens, once the home of Laura Ashley. Luxury meals available. *Closed Jan*.

Albert ✉ 80300

***Royal Picardie, Av du Général Leclerc, **t** 03 22 75 37 00, *www.royalpicardie.com* (*expensive–moderate*). Curiously grandiose modern stone building with comfortable rooms and a good restaurant. Tennis court. *Closed early Jan and early Aug*.

Bapaume ✉ 62450

La Paix, 11 Av Abel Guidet, **t 03 21 07 11 03 (*inexpensive*). Friendly hotel off the A1 north of Péronne, with restaurant (*moderate*).

scenes in polychrome stone from the early 16th century depict, on one side, the life of John the Baptist, on the other the life of St Firmin, credited with having brought Christianity to Amiens. As to the three great rose windows, although much of their glass is no longer original, they are breathtaking, made more of light than of stone.

On the way down to the riverside district, stop at **Place du Don**, a cobbled square with 16th-century houses containing antiques shops, restaurants and bars. Just off the square at 67 Rue du Don is the tiny shop of Jean-Pierre Facquier, the only remaining maker of the traditional Amiens puppets, the *Cabotans*. At the centre of each story is Lafleur, a roguish Mr Punch type, considered the archetypal Amiens and Picard caricature. Across the river, the engaging canalside quarter of **St-Leu** with its many-coloured houses was formerly the weavers' and dyers' district; now restaurants rule. The most eccentric trip to take is in a punt along the **Hortillonages**, the vegetable gardens to the east, watered by a whole grid of canals by the Somme. The association of allotment-holders runs tours of some of the over 50km of channels (*April–Oct daily from 2pm, depending on demand; call* **t** *03 22 92 12 18; adm*).

Back up in the centre of town, the large **Hôtel de Ville**, rebuilt after the war, stands in front of a square recently remodelled to an innovative, locally controversial design by Catalan architect Joan Roig, with intriguing inclined fountains. Walk around the town hall and you come to a solid 15th-century belfry, once a prison. Beyond, the **Musée de Picardie** (*open Tues–Sun 10–12.30 and 2–6; adm*) occupies a Second Empire wedding cake of a building, opened by Napoléon III in 1867, as the large 'N' stamped on the front makes pretty clear. Inside, around the giant main staircase, murals by Puvis de Chavannes present a fanciful vision of the prehistoric Picards. The museum contains a good number of artefacts from *Samarobriva*, and rooms of medieval sculptures in wood and stone, including an exquisite series of bas-reliefs of the life of Christ, from around 1500. Quite specific to Amiens are the Puys, paintings commissioned by city fraternities in the 16th century, gathering together large numbers of images of leading townspeople. Foreign artists represented include the likes of El Greco, Frans Hals, Fragonard and Boucher. Among the modern sections, the brash *Wall Drawing 711* stands out, a rotunda painted with mind-spinning patterns in 1992 by the American artist Sol LeWitt.

One particularly striking curiosity near the museum is the **Cirque Municipal**, a drum-like building with many ornate 19th-century details. Jules Verne married an Amiens woman and moved here in 1871. He busied himself with every aspect of local life, serving on the city council and in 1889 badgering his fellow councillors into giving Amiens this, one of the world's few permanent circus halls. Just east, the **Centre de Documentation Jules Verne** (*open Tues–Sat 9.30–12 and 2–6; adm*) is based where the great author lived, and crammed with information.

Into the Somme Battlefields

Across roughly a third of the *département* of the Somme, virtually every house was reduced to rubble in the Great War. The hugely devastating Battle of the Somme of 1916 and the fighting for this region right through the war caused massive loss of life, huge numbers of the war dead British, but many others from the Commonwealth, and from France. East of Amiens, vast areas still look remarkably empty. The dreadful density of war cemeteries recalls the hellish events. More than half a dozen **British cemeteries** lie along the N29 road or south of it. Just north, the big Commonwealth cemetery between Villers-Bretonneux and Corbie includes the **Australian National War Memorial**, commemorating the 1,200 Australians who perished in the 1918 action here, and the 10,797 Australians who died on the Western Front without a known place of death. **Villers-Bretonneux** itself was totally destroyed in the conflict, but was rebuilt with Australian aid.

Securely encased within the walls of a medieval castle, **Péronne**'s modern museum on the First World War, the **Historial de la Grande Guerre** (*open May–Sept daily 10–6; rest of year Tues–Sun 10–5.30; adm*), offers the best introduction in the whole area to the historical context and the campaigns of the Great War, with English-speakers well catered for. In fact the museum pays particular homage to the part played by the British Isles in the First World War. The response by some one million British and Irish men to Kitchener's call for voluntary enlistment is described as a miracle. Backed by

The Outbreak of the First World War

A fatal combination of festering wounds led to the devastation of the First World War. Early in the 20th century, paranoiac power politics had caused a split between the major European powers, the Triple Alliance of Austro-Hungary, Germany and Italy on the one side, the Triple Entente of France, Great Britain and Russia on the other. The spark for the war was lit in Serbia, a reluctant part of the Austro-Hungarian Empire. When Serbian nationalists assassinated Archduke Franz Ferdinand, heir apparent to the Austro-Hungarian throne, on 28 June 1914, the Austrian powers saw red. A month later they declared war on Serbia. Russia, regarding itself as the protector of the Serbs, mobilized its troops on 30 July. On 1 August Germany declared war on Russia and used the situation as a long-awaited excuse to attack France. The Schlieffen plan, devised as far back as 1895, was to storm through Belgium, taking the French army by surprise. On 2 August the invasion of Belgium began; on 3 August Germany declared war on France. The operation to conquer France was to last just six weeks; once achieved, the Germans would then concentrate on taking Russia. They were only prevented from pulling off this plan thanks to desperate French actions in 1914. But the Germans dug in, literally, and the appalling years of atrocious trench warfare followed. Britain entered the war on 4 August 1914, honouring its agreement to defend Belgium should its neutrality be violated.

the choral music of Benjamin Britten's *War Requiem*, the main film tells the story of the Battle of the Somme through the recollections of a British soldier, Harry Fellows. Like so many naïve volunteers, he left for France with a feeling of excitement, pleased at the thought of getting in some free foreign travel, little realizing the hell he was heading for. The postwar period isn't forgotten. In particular, reference is made to the Zone Rouge, the vast swath of land between Albert, Péronne, Villers-Cotterêts and Soissons where 80–100 per cent of buildings were destroyed.

The concentration of cemeteries and memorials close to the town of **Albert**, with its symbolic gilded Virgin atop its neo-Byzantine church, indicates the crucial importance this stretch of territory assumed in the years of relentless trench warfare. The vast triple-arched **Thiepval British memorial**, the largest British war memorial in the world, designed by Sir Edwin Lutyens, can be seen rising above woods for miles around. Its inhuman scale emphasizes the huge number of British men who went missing in these parts – almost 75,000. The great majority died between July and November 1916. The memorial's inauguration ceremony took place in 1932, but back in Britain some criticized the money being spent on the monument rather than on the large number of war-shattered, often unemployed men back in Britain. The piece is a depressing, coldly grandiose structure, individual names lost in huge long lists. Below the memorial, 300 French gravestones were added alongside 300 British ones as a symbol of the unified effort of the two armies. On a high ridge nearby, the **Ulster memorial** stands out, the tower a copy of Helen's Tower at Clandeboyne outside Belfast. A two-room museum recalls the Ulstermen's heroism here.

The **Beaumont-Hamel Parc Terre-Neuvien** is dedicated above all to troops of the 1st Newfoundland Regiment. The park, basically a field still puckered with craters and trenches, slopes gently down to 'Y' Ravine. On the first day of the Battle of the Somme, some Allied troops made it as far as here. Scottish soldiers are also remembered.

The rough old town of **St-Quentin** lies close to the source of the Somme. An impressive if somewhat maltreated Gothic basilica dominates one side of town, and proves a match for many of the cathedrals of northern France. Beyond the large main square with its lively Gothic-style town hall and exuberant bells, an elegant **museum** displays a fine collection of extraordinarily perceptive pastel portraits of 18th-century aristocrats by the great society artist Maurice Quentin de la Tour, who left his home town many of his works. St-Quentin lay in German hands through the First World War. The so-called Second Battle of the Somme of 1918, when the Germans captured tens of thousands of British prisoners, took place west of town.

North up the N44, an important **American war memorial** stands at the panoramic site of **Bellicourt**. Nearby is the **American Somme Cemetery** at **Bony**. Around 1,200 Americans broke through the German line here at the end of September 1918, only to find themselves cut off.

Southern Picardy

Geographically and administratively part of Picardy, emotionally part of the Ile de France, the areas around Soissons, Compiègne, Senlis and Beauvais are closely linked to the greater Paris region, and their magnificent churches vie with the Gothic giants of the Ile de France. Some of the châteaux are awesome too. Although the capital stands close by, most of this thickly forested area still feels delightfully rural.

Cathedrals and Châteaux from Laon to Noyon

Laon's Montagne Couronnée stands proudly on high above the A26 motorway to Reims, its hilltop crowned by a colossal Gothic **cathedral**. The old town's elevated position, 100 steep metres above the plains leading to Champagne, made it an obvious place to fortify, back at least to Gallo-Roman times. St Remigius, the famous Remi who became bishop of Reims, founded a bishopric here in the 5th century. The cathedral school developed into one of the most important centres of learning in France.

During a stormy period in 1111, a bishop was murdered and the cathedral burnt down, to be replaced by the gloriously grand Gothic design you see today. Most of the vast edifice was finished by 1230, although only four of the seven towers planned were included in the final construction. Unfortunately the sculptures on the façade were particularly heavy-handedly restored during the 19th century. Strain your eyes to make out the carved oxen high on the towers; they recall the legend that one of the exhausted beasts being used to transport the cathedral's building blocks from the Chemin des Dames up to Laon was replaced by an unusually energetic animal, sent down from heaven no less, to make the sure the job got done. Rarely will you see a more impressive Gothic interior, the vast tunnel of masonry in the shape of a Gothic lancet arch leading to the choir, its three windows surmounted by a large rose window glowing purple, blue and red. The architecture is exceptionally pure: the four

Getting Around

Paris-Charles-de-Gaulle **airport** lies just south of this area, Reims airport just east of it. A couple of **train** lines cross the area: Paris-Gare du Nord to Compiègne/St-Quentin, and Paris-Gare du Nord to Soissons/Laon.

Tourist Information

Laon: Parvis de la Cathédrale, t 03 23 20 28 62, *www.ville-laon.fr*.

Blérancourt: 2 Rue de la Chouette, t 03 23 39 72 17, *www.blerancourt.com*.

Noyon: Place de l'Hôtel de Ville, t 03 44 44 21 88, *www.noyon.com/tourisme*.

Soissons: 16 Place F. Marquigny, t 03 23 53 17 37, *www.ville-soissons.fr*.

Compiègne: Place de l'Hôtel de Ville, t 03 44 40 01 00, *www.compiegne.fr*.

Senlis: Place du Parvis Notre-Dame, t 03 44 53 06 40, *www.ville-senlis.fr*.

Ermenonville: 1 Rue René Girardin, t 03 44 54 01 58, *ot-ermenonville@wanadoo.fr*.

Chantilly: 60 Av du Maréchal Joffre, t 03 44 67 37 37, *www.chantilly-tourisme.com*.

Beauvais: 1 Rue Beauregard, t 03 44 15 30 30, *ot.beauvais@wanadoo.fr*.

Where to Stay and Eat

Laon ✉ 02000

★★★**La Bannière de France**, 11 Rue Franklin Roosevelt, t 03 23 23 21 44, *www.hoteldela*
bannieredefrance.com (*inexpensive*). Former coaching inn up in the old town, plus a duller modern wing. Comfortable rooms and good food (*expensive–moderate*). *Closed Christmas–21 Jan.*

★★**Les Chevaliers**, 3–5 Rue Sérurier, t 03 23 27 17 50 (*moderate–inexpensive*). By the town hall square up on the hilltop, the façade in the row of townhouses may be modern, the rooms in standard style, but the place is very well located. 14 rooms. *Closed early part of week in winter.*

Coucy-le-Château

★★**Le Belle Vue**, t 03 23 52 69 70 (*inexpensive*). Bright postwar building with its distinctive tower, up behind the ramparts, with restaurant (*moderate*). *Closed Christmas period.*

Courcelles-sur-Vesle ✉ 02220

★★★★**Château de Courcelles**, 8 Rue du Château, t 03 23 74 13 53, *www.chateau-de-courcelles.fr* (*luxury–very expensive*). Racine, La Fontaine, the Dumas and Jean Cocteau all stayed in this very clean-lined 17th-century white-stoned château by the Vesle river some 20km east of Soissons. One of the most refined stops in northern France, with superb restaurant, pool and tennis court.

Fère-en-Tardenois ✉ 02130

★★★★**Château de Fère**, Route de Fismes, t 03 23 82 21 13, *chateau.fere@wanadoo.fr* (*luxury–very expensive*). Luxurious 16th-century castle 26km southeast of Soissons

---

levels follow the same pattern all the way round. The side chapels look like monastic cells divided by Renaissance openings. In the choir glass, scenes from Christ's life feature alongside St Stephen's stoning and Théophile making his pact with the devil.

A hushed atmosphere generally reigns in the old streets of the walled city around the cathedral, packed with beautiful former religious buildings, clearly marked with explanatory panels. But the contents of the **Musée d'Art et d'Archéologie** (*open June–Sept Tues–Sun 11–6; rest of year Tues–Sun 2–6; adm*) have very little to do with Laon, the bulk of the collections made up of extraordinary items from ancient Mediterranean cultures amassed by an avid 19th-century collector. The three accomplished Le Nain brothers were, however, born in Laon in the 17th century, and highlight of the mediocre painting collection is *Le Concert* by Mathieu Le Nain. In the museum garden, the diminutive Romanesque Templars' chapel can't fail to delight, but be warned, it contains a sickening effigy of a corpse sprouting hair.

near the Oise-Aisne American war cemetery, with the ruins of a medieval castle to add to the picture. Excellent restaurant, pool and tennis court. *Closed Jan–mid-Feb.*

Noyon ✉ 60400
★★★Le Cèdre, 8 Rue de l'Evêché, **t** 03 44 44 23 24, *www.hotel-lecedre.com* (*inexpensive*). Modern brick hotel with modern bedrooms, but in lovely location by the cathedral.

Elincourt Ste-Marguerite ✉ 60157
★★★★Château de Bellinglise, Route de Lassigny, **t** 03 44 96 00 33, *chateaude bellinglise@wanadoo.fr* (*luxury–very expensive*). Stylish 16th-century brick château close to A1 motorway southwest of Noyon, rooms in the outhouses cheaper than in the château itself. Stylish restaurant. *Closed Christmas.*

Longpont ✉ 02600
★★Hôtel de l'Abbaye, 8 Rue des Tourelles, **t** 03 23 96 02 44 (*inexpensive*). Adorable inn in an adorable village with adorable abbey ruins. Simple rooms above the good provincial restaurant (*moderate*) and village bar.

Pierrefonds ✉ 60350
★★Hôtel des Etrangers, 10 Rue de Baudon, **t** 03 44 42 80 18, *www.hotel-pierrefonds.com* (*inexpensive*). One of the popular hotels, with the best view of lake and castle, enjoyed by the restaurant (*moderate*) too. *Restaurant closed Sun eve and Mon in winter.*

St-Jean-aux-Bois ✉ 60350
★★★Auberge a la Bonne Idée, 3 Rue des Meuniers, **t** 03 44 42 84 09, *www.a-la-bonne-idee.fr* (*moderate*). Lovely 18th-century inn in this pretty village in the forest west of Pierrefonds, with traditional restaurant. *Closed mid-Jan–mid-Feb.*

Compiègne ✉ 60200
★★Hôtel de France, 17 Rue Eugène Floquet, **t** 03 44 40 02 74, *contact@restauranthotelde france.fr* (*moderate*). Characterful, concave-fronted, timberframe hotel tucked behind the central square, with rooms crammed with facilities and a lively restaurant.

Senlis ✉ 60300
★★Hostellerie de la Porte Bellon, 51 Rue Bellon, **t** 03 44 53 03 05 (*moderate*). Charming centuries-old house on the edge of the historic centre. Restaurant with garden. *Closed 20 Dec–6 Jan.*

Ermenonville ✉ 60950
★★★Château d'Ermenoville, Rue René Girardin, **t** 03 44 54 00 26, *www.chateau-ermenon ville.com* (*luxury–moderate*). Stunning moated castle where Jean-Jacques Rousseau spent his last days.
★★Relais de la Croix d'Or, 2 Rue Prince Radziwill, **t** 03 44 54 00 04, *www.relais-delacroixdor.fr.st* (*inexpensive*). A characterful rustic, cheaper option, with restaurant (*expensive–moderate*). *Restaurant closed Mon and Tues.*

South of Laon, the charming name of the **Chemin des Dames** recalls the fact that this spectacular ridgeway was specially cleared for King Louis XV's daughters back in the 18th century. Lording it over the Aisne valley to the south and the plains of Champagne to the east, this strategic ridge has a military history going back to the Dark Ages, but in the First World War it became one of the most terrible bones of contention between the Germans and the French. In fact, it was along the Aisne valley from Compiègne to here that the terrible trench warfare of the First World War began. After the failure of the Germans' lightning attack in 1914, they turned the Chemin des Dames into one of the strongest points along the front. The ridge became the target of repeated disastrous French campaigns, the most absurd overseen by the madly ambitious new French commander in 1917, Nivelle. Over 1 million men and half a million horses were massed at the foot of the Chemin des Dames. Wave after wave of soldiers were sent to their deaths on the slopes of the impregnable ridge. Eventually, a number of the privates put up what now seems like a reasonable protest, but, because of the social and political implications, the French leadership called it a mutiny and came down hard on those they considered the troublemakers. A small number were even shot. They have never been pardoned. French leaders are still divided on the subject.

The Chemin des Dames (now the D18 road) is littered with First World War memorials. At the western end lies a German war cemetery. Some way east, a large French war cemetery and memorial chapel stand at the crossroads with the D967. Just south, on the D967, an exceptionally beautiful British war cemetery graces the slope at **Vendresse**. Continuing along the Chemin des Dames, the **Caverne du Dragon war museum** (*open May–Aug daily 10–6; Feb–April and Oct–Dec Tues–Sun 10–6; adm*) has a startling modern part on stilts, but it also drags you underground into former stone quarries where the horrors of the Great War in these parts are evocatively recalled.

The ruins of the **Abbaye de Vauclair** on the edge of forests a short way north offer a pause for more peaceful reflection. Continuing past an absurd recent statue of Napoleon, who enjoyed a misleading last victory here in 1815, the major **monument to the Basques** who fought particularly bravely in the Great War has more dignity.

Reaching the eastern end of the Chemin des Dames, you can enjoy stunning, dreamy views from the **Plateau de Californie** down on to the plains where Picardy and Champagne meet. But panels on the heights give nauseating details of the trench warfare here, while a disturbing recent monument displays copies of a bald head trapped in mesh. It looks like a Holocaust memorial, and of course the massacres of the Great War were a kind of holocaust too, perpetrated by the leaders on both sides. Down below, the spire of modern **Craonne** sticks out in the foreground, but the old village of that name was completely obliterated in the Great War. An arboretum has been planted among the substantial pits left by the brutal shelling, while the cemetery from before the conflict languishes in undergrowth.

Most of the war graveyards from the Chemin des Dames campaigns lie down in the Aisne valley – some sixteen French cemeteries, nine British, thirteen German and one Italian. **Craonnelle** has one of the most moving. Although the vast majority of the 2,000 tombs on its slope are marked by classic French crosses, they are interspersed not just with British and Belgian graves, but also with Muslim and Jewish ones.

Set on its defensive hilltop southwest of Laon, **Coucy-le-Château**, still surrounded by splendid ramparts, takes you back to different warring times, the Middle Ages. The **château** (*open May–Aug daily 9.30–12.30 and 2–6.30; Mar–April and Sept–Oct 10–12.30 and 2–6; rest of year 10–12.30 and 1.30–5; adm*) itself, one of the largest built in medieval France, has fared less well than the ramparts. However, it was brought back to life in Barbara Tuchmann's meticulously detailed, much respected historical novel *A Distant Mirror*, which tells the story of one of the most notable lords of Coucy, Enguerrand VII. This 14th-century heart-throb apparently so impressed Edward III of England that the king offered the Frenchman his daughter Isabelle's hand in marriage. Several ancestors of his also achieved fame or notoriety. Enguerrand III even tried to seize the French throne in the 13th century; exiled, he marked his defiance by making his castle twice the size of the Louvre in Paris.

Today, the remnants of the massive castle look forlorn at first sight, but bits and pieces give an idea of its grandeur in medieval times. The large round pile of rubble is what remains of the keep, one of the tallest ever erected in France, reaching over 150ft. In 1917 occupying Germans blew it up, along with the whole village outside the bailey, before fleeing. Much of the castle had in fact been destroyed earlier, in 1652, by order of France's chief minister Mazarin. However, the scale of the remnants of the two major halls gives a good notion of the medieval castle at its staggering apogee. The Salle des Preux, measuring roughly 200 by 50ft, was one of the largest medieval rooms ever built in France. Also explore the vast vaulted cellars below.

Due south of Coucy, in the Aisne valley, the city of **Soissons** played an important part in French history a very long time back. In 752 Pepin le Bref, the first of the dynamic early Carolingian monarchs and father of Charlemagne, was declared king here, putting an end to the lazy last rulers of the Merovingian dynasty. Although the Germans destroyed large parts of the city, several vast buildings prove the importance of the place through medieval times. The Gothic **cathedral** looks a bit grubby on the outside and is disappointingly surrounded by a large car park, but the edifice is impressive, with interesting features inside, including World War memorials. As to the medieval **Abbaye St-Léger**, also in the centre, it has been turned into part of the town's **museum** (*open Thurs–Tues 9–12 and 2–5, Sat and Sun 2–5; closed Wed; adm*). The abbey's former church contains beautiful pieces of medieval sculpture. Among the Ancien Régime works, Houdon's tenderly sad *Head of a Negress* was used at the Revolution as a symbol of the abolition of slavery in France. The most spectacular medieval building left in Soissons stands aloof outside the centre.

The sensational façade of the **Abbaye St-Jean-des-Vignes** (*open Mon–Sat 9–12.30 and 1.30–6, Sun 10–12.30 and 1.30–7; adm*) is in fact just a shell, but a breathtaking one, its two towers reaching over 230ft in height. The demolition in 1805 of the building which lay behind caused an outcry at the time; the decision was taken by Soissons' bishop, who wanted the stone to repair his cathedral. You can, however, still wander round the beautiful Gothic emptiness of the abbey refectory, the cellars, and the two remaining sides of the cloisters with their curious hybrid Gothic beasts.

Between Coucy and Noyon, the clipped wings of a once much greater dwelling are all that remain of the **Château de Blérancourt**, designed by royal architect Salomon de Brosse in the 17th century. A slick modern extension houses the quite fascinating **National Museum of French–American Friendship and Cooperation** (*open Wed–Mon 10–12.30 and 2–5.30; closed Tues; adm*), presenting paintings of America by French artists, and canvases of French scenes by American painters, including John Singer Sargent. The castle's links with the USA were forged when Anne Morgan, daughter of the fabulously wealthy American banker John Pierpoint Morgan, bought the place and in 1917 set up an American women's volunteer service to offer humanitarian aid to the French in the First World War. Her valiant efforts are also recalled here.

Moving west to the Oise valley, **Noyon** is a little-known cathedral city which, like Soissons, has a history quite out of proportion to its size today. Its origins go back to Roman times. St Médard and St Eloi were two of its famous Dark Ages bishops, very close to the Merovingian royals. In 768 Charlemagne came here to be crowned King of Neustria, taking in most of France and large portions of Germany. Noyon also puts in a claim, along with Senlis, to being the place where Hugues Capet was elected first Capetian king in 987. The sober Gothic **cathedral**, completed around 1220, is the centre of attention today; all the statuary in the deep western porches was ripped out at the Revolution. Inside, it is built on four impressive levels as at Laon; two ornate side chapels stand out. Outside, behind the cathedral, the library with its wooden-pillared colonnade is a surprising survivor from the 16th century.

In 1509, Noyon was the birthplace of that most formidable of early Protestants, Calvin, who would later make life so hard for the Catholic Church from the safer haven of Geneva. Many people think of him as purely Swiss, but his native town pays its respects to him at the **Musée Jean Calvin** (*open April–Oct Wed–Mon 9–12 and 2–6, closed Tues; rest of year Tues–Sun 10–12 and 2–5, closed Mon; adm*), on the site of the house of his birth. In the First World War, Noyon was in the unfortunate position, until 1917, of being the closest German-occupied town to Paris. Largely destroyed at the end of that conflict, and again in the Second World War, some pleasant quarters have been revived, while local history is recalled in the **Musée du Noyonnais** (*open April–Oct Tues–Sun 9–12 and 2–6; rest of year Tues–Sun 10–12 and 2–5; closed Mon; adm*).

Château-Filled Forests on the Ile de France Border

At the **Clairière de l'Armistice** in the **Forest of Compiègne** stands a replica of the **railway carriage** (*open April–Nov Wed–Mon 10–12 and 2–5.30; Dec–Jan Wed–Mon 2–5.30; closed Tues; adm*) in which Marshal Foch of France agreed to the armistice on 11 November 1918. On 22 June 1940, in one of his most symbolic acts of revenge on Germany's humiliation after the Great War, Hitler insisted that the French sign the armistice signalling their defeat at the hands of the Nazis in the same place. The original carriage was taken to Berlin during the war, where it was destroyed by bombing.

Surprisingly little known given its amazing grandeur, the positively imperial town of **Compiègne** is dominated by a magnificently pompous palace. This **château** (*open Wed–Mon 10–6; closed Tues; adm*) was built for Louis XV, but Compiègne had been a firm French royal favourite as far back as Carolingian times. Its abbey of St-Cornelius, now vanished, even served as the royal necropolis until St-Denis took over the role. In medieval times, it was in Compiègne in May 1430 that Joan of Arc was captured by Burgundian troops as she tried to storm the town. Building work began on the vast Ancien Régime château in 1738. Marie-Antoinette met the future Louis XVI here for the first time in 1770. In one of those bizarre historical links, her great-niece, Marie-Louise of Austria, would be brought to the castle in 1810 to be married to Napoleon. Later, in the mid-19th century, Napoléon III and Empress Eugénie held wildly extravagant house parties here. With well over 1,000 rooms, they had more than enough room to house their guests in what is one of the largest castles in France.

The displays inside concentrate on the two imperial periods. By 1811, Napoleon and Marie-Louise had had a son, François, and the life of the little family is evoked in a string of apartments. The boy became known as the Roi de Rome, even enjoying five days as Napoléon II in 1815. After his father's demise, he spent most of his short life in Vienna, dying of tuberculosis in 1832. On the long guided tour of the main **imperial**

apartments, you are regaled with *trompe-l'œils* by Sauvage, heroic wall paintings by Girodet, Bohemian crystal chandeliers, ravishing parquet floors, and the finest tapestries, some from Beauvais (*see* below). The **Museum of the Second Empire** contains an absurd number of portraits and family objects. In the **Musée de la Voiture**, a wide range of old carriages, early cars and bicycles line up for inspection. If it all gets too much, go for a walk in the splendid grounds, much loved by the town's inhabitants.

In the picturesque centre of town, one side of the impressive Hôtel de Ville, Napoleon might have enjoyed playing war games with the toy soldiers displayed in the **Musée de la Figurine Historique** (*open Mar–Oct Tues–Sat 9–12 and 2–5, Sun 2–5; closed Mon; adm*), although he wouldn't have appreciated the setpiece of the Battle of Waterloo. At the **Musée Vivenel** (*open same times; adm*), the artefacts from Egypt and ancient Greece eclipse the local archaeological finds. The church of St-Jacques, though, is a Gothic delight topped by a 17th-century dome. Joan of Arc is recalled in a melodramatic 19th-century statue by Frémiet on Place du 54e Régiment d'Infanterie.

The sensational picture-book **Château de Pierrefonds** (*open mid-May–mid-Sept daily 9.30–6; rest of year Mon–Sat 9.30–12.30 and 2–5.30, Sun 9.30–5.30; adm*) rises above a very pretty lakeside village on the southeastern edge of the forest of Compiègne. But the place turns out to be a pastiche of a Gothic castle. The original was built for Louis d'Orléans, brother of King Charles VI of France, in the late 14th century. It was the main fortification in a whole line commissioned by Louis to protect his Valois duchy. In the 16th century, Antoine d'Estrées, father of the beautiful Gabrielle d'Estrées whom King Henri IV took as his mistress, owned the castle, destroyed after he opted for the wrong side under Henri IV's son Louis XIII. Napoleon bought Pierrefonds' ruins for a pittance early in the 19th century, but it was by order of Napoléon III that Viollet-le-Duc, the architect who did so much (too much in many critics' eyes) to restore major dilapidated Gothic buildings around France, set about reconstructing the massive pile as a Second Empire residence from 1858 on. The 19th-century decorations, and in particular the sculptures, prove absorbing from the moment you enter the courtyard with its enormous lizard gargoyle. Most of the rooms lack furniture, but all their walls are highly decorated. The most impressive chamber, the Salle des Preuses, is dedicated to heroic women.

In the sometimes ghostly quiet old fortified quarter of **Crépy-en-Valois** to the south, the segment of castle remaining protects the **Musée de l'Archerie et de l'Art Sacré** (*open mid-April–11 Nov Wed–Mon 2.30–6.30; closed Tues; adm*). It offers a curiously medieval mix of displays, one on the military art of archery, the other on religious art, of course including images of St Sebastian shot through with arrows. The remnants of the **Abbaye St-Arnoul** contain a museum of local traditions going under the name of the **Musée du Mariage** (*open April–Christmas Sun 2–7*) owing to its main collection.

Senlis, Ermenonville and Around

Senlis' circular streets are fitted as tightly together as the rings of an onion. They are encased in ancient walls, parts of which date back, quite amazingly, to Gallo-Roman times. Senlis prospered under the Capetian kings, when the mighty cathedral at its heart was built. Philippe Auguste then ordered a second set of ramparts for the city, while his close friend Guérin was elected bishop and set up the Abbaye de la Victoire. In the Wars of Religion, the Huguenot contingent supported King Henri IV, but after him the town's royal links ceased, and it sank into a torpor. The **cathedral** was begun in 1155, one of the very first batch of French Gothic cathedrals. Two stern towers rise from the west front, only one of which was completed with a spiky Gothic spire. The sculptures on the west front are superb, and, unlike most of the other cathedrals of northern France, many are original. The large figures represent prophets, just sporting 19th-century heads. Note the importance given to the Virgin, placed on the same footing as Christ; this cathedral was apparently the first to devote a portal to Mary. Next door, in the **Hôtel de Vermandois** (*open Mon, Thurs and Fri 10–12 and 2–5, Wed 2–5, Sat and Sun 11–1 and 2–6; closed Tues; adm*)**,** the slide shows can help you appreciate the cathedral's carved figures up close. Inside the religious edifice, the nave may be very short by Gothic standards, its arches tentative, but for such an imposing structure it has a rare, warm feeling. The Flamboyant south transept has more elaborate pendant bosses and a window with tracery in the form of teardrops and flames.

Men flashing at you in the former bishops' palace make for one of the biggest surprises at the **Musée d'Art et d'Archéologie** (*open same times as Vermandois; adm*), packed with interesting things. The Gallo-Roman collections include not just the base of a grand monument to the Emperor Claudius and two extraordinary bronze crayfish, but also an alarming display of Gallo-Roman offerings to pagan gods from a shrine near Senlis; as well as countless hands, feet and heads, there's a host of male genitalia being exposed from under lifted tunics– apparently, the sick would go to the shrine with a carving of the body part from which they were suffering. The Gothic gallery contains magnificent dignified medieval statuary, none finer than the so-called 13th-century *Tête de Senlis*, in which the sculptor conveyed exceptional maturity and wisdom. The painting sections seem more prosaic. Nearby, the **Musée de la Vénerie** (*open same times as Vermandois; adm*), set in the grounds of the former castle, concentrates on the art of hunting, while the adjoining little **Musée des Spahis** (*open same times as Vermandois; adm*) explains the formation of this extraordinary North African cavalry regiment which fought for France, and was based in Senlis from the late 1920s to the early 1960s. Another curiosity to consider is the **Crypte of the church of St-Frambourg** (*open Sat and Sun 3–5; adm*), a restored royal chapel.

A clutch of quite contrasting tourist sights, some seriously cultural, others wildly entertaining, stand close together on the edges of the **Forest of Ermenonville** southeast of Senlis. The **Abbaye de Chaalis** contains the **Musée Jacquemart-André** (*museum open Mar–11 Nov daily 11–6; rest of the year Sun 11–5; park open daily 10–6; adm*), an art collection founded by the same Nélie Jacquemart-André as the Musée Jacquemart-André in Paris (*see* p.116). She transformed the elegant 18th-century religious buildings into her country home a decent period after the religious community had left. Although crammed with works, the place doesn't contain the same wealth of masterpieces as her house in the capital. However, in the elegant grounds, pay a visit to the small Gothic chapel, which conceals delicate ceiling frescoes of angels, apostles and evangelists by the 16th-century Italian artist Niccolo dell'Abbate, who had come over to France to help Primaticcio decorate the château of Fontainebleau.

Opposite the abbey, the extraordinary exotic landscape of dunes of **La Mer de Sable** (*open April–Sept; check complex opening times: www.merdesable.fr, t 03 44 54 00 96; adm*) was caused by deforestation in the 19th century. It has now been turned into a popular theme park with different quarters, from the American Wild West to China. For a more tranquil, elevated walk, visit the **Parc Jean-Jacques Rousseau** (*open April–Sept daily 2–6, rest of year 1–5; adm*) in **Ermenonville** itself. It seems fittingly ironic that the supremely influential 18th-century political theorist, often nowadays considered the most dangerous idealist who ever existed, should have ended up buried in such a posh park full of artifice, created by the Marquis René de Girardin. This great admirer of Rousseau generously received the man whose notions that men are born free but are everywhere in chains, that the goodness of human nature is only corrupted by society, and that the will of the common good must prevail, have been blamed for causing so many appallingly destructive attempts at creating utopias across the world. As it was, Rousseau was sick and insane when he came here, dying on 2 July 1778, shortly after his arrival. His tomb lies on an island, while follies around the grounds include the Temple of Philosophy. Back with more frivolous matters, off the A1 motorway a short way south of Senlis, **Parc Astérix** (*open April–Sept most days at least 10–6, but times are complex: t 01 60 77 04 04; adm*) has one of Europe's most terrifying roller-coasters, but also more comforting corners to please children who love the good-natured, feisty moustachioed cartoon Gauls.

Château de Chantilly

Museum open April–Oct Wed–Mon 10–6; Mar Wed–Mon 10–12.45 and 2–6; Nov–Feb Sat and Sun 10.30–12.45 and 2–5; park open Mar–Oct 10–6; adm.

The Château de Chantilly looks as rich and luscious as the whipped cream invented here. The Romans were the first to build a fort on what was then an island in a bog. Skipping rapidly to medieval times, the important Montmorency family erected their feudal castle here. This was rebuilt in the French Renaissance by the Anne de Montmorency, Grand Connétable, under kings François Ier and Henri II. His grand-daughter Charlotte caught the roving eye of King Henri IV, who thought the best way to have his evil way with her would be to marry her off to an obliging husband, Henri de Bourbon-Condé. The plan backfired when the groom refused to recognize the king's *droit de seigneur*, and the irascible royal showed his displeasure by exiling the young couple. They were able to return to Chantilly after the king's death and left the estate to their son, best known as the Grand Condé, who brought the château to the height of its fame, commissioning the gardens and fountains from Le Nôtre. The Renaissance château, however, was destroyed at the Revolution, then rebuilt, only to be destroyed again in that lesser revolutionary year, 1848. The elegant mess of a castle you see today is the fifth edition, with a delightful mirror of a lake.

The **Musée Condé** within boasts one of the best art collections in France outside the Louvre. It harbours some of the finest illuminated works of all the Middle Ages, the jewel in the crown the *Très Riches Heures du Duc de Berry* (*see* 'Bourges' for an introduction to the vile patron), the unparalleled masterpiece of early 15th-century illumination. You're only permitted to see well-made facsimiles, but you can still admire the detail of the fairytale interpretations of 15th-century French châteaux in the illustrations of the months. The splendid Italian Renaissance selection includes works by Botticelli, Filippino Lippi and Raphael. There are exceptional French canvases too, by the likes of François Clouet, Watteau and Poussin.

The grandson of the Grand Condé, convinced that he would be reincarnated as a horse, gave Chantilly one of the most palatial stables in the world, the **Grandes Ecuries**, now housing the **Musée Vivant du Cheval** (*open April–Oct Wed–Mon 10.30–6.30; rest of year Mon and Wed–Fri 2–5, Sat and Sun 10.30–6.30; closed Tues; adm*), where you can admire beautifully groomed steeds of nearly every conceivable breed. There are also dressage demonstrations daily, and over 30 rooms packed full of horsey artefacts and toys. Chantilly **racecourse** hosts some of the most prestigious meets in Europe. The town was also once celebrated for its black lace.

Along the Oise

Crossing into the Ile de France region, along the Oise valley skirting the capital to the northwest, **Royaumont** has a superbly preserved abbey; **Auvers' Maison Gachet** is dedicated to the memory of Van Gogh, who painted intensively in the area; while the artistic hero of **Pontoise** is superlative Impressionist **Pissarro**, given his own museum.

Beauvais

A bit out on a limb, north up the A16 motorway, among the flat cereal fields of western Picardy, the city of **Beauvais** may have been devastated by Second World War bombing, but it has still kept several spots of major cultural interest. You're actually only treated to half a cathedral here, but what it lacks in length it more than makes up for in height; Beauvais' **Cathedral St-Pierre** was a work of staggering vanity. This is the edifice with the tallest Gothic vaulting in the world, stretching over 150ft. Inside, you can suffer vertigo looking *up*! Begun in 1227, construction continued until the end of the 16th century. Unfortunately the pillars and buttresses proved inadequate to support the huge weight of the towering masonry; the nave kept on collapsing, and what remains is often clad in scaffolding. However, outstanding stained glass windows sparkle around the choir, while the mechanical clock proves another sizable treasure. The late-Gothic bishops' palace contains the renovated **Musée des Beaux-Arts** (*open July–Sept Wed–Mon 10–6; rest of year Wed–Mon 10–12 and 2–6; closed Tues; adm*). From a beautiful 1st-century Gaulish warrior via a comical late 15th-century ceramic knight, on past grandiose Italian works to pieces by the French Romantics, this museum serves up plenty of surprises. Better known across France is Beauvais' tradition of tapestry making, dating back to Louis XIV's reign, and celebrated in the modern **Galerie Nationale de la Tapisserie** (*open April–Sept Tues–Sun 9.30–12.30 and 2–6; rest of year Tues–Sun 10–12.30 and 2–5; adm*). The craft continues in town – to see how it has evolved, visit the **Manufacture Nationale de la Tapisserie** (*close to the railway station; open afternoons Tues–Thurs, guided tours at 2.15 and 3.30; adm*).

While out in these parts, press a little further west for the grand abbey church at **St-Germer de Fly**, with its own Sainte Chapelle made to house a relic of Christ, and the exceptionally quaint village of **Gerberoy**, both on the Normandy border.

The Northeast

p.528

NORD

BELGIUM

BELGIUM

SOMME

Givet

Haybes

Revin   Fumay

St-Michel   Rocroi   Monthermé

St-Quentin

Charleville-
Mézières   Sedan

Bazeilles

Poix-Terron   Avioth

A R D E N N E S   Mouzon   Longwy

Noyon   AISNE   Sissonne   Rethel   Montmédy

OISE   Coucy-le-   Laon   Vouziers   Buzancy   Stenay

Château   Craonne   Vilosnes

Aisne   Montfaucon   Fort de   Etain

Soissons   d'Argonne   Douaumont

Reims   ❸   Verdun

Villers-Cotterêts   Beaumont-   Les   Fresnes-   Lac de

La Ferté-Milon   Marfaux   sur-Vesle   Monthairons   en-W   Madine

Pourcy   ❶   Verzenay   Ste-   Hattonchâtel

Hautvillers   Verzy   Menehould

Château-   Champillon   Ambonnay   L'Épine   Beney-en-

Thierry   Cumières   Ay   Marne   Woevre

Épernay   MARNE   Châlons-en-Champagne   St-Mihiel

La Ferté-s/s-   Pierry   Le Mesnil-   MEUSE

Jouarre   Montmort   sur-Oger   Revigny

SEINE-ET-   Étoges   Vertus   Bar-le-Duc

MARNE   Bergèrest-lès-Vertus   Commercy

Mondemont-   Mont   Fère-   Vitry-le-

Montgivroux   Aimé   Champenoise   François   St-Dizier   Vaucouleurs

Sézanne   Lac de Der   Marne

Provins   Chantecoq   Wassy   Joinville   Domrémy

Romilly   Aube   Brienne-   Cirey-sur-   Grand

le-Château   Blaise   Vignory   Neufchâteau

AUBE   Lac du   Colombey-les-   Andelot

Temple   Arsonval   Deux-Églises

Troyes   ❷   Lac   Bar-sur-Aube   HAUTE-MARNE

Sens   d'Orient   Clairvaux   Chaumont

Fouchères   Bar-sur-Seine

Chaource   Essoyes   Arc-en-Barrois   Bourbonne-

Les Riceys   les-Bains

Vix   Langres

Mt-Lassois   Châtillon-   Recey

Laignes   sur-Seine   CÔTE-D'OR

p.137

p.618

p.618

ENGLAND   BELGIUM   GERMANY

English Channel   LUX.

FRANCE   SWITZ.

ITALY

SPAIN

The Northeast

40 km
20 miles

N

LUXEMBOURG

GERMANY

Sierck
Moselle
Thionville
Hayange
Briey
Forbach
SAARBRUCKEN
Metz 7
MOSELLE
St-Avold
Sarreguemines
Bitche
Wissembourg
Oberateinbach
Lembach
Meisenthal
Hunspach
Thiaucourt-
Regniéville
Pont-à-Mousson
Betschdorf
La Petite
Pierre
Soufflenheim
Château-
Salins
Graufthal
Haguenau
MEURTHE-
ET-MOSELLE
Sarrebourg
Saverne
Marmoutier
Marne
Toul
Nancy 4
St-Nicolas-de-Port
Lunéville
Dabo
Wangenbourg
BAS-
RHIN
Strasbourg 5
Haroué
Baccarat
Molsheim
Rosheim
Obernai
Mt-Ste-Odile
Barr
Le Hohwald
Mirecourt
Rambervillers
St-Dié
6
Sélestat
Vittel
Contrexéville
Épinal
VOSGES
Riquewihr
Kaysersberg
Gérardmer
Lac de Longemer
Turckheim
Munster
Colmar
Eguisheim
Neuf-Brisach
Bains-les-Bains
Remiremont
Rouffach
HAUT-RHIN
Plombières
Le Markstein
Guebwiller
Luxeuil
Grand
Ballon
HAUTE-SAÔNE
Ballon d'Alsace
Thann
Mulhouse
p.708 Ronchamp
TRE-DE-
BELFORT

Highlights

1 The Champagne wine routes
2 Troyes and its artistic treasures
3 Verdun's First World War memorials
4 Nancy's Ancien Régime and
  Art Nouveau glamour
5 Strasbourg's splendours
6 The absurdly cute Alsace wine route
7 The stained glass in Metz cathedral

Food and Wine

Champagne is synonymous with its sparkling wine, but also produces some fine cheeses, notably soft and creamy Chaource and Langres from the south of the region, while the **Ardennes** has become almost synonymous with pâtés made from game such as wild boar, venison or hare. **Lorraine** is famous for its creamy egg and bacon flan, quiche Lorraine. Pork specialities include *potée Lorraine*, which features all manner of pork cuts. Damsons, cherries and blueberries are widely grown, as well as *mirabelles*, little yellow plums which go into the region's best-known liqueur, Mirabelle de Lorraine. The vineyards around Toul produce some decent wines, including a rosé, vin gris. For those with a sweet tooth, there are buttery madeleines from Commercy and the alcohol-soaked *baba au rhum*.

Alsace offers *choucroute*, beer and some great white wines from riesling and gewurztraminer grapes. Neighbouring Germany influences much of the cuisine, with overgenerous portions of pork in many a dish; *bäeckoffe* is a copious, aromatic stew of pork, mutton and beef combined with large potatoes, onions and garlic marinated in riesling. *Foie gras* is also closely associated with Alsace. Extremely smelly Munster is the tastiest Alsace cheese. Among sweet specialities, gingerbread is popular, while Alsace's fruit brandies, (*alcools blancs*) are used to flavour puddings or as a *digéstif*.

Travel east from Paris and the landscapes unroll like a three-act play. The action opens with Champagne and its glamorous vineyards, where the *dramatis personae* include three rival sisters: jewel-like Troyes, bustling Reims and businesslike Epernay, the last the best place to visit the big champagne houses.

Act Two is the surprisingly pretty countryside of Lorraine, one of the French regions least known to English-speaking tourists, but packed with historical resonance for the French thanks to Joan of Arc, Verdun, General de Gaulle and the Cross of Lorraine. World-famous crystals Baccarat and Lalique are produced here. Lorraine also boasts several surprising cities that deserve to be better known, starting with Nancy and her Ancien Régime and Art Nouveau finery.

The Vosges, the red sandstone range that divides Alsace from Lorraine and the Rhine valley from the rest of France, add a theatrical backdrop to Act III: gorgeous little Alsace, a French curiosity – so full of *Kaffee and Kuchen* culture, and yet the Alsatians would be offended to be considered German. Strasbourg, Alsace's capital and now one of the capitals of the European Union, has one of the most uplifting of all Gothic cathedrals; Colmar holds the most devastating Crucifixion in Western art. Around them, absurdly picturesque timberframe and geranium-crazed wine villages lie below the forested Vosges slopes with their romantic ruined red castles.

Reims

So closely linked with the bubbly stuff, Reims (sometimes spelt Rheims in English) lies in the flat Vesle valley below some of Champagne's prettiest slopes. The cathedral, the Palais du Tau, the Basilique St Remi and the Musée Abbaye St Remi have been declared UNESCO World Heritage sites, while the wide shopping streets around make up in bustle for what they lack in beauty.

Settled by the Remi tribe in Celtic times, and an important city on the Roman Empire's eastern border, Reims' Christian history began in 496 (or 498) when Clovis, king of the Franks, was baptized by Bishop Remi, who at the same time generously granted the French kings the divine right to rule. Down the centuries, monarchs would come to be crowned here. Reims continued to grow in importance in the Middle Ages. The local sheep brought a thriving textile trade, and Reims cathedral would count as one of the greatest building enterprises of the 13th century. The drapers' city became a university town in 1547. In Napoleon's last desperate bid to regain power in 1814, Reims saw a late if futile victory, on 13 March. Through the 19th century champagne and textiles made the city fat and prosperous. So close to the front, much of Reims' historic centre was reduced to rubble in the First World War: during one week around Easter 1917, it was pounded by 25,000 shells. More destruction followed in the Second World War, if on a smaller scale. At least Reims had the honour of witnessing the signing of the Germans' unconditional surrender at Eisenhower's headquarters on 7 May 1945. In 1962 President Charles de Gaulle and the Chancellor Konrad Adenauer officially celebrated French and German reconciliation at Reims cathedral.

Known as the cathedral of angels, **Reims Cathedral** (1221–1311) is a staggering achievement, one of the most vertical and successful Gothic cathedrals ever built, and covered with dazzling sculpture. The central portal is dedicated to the Virgin, the left one to local Christian martyrs and to angels, including the much-photographed *Ange au Sourire*, with its slightly sickly smile. The right portal shows Christ of the Last Judgement. The statuary on the higher level is even more exceptional. The central scene of David and Goliath is extraordinary, and, up above, the row of kings has a truly splendid dignity. These figures, over 15ft in height, represent the kings of France; the baptism of Clovis takes centre stage. High up in the niches on the buttresses you can make out a row of massive open-winged angels, hence the cathedral's nickname. Most unusually, the brilliant carving continues on the inner side of the west façade. As you enter, look back to see a wall of niches filled with remarkable statues, including arresting knights in chainmail. Unfortunately a lot of the Gothic stained glass was destroyed in the First World War, but much has been restored, while Chagall produced the striking window in the end chapel of the choir.

Champagne Houses in Reims

Many champagne houses have their headquarters in Reims, but only a few are open to the public. The tours tend to be better in Epernay (*see* p.578).

Taittinger, 9 Place St-Nicaise, **t** 03 26 85 84 33. No need to book. *Open Mar–Nov Mon–Fri 9.30–12 and 2–5, weekends and hols 9–11 and 2–4,30; rest of year weekdays only; adm.*

Piper-Heidsieck, 51 Bd Henry Vasnier, **t** 03 26 84 43 44. Visits in little wagons. No need to book. *Open daily 9–11.45 and 2–5.15; closed Tues and Wed Dec–Feb; adm.*

Pommery, 5 Place du Général Gouraud, **t** 03 26 61 62 55. Book in advance.

Veuve Clicquot Ponsardin, 1 Place des Droits de l'Homme, **t** 03 26 89 53 90. Book.

Many of the figures on the cathedral façade turn out to be copies. The originals, superlative pieces of Gothic sculpting, are the glory of the museum in the former archbishops' palace, the **Palais du Tau** (*open July–Aug daily 9.30–6.30; mid-Mar–June*

Getting There and Around

From Britain, **drive** from Calais down the A26. Ryanair has flown to Reims **airport** in the past and may do so again one day. The **train** between Paris-Gare de l'Est and Reims takes 1hr 30mins. The A4 links the two cities. For **bus** information in Reims, call t 03 26 88 25 38.

Tourist Information

Reims: 2 Rue Guillaume de Machault, t 03 26 77 45 00, *www.tourisme.fr/reims*.

Shopping

Reims' main commercial centre covers Rue Carnot, Rue de Vesle, Rue Condorcet and Rue de Talleyrand. Food markets take place on Av Jean Jaurès (*Sun until 1pm*), and Place du Boulingrin (*Wed and Sat until 2pm*). There is a flea market the first Sun of every month.

Where to Stay

Reims ✉ **51100**
****Boyers' Les Crayères, 64 Bd Henry Vasnier, t 03 26 82 80 80, *www.gerardboyer.com* (*luxury*). Outrageously expensive, but the height of sophistication and luxury, both for the cuisine (*very expensive*) and the rooms, set in a grand little château built for the Pommery family early in the 20th century. *Restaurant closed Mon and Tues lunch.*
****L'Assiette Champenoise, 40 Av Paul Vaillant-Couturier, 51430 Tinqueux, t 03 26 84 64 64, *www.assiettechampenoise.com* (*luxury–expensive*) On the western edge of town, expanded from a 19th-century neo-Gothic mansion. It has 62 reasonably priced rooms and prides itself on its indoor pool and its high-quality cuisine.
****Grand Hôtel des Templiers, 22 Rue des Templiers, t 03 26 88 55 08, *www.perso. wanadoo.fr/hotel.templiers* (*very expen- sive–expensive*). This neo-Gothic hotel is still

expensive, but full of style. It even manages to fit in a pool. *Restaurant closed Mon and Tues lunch.*
***Hôtel de la Paix, 9 Rue Buirette, t 03 26 40 04 08, *www.bw-hotel-lapaix.com* (*moderate*). Large Best Western hotel down a few notches, with comfortable rooms in the heart of the action. Restaurant (*expensive*).
**Le Crystal, 86 Place Drouet-d'Erlon, t 03 26 88 44 44, *www.hotel-crystal.fr* (*moderate*). Well-located, relatively peaceful hotel with a flowery courtyard, but no restaurant.
**Azur Hôtel, 9 Rue des Ecrvées, t 03 26 47 43 39 (*inexpensive*). Central, cheap and well run.

Eating Out

There are innumerable brasseries and cafés along the main boulevards.
Au Petit Comptoir, 17 Rue de Mars, t 03 26 40 58 58 (*expensive*). Distinguished *bistrot* serving old-fashioned dishes and good- value champagne. *Closed Sat lunch, Mon lunch and Sun.*
Brasserie du Boulingrin, 48 Rue de Mars, t 03 26 40 96 22 (*moderate*). Famous Reims brasserie, Art Deco style with mural '*vendanges en champagne*'.

Entertainment and Nightlife

Opéra Cinema, 3 Rue T-Dubois, t 03 26 7 29 36. Shows non-dubbed films.
Cinéma Gaumont, 72 Place Drouet d'Erlon, t 03 26 47 32 02. Non-dubbed films every Tues.
Cactus Café, 47 Rue des Capucins, t 03 26 88 16 99. Mellow Tex-Mex bar. *Open daily 11am– 12.30am, Fri 11am–1.30am, Sat 4pm–1.30am; closed Sun.*
Le Gaulois, 2–4 Place Drouet d'Erlon. Cocktails and ice cream.

In the summer, as part of **Les Flâneries Musicales d'Été**, there are over 120 classical music concerts, many of which are free. Contact Reims Tourist Board for information.

Reims

N

250 metres
250 yards

To Laon

Musée de la Reddition

Chapelle Foujita

RUE DU CHAMP DE MARS

Mumm

Cimetière du Nord

PLACE DE LA RÉPUBLIQUE

BD LUNDY

Porte de Mars

Les Halles

Krug

RUE COQUEBERT

Train Station

Hautes Promenades

SQUARE COLBERT

BD FOCH

RUE DE MARS

RUE DU TEMPLE

Basses promenades

BD DU GENERAL LECLERC

RUE THIERS

RUE DE TALLEYRAND

Hôtel de Ville

RUE LINGUET

RUE DES TEMPLIERS

Louis Roederer

Lanson

BD LUNDY

AV. JEAN JAURES

RUE DE CERNAY

RUE DE CERNAY

PLACE DE L'HÔTEL DE VILLE

COURS J.B. LANGLET

RUE DU COLBERT

RUE JEANJACQUES ROUSSEAU

Hôtel Le Vergeur

Cryptoporticus

PLACE A. BRIAND

RUE DU CLOU DANS LE FER

PLACE DROUET-D'ERLON

PLACE DU FORUM

RUE CERES

PLACE ROYALE

SQUARE DES CORDELIERS

JE BUIRETTE

RUE DE VESLE

Eglise St-Jacques

RUE CARNOT

PLACE M. HERRICK

PLACE MARTYRS DE LA RESISTANCE

RUE CLOVIS

Grand Théâtre

Musée des Beaux-Arts

Cathedral

RUE VOLTAIRE

BD DE LA PAIX

BD ST-MARCEAUX

PLACE DU C. LUÇON

Palais de Tau

RUE LIBERGIER

RUE HINCMAR

RUE CHANZY

RUE DES CAPUCINS

RUE CLOVIS

Synagogue

RUE DU JARD

RUE CHANZY

RUE PONSARDIN

Ancien Port

To Paris

RUE DES CAPUCINS

RUE GAMBETTA

RUE DU BARBATRE

RUE DES COUTURES

Piper-Heidsieck

Charles Heidsieck

To Soissons, Dormans Chateau Thierry

RUE DES MOULINS

Ancien Collège des Jésuites

BD VICTOR HUGO

BD HENRI VASNIER

AUTOROUTE A4-E50

Canal

La Vesle

RUE SIMON

Musée St-Rémi

Taittinger

Basilique St-Rémi

Square St-Nicaise

RUE DES CRAYERES

Pommery

Ruinart

BD DIANCOURT

BD HENRI VASNIER

Esplanade du Sud

PLACE DES DROITS DE L'HOMME

AV DU GENERAL GIRAUD

Veuve Clicquot

To Metz

To Epernay

To Fort de la Pompelle and Chalons sur Marne

To Rethel

and Sept–mid-Nov daily 9.30–12.30 and 2–6; mid-Nov–mid-Mar daily 10–12 and 2–5; adm). The museum also houses beautiful tapestries and a splendid treasure that includes a 12th-century chalice used for royal coronations.

The **Musée des Beaux-Arts** *(open Wed–Mon 10–12 and 2–6; closed Tues; adm, free first weekend of month)* contains a rich collection in the drab surroundings of an 18th-century building that could do with a clean. Look for Cranach's studies of princes and dukes of the Holy Roman Empire, a splendid collection of Flemish masters, and 17th-century works by Philippe de Champaigne, Simon Vouet and Le Nain – the last painted scenes of everyday life. The 19th century is well represented by Boudin, Jongkind and Pissarro along with numerous paintings of trees by water by Courbet.

Reims' **shopping boulevards** lie at the northern end of town, with Cours J-B Langlet and Place Drouet D'Erlon the major arteries. East of here you will find the set-piece squares that more or less survived the bombardments: Place Royale is the most ordered, with a statue of Louis XV at its centre. Scrappier Place du Forum contains the vestiges of the Roman city, including the underground vaulted **cryptoporticus** *(open 15 June–15 Sept Tues–Sun 2–5).*

Be prepared to devote a couple of hours to **Hôtel Le Vergeur** *(open Tues–Sun 2–6; adm).* Heavily restored, the house dates from the Gothic period, and was built in what was once the bourgeois quarter of Reims. Nicolas Le Vergeur altered it to suit Renaissance tastes in the 16th century. In the 19th it belonged to the Veuve Clicquot-Ponsardin clan, but at the start of the 20th century it was bought by a German champagne heir, Hugues Krafft, who travelled around the world building up his art collection. He also recovered fragments of historic churches and homes in Reims destroyed in the First World War – models of the city show how it once looked.

Among the outer boulevards stands the Gallo-Roman **Porte de Mars**, sadly isolated by traffic at the end of Boulevard Foch. Beyond, the neo-Romanesque **Chapelle Foujita** *(open 2 May–Oct Thurs–Tues 2–6; closed Wed; adm)* is covered with wall paintings and stained glass by the Japanese artist Foujita, who converted to Christianity after a mystical experience in St-Remi, and began work on his chapel at the age of 80.

Tucked away behind the station, the **Musée de la Reddition** *(open Wed–Mon 10–12 and 2–6; closed Tues; adm)* contains the room in which the Second World War officially came to an end. On 7 May 1945, in a technical college serving as Allied headquarters, General Eisenhower had the commanders of the German army, navy and airforce sign their surrender; the news was announced on 8 May 1945. The museum concentrates on the events that led up to the German capitulation.

The main focus in the southern half of the centre is the **Basilique St-Remi**, a massive Romanesque church consecrated in 1049 by Pope Leo IX, which has just about managed to preserve its dignity among the surrounding apartment blocks. Supported by later Gothic buttresses, the interior is darkly atmospheric, cavernous even, with only a few small openings. Gothic additions are clearly visible in the ceiling vaults and in the choir, but rare Romanesque stained glass has been preserved in the choir, where you can see the grand tomb for St Remi, who figures along with Clovis and the 12 peers witnessing the coronation. These ornate statues only date from the 17th century and the tomb had to be put back together again after the Revolution.

The **Musée St-Remi** (*open daily 2–6.30; adm*), the region's archaeological and historical museum, occupies large parts of the monastery next door. Just one or two rooms were saved from the medieval monastery, including the chapterhouse. Gallo-Roman finds feature mosaics and a 4th-century sarcophagus. The cycle of tapestries of scenes from the life of St Remi is a Gothic delight, with devils dancing in the gardens.

Not far from St-Remi, the **Ancien Collège des Jésuites** (*guided tours Mon and Wed–Fri 10, 11, 2.15, 3.30 and 4.45; Tues, Sat and Sun 2.15, 3.30 and 4.45; adm*) has retained a good degree of its 17th-century grandeur, including the library and its extravagant Baroque woodwork. The former college also hosts art exhibitions, and has its own **Planétarium** (*open Mon–Fri 2–6; shows Sat, Sun and school hols at 2.45, 3.30 and 4.45; adm*).

Champagne Routes Between Reims and Troyes

The champagne vineyards are more attractive than the champagne towns, and there are hundreds of small champagne producers you can call on in the countryside. Epernay, however, has the densest concentration of major houses to visit, while the small town of Ay is packed with yet more. Follow the route marked '*Route touristique du Champagne*'.

The Making of Champagne – A Fragile and Explosive Affair

Between 25,000 and 30,000 hectares are devoted to true champagne vines, the majority of which lie around Reims and Epernay. Makers use three varieties of grapes, pinot noir, pinot meunier and chardonnay: pinot noir is considered the backbone of most champagne, imparting force and character; pinot meunier is known to give a faster maturing wine, and tends to feature in cheaper champagne; when a champagne is made using just chardonnay, the crisp, widely cultivated white grape variety, it is known as *blanc de blancs*.

Up until the first fermentation champagne is made like an ordinary white wine. At the vital second fermentation (the *méthode champenoise*), sugar is added, and the yeast that eats it up creates carbon dioxide – bubbles. For weeks, each bottle is turned a little each day (now mostly by machine) to coax the dead yeast up to the top. When the residue reaches the top, it is frozen, the bottle is opened and the dead yeast pops out (a process known as *dégorgement*). The bottle is topped up with a *liqueur d'expédition*, a little extra champagne mixed with sugar, the level of sweetness dictating whether the champagne will be *brut* (dry), *sec* (sweeter), or *demi-sec* (sweeter still). Tradition has it that we should thank the monk Dom Pérignon, buried at the abbey church of Hautvillers near Epernay, for mastering this tricky process. Most champagne is left to age for two or three years before coming on the market, but the most prestigious champagnes are kept back still longer. Vintage champagne is made using grapes from a single year. Champagne connoisseurs go for lesser-known names such as Bollinger and Billecart-Salmon, two of the superlative producers. Dom Pérignon is much the best-known top-quality champagne, the top blend of the house of Moët et Chandon.

Tourist Information

Epernay: 7 Av de Champagne, **t** 03 26 53 33 00, *www.ot-epernay.fr.*
Châlons-en-Champagne: 3 Quai des Arts, **t** 03 26 65 17 89.

Where to Stay and Eat

Beaumont-sur-Vesle ✉ 51360
La Table Champenoise, **t 03 26 03 92 45, *www.latablechampenoise.com* (*inexpensive*). A simple little hotel, although some rooms are a bit rough. The food (*expensive–moderate*) draws in the locals, and the wine list represents many smaller champagne producers.

L'Epine ✉ 51460
****Aux Armes de Champagne, 31 Ave du Luxembourg, **t** 04 89 88 40 91 (*expensive–moderate*). Very beautiful hotel near the Basilique L'Epine. Excellent cuisine (*very expensive–expensive*). *Closed Sun eve.*

Ambonnay ✉ 51150
Auberge St-Vincent, 1 Rue St-Vincent, **t 03 26 57 01 98, *www.auberge-st-vincent.*

com (*inexpensive*). Inn with a few comfortable rooms and a restaurant (*expensive–moderate*) with a chef who has revived and modernized traditional regional dishes. *Closed Sun eve and Mon and Feb.*

Champillon ✉ 51160
***Royal Champagne, **t** 03 26 52 87 11, *royalchampagne@wanadoo.fr* (*very expensive*). Old inns don't come much more luxuriously done up than this one, with its intoxicating views above this village just north of Epernay. The restaurant (*very expensive–expensive*) has a high reputation, the wine list a fabulous array of champagnes.

Cumières ✉ 51480
Le Caveau, Rue de la Coopérative, **t** 03 26 54 83 23, *www.restaurant-le-caveau.com* (*expensive–moderate*). Atmospheric restaurant in a cave in a village just west of Hautvillers. *Closed Sun, Mon eve and Wed.*

Epernay ✉ 51200
***Le Clos Raymi, 3 Rue Joseph de Venoge, **t** 03 26 51 00 58, *www.closraymi-hotel.com* (*expensive*). At last in the champagne wine capital a refined, stylish hotel, set back in its

Reims to Epernay

The **Montagne de Reims** natural park encompasses the hills southwest of Reims, its northern and eastern sides densely planted with vines. Tucked away at **Pourcy** you'll find the Maison du Parc, with details on its geology and wildlife in particular. Scattered to the north of Pourcy lie First World War cemeteries. Near **Marfaux**, British and German cemeteries have been quite shockingly laid back to back, the white crosses contrasting startlingly with the black ones next to them.

Verzenay's landmark is a comical lighthouse sticking out of a sea of steep vineyards. Built in 1909 and long abandoned, it was reopened in 1999 as an attractive **wine museum** which focuses on the vine-growers with films and commentaries, while the views down the slopes are utterly delightful.

Ay on the north side of the Marne looks rather friendlier than burly Epernay on the south side, and, although it is less well known, it's also packed with champagne houses. These include Gosset, which claims to be the oldest, with credentials going back to 1584, and the very exclusive Bollinger, whose headquarters stand by vine-covered slopes on the edge of the town.

Epernay's saving grace is its cluster of world-famous champagne houses (*see* over), seated around big courtyards on the Avenue de Champagne. **Hautvillers**, a short way northwest, is probably the prettiest and best kept of all the champagne villages. Its

own courtyard in one of the typical brick mansions built for wealthy Epernay merchants, in this case the Chandons. Just seven rooms. *Closed 15 Dec–1 Feb.*

Châlons-en-Champagne ✉ 51000

Well away from the vines, but it has some cheaper options.

★★Le Pot d'Etain, 18 Place de la République, **t** 03 26 68 09 09, *hotellepotdetain51@ wanadoo.fr (moderate)*. A pleasant old town house hotel.

★★Le Renard, 24 Place de la République, **t** 03 26 68 03 78, *www.le-renard.com (moderate)*. Modern rooms and a restaurant which spills out into the main square. Restaurant (*expensive–moderate*) *Closed Christmas. Restaurant closed Sat and Sun eve.*

Bergères-les-Vertus ✉ 51130

★★★Hostellerie du Mont-Aimé, 4–6 Rue de Vertus, **t** 03 26 52 21 31, *www.hostellerie-mont-aime.com (moderate)*. On the outside it just looks like a modest roadside village house that's been tarted up a bit, but inside the atmosphere is comfortable, the 30 rooms are sweet – set around the garden – and the cooking (*expensive–moderate*) is bright too. *Closed Feb hols and Sun eve.*

Etoges ✉ 51270

★★★Château d'Etoges, **t** 03 26 59 30 08, *etoges1@wanadoo.fr (expensive)*. This gloriously moated little castle is a classified historic monument, gorgeous to look at behind its walls, with its own smart gardens and own natural springs. Boats available to guests.

Montmort ✉ 51270

★★Le Cheval Blanc, Rue de la Libération, **t** 03 26 59 10 03 (*inexpensive*). Neatly kept by the roadside, an old-fashioned provincial hotel with reasonable prices. 19 rooms. There is a restaurant (*expensive–moderate*).

Sézanne ✉ 51120

★★Le Relais Champenois, 157 Rue Notre-Dame, **t** 03 26 80 58 03, *www.relaischampenois.com* (*inexpensive*). Doesn't look much, but the welcome and the decoration in the rooms is very bright, and the cuisine (*expensive–moderate*) makes the most of local produce.

★★Le Cézanne, 25 Rue Léon Jolly, **t** 03 26 42 77 77, *www.hotelfrance.fr* (*inexpensive*). Simple hotel with a good restaurant (*expensive–moderate*).

abbey, now owned by Moët et Chandon, was once home to the celebrated monk Dom Pérignon. His tombstone lies by the altar in the well-restored **abbey church**. The epitaph recalls his death in 1715 and his charitable rather thans his champagne work.

Around Epernay

Château-Thierry, some way west of Epernay along the Marne but still in champagne-producing territory, was the birthplace of the witty 17th-century poet La Fontaine, best known for his poems based on the classical animal fables of Aesop. The town has a museum devoted to his life, his works and his time.

The main champagne route leads south from Epernay. Take the famed **Côte des Blancs** along the D10 to **Vertus**, with busy wine villages along the way. South of Vertus, climb **Mont-Aimé** for the finest views of the Côte des Blancs and the Marne valley. Head for the further champagne vine slopes around Sézanne following a detour west round the marshes of St-Gond. Close to sleepy **Sézanne**, an enormous First World War memorial marks the hillside of **Mondement-Montgivroux**, a dramatic spot recalling the first French victory of the Marne in September 1914. It was one of the bloodiest confrontations of the war. The French managed to hold the line – at a pivotal moment, thanks to the taxis of Paris transporting troops to the front – causing the Germans to retreat and start digging their trenches.

> ## Champagne Houses in and around Epernay
> **Moët et Chandon**, Epernay (*open mid-Nov–Mar Mon–Fri 9.30–11.45 and 2–4.45; April–mid-Nov weekends only; adm*). Informative tour around the enormous cellars, plus a tasting of Napoleon's favourite champagne. Good shop.
> **Mercier**, Epernay, **t** 03 26 51 22 22 (*open Mar–Nov Tues and Wed; visits 9.30–11.30 and 2–4.30; adm*). A more relaxing house to visit, by train.
> **Leclerc-Briant**, 67 Rue Chaude Ruelle, Epernay, **t** 03 26 54 45 33. Call in advance to organize a tour down into the deep cellars (by rope!), or to visit at weekends.
> **Achille Princier**, 9 Rue Jean Chandon Moët, Epernay, **t** 03 26 54 04 06. 18th-century cellars and one of the oldest presses in Champagne.
> **G. Tribaut**, 88 Rue d'Eguisheim, Hautvillers, **t** 03 26 59 40 57. A good family-run estate.
> **Jean-Marie Rigot**, in Binson-et-Orquigny, **t** 03 26 58 33 38. Call ahead to make an appointment at this well-established family estate.
> **The Tarlants**, in Œuilly, **t** 03 26 58 30 60. Family estate (since 1687) on the south side of the river, which runs a B&B as well.
> **Château de Pierry**, at Pierry, **t** 03 26 54 05 11. *Dégustations* and visits to the castle. Call to arrange a visit.
> **Launois Père et Fils**, 2 Av Eugène Guillaume, Le Mesnil-sur-Oger, **t** 03 26 57 50 15. Atmospheric family estate. Call to confirm a good time to visit.
> **Drappier**, Rue des Vignes, at Urville beyond Troyes, **t** 03 25 27 40 15. Suppliers to Géneral de Gaulle and specialists in '*gros flaconnage*' – big bottles. 12th-century cellars excavated by the monks of Clairvaux.

Troyes

Troyes' splendid historic centre, shaped like a champagne cork, contains a clutch of late-Gothic to Renaissance churches and picturesque streets of timberframed or chequered façades. For centuries Troyes was known for textile production, although it is now famous for its cheap outlet stores. It also has an astounding fine arts collection.

Troyes' history goes back to Gallo-Roman times, but the first man to stand out was Bishop Loup in the 5th century, who offered himself up as a hostage to Attila and his Huns in return for the sparing of his city. Bishops kept power until the counts of Champagne took over in the 10th century, making Troyes their capital; their refined court produced one of the most celebrated poets of medieval Europe, Chrétien de Troyes, credited with writing the first Arthurian fiction featuring the Holy Grail. The importance of the Champagne counts dwindled when the last heir to the county, Jeanne, was married to the French king in 1284 and the region became part of the French royal domains. The Treaty of Troyes of 1420 saw the French royal heir, Charles, stripped of his rights and Henry V of England, married to Charles' sister Catherine, accepted as heir to the French crown. Henry V died in 1422. Joan of Arc would help stop Henry VI ruling both sides of the Channel by her support for the young Charles, and she played her part in freeing Troyes from the English.

The compact old city is divided in two by the canalized line of the Seine. North of the canal lies the quarter around the **Cathédrale St-Pierre-et-St-Paul**, a broad-shouldered Gothic giant that took centuries to complete. It was begun in the 13th century, when the choir and parts of the transepts went up, but the intricate façade shows all the signs of the Flamboyant late Gothic with its decorative pinnacles, buttresses and gargoyles. Joan of Arc is supposed to have witnessed the consecration of the cathedral with King Charles VII in 1429. Much of the fine detail and statuary were destroyed at the Revolution, leaving the Gothic niches empty. The interior is vast, grey and empty, relieved only by the stained glass. Next door, the former bishops' palace contains the **Musée d'Art Moderne** (*open Wed–Mon 11–6; closed Tues and public hols; adm*), a superb repository of works from 1850 to 1950, gathered by textile tycoon Pierre Lévy: there are portraits by Millet and Courbet, Fauvist canvases, especially by André Derain (a friend of Lévy); a disturbing portrait of the prostitute Yvette by the lesser known Chabaud; works by Soutine and Vuillard, and the Cubist Gris and Metzinger. Sculpture is well represented, especially with figures from Africa.

On the opposite side of the cathedral, the **Musée des Beaux-Arts** (*open Wed–Mon 10–12 and 2–6; closed Tues and public hols; adm*) occupies the enormous former abbey of St-Loup. By comparison with the modern art museum it looks dowdy, but it contains its share of treasures: beautiful Neolithic polished axe heads, the Gallo-Roman bronze Apollon de Vaupoisson, and some of the finest Merovingian jewellery and weapons in the country – the *Trésor de Pouan*, recovered from a 5th-century princess's tomb. The library claims to be one of the oldest public libraries in France (1651), and at the Revolution it received 50,000 works from Clairvaux abbey, including

Getting Around

Troyes has quite good **road** links with Paris via the A5, or by **rail**; trains from Paris-Gare de l'Est take *c.* 1 hr 20mins. The A26 from Calais is also convenient. Reims **airport** is 1hr away.

Tourist Information

Troyes: 16 Bd Carnot, **t** 03 25 82 62 70, *www. ot-troyes.fr*.

Where to Stay

Troyes ✉ 10000

★★★★Le Champ des Oiseaux, 20 Rue Linard Gonthier, **t** 03 25 80 58 50 (*very expensive–moderate*). Stylish timberframed hotel not far from the cathedral.

★★★★Le Relais St-Jean, 51 Rue Paillot de Montabert, **t** 03 25 73 89 90, *relais.st.jean@ wanadoo.fr* (*expensive–moderate*). Wonderfully located, delightfully beamed building, tucked away down a narrow street in the centre of the best part of town.

★★★★La Maison de Rhodes, 18 Rue du Linard, **t** 03 25 43 11 11 (*moderate*). Owned by the same family as the Comtes de Champagne. Newly opened and stylish.

★★Les Comtes de Champagne, 54–56 Rue de la Monnaie, **t** 03 25 73 11 70, *info@comtes-dechampagne.com* (*inexpensive*). A lovely hotel with a warm welcome and a strong sense of history, set in an historic building around an inner courtyard.

Eating Out

Le Valentino, 35 Rue Paillot de Montabert, **t** 03 25 73 14 14 (*expensive*). Refined restaurant next to **Le Relais St-Jean**, which shares the same picturesque charm and also has a lovely courtyard. *Closed 21 Aug–4 Sept; Jan; Oct–Easter Sat lunch, Sun eve and Mon*.

Le Jardin Gourmand, 31 Rue Paillot de Montabert, **t** 03 25 73 36 13 (*moderate*). First-class little restaurant. Excellent local dishes and original ice creams.

Les Crieurs de Vin, 4 Place Jean Jaurès, **t** 03 25 40 01 01 (*moderate*). Bistro/wine cellar run by two wine fanatics.

some unique manuscripts dating back to the 7th century. The fine arts section contains some interesting works, especially by the 17th-century maestro of realism, Philippe de Champaigne.

The church of **St-Nizier**, north of the cathedral, is hard to miss with its gaudy tiles. Largely reconstructed, it offers a fusion of Gothic and Renaissance, and contains a fine carved Entombment scene typical of the Troyes School. A short way south of the cathedral, the enormous former hospital or **Hôtel-Dieu** houses a splendidly preserved Ancien Régime pharmacy, now the **Musée de la Pharmacie** (*open Wed–Mon 10–12 and 2–6; closed Tues and public hols; adm*).

The star attractions of the lively southern section of historic Troyes are the sculptures and stained glass of a cluster of brilliant late-Gothic churches. Check their opening hours with the tourist office or at the doors, as these vary bizarrely from one church to the next. The most prominent, **St-Urbain**, cuts quite a dash with its gables and gargoyles in the centre of its own renovated square – it has the rare privilege in Troyes of not being hemmed in by houses. Commissioned by Pope Urban IV on the spot where his father had a cobbler's shop, the church was built in the second half of the 13th century, although it has been heavily restored and added to, and the main façade is a late-19th-century recreation. The interior is rather disappointing, with just a few bits of old stained glass, and some of Pope Urban's remains buried in the choir.

South of St-Urbain, Rue Emile Zola is the city's main commercial artery, but a short walk west, by the **covered market**, the soaring twisting slate-covered spire of **St-Remy** stands out. Like St-Urbain it has recently been scrubbed clean. Inside, the grisaille painted wood panels add 16th-century decoration to the Gothic forms. Beyond St-Remi is **Ste-Madeleine** which, although the original was built late in the 12th century, was so redone in the early 16th century that it looks a typical late-Gothic work, with a few Renaissance touches, and much heavy 19th-century renovating. A truly staggering Flamboyant Gothic rood screen dripping with stone decoration dominates the interior. The larger figures of the Crucifixion have a powerful simplicity. The whole work is attributed to the sculptor Jean Gailde and dated between 1508 and 1517. There are also fine stained-glass windows.

In the main shopping area, squeeze along the Ruelle des Chats, where the gables either side of the street virtually touch each other. In the thick of the action, the church of **St-Jean** is where the marriage of Catherine of France to the future King Henry V of England was celebrated on 2 June 1420. Long neglected, the battered Gothic edifice has been recently restored inside. It contains splendid stained-glass windows, some attributed to the local master craftsman Linard Gontier.

The church of **St-Pantaléon**, its fine architecture Gothic bent to Renaissance shapes, is full of virtuoso pieces. The interior has in fact been turned into something of a sculpture museum, some of the statues made specially for the church, such as the theatrical stone pair peering down from one gallery, while others were recovered from local churches destroyed at the Revolution.

Opposite, the **Musée Historique de Troyes et de la Champagne et Musée de la Bonneterie** (*open Wed–Mon 10–12 and 2–6; adm*) occupies the Hôtel de Vauluisant, one of the finest stone-fronted houses in Troyes, set around a courtyard hidden behind high walls. Splendid old statues and medieval decorated tiles feature inside, while a whole section is devoted to Troyes' bonnet- and sock-making traditions.

The elegant **Musée de l'Outil et de la Pensée Ouvrière** (*open daily 9–1 and 2–6.30; adm*) extends around the lovely chequered brick and limestone courtyard of the Hôtel de Mauroy. Once an orphanage, where orphans made bonnets and stockings, in 1746 it became the first place in Troyes to be mechanized. The museum is dedicated to the tools of craftsmen. Some of the most appealing are those of the glovemakers, with a collection of wooden hands, and those of the farriers' tools, decorated with horses.

The Côte des Bar and the Châtillonais

Chaource, south of Troyes, has a great masterpiece of the Champagne school of sculptors: a remarkable Entombment group hidden in a little corner chapel of its church. Rarely does art plunge you so directly into the drama of Christ's death – two guards stand menacingly on either side of the door, and the figures around the laid-out body show an intense, pale grief, their eyes fixed on the corpse. This group was made around 1515 by the anonymous Master of Chaource, sometimes known as the Master of the Sad Faces. The gilded 16th-century carved Nativity in an extravagant Renaissance side chapel is also beautifully executed.

In wine terms, the area around **Bar-sur-Seine** and **Les Riceys** is perhaps better known for the curiosity of its exclusive rosé wine than for champagne, but the champagne vineyards extend down the valley, producing a quarter of the champagne harvest.

The little town of **Essoyes** on the River Ource became home to Renoir, as this was the birthplace of Aline Charigot, one of Renoir's most important models and his wife. The couple bought a property here in 1885 and came frequently. Renoir painted many works around these parts, and Aline and Auguste are both buried in the cemetery. So too are their three sons, including Jean Renoir, the great French film director who emigrated to the United States during the Second World War. The great painter's workshop has been turned into a small museum, the **Atelier Renoir** (*open Easter–1 Nov daily 2–6.30; adm*), run by enthusiastic locals, although don't expect to see any of Renoir's art. Essoyes itself is a cheerful little place, proud of its champagne-making tradition. A pyramid of barrels stands in the middle of the river running through town, but the **Maison de la Vigne** (*open summer daily 2.30–6.30; adm*) proves dull.

Continuing south along the Seine valley, the main attraction is the most fabulous of Iron Age treasures, found in tombs on **Mont Lassois** above Vix. This was clearly an important strategic site at the end of the first Iron Age, or Hallstatt, period. A citadel was erected here, protected by a complex system of defences, and a number of major tombs dating from the end of the 6th century BC and the start of the 5th century BC have been excavated. The treasures are now housed in the **Musée du Châtillonnais** in nearby **Châtillon-sur-Seine**, (*open mid-June–mid-Sept daily 9–12 and 1.30–6; April–mid-June and mid-Sept–mid-Nov Wed–Mon 9–12 and 2–6, closed Tues; rest of year Wed–Mon 10–12 and 2–5, closed Tues; adm*). The staggering Vix bronze vase, as tall as a human being, is the highlight, discovered in 1953. Tongues stick out from the two fantastic handles, belonging to two scary figures with plaited hair. They are said to

Getting Around

To get to the Côte des Bar by public transport, you'll have to take a **bus** from Troyes.

Tourist Information

Aube-en-Champagne: 34 Quai Dampierre, t 03 25 42 50 00, *www.aube-champagne.com*.
Bar-sur-Seine: 33 Rue Gambetta, t 03 25 29 94 43, *www.ot-barsurseine.fr/otsi/index.htm*.
Bar-sur-Aube, Place de l'Hôtel de Ville, t 03 25 27 24 25, *www.barsuraube.net*.

Where to Stay and Eat

Chaource ✉ 10210

Maisons 'Aux Maisons', t 03 25 70 07 19, *www.logis-aux-maisons.com (moderate–inexpensive)*. Well known local hostelry with good modern rooms and excellent cuisine *(expensive–moderate)*.

Les Fontaines, 1 Rue des Fontaines, t 03 25 40 00 85 *(moderate)*. For a good country lunch.

Fouchères ✉ 10260

B&B **Le Prieuré**, Place de l'Eglise, t 03 25 40 98 09 *(inexpensive)*. Full of history and life, a priory-turned-farm with some simple, but characterful, excellent value rooms in a village on the west bank of the Seine between Troyes and Bar-sur-Seine.

Les Riceys ✉ 10340

★★Le Magny, Route de Tonnerre, t 03 25 29 38 39, *le-magny@wanadoo.fr (inexpensive)*. A pleasant cheap option. Restaurant *(expensive–cheap)*.

Arsonval ✉ 10200

La Chaumière, t 03 25 27 91 02 *(inexpensive)*. Right on the N19 but deceptive. Pleasant old house with grounds overlooking the Aube. Restaurant *(expensive–moderate)* serves kidneys and bacon *à la française* to die for.

represent Gorgons, with serpents for legs, while further snakes coil around their biceps. A frieze of charioteers runs round the vase's edge. The piece was probably made in Etruria, northern Italy. Other treasures from the tomb include a diadem torque, a unique work of Celtic jewellery with two tiny winged horses carved at either end. The Tumulus de la Garenne, discovered in 1846, also yielded startling treasures, not least of which was a chariot.

'The abbey is now a prison,' explains the sign at the entrance to **Clairvaux** just south of Bar-sur-Aube, a sad fate for one of the most powerful and influential monasteries of medieval Europe. This was the most important of the four daughters of Cîteaux and the strict reforming Cistercians, founded in 1115 by the austere and sour Bernard de Clairvaux, confidant of popes, tub-thumper for the Second Crusade and arch-enemy of progressive Peter Abelard. Because of him, the place gained the highest reputation for imposing Christian rigour, often as opposed to learning and art, both of which Bernard disdained. In 1808 the State decided to turn the place into a prison, although it is still possible to visit it to learn about the exceptional power the abbey and its founder once enjoyed. The Ministry of Culture is in the process of taking over.

The Upper Marne

If you follow the Marne back to its source from St-Dizier up into the most south-easterly corner of the Champagne region, one or two little surprises lie along the way.
La Boisserie at **Colombey-les-Deux-Eglises** *(open Feb–Dec Wed–Mon 10–12 and 2–5.30; closed Tues and Jan; adm)*, 16km due east of Bar-sur-Aube, is haunted by the

spirit of arguably the most important Frenchman of the 20th century, Charles de Gaulle, who retired here after leaving power both in 1946 and in 1969. He definitively retired from life here on 9 November 1970 and was buried in the village cemetery. He wrote in his memoirs of his attraction towards the calm, sad, wide horizons of the Champagne region and its unchanging, unpretentious villages, of which Colombey-les-Deux-Eglises is so typical. You only see a few rooms on the guided tour: the salon with plenty of photographs, the dining room, and the study where de Gaulle worked. A large Cross of Lorraine on the hill honours his importance in the fight to liberate France from the Nazis.

The **Château de Cirey-sur-Blaise** (*open 15 June–15 Sept daily 2.30–6.30; adm*), in the Blaise valley, may be linked with Voltaire, bright flame of the French Enlightenment, but he shares star billing with the exceptional Marquise du Châtelet, who was attracted to some of the most brilliant men of her age and seduced them, mind and body. She offered Voltaire refuge at her husband's pretty little Louis XIII-style brick château after his *Lettres anglaises* caused a furore at the French court. The marquise and Voltaire began their stormy relationship in 1733, and Voltaire was to stay here for long periods until 1749. However, all ended sadly when the marquise died in childbirth (not Voltaire's child) at the age of 42.

Old **Chaumont** on its hill is built in blindingly grey-white stone, with an enormous 19th-century railway viaduct (*you can walk along one level*) spanning the Suize valley

Tourist Information

Chaumont: Place du Général de Gaulle, t 03 25 03 80 80, *office-tourisme.chaumont@ wanadoo.fr*.

Langres: Square Olivier Lahalle, t 03 25 87 67 67, *office.tourisme.pays.de.langres@wanadoo.fr*.

Where to Stay and Eat

Arc-en-Barrois ✉ 52210

***Château d'Arc-en-Barrois, t 03 25 02 29 20, *chateau-darc@wanadoo.fr* (*luxury–very expensive*). Built for French royalty in the 19th century, walled off from the interesting village church, this is a very posh, clean-stoned château. The rooms are comfortable and stylish, the naff pictures an aberration. The large dining rooms (*expensive*) are decorated with naval paintings. *Restaurant closed end July and beginning Aug.*

Hôtel du Parc, 1 Place Moreau, t 03 25 02 53 07 (*moderate*). Also in the centre of the village, this former hunting lodge looks stylish too. Inside, it's a rustic, cheap inn. You can eat out on the terrace on warm sunny days (*expensive–moderate*). *Restaurant closed Tues.*

Chaumont and Chamarandes ✉ 52000

**Au Rendez-Vous des Amis, 4 Place du Tilleul, Chamarandes, t 03 25 32 20 20, *le-chateau-de-chaumont@wanadoo.fr* (*moderate*). By the church in this quiet village by the Marne just below Chaumont town, this well-flowered hotel looks simple on the outside but has 19 brightly redone rooms and serves good local cuisine (*expensive– moderate*). *Closed Aug; restaurant closed Fri eve and Sat.*

Langres ✉ 52200

**Le Cheval Blanc, 4 Rue de l'Estres, t 03 25 87 07 00, *info@hotel-langres.com* (*inexpensive*). With its medieval abbey buildings turned *auberge* at the Revolution, this lovely central hotel has five delightful little vaulted rooms, plus more conventional ones. The restaurant (*very expensive–moderate*) serves inventive food. *Closed Nov; restaurant closed Mon eve.*

Gray ✉ 70100

Château de Rigny, in Rigny 5km from Gray, t 03 84 65 25 01, *www.chateauhotels.com/ rigny* (*very expensive–moderate*). Small but stylish 17th-century château in beautiful gardens overlooking the Saône.

to one side. The old centre may be small, but it has character, despite the modern blocks pressing in round it. The town developed from a keep built by the counts of Champagne; below this, a small **museum** contains a mixed bag of archaeological bits, paintings, and a room devoted to the Bouchardon family of sculptors from Chaumont. However, the most intriguing art is hidden in the **Basilique St-Jean**, which develops from Gothic to Flamboyant Gothic as you walk from nave to choir, with a touch of Renaissance thrown in. Carved stone setpieces include a dramatic late 15th-century Entombment scene, a hilarious Tree of Jesse in stone, the kings perched on branches, and wildly pendant keystones in the choir. Many of the old town houses have a distinctive stair towers, and the grand 18th-century hôtels have splendid carriage gateways leading into their little courtyards.

Fortified **Langres**, dramatically situated on a hilltop near the source of the Marne, wasn't always such a backwater. St Benignus is said to have established a church here way back in the 2nd century. One of the earliest bishops, 4th-century St Didier, was martyred defending his city, but retained his dignity even after being decapitated – legend has it that he simply picked up his severed head and rode off. Located on the frontier with Lorraine, Franche-Comté and Burgundy, Langres long served as an important outpost of the French kingdom, hence the substantial fortifications. One of the best ways to appreciate the place is by walking around its **ramparts**; the recorded tour (*in French or English*) from the tourist office takes about two hours. Langres is also immensely proud of having been the birthplace, in 1713, of that great Enlightenment figure and author of the *Encyclopédie*, Denis Diderot, the son of a cutlery maker, although after his schooling here he rarely returned.

Into Lorraine via the French Ardennes

The Meuse River to Verdun

The Meuse, the major river of western Lorraine, flows in a gentle valley from the Langres plateau north. Here we follow its course from the Belgium border south through the French Ardennes back towards its source.

The French Ardennes, tucked between Champagne and Belgium, has taken tough knocks: the Germans invaded France here not once, not twice, but three times between 1870 and 1940. A little horn of French territory sticks up into Belgium north of Charleville, and here you'll find by far the most dramatic stretch of the Meuse in France, the river having to dig its way through tough rock. This is slate-mining country, and you can't fail to notice one enormous wall of slate just south of **Givet** near the Belgian border. Many of the houses in the old centre were built in an attractive mix of brick and local blue-grey stone. As well as walking along the quays, visit the **Centre Européen des Métiers d'Art** (*open Tues–Sat 10–12 and 2.30–6, Sun 2.30–6; closed Mon; adm*), a substantial craft centre.

Heading south, the little towns of Haybes, Fumay, Revin and Monthermé were all built in meanders in the Meuse and are linked by the road along the densely wooded high banks of the valley. **Fumay**'s small **Musée de l'Ardoise** (*open April–Oct daily 10–6; Nov–Mar daily 2–6; adm*) pays homage to the slate mines which closed in 1971.

The best way to appreciate the impressive star-shaped fortifications of **Rocroi**, west of Revin, is from the sky, but, should you fail to arrive by helicopter, a tour of the ramparts on foot is the next best thing. The streets of this model of a military town head out like the spokes of a wheel from the central square with its classical church, blue-tinted stone well and recently rebuilt covered market. The **Museé de la Bataille de Rocroi** (*open April–Oct daily 10–12 and 2–6; Nov–Mar daily 2–5; commentary in English; adm*), in a late 17th-century guard house, presents a short recorded show on the terrible battle fought outside the town in 1643, a pivotal moment in the long power struggle between the Hapsburgs and the Bourbons. In seven dreadful hours of fighting, some 10,000 men died. The French victory, which secured the kingdom, came in the year that Louis XIV inherited the throne.

Charleville's central **Place Ducale** has grand 17th-century brick façades topped by tall sloping slate roofs – more than a match for Paris' Place des Vosges (and designed by Clément Métezeau, brother of Louis, credited with the Parisian square). In one corner, the gorgeously presented **Musée de l'Ardenne** (*open Tues–Sun 10–12 and 2–6;*

Getting Around

A good **railway** line passes through the French Ardennes from Lille, via Charleville-Mézières and Sedan.

Tourist Information

Givet: Place de la Tour, **t** 03 24 42 03 54.
Rocroi: 14 Place d'Armes, B.P.50, **t** 03 24 54 20 06, *www.otrocroi.com*.
Charleville-Mézières: 4 Place Ducale, **t** 03 24 32 44 80.
Sedan: Place du Château Fort, B.P.322, **t** 03 24 27 73 73, *www.sedan-bouillon.org*.
Mouzon: Pl de l'Hôtel de Ville, **t** 03 24 26 10 63.
Stenay: 5 Pl R.-Poincaré, **t** 03 29 80 64 22.

Where to Stay and Eat

Givet ✉ 08600

Le Roosevelt, 76 Av Roosevelt, **t 03 24 42 14 14 (*inexpensive*). One of the most attractive choices overlooking the river, with 12 rooms, a terrace and a brasserie-style menu.
Le Val St-Hilaire, 7 Quai des Fours, **t 03 24 42 38 50, *hotel.val.saint.hilaire@wanadoo.fr* (*inexpensive*). 20 rooms. A lot of charm too to this 18th-century riverside house. Restaurant (*moderate*).

Charleville-Mézières ✉ 08000

Hôtel de Paris, 24 Av Corneau, **t 03 24 33 34 38, *hotel.de.paris.08@wanadoo.fr* (*inexpensive*). Decent option near the station. No restaurant. *Closed Aug*.

Le Sautoy ✉ 08350

B&B Domaine du Sautoy, **t** 03 24 52 70 08 (*moderate*). Delightful little fudge-coloured stone hunting lodge with towers, lost in dense woods north of Vrigne-aux-Bois between Charleville and Sedan, along a long, rough track surround by silence. The interiors have been lovingly redone by its new proprietors. The rooms are tastefully decorated and two have the added delight of a little round tower room.

Bazeilles ✉ 08140

Château de Bazeilles, **t** 03 24 27 09 68, *contact@chateau-bazeilles.com* (*moderate*). The rooms in this smart hotel just east of Sedan are set in the outbuildings of a Louis XV château. Stylish restaurant, **L'Orangerie** (*expensive–moderate*).

Stenay ✉ 55700

Les Tilleuls, 10 Rue Jeanne d'Arc, **t** 03 29 80 35 72 (*moderate*). Beer sometimes features in special dishes at this very satisfying restaurant in its agricultural setting. *Closed Mon*.

adm) has more style than substance, although the workings of the marionette scenes that appear on the hour below the large clock on another grand square incorporated into the museum are impressive; Charleville has an international reputation for its puppet gatherings. Along the main artery leading down to the Meuse, the grandiose 17th-century mill, built in similar style to Place Ducale, hosts temporary art exhibitions and houses the scrappy **Musée Rimbaud** (*open Tues–Sun 10–12 and 2–6; adm*). The precocious 19th-century literary bad boy ran away from Charleville at an early age to liberate himself and his poetry. He was none too complimentary about his home town, but it did inspire him, if only by representing so finely the values he rejected.

The historic centre of **Sedan** has suffered from war damage and economic depression. The grand old buildings in brass-coloured stone look tarnished and in need of a good polish. For the French, Sedan is still associated with one of the major disasters of the 19th century, when the Franco-Prussian War was lost, Napoléon III's Second Empire ended, and Alsace and part of Lorraine were annexed to Germany. The intimidating **fort**, one of the largest in Europe, was built mainly in the late 15th and mid-16th centuries. The **museum** (*open daily 10–6; adm*) clearly explains its architecture, its history and that of the town.

The Meuse valley looks more rustic as you head south, with an understated charm, the old stone buildings an appealing fudge colour. **Mouzon** is a quiet and attractive port on the Meuse, although much damaged in the world wars. Its powerful 13th-century **Notre-Dame** has large twin spires added at a later date, while the interior resembles a copy of Laon cathedral with its four levels of architecture. The 18th-century organ was saved at the Revolution and has recently been restored. On the tour, you're taken up to the wide gallery where pilgrims were allowed to sleep – one chapel on this level is dedicated to Thomas à Becket, who is said to have stayed here.

Slipping into Lorraine, sleepy **Stenay** tempts beer-lovers with its sprawling **Musée Européen de la Bière** (*open Mar–Nov daily 10–12 and 2–6; adm*), set in part of a 16th-century citadel. You can taste the local brews at the end of your visit.

Verdun, the First World War and Joan of Arc

Touring the Sites In and Around Verdun

Most of the war sites of Verdun lie north of the city. It makes sense to start a visit to the battlefields at the **Mémorial de Verdun** (*open mid-Mar–mid-Dec daily 9–6; mid-Jan–mid-Mar daily 9–12 and 2–6; adm*), a modern block of a museum on the site of Fleury-Devant-Douaumont, a village pounded into oblivion by artillery fire. Objects are displayed on two floors in a daunting clutter, around a mound of rubble recalling the destruction of the area. The big-screen film in the main hall clarifies the phases of the battles. The Mémorial also has information on war walks.

There is no more potent symbol to the French of the Great War's destruction than the **Ossuaire de Douaumont** (*open daily 9–12 and 2–5, sometimes later; adm*), its big tower, the Tour des Morts, marked by large crosses. It symbolizes an enormous shell. The Ossuaire was where the remains of 130,000 men, French and German, were

Verdun in the First World War

Verdun became the greatest symbol of French resistance in the First World War. The long-drawn-out battles over the city preceded those of the Somme through 1916 and were one of the very worst follies of the Great War. Before the First World War, Verdun lay in a key position close to the new French border with Germany following the disaster of the 1870 war with Prussia. In the German army's 1914 advance, it failed to take Verdun, although it gained a strong position around three sides of it. In the course of 1915 the German commander von Falkenhayn decided that a major offensive was needed at a weak spot on the western front, to bleed the enemy to death – Verdun was chosen for the attack. The plan initially worked: as the 1916 battle began, large numbers of French soldiers were rushed to the area. Verdun was to be defended at all costs: *'Ils ne passeront pas'* ('They will not pass'). A ceaseless chain of truck supplies was brought along from Bar-le-Duc via the road which became known as the **Voie Sacrée**, still marked with milestones carrying the hats of French soldiers. Pétain, then Nivelle, led the desperate defence, and by summer the main action had moved to the Somme. Because of the terrible German offensive, the territory north of the city became one of the worst killing fields in the whole war. Around 175,000 French soldiers and 165,000 German soldiers died, and roughly one million soldiers were wounded. Villages disappeared, wiped off the map, and even today you can wander round areas cratered by shellfire. The area is littered with military monuments, cemeteries and museums.

brought after the war. The names of French dead stretch down the long main gallery, well over 100 yards long. The tower contains a small museum and orientation tables to identify where the main campaigns took place. In the fields of cemeteries that stretch down the slope below, a little rose is planted in front of each dirty gravestone. A whole section of more curving tombstones is a reminder of all the North African fighters who fought for the Allies.

The dank **Fort de Douaumont** (*open daily 10–6; adm*), a bit further north, looks dismal when you wander through its echoing, dripping, underground darkness. There isn't much to see inside, but the ghosts of the First World War lurk tellingly here, in rooms with metal bed frames or basic washing facilities. This was the largest of 38 forts constructed after the Franco-Prussian war to protect Verdun. The guided tour describes the atrocious conditions experienced by the soldiers during the Great War. Built to take up to 800 soldiers, sometimes more than 3,000 were holed up here. At certain times it was hit by around 1,000 shells a day.

North of Verdun, and just north of Le Mort Homme and Cote 304, a fat white column rises out of the woods on the **Butte de Montfaucon**, honouring the victory of the 1st American Army here in the Meuse-Argonne campaign of autumn 1918. The village of Montfaucon vanished almost completely except for the ruins of a medieval church. The hundreds of rows of pure white gravestones – 14,246 – spilling down from the neo-Romanesque chapel at the immaculately kept **US war cemetery of Romagne** just north of the Butte de Montfaucon make a terrible sight, although under half of the Americans who died in the Meuse-Argonne campaign are buried here.

Verdun

The city of Verdun understandably looks rather scrappy, although the quays and upper cathedral quarter have been considerably restored. In 843 the Treaty of Verdun carved the massive Western European empire which Charlemagne had brought together into three, and it was not until the mid-16th century that the French crown gained the three bishoprics of Verdun, Metz and Toul. The Prussians briefly occupied Verdun during the Revolution, and the Germans took the citadel in the Franco-Prussian War, after a long siege. However, it was the massive German attack during the First World War which left the biggest scars.

The perhaps overtrendy **Centre Mondial de la Paix** (*open June–15 Sept daily 9.30–7; Feb–May and mid-Sept–Nov Tues–Sun 10–1 and 2–6; adm*) is located in the renovated, splendid bishops' palace. As you look at the thought-provoking objects on display, disturbing tapes play in the background – the sound of groaning or extracts from war-time letters. Next door, the interior of the **cathedral** is a mix of styles: Gothic side-aisles, a Renaissance nave, a wild Baroque baldaquin in the choir, and an impressive Romanesque crypt. Many of the capitals in the crypt illustrate scenes from the Great War. On the lurching tour of the **Citadelle Souterraine** (*open daily 9–12.30 and 1.30–6; adm*) in the lower town, the filmed scenarios skim over difficult First World War issues. The tour ends with an evocation of the choosing of France's unknown soldier, which took place in 1920. The body was buried at the Arc de Triomphe in Paris.

St-Mihiel and Bar-le-Duc

St-Mihiel really needs a clean-up if it is to be truly appreciated, but several fine Renaissance houses stand out along the town's streets, while the main historic building is the massive **abbey**, founded in the 8th century, and much rebuilt in the 17th. Its library has, unusually for France, preserved an extraordinarily rich collection of manuscripts and old books; the oldest date back to the 9th century. The virtuoso sculptor Ligier Richier was born in St-Mihiel at the start of the 16th century, when the town's merchants experienced a period of prosperity. One of his finest works, carved in walnut, stands in the abbey church. It represents the Virgin fainting, overcome with grief at the Crucifixion. The church of **St-Etienne** contains an astounding Entombment by Richier. This time Christ figures at the centre, but all the other characters are sculpted with extraordinary individuality.

The Battle of St-Mihiel in September 1918 was an extremely important victory for the American troops. Between 12 and 16 September 15,000 prisoners and 700 square kilometres were captured. The battle monument stands in perhaps the most beautiful spot in the Lorraine, east of St-Mihiel, on the **Butte de Montsec**.

Hattonchâtel, one of the prettiest villages in the whole region, stands on a rocky promontory a short way north. At one end a **château**, a copy of a 15th-century original, looks out over the plain below. The **church**, flanked by a tiny cloister, contains a retable of dramatic polychrome figures attributed to Ligier Richier, showing Christ carrying the cross, his crucifixion, and his entombment. East of Hattonchâtel, at **Beney-en-Woëvre** by Thiaucourt-Regniéville, a beautifully manicured US cemetery contains the graves of over 4,000 soldiers killed in the action at St-Mihiel.

Getting Around

To reach Verdun by **train** from Paris, change at Châlons-en-Champagne. To get to the battlefields without a car join a **guided bus tour** from the tourist office (*May–Sept daily 2pm*), or take a taxi: **t** 03 29 86 05 22/**t** 03 29 84 53 59/**t** 03 29 86 47 30/**t** 03 29 86 00 16.

Tourist Information

Verdun: Place de la Nation, B.P.232, **t** 03 29 86 14 18, *www.verdun-tourisme.com*.
St-Mihiel: Rue du Palais de Justice, **t** 03 29 89 06 47, *otsi@saint-mihiel.net*.
Bar-le-Duc: 5 Rue Jeanne d'Arc, **t** 03 29 79 11 13.

Where to Stay and Eat

Vilosnes ✉ 55110
★★Le Vieux Moulin, t 03 29 85 81 52 (*inexpensive*). A simple converted mill by the Meuse north of Verdun. Restaurant (*moderate*).

Verdun ✉ 55100
★★★Le Coq Hardi, 8 Av de la Victoire, **t** 03 29 86 36 36, *coq.hardi@wanadoo.fr* (*moderate*). The main hotel in the centre, plush behind its timberframe façade and slightly pricey, with a mix of styles. The smart restaurant (*very expensive–expensive*) serves classic cuisine. *Restaurant closed Sun eve and Fri.*

★★Le St-Paul, 12 Place St-Paul, **t** 03 29 86 02 16 (*inexpensive*). Less ostentatious but popular option with a restaurant (*moderate–cheap*).
L'Estaminet, 45 Rue des Rouyers, **t** 03 29 86 07 86. Café on the quays which serves some interesting local specialities.

Buzancy ✉ 08240
★★Le Saumon, Place Chanzy, **t** 03 24 30 00 42, *h-saumon@wanadoo.fr* (*inexpensive*). Lost in a typical downbeat village of the Ardennes *département*, north of the US Verdun memorials and cemeteries, this hotel is run with verve and has nice rooms and restaurant (*moderate*). *Restaurant closed Sun eve.*

Les Monthairons ✉ 55320
★★★Château des Monthairons, t 03 29 87 78 55, *accueil@chateaudesmonthairons.fr* (*expensive–moderate*). A very grand 19th-century château in its walled grounds 12 km south of Verdun (on the west bank D34), this hotel even has its private 'beach' on the Meuse riverbank. The place is stylish, the food (*expensive*) excellent. *Restaurant closed Mon and Tues lunch.*

St-Mihiel ✉ 55300
★★Hôtel Rive Gauche, Place de la Gare, **t** 03 29 89 15 83, *stephane@rive-gauche.fr* (*inexpensive*). The disused railway station well converted to new use, with a restaurant (*moderate*) attached.

Bar-le-Duc is known in French history as the supply centre for Verdun during the First World War, at the other end of the Voie Sacrée (*see* box, p.587). Its **Ville Haute**, sitting dramatically atop a high rock, was the seat of the local lords, who remained semi-independent of the rest of Lorraine for centuries. Beyond the vestiges of its castle lie streets crammed full of Renaissance mansions built from the beautiful local limestone. The church of **St-Etienne** contains more staggering works by Ligier Richier. His magnificent horror, *Le Transi*, was commissioned by Anne de Lorraine in memory of her husband René de Chalon, who died while besieging French troops at the town of St-Dizier. He is shown as a semi-decomposed figure, yet in defiant pose, one leg forward, one arm raised, proudly upright and grinning. Richier's Crucifixion scene shows Christ and the two thieves, fantastically executed.

The **Musée Barrois** in the castle, although recently reorganized, retains a 19th-century cluttered feel. The archaeological collections include a superb 2nd-century mother goddess and an intriguing stela representing a Gallo-Roman eye doctor. The variable collection of paintings features the *Temptation of St Anthony* by David

Teniers the Younger, and Jan Steen's *Beer Drinker*. In the attractive **Ville Basse**, or lower town, which spreads out either side of the Ornain river, a statue recalls the Michaux brothers who invented the pedal bicycle. Nowadays the town's absurd speciality is redcurrant jam made from currants whose pips are removed using a goose feather.

Domrémy and Joan of Arc

Joan of Arc was born in 1412 in the quaint village of Domrémy, in one of the prettiest spots along the Meuse. Her parents' house survives – quite comfortable for its day. The coats of arms over the door were added by Joan's great-grand- nephew, but then the house simply served as a storehouse for centuries, until the *département* rescued it in 1818. Joan lived at Domrémy for the first 18 years of her short life, and started hearing the voices of SS Catherine, Marguerite and Michael here. She raced off to the Loire (*see* 'Chinon' and 'Orléans') to help save the French kingdom from the English. Although abandoned by the French monarchs in her hour of need (*see* 'Rouen'), she was rehabilitated by the crown at the end of Charles VII's reign and a cult grew up around her. By the end of the 16th century the village had become celebrated as Domrémy-la-Pucelle (Domrémy-the-Virgin). Joan was canonized in 1920. The **Centre Johannique** opened in 1999 to set her story in its historical context. Dense earnest panels are devoted to the power politics of late-medieval France. However, Joan's character is rather surprisingly neglected. Her exceptional will and her passions come across clearly in the trial records which still exist, but these are passed over cursorily.

The **Basilique du Bois-Chenu**, 2km south of Domrémy, was built between 1881 and 1926 in striking black and white bands of stone, in one of the spots where Joan is said to have heard her saintly voices. The interior is richly decorated, notably with mosaics and with large colourful wall paintings depicting major episodes in the miraculous maid's life.

Gallo-Roman Grand

Over 20km southwest of Domrémy, the Gallo-Roman site at **Grand** long lay forgotten. Dedicated to Apollo, this was once one of the most important spa towns of Roman Gaul; Caracalla and Constantine are claimed to have visited. The amphitheatre on the edge of town has been modernized for modern shows. Better still is the sump-tuous carpet of a mosaic from a Roman basilica, one of the largest to have survived in France, displayed in a charming little museum. It is similar to one at the Baths of Caracalla in Rome. Finds from archaeological digs at Grand are nicely displayed in cabinets around the gallery, but the most famous discovery, of small wood-carved astrological tablets from Egypt, has been transferred to Epinal (*see* p.596).

Metz

Metz, modern capital of Lorraine, feels Gallic and Germanic at the same time. When Caesar came here he described it as one of the oldest settlements in Gaul. Up until the mid-16th century Metz was an important bishopric on the western edge of the

Getting There and Around

Metz has a small airport, but Luxembourg's airport is more useful for international flights. There are **train** links from Metz to Lille (and on to London-Waterloo), and Strasbourg.

Tourist Information

Metz: 2 Place d'Armes, **t** 03 87 55 53 76, http://tourisme.mairie-metz.fr.

Where to Stay and Eat

***Hôtel du Théâtre, 3 Rue du Pont St-Marcel, **t** 03 87 31 10 10, info@pont-saint-marcel.com (expensive–moderate). Modern hotel giving on to the central marina, with spacious, comfortable, well-equipped rooms. The restaurant, **Le Pont St Marcel** (expensive–moderate), serves regional cuisine.

***Le Royal Bleu Marine, 23 Av Foch, **t** 03 87 66 81 11, metz@bleumarine.fr (moderate). Comfortable hotel in a typical building near the station. Restaurant (moderate).

Grand Hôtel de Metz, 3 Rue des Clercs, **t 03 87 36 16 33, grandhoteldemetz@ wanadoo.fr (moderate). Stylish two-star on a pedestrianized street in the heart of town.

Cecil, 14 Rue Pasteur, **t 03 87 66 66 13, cecil.hotel@wanadoo.fr (inexpensive). A cheaper option near the station, in an elegant house with 39 rather dull rooms. No restaurant.

La Dinanderie, 2 Rue de Paris, **t** 03 87 30 14 40 (expensive–moderate). The best restaurant in town, by the Moselle, serving classic cuisine. Closed Sun and Mon.

Le Flo, 2 bis Rue Gambetta, **t** 03 89 55 94 95, flometz@id-net.fr (moderate). Classic brasserie with authentic Napoléon III décor. Local dishes well prepared and served.

Holy Roman Empire, the main centre of a semi-autonomous region known as the Trois Evêchés, including the areas of Toul and Verdun, which only fell to the French in 1552. The Germans reclaimed it as their own after the Franco-Prussian War and during the Second World War. American troops fought a courageous and difficult campaign to liberate Metz in late 1944.

One of the tallest in France, Metz's **cathedral** only lacks soaring spires to allow its silhouette to compete with the very greatest. The outside stone looks very yellow, while the green copper roofing dates from after a fire of 1877. The two pinnacled towers, the Tour de Mutte with its massive bell, and the Tour du Chapitre with its big carving of Christ, started going up in the 13th century, with the bulk of the nave. The west front rose window is a beautiful 14th-century design, but the portals are neo-Gothic. Much of the choir was only completed in the early 16th century. The scale of the massive darkly Gothic interior is daunting; two churches used to stand on this site. The view down to the altar offers an amazing unbroken perspective framed by sharply pointed vaults. The **stained glass** is phenomenal, covering all three levels, aisles, gallery and top windows. Much of it features individual figures rather than more complex stories; the most stunning examples are in the two transepts, sheer walls of stained glass. Chagall contributed striking modern windows in the 1960s.

Metz's main museum, **La Cour d'Or** (open daily 10–12 and 2–6; adm), has taken over a former 17th-century Carmelite monastery, under which excavations in the 1930s revealed Roman baths. The collections are extensive, but the Gallo-Roman rooms are not to be missed. A translucent onyx funerary vase stands out – the stone came from Egypt but the vase was fashioned by a master Roman craftsman – but the best Gallo-Roman item of all is the patched-up shrine to Mithra, a Persian god of light who gained popularity as Christianity was emerging. This shrine, found at Sarrebourg, depicted Mithra slaying the primordial bull with whose blood the world, according to Mithraism, was fertilized and regenerated. The fine arts are another highlight – the Dutch 17th-century portraits are particularly strong.

The lively shopping quarters of Metz march southwards from the cathedral. Head along Rue Tête d'Or to reach **Place St-Louis**, a stocky arcade running down one side. Up the hill the streets become quieter and more atmospheric. The **Moyen Pont**, down on the Moselle, offers the best views on to the river banks and its monuments. On the other side of the water lies the surprising enclosed **marina** surrounded by slickly converted industrial buildings. A separate section of town, the **Esplanade**, with its green spaces above the Moselle bank, stands on the site of Metz's former citadel. Here **St-Pierre-aux-Nonnains** puts in a claim to being the oldest surviving church in France. The big arsenal building has been spruced up and turned into a bright arts centre. Walks out from the centre of Metz take you to the medieval **Porte des Allemands**; to the grandiose imperial **Germanic quarter** around an impressive neo-Renaissance monster of a railway station; or to **St-Maximin**, with its stylized Afro-exotic stained-glass windows by Jean Cocteau.

Nancy

Bang in the middle of Lorraine, the region's historic capital bursts with life and culture. The city centre is composed of gilded squares which scream of 18th-century excess, creating a wonderful urban ensemble which has been placed on the UNESCO list of World Heritage Sites. The city blossomed in the early 20th century as the main centre of Art Nouveau in France, and Nancy's museums have superb collections.

Nancy began when Gérard d'Alsace, founder of the line of Lorraine dukes, chose this curious spot for a new castle, set between two marshes against the bank of the Meurthe river. A fire in 1228 destroyed much of the settlement, but it was recon-structed, and a wall was then built around the burgeoning town in the 14th century, recalled now only by the Porte de la Craffe. After the destruction of the Thirty Years' War, in the 17th century came more prosperous times. Stanislas Leczinski of Poland was appointed as last duke of Lorraine by his son-in-law, the French king, and from 1738 he had his magnificent capital at Nancy. Stanislas enjoyed the good life, with a huge appetite for women and food, and he also loved sumptuous architecture. Over a 30-year period he summoned fine architects and artists to create one of the great towns of 18th-century France. Although the ducal palace and tombs were vandalized at the Revolution, much of the town survives unscathed.

After France's humiliating defeat in the Franco-Prussian War Nancy remained French. Many leading families from annexed Alsace-Lorraine moved here, bringing a new wave of wealth. At the same time Emile Gallé, Daum and others introduced a new, splendidly languorous style, Art Nouveau. Although the town suffered some-what from bombing in the First World War, it escaped bad damage in the Second. Since then, major new quarters have been built on the Meurthe hillside, while a plethora of research and higher education institutes have created a centre of learning. In relatively sleepy Lorraine, Nancy appears all the more vibrant.

Getting There

Nancy has a small **airport**, and is connected by **trains** to Paris-Gare de l'Est.

Tourist Information

Nancy: Place Stanislas, **t** 03 83 35 22 41, *www.ot-nancy.fr*.

Where to Stay

Nancy ✉ **54000**

★★★★**Grand Hôtel de la Reine**, 2 Pl Stanislas, **t** 03 83 35 03 01, *nancy@concorde-hotels.com* (*very expensive–expensive*). In a superb location, the most luxurious hotel in Nancy looks on to the finest square in town. The rooms are in Ancien Régime style, as is the restaurant **Le Stanislas** (*expensive*), which serves refined cuisine. *Restaurant closed Sat lunch.*

★★★**Le Crystal**, 5 Place Maginot, **t** 03 83 17 54 00, *hotelcrystal@wanadoo.fr* (*moderate*). Recently upgraded to a three-star, a surprisingly comfortable hotel not far from the centre.

★★★**La Résidence**, 30 Bd Jean Jaurès, **t** 03 83 40 33 56, *hotel.laresidence.nancy@wanadoo.fr* (*moderate*). A bit out of the centre, south of the station, and run by someone mad about Images d'Epinal. Good value.

★★**Hôtel de Guise**, 18 Rue de Guise, **t** 03 83 32 24 68, *contact@hoteldeguise.com* (*inexpensive*). On a wonderfully atmospheric street in a great location close to the Musée Lorrain, packed full of old-fashioned, worn style.

★★**Le New York**, 63–65 Rue St-Nicolas, **t** 03 83 32 92 74 (*inexpensive*). Unexciting rooms, but close to the heart of town.

Eating Out

Le Capucin Gourmand, 31 Rue Gambetta, **t** 03 83 35 26 98 (*expensive*). A classic high-class exclusive restaurant. *Closed lunch Sat, Sun and Mon, and Feb hols.*

Le Comptoir du Petit Gastrolâtre, 1 Place de Vaudémont, **t** 03 83 35 51 94 (*expensive*). The friendly *patron* helps make this *bistrot* one of the most popular in town, though not the cheapest. Traditional local food. *Closed Sun, Mon lunch and Thurs eve, and 15–30 Aug.*

Mirabelle, 24 Rue Héré, **t** 03 83 30 49 69 (*expensive–moderate*). Charming restaurant, in a fantastic location between the two greatest squares in Nancy, with a superb value lunch. *Closed Sat lunch, Sun eves and Mon, and Aug.*

Les Bacchanales, 16 Rue de la Primatiale, **t** 03 83 37 37 77 (*moderate*). You can eat very well at this restaurant behind the cathedral. *Closed Sun and Mon.*

Méréville ✉ **54850**

★★★**Maison Carrée** 12 Rue du Bac, **t** 03 83 47 09 23, *hotel@maisoncarree.com* (*moderate*). A good modern option on the edge of the Moselle river a short way south of Nancy, but set in greenery and quite spacious and luxurious. 22 rooms. Restaurant (*expensive–moderate*). *Closed Dec–Feb; restaurant closed Sun eve and Mon.*

Rococo Nancy

Place Stanislas is wonderfully extravagant. French 18th-century architecture doesn't come much more ornate or striking than this. Stone urns and putti wrapped in protective nets top the balustraded façades of the square, which play second fiddle to the elaborate wrought-iron gates on the corners, framing sculptural scenes.

Looking on to the square, you will find the superb **Musée des Beaux-Arts** (*open Wed–Mon 10–6; closed Tues; adm*). A spectacular curving Baroque staircase leads up from the beautiful entrance hall to the 18th-century French paintings, hung against boldly coloured backgrounds. The basement contains stunning Art Nouveau glass. The pre-Revolutionary collections are divided by Italian, Flemish and French schools, each well represented. The most striking Italian works include Perugino's beautifully composed *Virgin with Children* and Caravaggio's *Annunciation*. Rubens' enormous and gloriously melodramatic *Transfiguration* is the star of the Flemish collection, showing Christ heading up to heaven on a swirl of cloud. This museum was the first to display a Manet, his *Automne*, and there are gorgeous works by Signac and Sérusier as well as others by Bonnard, Modigliano, Utrillo, Vlaminck and Valloton.

Splendid **Place de la Carrière** links Place Stanislas with the ducal palace. Its shape recalls its role as a medieval jousting ground. Stanislas had it remodelled by Héré, turning it into Nancy's second most glamorous square. Its southern entrance is through a blindingly white classical arch, a copy of an imperial Roman arch, erected in honour of Louis XV. At the other end, a row of dignified imperial busts adds decorative delight to the hemicycle. There are more outrageous wrought-iron gateways by Lamour too, and the lamps drip off their gilded brackets like outsized earrings.

The great Gothic, gargoyled façade of the ducal palace conceals the **Musée Lorrain** (*open May–Sept daily 10–6; rest of year Wed–Mon 10–12 and 2–5, closed Tues; adm*), a huge rambling historical museum. Its trump card is a collection of dramatic works by France's 17th-century master of chiaroscuro, Georges de La Tour; in the candlelit night of his canvases the figures seem silently absorbed in their tasks. De La Tour spent the last 30 or so years of his life at nearby Lunéville, where he died in 1652. Also seek out the fine Gallo-Roman glass, the Merovingian jewellery. and portraits of Lorraine dukes and dignitaries. A large late-medieval tapestry cycle made in Tournai is a violent morality tale against gluttony. Smaller rooms are devoted to the Revolution, Napoleon, the First World War and a collection of Jewish ceremonial objects. As if all this were not enough, the museum has an annexe, the **Musée d'Art et Traditions** in the former cloister of the Cordeliers, offering a celebration of Lorraine crafts and rural life. The church incorporated into the museum has some fine statues, but its most amazing feature is the **ducal mausoleum**, modelled on the Medici Chapel in Florence, with a dazzling decorated coffered ceiling above the black tombs.

Art Nouveau Nancy

Characterful old streets run between the Palais Ducal and Cours Léopold, another imposing square. At its northern end, enjoy a first taste of the city's Art Nouveau architecture. The main Art Nouveau quarter occupies a grid plan in the southwest corner of the centre, where the houses went up in the boom of the Belle Epoque, after French society had recovered from the trauma of the Franco-Prussian War. Emile Gallé, the founder of the Ecole de Nancy, was inspired by the Arts and Crafts movement in Britain, by oriental styles, and by his studies in botany, but the flourishing of Art Nouveau in Nancy involved the close co-operation and cross-fertilization of ideas of a large number of committed architects and artists. The tourist office's Art Nouveau itinerary locates individual addresses to look at. The architects of the school were Henri Gutton, George Biet, Lucien Weissenburger, Paul Charbonnier, Fernand César and Joseph Hornecker. In furniture Louis Majorelle and Eugène Vallin stand out; the latter commissioned the first Art Nouveau house in Nancy, in 1896. Another important figure, Victor Prouvé, applied himself to marquetry, sculpting, engraving, jewellery and bookbinding. Antonin Daum, like Gallé, produced exquisite glass.

The excellent **Musée de l'Ecole de Nancy** (*open Wed–Sun 10.30–6, Mon 2.30–6; closed Tues; adm*) is in an early 20th-century house crammed full of Art Nouveau delights. The woodwork by Majorelle and Vallin steals the show, with amazing pieces such as the Meuble à Blé, which uses 58 different woods. Beautiful lamps and vases from Gallé and Daum decorate many a corner, while Gallé's Dawn and Dusk bed, with a butterfly and moth at either end, has to be seen to be believed.

South of Nancy

Except for the occasional industrial blip, the Meurthe and Moselle valleys become increasingly rustic as you head up towards their sources in the southwestern Vosges.

The Upper Meurthe and Moselle Valleys

Soaring up as high as the factory chimneys southeast of Nancy, the bright white **Basilique St-Nicolas-de-Port** is an uplifting Gothic building, and all the more so for holding its own in such an industrial landscape. This pilgrimage church, built to house one of St Nicholas' fingers, dates from the late 15th and early 16th centuries.

Getting Around

You can get a **train** from Nancy to Lunéville, Epinal and Baccarat.

Tourist Information

St-Nicolas-de-Port: 13 bis Rue Anatole France, t 03 83 48 58 75, www.ot-saint-nicolas.fr.
Lunéville: Le Château, t 03 83 74 06 55.
Baccarat: Place du Général Leclerc, t 03 83 75 13 37, www.ville-baccarat.fr.
Epinal: 13 Rue de la Comédie, t 03 29 82 53 32.

Where to Stay and Eat

Lunéville and Rehainviller ✉ 54300
★★★Château d'Adoménil, Rehainviller, t 03 83 74 04 81, adomenil@relaischateaux.fr (*very expensive*). Tucked away on the north bank of the Meurthe a few km southwest of Lunéville, this is more a glorified manor than a château, with 14 spacious rooms and an inventive restaurant (*very expensive–expensive*). *Restaurant closed Mon and Tues lunch and Sun nights in winter.*
★★★Hôtel des Pages, 5 Quai Petits Bosquets, t 03 83 74 11 42 (*moderate*). Quiet, comfortable, but modern and on the wrong side of

the river from the Château de Lunéville. **Petit Comptoir** restaurant (*moderate*).

Senones ✉ 88210
★★★Au Bon Gîte, 3 Place Vautrin, t 03 29 57 92 46 (*inexpensive*). Friendly small hotel between Baccarat and St-Dié. Superb restaurant (*moderate*). *Closed 22 July–6 Aug; Feb hols; Sun eve and Mon.*

Les Thons ✉ 88410
Le Couvent des Cordeliers, t 03 29 07 90 84 (*moderate*). Amazing collection of medieval monastery buildings lost in the wilds, and housing a genuinely original restaurant. Gammon steaks grilled over an open hearth by the *patron*. A local favourite, so book ahead and ask for a table by the chimney. Visit the buildings and the museum. *Closed Dec–Feb and Mon, Tues and Thurs eve.*

Luxeuil-les-Bains ✉ 70300
★★★Beau Site, 18 Rue Georges Moulimard, t 03 84 40 14 67, beau-siteluxeuil@ wanadoo.fr (*moderate–inexpensive*). A bit of a suburban feel to this large house of a hotel with a mix of styles. But it's comfortable, serves good food (*expensive–moderate*) and has quite a lot of facilities. *Closed Nov–Feb Fri; Sat lunch and Sun eve.*

During the last war the church suffered from heavy bombardments,; it took the fortune of Camille Croue-Friedman, a native girl who married a wealthy American, to restore the building from the 1980s onwards. It now looks immaculate. The two magnificent towers, over 260ft tall, are topped by slate helmets. The scene in the central portal, of St Nicholas performing a miracle, is attributed to Claude Richier, brother of the more celebrated Ligier (*see* 'Bar-le-Duc'. The cleaned interior could scarcely look purer, but the building has a kink in it. The vertiginous tubular columns are decorated not with traditional capitals, but with ornamental rings. Two spectacular columns rise above the rest, stupendous palm trees of stone, at 92ft high said to be the tallest in France. Fine Renaissance stained-glass windows have also survived.

The modest town of **Lunéville** is in mourning for the loss of its great 18th-century château, destroyed in a recent fire along with its paintings, pottery and furniture. Known as the Versailles of the north, it is hoped to finish rebuilding in five years, better than before. The gardens and exterior can still be visited. The ornate church of **St-Jacques** near the château would look as if it had been lifted straight out of Baroque Rome were it not built from dried-red Vosges stone. The visual tricks of Baroque delight inside, with columns suffering from midriff bulges leading up to garlanded capitals. The nave balcony of curving and broken arches is backed by a *trompe-l'œil* scene.

Southwest of Lunéville, the village of Haroué boasts the beautiful **Château d'Haroué** (*open July–Aug daily 10–12 and 2–6; April–June and Sept–Oct daily 2–6; adm*), reflected in its moats. The magnificent wrought-iron gate was made by Lamour of Nancy fame, and the delightful putti were originally sculpted for Nancy's Place de la Carrière. Mainly built in 1720, Haroué has great style, with its colonnaded side wings topped by human and lion heads. Inside are portraits of the Beauvau-Craon family who built it; splendid tapestries depicting the triumphs of Alexander the Great, made from cartoons by Le Brun; and delightfully decorated apartments.

Epinal was devastated in the Second World War, and little remains of its mighty medieval castle and walls, but in the modern **Musée Départemental d'Art Ancien et Contemporain** (*open Wed–Mon 10–6; closed Tues; adm*) – one of the best museums in Lorraine – you can at least see them in a charming 17th-century fantasy bird's-eye view by Nicolas Bellot. *Job* by Georges de La Tour intrigues, and seek out too *L'Embarquement de St Paul à Ostia*, one of the few works in the region by perhaps the greatest artist Lorraine ever produced, Claude Gelée, nicknamed Le Lorrain. Rembrandt's dark *Mater Dolorosa* looks surprisingly modern, and Jan Breughel's *L'Hiver* is full of caricatures. The archaeological collection includes two tablets showing signs of the zodiac from Egypt. The top floor is taken up by contemporary art, including Gilbert and George's mock stained-glass window, while a whole section of the museum is devoted to the *Images d'Epinal*, simple prints with saturated colours produced in town since the late 18th century. The term *images d'Epinal* has now come to signify a hackneyed cliché in French. You can take a guided tour at **L'Imagerie d'Epinal** up river to see how the images are made and coloured.

Stop at **Baccarat** if you want to take home some beautiful crystal. A large shop near the museum sells top-quality pieces, even the smallest costing a small fortune, while there are other cheaper (but tackier) shops in town.

The Spa Towns of Southern Lorraine and Northern Franche-Comté

Vittel and Contrexéville are well known because of their widely marketed mineral waters, but this swath of specialist spa resorts includes many others, such as Bourbonne-les-Bains, Plombières-les-Bains, Luxeuil-les-Bains and even Bains-les-Bains. These towns enjoyed a glamorous period through the 19th century, and they are still very busy – mainly with patients of the generous French National Health Service, who are sent here on *cures*.

Slightly scruffy **Luxeuil-les-Bains**, just in Franche-Comté, has the most historic atmosphere. The local stone has a tinge of Vosges red to it, while many of the old windows date back to Gothic and Renaissance times. The Irish saint Columbanus set up a monastery here way back in the early 7th century, and the abbey dedicated to him still occupies the centre of town. Track-suited **Contrexéville** has retained the most glamorous feel of these spas, with a splendid old central building held up on mosaic columns; its neo-Byzantine forms date from 1912. Highlight is the circular room where you can taste the waters, a mosaic of flowers cascading down the dome above you. Picturesque little **Plombières**, lost in a valley in the Vosges, is known for the secret meeting held here in 1858 between Cavour and Napoléon III, which cemented the unification of Italy – France got Nice and Savoy. Architecturally it the place has retained in its centre a fine collection of 18th-century houses.

The Northern Vosges: Lorraine into Alsace

The Lorraine *département* of Moselle has been shedding its industrial image and now boasts two regional parks and nine 18-hole golf courses. The new **Museum of 17th–20th-century French Art** at **Vic-sur-Seilles** celebrates Georges de la Tour in his birthplace, the pride of the place being his *John the Baptist in the Desert*. **Sarreguemines**, on the Sarre, has an artistic legacy worth stopping for, centered on the ceramics industry, which flourished here in the 19th century. The star of its **Musée de la Faïence** (*open Wed–Mon 10–12 and 2–6; adm*) is the so-called winter garden decorated with large ceramic panels, smothered with decoration, commissioned in the early 1880s, a precursor of the Art Nouveau movement.

The **Simserhof Fort**, newly restored, offers an interesting introduction to the Maginot Line with electric trollies, film shows and modern museum facilities. The fortified town of **Bitche** came under terrible siege in the Franco-Prussian War from 1870 to 1871 – those 200 days and more of desperate defence are considered to have been its finest hour, and the story is well told on a tour inside the massive **hill fort**. Most of the fort is atmospherically empty, cold and dark, but the commentary evokes the dreadful conditions during the siege.

Much of the finest crystal and glass in France is produced in the Vosges woods south of Bitche. **Meisenthal** was the village where Emile Gallé worked for over 25 years and perfected his new techniques, bringing the curvaceous forms of Art Nouveau to France in the last decades of the 19th century. It is also where the first glass Christmas tree ornaments were made in the 1850s. The **Maison du Verre** (*open July–Aug Wed–Mon 2–6; rest of period Easter–1 Nov Wed–Mon 2–4; closed Tues; adm*) holds regular exhibitions, and contains one of Gallé's first designs – with flowers and luminous *clair de lune* blue – and some later works employing sophisticated enamel layering. You can also learn how glass and crystal are made, and take lessons, at the **Centre International d'Art Verrier** (*t 03 87 96 87 16*).

The densely wooded, red-stoned hills and mountains of the Vosges boast two regional parks, the Parc Naturel Régional des Ballons des Vosges in the south, the Parc Naturel Régional des Vosges du Nord in the north. After fortified northeastern Lorraine, the timberframe towns and villages of northern Alsace appear merry. Picturesque **La Petite-Pierre**, a favoured tourist spot, is home to the **Maison du Parc** which explains the fauna and flora of the Parc Régional des Vosges du Nord. The northern Vosges are more secretive than the more sensational southern Vosges, but hikers enjoy the wooded surrounds of La Petite-Pierre. A short way south, a delightful row of troglodyte houses with bright blue fronts are wedged into the rockface above the village of **Graufthal** (*open Sunday afternoons*). East of Bitche, the **Lac du Hanau** has many walking trails and red ruined castles on spurs, including the **Château de Falkenstein** – not to be confused with the even more sensational **Château de Fleckenstein**, nearby. (*Both are currently closed for repairs and restoration.*)

A walk up around the old ramparts of **Wissembourg** offers a delightful overview of this characterful border town with its steep-roofed timberframe buildings. Some church towers stick out, in particular two belonging to the enormous church of **St-Pierre et St-Paul**, the second largest Gothic church in Alsace. Gorgeous old stained-glass windows illuminate the choir, the oldest dating as far back as the 12th century. **Hunspach** a little south is a delightful farmers' village, all the immaculate black and white houses set around spotless courtyards.

Haguenau suffered wholesale destruction twice, first in Louis XIV's campaign to take Alsace, then in the Second World War. After the Sun King's troops had done their worst, a new 18th-century town went up, parts of which still stand today. The **Musée Historique** contains some splendid Celtic artefacts as well as more common Gallo-Roman finds. On the ground floor are pieces of medieval statuary rescued from the earlier ruined Haguenau. The **Musée Alsacien**, devoted to crafts and traditions, has good displays of Alsace pottery. If you're tempted, you could head off through the enormous **forest of Haguenau** in search of more contemporary stuff: **Betschdorf**, an amalgam of old villages on the northern side of the forest below Hunspach, specializes in grey and blue salt-fired stoneware; **Soufflenheim**, on the east side of the forest, deals in less exclusive tableware.

The surprisingly grand small town of **Saverne** has as its centrepiece a building that might be dubbed the Buckingham Palace of the Vosges – a vast red-stoned castle built for the Rohans of Strasbourg fame. The town bought it in the 1950s, filling it with amenities, including the archaeological, historical and art museums. The **Donation Louise Weiss**, the gift of the pioneering feminist journalist, includes drawings by Vlaminck and Van Dongen, and objects collected on her travels. Lovely old houses line the streets parallel to the palace. On the heights above Saverne, the dramatic remains of the **Château du Haut-Barr**, built in the 12th century and

Getting Around

Wissembourg, Hunspach and Haguenau have good **train** links with Strasbourg. Saverne lies on the line between Lille and Strasbourg.

Tourist Information

Wissembourg: 9 Place de la République, t 03 88 94 10 11, *www.ot-wissembourg.fr*.
Saverne: 37 Grand'Rue, t 03 88 91 80 47.

Where to Stay and Eat

La Petite-Pierre ✉ **67290**
***Au Lion d'Or, 15 Rue Principale, t 03 88 70 45 06, *phil.lion@liondor.com* (*moderate*). Really quite luxurious with 40 rooms, forest views and serious cuisine (*expensive–moderate*). *Closed 25 June–4 July and Jan.*
***Aux Trois Roses, 19 Rue Principale, t 03 88 70 45 02, *hotel.3roses@wanadoo.fr* (*moderate*). Another smart option. Restaurant (*expensive–moderate*). *Closed part of Jan; restaurant closed Sun eve and Mon.*

Obersteinbach ✉ **67510**
**Chez Anthon, 40 Rue Principale, t 03 88 09 55 01, *info@restaurant-anthon.fr* (*inexpensive*). With its lovely welcoming courtyard, a tasteful place to stay (just 9 rooms) and to eat (*expensive–moderate*); the

dining room has views on to the woods too. *Closed Jan; restaurant closed Tues and Wed.*

Lembach ✉ **67510**
Auberge du Cheval Blanc, 4 Route de Wissembourg, t 03 88 94 41 86, *info@au-cheval-blanc.fr* (*very expensive–expensive*). A highly reputed restaurant, one of the best in northern Alsace, and a pretty timber-frame picture in pink. Also rooms (*very expensive*). *Closed Mon, Tues, and Fri lunch.*

Wissembourg ✉ **67160**
Hostellerie du Cygne, 3 Rue du Sel, t 03 88 94 00 16, *hostellerie-cygne@wanadoo.fr* (*moderate–inexpensive*). In beautiful old timberframe houses in the historic centre. Restaurant (*expensive–moderate*). *Closed 2 weeks July; restaurant closed Sun eve, Wed and Thurs lunch.*
Le Châtelet, 65 Faubourg de Bitche, t 03 88 94 16 11 (*expensive–moderate*). A pretty little gastronomic restaurant in a picturesque spot by a weir on the edge of the old town.

Saverne ✉ **67700**
Taverne Katz, 80 Grand'Rue, t 03 88 71 16 56, *www.tavernekatz.com* (*expensive*). Excellent traditional restaurant with carved façade.
Villa Katz, t 03 88 71 02 02 (*moderate*). Newly opened sister establishment to above. 19th-century house beautifully converted into a small traditional hotel.

transformed in the 16th, overlook the Rhine plain and the Zorn valley. French troops brought most of the place down in 1648. The red architectural ruins merge with the fissured rocks on which they stand. There is a restored Romanesque chapel too, a restaurant in the ruins, and, best of all, the magnificent views. Do not miss the unique restored **telegraph signal station** 200 yards away. It formed part of the first modern communications system, built by Dr Chappe in 1794. A message from the army on the frontier reached Paris in 20 minutes – 400km away.

Strasbourg

Alsace's answer to Paris, its gorgeous historic centre set on an island on the Ill river, its cathedral one of the glories of European Gothic, Strasbourg of course has 'its' own parliament, that of the European Union, as well as being the seat of the quite separate Council of Europe, which includes the European Court of Human Rights. When the EU parliament is sitting, members move into town with their retinues, adding to the flocks of businessmen, students and tourists. Strasbourg still has one of the largest ports in France, along the Rhine, but the historic centre is so packed with riches – including three splendid art museums – that visitors rarely notice.

Strasbourg grew up as a port on the west bank of the Rhine. Through the Dark Ages it lay on the path of invaders from the east, suffering destruction after destruction, and from the 9th to the 17th centuries lay within the boundaries of the Holy Roman Empire. However, the city leaders retained a great degree of independence, first through a line of powerful bishops, then from the 14th century through the control of powerful trade guilds. Strasbourg was also a place where culture and intellectual advances often thrived. A lot is made of Gutenberg's years here working on the invention of the printing press, and the city drew some of the major figures of the Reformation: von Kaysersberg, Bucer and Calvin. The university opened in 1566; one of its most famous students was Goethe, who studied here from 1770 to 1771.

In 1681, Strasbourg became part of France, and joined the rest of Alsace, which had been French since 1648. It was an aristocratic French family, the Rohans, that most marked the city in the 18th century. Four Rohan cardinals succeeded each other as bishops of Strasbourg. In late April 1792, as the Army of the Rhine waited here to head into action, Rouget de Lisle composed a stirring song for the departing troops. The result was soon adopted by volunteers from Marseille, and henceforth became known as the *Marseillaise*, now the French national anthem. The Prussian bombardments during the Franco-Prussian War caused great damage to the centre and fires destroyed many houses. Once France had lost the war Strasbourg became capital of the annexed territory of Elsass-Lothringen, and only reverted to France at the end of the First World War. The town suffered badly from more bombing during the Second World War, but this time the historic centre emerged relatively unscathed.

The Cathedral and Around

What an overwhelming skyscraper of a medieval building Strasbourg's **cathedral** is. It was mainly built through the 13th and 14th centuries; the massive Romanesque choir went up first, followed in the mid-13th century by the Gothic nave. The soaring 466ft spire, one of the landmarks of the Rhine Valley, was completed in 1439. The fabulous west façade, designed by Erwin de Steinbach, is one of the greatest in the world. Work began around 1280 but it was not completed until well into the middle of the 14th century, after Erwin's death. The tiny-looking green wings of a row of high-perched angels stand out against the almost uniformly red sandstone façade. The central rose windows are stunning, the gabled doorways filled with sculpture. Climb up to the spire to admire views of Strasbourg's roofs and the Rhine valley. Inside, splendid stained-glass windows spread their mysterious light down the long nave. In contrast, the choir is lit by a single, small central opening. A startling nest of an organ loft, elaborately gilded, hangs precariously in the nave; while the pulpit is richly carved. Gem-like 14th-century glass illuminates the Chapelle Ste-Catherine. The transept beyond is held up by a fabulous central pillar known as the Angels' Pillar or Pillar of the Last Judgement, an exceptional piece of Gothic art with expressive figures of the evangelists, musical angels, and the Christ of the Last Judgement.

Strasbourg

To European Parliament
and Parc de l'Orangerie (1km)

250 metres
250 yards

N

PLACE DE LA RÉPUBLIQUE

AV DE LA LIBERTÉ

AV DE LA MARSEILLAISE

BD DE LA VICTOIRE

QUAI DES PÊCHEURS

RUE DE LA KRUTENAU

RUE DE ZURICH

PLACE DE ZURICH

RUE DE ZURICH

RUE DU JEU-DE-PAUME

RUE DE L'ABREUVOIR

Quai St-Etienne

L'III

Eglise St-Etienne

PLACE ST-ETIENNE

RUE ST-ETIENNE

RUE DE LA CROIX

RUE DES SOEURS

RUE DES VEAUX

RUE DES BATELIERS

QUAI DES BATELIERS

RUE DES ORPHELINS

PLACE D'AUSTERLITZ

PLACE D'AUSTERLITZ

RUE DE LA 1ERE ARMEE

Hôtel de Ville

BROGLIE

PLACE BROGLIE

RUE DES FRÈRES

PLACE DU MARCHÉ GAYOT

RUE DES ÉCRIVAINS

Cathedral

i

Palais Rohan

PLACE DU CHÂTEAU

Musée de l'Oeuvre Notre-Dame

RUE DU MAROQUIN

PLACE DU CORBEAU

RUE DES BOUCHERS

Musée Alsacien

P

RUE DES JUIFS

RUE BRÛLÉE

RUE DU TEMPLE NEUF

PLACE DU TEMPLE NEUF

RUE DU DOME

RUE DU SANGLIER

RUE DE L'OUTRE

RUE DES ORFÈVRES

RUE DES ARCADES

PLACE GUTENBERG

i

RUE DU VIEUX MARCHÉ AUX POISSONS

QUAI STURM

Palais de Justice

RUE DE LA FONDERIE

P

RUE DE LA NUEE BLEUE

UE DU FAUBOURG DE PIERRE

QUAI FINKMATT

QUAI KELLERMANN

Eglise St-Pierre-le-Jeune

PLACE DE L'HOMME-DE-FER

P

P

PLACE KLEBER

RUE DES FRANCS-BOURGEOIS

RUE DE LA DIVISION LECLERC

RUE STE-HELENE

RUE DU BOUCLIER

RUE DE LA MONNAIE

Eglise St-Thomas

PLACE ST-THOMAS

Eglise St-Louis

FOSSE DES TANNEURS

RUE DES DENTELLES

RUE DES MOULINS

QUAI FINKWILLER

RUE HUMANN

Hôpital Civil

GRAND RUE

RUE DU 22 NOVEMBRE

QUAI DE PARIS

QUAI KLEBER

RUE DE SEBASTOPOL

Les Halles

P

P

P

RUE DU FAUBOURG DE SAVERNE

QUAI ST-JEAN

QUAI DE TURCKHEIM

Eglise St-Pierre-le-Vieux

QUAI ALTORFFER

PONTS COUVERTS

L'III

QUAI PETITE FRANCE

PETITE FRANCE

Barrage Vauban

Musée d'Art Moderne et Contemporain

P

Hôtel du Département

BD DU PRÉSIDENT WILSON

RUE DU FAUBOURG NATIONAL

RUE DU MAIRE-KUSS

RUE STE-MARGUERITE

RUE DE WASSELONNE

Train Station

PLACE DE LA GARE

P

i

BD DE METZ

RUE DE MOLSHEIM

Getting There and Around

There are direct **flights** daily to Strasbourg from the UK with Air France. You can also fly in from Paris and other French airports. The Strasbourg-Entzheim airport lies 15km southwest of the city centre; buses into the centre run Mon–Fri roughly every 30mins. There are **trains** from Paris-Gare de l'Est to Strasbourg city centre (at least 4hrs).

Tourist Information

Strasbourg: 17 Pl de la Cathédrale, **t** 03 88 52 28 28, **f** 03 88 52 28 29, *www.ot-strasbourg.fr*. There are offices at Pl de la Gare, **t** 03 88 32 51 49, and Pont de l'Europe, **t** 03 88 61 39 23. Take a relaxing vedette or riverboat cruise around central Strasbourg from the terraces on the riverside of the Palais Rohan.

Shopping

The major shopping streets lie on the central island. There is a food market on Bd de la Marne (*Tues and Sat am*) and a flea market on Rue du Vieux-Hôpital (*Wed and Sat*).
The Bookworm, 3 Rue de Pâques. English-language bookshop,
Christian Maître Chocolat, 12 Rue de l'Outre. Traditional-style chocolates, such as pralines, marzipan, liqueur chocolates, flavoured truffles and the Alsatian speciality, chocolate 'chestnuts'.

Where to Stay

Strasbourg ✉ 67000

You should book well ahead if you want to stay in Strasbourg, which is very popular and packed out when the European Union Parliament is sitting.

★★★★Régent Contades, 8 Av de la Liberté, **t** 03 88 15 05 05, *www.regent-hotels.com* (*luxury–very expensive*). Spacious, luxurious hotel with old-fashioned style in an imposing building in the Prussian quarter just east of the central island, constructed in the late 19th century. 24-hour room service.

★★★★Régent Petite France, 5 Rue des Moulins, **t** 03 88 76 43 43, *www.regent-hotels.com* (*luxury–very expensive*). Sister hotel with a contemporary feel in big converted old buildings in the delightful Petite France district. Dull exterior but exciting and recently done up hotel, if still more outrageously expensive than its older relative. Restaurant (*expensive*). *Closed June–Sept Mon; Oct–May weekends*.

★★★Baumann, 16 Place de la Cathédrale, **t** 03 88 32 42 14, *baumann@maison-kammerzell.com* (*expensive*). Near the

The splendid **Musée de l'Œuvre Notre-Dame** (*open Tues–Sun 10–6; adm, but free 1st Sun of month*) has dozens of rooms devoted to medieval and Renaissance art, and religious art in particular, including the Romanesque cloister from Eschau. The museum also lays claim to the oldest known piece of figurative stained glass, the Wissembourg head of Christ, dated to around 1070.

Museums in the Palais Rohan

All open Wed–Mon 10–6; closed Tues; adm.

The outrageous bishops' residence, the **Palais Rohan**, was badly damaged in 1944, and the restoration of the ground-floor apartments was only completed in 1980. A trio of major museums is housed within. The **Musée Archéologique** down in the basement covers Alsace culture from 600,000 BC to AD 800. There are some interesting Neolithic engravings, but the Gallo-Roman section is the best, with a monumental 3rd-century head of a cross-eyed emperor and fine carved stelae. An early-Christian engraved glass depicts the sacrifice of Isaac with startling sophistication; some of the Dark Age weapons share the high standard of craftsmanship.

cathedral, a fabulous many-storeyed timber-frame house built in the 15th and 16th centuries, with sumptuous interior decoration. A small number of lovely rooms, but known above all for its restaurant and the reputed *choucroute Baumann*, named after the proud proprietor. *Closed Feb hols.*

★★★**Hôtel Cardinal de Rohan**, 17–19 Rue du Maroquin, B.P.39, Cathédrale, t 03 88 32 85 11, *info@hotel-rohan.com* (*expensive*). A charming, comfortable hotel in a prime location close to the cathedral, but perhaps just a tad too close to the major tourist path.

★★★**Maison Rouge**, 4 Rue des Francs-Bourgeois, t 03 88 32 08 60, *info@maison-rouge.com* (*expensive*). Large, but the rooms have individual style.

★★★**Beaucour**, 5 Rue des Bouchers, t 03 88 76 72 00, *beaucour@hotel-beaucour.com* (*expensive–moderate*). Appealing group of timberframe façades just on the south side of the Ill close to the Pont du Corbeau, also owned by Baumann. A bit overdone for some tastes and very pricey, but the rooms are extremely comfortable and really luxurious for a three-star.

★★**Suisse**, 24 Rue de la Rape, t 03 88 35 22 11, *www.hotel-suisse.com* (*moderate*). In a great location opposite the cathedral, with a stylish blue façade behind the terraces.

★★**Hôtel de l'Ill**, 8 Rue des Bateliers, t 03 88 36 20 01 (*moderate*). In a great location just

south of the main island, close to the church of Ste-Madeleine.

★★**Couvent du Franciscain**, 18 Rue du Faubourg de Pierre, t 03 88 32 93 93, *www.hotel-franciscain.com* (*inexpensive*). Just north of the main island, good value.

Ostwald ✉ 67540

★★★★**Château de l'Ile**, 4 Quai Heydt, t 03 88 66 85 00, *www.grandes-etapes.fr* (*very expensive*). Highly reputed hotel southwest of the centre, midway to the airport, in a meander of the Ill. All mod cons; sumptuous cuisine (*expensive*). *Closed Sat lunch, Sun eve, Mon.*

Eating Out

Buerehiesel, 4 Parc de l'Orangerie, t 03 88 45 56 65 (*very expensive*). Absolutely fabulous cuisine in a ridiculously pretty old Alsatian house. *Closed Tues and Wed, and Aug.*

Au Crocodile, 10 Rue de l'Outre, t 03 88 32 13 02 (*very expensive*). Another starry reputation for superlative light but classic cuisine. *Closed July.*

Chez Yvonne, 10 Rue du Sanglier, t 03 88 32 84 15 (*expensive*). Famous *winstub* on the main island with great cuisine and atmosphere. *Closed Sun and Mon lunch.*

L'Arsenal, 11 Rue de l'Abreuvoir, t 03 88 35 03 69 (*expensive–moderate*). Refined, light and

Poverty and meekness were not words in a Rohan's vocabulary. On the ground floor the formal apartments of the **Musée des Arts Décoratifs** count among the most ostentatious anywhere in France, with gilded, stuccoed ceilings and painted allegories. The Salle du Synode treated visiting bishops to a *trompe-l'œil* painting of the goddess Ceres. The Salon des Evêques, decorated with images of the virtues, doubled as the games room under the Rohans. The Chambre du Roi, exquisitely gilded, is where Louis XV stayed in 1744, and Marie-Antoinette in 1770. Copies of works by Raphael adorn this room and the Salon d'Assemblée. A whole series of further chambers display ceramics, of which Strasbourg became a major producer from the late 17th century. At first decorated with simple blue patterns, big purple and pink flowers came to dominate.

The **Musée des Beaux-Arts** is one of France's great provincial museums. The major European schools are covered, the Italian, Flemish and 17th-century French paintings exceptionally rich. One of the oldest and finest works is a small Giotto *Crucifixion*. Botticelli, Piero di Cosimo, Del Sarto and Correggio are all here, but look out too for lesser-known artists such as Barocci and Negretti, and Flemish masterpieces. Among

modern Alsatian cuisine in an interesting interior in a timberframe building in the Krutenau quarter. *Closed Sat eve exc Sept–June, and Aug.*

L'Ami Schutz, 1 Ponts-Couverts, **t** 03 88 32 76 98 (*expensive–moderate*). Strasbourg institution in a medieval setting in Petite France, with a well-located terrace and Alsatian specialities.

Le Festin de Lucullus, 18 Rue Ste-Hélène, **t** 03 88 22 40 78 (*expensive–moderate*). Fine fresh cooking at a reasonable price near the centre of the main island. *Closed Sun and Mon exc Dec, and Aug.*

La Choucrouterie, 20 Rue St-Louis (just south of the main island, opposite the church of St-Thomas), **t** 03 88 36 52 87 (*moderate*). An extremely popular and lively place to try *choucroute*, in a converted 18th-century posting inn. Musical evenings, especially gypsy bands, by arrangement.

There's an appealing choice of places to eat on the Place du Marché Gayot.

Entertainment and Nightlife

There are often free concerts in Parc des Contades and Parc de l'Orangerie.

Le Bateau Ivre, Quai des Alpes, **t** 03 88 61 27 17. A spacious, elegant boat, moored on the quay near the city centre, a popular spot for the trendy and fashionable.

Les 3 Brasseurs, 22 Rue de Veaux, **t** 03 88 36 12 13. Unusual brasserie. Beer brewed on the premises, *tarte flambée*. Concerts in the cellars Fri and Sat.

Café P'tit Max, 4 Place de l'Homme de Fer, **t** 03 88 23 05 00. A pillar of Strasbourg nightlife, with singers and dinner concerts (*Tues, Thurs and Fri eves*). *Open all day until 1/1.30am.*

Bar du 7e Art, 18 Rue du 22 Novembre. The movie-lover's bar, linked to the Etoile Cinema, a relaxed place where movie buffs can read newspapers and sip coffee. *Open daily 8am–1.30am, Sun 2.30pm–11.30pm.*

Le Café du TNS, 1 Av de la Marseillaise. The National Theatre of Strasbourg café with a striped ceiling and stylish, subdued designer furniture, all black and white. Brunch-type breakfasts, fresh sandwiches and exquisite regional dishes. *Open daily 8am–1am.*

Opéra Café, 19 Place Broglie. Attractive Baroque-style café in the beautiful Opera House. Attracts a fashionable, artsy crowd. Limited menu available at lunchtime. *Open daily 11am–3am, Sun from 2pm.*

Les Aviateurs, 12 Rue des Soeurs, **t** 03 88 36 52 69. Stronghold of the eternally attractive Michèle Noth, Strasbourg's night queen. Now run by her son. Great atmosphere, great place to meet. *Open daily 6pm–4am.*

the French masterpieces, look out for Philippe de Champaigne's piercing portrait of Cardinal Richelieu and de Largillère's seductive *La Belle Strasbourgeoise* (1703).

Elsewhere around Strasbourg

The labyrinthine **Musée Alsacien** (*open Wed–Mon 10–6; closed Tues; adm*) lies on the southern quay of the Ill. Three substantial houses have been knocked into one to make a rambling museum of popular arts and crafts, a good introduction to traditional life in Alsace. Don't miss the fantastical prophylactic masks.

The major shopping streets lie on the central island, west of the cathedral quarter. In the centre of **Place Gutenberg**, the green statue, a 19th-century work by David d'Angers, honours the inventor of the printing press. Rue des Arcades leads up to **Place Kléber** which commemorates a more controversial figure. Born in Strasbourg, Jean-Baptiste Kléber is remembered above all as a ruthlessly determined general who fought for the Revolution and then for Napoleon, notably in Egypt.

Tourists flock to the line of smaller islands, and the quarter which goes by the curious title of **Petite France**. The waterways here reflect some splendid timberframe houses, where millers, tanners and fishermen once lived. The **Barrage Vauban** is a covered walkway, a remnant of the fortifications Vauban planned for the city. From its roof there are great views over Petite France to the cathedral. On the opposite side you also get an excellent view of Strasbourg's slick new modern art museum, a sculpture of a horse calmly perched on its roof. This, the **Musée d'Art Moderne et Contemporain** (*open Tues, Wed, Fri and Sat 11–7, Thurs 12–10, Sun 10–6; closed Mon; adm*), opened in November 1998 as the focal point of a whole new quarter. The collection starts in the last decades of the 19th century: there are paintings by Monet, Renoir, Boudin, Emile Bernard, Burne-Jones and Klimt, followed by Vlaminck, Gris and Picasso. A special place is reserved for Jean Arp, born in Strasbourg and a founding figure of the Dada movement, there's space for contemporary installations.

East and north of the cathedral, **Place du Marché Gayot** is a popular haven of restaurants and cafés. Cross the northern branch of water embracing Strasbourg's central island and **Place de la République** is dominated by the imposingly pompous German structures of the late 19th century. The Prussian architecture extends outwards to the university and the Orangerie, a park originally designed by Le Nôtre at the end of the 17th century. The **European quarter**, on the banks of the River Ill, includes the European Parliament, the Council of Europe and the European Court of Human Rights, designed by Richard Rogers. They are all remarkable buildings.

The Alsace Wine Route

The enchanting Alsace wine route runs almost directly south along the bottom slopes of the Vosges from Strasbourg down to the Thann area. It's an easy route to follow, but at certain times of year it can become frustratingly busy with tour buses. The wine villages are almost all as beautiful as each other, often with round ramparts and old gateways embracing colourful timberframe, orange-roofed houses. Above, in the steep, wooded Vosges slopes, crumbling medieval castles peer down across the Rhine plain. The one château to have been completely restored is Haut-Koenigsbourg, rebuilt for Kaiser Wilhelm II in the early 20th century, a symbol of Germany's authority over Alsace at that time. Terrible traces of the two world wars remain in Le Linge's First World War trenches and in the Nazi concentration camp of Le Struthof, the only one on French territory.

Northern Wine Route: Strasbourg to Kaysersberg

The main Alsace wine route starts due west of Strasbourg, at the base of the Vosges. **Marlenheim** counts as the first northerly stop, a well-known wine-producing parish. Next, **Molsheim** is a wealthy town which has sprawled out beyond its red walls. During the 17th century it became perhaps the most important religious centre in Alsace, when the Archduke Leopold of Austria, also bishop of Strasbourg, founded the Jesuit University here in 1618, which lasted until 1702, when a Rohan cardinal transferred it to Strasbourg to counteract the Protestant influences there. The

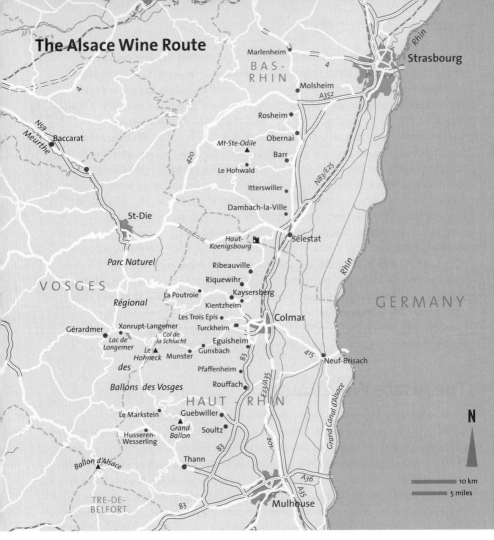

The Alsace Wine Route

Strasbourg

Marlenheim

BAS-RHIN

Molsheim
A352

Rosheim

Baccarat

Obernai

Mt-Ste-Odile ▲

Barr

Le Hohwald

Itterswiller

Dambach-la-Ville

St-Die

Haut-Koenigsbourg ⊞

Sélestat

Parc Naturel

Ribeauvillé

Riquewihr

VOSGES

Régional

La Poutroie

Kaysersberg

Kientzheim

Les Trois Epis ●

Colmar

Gérardmer

Xonrupt-Langemer

Turckheim

Col de la Schlucht

Eguisheim

Lac de Longemer

Le ▲ Hohneck

Gunsbach

Munster

des

Pfaffenheim

GERMANY

Ballons des Vosges

Rouffach

HAUT-RHIN

Le Markstein

Guebwiller

Grand Ballon ▲

Soultz

Husseren-Wesserling

Neuf-Brisach

Thann

Ballon d'Alsace ▲

TRE-DE-BELFORT

Mulhouse

N

10 km
5 miles

Rhin
Meurthe
Grand Canal d'Alsace

Musée de la Chartreuse, in the priory of what was an enormous charterhouse, is the local history museum. In 1909 the Italian Ettore Bugatti set up his celebrated car factory at Molsheim. The museum contains a few old models, and Bugattis are still built on the outskirts of town. The **Metzig** is the most celebrated of the old houses in town – a Flemish-style, high-gabled house built for the butchers' corporation.

An inordinate number of gift shops hint at the popularity of **Obernai**, a residence of the dukes of Alsace and the major centre for brewing Kronenbourg beer. A soaring, isolated medieval tower, the **Kappelturm**, remains from a mostly destroyed church, although the choir still stands nearby. The massive church of **Sts Peter and Paul** is a showy 19th-century neo-Gothic giant, standing by an early 20th-century fountain dedicated to Ste Odile (*see* box).

The vestiges of an immense ancient wall known as the **Mur Païen** wind their way around the top of **Mont Ste-Odile**, still a significant religious site. The main convent burned in the 16th century, so the church and other buildings have been rebuilt. As well as the church with its ornate 18th-century decorations, pilgrims visit the 11th-century **Chapelle de la Croix**, once containing Etichon's sarcophagus, and the 12th-century **Chapelle Ste-Odile**, claiming still to hold his daughter's relics in an 8th-century tomb. The views from the hillside are splendid.

Barr, back on the wine route, has a curious Norman feel to its timberframe centre and suffers less from the tourist hordes than Obernai. You can climb up to the splendid ruins of the castle of Haut-Andlau and the nearby Château de Spesbourg.

The concentration camp of **Le Struthof** (*open July–Aug daily 10–5, rest of period Mar–24 Dec daily 10–11.30 and 2–4; adm*) is hidden high up in the Vosges, beyond the little ski resort of **Le Hohwald**. This was the only Nazi death camp on French territory, close to a stone quarry which the Nazis wanted to exploit. Brace yourself for the horror stories in the museum. It was mainly French Resistance fighters and political protestors who were imprisoned and exterminated here. The so-called *Nacht und Nebel* (Night and Fog) deportees were openly destined for extermination. The camp was built to hold 2,000, but when it was evacuated in September 1944, there were some 7,000 people imprisoned here, and the last recorded number for a prisoner was 17,045, so it is thought that over 10,000 were killed in this tranquil spot. A towering monument unfurls above the camp. Watchtowers mark its barbed wire limits. Some of the internment blocks remain on the terraced hillside. The simple museum has harrowing photos and displays. At the bottom of the camp lies the pit where the remains of the dead were incinerated, while a gas chamber still stands down the road.

Preserving several fortified gateways, its picturesque houses laden with flowers, **Dambach-la-Ville** is a prosperous wine village, one of the largest producers of riesling. Legend has it that a bear enjoying grapes from a wild vine nearby showed the locals the viticultural way, as is recalled on a Renaissance fountain in the centre. A path through the vines leads to the **Chapelle St-Sébastien**. Outside, the ossuary is still packed with bones, while inside you can hardly miss the twisted columned, wildly

Ste Odile, Persecuted Patron Saint of Alsace and the Blind

Obernai was the birthplace of Ste Odile. She was born blind, much to the anger of her father, Duke Etichon of Alsace. He ordered her to be killed. Rescued by her wetnurse, she was brought up religiously. When Bishop Erard baptized her, she recovered her sight. Eventually her mother and brother revealed her existence to Etichon, but, on finding out, the violent man murdered his son with his own hands. Filled with remorse, he tried to make up for his sins by offering Odile in marriage to a fine knight, but she refused, wanting to lead a religious life. Infuriated beyond reason yet again, the duke chased after Odile to kill her, but, miraculously, a rockface opened up between them and saved her. Her father finally gave in and offered her the Hohenbourg, now Mont Ste-Odile, on which she built two convents. The mountain became a major pilgrimage site, visited by Holy Roman Emperors from Charlemagne on. Odile was made patron saint of Alsace at the start of the 19th century; she is also patron saint of the blind.

Getting Around

Sélestat is well served by **trains**, on the Strasbourg-Colmar-Mulhouse line. A branch line from Strasbourg also stops at Molsheim, Rosheim, Obernai, Barr and Dambach.

Tourist Information

Obernai: Place du Beffroi, **t** 03 88 95 64 13, *www.obernai.fr*.

Sélestat: Commanderie St-Jean, Bd du Général Leclerc, **t** 03 88 58 87 20, *www.selestat-tourisme.com*.

Ribeauvillé-Riquewihr: 1 Grand'rue, **t** 03 89 73 62 22, *www.ribeauville-riquewihr.com*.

Kaysersberg: 39 Rue Charles de Gaulle, **t** 03 89 78 22 78, *www.kaysersberg.com*.

Where to Stay and Eat

Itterswiller ✉ 67140

★★★Arnold, 98 Route des Vins, **t** 03 88 85 50 58, *arnold-hotel@wanadoo.fr* (*expensive*). Very attractively located among the vines, a large, comfortable hotel and restaurant (*expensive–moderate*) serving copious Alsace dishes. *Closed 1st half Feb; restaurant closed Sun eve and Mon.*

Dambach-la-Ville ✉ 67650

★★Le Vignoble, 1 Rue de l'Eglise, Dambach-la-Ville, **t** 03 88 92 43 75 (*inexpensive*). Very

sweet converted timberframe barn. *Closed Christmas–16 Mar and Sun eve out of season.*

Obernai ✉ 67210

★★La Cloche, 90 Rue Général Gouraud, **t** 03 88 95 52 89, *hotel.lacloche@wanadoo.fr* (*inexpensive*). 14th-century house with an excellent restaurant and good rooms. *Closed part Jan; restaurant closed Sun eve in winter.*

Sélestat ✉ 67600

★★★Abbaye La Pommeraie, 8 Av du Maréchal Foch, **t** 03 88 92 07 84, *www.relaischateaux.fr/pommeraie* (*expensive*). No asceticism these days in this luxurious hotel which has grown out from the buildings of a Cistercian abbey. It even has two restaurants (*very expensive–expensive*). Main restaurant closed Sun eve and Mon am.

Thannenkirch ✉ 68590

★★Auberge de la Meunière, 30 Rue Ste-Anne, **t** 03 89 73 10 47, **f** 03 89 73 12 31, *info@aubergelameuniere.com* (*inexpensive*). A delightful small hotel with 23 rooms in this village close to but tucked away from the overtouristy wine route. Restaurant (*expensive–moderate*). *Closed Christmas–24 Mar; restaurant closed Mon and Tues lunch.*

La Poutroie ✉ 68650

Les Aliziers, **t** 03 89 47 52 82, *www.aliziers.com* (*moderate*). 3km up a steep narrow lane behind the church. Stunning views and

carved wooden altarpiece. It's a more demanding walk up to the ruins of the **castle of Bernstein**, yet another victim of the Thirty Years' War.

An irritating row of towering red and white masts dominates the Rhine plain by **Sélestat**, which may have lost most of its medieval fortifications, but remains an attractive old town. Vying for attention, the churches of **Ste-Foy** and **St-Georges** stand close to each other. The first, with its twin towers and pyramidal structure over the crossing, has been much played about with since it originally went up in the 12th century. The nave looks surprisingly small behind the bold exterior. A few statues adorn the mysterious crypt, while a Baroque pulpit recalls the times when Jesuits took over. The second church has a massive central entrance tower and long, long, Gothic nave; the splendid flat choir end has kept some original windows. The **Bibliothèque Humaniste** (*open Mon and Wed–Fri 9–12 and 2–6, Sat 9–12; July and Aug also Sat and Sun 2–5; adm*) recalls the time when the town boasted one of the finest schools in Europe. Books were rare and precious, but various masters, former pupils

excellent food in this hotel and restaurant (*moderate*) that grew out of an old farm. *Closed Jan; restaurant closed Mon eve and Tues in winter.*

Riquewihr ✉ 68340

Riquewihr is an excellent place to stay, despite the crowds, with a half-dozen good hotels, although you may feel like you're in a fake tourist tinsel village rather than a genuine traditional wine-making community. However, prices are surprisingly reasonable.

**La Couronne, 5 Rue de la Couronne, t 03 89 49 03 03, *www.hoteldelacouronne.com* (*expensive–moderate*). A charming hotel with splendid 16th-century timberframe walls and beamed rooms.

***A l'Oriel, 3 Rue des Ecuries Seigneuriales, t 03 89 49 03 13, *oriel@club-internet.fr* (*moderate*). 19 rooms in a 16th-century building inside the walls.

**Le Sarment d'Or, 4 Rue du Cerf, t 03 89 47 92 85, *www.riquewihr-sarment-dor.com* (*moderate–inexpensive*). A rival in cuteness to the above, also set along the ramparts, with 17th-century interiors and cosy rooms. Quite inventive Alsace food in the restaurant (*expensive–moderate*). *Closed Jan; restaurant closed Sun eve, Tues lunch and Mon.*

**St-Nicolas, 2 Rue St-Nicolas, t 03 89 49 01 51, *www.saintnicolas.fr* (*inexpensive*). By the Sarment d'Or inside the walls. Restaurant (*expensive–moderate*). *Closed 2 Jan–15 Mar and 15–30 Nov; restaurant closed Mon lunch.*

***Le Schoenenbourg, Rue du Schoenenbourg, t 03 89 49 01 11 (*very expensive–moderate*). Just outside the village walls, close to the naff pond but right next to vineyards. Not as charming as the others, but a comfortable modern hotel with modern facilities. Restaurant (*very expensive–expensive*). *Closed 15 Jan–15 Feb; restaurant closed Mon–Sat lunch.*

Illhaeusern ✉ 68970

****Auberge de l'Ill and Hôtel des Berges, Rue de Collonges du Mont d'Or, t 03 89 71 89 00, *auberge-d-l-ill@auberge-d-l-ill.com* (*luxury–very expensive*). The most fabled restaurant (*very expensive*) in Alsace in a village by the Ill river east of Riquewihr. The regional cuisine and the wine list are absolutely stunning. Impeccable rooms too. *Closed Feb; restaurant closed Tues and Wed.*

Kaysersberg ✉ 68240

Hôtel Constantin, 10 Rue Père Kohlman, t 03 89 47 19 90, *reservation@hotelconstantin.com* (*moderate–inexpensive*). Fine old Alsace house welll restored with good rooms. Eat at **Relais du Château** (*cheap*) next door, owned by the same family. Good traditional food.

Auberge St Alexis, t 03 89 73 90 38 (*cheap*). A farm lost in the hills 6km from Riquewihr by road, or a hearty walk from Kayserberg, with great views of the Vosges. Excellent traditional food. Book ahead – the locals come here in force. *Closed Fri and after 8pm.*

and locals donated their volumes. Some were so valued that they were chained up to stop thieving. The greatest bequest of all came from Beatus Rhenanus of Sélestat, who studied for some time in Paris and was a close friend of Erasmus. This is one of the few great collections of humanist works to have survived in Europe and is well-explained to English-speaking visitors. The collection contains the first written reference to America in the *Cosmographiae Introductio*, published in 1507.

The most spectacular castle in Alsace, visible across the Rhine plain at the top of its precipitous wooded mountain, the **Château du Haut-Koenigsbourg** (*open Nov–Feb daily 9.45–12 and 1–5; Mar and Oct daily 9.45–5; April, May and Sept daily 9.30–5.30; June–Aug daily 9.30–6.30; closed 1 Jan, 1 May and 25 Dec; adm; audioguide in English*) was rebuilt as a pastiche of a medieval castle thanks to Kaiser Wilhelm II at the very start of the 20th century, when Alsace was annexed to Germany. Bodo Ebhardt, a young German architect, was called upon to recreate the late medieval fort. The sheer verticality of its walls and towers and the dramatic location make it an exciting place

The Opinionated Wines of Alsace

Alsace wines are like very opinionated guests around a dinner table: they have powerful, challenging, competitive characters. Single grape varieties give distinctive qualities to the different wines. Almost all the production is dry and white, and most of the bottles contain wine from just one of the eight or nine grape varieties grown across the region. The very best wine-making regions are in the Haut-Rhin or southern half of Alsace. *Grand cru* Alsace wines can be made from riesling, the most typical variety, gewurztraminer, pinot gris and muscat. Other common varieties are sylvaner, pinot blanc, auxerrois and chasselas. Riesling tends to taste dry and clean, wine experts talking of gunflint, minerals and masculinity. Gewurztraminer is sweeter, but spiciness is its essential quality, from smoky frankfurters to perfumed lychees. More fragile muscat produces dry, crisp, but delicately fruity wines.

(come early to avoid the crowds). The mock medieval reaches the height of absurdity in the Salle du Kaiser, smothered in ornate woodwork and coats of arms. On the clearest days the views from the château reach the Alps.

Three ruined medieval castles built by the Ribeaupierre family, one of the most powerful in Alsace, survey the wine village of **Ribeauvillé**. Although the village was bombed in the Second World War it has recovered remarkably well. The hike to see all three castles takes a good three hours. The **castle of St-Ulrich** was once the Ribeaupierres' magnificent seat; the form of a splendid Romanesque hall can be made out and you can climb a couple of formidable towers that have survived. From the heights you will spot the picturesque ruins of the former **castle of Girsberg**. The name has been adopted by one of Ribeauvillé's wines, a highly reputed *grand cru* riesling. There are also fine views from the **Château du Haut-Ribeaupierre**.

The archetypal Alsace picturebook wine village, **Riquewihr** often gets totally overrun by its admirers. Behind the fortifications, the 16th- and 17th-century vintners' houses look immaculate. In summer, a *son-et-lumière* show telling the history of Riquewihr takes place around the château. Head down the Rue des Juifs to the former Jewish quarter and you come to the ramparts and the **Musée de la Tour des Voleurs**, the former village prison. Riquewihr is home to many celebrated wine houses, its slopes producing some of the finest riesling in Alsace.

Kientzheim, an open little village peering over simple red walls, occupies an inordinately large place in the Alsace wine world: the Confrérie St-Etienne, which oversees the control of the quality of the wines, meets at its château. Its museum in the outhouses of the castle is devoted to wine-making in the region, with lots of old tools enjoying a pleasant retirement.

Birthplace of the 1952 Nobel Peace Prize winner Albert Schweitzer, **Kaysersberg** is a self-important town full of splendid old houses. An exceptional timberframe collection runs alongside the boulder-strewn river Weiss. The name of the place, the Emperor's Hill, derives from Gallo-Roman times, when a major route between Gaul and the Rhine valley passed this way. In the 13th century, Emperor Frederick II bought the village and paid for fortifications to keep out the dukes of Lorraine. The **Centre**

Culturel Albert Schweitzer occupies a house next to the one in which he was born. In 1896, at the age of 21, the precocious student of philosophy, theology and the organ decided that he would devote himself to science and art until he was 30, and that after that he would serve humanity.

Colmar

For the very best timberframe show in Alsace, head for Colmar, Strasbourg's rival as tourist capital of the region. Red-tinged Gothic churches and stupendous Gothic paintings are the main attractions, the Musée d'Unterlinden famously housing Grünewald's harrowing Issenheim altarpiece.

Set in the Rhine plain by the Lauch river, Colmar grew up around a Carolingian villa visited several times by Charlemagne and his sons. The prosperous place became a free imperial city in 1226. In the mid-15th century the emperor's representative in Alsace, the Archduke Sigismond, temporarily gave up part of his province to Charles the Bold of Burgundy in exchange for much-needed funds. The Burgundian appointed Pierre de Hagenbach to rule Colmar, and his cruelty towards the locals was eventually repaid when he had his head chopped off. After Swedish troops briefly took Colmar in the Thirty Years' War, French forces stepped in from 1635, but Germany took back Alsace in 1871. In the last war, the Germans held on fiercely to the town, but luckily the centre survived relatively unharmed.

The fountain splashes in the unkempt cloister garden as you wander round the **Musée d'Unterlinden** (*open April–Oct daily 9–6; rest of year Wed–Mon 10–5; closed Tues; adm*). The convent was founded in the 13th century and up to the Revolution was renowned for its strict rule and strain of Christian mysticism. It now contains one of the finest collections of Rhenish art of all, a whole series of north European master-pieces including Hans Holbein's portrait of a sour woman and Lucas Cranach's study of Melancholy. It is impossible to avoid being shocked into reflection by the greatest piece in the museum, Grünewald's **Issenheim altarpiece**, a harrowing work on the intensity of suffering and Christian redemption, brilliantly displayed in the former convent church. The outer panels depict a gruesome crucifixion scene. Christ's body is covered with gaping bleeding sores, his fingers are contorted, rigid with suffering, while a disturbing growth emerges from one of his feet. He wears a heavy crown of thorns and hangs, mutilated and dead, against a black backdrop. The figure of St Sebastian is reckoned by some to be a portrait of the artist. The second layer of painted panels depicts the Annunciation to the Virgin and the resurrected Christ. The temptations of St Anthony, the most disturbing scenes of all, are saved until last.

The **Eglise des Dominicains** (*small adm*), topped by a patterned roof of green diamond tiles, is held up by some of the tallest Gothic columns in France, soaring uninterrupted by capitals to pointed vaults. The first stone was laid in 1283, but the building is essentially 14th and 15th century. The church is home to the most famous Virgin in Alsace, Schongauer's *Virgin in the Rose Bower*, which is utterly dwarfed by the vast Gothic edifice, despite Mary being represented more than life-size. The depic-

Getting Around

Colmar's **airport** is for special business services only, **t** 03 89 20 22 90. Colmar is on the **train** line through Alsace from Strasbourg to Mulhouse and Basel. The train from Strasbourg takes *c.* 30mins.

Tourist Information

Colmar: 4 Rue des Unterlinden, **t** 03 89 20 68 92, *www.ot-colmar.fr.*

Where to Stay

Colmar ✉ 68000

★★★**Le Colombier,** 7 Rue de Turenne, **t** 03 89 23 96 00, *info@hotel-le-colombier.com (very expensive–expensive).* Very charming, cleanly restored and historic timberframe hotel with 24 rooms in the quieter quarter of the Little Venice district. No restaurant. *Closed Christmas.*

★★★★**Les Têtes,** 19 Rue des Têtes, **t** 03 89 24 43 43, *les-tetes@rmcnet.fr (expensive).* An unforgettable hotel in an unmissable 17th-century house covered in little figures in the busy centre of town; once a wine exchange. The 18 rooms and restaurant (*very expensive–expensive*) are luxurious. *Closed Feb hols; restaurant also closed Sun eve, Mon and Tues.*

★★★★**Romantik Hôtel Le Maréchal,** 4–6 Place des Six-Montagnes-Noires, **t** 03 89 41 60 32, *marechal@calixo.net (expensive–moderate).*

Occupying a fabulous timberframe house in the Little Venice district, a luxurious hotel set back in its own courtyard. The restaurant (*very expensive–expensive*), with its dining room giving on to the water, serves exciting updated regional cuisine.

★★★**St-Martin,** 38 Grand'Rue, **t** 03 89 24 11 51, *colmar@hotel-saint-martin.com (expensive–moderate).* By the Schwendi fountain, the appealing old façade of this hotel looks over one of the most central spots in Colmar.

★★**Colbert,** 2 Rue des Trois-Epis, **t** 03 89 41 31 05 (*inexpensive*). Near the station, lively, friendly and comfortable.

Eating Out

Au Fer Rouge, 52 Grand'Rue, **t** 03 89 41 37 24 (*very expensive–expensive*). The finest address for classic regional cuisine. *Closed Sun and Mon exc May, June, Sept, Oct and Dec.*

Le Caveau St-Pierre, 24 Rue de la Herse, **t** 03 89 41 99 33 (*moderate*). Characterful Little Venice restaurant with a terrace by the water, serving good-value Alsatian dishes. *Closed Sun eve, Mon and Fri lunch.*

Les Tanneurs, 12 Rue des Tanneurs, **t** 03 89 23 72 12 (*moderate*). In the same area, also with a terrace; try trout in riesling sauce. *Closed Mon and Thurs lunch.*

Winstub à la Ville de Paris, 4 Place Jeanne d'Arc, **t** 03 89 24 53 15 (*moderate*). In a house with a typical timberframe façade. *Closed Mon eve and Tues.*

---

tion of the Virgin in a garden was a popular theme, but no artist produced a more intense version than this.

Don't miss the concentration of superlative historic houses along the **Rue des Marchands** just off the Place de la Cathédrale, especially where it meets Rue Mercière and Rue Schongauer. The **Maison Pfister** boasts wonderful wooden galleries with Renaissance paintings below Old Testament figures, evangelists and symbols of Christian virtues. The beautiful naked buttocks of Patriotism may entice you into the courtyard of the **Musée Bartholdi** (*open Mar–Nov Wed–Mon 10–12 and 2–6; adm*) at 30 Rue des Marchands. This museum occupies the opulent 18th-century house where the sculptor was born in 1834. Many of his works celebrated leading lights in the history of Colmar and Alsace, including General Rapp, a strong-headed Colmarien who served as aide-de-camp to Napoleon. Bartholdi is best known as the sculptor of the Statue of Liberty, and the second floor concentrates on its making. A room on the ground floor is devoted to Jewish history in Colmar.

In Place de l'Ancienne Douane, the imposing **Koifhus** was Colmar's late 15th-century customs house and warehouse. The delightful Place du Marché aux Fruits is overseen on one side by the 18th-century **Palais de Justice**, where the Conseil Souverain d'Alsace, a regional parliament, sat before the Revolution. The enormous Gothic **St-Mathieu**, now Protestant, originally served a Franciscan monastery. A masonry screen divides the nave and choir, while the gallery running round the nave is decorated with panels depicting the miracles of Christ.

South of the Place du Marché aux Fruits, the stunning timberframe houses lead you to the ravishing waterways of Colmar's **Petite Venise**. Take a punt out on the water and watch the façades and the tourists peeping between the railings, hung with colourful hanging baskets.

Southern Wine Route: Colmar to Thann

Gorgeous wine villages lie along the slopes from Colmar down to Thann. Haughty but tattered medieval castle towers peer down from the Vosges heights above. The small towns along the way tend to be quiet, despite their rich religious legacies. Roads west of these towns and villages lead rapidly up into the Ballons des Vosges, the big pudding-shaped mountains of southern Alsace, dotted with tiny ski resorts.

For the benefit of the tourists, triangular old **Turckheim** is still 'patrolled' by a loud nightwatchman every evening between May and October. Within its three gateways, central Place Turenne is named after the French general who masterminded a tough winter campaign in these parts between 1674 and 1675 against the imperial army and won Alsace for Louis XIV. Beyond the Flemish-gabled Hôtel de Ville rises the church spire, as colourful as the village houses with its green diamond patterning. Even the hospital looks utterly enchanting. The village **museum** is devoted to the battle for the Colmar pocket in the Second World War.

Delightful circular old timberframe streets surround the centre of **Eguisheim**, disputed birthplace of Pope Leo IX, alias Bruno d'Eguisheim. His statue stands above a fountain. Painted medallions on the ceiling of a neo-Romanesque **chapel** nearby tell events in his life. He was elected pontiff in 1048, and is said to have tried hard to encourage peace in Europe. The soaring 13th-century Gothic tower of the main church is regularly graced by a nesting stork.

More lovely wine villages lie south. A single red stone tower stands out at **Gueberschwihr**, the remnants of the Romanesque church. Surrounded by tall hedges of vines, **Pfaffenheim** has delightfully powdery coloured houses. **Rouffach** makes a more substantial stop and is less overrun by tourists. Its architectural legacy is of dignified Rhenish Renaissance buildings, and with its array of scrolled gables, the centre looks Flemish.

Popular routes head up steeply into the Vosges west of Colmar. From Turckheim, one road quickly rises to **Les Trois-Epis**. In the late 15th century, a travelling smith was

Getting Around

Some **trains** between Colmar and Mulhouse stop at Rouffach. Take the local line west from Colmar to Turckheim, Gunsbach and Munster. Another local line from Mulhouse heads west to Thann and various other little stations.

Tourist Information

Turckheim: Corps de Garde, **t** 03 89 27 38 44, *www.turckheim-alsace.com.*
Eguisheim: 22A Grand'rue, **t** 03 89 23 40 33.
Munster: 1 Rue du Couvent, **t** 03 89 77 31 80. *www.la-vallee-de-munster.com.*
Guebwiller: 5 Place St-Léger, **t** 03 89 76 10 63, *www.tourisme-guebwiller-soultz.com.*

Where to Stay and Eat

Eguisheim ✉ 68420
★★★**Hostellerie du Château**, 2 Rue du Château, **t** 03 89 23 72 00 (*expensive–moderate*). 12 rooms. Smart and expensive, by fountain and chapel. *Closed Jan.*
★★**Hostellerie du Pape**, 10 Grand-Rue, **t** 03 89 41 41 21, *info@hostellerie-pape.com* (*moderate*). Special for a two-star. The restaurant (*expensive–moderate*) is atmospheric too. *Closed Jan; restaurant closed Mon and Tues.*

Rouffach ✉ 68250
★★★★**Château d'Isenbourg**, **t** 03 89 78 58 50, *isenbourg@grandesetapes.fr* (*luxury–expensive*). Dominating the vineyards, flanked by a curious tower, this place once belonged to those decadent bishops of Strasbourg. Now

its posh 19th-century frame offers 40 luxurious rooms and two fine restaurants (*very expensive–expensive*), one set in a vaulted cellar. *Closed 16 Jan–10 Mar; restaurant closed Wed and Sat lunch.*

Guebwiller ✉ 68500
★★★★**Château de la Prairie**, Allée des Marronniers, **t** 03 89 74 28 57, *prairie@ chateauxhotels.com* (*moderate*). Elegant little 19th-century château, with 20 luxurious rooms. More French than Alsatian.

Guebwiller-Murbach ✉ 68530
★★★★**Hostellerie St-Barnabé**, 53 Rue de Murbach, **t** 03 89 62 14 14, *hostellerie. st.barnabe@wanadoo.fr* (*expensive–moderate*). Excellent hotel on the quiet road between Guebwiller and Murbach. Fine cuisine too (*expensive*). *Closed Jan; restaurant closed Wed lunch.*

Soultz/Jungholtz-Thierenbach ✉ 68500
★★★**Résidence Les Violettes**, Jungholtz-Thierenbach, **t** 03 89 76 91 19, *lesviolettes2@ wanadoo.fr* (*expensive*). 25 rooms. Set against a backdrop of trees above Soultz, this well-run hotel is immaculately kept inside and out. Restaurant (*very expensive*). *Restaurant closed Mon.*

Thann ✉ 68800
★★★**Hôtel du Parc**, 23 Rue Kléber, **t** 03 89 37 37 47, *hduparc@hrnet.fr* (*very expensive–expensive*). The bright yellow façade of this romantic hotel hides Italian touches inside. Restaurant (*expensive*).

halted here by a figure of the Virgin, who warned him that unless the locals mended their wicked ways they would be struck by the plague. If they repented, then they would know prosperous times, symbolized by three ears of corn she proffered in her right hand. The locals chose to change. The corny story has made Les Trois-Epis surprisingly popular, although the resort itself is a bit dull. Walkers use it as a base for hikes up to the glacial lakes, the **Lac Noir** and the **Lac Blanc**.

The trenches of **Le Linge** seem lost in the most unlikely of locations high up in the Vosges, but bitter fighting raged here in 1915 and 1916. A war museum recalls the campaign, and the trenches are remarkably preserved with their stone walls, white crosses rising out of the ground between them marking bodies found in recent decades. Even today some areas are out of bounds.

Munster carries its Irish name because monks came here from the Emerald Isle in the 7th century to evangelize the region. The abbey closed at the Revolution, and much of the village was destroyed in the First World War. Its fame now rests on smelly cheese. A wing of the abbey holds the headquarters of the **Parc Naturel Régional des Ballons des Vosges**. Gunsbach just down from Munster was where Albert Schweitzer (*see* pp.610–11) spent his childhood and had a house built for himself in 1928. Although he worked so much in Africa, he returned here regularly, and his study has been left more or less as it was when he died.

Heading higher into the Vosges, a little south of the **Col de la Schlucht** pass you come to **Hohneck**, one of the very highest peaks in the Vosges at 4,467 ft. Cars wind up to the simple hotel-restaurant close to the summit, which means it's hardly tranquil, but massive views open up in all directions from the mountain's bald pate.

The popular resorts of **Gérardmer**, just in Lorraine, and **Xonrupt-Longemer**, lie next to the prettiest lake in the Vosges, **Lac de Longemer**, pines coming right down to the water's edge. This glacial 'sea' is the venue for all sorts of water sports, and you can take a boat cruise or a *pédalo* to enjoy it at a gentle pace.

Back on the Rhine side of the Vosges, along the Alsace wine route, a trio of splendidly different churches in red Vosges stone mark **Guebwiller**. It may not be the prettiest town in the region, but it isn't swamped by tourists, and has plenty of character, overseen on one side by extremely steep terraced vineyards. The three churches all lie just off the Rue de la République. **St-Léger** is the oldest, its Romanesque-Gothic façade flanked by twin towers, striking criss-cross patterning decorating its gable. The long Gothic **Sts Peter and Paul** formed part of a Dominican abbey. Now a cultural centre, its choir features an exhibition on the Dominicans in Alsace, while the nave serves as a concert venue. Most startling of Guebwiller's churches is the giant neoclassical **Notre-Dame**. Built from 1760 to 1785 for the last prince-cum-abbot of Murbach abbey above Guebwiller, the architecture may seem sober on the outside, but the interior looks like an enormous terracotta masterpiece ready for firing in the kiln. Stunning Corinthian columns hold up the vast nave, and the choir has a Baroque cascade of a centrepiece illustrating the Assumption of the Virgin.

The **Grand Ballon**, the highest mountain in the French Vosges at 4,671ft, is a sensational viewing point. You can climb up to the base of the radar station and walk round the open-air gallery with viewing tables. On clear days you can see as far as the Alps, and on most days the views down over the last black edges of the Vosges to the vast plain from Belfort to the Rhine are breathtaking.

Flanked by vine slopes and a fragment of old castle, **Thann** has a Gothic church teeming with statuary and carved figures. Even the high buttresses are embellished. The witch's eye – a tower fallen on its side intact – is a local landmark.

The best place to appreciate the romantically wooded Thur valley is **Husseren-Weserling**, a pretty village in which a large textiles factory still produces high-quality fabric which you can buy from the factory shop. The textile tradition goes back to the Ancien Régime, when the village had the only textile factory in Alsace given the French royal seal of approval. A new, slickly presented **textile museum** has been opened alongside the factory.

One Marquis de Pezay, in 1770, summed up the spot you'll find yourself in by climbing to the top of the **Ballon d'Alsace**: one foot in Alsace, the other in Lorraine, with Franche-Comté just an arm's length away. A belligerent equestrian statue of Joan of Arc indicates that, officially at least, the Ballon d'Alsace lies just in Lorraine.

The combination of beautiful houses gathered from across Alsace, well-tended gardens, farm animals and traditional craftspeople is a recipe for mass tourist success at the **Ecomusée d'Alsace** outside **Pulversheim**. This artificial village was deliberately put up in a deserted area, which it has successfully revived. From the tallest old building, a stocky timberframe tower, you can see the Vosges in the distance as well as the storks 'encouraged' to settle on the chimneys. You are free to wander, but the explanatory panels and the demonstrations are only in French and German, although there is a guide to the site in English.

Below the Southern Vosges: Mulhouse

Historically, Mulhouse long lay out on a limb. While the rest of Alsace became French in the 17th century, the Republic of Mulhouse joined the Swiss Confederation, and only in 1798 decided to join the French Republic. This was the birthplace of the Jewish army officer **Alfred Dreyfus**, who was so infamously framed by the French army at the close of the 19th century, although it was of course annexed to Germany for most of his troubled life. Mulhouse today boasts a host of museums.

Outside the centre, the best known is the massive **Musée National de l'Automobile (Collection Schlumpf)** (*open daily 10–6; adm*) which gives pride of place to its Bugatti collection. Train-lovers might prefer the equally large **Musée Français du Chemin de Fer** (*open April–Sept daily 9–6, otherwise till 5; adm*). A state-of-the-art electricity museum, the **Musée Electropolis** (*open July–Aug daily 10–6; rest of year closed Mon; adm*) stands next door. The **Musée du Papier-Peint at Rixheim** (*open June–mid-Sept daily 9–12 and 2–6; otherwise Wed–Mon 10–12 and 2–6; closed Tues; adm*) is a charming museum, dedicated to the French people's long love affair with wallpaper.

Mulhouse has a lively old heart too. The Protestant **Temple St-Etienne** contains a stunning collection of 14th-century stained-glass windows, with a gallery that enables you to admire it close up. In the town hall, a wildly decorated 16th-century piece of Rhine architecture, the **Musée Historique** (*open May–Sept Wed–Mon 10–12 and 2–6; rest of year till 5; adm*) offers a ramble through local history. The **Musée des Beaux-Arts** (*open mid-June–Sept Wed–Mon 10–12 and 2–6; rest of year till 5; adm*) has sections on local painters. When you're all museumed out, escape into Mulhouse's pretty orchardy countryside, the **Sundgau**, producing fruit and heady fruit liqueurs.

Getting Around

There are direct **flights** to Basel-Mulhouse, **t** 03 89 90 25 77, from Edinburgh and New York (Newark). Mulhouse is on the **train** line from Paris-Gare de l'Est to Basel in Switzerland.

Tourist Information

Mulhouse: 9 Av Foch, **t** 03 89 35 48 48, *www.tourism-mulhouse.com*.

Burgundy and Beyond

Burgundy

pp.568–9

pp.568–9

pp.266–7

pp.374–5

p.708

pp.660–61

20 km
10 miles

N

Highlights

1 Religious halts around the Yonne
2 Medieval thought in stone at Vézelay and Autun
3 Dijon's many fruitful delights
4 The Côte d'Or golden wine route
5 The Loireside surprise of Nevers and La Charité

Food and Wine

The Burgundians are very proud of their culinary traditions, which often combine alcohol with food. *Bœuf bourguignon* and *coq au vin* are famed regional dishes, while wine sauces are a great favourite. *Œufs en meurette* is a delicious recipe in which wine is combined with eggs. Bacon, pork, onions and mushrooms are often thrown into traditional Burgundian sauces; mushrooms are still quite easy to find in the region's many woods. Snails too are a regular feature on local menus. White Charolais cattle graze across large parts of southern Burgundy. The flatlands of the Bresse produce the white-plumed blue-stockinged *poulets de Bresse*, chickens with a formidable culinary reputation, and their own AOC.

Dijon is of course reputed for mustard, gingerbread and blackcurrants, which go into making the intense liqueur, *crème de cassis*.

Most Burgundy wines grow on the eastern side of the region, along the slopes of the Saône valley. Heading south from Dijon past Beaune, the Côte de Nuits and the Côte de Beaune combine to make the legendary Côte d'Or. Continuing southwards, the Côte Chalonnaise and the Mâconnais also yield splendid wines, sold at more reasonable prices. Then comes brash Beaujolais of the famous young fresh wines. Chablis, in the northwest of Burgundy, produces a popular white wine. In the west is Pouilly-sur-Loire with its noted white Pouilly-Fumé. One of Burgundy's finest cheeses, Epoisses, is matured in a marc, or liqueur.

Lush Burgundy (Bourgogne to the French) is synonymous with wine, and remains surprisingly rural. But there were three periods when Burgundian doings profoundly changed the history not just of France but also of western Europe. First, as the Astérix comics remind their readers, this is where the Gauls met with their decisive defeat against Caesar, at Alésia in 52 BC. The second period came in early medieval times, when powerful monastic orders took root at Cluny and Cîteaux and then spread their influence across the continent. The third period, in the 14th and 15th centuries, saw the proud dukes of Burgundy, difficult, dangerous cousins of the kings of France, swallow up Flanders and Holland as well as parts of northern France. Dijon flourished as their capital. Beaune, the historic capital of the earlier Capetian dukes, now has the distinction of being capital of the wine trade. Later castles decorate the land.

South of diminutive modern-day Burgundy are the Bourbonnais, home of the notorious spa town of Vichy, and bibulous Beaujolais. On the opposite side of the Saône, the flat, watery Bresse is the last area that has sneaked into this chapter.

Northwestern Burgundy

The Yonne river starts in the wooded hills of the Morvan and flows northwest to join the Seine near Fontainebleau. Along the way stand two mighty cathedral cities, Sens and Auxerre, although they have been somewhat eclipsed by much smaller Vézelay and Avallon. Pontigny and vinous Chablis make popular stops along the Serein river. The fine châteaux of Tanlay and Ancy-le-Franc lie by the Armançon.

Getting Around

This is the area of Burgundy closest to Paris-Orly **airport**, from where the A6 or A5 swiftly bring you here. Sens has a **railway** station on the TGV line from Melun, southeast of Paris, heading for Marseille. Auxerre, Avallon and Tonnerre also have useful railway stations.

Tourist Information

Sens: Place Jean Jaurès, **t** 03 86 65 19 49, *www.office-de-tourisme-sens.com.*

Auxerre: 1–2 Quai de la République, **t** 03 86 52 06 19, *www.ot-auxerre.fr.*

Vézelay: Rue St-Pierre, **t** 03 86 33 23 69, *www.vezelaytourisme.com.*

Avallon: 4 Rue Bocquillot, **t** 03 86 34 14 19.

Chablis: 1 Quai du Biez, **t** 03 86 42 80 80, *www.chablis.net.*

Tonnerre: 12 Rue François Mitterrand, **t** 03 86 55 14 48, *www.tonnerre.fr.*

Where to Stay and Eat

Joigny ✉ 89300

★★★★La Côte St-Jacques, 14 Fbg de Paris, **t** 03 86 62 09 70, *lorain@relaischateaux.fr* (*luxury–expensive*). Overlooking the Yonne river, one of the most sumptuous hotels in Burgundy with some of the finest cuisine in France. *Closed Jan.*

★★★Le Rive Gauche, Rue du Port au Bois, **t** 03 86 91 46 66, *lorain@dial.oleane.com* (*moderate*). Less exciting, but run by the same family and very comfortable. *Restaurant closed Sun eve Nov–Feb.*

Auxerre ✉ 89000

★★★Le Parc des Maréchaux, 6 Av Foch, **t** 03 86 51 43 77, *contact@hotel-parcmarechaux.com* (*moderate*). Elegant 19th-century property, tucked away just outside the historic centre.

A wonderful and not too pricey hotel. 25 stylish, relaxing rooms named after Napoleonic marshals.

★★★Le Maxime, 2 Quai de la Marine, **t** 03 86 52 14 19, *hotel-maxime@ipoint.fr* (*moderate*). The posh option on the busy but picturesque road down beside the river Yonne. Restaurant.

★★Le Seignelay, 2 Rue du Pont, **t** 03 86 52 03 48 (*inexpensive*). Sweet-looking hotel in the historic centre, with timberframe front, courtyard and restaurant (*moderate*).

Jean-Luc Barnabet, 14 Quai de la République, **t** 03 86 51 68 88 (*expensive*). A 17th-century coaching inn with delightful cuisine. *Closed Sun eve, Mon, and Tues lunch.*

Le Jardin Gourmand, 56 Bd Vauban, **t** 03 86 51 53 52 (*expensive*). An artist of a chef serving experimental but refined fare. *Closed Tues and Wed, and 2 weeks Nov.*

Vincelottes ✉ 89290

Auberge Les Tilleuls, 12 Quai de l'Yonne, **t** 03 86 42 22 13 (*inexpensive*). A riverside inn with plain rooms and a popular restaurant (*expensive–moderate*) which has a curious terrace by the water. *Closed Wed eve, Thurs out of season, and 20 Dec–20 Feb.*

Vézelay ✉ 89450

★★★Le Pontot, Place du Pontot, **t** 03 86 33 24 40 (*expensive*). With its secret garden and protecting fortified walls, the kind of delightful, exclusive place where even if you aren't staying you'll wish you could have a good look round. Very comfortable and very close to the church. *Closed 16 Oct–19 April.*

★★★La Poste et le Lion d'Or, Place du Champ de Foire, **t** 03 86 33 21 23, *lion.dor.vezelay@wanadoo.fr* (*moderate*). Most comfortable option in the busy lower part of the village, with a lovely terrace. *Closed 12 Nov–31 Mar.*

★★Le Compostelle, Place du Champ de Foire, **t** 03 86 33 28 63, *le.compostelle@wanadoo.fr*

Sens

Sandwiched between the Ile de France and Champagne, Sens was a major Gallo-Roman town called *Agedincum*. The first bishops established themselves here in the 4th century, and by the 8th century they styled themselves archbishop of the Gauls and the Germans. Up to the 12th century they reserved the right to crown new kings of France. One medieval chronicler referred to the archbishop of Sens, who governed

(*inexpensive*). Popular, with 18 modern rooms, many with good views of the countryside. *Closed Feb.*

Cabalus, Rue St-Pierre, **t** 03 86 33 20 66 (*inexpensive*). Atmospheric B&B in the former medieval hostelry of the abbey. The rooms are artistically sparse and charitably cheap. The café downstairs is charming.

St-Père-sous-Vézelay ✉ 89450

***L'Espérance, **t** 03 86 33 39 10, *marc-meneau @wanadoo.fr* (*very expensive*). You can't get a more luxurious place to stay around Vézelay. The conservatory dining room is a Mecca for food-lovers (*very expensive*). Marc Meneau has opened a new, cheaper restaurant, **L'Entrevigne** (*moderate*) next door; try Sunday brunch. *Closed Feb; restaurant closed Tues lunch and Wed eve. Book.*

***Le Crispol, Hameau de Fontette, **t** 03 86 33 26 25, *crispol@wanadoo.fr* (*moderate*). A smart, small modern hotel, well located on a hill with views of Vézelay. Restaurant (*expensive–moderate*). *Closed Jan–Feb.*

Avallon ✉ 89200

****Hostellerie de la Poste, 13 Place Vauban, **t** 03 86 34 16 16, *www.hostelleriedelaposte. com* (*expensive*). A central 18th-century posting inn, with its own cobbled courtyard and modern interiors. Restaurant. *Closed Dec; restaurant closed Sun eve and Mon.*

***Hostellerie du Moulin des Ruats, Vallée du Cousin, **t** 03 86 34 97 00, *ruats@chateauxhotels.com* (*moderate*). Former flour mill by the river in the valley south of Avallon. Well converted too, with a very pleasant restaurant (*expensive*). *Closed mid-Nov–mid-Feb; restaurant closed Mon, and eves Tues–Sat.*

Le Moulin des Templiers, Vallée du Cousin, **t 03 86 34 10 80, *www.hotel-moulin-des-templiers.com* (*inexpensive*). Des Ruat's smaller neighbour: another comfortable mill with 12 rooms. Breakfast in the garden.

Avallon Vauban, 53 Rue de Paris, **t 03 86 34 36 99, *www.avallonvaubanhotel.com* (*inexpensive*). Nicely done-up old coaching inn in the centre of town, with good restaurant and garden.

Vault-de-Lugny ✉ 89200

****Château de Vault de Lugny, 11 Rue du Château, **t** 03 86 34 07 86, *www.lugny.com* (*very expensive*). A splendid place with a medieval look, surrounded by a moat. A dozen superb rooms with antique furnishings and four-posters. Restaurant for residents only (*dinner only*). *Closed Nov–Mar.*

Chablis ✉ 89800

***Hostellerie des Clos, 18 Rue Jules Rathier, **t** 03 86 42 10 63, *host.clos@wanadoo.fr* (*moderate*). The posh option, with 26 spacious and modern rooms. Fine restaurant reputed for its Burgundian dishes (*very expensive–expensive*).

Relais de la Belle Etoile, 4 Rue des Moulins, **t 03 86 18 96 08 (*moderate*). Very attractive building in the historic centre.

Ligny-le-Châtel ✉ 89144

Relais St-Vincent, 14 Grande Rue, **t 03 86 47 53 38, *relais.saint.vincent@libertysurf.fr* (*inexpensive*). Appealing timberframe old house with country cooking (*moderate*).

Ancy-le-Franc ✉ 89160

Hostellerie du Centre, 34 Grande Rue, **t 03 86 75 15 11, *hostellerieducentre@ diaphora.com* (*inexpensive*). A comfortable traditional option with 22 rooms. Restaurant (*moderate*). *Closed 15 Nov–15 Mar.*

Noyers ✉ 89310

La Vieille Tour, Place du Grenier à Sel, **t** 03 86 82 87 69 (*inexpensive*). A relaxing and atmospheric cheap hotel in an historic house in the village. *Closed Oct–Mar. Book.*

ecclesiastically over Paris and Chartres and five other major bishoprics, as 'a second pope', and briefly (1163–4), the real Pope Alexander III resided here. Thomas à Becket spent several years in exile at Sens too. It wasn't until the 1620s that Paris was finally granted its own archbishopric.

The **Musée de Sens** (*open June–Sept daily 10–12 and 2–6; rest of year Mon, Tues, Thurs and Fri 2–6, Wed, Sat and Sun 10–12 and 2–6; adm, free 1st Sun of month*) occupies the truly palatial archbishops' palace adjoining the cathedral. On one side stands the long Gothic hall where the bishops would meet, its roofs covered in patterned tiles, a Burgundian trademark. Justice was meted out here, and the prison area contains centuries-old prisoners' graffiti. The brick and limestone façades of the other two sides of the courtyard are decorated with rich Renaissance motifs. Downstairs you can discover one of the best Gallo-Roman collections in France. The main religious treasures of the museum were acquired by medieval bishops of Sens, jewelled reliquaries only upstaged by saintly vestments probably woven in Persia or Byzantium. But the most famous cloth of all belonged to Thomas à Becket. His ceremonial garb, including an enormous alb, or linen piece, and his rather worn liturgical slippers, were considered extremely important relics after his assassination in Canterbury cathedral.

The **cathedral of St Stephen** has formidable credentials. Work began on it in the 1130s in Romanesque style, but from as early as the 1140s new Gothic forms were adopted, as at St-Denis in Paris. The architect, William of Sens, went on to remodel the choir end of Canterbury cathedral, helping export Gothic to England. The imposing west front is dedicated to St Stephen, shown in a dour statue, with the central portal tympanum also devoted to him. The other portals show scenes from the lives of John the Baptist and the Virgin. Inside, the vast Gothic nave is grimly grey, but some of the stained-glass panels count among the finest in Burgundy.

South along the Yonne

The old streets of **Joigny** rise sharply above the Yonne south of Sens. Some extraordinary carved timberframe houses stand out along the close-packed streets, one decorated with a Tree of Jesse, another with an equestrian figure who also features on the Gothic church of **St-Thibault**, dedicated to St Theobald of Provins, who went a-wandering all round Europe. It contains naive Renaissance touches: carved medallions and grotesques and a choir dripping with pendant bosses; the remarkable Smiling Virgin was carved in the 14th century. The nearby Renaissance church of **St-André** has an ornate entrance lintel with a striking figure of St Andrew on his skewed cross. From the Renaissance **Château de Gondi** above, you get extensive views along the Yonne valley. Vines grow on the still higher slope, the Côte St-Jacques, known above all for producing a Vin Gris (a rosé). Down on the water, you'll find Joigny's river port.

Auxerre

The cathedral of Auxerre rises like a great Gothic vessel moored on the Yonne. A second enormous church, dedicated to St Germain, rises like another medieval ocean-liner docked by the river. Auxerre (Gallo-Roman *Autessiodurum*), long an important centre, lay on one of the main routes through Gaul linking Lyon with Boulogne, and the Mediterranean with the Channel.

The **Cathédrale St-Etienne** provides a splendid example of the Rayonnant Gothic style: sophisticated, yet simple in its sense of order. The cathedral dominates the roofscape of the town, harmoniously covered with the same earthen tiles as the buildings around it. Only one tower rises from the west front; the other one fell down in 1217, just two years after construction. Coming to the façade, you are greeted by superb portals full of sculptures, even if many were cruelly hacked at the Revolution.

Inside, the rhythm of the plain Gothic bays is impressive; the huge vaults of the crossing look slightly bowed by the pressure of their role. Each transept is embellished by a rose window containing Renaissance glass. In the ambulatory, the deep blue stained-glass windows are dense with biblical and saintly scenes separated by wonderful blood-red rings. The crypt, from an earlier Romanesque cathedral, is a wonky structure resting on simple rounded arches. The end chapel contains a couple of remarkable frescoes based on the Book of Revelations: Christ riding a white horse, accompanied by four angels on horseback, and a Christ in Majesty.

Just a short walk from the cathedral stands the **Abbaye St-Germain**. Germain was born in Auxerre in 378, and took up the torch from St Martin (*see* 'Tours') in the race to convert Gaul to Christianity. As bishop of Auxerre he greatly encouraged Christian learning in the city. Germain also travelled extensively: he probably studied for a time in Rome, and made it as far west as Wales and as far east as Ravenna in Italy, where he died in 448. The empress there had his body sent back to Auxerre, where it was placed in a small oratory which the bishop had had prepared for himself. Clothilde, wife of Clovis, founded the abbey some time around the beginning of the 6th century. In the 9th century Count Conrad of Auxerre had a new edifice constructed, including what is now the best-preserved Carolingian crypt in France. A later Romanesque abbey built around this burned down in the 13th century, except for the Tour St-Jean. The whole messy complex is now the **Musée d'Art et d'Histoire d'Auxerre** (*open June–Sept Wed–Mon 10–6.30; rest of year Wed–Mon 10–12 and 2–6; closed Tues; adm*).

There are regular guided tours of the crypt. The *confessio* at the centre, held up on columns taken from a Gallo-Roman building, contains a decoy sarcophagus of St Germain; a hole shows where the real one could be hidden in times of emergency. The north side of the crypt is decorated with 9th-century frescoes, the oldest Christian ones in France, but the scenes are very faded. The rest of the museum is spread out around the chalky-white classical 17th-century cloisters.

St-Pierre, also rising haughtily above the Yonne river and city roofs, has a lovely square Flamboyant Gothic tower, but inside the style is sober round-arched classicism. The rest of Auxerre's historic centre proves a delight to wander round. It has the second largest area of protected old streets in Burgundy after Dijon, tightly bound by boulevards which follow the lines of the former fortifications.

Vézelay

Vézelay, a very pretty but overhyped fortified hilltop village, is dominated by a famed church, **La Madeleine**, which grew into a great pilgrimage centre on the back of a big Christian fib. The first abbey of Vézelay was founded in the 9th century. The story goes that an early abbot sent a monk to Provence to save the relics of Mary Magdalene (*see* 'Stes Maries de Mer', pp.778–80) from Saracen raids, and around the year 1000 the rumour spread that Mary Magdalene's bones now rested in Vézelay, a story sanctioned by the papacy in 1058. The overexcited abbots also put in claims to having relics of Martha and Lazarus. Work on the splendid abbey church began around 1096, and most of it was built in the 12th century. The best sculptors carved the capitals and tympanums. Important figures visited the abbey, exploiting its renown for their own advancement; most notoriously, St Bernard set the Western Christian world alight in 1146 with his preaching here in favour of a Second Crusade.

As well as serving as a crusading centre, Vézelay became one of the four major starting points in France for the pilgrimage to Santiago de Compostela. In 1217 St Francis also sent a couple of trusted friars to set up the first Franciscan monastery in France here. Louis IX, known as St Louis, came on several occasions to Vézelay as a pilgrim. But before the end of the 13th century the abbey would be discredited: the monks at St-Maximin in Provence had been instructed to try to find Mary Magdalene's remains in their abbey, which they promptly claimed to have done. During the Revolution most of Vézelay's abbey buildings were brought down, and a fire in 1819 saw the church fall into ruin. Its restoration by Viollet-le-Duc began in 1840.

After the disappointment of the stilted carving on the outer façade, the interior is very striking. In the celebrated tympanum, energy emanates from the massive, confident Pentecostal Christ surrounded by his apostles, chatting in animated fashion, and spreading the Good Word to a curious representation of the peoples of the world: Jews, Arabs, Byzantines, Ethiopians, Phrygians, Armenians and Scythians can all be identified in the cavalcade, along with giants, pygmies and 'the ones with big ears'.

The vast Romanesque nave appears to have been transported from Moorish Spain. Different coloured stone makes for a decorative patterning, and there is a fabulous array of capitals on the columns. Pick up the detailed guide to the capitals. Violence is a main theme: try counting the number of swords and daggers drawn.

Along Vézelay's main village street, art exhibitions, wine shops and other tourist boutiques occupy the magnificent cellars below many of the houses. A walk around the medieval ramparts offers calm, splendid views all round.

Around Vézelay

Down in the valley below Vézelay, **St-Père** makes a quieter stop. An abbey existed here first, but its destruction by Viking raiders led to the establishment of Vézelay's on its more easily defended hilltop. But St-Père has a delightful Gothic church of its own, **Notre-Dame**, with an elaborate screen of a façade decorated with statues. A lovely three-tiered tower rises from above this. The interior is luminous, the vaults finished by charmingly decorated key stones. Set back in a little courtyard, the **archaeological museum** (*open April–Oct daily 10–12.30 and 1.30–6.30; adm*) contains a few remarkable finds from the nearby **Fontaines Salées**, which were being exploited at least 2,500 years ago and remain as salty as ever.

Beautiful hilltop **Avallon** remains relatively peaceful thanks to its neighbour Vézelay's all-consuming fame. Its old streets are still contained in remnants of medieval walls, looking dramatically over the narrow Cousin valley. On this side stand intriguing vestiges of the Romanesque church of **St-Lazare** which was supposed to contain a relic of Lazarus. In a section of town wall nearby, the collections of the **Musée de l'Avallonnais** (*open May–Oct Wed–Mon 2–6; closed Tues; adm*) reveal that civilization on this rocky outcrop dates back to Gallo-Roman times and beyond. The **Musée du Costume** (*open early April–Oct daily 10.30–12.30 and 1.30–5.30; adm*) offers elaborate displays on period fashions inside a well-to-do bourgeois townhouse from the Ancien Régime.

The splendid 12th-century **Château de Bazoches** (*open Easter–early Nov daily 9.30–12 and 2.15–6; adm*) surveys an unspoilt valley on the northern edge of the Morvan and commands views up to hilltop Vézelay. The castle dates in large part from the second half of the 12th century. Richard Cœur de Lion and Philippe Auguste are said to have stayed here before heading out on the Third Crusade, but the man most associated with Bazoches is Sébastien Le Prestre de Vauban, the great military strategist. Vauban was born in modest circumstances in nearby St-Léger-de-Forcheret. Through brilliance and hard work he became one of the key figures in the reign of Louis XIV, devoting most of his life to planning meticulous sieges and fortifications. The successful taking of Maastricht in 1672 was one of his finest military achievements. In reward, Louis XIV gave Vauban a grant of 80,000 *livres*, with which the Morvan-boy-made-good was able to buy the local château and see to its refurbishment.

The castle has been lovingly restored in recent decades. The tour takes you round elegant rooms, where the 17th-century Aubusson tapestry with peacocks and the Chinese lacquer work stand out. Splendid portraits depict royalty. Vauban had the long gallery constructed specially to serve as an office to draw up plans for his fortifications; there are scale models, and explanations of his theories on defence. Vauban died in Paris, but was buried in Bazoches church.

East of Bazoches, the unremarkable village where Vauban was born honours its most famous son well. For a start it has changed its name from St-Léger-de-Forcheret to **St-Léger-Vauban**. It has also created a small museum, the pleasingly didactic **Maison Vauban** (*open late Mar–early Nov daily 10–12.30 and 2–6.30; adm*). Vauban was a bold political thinker as well as a military strategist, who wrote on economics, taxation, social questions, land management and the French colonies. While an ardent royalist, he argued against the abuse of privileges and for a lessening of the tax burden on the poor – he was a caring patriot, ahead of his times.

The Serein and Armançon Valleys

Chardonnay (*see* box, over) has brought success to the little wine town of **Chablis**, which sits below the hills of the Serein east of Auxerre. Swanky estates lie behind gates on the outskirts, but the vats belonging to the cooperative don't look too pretty.

Along the Serein north of Chablis, Cistercian **Pontigny** was founded in 1114, the second of the four so-called daughters of Cîteaux (*see* p.641). Thomas à Becket found refuge here in 1164, while Edmund Rich (St Edme in these parts), an intriguing figure who fought against Henry III for the independence of the English Church, was buried here. Pontigny witnessed a 20th-century intellectual flowering when the philosopher Paul Desjardins drew literary figures here for his Décades meetings between the wars.

For a Cistercian building, Pontigny's church façade has a certain stylishness. Inside, however, all is sobriety – Romanesque moving towards Gothic, vast, uncluttered and

Chablis

Chablis is generally considered to produce a wonderfully crisp chardonnay (the variety is sometimes known in the area as Beaunois). Chablis is only a small wine-producing area: under 3,000 hectares of land have been designated as suitable for producing the *appellation* wines, of which there are four: Petit Chablis, Chablis, Chablis Premier Cru and Chablis Grand Cru, in ascending order of merit. A mere 100 or so hectares are deemed capable of producing the best quality Grand Cru Chablis – the very finest vineyards lie on exclusive terrain northeast of town.

pure. The Baroque additions come as a bit of a surprise: on a screen with paintings of a stormy *Annunciation* and *Flight into Egypt*; with the feathery-looking putti floating on the ornately carved choir stalls; and in an extraordinary stone baldaquin at the end of the choir, serving as melodramatic setting for St Edmund's reliquary chest.

East of Chablis in the Armançon valley, **Tonnerre** boasts one of the oldest and largest medieval hospitals in France, as well as arguably the finest washhouse. With its mysterious watery pool emerging straight out of the ground, the **Fosse Dionne** is tucked away in a quiet corner of the old town. The covered colonnade adds to the feeling that this is a place of devotion, rather than somewhere to clean dirty linen.

The massive **Hôtel-Dieu** (*open June–Sept Wed–Mon 10.30–12.30 and 1.30–6.30; rest of period early April–Oct weekends and public hols 10–12 and 1.30–6.30; adm*) was built at the end of the 13th century, thanks to generous donations from Marguerite of Burgundy, the young widow of Charles d'Anjou, King of Sicily and Naples, who with-drew to Tonnerre when her husband died. A splendid timberframe ceiling covers the length of the building, in which the sick would have been looked after in beds placed in alcoves along the walls. The hospital museum preserves some of its founding documents, and displays gruesome old surgical instruments.

The **Château de Tanlay** (*open April–15 Nov Wed–Mon, visits at 9.30, 10.30, 11.30, 2.15, 3, 3.45, 4.30 and 5.15, plus one at 5.45 in July and Aug; closed Tues; adm*), a short way east of Tonnerre, oozes style and excess. Built in light local limestone, topped by black slate roofs, this innovative château was begun in the middle of the 16th century. The two side wings end with big-breasted cupolas, and the central section is flanked by two striking, pilaster-decorated towers. Not surprisingly, the interiors have their excesses and eccentricities too, including some magnificently grotesque fireplaces. The high-point is the so-called Tour de la Ligue, whose ceiling is covered with nude figures painted in the 16th-century Fontainebleau style. Catherine de Médicis features as Juno, Diane de Poitiers, her rival in Henri II's affections, as Venus, while the king himself appears, appropriately enough, as a two-faced Janus.

Along the Armançon from Tanlay, the sober **Château d'Ancy-le-Franc** (*open Easter–11 Nov, visits at 10, 11, 2, 3, 4 and 5, Easter–15 Sept till 6; adm*) was built according to the plans of Sebastiano Serlio in the mid-16th century for Antoine III de Clermont, Diane de Poitiers' brother-in-law. The plainish frame hides a riot of wall paintings, by the likes of Primaticcio, Nicolo dell'Abbate and the Burgundians André Meynassier and Philippe Quantin. In the Chamber of Judith and Holofernes, the biblical scenes take place against superb backgrounds; the Cabinet du Pasteur Fido features original wood panelling, and shepherds and shepherdesses by Philippe Quantin; and the Salon Louvois has superb gilded Renaissance grotesques on its coffered ceiling. The highlight is the splendid battle scene between Pompey and Caesar by dell'Abbate, full of terrible action. The Chambre des Fleurs, with its floral panels, and the Chambre des Muses, in which Primaticcio represents the liberal arts, introduce a calmer note.

The Morvan and Autun

Land of lakes, logging and, above all, endless wooded hills, the Morvan might be the geographical heart of Burgundy, but in tourist terms it lies off the beaten track. Château-Chinon is its main town, where the late President Mitterrand (nicknamed *Tonton* (uncle) or simply *Dieu* (God)) was long-time mayor, with a finger in every pie. The creation of the Parc Régional du Morvan in the 1970s has helped tourism develop, and a few little museums or *maisons* now highlight the park's main features.

The Maison du Parc at **St-Brisson** is a good place to pick up information on the area. The **Musée de la Résistance en Morvan** (*open June–mid-Sept Sat–Thurs 10–12.30 and*

Getting Around

This area is not easily accessible by public transport, but Autun has a **railway** station.

Tourist Information

St-Brisson: Maison du Parc, **t** 03 86 78 79 00.
Saulieu: 24 Rue d'Argentine, **t** 03 80 64 00 21.
Château-Chinon: Place Notre Dame, **t** 03 86 85 05 58, *otsi.chateau-chinon@wanadoo.fr*.
Autun: 2 Av Charles de Gaulle, **t** 03 85 86 80 38, *www.autun.com*.
Le Creusot: Château de la Verrerie, **t** 03 85 55 02 46, *www.creusot.net*.

Where to Stay and Eat

Saulieu ✉ 21210
★★★★**La Côte d'Or/Bernard Loiseau**, 2 Rue d'Argentine (N6), **t** 03 80 90 53 53 (*luxury–expensive*). Swanky hotel whose restaurant (*very expensive*), despite the tragic death of Bernard Loiseau, is still a Mecca for foodies. A few luxury and a few more modest rooms. *Closed 3 weeks Jan.*

St-Léger-sous-Beuvray ✉ 71990
★**Hôtel du Morvan**, **t** 03 85 82 51 06, *hotel.du. morvan@wanadoo.fr* (*inexpensive*). Basic,

pleasant little country hotel at the foot of Mont Beuvray.

Autun ✉ 71400
★★★★**Hôtel St-Louis et de la Poste**, 6 Rue de l'Arbalète, **t** 03 85 52 01 01, *louisposte@ aol.com* (*expensive–moderate*). Extremely nicely done rooms, not outrageously expensive, set around a courtyard where you can eat in summer (*expensive*). Napoleon stayed here. *Restaurant closed Sat lunch.*
★★★**Les Ursulines**, 14 Rue de Rivault, **t** 03 85 86 58 58, *welcome@hotelursulines.fr* (*moderate*). Once a convent, the 17th-century buildings have been transformed into a very comfortable hotel, just within the Gallo-Roman city walls at the top of the old town. The restaurant has character too.
★★★**Hostellerie du Vieux Moulin**, **t** 03 85 52 10 90 (*inexpensive*). Delicious food and wine at this quiet riverside address just out of town, surrounded by trees: lentils in truffle juice, the tenderest Burgundy *escargots* with mushrooms. But the rooms are badly in need of renovation. *Closed Dec–Mar; restaurant closed Sun eve and Mon out of season.*
★★**La Tête Noire**, 3 Rue de l'Arquebuse, **t** 03 85 86 59 99 (*inexpensive*). Characterful building, but there's a supermarket below it. Pleasant refurbished rooms and the restaurant isn't bad (*moderate*).

2–6, closed Fri; early April–May and mid-Sept–early Oct Sat, Sun and hols 10–12.30 and 2–6; adm) keeps alive the wretched stories of the wartime deportees, the martyred villages of the area, and the Resistance cells in the hills. **Saulieu**, somewhat spoilt by the busy road passing through it, is an eastern gateway into the park. The medieval **Basilique St-Andoche** is dedicated to an evangeliser from the Middle East martyred here in early Christian times. It has been messed about with down the centuries, but the nave's Romanesque capitals, carved by the Cluny school, still make for an impressive show. The adjoining **Musée Pompon** (*open April–Sept Wed–Mon 10–12.30 and 2–6; closed Tues; adm*) is named after a 19th-century animal sculptor of some repute born here and taught by Rodin, though his smooth style is very different.

South of St-Brisson, above the artificial **Lac de Settons**, several villages, notably Montsauche and Planchez, were completely destroyed by the Nazis in 1944 and have been rebuilt since the war. The town of **Château-Chinon** stands in a fine location, but it is not an attractive place. Mayor Mitterrand helped establish two big museums: the stylish **Musée du Costume** (*open July–Aug daily 10–1 and 2–7; Sept–June Wed–Mon 10–1 and 2–6, closed Tues; adm*); and the **Musée du Septennat** (*open same times; adm*), a hilarious absurdity, showing off ostentatious and outrageous gifts from around the world donated to Mitterrand during his time as president of France.

Bibracte, high up on Mont Beuvray, has officially been designated a site of national importance. It was the main fortified oppidum of the Aedui, the local Celtic tribe, and is one of the rare pre-Roman towns of which any vestiges remain in France. In recent times Mitterrand came, saw and inaugurated. A slick modern museum, the **Musée de Bibracte** (*open July–Aug daily 10–7; mid-Mar–June and Sept–mid-Nov Wed–Mon 10–6; closed Tues; adm*), explains the oppidum and puts it in the wider context of its Celtic times. Disappointingly few of the objects unearthed here are on display, but you can visit the archaeological digs free. Sections of ramparts and a gateway have been reconstructed; the location of the main street has also been identified. You'll need to use a great deal of imagination to recreate the oppidum; confusingly, the most substantial ruins up here formed part of a 15th-century Franciscan monastery. But the setting is majestic and, beyond a splendid beech wood, spectacular views open out on to the city of Autun and down over southern Burgundy.

Autun

Sloping up from the river Arroux, this city was one of the greatest of Roman Gaul. Two well-preserved monumental gateways stand strangely isolated on the edge of town, along with the more subdued remnants of a large theatre and a tower of the so-called Temple de Janus, now thought to have been dedicated to Mars. Built in the 1st century AD to control the territory of the Aedui tribe, the city lay along the Roman road between Lyon and Boulogne. It grew into an important centre of learning, renowned for its school of rhetoric. In medieval times the bishopric managed to secure what were claimed to be the relics of Lazarus, a major pull for pilgrims. The town would be greatly altered by the wealthy Rolin family in the 15th century.

It makes chronological sense to visit the archaeological, historical and art collections of the **Musée Rolin** (*open June–Aug Wed–Mon 10–12 and 2–6; rest of year*

Wed–Mon 2–5; closed Tues; adm) first to get some inkling of the grand Gallo-Roman city that once stood here. After the impressive classical pieces, go on to admire the Romanesque section, including the renowned and powerful depiction of Eve's temptation, a work attributed to the great Gislebertus, generally regarded as the finest French Romanesque sculptor, and one of the few whose name has survived. The museum also contains some excellent paintings from the late 15th and early 16th centuries. The most famous features Cardinal Jean Rolin – baggy eyes, wrinkles and all – thought to be by the Master of Moulins (*see* p.633).

The cathedral of **St-Lazare**, built to hold the relics of Lazarus, has a Romanesque body wearing a Flamboyant Gothic coat, commissioned by Cardinal Rolin. The soaring spire, the side chapels and the choir are all elaborate Gothic. Viollet-le-Duc's team got their hands on the west front in the 19th century and it shows. The tympanum, although spoilt by all the plaster around it, is decorated with one of the most celebrated works of Romanesque sculpture in France, signed by Gislebertus. The elongated figures play out their parts in the Last Judgement as St Michael and Satan weigh souls. The cathedral's capitals are superb, but you need a torch to illuminate them. You can appreciate some of the best close up by climbing from the choir to the chapterhouse. The most delightful one depicts the dream of the Magi, the three kings tucked up cosily together in bed, an angel coming to touch one on the hand.

Western Burgundy: the Puisaye and Nivernais

West of the Yonne and the Morvan hills, the quiet wooded countryside of the Puisaye and the Nivernais rolls down to the Loire. Colette spent her childhood in the Puisaye; many of the villages dream away in the past, but the number of tourist attractions has grown rapidly. The Loire forms the frontier between Burgundy and the Berry in the Nivernais. Nevers is famed for its pottery traditions, but also for its historic centre, and for the preserved body of Bernadette of Lourdes.

The Puisaye

Heading down from the busy Yonne river and Joigny into the Puisaye, try to make a detour to see the late-medieval wall paintings of skeletons in the church at **La Ferté-Loupière**: flesh-coloured and big-eyed, one eyes a baby in a cot while some of his colleagues play musical instruments and others adopt saucy poses. A short way south, the church of **Villiers-St-Benoît** contains a depiction of three lords meeting three skeletons from a medieval fable, a reminder that death may pounce at any time. Here the **Musée d'Art et d'Histoire de Puisaye** (*open Feb–15 Dec Wed–Mon 10–12 and 2–6; adm*) is set in a pretty 18th-century Puisaye home, resembling an elegant but cluttered roadside antiques shop.

The **Château de St-Fargeau** (*open April–early Nov daily 10–12 and 2–7; adm*), in little St-Fargeau, capital of the Puisaye, looks old-fashioned and messy while boasting possibly the largest towers of any château in France, thick and dumpy. Most of what

Getting Around

Cosne and Nevers have **railway** stations.

Tourist Information

St-Fargeau: Maison de la Puisaye, 3 Place de la République, **t** 03 86 74 15 72.
St-Sauveur-en-Puisaye: Parking du Château, **t** 03 86 45 61 31, *sier-stsauveur@wanadoo.fr*.
La Charité-sur-Loire: Place Ste-Croix, **t** 03 86 70 15 06. *www.ville-la-charite-sur-loire.fr*.
Nevers: Palais Ducal, **t** 03 86 68 46 00, *www.ville-nevers.fr*.

Where to Stay and Eat

Villiers-St-Benoît ✉ 89130

★★Relais St-Benoit, Rue Paul Huillard, **t** 03 86 45 73 42, *(inexpensive)*. Small inn with 6 rooms and a restaurant *(moderate)*. *Closed Feb, Sun eve, and Mon.*

Donzy ✉ 58220

★★Le Grand Monarque, 10 Rue de l'Etape, **t** 03 86 39 35 44, *grandmonarque@hotmail.com (inexpensive)*. Pleasing golden stone building with a slightly run-down charm but up-to-date décor. Restaurant *(moderate)*. *Closed Sun eve and Tues exc hols.*

La Charité-sur-Loire ✉ 58400

★★★Le Grand Monarque, 33 Quai Clémenceau, **t** 03 86 70 21 73, *le.grand.monarque@wanadoo.fr (moderate)*. Small hotel with good view of the Loire and excellent food. *Restaurant closed Fri eve and Sun in winter.*

Tintury

Guény, Fleury La Tour, **t** 03 86 84 12 42 *(inexpensive)*. Big, tranquil lakeside farmhouse with simple large B&B rooms in the quiet Nièvre countryside between Nevers and Château-Chinon. A really restful retreat. The retired farmer and his wife are very jolly.

you see today dates back to the 15th century, ordered for Antoine de Chabannes, favourite of Charles VII. When Louis XIV's awkward cousin Anne-Marie-Louise d'Orléans, alias La Grande Mademoiselle, was exiled here, she ordered Louis Le Vau to give the pile greater panache. The inner castle therefore looks more stately, but the displays inside are amateurish, and many of the rooms stand in a state of disrepair. You can wander freely around some rooms, but on the guided tour you are shown a few restored chambers – the dining room is the *pièce de résistance* with its curved corners, caramel wood panelling and marble fireplace. Restoration work began at the end of the 1970s, after the passionate M. Guyot acquired the property. It is partly financed by the spectacular summer evening shows which tell the story of the castle. Don't miss the tour of the attics, on a path measuring half a kilometre, taking you around the impressive oak timbers beneath the castle roofs.

In **St-Sauveur-en-Puisaye**, the wonderfully evocative new **Musée Colette** (*open April–Oct Wed–Mon 11–7; Mar, Nov and Dec weekends and public hols 2–6; adm*) is housed in the village château and pays homage to the taboo-breaking author, drama queen and animal lover. (Her bisexuality, sometimes shockingly right-wing views and neglect of her daughter go unmentioned.) Inside, the spaces are covered with photos. Several rooms from her flat in Paris have been recreated. At the top of the stairs a big slide show concentrates on Colette's eyes, making you feel as if the author's spirit watches over the museum. In the library, each of the specially created cardboard books contains just one short, sweet, pithy quote.

In 1982 a dry spell made the whitewash peel off the walls of the church in sleepy little **Moutiers-en-Puisaye**, revealing the traces of a series of excellent medieval wall paintings. For 10 years work was carried out to bring the paintings back to life. Scenes from Christ's life and the Old Testament feature down the nave; in the choir two big figures carry a rock in each hand, ready to stone St Stephen as if in a fairground game.

M. Guyot, the restorer of the Château de St-Fargeau, is also responsible for an extraordinary building enterprise at **Guédelon** (*www.guedelon.org; open July–Aug daily 10–7; April–June Thurs–Tues 10–6, closed Wed; Sept–mid-Nov Thurs–Tues 10–5.30, closed Wed; adm*) just below St-Sauveur-en-Puisaye, where he and his team of volunteers are recreating a 13th-century fort from scratch, using 13th-century techniques. The project, started in 1996, will take 25 years to complete. Perhaps the most fascinating aspect is watching the masons painstakingly preparing the individual stones. You can also see specialist craftsmen at work, while peripheral activities include the copying of illuminated manuscripts, all the workers in period costume.

Below Guédelon, the charming, turreted **Château de Ratilly** (*open 15 June–15 Sept daily 10–6; Easter–15 June and 15 Sept–Oct daily 10–12 and 3–6; Nov–Easter Mon–Sat 2–5; adm*) – a real 13th-century castle – lies hidden in the woods. It is now a pottery centre with potters at work, a permanent collection, and exhibitions and concerts in summer. The simple château in nearby **St-Amand-en-Puisaye** also houses a pottery museum, and there are plenty of opportunities to buy a pot to take home.

The Nivernais, or Nièvre

La Charité-sur-Loire

Historic La Charité-sur-Loire has remained pickled in the past, except for the odd old 20th-century advertisement fading on the wall by the priory. Large numbers of pilgrims used to cross the Loire here on the long trail to Santiago de Compostela, and the *bons pères* gave them free room and board. This charity helped the town to develop, as the merchants outside the priory walls did a roaring trade. After the Revolution, however, the religious buildings were terribly neglected.

The church of **Notre-Dame** (1059–1135), built by monks from Cluny, was one of the most splendid of medieval France, and, although now truncated and battered, it remains an atmospheric place, best visited on a guided tour. The scale of the enterprise was awesome. The soaring entrance tower survives; a courtyard now lies between the tower and the church, large parts of which fell down in a 16th-century fire. The much-reduced plain nave in the Cluniac style, held up by rounded Romanesque arches, leads on to lofty transepts and a crossing supported on huge Gothic vaults. The crossing is topped by a tower, on the outside of which stand curious statues in pairs. The choir end and the end chapels are richly carved.

Recent excavations beyond the choir seem to indicate that an enormous second church once stood next to Notre-Dame. The sorry remnants of the medieval chapterhouse and two later courtyards lie forlornly to the side, all in dire need of restoration. One large space is given over to the **Cellier du Goût**, on the history of taste. The separate **Musée Municipal** holds interesting finds from the priory excavations, as well as works from various 19th- and 20th-century art movements.

Nevers

The charming old centre of Nevers is still relatively undiscovered, although it has been known for some time for its pottery and as a place of pilgrimage to see the body of St Bernadette of Lourdes. The elegant main monuments of this Loireside city stand on a broad, flat plateau, the château somewhat stealing the show from the cathedral.

At the beautiful beige-stoned **Palais Ducal** – the castle – iround towers from the medieval castle survive on the north side, but the bulk of the building dates from the 16th century, when the de Clèves family lived here and, through marriage, the son of one duke of Mantua became lord of Nevers. He encouraged pottery manufacturers to settle, and today a few still follow Italian traditions. The swan, symbol of the de Clèves, appears in several carvings, and is one of the most popular motifs on Nevers pottery.

One end of the **cathedral of St-Cyr and Ste-Juliette** is defensively Romanesque, the other openly Gothic: two churches facing in different directions were joined to form this one massive whole. Walk round the outside to appreciate the rich decoration. Inside, a vast, black-eyed, rosy-cheeked and youthful Christ in Majesty looks down from the Romanesque apse. The perspective of this extraordinary painting creates unexpected effects. From a distance, the almond-shaped mandorla takes on the shape of a globe, with Jesus appearing like a single huge continent upon it. The nave is Gothic: comical straining figures are carved at the base of the pillars of the triforium arcade. The carved angels have a much easier time floating happily above. The bulk of the stained glass is modern, replaced after Second World War bombing.

A blue line on the pavements indicates a trail through the **pottery quarter** below the plateau. Fayencerie Gonzague, 8 Rue des Récollets, is outstanding. More tempting boutiques can be found on Rue du 14 Juillet and Rue de la Porte du Croux. Gerard Montagnon is one of the rare *maîtres-faïencier* still using traditional methods. Look out too for Leatitia Welsch and Christine Girande.

The **Porte du Croux** holds the **Musée de la Porte du Croux** (*t 03 86 68 46 00; open by arrangement only*), which includes local Gallo-Roman pieces and Romanesque fragments saved from the church of St-Sauveur. Outside the ramparts, the **Musée Frédéric Blandin** (*open Wed–Mon May–Sept 10–6.30; rest of year 1–5.30, but Sun 10–12 and 2–5.30; adm*) is mainly devoted to the development of Nevers pottery, but it also serves as the town's fine arts museum. Some rooms occupy the former medieval **abbey of Notre-Dame**. A wonderful array of typical blue Nevers pottery is displayed in the restored vaulted chapterhouse.

The **convent of St-Gildard** lies across the municipal garden. Bernadette arrived here in 1866, some eight years after her visions at Lourdes (*see* p.501) and lived at the convent under the name of Sister Marie-Bernard until her death in 1879. Up to half a million pilgrims a year come to see her glistening, wax-coated body.

Southwest of Nevers, along an enchanting curve of the Allier river just before it joins the Loire, **Apremont-sur-Allier** makes a gorgeous halt, the pristine village cleansed for the massively wealthy industrialist Eugène Schneider in the 1930s. He had the huge **château** (*open Easter–mid-Sept daily 2–6*) above the village restored with modern comforts. The superb **Parc Floral** (*open Easter–mid-Sept 10–12 and 2–7*) spreads up the slope.

The Bourbonnais, or Allier

The Bourbonnais was roughly converted into the *département* of the Allier at the Revolution, and although now part of the Auvergne, it is more akin to Burgundy.

The Bourbon dukes were renowned for their semi-independence in the late-Gothic period. **Moulins**, their capital between the early 14th and the early 16th centuries, held one of the most sumptuous courts of any of the French provinces of that time. The town has an attractive mix of architectural styles: grand buildings in stone, patterned ones in brick, timberframe ones, and some covered in colourful plaster. The **cathedral**, rebuilt in striking white stone with black decorative additions in the 19th century, contains one of the great masterpieces of late-Gothic painting, a superlative triptych by an artist known simply as the Maître de Moulins. Groups are only allowed into the sacristy to see the triptych every 20 minutes. The reason for all the fuss – floating on a chair in the midst of a spectacular rainbow – is the gorgeous slip of a Virgin, a girl suddenly faced with more than just the serious responsibility of motherhood, who looks with maternal concern at her new-born son. The magnificent stained-glass windows in the choir seriously rival the triptych; along with their wealthy donors, they feature a collection of gruelling martyrdoms, and some of the most painful episodes in Christ's life.

The daunting and dilapidated **medieval castle** (*open June–mid-Oct; adm*) of the Bourbon dukes stands opposite the cathedral. In recent times it served as a prison until 1983, while the Nazis used it as an internment centre during the Second World War. Some 10,000 Jews passed through here on their way to deportation and death.

Getting Around

Moulins and Vichy both have **railway** stations. Clermont-Ferrand not far south has direct **flights** on Ryanair to and from London.

Tourist Information

CDT Allier: Parc de Bellevue, B.P.65, ✉ 03402 Yzeure, t 04 70 46 81 50, *http://cdt.pays-allier.com*.
Moulins: 11 Rue F.-Peron, t 04 70 44 14 14, *o.t.moulins@wanadoo.fr*.
Vichy: 19 Rue du Parc, t 04 70 98 71 94, *www.vichy-tourisme.com*.

Where to Stay and Eat

Moulins ✉ 03000
Grand Hôtel du Dauphin, t 04 70 44 33 05 (*inexpensive*). Comfortable coaching inn turned modern hotel right in the centre.

Le Grand Café, 49 Place d'Allier (*moderate–cheap*). Traditional brasserie, with fine listed *fin de siècle* interior, partly decorated by the young Coco Chanel before she was famous.

St-Pourçain-sur-Sioule ✉ 03500
Le Chêne Vert, Bd Ledru-Rollin, t 04 70 45 40 65, *hotel-chenevert@wanadoo.fr* (*inexpensive*). Traditional provincial hotel with reasonable rooms and excellent regional food (*expensive–moderate*). Closed Jan; restaurant closed Sun eve, Mon, and Fri lunch.

Vichy ✉ 03200
****Aletti Palace**, 3 Place Joseph Aletti, t 04 70 31 78 77, *aletti.palace.best.western@wanadoo.fr* (*expensive*). By the casino and seat of the Vichy government, a big Belle Epoque posh hotel with a restaurant.
***Le Pavillon D'Enghien**, 32 Rue Callou, t 04 70 98 33 30 (*moderate–inexpensive*). First-class hotel and restaurant in a fine old 19th-century residence in the spa area.

Before heading down the slope to the town's shopping district, walk up Rue de Paris, which features some remarkably fine courtyards along its way. Below the cathedral, the sloping Place de l'Hôtel de Ville is surrounded by a charming hotchpotch of architectural styles, an orangey-red stone belfry rising above the mêlée. The major shopping artery, Rue d'Allier, leads to lively Place d'Allier.

The beige stones and brown roofs typical of the Bourbonnais look at their best in the small town of **Souvigny**, just southwest of Moulins. The former **abbey church of St Peter** and the monastic gateways dominate the centre. Their grandeur seems quite out of keeping with the little place, but Souvigny was an *haut lieu* of the Cluniac Benedictine order and of the lordly Bourbon family. Two of Cluny's greatest and longest-serving abbots, Mayeul and Odilon, died and were buried here. Much later, the great Bourbon dukes chose it as their burial place. The **abbey** is a startling five-aisled mix of Romanesque and Gothic, teeming with architectural and decorative curiosities. The long nave has a kink, said to have been built deliberately to reflect the bend of Christ's head on the cross. The windows in the choir end are in Gothic style, as are those of the first storey, but the aisles have rounded Romanesque arches, with carved capitals featuring bearded figures. Many of the heads of the tomb effigies have been chopped off, but the finely draped bodies remain. The two grand Bourbon tombs lie behind lacy Gothic stone bars.

Vichy

Vichy is a town of two halves. One side of the Allier river you have Belle Epoque Vichy, the Vichy of palatial hotels and grand town houses. This is the chic Vichy of the elderly and the sickly *curistes* who come to drink the hot eggy waters for their health. This is also the Vichy where Pétain installed his government in the unoccupied zone during the Second World War. The other side of the river is young and sports-mad Vichy, where all manner of hearty events take place, and France's future gym teachers are put through their paces. The Allier here resembles a lake, and is good for rowing.

There may not be much to do in Vichy besides drinking the waters or playing sports, but the place has a mesmerizing quality. Virtually every building in the centre holds some interest, with every possible pastiche present – mock Gothic, mock Arabic, mock Venetian, mock Spanish – plus plenty of Art Nouveau and Art Deco. Grand set pieces include the mock Mannerist **Palais des Congrès**, which opened as the first grand casino in France in 1865, and the **Centre Thermal des Dômes**, with its gilded Arabic-style cupola. Between the two stretches the **Parc des Sources**, a civilized public garden with a delightful tree-lined covered walkway. The park's **Halle des Sources** is the best-known centre for taking the waters. Six thermal springs bubble up here like mini Jacuzzis; you can try them for a small fee.

South of the thermal establishments and shops, the little quarter around **St-Blaise** is more historic. St-Blaise itself is a curious hybrid: a showy 20th-century church with rounded nave and choir, containing glittering mosaics and big panels of gaudy stained glass, was added on to the medieval church sheltering Notre-Dame des Malades, a dark wood Virgin venerated by the sick. The **Parc des Célestins** nearby is fronted by an ostentatious oval pavilion. The thermal spring water here is free .

The Auxois

Moving right back into Burgundy, 40km northwest of Dijon stands the unshakeably sober Cistercian abbey of Fontenay, a UNESCO World Heritage Site. Nearby, Mont Auxois was the site of Alésia, where in 52 BC the Gauls under Vercingétorix met with their final defeat against Caesar.

The **abbey of Fontenay** (*open daily 10–12 and 2–5; adm*), hidden in its shallow valley, is one of the best-preserved and earliest Cistercian monasteries in Europe. In 1118 the future St Bernard of Clairvaux sent out his cousin Godefroy de la Roche-Vanneau to found a new Cistercian community. When it became established a new monastery was commissioned and work began on the church in the 1130s. Pope Eugenius III, a former protégé of Bernard's, came to consecrate it in 1147. The rest of the complex, including the forge, was completed by the end of the century. At its height, the abbey had 300 monks, but it waned after the 16th century. Sold off at the Revolution, it was turned into a paper works, which it remained through the 19th century. Yet from its inception Fontenay was an industrial centre, iron-working its speciality. The place – rare because of its state of preservation – was in fact a relatively modest monastery. The rigorous Cistercian rule of prayer and work was strictly adhered to. Now well restored, of the original complex the only major building missing is the refectory. The church is the very model of Cistercian simplicity and severity. There is, however, a superb view down the nave to the straight-ended apse. The chapterhouse was one of the few places where the monks would talk, discussing matters affecting the abbey.

The unpretentious old village of **Alise-Ste-Reine** clings to the steep slope below the flat summit of Mont Auxois. This hill, known to the Romans as Alésia, witnessed the last great stand of the Celts against Caesar. As Caesar conquered Gaul to further his political career back home, the native settlement on this hilltop became the fatal hideout for the Gaulish troops united in rebellion under Vercingétorix. Vercingétorix had carried off a memorable victory over the Romans at Gergovie (*see* p.698). Caesar had then headed north. Vercingétorix raced after the Romans and attacked them near Dijon. Unfortunately, Caesar's legions not only survived the surprise attack, but emerged victorious. Vercingétorix and his men sought refuge on the height of Alésia. Caesar pursued them and had his men build a double line of fortifications round the base of Mont Auxois. The Romans, who included Mark Antony and Brutus among their number, then laid siege. Vercingétorix was forced to surrender after six weeks. He was be sent to Rome to be paraded in front of the crowds before being strangled, and in Gaul serious resistance to Rome came to an end. A 19th-century statue on top of Mont Auxois pays homage to Vercingétorix.

A few still dispute whether Mont Auxois was actually the place where Vercingétorix was defeated, but what is beyond doubt is that the remains of an important **Gallo-Roman settlement** (*open July–Aug daily 9–7; late-Mar–June and Sept–Oct daily 10–6; adm*) have been discovered around the hilltop. This grew up after the infamous siege, with all the trappings you would expect, including basilica, forum, temples and a theatre capable of seating 5,000 spectators. The remains are hard to make out on the ground, but the old-fashioned-looking **museum** (*open same times; adm*) in the village

Getting Around

The Paris **train** to Dijon stops at Montbard, from where there's a **bus** to Semur-en-Auxois.

Tourist Information

Flavigny-sur-Ozerain: t 03 80 75 81 21, or t 03 80 75 83 32.
Semur-en-Auxois: 2 Pl Gaveau, t 03 80 97 05 96.

Where to Stay and Eat

Fain-les-Montbard ✉ 21500
***Château de Malaisy, t 03 80 89 46 54, ch-malaisy@club-internet.fr (moderate).

A clean-lined and neatly restored 17th-century manor 6km southeast of Montbard. Impeccably kept, with a good restaurant (expensive–moderate).

Semur-en-Auxois ✉ 21140
**Les Cymaises, 7 Rue de Renaudot, t 03 80 97 21 44, hotel.cymaises@libertysurf.fr (inexpensive). Adorable hotel with 18 rooms in an 18th-century town house. Closed mid-Jan–Feb, Nov, part of Dec.
***Hostellerie d'Aussois, Rte de Saulieu, t 03 80 97 28 28, info@hostellerie.fr (moderate). Modern hotel and restaurant with views on to the old town or the countryside. Restaurant. Closed Dec–Feb; restaurant closed Sun eve.

contains some revealing finds. In particular, Gallo-Roman Alésia became an important place for bronze craftsmen, praised by Pliny the Elder, and impressive pieces were recovered from the digs, including some beautiful heads.

The name of Alise-Ste-Reine indicates the importance in these parts of the early Christian saint, Reine or Regina, martyred here in 262 AD after espousing Christianity and refusing to marry the Roman governor Olibrius. Her relics were kept on the hill for many centuries after her death, but were moved to the nearby hilltop site of **Flavigny-sur-Ozerain** in the 860s. The smell of aniseed often wafts across the fortified village – the tradition of making aniseed sweets here also goes back as far as the 9th century. Flavigny has a potentially fine array of old gateways and houses in need of restoration. The former abbey of St-Pierre looks particularly battered, and the ugly aniseed sweet factory has taken over many of its 17th-century buildings. Among the fragments of the abbey cower the dingy remnants of the Carolingian crypt.

The charmingly acerbic **Château de Bussy-Rabutin** (open April–Sept daily 9.30–11.30 and 2–5, plus daily visit June–Aug at 6; Oct–Mar Wed–Mon and Wed 10–11 and 2–3; adm), in a little valley northeast of Alise-Ste-Reine, deserves a detour for the very lively guided tour. The castle is surrounded by pretty gardens, and substantial late-Gothic round towers mark the corners of the moated building. The wings were redone in Renaissance style for the Comte de Rochefort in the 16th century. Having lost his fortune, his principal creditor, François de Rabutin, acquired the castle and commissioned the redesign of the central section in the first half of the 17th century. The lovable but uncontrollable courtier and scandalmonger Roger de Rabutin was François de Rabutin's grandson, and the mordant paintings in the castle reflect his colourful life. Born in 1618, Roger was destined for a military career, and he served in the Thirty Years' War. He gained a reputation for his scurrilous verse, while his actions were invariably excessive too. Roger's pen would be his downfall. When he insulted Louis XIV he was exiled to his estates in Burgundy where he whiled away the months writing naughty and thinly disguised sketches of Louis XIV's courtiers, L'Histoire

Amoureuse des Gaules. Bitterness mixed with his wit, Roger commissioned local artists to paint allegories of the goings-on in court at his château.

Four sturdy round towers rise above the river at **Semur-en-Auxois**, a small town set on its spur above a meander in the Armançon, west of Alise-Ste-Reine. This served as an important fortress for the dukes of Burgundy. The church of Notre-Dame is the town's focal point. Much of the statuary on the main Gothic portal was hacked away at the Revolution, but the north doorway has retained its touching scenes of the life of Doubting Thomas. Side chapels in Flamboyant Gothic and Renaissance styles lie off the surprisingly tall and slender nave. The restored Gothic stained-glass windows show drapers and butchers at work. The **Musée Municipal** (*open June–Sept Wed–Mon 10–12 and 2–6; closed Tues; adm*) contains extensive collections of sculpture.

Surrounded by a dry moat, the **Château d'Epoisses** (*grounds open daily 9–7; interior open July–Aug Wed–Mon 10–12 and 3–6; adm*) west of Semur is cut off from its village by a double line of fortifications. In the medieval outer bailey stand a solid dovecote and a simple church containing a 16th-century pietà and a Christ attributed to the great 16th-century sculptor Germain Pilon. What remains of the castle is still substantial, with many towers. One is named after a 6th-century queen of Burgundy, Brunehaut, another, the most remarkable, with its layering of different-coloured stone, after the Grand Condé who owned the château for a time.

Lovely valleys of oaks, with Charolais cows grazing in the meadows, lead to the **source of the Seine**, which has been turned into what looks like a 19th-century city park in the middle of nowhere, ordered by Napoléon III and Haussmann. In a grotto around where the first waters of the Seine emerge from the ground, the recumbent statue represents Sequana, the residing Gallo-Roman goddess.

Dijon

Most people will be familiar with culinary Dijon, its mustard and its *crème de cassis*, the intense blackcurrant liqueur mixed with white wine to create a drink known as a Kir (named after Resistance hero and one-time mayor of Dijon, Chanoine Kir), not to mention the fabulous local wines. But first-time visitors will be surprised by this splendid Burgundian city, where the culinary even extends to the architecture, the finest façades weighed down with stone garlands of fruit.

There was a Gallo-Roman settlement here, *Divio*, and early Christian activity is traced to a misty figure known as St Bénigne or Benignus. In 989, Mayeul, the great abbot of Cluny, sent a brilliant Italian protégé, William of Volpiano, to the abbey of St-Bénigne to restore the Benedictine rule there. The first Capetian duke of Burgundy, Robert Ier, chose Dijon as his capital in the first half of the 11th century. A terrible fire ravaged much of the town in 1137, causing it to be rebuilt. The powerful Valois line of Burgundy dukes – Philippe le Hardi and his three successors, Jean sans Peur, Philippe le Bon and Charles le Téméraire – were the most significant of all lords of Dijon, a ruthless major European dynasty with a fabulous court. Their rule came to an end in 1477, with overambitious Charles' death in battle in Lorraine, and from 1482 Burgundy

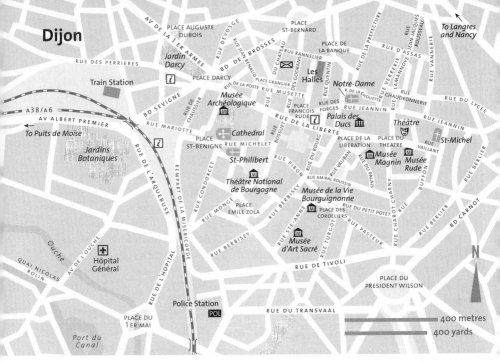

Dijon

Train Station

RUE DES PERRIERES

A38/A6
AV ALBERT PREMIER
← To Puits de Moïse

Jardins Botaniques

Ouche

QUAI NICOLAS ROLIN

Hôpital Général

Port du Canal

PLACE DU 1ER MAI

Police Station
POL

AV DE LA 1ère ARMEE

PLACE AUGUSTE DUBOIS

Jardin Darcy

i

PLACE DARCY

BD SEVIGNE

RUE DE LA CHAUSSIER

RUE MARIOTTE

RUE DE L'ARQUEBUSE

RUE CONDORCET

REMPART DE LA MISERICORDE

RUE MONGE

AV DE L'OUCHE

RUE DE L'HOPITAL

AV DE DEVOSGE

RUE JEAN RENAUD

BD DE BROSSES

DU CHATEAU

PLACE GRANGIER

RUE DE LA POSTE

RUE MUSETTE

Musée Archéologique
M

PLACE ST-BENIGNE

Cathedral

RUE MICHELET

St-Philibert

Théâtre National de Bourgogne

PLACE EMILE ZOLA

RUE BERBISEY

RUE BERBISEY

RUE STE-ANNE

RUE RANNELIER

PLACE ST-BERNARD

PLACE DE LA BANQUE

Les Halles

PLACE FRANCOIS RUDE

RUE DES FORGES

RUE DE LA LIBERTE

RUE DU BOURG

RUE PIRON

RUE QUENTIN

Notre-Dame

PLACE DES CORDELIERS

Musée de la Vie Bourguignonne
M

Musée d'Art Sacré
M

RUE DE LA PREFECTURE

RUE D'ASSAS

RUE DE LA CHOUETTE

RUE JEANNIN

Palais des Ducs
m̂

PLACE DE LA LIBERATION

RUE VAUBAN

RUE DU PALAIS

RUE AMIRAL ROUSSIN

RUE VAILLANT

RUE DU PETIT POTET

RUE PASTEUR

RUE TURGOT

RUE DE TIVOLI

RUE JEAN-JACQUES ROUSSEAU

RUE VANNERIE

RUE VERRERIE

LAMANNOYE

RUE CHAUDRONNERIE

RUE DU LYCEE

RUE JEANNIN

Théâtre

St-Michel

PLACE DU THEATRE

Musée Magnin
M

Musée Rude
M

RUE CHABOT CHARNY

BUFFON

RUE BERLIER

RUE BERLIER

RUE BERLIER

BD CARNOT

To Langres and Nancy ↗

PLACE DU PRESIDENT WILSON

RUE DU TRANSVAAL

N

400 metres
400 yards

became a possession of the French monarchy. Louis XI created a regional Parlement here; many great houses were built for its members.

The **Musée Archéologique** (*open June–Sept Wed–Mon 10–8; rest of year Wed–Mon 9–12 and 2–6; closed Tues; adm; free Sun*) is housed in an impressive wing of the medieval abbey next to the cathedral. The prehistoric finds include glittering jewellery, most spectacularly the Blanot treasure. The Gallo-Roman collections feature votive offerings left to Sequana, goddess of the Seine. The medieval carvings are the most beautiful artefacts on display, with wonderful representations of St Benigné.

The great medieval church dedicated to St Bénigne has only been a **cathedral** since 1731. Virtually nothing remains of the 11th-century original, except the crypt (*small fee*) which is damp and badly restored, yet deeply atmospheric. Some of the capitals show fascinating primitive Carolingian figures. The vast Gothic building above was begun around 1280. After the colourful roofs outside, the wide interior looks extremely sober, although the shift from the pink-tinged stone of the nave to the golden-orange stone of the choir is striking. A few embellishments from the Ancien Régime add visual interest, including statues on the columns, some elaborate tombs in the side aisles, and a wild baptismal font.

The pompous **Palais des Ducs** was reshaped in the late 17th century at the same time as the charming semi-circular Place de la Libération. It now holds the town hall and the enormous **Musée des Beaux-Arts** (*open Wed–Mon 10–6; adm*). The chapter-house contains some fabulous Burgundian statuary and precious religious items. But the most famous pieces lie in the Salle des Gardes on the first floor: the famed tombs of the dukes of Burgundy, especially Claus Sluter's magnificent work for Philippe le Hardi. One of the finest of all medieval sculptors, Sluter also trained his nephew

Claus de Werve. The master carved most of the mourning monks, known as *pleurants*, around the base of the tomb; de Werve completed the collection. The tomb of Jean sans Peur and his wife Marguerite of Bavaria by Spaniard Juan de la Huerta and Antoine Le Moiturier of Avignon copied the style of the first tomb. The retables made for the ducal charterhouse by the Flemish artists Melchior Broederlam of Ypres and Jacques de Baerze are also stupendous.

The room devoted to Flemish painters offers further delight, with a famed Nativity scene by Robert Campin or the Master of Flémalle. The riches continue in the Dutch,

Getting There and Around

Dijon-Bourgogne **airport**, t 03 80 67 67 67, *www.dijon.aeroport.fr*, lies 6km southeast of town; Ryanair have flown there and may again. By **train** there is a TGV from Paris-Charles de Gaulle airport (*c.* 1hr 55 mins) or from Lille (2hrs 50mins), but there is only one service a day on each line. Trains from central Paris to Dijon leave from the Gare de Lyon.

Tourist Information

Dijon: Place Darcy or 34 Rue des Forges, t 03 80 44 11 44, *www.dijon-tourism.com*.

Shopping

Rue de la Liberté is the main shopping street in the centre. Look out for Pâtisserie Vannier, one of the very finest in town, and Maille, a household name in France for mustard. Boutiques spread into the streets off **Rue de la Liberté**. **Place de la Libération** has upmarket food and wine stores. See also **Les Halles** covered market for culinary specialities. For antiques look at **Rue Verrerie** and **Rue Comte**.

Where to Stay

Dijon ✉ 21000

★★★★Hostellerie du Chapeau Rouge, 5 Rue Michelet, t 03 80 50 88 88, *chapeaurouge@bourgogne.net* (*expensive*). Good hotel with old stone façade on the edge of the historic heart of Dijon. Actually quite reasonably priced, with 30 rooms and exquisite cuisine (*expensive–moderate*).

★★★Hôtel Wilson, Place Wilson, t 03 80 66 82 50, *hotelwilson@wanadoo.fr* (*moderate*).

27 comfortable rooms set around a charming little courtyard. No restaurant.

★★★Hôtel du Nord, Place Darcy, t 03 80 50 80 50, *hotelnord@bourgogne.net* (*moderate*). Central, with well-equipped rooms, a fine restaurant (*expensive–moderate*) and a cellar for Burgundy wine tastings.

★★Le Jacquemart, 32 Rue Verrerie, t 03 80 60 09 60, *hotel@hotel-lejacquemart.fr* (*inexpensive*). Delightful, well-run, old-style but stylish hotel in the centre. A real bargain.

★★Le Sauvage, 64 Rue Monge, t 03 80 41 31 21, *hoteldusauvage@free.fr* (*inexpensive*). Lovely hotel with timberframe walls and courtyard; practical for parking.

★★Le Palais, 23 Rue du Palais, t 03 80 67 16 26, *hoteldupalaisdijon@wanadoo.fr* (*inexpensive*). Appealing hotel in an 18th-century limestone building, well located in the centre of the city.

Eating Out

Le Pré aux Clercs/Jean-Pierre Billoux, 13 Place de la Libération, t 03 80 38 05 05 (*very expensive–expensive*). Splendid restaurant, set in the semi-circle of architecture in front of the ducal palace. Renowned in particular for poultry. *Closed Sun eve and Mon.*

Au Moulin à Vent, 8 Place François Rude, t 03 80 30 81 43. Typical Burgundian cuisine served in a friendly and lively atmosphere. *Closed Sun eve and Mon.*

Le Cézanne, 40 Rue Amiral Roussin, t 03 80 58 921 92 (*expensive*). Charming small-scale restaurant in an old house in an old street, with a small terrace. *Book in advance. Closed 2nd half Aug, Mon lunch and Sun.*

Le Passé Composé, 13 Place Emile Zola, t 03 80 50 06 66. Simple but good; traditional and Provençal cuisine. *Closed Sun and Mon.*

German, Swiss, Italian and French Ancien Régime collections, but the 19th- and 20th-century works prove a bit disappointing; a few pieces by the monumental Burgundian 19th-century sculptor François Rude stand out.

Rude has also been given his own museum, the **Musée Rude** (*open June–Sept Wed–Mon 10–12 and 2–5.45; adm*), in the converted church of St-Etienne east of the Palais des Ducs, on the same square as the classical **theatre**. Beyond, the virtuoso façade of the church of **St-Michel** makes a great Renaissance song and dance.

Dijon's grand quarter just north of the Palais des Ducs contains truly spectacular mansions. Rue des Forges boasts some of the very finest. The **Maison Maillard**, built from the second half of the 16th century for one of Dijon's mayors, Jean Maillard, wins the prize for most overdressed house of all, the façade groaning under a bumper crop of garlands. Nearby, three rows of hefty gargoyles, with floral decoration stuffed between their contorted figures, decorate the Gothic church of **Notre-Dame** which more than holds its own amongst all the neighbourhood's excesses. The portal sculptures were unfortunately hacked to bits, but the plethora of stone carvings above remain. Green *jacquemarts*, or bell strikers, add a carnival touch to the bell tower.

The streets north and east of Notre-Dame have more fabulous town houses: along Rue de la Chouette, the **Hôtel de Vogüé** vies with the Maison Maillard for the accolade of finest in town. It exudes refinement, its pink-stoned arch leading into an exquisite courtyard embellished with enchanting carvings. Rue Jeannin, Rue Verrerie, Rue Chaudronnerie, Rue Lamannoye, Rue Jean-Jacques Rousseau and Rue Vannerie contain more wonderful buildings. Just to the west is the covered market, one of the first works of Gustave Eiffel; the area is a sort of mini-Covent Garden.

To the south of the Palais des Ducs, semi-circular Place de la Libération is the most elegant place to shop. Hidden away down Rue des Bons Enfants, the **Musée Magnin** (*open Tues–Sun 10–12 and 2–6; adm*) allows you into one of Dijon's great houses without an invitation to dinner. It is crammed full of small works of art collected in the late 19th century and early 20th century by Maurice Magnin and his sister Jeanne.

Two lesser-known museums stand next to each other on Rue Ste-Anne. The **Musée d'Art Sacré** (*open Wed–Mon 9–12 and 2–6; closed Tues; adm, free Sun*) occupies the domed circular church of the Bernardines, a dramatic setting for some absorbing religious works. The **Musée de la Vie Bourguignonne** (*open Wed–Mon 9–12 and 2–6; adm, free Sun*) has taken over other buildings of the former convent, set around a classical cloister. The rambling collection includes 19th-century Burgundian costumes and interiors, recreated old shops and builders' crafts. Some way west, the **Musée Amora** or **Musée de la Moutarde** (*48 Quai Nicolas Rolin; guided tours mid-June–mid-Sept Mon–Sat at 3pm only; adm*) will fill you in on the story of mustard-making.

Among the sprawling buildings of the **psychiatric hospital** a kilometre west of Place Darcy, you can go in search of some of the finest statues to be have survived from the great 14th-century ducal period, on the so-called **Puits de Moïse** (the Moses Well). Six life-size figures were carved round the base of what must once have been a superlative calvary made to sit in the cloisters of the **Chartreuse de Champmol**, built for the dukes of Burgundy. The ducal tombs have been moved to the central Musée des Beaux-Arts (*see above*), but the vestiges of the calvary have stayed put. The work of

Claus Sluter again, executed between 1395 and 1405, they are regarded as one of the very finest groups of Gothic sculpture ever made.

The Côte d'Or

This is one of the most famous stretches of vineyards in the world, running for some 56km south from Dijon, past Beaune, to Santenay (near Chagny). Many of the best wines in the world are made here and rival the top Bordeaux for the position of most absurdly prized and priced wines on the planet. The great red wines are made using pinot noir, the great whites using chardonnay. A little red is produced using gamay, a little white using aligoté. The Côte de Nuits production is almost entirely of the finest possible reds; the Côte de Beaune yields both fabulous reds and whites.

The Côte de Nuits

This section of the Côte d'Or has been dubbed the Champs-Elysées of Burgundy. Along the D122 or **Route des Grands Crus**, lies a string of villages which produce arguably the most envied red wines in the world: Gevrey-Chambertin followed by Chambolle-Musigny, Clos de Vougeot and Vosne-Romanée. The most celebrated estate around **Gevrey-Chambertin** is the Clos de Bèze, which produced Napoleon's favourite wine. You can go on an entertaining tour of the **Château de Gevrey-Chambertin** (*open Fri–Wed 10–12 and 2–6; closed Thurs; adm*), with a tempting range of wines on offer. A pretty road leads up into the **Hautes-Côtes de Nuits** from Gevrey-Chambertin. Head for the **Vergy** hilltop for extensive views of the area.

The **Château du Clos de Vougeot** (*open April–Sept Sun–Fri 9–6.30; Oct–Mar Sun–Fri 9–11.30 and 2–5.30, Sat till 5; adm*) stands as a stately symbol for the whole Côte de Nuits, in the midst of the world-renowned Clos Vougeot. The solid, square castle was built for the monks of Cîteaux, who planted vines here and made wine on the spot until the Revolution. Clos Vougeot wine hasn't been made at the château since 1913, but since the war the castle has been the headquarters of the Confrérie des Chevaliers du Tastevin which promotes Burgundy wines.

Nuits-St-Georges is packed with cellars selling fine wines; a good address at which to pick up relatively reasonably priced bottles is **Le Cavon de Bacchus** (*t 03 80 61 15 32*). The local community shows its devotion to the god of wine with regular wine festivities, including a celebrated wine auction on the Sunday before Palm Sunday. Nuits-St-Georges has strong connections with Cîteaux, and the **local history museum** (*open 2 May–Oct Wed–Mon 10–12 and 2–6; adm*) contains an 18th-century model of the famous abbey. A new **museum** (*open April–Oct daily 10–1 and 2–7; Nov–Mar Tues–Sat 10–1 and 2–6*) deals with the noble *cassis* – blackcurrant – in all its aspects.

Cîteaux

Open mid-May–mid-Oct Tues–Sun 9–6, guided tours 9.15, 11, 1.45 and 4.15; adm.

Take a good look, because little remains of Cîteaux, the birthplace of that most austere of religious orders, the Cistercians. The revived abbey was in fact also largely

Getting Around

Gevrey-Chambertin, Vougeot and Nuits-St-Georges have **railway** stations on the Dijon–Beaune line, and there are regular services to Chagny on the Dijon-Mâcon line. Otherwise, to reach the villages along the Côte you can take a **bus** from Dijon or Beaune.

Tourist Information

Gevrey-Chambertin: Place de la Mairie, **t** 03 80 34 38 40, *www.ot-gevreychambertin.fr.*
Nuits-St-Georges: Rue Sonoys, **t** 03 80 62 01 38.
Meursault: Place de l'Hôtel de Ville, **t** 03 80 21 25 90, *www.ot-meursault.fr.*
Chagny: 2 Rue des Halles, **t** 03 85 87 25 95.
Nolay: Maison des Halles, **t** 03 80 21 80 73, *www.nolay.com.*

Where to Stay and Eat

Gevrey-Chambertin ✉ 21220

★★★**Arts et Terroirs**, 28 Route de Dijon, **t** 03 80 34 30 76, *arts-et-terroirs@wanadoo.fr* (*moderate*). Painting and culture on the agenda at this hotel in an old home done out with panache.
★★★**Les Grands Crus**, Route des Grands Crus, **t** 03 80 34 34 15, *hotel.lesgrandscrus@ipac.fr*

(*moderate*). Modern-looking but comfortable, among the vineyards. *Closed Dec–Feb.*
Les Millésimes, 25 Rue de l'Eglise, **t** 03 80 51 84 24 (*very expensive*). One of Burgundy's legendary restaurants with what's regarded as just about the best wine list in the region and delicious seafood. *Closed 12 Dec–25 Jan, Wed lunch and Tues.*
Rôtisserie du Chambertin, Rue du Chambertin, **t** 03 80 34 33 20 (*expensive*). Splendid food, and staggering wines at staggering prices. **Le Bon Bistro** (*moderate*) next door is now part of the establishment. *Closed Sun eve and Mon exc bank hols.*

Saulon-la-Rue ✉ 21910

★★**Château de Saulon-la-Rue**, **t** 03 80 79 25 25, *saulon@chateauhotels.com* (*moderate*). Appealing 17th-century château in large grounds with comfortable sitting rooms and a stylish pool and terrace. Restaurant (*expensive*).

Morey-St-Denis ✉ 21220

★★★**Castel de Très Girard**, 7 Rue Très Girard, **t** 03 80 34 33 09, *info@castel-tres-girard.com* (*expensive*). Walled 18th-century manor offering a calm retreat, set among vineyards, with a pool. Wide selection of wines in the gastronomic restaurant. *Closed 2 weeks Feb; restaurant closed Mon, and Tues lunch.*

responsible for giving birth to the great vineyards which were tended for so many centuries by the monks.

The first abbey was founded in 1098 by Robert, a monk from the Benedictine abbey of Molesme, who would be succeeded by his right-hand man Alberic. An English religious man, Stephen (Etienne to the French) Harding, became the third abbot after Alberic's death in 1109. Harding was responsible for developing the vibrant intellectual and cultural aspects of the monks' religious life at the parent abbey, encouraging the highest standards in copying texts and illuminating manuscripts, as well as in music. The future St Bernard joined the abbey in 1113; he would be sent out from Cîteaux by Stephen to found Clairvaux (*see* p.582). The Cistercian order reached its height in the 13th century, becoming the largest in Europe.

Most of the great abbey was destroyed after the Revolution, but a few scattered old buildings remained standing and, after a long period of neglect, some of these have been restored. It is once again a living community, the monks provided with one old wing and a modern church. The guided visit around the sad remnants of this once hugely important abbey is one of the most intelligently conceived tours in Burgundy.

Caveau St-Nicolas, 13 Rue Haute, **t** 03 80 58 51 83 (*inexpensive*). Run by a former travelling salesman who likes a good joke, a simple but sweet B&B tucked away in a cul-de-sac.

Chambolle-Musigny ✉ 21220
★★★★Château-Hôtel André Ziltener, Rue de la Fontaine, **t** 03 80 62 41 62, *chateau.ziltener@ wanadoo.fr* (*very expensive*). Splendid, exclusive little hotel hidden behind walls, with its own wine cellars. *Closed Dec–14 Mar.*

Curtil-Vergy ✉ 21700
Hôtel Manasses, **t** 03 80 61 43 81 (*expensive*). Good combination of ancient and modern, overlooking vineyards. Patronized by the Prince of Wales and owned by the ebullient Yves Challey, of TV fame.

Gilly-lès-Citeaux ✉ 21640
★★★★Château de Gilly, **t** 03 80 62 89 98, *gilly@ grandesetapes.fr* (*luxury–expensive*). High-class luxury at this former abbots' country pile. Excellent cuisine. *Closed Feb.*

Châteauneuf-en-Auxois ✉ 21320
★★Hostellerie du Château, **t** 03 80 49 22 00. *info@hostellerie-chateauneuf.com* (*inexpensive*). Some of the 17 rooms have a brilliant valley view by the spectacular castle. Dining *à la carte* (*expensive–moderate*). *Closed*

Jan–15 Feb; restaurant closed Mon and Tues exc July and Aug.

Meursault ✉ 21190
Les Magnolias, 8 Rue Pierre Joigneaux, **t** 03 80 21 23 23 (*expensive*). Lovely 18th-century manor with its own courtyard and charming rooms. *Closed Dec–15 Mar.*
Le Chevreuil, Place de l'Hôtel de Ville, **t** 03 80 21 23 25 (*expensive–moderate*). A good restaurant serving Burgundian classics.

Puligny-Montrachet ✉ 21190
★★★Le Montrachet, 10 Place des Marronniers, **t** 03 80 21 30 06, *info@le-montrachet.com* (*moderate*). Unexciting hotel, but a special restaurant (*very expensive– expensive*). *Closed 30 Nov–10 Jan.*

Chagny ✉ 71150
★★★★Lameloise, 36 Place d'Armes, **t** 03 85 87 65 65 (*expensive*). Traditional hotel with variable *haute cuisine* (*very expensive*). *Closed 20 Dec–25 Jan; restaurant closed Tues lunch, Thurs lunch and Wed.*

Bouilland ✉ 21420
★★Hostellerie du Vieux Moulin, **t** 03 80 21 51 16 (*expensive*). Well away from the crowds. Cuisine of the highest quality, the rooms more modest. *Closed Mon lunch, Wed, Thurs.*

Texts give glimpses of Cistercian thinking, and the rules of the order along with its five pillars are clearly explained; you are even asked to observe a degree of silence.

The Côte de Beaune

This is one of the top white wine territories in the world, although the estates of **Aloxe-Corton** have the distinction of producing both red and white wines of supreme quality. The village château has an outrageous colourfully tiled roof. Charlemagne is said to have owned vineyards here, hence the magical name Corton-Charlemagne in white wines. The *appellation* stretches into neighbouring **Pernand-Vergelesses** whose church dates from the Romanesque period. The grand **Château de Savigny-lès-Beaune** contains the **Musée de la Moto, de l'Aviation et de la Voiture de Course** (*open 15 Jan–Dec daily 9–12 and 2–6, but 5 in winter; adm*), a large collection of vintage cars, motorbikes and planes gathered together by a vinegrower. The fighter planes make a curious sight parked next to vines in the noble grounds. The village of Savigny-lès-Beaune has plenty of delightful old wineries.

A detour takes you up the gorgeous and quiet wooded Rhoin valley from Savigny-lès-Beaune to **Bouilland**, the limestone clifftop of a Burgundian *combe* (a steep

indented valley) sticking out above the trees. Not far from Bouilland, the ruins of the **Abbaye Ste-Catherine** rise as high as the tall trees which surround it. The Romanesque to Gothic abbey church stands romantically roofless.

The Côte de Beaune vineyards continue south of Beaune. Pommard and Volnay both produce top quality red wines. In Pommard, the **Domaine Coste Caumartin** (*Rue du Parc, t 03 80 22 45 04*), in the same family since the Revolution, is a down-to-earth but serious wine-making estate run by charming people. The villages of **Meursault, Puligny-Montrachet** and **Chassagne-Montrachet** are synonymous with superlative white wines. The famous estates are discreet here. In Puligny-Montrachet, **Le Caveau de Monsieur Wallerand**, Rue de Pouisseul, is a good little wine shop.

Get away from the main Côte de Beaune wine route by heading into the delightful hills of the **Hautes-Côtes de Beaune** west of Puligny and Chassagne-Montrachet. The **Château de la Rochepot** (*open April–Oct Wed–Mon 10–11.30 and 2–5.30; adm*) offers the most dramatic silhouette in the area, its towers with coloured Burgundian tiles rising above a sleepy village. The original fort dated from the 12th century, but was completely transformed by the Pot family in the 15th century. Much of the castle was brought down at the Revolution, and rebuilt in the 19th century. It's full of mock-medieval charm inside, with period furniture and weapons on display.

Seek out the picturesque vineyards route via the **Vallon de la Tournée** from La Rochepot to reach **Nolay**, a village with a tatty appeal set in a bowl of flat-topped hills. The central square with its wooden market place, big church and timberframe houses is charmingly unrestored. A short way south, below Mont de Sène, **Dezize-lès-Maranges** benefits from an enviably picturesque location, with approachable wine estates. The vineyards rise high up the sides of dramatic **Mont de Sène**, also known as the Montagne des Trois Croix because of the three crosses at the top.

Beaune

Chock-a-block with wine cellars, wine-lovers and hotels and restaurants, Beaune seems to have sold its soul to Bacchus. It is the main centre for the marketing of the great wines of Burgundy. These have benefited from rich US and Japanese buyers who have pushed the prices to obscene levels. But Beaune also boasts the famous charitable foundation of the Hospices de Beaune which has become the proprietor of a large number of the best vineyards.

The **Hospices de Beaune** (*open late Mar–late Nov daily 9–6.30; rest of year daily 9–11.30 and 2–5.30; adm*) buildings were commissioned by the massively wealthy Nicolas Rolin and his wife after the local population had suffered poverty, famine and disease in the wake of the Hundred Years War. Begun in 1443, it was probably designed by a Flemish architect, Jehan Wiescrère. It was meant initially to accommodate the poor, who were to be cared for by religious sisters, but its reputation was such that merchants and nobles also came to be treated here. It served as a hospital right up until 1971 when it was turned into a museum, devoted mainly to hospitals in medieval times. These were as much involved with treating the soul as the body. Wondrous works of art were often commissioned.

Getting Around

Beaune is a little over 2hrs from Paris-Gare de Lyon by **train**. There are also regular train services to and from Dijon.

Tourist Information

Beaune: 1 Rue de l'Hôtel Dieu, **t** 03 80 26 21 30, *www.beaune-burgundy.com*.
Safari-Tours, run via the Beaune tourist office, offer a good if pricey introduction (in English) to selected vineyards.

Shopping

There are numerous wine merchants' houses or *négociants* you can visit in Beaune, invariably with impressive cellars under their houses. Expect to pay an entrance fee.
Caves Patriarche Père et Fils, 7 Rue du Collège, **t** 03 80 24 53 78. Boasts the largest medieval cellars in town.

For a more exclusive tasting, you could arrange a visit to a more small-scale merchant house who will expect you to be serious about buying. Ask at the tourist office.
Maison Champy, 5 Rue du Grenier à Sel, **t** 03 80 25 09 99. Claims to be the oldest of the great Burgundy wine companies, founded in 1720. Run by a team of experts headed by Henri and Pierre Meurgey. The house has seven hectares of its own vines and buys in other wines to sell.
Denis Perret, Rue Carnot. An excellent wine shop that represents some of the really top-class Burgundy *négociants*.
Le Tast' Fromage. Sells superlative Epoisses, Chambertin and Cîteaux cheeses.

Where to Stay

Beaune ✉ 21200
★★★★**Le Cep**, 27 Rue Maufoux, **t** 03 80 22 35 48, *resa@hotel-cep-beaune.com* (*very expensive*). A Renaissance town house in an arcaded courtyard. Attached to it, **Bernard Morillon**, **t** 03 80 24 12 06 (*very expensive–expensive*), has a splendid old dining room for classic Burgundian cuisine. *Closed Jan, Tues lunch, Wed lunch and Mon.*
★★★★**Hôtel de la Poste**, 5 Bd Clemenceau, **t** 03 80 22 08 11 (*expensive*). Big hotel with relatively small rooms with views of the ramparts or some vines. Wine-tasting cellar and restaurant. *Closed Feb.*
★★★**Central**, 2 Victor Millot, **t** 03 80 24 77 24 (*moderate*). A satisfying address, both for its central location, its good-value, comfortable rooms and its original cuisine in the **Cheval Blanc**, **t** 03 80 24 69 70 (*moderate*). *Closed 22 Nov–19 Dec; restaurant closed Wed.*
★★★**Grillon**, 21 Rte de Seurre, **t** 03 80 22 44 25, *joel.grillon@wanadoo.fr* (*inexpensive*). Substantial town house with a garden; reasonably priced and charming. Cellars below. *Closed Feb.*

Eating Out

Le Verger, 21 Route de Seurre, **t** 03 80 24 28 05 (*moderate*). In the Grillon hotel's garden, in a striking building, a restaurant run with love. *Closed Feb, Wed lunch and Tues.*
Ma Cuisine, Passage Ste-Hélène, **t** 03 80 22 30 22 (*moderate–inexpensive*). A husband and wife team run this bright little restaurant. *Book in advance. Closed school hols, Aug, Sat, Sun, and Wed lunch.*

Within the courtyard, the building is highly decorated: the famed coloured tiles form complex diamond patterns on the roofs; ornate pinnacles rise from the dormers; carved angels glide down from the gables. Inside, the enormous paupers' ward is extremely impressive with its neat, crimson-covered beds. The carvings on the ceiling may represent leading figures in 15th-century Beaune. The chapel area at one end was always an integral part of the paupers' ward, where **Van der Weyden's polyptych** originally stood. This sublime work now takes pride of place in a separate room. On the outer panels the donors look miserable; Nicolas Rolin holds his helmet, a red-faced angel blowing its trumpet by his side. An Annunciation scene is depicted above. The great main scene depicts the Christ of the Last Judgement sitting on a rainbow, holding the lily, symbol of purity, and the sword, symbol of punishment. Magnificent purple-clad angels blow their trumpets to either side. Below, the androgynous St Michael with his intense gaze and brilliant peacock-coloured wings weighs souls. To the left of him, the Virgin, apostles and saints pray to Christ. To the right John the Baptist is accompanied by further apostles and three female saints. A magnifying glass has been set up for you to appreciate the detail.

Romanesque **Notre-Dame** contains some late-Gothic art treasures including a series of tapestries depicting the life of the Virgin. The **Musée des Beaux Arts** (*open April–Oct daily 2–6; adm*) presents lesser Flemish works of art and scenes by the local 19th-century painter Félix Ziem. The **Musée du Vin de Bourgogne** (*open daily 9.30–6; Dec–Mar closed Tues; adm*) occupies a property once owned by the dukes of Burgundy.

On the A6 just to the south is the very popular **Archéodrome de Bourgogne** (*open Feb–Oct daily 10–5; adm*), a fascinating collection of reconstructions from earliest times, including a section of the defences of Alésia, as described by Julius Caesar.

Down the Saône

The Côte Chalonnaise, west of Chalon-sur-Saône, is a natural extension of the Côte d'Or. Its 4,000 hectares of vines produce some delightful burgundies, cheaper than their northern cousins. The Mâconnais is planted with more hectares of vines than any of the other wine areas in Burgundy, some 6,500, although that still pales into insignificance when compared with the vast extent of the vineyards of Beaujolais to the south. The Saône riverside towns of Tournus and Mâcon are good starting points for trips westwards into lovely countryside marked by the legacy of the abbey of Cluny.

The Côte Chalonnaise and the Mâconnais

The Côte Chalonnaise begins where the Côte de Beaune left off. A winding route along little roads will lead you along the vine slopes from Chagny to Chalon. **Bouzeron** offers an aligoté white wine surprise. Above **Rully**, a medieval **château** is the most spectacular wine-making property of the Côte Chalonnaise, still owned by descendants of its 13th-century builders. Wine-lovers should then wend their way to little **Mercurey**, with five Premier Cru vineyards. **Givry** boasts a late-18th-century church by Emiland Gauthey with extravagant domes. Tatraux-Juillet is a wine *domaine* to look out for at Poncey, west of town.

Chalon-sur-Saône may be fairly industrial, with drab quaysides, but the old town has dashes of colour and the odd fancy façade, particularly on Rue du Châtelet. The **Musée Niepce** (*open July–Aug Wed–Mon 10–6; rest of year Wed–Mon 9.30–11.30 and 2.30–5.30; adm*) on the quays is devoted to the pioneering local man who made the first photograph of all time, and to the history of photography. On Place St-Vincent, the main square in the old town, timberframe houses look on to the cathedral with its sharp-edged rectangular towers. Romanesque faces peer out of the odd capital, but the style of the interior is three-storey Gothic. The chaotic displays of the **Musée Denon** (*open Wed–Mon 9.30–12 and 2–5.30; adm*) stand across the square from the cathedral behind a classical façade.

Getting Around

There's a faster **train** service from Paris-Gare de Lyon to Mâcon (*c. 1hr 40mins*) than to Chalon-sur-Saône further north (*2hrs 30mins*). Mâcon has two separate train stations, the TGV station Mâcon-Loché and the central Mâcon-Ville. Regular trains between Dijon and Mâcon serve Chalon-sur-Saône and Tournus.

Tourist Information

Chalon-sur-Saône: Square Chabas, Bd de la République, **t** 03 85 48 37 97, *www.chalon-sur-saone.net*.
Tournus: 2 Place Carnot, **t** 03 85 51 13 10.
Mâcon: 1 Place St-Pierre, **t** 03 85 21 07 07, *www.macon-tourism.com*.

Where to Stay and Eat

Rully ✉ 71150

Le Vendangerot, 6 Place Ste Marie, **t 03 85 87 20 09 (*inexpensive*). A simple but satisfying hotel-restaurant in the centre, with good wines (*moderate*). *Closed mid-Jan–Feb; restaurant closed Tues lunch and Wed lunch*.

Mercurey ✉ 71640

***Le Val d'Or, Grande Rue, **t** 03 85 45 13 70, *www.levaldor.com* (*moderate*). A 19th-century coaching inn with comfortable rooms and Burgundian fare (*expensive*). *Closed Christmas–mid-Jan, 3 wks Mar/April; restaurant closed Mon, and Tues lunch*.

Chalon-sur-Saône ✉ 71100

***St-Georges, 32 Av Jean Jaurès, **t** 03 85 48 27 05 (*moderate*). The best place in Chalon, set in an appealing old building. There's a

cheaper *bistrot* as well as the reputed restaurant (*expensive–moderate*).
Hôtel St-Jean, 24 Quai Gambetta, **t 03 85 48 45 65 (*inexpensive*). Restful rooms overlook the calm river. Good value.

Buxy ✉ 71390

Hôtel Fontaine de Baranges, **t 03 85 94 10 70, *Hotel.Fontaine.de.Baranges@wanadoo.fr* (*moderate*). Nicely done up 19th-century house with balconies to the rooms.
Aux Années Vins, Place du Carcabot, **t** 03 85 92 15 76 (*expensive–moderate*). A well-run restaurant with tempting menus. Doubles as an interesting wine shop. *Closed Tues, Wed lunch, and part of Jan and Sept*.

Tournus ✉ 71700

****Hôtel Greuze, 5 Place de l'Abbaye, **t** 03 85 51 77 77 (*luxury–very expensive*). Beautifully restored old house near the abbey with 21 rooms . *Closed mid-Nov–mid-Dec*.
***Le Domaine de Trémont, Route de Plottes, **t** 03 85 51 00 10, *tremont@chateauhotels.com* (*expensive–moderate*). A restful and exclusive address south of town.
Hôtel de Saône, Rive Gauche, Quai Georges Bardin, **t 03 85 51 20 65 (*inexpensive*). Quietly set by the river, with a terrace looking on to it. *Closed mid-Oct–mid-Mar*.
Greuze, Rue Albert Thibaudet, **t** 03 85 51 13 52 (*very expensive–expensive*). A bastion of the finest traditional Burgundian cuisine and wine. *Closed mid-Nov–mid-Dec*.

Mâcon ✉ 71000

***Bellevue, 416 Quai Lamartine, **t** 03 85 21 04 04, *Bellevue.Macon@wanadoo.fr* (*expensive–moderate*). Solid, respectable old hotel with satisfying cuisine. *Closed mid-Nov–Dec; restaurant closed Tues lunch and Sun*.

Around Tournus, Roman-style terracotta tiles start to put in an appearance on the roofs, a sign that you are approaching southern France. **Tournus** is a little town sandwiched between a busy main road and a dull bank of the Saône river. However, its **abbey church** was at the centre of a melodramatic tale. Running away from the Vikings with the relics of the influential Philibert (*see* 'Noirmoutier', p.338, and 'Cunault', p.317), a religious community eventually joined an existing monastery here, with some inevitable clashes. The church dates from the Romanesque reconstruction. You can still make out the form of the oval defensive enclosure around it, fortified gates and all. The west front openings look like loopholes. Some patterning in the Lombard tradition adds meagre visual relief to the façade. The narthex is flanked by two bodyguards of towers. Walk inside and you will see that the narthex has the dimensions of a separate church, held up on enormous columns. Further staggeringly high columns hold up the nave. Made of pink stone, they have been set out so as to resemble brick. The choir, the last part of the church to be built, in contrasting white stone, seems dwarfed by the scale of the nave. In the pretty houses encircling the church, craft and tourist shops sell wicker baskets and pottery, while black coiffes with veritable chimney tops steal the show in the **local history museum**. The town's most famous son is that tear-jerker of a pre-Revolutionary painter, Greuze.

Macho **Mâcon** has been expanding along the flat west bank of the Saône for some time now. It was the home of the Romantic poet-cum-politician Alphonse Lamartine, whose statue stands on the central quayside. The **Musée Lamartine** (*open Wed–Mon 10–12 and 2–6, Sun pm only; adm*), in a splendid pre-Revolutionary stone mansion, tells his story. Having enjoyed a fairly happy childhood, Lamartine went on to lead a dissolute student life but in later life was haunted by the death of his daughter. His first volume of poetry, *Méditations*, was published in 1820; a decade later *Harmonies poétiques et religieuses* caused him to be elected to the Académie Française. A liberal thinker and politician, he believed that politics should mainly be concerned with trying to solve the problem of poverty, and championed the separation of Church and state as well as press freedom.

The **Musée des Ursulines** (*open same hours; adm*) occupies a former convent but offers an extensive introduction to the Mâconnais from prehistory to the present. Not much remains of Mâcon's medieval **cathedral**, but you can make out some of the fine detail of the Last Judgement scenes on the tympanum of the 12th-century narthex. The sober replacement cathedral went up in the early 19th century. The unmissable Hôtel-Dieu opposite, still a hospital, was the work of Soufflot, he who designed the Panthéon in Paris.

The wines of the Mâconnais are on sale in town, but the **Maison Mâconnaise des Vins** is a short drive north of the centre, on the busy N6. This large establishment represents the wines of some 20 *appellations*.

The Charollais and the Brionnais

Among the splendid hills of this most southerly section of Burgundy lie the vestiges of what was once the greatest early medieval abbey in Europe – Cluny. For a touch of Ancien Régime decadence, head for the Château de Cormatin, and for sheer indulgence don't miss the gorgeous wine villages of the charming Mâconnais countryside.

Towards Cluny

Two routes from the Saône-side vineyards to Cluny offer many distractions along the way. The northerly one goes west from Tournus past wooded hilltop villages, including **Brancion** (*small fee to enter the village*), the prettiest one in Burgundy,

Getting Around

A local **railway** line from Le Creusot, which is linked to Paris by TGV, serves Paray-le-Monial, Marcigny, Pouilly-sous-Charlieu and Roanne.

Tourist Information

Cluny: 6 Rue Mercière, **t** 03 85 59 05 34, *cluny@wanadoo.fr.*

Charolles: Rue Baudinot, **t** 03 85 24 05 95, *www.institut-charolais.com.*

Paray-le-Monial: Av Jean-Paul II, **t** 03 85 81 10 92, *ot.paray@wanadoo.fr.*

Charlieu: Place St-Philibert, **t** 04 77 60 12 42, *www.ville-charlieu.fr.*

Where to Stay and Eat

Salornay-sur-Guye

M Forestier et M Berclaz, t 03 85 59 91 56 (*moderate*). A couple of young Swiss guys have done up this large B&B – in a quiet village 12km north of Cluny. They'll also provide lively and intelligent conversation.

St-Vérand ✉ 71570

★★★**Auberge du St-Véran**, La Roche, **t** 03 85 23 90 90, *direction@auberge.saintveran.com* (*moderate–inexpensive*). Utterly enchanting small, simple wine village hotel with 11 rooms and a restaurant (*expensive–moderate*) to match. *Closed Jan, Mon, and Sept–June Tues.*

Berzé-la-Ville ✉ 71960

★★**Le Relais du Mâconnais**, La Croix Blanche, **t** 03 85 36 60 72, *www.ifrance.com*

(*moderate*). Peaceful rooms and a sensational restaurant (*expensive*).

Igé ✉ 71960

★★★★**Château d'Igé, t** 03 85 33 33 99, *ige@relaischateaux.com* (*expensive*). Just east of Cluny, with vaulted rooms, a beamed dining room, and a history going back to medieval times. Good cuisine. *Restaurant closed lunch Mon–Thurs exc hols.*

Cluny ✉ 71250

★★★**Hôtel de Bourgogne**, Place de l'Abbaye, **t** 03 85 59 00 58 (*moderate*). Right by the former abbey, with new owners. Check to see your room's been renovated. The restaurant (*expensive–moderate*) is plush and old-fashioned. *Closed Dec–Feb; restaurant closed Wed and Tues.*

Paray-le-Monial ✉ 71600

★★★**Terminus**, 27 Av de la Gare, **t** 03 85 81 59 31, *terminus-paray@club-internet.fr* (*inexpensive*). Comfortable rooms and restaurant (*dinner only; moderate*). *Closed Sun eve out of season, and 2 wks Nov.*

★★**Grand Hôtel de la Basilique**, 18 Rue de la Visitation, **t** 03 85 81 11 13, *resa@hotel basilique.com* (*inexpensive*). More characterful. Restaurant (*moderate*). *Closed 1 Nov–14 Mar.*

Sermaize near Poisson ✉ 71600

Mathieu, t 03 85 81 06 10 (*inexpensive*). Among gorgeous pastures dotted with Charolais cows, due south of Paray-le-Monial, a gentle, retired farming couple greet you at the round stairtower to their adorable medieval stone farmhouse B&B. Charming rooms with old stone features.

which has done well in protecting itself from the tourist hordes. While a good number of houses remain from the 15th century, the medieval castle has fallen into picturesque disrepair. For a small fee you can wander round its mostly empty chambers and climb to the top of its keep. From here you get a lovely view of the village church at the top of the hill which contains some of the gentlest of medieval frescoes.

Bears and lions once favoured the **Grottes d'Azé** (*open April–Sept daily 10–12 and 2–6; adm*). Now tourists come to cool down in these caves south of Brancion, reached via picturesque winding roads. The archaeological finds at the caves also show the traces of many humans from down the millennia. The guided tour takes you past an underground river and pretty pools.

The recently restored **Château de Cormatin** (*open May–Sept daily 10–12 and 2–6.30; rest of period Easter–11 Nov daily 10–12 and 2–5.30; adm*) is surrounded by playful Baroque-style gardens, with a labyrinth, chequerboard effects, and the odd folly. It was built for Antoine du Blé d'Huxelles, between 1605 and 1616; his son ordered the extravagant banquet of 17th-century interiors, with Mannerist paintings, gold-leaf, painted flowers, and garlands and grotesques on the ceiling. The *pièce de résistance* is the small study, a gem of a blue and gold room, made to glitter by candlelight.

The second route to Cluny takes you west from Mâcon, into the irresistible countryside of the Mâconnais and its vineyards. The orange-stained **Roche de Solutré**, a massive outcrop of limestone watching over the frontier with Beaujolais, commands the landscape. In the 19th century, the remains of thousands of wild horses were found at the base of the Roche; these Solutré finds gave their name to the Upper Paleolithic Solutrean era (20,000–16,000 BC). The **Musée de la Préhistoire** (*open June–Sept daily 10–7; Feb–May and Oct–Nov Wed–Mon 10–12 and 2–5; adm*), just below the outcrop, explains the theories behind the local prehistoric men's wiles to catch these horses.

The Solutré rock overlooks the orange-stone villages of Mâconnais wine country. Two of these, **Pouilly** and **Fuissé**, have given their name to a highly regarded white wine produced in a handful of parishes here. Goyon at Solutré is one Pouilly-Fuissé producer worth seeking out. It is hard to find a prettier wine village than nearby **Chasselas**, which shares its name with a well-known sweet table grape, but also produces good Mâconnais wines. North of Solutré a clutch of utterly charming Mâconnais villages have strong connections with Lamartine (*see* 'Mâcon'), hence its tourist label – the Val Lamartinien. The irresistible **Château de Pierreclos** (*open daily 9.30–6; adm, you may need to shout to attract the attention of the feisty Mme Pidault – she's often serving customers in the wine cellars*) dominates its village. The medieval structure was brought up to date in the 16th century. You can visit the vaulted cellars and one or two reception rooms, as well as buying Mâcon wines and liqueurs.

Milly-Lamartine has changed its name to reflect the fact that the poet spent his childhood here. The Lamartine home is a wine property dating back to the 17th century, set around an enchanting courtyard; if you arrive at the right moment the courteous owner will let you try his wines and show you around. The chapel at **Berzé-la-Ville** is famous as one of the rare places to have preserved Cluniac wall paintings, dating from no later than the 12th century. The colours and size of the 15ft high Christ in Majesty are striking. He has a middle-aged wise face, with wide eyes, inspired by Byzantine art. The medieval château at **Berzé-le-Châtel**, just north, is a superb structure in earth-brown stone, surveying the southern approaches to Cluny. Now an elegant residence, you can wander round its terraces.

Cluny

Boasting the largest church in Europe through the Middle Ages, and for some time home to the most powerful abbey in Europe, Cluny saw its sublime **abbey church** hammered to bits at the French Revolution. Begun in 1085, completed about 1130, it

The Powerhouse of Early Medieval Monasteries

The abbey was founded in 910 after Bernon, abbot of Baume-les-Messieurs in the Franche-Comté, was given land here. Bernon wanted to encourage the strict observance of the Benedictine Rule, but, most importantly, the Cluny abbey charter gave it total independence from all authorities except for the papacy. The abbots turned into powerful feudal landowners and ended up running an immense network of foundations across Europe.

Maieul of Avignon became abbot in 965. Admired and respected, he emphasized the importance of charity and commissioned the church known as Cluny II. His successor, Odilo, ruled the order for 55 years, from 994 to 1049, when Cluny grew into the most important abbey in Europe. Odilo insisted on the rigorous spirit of monasticism, fought against abuses and forged very close ties with the papacy in Rome. He advanced the importance of Mary in medieval theology and also instituted All Souls' Day on 1 November to commemorate the dead. By the end of his time, there were around 60 monasteries under Cluny's control.

Hugues de Semur, later St Hugues de Cluny, held the post of abbot for a record 60 years, from 1049 to 1109, and ordered the building of the vast Cluny III and a new monastic ensemble as the headquarters of the order. Under him the number of Cluniac dependencies exploded perhaps to as many as 2,000 institutions. Kings, emperors and even popes came to Cluny to seek advice. In the 12th century Cluny was starting to go downhill. St Bernard railed against the decadence of the Cluniac order in this period; he would develop the much stricter Cistercian order in response.

was at 613ft the largest church in Europe until St Peter's in Rome went up in the 16th century.

The **Musée Ochier** (*open July–Sept daily 9–6; mid-Feb–June and Oct daily 10–12 and 2–5; Nov–mid-Feb daily 10–12 and 2–4; adm*) will help you visualize the scale of the medieval abbey. It also has a wonderful collection of carved stone sculptures. From the museum you can take a 1½ hour-guided tour of the abbey vestiges; or you can visit them at your own pace. The narthex by itself would have been the size of a mighty church. Head to the granary building for the highlight of the tour, beautifully carved and displayed capitals rescued from Cluny III's choir end. The most striking one depicts Adam and Eve desperately trying to hide from God behind big leaves.

A few kilometres north is **Taizé** (*www.taize.fr*), a noted religious centre visited by tens of thousands of young people from all over the world.

Paray-le-Monial

To see a small-scale model of Cluny III, visit Paray-le-Monial. The exterior decoration is concentrated on the two transept doors, with their chevrons and chequered effects, their Romanesque beasts and vines in stone. The church was planned under the great Cluniac abbot Hugues de Semur, who was overseeing the construction of the mighty Cluny III at exactly the same time. The entrance to the nave lies curiously off centre. The nave itself is tall and dark, the main arches in Gothic style with egg-patterned borders, the two levels of arcades above having round Romanesque arches. The architecture is divided up along its length by Roman-style channeled pilasters and columns. Experts say that this interior reflects the plan of Cluny III the most clearly of any church in France.

Paray's church was dedicated to the Virgin Mary, but the visions of an extraordinary woman in the 17th century eventually changed that. Marguerite-Marie Alacoque was the daughter of a Charollais lawyer who felt a strong religious calling. In 1671 she entered a convent where she said she received several visitations from Christ exhorting her to encourage a cult devoted to his Sacred Heart, a symbol of his love for mankind. Her fellow nuns and Louis XIV pooh-poohed her 'delusions', and it was only after the French Revolution that the need for religious fervour encouraged a wider interest in the cult she had started. The first important pilgrimage to Paray-le-Monial in honour of the Sacred Heart took place in 1873 and the annual event has been going strong ever since. Marguerite-Marie was canonized in 1920. A good number of religious orders now have communities in town, and the pilgrimage to Paray apparently ranks second in importance in France after Lourdes. You can visit the 17th-century **Chapelle de la Visitation** where Marguerite-Marie experienced her major visions.

The Brionnais to Charlieu

The southwest section of Burgundy, the triangular Brionnais, rolls down east of the Loire below Paray-le-Monial, from Charolles to Charlieu. This is the closest Burgundy comes to the Massif Central, the Monts de la Madeleine west of the Loire forming a distant deep-blue backdrop. Set in a lovely countryside of rural hedgerows, these quiet parts are known above all for their Romanesque churches dating from the late 11th and early 12th centuries, when the abbey of Cluny was at the height of its powers.

Rarely will you see so much elation portrayed in Christian art as on the tympanum of the golden-tinged stone church of **Montceaux-l'Etoile**. Christ seems to be stepping out of his mandorla like a showbiz queen making her entrance on stage. His shapely front leg is scarcely disguised by drapery. Below, the crowded apostles join in, lifting their hands high with wild excitement. Inside, second-rate 18th-century decorators were allowed in, plastering sickly putti on the ceiling. **Anzy-le-Duc**, a short way south, has one of the most important churches of the Brionnais, part of a former priory going back to the 11th century. An octagonal tower with twin arcaded layers rises from the church itself. On the outside, the carved figures on the tympanum have had their faces hacked off, but the Virgin and apostles along the lintel still stand in expressive poses. From the priory courtyard, admire the row of *modillons*, offering a great display of medieval creatures and faces. Inside some truly weird and wonderfully monstrous capitals line up along the nave columns. St Michael, carrying a big shield, fights a hideously deformed creature. A musician plays the flute, his wild hair like flowing unkempt foliage. One strange couple are joined at the hip.

Once a sturdy fortified hill village, **Semur-en-Brionnais** has now been reduced to a bucolic tourist one. The remnants of a medieval castle stand in the centre; squeeze through its tight corridors and staircases on a self-guided tour. Hugues de Semur, the great abbot of Cluny, came from the lordly family whose home this was. Not surprisingly then, the place was endowed with a Cluniac-style church; it now looks a bit of a shambles, having suffered neglect and been heavily restored. The lovely crossing tower is its finest feature. The tympanum represents Christ in Majesty, but the lintel scene is less familiar, representing the life of St Hilaire, the Poitevin saint (*see* 'Poitiers', pp.347–51) to whom the church was dedicated. Crude carvings decorate the apse.

Charlieu, at the southern tip of the Brionnais triangle, boasts the greatest golden-stoned religious legacy in the area. Although most of the once especially splendid abbey church of **St-Fortunat** was destroyed at the Revolution, the remnants of the entrance are covered with some of the finest Romanesque carving produced in 12th-century France. A fleecy Paschal lamb in high relief peers down, half-wise, half-dumb, over the main portal. Bands of floral and geometrical patterns like finely designed cloth embellish the arch. Below, many of the figures have been decapitated, but their liveliness lives on. On the smaller portal, the wedding scene at Cana unfolds. The other main scene represents the Transfiguration, with Moses, Elijah, Peter, James and John as witnesses. Bits and pieces of the rest of the abbey have been transformed into museum spaces. On Charlieu's main square, the 13th-century **St-Philibert**, with its three tympanum reliefs on the façade, survived the Revolution rather better.

Charlieu has long had a reputation for producing luxury silk, as recalled at the **Musée de la Soierie** (*open July–Aug daily 10–7; rest of year Tues–Sun 2–6; closed Jan; adm*), which has taken over the central 18th-century hospital. A good video in French explains silk-weaving, while the tour guides take pleasure in getting the old looms to clatter into action. A corridor of haute couture silk dresses made in Charlieu includes a leopard-silk number made by Yves St-Laurent for Catherine Deneuve. Back outside, several of the substantial crossed timberframe townhouses have been turned into tempting shops. In the western outskirts, the 14th-century **Couvent des Cordeliers** calls for a last religious halt. The church is typically Franciscan, big and plain, but decorated with worn fragments of Gothic paintings. In the cloisters, most of the capitals simply bear floral motifs, but one side is enlivened by cautionary tales in stone.

Beaujolais and the Bresse

Stepping outside Burgundy, the Beaujolais and the Bresse stretch down either side of the Saône river to the outskirts of Lyon.

Beaujolais

The massed ranks of vines rising above the west bank of the Saône between Mâcon and Lyon produce the extraordinarily well-known wines of Beaujolais. The area lies almost entirely outside Burgundy, but this gorgeous rectangle of land, a mere 60 by 20 kilometres, makes almost as much wine as the whole of Burgundy's vineyards put together. Beaujolais is meant to be drunk young, but not that young; the rush to produce Beaujolais Nouveau each November is a marketing coup that cuts both ways – while becoming known across the world, the area has suffered from a reputation for poor-quality vinification. There are many excellent Beaujolais wines, of course. The best ten *crus*, from the northern Beaujolais, have each been given their own AOC to

Getting Around

Lyon's **airport** lies close by. Romanèche-Thorins and Villefranche-sur-Saône have reasonable **rail** links with Paris and Dijon as well as Lyon. Bourg-en-Bresse is on the Paris-Gare de Lyon–Geneva line.

Tourist Information

Beaujeu: Square de Grandhan, t 04 74 69 22 88, www.beaujeu.com.
Villefranche-sur-Saône: 96 Rue de la Sous-Préfecture, t 04 74 07 27 40, www.villefranche.net.
Châtillon/Beaujolais des Pierres Dorées: Place de la Mairie, t 04 78 47 98 15, www.beaujolais.com.
Bourg-en-Bresse: 6 Av Alsace Lorraine, t 04 74 22 49 40, www.bourg-en-bresse.org.
Châtillon-sur-Chalaronne: Place du Champ de Foire, t 04 74 55 02 27, www.tourisme-en-dombes.org.
Pérouges: t 04 74 61 01 14, www.perouges.org.

Where to Stay and Eat

St-Amour-Bellevue
L'Auberge du Paradis, t 03 85 37 10 26 (*moderate*). Lots of angels amongst the sweet decorations of this characterful little restaurant. *Closed Mon and Tues, and Jan.*

Juliénas ✉ 69840
★★Chez La Rose, t 04 74 04 41 20, www.chez-la-rose.fr (*inexpensive*). Appealing hotel with comfortable rooms in this lively Beaujolais village, with capacious dining room (*expensive–moderate*) in which to savour local classics. *Restaurant closed Mon, and lunchtimes Tues, Thurs and Fri.*

Fleurie ✉ 69820
★★★Hôtel des Grands Vins, La Chapelle des Bois, 1km south by D119E, t 04 74 69 81 43 (*moderate*). In the midst of the vines with 20 decent rooms, plus wines for sale. Pool. *Closed Dec and Jan.*
Le Cep, Place de l'Eglise, t 04 74 04 10 77 (*expensive–moderate*). One of the best restaurants in the Beaujolais. *Must book. Closed Sun and Mon, and Dec and Jan.*

Chiroubles ✉ 69115
La Terrasse du Beaujolais, t 04 74 69 90 79 (*expensive–moderate*). A restaurant in a wonderful location above the vineyards, with tremendous views. *Closed Mon, and eves outside July and Aug, plus early Dec–Feb.*

Beaujeu ✉ 69430
★★Anne de Beaujeu, 28 Rue de la République, t 04 74 04 87 58 (*inexpensive*). Classic provincial rooms, grand dining room (*expensive–moderate*) and garden. *Closed late Dec–late Jan; restaurant closed Sun pm, Mon, and Tues lunch.*

Vaux-en-Beaujolais ✉ 69460
★★Auberge de Clochemerle, Rue Gabriel Chevallier, t 04 74 03 20 16, www.georgeslegarde.com (*inexpensive*). In this village of popular literary renown, rooms in a modern annexe, but traditional restaurant (*expensive–moderate*) in an old house with lovely terrace. *Closed late July–mid-Aug; restaurant closed Tues and Wed.*

Bagnols-en-Beaujolais ✉ 69620
★★★★Château de Bagnols, t 04 74 71 40 00, info@bagnols.com (*luxury*). Stupendous hotel rooms in a medieval hillside castle in a village above the vineyards, reached by a drawbridge. A splendid stone fireplace oversees the superb restaurant (*very expensive*). Pool. *Closed Jan–Mar; restaurant closed Sun pm, Mon, and Tues lunch in winter.*

Vonnas ✉ 01540
★★★★Georges Blanc, t 04 74 50 90 90, blanc@relaischateaux.fr (*luxury–very expensive*). For culinary brilliance, plus chic contemporary rooms. Pool and tennis court. *Restaurant closed Mon, Tues, and Wed lunch*
L'Ancienne Auberge, t 04 74 50 90 50 (*expensive–moderate*). An extra Blanc inn done in 1900s feel, offers simpler traditional cuisine at much more reasonable prices. *Closed Jan.*

Mionnay ✉ 01390
★★★★Alain Chapel, t 04 78 91 82 02, chapel@relaischateaux.fr (*expensive*). Another legendary French restaurant (*very expensive*), as well as luxury rooms. *Closed Jan; restaurant closed Mon, Tues, and Fri lunch.*

mark them out, and can keep a few years. Virtually every village across the whole Beaujolais area has a general wine-selling cellar. Or pick out individual properties making and bottling their own wine; some have grouped together into an association of impassioned Beaujolais makers, Secrets de Terroir, wishing to receive visitors.

The names of the lovely, vine-surrounded villages of the very fragrant top Beaujolais *appellations* trip prettily off the tongue. **St-Amour**, the most northerly, is the only one to lie within the boundaries of modern-day Burgundy. **Juliénas** has plenty of life and a clutch of restaurants. Down from **Chénas**, at **Romanèche-Thorins**, a major winehouse has transformed warehouses into a major modern wine museum, **Le Hameau du Vin** (*open daily 9–6; adm*), with ambitious presentations on wine-making down the ages before you arrive at the vast tasting and shopping areas. Back on the slopes, **Fleurie** benefits from a particularly open position. **Chiroubles** stands in a delightful location too, below a theatre of vines. Then **Morgon**, **Régnié** and **Brouilly** follow, Mont Brouilly offering great views all round.

Just west of the rather misleadingly named Belleville, **Capvignes** counts among six **Pôles Oenologiques**, imaginative new tourist centres highlighting Beaujolais viticultural traditions. This one is set in the restored little Château de Bel-Air at the back of a modern viticultural college. The other side of Belleville, another Pôle Oenologique and major Beaujolais wine-tasting centre has been placed, without any French irony, right by the busy N6 road at St-Jean-d'Ardières just north of town. **La Maison des Beaujolais** (*open mid-Jan–mid-Dec daily 9am–10pm; adm*) caters well to the masses.

Hidden in the hills to the west, the little town of **Beaujeu** was historic capital of Beaujolais. It looks crammed along its narrow valley bottom, the steep slopes above reserved for vineyards. The lively guided tour round the Pôle Oenologique of **Les Sources du Beaujolais** (*open May–Sept daily 10–7; Mar–April and Oct–Dec Wed–Mon 10–12 and 2–6; adm*) reveals the history of Beaujeu and the Beaujolais. Apparently Beaujolais wine has the giant Claude Brosse to thank for an early marketing coup. He took a cartload to Versailles in the 1680s. When the crowd of royal suitors was ordered to kneel, Brosse stood out from the others, still the height of an average man on his knees. The king, intrigued, tasted the merchant's wine, and the fashion was born for drinking Beaujolais in the highest circles. You too are treated to a wine-tasting at the end of the tour. Beaujeu's **Musée Marius Audin** (*same ticket*) is a more traditional local history museum on the same square. The outstanding stone sculptures displayed inside were rescued from Beaujeu's old château and church. You are also reminded here that Beaujeu hospital was the first in France to initiate charitable wine auctions to raise funds, before the more famous ones at Beaune got under way.

Vaux-en-Beaujolais has a special place in many a Frenchman's heart, as the inspiration for Gabriel Chevallier's *Clochemerle*, a classic novel from the 1930s poking fun at French village life in mock-pompous fashion. Down in the Saône valley, apartment blocks signal Beaujolais' modern capital, **Villefranche-sur-Saône**. The city's cultural life has been given a boost with the opening of the stylish **Musée Paul Dini** (*open Wed–Fri 11–6.30, weekends 2–6.30; adm*), a former grain exchange cleverly transformed to display the many hundreds of works by artists from Lyon and the Rhône-Alpes region from 1875 to the present day, avidly collected by the Dinis.

In the vinous Beaujolais hills west of Villefranche, the look of the villages lightens with the shift from granite to golden sandstone, and the wine lightens somewhat too. This area of glowing villages has been justly nicknamed **Les Pierres Dorées**. There's a touch of Italy in the air. As well as having houses built in the rich ochre stone, many of the villages are beautified by a dominating château. Meander through **Cogny**, **Jarnioux** and **Ville-sur-Jarnioux** for **Theizé**, its imposing **Château de Rochebonne** (*open May–Oct Wed–Mon 2–6; adm*) transformed into another Pôle Oenologique. The villages of **Oignt**, **Bagnols**, **Charnay** and **Châtillon** look particularly dramatic, castle towers silhouetted on their heights. Beside more modest **St-Jean-des-Vignes**, the modern cement **Espace Pierres Folles** (*open Mar–Nov Mon–Tues and Thurs–Fri 9–12 and 2–6, Wed and weekends 2–6; adm*), the most southerly of the Beaujolais' Pôles Oenologiques, focuses on the geology of the region, extraordinarily rich in fossils.

The Bresse and the Dombes

East of the Saône, the flat, fertile lands of the Bresse straddle the modern regions of Burgundy and the Rhône-Alpes. In France, the name not only conjures up images of adorable timberframe farms with cute chimneys known as *cheminées sarrasines* and decorative arrangements of corn on the cob, but also blue-legged white-robed *poulets*, considered the finest chickens in the country, sold under a specific AOC label. Start at the **Ecomusée de la Bresse Bourguignonne** in the **Château de Pierre-de-Bresse** (*open daily 2–6; adm*). This stupendous moated castle was built for the Thyard family in the 17th century, to classic French design; one wing presents the history and traditions of the Bresse. Talking of wings, the town of **Louhans** goes wild on chicken market day. It also offers an arcaded main street, historic hospital pharmacy, and the church of St-Pierre with its colourfully tiled roof. Heading into the Rhône-Alpes region, some of the finest old Bressan farms are to be found around **St-Trivier**. South, along the N79 road linking Mâcon and Bourg-en-Bresse, the **Musée de la Bresse** by St-Cyr-sur-Menthon provides a major showcase for Bressan culture.

The centre of **Bourg-en-Bresse**, former capital of the whole region, has a few historic streets and a central church containing carved choir stalls depicting elegant saints, comical jesters and fighting dogs and dragons. This, though, is quite eclipsed by the triple-cloistered **abbey of Brou** (*open daily 9–12 and 2–5; adm*), one mile outside the centre. Under its multicoloured roof, the church (1513–32) was a tour de force of Flamboyant Gothic by Flemish architect Loys Van Boghem. The abbey's founder, Marguerite of Austria, is depicted with her husband Philibert de Savoie on the tympanum of the main façade with its intriguing tracery patterns. Inside, the carved rood screen hints of the splendours to come in the choir. The stalls carved with biblical scenes have an almost neurotic intensity. Few more elaborate and dignified lordly tombs have survived in France than those of Marguerite and Philibert. The couple are each represented twice in idealized form, above in finery, below in their death shrouds. The couple are depicted again in the splendid stained glass, and, in less idealized fashion, in portraits in the excellent **fine arts museum** spreading out around the cloisters and in the former monastic cells.

Southwest of Bourg, the Dombes, an extension of the flatlands of the Bresse, is dotted with hundreds of lakes. At **Châtillon-sur-Chalaronne**, a really fine mix of timberframe and brick houses cluster round the splendidly dark covered market, held up on a forest of wooden pillars. The Flemish-looking church is very grand too. The modern **Musée Traditions et Vie** (*open April–Sept Tues–Sun 10–12 and 2–6; Oct weekends only, same times; adm*) presents scenes of local rural life at the start of the 20th century. Another little museum is dedicated to model trains. A short walk up the hill stand the remnants of a castle.

Wild birds are attracted in large numbers to this lakeland area, but at the extremely popular **Parc des Oiseaux** (*entrance July–Aug daily 9.30–7.30; May–June and Sept 10–6.30; rest of year 10–5; adm*) by **Villars-les-Dombes**, birds from across the world, including even condors, are kept behind bars, admittedly in truly spacious, impressive modern aviaries. Even more popular **Pérouges**, a famously picturesque village above the Ain, is often swamped by flocks of tourists. Despite the industrial sprawl from Lyon, Pérouges remains particularly well protected by its ramparts, the surprising, stern church incorporated into them, and even provided with gun holes. Weaving and wine-making were once the source of the villagers' wealth. The houses are made of the same stones as the cobbled streets; many date from the 15th century, although a few timberframe structures go back even further. Take refuge from all the craft shops in the **Musée du Vieux Pérouges** (*open Easter–Oct; adm*) which fits together pieces of local history and provides wide views of the surrounding area from its tower.

The town of **Trévoux** may be much less well-known than Pérouges in these tourist times, but it is of greater historic importance. Overseeing the Saône river a little north of the Lyon, shielded from the big city by the beautiful Mont d'Or, it served as capital of the thorny independent principality of the Dombes from 1424 through the Ancien Régime. In the 18th century it became a major publishing centre, and even had its own Parlement, or law courts, from 1676 to 1771, although the Dombes was fully incorporated into the French kingdom in 1762. Grand old mansions climb the steep slopes to the plain Parlement building; pompous classical paintings inside can still be seen when the court isn't sitting. The remnants of a medieval castle languish further up.

Given the kiss of life by the dynamic and determined Marc Simonet-Lenglart and his partner (*see* also their sumptuous restoration of the Château de Cormatin, p.651), the early 17th century **Château de Fléchères** (*open July–Aug daily 10–12 and 2.30–6; April–June and Sept–mid-Nov weekends and public hols 10–12 and 2.30–6; adm*), just north of Trévoux and Fareins, by the Saône, looks in fine condition once more, fully recovered from a period of sad neglect: wood panelling and wood flooring restored, the place refurnished. Most excitingly, the new owners discovered whole expanses of original Italianate murals hidden under whitewash; Pietro Ricci of Lucca, a pupil of Guido Reni, spent the year of 1632 at Fléchères decorating the interiors. The action-packed works include depictions of a fantasy hunt. The most engrossing cycle portrays the labours of Hercules. Even if the classical hero looks a bit brutish, he shows immense physical energy carrying out his near-impossible tasks.

Straight Down the Rhône Valley

Although this stretch of river is blighted in parts by heavy industry, the vineyards desperately holding on to the slopes produce some of the greatest wines in southern France, while the dusty old riverside towns prove to have surprisingly sweet hearts.

Lovably tatty old Vienne, south down the Rhône from Lyon, was a very important place in Gallo-Roman and early Christian times, built on the site of the main settlement of the Celtic Allobroges tribe. It enjoyed a period of immense trading prosperity from the 1st century AD to the 3rd, as did **St-Romain-en-Gal** just across the river. In fact, head there first to appreciate the magnificence of the area's ancient legacy at the superlative modern **Musée et Sites Archéologiques** (*open Wed–Mon 10–6; closed Tues; adm*), presenting fabulous finds. The traders ordered sumptuous dwellings, and over 250 mosaic floors have been uncovered either side of the river, making this one of the most prolific areas for such art in the Roman world. The museum displays them beautifully. Some are highly coloured, others black and white. Some tell stories from Greek mythology, others feature decorative geometrical motifs. There are also outstanding Gallo-Roman mural paintings, models of Vienne and St-Romain-en-Gal in ancient times, and all the other archaeological finds typically associated with Roman towns – amphorae, statues of gods, tools – creating a highly evocative picture of Vienne's Gallo-Roman life. Don't miss the luxurious latrines rescued for posterity.

Across the river, **Vienne** seems quite overwhelmed by the weight of its dense cultural legacy. On top of the riverbank, the ruined medieval bishops' castle looks wearily down on the town; the 19th-century church with accompanying massive statue of the Virgin looks more confident, but boldest of all is the modern hospital on the heights. Vienne's **Roman theatre** (*open daily 9.30–1, summer also 2–6; adm*) was fitted snugly and discreetly into the hillside, yet with almost 50 tiers this counts among the largest built in Gaul. A few marble slabs in the stalls show how sumptuous the decorative finish was. Today the place hosts the Vienne summer jazz festival. Remnants from here, plus other wonderful classical fragments, have been dumped in the battered church of **St Peter**, forming a neglected but fascinating **Musée Archéologique** (*open 9.30–1, summer also 2–6; adm*). Vienne's most extraordinary Roman vestige stands in the heart of town, the **Temple of Augustus and Livia**. Its columns may look chipped and shoddy, but the building still stamps Roman imperial authority on the centre of town.

Vienne developed into an important Christian centre down the centuries, as its medieval churches help recall. The former **Cathédrale St-Maurice** resembles Lyon's muscular main church from the front. Among the delightful decorations in the three Gothic portals, look out for the adorable musical angels. The scenes in the central doorway illustrate events in Christ's life prefigured in the Old Testament. Inside, Gothic bays were added on to the earlier Romanesque ones down the nave, with their amusing carved decorations. Leave by the north door to admire more wonderful carving. The other main Christian stop is the **Cloître St-André-le-Bas** (*open 9.30–1, summer also 2–6; adm*), its greying Romanesque cloister held up on elegant columns, while contemporary art shows occupy further spaces.

The **Musée des Beaux-Arts et d'Archéologie** (*open daily 9.30–1, summer also 2–6; adm*), looks very old-fashioned, but, as elsewhere in Vienne, you'll enjoy the art if you're prepared to look beyond the neglected environment. The streets and squares

Getting Around

Valence is a mere 2hrs 30mins from Paris by TGV fast **train**. Vienne, Tain-l'Hermitage and Montélimar have regular rail links with Lyon.

Tourist Information

Vienne: Cours Brillier, t 04 74 53 80 30, *contact@vienne-tourisme.fr*.
Condrieu: Place du Séquoia, t 04 74 56 62 83.
Tournon-sur-Rhône: Hôtel de la Tourette, t 04 75 08 10 23, *tournon-sur-rhone@fnotsi.net*.
Valence: Parvis de la Gare, t 04 75 44 90 40, *www.tourisme-valence.com*.
Montélimar: Allées Provençales, t 04 75 01 00 20, *montelimar.tourisme@wanadoo.fr*.

Where to Stay and Eat

Vienne ✉ 38200

★★★★**La Pyramide**, 14 Bd Fernand Point, t 04 74 53 01 96, *pyramide@relaischateaux.com* (*very expensive*). Bright modern Provençal chic in the rooms, but known above all as a temple of *haute cuisine* (*very expensive–expensive*) – the street is even named after Fernand Point, the legendary chef who made its name. *Closed Feb–mid-Mar; restaurant closed Tues and Wed.*
★★**Hôtel de la Poste**, 47 Cours Romestang, t 04 74 85 02 04 (*inexpensive*). A reasonable option in the centre.

Estrablin ✉ 38780

★★★**La Gabetière**, 8km east of Vienne off the D502, t 04 74 58 01 31 (*inexpensive*). Delightful 16th-century manor with pool.

Chonas-l'Amballan ✉ 38121

★★**Domaine de Clairefontaine/Les Jardins de Clairefontaine**, t 04 74 58 81 52, *domaine.de.clairefontaine@gofornet.com* (*moderate–inexpensive*). Set back in large gardens on the Rhône's east bank, partly a former country retreat of the bishops of Lyon, now a characterful old-fashioned hotel

with reputed restaurant (*very expensive–expensive*), plus more sumptuous rooms in Les Jardins. Tennis court. *Restaurant closed Mon and Tues, and mid-Aug, and mid-Dec–mid-Jan.*

Condrieu ✉ 69420

★★★★**Hôstellerie Beau-Rivage**, 2 Rue du Beau-Rivage, t 04 74 56 82 82, *infos@hotel-beaurivage.com* (*expensive*). Luxury hotel right by the Rhône, with pleasing rooms even if the architecture's a bit of a mixed bag. Fine traditional restaurant with terrace overlooking the river.

Tournon-sur-Rhône ✉ 07300

Le Chaudron, 7 Rue St-Antoine, t 04 75 08 17 90 (*moderate*). On a pedestrian street, restaurant reputed for its Ardèche specialities and excellent wines. *Closed Thurs eve, and Sun, and most Aug and Christmas hols.*

Tain-l'Hermitage ✉ 26600

Rive Gauche, 17 Rue Joseph Péala, t 04 75 07 05 90 (*expensive*). Exciting modern restaurant with liner decoration, looking across the Rhône. *Closed Sun eve and Mon, and some Weds, and most Jan.*

Soyons ✉ 07130

★★★★**Domaine de la Musardière** and ★★★**La Châtaigneraie**, t 04 75 60 83 55, *info@provencehotel.fr* (*very expensive–expensive*). Two very good sister establishments side by side just off the N86. The Musardière has a good restaurant (*expensive*). Swimming pool and tennis court. *Restaurant closed Mon in winters, and Jan.*

Baix ✉ 07210

★★★★**La Cardinale et sa Résidence**, Quai du Rhône, t 04 75 85 80 40 (*luxury–very expensive*). Farm converted into a very smart, bright hotel, with pool; 3km away, the restaurant (*expensive*) in a grand old house has lovely views of the Rhône. *Restaurant closed lunch Mon–Sat July–Aug, and Mon–Wed lunch in winter.*

outside are vibrant and appealing. South of the centre, one last Gallo-Roman remain worth seeking out is the **Aiguille**, long claimed, in one of those more far-fetched Christian legends, to have been the tomb of Pontius Pilate. In fact the imposing arch topped by a pyramid probably formed the centrepiece of a Roman circus.

A string of very fine little winemaking *appellations* clings to the Rhône's west bank between Vienne and Valence. Tending these steep vines is quite a feat, but the well-drained plants lap up the sunshine to produce superlative wines. Syrah grapes yield heady red wines, the viognier, marsanne and roussanne varieties liquorous whites. North to south, you pass through the exclusive vineyards of Côte Rôtie, Condrieu (and tiny Château-Grillet), St-Joseph, Cornas and St-Péray. Hermitage and Crozes-Hermitage spread around the vine-covered hill of **Tain-l'Hermitage** on the east bank. From the latter's **Cave Coopérative**, take the **Route des Belvédères** for delicious views.

Opposite, towards the southern end of the St-Joseph area, the château at **Tournon-sur-Rhône** stands on solid rock surveying the river at its feet. Towers mark the line of the town's former ramparts. Highlight of the **castle museum**'s tour (*open June–Aug daily 10–12 and 2–6; late-Mar–May and Sept–Oct Thurs–Mon 10–12, Wed 10–12 and 2–5; closed Tues; adm*) is the triptych in the chapel, Christ ascending to heaven in a ball of flaming light. Rhône mariners are also recalled inside. Down below, venture into the darkness of the big plain Gothic church of **St-Julien** to view its touching murals. A steam train runs up from Tournon into the rugged northern Ardèche hills.

Below Tournon, follow the Route Panoramique to get a spectacular view in all directions from the heights of **St-Romain-de-Lerps**. **Cornas** back by the river produces splendid meaty red wines. Its white sibling, **St-Péray**, centred round the sweet little town of the same name, comes sparkling as well as still. The spectacular bone-white ruins of the medieval castle of **Crussol** sit like a huge battered snail's shell on the steep hillside above; amazing views east past Valence to the barrier of the Vercors mountains are the reward if you make it up its slippery sides.

Valence has pleasant pedestrianized old streets in its historic heart, the odd ornate façade standing out, notably the sensational Maison des Têtes, from which carved heads protrude. The Romanesque **cathedral** has been savaged by time and renovations. A bust recalls the death of Pope Pius VI in Valence in 1799, dragged here by Napoleon. Somewhat ironically, fiery red chalk drawings of Italy by the 18th-century artist Hubert Robert are the highlight in the **fine arts museum**. For thriving contemporary artistic communities, head south for the villages of **Cliousclat** and **Mirmande**.

Although its compact historic kernel may be caught between major nuclear installations along the Rhône, **Montélimar** conjures up very sweet images to French children. The almonds essential in making its famous nougat were first imported in the 16th century, but the area has always been able to produce the honey needed for the recipe. Shops selling nougat have sprung up along the treeless main roads into town. The old centre hides behind layers of plane trees and proves a surprisingly gentle place. Façades have recently been repainted in powdery colours, and one of the brightest buildings converted into the curious **Musée de la Miniature** (*open July–Aug daily 10–6; Feb–June and Sept–Dec Wed–Sun 2–6; adm*), dedicated to miniature works of art. Steep paths lead up to the semi-ruined, severe feudal **Château des Adhémars** (*open April–Oct daily 9.30–11.30 and 2–5.30; Nov–Mar closed Tues; adm*), aloof above the old town, but now given over to striking contemporary art exhibitions.

West of the Rhône, a surprisingly magnificent if little-known medieval cathedral crowns the hill of **Viviers**, long a deeply religious centre. From the outside, the Gothic choir looks as if it's wearing a tiara of stone. The interior is a staggering, vast, aisleless space. A series of rich tapestries showing scenes of Jesus' life adorns the choir.

East of the Rhône from Lyon into the Drôme

East of the Rhône below Lyon, sensationally unspoilt hills roll down from the Chartreuse and Vercors ranges. The Isère and Drôme, two major tributaries of the Rhône, weave their way through fertile valleys to join their master. Nature and semi-restored hill villages are the main tourist sights in these parts, but there are eccentric cultural surprises to entertain you along the way, plus the odd grand hilltop castle.

The Western Isère and Western Drôme

Music-lovers make the pilgrimage east from Vienne to the birthplace in 1803 of the great composer Berlioz. The pleasant valleyside town of **La Côte-St-André** stands above the stunningly flat Plaine de Bièvre with its seemingly unbroken patchwork of fields. Here the family's very comfortable, spacious 18th-century home on the main street has been turned into the **Musée Hector Berlioz** (*open Wed–Mon 9–12 and 3–6; adm*), recently renovated with verve to reflect the passionate nature of this supremely lyrical composer. He was also a deep romantic in his private life, and a sparkling correspondent. A major Berlioz music festival takes place in town every summer.

The intimidating **Château de Virieu** (*open July–Aug Tues–Sun 2–6; Easter–June and Sept–Oct weekends and public hols 2–6; adm*) stands high above the little town grovelling at its feet, its many towers and roofs covered with tiles typical of Dauphiné, like brown fish scales. The formidable place has never been disturbed by wars, and the entrance looks so forbidding you can understand why. Enter the inner courtyard via the wooden door covered with over 1,000 sharp nails, and you are greeted by five cannons pointing towards you, a gift from Louis XIII when he visited. The military theme continues through the handful of chambers you are shown, even featuring in the marquetry furniture in the most elegant room. Close by, a few pleasant little family resorts lie around the emerald-blue waters of the **Lac de Paladru**.

Joining the Isère river below **Voiron**, known as the place where Chartreuse liqueurs are made, the valley is lined with remarkably beautiful walnut orchards producing *appellation d'origine contrôlée* nuts. This area has a further culinary speciality, melting St-Marcellin cheese. Meandering along the delightful country lanes north of **St-Marcellin** town you will see big white milk-producing cattle grazing by solid farms with wide-brimmed roofs designed to cope with harsh wintry conditions.

At **Pont-en-Royans**, located below a near vertical wall of the Vercors range, the cluster of old riverside houses look as if they are about to jump into the clear waters of the Bourne rushing down from the heights. Jets of water freshen the air at the wonderfully playful **Musée de l'Eau** (*open July–Aug daily 10–6; rest of year Tues–Sun outside school hols 10–12 and 2–5.30; adm*), a brilliantly designed modern museum which offers the most appealing of introductions to the ecology of the Vercors range and to the theme of water power. At the end of the refreshing visit, taste H_2O vintages from around the world at the water bar.

No amount of water could soothe the agonizing burning pains and dreadful convulsions suffered by the patients in what is now the beautifully peaceful former religious foundation of **St-Antoine-l'Abbaye** west of St-Marcellin. In medieval times, ergotism, a terrible wheat-borne fungal illness, could ravage communities, and a religious order called the Antonins developed here in the 13th century to look after those afflicted by the terrible illness that became known as St Anthony's Fire. The place contained relics of St Anthony, one of the greatest figures of the early Christian centuries, reputed to have experienced torment during his days as a hermit in the desert. Although his sufferings were mainly psychological, he was adopted as the patron saint of the medieval order that spread across Europe. Work began on a great Gothic church here in the 13th century, but it would not be completed until the 15th. This was the most successful period in the abbey's history; from the 16th century it went into decline. A large portion of the complex of buildings has survived, however, and is slowly being restored. The church contains many riches, including wall paintings. In the choir, a tapestry cycle of finest Aubusson work depicts scenes in the life of Joseph. The **Musée de St-Antoine-l'Abbaye** (*open July–Aug daily 11–12.30 and 1.30–6; rest of year Wed–Mon 2–6; closed Tues; adm*), in adjoining buildings, houses a permanent collection on the Antonins and presents a changing programme of contemporary art exhibitions.

The valleys in these parts yield large rounded glacial pebbles, put to good effect in the characteristic square farmhouses, the stones often laid out in pleasing herringbone patterns. They were also employed in one of the strangest works of naïve architecture created in France, the **Palais Idéal du Facteur Cheval** (*open 15 April–15 Sept daily 9–7; Feb–14 April and 16 Sept–16 Nov 9.30–5.30; Dec–Jan 10–4.30; adm*), set in the back garden of an ordinary house in the Drômois village of **Hauterives**. The local postman Ferdinand Cheval fell in love, almost literally, with the stones of the area; having tripped over one in 1879, he picked it up, took it home, and began on a crazy building programme that would last 34 years. After the grottoes came a tomb for the family, in Egypto-Christian style, followed by a Hindu temple guarded by giants. Bizarre creatures and twisted vegetation popped out all over the complex. Models of great buildings from around the world were stuck on here and there. Cheval's folly has become one of the region's big attractions. On the back of it, **L'Art en Marche** (*open daily 10–12 and 2–6; adm*) presents quite an array of more recent naïve art.

Shoe addicts should leg it straight south for riverside **Romans-sur-Isère**, a bustling town where many shoe manufacturers are based. The place is crammed with shoe shops. The startling **Musée International de la Chaussure** (*open July–Aug Mon–Sat 10–6.30, Sun 2–6; Feb–June and Sept–Dec Tues–Sat 9–11.45 and 2–5.45, Sun 2–5.45; adm*) has taken over an immense former convent in the centre and offers surprising insights into the customs of past centuries and cultures via the history of footwear.

Getting Around

Romans-sur-Isère and St-Marcellin have railway stations on the line from Valence to Grenoble. Crest and Die are on the line from Valence to Gap and Briançon.

Tourist Information

La Côte-St-André: Pl Berlioz, t 04 74 20 61 43, *office-tourisme@cc-bievre-liers.fr.*

Pont-en-Royans: Grande Rue, t 04 76 36 09 10, *ot.gorgesdelabourne@wanadoo.fr.*

St-Antoine-l'Abbaye: t 04 76 36 44 46, *stantoine.tourisme@wanadoo.fr.*

Hauterives: Pl de la Galaure, t 04 75 68 86 82.

Romans-sur-Isère: t 04 75 02 28 72.

Crest: Place du Dr Maurice Rozier, t 04 75 25 11 38, *www.vallee-drome.com/ot-crest.*

Dieulefit: 1 Place de l'Eglise, t 04 75 46 42 49, *ot.dieulefit@wanadoo.fr.*

Grignan: t 04 75 46 56 75, *ot.paysdegrignan/ tourisme@wanadoo.fr.*

St-Paul-Trois-Châteaux: t 04 75 96 61 29, *www.st.paul-3-chateaux-tourisme.com.*

Suze-la-Rousse: t 04 75 04 81 41, *http://perso.wanadoo.fr/ot.suzelarousse.*

Nyons: t 04 75 26 10 35, *ot.nyons@wanadoo.fr.*

Buis-les-Baronnies: 2 Place du Quinconce, t 04 75 28 04 59, *www.buislesbaronnies.com.*

Where to Stay and Eat

St-Antoine-l'Abbaye ✉ 38160

Auberge de l'Abbaye, Mail de l'Abbaye, t 04 76 36 42 83 (*expensive–moderate*). Facing the abbey, restaurant serving excellent reasonably priced food. *Closed Tues out of season, and most Jan.*

Hauterives ✉ 26390

★★Le Relais, t 04 75 68 81 12 (*inexpensive*). Smart traditional house of pebbles, rooms nicely renovated, with decent traditional cuisine (*moderate*). *Closed 15 Jan–end Feb; restaurant closed Sun eve outside July–Aug, and Mon.*

Grignan ✉ 26230

★★★★Manoir La Roseraie, Route de Valréas, t 04 75 46 58 15, *roseraie.hotel@wanadoo.fr* (*very expensive*). Exclusive 19th-century property in walled grounds with pool and tennis court below the village. Stylish restaurant (*expensive*). *Closed half Dec and early Jan–mid-Feb; restaurant closed Tues and Wed out of season.*

★★★Au Clair de la Plume, Place du Mail, t 04 75 91 81 30 (*expensive*). Romantic pink hotel in 18th-century village house, rooms overlooking a delightful garden where teas are served. *Closed late-Jan–Feb.*

Le Poème, Montée du Tricot, t 04 75 91 10 90 (*moderate*). Intimate address serving delicious dishes such as the *brandade de morue* with summer truffles.

Dieulefit ✉ 26220

Auberge des Brises, Route de Nyons, t 04 75 46 41 49 (*moderate*). Stylish country cooking under shady lime trees 1.5km outside town. *Closed Tues, plus Mon eve and Wed out of season, and mid-Jan–mid-Mar.*

The Drôme River Valley and the Southern Drôme

Following the Drôme valley east from the Rhône, the odd village stands precariously perched over the waters. Occasionally, adventurous types are allowed to abseil down the side of the 170ft of sheer masonry of **Crest's** keep (*open June–Sept daily 10–7; Mar–May and Oct–Nov Wed–Mon 2–6; rest of year Sat and Sun 2–5; adm*). The medieval donjon, dating from the 12th century, is massive inside, and said to be the tallest surviving one in France. It long served as a prison and still retains prisoners' graffiti scratched on its walls. From its towering height are splendid views east to the Vercors.

East of Crest, the vines produce a perfumed sparkling apéritif wine, **Clairette de Die** – discover it along with a somewhat overpoetic presentation of its origins at the huge **Jaillance** cellars outside Die. Dwarfed by the massive yellow limestone Montagne de Glandasse, the southern rampart of the Vercors range, reaching nearly 5,000ft, it's

Le Poët-Laval ✉ 26160

***Les Hospitaliers**, t 04 75 46 22 32, *hotel-les-hospitaliers.com* (*expensive–moderate*). Wonderful little hotel in semi-ruined hillside village by Dieulefit. Delicious cuisine on a very limited menu (*expensive*). Pool. *Closed mid-Nov–mid-Mar; restaurant closed Mon and Tues out of season.*

Vinsobres

Le Bistrot, t 04 75 27 61 90 (*moderate–cheap*). Village restaurant spreading out appealingly round a simple fountain.

Nyons ✉ 26110

***Le Colombet**, Place de la Libération, t 04 75 26 03 66 (*moderate*). Pleasant traditional French provincial hotel with restaurant (*moderate*) at the heart of the action. *Closed late Nov–late Jan.*
Le Petit Caveau, 9 Rue Victor Hugo, t 04 75 26 20 21 (*expensive*). Restaurant in a very old vaulted room. The chatty waitress doubles as wine expert and is married to the chef, whose cuisine is full of Provençal herbs. *Closed Sun eves and Mon exc hols, plus Thurs out of season.*

Aubres ✉ 26110

***Auberge du Vieux Village**, Route de Gap, t 04 75 26 12 89, *auberge.aubres@wanadoo.fr* (*moderate*). Built on the castle ruins of a hilltop village just east of Nyons, some of the rooms have their own terraces as well as fantastic views. The restaurant has a terrace where you'll feel on top of the world. Pool. *Closed Dec.*

Les Pilles/Condorcet ✉ 26110

La Charrette Bleue, Route de Gap, t 04 75 27 72 33 (*moderate*). Cheerful roadside restaurant serving reliably excellent Provençal cuisine. *Closed Wed, and Sun eve and Tues out of season, plus mid-Dec–Jan.*

Valouse ✉ 26110

***Le Hameau de Valouse**, t 04 75 27 72 05, *egauhdv@alo.com* (*moderate–inexpensive*). Delightful restored huddle of stone houses turned into a peaceful hotel just off the amazing mountainous eastern route between Dieulefit and Nyons. Pleasant restaurant (*moderate*) with large terrace. Pool. *Closed Nov–Feb; restaurant closed Mon eve and Tues out of season.*

Mérindol-les-Oliviers ✉ 26170

Auberge de la Gloriette, t 04 75 28 71 08 (*moderate*). South of Nyons, off the road to Vaison-la-Romaine, dream of a Provençal cliché, an inn where pottery cats stretch out in the shade of splendid trees by a splashing fountain. The pies, pizzas and tarts cooked in the wood-burning oven are superlative, as are the views. The place has a few quite pleasant modern B&B rooms (*inexpensive*) at the back. *Closed Jan–early Feb; restaurant closed Sun, plus Thurs out of season.*

Buis-les-Baronnies ✉ 26170

**Sous l'Olivier, Quartier du Menon, t 04 75 28 01 04 (*inexpensive*). Pleasant rooms, pool, tennis court and sauna, plus inexpensive restaurant. *Closed Nov–mid-Mar.*

---

hard to believe such a tiny place as **Die** was long a cathedral city. And one with Roman roots. Gallo-Roman traces remain in this colourful town, such as the **St-Marcel arch**. Further vestiges are displayed in the little town **museum**. The separate 'mosaic of the bishop's palace' isn't Roman, as you might expect, but a medieval work providing a rare glimpse into Christian fantasies about the cosmos. The former **cathedral**, built in blindingly white stone, has an interior filled with Romanesque darkness.

Half-restored villages, sometimes with the battered ruins of a medieval castle perched above, hide out in the hills south of the Drôme river. The mountainous backdrops look like sets for Cowboys and Indians films, but, in the valleys, lavender fields presage Provence. Along the stunning D538 via Saou and Bourdeaux, the upturned beaks of the peaks of the Trois Becs cry out greedily for attention. Climb the D156 road around them for distant views eastwards to the highest peaks of the Alps.

In the mesmerizing countryside east of Montélimar and Donzère, elegant pyramidal mountains slope down to olive groves and cherry and apricot orchards, while the flats are carpeted with vines and lavender. Between Montélimar and Dieulefit, seek out the old hilltop villages such as **La Bégude-de-Mazenc** and **Le Poët-Laval**, the latter still beautiful if semi-ruined, its small museum recalling the sufferings experienced in this region for adopting Protestantism, including a rare preserved Protestant chapel.

Dieulefit, 'God made it', has made it rich through modelling clay of its own. The streets of this hippy-chic town are filled with potters. The traditional style is of simple glazes in blue, green, yellow or caramel – typically Provençal – but a clutch of more experimental artists have also opened up shop. The **Maison de la Terre** holds pottery exhibitions. The outskirts of town are the rather curious location for a Club Med holiday village, drawing a surprisingly glamorous crowd to the local cafés.

The irresistible D538 route leads south to the aristocratic French Renaissance **Château de Grignan** (*open April–Oct daily 9.30–11.30 and 2–5.30; Nov–Mar closed Tues; adm*), standing aloof on its rock above the village, houses running around its feet. The castle may have lost its head at the Revolution, but this remains an imposing pile with fascinating Ancien Régime connections. Mme de Sévigné, the court socialite and prolific letter-writer of Louis XIV's day, spent three long periods here. Her daughter, Françoise-Marguerite, was also quite a character, and a fine catch, regarded as one of the brightest beauties of the time. In 1669 she married François, Comte de Grignan, who forked out vast amounts on lavish entertainment. The couple's daughter Pauline was forced to sell the family castle in 1732 to pay off his debts. On a tour around some 20 modestly furnished rooms you are also told stories of the castle's other significant owners. Afterwards, go out on to what is surely one of the most decadent, glorious terraces in southern France, placed on the flat roof of the substantial church below.

Down in the touristy village streets, beautiful old roses perfume the air. The appealing **Musée de la Typographie et du Livre** (*open Tues–Sun 10–12.30 and 2–6; adm*) celebrates the art of book-making and famous correspondents, including Mme de Sévigné, who is buried in the vast Gothic cave of a church pressed against the hillside.

The lands south of Grignan are the most prolific truffle-producing territories in France, whole patches of truffle oaks planted in neat rows to encourage the crop. The superbly fortified square village of **Richerenches**, near Valréas, holds the most important truffle fair in France in midwinter. The place originally grew up as both a training and retirement centre for the massively rich banking crusaders, the Knights Templars, as recalled in the village.

An ancient little city still surrounded by medieval walls, the heart of **St-Paul-Trois-Châteaux** contains several intriguing elements, including a **Maison de la Truffe** (*open May–Sept Tues–Sun 9–12 and 3–7; Oct and Mar–April Tues–Sun 9–12 and 2–6; Nov–Feb Sun only 9–12 and 2–6; adm*), although details on the area's 'black diamond' get overtechnical – do listen to the useful CD in English for help. This centre stands at the back of the **cathedral**, full of astonishing details, like the masons' marks clearly visible on the stones around the outside of the choir, and the Gallo-Roman pieces incorporated into the west front. Inside, patches of naive murals and mosaics add to the captivating atmosphere. Also explore the maze of streets off the main square.

A sea of vines extends across the southwestern corner of the Drôme touching on Provence, producing excellent, sun-drenched, good-value Coteaux du Tricastin and Côtes du Rhône wines. As at Grignan, a massive **château** (*open April–Oct daily 9.30–11.30 and 2–5.30; Nov–Mar closed Tues; adm*) stands on its rock at **Suze-la-Rousse**, intimidating the village below. The crenellated medieval castle may look intimidating on the outside, but a staggering display of Renaissance features decorates the inner courtyard, bearing the symbols of power of the 16th-century owners, one of whom, François de la Baume, became governor of Provence. Part of it is now occupied by the **Université du Vin**, which has installed ultra-modern wine-tasting facilities and runs oenological courses. Even if you don't want to study wine, you can enter the sensational courtyard, and visit a string of rooms, sadly mostly empty.

The intensity of vines planted along the flat valley from Suze to Nyons indicates that this is major Côtes du Rhône wine-producing territory. The villages each boast an enormous wine cooperative, but consider visiting individual estates. Delicious hilltop **Vinsobres**' hilariously inappropriate-sounding name for a village devoted to wine-making in fact derives from the Latin for 'above the vines'.

Olives are the main crop associated with **Nyons**, although vineyards also abound around town, along with cherry and apricot orchards. The gourmet Tanche olives have been granted the distinction of their own *appellation d'origine contrôlée*. This friendly place hosts the **Institut du Monde de l'Olivier** (*open Mon–Thurs 8.30–12.30 and 1.30–5.0; adm*), with exhibitions on olive-related subjects, and has a rather sorry olive museum. Down by the stunning single arch of Nyons' medieval bridge, which spans the turquoise waters of the Eygues, the atmospherically restored **Moulins à Huile** (*open July–Aug daily exc Sun pm, visits at 10.30, 11.30, 3, 4 and 5; Feb–June and Sept–Dec Tues–Sat, visits same times; adm*) proves more engaging. Along the riverside, you'll find a lavender distillery often still in action. Up beyond the main old arcaded square, the old town is a secretive place, with steep little alleys leading up to the crenellated **Tour Randonne**. At the tourist office, get maps of the olive trail leading into the hills.

From the Tour Randonne, Nyons looks like a stopper wedged into the narrow entrance to the gorgeous **Baronnies** mountains to the east. Bald-topped Mont Ventoux and Montagne de Lure, guardians of northwestern Provence, loom over this quiet range – the Baronnies mark the historic boundary between the Dauphiné region and Provence. Down in the valleys are yet more cherry and apricot orchards, while the vines produce pleasant Coteaux des Baronnies wine. Lavender also finds space to grow. Crumbling, semi-abandoned, semi-restored villages cling to the hillsides. In summer you may encounter a lone goatherd guarding his or her flock; these parts produce excellent goat's cheese, *picodons*. Villages such as **Ste-Jalle** or the high-perched **Le Poët-Sigillat** stand in exceptionally gorgeous landscapes. The laid-back town of **Buis-les-Baronnies** attracts a fair crowd of hippies young and old, with plenty of plane-tree shade for all to lounge under beyond the tightly packed streets of the centre. It is claimed that Hannibal may have passed through here to surprise Rome, and that his elephants drank at the fountains. The healthy local special brew comes from the pretty linden or lime trees which line so many of the area's roads; their young leaves and flowers are gathered and dried to make *tilleul* infusion.

Two spectacular routes lead east from Buis. The more northerly takes you via the **Ouvèze valley** and the **Méouges gorge**. The more southerly route through the **Derbous and Jabron valleys** passes along delectable roads in the shadow of the brooding masses of Mont Ventoux and Montagne de Lure. The tiny village of **Brantes** faces the dark side of Mont Ventoux with foolhardy yet admirable defiance, while **Montbrun-les-Bains**' highly picturesque castle ruins stand on a gentler spine of rock. Press east to that dramatic gateway to Provence, **Sisteron**, the natural sliding doors of rock topped by a precipitous fort.

West of the Rhône Valley into the Ardèche

The Monts du Lyonnais and Mont Pilat

Fragments of Roman aqueducts scattered across the rolling hills of the **Monts du Lyonnais** recall how these well-watered hills due west of Lyon helped maintain the greedy needs of the great Gallo-Roman *Lugdunum*. Essentially a continuation southwards of the Beaujolais hills, the Monts du Lyonnais do produce small quantities of palatable wines of their own, the Coteaux du Lyonnais. The patches of vines begin

Getting There and Around

Ryanair operates cheap **flights** to St-Etienne's airport at Andrézieux-Bouthéon north of town. The Ardèche has a few tourist **trains**, but for public transport you have to rely on the rare **bus**. To reach central and southern Ardèche, best go from Montélimar. One bus line from there serves Vogüé, Ruoms and Vallon-Pont-d'Arc, another Aubenas, Vals-les-Bains, Joyeuse and Les Vans. There's also a bus line from Valence via Privas, Aubenas and Vals-les-Bains to Lalevade d'Ardèche.

Tourist Information

Pélussin: Maison du Parc du Mont Pilat, t 04 74 87 52 00, *www.parc-naturel-pilat.fr*.
St-Etienne: 16 Av de la Libération, t 04 77 49 39 00.
Privas: Place Charles de Gaulle, t 04 75 64 33 35, *privas@fnotsi.net*.
Vals-les-Bains: t 04 75 37 49 27, *vals-les-bains@fnotsi.net*.
Aubenas: t 04 75 89 02 03, *aubenas@fnotsi.net*.
Largentière: t 04 75 39 14 28, *largentiere@fnotsi.net*.
Joyeuse: t 04 75 39 56 76, *joyeuse@fnotsi.net*.
Les Vans: t 04 75 37 24 48, *les-vans@fnotsi.net*.

Ruoms: t 04 75 93 91 90, *ruoms@fnotsi.net*.
Vallon-Pont-d'Arc: t 04 75 88 04 01.
St-Martin-d'Ardèche: t 04 75 98 70 91, *st-martin-dardeche@fnotsi.net*.

Where to Stay and Eat

Ste-Croix-en-Jarez ✉ 42800
*Le Prieuré, t 04 77 20 20 09 (*inexpensive*). Four simple, atmospheric rooms set in the gateway into the abbey-village, with a big restaurant below (*moderate*). *Closed Jan–mid-Feb; restaurant closed Mon*.
Auberge de Vernolon, t 04 77 51 56 58 (*inexpensive*). Basic but good-value B&B rooms, with fine views, plus a spacious barn hung with striking modern art where rustic country cooking is served. Book in advance. *Restaurant closed Mon–Fri exc July and Aug*.

St-Agrève ✉ 07320
***Domaine de Rilhac, t 04 75 30 20 20 (*moderate*). An old stone farm in countryside 2km south of town converted into the most charming small hotel in the area. Tasty cuisine too (*expensive–moderate*). *Closed Jan–Feb; restaurant closed Tues eve, Wed, and Thurs lunch*.

around **L'Arbresle**, an old textile town, its quaint little historic heart signalled by three towers. Fans of Le Corbusier's modernist blocks wander around the secluded, neglected **Couvent des Tourettes** (*guided tours July–Aug daily; mid-April–June and Sept–Oct weekends; adm*) above Eveux, a stark convent on stilts, with playful elements added on to the fortress-like church.

The explosion in the Rhône Valley's chemical industry was set off in the quiet village of **St-Pierre-la-Palud**. The thick seam of pyrites here had already been exploited for its copper by France's greatest wheeler-dealer of the 15th century, Jacques Cœur (*see* 'Bourges', p.271), but in the mid-19th century the Perret brothers worked out how to extract sulphuric acid from the minerals, to be put to all manner of uses in the chemical industry. The **Musée de la Mine** (*open Mar–Nov weekends and public hols 2–6, plus July and Aug Tues and Thurs at 3; adm*) tells the serious industrial story. Going back to nature, south of St-Pierre, learn about the lives of wolves at the **Parc de Courzieu** (*open Mar–Oct daily 10–7; adm*), which keeps a lazy pack in captivity, and puts on displays of falconry in the afternoons. At **Yzeron**, the **Maison de l'Araire** (*open April– Nov Wed–Sun 2–6; adm*) covers Roman aqueducts, textiles and rural life. Outside the attractive old village of **Taluyers**, the Domaine du Caveau de St-Marc is one of the best Coteaux du Lyonnais properties to visit, making the whole range of local wines.

Lamastre ✉ 07270

★★★**Château d'Urbilhac, t** 04 75 06 42 11 (*expensive*). Very comfortable 19th-century château in mock-16th-century style. Spacious rooms and an extensive terrace for outside dining. Pool and tennis court. *Closed mid-Sept–May; restaurant closed weekday lunch plus Tues eve.*

Antraigues-sur-Volane ✉ 07530

★★**Auberge La Castagno**, Pont de l'Huile, **t** 04 75 88 25 01 (*inexpensive*). A pleasant, comfortable hotel with 10 rooms.

Remise, Pont de l'Huile, **t** 04 75 38 70 74 (*moderate*). Passionate chef serving fresh regional cuisine in a converted barn. *Closed Fri, and Sun eve out of season, late June, early Sept and mid-Dec–early Jan.*

St-Julien-du-Serre ✉ 07200

B&B Mas de Bourlenc, t 04 75 37 69 95 (*inexpensive*). Lost in the hills a few kilometres above Aubenas, with splendid views. Run by a charming young couple.

La Garde-Guérin ✉ 48800

★★**La Régordane, t** 04 66 46 82 88 (*inexpensive*). Cosy small hotel in this huddled village. Fare (*moderate*) to give you strength for local walks. *Closed Oct–mid-April; restaurant closed Tues lunch outside July–Aug.*

Les Vans ✉ 07140

★★**Mas de l'Espaïre, t** 04 75 94 95 01, *www. hotel-espaire.fr* (*moderate*). Spacious rooms in a tranquil silk farm just 6km south of town, meals for guests only. There is a shaded terrace leading to a pool. *Closed mid-Nov–mid-Mar.*

★★**Le Carmel, t** 04 75 94 99 60, *lecarmel@ wanadoo.fr* (*moderate*). A delightful rambling converted convent above the centre, run with real passion by the owners. Fine menu (*moderate*). *Closed most mid-Nov–Mar.*

Le Grangousier, Rue Courte, **t** 04 75 94 90 86 (*moderate*). Regional fare in fabulous historic house. *Closed Tues and Wed exc July–Aug, and mid-Nov–Feb.*

Barjac ✉ 30430

★★★**Le Mas du Terme**, Route de Bagnols-sur-Cèze, **t** 04 66 24 56 31, *welcome@mas-du-terme.com* (*expensive–moderate*). Vine-surrounded 18th-century silk farm tastefully converted into a relaxing country hotel 3km outside the village. Good cuisine (*expensive*). Pool. *Closed Nov–Mar.*

The pine-crested **Mont Pilat** range, a protected regional nature park, rises magnificently indifferent and unchanged above the industrial Gier valley leading to St-Etienne and the industrial Rhône valley just south of Lyon. It offers an uplifting, bucolic haven. Among the glorious winding roads of the northern Pilat, **Ste-Croix-en-Jarez** is the most intriguing destination, a defensive 13th-century monastery turned village after the Revolution. Although religious elements such as the cloisters have disappeared, the monastic plan remains clear, while paintings of exemplary monks still adorn the church. Nearby **Pélussin** hosts the **Maison du Parc**, offering information on the range's environment and traditions. The D19 road to the east runs along a high fertile balcony of a plateau, the industrial Rhône invisible below, the Pilat's heights dominating above. Quiet pine-forested roads lead to the highest peaks of the Pilat, the **Crêt de l'Œillon** and the **Crêt de la Perdrix**, popular for cross-country skiing in midwinter, with magnificent views all round. Further west, from **Mont Chaussitre**, a splendid array of Auvergne volcanoes marks the horizon. To the north, the village of **Rochetaillée** lies, with its ruined château, along a precipitously thin crest. From here you can plunge down into industrial **St-Etienne**, not an obvious tourist destination, although a substantial **mining museum** (*open Wed–Mon 10–11.30 and 2–5.30; closed Tues; adm*) run by former mine-workers recalls what was until recently the main industry of these parts, while the grandly restored **Musée d'Art et d'Industrie** (*open Wed–Mon 10–6; closed Tues; adm*) covers with verve the other strong local traditions of arms-, cycle- and ribbon-making. On the eastern ringroad, the town's excellent **modern art museum** (*open Wed–Mon 10–6; closed Tues; adm*) looks like a stylish big black-tiled bathroom centre. Most apt in this context, the tubular-industrial works of Léger stand out, but look out too for major provocative works by Picasso, Dubuffet and Surrealists' favourite, Victor Brauner, still shocking with his crude sexual images.

The Ardèche

Moving down into the northern Ardèche, the splendid valleys with their semi-abandoned terraces and semi-moribund villages far eclipse the messy towns. **Annonay** is really only worth a stop if you want to pay homage to the Montgolfier brothers, the hot-air balloon pioneers who hailed from here, although the safari-zoo at Peaugres draws in tourist crowds.

The rivers that start off to the southwest on the slopes of Mont Mézenc and Mont Gerbier de Jonc (*see* p.693) hurtle down at breakneck speed towards the Rhône through chicanes of gorges. Driving along these routes is exhilarating: try the **Eyrieux valley** from Le Cheylard to Privas. **St-Pierreville**, a bit west, stands in a tremendous location surrounded by mountains, its **Maison du Châtaignier** (*open July–Aug Mon–Fri 11–12.30 and 2.30–6; June and Sept–Nov Wed and Sun 2–6; adm*) filling you in on the importance of the Ardèche's chestnuts, in the past essential fare for families and farm animals alike. Get enjoyably lost meandering round the spectacularly beautiful roads around St-Pierreville; the Glueyre valley is lined with the finest of old terraces planted with chestnut trees. **Privas** has a nice little heart made up of small sloping squares.

South of Le Cheylard, the route along the valleys of the Dorne and the Volane leads to Aubenas. The small hilltop village of **Antraigues** is surrounded by particularly startling towering rocky slopes covered in green lichen; this isolated place became an important centre for the Ardèche Resistance movement in the Second World War. The busy spa town of **Vals-les-Bains** produces a dramatic natural jet of water every six hours, plus an endless supply of sparkling water, a great commercial success across France long before most of its upstart – now more successful – rivals in the Auvergne.

Below Vals, the Volane joins the Ardèche, which has raced down from its source in the Massif Central to here at breakneck speed. Just west, the Bourges also joins the Ardèche river, below the dramatic ruined **Château de Ventadour** (*being restored for visits*). Nearby, **Neyrac-les-Bains** must be the smallest spa resort in France, its pleasant facilities adapted to relaxation treatments. **Aubenas** runs along a dramatic crest east above the Ardèche, with great views north and south. The town's melodramatic silhouette is dominated by a Gothic castle covered with turrets and Burgundian-style colourful tiles, and by a church with a wide cupola. Although the castle dates back as far as the 12th century, the interiors reflect 18th-century good living.

The hugely touristy gorges of the Ardèche river lie south of Aubenas, but, southwest of town, go in search of the wilder Ardèche, recently designated a regional nature park. Head for the high drama of **Largentière**, the castle with its square-sided series of towers stamping its military authority on the town. Even with its soaring spire, the Gothic church below can't compete. But beyond the lively shopping streets and the boulder-strewn river waters, the temple-like law courts put on a grand show. So, in season, do the 600 varieties of roses at the **Roseraie de Berty** outside town.

Hilltop **Joyeuse** has played on its name ('Happy'), opening an appealing little centre featuring cutting-edge contemporary cartoonists in one of the nicest houses up by the church, right by whose entrance stands the **Musée de la Châtaigneraie** (*open July–Aug Tues–Sat 10–12.30 and 3–7, Sun and Mon 3–7; 15 Mar–June and Sept–15 Nov Tues–Sat 9–12 and 2–6, Sun and Mon 2–6; adm*), celebrating chestnuts and chestnut trees in all their forms and transformations, including some comically eccentric pieces of rural furniture. Dark passageways lead down through the old ramparts into the lower, shopping part of town. Northwest of Joyeuse, the hardier tourist might venture into the trickier mountain terrain of the Drobie valley.

Southwest of Joyeuse, the laid-back town of **Les Vans**, its main square seemingly provided with a café for every inhabitant, has sprawled across a fertile bowl of land in the Chassezac valley. Several picturesque villages with Romanesque churches and ruined castles stand in the hills around: **Chambonas** to the north, **Naves** to the west, and **Banne** to the south, close to the mysterious, massive boulder-strewn woods of **Païolive**. Climbing the Chassezac valley up towards the Cévennes national park, branch off to visit the dramatic village of **Thines**, superbly preserved in time at the end of its high valley, and only reachable by foot. Venture on to the northeastern plateau of the Cévennes via Villefort for the much more open, wonderfully preserved village of **La Garde-Guérin** – nothing, not even its tough granite walls, can protect it from the biting winds that sweep across the high plain.

Moving to the major tourist territory of the central and southern Ardèche river valley below Aubenas, splendid riverside villages and dramatic river gorges and caves are the main attractions. **Vogüé**'s square castle, still owned by an aristocratic family, stamps its personality on its delightful old village. Canoeists proliferate from here on south as soon as the season commences. **Balazuc**'s maze of narrow lanes, the odd craft shop tucked away in a corner, climb steeply up from the intriguing rock formations on the river bank. The main street in the more substantial old grid-planned, fortified town of **Ruoms** is a tourist trap, but the rest of the old place has been spared. A good new wine museum, **Vinimage** (*open April–Oct Tues–Sun 10–12.30 and 2–6.30; adm*), forms part of the Ardèche winemakers' effort to improve the image of the region's wines, underlining their search for improved quality. You get to taste, too!

A short way west, **Labeaume** is the most dramatic village of the lot, on one bank of the Beaume river. A small restored castle perches on an unlikely natural spindle of rock above the quaintly restored stone houses below. For the hotter half of the year, towering plane trees form a vast canopy of shade down beside the river. On the other bank, a row of elephant-man rocks add a surreal feel. Also west from Ruoms, but along the road to St-Alban-Auriolles, at the **Mas de la Vignasse** (*open July–Aug daily 11–1 and 2–7; April–June and Sept daily 2–6; adm*) you are treated to a presentation of 19th-century agricultural life in these parts, plus memorabilia on the life of one of the best-loved writers of 19th-century France, Alphonse Daudet, whose mother's family hailed from this farm.

Vallon-Pont-d'Arc is the traditional main starting point for a trip down the breathtaking **Gorges de l'Ardèche**. Hundreds of thousands of people do the journey by canoe every year, although the road that follows the gorges from high up in the scrubland on the northern side offers vertiginous glimpses down the vertical slashes of apricot and grey rock to the river hundreds of feet below. Vallon itself is a pretty enough town, but almost always packed out with tourist crowds. Sensational prehistoric cave paintings were found nearby in the mid-1990s – arguably the finest cave art ever found, with a greater diversity of animals even than at Lascaux. A replica of the cave is now being created; in the meantime, an excellent half-hour film at the **Exposition de la Grotte Chauvet** (*open June–Aug Tues–Sun 10–1 and 3–8; 15 Mar–May and Sept–15 Nov Tues–Sun 10–12 and 2–5.30; adm*) shows the paintings in all their glory. Prides of prehistoric lions, gatherings of prehistoric bears and an unforgettable array of prehistoric rhinos feature alongside horses and mammoths.

To avoid the main tourist hordes along the gorges themselves, branch south for **Labastide-de-Virac**, topped by the pleasingly rustic **Château des Roure** (*open July–Aug daily 10–7; Easter–June and Sept Thurs–Tues 2–6; closed Wed; adm*), in which you can learn of the area's history, and the particular importance of silk-worm farming.

Among the hundreds of grottoes and major potholes (*avens*) discovered in the limestone of the southern Ardèche, the **Aven d'Orgnac** (*open July–Aug daily 9.30–6.30; April–June and Sept 9.30–5.30; Oct–Nov 9.30–5.45; Feb–Mar 10.30–4.45; adm*) is the most celebrated, almost lost among scrub and poor vinelands below Labastide. The extraordinary stalagmites of the vast cavern have nicknames which reflect their eccentric forms. Alongside the *aven* stands a substantial modern museum of prehistory.

So to the breathtaking gorges of the Ardèche east of Vallon. Before the road climbs way up high above the northern bank of the river, it takes you past small cliffside caves and the sensational **Pont d'Arc**, a natural bridge of rock under which colourful canoes pass like shoals of bright fish. Swimmers also take to the fresh river waters in summer. Visiting the **Grotte de la Madeleine** (*open July–Aug daily 9–7; April–June and Sept–Oct 10–6; adm*) along the road way above the river gives you the bonus of one of the most sensational views down into the Ardèche gorges. You then plunge into deep caverns of staggering proportions. To the north, the **Aven de Marzal** (*open April–Sept daily; adm*) is much more restricted, the stairs down far more vertiginous, definitely not for those prone to vertigo. But if you stay above ground there's a small museum on potholing, plus the Zoo Préhistorique, with some quite large models of dinosaurs growling in the undergrowth. A little further north, close to **St-Remèze**, all is spick and span at the new **Musée de la Lavande** (*open April–Sept daily 10–7; adm*), surrounded by lavender fields. East of the Aven de Marzal, at **Bidon**, the **Musée de la Vie** (*open April–Nov daily 10–6; adm*) offers an appealing introduction to the region's geology.

The **Grotte de St-Marcel-d'Ardèche** (*open July–Aug daily 10–6.30; Mar–June and Sept 10–5.30; Oct–Nov 10–5; adm*) is *not* at the pretty village of that name, but some way off, right by the gorges. Reached by easy if numerous steps, the caverns are beautifully lit, the highlight of the tour the stunning series of natural pools known as *gours*, although the lighting engineer got a bit carried away here. At the end of the gorges, the villages of **St-Martin-d'Ardèche** and **Aiguèze** compete in prettiness either side of the river, the former more popular, with lots of cheap eateries and canoeing centres, the latter more atmospherically historic, its battlements merging with the rock.

The Upper Loire Valley, and the Secretive Dore

The Upper Loire and the Forez Between Roanne and St-Etienne

Dark pine-forested slopes divide the upper Loire from the Dore valley, a black barrier to the Auvergne. These slopes and the flat bucolic plain of the Loire below were ruled by the counts of Forez, based at Montbrison, through much of the Middle Ages. The many medieval castles show what a hard job the counts had protecting their territories, and battling with the local lords. Eventually the mighty dukes of Bourbon gained possession of these lands through marriage, until one of their line backed the Holy Roman Emperor Charles V against King François Ier – the French king responded by confiscating his lands, and the Forez came under direct royal control.

Sticking to the Loire river, culinary pilgrims stop opposite **Roanne**'s train station to sample the fabulous Troisgros restaurant, but beyond this foodies' pilgrimage stop, and the well-displayed archaeological and art museum in one of the grandest town houses, this treeless industrial centre won't incite you to linger. South of Roanne, hug the banks of the great river, to be viewed from close quarters as it's been dammed here. The spectacular 13th-century **Château de la Roche** (*open Aug daily 10.30–12 and 2–7; rest of year daily 2–6; adm*) stands in the midst of the waters, joined to the bank by a low walkway. The recently restored interiors include exhibitions on Loire river trading and the Villerest dam. On the opposite bank, seek out quiet **St-Maurice-sur-Loire** which, along with a 12th-century round keep, has a charming church containing cartoon-like 13th-century wall paintings.

Getting Around

By **train**, go to St-Etienne and then change for Montbrison and Le Puy. Thiers is on the line between Lyon and Clermont-Ferrand.

Tourist Information

Montbrison: Cloître des Cordeliers, t 04 77 96 08 69.

Thiers: Château du Pirou, t 04 73 80 65 65, *office.tourisme.thiers@wanadoo.fr*.

La Chaise-Dieu: Place de la Mairie, t 04 71 00 01 16, *www.tourisme.fr/lachaisedieu*.

Le Puy-en-Velay: Place du Breuil, t 04 71 09 38 41, *www.ot-lepuyenvelay.fr*.

Le Monastier-sur-Gazeille: 32 Rue St-Pierre, t 04 71 08 37 76.

Where to Stay and Eat

Roanne ✉ 42300

★★★★Troisgros, Place de la Gare, t 04 77 71 66 97, *troisgros@avo.fr* (*luxury–very expensive*). One of the most renowned, exciting restaurants (*very expensive*) in France. Extremely stylish contemporary rooms, and fabulous dining room. *Closed early Aug; restaurant closed Tues and Wed.*

St-Maurice-sur-Loire ✉ 42155

L'Echauguette, Rue Guy de la Mure, t 04 77 63 15 89 (*inexpensive*). Wonderful B&B in lovely village, with views on to the gorges.

La Chaise-Dieu ✉ 43160

★★Hôtel de l'Echo et de l'Abbaye, Place de l'Echo, t 04 71 00 00 45 (*inexpensive*). Delightfully run small hotel and restaurant right in the abbey complex, its pleasant restaurant (*expensive–moderate*) with terrace. *Closed mid-Nov–Easter; restaurant closed Wed outside July and Aug.*

St-André-de-Chalencon ✉ 43130

★★Relais des Seigneurs, Place de l'Eglise, t 04 71 58 41 41 (*inexpensive*). Caringly renovated little hotel by the church. Special evenings in the restaurant arranged around regional themes at which tourists can meet the locals. A real find.

Polignac ✉ 43000

L'Auberge du Donjon, t 04 71 09 53 63 (*inexpensive*). Simple inn at the foot of the castle ruins. **Restaurant de la Tour**, t 04 71 09 68 30 (*moderate*), below, has panoramic views.

Espaly St-Marcel ✉ 43000

★★L'Ermitage, 73 Av de l'Ermitage, t 04 71 07 05 05, *hotel.ermitage@free.fr* (*inexpensive*). Tremendous views on to Le Puy-en-Velay from the hillside west out of town. Nicely renovated big rooms and a restaurant (*moderate*). *Closed Jan and Feb; restaurant closed Sat lunch, Sun eve and Mon.*

Le Puy-en-Velay ✉ 43000

★★★Régina, 34 Bd Maréchal Fayolle, t 04 71 09 14 71, *www.hotelrestregina.com* (*inexpensive*). Completely modernized hotel on the boulevards, with good cuisine (*moderate*).

★★Le Bristol, 7 Av Maréchal Foch, t 04 71 09 13 38, *guy.mallet2@wanadoo.fr* (*inexpensive*). Fairly smart, good value again, and with a friendly boss and restaurant.

Tournayre, 12 Rue Chênebouterie, t 04 71 09 58 94 (*expensive–moderate*). Swish restaurant in an historic house with vaulted dining room for Auvergnat specialities. *Closed Sun eve, Mon, Wed eve, plus Jan and early Sept.*

L'Olympe, 8 Rue du College, t 04 71 05 90 59 (*expensive–moderate*). Stylish little restaurant up in a quiet little historic street. *Closed Sat lunch, Sun eve and Mon, and half Mar and early Sept.*

Le Bateau Ivre, 5 Rue Portail d'Avignon, t 04 71 09 67 20 (*moderate*). Cosy restaurant devoted to Auvergnat traditions. *Closed Sun and Mon, 1 week June, 10 days Nov.*

Chaspinhac ✉ 43700

La Paravent, t 04 71 03 54 75 (*inexpensive*). Pleasant old B&B, just outside Chaspinhac, with spacious, simple rooms. Run by a woman who's passionate about the area.

Arlempdes ✉ 43490

★Hôtel du Manoir, t 04 71 57 17 14 (*inexpensive*). An appealing old stone block of a hotel below the castle in this picturesque village, its restaurant (*moderate*) with a fine view. *Closed Nov–early Mar.*

In the partly walled rustic old village of **Pommiers**, a Romanesque church sits proudly above the vegetable plots. The dark interior conceals delicate Gothic wall paintings. To the south the Loire valley opens out. The ark of a building at the **Ecopôle** (*open daily 2–6; adm*) close to the river by **Chambéon** (below Feurs) presents the flora and fauna of this stretch of the Loire most imaginatively. In the broad valley bottom, worn-down old volcano chimneys protrude like islands on a calm sea. The fortified **priory of Montverdun**, built in forbidding black stone, stands guard on one pinnacle.

The **Château de la Bastie-d'Urfé** (*open July–Aug daily 10–12 and 1–6; April–June and Sept–Oct 10–12 and 2.30–5.30; Nov–Mar Wed–Mon 2–5, closed Tues; adm*) just below was splendidly transformed from medieval manor into early French Renaissance château for Claude d'Urfé, close friend of King François Ier, fighting with him in Italy, and then serving as diplomat there for his son King Henri II. The attempts at perspectival arches and the shell-plastered grotto with its saucy statues count among many architectural pleasures, but the high point is the chapel, dedicated to the Trinity, with sumptuous, recently restored paintings, marquetry, tiles and stucco ceiling. Claude's great-nephew Honoré, brought up at La Bastie d'Urfé, wrote a famous pastoral novel, *L'Astrée*, which made the castle famous across Europe; tapestry cycles illustrate scenes from this bestseller which set a trend for nobles playing at being shepherds and shepherdesses. Now in summer, the courtyard doubles as a general theatre and concert venue.

The pleasant historic town of **Montbrison**, long home to the counts of the Forez, comes fully to life for its Saturday markets. The counts ordered the big Gothic church, and the Salle La Diana, plastered in painted coats of arms. **St-Romain-le-Puy**'s amazing **priory church** (*open April–Oct daily 2.30–6.30; adm*) stands out on a volcanic rock like a Mont-St-Michel of the Loire plains south of town. Dating mainly from the late 10th and early 11th centuries, its battered body has undergone a fair deal of surgery since. An amusing frieze of crudely carved animals outside the apse offers a ritual message to the initiated; further startling fragments of bizarre carvings and medieval wall paintings await in the maze within. The historic hillside town of **St-Galmier** on the opposite side of the Loire has preserved its old-style charm thanks in part to the wealth derived from its Badoit sparkling water springs.

The Monts de la Madeleine and Monts du Forez

As an alternative to following the bottom of the Loire valley, west of Roanne, take the delightful rustic hillside roads through fortified villages along the Monts de la Madeleine and Monts du Forez, separating the Loire valley from the Auvergne region.

Start in the **Monts de la Madeleine**, on the old medieval frontier with the once mighty Bourbon duchy. **Le Crozet** has a tight historic centre defensively surrounding its hilltop church and keep. **Ambierle** looks out more confidently from its hillside position. The gorgeous Gothic church has a none-too-shy Burgundian-style roof. The uplifting interior boasts a staggering number of aristocratic coats of arms; the local lords even made their presence felt on the column capitals. The noble decoration doesn't stop there: below the choir's splendid stained glass, a sumptuous Gothic altar painting depicts two grand couples kneeling below their patron saints. In a plain former religious school behind a plain garden with lovely views over the Loire plain, the **Musée Alice Taverne** (*open Feb–Nov daily 10–12 and 2–6; adm*) packs countless rooms with traditional everyday objects rescued from neglect from local houses by an impassioned local ethnographer. Seventeen towers once protected the hilltop fort of **St-Haon-le-Châtel**. Seek out their vestiges in the village's well-flowered streets.

Moving south of the A72 motorway into the **Monts du Forez**, walk to the abandoned vestiges of the **Château d'Urfé** for wide views of the region from up in its ruins. Simple Gothic arches lead into hilltop **Cervières**, prettily neglected by time, surveying the wooded slopes of the Haut-Forez. Even if the castle has disappeared, a truncated church survives, containing a remarkable, big-cheeked peasant of a Mary. Opposite, the **Maison des Grenadières** (*open April–Oct Wed–Mon 2.30–6, closed Tues; rest of year weekends 2.30–6; adm*) is dedicated to the local tradition of embroidering military badges for the French forces. South by **Jeansaignière**, in the **Parc de la Drosera** (*open Mar–mid-Nov from 10am; adm*) follow a curious hillside trail past miniature models of the principal buildings of the region, explained in detailed panels. A very solid castle receiving much-needed restoration work oversees the fresh-feeling village of **Chalmazel** below its straight single ski slope carved out of the forests. The cheese-obsessed village of **Sauvain**, with its cheese shops and **cheese museum** (*open July–Aug Tues–Sun 2.30–6; closed Mon; adm*), offers superb views across the Loire valley. To the east, the impressive hilltop ruins of the **Château de Couzan**, built for the Damas family, difficult rivals of the counts of Forez, stand in even more sensational a location above the valley. Follow the twisting high road south through peaceful villages with yet more dramatic views: **St-Bonnet-le-Courreau**, **Roche**, **Gumières** and **Montarcher**, the last a tiny, tight hilltop village with exquisite views from the welcoming entrance to its church, which seems to grow straight out of the highest rock.

Finish the high Forez trail with the high drama of **St-Bonnet-le-Château**. *Boules*-lovers from far and wide visit this historic hillside town, home to one of France's major makers of metallic bowls and its **Musée International Pétanque et Boule** (*open April–Oct Mon–Fri 2.30–5.30, Sat and Sun 3–6; adm*). In this appealing centre, glean all sorts of information on the sport, from antiquity to the major schism between *boules* and *pétanque*. The southern tradition of the loser kissing Fanny's bottom is also explained with gravitas. On a more elevated note, the main **church** looks out soberly from a terrace with absolutely superb views. The interior looks dignified , but on the guided tour you are shown the skeletons in the church's cupboard; the leathery mummies died of natural deaths. In delightful contrast, the lower chapel conceals some of the most graceful of all medieval wall paintings in southeastern France.

The Dore Valley

The secretive, steep-sided Dore valley sandwiched between the upper Loire and the upper Allier lies hidden from view by the unspoilt, steep heights of the Monts du Forez on one side and the Livradois on the other. Balanced on something of a knife-edge of a slope, the knife shops, knife museum and knife house of **Thiers** all make the town's speciality pretty obvious: this is the largest knife- and cutlery-producing centre in France, the tradition dating back to the 14th century, celebrated at the **Musée de la**

Coutellerie and **Maison des Couteliers** (*open July–Aug 10–6.30; June and Sept 10–12 and 2–6; Feb–May and Oct–Dec daily exc Mon 10–12 and 2–6; adm*). Thiers' other striking speciality is its many houses with crossed timberframe façades.

South of Thiers, the **Château d'Aulteribe** (*open mid-June–mid-Sept 10–12 and 2.30–6.30; rest of year weekends 2.30–5.30; adm*) lies well hidden behind a curtain of woods. This late-Gothic edifice, long the property of the Lafayette family, was transformed into a luxurious dwelling in the 19th century for the Onslow-de Pierres. Edward Onslow, a British diplomat, met his wife-to-be in Clermont-Ferrand in 1781. They had a son, Georges, who became an accomplished Romantic composer (CDs are on sale here). The last marquis died without heir, leaving the property to the state in the 1950s. Highlights of the rich art collections installed inside since include many accomplished portraits of French royalty.

The small town of **Ambert** just above the Dore is now most closely associated with a blue cheese, Fourme d'Ambert, the Auvergne's pale version of Roquefort; a **cheese museum** (*open July–Aug daily 9–7; rest of year Tues, Thurs, Fri and Sat 9–12 and 2–7; adm*) stands in the centre of town, along with attractive timberframe houses with distinctive crossed beams as at Thiers, plus a late-Gothic **church** crawling with gargoyles. However, for centuries Ambert was best known for producing paper for the Lyon printing business, and an excellent **museum** (*open July–Aug daily 9–8; rest of year daily 9–12 and 2–6; adm*) on the subject has been set up in an old paper mill at **Moulin Richard-de-Bas** below town. Little **Arlanc** goes global with its startling **Jardin Pour la Terre** (*open July–Aug daily 10–7; May–June and Sept daily 2–7; adm*), plants from around the planet placed around gardens in the shapes of the continents.

God's Seat – the name of **La Chaise-Dieu** indicates the elevated religious calling of this place, perched on an isolated high plateau beyond the source of the Dore. A Benedictine abbey was first founded here in the middle of the 11th century by Robert de Turlande, a canon from Brioude (*see pp.700–701*). Robert obtained papal protection for the abbey, and a century after its foundation this mother abbey ruled over one of the most powerful monastic orders in France. After a crisis in the early 14th century, however, it had to be rescued by one of its former monks promoted to high places, Avignon pope Clement VI. He ordered the rebuilding of the church, designed by Hugues Morel, in 1343, and his nephew and successor, Pope Gregory XI, saw to its completion after Clement VI had been buried in the abbey church. Receiving lavish decorations in the 16th century, the place became the target of the Huguenots, before going on to be milked for the wealth of its territories by various major political figures, including Richelieu and Mazarin. The monks left at the Revolution, and the place was pretty well abandoned through the 19th century. Slowly restored, it has found a new lease of life since the 1960s, when the leading pianist Georges Cziffra began the now prestigious Festival de Musique Française here.

The **abbey church**, named after the founder, looks a defensive Gothic edifice, with its stocky square towers. But exceptional decorations enliven the sober interior, including a fine wood-carved Baroque organ held up by carved figures and covered in putti. The short nave ends with a rood screen topped by a statue of Christ. Beyond, an intensely detailed cycle of tapestries made in Arras and Brussels runs round the chancel, the figures in the biblical scenes wearing the most exquisite late-Gothic attire. The richly carved stalls below also teem with figures. In the middle of the chancel lies the tomb of frog-eyed Clement VI, tiny tame lions lying at his feet. Other parts of the abbey have survived, including remnants of the cloister, while the monks' library now contains the abbey's treasury. The extraordinary Italianate Tour Clémentine, rising at a strange angle from the end of the choir, houses the sacristy.

In adjoining **Place de l'Echo**, test out the echoing corners of the chamber after which the square is named. The **waxworks museum** presents tableaux from local history, and the **Musée du Bois** celebrates the woodworking traditions of these parts.

The Upper Loire from St-Etienne to Le Puy-en-Velay

Back west of St-Etienne (*see p.682*), the Loire passes through another set of gorges below St-Just-St-Rambert. You get head-spinning views of them by clambering round the precarious ruins of the **Château d'Essalois**. Down below, on the dammed river, the vestiges of medieval **Château de Grangent** make an enchanting picture. **Chambles**, the hilltop village south of Essalois, has equally stunning views. Pressing south via Aurec-sur-Loire, high above Bas-en-Basset, you can only reach the aloof **Château de Rochebaron** by a long, steep hillside walk. Enthusiasts have been cleaning up this isolated medieval fort in recent years. **Retournac**, back down by the Loire, has recently revived its lace-making traditions, opening a museum on the subject. A detour west takes you past the sweet village of **St-André-de-Chalençon** to the exceptional hamlet of **Chalençon** with its adorable chequered church lost in its wooded valley.

Continuing down towards the source of the Loire, the darkly picturesque **Château de Lavoûte-Polignac** (*open July–Sept daily 10–12.30 and 2–6.30; June daily 2–5; May weekends and hols 2–5; Easter hols daily 2.30–5; adm*) stands guard over a meander in the river, one of the major centres of the powerful Auvergnat Polignac family, described by historian Simon Schama as one of the most hated aristocratic clans in France at the Revolution. Abandoned during that period, the castle was restored in the late 19th century. It now looks sorry for itself inside, but the guided tour offers an absorbing insight into the family. Although in an even more ruined state, the same family's medieval **Château de Polignac** (*open June–Sept daily 10–7; Easter–May and Oct 2–6; adm*) still commands respect on top of its volcanic platform. This tremendous stage-set was the family base until they moved to Lavoûte in the 18th century. Its towering keep is 15th century, but some of the substantial walls date back to early medieval times. From here you can look down on the cathedral city of Le Puy-en-Velay, set in the Velay basin, surrounded by conical mountains. A short detour west takes you to the better-preserved **Château de St-Vidal** (*open July–Aug daily 2–6.30; adm*), a bit like a children's picture-book image of a medieval fort with its square shape and round corner towers, all built in the forbidding local black volcanic rock.

Le Puy-en-Velay

The improbably thin fingers of volcanic rock sticking outrageously into the air make the skyline of Le Puy-en-Velay quite unforgettable. The heaven-pointing heights seemingly encouraged religious veneration in distant, prehistoric times. On one of

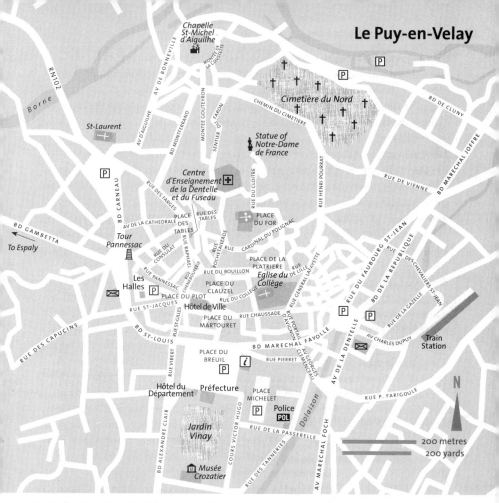

Le Puy's pinnacles, a rock known as the Feverish Stone, thought possibly to have formed part of a neolithic dolmen, became a particularly significant place of worship in Gallo-Roman times. At the end of the 4th century, as Christianity spread across the Velay, Le Puy was apparently one of the places where the cult of the Virgin Mary first flourished in France; she was said to have worked many miracles here, and the first church dedicated to her is thought to have been built in the late 5th century.

Tradition has it that Bishop Gothescalk set out in 950 on the first major pilgrimage from Le Puy to Santiago de Compostela in northern Spain. During the Middle Ages, the place developed into one of the four most important gathering points in France for this hugely popular spiritual journey, and a whole administrative city was built to deal with the pilgrims. The craft of lace-making, probably established in the 15th century, became a second source of renown and revenue for Le Puy. Although the trade was largely mechanized in the 19th century, up until the First World War large numbers of women in the region were still employed producing hand-made *dentelle*.

One of the most memorable streets in France, steep, many-stepped **Rue des Tables**, leads up to the **cathedral**. Its huge, gaping black porch, like the mouth of a biblical leviathan, waits wide open below the sheer wall of the late-12th-century façade embellished with patterns of alternating coloured stones and columns, a virtuoso display of Romanesque decoration. Rising to the left of the cathedral façade stand the imposing Hôtel Dieu, or hospital, and a castle-like building surrounding the cathedral cloister. The whole complex looks like a very well-defended holy citadel.

Enter via that massive porch, itself the size of a decent church and a piece of extraordinarily bold architecture, built out from the hilltop to allow the cathedral to be extended. Pilgrims in centuries past would have found themselves popping up out of the floor in the centre of the nave; nowadays you have to go up via side stairs. The cathedral interior was restored with a disappointingly heavy hand in the 19th and 20th centuries. Pilgrims still venerate the curious Black Virgin on the high altar. The original was said to have been brought back from the Orient by a medieval French king, possibly as a gift from a Middle Eastern ruler – it's now thought she may in fact have been a representation of the ancient Egyptian goddess Isis. The original was destroyed at the Revolution; the copy shows Jesus popping his head out of his mother's clothing like a baby kangaroo. In the north aisle, an evocative 17th-century painting depicts a procession of the Virgin through the town in thanks for her supposed intercession during an outbreak of the plague. The sacristy houses a mixed bag of further religious curiosities. A labyrinth of buildings surrounds the cathedral. The **Chapelle du St-Sacrement** once served as the library of the cathedral school. In the 16th century one wall was decorated with marvellous depictions of the liberal arts as enthroned women in period attire. You have to pay to visit the overrestored **cloisters** (*open July–Aug daily 9–6.30; mid-May–June and most Sept 9–12 and 2–6.30; rest of year 9–12 and 2–5; adm*) and the rooms around it, housing a museum of religious art (*same ticket as for cloisters*). The most striking features include the medieval wall paintings in the chapterhouse and a 16th-century embroidered coat made for the Black Virgin, featuring a splendid Tree of Jesse depicting Christ's lineage.

Gather your energies to mount the enormous sickly pink **Notre-Dame de France** (*open mid-Mar–Sept daily 9–7; rest of year 10–5; adm*) stuck on top of the nearby **Rocher Corneille** in the 19th century. So striking from a distance, this Virgin turns out to be a bit of a monstrosity close up. Designed by Jean-Marie Bonnassieux, she measures over 50ft in height and weighs in at over one hundred tons.

Back down at Place des Tables, head along Rue Raphaël. The **Centre d'Enseignement de la Dentelle au Fuseau** (*open mid-June–mid-Sept weekdays 9–12 and 1.30–5.30, Sat 9.30–4.30; rest of year weekdays 10–12 and 2–5; adm*) presents a video on the history of lace-making in Le Puy-en-Velay, and small exhibitions of pieces. Little Rue Rochetaillade nearby boasts some of the oldest houses in town. Also take a good look along Rue Cardinal de Polignac, lined with fine mansions. Down below Place de la Platrière, the former Jesuit Eglise du Collège adds a twist of Baroque. Adjoining Place du Clauzel and Place du Martouret form the heart of the old town. The neoclassical **Hôtel de Ville** was completed in 1766, in time to witness the guillotining of over 40 people, including 18 priests, and the burning in 1794 of the original Black Virgin. On the other side of the town hall, imposing Rue Pannessac curves away from Place du Plot towards the stocky gateway of the **Tour Pannessac**, a remnant of medieval defences. Most of these ramparts have long been replaced by boulevards. A grandiose area was laid out in the 19th century, stretching from **Place du Breuil** through the shaded *boules*-players' **Vinay Gardens** to the substantial **Musée Crozatier** (*open mid-June–mid-Sept daily 10–12 and 2–6; May–mid-June and late Sept Wed–Mon 10–12 and 2–6; rest of year Mon and Wed–Fri 10–12 and 2–4, Sun 2–4, closed Tues; adm*), generously paid for by the wealthy sculptor Charles Crozatier. The place is crammed with a confusion of artefacts, with regional arts and lace well represented. By the boulevards just west of the centre, the church of **St-Laurent** stands out close to the Borne river. St Dominic, founder in Toulouse of the Inquisition, came here in the 13th century and a Dominican monastery was set up. In the first half of the Hundred Years War the fearsome French leader Bertrand du Guesclin died besieging Châteauneuf-de-Randon not far to the south, which explains why his entrails and effigy ended up inside.

Two hundred and sixty steps lead up another staggering pinnacle of rock to the crooked little **Chapelle St-Michel d'Aiguilhe** (*open May–Sept daily 9–6.30; mid-Mar–April and Oct–mid-Nov 9.30–12 and 2–5.30; Feb–mid-Mar, plus Christmas hols 2–7; adm*), isolated high above another atmospheric corner of town. Before the climb, say a quick prayer at the simple **Oratoire St-Grégoire** below and visit the **Espace St-Michel**, which briefly explains the geology of the area and the cult of St Michael. The story goes that Bishop Gothescalk had the extraordinary chapel built in the bellicose archangel's honour on his return from his pilgrimage to Santiago; the architecture certainly appears to contain several Spanish-Moorish touches. In the cramped, contorted, cave-like interior, various nooks and crannies contain intriguing religious items.

If captivated by the pinnacles of Le Puy, head out to **Espahy** to look at the enormous Joseph (*open July–Aug 2–7; adm*), surrounded by more sickly 19th-century religious confections. As with Notre-Dame de France, you can climb inside the outsized body.

The Last Leg of the Loire: from Le Puy-en-Velay to its Source

Follow the D37 out of Le Puy's eastern suburb of Brives-Charensac to start on a spectacular route along the Loire valley to its source, a string of ruined medieval forts marking the way. Detour east to marvel at the dark purples, blacks and oranges of **Le Monastier-sur-Gazeille**'s exceptional church, a remnant of the most important abbey in the Velay in medieval times. The stocky castle behind may be less colourful, but with its black volcanic sides and its crinkly red-tiled roofs it has character too. The insubstantial local history museum inside has one section devoted to Robert Louis Stevenson, who stayed for a month here in 1878 before heading off on his travels with a donkey through the Cévennes. Back by the Loire, **Arlempdes** stands in a wonderfully dramatic location, the remnants of its fort clinging to the back of a monster of a rock with the skin of a great wrinkled elephant. Here, the Loire makes an important turn; its source is to the east. Make a detour for the almost perfectly round **Lac d'Issarlès**, this natural wonder created by water collecting in an old volcanic crater. The first waters of the Loire dribble down the sides of the pyramid top of **Mont Gerbier de Jonc** (*fee*). This mountain looks almost man-made, seemingly built up of a great mound of boulders, snow-covered or stained with green lichens depending on the season. Still more impressive is Mont Gerbier's larger brother, **Mont Mézenc**, to the north.

Clermont-Ferrand and the Monts Dômes

Heading into the heart of the Auvergne region, from far down in the Allier valley, the crater tops of the Monts Dômes look like so many giant eggs which have had their tops chopped off for a godly family's breakfast. They form the sensational backdrop to the compellingly dark capital of the Auvergne, Clermont-Ferrand, and to the spa and spring-water towns on the slopes around it, the best known being Volvic. Around here, the Gauls won their one great victory against Caesar.

Clermont-Ferrand

Black is the colour of Clermont-Ferrand's gorgeous heart, and of its cathedral, dwarfed by the silhouettes of the spectacular Monts Dômes. It is also the colour of the Michelin tyres indelibly linked with the city's industrial growth in the last century.

One of the most powerful Gaulish tribes, the Arveni, held spectacular feasts and planned their military campaigns on the heights above the broad Allier valley around Clermont. *Nemessos* was the name of their main settlement in the area. When their greatest leader Vercingétorix managed to unite the Gauls against Caesar's invasion in 52 BC, the Roman megalomaniac met with a rare defeat in his attempted siege of Gergovie, south of Clermont. Unfortunately, encouraged by this stunning victory, Vercingétorix pursued Caesar northwards, only to be defeated on another dramatic hilltop, Alésia in Burgundy (*see* p.635). The Gallo-Roman city then developed lower down the slopes of the Monts Dômes. The name Clermont appears on records from the 8th century. By the 11th century it was a vibrant city, run by its powerful bishops. At the Council of Clermont in 1095, the place received over 300 major European religious representatives, and it was here, in one of the most decisive moments for the militant medieval Church, that Pope Urban II proclaimed the First Crusade, setting in motion the beginning of centuries of cruel warring between Europe and the Middle East over Jerusalem and the so-called Christian Holy Land. A large number of knights also present at the Council responded to Urban II's call with wild enthusiasm, fixing red crosses on their clothes as a symbol of their mission.

While the bishops held sway in Clermont, they often came up against the counts of Auvergne, who had a fortress built on a neighbouring slope – Montferrand, as it was known, expanded into a separate *bastide* town in the 13th century. The merchants of both towns then started to assert their independence, and gained still more when Queen Catherine de Médicis took power away from the Clermont bishops.

In the 17th century, the city saw the birth of a French genius, the scientist and philosopher Blaise Pascal, who conducted some of his most famous experiments on the top of the Puy de Dôme. But the name most associated with Clermont-Ferrand (the two towns were merged in the 18th century) is Michelin. The company profited enormously from the growth of the car industry, and boasts one of the most famous corporate logos in the world, Bibendum, the chubby Michelin man with his cheerful rolls of tyre fat. The past few decades have seen a dramatic reduction in tyre production in Clermont-Ferrand, but the creation of an enormous university has somewhat compensated for the industrial decline.

Getting There and Around

Clermont-Ferrand's airport, at Aulnat, is 7km east of the city; Ryanair has flown there in the past and may do again one day. By **train**, Clermont-Ferrand can take just 3hrs 30mins from Paris; the fastest direct trains from Lyon-Perrache take 2hrs 30mins.

Tourist Information

Clermont-Ferrand: Place de la Victoire, t 04 73 98 65 00, www.ot-clermont-ferrand.fr.
Riom: 16 Rue du Commerce, t 04 73 38 59 45, www.riom.auvergne.com.
Volvic: 23 Place de l'Eglise, t 04 73 33 58 73, www.volvic-tourisme.com.

Where to Stay and Eat

Clermont-Ferrand ✉ 63000
★★★**Hôtel de Lyon**, 16 Place de Jaude, t 04 73 93 32 55, hotel.de.lyon@wanadoo.fr (moderate). Overlooking the major shopping square close to the historic centre, slightly jaded big rooms with modern facilities above a string of lively restaurants.
★★**Dav'Hôtel**, 10 Rue des Minimes, t 04 73 93 31 49, contact@ davhotel.fr (inexpensive). Just tucked away off Place de Jaude, on a street with a choice of ethnic restaurants, appealing simply decorated rooms.
Le Bougnat, 29 Rue des Chaussetiers, t 04 73 36 36 98 (moderate). An atmospheric Auvergnat address, on a popular street

for restaurants, serving hearty, good-value regional fare.
Restaurant Riquier, 11 Rue de l'Etoile, t 04 73 36 67 25 (moderate). Delightful terrace, stylish interior and good-value regional dishes.

Chamalières ✉ 63400
★★★**Hôtel Radio**, 43 Av Curie, t 04 73 30 87 83, resa@hotel-radio.fr (expensive–moderate). Art Deco hotel perched up high, with great views down on Clermont. Lovely modern rooms and ambitious cuisine (very expensive–expensive). Closed most Jan, and April–mid-May; restaurant closed Sat lunch, Sun, and Mon lunch.

Pérignat-lès-Sarliève ✉ 63170
★★★**Hostellerie St-Martin**, t 04 73 79 81 00, reception@hostellerie-st-martin.com (expensive–moderate). Lovely country retreat in former Cistercian abbey some 6km southeast of Clermont, with smart restaurant. Pool and tennis court. Restaurant closed Sun eve out of season.

Royat ✉ 63130
Le Paradis, t 04 73 35 85 46 (expensive). A real eagle's eyrie of a restaurant above Royat in a roughly redone block of a medieval castle, with fantastic views.

St-Saturnin ✉ 63450
B&B Château de St-Saturnin, Place de l'Ormeau, t 04 73 39 39 64 (expensive). A spectacular historic castle in which to stay. Extremely comfortable rooms.

The huge, black **cathedral** soars up from the grand old city. Its twin spires, although built in Gothic style, were in fact only added in the 19th century, to plans by Viollet-le-Duc. The rest of the structure is original, built in the second half of the 13th century and the 14th century. Inside, stained-glass windows set within decorative squares illuminate the transepts and choir. The chapels radiating out from the choir ambulatory contain decorative riches, the most famous of which is the gilded statue of the Virgin and child in the lady chapel. The crypt actually dates from an earlier Romanesque church. The Bayette tower leads to the richly endowed cathedral treasury and, if you climb all its steps, to a panoramic view over the orange-red rooftops.

Substantial, vibrant café-lined squares spread out around the cathedral, giving you space to stand back and admire its powerful form and its rows of gargoyles. A statue of Urban II on Place de la Victoire recalls the rabble-rousing, war-mongering pontiff.

The Maison du Tourisme houses the tourist office and the **Espace Art Roman** (*open June–Sept Mon–Sat 8.30–7, Sun 9–12 and 2–6; Oct–May Mon–Fri 8.45–6.30, Sat 9–12 and 2–6, Sun 9–1; adm*), a modern presentation of the contemplative yet colourful Romanesque art which flowered so finely in the Auvergne.

Explore the bold black-stoned streets and squares all around the cathedral, their corners embellished by fountains. **Rue des Gras**, a grand, wide street lined with old mansions turned into shops, slopes down from the cathedral entrance. A Chinese face above one doorway signals the entrance to the old-fashioned **Musée Ranguet**, which presents local traditions and crafts, with a section devoted to Pascal and his inventions, including one of the earliest mechanical calculators. The modern covered **market** lies nearby, a childlike piece of architecture made up of colourful building blocks. Just north of the cathedral, the **Hôtel de Ville** makes its own dramatic statement with its enormous black columns. Down Rue du Port, with its fashionable shops, seek out the elaborate black and white façade of the sunken church of **Notre-Dame-de-Bon-Port**. This major mosaic of a building dates back to the Romanesque period.

Above the **Jardin Lecoq**, Clermont's pretty main formal public garden, the twin **Musée Bargoin** and **Musée du Tapis d'Art** (*open Tues–Sun 10–6; adm*) occupy serious purpose-built Belle Epoque buildings. These contain some fascinating displays, including ancient Celtic finds and vestiges of the Gallo-Roman city, with statuettes, fragments of mosaics, funeral stelae, sarcophagi, and even a Gallo-Roman tunic. One outstanding section consists of ex-votos found up at the Roches spring at Chamalières. The magnificent carpet collection comes from the Middle East, presenting a rather more positive meeting of East and West than the Crusades.

The finest museum in Clermont-Ferrand lies out in **Montferrand**. This quarter's centre doesn't have anything like the immediate appeal or cohesive character of historic Clermont, but the grid of old streets close to the **Musée des Beaux-Arts** (*open Tues–Sun 10–6; adm*) has been well restored. The slick museum has taken over a former Ursuline convent which also served as a barracks later – but, within, the spaces have been superbly adapted to hold the biggest collection of fine arts in the Auvergne. The medieval collection includes wonderful rare objects such as an olifant from the cathedral, a kind of trumpet decorated with delicate Romanesque carvings. Two portraits stand out in the Renaissance section, a Clouet woman wearing a huge period ruff and big earrings, and a Bronzino portrait of a rather effeminate young man who looks as though he might have been envious of her attire. In the 17th-century collection, Philippe de Champaigne is represented by a beautiful angel of the Annunciation, and a masterly portrait of Vincent Voiture.

On the Slopes Around Clermont-Ferrand

Drive up from Clermont to drink in the markedly grand Belle Epoque atmosphere of the old spa resort of **Royat** on the extremely steep slopes just above town, elegant gardens scattered around the mansion blocks. Once Napoléon III's wife Eugénie came, kings, princes and princesses followed. The fortified church of **St-Léger** shows that the place had a life back in medieval times, but the spring waters were also known to the Arveni.

Sober as a judge, the darkly historic town of **Riom** north of Clermont has been the seat of the Auvergne's law courts for centuries. Thanks to the wealth of its lawyers, the place is packed with grand mansions, and in the Middle Ages it rivalled Clermont. Its roots go far back too, to the 5th century at least, when its first priest, snake-frightener and fire-extinguisher Amable, made quite a reputation for himself; but it seems its name derives from the Latin *Ricomagum*, indicating that it was the site of another Gallo-Roman settlement. The plan of the fortified town was laid out in the 13th century. In the 14th, Jean Duc de Berry, one of King Jean II of France's extravagant sons (*see p.271*), was given the Auvergne as an apanage. In Riom, he ordered a sumptuous palace, virtually all of which has vanished apart from the **Sainte-Chapelle** (*open July–Aug Mon–Fri 10–12 and 2.30–5.30; June and Sept Wed–Fri 3–5; May Wed 3–5; adm*), built to house a supposed piece of Christ's cross. The lofty, aisleless Gothic chapel with its large expanses of windows was later incorporated into the substantial 19th-century law courts. Heavily restored, the main interest now is its surviving 15th-century stained glass. The **Musée Francisque Mandet** (*open June–Sept Wed–Mon 10–12 and 2.30–6; rest of year Wed–Mon 10–12 and 2–5.30; closed Tues; adm*), the fine arts museum, spreads across two substantial granite houses. Paintings feature in the first building, including a few hilarious Dutch scenes. Local artists are well represented, notably by Alphonse Cornet of Riom. A surprise section presents modern designer objects. The second building takes you back to antiquity with a recent bequest left to the town by a lawyer from Riom who amassed an impressive collection of art from ancient cultures. The **Musée Régional d'Auvergne** (*open same times; adm*) close by contains an extensive collection of much more prosaic but well-presented objects associated with traditional Auvergnat life. Further fine Ancien Régime mansions stand out along the main streets, one displaying startling medallions of topless women, while fountains embellish many a corner. The elaborate belfry has a permanent exhibition on the history of Riom. The town hall boasts a couple of statues by Rodin and a copy of a letter signed by Joan of Arc, asking the good citizens of Riom to help fund her campaigning – apparently they were slow to respond.

In neighbouring **Mozac**, the curious black-freckled church conceals amazing medieval treasures, notably some of the most exquisite capitals in southeastern France. They date from the Romanesque period, when most of the church was built, although it has been much altered since. Marvel too at a staggering Limoges 12th-century reliquary chest, made for the bones of St Calmin; semi-precious stones decorate the collars and books of the apostles represented on it.

The small hillside town of **Volvic**'s Romanesque church has been heavily restored, although a few bold carved capitals remain inside. You can tour the town's little art museum, and even go round the Volvic water-bottling plant, but the best place to visit here is the **Maison de la Pierre** (*open March–mid-Nov daily 10–12 and 2–5; adm*), its caverns long exploited for quarrying, which apparently began in the middle of the 13th century to provide the stone for the cathedral of Clermont. The **Château de Tournoël**, a shell of a medieval castle above Volvic, stands in a dramatic position with plunging views across the whole of the Limagne, the picturesque Allier plains east of Clermont-Ferrand.

Following the slopes south of Clermont-Ferrand, the plateau of **Gergovie** is where the Gauls under Vercingétorix famously stood up to Caesar's army, as readers of the Astérix books are so frequently reminded. This place provides another eagle's eye view across the Allier and the eastern Auvergne. The **Maison de Gergovie** (*open July–Aug 10–7; May–June and Sept–Oct 10–12.30 and 2–6; Mar–April and Nov weekends and public hols 2–6; adm*) deals briefly with the geology – going back to a volcanic eruption around 17 million years ago – as well as archaeology and the Celtic triumph story.

The Monts Dômes

Up among the volcano-tops of the high plateau of the Monts Dômes, you lose sight of the slopeside towns and the Allier valley below. But climb to the crowning point of the range, the huge pudding of the **Puy de Dôme**, and you can take in one of the greatest 360° views in France, peering down like a divinity on to the crater domes below, lines of mountains disappearing mistily into the distance in every direction. The summit was a sacred site to the Celts, who had a shrine to Lug here, while in Gallo-Roman times a temple to Mercury was built. There are still a few vestiges of it on the top; the size of the blocks suggests it must have been an impressive structure, perhaps one of the largest temples in Gaul. A monumental statue of Mercury made by the Greek sculptor Zenodore may have been raised on the summit. The temple was destroyed in the Dark Ages, replaced by a Christian chapel which survived until the 18th century. Unfortunately, the Puy de Dôme site has suffered some indignities since. The military has planted a dirty great syringe of a mast on the very pinnacle, and a few tacky tourist attractions have been set up near its foot. You also have to pay a toll to take the road up to the summit, and at busy times you'll be forced to park at the bottom and take a shuttle bus to and from the peak. But the view, a panorama of extinct volcanic craters, will still blow you away.

Well hidden in what was a former military camp with a warren of hidden galleries used to stock weapons, **Vulcania** (*open June–early Sept daily 9–7; late Feb–May and early Sept–mid-Nov Wed–Sun 10–6; adm*) is an extremely ambitious new tourist centre created at the behest of former French president and lover of his Auvergnat region, Valéry Giscard d'Estaing. The place lies by the wood-covered Puy de Côme, the top of the Puy de Dôme not far off, but looking much less daunting than it does down in the Allier valley. The sensitively landscaped car parks make a good first impression, although the zones are named after Italian volcanoes, giving an early indication that Vulcania is not primarily concerned with the craters of the Auvergne.

The extraordinary exhibition spaces are almost entirely concealed underground, in basalt corridors. Just a large building containing restaurants, and a large artificial cone with a glittering golden interior, stand out. Descending into the extremely well-presented chambers, three major zones of permanent exhibition spaces lie off the central tropical garden with giant ferns from New Zealand, one presenting the different planets and their volcanoes (Venus certainly doesn't sound romantic when you learn that it is almost entirely covered with volcanic spots), another focusing on the different types of volcanoes that exist, and the third looking at man's relationship with volcanoes. Each has a smart little theatre space, where the theme of the zone is succinctly presented in sympathetic manner, but each also has corners packed with interactive screens and panels. High-tech presentations in museums don't come much better than this, and the English-language coverage is first-rate.

It just comes as such a surprise that so little attention is paid to the Auvergnat volcanoes. The thing is, these are now a peaceful lot. Clearly, it was decided that the public required something more sensational. So virtually all the attention is devoted to still-active volcanoes. Much focus is on the major explosive craters of the 20th century, notably Mount Pelée on Martinique, St Helen's, Pinutobo, Montserrat and highly volatile Japanese volcanoes, while in one corner you can select videos on over 30 active craters around the world. Homage is paid to the Kraffts, a daredevil couple who carried out their research into volcanoes with foolhardy passion, eventually dying in an eruption. The destructive force of volcanoes is underlined time and again. Some of the film footage is explosive, of course, especially in the main cinema hall, one of several areas featuring changing exhibitions. In the end, it is also shown that explosions can eventually have some positive effects, for example creating very fertile soil, and bringing precious minerals in the earth's crust to the surface – but the film footage of mine workers being exploited is shocking.

Very close to Vulcania, at the **Puy de Lemptegy Volcan à Ciel Ouvert** (*open July–Aug daily 9.30–6; April–June and Sept–Oct 9.30–5; early Feb–Mar 2–4.30; adm*), the expert guides *do* concentrate on the volcanoes of the Auvergne, and you get the chance to walk round a volcano crater, admittedly one that has long been transformed into a quarry, but extremely interesting for all that. While waiting for the guide, take an initial lesson in local vulcanology either by watching the slide film (with English commentary sometimes available) or touring the exhibition; that way, you'll be more familiar with the technical terms the guides use on the long tour. Roughly speaking, the Monts Dôme consist of around 70 volcanoes, the intense line of them caused by the movement in the earth's plates as the Alps formed and grew. The Monts Dôme volcanic line was active from around 80,000 to 10,000 years ago; none is active now. The guides illustrate the three different types of volcano tops that mark the landscape simply by pointing around the horizon: the strombolian ones with cones, the pelean ones with domes, and the maars with wide craters.

Walking tracks have been laid through the volcanoes of the Monts Dômes, and you may find this the most atmospheric way of all to discover these exceptional landscapes. The Monts Dore, a volcanic range with a quite different character from the Monts Dômes, rise just to the south, but first we travel from Clermont-Ferrand down towards the source of the Allier river.

The Upper Allier

The views are thrilling along the first part of the Allier south of Clermont-Ferrand, the silhouettes of the Monts Dômes and Monts Dore standing out to the west, those of the less well-known but beautiful Monts du Livradois forming the backdrop to the east. Meander around the enchanting villages set on the gentle slopes around the Allier between Clermont and Issoire, such as **Montpeyroux**.

Getting Around

The Clermont-Ferrand–Nîmes line passes via Issoire, Brioude and through the Allier gorges to Langogne and beyond.

Tourist Information

Issoire: Pl du Général de Gaulle, t 04 73 89 15 90.
Brioude: Place Lafayette, t 04 71 74 97 49.
Lavoûte-Chilhac: Place du Monument, t 04 71 77 46 57.
Pradelles: Place du Foirail, t 04 71 00 82 65.

Where to Stay and Eat

Sarpoil ✉ 63490

La Bergerie de Sarpoil, t 04 73 71 02 54 (*expensive–moderate*). The young chef in this prettily restored building has built up his success on experimental cuisine. *Closed Sun eve, Tues and Wed exc July–Aug, plus Jan.*

Lavaudieu ✉ 43100

B&B La Maison d'à Côté, t 04 71 76 45 04 (*inexpensive*). A lovely typical stone house with beautiful terraces by the old bridge in this delightful village.
Auberge de l'Abbaye, t 04 71 76 44 44 (*moderate*). Quaint village restaurant serving traditional fare. *Closed Mon, plus Sun eve outside summer season.*
Court La Vigne, t 04 71 76 45 79 (*moderate–cheap*). Also appealing, offering good-value regional food. *Closed Tues and Wed, and Dec and Jan.*

St-Haon ✉ 43340

✶✶Auberge de la Vallée, t 04 71 08 20 73, *aubergevallee43@aol.com* (*inexpensive*). Simple and fun, on the church square, with comfortable rooms and a pleasant restaurant (*moderate*). *Closed Jan–mid-Mar; restaurant closed Sun eve and Mon in winter.*

Langogne ✉ 48300

✶✶✶Domaine de Barres, t 04 66 69 71 00 (*moderate*). A very elegant 18th-century manor by the lake of Naussac, surrounded by a golf course. The interior has been transformed in contemporary style. Excellent value for such comfort, including a covered pool. Gastronomic cuisine too (*expensive*).

Down on the flat by the river, the lively heart of **Issoire** may now be encircled by busy boulevards, but boasts the ornate Romanesque church of **St-Austremoine**, built in the 12th century to serve a Benedictine monastery. Outside, the exuberant east end is decorated with chequered patterns and medallions depicting signs of the zodiac. Much of the colour inside was added in a major 19th-century neo-Romanesque redecorating campaign. Original medieval capitals survive, including the Last Supper scene, the tablecloth a frilly addition right round the column. In the narthex a splendid Last Judgement fresco from the 15th century portrays Christ sitting on a rainbow. The 13th-century Limoges reliquary chest of the mystery saint after whom the place is named lies in the crypt. The **Centre d'Art Roman** by the church puts on good exhibitions explaining Romanesque art and architecture. Although much of the historic town was destroyed in the 16th-century Wars of Religion, the **Tour de l'Horloge** (*open June–Sept Tues–Sat 10–12 and 2–7, Sun 2–7; Oct–May Tues–Sun 2–7; closed Mon; adm*) recalls highpoints of the Renaissance period here.

High up on the other bank of the Allier southeast of Issoire, **Usson** stands perched on extraordinary basalt columns resembling huge organ pipes. The village castle was demolished by Richelieu, but the late-medieval church (*rarely open*) has uplifting views, and there is a small museum on local customs.

In the atmospheric town of **Brioude** south along the Allier, the alarmingly deep ochres of the **Basilique St-Julien** derive from the local sandstone, appropriately bloody in colour, as this is where St Julian was martyred in the 4th century. Great powers being ascribed to his relics, his tomb quickly became an important place of pilgrimage, and he was made patron saint of Auvergne. Curiosities abound inside the fascinating, wonderfully quirky medieval church dedicated to him: a frighteningly emaciated Christ looking like an Auvergnat peasant; a black Virgin in the ambulatory; even the cobblestone floor, with its petal patterns, added in the 16th century. Strain your neck to make out the capitals alarmingly carved with winged monsters, animals making music, knights jousting and a surprising number of naked figures, then take the guided tour to appreciate the paintings of Christ, a host of angels and other scenes high up in the narthex. Brioude's specialities are reflected in its tourist attractions. The **Hôtel de la Dentelle** (*open April–Oct Mon–Fri 9–12 and 2–6, or 7 in July and Aug, Sat and public hols 3–6; adm*) presents the strong tradition of lace-making, but emphasizing contemporary creativity. The **Maison du Saumon** (*open May–Sept; t 04 71 74 91 43 for times; adm*) celebrates the fish that migrate up and down the Allier.

With its rustic wooden balconies and porches, its old houses in orange- and red-tinged stone and its delightful little river running past the village vegetable plots, **Lavaudieu** would be charming even without its intriguing cultural attractions. Its abbey was founded as an establishment for women by Robert, the man who created La Chaise-Dieu (*see* p.689). The curiously truncated octagonal steeple of the Romanesque **abbey church** lost its top at the Revolution, to be replaced by the strange umbrella of a structure protecting it today. Inside, unusually colourful medieval frescoes stand out, painted high up above the arches. One rare scene may be an allegory of the Black Death which struck in the middle of the 14th century. Look out too for the violent depiction of the martyrdom of St Ursula and her companion virgins. The sensational medieval sculpture of an oriental-looking Jesus, the Christ of Lavaudieu, is only a copy; the original head has ended up in the Louvre, the body in New York's Metropolitan Museum. Coiled and crinkled columns hold up the **abbey cloister** (*open mid-June–mid-Sept daily 10–12 and 2–6.30; Easter–mid-June and mid-Sept–Oct Wed–Mon 10–12 and 2–5, closed Tues; adm; ticket also valid for the little museum of local arts, crafts and traditions opposite the church*). In the refectory, a very large Christ in Majesty presides above the Virgin flanked by angels and saints.

A handful of craftspeople work year-round in Lavaudieu creating and restoring stained glass. Follow their work on the short but fascinating guided tour at the **Carrefour du Vitrail** (*open May–Oct daily 9.30–12 and 2–6.30; adm*) which explains how the lead and glass are prepared and put together, as well as outlining the history of stained-glass-making in France. Someone has calculated that France can lay claim to some 65 per cent of the historic stained glass in the world. Apparently fragments have been found dating back to the 8th century, but the craft only really took off from the end of the 12th century. Its most glorious flowering came in the Gothic period, but in the 16th century the craft waned, only to experience a revival in the 19th century.

The US and French flags fly over the **Château de Chavaniac-Lafayette** (*open July–Aug daily 9–6; Mar–June and Sept–mid-Nov Wed–Mon 10–12 and 2–6, closed Tues; adm*) which, like the village, has changed its name to honour the revolutionary general born here in 1757. In 1916 the castle was bought by the La Fayette Memorial Inc. Since then it has been well cared for and well furnished, and contains Lafayette memorabilia. The idealistic young aristocrat sailed to America to aid the colonists in 1777, and found himself commanding the troops that trapped the British army at Yorktown, thus ending the war. Back in France, he was an early leader of the Revolution, and wrote a first draft of the *Declaration of the Rights of Man* – though when the radical Jacobins took power he had to flee to avoid the guillotine before finding favour again with the restoration of the monarchy. After the tour, relax in the landscaped gardens.

Dramatic twisting roads take you down the gorges of the Allier towards the large artificial lake of Naussac. **Lavoûte-Chilhac**'s wonderful curve of houses follows one meander in the river; its big Gothic church is reached via a concave crescent of buildings, part of a former Benedictine abbey. The wide, aisleless church contains some amusing carved stone figures. The **Maison des Oiseaux** is dedicated to the bird life of the gorges.

Surrounded by wrinkly rocks, and very popular with canoeists, **Pradelles** is one of the liveliest villages in the Allier gorges, its lovely chapel containing very faded frescoes. Amusing rock formations will entertain you on the way south, past **Monistrol-d'Allier** and **St-Didier-d'Allier**, both worth seeking out for their superb locations. A detour west takes you towards the pretty deserted Montagne de la Margeride and the pleasantly sleepy town of **Saugues**, but this place has a troubled past, as some of its monuments recall. The medieval keep known as the **Tour des Anglais** is named after the English mercenaries who ruled the area by terror after the Hundred Years War; it now serves as an artists' exhibition space. The **Musée Fantastique de la Bête du Gévaudan** tackles the horrifying 'Beast of the Gévaudan' which devoured 99 victims, mostly women and children, in these parts in the 1760s. The appalling mystery has never been solved, although a fantastical French cinema epic of 2000 turned it into a vile tale of satanic ritual and murder.

Into the Monts Dore

The Monts Dore, like the Monts Dômes, form part of the Parc Régional Naturel des Volcans d'Auvergne, but their explosive past is nowhere near as obvious – they look more like conventional mountains. Most of the volcanoes in these parts were active around 2 million to 3.5 million years ago, although the youngest, such as Montchal and Montcineyre, are only around 6,000 years old. The **Puy de Sancy**, the tallest summit at almost 6,200ft, dominates the countryside for vast distances around with its sharp triangular top. Steep, claustrophobic valleys characterize the landscapes below.

Heading up to St-Nectaire from the Allier, seek out intriguing villages such as **St-Saturnin**, **Champeix** or **St-Floret**. **St-Nectaire**, squeezed into the Chambon valley, is dominated by its well-known Romanesque church. Dedicated to a companion of St Austremoine (*see* 'Issoire', p.700), it was built for a Benedictine priory attached to the abbey of La Chaise-Dieu (*see* p.689). Inside, entertaining capitals depict lively biblical scenes. The treasury preserves an unusual medieval reliquary arm, said to

Getting Around

Not much by way of public transport in this mountainous region.

Tourist Information

Le Mont-Dore: Av Libération, t 04 73 65 20 21.
La Bourboule: Place de la République, t 04 73 65 57 71.

Where to Stay and Eat

Le Mont-Dore ✉ 63240

**Le Castelet, Av Michel Bertrand, t 04 73 65 05 29, *castelet@compuserve.com* (*inexpensive*). Many of the hotels in this resort cater to spa-goers, this one less so. Reasonable restaurant (*moderate*). Pool. *Closed late Mar–mid-May and late Sept–late Dec.*

B&B Closerie de Manon, t 04 73 65 26 81 (*inexpensive*). A charming place to stay in a typical house between Le Mont-Dore and La Bourboule.

Le Bougnat, 23 Av Georges Clemenceau, t 04 73 65 28 19 (*moderate*). A young team cooking up tasty local dishes in a lovely stable-turned-restaurant. *Closed Mon and Tues, and mid-Nov–mid-Dec.*

La Bourboule ✉ 63150

**Les Fleurs, Av Gueneau de Mussy, t 04 73 81 09 44 (*inexpensive*). Chalet of a hotel. Many rooms have balconies and views.

**Aviation, Rue de Metz, t 04 73 81 32 32, *aviation@nat.fr* (*inexpensive*). Good choice of rooms and facilities. Restaurant (*moderate*). *Closed Oct–mid-Dec.*

contain offcuts of St Nectaire. Below the church, the dark village has a few thermal spa establishments, but the area is better known to visitors for its grassy cheese, on sale in many shops. Uncover medieval underground living here at **Les Mystères de Farges** (*open July–Aug daily 10–7; May–June, Sept and school hols 10–12 and 2–7; adm*).

To escape from the Chambon valley, climb north to **Les Arnats** for sensational views of the Monts Dore, and, closer by, of the **Château de Murol** (*open April–Oct daily 2–5, plus special theatrical visits July and Aug mornings Sun–Tues and Thurs–Fri; adm*), an impressively sinister-looking ruin of a medieval castle high above the valley, the extraordinary defensive architecture taking the form of a circle within a circle.

The D5 continues to **Besse-en-Chandesse**, on the southern side of the Monts Dore, a grey, fortified village which sits in a landscape of stark volcanoes and pastures. It's a popular tourist stop, with hotels and boutiques aplenty. The Romanesque church with decorative capitals turns Gothic at the choir. The modern ski resort of **Super-Besse** stands a bit higher up to the west, set under volcanic peaks, with wide south-facing slopes in a splendid location. From here you can take a chair lift up to the **Puy Ferrand** (nearly 6,000ft), just below the Puy de Sancy, affording fabulous views. South of Besse, walkers can appreciate a string of curious high lakes set in volcanic craters. The best-known and easiest to reach is the circular **Lac Pavin**, surrounded by woods.

The Dordogne river starts on its long journey to the Altantic from the north side of the Monts Dore, on the **Puy de Sancy**. A steep, dramatic road takes you from Le Mont-Dore up close to the peak, a cablecar operating for the final section. The spa town of **Le Mont-Dore** far down below has a lively summer season for rheumatics, asthmatics and ramblers lasting from May to October. The Celts apparently enjoyed the thermal waters here even before the Romans built their substantial baths. Forgotten by the outside world for centuries, the waters were rediscovered in the time of Louis XIV;

emerging from the lava at between 38°C and 44°C, they are said to be particularly helpful for respiratory problems. Vestiges of the Roman baths survive in the outrageous pastiche 19th-century **Etablissement Thermal**. To the north, the little village of **Orcival** is often overwhelmed by tourists, but the dominating presence is the **Basilique Notre-Dame**. With its octagonal tower and the tiers of its choir end, it was built in the 12th century as a dependency of the abbey of La Chaise-Dieu. One of the finest works of the Auvergnat Romanesque, it is in fact somewhat less lavishly decorated than some others. The one truly remarkable art work inside is an icon-like, silver-coated statue of the Virgin and Child in severe Auvergnat style.

La Bourboule, back down along the Dordogne valley, is Le Mont-Dore's rival – a faded 19th-century spa with several grandiose buildings including its baths, the Grands Thermes, and its casino. Hillside **Murat-le-Quaire**, further up the slopes, presents a picture of a typical agricultural village, although these have suffered terribly from changes in agriculture since the war; only two working farms are left in the parish. The **Musée de Toinette** pays its respects to rural life and traditions. The most popular walk from here takes you to the curiously flat-topped old volcano of **La Banne d'Oranche**, another of the many wonderful viewing points over the volcanic landscapes. The Dordogne river carves its tortuous way west through the steep and wooded **Gorges d'Avèze** to enter the Limousin (*see* **The Southwest**, p.377ff).

Cantal

Below the Monts Dore, the Cantal region is basically one huge dormant volcano, the largest one in Europe, with sweet valley roads spilling down its sides like rivulets of sauce trickling down a vast pudding. The top has been worn away to reveal a cluster of volcanic plugs, notably the Puy Mary, the Puy Griou and the Plomb du Cantal, but you can still get a good sense of the shape of the vast volcano from its sloping sides or *planèzes*. Even in the height of summer the high pastures are lush and green, with the handlebar-horned Salers cows adding their ruddy character to the landscapes.

One of the most delightful routes up into the centre of the Cantal volcano is via the winding Cheylade valley from **Riom-ès-Montagne**, a sweet village best known for producing cheese and gentian bitters. Its medieval church sports a couple of naughty capitals: one appears to depict a religious figure cutting off a lustful man's member. The lush pastures and open horizons above are interrupted only by the odd worn-down volcano plug. The pilgrimage stop of **La Font-Sainte** stands lost in an Irish-looking landscape, the sound of jangling cow bells often ringing in the air. Reaching delightful **Cheylade**, its church has one of the most flowery ceilings imaginable: angels and naïve animals also feature. A fair walk takes you up to the top of the **Puy Mary**, the highest peak in the Cantal (at over 6,000ft) from where you get a magical view of the whole volcanic structure and far beyond.

It's a long way round by road from the Puy Mary to the Plomb du Cantal. A route round to the east takes you via **Dienne**, whose Romanesque church stands aloofly on its terrace outside the village. **Murat** slopes prettily down the Alagnon valley, with

Getting There and Around

Airlinair, **t** 04 71 63 56 98, **flies** from Paris to Aurillac-Tronquières. Aurillac **train** station is on a line from Paris-Gare de Lyon. St-Flour station can be reached by train from Clermont-Ferrand. A local rail line runs across the Cantal from Brioude to Aurillac.

Tourist Information

Riom-ès-Montagnes: Place Charles de Gaulle, **t** 04 71 78 07 37, *www.riom-montagnes. auvergne.net.*
Murat: 2 Rue Faubourg Notre-Dame, **t** 04 71 20 09 47, *www.ville-de-murat.com.*
St-Flour: 17bis Place d'Armes, **t** 04 71 60 22 50, *www.saint-flour.com.*
Chaudes-Aigues: 1 Av Georges Pompidou, **t** 04 71 23 52 75, *www.chaudes-aigues. auvergne.net.*
Mauriac: 1 Rue Chappe d'Auteroche, **t** 04 71 67 30 26, *www.mauriac.auvergne.net.*
Salers: Place Tyssandier d'Escous, **t** 04 71 40 70 68, *www.pays-de-salers.com.*
Aurillac: Place du Square, **t** 04 71 48 46 58, *www.iaurillac.com.*

Where to Stay and Eat

St-Flour ✉ 15100

★★**Hôtel des Roches**, Place d'Armes, **t** 04 71 60 09 70, *fillesgauthier@wanadoo.fr* (*inexpensive*). The spacious rooms overlooking the cathedral make up for the dull modern decoration. Traditional cuisine (*moderate–cheap*). *Restaurant closed weekends out of season.*

Lanau ✉ 15260

★★**Auberge du Pont de Lanau**, **t** 04 71 23 57 76, *aubergedupontdelanau@wanadoo.fr* (*inexpensive*). By the main road south from St-Flour to Chaudes-Aigues, but a charming inn, offering innovative regional cuisine (*expensive–moderate*). *Closed late-Dec–Jan; restaurant closed Mon lunch.*

Salers ✉ 15140

★★**Hôtel des Remparts**, Esplanade de Barrouze, **t** 04 71 40 70 33, *hotel.remparts@wanadoo.fr* (*inexpensive*). Extremely attractive typical architecture, rooms with views, plus restaurant (*moderate–cheap*) with terrace. *Closed mid-Oct–mid-Dec.*

Le Theil ✉ 15140

★★★**Hostellerie de la Maronne**, **t** 04 71 69 20 33, *hotelmaronne@cfi15.fr* (*expensive–moderate*). Special 19th-century manor in a beautiful valley, with spacious rooms and excellent cuisine (*dinner only; expensive*). *Closed Nov–Mar.*

Tournemire ✉ 15310

Auberge de Tournemire, **t** 04 71 47 61 28, *louisfert@wanadoo.fr* (*inexpensive*). Delightful location looking down on the valley. Simple cheap rooms and hearty Auvergne cooking (*moderate*). *Closed mid-Jan–early Feb.*

irregular old slates on the roofs of its old houses. Pine forests surround the lower resort of **Le Lioran**, but it's from the ski resort of **Super-Lioran** that you can take the cablecar to the top of the **Plomb de Cantal** for more fantastic views.

Extraordinarily perched high up on a large almond-shaped rock overlooking the Ander and Lescure valleys, **St-Flour** is a seductively severe little city. The Gothic **cathedral** with its twin towers dominates the upper town. The former **bishops' palace** has been converted into the town hall and town museum, the **Musée de la Haute-Auvergne** (*open mid-April–mid-Oct daily 10–12 and 2–6; rest of year daily exc Sun and public hols 10–12 and 2–6; adm*), interesting religious displays including a number of wood-carved saints and the cathedral's treasure. Other sections are devoted to regional folklore and traditions. The grandest old mansion in town, the grey Renaissance Maison Consulaire, contains the **Musée Douët** (*open mid-April–mid-Oct daily 10–12 and 2–6; rest of year Mon–Sat same times; adm*), with diverse collections of decorative arts. Close to St-Flour, the massive metal arch of the **Viaduc de Garabit** is so bold it comes as no surprise to discover it was built by Gustave Eiffel, in the early 1880s. **Chaudes-Aigues**, an unexpectedly lively little spa town a bit further south, pulls in the crowds in summer. It claims to have the hottest spa waters in Europe, coming out of the rock at 82°F (26°C).

Yet more picturesque valleys slide down the western side of the Cantal volcano from the Puy Mary. The Vallée du Falgoux takes you northwest to **Mauriac**, a cheerful Auvergnat town. Both its **Basilique Notre-Dame-des-Miracles** and the **Hôtel d'Orcet** have remarkable Romanesque carved doorways, and the basilica a colourful carved font. The Maronne valley leads you to **Salers**, an imposingly dour, deep grey fortified hilltop village surrounded by low walls, suspiciously surveying the wide vistas around. A splendid array of corner towers and stair towers compete for your attention on the central square, and you can visit the interiors of several of the finest old houses. Local cheese-making is well covered at **Les Burons de Salers** (*open April–11 Nov daily 10–7; adm*) between Salers and Le Puy Mary.

The Doire valley, harder to reach from the Puy Mary, leads you to the impressive hill-side village of **Tournemire** and the adjoining **Château d'Anjony** (*open Feb–mid-Nov daily exc Sun in July and Aug 2–6.30; adm*), built in the 15th century for Louis II d'Anjony, a companion in arms to Joan of Arc. One tower contains a chapel with wall paintings depicting the life of Christ, but still better frescoes are devoted to chivalric scenes and 16th-century Michel d'Anjony and his wife. Tournemire and its castle benefit from similar views on to the deep verdant valley, with cows and horses grazing on its slopes and speckled-stone villages lying far below.

The Mandailles valley takes you directly southwest to **Aurillac**, the quiet, attractive capital of the Cantal *département*. It lays claim to being the home town of France's first-ever pope, Sylvester II, who made his meteoric rise from shepherd to pontiff at the end of the 10th century. His statue stands in a prominent position on Place Gerbert by the river Jordanne and the old town centre; behind him stretches a pretty row of riverside houses. The small centre has many fine façades, and a **waxworks museum** (*open mid-May–mid-Sept daily exc Sun am 10–12 and 3–7; adm*) featuring Sylvestre among other historic figures. In a separate part of town the **Musée d'Art et d'Archéologie** (*open Feb–Oct daily exc Sun and Mon 10–12 and 2–6; adm*) presents local archaeological finds, paintings of various European schools and an array of traditional Cantal interiors. But on Place St-Géraud the Château St-Etienne houses the **Muséum des Volcans** (*open mid-June–mid-Sept Mon–Sat 10–6.30, Sun 2–6.30; rest of year Tues–Sat 2–6; adm*), bringing you back to the heart of the matter in the Auvergne, volcanoes, and in particular the formation of the vast one on which you're standing.

The Alps and the Jura

The Alps and the Jura

pp.568–9

Belfort
Montbéliard
Audincourt
Montbéliard

HAUTE-SAONE
Saône
E23
E54/A36
A36
Dijon
COTE-D'OR
A38
A39
Besançon
Nancray
Doubs
St-Hippolyte
Gournois
Baume-les-Dames
Pierrefontaine
DOUBS
Villers-le-Lac
Dole
Quingey
Bonnevaux-le-Prieuré
Arc-en-Senans
Cléron
Ornans
Mouthier
Beaune
Arbois
472
Lods
Montbenoît
Salins-les-Bains
Pontarlier
Chalon-sur-Saône
Poligny
Château-Chalon
JURA
Malbuisson

p.618

Louhans
Lons-le-Saunier
Champagnole
Clairvaux-les-Lacs
Bonlieu
Lac de Chalain
Lac de Narlay
Pic de l'Aigle
Lausanne
SAONE-ET-LOIRE
St-Amour
Morans-en-Montagne
St-Claude
Lac Léman (Lake Geneva)
Evian-les-Bains
Thonon-les-Bains
Abondance
Châtel
St-Julien
Parc Nat. Reg. du Haut Jura
Gex
Divonne
Yvoire
Avoriaz
Mâcon
Treffort
HAUTE
SAVOIE
Geneva
Annemasse
Les Gets
Bourg-en-Bresse
Nantua
Cruseilles
Bonneville
Flaine
Argentière
Roanne
Ambronay
Ambérieu-en-Bugey
Thorens-Glières
Chamonix-Mont-Blanc
BEAUJOLAIS
Artemare
Annecy
Thônes
St-Gervais
Mont Blanc
Belley
Menthon
Megève
Lac d'Annecy
Hautecombe
Ugine
Beaufort
LYON
Izieu
Aix-les-Bains
Conflans
La Rosière
St-Genix
Le Bourget
Albertville
Bourg-St-Maurice
RHONE
Chambéry
Val d'Isère
St-Etienne
Vienne
Entremont-le-Vieux
Moûtiers
Courchevel
Bonneval
Mt Pilat
St-Pierre-d'Entremont
Allevard
SAVOIE
Parc National de la Vanoise
Bessans
St-Etienne-de-St-Geoirs
Voiron
Val-Thorens
Lanslebourg
HAUTE-LOIRE
St-Jean-de-Maurienne
Aussois
Modane
Grenoble
Uriage
Valloire
Villard-de-Lans
Vizille
Chamrousse
L'Alpe-d'Huez
Montgenèvre
La Chapelle-en-Vercors
Le Bourg d'Oisans
Les Deux-Alpes
Chantemerle
Valence
Vassieux-en-Vercors
Venosc
Briançon
L'Obiou
Parc National des Ecrins
Vallouise
Château-Queyras
Abriès
Aiguilles
Queyras
HAUTES-ALPES
Guillestre
Ceillac
M Viso
Gap
Vars
Les Orres
Embrun
Barcelonnette
Le Sauze
Pra-Loup
ITALY

pp.660–1

pp.760–61

ENGLAND
English Channel
BELGIUM
GERMANY
LUX.
FRANCE
SWITZ.
ITALY
SPAIN

20 km
10 miles

N

Highlights

1 Besançon, caught in the Doubs' meander
2 The Jura wine and salt routes
3 The overwhelming peak of Mont-Blanc
4 Savoy's great lakes and their towns:
   du Bourget, Annecy and Léman

Food and Wine

Most people imagine devouring a rich **cheese** fondue after a long day's skiing when they think of this region. But two of the best local cheeses are so fine they should be eaten just as they are: Comté, made in the Franche-Comté, and Beaufort, made in Savoy. *Tomme* is a general name for the traditional rounded cheese of Savoy; *tommes* vary a great deal in flavour. Tome des Bauges is distinguished from the rest by having an *appellation d'origine contrôlée* as well as just one 'm'. Reblochon from the Aravis range tastes excellent in a *tartiflette* – served with layers of potatoes, garlic and herbs. Bleu de Gex is probably the best blue cheese of these regions. The Franche-Comté's soft Morbier cheese tries to give itself extra character by adding a line of ash through the middle. Sticky Cancoillotte, also from Franche-Comté, with only 5 per cent fat, is excellent hot or cold with steamed potatoes. But the best way of serving potatoes in these parts bears the name of one of the old Alpine regions – *gratin dauphinois*, slices of potatoes baked with eggs, milk and grated cheese.

Meats are often served in stews, or with rich, mushroom sauces. Game such as venison, wild boar, hare and woodcock is still hunted in these wooded mountainous parts and chefs will often seek out wild *champignons* or wild herbs and berries with which to flavour their dishes. Pork *saucissons* and smoked hams traditionally lasted well through the long mountain winters. River and lake fish often appear on the menus, as do *écrevisses*, the prized crayfish plucked from the local streams.

Some distinctly surprising **wines** and some positively dangerous **liqueurs** are produced in the Jura and the Alps. Along the gorgeous Jura wine route, the *vignerons* make some rather weird numbers (*see* p.718). Vinegrowers in the Bugey down close to the Rhône produce light, but very perfumed wine. The Vins de Savoie from sloping vineyards along the Rhône and Isère valleys, or by Lake Geneva, vary in quality.

Absinthe, long made in the Franche-Comté, from wormwood macerated in brandy, was banned some time ago for its mind-rotting effects, but has been making a diluted come-back recently. Chartreuse, a dangerous green liqueur made to a secret recipe of the Carthusian monks, comes from the mountain range of the same name, near Grenoble. Jura kirsch, produced from cherries, is a rather friendlier liqueur.

When Hannibal led his elephants on history's most dramatic expedition through the French Alps in 218 BC the mountains were regarded as an almost impossibly dangerous obstacle to surmount. And daunting they long remained, although the Romantics transformed perceptions of them, seeing the enormous peaks and troughs of the Alps as a reflection of life itself, with its exhilarating heights and abysmal depths. Today the French Alps have undergone another metamorphosis, into one of Europe's favourite playgrounds.

This chapter starts with the quieter Jura mountains of the Franche-Comté, the 'Free County', where Besançon and other elegant Comtois towns still seem to thrive on their own semi-independence. After the discreet but delightful Jura wine, salt, lake and forest routes come the sensational French Alpine regions of Savoy and the Dauphiné, stretching between Lake Geneva and Provence. In their eastern portions you'll find many of the most famous ski resorts and many of the highest places in

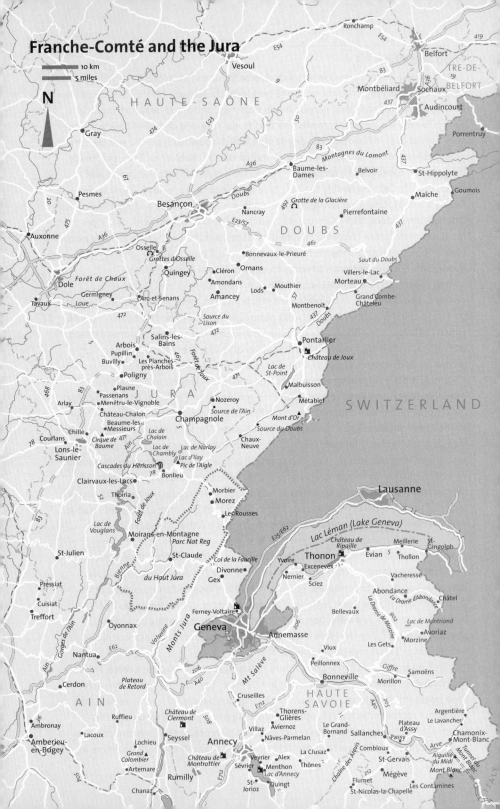

Franche-Comté and the Jura

10 km
5 miles

N

Ronchamp

Belfort

TRE-DE-BELFORT

E54

419

Vesoul

Montbéliard   Sochaux

HAUTE-SAÔNE

Audincourt

Porrentruy

Gray

83

437

437

Pesmes

Montagnes du Lomont

Baume-les-Dames

Belvoir

St-Hippolyte

Maîche

Goumois

A36

Besançon

Nancray

492   Grotte de la Glacière

Pierrefontaine

DOUBS

437

Auxonne

A36

461

Saut du Doubs

Osselle

Grottes d'Osselle

Bonnevaux-le-Prieuré

Villers-le-Lac

Morteau

Forêt de Chaux

Quingey

Cléron   Ornans

Germigny

Arc-et-Senans

Amondans

Lods   Mouthier

Grand'Combe-Châteleu

Dole

Amancey

Tavaux

Loue

472

Montbenoît

Source du Lison

Pontarlier

472

Château de Joux

Salins-les-Bains

Arbois

Pupillin

Buvilly

Les Planches-près-Arbois

Lac de St-Point

Malbuisson

Poligny

Plasne

Nozeroy

Métabief

Passenans   Menétru-le-Vignoble

Source de l'Ain

Mont d'Or

SWITZERLAND

Arlay

Château-Chalon

Champagnole

Source du Doubs

Chille

Beaume-les-Messieurs

Courlans

Cirque de Baume

Lac de Chalain

Chaux-Neuve

Lons-le-Saunier

Lac de Chambly

Lac de Narlay

Cascades du Hérisson

Lac d'Ilay   Pic de l'Aigle

Clairvaux-les-Lacs

Bonlieu

Lausanne

Thoiria

Morbier

Morez

Les Rousses

Lac Léman (Lake Geneva)

Lac de Vouglans

Moirans-en-Montagne Parc Nat Reg

Château de Ripaille

Meillerie

St-Gingolph

St-Julien

Forêt de Joux

du Haut Jura

St-Claude

Col de la Faucille

Yvoire

Thonon   Evian

Thollon

Pressiat

Divonne

Nernier   Excenevex

Vacheresse

Gex

Sciez

Abondance

Châtel

Cuisiat

Treffort

Bienne

Bellevaux

Lac de Montriond

St-Julien

Oyonnax

Ferney-Voltaire

Geneva

Annemasse

Les Gets

Avoriaz

Morzine

Nantua

Monts Jura

Viux

Giffre

Samoëns

Cerdon

Plateau de Retord

Mt Salève

Peillonnex

Bonneville

Morillon

AIN

Cruseilles

HAUTE-SAVOIE

Ambronay

Ruffieu

Château de Clermont

Thorens-Glières

Le Grand-Bornand

Argentière

Le Lavancher

Lacoux

Villaz   Aviernoz

Sallanches   Passy

Plateau d'Assy

Chamonix-Mont-Blanc

Ambérieu-en-Bugey

Lochieu

Seyssel

Nâves-Parmelan

La Clusaz

Combloux

Grand Colombier

Annecy

Veyrier   Alex

St-Gervais

Aiguille du Midi

Artemare

Château de Montrottier

Sévrier   Menthon

La Dranse d'Abondance

Mont Blanc

Rumilly

St-Jorioz

Lac d'Annecy

Thônes

Mégève

Tunnel du Mont Blanc

Chanaz

Duingt

Flumet

Les Contamines

St-Nicolas-la-Chapelle

Europe, topped by Mont Blanc, rising like an otherworldly meringue high above the other peaks on the Italian frontier. Approached from the Rhône valley, the sheer and weird limestone tops of the prealpine ranges of the Bauges, the Chartreuse and the Vercors present a formidable jagged wall. They loom above the most interesting towns and romantic lakes in the French Alps: Grenoble, Annecy and Lac d'Annecy, Chambéry and Aix-les-Bains close to Lac du Bourget. East of Grenoble start the major resorts of the southern French Alps, on the edges of the serrated Ecrins national park. In neighbouring Queyras regional park, the lofty old villages and towns all wear sundials, testimonials to the inordinate amount of sunshine they receive.

Franche-Comté

The Old Capitals of the Franche-Comté

Attractive **Dole** on the Doubs river is the western outpost of the Franche-Comté. Regional capital in the Middle Ages, it later bagged the Parlement and university. But the French bashed it repeatedly: Louis XI's troops in 1479, then Louis XIV's, who brought down the fortifications. Dole's enormous Gothic centrepiece, the **Collégiale Notre-Dame**, survived for you to admire the fine stone apostles in the rather bare interior. The streets heading off from the Collégiale have tempting shops occupying some of the best town houses, several sporting elegant stair towers. In the former tanners' quarter by the Doubs, the **Maison Natale de Pasteur et Musée Pasteur** (*open July–Aug Mon–Sat 10–6, Sun 2–6; April–June and Sept–Oct Mon–Sat 10–12 and 2–6, Sun 2–6; adm*) was where that most important of pioneering scientists, Louis Pasteur, was born in 1822. As well as learning about his family life, explore the enormous significance to medicine of his work on bacteria and vaccination. The **Musée des Beaux-Arts** (*open July–Aug Wed–Sun 10–12 and 2–6; rest of year Tues–Sun 10–12 and 2–6*) features local archaeology, paintings by local maestro and major 19th-century provocateur Courbet, and experimental landscapes by Auguste Pointelin.

Due north of Dole, the fortified old village of **Pesmes** stands prettily above the Ognon river. The wide main street leads down to the surviving main gateway and a treasure trove of a Gothic church, signalled by a typical Comtois tower, resembling a helmet, covered in deep-brown tiles.

Besançon

Under the Holy Roman Empire, the Franche-Comté was a fairly independent state, and **Besançon** a city state within it. With Hugues de Salins, archbishop in the 1030s, the place was already declared a 'free and imperial city', while in 1290 it became a *commune* with far-reaching powers. But when the late medieval Burgundian dukes imposed their authority on the region, rival Dole gained in importance. Between the 1470s and the 1670s the Franche-Comté came under the control of the Holy Roman Empire once again, and under Habsburg rule Besançon became one of the mightiest cities in the Empire. But throughout the 17th century the French coveted it, until

Louis XIV took the region in lieu of the dowry he had been promised at his marriage to Maria Theresa of Spain. Imperial forces briefly won back Besançon, but in 1678 the Franche-Comté was officially made a part of France by the Peace of Nijmegen, and Besançon became undisputed capital of the region: the Parlement and university were moved here from Dole. Famous 19th-century sons include Victor Hugo and the Lumière brothers; as to the Comte de Chardonnet, he revolutionized the clothes industry by inventing 'artificial silk', rayon.

From the quays opposite the historic centre, admire Besançon's dramatic location, caught in its noose in the Doubs. Then take the Grande-Rue which cuts through the heart of town, lined with mansions in the characteristic blue-tinged stone of the area, relieved from time to time by grand squares. The **Musée des Beaux-Arts et d'Archéologie** (*Place de la Révolution; open Wed–Mon 9.30–12 and 2–6; closed Tues; adm, free Sat pm*) occupies the 19th-century corn market on a square to one side. The extensive painting sections include works by the likes of Titian, Bronzino and Bellini, Cranach and Zurbarán. Courbet contributes a brooding self-portrait and a huge snowy deer hunt showing the bright Jura of midwinter. Back along the Grande-Rue, behind the colourful 16th-century town hall, the **Palais de Justice**, by the Dijon archi-

Getting There and Around

Dole is on the main **rail** line from Paris-Gare de Lyon to Bern and Zurich. There are more stops on the Paris-Gare de Lyon–Besançon line.

Tourist Information

Dole: 6 Place Jules Grévy, **t** 03 84 72 11 22, *www.dole.org/sitedole*.
Besançon: Parc Micaud, **t** 03 81 80 92 55, *www.besancon.com*.

Sports and Activities

In Besançon, take a **boat trip** along the Doubs from the Pont de la République with **Vedettes Bisontines, t** 03 81 68 13 25.

Where to Stay and Eat

Dole ✉ 39100
★★La Cloche, 2 Place Grevy, **t** 03 84 82 06 06 (*inexpensive*). Central, pretty comfortable, and being renovated.
La Romanée, 13 Rue des Vieilles Boucheries, **t** 03 84 79 19 05 (*inexpensive*). Near the cathedral, serving good Jura cooking in stone-vaulted rooms. *Restaurant closed Sun eve and Wed exc July and Aug.*

Besançon ✉ 25000
★★★Castan, 6 Square Castan, **t** 03 81 65 02 00, *art@hotelcaston.fr* (*expensive*). Wonderfully set in Ancien Régime buildings by the cathedral. *Closed 3 weeks Aug.*
★★Granvelle, 13 Rue du Général Lecourbe, **t** 03 81 81 33 92 (*inexpensive*). Set back in its own courtyard near the cathedral.
★★★Hôtel du Nord, 8 Rue Moncey, **t** 03 81 81 34 56, *hoteldunord@wanadoo.fr* (*inexpensive*). Central and appealing.
Mungo-Park, 11 Rue Jean Petit, **t** 03 81 81 28 01 (*very expensive–expensive*). Inventive and tasty regional cuisine. *Closed Sun, Mon, and part Aug and part Nov.*
La Tour de la Pelote, 41 Quai de Strasbourg, **t** 03 81 82 14 58 (*expensive*). A well-known rendezvous in a 16th-century riverside tower.
Brasserie du Commerce, 31 Rue des Granges, **t** 03 81 81 33 11 (*expensive*). The interior is a listed monument, and the food is excellent, served here since 1873.
Le Chaland, Promenade Micaud, near Pont Bregille, **t** 03 81 80 61 61 (*expensive–moderate*). Fun, on a barge on the Doubs. *Closed Sat lunch.*
Le Vauban, Citadelle, **t** 03 81 83 02 77 (*moderate*). Decent restaurant, in vaulted chambers, with a terrace enjoying a great view. *Restaurant closed Sun, and Mon eve.*

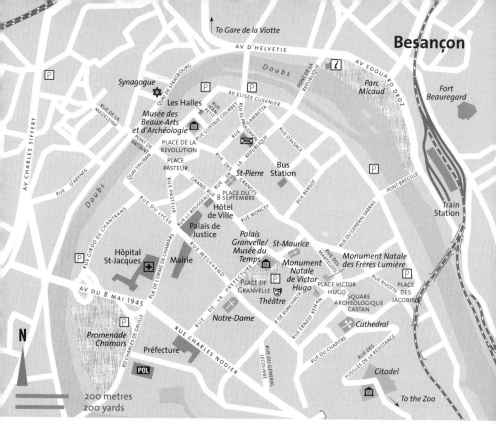

Besançon

tect Hugues Sambin, was where the Franche-Comté Parlement used to meet. Take a short detour along Rue de l'Orme de Chamars to the **Hôpital St-Jacques**, whose chapel, **Notre-Dame-du-Refuge**, is full of flirtatious Baroque playfulness.

The substantial Renaissance façade of the **Palais Granvelle** stretches down one side of the Grande-Rue. The courtyard with its basket-handle arcades has recently been polished up, and the smoothly running **Musée du Temps** (clock museum; *open Wed–Sun 1–7; closed Mon and Tues*) now operates within. Behind the Palais Granvelle, in Rue Megevand, cast an eye over the bold **theatre**, designed by Claude-Nicolas Ledoux (*see pp.715–6*), and the partly Romanesque church of **Notre-Dame**.

The birthplaces of Victor Hugo and the Lumière boys look out on to little Place Victor Hugo, in a pretty corner of town. In the shaded **Square Archéologique Castan** you can make out the remnants of a Roman pool in the darkness. Head through a fine remnant of Besançon's Gallo-Roman predecessor *Vesontio* – a blackened coffered gate, known as the **Porte Noire** – to reach the **cathedral**, whose colourful dome rises above the quarter. A splendidly romantic St John features in the Baroque swirl over the entrance, and the gilded rays, capitals and frames of the Chœur du St-Suaire make an outrageous Baroque show inside. The *Virgin and Saints* by Fra Bartolomeo is generally considered the cathedral's finest painting.

To reach the **citadel** (*open July–Aug daily 9–7; Easter–June and Sept–Oct daily 9–6; Nov–Easter daily 10–5; adm*) above the cathedral, take the free summer bus, or the tourist train if you're daunted by the extremely steep climb. It has four museums in its many-layered defences: the **Espace Vauban**, concentrating on the history of the citadel and its architect; the **Musée Comtois**, which covers the traditions and folklore of the Franche-Comté; the **Musée de la Résistance et de la Déportation**, dealing with the Second World War; and the **Musée d'Histoire Naturelle**. The **zoo**, curiously installed among the fortifications, includes an Insectarium, a Noctarium, and the modernized Aquarium Georges Besse. Best of all is the view.

Along the Jura Wine and Salt Routes

Salins-les-Bains may offer a surprisingly attractive picture of a former salt-making town, but Arc-et-Senans' Saline Royale is truly sensational, a UNESCO World Heritage Site. The beautiful Jura wine route is a real find too, extending south from Salins-les-Bains to arcaded Lons-le-Saunier, passing gorgeous slopeside villages. First, though, to the quiet provincial backwater from which Gustave Courbet stirred French society.

From Besançon to Ornans and the Loue

A short way southeast of Besançon, appealingly tottering old terraces lurch over the Loue at **Ornans**. The place and the river provided much inspiration for one of the most provocative painters of the 19th century, Gustave Courbet (1819–77), whose home has been turned into the **Musée Courbet** (*open daily 10–12 and 2–6; Nov–Mar closed Tues; adm*). Founder of the so-called Realist school, Courbet was a vociferous critic of the art establishment and its obsessions with the Beautiful and the Ideal. His unflinching depictions of modest people in mundane settings (many on display here) were deeply controversial in his day; the Empress Eugénie compared his fleshy naked women bathing in the local waters to cart horses.

East of Ornans along the Loue valley, the river gushes through lovely **Lods**, where the local museum recalls the valley's wine-making traditions – which were wiped out by the phylloxera epidemic of the late 19th century. **Mouthier-Haute-Pierre**, set in a curve in the river, proclaims itself capital of kirsch, the cherry liqueur still made in these parts. The walk to the **Source de la Loue** takes you to one of Courbet's favourite spots.

West of Ornans, the village and château of **Cléron** make a particularly striking ensemble. Tucked into the bank of the Doubs west of Quingey, the **Grottes d'Osselle** (*open June–Aug daily 9–7; April–May daily 9–12 and 2–6; Sept daily 9–12 and 2–5; Oct Mon–Fri 2.30–5, Sun 9–12 and 2–5; adm*) offer a refreshing summer stop. Discovered as far back as the 13th century, this may have been the first cave system to be explored in France; its many grottoes are full of colourful columns and pools.

Salins-les-Bains and the Saline Royale at Arc-et-Senans

Dramatically guarded by a fort perched either side of the steep valley of the Furieuse river, **Salins-les-Bains**, in the 17th century one of the most important towns in the Franche-Comté, looks a bit frayed at the edges now, but retains some grandiose buildings. Visit the **Salines** (*open July–Aug daily 9–7; Mar–June and Sept–Oct Wed–Mon 10–12 and 2–6; adm*), the salt works exploited since Roman times. In medieval

White Gold

Salt was a very precious commodity up to the Revolution: it was a vital ingredient in preserving food for every household and was heavily, compulsorily, ruthlessly taxed. The *gabelle* (salt tax) was imposed from the 14th century, and those who produced the stuff and levied the *gabelle* could make vast fortunes. This corner of the Franche-Comté was lucky to be located on seams rich in salt left over from a distant geological time, when the region lay under the sea. The extraction of salt was a lucrative but painstaking business here. The sedimentary deposits had to be drawn up from far beneath the ground, and then the brine had to be evaporated to produce usable salt. The main salt-producing centre was moved from Salins-les-Bains to Arc-et-Senans just before the Revolution as the woods around Salins had been depleted.

times they were exploited by the Chalon family. Most of the buildings were demolished when the works closed in 1962, but the tour takes you into enormous medieval caverns to see the centuries-old pump bringing salt waters up from some 780ft below ground. In these sulphurous-smelling quarters, imagine the infernal work of those employed down here. You're invited to a *dégustation*, but you won't want much: it's ten times saltier than ordinary seawater and saltier even than the Dead Sea.

Walk along the main street, lined with fine mansions, as far as the elegant arcaded 18th-century town hall. Behind rises the fat dome of the slightly earlier chapel of **Notre-Dame de la Libératrice**, a cage of ribs holding up the ceiling. A small **thermal establishment** (*open daily 3.30–6.30; adm*) still operates in the centre. Two churches lie up the slopes either end of town. A beautiful route east into the hills takes you to the **Source du Lison**, springing fully formed from below dramatic walls of rock.

The staggeringly bold buildings of the **Saline Royale** (*open July–Aug daily 9–7; April–June and Sept–Oct daily 9–12 and 2–6; rest of year daily 9–12 and 2–5; adm*) stand to one side of quiet, unassuming **Arc-et-Senans** on the north bank of the Loue. Planned by the visionary architect Claude-Nicolas Ledoux, built between 1775 and 1779, they form one of the grandest architectural set pieces in eastern France, classified a World Heritage Site by UNESCO. The Saline Royale wasn't actually owned by the crown, but was granted the exclusive royal privilege to exploit the local seams. Ledoux was commissioned to construct a magnificent new salt-producing centre, along with a new town for the workers. His ideal city, Chaux, was never completed, but the hemicycle of buildings that did go up is one of the greatest expressions of neoclassicism in Ancien Régime France, with imposing Italianate columns and bold decorative details; a recurring theme is of water pouring from pots, symbolizing the blessed brine. The magnificent **Maison du Directeur**, the stocky building which acts as the focal point, boasts the most amazing columns of all, built from chunky square and rounded blocks, the latter resembling Comté cheeses in stone. The place now houses the **Lieu du Sel**, an exhibition on the salt industry in France down the ages. You can also visit the **Bâtiments des Sels**, where the salt was extracted from the brine.

Ledoux, one of the most fascinating architects of the 18th century, worked for the likes of Madame du Barry, Louis XV's powerful mistress. Models of his other projects are superbly displayed in the Tonnellerie, the former barrel-makers' building, now

Getting Around

A **bus** service links Dole to Lons-le-Saunier (**t** 03 81 46 40 44).

Tourist Information

Arc-et-Senans: **t** 03 81 57 43 21.
Arbois: 10 Rue de l'Hôtel de Ville, **t** 03 84 66 55 50, *www.arbois.com*.
Poligny: Cour des Ursulines, **t** 03 84 37 24 21.
Baume-les-Messieurs: Mairie, **t** 03 84 44 61 41.
Lons-le-Saunier: Place du 11 Novembre, **t** 03 84 24 65 01.

Where to Stay and Eat

Ornans ✉ **25290**
★★★**Hôtel de France**, 51 Rue Pierre Vernier, **t** 03 81 62 24 44, *hoteldefrance@europost.org* (*inexpensive*). Agreeable if old-style central hotel-cum-restaurant close to the river. *Closed mid-Dec–mid-Feb; restaurant closed Sun even and Mon exc school hols.*

Bonnevaux-le-Prieuré ✉ **25620**
★★★**Moulin du Prieuré**, **t** 03 81 59 21 47, *moulin prieure@chateauxhotels.com* (*moderate*). Restful small country hotel near Ornans in a converted mill, with well-equipped little modern chalets. *Closed mid-Nov–Jan; resta-raunt closed Tues and Wed out of season.*

Lods ✉ **25930**
★★**La Truite d'Or**, Rue du Moulin Neuf, **t** 03 81 60 95 48, *latruite-dor@wanadoo.fr* (*inexpensive*). A nice, good-value place. Restaurant (*expensive–moderate*). *Closed 15 Dec–25 Jan; restaurant closed Oct–April Sun eve and Mon.*

Amondans ✉ **25330**
Restaurant du Château d'Amondans, 9 Rue Louise Pommery, **t** 03 81 86 53 14, *www.chateau-amondans.com*. Great dishes, including fish, in a restored castle. *Booking essential. Closed Sun eve and Wed out of season, and Jan–Mar.*

Germigney ✉ **39600**
★★★★**Château de Germigney**, **t** 03 84 73 85 85 (*luxury–expensive*). A gorgeously converted 18th-century manor along the Loue valley; probably the best hotel in the Franche-Comté. Divine rooms, dining rooms, a splendid terrace for summer dining (*very expensive–expensive*), pool, etc.

Salins-les-Bains ✉ **39110**
★**Hôtel des Deux Forts**, Place du Vigneron, **t** 03 84 37 90 50 (*inexpensive*). Basic, old-fashioned *Logis de France* in a characterful old house.

Arbois ✉ **39600**
★★★★**Jean-Paul Jeunet**, 9 Rue de l'Hôtel de Ville, **t** 03 84 66 05 67, *jeunet@reception*

converted into the **Musée Ledoux**. At the Revolution, when the *gabelle* was abolished and salt suddenly became cheap, Ledoux found himself in a dangerously ambiguous position as a friend of Ancien Régime notables. While in prison he set about writing a book which he hoped would justify his work for posterity; only one volume of the planned five was published before his death in 1806. His Saline Royale continued to operate through the 19th century, but the depletion of its spring and new means of salt production meant that the works fell into decline.

Along the Jura Wine Route

Set among dense vineyards, the brown roofs and yellow and grey stones of **Arbois**, capital of Jura wines, look particularly attractive. The restored remnants of the **Château Pécaud** have been converted into the **Musée des Vins de Franche-Comté** (*open July–Aug daily 10–12 and 2–6; April–June and Sept–Oct daily 9–12 and 2–6; rest of year Wed–Mon 2–6, closed Tues; adm*), where you can learn about local wine history, traditions and making, while neatly kept vines outside illustrate the care of the

france.com (*moderate*). Very smart address in the centre, but the restaurant (*very expensive–expensive*) is the main attraction. *Closed Dec and Jan; restaurant closed Oct–June Wed lunch and Tues.*

Les Planches-près-Arbois ✉ 39600
★★★**Le Moulin de la Mère Michelle, t** 03 84 66 08 17, *moulin@mere-michelle.com* (*expensive–moderate*). Thoroughly enchanting converted mill tucked below limestone cliffs close to a waterfall.

Poligny ✉ 39800
★★★**Domaine de la Vallée Heureuse**, Route de Genève, **t** 03 84 37 12 13 (*expensive–moderate*). A converted 18th-century mill, with small, cosy rooms. *Closed mid-Nov–mid-Dec; restaurant closed Wed lunch and Thurs lunch out of season.*
★★**Hôtel de Paris**, 7 Rue Travot, **t** 03 84 37 13 87 (*inexpensive*). Reasonable, central and old-fashioned. *Closed Nov–Jan.*

Monts de Vaux ✉ 39800
★★★**Hostellerie des Monts de Vaux, t** 03 84 37 12 50, *mtsvaux@hostellerie.com* (*expensive*). Exclusive hotel, pleasingly set in a converted stagecoach inn, with restaurant (*very expensive–moderate*). *Restaurant closed Nov and Dec; July–Aug Tues lunch; Sept–June Wed lunch.*

Passenans ✉ 39230
★★**Domaine de Revermont, t** 03 84 44 61 02 (*inexpensive*). Well-located large modern hotel by the vineyards, with pleasant rooms and restaurant. *Restaurant closed Jan and Feb; Oct–Mar closed Sun eve and Mon.*

Les Bordes ✉ 39230
La Maison du Haut St-Lothain, t 03 84 37 31 08, *www.maisonduhaut.com* (*inexpensive*). Great-value farmhouse rooms and excellent food (*moderate–cheap*). Not for the stuffy. *Booking essential.*

Baume-les-Messieurs ✉ 39210
Des Grottes, t 03 84 44 61 59 (*moderate*). Delightful restaurant by a waterfall, with simple menus. *Closed eves, Wed exc July and Aug, and Nov–Easter.*

Chille ✉ 39570
★★**Parenthèse et Thélème, t** 03 84 47 55 44, just 3km northeast of Lons-le-Saunier (*expensive–moderate*). Nice rooms in inviting large house with garden. *Restaurant closed Sun eve and Mon lunch.*

Courlans ✉ 39570
Auberge de Chavannes, t 03 84 47 05 52 (*expensive*). Reputed and refined little restaurant, 6km west of Lons-le-Saunier. *Closed 27 Jun–5 Jul; Jan; Sun eve, Tues lunch and Mon.*

vineyards. The major monument in Arbois, an orange-tinged bell tower, was tacked on to the Romanesque Gothic **St-Just** in the 16th century. The wonky nave contains ornate wood carving, including on the elaborate organ and pulpit. The town's central Place de la Liberté is lined with beautiful 18th-century buildings. Head up Rue Jean Jaurès to the **Musée Sarret-de-Grozon** (*contact tourist office for opening times*), which displays typical bourgeois interiors of the period. Louis Pasteur spent his childhood in Arbois, and he kept his father's home here as a holiday retreat afterwards, complete with laboratory. The **Maison Pasteur** (*contact tourist office for opening times*) has been lovingly restored. Learn how close he was to his family, and how he developed into one of the most important scientists in history, still finding time to work with the local vine-growing community on their problems. He was honoured with a state funeral.

South of Arbois a delectable country road leads to **Les Planches-près-Arbois**, a delightful village at the foot of a typical *reculée*, a bite out of the Jura plateau, with walls of limestone rising above the village. Another enchanting road takes you along the vine slopes via **Pupillin**, which has a well-regarded wine cooperative, to **Buvilly**.

Strange Wines

Jura wines are a real peculiarity, and are an acquired taste. Nutty *vin jaune*, the region's best-known white, comes from savagnin grapes grown around Arbois and Château-Chalon. *Vin de paille* is a sweet white wine made by drying the grapes on straw before they're pressed, causing the sugar levels to be very high. Both can be kept for years, but are expensive, the amounts produced being small. Many of the ordinary whites come from chardonnay grapes; try the lightly sparkling Chardonnay Crémants de Jura. If you want to play it safe among the reds, look for Pinot Noir; more unusual reds come from the local poulsard and trousseau grapes.

The small town of **Poligny** was once an important Catholic centre, but now its religious institutions have found other uses – for wine, theatre, and so on. Big Gothic **St-Hippolyte** still serves as a church, while the newly renovated **Maison du Comté** (*for hours, call* **t** *03 84 37 23 51; adm*) is devoted to a local demigod, Comté cheese. South of Poligny, take the route along the vine slopes via a string of adorable villages: **Plasne**, **Passenans**, **Frontenay** and **Menétru-le-Vignoble**, with the hilltop village of **Château-Chalon** the crowning glory. Only fragments of its medieval abbey remain today, along with the stocky church of St-Pierre with its thick stone ribbing, its baptistry behind bars, its curious paintings and its well-displayed treasury. Enjoy lovely views along the vine slopes from the belvedere. *Vin jaune* originated in this area.

A short way south, utterly picturesque **Baume-les-Messieurs** is guarded by a dramatic array of limestone outcrops that frame its historic **abbey**, said to have been founded by the Irish saint Columban. It was developed in the 9th century by abbot Bernon, who went on to found Cluny (*see* pp.651–2); from the 16th century, the monks came from the aristocracy, hence the village's posh suffix. You can wander round the abbey's cobbled squares by yourself, or take a guided tour.

The arcades of Rue du Commerce impart a sense of style to the heart of **Lons-le-Saunier**, another salty spa town known as far back as Roman times. Its **Musée des Beaux-Arts** (*open Mon and Wed–Fri 10–12 and 2–6, Sat and Sun 2–6; closed Tues; adm*) is a likable small museum, housing two engrossing Breughel the Youngers. But the main emphasis is on pure white statues, mostly by the Jura sculptor Jean-Joseph Perraud. The relatively undistinguished life of Rouget de Lisle, composer of the French national anthem, is celebrated in the little **Musée Rouget de Lisle** in his birthplace on Rue du Commerce. The clock tower in Place de la Liberté plays the *Marseillaise* hourly.

The Big Loop in the Doubs

Here we follow the enormous loop in the Doubs from Besançon back to its source, first heading up into the northeastern corner of the Franche-Comté, then along the picturesque border with Switzerland, where chalets sit below wooded ridges. At its most northerly points, the Doubs draws two big snail's horns on the map. One horn gets caught around the Germanic industrial town of Montbéliard, while the other heads around Ste-Ursanne in Switzerland.

Getting Around

Belfort is on the **train** line from Paris-Gare de l'Est to Basel in Switzerland. Pontarlier has a station on the line to Bern. A line leads from Besançon to Morteau and Villers-le-Lac.

Tourist Information

Montbéliard: 1 Rue Henri Mouhot, t 03 81 94 45 60, *www.montbeliard.com*.
Belfort: Av Clemenceau, t 03 84 55 90 90, *www.ot-belfort.fr*.
Villers-le-Lac: Rue Berçot, t 03 81 68 00 98, *www.villers-le-lac.com*.
Montbenoît: Rte de Pontarlier, t 03 81 38 10 32.
Pontarlier: 14 bis Rue de la Gare, t 03 81 46 48 33, *www.pontarlier.org*.
Malbuisson: t 03 81 69 31 21.

Sports and Activities

Boat trips to the **Saut du Doubs** leave from Villers-le-Lac. Contact the Saut du Doubs Bateaux Mouches, t 03 81 68 13 25; or CNFS Vedettes Panoramiques, t 03 81 68 05 34.

Where to Stay and Eat

Montbéliard ✉ 25200

★★★**La Balance**, 40 Rue de Belfort, t 03 81 96 77 41, *hotelbalance@wanadoo.fr* (*moderate*). Suiting the new image of this town, in a soft-coloured historic house just below the castle, a very comfortable hotel, rooms renovated in style.
Chez Joseph, 17 Rue de Belfort, t 03 81 91 20 02 (*expensi ve*). A neat little restaurant nearby in the old heart of town. *Closed Sat lunch and Sun, and Aug lunch*.

Belfort ✉ 90000

★★★**Grand Hôtel du Tonneau d'Or**, 1 Rue Reiset, t 03 84 58 57 56, *tonneaudor@tonneaudor.fr*

(*moderate*). A luxurious mix of Belle Epoque and modern styles. Restaurant (*moderate*). *Closed Sat and Sun, and Aug*.
★★★**St-Christophe**, Place d'Armes, t 03 84 55 88 88 (*inexpensive*). Characterful, overlooking a central square.
Auberge des Trois-Chênes, 29 Rue de Soissons, t 03 84 22 19 45 (*moderate–cheap*). Recently renovated; a local favourite, especially for fish. *Closed Mon, Tues and Wed eves, and Aug*.

St-Hippolyte ✉ 25190

★★★**Hôtel Bellevue**, Route Maîche, t 03 81 96 51 53 (*inexpensive*). Reliably good option, with restaurant, in a popular spot. *Restaurant closed 21–27 August; Sun eve and Mon exc July and Aug*.

Goumois ✉ 25470

★★★**Taillard**, t 03 81 44 20 75, *hotel.taillard@wanadoo.fr* (*moderate–inexpensive*). A very well-run white chalet on the wooded slopes of this lovely spot along the Doubs. Delightful rooms with balconies. Good cooking too (*expensive*). *Open 6 Mar–Nov. Restaurant closed Wed lunch exc July and Aug; Mar, Oct and Nov Wed eve*.
★★**Le Moulin du Plain**, t 03 81 44 41 99 (*inexpensive*). At the bottom of the valley, a comfortable hotel with restaurant, a fisherman's paradise (*moderate*). *Closed Nov–Feb*.

Malbuisson ✉ 25160

★★★**Hôtel du Lac**, Grande Rue, t 03 81 69 34 80, *www.lelac-hotel.com* (*expensiive–inexpensive*). Many rooms have views on to the lake of St-Point in this colourful, well-respected family-run hotel. Excellent dinners (*expensive–moderate*). *Restaurant closed 15 Nov–17 Dec Mon–Fri*.
★★★**Le Bon Accueil**, 10 Grande Rue, t 03 81 69 30 58 (*moderate*). Another good address, with fine regional cuisine (*expensive*). *Restaurant closed Tues lunch and Mon, Sun eve exc July and April; 3–11 April; and 18 Dec–18 Jan*.

Ruled by the Württemberg family between 1397 and 1793, **Montbéliard** still feels rather Germanic: from the time of the Reformation it was strongly marked by Protestantism and claims the oldest Protestant church still standing in France. At the start of the 17th century the architect Schickhardt was taken round Italy by Friedrich I of Württemberg to prepare him for beautifying Montbéliard, and his efforts add grace to the town centre. Montbéliard's recent rejuvenation has included a refurbishment of the fine arts museum in the **castle**. The streets below have also been spruced up and given new soft-coloured façades.

East of the centre, industrial **Sochaux** is best known as the home of Peugeot cars; its museum tells the story of car-making through the 20th century. It is also possible to tour the Peugeot factory next door at times. South of Sochaux, in the quiet residential quarters of **Audincourt**, Fernand Léger's tubular figures and the flaming ones of Jean Bazaine decorate the glowing stained-glass windows of the **Eglise du Sacré-Cœur**. The baptistry is a sheer delight – it's like walking inside a bag of giant, vibrantly coloured boiled sweets.

North of Montbéliard, the town of **Belfort** spreads out in France's vulnerable gap between the Franche-Comté and the Vosges, the Trouée de Belfort, an all too tempting natural corridor for invading troops coming from the east. Part of the Prussian army advanced this way in 1870, but the French under Colonel Denfert-Rochereau put up a brave defence. They survived a siege of just over 100 days and only emerged from the citadel once the armistice had been signed.

Belfort strongly resists any connection with Alsace, but much of the centre – including the castle, the citadel within which it stands, the town's basilica and even its famous lion, sculpted as a symbol of Belfort pride to commemorate the resistance to the Prussians – is built in red Vosges sandstone, so it does *look* a chip off the Alsatian block even if it is very distant in spirit. The French flag flies prominently from the top of the château at the top of the **citadel**. Its **museum** houses archaeological finds as well as photos of the destruction caused by the Prussian bombardments. A copy of Vauban's 1687 model of the a Belfort citadel shows how the complete fortifications once looked. The fine arts sections have Dürer prints, a school of Rubens *Resurrection*, ghostly works by Carrère, and Rodin sculptures. The Belfort lion, sculpted by Bartholdi of Statue of Liberty fame (*see* 'Colmar', pp.612–13), sits defensive and menacing under the castle. In the town below, the red sandstone mass of the neoclassical 18th-century **cathedral** calls out for the most attention. In the grand squares beyond you will find statues to victory, including the theatrical set piece of Bartholdi's group of the Defenders of Belfort.

Like a giant single-winged bird that has landed on the steep slope above the village of **Ronchamp** northwest of Belfort, Le Corbusier's great **Chapelle Notre-Dame du Haut** (*adm*) is surely his best-loved and best-lasting work in France, a wonderful flight of fancy. Built in 1955, it contains elements that you would expect to find in medieval French architecture: rounded castle-like towers and a tight array of window openings as if made for weapons. The most remarkable element is perhaps the grey concrete roof curving over the whitewashed walls. An outdoor altar and pulpit stand below a single window featuring a statue of the Virgin and Child. From inside, set against the single source of light along the end wall, your attention is brilliantly concentrated on this group. In each of the secretive towers a Bible is left open for visitors to read.

Ignoring its little detour into Switzerland, rediscover the Doubs at pretty **Goumois**, which has a bridge spanning France and Switzerland. South of here the valley forms a dramatic border between the two countries. The **Saut du Doubs** is the most famous waterfall in the Franche-Comté, and the best way of appeaciating it is by boat from scruffy **Villers-le-Lac** (*see* box, p.710). So close to the Swiss border, it's no surprise that this is clock-making territory. At Villers, the **Musée de la Montre** (*open school hols Wed–Mon 10–12 and 2–6; closed Tues; adm; the museum is staffed by apprentices and can be opened also by appt, t 03 81 68 08 00*) goes back to the 16th-century origins of the craft. **Montbenoît**, sitting beside rocky cliffs above the Doubs, boasts an important abbey, significant portions surviving from the 12th century. The late-Gothic cloisters and church choir are very attractive, but the decorative highlights were added in the 16th century for abbot Ferry Carondelet, an art-lover much influenced by his trips to Italy. The carved stalls show lively scenes of women dominating men.

Pontarlier, where absinthe-making is undergoing something of a revival, lies at the meeting point of several valleys, its strategic location underlined by the daunting **Château de Joux** (*open July–Aug daily 9–6; Feb school hols–June and Sept daily 10–11.30 and 2–4.30; Oct–Feb school hols daily 10–11.15 and 2–3.30; adm*), a little way south, a formidable fort built on a jagged ridge. Five layers of ramparts encircle the remnants of medieval fortifications going back to the 11th century. One courtyard serves as the setting for theatrical performances on summer evenings. On the guided tour you're taken to a **Musée d'Armes Anciennes**, and rooms and cells connected with three remarkable prisoners: Berthe the châtelaine, who, being informed that her husband was killed in the Crusades, took a friend as a lover, only to have her husband return alive, well and angry; the young troublemaking Mirabeau of Revolutionary fame, imprisoned here by his own father until he charmed a local married woman into taking all her husband's money and eloping (they were caught); and, most famous of all, Toussaint Louverture, a black general inspired by the French Revolution, who achieved independence for Haiti (the first independent black state in the modern world, in 1804), but was captured by order of Napoleon, and brought to Joux to end his days in misery. Be warned that the visit involves a lot of climbing.

After the Château de Joux, the long, thin **Lac de St-Point** has restful, gentle slopes dotted with chalet resorts slipping down to small lake ports. For real drama climb to the top of the **Mont d'Or**, which has the best views in the Franche-Comté, down on to the Swiss plains, and across to the distant white tops of the Alps.

Central and Southern Jura

Head down to the big lakes of the central Jura via **Nozeroy**, which looks like a Burgundian hilltop village that got away. It lies in beautiful agricultural country between Lons-le-Saunier and Pontarlier, and was a stronghold of the Chalon salt family; Jean l'Antique de Chalon had the first castle built here in the 13th century. The medieval village beside it went up on a grid plan, entered by major gateways. A Gothic church hides behind a neoclassical façade, with paintings inside celebrating St Augustine, the hermit St Anthony with his pig, and François de Sales (*see* 'Annecy'). Continue south for a cluster of major lakes; from the heights of the **Belvédère des Quatre Lacs**, look down on the waters of Maclu and Petit Maclu, Ilay and Narlay. For

Getting There and Around

Geneva international **airport** lies close by, while a **railway** line from Geneva crosses through the Bugey and heads up through the central Franche-Comté, with stations at St-Claude, Morez, Morbier and Champagnole.

Tourist Information

Clairvaux-les-Lacs/Pays des Lacs: 36 Grande Rue, t 03 84 25 27 47.
Moirans-en-Montagne: 2 Place Robert Monnier, t 03 84 42 31 57.
St-Claude: 19 Rue du Marché, t 03 84 45 34 24.
Ferney-Voltaire: 26 Grand'Rue, t 04 50 28 09 16, www.ferney-voltaire.net.
Nantua: Place de la Déportation, t 04 74 75 00 05, www.ville-nantua.com.
Seyssel: Maison de Pays, Chemin de la Fontaine, t 04 50 59 26 56, otseyssel@wanadoo.fr.
Belley: 34 Grande Rue, t 04 79 81 29 06, ot_belley@club-internet.fr.

Activities

If you take cheese seriously, visit a *fruitière*, the regional name for a cheese-making holding. The **Fruitière 1900 at Thoiria** (*open July–Aug; demonstration at 9am – small adm*) still makes Comté the old-fashioned way.

Where to Stay and Eat

Bonlieu ✉ 39130

★★Auberge de la Poutre, t 03 84 25 57 77 (*inexpensive*). The rooms are a right old confusion of tastes and colours, but the chef is a great ambassador of Jura food and wine (*moderate*). *Closed 11 Nov–11 Feb; restaurant closed Sun eve, Wed eve and Mon.*

Les Rousses ✉ 39220

★★★Hôtel de France, t 03 84 60 01 45 (*moderate*). A warm and welcoming big family-run chalet in the middle of this pleasant little mountain resort. *Closed 24 April–12 May and 20 Nov–15 Dec.*

Col de la Faucille ✉ 01170

★★★La Mainaz, t 04 50 41 31 10 (*moderate*). Well-located hotel high up off the roadside east of the pass, with wonderful views down on Lake Geneva and the Alps. Also enjoy the vistas from the large dining room. *Closed 28 Oct–8 Dec; Sun eve and Mon exc school hols.*

Divonne-les-Bains ✉ 01220

★★★★Château de Divonne, 115 Rue des Bains, **t** 04 50 20 00 32, www.chateau-divonne.com (*expensive*). The most luxurious hotel in this casino spa town with choice of restaurants. *Closed Jan.*

Ferney-Voltaire ✉ 01210

★★Hôtel de France, 1 Rue de Genève, **t** 04 50 40 63 87, hotelfranceferney@wanadoo.fr (*moderate*). Attractive-fronted house where Voltaire's secretary lived, now with pleasant hotel rooms and a good rustic restaurant with terrace (*moderate*). *Closed late Dec–early Jan; restaurant closed Sun and Mon.*

Artemare ✉ 01510

★★Hôtel Michallet, Rue de la Poste, **t** 04 79 87 39 33 (*inexpensive*). Pleasant, traditional country town hotel with restaurant (*moderate*). *Closed Christmas–mid-Jan; restaurant closed Sun pm and Mon.*

Contrevoz ✉ 01300

Auberge de Contrevoz, La Plumardière, **t** 04 79 81 82 54, auberge.de.contrevoz@wanadoo.fr (*moderate*). Delightful country restaurant with terrace, 8km northwest of Belley, serving refined cuisine.

even more spectacular views, climb the frittered grey limestone layers to the nearby **Pic de l'Aigle**. A footpath of slippery stones leads along the beech-shaded **Cascades du Hérisson**, the big steps this river takes down from the Jura plateau.

Near where the Hérisson joins the Ain river, enjoy a dramatic view down on to **Lac de Chalain** from the belvedere on its eastern side. The most touristy lake in the area, the beautiful site is swamped by campers in summer, with a busy strip of beach and turquoise waters full of pedalos. In the early 1900s a drought revealed the vestiges of a Neolithic settlement, hence the copies of a couple of Neolithic houses on stilts.

Wood-working has long been a speciality in these parts, and appealing **Moirans-en-Montagne** is devoted to the craft, specializing in toys. In the bright blue **Musée du Jouet** (*open July–Aug daily 10–6.30; Feb–June Mon–Fri 10–12 and 2–6, Sat and Sun 2–6; adm*), with its outsized games and puppet show, children rule the roost.

Wooded valley roads lead to **St-Claude**, its large white cathedral looking half-church, half-château. The façade displays a sober grandeur, although the few large putti seem to have freshly coiffed bouffant hair. Particular homage is paid to saint Claude, a lordly 7th-century archbishop of Besançon who gave up the good life to became an abbot here. The most famous pilgrim to the tomb of St Claude was Anne de Bretagne, married to two French kings. She had had problems conceiving, but after her visit gave birth to a daughter – named Claude – who went on to marry King François Ier. By the cathedral the old-fashioned **Musée du Diamant et de la Pipe** (*open May–Sept Mon–Sat 9.30–12 and 2–6.30; Oct and Christmas–April Mon–Sat 2–6; closed Nov, Dec and Sun; adm*) dwells on the town's two major industries. Ask at the tourist office about visiting a pipe-maker or diamond-cutter.

Heading east from St-Claude beyond the boundaries of modern Franche-Comté, from the **Col de la Faucille** you can embark on the GR9, a splendid walking path along the highest crest of the Jura range, the **Monts Jura**, with unforgettable views of the Alps. Or plunge down into the **Gex**, the sloping slice of French land closely observing the Swiss enclave of Geneva from the north. **Divonne** long attracted Swiss wealth because of its naturally bubbly spa waters and its casinos, although a recent loosening of the Helvetian gambling laws has affected its fortunes.

That most provocative of French Enlightenment writers, Voltaire spent much of his life living on France's frontier, ready to slip into exile should he antagonize the royal authorities too much. He hardly slummed it. The **Château de Ferney** (*contact t 04 50 28 09 16 for times of visits*) was rebuilt in classical style for him, and from 1760 became his favourite residence. On the intelligent tour you're given a picture of Voltaire's life here with his niece-cum-lover. He entertained lavishly, but also provided for the local community and encouraged local enterprise. The place puts on many cultural events.

The Bugey

The Bugey is the name for the gorgeous triangular tip of the Jura range sticking like an arrowhead into the Rhône valley. It extends roughly from Nantua in the north to its sharp point at Izieu in the south. This area was long ruled over by the mighty lords of the northwestern Alps, the counts, and later dukes, of Savoy, until it was ceded, along with the flatlands of the Bresse to the west (*see* p.657) to King Henri IV of France, at the beginning of the 17th century.

On the edge of a shockingly bright glacial lake popular for summer swimming and boating, and overseen by limestone cliffs, **Nantua** is one of the Bugey's most appealing semi-forgotten towns. The settlement grew up around an 8th-century abbey and the church of St Michael, with its hammered Romanesque doorway and disconcertingly curving pillars. The nave slopes up towards a Gothic choir, where the striking painting by Delacroix depicts a foreshortened St Sebastian. Nearby, a former prison has been effectively turned into the very thorough **Musée de l'Histoire de la Résistance et de la Déportation** (*open May–Sept daily 10–12.30 and 2–6; adm*).

Some staggeringly steep vineyards are defiantly tended around the Bugey, producing extraordinarily perfumed wines. For the most spectacular array of *vignobles d'altitude*, head southwest from Nantua for **Cerdon**. The church is perched above the village, its cemetery happily surrounded by vines. Down below, several tourist attractions are strung along the long, tight village streets. And far above, you can either visit the Cerdon cave, or take an exhilarating cablecar ride down into the valley.

The river Ain flowing through **gorges** a little further west has been tamed since the war by a series of dams, creating what amounts to a series of lakes, popular with campers and for watersports. You come out at **Ambronay**, an attractive slope-side town, with its abbey church founded in the 800s. The restored lintel over the main entrance shows an engrossing Resurrection scene and a pretty Virgin. The cool Gothic interior contains old stained glass, soberly carved wooden stalls and a remarkable stone Crucifixion. A door leads into the beautiful Gothic cloister.

Almost parallel to the Ain gorges, the **Revermont**, the name for the most westerly line of hills looking down over the wide flat plain of the Bresse, has pretty villages to potter through, including **Pressiat** below **Mont Myon**, colonized by hang-gliders; **Cuisiat**, with a cute museum on the Revermont in the former village school; **Treffort** on its steep slope; and **Meillonas**, known for its potters.

Head southeast of Nantua for some spectacular views over Savoy from the roads around the **Plateau de Retord**. The lovely country route south takes you through a string of appealingly unpretentious villages like the Abergements and Ruffieu. Contemporary art lovers should try seeking out the amazingly well-hidden centre at **Lacoux** (west of Hauteville-Lompnes; *www.cac-lacoux.com*). Head into the hills to the east for **Lochieu**'s **Musée du Bugey-Valromey** (*open April–early Nov Thurs–Mon 2–6; adm*) spread out around a fine Renaissance house, with a section on outstanding contemporary woodcraft as well as historic pieces. Alarmingly precipitous roads climb up east to the **Grand Colombier**, the enormous-backed eastern mountain of the Bugey, from which the views are amazing, including on to the Lac du Bourget.

If you avoid the Grand Colombier, continue south towards Belley and don't miss the picturesque wine village of **Vongnes**, whose reds not only employ gamay and pinot noir, but also the rarer manicle and mondeuse. The place has a free **wine museum** (*open daily 9–12 and 2–7*). Also seek out the unspoilt traditional village of **Aignoz**, where the **Maison du Marais de Lavours** (*open June–Aug daily 10–7; April–May 2–6.30; Feb–Mar and Sept–Nov weekends only 2–6; adm*) reveals the frog-eat-frog world of this beautiful marsh in the most engaging style.

Another extraordinarily beautiful route takes you along the Bugey's eastern frontier, marked by the Rhône, down to Belley, below the enormous brooding presence of the Grand Colombier. Vineyards line the way, and typical wine villages, such as **Seyssel**, actually two settlements sharing the same name, but separated by the Rhône. Both sides have a characterful, feisty air, sitting in the shadow of massive backs of mountains either side. Rhône boatmen used to halt here, and the quays have been restored.

Gorgeous country roads lead down to **Belley**. Along the curving main street stands the house of Brillat-Savarin, the town's most famous son, whose work *La Physiologie du Goût* (1826) is a peculiarly French concoction, a celebrated meditation on the art of good living and cuisine. The idyllic village of **Izieu**, at the very bottom of the Bugey, was the setting for an horrific event, recalled in the harrowing **Musée Mémorial** (*open July–Aug Thurs–Tues 10–6.30; rest of year Thurs–Tues 10–5; closed Wed; adm*), in an isolated farm on the hillside. During the war this place became a secret refuge for Jewish children. But on 6 April 1944 the Gestapo came and took away 44 children and their handful of teachers; 47 would die in Auschwitz; three others would be shot in Estonia; and just one survived. The barn has been converted into a museum that confronts the terrible ghosts of France's anti-semitism.

Into Savoy via its Great Lakes

Below Lake Geneva and east of the Rhône rise the greatest heights in Europe, the mountains of Savoy. The town of Chambéry in the west long served as capital of this independent region; Savoy only officially became a part of France in 1860, by over-whelming male vote. Nowadays the region is somewhat confusingly divided into two *départements*, Savoie to the south and Haute Savoie to the north.

Chambéry

In Alpine-fresh Chambéry, the long backs of mountains and the odd jagged peak are visible at the end of many a street. Symbols of Savoy pride stand out around town, notably the regional flag, a white cross on a red background, similar to the Swiss one (spot the difference), plus a bellicose heraldic black lion, while various melodramatic monuments pay homage to Savoyard heroes. Chambéry first acquired political impor-tance during the 13th century, when it was suddenly made regional capital, after Count Thomas I of Savoy bought the place. Incidentally, in the 13th century, Pierre II of Savoy ordered the building of the Savoy Palace in London (now site of the Savoy Hotel), and his brother Boniface became Archbishop of Canterbury.

A line of counts by the name of Amédée saw to the development of town and region from the 14th century. For a time, the house of Savoy controlled an Alpine terri-tory and lucrative Alpine passes all the way from Lake Geneva to the Mediterranean. Amédée VIII acquired Geneva and Piedmont for the family before abdicating.

Most famously, in 1453 the dukes of Savoy came by a shroud said to have covered Christ's dead body. Displayed in Chambéry, it drew large numbers of pilgrims. But the expansionist French monarchy was pressing at the gates. In 1536, King François Ier briefly took Chambéry. The then duke fled to Turin. Duke Emmanuel Philibert regained Savoy's independence in 1559, but by 1562 Turin officially became capital of the duchy, and the shroud was moved there in 1578.

French troops continued to harass Chambéry, while in the 1740s a Spanish army devastated parts of the town. Victor-Amédée III had much of the castle rebuilt. The French came back in force during the Revolution and made Chambéry capital of the

Savoy, Lake Geneva, Mont Blanc and the Isère and Arc Valleys

large if shortlived *département* of Mont-Blanc. Several colourful Chambériens stand out from this period. Adèle de Bellegarde, enthused by the Revolution, was painted by the major painter of the period, David, in one of his best-known works; she later became the face of Marianne, symbol of the French Republic. In contrast, Joseph de Maistre railed against the Revolution in his writings, although his brother Xavier devoted himself to more frivolous literature, including the delightfully titled *Voyage*

Around My Bedroom. After Napoleon's defeat, the Savoyards regained control of their territories. Meanwhile, adventurer General Benoît de Boigne had avoided the European upheaval altogether, fighting in India and making a fortune, part of which he ploughed back into civic provisions for Chambéry. But the long-proud independence of Savoy was reaching its end. First incorporated into a united Italy, the limited number of Savoyard men with the vote then agreed overwhelmingly to a political arrangement made between Emperor Napoléon III and Cavour, and Savoie became French.

The compact historic kernel of Chambéry is encased in broad, busy boulevards. Start with the majestic, white-stoned Gothic **castle** of the dukes of Savoy (*open July and Aug Mon–Sat for tours at 10.30, 2.30, 3.30 and 4.30; Sept daily tour at 2.30 only; adm*) with its imposing machicolated tower. Another striking part of the complex, the aloof-looking **Sainte Chapelle**, is where the Turin shroud once lay. Despite a damaging

Getting There and Around

Book cheap **flights** from Southampton to Aix-les-Bains/Chambéry with Flybe (*see* **Travel**) Chambéry, Aix-les-Bains and Annecy are all well served by regular **trains** from Paris-Gare de Lyon.

Tourist Information

Chambéry: t 04 79 33 42 47, *www.chambery-tourisme.com*.
Aix-les-Bains: Rue Jean Monard, B.P.132, t 04 79 88 68 00, *www.aixlesbains.com*.
Annecy: 1 Rue Jean Jaurès, Centre Bonlieu, t 04 50 45 00 33, *www.lac-annecy.com*.

Boats and Flights over the Lakes

For **boat trips** on Lac d'Annecy, try **Compagnie des Bateaux du Lac d'Annecy**, t 04 50 51 08 40, *www.annecy-croisieres.com*, the **Groupement des Loueurs de Bateaux de Haute-Savoie**, t 04 50 66 01 75, or **Bateaux Dupraz**, t 04 50 52 42 99, *www.bateauxdupraz.com*. For Lac du Bourget, contact the **Bateaux du Lac du Bourget et du Haut-Rhône**, t 04 79 88 92 09, *www.gwel.com*.

For helicopter **flights** from the lakeside airports, a magical if expensive way of touring the area, try: **Héli-Alpes**, t 04 50 27 35 45; or **Hélijet**, t 04 79 54 46 30. **Ski Vol**, t 04 79 08 41 72, and **Takamaka**, t 04 50 45 60 61, offer balloon trips. For parachuting, try *www.veloce-skydive.com/chambery*, t 04 79 54 42 93.

Where to Stay and Eat

Chambéry ✉ 73000
★★★★**Château de Candie**, Rue du Bois de Candie, t 04 79 96 63 00, *candie@icor.fr* (*luxury–expensive*). Beautifully furnished converted fortress above town. The modern dining room (*expensive*) serves up *trompe-l'œil* decorations with refined cuisine. Pool. *Restaurant closed Mon, Tues lunch and Sat lunch June–July, plus Sun pm rest of year.*
★★★**Les Princes**, 4 Rue de Boigne, t 04 79 33 45 36, *hoteldesprinces@wanadoo.fr* (*moderate–inexpensive*). A reliable, comfortable, very central option with themed rooms.
★★**Le Savoyard**, 35 Place Monge, t 04 79 33 36 55, *savoyard@noos.fr* (*inexpensive*). Cheerful big-fronted hotel on a main boulevard, with a restaurant (*moderate*) serving reliable Savoy classics. *Restaurant closed Sun.*
★★**Les Pervenches**, Chemin des Charmettes, t 04 79 33 34 26, *www.pervenches.net* (*inexpensive*). Delightful country location close to Rousseau's house 2km above town, old-fashioned rooms and appealing traditional restaurant (*moderate*) with terrace. *Restaurant closed Sun pm and Mon.*
Le Saint Réal, 86 Rue St-Réal, t 04 79 70 09 33 (*very expensive–expensive*). Brilliant restaurant in a 17th-century building in the heart of town, its smart bourgeois décor overseen by portraits. *Closed Sun.*
Le Tonneau, Rue St-Antoine, t 04 79 33 78 26 (*expensive–moderate*). Right in the centre, more excellent traditional cuisine, but a more relaxed brasserie atmosphere. *Closed Sun pm and Mon.*

fire, the chapel has preserved some fine 16th-century stained glass. Place du Château below is overseen by particularly grand mansions and the arresting statue of the passionate de Maistre brothers. Rue de Boigne, a major arcaded shopping avenue of pink fronts, leads straight as an arrow from this statue to Chambéry's most famous monument, the amusing column of the elephants topped by Benoît de Boigne.

Picturesque historic streets lead away from Place du Château. Take stocky Rue Juiverie or curving Rue Basse du Château. Place St-Léger is the most vibrant square in the centre, with its pinkish cobbles, its fountains and its characterful façades, their shutters bringing to mind Alpine chalets. Explore the maze of alleyways that lead off the square; you may stumble across the odd *trompe l'œil* decoration, a Chambéry speciality. One end of Place St-Léger, Rue Croix d'Or, lined with some of the grandest old houses in town, has a fine selection of shops. These continue along Rue d'Italie

La Maniguette, Rue Juiverie, t 04 79 62 25 26 (*moderate*). Trendy restaurant serving a very interesting single menu. *Closed Sun, Mon and Tues lunch, plus most of Aug.*

L'Hypoténuse, Carré Curial, t 04 79 85 80 15 (*moderate*). Stylish restaurant in this quite intriguingly eccentric cultural quarter. *Closed Sun and Mon, spring hols and late July–mid-Aug.*

Le Bistrot, 6 Rue du Théâtre, t 04 79 75 10 78 (*moderate–cheap*). Excellent deal for Savoie specialities. *Closed Sun and Mon lunch.*

Challes-les-Eaux ✉ 73190

★★★**Château des Comtes de Challes**, 247 Montée du Château, t 04 79 72 86 71 (*very expensive–moderate*). Variety of rooms, some magnificent, in a fortified medieval manor and its outbuildings, with fine views above this small spa town 6km southeast of Chambéry. Restaurant (*expensive*). Pool.

Le Bourget-du-Lac ✉ 73370

★★★★**L'Orée du Lac**, La Croix Verte, t 04 79 25 24 19 (*expensive*). Charming manor at the southern end of the lake, with comfortable rooms and watersports.

Aix-les-Bains ✉ 73100

★★★**Le Manoir**, 37 Rue Georges 1er, t 04 79 61 44 00, Hotel-le-Manoir@wanadoo.fr (*very expensive–moderate*). Swanky address close to the centre and the new Thermes, restaurant and terrace giving on to the exclusive garden. Indoor pool. *Closed mid-Dec.*

★★★**Astoria**, 7 Place des Thermes, t 04 79 35 12 28, hotel.astoria-savoie@wanadoo.fr

(*moderate*). In the heart of town, stylish rooms beyond the Art Deco entrance and restaurant. *Closed early Dec.*

★★**Au Petit Vatel**, 11 Rue du Temple, t 04 79 35 04 80, www.petit-vatel.com (*inexpensive*). Old-style charm and simple rooms, by the Anglican church which Queen Victoria attended. Traditional regional cusine (*moderate*). *Closed Jan.*

★★**Davat**, 21 Chemin des Bateliers, Le Grand Port, t 04 79 63 40 40 (*inexpensive*). Pleasant traditional hotel by the lake. Meals served in the garden on warm days. *Closed Jan and Feb; Sun eve and Mon.*

Talloires ✉ 74290

★★★★**Auberge du Père Bise**, t 04 50 60 72 01, reception@perebise.com (*luxury*). In a village packed with brilliant four-star (and three-star) hotels, this is the most exceptional, with private lakeside beach. Sumptuous rooms with views. Lake fish is beautifully dressed up in the first-rate restaurant (*very expensive*). *Closed Christmas–mid-Mar; restaurant closed Tues lunch and Fri lunch in season, Tues and Wed out of season.*

★★★★**L'Abbaye**, Chemin des Moines, t 04 50 60 77 33, abbaye@alp-link.com (*luxury–very expensive*). Former Benedictine abbey now with piano bar, solarium, and a private beach at the end of the gorgeous garden! Rooms are set around a graceful 17th-century cloister, some adorned with beautiful tapestries. Good restaurant (*very expensive– expensive*). *Closed late Dec and most Jan.*

★★★**Villa des Fleurs**, Route du Port, t 04 50 60 71 14, lavilladesfleurs@wanadoo.fr

beyond the fancy 19th-century theatre, lit up at night to flattering effect, like so much of central Chambéry.

In a square tucked away from immediate view between Place St-Léger and Rue Croix d'Or, Chambéry's **cathedral** originally formed part of a Franciscan abbey, built in the late-Gothic period in rather sober style, apart from the Flamboyant door. But brace yourselves for the dizzying *trompe-l'œil* tracery splashed all over the interior, like the campest neo-Gothic wallpaper, the 19th-century work of Vicario. Fragments of older wall paintings have survived, while the treasury includes beautiful items.

The substantial regional museum, the **Musée Savoisien** (*open Wed–Mon 10–12 and 2–6; closed Tues and public hols; adm*), sprawls across the rest of the former Franciscan monastery. It contains displays going back to prehistoric communities that settled along the nearby Lac du Bourget some 3,000 years ago. The Gallo-Roman section

---

(*moderate*). 100m from the water, a more secretive chalet hotel with cute rooms and serving good lake fish (*expensive*). *Closed mid-Nov–mid-Dec and late Jan; restaurant closed Sun pm, Mon, and Tues lunch.*

Veyrier-du-Lac ✉ 74290
★★★★Auberge de l'Eridan, 13 Vieille Route des Pensières, **t** 04 50 60 24 00, *contact@marc veyrat.fr* (*luxury*). Fabulous lakeside hotel, and fabulously expensive. Extremely luxurious rooms. Owner Marc Veyrat is one of the country's star chefs (*very expensive*). *Closed Nov–mid-May; restaurant closed weekday lunchtimes, Mon pm, and Tues pm outside July–Aug.*

Annecy ✉ 74000
★★★★L'Imperial Palace, Allée de l'Impérial, **t** 04 50 09 30 00, *www.hotel-imperial-palace.com* (*luxury*). Impressive white palace of a luxury hotel unmissable behind the lakeshore north of the centre, with flash casino and conference centre, plus four restaurants with lake views, **La Voile** (*very expensive–expensive*) the most exclusive, the others with more reasonable prices.
★★★Palais de l'Isle, 13 Rue Perrière, **t** 04 50 45 86 87, *www.hoteldupalaisdelisle.com* (*moderate*). Sensationally located in wonderful house on the main (sometimes noisy) central canal, tight stairways leading to modern rooms.
★★★Les Trésoms, 3 Bd de la Corniche, **t** 04 50 51 43 84, *www.lestresoms.com* (*very expensive–moderate*). Charming big house with Art Deco touches, up on the slope south of

the historic centre, many rooms with views of the waters. Panoramic restaurant, **La Rotonde**, looking on to the garden. Pool.
★★Nouvel Hôtel, 37 Rue Vaugelas, **t** 04 50 45 05 78, *www.nouvelhotel.com* (*moderate–inexpensive*). Actually in a stylish Art Deco building, with well-kept rooms, in the shopping quarter towards the station.
★Central, 6 Rue Royale, **t** 04 50 45 05 37, *www.lac-annecy.com* (*inexpensive*). Bargain, central, calm.
L'Atelier Gourmand, 2 Rue St-Maurice, **t** 04 50 51 19 71 (*very expensive–moderate*). More exclusive address; the chef also puts his art on the walls. *Closed Sun pm, Mon, and Tues lunch, plus late Aug and early Jan.*
Ciboulette, Cour du Pré Carré, 10 Rue Vaugelas, **t** 04 50 45 74 57 (*very expensive–moderate*). This gastronomic address is set in an exclusive courtyard off one of the main arcaded streets lined with more basic restaurants. *Closed Sun and Mon, and most July.*
Auberge de Savoie, 1 Place St-François de Sales, **t** 04 50 45 03 05 (*expensive–moderate*). Annecy's canalsides are packed with touristy restaurants; at this excellent address at the heart of the action, sample lake fish. *Closed Tues and Wed, and early Jan, late April–early May and late Aug–early Sept.*

Aviernoz ✉ 74570
★★Auberge Camelia, **t** 04 50 22 44 24, *info@ hotelcamelia.com* (*inexpensive*). Run by a friendly British couple who have fallen in love with the region and will do their best to ensure that you do too, this simple village hotel is a real find.

contains lots of little finds too. Moving swiftly through the layers of Savoy civilization, one level is devoted to paintings, many of which have connections with the region, the explanations filling in pieces of Savoyard history. A large separate room is devoted to the fragments of a 13th-century mural recently rescued from a fort in the area – its secular illustrations, including an attack on a castle, are rare in medieval art.

Boulevard du Théâtre behind the museum leads to the **De Boigne column**, with its curious bottomless elephants. Bd de la Colonne heads on to several grandiose buildings, including the **Musée des Beaux-Arts** (*open Wed–Mon 10–12 and 2–6; closed Tues and public hols; adm*), opposite the law courts. Its Italian collections are particularly rich, a strong reminder of Savoy's connections across the Alps. Rue Denfert-Rochereau goes from the theatre out to the recently transformed **Quartier Curial** by the boulevards. An attempt has been made to freshen up a massive arcaded barracks, while the curves of the theatre are a striking contemporary creation by architect Mario Botta.

A steep two miles up from this part of the town takes you into almost unspoilt countryside by the **Maison des Charmettes** (*open Wed–Mon 10–12 and 2–6; Oct–Mar 10–12 and 2–4.30; closed Tues and public hols; adm*), country home of Chambéry's most famous 18th-century resident, Jean-Jacques Rousseau, and still surrounded by little sloping orchards, with open views of the mountains. The brilliant young man had run away from an unhappy situation in Geneva at the age of 16 and was taken into the rather more mature bosom of one Madame de Warens, an immensely influential figure in his life, also his first lover. They lived both in Chambéry and here from 1731 until 1736. In these idyllic surroundings, he spent some of his happiest times and, most importantly, developed his *magasin d'idées* from which his radical thinking sprang through his voracious studies. The simple interiors and garden somehow reflect Rousseau's idealizing works, credited with bringing the world the rights of man, and damned for serving as creed of the vilest 20th-century totalitarian regimes.

To Lac du Bourget and Les Bauges

Charming **Lac d'Aiguebelette** just west of Chambéry makes a delightful introduction to Savoy's lakes, more peaceful than its larger cousins, motor boats forbidden, making it a popular place to swim, boat and row in summer.

Just north of Chambéry, much more dramatic **Lac du Bourget** is the largest natural lake in France, a long expanse of water left over from the last ice age, surrounded by striking mountains. The centre of **Le Bourget-du-Lac**, after which the whole lake is named, has known better days. Its medieval priory has survived, though, its church containing an exceptional 13th-century frieze. Count Thomas II of Savoy had a castle built nearby, its ruins now undergoing restoration. But the main interest for the moment is the port and resort, with its variety of water activities.

A road from the resort leads up towards the most distinctive peak overlooking the lake, the sharp **Dent du Chat**. For the best views, walk the track to the nearby **Molard Noir**. A magically beautiful wine route runs along the western slope of the Mont de la Charvaz, via **Billième**, **Jongieux** and **Lucey**, but here you look down on the ribbon of the Rhône. Rejoin the lake via peaceful, pastoral **St-Pierre-de-Curtille**, but for an unforgettable view down Lac du Bourget climb to the belvedere at **Ontex**.

Back right beside the lake, the impressive **Abbaye de Hautecombe** (*open Wed–Mon 10–11.30 and 2–5; closed Tues*) sits on a promontory protruding into the waters. A Cistercian foundation dating back to 1135, two of its abbots became popes in the 13th century, Celestine IV – for just 17 days – and Nicholas III – for slightly longer. In the 14th century, a chapel was constructed here to house the tombs of the counts and dukes of Savoy. Many members of the family would be buried inside, up until the start of the 16th century, when the abbey fell into decline. However, Charles-Félix of the house of Savoy had them sumptuously restored in neo-Gothic style, while a religious community was reinstalled. You can visit some of the extravagant neo-Gothic parts. The last king of Italy, Umberto II of the house of Savoy, was buried here in 1983.

The Lac du Bourget's main settlement, **Aix-les-Bains**, slopes up the eastern side of the waters. Its hot sulphurous waters were celebrated by the Celtic Allobroges and it boasted splendid baths in Roman times. In the early 1600s King Henri IV cavorted here, while in the 18th century grand new spa buildings went up. Napoleon's family enjoyed taking the waters, but the best-remembered French visitor was the sickly young Romantic poet Lamartine, who came in October 1816 and met Julie Charles, a young married woman suffering from tuberculosis. They fell madly in love, and promised to meet again the following season, but Julie was too ill and died before the end of 1817; the forlorn Lamartine immortalized her in his poetry, notably 'Le Lac', under the name of Elvire. Another famous visitor to Aix-les-Bains on several occasions from 1885 went by the subtle pseudonym of Countess of Balmoral. She was none other than Queen Victoria, and a whole English colony followed in her wake.

Central Aix-les-Bains is something of an architectural jumble now, although it retains a certain style and flair, and that curious spa mixture of sickness and jollity. Opposite the mistreated Art Deco facade of the Thermes Nationaux stand the remnants of two major **Roman monuments**, the Arch of Campanus and the Temple of Diana. On the guided tour of the town you're taken inside the rather grim if grand **Thermes Nationaux**, which specialize in treatments for rheumatism, to peer at the dark remnants of the Roman baths beneath. Peek inside the **Grand Casino** not far from the Hôtel de Ville; some of the original mosaics and stained glass are still in place above the fruit machines in this outrageous Belle Epoque extravaganza, its theatre first place in France to witness Wagner's *Tristan and Isolde*, in 1897.

The swanky modern **Thermes Chevalley** have opened above the old thermal centre, catering in part for those in search of luxury treatments. The **Musée Faure** (*open 6 Jan–19 Dec Wed–Mon 10–12 and 1.30–6; closed Tues and public hols; adm*), also up on the hillside, contains an unusual selection of Impressionist works and a whole room of sculptures by Rodin, plus some rather miserable memorabilia of Lamartine. At Aix's **lakeshore**, some distance from the centre, you'll find a long beach, all manner of boats for going cruising on the lake, restaurants, and rather rampant urbanization.

For much more charming little ports, head for the quieter, wilder, northern end of Lac du Bourget to explore the string of gorgeous havens tucked into crannies on the waters' edge: **Châtillon**, the marina hidden below a hilltop castle; **Portout**, with a brand-new marina; and **Conjux**, a village of lake fishermen. For one of the most breathtaking views down the whole of the Lac du Bourget, head up the mountain road from Chaudieu behind Châtillon to **La Chambotte's** belvedere. This is a sight to be taken with scones for tea, a tradition kept up here since Queen Victoria's day.

Chanaz may not lie by the lake, but it has another highly touristy port, along the deep green canal linking Lac du Bourget's waters with those of the Rhône. The calm boat trip along the canal, the waterside restaurants and terraces, the craft shops, and an old nut mill run by a passionate enthusiast all make this a popular stop.

Press directly north from the lake to enjoy another set of lovely wine villages above the Rhône, caught between the spines of the Grand Colombier on one side and the Gros Foug on the other. **Ruffieux** has a large cooperative. A beautifully laid-out new park allows you to appreciate the Rhône close up and looking at its best at the confluence with the Fier, below Châteaufort. Pass on the eastern side of Seyssel (*see* p.724) to head up to Clermont via Droisy, with dreamy glimpses of to Mont Blanc.

The **Château de Clermont** (*open mid-June–mid-Sept daily 10.30–12.30 and 1.30–6.30; early May–mid-June and mid-Sept–early Oct weekends and public hols 2–6; adm*) was transformed in the 16th century from a sturdy Savoyard home into a more graceful Renaissance residence for Monseigneur Gallois de Regard, a local religious figure who spent much of his life at the Vatican. On his return, he had his home done out in sumptuous contemporary fashion. The place remains devoted to the Renaissance. In summer, the double balustraded arcades serve as a backdrop to cultural events.

Closer to Annecy, the medieval **Château de Montrottier** (*open June–Aug daily 10–12 and 2–7; mid-Mar–May Wed–Mon 10–12 and 2–6, closed Tues; adm*) stands out on its hill. The views are especially grand from the top of the round 15th-century keep. Lower down you're shown around the collections of Léon Marès, who bequeathed all to the Académie Florimontane (Annecy's cultural association). Among the jaded displays of weapons, tapestries and Napoleonic objects, the finest works are the Vischers' Renaissance-style bronzes of the Battle of the Centaurs, commissioned by the super-rich Fuggers of Augsburg, but rejected because they featured too many buttocks. Nearby, the path along the edge of the narrow and precipitous **Gorges du Fier** (*open mid-June–mid-Sept daily 9–7; mid-Mar–mid-June and mid-Sept–mid-Oct daily 9–12 and 2–6; adm*) is best avoided by those who suffer from vertigo.

An alternative route from Lac du Bourget to Lac d'Annecy takes you through the highly picturesque, peaceful prealpine range of **Les Bauges**. Take the winding road east from Aix up to **Mont Revard** to be rewarded with the most sensational view of the whole lake, and of mountains far and wide. The plateau here is excellent for cross-country skiing, with over 150km of pistes laid out around **La Féclaz**.

Les Bauges, basically extending from Lac du Bourget to Lac d'Annecy, has been a regional nature park since 1995, but feels like a mountain range a bit lost in time. The delectable Aillon valley cuts through the heart of its quiet, wooded heights. See exactly how the reputed Tome des Bauges is made at **Aillon-le-Jeune** old village, the new little ski resort tucked away out of sight. To the west, craftspeople have set up shop in pretty **Noyer**, while to the east **Le Châtelard** has further craft shops, although **La Compôte** proves prettier, with its traditional barns. Hang-gliding and mountain-walking are popular. Down at **Ecole**, the modern **Maison Faune et Flore** presents the natural world in Les Bauges. Another Savoy wine route follows the slopes between the eastern heights of Les Bauges and the Isère river to Albertville (*see* p.743), passing via the **Château de Miolans**. Up at **Tamié**, monks make their own cheese in their abbey opposite a 19th-century fort, all in a magnificent location.

Lac d'Annecy

The most romantic lake in France, layers of peaks receding into the distance beyond huge molar-tooth mountains in the middle distance, sensational Lac d'Annecy draws a glamorous crowd. It may be one of the largest lakes in the country, but the single road around it, and the sheer number of visitors, mean the lakeside often feels cramped. You might arrive by the dramatic northerly ridge of the Les Bauges, the **Montagne du Semnoz** on the western side, or via the **Col de la Forclaz,** the still more perilous route on the eastern side.

Annecy

The beautiful canal-crisscrossed old city hides in the northwestern corner by the lake, although modern Annecy has sprawled right across the north side of the waters. Annecy's medieval castle sits on a more discreet height than its church of the Visitation, while a few big modern blocks are even more prominent. The medieval town grew up around the castle, dating back as far as the 12th century. It was purchased in 1401 by Amédée VIII of Savoy, and from the mid-15th to the mid-17th centuries lordship of Annecy was reserved for various junior members of the house of Savoy. With the splits caused by the Reformation in the 16th century, Annecy suddenly acquired greater importance. Geneva had become the stronghold of Calvinism, and the city's monastic communities were expelled. Many moved to Annecy, which became the seat of a new bishopric for Geneva. The most famous of these Geneva bishops in exile was the charismatic François de Sales (1567–1622), who devoted his life to gentle but persuasive preaching of a virtuous Catholic life. In 1610 he established the charitable Order of the Visitation with Jeanne de Chantal (grandmother of super-socialite Mme de Sévigné – *see* p.678). François de Sales was buried in Annecy, canonized in 1665, and proclaimed patron saint of writers and journalists in 1923.

The lake, however, had grown increasingly polluted as the 20th century progressed. Then the dynamic mayor Bosson (to be succeeded by his son) set about reviving it. The lake waters are now considered among the clearest and healthiest in Europe. To appreciate the lake in its full glory, first take a trip out on its waters.

Back among the tourist-packed canals and arcades of central Annecy, start a tour of the historic city on the **Pont sur le Thiou**, from where the town's most celebrated building, the **Palais de l'Isle**, resembles a stone vessel moored in the water. It dates back to the 12th century, and has served as a residence, prison, mint and law courts. It now contains the **Musée de l'Histoire d'Annecy** (*open June–Sept daily 10.30–6; Oct–May Wed–Mon 10–12 and 2–5; adm*), offering a light introduction to local history.

Also unmissable from the Pont sur le Thiou, the grand scrolled 17th-century front of the church of **St-François de Sales** signals where the first monastery of the Order of the Visitation was located, the place where both François de Sales and Jeanne de Chantal were buried. During the Revolution the church was badly damaged and their tombs demolished. A short way north, the Dominican Gothic barn of **St-Maurice** is the oldest church in Annecy, but only dating from 1422. Look out for the creepy funeral picture for Philibert de Monthouz and the splendid *Deposition* by Pourbus the Elder.

Head along Rue Grenette and Rue Jean-Jacques Rousseau for the **Cathédrale St-Pierre**, with a striking Gothic-to-Renaissance façade. Built for the Franciscans in 1535, it was converted into the bishops' seat with the move from Geneva. Dramatic chiaroscuro paintings stand out, one showing the liberation of St Peter by Mazzola, another Christ's deposition, attributed to Caravaggio. The **bishops' palace** now houses a major school of music and the Académie Florimontane, the high-minded literary institution co-founded by François de Sales to promote goodness and beauty in art. A slightly leaning Romanesque-style bell tower signals the fourth central church of note, imposing **Notre-Dame-de-Liesse**, rebuilt after the Revolution and given a classical front topped by a gilded statue of the Virgin and Child. Among the arcaded streets round and about, don't miss Rue du Pâquier and the **Hôtel de Sales**, the latter one of the finest mansions in town, embellished with figures of the seasons.

South of the Thiou, arcaded **Rue Ste-Claire** curves irresistibly around the base of the castle rock. This was the main thoroughfare of medieval Annecy, guarded by the **Porte Ste-Claire**. The **Château d'Annecy** (*open June–Sept daily 10.30–6; Oct–May Wed–Mon 10–12 and 2–5; adm*) lies a short walk up the hill, but a world away from the tourist crowds. The enormous 13th-century Tour de la Reine forms the oldest part of a massive ensemble. The 14th–15th-century Gothic Logis Vieux and the 16th-century Renaissance Logis Nemours contain a **regional museum** filled with religious statues and chocolate-box views of Annecy. Many of the spaces are impressive, notably the kitchen with its double fireplace, and the guards' room. The **Observatoire Régional des Lacs Alpins**, set apart in the 15th-century Logis Perrière closing off one end of the huge courtyard, explains the formation of the region's lakes and their ecology.

The **Conservatoire d'Art et d'Histoire** (*open Mon–Fri 10–12 and 2–6*) a bit further out occupies the big plain Grand Seminary building where trainee priests continued to be educated up to 1970. It now contains a mixed bag of art, including a beautiful exotic faces sculpted by Evariste Jonchère on his early 20th-century travels, and contemporary works from the Lyon school. Most excitingly, a new section devoted to early, pre-cinema developments in moving images has been installed in the former chapel, allowing you to experiment with the machines dreamt up by inventors like Joseph Plateau, Emile Reynaud or Jules Etienne Marey. Proud on its higher height, the showy white **church of the Visitation**, consecrated in 1949, holds relics of François de Sales and Jeanne de Chantal, and forms part of the monastery of La Visitation.

Back down at the lake, the **waterside** offers many pleasures, including a narrow beach (*adm*) just south of town, and the shady Jardins de l'Europe. Walk along the lake to the massive, unmissable Imperial Hotel; some of the best views of all open up as you approach the wedding-cake building, in front of which is another beach (*adm*).

Around the Lake

Following the lake's west bank down from Annecy, at **Sevrier**, with its spectacular views of the toothy mountains on the opposite side of the waters, the beach (*adm in* *summer*) and marina inevitably attract the most attention. But, up by the smart slim neo-Gothic church aloof on its terrace, old Savoyard traditions are recalled in the enthusiastically run **Musée du Costume Savoyard** (*open mid-June–mid-Sept Tues–Sat 10–12 and 2.30–6.30, Sun 2.30–6.30; May–mid-June and late Sept Tues–Sun 2–6; closed Mon; adm*), while just off the major road through Sevrier the Paccard foundry cele-brated at the **Musée de la Cloche** (*open June–Sept Mon–Sat 10–12 and 2.30–6.30, Sun 2.30–6.30; rest of year daily Tues–Sat 10–12 and 2.30–5.30, Sun 2.30–5.30; adm*) has been making bells for eight generations, although not on the same spot. Numerous copies of the Philadelphia liberty bell have been cast by Paccard.

St-Jorioz has a quite good expanse of beach, while **Duingt** is overseen by an aristo-cratic château owned by the de Sales family in medieval times. Nature lovers might enjoy exploring the marshy reedbeds at the southern end of the lake by **Doussard**.

Moving to the eastern shore of Lac d'Annecy, lakeside resorts don't come more chic than **Talloires**, with its swanky port and fabulous array of waterside hotels and restaurants. The **Roc de Chère** promontory to the north is so rich in flora it's been turned into a nature reserve. Just beyond it, delightful **Menthon-St-Bernard** is over-seen by the many-towered **Château de Menthon** (*open July–Aug daily 12–6; May–June and Sept Fri, weekends and public hols 2–6; adm*), which claims to have been the birth-place of St Bernard at the end of the 10th century. This is the saint who did a great deal to encourage piety in the western Alps and cared for mountain travellers, most famously by setting up monasteries at the Petit Bernard and Grand Bernard passes, where the big dogs named after him are trained to help in Alpine rescues.

Press east towards Thônes. By the time you reach **Alex**, the valley is already tight-ening its grip, the pretty village awed by a massive wall of limestone opposite. The **Château d'Arenthon** (*open July–Oct Wed–Fri 2–7, weekends 11–7; Feb–May Thurs–Sun 2–7; adm*), a tough-looking building on the edge of the village, has been given a bold make-over recently, turned into a centre for contemporary art exhibitions. The star-tling transformation was carried out for the Salomon family, renowned in the French Alps for making its fortune through ski manufacturing.

Continuing along the tightening valley towards Thônes, the atmosphere darkens as you reach the **Nécropole Nationale de Morette**, a moving Second World War ceme-tery, and **Musée de la Résistance** (*open June–mid-Sept daily 10–12 and 2–7*) alongside, which follows in detail the harrowing anti-Nazi campaigns in these parts; British servicemen played a crucial role. **Thônes** itself has a rather cheerful, open feel, a meeting place at the junction of several valleys. It has a couple of small museums celebrating local traditions. You now stand in the shadow of the Aravis chain, rising to around 8,200ft, forming a massive north–south barrier before the Mont Blanc range.

Avoiding the Aravis and heading north from Annecy towards Lake Geneva, take the picturesque high road via Dingy, Nâves-Parmelan, Villaz and Aviernoz to the **Château de Thorens** (*open July–Aug daily 2–7; adm*), its lovely restored towers covered with earth-coloured tiles. The castle was owned by François de Sales the Elder, who had a good eye for art, and acquired beautiful pieces, including a series of early 16th-century Antwerp tapestries. As well as containing many memories of St François de Sales, a couple of rooms are devoted to the Sales' distant descendant, Count Cavour, the headstrong Italian politician who negotiated the ceding of Savoy to France in 1860 in exchange for military help to expel the Austrian army from northern Italy.

From the Château de Thorens a road leads up to the high **plateau of Glières** where a large monument pays homage to the improbably successful actions of a band of around 500 *maquisards* during the winter of 1944. The high meadows of the Glières plateau now provide opportunities for summer walking to the sound of cow bells.

Lake Geneva and Haute-Savoie's Ski Resorts

Lake Geneva, or Lac Léman?

Reaching the great crescent of water of Lake Geneva, or Lac Léman as the French always refer to it, you may feel more as if you've arrived at the edge of a sea rather than by a lake. Virtually the whole of the southern side of Lac Léman is French, although the Genevan enclave sticks its defiant Swiss tongue out at the western end of the waters. We avoid the great Protestant city here and suggest you take the spectacular road along the crest of the **Mont Salève** coming up from Annecy as the most beautiful bypass – and from on high, you do get a splendid view on to Geneva, the arc of its giant lake fountain often clearly visible.

Following the French side of the lake, the string of beautiful resorts tips right over into tweedom. **Nernier** occupies a particularly lovely promontory, while **Yvoire** looks as cute as a fairytale village, with its shiny silver church tower, the old stone houses below smothered in flowers in summer. Visitors swarm around the tourist bazaar. A picture-book castle dominates the lakeside here; for a sensuous floral experience, visit its **Jardin des Cinq Sens** (*open mid-April–mid-Sept daily 10–7; mid-Sept–mid-Oct daily 1–5; adm*). **Excenevex**, just south of Yvoire, boasts the largest, nicest beach on the French side, as well as some of its very poshest villas.

More substantial **Thonon-les-Bains** was once capital of the local Chablais area stretching south from Lake Geneva, and much favoured by the lords of Savoy. The town is split in two by its cliff. Down below, it has a good beach, a sizeable marina and a few old fishermen's cottages. Connected to the lake by a cablecar, the historic and shopping quarters stand aloof on their promontory. Right on the cliff edge, regional culture is celebrated in a grand house containing the **Musée du Chablais** (*open July–Aug daily 10–12 and 2.30–6.30; rest of year during exhibitions Wed–Sun 2.30–6.30; adm*). Nearby lie the interconnecting churches of **St-François de Sales** and **St-Hippolyte**, vying for attention with their over-elaborate decorations. The older, a Gothic structure whose interior was smothered with Baroque decorations in the 17th century, witnessed François de Sales preaching to the recalcitrant people of Thonon and winning them over. Maurice Denis covered the later one with bold biblical scenes, distinguished by his distinctive pinks and mauves.

Surrounded by vineyards on the flat east of town, the impressive **Château de Ripaille** (*www.ripaille.com; open Feb–Nov daily; adm*) served as a hunting lodge for the counts of Savoy. Amédée VIII enlarged it, and retired here with six like-minded gentlemen to devote himself, up to a point, to the holy life, but drawing the line firmly

Getting There and Around

Geneva **airport** is of course very close by. You can reach Thonon and Evian easily by **train** from Geneva, or from Annecy, Aix-les-Bains or Chambéry to Bourg-St-Maurice. Another train line via Chambéry serves the Arc valley.

Tourist Information

Yvoire: Place de la Mairie, t 04 50 72 80 21, *www.presquile-leman.com*.
Thonon-les-Bains: t 04 50 71 55 55, *www.thononlesbains.com*.
Evian-les-Bains: t 04 50 75 04 26, *www.eviantourism.com*.
Abondance: t 04 50 73 02 90.
Morzine: t 04 50 74 72 72, *www.morzine-avoriaz.com*.
Avoriaz: t 04 50 74 02 11, *www.avoriaz.com*.
Samoëns: t 04 50 34 40 28, *www.samoens.com*.

Where to Stay and Eat

Yvoire ✉ 74140
★★★**Le Pré de la Cure**, t 04 50 72 83 58, *leprede lacure@wanadoo.fr* (*moderate*). Modern but picturesque hotel just outside the main gateway, with excellent restaurant. Pool. *Closed mid-Nov–early Mar*.
★★★**Hôtel du Port**, t 04 50 72 80 17, *hoteldu port.yvoire@wanadoo.fr* (*expensive*). Irresistible, flower-covered house by the port and the castle with just four rooms, but a more generous restaurant. *Closed mid-Oct–early Mar; restaurant closed Wed out of season*.

Sciez-sur-Léman ✉ 74140
★★★★**Château de Coudrée**, Bonnatrait, t 04 50 72 62 33, *coudree@chateauxhotels.com* (*luxury–expensive*). Magical lakeside location, a 12th-century keep encased within the outer wings of the castle. Classic cuisine. Pool and tennis court. *Closed Nov–early Dec*.

Anthy-sur-Léman 74200
★★★**Auberge d'Anthy**, t 04 50 70 35 00, *auberge.danthy@wanadoo.fr* (*inexpensive*). Excellent value for this renovated family inn, with fine restaurant, in a quiet lakeside village west of Thonon.

Evian-les-Bains ✉ 74500
Evian has several extremely luxurious hotels, notably the outrageously ostentatious and very expensive linked ★★★★**Royal** and ★★★★**Ermitage**, (for both, t 04 50 26 85 00), with all manner of facilities and restaurants.
★★★★**La Verniaz et ses Chalets**, Av d'Abondance, Neuvecelle-Eglise, t 04 50 75 04 90, *verniaz@ relaischateaux.fr* (*very expensive*). Luxurious purpose-built rooms spread out in chalets in the well-tended gardens in this plush property above Evian. Very good restaurant-rôtisserie (*expensive*) with excellent lake fish. *Closed mid-Nov–early Feb*.
★★**Hôtel de France**, 59 Rue Nationale, t 04 50 75 00 36, *hotel-france-evian@wanadoo.fr* (*moderate–inexpensive*). Decent option on the main pedestrian shopping street.

Thollon-les-Memises ✉ 74500
★★**Bon Séjour**, t 04 50 70 92 65, *www.bon-sejour.com* (*inexpensive*). Sweet old-styled family hotel a bit above the lakeside village of Meillerie.

Morzine ✉ 74110
★★★**La Bergerie**, Rue du Téléphérique, t 04 50 79 13 69, *hotelbergerie.com* (*expensive–moderate*). In a resort with several good chalet-hotels, this one is very jolly. Pool. *Closed mid-Sept–mid-Dec and mid-April–June*.

Samoëns ✉ 74340
★★**Le Moulin du Bathieu**, t 04 50 34 48 07, *moulin-du-bathieu@wanadoo.fr* (*moderate*). Picturesque chalet up among peaceful meadows (follow signs for Samoëns 1600). Savoyard cuisine. *Closed May and Nov–Dec*.

at the table, hence, apparently, the French expression '*faire ripaille*' for enjoying a banquet. However, as the Great Papal Schism was creating havoc in the Church, Amédée was elected anti-pope Felix V at the Council of Basle of 1439. Resigning nine years later, he helped end the dreadful division in the Church of Rome. Carthusian monks settled here from the early 17th century to the Revolution; on the tour you're shown their kitchens and wine press. But the bulk of the interiors were redecorated in the 19th and 20th centuries in mock Gothic style with an Art Nouveau twist.

The year 1789 was revolutionary for **Evian**; that is the year when its mineral water was 'discovered'. The place grew into a highly fashionable spa resort, attracting the extremely wealthy. Now the marina draws more than its fair share of glamorous boats, while the waterside promenade parterres are immaculately manicured for all. The town behind proves a bit of a jumble, but is undergoing major renovations. Along the front, the irreverent **casino** mocks the shape of a Greek-cross church and is only separated from the real town church by an elaborate mock-Renaissance villa, now the **town hall**, originally built for the Lumière family of cinema fame – enter for a free peek at a Belle Epoque decorative extravaganza. The place was just slightly damaged in the anti-globalization protests over the 2003 Evian G8 summit. The luxury hotels now stand aloof on the hillside, but remnants of the lakeside's palatial blocks can still be made out on the front, along with the jaded old thermal establishment – a much more contemporary glass-covered Thermes has made it redundant. Up on the main pedestrian street, the **Art Nouveau Evian Buvette Thermale** (*open mid-June–mid-Sept daily 10.30–12.30 and 3–7; early May–mid-June and late Sept daily 2.30–6.30*) cuts a dash. On the street above you can top up on Evian water for free, at one of the public fountains. You can also book a visit to the Evian bottling plant out of town.

A trip out on a boat is one of the highlights of a visit to Lac Léman. From Evian you can choose from all manner of cruises, or just take a short boat trip to the **Pré Curieux** (*visits May–Sept Wed–Sun 10.15, 1.30 and 3; adm*), a lakeside garden cleverly set out to show the different aspects of watery ecosystems, from torrents to marshes.

Further pretty ports cling to the lakeside beyond Evian, notably **Meillerie** and **St-Gingolph**, but they are more cramped, as the mountains virtually descend right into the water. St-Gingolph is in fact divided between two countries; just on the Swiss side (you don't need to cross customs), a **museum of boating** on Lake Geneva (*open mid-June–mid-Sept daily 2–5.30; adm*) occupies part of the castle.

The Northern Ski Resorts of Haute-Savoie

Picturesque roads south from Lake Geneva wind up to the most northerly ski resorts of the French Alps. The Dranse d'Abondance valley takes you via the historic town of **Abondance**, overseen by its **abbey** (*open May–Oct daily 10–12 and 2–5; Christmas–April daily 10–12 and 2–4; adm*), one of the most important in the Alps in medieval times. Its cloisters have striking remnants of 15th-century frescoes mixing Gothic elegance and naïveté. The treasury museum contains an amusing clutter of religious objects. In the well-located ski resort of **Châtel** by the Swiss border, the pleasing south-facing chalets receive the sun late into the afternoon.

Follow the Dranse de Morzine valley from Thonon to reach a clutch of resorts. **Les Gets** has a friendly array of chalets, while chic boutiques line the main street of **Morzine**, but somehow the centre lacks character despite the church with its spiked onion dome. In summer, mountain-bikers swarm over the slopes. **Avoriaz** is just about the most dramatic of all the modern French Alpine resorts. This high-energy centre lies at the heart of the Portes du Soleil skiing area, which is lively all year round, making the narrow hairpin bends down to the emerald-green **Lac de Montriond** all the more dangerous, as they're often crawling with cars.

The surprisingly wide, fertile **Giffre valley** to the south, peppered with fruit trees and waterfalls, has a scattering of delightful old hamlets, including those of **Morillon** and **Sixt-Fer-de-Cheval**, but all are outdone by higgledy-piggledy **Samoëns**, reached most dramatically from Morzine via the lofty **Col de Joux** and overseen by the massive pyramidal tops of the Tuet and Criou. Beyond the covered market lies the church, its door guarded by two Chinese-looking lions, a feature adopted from northern Italy. To one side rises the delightful **Alpine garden** created by a local girl made good, co-founder of the celebrated Seine-side Samaritaine department store in Paris. Continue east and you come up against the huge **Cirque du Fer à Cheval** (*fee for cars*), perhaps the most overwhelming dead end in the Alps, a score of sensational waterfalls dropping from the great heights that encircle you.

Sticking closer to Thonon, for quieter, traditional Alpine scenery, hamlets and small museums, head up to **Bellevaux** or **Habère**, and continue down via **Viuz**. The Baroque church of **Peillonnex** nearby is exceptionally well presented, standing on its terrace above the great Arve valley linking Geneva to Mont Blanc.

To Mont Blanc and Chamonix

And so to Europe's greatest summit, Mont Blanc, whose peak can surprise you from 100km away and more. It rises far above the surrounding mountains like a vast, other-worldly meringue, a blinding white all year round. As you get closer, the much sharper summits of the Aiguilles (Needles) surrounding the summit come into focus.

Approach the awesome range either along the busy Arve valley from Geneva, or take the prettier route from the Lac d'Annecy via the Aravis chain, a major wall of mountains south of the Arve. The resort of **La Clusaz** may be modern, but it looks extremely appealing, its chalets climbing up out of a steep bowl. Head north for the more traditionally picturesque resort of **Le Grand-Bornand**. Or, south of La Clusaz, the road via the **Col des Aravis** with its view of Mont Blanc and cutesy chapel takes you to **Mégève**. In this, one of the oldest-established resorts in the French Alps, you'll find the Hermès boutique handily close to the church, the latter filled, appropriately enough, with gilded Baroque altarpieces. This place caters mainly to the mega-rich, a kind of St-Tropez of the snows. However, Mont Blanc lies tantalizingly out of sight.

Just beyond, on the steep slopeside villages of **Cordon** or **Combloux** high above the Arve, on clear days you get an overwhelming, unimpeded view of Mont Blanc totally filling the end of the valley. Highly popular **St-Gervais-les-Bains** is the tradtional base for the ascent of the summit, although you can't actually see much of Europe's ulti-mate mountain from this cheerful resort with its large Belle Epoque hotels spreading across from the Baroque church. Down the valley, a long, lush, shaded public garden leads to the revived spa centre. But most visitors come to join the mountaineers on the highest train journey in France, the wonderful **Tramway du Mont Blanc** (*reserva-tions, t 04 50 47 51 83 or t 04 50 53 22 75*) up to the Nid d'Aigle (over 2,300m) by the Bionnassay glacier, where you can go walking. For a more peaceful drive through the

Getting Around

Chamonix has a **train** station, with slowish connections to the rest of France.

Tourist Information

Mégève: t 04 50 21 27 28, *www.megeve.com*.
Combloux: B.P. 38, t 04 50 58 60 49, *www.combloux.com*.
Chamonix-Mont-Blanc: B.P.25, t 04 50 53 00 24, *www.chamonix.com*.

Where to Stay and Eat

La Clusaz ✉ 74220

★★★**Carlina**, t 04 50 02 43 48, *info@hotel-carlina.com* (*expensive–moderate*). In this modern resort crammed with 3-star hotels, this many-gabled modern chalet has rooms with lovely balconies, plus an indoor pool.

Mégève ✉ 74120

★★★★**Hôtel du Mont Blanc**, Place de l'Eglise, t 04 50 21 20 02 (*luxury–very expensive*). Legendary luxury central address. Pool. *Closed May–mid-June.*

★★**Chalet des Ours**, 39 Chemin des Roseaux, t 04 50 21 57 40, *chaletdesours@aol.com* (*moderate*). Delightful good-value choice. Small restaurant. *Closed May and Oct; restaurant closed Thurs pm.*

Combloux ✉ 74920

★★★**Au Cœur des Prés**, t 04 50 93 36 55 (*moderate*). A garden-surrounded chalet, many of its balconied rooms with splendid views. Good restaurant. *Closed early April–May and late Sept–mid-Dec.*

St-Nicolas-de-Véroce ✉ 74190

L'Etape, t 04 50 93 20 95 (*inexpensive*). 3km above the village, a chalet in stunning location looking to Mont Blanc, the rooms simple but very pleasant, the place run with great charm. Good family cooking too.

Chamonix-Mont Blanc ✉ 74400

★★★★**Auberge du Bois Prin**, 69 Chemin de l'Hermine, Les Moussoux, t 04 50 53 33 51, *boisprin@relaischateaux.fr* (*expensive*). Wonderfully located, splendid little family-run chalet above town close to the Brévent cablecar. Restaurant (*expensive*). *Closed late April–early May and Nov; restaurant closed lunch Mon and Wed.*

★★★★**Le Hameau Albert 1er**, 119 Impasse Montenvers, t 04 50 53 05 09, *infos@hameaualbert.fr* (*luxury–expensive*). Luxury hotel, not in the most obviously appealing location down in town, but surrounded by a sumptuous garden, and with a splendid restaurant (*very expensive–expensive*). *Closed mid-May and Nov; restaurant closed Wed, and Thurs lunch.*

★★★**La Croix Blanche**, 87 Rue Vallot, t 04 50 53 00 11, *croix-blanche@chamonixhotels.com* (*moderate*). At the heart of the resort's action, with good rooms and the best terrace. *Closed May–mid-June.*

★★**L'Eden**, 35 Route des Goudenays, t 04 50 53 18 43, *relax@hoteleden-chamonix.com* (*expensive–moderate*). A stylish, well-established house out in quieter Les Praz by the golf course, with restaurant. *Closed most Nov; restaurant closed lunch.*

★★**Le Faucigny**, 118 Place de l'Eglise, t 04 50 53 01 17, *www.hotel.faucigny-chamonix.com* (*moderate–inexpensive*). Central, plain family hotel, some mountain views. *Closed Nov.*

Arve valley, offering the finest views of Mont Blanc, take the high road via Passy, Plateau d'Assy and Servoz north of the river. Or head up to **St-Nicolas-de-Véroce**, which has one of the most captivating churches in the area, its cemetery looking across to Mont Blanc's summit. There are further chapels to discover on the way to **Les Contamines-Montjoie**, a rather exclusive ski resort hidden down its own valley.

Back in the Arve valley, approaching Chamonix, **Les Houches** offers a couple of exhilarating cablecar rides up the mountains for great views. And its **Parc Animalier du Merlet** (*open May–Sept 10–6; adm*) allows you to see mountain wildlife such as ibex, chamois and marmots at close quarters.

Coming Face to Face with Mont Blanc

Chamonix-Mont-Blanc is a mountain Mecca, a resort of dreams, high dramas and tragedies. Some claim that a group of Englishmen put Chamonix on the map in the 1740s. Mountaineering fever gripped the village from 1760, when one Monsieur de Saussure offered a reward to the first person to get to the top of Mont Blanc, then otherwise known as the *Montagne Maudite* (Cursed Mountain). Messrs Paccard and Balmat were apparently the first to climb it, in 1786, as statues of rather maddened-looking figures recall in the centre of town, by the leaping waters of the Arve. De Saussure followed the next year, as did Colonel Beaufoy, the first Englishman. There's some dispute over the first woman to climb Mont Blanc. Marie Paradis reached the top in 1809, but was carried much of the way by friends, so the honour goes to Henriette d'Angerville. Many died trying, their frozen bodies often only discovered decades later. Chamonix is still associated with danger. In 1999 heavy snows led to more avalanches than usual, and many more deaths. A fire in the Tunnel du Mont-Blanc the same year killed over 40 people, instigating an array of new safety features.

Now the third most visited natural site in the world, given the millions of visitors clambering around the Mont Blanc range every year, accidents are very rare. But if you want to climb to the summit you must be accompanied by a professional guide or organize your expedition with the authorities. You might contact the experts of the Compagnie des Guides de Chamonix, **t** 04 50 53 00 24, or go to the town's website.

Any close encounter with the majestic meringue proves an unforgettable experience. However, special trips are expensive, and the weather here is unpredictable, so consider staying a few days for a better chance of seeing the spectacular summit. You might try a magical tour of Mont Blanc by **hot-air balloon** (Objectif Ballons du Mont-Blanc, **t** *04 50 58 08 46, www.alpes-montgolfiere.com*) or by **helicopter** (**t** *04 50 54 13 82, www.helico.fr*). For yet more exhilaration, there are several **paragliding companies** (e.g. Les Ailes du Mont-Blanc, **t** *04 50 53 96 72, www.lesailes dumontblanc.com;* Kaïlash Adventure, **t** *06 83 29 43 67, www.kailashadventure.com;* or Summits Parapente, **t** *04 50 53 50 14, www.summits.fr*). Easier options for less adventurous mortals include several exhilarating **cablecar** and **train** trips up the slopes around Chamonix. Many are run by the Compagnie du Mont-Blanc (*www.compagniedumontblanc.fr*).

The **Aiguille du Midi** (*reservations, **t** 04 50 53 30 80 or **t** 04 50 53 22 75*) is the closest most visitors come to the top of Mont Blanc. The cablecar and lift take you up in three stages. The first viewing platform isn't of much interest, but the second is stupendous, and the third even better, at 3,842m (*c.* 12,000ft), still almost 1,000m below the summit. The climbers seem ant-sized. From level two the most magical of all cablecar rides whisks you over sparkling glaciers to the Hellbronner peak on the Italian border.

The journey by little red mountain train to the **Mer de Glace glacier** (*from Montenvers station behind Chamonix railway station; **t** 04 50 53 12 54/**t** 04 50 53 22 75*) is less spectacular, taking you up to just under 2,000m. In summer the Mer de Glace can look decidedly grubby, with stone débris covering the surface. Its main attraction is an ice grotto, carved afresh each year. Further up, there are displays on crystals and fauna, and a café from which you can watch parties walking on the glacier; contact the tourist office well in advance if you want to join them.

Many locals will tell you that the finest views of Mont Blanc are to be had from the heights west of town. Either take the cablecar up to **Le Brévent** (*reservations, t 04 50 53 13 18 or t 04 50 53 22 75*) at just over 2,500m, or go to **Les Praz**, just north of Chamonix, to take the cablecar for **La Flégère** (*reservations, t 04 50 53 18 58 or t 04 50 53 22 75*). This side of the Arve is for skiers too. In 1924 Chamonix hosted the first ever Winter Olympics, and the winter sports facilities have kept up with the times. Just don't expect to be alone. In summer, glacier walks, rock-climbing, canyoning, white-water rafting on the Arve and mountain-biking are all possible (*contact tourist office*), while the walking possibilities are endless. The Compagnie des Guides puts on a whole programme of special mountaineering activities for youngsters (*contact Cham Aventure, Maison de la Montagne – office by the Baroque church – t 04 50 53 55 70*), all monitored by professionals.

The **Musée Alpin de Chamonix** (*open summer 2–7; winter 3–7; also school hols 10–12; adm*) has taken over one of the many huge but dilapidated Belle Epoque hotels scattered around the centre of Chamonix, recalling the resort's glamorous heyday. The displays go into detail on the many major events to have taken place in these parts, from the conquest of Mont Blanc to the Olympic Games. Separate temporary exhibitions on Alpine themes are held in the slick modern architecture of the **Espace Tairraz** beyond the richly gilded interior of the town's Baroque church.

Huge glaciers curve menacingly down the mountainsides towards the small centre of **Argentière**, an old settlement as well as a ski resort, its churches nestling close to the source of the Arve. Although the place is very highly regarded among experienced skiers for its challenging slopes, anyone can get up close to the glaciers, even in summer, by taking the cablecar up to the **Aiguille des Grands Montets** (*reserve tickets in advance, t 04 50 54 00 71*); the magical view up the white valley ends with **Mont Dolent**, whose summit marks the point where France, Switzerland and Italy meet.

The atmosphere changes heading for Vallorcine, entering the **Réserve Naturelle des Aiguilles Rouges**. The **chalet** (*open June–mid-Sept*) at the **Col des Montets** offers slightly old-fashioned displays on the geology, flora and fauna of the big green boulder-strewn valley, a world apart from the glacial grandeur of the Arve, but with great walking, and more traditional communities on the way to the Swiss frontier.

The Isère and Arc Valleys Circling the Vanoise

The second greatest French Alpine range, the Massif de la Vanoise, rises immediately south of the Mont Blanc range. Encircled by the Isère river to the north and the Arc river to the south, the centre of the Vanoise is a national park. Its highest peaks reach well over 3,500m, aloof, far above the highest pistes – many of the most reputed ski resorts in the world stand along the sensational slopes of the jagged upper Isère valley, although most look architectural messes. The less well known but equally spectacular (and intimidating) Arc valley may be more heavily fortified and heavily industrialized in parts, but it conceals the odd little ski resort, and a surprisingly exuberant legacy of naively decorated Baroque churches, while St-Jean-de-Maurienne boasts an intriguing cathedral.

Getting Around

Albertville, Moûtiers, Aime-La Plagne, Bourg-St-Maurice and St-Jean-de-Maurienne have excellent **rail** connections, being on TGV lines. Moûtiers, Aime and Bourg are even on a direct ski train link with London in winter, for which you can contact Eurostar, *see p.65.*

Tourist Information

Albertville: t 04 79 32 04 22, *www.albertville.com.*
Beaufort: t 04 79 38 37 57, *www.areches-beaufort.com.*
Moûtiers: t 04 79 24 04 23, *www.ot-moutiers.com.*
Val-Thorens: t 04 79 00 08 08, *www.valthorens.com.*
Méribel: t 04 79 08 60 01, *www.meribel.net.*
Courchevel: t 04 79 08 00 29, *www.courchevel.com.*
Pralognan-la-Vanoise: t 04 79 08 79 08, *www.pralognan.com.*
La Plagne: t 04 79 09 79 79.
Les Arcs: t 04 79 07 12 57, *www.lesarcs.com.*
La Rosière: t 04 79 06 80 51.
Val d'Isère: t 04 79 06 06 60, *www.valdisere.com.*
Bessans: t 04 79 05 96 52, *www.bessans.com.*
Lanslebourg: t 04 79 05 91 57, *www.haute maurienne.com.*
Aussois: t 04 79 20 30 80, *www.aussois.com.*
St-Jean-de-Maurienne: t 04 79 83 51 51, *www.saintjeandemaurienne.com.*

Where to Stay and Eat

Albertville ✉ 73204

***Million, t 04 79 32 25 15, *www.hotel million.com* (*very expensive–expensive*). Excellent central hotel. Spacious rooms. Exquisite restaurant. *Closed early May; restaurant closed Sat lunch, Sun pm and Mon.*

St-Nicolas-la-Chapelle 73590

**L'Eau Vive, t 04 79 31 60 46, *www.hotel-eauvive.com* (*inexpensive*). Appealing chalet, simple restaurant (*moderate*), lively owners; Monsieur is a mountain guide. *Closed Easter–May and Oct–mid-Dec.*

La Rosière ✉ 73700

**Plein Soleil, t 04 79 06 80 43 (*inexpensive*). Fabulous views from this cheerful little hotel at the side of the resort.

Val d'Isère ✉ 73150

****Christiana, t 04 79 06 08 25, *welcome@hotel-christiania.com* (*luxury*). Height of luxury in this valley-bottom resort. Restaurant (*moderate*) and terrace with good mountain views. Indoor pool. *Closed early Dec–mid-April.*
La Becca, Le Laisinant, **t 04 79 06 09 48, *info@labecca.fr.st* (*expensive*). Appealing option in a quieter hamlet up towards the Iseran pass, with pleasing restaurant. *Closed early May–June and late Aug–Nov.*

Aussois ✉ 73500

***Hôtel du Soleil, 15 Rue de l'Eglise, **t** 04 79 20 32 42 (*moderate*). Cosy rooms in the centre; mountain views and outdoor Jacuzzi. Restaurant, evenings by reservation only. *Closed mid-April–mid-June and Oct–mid-Dec.*
Les Mottets, 6 Rue des Mottets, **t 04 79 20 30 86, *infos@hotel-lesmottets.com* (*inexpensive*). Plain-looking central hotel with merry Alpine painting and good family cooking (*moderate*). *Closed May and Nov–mid-Dec.*

Valloire ✉ 73450

Christiania, Rue de Tigny, **t 04 79 59 00 57, *info@christiania-hotel.com* (*inexpensive*). Cheerful to brash, a popular stopping point in this lively resort, with traditional restaurant (*moderate*). *Closed late April–mid-June and mid Sept–early Dec.*

The Upper Isère and Tarentaise, plus the Beaufortain

Set on a big elbow in the Isère, industrial **Albertville**'s main claim to fame is having hosted the Winter Olympics in 1992, as recalled in the Maison des Jeux. A fairly modern creation, the town was named after its founder in 1836, Charles-Albert of Savoy. The grandiose administrative buildings left from that time were upstaged by the rebuilding of central Place de l'Europe for the Olympics, in extravagant apricoty-pink Italian neo-fascist style. On the nearby hillside, looking down its nose at Albertville, the much older, almost overprettified village of **Conflans** now uses its 14th-century buildings to house craft shops and restaurants. From the esplanade, wide views open up of the Isère valley beyond the 16th-century castle of Manuel de Locatel. Admire the Baroque wood carving in the church.

Northeast of Albertville, the exquisite cheese-making area around **Beaufort** produces delicious big round *fromages* with concave sides, which you can learn about and taste at the cooperative in the well-built town with its muscular Baroque church. Just north, heavenly **Hauteluce**, high above the Dorinet river, proves one of the prettiest places in Savoy, 'sitting under the gaze of Mont Blanc'. The onion steepled Baroque church is hard to resist, while an **Ecomusée** recalls traditional Savoyard ways. Up by the high pass of the Col des Saisies, the well-planned modern resort of **Les Saisies** was built for cross-country skiing.

Then you arrive at the pleasant little towns and resorts of the **Val d'Arly** below the Aravis range. **Flumet** at a crossroads down in the valley has a defensive medieval heart. **Crest-Voland** up high, a charming resort in summer as well as winter, looks far down the Isère valley to the Bauges and Belledonne ranges. Across at **St-Nicolas-la-Chapelle**, gilded Baroque and some shockingly bloody paintings fill the church.

South of Beaufort, a tortuously beautiful road leads to the picturesque traditional Alpine villages of **Arèches** and **Boudin**. The steep wood-surrounded pastures here, and the more open ones around the big, bare **Lac de Roselend**, ring with the sound of cow bells in summer. Then you can take an austere, almost treeless, houseless and completely resortless shortcut avoiding the Isère valley's huge meanders by going via the **Col de Méraillet**, with its superlative views of Mont Blanc, to Bourg-St-Maurice.

Back at another big elbow turn in the Isère, historic **Moûtiers** has a pleasingly Italianate heart. A fine stone bridge spans the bounding river close to the **cathedral**, a mix of Romanesque and Gothic. Moûtiers, seat of one of the most important bishoprics in Savoy, was clear capital of the Tarentaise area for centuries until the ski resorts took pride of place. The **bishops' palace** now houses a tempting **museum** (*open Mon–Sat 9–12 and 2–6; adm*) of Baroque art and local traditions.

Val-Thorens lies far up its own separate Alpine valley, but an exceptional number of ski lifts strung out along its length link it with other valleys. With famous neighbours Méribel and Courchevel, this area – **Les Trois Vallées** – boasts the largest interconnecting network of ski runs in the world. Exclusive **Méribel**, its heliport tucked away down its own private wooded valley, is the Isère resort with the most style. The high road connecting Méribel and Courchevel passes through that rarity in these parts, a genuine old settlement, **Méribel-Village**. The messy resort of **Courchevel** has centres on three levels; the lowest, Courchevel 1550, is much the nicest and most glamorous.

Especially delightful small resorts hide out east of Courchevel, on the edge of the Vanoise national park. **Champagny-en-Vanoise** is made up entirely of chalets, with an orangey church crowning its hillock. Pink putti swarm within. A precipitous road leads to **Champagny-d'en-Haut** and a delightful flat valley strung with old hamlets. Walking paths head into the park, its massive peaks snow-covered year-round.

More paths start at **Pralognan-La-Vanoise**, further still into the park. The resort is known for cross-country skiing, and walking and climbing in summer.

Back in the main Isère valley, the town of **Aime** has an inordinately long history for these parts, with stones bearing Roman inscriptions in the crypt of the severe 11th-century Romanesque church with its few fragments of frescoes. Above town, **La Plagne**, a major ski resort, consists of a handful of centres built in different styles. At **La Roche** you can't miss the huge worm of a bobsleigh track used for the Olympics.

Bourg-St-Maurice, popular with canoeists in summer, serves in winter as the main gateway for the massive modern string of resorts of **Les Arcs**. Here, the Kilomètre Lancé is legendary among skiers for recording-breaking speeds. High above **Séez**, which contains more Baroque attractions, secretive **La Rosière** has the most spectacular location of all the Isère ski resorts, overlooking a sharp turn in the river's course. At the nearby **Col du Petit St-Bernard**, a once-important route into Italy, the rather grim-looking remnants of St Bernard's medieval Hospice du Petit-St-Bernard are being restored. In summer, try the vertiginous route south from La Rosière, past the whitewashed church of **Le Châtelard**, standing out like a beacon on the slopes, and the pretty hamlet of **Le Moulin**, to the stepped chalets of **Le Miroir**.

Down by the big, artificial Lac de Chervil, a road leads up to **Tignes**, its fortresses of ski apartments built in a wide open bowl surrounded by sensationally snowy peaks which offer almost year-round skiing. **Val d'Isère**, the final, exclusive resort set deep at the end of the valley, has more style, and a glamorous reputation. Above town, hardy walkers head out early to spot ibex and chamois in the **Gran Paradiso Park**. The Route des Grandes Alpes, linking Lake Geneva with the Mediterranean, takes you south of Val d'Isère via the **Col de l'Iseran**, Europe's highest road pass at 2,764m (over 9,000ft).

The Arc Valley and the Maurienne

Separated by the enormous bulk of the Vanoise range, the rivers Isère and Arc meet a short way south of Albertville. But the Arc river starts on the southern side of the Col d'Iseran by the Italian frontier. The old villages near its source have preserved some delightful churches. **Bonneval-sur-Arc** has quaint houses covered with slabs tinged orange with lichen in summer, many turned into tourist shops. **Le Villaron**, an irresistible old Alpine hamlet, is only accessible by foot. Across the Arc, the Avérole valley offers a calm walking retreat, covered in a profusion of flowers in summer. Although destroyed in large part in the war, **Bessans**' church and chapel mercifully survived on a hillock above town. The **Chapelle St-Antoine** (*small fee*) is covered in vibrant paintings. One outer side is decorated with worn frescoes. Inside, the 40 naively painted panels represent episodes in Christ's life, but the tight-lipped participants sport late Gothic fashions. The church contains a colourful array of statues of saints, although the main woodworking tradition in the village is of carving devils.

At **Lanslevillard**, the **Chapelle St-Sébastien** is covered head to toe with further engrossing naive frescoes of the lives of Christ and Sebastian. Lanslevillard's larger twin, **Lanslebourg**, has less charm, but its **Espace Baroque Maurienne** in a converted church offers a good introduction to local Baroque. Pick up the keys to an array of local hillside chapels here. The historic route up to Italy via the **Mont Cenis** passes beside a big barren-sided lake. West of Lanslebourg, the Arc valley becomes industrial and the slopes bristle with **forts**, many of which you can visit. Most were built to defend Savoy from France, the most sensational, that of **Esseillon**, with half a dozen levels of fortifications stepping down the mountainside. As to **Fort St-Gobain**, it formed part of the 1930s French Maginot line. The village of **Avrieux** among these forts boasts one of the most extravagant Baroque churches in the valley. **Aussois**, a high sunny resort above, dominated by the dramatic **Dent Parrachée**, faces the summits of the Italian frontier, but mainly serves as a starting point for reaching the Vanoise park from the south. In the old village, a hell-fire Last Judgement greets you at the entrance to the Baroque church, but it's all floating putti within.

Don't dismiss **St-Jean-de-Maurienne** because of the huge Péchiney works down in the valley. The historic town has many dignified monuments worthy of your attention below mountainsides marked by high crosses. Beside a soaring bell tower stands one of the most intriguing **cathedrals** in the region, given a classical front, but mainly dating from medieval times. It held revered relics, three supposed fingers of St John the Baptist, brought back by 6th-century saint Thècle. A few highly carved stones from a Carolingian cathedral were incorporated into the Romanesque structure. Then ambitious bishops transformed the building in the late-Gothic period. Staggering religious decorations from this period adorn the choir, a towering ciborium, and walnut stalls carved with 300 images. Going via the Gothic cloister, an entrance leads down to the crypt, containing rough Carolingian carvings. Opposite the cathedral, the massive **bishops' palace** stands out in vibrant colour, one part housing a museum of local history. On the edge of the centre, the **Opinel knife centre** and the **Mont Corbier mountain-herb liqueur distillery** make further local attractions.

While the bishops of St-Jean ruled the roost for so long in town, the local lords observed them from their perch across the Arc valley, at **Le Châtel**, now an enchanting mountainside village. This eyrie was the birthplace of the mighty house of Savoy. Humbert aux Blanches-Mains (his hands white because of his rare honesty) came from these parts, and is the man considered as the father of the dynasty, taking command not just of the Maurienne, but also of Savoy in the early 11th century.

West of St-Jean, follow a head-spinning loop of mountain roads round the eastern side of the Belledonne range, old Savoyard villages and small new ski resorts along the way. Before the Arc joins the Isère some way north of St-Jean, the museum in slope-side **Argentine** celebrates local traditions and the valley seasons.

Grenoble

Encircled by jagged mountain ranges, set at a flat junction of valleys leading off towards Savoy and Switzerland to the north, Provence and Italy to the south, and the Rhône Valley to the west, Grenoble was an obvious location for the commercial, cultural and intellectual capital of the Dauphiné region. Tarnished with a reputation for being uncompromisingly modern and industrial, it turns out to be a cosmopolitan place, with wonderful squares, and as many museums as there are months of the year.

Getting There

Grenoble is just under 3hrs from Paris-Gare de Lyon. Ordinary **trains** between Grenoble and Lyon take around 2hrs. The regional **airport** of Grenoble-St-Geoirs (**t** 04 76 65 48 48) is around 40km northwest of the city but it is handy for the Alpine resorts.

Tourist Information

Grenoble: 14 Rue de la République, **t** 04 76 42 41 41, *www.grenoble-isere-tourisme.com*.

Where to Stay and Eat

Grenoble ✉ 38000

★★★★Park Hôtel, 10 Place Paul Mistral, **t** 04 76 85 81 23, *www.park-hotel-grenoble.fr* (*luxury–very expensive*). Looking out on to the picturesque Paul Mistral park, the luxury option in central Grenoble, with refined restaurant (*expensive–moderate*).

★★★Hôtel d'Angleterre, 5 Place Victor Hugo, **t** 04 76 87 37 21, *www.hotel-angleterre.fr* (*expensive–moderate*). Pleasant and central, opposite a garden.

★★Splendid, 22 Rue Thiers, **t** 04 76 46 33 12, *info@splendid-hotel.com* (*moderate–inexpensive*). Southwest of the centre, with imaginatively decorated rooms.

★★L'Europe, 22 Place Grenette, **t** 04 76 46 16 94, *hotel.europe.gre@wanadoo.fr* (*inexpensive*).

Good central location, in a Haussmann-style block with wrought-iron decoration but modern rooms.

L'Escalier, 6 Place Lavalette, **t** 04 76 54 66 16 (*expensive*). Excellent restaurant in characterful house close to the art museum, serving classic French cuisine. *Closed Sat lunch, Sun, and Mon lunch.*

Auberge Napoléon, 7 Rue Montorge, **t** 04 76 87 53 64 (*expensive*). Stylish, excellent little restaurant where the Emperor once ate, by the central garden. *Closed Sun and all lunchtimes exc Sat, plus early Jan, early May and late Aug–early Sept.*

L'Arche, 4 Rue Pierre Duclot, **t** 04 76 44 22 62 (*moderate*). Good regional cuisine at a reasonable price, plus a terrace. *Closed Sun.*

Eybens ✉ 38320

★★★Château de la Commanderie, 17 Av d'Echirolles, **t** 04 76 25 34 58, *resa@commanderie.fr* (*expensive–moderate*). Little castle in lovely grounds south of Grenoble. Stylish rooms and a terrace for summer dining (*expensive*). *Closed late Dec–early Jan; restaurant closed Sat lunch, Sun pm and Mon.*

Bresson ✉ 38320

★★★★Chavant, **t** 04 76 25 25 38, *chavant@chateauxhotels.com* (*expensive*). Reputed family village hotel a bit south of town, with great restaurant (*expensive*) and garden, plus pool. *Closed 25–31 Dec; restaurant closed Sat lunch, Sun pm and Mon.*

Grenoble's Gallo-Roman predecessor was insignificant compared to magnificent Vienne on the Rhône (*see* p.671), under whose authority it lay, but by the 3rd century it was surrounded by substantial oval walls. Christianity got an early footing here. In the early medieval period, the bishops battled with local lords to rule the city. The mighty counts of Albon took control of Grenoble, overseeing the southern Alpine lands from the Rhône to Savoy. One of their number, Guiges IV, was given the name of Dauphin (Dolphin), which was adopted by his descendants, the region they ruled becoming known as the Dauphiné. The Dauphin Humbert II established his council and treasury at Grenoble. Humbert III, however, wasted the family fortune and was forced to sell the region – so the French king Philippe V bought the Dauphiné in 1349, giving it to his eldest son. From that time on, the heir to the French throne would be known as the Dauphin. Only one of their number, the future King Louis XI, actually ruled the region before becoming monarch; it was he who created the Dauphiné Parlement or law courts in 1453.

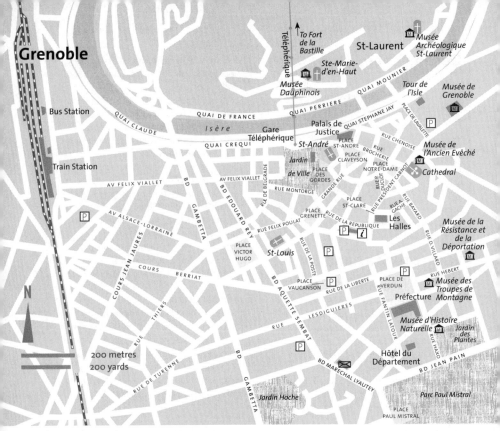

The 16th-century Wars of Religion caused bitter fighting in the region, the fanatical Catholic Baron des Adrets wreaking devastation. But the leading Protestant Lesdiguières put his stamp firmly on Grenoble, securing it in 1590 on behalf of King Henri IV, extending the ramparts, ruling the city with firmness and defending the Dauphiné against Savoy. The Catholic Church hit back in the 17th century by building religious communities around town. This period proved prosperous for the city's merchants. Despite its image of aristocratic elegance, as the Ancien Régime cracked up, Grenoble became a hotbed of sedition. The celebrated Journée des Tuiles of 7 June 1788 was named after a riot in town brought about by the monarchy's attempt to close France's regional Parlements; protesters threw tiles from the rooftops at royal troops. The event has been interpreted by some historians as an important warning rumble of the Revolution. The three Estates of the Dauphiné gathered to call for a national meeting of the French Estates. Local boy Henri Beyle, better known by his pseudonym Stendhal, recorded his impressions of the Revolution in Grenoble before he went on to become one of France's greatest 19th-century novelists.

In fact, the Revolutionary period passed off relatively peacefully in Grenoble, but through the 19th century the place was massively fortified, notably with the building of the Fort de la Bastille high above the Isère. Industrialization and working-class struggles came early. But so did skiing. The first attempts to introduce the sport in France took place at Chamrousse east of town. A major centre for the production of arms in the First World War, Grenoble's chemical industries developed enormously through the 20th century. During the Second World War, Grenoble, as with much of the French Alps, was occupied by the Italians. Although Pétain and other Vichy notables were warmly greeted when they came to the city, Grenoble became the main centre of resistance in the Alps and was awarded the Croix de la Libération. A large university town, Grenoble is now renowned for its European research facilites. The chemical industry has also developed along its valleys. But pleasure is never far away: the city hosted the Winter Olympics in 1968 and it is the major gateway to the Alpine resorts in the Parc National des Ecrins.

On a tour of Grenoble, head first for the grand **Place Notre-Dame**, in the quarter where the bishops of Grenoble held sway in medieval times. The **cathedral** looks as if it's had to fight to stay on the square, with town houses shouldering in beside it. The stocky front is topped by a mighty, square brick bell tower which went up in the early 13th century. From inside the edifice you can visit the adjoining church of **St-Hugues**, a grim and messy early Gothic building. While a new tramway was being built around here in the 1980s, vestiges were unearthed of earlier episcopal buildings (including a rare 5th-century baptistry), plus Gallo-Roman walls, all now well housed in the splendidly presented **Musée de l'Ancien Evêché** (*open Thurs–Mon 10–7, Wed 10–10; closed Tues; adm*). The section on the Dark Ages boasts the rare Vézeronce helmet. You can then follow a clear path through the history of the Dauphiné, including the foundation of three major religious orders in the 11th century – the Antonine, the Chalais (absorbed by the Cistercian's), and the Chartreuse or Carthusian, the last founded by St Bruno in the Chartreuse range just north of the city.

The even swisher modern **Musée de Grenoble** (*open Thurs–Mon 10–7, Wed 10–10; closed Tues; adm*), the fine arts museum, stands on the eastern edge of the historic centre, near the river. Among the highlights are Perugino's *St Sebastian*, Giuseppe Cesari's *Portrait of an Architect*, Rubens' *Pope Gregory Surrounded by Saints*, and French works by Philippe de Champaigne, Vouet and Claude Lorrain, plus a series of sumptuous New Testament scenes by Zurbarán. David's 1780 *Tête de femme* looks like a precursor of Lucien Freud. Henri Fantin-Latour, an accomplished 19th-century artist from Grenoble, is reserved his own space. The museum also boasts one of the finest modern art collections in France outside Paris, with major sculptures in the garden.

West of the museum lie the liveliest, most atmospheric streets of the city. Splendid residences built for members of the Parlement stand along Rue Chenoise and Rue Brocherie, which lead to the town's prettiest square, Place St-André, overseen by the former **Parlement du Dauphiné** and the church of **St-André**. You might pause to watch the world go by from the terrace of the Café de la Table Ronde, which claims to be the second-oldest café in France. Adjoining Place des Gordes leads to the **Jardin de Ville**, a leafy garden created for Lesdiguières.

South of the historic core of Grenoble, a whole grand 19th-century city went up mimicking Parisian Haussmann-style, but with many of the façades built in ground-breaking moulded cement. The most impressive set piece in the grid is the immense Place de Verdun, overseen by imposing civic and army buildings in a variety of pastiche styles, although the departure of Napoleon's statue, which once stood in the middle, has left an empty feel. Not far off, the **Musée de la Résistance** is a very sobering, serious Second World War museum, with modern presentations. South beyond the good **Muséum d'Histoire Naturelle** you come to the best gardens in town. The **Tour Perret**, a cement skyscraper by one of the pioneers in the genre, went up for a 1925 international exhibition on *houille blanche* ('white coal' as the French call hydroelectric power). There are also memories of the Winter Olympics here.

North across the Isère's steely grey waters, Grenoble's oldest church has been converted into the **Musée Archéologique St-Laurent** (*open Wed–Mon 9–12 and 2–6; closed Tues; adm*). So many layers of Christian buildings have been discovered one on top of another here that the architecture is deeply confusing. In the 4th century, a Christian necropolis was established on the spot, just outside the city, protected from the floods of the Isère. At the end of the 5th century a rectangular chapel went up. A rare little funerary church in the shape of a cross, with trefoil ends to each arm, was then built on the site in the 6th century. This was transformed in the 8th and 9th centuries, with a whole new church built on top. Following all this, in the 11th and 12th centuries the church was transformed as part of a Benedictine priory. Confused? Through the church's now floorless nave, amid a jumble of gaping tombs, start identifying the different periods. Alarming swastikas feature among the early 20th-century decorations on the ceiling; when they were painted in 1910 they were merely taken as ancient solar symbols. In the maze of corners you can then visit down in the museum, don't miss the crypt of St-Oyand; wolfish monsters and birds feature among the foliage of the beautiful Carolingian capitals. Outside, the narrow **St-Laurent quarter**, with its massive 14th-century gateway, its 19th-century fortifications and its Italian and ethnic restaurants, has a more laid-back, alternative feel than central Grenoble.

A steep track up the hill takes you to the **Musée Dauphinois** (*open May–Oct Wed–Mon 10–7; Nov–April Wed–Mon 10–6; closed Tues; adm*), set in a huge former convent, Ste-Marie-d'en-Haut, built during the Counter-Reformation by François de Sales' and Jeanne de Chantal's Order of the Visitation. Its nuns came from wealthy families, and the architecture has a spacious air, although the interiors have been much transformed, having served since the Revolution as prison, school, barracks and housing centre before being turned into a museum. However, the Baroque chapel has survived intact, covered head to toe with paintings depicting François de Sales' life (*see* 'Annecy', p.733). The gilded retable with twisted columns is topped by a figure of God looking like a wild-eyed preacher. The museum has two interesting permanent collections, one on Alpine village life, the other devoted to the history of skiing, while temporary exhibitions on aspects of the Dauphiné are mounted in the other spaces.

The bubble cars taking you over the metallic grey-green waters of the Isère are the best way to reach **Fort de la Bastille**, which guards the city from the north. From here you'll see how far Grenoble has sprawled down all the flat valleys around, and how dramatically it's surrounded by high peaks.

A couple of very smart addresses are worth seeking out in Grenoble's rampant suburbs. The **Musée Hébert** occupies an Ancien Régime villa with views of the Belledonne peaks. As it was being restored recently, bold, rough *trompe-l'œil* scenes were discovered in many of its rooms. But the place is dedicated to a 19th-century artist, son of a wealthy Grenoble lawyer. Although Hébert spent much of his life in Paris and Italy, his family left many of his works to the city. They include gorgeous male and female figures, somewhat in pre-Raphaelite style, including the most sensual of Joan of Arcs. While none of Hébert's major works depicted his native land, his watercolours did.

The **Château de Sassenage** (*t 04 76 27 54 44, www.domaine-de-sassenage.com; garden open July–Aug Tues–Sun 2–6; château open for many cultural events*) has kept its aristocratic head above the engulfing suburbs west of town. It sits below the soaring Vercors heights, looking across to the big-veined Chartreuse mountains. This spot was the seat, for almost 1,000 years, of one of the mightiest families in Dauphiné history, lords of the Vercors and surrounding territories. The medieval castle was abandoned for a grand Ancien Régime edifice reminiscent of a Loire château. The interiors reflect 17th-century good living in the Dauphiné, with interesting regional furniture and paintings, well explained on an intelligent tour.

Prealpine Mountain Ranges around Grenoble

The savage-looking, densely forested **Chartreuse range**, where the Carthusian monks went to seek the hard life and the mountain herbs, stretches between Grenoble and Chambéry, marked at either end by a huge tooth of a mountain, the Dent de Crolles in the south, the Mont Granier in the north. A very steep road climbs from Grenoble via Corenc to the **Fort du St-Eynard**, one of a rash of dramatic forts built by the French military after the disastrous rout by the Germans in the Franco-Prussian war of 1870. The precipitous view on to Grenoble induces vertigo.

St-Pierre-de-Chartreuse consists of a scattering of charming hamlets, including a little ski resort. The village of **St-Hugues-de-Chartreuse** lies contentedly in a more open valley; its church, converted into a **Musée Départemental d'Art Sacré Contemporain** (*open Wed–Mon 9–12 and 2–7; closed Tues*), contains an intriguing cycle of paintings and decorations, the work of the artist Arcabas, who came here on three separate occasions, in 1952, 1973 and 1985. The display ends with the superb drama of the Last Supper. You can't visit the Couvent de la Grande Chartreuse, headquarters of the Carthusian order of monks, but you can get an excellent picture of the order's history and punishing monastic life at the **Musée de la Grande Chartreuse** at La Correrie (*open April–Oct daily 9.30–6.30*) west of St-Pierre-de-Chartreuse.

Head for the northern half of the Chartreuse via the **Col du Cucheron**. At St-Pierre-d'Entremont, nub of these mountains, the tourist office doubles as a Relais du Parc, presenting a good brief overview of the range and its sights, and a good local craft shop. Some way west of the village, the two **Grottes des Echelles** lie to the side of a Roman way leading out of the Chartreuse, while to the east the **Cirque de St-Même** ends in a theatrical dead end of mountains. North, follow the Entremont valley which cuts through the range to Chambéry. Below the terrifyingly beautiful, mesmerizing **Mont Granier**, a huge cache of bears' bones was recently discovered in a cave below the summit; the reasons behind this high spot of hibernation are nicely explained at the new **Musée de l'Ours** (*open July–Aug Wed–Mon 10–12.30 and 3–7; May–June and Sept Wed–Mon 3–7; rest of year Wed–Fri and Mon 3–7; closed Tues; adm*) in **Entremont-le-Vieux**. From beyond the **Col du Granier**, wonderful views open up on to the Lac du Bourget (*see p.730*).

Across the Isère valley from the Chartreuse range, spreading northeast from Grenoble, the **Belledonne mountain range** offers the more conventional picture of almost eternally snow-tipped triangular Alpine peaks. Geologists say they count among the oldest rocks in France, perhaps dating back 700 million years. Starting from Grenoble, reach the southern end of the Belledonne through the still quite elegant old spa resort of **Uriage**. **Chamrousse** far above counts among the very earliest ski resorts in France. Although not well known these days, it hosted Winter Olympic downhill competitions in 1968, when the legendary skier, Jean-Claude Killy, won three gold medals. Follow the D280 from Uriage up to Allevard, the road known as the **Route des Balcons**, passing steep orchards and the odd vineyard below, sharp snowy peaks above. Branch off for **Prapoutel** and **Pipay**, two out of the three little resorts making up the Belledonne skiing terrain of **Les Sept-Laux**. From **Allevard**, a 19th-century spa resort, head into the heart of the range along the picturesque road

Getting Around

These mountain ranges aren't at all easy to explore without your own transport. Ask about bus services. VFD **buses, t** 08 20 833 833, run to Vizille from Grenoble bus station.

Tourist Information

St-Pierre-de-Chartreuse: **t** 04 76 88 62 08, *OT@st-pierre-chartreuse.com*.
Uriage: 5 Av des Thermes, **t** 04 76 89 10 27, *info@uriage-les-bains.com*.
Chamrousse: t 04 76 89 92 65, *infos@ chamrousse.com*.
Villard-de-Lans: 105 Chemin de la Patinoire, **t** 04 76 95 10 38, *info@ot-villard-de-lans.fr*.
Corrençon-en-Vercors: Place du Village, **t** 04 76 95 81 75.
Vizillle: Place du Château, **t** 04 76 68 15 16, *info@ot-vizille.com*.
Mens: t 04 76 34 84 25, *ot.mens@wanadoo.fr*.

Where to Stay and Eat

Vizille ✉ 38220
★★★**Château de Cornage, t** 04 76 68 28 00 (*moderate*). Grand *bourgeois* house in the Cornage hillside area north of the centre, plus fine cuisine.

Uriage ✉ 38410
★★★★**Grand Hôtel, t** 04 76 89 10 80, *grand hotel.fr@wanadoo.fr* (*expensive–moderate*). A grand Second Empire establishment with modern hydrotherapy centre and fabulous restaurant (*very expensive*). *Closed Jan; restaurant closed July–Aug Wed, and Thurs lunch; rest of year closed Sun, Mon, and Sun–Thurs lunch; also closed late Aug.*

St-Pierre-de-Chartreuse ✉ 38380
★★★**Beau Site, t** 04 76 88 61 34, *hotel. beausite@libertysurf.fr* (*moderate–inexpensive*). Good option in this village with a number of pretty hotels. Restaurant (*moderate*). Pool. *Closed mid-April–early May and mid-Oct–mid-Dec; restaurant closed Sun pm, Mon and Tues.*

Villard-de-Lans ✉ 38250
★★★**Le Christiania, t** 04 76 95 12 51, *hotel-le-christiania* (*expensive–moderate*). Big, modern, family-run chalet with well-furnished rooms. Gastronomic cuisine. Covered pool. *Closed mid-April–mid-May and late Sept–mid-Dec.*
★★**Villa Primerose**, 147 Av des Bains, **t** 04 76 95 13 17, *www.hotel-villa-primerose.com* (*inexpensive*). Bargain charming hotel. *Closed late April and Oct–mid-Dec.*

Grenoble, the Southern Alps and the Ecrins

SAVOIE

Col du Granier
Entremont-le-Vieux
St-Pierre-d'Entremont

Voiron   Col du Cucheron   Allevard
St-Pierre-de-Chartreuse

St-Etienne-de-St-Geoirs
Tullins

ISÈRE

Massif de la Chartreuse

Le Pleyney
Pipay
Prapoutel
Fort du St-Eynard

Grenoble
St-Marcellin   Eybens   Uriage
Parc   Bresson   Chamrousse
Vizille

Pont-en-Royans
Villard-de-Lans
Correncon-en-Vercors   National
Combe Laval   Grands Goulets
Gorges de la Bourne
La Ch-en-du Vercors

Vassieux-en-Vercors   Le Grand
Vercors   Veymont
Col de Rousset

Die
Châtillon-en-Diois

DRÔME

Col de Cabre

Col de Menée
Col de Grimone
Col de la Croix Haute   Col du Festre

Mont   Corps
Mens   Aiguille
L'Obiou

Vieux Chaillol

Col Bayard

Gap

Barrage de Serre-Ponçon

Durance

ALPES-DE-HAUT-PROVENCE

Le Pleyney
Pipay
Prapoutel

La Chambre

Chaîne de Belledonne

Grandes Rousses

L'Alpe-d'Huez
La Grave
Le Bourg-d'Oisans
Les Deux-Alpes
Venosc   La Meije

St-Christophe-en-Oisans

Massif des Ecrins
Glacier Blanc
Les Ecrins
Glacier Noir   Mt-Pelvoux
Parc National   Serre
des Ecrins   Chevalier

Valouise

Méribel
Pralognan-la-Vanoise
Le Châtel   Val-Thorens
St-Jean-de-Maurienne
Avrieux   Aussois

Parc National
de la Vanoise
Bessans
Lanslevillard
Dent Parrachée   Lanslebourg
Col du Mt Cenis
Modane

Valloire

Col du Galibier
Névache
Col du Lautaret
Le Monetier   Plampinet
La Salle
Chantemerle
Serre   Briançon
Chevalier   Montgenèvre   Col de Montgenèvre

HAUTES-ALPES

ITALY

Col d'Izoard   Parc Nat Reg   Abriès
Aiguilles
Château-Queyras
St-Véran
du Queyras
Mont-Dauphin   Guillestre   Ceillac
Risoul   Vars
St-André-d'Embrun   Les Claux
Embrun   St-Sauveur   Col de Vars
Les Orres

Barcelonnette
Pra-Loup   Le Sauze
Super-Sauze
Le Chapeau de Gendarme

N

10 km
5 miles

up the Bréda valley, past pleasant Alpine villages to the ski resort of **Le Pleyney**, the third of Les Sept-Laux's trio.

With its violently torn peaks and its terrible memories of the Second World War, the natural fort of the **Vercors range**, stretching southwest from Grenoble, is only reachable by disturbing roads from whichever way you approach. The villages up top long remained cut off from the outside world. But once you've scaled the Vercors' walls, the high plateaux prove generally flat. Below the long Montagne de Lans heading down from Grenoble lie a string of family ski resorts. **Villard-de-Lans**, surrounded by meadows, is a place that is becoming as busy in summer as in winter. The highest line of Vercors mountains reach over 2,000m. The only way to get close to them is by taking the GR91 hiking trail from the mountain resort of **Corrençon-en-Vercors**. West of Villard, the road plunges through the **Gorges de la Bourne**. The sensational entrance to the **Grottes de Choranche** hangs to a lip of rock sticking out from a massive sheer face of forested mountainside. Two streams converge inside the caves; the main wonder are the *fistuleuses*, which resemble spaghetti glued to the ceiling.

Terrifying roads lead south from the Bourne valley. The most notorious takes you along the side of the Vernaison gulley via the **Petits** and **Grands Goulets**, headspinning distances above and below. The rival route takes you via the **Combe Laval**, with tremendous canyon views. **La Chapelle-en-Vercors** was one of the villages martyred by the Nazis in 1944 as they tried to wipe out the Resistance groups hiding on the high plateaux. **Vassieux-en-Vercors** was another. Some 600 Resistance fighters, along with around 200 villagers, were assassinated by SS soldiers who flew in silently in gliders. The horror is retold both at the passionately run, old-fashioned **Musée de la Résistance** in the reconstructed village, and up at the new-fangled **Mémorial de la Résistance**, snaking down the ridge. Opposite the great arc of the **Grand Veymont**, the highest peak in the Vercors at 2,341m.

East below the Vercors lies the quietly dramatic **Drac valley** and the mountain-locked land of the **Trièves**. Head this way from Grenoble via the brutally massive **Château de Vizille** (*open June–Aug Wed–Mon 9am–10pm; April–May and Sept–Oct Wed–Mon 9–7; rest of year Wed–Mon 10–5; closed Tues; grounds free; adm for château*). Set in splendid grounds, this intimidating castle was built from 1600 to 1619 for Lesdiguières (*see* 'Grenoble', p.748), and houses an engrossing **Museum of the French Revolution** (*open April–Oct Wed–Mon 10–6; rest of year exc public hols and Tues 10–5; adm*). On 21 July 1788 it hosted the celebrated meeting of the representatives of the three Estates of the Dauphiné in a ground-breaking act of independent cooperation between nobles, Church and bourgeoisie. The entrance hall contains a useful timechart, while throughout, paintings and models are fused with text in most telling fashion to illustrate the stages of the Revolution.

Follow the Drac valley south, perhaps via the bucolic western road under the gaze of the Vercors' highest heights, or via the old-fashioned train running high on the river's eastern bank. The once formidable river, compared in legend to a *drac*, or dragon, has been tamed by dams at various points, allowing people to practise watersports in the violently bright waters. In the hills high above the east bank, the towns conserve memories of their coal-mining past. Pleasantly laid-back **Mens** hasn't spruced itself up yet, but has charm, what with its little fountains, its covered market, its churches, and the delightful Belle Epoque Café des Arts whose walls are covered with local landscapes. **Terre Vivante** (*open May–Oct; adm*), well hidden in the countryside out of town, proves an amazingly well-run ecological park encouraging environmentally friendly practices with exceptional good sense.

In this area, the extraordinary bald **Mont Aiguille** stands out particularly clearly, totemic symbol of the Trièves. Although called the Needle in French, it looks much more like a vast exposed tooth. At the close of the 15th century, King Charles VIII passed this way on his Italian campaigning. On a whim, seemingly in a mood to conquer all he saw, he ordered Antoine de Ville, one of his lords, to organize the ascent of this inaccessible-seeming summit, which was achieved with an elaborate use of ladders. This is often claimed in France to be the first example of mountaineering. The 20th-century writer Jean Giono, well known in France for his evocative novels on traditional rural life, set several of his books in the Trièves, hence the centre planned in his memory near the Mont Aiguille.

Southern Alpine Resorts around the Ecrins

This section takes you east from Grenoble and around the Ecrins, the third major range of the French Alps, its highest peaks almost touching 4,000m. This is an exceptionally sunny part of France – Briançon boasts 300 sunny days a year and has a passion for sundials to prove it. The delightful Italianate towns have impressive fortifications, a legacy of invasion and conflict.

East of Grenoble, a winding road leads up from the deep Romanche valley to the Oisans range. High above lively **Le Bourg d'Oisans**, the big modern resorts of **L'Alpe d'Huez** and **Les Deux Alpes** are renowned for their high, open skiing slopes, and both have a bustling summer season. Although the two are an architectural chaos, L'Alpe d'Huez has a bit more style, its views across to the Massif des Ecrins hard to match. Its remarkably unspoilt 'Route Pastorale' leads back down to the Romanche. Other

Getting Around

A **rail** line from Livron in the Rhône Valley serves Briançon. Trains are infrequent.

Tourist Information

La Grave/La Meije: t 04 76 79 90 05.
Serre-Chevalier: t 04 92 24 98 98, *www.serre-chevalier.com*.
Briançon: 1 Place du Temple, t 04 92 21 08 50, *www.ot-briancon.fr*.
Guillestre: Place Joseph Salva, t 04 92 45 04 37, *www.pays-du-guillestrois.com*.
St-Véran: t 04 92 45 82 21, *www.saintveran.com*.
Barcelonnette: Place Sept Portes, t 04 92 81 04 71, *www.barcelonnette.com*.
Embrun: Place Général Dosse, t 04 92 43 72 72, *www.embrunais-serreponcon.net*.

Where to Stay and Eat

La Grave ✉ 05320
**La Meijette, t 04 76 79 90 34 (*moderate–inexpensive*). Most appealing of the collection of hotels crammed in here, with views from the restaurant terrace (*moderate*). *Closed May and late Sept–Feb; restaurant closed Tues outside July–Aug.*

Le Monêtier-les-Bains (Serre-Chevalier) ✉ 05220
***Auberge du Choucas, 17 Rue de la Fruitière, t 04 92 24 42 73, *auberge.du.choucas@wanadoo.fr* (*very expensive–expensive*).

An 18th-century village farm converted into a very comfortable hotel, plus inventive cuisine (*expensive*). *Closed most May and Nov–mid-Dec; restaurant closed lunchtimes Mon–Thurs out of main summer season.*
**Alliey, t 04 92 24 40 02, *hotel@alliey.com* (*moderate*). Family-run hotel with cosy rooms. Dinner only. *Closed late April–late June and Sept–mid-Dec.*

Briançon ✉ 05100
**Edelweiss, 32 Av de la République, t 04 92 21 02 94, *hotel.edelweiss.briancon@wanadoo.fr* (*inexpensive*). Not far from the Haute Ville, a family hotel with a little garden. Some rooms have views.
**Auberge du Mont Prorel, 5 Av René Froger, t 04 92 20 22 88, *www.skisunrosbif.com* (*inexpensive*). Pleasant chalet hotel with a little garden by one of the closest ski lifts to town.
La Caponnière, 12 Rue Commandant Carlhan, t 04 92 20 36 77 (*moderate*). Warm surroundings, quite refined cuisine, and a terrace.
Le Valentin, 6 Rue Mercerie (Petite Gargouille), t 04 92 21 37 72 (*moderate*). A darkly atmospheric vaulted dining room in which to try local specialities.

Embrun ✉ 05200
**Hôtel de la Mairie, Place de la Mairie, t 04 92 43 20 65 (*inexpensive*). On a beautiful square in the old town. The restaurant (*moderate*) with terrace serves tasty regional food. *Closed most May, Oct and Nov; restaurant closed Sun pm and Mon in winter.*

atmospheric routes in the Oisans avoid the two major resorts altogether. Follow the road up the **Vénéon valley**, alongside a turquoise stream, deep into the Ecrins range. At picturesque **Venosc** you can buy good woodwork and pottery. Beyond St-Christophe-en-Oisans at **Les Etages** you're rewarded with fantastic views of the highest peaks in the range.

Continuing east along the Romanche valley, **La Grave** faces the highest peak of the Ecrins, the monumental **La Meije** (just under 4,000m), brought closer by a fabulous cablecar ride. The **Col du Lautaret** is the major pass through the northern Dauphiné, allowing you to head over from the Romanche to the Guisane valley in the eastern Ecrins. The **Jardin Alpin** grows plants from around the globe. The **Col du Galibier**, just north of the **Col du Lautaret**, is the amazing pass (2,645m) traditionally regarded as linking the northern and southern French Alps. The road may often be closed, but on a good day it offers one of the finest, widest views in the Alps.

The ski resorts of **Serre-Chevalier** are strung along the Guisane valley from Le Monêtier-les-Bains to Briançon. The slopes cater for all levels of skiers. **Le Monêtier-les-Bains** (alias Serre-Chevalier 1500) is both a resort, a spa and an old monastic centre; a church here houses the **Musée d'Art Sacré**, containing statues and finery from some 30 churches in the region. **Villeneuve** (Serre-Chevalier 1400) looks a bit brutal, built below the pretty village of Le Bez, but it has the most facilities of the resorts, including the longest chairlift in the world. From **Chantemerle**, another modern resort adjoining Villeneuve, you can take cablecars up to the peak of Serre-Chevalier itself.

The resort just west of Briançon, known as **Serre-Chevalier 1200**, stands in the shadow of historic **Briançon**, whose Ville Haute is claimed to be Europe's highest town at some 1,320m. A settlement has existed up here since early medieval times, surveying the junction of five valleys. The heights around bristle with a formidable array of forts built down many centuries. You can climb up the various levels of the **Fort du Château** to look down on the roofs of the upper town. You have to penetrate several layers of fortifications just to enter the beautiful **Ville Haute** and arrive at the top of Grand'Rue, also known as the **Grande Gargouille** – referring to the water streaming down its central channel. Lined with fine Italian style houses, it leads to the colourful main square, Place d'Armes, featuring two elaborate sundials, a very common feature in this exceptionally sunny area, their Latin inscriptions always carrying a sting in the tail. The **Petite Gargouille**, likewise provided with a channel running along its length, descends parallel to the Grande Gargouille. Dominating Place du Temple off the Petite Gargouille rise the twin towers of the 17th-century **Collégiale Notre-Dame**, with its deeply attractive orange and stone façade. But even this church, its backside sticking indecorously out over the ramparts, has a military air, the tops of its towers (with sundials of course) resembling helmets. Of the previous Romanesque church, only the two worn pink marble lions at the doorway were saved. Inside, elaborate paintings adorn the choir, as do gilded busts and statues.

From the open terrace looking out from the Ville Haute's rocky perch, you can look down on the messy modern town. On one side of the terrace rises the former governors' palace, on the other the **Maison du Parc** (*open July–Aug daily 10–7; rest of year*

Tues–Sat 10–12 and 2–7; closed late Sept–late Oct; recorded commentary in English), which presents the Ecrins national park, its wildlife and traditional communities. The disused Franciscan church of **Les Cordeliers** nearby was only handed over to the town by the military authorities in 1980. The friary of which it was a part was planted here in the late 14th century, to combat heresy in the valleys around. It was taken over by the army at the Revolution and largely destroyed, apart from the church, which was transformed into a military hospital. The town has now converted it into a cultural centre. Inside, don't miss the couple of comical curly-haired Lombard lions at the base of the columns and the superbly frescoed chapel from the 1460. Inevitably, there's a sundial painted on the outside of the church, added in 1795, but the bizarre date given – 5795 – apparently indicates that it was ordered by a masonic lodge, whose timing begins with the destruction of King Solomon's temple in 4000 BC.

The busy road east out of Briançon takes you into Italy via **Montgenèvre**, a workaday ski resort, its main street lined with restaurants and tourist boutiques. For a particularly picturesque excursion nearby, head up the Vallée de la Clarée running parallel to the Italian border, strung with unkempt villages. **Névache** looks particularly charmingly scruffy , with its quirky church and its sundials. Wild roses grow in profusion in summer along the boulder-strewn way to **Laval**, an excellent place for walks.

An alternative detour west into the Ecrins leads you via the lively village of **Vallouise** to the **Pré de Madame Carle** in the shadow of formidable **Mont Pelvoux**, the second highest peak of the Ecrins range. The walks up to the **Glacier Blanc** and **Glacier Noir** are very popular. You may spot chamois and marmots in these parts.

Dramatically perched on their rocks, Guillestre and Mont-Dauphin stand at the wide junction of the Durance and Guil valleys. At **Guillestre** you can still make out the 14th-century walls, and old gateways lead into the dense network of streets. Two adorable Romanesque lions welcome you into the church of Notre-Dame-d'Aquilon. The very grand star-shaped fortifications of **Mont-Dauphin**, aloof on their platform of rock to the west, went up from 1692. Most of the place, named in honour of the heir to the French throne, has survived, but some parts, such as the church, were never completed, and others suffered from bombardments in 1940. The French army only left in 1980. Since then, a craft community has taken root here.

The **Parc Naturel Régional du Queyras**, whose mountain slopes come out in an exceptional blossoming of alpine and Mediterranean plants in season, extends east towards Italy. You can reach it in summer via the vicious pinnacles of the **Col d'Izoard**, or at any time via the **Guil valley** and its daunting gorges where coaches often get stuck. This way, you hit upon the startling glacial hill of **Château-Queyras**, topped by a picture-book fort. Parts of the medieval castle have survived, including a keep; it was won by the Protestants in 1587, and a century later Vauban added impressive new layers of defences for King Louis XIV. With its old wooden chalets sporting long balconies for drying crops, with its wood-working shops and its wooden fountains, **St-Véran** counts among the very prettiest traditional villages in all the French Alps. It also claims to be the highest village in Europe to be inhabited year-round, at c.2,000m. At the **Musée Soum**, in the neat little rooms of a 17th-century house, learn something of the harsh living conditions of the past. Another much more rustic house has been lovingly preserved by a local family as the **Musée de l'Habitat Ancien**. The dark interiors are full of roughly labelled clutter, including such delights as marmot grease, used as a fuel for light, for curing rheumatic pain, and for polishing shoes. In winter the family would sleep in the same room as the horses and pigs, whose heat and manure were much appreciated. Many other houses have been turned into souvenir shops. The extraordinary church, largely rebuilt at the end of the 17th century, retains its Romanesque lions and a few old capitals carved with primitive little figures.

Continuing along the Guil valley, you pass through **Aiguilles**, with its old stone houses and the headquarters of the Queyras nature park, and **Abriès**, its delightful church containing Baroque retables and choir ribs covered with garlands of grapes. Beyond Abriès, a very popular walk takes you through enchanting Alpine meadows to belvederes over the huge coal-like faces and triangular peak of the **Monte Viso** in Italy.

South of Guillestre you come to the ski resorts of **Vars**. Here professionals take on the most famous record-breaking piste in France, where speeds of over 200km an hour have been achieved. Beyond the Col de Vars, the **Ubaye valley** offers relatively unspoilt Alpine countryside. Colourful **Barcelonnette** is the main attraction, with its Spanish touches. The name dates from 1231 when it was founded by the count of Provence and Barcelona. Its narrow old streets are lined with houses in fruity tones, and by chic boutiques and cafés. A surprising trading link was established between Barcelonnette and Central America in the 19th century, bringing wealth to the area. The **Musée de la Vallée**, in a merchant's villa, covers the town's history.

West of Barcelonnette, the sprightly river is busy with white-water rafters in summer. Two ski resorts lie just south of town. You can easily make out **Pra-Loup**, high on a wooded ridge. While best known for its snow fields in winter, in summer it stays lively thanks to paragliding and other sporting activities. **Le Sauze** and **Super-Sauze** are modest ski resorts, Le Sauze with an older pedigree and more charm. In summer you can walk to the noticeably curiously shaped mountain tops of Chapeau de Gendarme (Policeman's Hat) and Pain de Sucre (Sugarloaf).

Southwest from Guillestre, follow the early stretches of the Durance before it turns into one of the major rivers of Provence. The alarmingly bright blue waters of the huge manmade **Lac de Serre-Ponçon** are popular for watersports. In a sensational location high above the lake, the historic town of **Embrun** contains many enchanting Italianate features, including even frescoes in its tourist office. Fountains splash away on the string of squares in the centre of this high-perched town. The best views are to be had from the top of the medieval **Tour Brune**, holding exhibition spaces in its vertiginous chambers. The **cathedral** next door is a gem. The use of coloured stone reflects the northern Italian influence in these parts, as do the wonderful worn lions guarding the porch. Inside, many further treasures await discovery, although your eyes will first be drawn to the great zebra pelt of a ceiling.

Provence and the Côte d'Azur

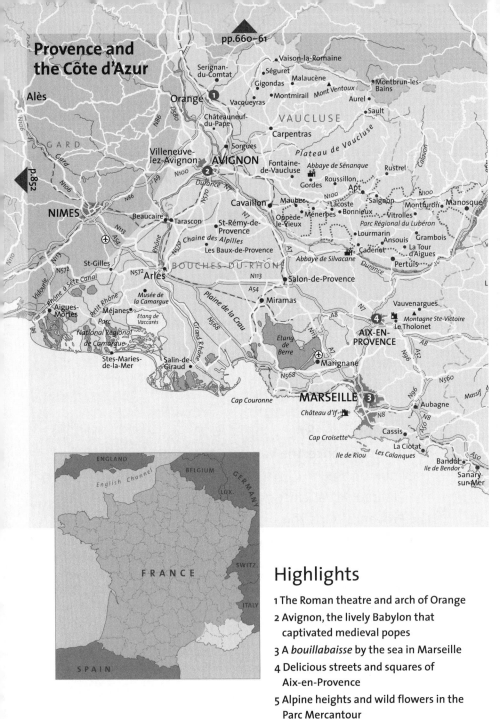

Provence and the Côte d'Azur

pp.660–61

p.852

Alès

Orange **1**

Serignan-du-Comtat
Vaison-la-Romaine
Séguret
Gigondas Malaucène
Montbrun-les-Bains
Montmirail Mont Ventoux
Vacqueyras
Aurel
Châteauneuf-du-Pape
Sault

VAUCLUSE

Carpentras

Sorgues
Villeneuve-lez-Avignon
AVIGNON **2**
Plateau de Vaucluse
Fontaine-de-Vaucluse
Abbaye de Sénanque
Rustrel
Gordes Roussillon
Apt
N100
Maubec Lacoste Saignon
Montfuron Manosque
Cavaillon
Ménerbes Bonnieux Vitrolles
Oppède-le-Vieux
Parc Régional du Lubéron
Ansouis Grambois
Lourmarin
La Tour
d'Aigues
Cadenet
Abbaye de Silvacane Pertuis

NIMES

GARD

Beaucaire Tarascon
St-Rémy-de-Provence
Chaine des Alpilles
Les Baux-de-Provence

St-Gilles

BOUCHES-DU-RHÔNE

Arles

Salon-de-Provence
Miramas

Aigues-Mortes
Méjanes
Parc
National Régional
de Camargue
Musée de
la Camargue
Etang de
Vaccarès
Plaine de la Crau

Vauvenargues
Montagne Ste-Victoire
Le Tholonet
AIX-EN-PROVENCE **4**

Etang
de
Berre

Stes-Maries-de-la-Mer
Salin-de-Giraud
Marignane

Cap Couronne

MARSEILLE **3**
Aubagne

Château d'If

Cap Croisette
Cassis
Massif
La Ciotat
Ile de Riou Les Calanques
Bandol
Ile de Bendor
Sanary-sur-Mer

ENGLAND
BELGIUM GERMANY
English Channel
LUX.

FRANCE
SWITZ.
ITALY

SPAIN

Highlights

1 The Roman theatre and arch of Orange
2 Avignon, the lively Babylon that captivated medieval popes
3 A *bouillabaisse* by the sea in Marseille
4 Delicious streets and squares of Aix-en-Provence
5 Alpine heights and wild flowers in the Parc Mercantour
6 Nice, for a hundred reasons

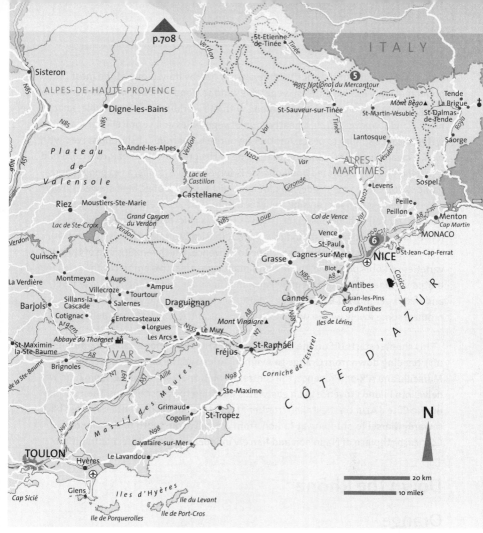

First settled by the ancient Greeks, Provence was the beloved Provincia of the Romans. Even the medieval popes and cardinals in Avignon fell prey to its sensuous *dolce vita*; the voluptuous Mediterranean light inspired Van Gogh, Cézanne, Renoir, Matisse, and the Fauves. After a century of hosting the consumptive and the wealthy in the winter, the Roaring 20s introduced a new fad for turning brown by the sea. The French invented paid summer holidays for everyone in 1936, and the rest is history.

Today, after Paris, Provence and the Côte d'Azur – the French Riviera – are the most visited regions in France. Endowed with a sunny climate, naturally air-conditioned by the mistral wind, replete with dramatic scenery and beaches, fascinating Roman and medieval remains, top-notch art museums, fantastic restaurants and hotels, this 'California of Europe' has its down sides as well: too many holiday villas, too many people, high prices, and too many shop selling lavender soap or *santons*, the omnipresent Provençal crèche figurines. Pick and choose here, and come on the cusp of the season, and you'll better understand what started all the fuss in the first place.

Food and Wine

The sunny cuisine of the south, influenced by nearby Italy, is one of the most popular in France: olive oil, fresh vegetables and seafood are basic ingredients. Ravioli and gnocchi were invented in Nice, along with the world-famous ratatouille, salad niçoise and *soupe au pistou*, a hearty soup of vegetables and vermicelli, served with *pistou*, a sauce similar to pesto. Another favourite is *bourride*, a fish soup served with *aïoli*, a creamy garlic mayonnaise that is one of the great symbols of Provence, while Marseille's justly celebrated *bouillabaisse* is served with a *rouille*, a red pepper and garlic sauce. On the meat side, look for lamb dishes and *daubes*, beef stewed slowly in red wine; vegetarians can sink their teeth into stuffed vegetables or courgette flowers (*farcies*) or delicious snacks such as *socca*, a chickpea-flour pie, tapenades (olive paste, served on toast) and *pan-bagnat* (basically a salade niçoise sandwich).

The Greeks introduced the syrah grape to Provence, which remains one of the chief varieties of Côtes du Rhône, the region's main wine area; this embraces the celebrated vintages of Châteauneuf de Pape and Gigondas among the reds, rosé Tavel, and the sweet muscat Beaumes-de-Venise. Ancient, small vineyards along the coast produce some lovely wines: white Cassis, Bandol, and rare Palette and Bellet.

This chapter starts off on the mighty Rhône (where the **Rhône Valley** chapter left off), heading down from Orange to Avignon, Arles and the Camargue. Next comes Marseille and Aix-en-Provence, the centres of Metropolitan Provence. From here we delve into inland Provence in an eastwards direction towards the Alps. Then we pick up the Côte d'Azur on the Italian frontier at Menton and head relentlessly west back towards Marseille, stopping at Toulon, from where we dip south to the island of Corsica, birthplace of Napoleon and fiercely independent in culture and tradition.

Down the Rhône

Orange

Orange is a miasmic provincial town with a few cosy corners among the prevailing drabness. Fate, or the lack of a bypass road, has made its streets a kind of Le Mans for heavy lorries. Twice electing a National Front mayor hasn't helped it either, despite his superficial attempts to gentrify the town, earning him the nickname 'the flowerpot mayor'. Nevertheless the prosperous Roman colony that was Orange left it two ancient monuments unmatched in France. The most unusual page of the city's history, however, was an odd chance that would let Orange lend its colour to the Dutch, the Northern Irish, the Orange Free State and Orange, New Jersey. In 1530, the city became the property of the German House of Nassau, just in time for the Reformation. The Nassaus declared for Protestantism, and Orange rapidly became the dissenters' chief stronghold in Provence. Soon after, William of Nassau – William of Orange – became the first *stadhouder* of the United Provinces and led the fight for Dutch independence. French rule, won by Louis XIV, was a disaster, particularly after the Revocation of the Edict of Nantes, and the city has never really recovered.

The architects of the Roman **Théâtre Antique** (*open April, May and Sept 9–7; June–Aug 9–8; Mar and Oct 9–6, Dec–Feb 9–5; adm*) might be distressed to hear it, but these days the most impressive part of this huge structure is its back wall. If the old prints in the municipal museum are accurate, this rugged, elegant sandstone cliff facing Place des Frères-Mounet was originally adorned with low, temple-like façades. In its present state, it resembles a typical Florentine Renaissance palace, without the windows. Unlike Greek theatres, which always opened to a grand view behind the stage, those of the Romans featured large stage buildings, serious architectural compositions of columns, arches and sculptured friezes. This is what the great exterior wall is supporting; Orange's stage building (115ft high) is one of two complete specimens that remain to us (the other is at Aspendos in Turkey). Of the decoration, a statue of Augustus remains in the centre. The theatre hosts an annual festival of opera and choral music, **t** 04 94 34 24 24. Other fragments, including an exceptional frieze of satyrs and Amazons, are stowed opposite in the truly fascinating **Musée Municipal** (*same hours and ticket as amphitheatre*).

Rue Victor-Hugo follows the route of the ancient Roman *cardo major* to Orange's other Roman attraction. The **Triumphal Arch**, built around AD 20, celebrates the conquests of the Second Gallic Legion with almost abstract scenes of battling Romans and Celts. This is the epitome of the Provençal-Roman style: excellent, careful reliefs, especially in the upper frieze, with a touch of Celto-Ligurian strangeness.

Châteauneuf-du-Pape

You'll begin to understand why Châteauneuf's wines are so expensive when you pass through the vineyards between Orange and Avignon. Blink and you'll miss them. Every available square inch is covered with vineyards of a rare beauty, so immacu-

Getting There and Around

The **train** station on Av Frédéric Mistral, **t** 04 90 11 88 64, has direct connections to Paris, Avignon, Arles, Marseille, Nice and Cannes. **Buses** depart from Cours Portoules, **t** 04 90 34 15 59, for Carpentras, Vaison-la-Romaine and Avignon, and Séguret.

Where to Stay and Eat

Orange ✉ **84100**

Arène, Place de Langes, **t** 04 90 11 40 40 (*moderate*). Pleasant, on a quiet square.

★★St-Florent, 4 Rue du Mazeau, **t** 04 90 34 18 53 (*inexpensive*). A decent budget choice.

Leyaca, 24 Place Sylvain, **t** 04 90 34 70 03 (*moderate–cheap*). Pretty, with appetising menus. *Closed Tues eve, Wed, and Nov.*

Châteauneuf-du-Pape ✉ **84230**

★★★Château des Fines Roches, 2km south on the D17, **t** 04 90 83 70 23, *www.chateaufines roches.com* (*expensive*). For a luxurious stay, there's this imposing but fake crenellated castle with gardens, set among the vineyards. *Closed mid-Dec–Feb.*

★★★★La Sommellerie, D17 near Roquemaure, **t** 04 90 83 50 00 (*moderate*). In a restored 18th-century sheepfold, with rooms overlooking the small pool or vines; the restaurant serves delicately perfumed dishes and fish. Don't miss his reproductions of Van Gogh's paintings – in spun sugar (*expensive*). *Closed Mon lunch in winter.*

La Mère Germaine, Place de la Fontaine, **t** 04 90 83 54 37 (*inexpensive*). Recently renovated rooms, and a gourmet restaurant (*expensive–moderate*) serving tantalizing lamb. *Closed Tues eve in winter, Wed, and Feb.*

lately precise and luxuriant they resemble bonsai trees. The very attractive village that gives the wine its name has not resisted the temptation to become the Midi's foremost oenological tourist trap; along the main street there are few grocers or boutiques, but plenty of wine shops. Brave the hordes and visit the 14th-century **castle**, which the Avignon popes used as a summer residence, to see the huge plain below you, and the Rhône muscling away to the west on its way south to Avignon, or wait till dusk if you can, for a magnificent sunset.

Avignon

Avignon has known more passions and art and power than any town in Provence, a mixture of excitement whipped to a frenzy by the mistral. But even the master of winds has never caused as much trouble as the 14th-century papal court, a vortex of mischief that ruled Avignon for centuries, trailing violence, corruption and debauchery in its wake.

History

Philip the Fair of France, having just bribed the conclave to elect a Frenchman, Clement V, as pope, also suggested that he flee the anarchy of 14th-century Rome for the safer havens of the Comtat Venaissin, a piece of papal turf picked up after the Albigensian Crusade. Clement V always intended to return to Rome, but when he died the French cardinals elected a former archbishop of Avignon, John XXII (1316–34), who moved the Curia into his old episcopal palace. Although he enlarged the palace with the proceeds, it still wasn't roomy enough for his successor, Benedict XII (1334–42), who replaced it with another palace, or for Clement VI (1342–52), who added another. Meanwhile all the profits that the 14th-century papal machine generated went to Avignon instead of Rome, and overcrowding, debauchery, dirt, luxury, plague, blackmail and crime came with the deal. In 1377 St Catherine of Siena convinced the seventh Avignon pope, Gregory XI, to return to Rome. The pope came, he saw, he sickened, but before he could pack his bags to return to Avignon, he died. The Roman mob seized their chance, and physically forced the cardinals to elect an Italian pope who would re-establish the papacy in Rome. When the French cardinals escaped the Romans' clutches, they sparked off the Great Schism by electing a French anti-pope, Clement VII, and went back to Avignon. Finally, the Church decided on one pope, and the Comtat Venaissin was eventually incorporated into France during the Revolution in a blood rite of atrocities. But even as part of France, Avignon has maintained its lively international character. In 1946, actor Jean Vilar founded the Avignon Festival, the liveliest and most popular event on the entire Provençal calendar.

The Famous Half-Bridge

From the Rhône, Avignon is a brave two-tiered sight: in front rise the sheer cliffs of the **Rocher des Doms**, inhabited since Neolithic times, and behind it the sheer manmade cliffs of the Palais des Papes. The ensemble includes the **walls** that the popes

Getting There and Around

Avignon's **airport** is at Caumont, **t** 04 90 81 51 15. The **Eurostar**, **t** 08705 186 186, *www.eurostar.co.uk*, runs from London in summer, taking 6½ hours.

The **train** station is outside the Porte de la République. Avignon is on the Paris–Marseille TGV line, and has frequent links to Arles, Montpellier, Nîmes, Orange, Toulon and Carcassonne. The **bus** station is next door (Bd St Roch, **t** 04 90 82 07 35). There are buses to Carpentras, Cavaillon, St-Rémy and Orange, Arles, Nîmes, one early-morning run to Nice, Aix and Cannes, along with others to Aix and Fontaine-de-Vaucluse, Marseille, and services to the Pont du Gard, Uzès and Châteauneuf-du-Pape. For Villeneuve lez Avignon, take city bus no.11 from in front of the post office.

For a **taxi**, call **t** 04 90 82 20 20.

You can take the **tourist excursion boat** *Le Cygne* from Beaucaire, **t** 04 66 59 35 62, or have a **lunch or dinner cruise** on *Le Miréio*, based at Allées de l'Oulle, **t** 04 90 85 62 25. In July and August, the **Bateau-Bus** makes regular trips between Avignon and Villeneuve, starting from the Allées de l'Oulle.

Inexpensive **car hire** firms are VEO, 51 Av Pierre Sémard, **t** 04 90 87 53 43, and Eurorent, 3 Av Saint Ruf, **t** 04 90 86 06 61.

Tourist Information

Avignon: 41 Cours Jean Jaurès, **t** 04 32 74 32 74, *www.ot-avignon.fr*.
Villeneuve lez Avignon: Place Charles David, **t** 04 90 25 61 33.

Where to Stay

Avignon ✉ 84000

Avignon gets full to the brim in July and August: it's imperative to book ahead. Note that there are also a huge number of chain hotels around the suburbs.

Luxury–Expensive

★★★★Hôtel d'Europe, 12 Place Crillon, **t** 04 90 14 76 76. Oldest, and still classically formal with Louis XV furnishings, converted to an inn in the late 1700s. Napoleon stayed here, as did the eloping Browning and Barrett. *Restaurant closed Sun, and Mon lunch.*

★★★★Hôtel Clarion/Cloître St-Louis, 20 Rue du Portail Boquier, **t** 04 90 27 55 55, *www.cloitre-saint-louis.com*. Built in 1589 as part of the Jesuit school of theology, the beautiful cloister is an island of tranquillity. Rooms are austerely modern; meals are served under the portico or by the rooftop pool.

★★★★La Ferme Jamet, Chemin de Rhodes (off Pont Daladier), **t** 04 90 86 88 35, *fermja@club-internet.fr*. A 16th-century farmhouse on the Ile de la Barthelasse; rooms range from traditional Provençal to a Gypsy caravan, around a tennis court and a pool.

Moderate

★★Hôtel du Palais des Papes, 2 Place du Palais, **t** 04 90 86 04 13. Best views of the palace, modern soundproofed rooms, air conditioning and restaurant.

★★St-Roch, 9 Rue Mérindol, **t** 04 90 16 50 00. Quiet with a delightful garden just outside the walls of Porte St-Roch.

★Splendid, 17 Rue A. Perdiguier, off Rue de la République, **t** 04 90 86 14 46, *www.avignon-splendid-hotel.com*. Recently renovated.

Inexpensive

★Mignon, 12 Rue Joseph Vernet, **t** 04 90 82 17 30, *www.hotel-mignon.com*. Bright and charming with modernized but rather small rooms.

Eating Out

Expensive–Moderate

Hiély-Lucullus, 5 Rue de la République, **t** 04 90 86 17 07. Avignon's gourmet bastion for the past 60 years. The kitchen never disappoints

wrapped around Avignon. From the walls, four arches of a bridge leapfrog into the Rhône, sidle up to a waterbound two-storey Romanesque chapel and then stop abruptly mid-river. This is the famous **Pont St-Bénézet**, or simply the Pont d'Avignon, begun in 1185 (*open April–June and Oct daily 9–7; Nov–Mar daily 9.30–5.45; adm*).

with its *tourte* of quail and *foie gras*, a legendary *cassoulet de moules aux épinards* and, for dessert, *meringue glacée au chocolat ou café*, accompanied by carafes of Châteauneuf-du-Pape or Tavel. *Closed Tues, Wed, and last 2 weeks Feb.*

Moderate

La Fourchette, 17 Rue Racine, **t** 04 90 85 20 93. Hiély-Lucullus' sister restaurant serves as good for less: a choice of 12 desserts and wine by the carafe. *Closed Sat lunch and Sun, end Aug, and last 2 weeks Feb.*

Le Bain Marie, 5 Rue Pétramale, **t** 04 90 85 21 37. Popular and serves traditional French fare. *Closed Sat lunch, Sun, Mon lunch.*

Le Petit Bedon, 70 Rue Joseph Vernet, **t** 04 90 82 33 98. Quickly becoming an Avignon institution for well-prepared dishes seldom found elsewhere, like *lotte au Gigondas*, angler-fish in wine. *Closed Sun and Mon.*

Woolloomoolloo, 16 bis Rue des Teinturiers, **t** 04 90 85 28 44. Go global with a feast of 'world cuisine' and live music.

Terre de Saveur, Rue St-Michel, **t** 04 90 86 68 72. For lunch, pop into this vegetarian-orientated place which serves up omelettes and pasta dishes, many recipes using wild mushrooms. *Open lunch only except also Fri and Sat eves.*

Around Avignon

***Hostellerie L'Hermitage-Meissonnier, 30 Av de Verdun, 4km west of Avignon at Les Angles, **t** 04 90 25 41 02 (*moderate*). Sixteen luxurious rooms and a restaurant (**t** 04 90 25 41 68) specializing in Provençal cuisine of the highest order – even the tomatoes taste better here, especially if you eat out in L'Hermitage's lovely garden. *Closed Sun eve and Mon; July and Aug Mon lunch only.*

****Hostellerie les Frênes, 645 Av les Vertes-Rives, Montfavet, 5 km east (follow the Avenue d'Avignon), **t** 04 90 31 17 93,

www.lesfrenes.com (*luxury–expensive*). A Relais et Châteaux place, set around a beautiful garden and pool; the rooms are furnished with antiques. Half-board is mandatory in season, but the food is as marvellous as the setting.

Villeneuve lez Avignon ✉ 30400

****Le Prieuré, Place du Chapître, **t** 04 90 15 90 15, www.leprieure.fr (*expensive*). Sleep in a 14th-century *livrée*, where the rooms are furnished with antiques, or in the comfortable annexe by the pool; garden, tennis, and a restaurant that does delightful things with seafood and truffles. *Closed Nov–Mar.*

****La Magnaneraie, 37 Rue Camp-de-Bataille, **t** 04 90 25 11 11 (*expensive*). Modern rooms in a former silkworm nursery, or in an annexe; with a pool, gardens, and Le Prieuré's rival for the best restaurant in town (*expensive*).

L'Atelier, 5 Rue de la Foire, **t 04 90 25 01 84, hotel-atelier@libertysurf.fr (*moderate*). Charming 16th-century building with a lovely walled garden and beautifully austere rooms.

Les Jardins de la Livrée, 4 bis Rue Camp de Bataille, **t** 04 90 26 05 05 (*moderate*). Charming *maison particulière* with a walled garden and pool. The restaurant is good too; try the cannelloni stuffed with salmon. *Closed Sun eve and Mon in winter.*

Les Ecuries des Chartreux, 66 Rue de la République, **t** 04 90 25 79 93, www.avignon-et-provence.com/ecuries-chartreux (*moderate*). A delightful 17th-century oasis with three studios, a lovely garden and full breakfast included.

Aubertin, 1 Rue de l'Hôpital, **t** 04 90 25 94 84. Intimate place to savour red mullet tartines, with *pistou* and fried aubergines. Book. *Closed Sun, and Mon lunch in winter.*

La Maison, 1 Rue Montée du Fort St-André, **t** 04 90 25 20 81 (*moderate*). An old favourite, with a traditional menu. *Closed Wed and Aug.*

Originally 22 arches and half a mile long, the bridge enriched Avignon with its tolls, but in 1660 the Avignonnais got tired of the constant repairs it demanded and abandoned it to the monsters of the Rhône; now only four arches remain. Mid-river **Ile de la Barthelasse**, formerly a hunting reserve.

The Palais des Papes

Open April–June and Oct daily 9–7; Nov–Mar daily 9.30–5.45; adm.

After crossing the **Cour d'Honneur**, the great courtyard dividing Benedict XII's stern Cistercian Palais Vieux (1334–42) and Clement VI's flamboyant Palais Neuf (1342–52), the tour begins in the **Jesus Hall**, decorated with monograms of Christ and now containing a hoard of maps and curios. The most valuable loot would be stored behind walls 10ft thick in the windowless bowels of the **Angels' Tower**.

Next is the **Consistory**, where the cardinals met and received ambassadors; its lavish frescoes and ceiling burned in 1413, and it now displays 19th-century portraits of Avignon's popes and Simone Martini's fresco of the *Virgin of Humility*. In the **Chapelle St-Jean**, dedicated to both Johns, the Baptist and the Evangelist, Matteo Giovannetti of Viterbo, a trecento charmer who left the bulk of his work in Avignon, did the frescoes for Clement VI: saints floating overhead in starry blue landscapes (recall that at the time ultramarine blue paint was even more expensive than gold). The tour continues to the first floor and the huge banqueting hall, or **Grand Tinel**, hung with 18th-century Gobelin tapestries. The adjacent **Upper Kitchen** was large enough to produce Clement VI's coronation feast. Off the Grand Tinel, more delightful frescoes by Matteo Giovannetti decorate the **Chapelle St-Martial**.

The tour continues to the pope's **Antechamber**, where he would hold private audiences, and then on to the **Pope's Bedroom**, covered with murals of spiralling foliage, birds and birdcages. It leads directly into the New Palace and the most delightful room in the entire palace, the **Chambre du Cerf**, Clement VI's study. In 1343 he had Matteo Giovannetti (probably) lead a group of French painters in depicting outdoor scenes of hunting, fishing, and peach-picking. The arrows direct you next to the **Sacristy**, crowded with statues of kings, queens and bishops escaped from Gargantua's chessboard, followed by Clement VI's **Great Chapel**, longer even than the Grand Tinel and just as empty. A grand stair leads down to the flamboyant **Great Audience Hall**, where a band of Matteo Giovannetti's Prophets remain intact.

Around the Palace: Notre-Dame-des-Doms

To the left of the palace is Avignon's cathedral, **Notre-Dame-des-Doms**, built in 1150, its landmark square bell tower ridiculously dwarfed by a gilt statue of the Virgin added in 1859 in an attempt to make the church stand out next to the papal pile. Next to the cathedral, ramps lead up to the oasis of the **Rocher des Doms**, once a *citadela* and now a garden enjoying views of the Rhône and Mont Ventoux.

Musée du Petit Palais

At the end of Place des Papes, the Petit Palais once housed the cardinal legate and now holds Avignon's medieval art (*open Wed–Sun 9.30–1 and 2–5.30; June–Sept daily 10–1 and 2–6; adm*). There are fascinating fragments of the 35ft, 8-storey **Tomb of Cardinal Jean de Lagrange** (1389), from Avignon's church of St-Martial, and six rooms glowing with the golden 14th- and early 15th-century Italian Madonnas. The museum's best-known work, Botticelli's *Virgin and Child*, is a tender, lyrical painting of

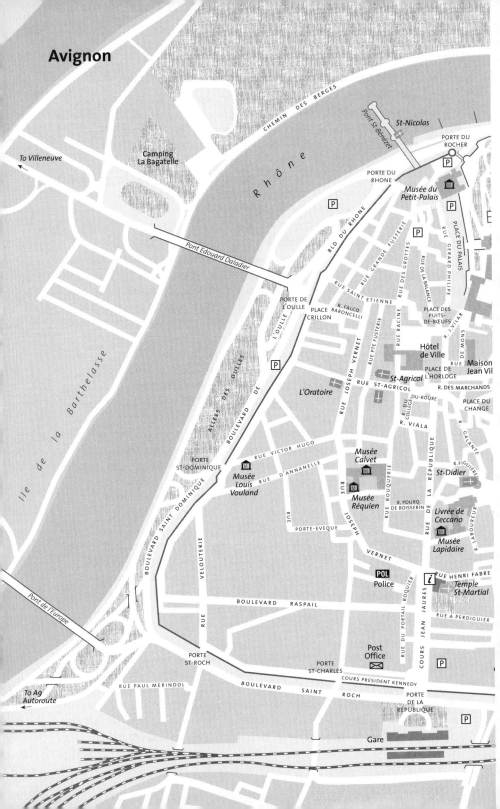

Avignon

To Villeneuve

CHEMIN DES BERGES

Pont St-Bénézet

St-Nicolas

PORTE DU ROCHER

Rhône

Camping La Bagatelle

PORTE DU RHONE

Musée du Petit-Palais

Pont Edouard Daladier

BLD DU RHONE

PLACE DU PALAIS

RUE GRANDE FUSTERIE

RUE DES GROTTES

RUE GERARD PHILIPE

RUE DE LA BALANCE

RUE SAINT ETIENNE

PORTE DE L'OULLE

R. FALCO

PLACE CRILLON BARONCELLI

RUE RACINE

PLACE DES PUITS-DE-BŒUFS

R. J. VILAR

RUE PTE FUSTERIE

Hôtel de Ville

RUE DE MONS

Ile de la Barthelasse

L'OULLE

RUE JOSEPH VERNET

RUE ST-AGRICOL

St-Agricol

PLACE DE L'HORLOGE

Maison Jean Vil

R. DES MARCHANDS

ALLÉES DES OULLES

L'Oratoire

RUE DU COLLÈGE

DU-ROURE

PLACE DU CHANGE

BOULEVARD DE

R. VIALA

R. GALANTE

RUE VICTOR HUGO

RUE D'ANNANELLE

Musée Louis Vouland

Musée Calvet

RUE BOUQUERIE

RUE DE LA RÉPUBLIQUE

R.FIGUIERE

St-Didier

PORTE ST-DOMINIQUE

Musée Réquien

R. POURQ. DE BOISSERIN

Livrée de Ceccano

R.LABOUREUR

BOULEVARD SAINT DOMINIQUE

RUE JOSEPH

PORTE-EVEQUE

RUE

VERNET

Musée Lapidaire

VELOUTERIE

POL Police

RUE HENRI FABRE

i

Temple St-Martial

RUE

BOULEVARD RASPAIL

RUE DU PORTAIL BOQUIER

COURS JEAN JAURES

RUE A PERDIGUIER

Pont de l'Europe

PORTE ST-ROCH

PORTE ST-CHARLES

Post Office

Gare

PORTE DE LA RÉPUBLIQUE

To Ag Autoroute

RUE PAUL MERINDOL

BOULEVARD SAINT ROCH

COURS PRESIDENT KENNEDY

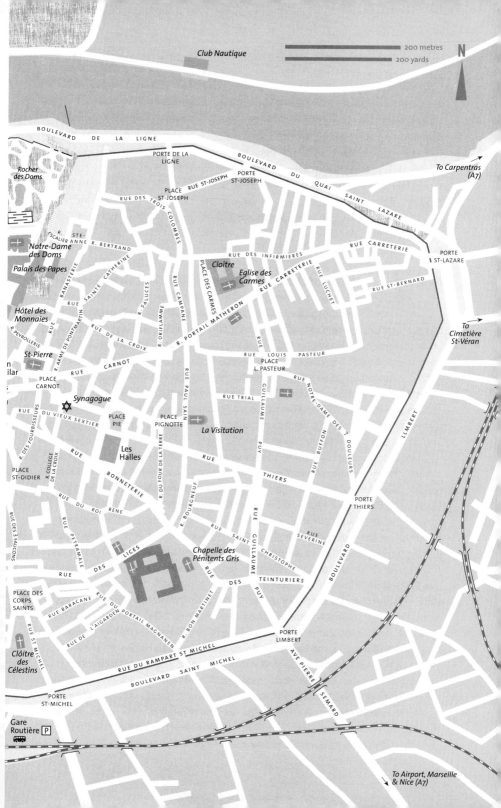

Club Nautique

200 metres
200 yards

N

To Carpentras
(A7)

BOULEVARD   DE   LA   LIGNE

PORTE DE LA
LIGNE

BOULEVARD   DU   QUAI   SAINT   LAZARE

Rocher
des Doms

PORTE
ST-JOSEPH

PLACE
ST-JOSEPH   RUE ST-JOSEPH

RUE CARRETERIE

PORTE
ST-LAZARE

RUE DES TROIS COLOMBES

RUE DES INFIRMIERES

R. STE-
SCALIER ANNE   R. BERTRAND

RUE ST-BERNARD

Notre-Dame
des Doms

Cloître

Eglise des
Carmes

RUE CARRETERIE

RUE LUCHET

Palais des Papes

BANASTERIE

PLACE DES CARMES

RUE CAMPANE

RUE SAINTE CATHERINE

Hôtel des
Monnaies

R. ARME DE PONTMARTIN

RUE

R. ORIFLAMME

R. SALUCES

R. PORTAIL MATHERON

RUE LOUIS   PASTEUR

R. PEYROLLERIE

RUE DE LA CROIX

PLACE
L. PASTEUR

To
Cimetière
St-Véran

St-Pierre

CARNOT

RUE NOTRE-DAME DES 7

ilar

RUE

RUE TRIAL

RUE GUILLAUME

RUE BUFFON

DOULEURS

PLACE
CARNOT

RUE PAUL SAIN

PLACE
PIGNOTTE

La Visitation

PUY

LIMBERT

Synagogue

DU VIEUX SEXTIER

PLACE
PIE

RUE DES FOURBISSEURS

RUE

R. COLLEGE
DE LA CROIX

Les
Halles

BONNETERIE

RUE DU FOUR DE LA TERRE

RUE

THIERS

RUE SEVERINE

PORTE
THIERS

PLACE
ST-DIDIER

RUE DU ROI
RENE

R. BOURGNEUF

RUE SAINT

RUE

RUE
CHRISTOPHE

BOULEVARD

RUE DES 3 FALCONS

RUE PETRAMALE

LICES

Chapelle des
Pénitents Gris

RUE GUILLAUME

DES

PUY

RUE   DES

TEINTURIERS

PLACE DES
CORPS
SAINTS

RUE

DES

RUE BARACANE

RUE DU

RUE DE L'AIGARDEN PORTAIL MAGNANEN

R. BON MARTINET

PORTE
LIMBERT

RUE ST-MICHEL

Cloître
des
Célestins

RUE DU RAMPART ST MICHEL

BOULEVARD   SAINT   MICHEL

AVE PIERRE

SEMARD

PORTE
ST-MICHEL

Gare
Routière P

To Airport, Marseille
& Nice (A7)

his youth. Rooms 17–19 are devoted to works by French artists in Avignon, who after 1440 formed one of the most important schools of French Renaissance art.

Place de l'Horloge and Quartier des Fusteries

Just below the Place du Palais, an antique carousel spins in the lively centre of old Avignon: **Place de l'Horloge**, site of the old Roman forum. The windows on the east side of the square are filled with *trompe-l'œil* paintings of historic personages. Behind the Hôtel de Ville lies the **Quartier des Fusteries**, named for the wood merchants and carpenters who had their workshops here in the Middle Ages, replaced in the 18th century with *hôtels particuliers*. From the Quartier des Fusteries, the steep pictur-esque lanes of the **Quartier de la Balance** wind back up to the Place du Palais. Off Place de l'Horloge, Rue St-Agricol is named after the Gothic church of **St-Agricol** (1326); its treasure is the *Doni Retable*, a rare Provençal work from the Renaissance.

Avignon's Smaller Museums

At the end of Rue St-Agricol curves Rue Joseph Vernet, lined with 18th-century *hôtels particuliers*, antique shops, pricey restaurants and cafés. The kind of overly ornate, spindly furniture, porcelains and knick-knacks that originally filled these mansions is on display nearby in Rue Victor Hugo's **Musée Louis Vouland** (*open May–Oct Mon–Sat 10–12 and 2–6, Sun 2–6; Nov–April daily 2–6; adm*). At 65 Rue Joseph Vernet, a fancy *hôtel particulier* houses the **Musée Calvet** (*open 10–1 and 2–6; closed Tues; adm*), which offers something for every taste: 6,000 pieces of wrought iron, Greek sculpture, 18th-century seascapes by Avignon native Joseph Vernet, mummies, tapestries, prehistoric statue-steles, dizzy kitsch paintings of nude men, and an excellent collection of 19th- and 20th-century paintings.

Adjacent to the Calvet museum, the **Museum Requien** is Avignon's fuddy-duddy natural history collection (*open Tues–Sat 9–12 and 2–6*), where a 81lb beaver found in the Sorgue steals the show. At 5 Rue Violette the **Lambert Collection**, situated in the Hôtel de Caumont (*open Tues–Sun 11–6*), features modern art in an 18th-century mansion. At 27 Rue de la République, in the chilly 17th-century Jesuit chapel, are the sculptures of the **Musée Lapidaire** (*open Wed–Mon 10–1 and 2–6; closed Tues; adm*). It's worth popping in for the 2nd-century BC (or Merovingian) man-eating *Tarasque de Noves*; or for its statues of Gallic warriors. There is good Renaissance sculpture as well, but the best is in the nearby church of **St-Didier** (1359), just to the north in Place St-Didier: Francesco Laurana's polychrome reredos of Christ bearing the Cross, called Notre-Dame du Spasme for the spasm of pain on Mary's face.

Nearby, at 5 Rue Laboureur are the treasures of a serious art collector named Jean Angladon-Dubrujeaud, the **Fondation Angladon-Dubrujeaud** (*open Dec–Mar Wed–Sun 1–6; April–Nov Tues–Sun 1–6; adm*), with a fine assortment of modern painting never before seen: works by Modigliani, Picasso, Manet, Degas and Cézanne, as well as the only Van Gogh on display in Provence, called *Les Wagons de chemin de fer*. The **Musée du Mont de Piété**, 6 Rue Saluces (*open Mon–Fri 8.30–12 and 1.30–5.30*), the oldest pawnbroker's in France, now houses not only the town archives, but the *conditions des soies*, or silk-conditioning equipment, once the wealth of Avignon.

The Eastern Quarters

Rue des Teinturiers, the most picturesque street in Avignon, was named after the dyers and textile-makers who powered their machines on water-wheels in the Sorgue, two of which survive. Rue des Teinturiers turns into Rue Bonneterie on its way to Avignon's shopping district. Just beyond Place Carnot, **St-Pierre**'s flamboyant façade boasts a set of beautifully carved walnut doors (1551). From Place St-Pierre, Rue Carnot continues to the charming Place des Carmes, dominated by the 14th-century **Eglise des Carmes**, Avignon's biggest church, with a pretty cloister.

Villeneuve lez Avignon

The 10th-century abbey of St-André above Villeneuve lez Avignon was one of the mightiest monasteries in the south of France, and in 1226, when Louis VIII besieged pro-Albigensian Avignon, the abbot offered the king co-sovereignty of the abbey in exchange for royal privileges. But Villeneuve was soon invaded in another way, by cardinals wishing to retreat across the Rhône from the wanton, squalid Avignon of the popes. Today a dormitory suburb, Villeneuve still maintains a separate calm.

In 1307, when Philip the Fair ratified the deal that made Villeneuve royal property, he ordered that a citadel should be built on the approach to Pont St-Bénézet and named after guess who – the **Tour Philippe-le-Bel** (*open Oct–Mar daily 10–12 and 2–5.30; April–Sept daily 10–12.30 and 3–7; closed Mon out of season, and Feb*). From here, Montée de la Tour leads up to the 14th-century **Collégiale Notre-Dame** (*open Oct–Mar daily 10–12 and 2–5.30, April–Sept daily 10–12 and 3–7*), now Villeneuve's parish church. The church's most famous work, a beaming, swivel-hipped, polychrome ivory statue of the Virgin carved in Paris out of an elephant's tusk *c.* 1320, has been removed to safer quarters in the nearby **Musée Pierre-de-Luxembourg** (*same hours as Tour Philippe-le-Bel; adm*). The museum's other prize is the masterpiece of the Avignon school: Enguerrand Quarton's 1454 *Couronnement de la Vierge*, one of the greatest works of 15th-century French painting, commissioned for the Charterhouse (*see* below). Unusually, it portrays God the Father and God the Son as twins.

In Rue de la République rises what was the largest and wealthiest charterhouse in France, the **Chartreuse du Val-de-Bénédiction** (*open April–Sept daily 9–6.30; Oct–Mar daily 9.30–5.30; adm*). In 1792, the Revolution forced the monks out, and the charterhouse was sold in 17 lots. Now beautifully restored, it hosts seminars, exhibitions and performances, especially during the Avignon festival. In the Tinel's chapel are 14th-century frescoes by Matteo Giovannetti and his school. The star attraction is **Innocent VI's tomb**, with an alabaster effigy under a Gothic baldachin.

St-Rémy-de-Provence

Enclosed by a garland of boulevards lined with plane trees, St-Rémy's tranquil charms have attracted its share of the famous. Nostradamus was born here, Gertrude Stein spent years here, Princess Caroline drops in for visits (St-Rémy used to belong to the family), and Vincent Van Gogh spent his tragic last year in St-Rémy's asylum. Nowadays St-Rémy is home to a good many artists, and there are always exhibitions going on. The newest attraction is the bizarre-looking organ in the church of **St-Martin** on Bd Marceau, built only in 1983 and said to be one of the finest in the world. Older attractions are two fine Renaissance palaces, both around Place Flavier. The Hôtel Mistral de Mondragon (1550) contains the **Musée des Alpilles** (local folk life and arts) with a special section on Nostradamus (*closed, due to reopen 2004*); the Hôtel de Sade has a small but interesting **Musée Archéologique** (*guided tours in French every hour, open daily 10–12 and 2–5; July and Aug till 7; adm; combined ticket with Glanum and Musée des Alpilles available*). St-Rémy is the medieval successor to the abandoned Roman town of Glanum; finds on display here include architectural fragments, statues and reliefs of deities from Hermes to the Phrygian god Attis, and Roman glass and jewellery. The Grimaldi representative in St-Rémy lived in the beautiful 18th-century Hôtel Estrine, in Rue Estrine, now the **Centre Vincent Van Gogh** (*open Tues–Sun 10.30–12.30 and 2.30–6.30; adm*).

Les Antiques, and Van Gogh's Asylum

Just a 15-minute walk from the centre of St-Rémy, south on the D5, stand two remarkable Roman relics. Originally they decorated the end of the Roman road from Arles to Glanum, the ruins of which lie just across the D5. The **Triumphal Arch** was probably built in the reign of Augustus; its elegant form and marble columns show the Greek sensibility of the artists, far different from the strange Celtic-influenced arches of Orange and Carpentras. Next to it, the so-called **Mausoleum** was really a memorial to Caesar and Augustus, erected by their descendants in the early 1st century AD. There is nothing else quite like this anywhere; the excellent reliefs on the base show mythological scenes.

Just across the road from Les Antiques, a shady path leads to the **monastery of St-Paul-de-Mausole** (*open April–Oct daily 9.30–7; Nov–Mar daily 10.30–1 and 1.30–5; adm*), in a beautiful setting with gardens all around. Founded in the 900s, the monastery buildings were later purchased for use as a private hospital. This is the place Vincent Van Gogh chose as a refuge from the troubles of life in the outside world, in May 1890, not long after he chopped off his ear. He spent a year here, the most intense and original period of his career, painting as if possessed – 150 canvases and over 100 drawings, including many of his most famous works, such as the *Nuit étoilée* ('Starry Night') and *Les Blés jaunes* ('Cornfield and Cypress Trees').

Glanum

Open April–Sept daily 9–7; Oct–Mar daily 9–12 and 2–5; adm.

Glanum began as a Celtic settlement before the Romans under Marius snatched it around 100 BC. More than anywhere else in France, this is the place to feel really at home in the Roman world. But you'll have to work for it; only the foundations remain, and recreating Glanum will require a bit of imagination (see the museum in the Hôtel de Sade first). From the entrance, to the left are the **Maison des Antes** and the **Maison d'Atys**, two wealthy homes built around peristyle courtyards. The latter had

Getting Around

Although there are no trains, St-Rémy has a decent coach service. All leave from Place de la République, across from the church: at least one a day to Tarascon and Aix; more frequently to Avignon. You can easily walk to Les Antiques and Glanum, but buses from St-Rémy to Les Baux only run July and Aug. The latter is better connected to Arles, with four or five buses a day.

Tourist Information

St-Rémy: Place Jean-Jaurès, t 04 90 92 05 22, *www.saint-remy-de-provence.com*.

Where to Stay and Eat

St-Rémy ✉ 13210

****Le Vallon de Valrugues, Chemin de Canto Cigalo, t 04 90 92 04 40, *www.valrugues-cassagne.com* (*luxury–expensive*). On the outskirts. Lovely Provençal-style rooms, pool, Jacuzzi, and delicious meals, including lots of seafood and truffles in season.

****Château des Alpilles, D31, t 04 90 92 03 33, *www.chateaualpilles.com* (*expensive*). Outside the busy one-way rush of traffic round the centre, yet just a few steps out of town, in a park, with a tennis court and pool.

It's all mirrors, period furniture and creature comforts; the restaurant caters for hotel guests only. *Closed mid-Nov–mid-Feb.*

***Hôtel l'Atelier de l'Image, 5 Av Pasteur, t 04 90 72 51 50, *www.hotel-photo.com* (*luxury–expensive*). A slick but comfortable hotel-cum-photography retreat, with an immense pool, internet access in every room and darkroom space.

***Castellet des Alpilles, 6 Place Mireille, t 04 90 92 07 21, *www.castelletalpilles.com* (*moderate*). An old country mansion, with pretty rooms and a lovely terrace under a century-old cedar. *Closed Nov–Easter.*

**Villa Glanum, 46 Av Van Gogh, t 04 90 92 03 59 (*moderate–inexpensive*). Near the ruins, family-run and has some surprising amenities for its price: a pool and garden. *Closed Nov–mid-Mar.*

La Maison Jaune, 15 Rue Carnot, t 04 90 92 56 14 (*moderate*). With panoramic terrace. *Closed Sun eve and Mon in winter, Mon and Tues lunch in summer, plus Jan and Feb.*

L'Assiette de Marie, 1 Rue Jaume Roux, t 04 90 92 32 14 (*moderate*). Vegetarians (and others) will find joy among the bric-a-brac; try the home-made pasta. Good wine list. *Closed Thurs, and Mon–Fri lunch, plus Jan.*

Le Bistrot des Alpilles, 15 Bd Mirabeau, t 04 90 92 09 17 (*moderate*). A cheaper place where you'll get generous fresh pasta, great desserts and a pleasant terrace. *Closed Sun.*

apparently been transformed into a sanctuary of Cybele and Attis; this cult was one of the most popular of the mystery religions imported from the east in imperial times. Across the street are remains of a fountain and the *thermae* (baths), with mosaics, a *palaestra* (exercise yard) and a pool. Next door is a building with an exedra that was probably a temple. In this part of the street the **sewers** have been uncovered. The **forum** wasn't very impressive, by Roman standards, and it is hard to make anything out today from the confusion of buildings from various ages that have been excavated. Beyond it, to the right, are foundations of temples; to the left are bases of another fountain and a monument. The street closes at a **gate** from Hellenistic times; the **nymphaeum** is beyond it, to the left.

The Chaîne des Alpilles and Les Baux-de-Provence

In a matter of minutes the five twisting kilometres from St-Rémy to the heart of the Alpilles take you to another world. This world, incredibly, is at most 16km across, and a stone's throw from the swamps of the Camargue and the sea. It is made of thin, cool

Where to Stay and Eat

Les Baux ✉ 13520

★★★★**L'Oustau de Baumanière**, Route d'Arles, t 04 90 54 33 07, *www.ousteaudebauman iere.com* (*luxury–expensive*). In magical surroundings in the Val d'Enfer, a restored farmhouse with all the amenities, and a two-Michelin-star restaurant and spectacular terrace view. There are sumptuous desserts and a formidable wine list (over 100,000 bottles) of Provençal treasures.

A memorable splurge, if you can bear the disdainful hauteur. *Closed Jan and Feb.*

★★★★**Cabro d'Or**, D27, t 04 90 54 33 21, *www.lecabrodor.com* (*luxury– expensive*). Charming place that offers similar facilities. *Closed Mon in winter and Tues lunch all year.*

★★★**Mas d'Aigret**, below Les Baux (east on the D27), t 04 90 54 20 00, *contact@masdaigret. com* (*moderate*). Some rooms have great views, others open on to the gardens; the *chambres troglodytes* are actually hewn from the rock face. There is a pool, too.

breezes and brilliant light; its colours are white and deep green – almost exclusively – in an astringent landscape of limestone crags and patches of scrubby maquis.

In the Middle Ages, **Les Baux**, a steep barren plateau in the centre of the Alpilles, made the perfect setting for the most feared and celebrated of Provence's clans, Seigneurs des Baux, great patrons of the troubadours. By waging incessant warfare on all comers, and occasionally on each other, they gradually became a real power in the region until their castle was demolished by Richelieu in 1632. The village below the castle has been rebuilt in the worst way, and whatever spark of glamour survives here, you will have to run the gauntlet of shops peddling trinkets to reach it.

Up the Rue de la Calade you come to the Place de l'Eglise, where the 16th-century Hôtel des Porcelet has now become the **Musée Yves Brayer** (*open April–Sept daily 10–12.30 and 2–6.30; Oct–Mar till 5.30; closed Jan–mid-Feb; adm*). Brayer (1907–90), a respected figurative painter, left his major works here, pictures of Spain and Italy as well as Provence; you can get a preview of his work in the 17th-century **Chapelle des Pénitents Blancs** opposite (*same hours*). Also in the village are the **Hôtel Jean de Brion** and the **Hôtel de Manville**, on the Grand-Rue. The first houses the **Fondation Louis Jou** (*t 04 90 54 34 17; open April–Oct Fri–Mon 2–5, Tues–Thurs and Nov–Mar by appt only; adm*), containing Jou's engravings, as well as ones by Dürer, Rembrandt and Goya. The second is the Hôtel de Ville. The **citadel** (*open daily 9–6.30, till 8.30 in summer, till 5 in winter; adm*) has a new museum: the **Musée d'Histoire des Baux**.

Further up, the ambience changes abruptly – a rocky chaos decorated with fragments of once-imposing buildings. The path leads through this 'Ville Morte' to the tip of the plateau, where there is a grand view over the Alpilles. Turning back, the path climbs up to the **château** itself, with bits of tower and wall everywhere, including the apse of a Gothic chapel cut out of the rock, and the long eastern wall that survived Richelieu's explosives, dotted with carved windows. The only intact part is the donjon.

Three kilometres further on, the **Val d'Enfer**, the wildest corner of the Alpilles, is a weird landscape of eroded limestone, caves and quarries. The quarries host one of Les Baux's big attractions: the **Cathédrale des Images** (*open Mar–Sept daily 10–7; Oct–Feb daily 10–6; adm*), a slick show where thirty projectors bounce giant pictures over the walls; the theme of the show changes annually.

Arles

Despite a general scruffiness that seems more intentional than natural, modern Arles, sitting amidst its ruins, is still somehow charming. For all the tourists it gets, no town could seem less touristy.

In 49 BC, the local Ligurians, tired of getting raw deals from the Greeks in Marseille, readily gave Caesar the boats he needed to punish and conquer Marseille for siding with Pompey. In return Arles was rewarded the spoils and, most important of all, got all the business that had previously gone through Marseille. At the crossroads of Rome's trading route between Italy and Spain and the Rhône, Arles grew rapidly, each century adding more splendid monuments. On the whole, the Dark Ages were not so dark in Arles; from 879 to 1036 it served as the capital of Provence-Burgundy (the so-called 'Kingdom of Arles'), a vast territory that stretched all the way to Lorraine. Most importantly, Arles was a centre of power for Christianity and one of the bases of the counts of Provence. The city's special history ended in 1239 when Raymond Bérenger, count of Provence, evicted Arles' imperial viceroy. As the city declined even the sea abandoned it, leaving the port stranded between marshes and the rocky Crau plain.

The Arènes and Théâtre Antique

As enormous as it is, the Roman **Arènes** (*open Oct–April daily 9–6; May–Sept daily 9–6.30*), 10ft wider than its rival at Nîmes, originally stood another arcade higher, and was clad in marble. An enormous awning operated by sailors protected the audience. From the Middle Ages on it sheltered a poor, crime-ridden neighbourhood with two churches and 200 houses, built from stones prised off the amphitheatre's third storey. These were cleared away in 1825, leaving the amphitheatre free for bullfights, and able to pack in 12,000 spectators. But a different fate was in store for the **Théâtre Antique** (*same hours as Arènes*), just south of the Arènes: in the 5th century, in a fury usually reserved for pagan temples, Christian fanatics pulled it apart stone by stone. A shame, because the fragments of fine sculpture they left in the rubble suggest that the theatre, once capable of seating 12,000, was much more lavish than the one in

The Arles of Van Gogh

When Vincent Van Gogh arrived in Arles in 1888 he found a shabby, ugly town. But he decided to stay, and painted the Arles around him: the Café de Nuit with its hallucinogenic lightbulb, the Maison Jaune and the Pont de Langlois (part of a ghastly irrigation project) with colours intense in their chromatic contrasts. Van Gogh's dream was to found an art colony at Arles, and he begged his overbearing friend Gauguin to join him, but when Gauguin finally arrived in October he found little to like there. The tension between the two men reached such a pitch in December that the overwrought Van Gogh confronted Gauguin in the street with a razor. Gauguin stared him down and Van Gogh, despising himself, went back to his room and cut off his own ear. Arles breathed a sigh of relief when Van Gogh committed himself to the local hospital, and then to the hospital in St-Rémy. Van Gogh's output in Arles was prodigious, but not a single one remains in the city today.

Getting There and Around

Arles' **train** station is on the northern edge of town, on Av Paulin Talabot. Arles has frequent connections to Paris, Marseille, Montpellier, Nîmes, Aix-en-Provence, and Perpignan; also frequent trains to Avignon and a less frequent service to Orange.

The **bus** station is just across the street, **t** 04 90 49 38 01. There are several daily buses to Stes-Maries-de-la-Mer in the Camargue, to Salon, Aix and Marseille, to Avignon, to Nîmes and a couple to St-Gilles; in July and August, there are services to Aigues-Mortes. For a **taxi** day or night, call **t** 04 90 96 90 03.

Tourist Information

Arles: Esplanade Charles de Gaulle, **t** 04 90 18 41 20, *www.arles.org*, and in the train station, **t** 04 90 49 36 90. If you intend to see more than two of Arles' museums, stop here to purchase the €12 global ticket (or you can also pick one up at any of the museums). The tourist office also sells tickets for various city tours in English.

Where to Stay

Arles ✉ 13200

★★★★**Jules César**, Bd des Lices, **t** 04 90 52 52 52, *www.hotel-julescesar.fr* (*luxury*). The luxurious grand-daddy of hotels in Arles occupies a former Dominican monastery with a Caesar-ish temple porch tacked on. The rooms are vast, air-conditioned and furnished with Provençal pieces; the pool is heated and the gardens beautiful. *Closed Nov–23 Dec.*

★★★★**Nord Pinus**, Place du Forum, **t** 04 90 93 44 44, *www.nord-pinus.com* (*luxury*). With columns from a Roman temple embedded in its façade, the favourite of Stendhal, Mérimée and Henry James now draws top matadors; the premises are full of bull-fighting paraphernalia. *Closed Dec–mid-Feb.*

Orange. South of the theatre runs the **Boulevard des Lices** ('of the lists'), the favourite promenade of the Arlésiens since the 17th century.

Place de la République: St-Trophime and the Crypto-portiques

From there, Rue Jean Jaurès (the Roman *cardo*) leads to the **Place de la République**, a harmonious square on the Roman model. Overlooking it is the Romanesque cathedral of **St-Trophime**. The original church was built in the 5th century, and the great **portal** was added in the 12th century. Its reliefs describe the Last Judgement. After the sumptuous portal, the spartan nudity of the long, narrow nave is as striking as its unusual height. Aubusson tapestries from the 17th century hang across the top. Around the corner in Rue du Cloître is the entrance to St-Trophime's **cloister** (*same hours as the Arènes*). No other cloister in Provence is as richly and harmoniously sculpted as this, carved in the 12th and 14th centuries by the masters of St-Gilles.

Sharing Place de la République with St-Trophime is Arles' palatial **Hôtel de Ville**, built in 1675 after plans by Hardouin-Mansart. Just around the corner on Rue Balze are the subterranean barrel-vaulted double galleries built as foundations for the forum, the **Crypto-portiques** (*same hours as Arènes; adm*). With the ramparts, this cryptoporticus was the first large construction of the Roman colony.

The Muséon Arlaten, Réattu Museum and Musée de l'Arles Antique

The indefatigable Frédéric Mistral – poet, founder of the Félibrige literary school, and the first (and only) writer in a minority language to win the Nobel Prize for literature – began his collection of ethnographic items from Provence in 1896. In 1904 he set up

***D'Arlatan**, 26 Rue du Sauvage, t 04 90 93 56 66 (*expensive*). Near the lively Place du Forum, the 12th–18th-century home of the Comtes d'Arlatan has been converted into a magnificent hotel. If you're alone and can do without a TV and your own bathroom, ask for moderately priced rooms 24 and 38. There's an outdoor pool in the garden. *Closed Jan.*

**St-Trophime, 16 Rue de la Calade, t 04 90 96 88 38 (*moderate*). In an old house with a central court. *Closed mid-Nov–Jan.*

**Calendal, 5 Rue de la Porte, t 04 90 96 11 89, www.lecalendal.com (*moderate*). Rooms overlook a garden with palms. *Closed Jan.*

**Hôtel du Musée, 11 Rue du Grand-Prieuré, t 04 90 93 88 88, www.hoteldumusee.fr (*moderate*). A 17th-century residence opposite the Musée Réattu. Quiet, subtly chic, and above all friendly. *Closed Jan–mid-Feb.*

**Hôtel Le Cloître, 16 Rue du Cloître, t 04 90 96 29 50, www.members.aol.com/hotel cloitre (*inexpensive*). Friendly, well-priced hotel in a 12th-century building that was part of the medieval cloister. Clean, bright rooms, and almost on the doorstep of the Roman arena.

*Terminus et Van Gogh, 5 Place Lamartine , t 04 90 96 12 32 (*inexpensive*). Bright and welcoming.

Eating Out

Lou Marquès, in Jules César. Arles' elegant citadel of traditional *haute cuisine* (*expensive*), featuring dishes such as *croustillant de St-Pierre* and *carré d'agneau*, and an excellent wine cellar. *Closed Mon, and Sat lunch.*

Le Jardin de Manon, 14 Av des Alyscamps, t 04 90 93 38 68 (*moderate*). *Cuisine provençale* on a pretty terrace. *Closed Wed.*

Le Mejan/Actes Sud, Quai Marx-Dormay, t 08 36 68 47 07 (*moderate–cheap*). Great couscous, with a hammam in the back for real pampering. Very lively at night, with a cinema and concerts in the adjoining buildings. *Closed Sun, exc July.*

the **Muséon Arlaten**, 29 Rue de la République (*open April, May and Sept daily 9.30–12.30 and 2–6; June–Aug daily 9.30–1 and 2–6.30; Oct–Mar closed Mon; adm*). Mistral's aim was to record the details of everyday life in Provence for future generations. The evolution of the traditional Arlésienne costume was one of his obsessions. Strangest are the life-size dioramas: a Christmas dinner at a *mas*, with a table groaning with wax food, a reed-thatched *cabane des gardians*, and a visit to a new mother and her infant. A **statue of Mistral**, looking uncommonly like Buffalo Bill, stands on Place du Forum.

After the Revolution an academic painter named Jacques Réattu purchased the Priory of the Knights of Malta, and his daughter made it into the **Musée Réattu**, Rue du Grand Prieuré (*same hours as Arènes; adm*). Besides Réattu's own contributions, there are works by Théodore Rousseau and followers of Lorrain and Salvator Rosa. In 1972, the museum was jolted awake with a donation of 57 drawings from Picasso, in gratitude for the many bullfights he enjoyed in Arles.

Arles' newest museum, the **Musée de l'Arles Antique** (*open Mar–Oct daily 9–7; Nov–Feb daily 10–5; adm*), at Presqu'île du Cirque Romain, Avenue de la 1ère D.F.L., is situated in an eerie wasteland slightly out of town (*follow the Boulevard des Lices to its western end, and pass under the motorway*) and contains the collected contents of several of Arles' old museums. Architectural models bring the Roman city back to life; here you'll see how the Roman sailors wired up the sailcloth awning to shade the amphitheatre, how the city centre – the Forum and temples – looked to the man in the street, and much more. Also in the museum are the contents of the former Musée d'Art Chrétien, with a superb collection of 4th-century Christian sarcophagi.

The Alyscamps

Because of the legend of St Trophime, who was said to be a disciple of St Paul himself, the Alyscamps (*follow Rue E. Fassin from the Boulevard des Lices, eastwards; a 10min walk from the centre; same hours as the Arènes; adm*) was one of the most prestigious necropolises of the Middle Ages. Burial here was so desirable that bodies sealed in barrels with their burial fee attached were floated down the Rhône. At its greatest extent the necropolis stretched for 2.5km and contained 19 chapels and several thousand tombs, many of them packed five bodies deep. Now, only one romantic, melancholy lane lined with empty, mostly plain sarcophagi remains.

The Camargue

To its handful of inhabitants the Camargue was the *isclo*, the 'island' between the two branches of the Rhône. The river's course has taken many different forms over the millennia, and the present one, with its two arms, has created a vast marshland – France's salt cellar, a treasure-house of water-fowl and the home of some of its most exotic scenery. The Grand and Petit Rhônes build separate deltas, leaving the space in between a soupy battleground where land and sea slowly struggle for mastery.

From the 1600s, cowboys (*gardians*) have created large ranches to exploit the two totem animals of the Camargue: the native black longhorn cattle that thrive on salt grass, always the preferred stock for Provençal bullfights; and the beautiful white horse, believed to have been introduced by the Arabs in the Dark Ages. A true cowboy culture grew up, a romantic image dear to the Provençaux. The government made a Regional Park of the area in 1970. The Regional Park's **Musée de la Camargue** (*open Oct–Mar Wed–Mon 10.15–4.45; April–June and Sept daily 9.15–5.45; July and Aug daily 9.15–6.45; adm*) occupies what not long ago was a working cattle and sheep ranch, 9km southwest of Arles on the D570. The buildings are well restored and documented, giving a feeling of what life was like a century ago. Outside, are marked nature trails.

For motor tourists, the way to see the best of the Camargue is to take the D37, a left turn 4km south of the museum. After another 4km, a side road leads to the **Domaine de Méjanes**, with horse-riding and canoes; on summer weekends the gardians put on shows of cowboy know-how, and occasionally bullfights. Further on, the D37 skirts the edges of the **Etang de Vaccarès**, the biggest of the lagoons and centre of the Camargue wildlife preserve. In some places you can see flocks of flamingos year-round. The scenery changes abruptly at **Salin-de-Giraud**, a 19th-century industrial village devoted to the largest saltworks in Europe: a staggering 110 square kilometre network of pans, annually producing 800,000 tonnes of salt. There's a nature centre on the D36, **La Palissade** (*open daily 9–5*).

Les Stes-Maries-de-la-Mer

Set among the low sand-dunes, lively Stes-Maries-de-la-Mer has an open-armed approach to visitors that long predates any interest in the Camargue, for this is one of Provence's holiest places. The pious story behind it all was promoted to the hilt by the

Getting Around

By train and bus: The only public transport to the centre of the Camargue begins at the bus station in Arles: one or two buses a day each to Stes-Maries-de-la-Mer and Salin-de-Giraud. In July and Aug there are direct services from Stes-Maries to Aigues-Mortes and Montpellier (**t** 04 67 92 01 43) and others to St-Gilles and Nîmes (**t** 04 66 29 52 00). There are also one or two SNCF trains to St-Gilles from Arles. St-Gilles has regular bus connections to Nîmes, and a few to Arles.

On horseback and by bike and jeep: The Camargue is really quite small – it's never more than 40km from Arles to the coast. It is perfect country for cycling, and there are a few places in Stes-Maries-de-la-Mer to rent some wheels; try Le Vélociste, Place des Remparts, **t** 04 90 97 83 26 (*open Sept–June*). Horses are even more popular; there are many places to hire one, including, at l'Etang de l'Estagel, L'Etrier, **t** 04 66 01 36 76. Destination Camargue, **t** 04 90 96 94 44, organizes day and half-day trips by jeep.

By boat: Blue-Line, **t** 04 66 87 22 66, and other firms in St-Gilles rent boats fit for a few days' trip through the Petite Camargue. At Stes-Maries and St-Gilles there are excursion boats that make short cruises around the Camargue. From Stes-Maries, the paddle steamer *Tiki III*, **t** 04 90 97 81 68, *www.tiki3.fr*, offers an hour-long cruise on the Petit Rhône (*end Mar–Sept*).

Where to Stay and Eat

Les Stes-Maries-de-la-Mer ✉ 13460

★★★Le Pont des Bannes, 3km north on the D570, **t** 04 90 97 81 09, *www.pontdes-bannes.com* (*expensive*). You can sleep comfortably in a *cabane de gardian* with a pool, garden and stables for the total Camargue experience. *Closed mid-Jan–Feb.*

Similar facilities may be had at the annexe, **★★★Le Mas Sainte-Hélène**, Chemin Bas-des-Launes, **t** 04 90 97 81 09 (*expensive*), spread out along an islet in the Etang des Launes.

★Le Delta, Place Mireille, **t** 04 90 97 81 12 (*moderate–inexpensive*). Good value for the price, and central.

Le Brûleur de Loups, Av Gilbert-Leroy, **t** 04 90 97 83 31 (*moderate*). With a terrace overlooking the beach and more delights from the sea, with a focus on lobster. *Closed mid-Nov–Dec, Tues eve and Wed.*

Hostellerie du Pont de Gau, 4 km north on the Route d'Arles, **t** 04 90 97 81 53 (*moderate*). Jolly Provençal décor and a delicious *bouillabaisse*. *Closed Jan–mid-Feb.*

Le Mangio Fango, Route d'Arles, **t** 04 90 97 80 56 (*moderate*). Get a table on their skeeter-free patio for excellent Camargue bull stew. *Closed Wed.*

Aigues-Mortes ✉ 30220

★★★St-Louis, 10 Rue de l'Amiral Courbet, just off Place St-Louis, **t** 04 66 53 72 68 (*expensive*). Gracious and welcoming in a beautifully furnished 18th-century building.

Hermitage de St-Antoine, 9 Bd Intérieur Nord, **t** 04 06 03 04 05, *www.hermitagesa.com* (*moderate–inexpensive*). A delightful *chambre d'hôte* with three rooms, all with bathrooms. It has a tranquil patio, serves full English breakfast, and has a genial Australian host.

La Camargue, 19 Rue République, **t** 04 66 53 86 88 (*moderate*). The Gypsy Kings got their start here, but even in their absence this is the liveliest place in town, with flamenco guitars strumming in the background; seafood and grilled meat.

Maguelone, 38 Rue République, **t** 04 66 53 74 60 (*moderate*). Nearby, bright and blue, with a menu based on local ingredients: *matelote d'anguilles, bourride de lotte* and a *St-Marcel au chocolat croustillant aux coings*. *Closed two weeks Jan.*

---

medieval Church: after Christ was crucified, his Jewish detractors took a boat without sails or oars and loaded it with three Marys – Mary Salome (mother of the apostles James and John), Mary Jacobe, the Virgin's sister, Mary Magdalene, Martha and her resurrected brother Lazarus, St Maximin and St Sidonius. As this so-called Boat of Bethany drifted offshore, Sarah, the black Egyptian servant of Mary Salome and Mary Jacobe, wept so grievously that Mary Salome tossed her cloak on the water, so that

Sarah was able to walk across on it and join them. The boat took them to the Camargue, to this spot where the elderly Mary Salome, Mary Jacobe and Sarah built an oratory, while their younger companions went to spread the Gospel. In 1448, during the reign of Good King René, the supposed relics of the two Marys were discovered, greatly boosting the local pilgrim trade. Today Stes-Maries-de-la-Mer is best known for the pilgrimage of Mary Jacobe on 24 and 25 May. This attracts Gypsies from all over the world, who have canonized her servant Sarah as their patron saint.

Built in 1130, the **church** is the most impressive fortified church in Provence: a crenellated ship with loopholes for windows in a small pond of white villas with orange roofs. Inside are wells that supplied the church-fortress in times of siege; pilgrims still bottle the water to ensure their protection by St Sarah. The capitals supporting the blind arches of the raised choir are finely sculpted in the style of St-Trophime. Under the choir is the **crypt**, where the relics and statue of St Sarah in her seven robes are kept. From April to mid-November, you can take a stroll below the **bell tower**, with views stretching across the Camargue (*open daily 10–12.30 and 2–6.30*).

To the south in Rue Victor-Hugo the **Musée Baroncelli** is devoted to zoology, archaeology and folklore. It is named after the Félibre Marquis Folco de Baroncelli-Javon (1869–1943), who abandoned all at the age 21 to live the life of a *gardian*.

St-Gilles-du-Gard

West of Arles, the N572 takes you through the drier parts of the Camargue. After crossing the Rhône (you're now in the **Petite Camargue**), it approaches **St-Gilles**, originally a port and the only town for miles in any direction. The cradle of the powerful counts of Toulouse, it had a pilgrimage chapel holding the relics of an 8th-century Greek hermit who lived on doe's milk. Beginning in 1116, this was rebuilt as an **abbey** in one of the most ambitious projects in medieval Provence. During the Wars of Religion the Protestants thought it would look better as a fortress. Rebuilt on a smaller scale in 1650, it suffered further indignities but the **façade** remains, miraculously, one of the great ensembles of medieval sculpture, the masterpiece of the 12th-century school of Provence. The other great sight is '**the screw**', the Vis de St-Gilles, a spiral stair of *c.* 1142 that once led to a bell tower, a tremendous *tour de force* of stones cut so precisely as to form a self-supporting spiral vault.

Aigues-Mortes

In 1241, the Camargue was the only bit of Mediterranean coast held by France. To solidify this precarious strip, Louis IX (Saint Louis) began construction of a new port. In 1248, the port was complete enough to hold the 1,500 ships that carried Louis and his knights to the Holy Land, on the Seventh Crusade. His successor, Philip III, finished Aigues-Mortes and built its great walls, over a mile in length. Aigues-Mortes means 'dead waters', and it proved to be a prophetic name: the sea deserted Aigues and the port went into decline after 1350. Forgotten and nearly empty a century ago, Aigues now makes its living from tourists, and from salt; half of France's supply is collected here, at the enormous 10,000ha Salins-du-Midi pans south of town in the Petite Camargue (ring t 04 66 73 40 00 to visit between Mar and Oct).

Marseille

Founded by Greek colonists in 600 BC, Massalia (Marseille) boomed from the start. Conquered by Caesar for siding with Pompey, Marseille nearly went out of business. However, in the 11th century, when the Crusaders showed up looking for transport to the Holy Land, Marseille grew fat on the proceeds. It was Europe's greatest port in the 18th century, when its workers did their share in upholding the Revolution: as 500 volunteers set off in July 1792, someone suggested singing the new battle song of the Army of the Rhine. By the time they reached Paris, the 'song of the Marseillais' was perfected and became the hit tune of the Revolution, and subsequently the most rousing and bloodcurdling of national anthems.

Today amid Provence's carefully nurtured image of lavender fields, rosé wine and *pétanque*, Marseille is the great anomaly, the second city of France and the world's eighth largest port. Like New York, it has been the gateway to a new world for hundreds of thousands of new arrivals – especially Corsicans, Armenians, Jews,

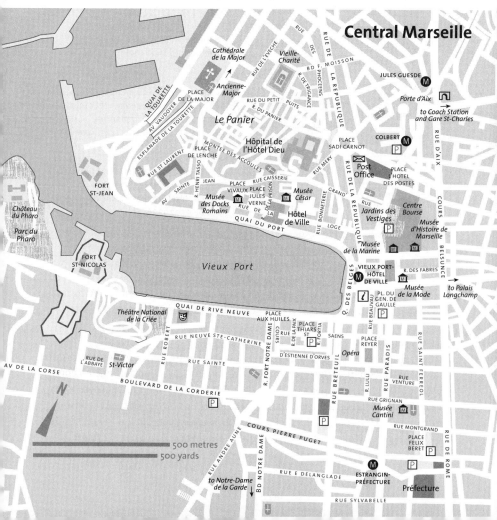

Getting There and Around

By plane: Marseille's airport (BA, Air France, easyJet) is to the west at Marignane; call **t** 04 42 14 14 14 for flight information. A bus every 20mins (**t** 04 91 50 59 34) links the airport with the train station, Gare St-Charles, taking 25mins.

By train: There are connections to nearly every town in the south from the main station, Gare St-Charles, 4e, and the TGV will get you to Paris in 4hrs 40mins.

By métro and bus: Marseille runs an efficient bus network and two métro lines. Pick up the useful *plan du réseau* at the tourist office or at the RTM (Réseau de Transport Marseillais) information desk by the Bourse, 6–8 Rue des Fabres, 1er, **t** 04 91 91 92 10. Tickets are valid for an hour, and transferable between the bus and métro, or you can buy a day pass.

At night a number of buses (Fluobus) run from the Canebière across town.

The coach station, **t** 04 91 08 16 40, is behind the train station at 3 Place Victor Hugo, with connections to Aix, Cassis, Nice, Arles, Avignon, Toulon and Cannes.

RTM's guided tour bus, the Histobus, leaves from the Vieux Port at 2pm, Sun in winter, daily in summer.

By taxi: t 04 91 02 20 20.

Car hire: Some car hire firms are in the Gare St-Charles, including Avis, **t** 04 91 64 71 00. Others include Hertz, 16 Bd Charles Nédelec, 1er, **t** 04 91 14 04 24, and Thrifty, Place Marseillaises, 1er, **t** 04 91 95 00 00.

Tourist Information

Marseille: 4 La Canebière, by the Vieux Port, 1er, **t** 04 91 13 89 00, *www.marseille-tourisme.com*.

Shopping

Rue St-Ferréol and Rue Paradis are the main shopping streets. Marseille holds a remarkable market of clay Christmas crib figures, the Foire aux Santons (end Nov–Jan); at other times, you can find *santons* at **Marcel Carbonel**, 47 Rue Neuve Ste-Catherine, 7e, near St-Victor.

For the best in Provençal food and wine, try **Georges Bataille**, 18 Rue Fontange, 6er.

Where to Stay

Marseille ✉ 13000

Marseille's top-notch hotels are the bastion of expense-account businessmen and women, while its downmarket numbers attract working girls of a different kind.

★★★★**Le Petit Nice Passédat**, off Corniche Kennedy, at Anse de Maldormé, 7e, **t** 04 91 59 25 92, *www.petitnice-passedat.com* (*luxury*). Marseille's most refined, exclusive hotel, the Relais et Châteaux former villa overlooking the Anse de Maldormé, with a fine restaurant, **Le Passédat** (*see* below).

★★★**New Hôtel Bompard**, 2 Rue des Flots Bleus, 7e, **t** 04 91 92 22 22, *www.new-hotel.com* (bus 61 from ⓜ Joliette or St-Victor) (*expensive*).

Greeks, Turks, Italians, Spaniards and Algerians. On the down side, Marseille suffers from disproportionately high unemployment and the National Front has generally picked up about a third of the vote here. On the up side, the city is undergoing a vast renovation programme of 3,000 historic buildings, and has a new sparkle.

The Vieux Port

Marseille's Vieux Port is now a huge pleasure port with over 10,000 berths; its cafés have fine views of the sunset, though in the morning the action and smells centre around the Quai des Belges and its boatside **fish market**. From the Quai des Belges *vedettes* sail to the Château d'If and Frioul islands (*see* p.787), past the two bristling fortresses that still defend the harbour: to the north **St-Jean**, built in the 12th century by the Knights of St John, and to the south **St-Nicolas**, built by Louis XIV to keep a close eye on Marseille rather than the sea.

Modern and quiet, set in its own peaceful grounds, with rooms overlooking a garden; the bungalows have their own kitchenette.

***Mercure Vieux Port, 4 Rue Beauvau, 1er, **t** 04 91 54 91 00, *www.accorhotels.com* (*expensive*). Overlooking the Vieux Port. Where Chopin and George Sand canoodled – wood-panelled and comfortable with air-conditioned, soundproofed rooms (but no restaurant).

Le Corbusier, 280 Bd Michelet, 8e, **t 04 91 16 78 00 (*moderate*). Incorporated into the Unité d'Habitation, this hotel restaurant, now slightly worn, is a special treat for students of architecture, if only for the fanstastic view. Book to get one of its 22 rooms.

Péron, 119 Corniche Kennedy, 7e, **t 04 91 31 01 41, near the Plage des Catalans (*moderate*). An unusually decorated, old-fashioned family hotel.

Le Richelieu, 52 Corniche Kennedy, 7e, **t 04 91 31 01 92 (*moderate*). Ask for a room with a sea view. Outdoor breakfast terrace.

Azur, 24 Cours Roosevelt, 1er, **t 04 91 42 74 38, *www.azurhotel.fr* (*moderate*). Average rooms, with some frills, such as colour TV and garden views (Ⓜ Réformés).

*Montgrand, 50 Rue Montgrand, 6e (off Rue Paradis, behind the Opéra), **t** 04 91 00 35 20 (*inexpensive*). Good budget choice in a safe part of town.

*Little Palace, 39 Bd d'Athènes, 1er, **t** 04 91 90 12 93 (*inexpensive*). Near the Gare St-Charles, at the foot of the grand stair.

Eating Out

The Marseillais claim an ancient Greek – even divine – origin for their ballyhooed *bouillabaisse*: Aphrodite invented it to beguile her husband Hephaestos to sleep so that she could dally with her lover Ares – seafood and saffron being a legendary soporific. Good chefs prepare it just as seriously, and display their *Charte de la Bouillabaisse* guaranteeing that their formula more or less subscribes to tradition: a saffron- and garlic-flavoured soup cooked on a low boil (hence its name), based on *rascasse, fielas* (conger eel), *grondin* (gurnard) and *St-Pierre* (John Dory). When served, the fish is cut up before you and presented on a side dish of *aïoli* or *rouille*, a paste of Spanish peppers.

Le Petit Nice Passédat (*see above*, 7e) (*very expensive*). A haughty gourmet citadel offering ravishing food in its exotic garden. *Closed Sun and Mon in winter, Sun and Mon lunch in summer.*

Michel-Brasserie des Catalans, 6 Rue des Catalans, 7e, **t** 04 91 52 30 63 (*very expensive*). The best and certainly swankiest *bouillabaisse* is served here, to politicians and showbiz people.

Miramar, 12 Quai du Port, 2e, **t** 04 91 91 10 40 (*expensive*). Serves up a reliable, traditional *bouillabaisse* by the Vieux Port; **Oscar**, next door (*moderate*) does an excellent *bouillabaisse*, too. *Closed Sun, Mon lunch and Aug.*

Chez Fonfon, on the little fishing port at Vallon des Auffes, 7e, **t** 04 91 52 14 38 (*expensive*). Overlooking the Château d'If and Frioul, you

A bronze marker in the Quai des Belges pinpoints the spot where the Greeks first set foot in Gaul. And yet Marseille concealed its age until this century, when excavations for the glitzy shopping mall, the Centre Bourse, revealed the eastern ramparts and gate of Massalia, dating back to the 3rd century BC, now enclosed in the Jardin des Vestiges. On the ground floor of the Centre Bourse, the **Musée d'Histoire de Marseille** (*open Mon–Sat 12–7; adm*) displays models, everyday items from ancient times, mosaics and a 3rd-century BC wreck of a Roman ship, discovered in 1974. Elaborate antique models of later ships and items related to trading history are the main focus of the **Musée de la Marine**, in the nearby Bourse (*open daily 10–6; adm*).

Le Panier

The quarter rising up behind the north end of the Vieux Port is known rather oddly as the Panier or 'Basket' after a popular 17th-century cabaret, although its irregular

can feast on a renowned *bouillabaisse* from a charter member. *Closed Sun, Mon lunch and Jan.*

L'Epuisette, near Chez Fonfon, 7e, t 04 91 52 17 82 (*expensive*). A Marseille institution for its seafood. *Closed Sat lunch, Sun eve, Mon.*

Les Mets de Provence Chez Maurice Brun, second floor, 18 Quai de Rive Neuve, 7e, t 04 91 33 35 38 (*expensive*). 50-year-old restaurant with a large three-course lunch menu that starts with eight different *hors-d'œuvre*. *Closed Sat lunch, Sun, Mon lunch.*

Les Arcenaulx, 25 Cours d'Estienne d'Orves, 1er, t 04 91 59 80 30 (*moderate*). A favourite in the old arsenal; fresh market fare. *Closed Sun.*

Le Giraffe, 8 Rue Sainte, 1er, t 04 91 33 21 43 (*moderate*). A new, funky space to sample *nouveau provençal* cuisine. *Closed Sun.*

Le Marseillois, Quai de Port, 2e, a sailing boat moored stern-on, t 04 91 90 72 52 (*cheap*). Plenty of atmosphere.

Au Roi du Couscous, 63 Rue de la République, 2e, t 04 91 91 45 46 (*cheap*). The best couscous in town. *Closed Mon.*

Entertainment and Nightlife

Marseille has lively after-dark pockets, especially around Place Thiers, Cours Estienne d'Orves and Cours Julien. In the last decade, most of the cultural excitement in Marseille has been generated in its theatres – it has more seats per capita than Paris.

Théâtre National de la Criée, 32 Quai de Rive Neuve, 7e, t 04 91 54 70 54. Performances directed by Marcel Maréchal to wide critical acclaim since 1981.

Théâtre Les Bernadines, 45A Rue d'Aubagne, 1er, t 04 91 54 04 57. Experimental dance and theatre.

Théâtre du Merlan, Av Raimu, 14e, t 04 91 11 19 30. There's more of the same at Marseille's second national theatre, in the city's northwest quarter.

Opéra Municipal, Place Reyer, 1er, t 04 91 55 14 99. Italian opera and occasional ballets from the **Ballet National de Marseille** (Roland Petit), 20 Bd Gabès, 8e, t 04 91 32 72 72.

Nightlife in Marseille is concentrated in several distinct zones. Place Jean-Jaurès/Cours Julien and around is the trendiest place.

Espace Julien, 39 Cours Julien, 6e, t 04 96 12 23 40. Jazz, rock and reggae, and a café with live music many nights of the week.

Chocolat Théâtre, 59 Cours Julien, 6e, t 04 91 42 19 29. More music, along with chocolates, pastries and *plats du jour*. *Closed Sun.*

Metal Café, 20 Rue Forbia, 1er, t 04 91 54 03 03. Temple of rock.

Le Trolleybus, 24 Quai de Rive Neuve, t 04 91 54 30 45. A great place for a drink or a dance.

Bars and Latin clubs have also sprouted up along the seafront at the Plage de Borély, 8e.

Café de la Plage, 148 Av Pierre-Mendès-France, t 04 91 71 21 76. Trendy café, with karaoke nights.

weave of winding narrow streets and stairs dates from the ancient Greeks. During the war this warren of secret ways absorbed hundreds of Jews and other refugees from the Nazis hoping to escape to America. In January 1943, Hitler cottoned on and, in collusion with the French police and local property speculators, ordered the dynamiting of the lower Panier. Two buildings were protected: the 17th-century **Hôtel de Ville** on the quay, and behind it, in Rue de la Prison, the **Maison Diamantée**, Marseille's 16th-century Mannerist masterpiece, named after the pyramidical points of its façade. It holds the **Musée du Vieux Marseille** (*open for temporary exhibitions*). The dynamite that blew up the lower Panier was responsible for revealing the contents of the **Musée des Docks Romains**, 2 Place Vivaux (*open winter Tues–Sun 10–5; summer Tues–Sun 11–6; adm*), built over a stretch of the vast 1st-century AD Roman quay.

The Panier retains its original crusty character atop the well-worn steps of **Montée des Accoules** and around **Place de Lenche**, once the market or *agora* of the Greeks.

Signs point the way through the maze to the top of Rue du Petit-Puits and the elegant **Vieille-Charité**, designed by Pierre Puget, a student of Bernini and court architect to Louis XIV – and a native of the Panier. Built by the city fathers between 1671 and 1745 to take in homeless migrants from the countryside, this is one of the world's most palatial workhouses: three storeys of arcaded ambulatories in pale pink stone, overlooking a court with a sumptuous elliptical chapel crowned by an oval dome. It has now been restored as a cultural centre. The Charité's middle gallery on the second floor houses the excellent **Musée d'Archéologie Méditerranéenne** (*open winter Tues–Sun 10–5; summer Tues–Sun 11–6; adm*), featuring a remarkable collection of Egyptian art (second in France, after the Louvre) and beautiful works from ancient Cyprus, Susa, Mesopotamia, Greece and pre-Roman and Roman Italy. The Charité also houses the **Musée d'Arts Africains, Océaniens et Amérindiens** (*open winter Tues–Sun 10–5; summer Tues–Sun 11–6; adm*), with a fascinating collection of ritual artefacts.

South of the Vieux Port: Quai de Rive Neuve and St-Victor

At 19 Rue Grignan, an *hôtel particulier* houses the modern art collection of the **Musée Cantini** (*open mid-Sept–May Tues–Sun 10–5; June–mid-Sept Tues–Sun 11–6; adm*). Permanent displays include Paul Signac's shimmering *Port de Marseille*, and the first Cubist views of L'Estaque that Dufy painted with Braque in 1908; most of the Cantini's post-1960 works have been moved into the new Musée d'Art Contemporain.

On **Quai de Rive Neuve** you'll find ship chandlers' shops, restaurants, and the national theatre, **La Criée**, installed in a former fish auction house. Further along the *quai*, steps lead up to battlemented walls and towers good enough for a Hollywood castle, defending one of the oldest Christian shrines in Provence, the **Abbaye St-Victor**. St-Victor was founded in AD 416 by St Jean Cassien, formerly an anchorite in the Egyptian Thebeaid. Cassien excavated the first chapels into the flank of an ancient stone quarry near a Hellenistic necropolis, which he expanded for Christian use. In the 11th century, when the monks of St-Victor adopted the Rule of St Benedict, they added the church on top, turning the old chapels into a labyrinthine **crypt** (*open daily 8.30–6.30; adm*), with ceilings ranging from six to 60ft high. Some of the beautifully sculpted sarcophagi date from the 3rd century AD and were found to contain seven or eight dead monks crowded like sardines, proof of the popularity of an abbey that founded 300 monastic houses in Provence and indeed Sardinia.

Below St-Victor is Louis XIV's **Fort St-Nicolas**, and beyond that, the **Château du Pharo** (bus no.83 from the Vieux Port), built by Napoléon III. The prize 360° view is from Marseille's watchtower hill – an isolated limestone outcrop towering 531ft above the city, crowned by **Notre-Dame de la Garde** (*bus no.60, from Place aux Huiles on Quai de Rive Neuve*), a neo-Byzantine/Romanesque pile with an unfortunate resemblance to a locomotive topped in turn by France's largest golden mega-Madonna, 33ft high.

La Canebière

They used to make rope here, and the hemp they used has given its name to Marseille's most famous boulevard. This was the high street of French *dolce far niente*, which could swagger and boast that 'the Champs-Elysées is the Canebière of

Paris'. In its day it sported grand cafés, fancy shops and hotels where travellers of yore had their first thrills before sailing off to exotic lands, but these days La Canebière has suffered from an overabundance of banks, airline offices, traffic and pizza stands.

Palais Longchamp and Environs

In 1834 Marseille suffered a drought so severe that it dug a canal to bring in water from the Durance. This 80km feat of aquatic engineering ends with a heroic splash at the **Palais Longchamp**, a delightfully overblown nymphaeum and cascade, populated with stone felines, bulls and a buxom allegory of the Durance, presently under restoration (Ⓜ *Longchamp-Cinq-Avenues; bus no.80 from La Canebière*). Behind the palace stretch the prettiest public gardens in Marseille; in the right wing of the palace itself, some of the same creatures are embalmed in the **Musée d'Histoire Naturelle** (*open winter Tues–Sun 10–5; summer Tues–Sun 11–6; adm*).

The left wing of the Palais Longchamp houses the **Musée des Beaux Arts** (*open winter Tues–Sun 10–5; summer Tues–Sun 11–6; adm*). Local talent is represented by Baroque sculptor, architect and painter Pierre Puget (1671–1745); Françoise Duparc, a follower of Chardin (1726–76), who worked most of her life in England; and the satirist Honoré Daumier (1808–97), who went to prison for his biting caricatures of Louis Philippe's toadies. Here, too, is Van Gogh's roving, bohemian precursor, Adolphe Monticelli (1824–86), who sold his paint-encrusted canvases of fragmented colour for a day's food and drink in the cafés along the Canebière.

Heading South: Le Corbusier

To pay your respects to Modular Man, take bus no.21 from the Bourse down dreary Bd Michelet to the Corbusier stop. In 1945, at the height of Marseille's housing crisis, the French government commissioned Le Corbusier to build an experimental **Unité d'Habitation**, derived from his 1935 theory of 'La Cité Radieuse'. Le Corbusier thought the solution to urban *anomie* and transport and housing problems was to put living-space, schools, shops and recreational facilities all under one roof, balanced on concrete *pilotis*, or stilts; the ground level was reserved for parking.

For a city like Marseille, where people enjoy getting out and about at ground level, the building was a ghastly aberration. But architects were entranced; for the next 30 years thousands of buildings in every city in the world went up on *pilotis*. Of the original extras, only the school, the top-floor gym, and the communal hotel for residents' guests (*see* 'Where to Stay') have survived. The hotel offers tours on appointment.

Marseille's Corniche and Parc Borély

From the Vieux Port, you can catch bus no.83, and pass the Parc du Pharo to **Corniche Kennedy**, a dramatic road overlooking a dramatic coast – now improved with artificial beaches, bars, restaurants, villas and nightclubs. Amazingly, until the road was built in the 1850s, the first cove, the picture-postcard **Anse des Catalans**, was so isolated that the Catalan fisherfolk who lived there could hardly speak French. This now has the most popular (and the only real) sandy beach. From the bus stop Vallon des Auffes you can walk down to the fishing village of **Anse des Auffes** ('of the ropemakers').

As soon as the corniche was built, the wealthy families of Marseille planted grand villas along it. The corniche then descends to the artificial **Plages Gaston Deferre**, where a copy of Michelangelo's *David* holds court at the corner of Av du Prado. Beyond him opens the cool green expanse of **Parc Borély**, with a botanical garden (*open summer Mon–Fri 1–4.45, Sat and Sun 3–6.45; winter Mon–Fri 1–4.45, Sat and Sun 2–4.45*), duck ponds and the **Château Borély**, an 18th-century palace built according to the strictest classical proportions for a wealthy merchant. Behind it, Av de Hambourg leads into Ste-Anne, another former village, where César's Giant Thumb emerges at the Av d'Haïfa, signalling the vast new **Musée d'Art Contemporain** at No.69 (*open winter Tues–Sun 10–5; summer Tues–Sun 11–6; adm*), with a large collection of post-war art (New Realists, Arte Povera, 'individual mythologies' and more).

The *Calanques* and Grotte Cosquer

To continue along the coast from Parc Borély, you'll need to change to bus no.19, which passes by another beach and the **Musée de la Faïence**, 157 Av de Montredon (*open winter Tues–Sun 10–5; summer Tues–Sun 11–6; adm*). More *calanques* follow until the road gives out and the GR98 coastal path to Cassis begins. In 1991, the beautiful jagged **Calanque de Sormiou** made national headlines when local diver Henri Cosquer discovered a subterranean cave above sea level, covered with paintings. The **Grotte Cosquer** (named in honour of its discoverer) is now recognized by prehistorians as a contemporary of Lascaux (c. 27,000 BC). To protect the art, the cave has been walled up, but reproductions are on display at the Exposition Grotte Henri Cosquer.

The Château d'If and Frioul Islands

If in French means yew, a tree associated with death, and an appropriately sinister name for this gloomy precursor of Alcatraz built in 1524 (*open daily 9.30–6.30 exc in rough seas; boats, t 04 91 55 50 09, from the Quai des Belges; departures summer hourly 9–6; winter 9–5*). Even when Alexandre Dumas was still alive, people wanted to see the cell of the Count of Monte-Cristo, and a cell, complete with escape hole, was obligingly made to show to visitors. Real-life inmates included a Monsieur de Niozelles, condemned to six years in solitary confinement for not taking his hat off in front of Louis XIV; and, after the revocation of the Edict of Nantes, thousands of Protestants. The other two islands in the archipelago are **Pomègues** and **Ratonneau**.

Aix-en-Provence

Elegant and honey-hued, the old capital of Provence is splashed by a score of fountains, a charming reminder that its very name comes from its waters, *Aquae Sextiae*. If tumultuous Marseille is in many ways the great anti-Paris, Aix-en-Provence is the stalwart anti-Marseille – bourgeois, cultured, aristocratic, urbane, slow-paced, convivial, and famous for its university.

Aix was chosen as the capital of Provence by the counts of Provence in the early 13th century. In 1409 Louis II d'Anjou endowed the university; and in the 1450s Aix was the

Getting There and Around

The **train** station is on Rue G. Desplaces, at the end of Av Victor-Hugo; there are hourly connections to Marseille, and less often to Toulon. The coach station is in Av de l'Espace, t 04 42 91 26 80, with **buses** to Marseille and direct to the airport, and others to Avignon, Cannes, Nice, Arles and more. For a **taxi**, t 04 42 27 71 11. **Bike hire** is available at Cycles Zammit, 27 Rue Miguet, t 04 42 23 19 53.

Tourist Information

Aix-en-Provence: Place du Gén. de Gaulle, t 04 42 16 11 61, *www.aixenprovencetourisme.com*.

Shopping

The traditional souvenirs of Aix are its almond and glazed melon confits, *calissons*, which have been made here since 1473; buy them at **Béchard**, 12 Cours Mirabeau, t 04 42 26 06 78; or **Confiserie Brémond**, 16 Rue d'Italie, t 04 42 27 36 25. **Le Provence**, 6bis Rue Aude, t 04 42 93 04 54, has local, world-renowned pottery. The better grocers sell the prize-winning *huile d'olive du pays d'Aix*. Visit the markets on Tues, Thurs and Sat am in Place des Prêcteurs and Place de la Madeleine.

Where to Stay

Aix-en-Provence ✉ 13100

Book as early as possible for the festival.
★★★★**Villa Gallici**, Av de la Violette, t 04 42 23 29 23 (*luxury*). A member of the Relais et Châteaux group, with all the warm

atmosphere of an old Provençal *bastide*; charming rooms, garden, parking and pool.
★★★★**Le Pigonnet**, 5 Av du Pigonnet, on the outskirts, t 04 42 59 02 90 (*expensive*). A romantic old *bastide* with rose arbours, pool, lovely rooms furnished with antiques, an excellent restaurant and views out over the Aix countryside.
★★★**Hôtel des Augustins**, 3 Rue de la Masse, just off Cours Mirabeau, t 04 42 27 28 59 (*expensive*). A 12th-century convent, with soundproofed rooms.
★★★**Grand Hôtel Nègre-Coste**, 33 Cours Mirabeau, t 04 42 27 74 22 (*expensive*). Renovated, in an elegant 18th-century mansion, that still hoists guests in its original elevator. No restaurant.
★★★**Mercure Paul Cézanne**, 40 Av Victor Hugo (two blocks from the train station), t 04 42 26 34 73, *mercure.paulcezanne@free.fr* (*moderate*). Exceptional little hotel, well priced, furnished with antiques and serving delicious breakfasts.
★★★**Le Manoir**, 8 Rue d'Entrecasteaux, t 04 42 26 27 20, *www.hotelmanoir.com* (*moderate*). Built around a 14th-century cloister.
★**Artea**, 4 Bd de la République, near the bus station, t 04 42 27 36 00, *www.hotel-artea.fr* (*moderate*). The home of composer Darius Milhaud (who grew up in Aix) is now a comfortable hotel.
★★★**Le Prieuré**, Route des Alpes, 2km from the centre, t 04 42 21 05 23 (*inexpensive*). In a charming 17th-century priory overlooking a garden designed by Le Nôtre.
★★**France**, 63 Rue Espariat, t 04 42 27 90 15 (*inexpensive*). Well-priced and old-fashioned.
★**Paul**, 10 Av Pasteur, near the cathedral, t 04 42 23 23 89 (*inexpensive*). Good budget old-fashioned hotel with garden.

setting for the refined court of Good King René, fondly remembered, not for the way he squeezed every possible sou from his subjects, but for the artists he patronized, such as Francesco Laurana, Nicolas Froment and the Maître de l'Annonciation d'Aix, and the popular festivities he founded, especially the masquerades of the Fête-Dieu. When René died in 1486, France absorbed his realm but maintained Aix's status as the capital of Provence, seat of the unpopular king-appointed Parlement.

In 1789, the tumultuous Count Mirabeau became a popular hero in Aix when he eloquently championed the people and condemned Provence's Parlement as unrepresentative; in 1800, Provence's government was unceremoniously packed off to Marseille.

Aix

Near Aix

★★★**Relais Ste-Victoire**, 10km from Aix, off the N7 in Beaurecueil, **t** 04 42 66 94 98, *relais-ste-victoire@wanadoo.fr* (*expensive–moderate*). Ravishing place to stay or eat, complete with pool, tennis courts, a gourmet restaurant with a lovely veranda and, above all, tranquillity. Air-conditioned rooms with terraces. *Book early*.

★★**Arquier**, 10km west from Aix along the D64, in the Arc Valley next to the 19th-century Aqueduc de Roquefavour, **t** 04 42 24 20 45 (*inexpensive*). Peaceful rooms in a wooded setting, with a restaurant (*moderate*) and terrace along the river.

Eating Out

Clos de la Violette, 10 Rue de la Violette (just north of the cathedral), **t** 04 42 23 30 71 (*expensive*). Under the masterful touch of Jean-Marc Banzo, a lovely place that has long been considered the best in Aix, and does wonderful things with seafood and Provençal herbs. *Closed Sun and Mon lunch*.

Le Bistro Latin, 18 Rue de la Couronne (just north of Place du Général de Gaulle), **t** 04 42 38 22 88 (*moderate*). Imaginative variations on local themes such as lentil and sausage terrine. *Closed Sun and Mon lunch*.

Chez Maxime, 12 Place Ramus, **t** 04 42 26 28 51 (*moderate*). Dine on a shady terrace or by a cosy fireside on delicious meat or fish dishes, accompanied by a list of 500 wines. *Closed Sun and Mon lunch*.

Trattoria Chez Antoine, 3 Rue Clemenceau (just off Cours Mirabeau), **t** 04 42 38 27 10 (*moderate*). Intimate, laid-back, and good for fresh pasta.

La Vieille Auberge, 63 Rue Espariat, **t** 04 42 27 17 41 (*moderate*). Cosy and popular and serves tasty gourmet Provençal dishes by an award-winning chef.

Le Petit Verdot, 7 Rue d'Entrecasteaux, **t** 04 42 27 30 12 (*moderate*). An authentic typical bistro where red wines by the glass are accompanied by ancient jazz records and simple dishes or *charcuterie. Open eves only*.

Laurane et Sa Maison, 16 Rue Victor Leydet, **t** 04 42 93 02 03 (*moderate*). For Provençal cuisine at its best in a cosy atmosphere. Popular with locals, so book ahead.

L'Hacienda, 7 Rue Mérindol (near Place des Cardeurs), **t** 04 42 27 00 35 (*cheap*). Eternally popular, offering the best deal in town. Provençal at lunch, Tex-Mex by night. *Closed Sun and Mon*.

Entertainment and Nightlife

Outside the festival season, the large student population keeps a number of jazz clubs in business.

Hot Brass, Chemin de la Plaine-des-Verguetiers, west of the centre, **t** 04 42 21 05 57. Jazz club.

L'IPN, 23 Cours Sextius (downstairs). For a good stomp.

Le Richèlm, 24 Rue Verrerie, **t** 04 42 23 49 29. A private club – you may have to dress up to get in.

Club 88, at La Petite Calade north on the RN7, **t** 04 42 23 26 88. Club outside town.

Le Scat, Rue de la Verrerie, **t** 04 42 23 00 23. Live music at weekends.

Cours Mirabeau and Musée Granet

Canopied by its soaring plane trees, decked with fountains and flanked by cafés, banks, *pâtisseries*, and *hôtels particuliers* of the 17th and 18th centuries, **Cours Mirabeau** is the centre stage for Aixois society, though at the moment extensive roadworks make it a bit of an eyesore. Laid out in 1649, it begins in Place du Général de Gaulle and includes the house where Cézanne grew up (No.55); at the far end is the **Fontaine du Roi René**, with a statue of the good monarch.

South of Cours Mirabeau, the **Musée Granet** (*Place St-Jean-de-Malte; open daily 10–12 and 2–6; closed Tues; adm*) houses Aix's art and antiquities, including 17th-century portraits of Aixois nobility, and eight small canvases by Cézanne.

Vieil Aix

North of Cours Mirabeau, the narrow lanes and squares of Vieil Aix concentrate some of Provence's finest architecture and shopping, especially off the elegant cobbled and fountained Place d'Albertas. In the adjacent Place des Prêcheurs stands the church of **Ste-Marie-Madeleine**, which has a pleasant Second Empire façade and paintings by Rubens and Van Loo, although the show-stopper is the central panel of the *Triptych of the Annunciation*, a luminous esoteric work of 1445, attributed to Barthélémy d'Eyck. Aix's flower market lends an intoxicating perfume to Place de la Mairie, a lovely square framed by the stately, perfectly proportioned **Hôtel de Ville** (1671) and the flamboyant **Tour de l'Horloge** (1510), with clocks telling the phase of the moon and wooden statues that change with the season. From here, Rue Gaston de Saporta leads to the **Musée du Vieil Aix** at No.17 (*open winter Wed–Mon 10–12 and 2–5; summer 10–12 and 2.30–6; closed Tues; adm*). It stores some quaint paintings on velvet, a bevy of *santons* in a 'talking Christmas Crib' and 19th-century marionettes.

Cathédrale St-Sauveur and the Tapestry Museum

Rue Gaston de Saporta continues north to Place de l'Université, once part of the forum of Roman Aix, and the **Cathédrale St-Sauveur**, a dignified patchwork of periods and styles. The interior has naves for every taste: from right to left, Romanesque, Gothic and Baroque. The cathedral's famous treasure, Nicolas Froment's *Triptyque du Buisson Ardent* (1476), is under restoration, but there is a replica in the foyer.

At the back of the cathedral, the 17th–18th-century residence of Aix's archbishops, **L'Archevêché**, is the setting for the festival's operas. It also houses the **Musée des Tapisseries** (*open daily 10–11.45 and 2–5.45; closed Tues; adm*), containing three sets of lighthearted Beauvais tapestries, hidden under the roof during the Revolution.

Around Aix: Cézanne and the Montagne Ste-Victoire

Paul Cézanne spent an idyllic childhood roaming Aix's countryside with his best friend, Emile Zola, and as an adult painted those same landscapes in a way landscapes had never been painted before. The **Atelier Cézanne**, 9 Av Paul Cézanne (*open winter daily 10–12 and 2–5; summer daily 10–12 and 2.30–6; adm*), the studio he built in 1897, has been rather grudgingly maintained as it was when the master died in 1906.

The rolling countryside around Aix is the quintessence of Provence for those who love Cézanne: the ochre soil, the dusty green cypresses, the simple geometry of the old *bastides* and villages and the pyramidal prow of the blueish limestone **Montagne Ste-Victoire**. This is encircled by the striking 60km **Route Cézanne** (D17), beginning along the south flank in the wooded park and Italianate château of **Le Tholonet** (3km from Aix; take the bus from La Rotonde). The ascent of the Montagne Ste-Victoire takes about two hours (bring sturdy shoes, a hat and water) and there's a 17th-century stone refuge with water and a fireplace if you want to spend a night. Crowning the precipitous west face, the 55ft **Croix de Provence** (which Cézanne never painted) has been here, in one form or another, since the 1500s. Northerly approaches to the summit of Ste-Victoire begin at Les Cabassols or **Vauvenargues**. The 14th-century Château de Vauvenargues was purchased by Picasso, and he is buried here.

Northern Provence: the Vaucluse

Some of the Midi's most civilized countryside and loveliest villages are in the Vaucluse. These have not passed without notice, of course, and the region is now what the Côte d'Azur was forty years ago. Vaucluse's two cities, Orange and Avignon, will be found on pp.762–71. The remainder divides neatly into two areas: the mountainous Luberon, a *pays* of especially pretty villages; and Provence's northern wall.

The Luberon

As is the case with many a fair maiden, the Luberon's charms are proving to be her undoing. This is Peter Mayle country, the stage set for his surprise bestseller *A Year in Provence*. The trickle of outsiders who began settling here in the 1950s, permanently or in holiday homes, has now become a flood. In danger of being destroyed by a rash of outsiders and unplanned holiday villas, the Parc Régional du Luberon was founded

Getting Around

Public transport is woefully inconvenient in the Luberon; it's possible to get around the villages, but just barely. Apt is on an SNCF branch line, with a few **trains** daily to Cavaillon and Avignon. **Buses** from Apt, **t** 04 90 74 20 21, leave from the Place de la Bouquerie by the river; there are one or two daily to Roussillon, Avignon and Aix, stopping at Bonnieux and Lourmarin; also one to Digne.

Cavaillon is on the main Avignon–Marseille rail line, and there are also buses to L'Isle-sur-la-Sorgue and Carpentras, to Apt and Avignon, and very occasionally to Bonnieux and other western Luberon villages.

Where to Stay and Eat

La Tour d'Aigues ✉ 84240

Les Fenouillets, just outside the village on the D956, **t 04 90 07 48 22 (*inexpensive*). Rooms are simple, but there's a pool nearby, and an inexpensive restaurant with outdoor tables, a good bet for lunch.

Lourmarin ✉ 84160

Lourmarin has some of the best restaurants.

****Le Moulin, Rue du Temple, **t** 04 90 68 06 69, *moulin@provence-luberon.net* (*expensive*). A one-time olive mill with views over the château and nearby hills, now Provençal

meets Art Nouveau in its tasteful decoration, and the restaurant serves attractive and delicious Provençal dishes. *Book early. Closed mid-Jan–Feb.*

***Le Mas de Guilles, t 04 90 68 30 55, *www.guilles.com* (*expensive*). Just east of the village, an immaculately restored farmhouse, with tennis court, pool and gardens. *Closed Nov–Dec.*

L'Hostellerie le Paradou, Route d'Apt, **t 04 90 68 04 05 (*moderate*). In a dreamy setting north of Lourmarin on the D943, at the entrance to the Combe de Lourmarin, with a rocky pool and a restaurant. *Half-board only in summer.*

La Fenière, Rte de Lourmarin-Cadenet, **t** 04 90 68 11 79 (*expensive*). Expert, innovative cooking with old Provençal favourites: batter-fried courgette flowers and a hearty *daube. Closed Sun eve and Mon, and Tues lunch.*

Le Bistrot, Av Raoul Dautry, **t** 04 90 68 29 74 (*moderate*). A choice of well-priced Provençal or Lyonnais cuisine. *Closed Thurs, and Mon lunch July–Aug.*

La Récréation, 15 Rue Philippe de Girand, **t** 04 90 68 23 73 (*moderate*). Fresh organic Provençal fare and good lamb dishes with garlic on the terrace. *Closed Wed.*

Apt and Around ✉ 84400

***Auberge du Luberon, 17 Quai Léon Sagy, **t** 04 90 74 12 50, *www.auberge-luberon-*

in 1977; it is now ranked as a UNESCO Biosphere Reserve. Park information is available from the **Maison du Parc du Luberon**, 1 Place Jean Jaurès in Apt, with exhibits, slide shows and a gift shop (*t 04 90 04 42 00, www.parc-du-luberon.com*).

The southern end of the Park, the Pays d'Aigues, is the sleepier corner of the Luberon, a rolling stretch of good farmland sheltered by the Grand Luberon mountain to the north. Of the smaller villages, a few stand out: **Grambois** to the northeast is a neatly rounded hilltop hamlet, a Saracen stronghold in the 8th–10th century and later one of the twelve citadels of Provence. **Ansouis**, north of Pertuis on the D56, is a *village perché* built around the sumptuously furnished Château de Sabran (*open April–Oct daily 2.30–6; Feb and Mar closed Mon; Nov–Jan Sat and Sun only 2.30–6; adm*). For an airier, more pleasant castle without the bric-a-brac, there's **La Tour d'Aigues**, an elegant if roofless Renaissance shell just to the east. Heading west, and still on the south flank of Montagne du Luberon, **Cucuron** was used as the set for *Le Hussard sur le toit* (*The Horseman on the Roof*), the film adaptation of a novel by Jean Giono. Further west, into the heart of the Luberon, **Lourmarin** was the last home of Albert

peuzin.com (*moderate*). Rooms and a good restaurant (*expensive*) on the river; the speciality is rabbit with figs, and dishes with *confit d'Apt. Closed Nov–mid-Dec.*

★★**Relais de Roquefure**, on the N100, 4km west, t 04 90 04 88 88 (*moderate*). An old stone-built inn with a pool and an inexpensive restaurant. *Closed Jan–mid-Feb.*

★★**Le Palais**, Place Gabriel-Péri, t 04 90 04 89 32 (*inexpensive*). A simple but comfortable and friendly budget choice. *Closed Nov–Feb.*

Bernard Mathys, 5km northwest in Gargasa, t 04 90 04 84 64 (*expensive–moderate*). A lovely restaurant in an 18th-century house for a delightful meal with all the trimmings; the vegetables are especially ravishing. *Closed Tues and Wed, mid-Jan–mid-Feb.*

Auberge du Presbytère, Place de la Fontaine in Saignon, t 04 90 74 11 50 (*expensive–inexpensive*). Two 10th- and 11th-century buildings with a magnificent view over the Luberon, charming rooms and an intimate restaurant (*moderate*); book. *Closed mid-Nov–mid-Feb.*

Roussillon ✉ 84220

★★★**Mas de Garrigon**, just outside the village, t 04 90 05 63 22 (*expensive*). One of the few real luxury places in Roussillon, a well-restored farmhouse with all the amenities, lovely rooms and a gourmet restaurant; but both, unfortunately, are woefully overpriced. *Restaurant closed Nov and Dec; half-board only in summer.*

★★**Rêve d'Ocres**, Route de Gordes, t 04 90 05 60 50 (*moderate*). Adequate and much cheaper, with convenient parking. *Closed Nov–Feb.*

Le Val des Fées, Rue R. Casteau. t 04 90 05 64 99. For a simple meal, with lovely views over the ochre from its terrace (*moderate*).

Bonnieux ✉ 84480

★★★**Hostellerie du Prieuré**, t 04 90 75 80 78 (*expensive–moderate*). Lovely old hotel in a 17th-century priory in the village centre; the rooms have a view and there's a garden and a gourmet restaurant. *Closed Nov–Mar.*

★★**Hôtel Le César**, Place de la Liberté, t 04 90 75 96 35, *www.hotel-cesar.com* (*moderate–inexpensive*). An 18th-century hotel with comfortable rooms in the village centre. Avoid the street side and ask for rooms with the fantastic views over the Luberon.

Le Fournil, on lovely Place Carnot, t 04 90 75 83 62 (*moderate*). A dining room excavated in the cliff and light fresh fare. *Closed Mon and Jan–Feb.*

Ménerbes ✉ 84560

★★★**Le Roy Soleil**, Le Fort, along the Route des Beaumettes, t 04 90 72 25 61 (*expensive*). In a 17th-century building in an olive grove overlooking Ménerbes, with a pool and tennis and excellent restaurant. *Closed Dec–mid-Mar.*

Camus, and he is buried in the cemetery. This is an unusual village, densely packed almost to the point of claustrophobia; many of its houses have tiny courtyards facing the street – too cute for its own good, as its villages are beset by tourists.

South of the Durance and 7km from Cadenet is the **Abbaye de Silvacane** (*open April–Sept daily 9–7; Oct–Mar Wed–Mon 10–1 and 2–5; closed Tues; adm*). A Benedictine community had already been established here when the Cistercians arrived in 1147, and made the land flourish until bad frosts in the 1300s killed all the olives and vines. The church is austere and uncompromising; even the apse is a plain rectangle. The cloister now contains a herb garden, around a lovely broken fountain. Note the capitals on the arcades, carved, oddly, with maple leaves.

The narrow roads south of the N100 in the northern Luberon are some of the most beautiful in the region, passing through **Vitrolles** or through **Montfuron**, with its lofty ruined castle, on their way to the Pays d'Aigues. The summit of the Grand Luberon, the **Mourre Nègre**, has views that take in all of the Vaucluse and beyond. **Saignon**, 5km southeast of Apt, is a beautiful *village perché* between two crags, boasting a well-preserved 12th-century church of Ste-Marie.

Apt

The capital of the Luberon (pop. 15,000 and growing) also claims to be the 'World Capital of Candied Fruits'. Everyone comes here for the huge Saturday market, but no one has ever admitted to liking the place. Apt has a good, well-laid-out **Musée d'Histoire et d'Archéologie**, 27 Rue de l'Amphithéâtre (*open June–Sept Mon–Sat 10–12 and 2–5, Sun 2–6; Oct–May Mon, Wed, Thurs and Fri 2–5, Sat 10–12 and 2–5; adm*), with archaeological finds going back to the Palaeolithic period, recent Roman and medieval finds from the town centre and a display of Apt's once-flourishing craft of faïence, which had its heyday in the 18th century.

Red Villages North of Apt

Rustrel, northeast of Apt on the D22, was an ochre-quarrying town until 1890. The huge ruddy mess they left is called the **Colorado**; there are hazily marked routes around it for tourists and a map for sale in a kiosk in the car park. **Roussillon**, to the southwest, occupies a spectacular hill-top site, and so it should, for centuries of mining have removed nearly everything for miles around. The Association Terre d'ocres, an organization that wants to get the ochre business going again, has an information centre in the village, and can direct you on a walk through the quarries.

West of Apt, and south of the N100, is a string of truly beautiful villages that have become the high-rent district of the Luberon, one of the poshest rural areas in France. Don't come here looking for that little place in the country to fix up; it's all been done, as long as 40 years ago, first by the Parisians and then by a wave of outsiders, including many Americans. Biggest and busiest of the villages, **Bonnieux** is also one of the loveliest, a belvedere overlooking all the Petit Luberon. **Lacoste**, west of Bonnieux on the D109, is a trendy *village perché*. Overlooking the village is a gloomy ruined castle, once home of no less a personage than the Marquis de Sade, and recently bought and restored by Pierre Cardin. Continuing along the D109, you come to **Ménerbes,** honey-coloured, artsy and cuter than cute (with an attitude to match). As the former home of Peter Mayle it attracts a constant stream of fans. From here the D188 continues through grand scenery almost to the top of the Petit Luberon, and **Oppède-le-Vieux,** with its even gloomier ruined castle. To the west, **Maubec** with its Baroque church may be the Luberon village of your dreams.

The large town of **Cavaillon,** famous for its melons, has an undistinguished Roman arch, a small archaeological museum, an odd-shaped, rather forbidding cathedral, and an ornate 18th-century synagogue, as well as a big market on Mondays and a melon festival in early July.

The Plateau de Vaucluse

The Plateau de Vaucluse is the high ground that runs between the Luberon and Mont Ventoux to the north. The striking *village perché* of **Gordes** used to make its living from olives. Today, Gordes has found something easier and more profitable: art tourism, with exhibits and concerts in the summer. Gordes was a fierce Resistance stronghold in the war and suffered for it, with wholesale massacres of citizens and the destruction of much of the village. All the damage the Nazis did has been repaired; the village centre, all steep, cobbled streets and arches, is extremely attractive. The château (*open 10–12 and 2–6; adm*) has a superb Renaissance fireplace, the second largest in France, and a hodgepodge of art. The **Village des Bories** just south of Gordes, off the D2 (*open daily 9–sunset; adm*) has a collection of *bories*, or dry-stone huts, restored as a rural museum.

The **Abbaye de Sénanque,** the loveliest of Provence's Cistercian Three Sisters, lies 4km north of Gordes on the D177, built in the warm golden stone of the Vaucluse and set among lavender fields and oak groves. The **church** (*open Feb–Oct Mon–Sat 10–12 and 2–6, Sun 2–6; Nov–Jan Mon–Fri 2–5, Sat and Sun 2–6; adm*), begun about 1160, shows the same early Cistercian seriousness as Silvacane. Most of the monastic buildings have also survived, including a lovely **cloister,** the *chauffoir,* the only heated room, where the monks transcribed books, and a refectory.

Fontaine-de-Vaucluse

The little Vaucluse river called the Sorgue makes its daylight debut at **Fontaine-de-Vaucluse.** In the spring, and occasionally in winter, it pours out at a rate of as much as 200 cubic metres per second. The Fontaine is exquisite, but the 540 or so residents of the town of Fontaine-de-Vaucluse have not been able to keep it from becoming one of Provence's more garish tourist traps. Incredibly, many of the attractions are worthwhile. Norbert Castaret's **Musée de Spéléologie (Le Monde Souterrain)** (*open daily 9.30–12 and 2–6; June–Sept 9.30–7; closed mid-Nov–Feb; adm*) is a 'subterranean world' museum of underground rarities and informational exhibits overseen by France's best-known cave explorer.

Most surprising of all, in a sharp modern building, is the **Musée d'Histoire 1939–1945** (*open Jan–April daily 10–12 and 2–5; May–June and Sept–Oct till 6; July–Aug*

Getting Around

Carpentras is the node for what little there is of **coach** transport in the northern Vaucluse, with good connections to Avignon and Orange, one to Marseille; also one or two a day to Vaison-la-Romaine, Beaumes-de-Venise and Gigondas. There are also several daily SNCF **trains** to Orange and Avignon.

Where to Stay and Eat

Gordes ✉ 84220

★★Auberge de Carcarille, southwest of town on the D2, t 04 90 72 02 63 (*expensive–moderate*). An honest establishment outside the village, a carefully restored *mas* with pretty rooms, some with balconies, and a reasonable restaurant specializing in fish and game. *Half-board only in summer.*

Le Bouquet des Basilic, Route de Murs, t 04 90 72 06 98 (*moderate–cheap*). Fresh, organic and veggie-orientated food, good lunches and puddings. *Closed Thurs.*

Fontaine-de-Vaucluse ✉ 84800

★Hostellerie Le Château, t 04 90 20 31 54, (*rooms expensive, restaurant moderate*). In Fontaine's old *mairie*, with a terrace overlooking the Sorgue. Excellent old-fashioned cooking includes delicate sautéed frogs' legs and *rouget à la tapenade*. Five rooms.

★★Le Parc, near the river and centre at Les Bourgades, t 04 90 20 31 57 (*inexpensive*). Simple but pretty hotel; its restaurant (*moderate*) serves some of the best Italian food in Provence. *Closed Nov–mid-Feb; restaurant closed Wed.*

Carpentras ✉ 84200

★★Le Fiacre, 153 Rue Vigne, t 04 90 63 03 15 (*moderate–inexpensive*). For something cosy in the centre, an elegant old hotel in an 18th-century building. The small top-floor room offers a fantastic view of Mont Ventoux.

★Hôtel du Théâtre, 7 Av Albin Durand, t 04 90 63 02 90 (*inexpensive*). The budget choice; the friendly proprietor may try to corner you into a game of chess.

Le Vert Galant on Rue des Clapiès, t 04 90 67 15 50 (*expensive– moderate*). For original cooking and fresh seafood. *Closed Sun, and Mon lunch.*

Malaucène ✉ 84340

★★Hostellerie La Chevalerie, Rue des Remparts, t 04 90 65 11 19 (*moderate*). Peaceful and comfortable rooms; the restaurant has a charming terrace. *Closed Wed, and Tues eve out of season.*

★★L'Origan, Cours Isnards, t 04 90 65 27 08 (*inexpensive*). Clean, central, and shipshape; the restaurant offers some hearty cooking – dishes such as guinea-fowl with *morilles*. *Closed Nov–mid-Mar, and Mon.*

Domaine des Tilleuls, Rte de Mont Ventoux, t 04 90 65 22 31 (*moderate*). A new B&B hotel with spacious, austerely decorated rooms and a large garden with a pool.

La Maison, Hameau de Piolon, outside Beaumont-du-Ventoux, t 04 90 65 15 50 (*moderate*). The best cooking in the area, with only one menu, though it has a wide selection of dishes, many with a touch of the

---

daily 9–7; Nov, Dec and Mar Sat and Sun only 10–12 and 2–5; adm), a government-sponsored institution that recaptures the wartime years vividly with two floors of explanatory displays, newsreels and magazines, weapons and other relics. As at Gordes, Resistance life around Fontaine-de-Vaucluse was no joke. On the way out, peek in at the **Musée Pétrarque** (*open Mar–Oct 10–12 and 2–6; closed Tues and Oct–Feb; adm*), a subdued look at the life and times of the poet during his stay in the town in the early 1300s.

Carpentras

Perhaps because of its long period under papal rule and its own bishops, Carpentras has character and a subtle but distinct sense of place. It's a lively town, especially

southwest; try the *pintadeau en croûte*. Also has three rooms. *Closed Nov–Mar and Mon and Tues; July–Aug eves and Sun lunch only.*

Around Mont Ventoux ✉ 84390

★★★**Hostellerie du Val de Sault**, Ancien Chemin d'Aurel, Sault, t 04 90 64 01 41, *valdesault@aol.com* (*luxury– moderate*). Handsome hotel 2,493ft up, facing Mont Ventoux, with only 11 rooms and five suites surrounded by trees and gardens, and equipped with a pool, gym, *salle de pétanque* and restaurant. *Closed mid-Nov–Mar. Half-board in summer.*

Chalet-Reynard, on Ventoux, at the corner of the D164 and D974, t 04 90 61 84 55 (*moderate–cheap*). The only restaurant for miles, a cosy, wood-lined bar where the local lumberjacks tuck into boar and a *pichet de rouge* at lunchtime. *Closed Tues, and Oct–April.*

Beaumes-de-Venise/ Vacqueyras ✉ 84190

★★★**Hôtel Montmirail**, once part of the spa, t 04 90 65 84 01, *www.montmirail.com* (*moderate*). Secluded hotel with pool, garden and restaurant. *Closed mid-Oct–mid-Mar.*

Auberge St-Roch, Av Jules Ferry, in Beaumes, t 04 90 65 08 21 (*moderate*). Modest restaurant: seafood and local dishes. *Closed Dec.*

★**Hôtel Restaurant des Dentelles**, Vacqueyras, t 04 90 65 86 21 (*inexpensive*). Two-star comfort; so-so restaurant.

Gigondas ✉ 84190

★★**Les Florets**, Route des Dentelles, 2km outside the village, t 04 90 65 85 01 (*expensive–moderate*). In the middle of a vineyard, simple rustic rooms and peace and quiet. *Closed Jan–mid-Mar.*

Le Mas de Bouvau, Route de Cairanne, just west of Gigondas in Violès, t 04 90 70 94 08 (*inexpensive*). Charming family-run hotel-cum-restaurant in the vines, serving specialities from southeast France: duck *confit*, *magret*, *foie gras*, pigeon and rabbit. *Closed Sun eve and Mon.*

L'Oustelet, Place Gabriel Andéol, t 04 90 65 85 30 (*expensive*). In a neoclassical building, serving good beef in wine. *Closed Sun Mon, and mid-Nov–Jan.*

La Farigoule, Le Plan de Dieu, Violès, t 04 90 70 91 78 (*inexpensive*). Pleasant B&B in an old farmhouse; they also rent bikes. *Closed Nov–Mar.*

Séguret ✉ 84110

★★★**Domaine de Cabasse**, on the D3 towards Sablet, t 04 90 46 91 12, *www.domaine-de-cabasse.fr* (*moderate*). Part of a Côtes-du-Rhône estate on the D23 towards Sablet; comfortable rooms with terraces, a pool, and an excellent restaurant that has truffles in season, vegetables from their farm, and other extravagant dishes year-round. *Closed Nov–Mar.*

★★★**La Table du Comtat**, in the village, t 04 90 46 91 49 (*expensive*). Well known for refined dishes such as *julienne de truffe en coque d'œuf. Closed Oct–June Tues and Wed.*

Le Mesclun, also in the village, t 04 90 46 93 43 (*moderate*). For simpler fare, and an *à la carte* selection of local delights. *Closed Sun eve and Mon.*

when the gorgeous produce of the Comtat Venaissin, 'The Garden of France', rolls in for the Friday market.

Undoubtedly the **Cathédrale St-Siffrein** (*open daily 10–12 and 2–6; closed Sun pm*) is one of the most absurd cathedrals in Christendom. So many architects, in so many periods, and no one has ever been able to get it finished and get it right. Begun in the 1400s, remodellings and restorations proceeded in fits and starts until 1902. Some of the original intentions can be seen in the fine Flamboyant Gothic portal on the southern side, called the **Porte Juive** because Jewish converts were taken through it, in suitably humiliating ceremonies, to be baptized. Just above the centre of the arch is Carpentras' famous curio, the small sculpted *Boule aux Rats* – a globe covered with rats – probably a joke on an old fanciful etymology of the town's name: *carpet ras*, or 'the rat nibbles'. The 28ft Roman **Triumphal Arch**, tucked in a corner between the Cathedral and the Palais de Justice (1640), was built about the same time as that of Orange, in the early 1st century AD. Anyone who hasn't yet seen Orange's would hardly guess this one was Roman at all. Of all the ancient Provençal monuments, this shows the bizarre Celtic quality of Gallo-Roman art at its most stylized extreme.

Behind the cathedral and palace, two streets north up Rue Barret, is the broad Place de l'Hôtel de Ville, marking the site of Carpentras' Jewish Ghetto. Before the Revolution, over 2,000 Jews were forced to live walled in and obliged to pay a fee any time they wanted to leave. All that remains of the old ghetto is the **synagogue** at the end of the square. Built in 1741, it has a glorious decorated interior in the best 18th-century secular taste (*open Mon–Thurs 10–12 and 3–5, Fri 10–12 and 3–4*).

Mont Ventoux

Wind-swept **Mont Ventoux**, a bald, massive humpbacked massif, is the northern boundary stone of Provence. The base for visiting the mountain is **Malaucène**, a friendly village on the road from Carpentras to Vaison. Further up the mountain, the almost permanent winds make themselves known and vegetation becomes more scarce. Coming down the eastern side of the mountain takes you into one of the least-visited backwaters of Provence, a land of shepherds, boar and *cèpes*.

Les Dentelles de Montmirail

Montmirail's 'lace' is a small crown of dolomitic limestone mountains, opposite Mont Ventoux on the other side of Malaucène. This is superb walking country, and superb wine country. The D90 takes you into the Côtes-du-Rhône region, beginning with **Beaumes-de-Venise**, the metropolis of the Dentelles. There's a ruined castle to explore, and a small archaeological museum. **Vacqueyras** is a dusty little crossroads devoted entirely to wine. A few kilometres north, **Gigondas**, like so many wine villages in the south, is much smaller than its fame: sweet and small, overlooking the immaculate vineyards, full of shops to *déguster* the eponymous red nectar. Most of the tourists home in on **Séguret**, built on a terrace over the vine-striped Ouvèze plain.

Vaison-la-Romaine

Vaison, in all its 2,400 years, has never been able to make up its mind which side of the River Ouvèze it wanted to be on. Locals have always been wary of the river's mighty potential for destruction, and Vaison began on the heights south of the Ouvèze as a Celtic *oppidum*. In the late 2nd century BC, the Romans took control, and moved the town down the hill, where it prospered spectacularly for the next five centuries. In perhaps the 700s, the counts of Toulouse acquired the site of the old *oppidum* and built a castle on it. Most people abandoned the Roman town for the safety of the heights, the beginnings of what is now the Haute-Ville. In the 1900s, on the move once more, the Vaisonnais were abandoning the Haute-Ville for the river bank, though there was a huge flood in 1992 that drowned 30 people.

Between 1907 and 1955 a local abbot uncovered almost 11 hectares of **Roman Vaison's foundations** (*open Nov–Jan Wed–Mon 10–12 and 2–4.30; Mar–May and Oct*

Tourist Information

Vaison-la-Romaine: Place du Chanoine Sautel, t 04 90 36 02 11, *www.vaison-la-romaine.com*.

Where to Stay and Eat

Vaison-la-Romaine ✉ 84110

***Le Beffroi**, Rue de l'Evêché, up in the Haute-Ville, t 04 90 36 04 71, *www.le-beffroi.com* (*expensive–moderate*). Picturesque 16th-century house, furnished to match. A bargain for its quality. *Closed mid-Jan–mid-Mar*.

La Bastide de Vaison, west of Vaison on the D977, t 04 90 36 03 15 (*moderate*). Modernized old farmhouse with a pool. *Closed mid-Nov–April*.

Le Burrhus, 1 Place Montfort, t 04 90 36 00 11 (*inexpensive*). Comfortable rooms with an Art Deco touch, and a shady terrace. *Closed mid-Dec–mid-Jan.*

La Fête en Provence, Place du Vieux Marché in the Haute-Ville, t 04 90 36 36 43, *www.la-fete-en-provence.com* (*expensive–moderate*). A hidden hotel which serves its own *foie gras de canard*, followed by a *magret* of lamb with olives. *Closed mid-Nov–mid-April, and Wed.*

Le Brin d'Olivier, 4 Rue du Ventoux, t 04 90 28 74 79 (*expensive–moderate*). Vaison was something of a gastronomic desert until 1995, when Olivia and Didier Rogne opened this intimate, romantic restaurant with an inner courtyard, the ideal place to feast on Olivia's fresh, imaginative Provençal cuisine, where fresh herbs hold pride of place. *Closed Wed, Thurs and Sat lunch out of season.*

daily 10–12.30 and 2–6; June–Sept daily 9.30–6.15; Feb and Oct daily 10–12.30 and 2–5.30; Site Puymin open July and Aug daily 9.30–6.45; same adm for both, also includes cathedral cloister). There are two separate areas, the **Quartier de la Villasse** and the **Site Puymin**. The Villasse is the smaller of the two areas; from the entrance, a Roman street takes you past the city's **baths** (the best parts are still hidden under Vaison's post office) and the **Maison au Buste d'Argent**, a truly posh villa with two *atria* and some mosaic floors. It has its own baths, as does the adjacent **Maison au Dauphin**; beyond this is a short stretch of a **colonnaded street**. The Puymin quarter has more of the same: another villa, the **Maison des Messii**, is near the entrance. Beyond that, however, is an *insula*, or block of flats for the common folk, as well as a large, partially excavated quadrangle called the **Portique de Pompée**, an enclosed public garden with statuary that was probably attached to a temple. On the opposite side of the *insula* is a largely ruined *nymphaeum*. From here you can walk uphill to the **theatre**, restored and used for summer concerts, and the **museum**, with the best of the finds from the excavations.

The fascinating **Cathedral of Notre-Dame-de-Nazareth**, west of the ruins on Av Jules Ferry, was begun in the 6th century. Its **apse** is the oldest part; the rest of the structure dates from a rebuilding that began in the 1100s. Among its many mysteries is a rectangular **maze**, near the top of the façade, and a triangular figure that may be a mystic representation of the sun. The nave is Romanesque at its best, and the arcaded apse is magnificent.

The **Haute-Ville** – the medieval town – is a splendid sight atop its cliff, a honey-coloured skyline of stone houses under the castle of the counts of Toulouse. Almost abandoned at the turn of the century, it is becoming quite chic now, with restorations everywhere. You reach it by crossing the Ouvèze on a **Roman bridge**.

The Provençal Alps

The Alpes-Maritimes

These are real Alps – arrogant crystalline giants, which make their contempt felt as you crawl through the valleys beneath. The best parts have been set aside as the **Parc National du Mercantour**. Established only in 1979, the Parc consists of a central 'protected zone', a narrow strip of the most inaccessible areas, including the Vallée des Merveilles with its prehistoric rock carvings, and a much larger 'peripheral zone' that includes all the villages from Sospel to St-Etienne-de-Tinée and beyond. The

Getting Around

In all the hinterlands of Provence, this is the region most difficult to navigate by **car**, and the most convenient for public transport.

One of the best ways to see the Vallée de la Roya is from that alpine rarity – a **train**. The railway line from Nice that runs to Cuneo in Italy offers spectacular scenery and serves all of the local villages: L'Escarène, Sospel, Breil, St-Dalmas and Tende.

Sospel also has daily **buses** to and from Menton, which take 20 minutes. There is a range of buses from Sospel into the smaller valleys (t 04 93 04 01 24).

St-Martin-Vésubie can be reached by coach from the bus station in Nice (Cars TRAM, t 04 93 89 47 14); buses for St-Sauveur and St-Etienne in the Tinée also leave from here.

Park information: Parc National du Mercantour, 23 Rue d'Italie, Nice, t 04 93 16 78 88, *www.parc-mercantour.fr*.

Where to Stay and Eat

St-Martin-Vésubie ✉ 06450

★★La Bonne Auberge, Place Félix Faure, t 04 93 03 20 49 (*inexpensive*). A welcoming and pretty place with nice rooms and a cosy cellar restaurant (*moderate*). *Closed mid-Nov–Jan.*

★Hôtel des Alpes, across the square, t 04 93 03 21 06 (*inexpensive*). If the *auberge* is full, settle here. *Closed Jan.*

Le Cavalet, outside St-Martin in Le Boréon, t 04 93 03 21 46 (*moderate*). Simple abode in a dreamy lakeside setting, at the forest edge, with excellent restaurant. *Closed Nov.*

Sospel ✉ 06380

★★Hôtel des Etrangers, 7 Av de Verdun, t 04 93 04 00 09, *sospel@ifrance.com* (*moderate*). Only marginally the most expensive, and has a pool. *Closed Dec–Feb.*

★★L'Auberge Provençale, Route de Menton, a mile from the centre, t 04 93 04 00 31, *aubpro@aol.com* (*moderate*). Also has a terrace with a magnificent view over Sospel. *Closed Thurs, and mid-Nov–mid-Dec.*

Domaine du Paraïs, off the D2566 towards Moulinet at La Vasta (you need a car), t 04 93 04 15 78 (*moderate*). A villa taken over by officers during the war, which has now been proudly restored as a *chambre d'hôte*.

L'Escargot d'Or, 3 Bd de Verdon, t 04 93 04 00 43 (*moderate*). The best place to eat in Sospel, specializing in meat fondues. Ring to reserve, and to check they're open out of season – they'll close if they anticipate a quiet night.

Saorge ✉ 06540

Lou Pountin, Rue Revelli, t 04 93 04 54 90 (*cheap*). Excellent pizzas. *Closed Wed.*

La Brigue ✉ 06430

★★Le Mirval, Rue St-Vincent Ferrier, t 04 93 04 63 71 (*inexpensive*). The best choice here; some rooms have views, and the management can arrange a trip (expensive) into the Vallée des Merveilles. *Closed Nov–Mar.*

Levens ✉ 06450

La Vigneraie, 82 Rte de St-Blaise, t 04 93 79 70 46 (*cheap; full board inexpensive*). Friendly *auberge* on the Nice road below the village. Comfortable rooms, and renowned for its Sunday lunch. *Closed mid-Oct–Jan.*

most spectacular alpine fauna, and the sort you're most likely to see, are the birds of prey: golden eagles, falcons and vultures. A recent addition, reintroduced from the Balkans after becoming extinct here, is the lammergeyer. On the ground, there's the ubiquitous stoat or ermine, the bulkier marmot, and plenty of boars, foxes, mouflons (wild mountain sheep), chamois and *bouquetins* (ibex). Half the flowers of the whole of France are represented here. The symbol of the park is the spiky *Saxifrage multiflora*, one of 25 species found nowhere but here. Edelweiss also exists here.

The Valleys of the Vésubie and the Tinée

The Vésubie flows into the Var near **Levens**, a big walled village high on a small plain with a big church and a scattering of small private art galleries. Beneath it, the main road up the valley, the D2565, follows the scenic **Gorges de la Vésubie**. At the top of the valley, **St-Martin-Vésubie** is the only town for a great distance in any direction, and a base for tackling the upper part of the Mercantour. It's as unaffectedly cute as a town can be; in the delightful and shady town square is an old fountain where the mineral waters of its spa used to flow.

There's nothing splashy or spectacular about the Tinée, serenely beautiful even by alpine standards. In the lower part of the valley, the scenery is as much indoors as out; prosperity in the 15th and 16th centuries allowed the villages of the Lower Tinée to decorate their modest churches with fine Renaissance frescoes by artists of the Nice school. You will find examples in the chapels of **La Tour** and **Clans**. Continuing up the valley, the next stop is **St-Sauveur-sur-Tinée**, throbbing metropolis of the valley, with its 496 souls. The uppermost part of the Tinée, following the D2205, runs through the northern half of the Parc Mercantour. Near the source of the Tinée river is **St-Etienne-de-Tinée**, which has two painted rural chapels.

The Vallée de la Roya

Along the road from Nice, **Sospel** greets you with rusty cannons and machine guns, pointing out over the road from Fort St-Roch (*open July–Sept Tues–Sun 2–6; April and May weekends only*). The fortress, almost entirely underground, shows only a few blockhouses, in a sort of military Art Deco; it dates from a 1930s counterpart of the Maginot Line. In the last war the town suffered considerable damage, now entirely, and lovingly, restored, including Sospel's landmark, the Pont Vieux, the base of which dates back to the 10th century. The tiny tower in the middle of the bridge was the toll on the salt road; in the Middle Ages, salt from the flats of Toulon and Hyères was taken by boat to Nice, and from there by convoys of mules to Piedmont and Lombardy. Make sure you take a wander around the winding streets of the old town, and arcaded Place St-Nicolas with a 15th-century fountain across the bridge.

The Vallée de la Roya is a cul-de-sac: if you travel north beyond Saorge on the N204, there's no way out unless you retrace your steps or continue through the tunnel to Cuneo, Italy. The mountains close in immediately, with the **Gorges de Bergue et de Paganin**; these end at the village of **St-Dalmas-de-Tende**, the gateway to the western offshoot of the **Vallée des Merveilles**. From about 1800 BC, the Ligurian natives of these mountains began scratching pictures and symbols on the rocks. They kept at it for the next 800 years, until over 100,000 inscriptions decorated the valley. Most defy any conclusive interpretation – circles, spirals and ladders or chequerboard patterns of the kind found all over the Mediterranean. Why they were made is an open question; one very appealing hypothesis is that this valley, beneath Mont Bégo, was a holy place and a pilgrimage site, and that the carvings can be taken as *ex votos* made by the pilgrims. As the prime attraction of the Parc Mercantour, the valley gets its share of visitors these days. Besides the carvings, the landscape itself is worth the hike, including a score of mountain lakes, mostly above the tree line, all in the shadow of the rugged, uncanny **Mont Bégo**, highest of the peaks around the Roya.

Tende, a dour slate-roofed *bourg*, is the only town in the Upper Roya. No longer a dead end since the road tunnel through to Italy was built, it has become a busy place by local standards. On Av du 16 Septembre 1847, the **Musée des Merveilles** (*www.museemerveilles.com; open Mar–mid-Oct daily 10–6; mid-Oct–Feb daily 10–5; closed Tues; adm*) has copies and photos of the rock engravings.

East of St-Dalmas-de-Tende, the D143 takes you to **La Brigue**, in a minute region (partly in Italy) that grows apples and pears and raises trout. It has some fine paintings in the late Gothic church of St-Martin: three altarpieces by Ludovico Brea and his followers, along with Italian paintings from the 17th and 18th centuries. Even better are Giovanni Canavesio's wonderful Renaissance frescoes at **Notre-Dame-des-Fontaines**, a rural chapel 4km from La Brigue. Done in the 1490s, these include 26 large scenes of the Passion of Christ in the nave, and on one of the side walls a tremendous *Last Judgement*, a gentle reminder that God wasn't joking. The frescoes in the choir itself are by another hand, Giovanni Baleison, done in the 1470s in a more old-fashioned style that still shows the influence of Byzantium.

The Alpes de Haute-Provence

There is something of the Wild West in this *département*, complete with lofty plateaux and canyons. Provence's wide open spaces are full of lavender fields and fresh air, a place to white-water raft, hang glide, ride, climb or hike.

Castellane, south of Lac du Castillon, is the capital of the Grand Canyon du Verdon, the base for visiting one of the greatest natural wonders in Europe. There is a pretty *mairie* and a church, where the 597ft ascent up the Castellane's landmark square rock begins. The most surprising thing about the **Grand Canyon du Verdon** is that it was not 'discovered' until 1905. The name 'Grand Canyon' was a modern idea; when the French became aware of its existence, comparisons with Arizona were inevitable. It does put on a grand show: sheer limestone cliffs following the meandering course of the Verdon; in many places there are vast panoramas down its length. There are roads along both sides, though not for the entire distance. The best views are from the Corniche Sublime (D71) on the south side; if you want to explore the bottom, ask about trails and the best approaches (it's a long trek) at the Castellane tourist office.

Directly west of the Canyon, a less spectacular section of the Verdon has been dammed up, forming the enormous **Lac de Ste-Croix**; there is another dam further

Getting Around

Buses are so rare they aren't worth the trouble, but it can be fun seeing this region by the scenic, recently modernized narrow-gauge rail-line familiarly called the **Train des Pignes**, from Nice to Digne; it follows the Var, and a few trains stop at villages along the way. This is not the SNCF, but a separate line called Chemin de Fer de Provence.

Where to Stay and Eat

Castellane ✉ 04120

★★★**Hôtel du Commerce**, Place de l'Eglise, t 04 92 83 61 00 (*moderate*). Friendly and comfortable. *Closed Nov–April.*

★★**Grand Canyon**, 14km east of the village of Aiguines, at the Falaise des Cavaliers, t 04 94 76 91 31 (*expensive– moderate*). The best views of the canyon, looking 300m down on to the Verdon from its glassed-in restaurant terrace. *Closed Nov–April.*

★★**La Forge**, t 04 92 83 62 61 (*inexpensive*). At the foot of the rock next to the church, with a terrace from which to view the village and the walkers going up and down the *roc*. *Closed mid-Dec–Jan.*

Moustiers-Ste-Marie ✉ 04360

★★★★**La Bastide de Moustiers**, just outside the village at La Grisolière, t 04 92 70 47 47 (*expensive*). After a day's tramping through the Grand Canyon, you can sleep in comfort and splurge for a memorable dinner at celeb-chef Alain Ducasse's 17th-century hotel with 12 individually fashioned rooms, Jacuzzi, pool, riding stable, etc. The food is predominantly local, picked from the kitchen garden, and innovative. *Restaurant closed Jan and Feb.*

★★**Belvédère**, t 04 92 74 66 04 (*inexpensive*). Up in the village. *Closed mid-Nov–Jan.*

Les Santons, Place de l'Eglise, t 04 92 74 66 48 (*expensive–moderate*). Enjoys a gorgeous setting on top of the village overlooking the torrent; the refined Provençal cooking matches the views. *Closed Mon eve and Dec–Jan; book.*

Quinson ✉ 04500

★★**Relais Notre-Dame**, in the middle of the Gorges du Verdon at Quinson, t 04 92 74 40 01 (*inexpensive*). A garden and pool, but most importantly a real, warm welcome and very good food. *Closed mid-Dec–mid-Mar.*

Digne ✉ 04000

★★★★**Hôtel du Grand Paris**, 19 Bd Thiers, t 04 92 31 11 15, *grandparis@wanadoo.fr* (*expensive– moderate*). Distinguished hotel in a restored 17th-century monastery, with an excellent restaurant featuring classic cuisine with truffles. *Closed mid-Dec–mid-Mar.*

★★**Hôtel de Provence**, 17 Bd Thiers, t 04 92 31 32 19 (*inexpensive*). Central and comfortable, and has a good restaurant.

downstream, and the next 40km of the river valley are under water too: the **Gorges du Verdon**, in parts as good as the Canyon, but sacrificed forever to the beaverish Paris planners. In **Quinson**, visit at least the exterior of the new Norman Foster-designed **Musée de Préhistoire des Gorges du Verdon**, in the village centre (*open Feb–mid-June and mid-Sept–mid-Dec Wed–Mon 10–6; mid-June–mid-Sept daily 10–8*), which claims to be the biggest of its kind in Europe.

The **Plateau de Valensole**, north of the Verdon and the Lac de Ste-Croix, is a hot, dry plain of olive and almond trees, and one of the big lavender-growing areas of Provence – come in July to see it in full bloom. **Riez**, in the middle, is an old centre for lavender-distilling, now adapted to tourism. Ruined medieval houses have been restored, and artists and potters have moved in. At the west edge of town are four standing columns of a Roman Temple of Apollo, and a 6th-century baptistry that is one of the few surviving monuments in France from the Merovingian era.

To the east, some 15km on the D952, **Moustiers-Ste-Marie** gets all the attention, spectacularly hanging on the west cliffs of the Grand Canyon du Verdon. Another popular base for visiting the Canyon, Moustiers was Provence's main centre for painted ceramics; the blue and yellow faïences were often works of art in their own right. Today potters, some talented and some pretty awful, clutter the village streets, capitalizing on the perfect clay of the region (and on the tourists).

Another of Moustiers' distinctions is the **Cadeno de Moustié**, a 783ft chain suspended between the tops of two peaks overlooking the village. A knight of the local Blacas family, while a prisoner of the Saracens during the Crusades, made a vow to put it up if he ever saw home again.

Digne means 'worthy'. The capital of the Alpes de Haute-Provence *département*, and the only city in a long stretch of mountains between Orange and Turin, it has one thriving boulevard of cafés and touristic knick-knackery mixed with smart shoe-shops, posh chocolates and bookshops. Out of town is something entirely unexpected: the **Fondation Alexandra David-Neel** (*27 Av du Maréchal Juin; guided tours with her former secretary; July–Sept daily at 10.30, 2, 3.30 and 5; otherwise at 10.30, 2 and 4*), the former home of a truly remarkable Frenchwoman who settled here in her 'Himalayas in miniature' after a lifetime exploring in Tibet. There are exhibits of Tibetan culture, photographs and crafts on sale; the Dalai Lama has visited twice.

Villages of the Central Var

West of the military town of Draguignan are some of Provence's loveliest and most typical landscapes. Though this area gets its share of summer folk, it isn't as chic or colonized as the Luberon. **Lorgues** is the first village, with a complete ensemble of 18th-century municipal decorations: a fountain, the dignified church of St-Martin, and the inevitable avenue of plane trees, one of the longest and fairest in Provence. Further north, there are a number of pretty villages around the valley of the Nartuby: **Ampus**, **Tourtour**, over-restored but up on a height with views down to the sea, and **Villecroze**, with its vaulted lanes, built up against a tufa cliff.

Aups was a Ligurian settlement, and a Roman town. It has a reputation for being different; a monument in the town square records Aups' finest hour, when the citizens put up a doomed republican resistance to Louis Napoléon's coup of 1851. Like the other villages, it has not completely escaped Riviera modernism. The **Musée Simon Ségal** (*open mid-June–mid-Sept daily 10–12 and 4–7; adm*), founded by the eponymous Russian artist, has his and other 20th-century works. **Salernes**, south of Aups, has been known for over 200 years for its small, hexagonal terracotta floor-tiles called *tomettes* that are as much a trademark of Provence as lavender. Further west, **Sillans** has lately been calling itself Sillans-la-Cascade, to draw attention to the 118ft waterfall just south of the village (it dries up in summer).

South of Salernes, **Entrecasteaux** is dominated by a 17th-century castle, completely restored in the 1970s by a Scotsman named McGarvie-Munn. Further south, the artificial **Lac de Carcès** has been a favourite with fishermen since the dam was built in the 1930s. To the east are the biggest bauxite mines in France, which are playing hell with one of the most impressive medieval abbeys in Provence. This is the **Abbaye du**

Where to Stay and Eat

Lorgues ✉ 83510

Chez Bruno, Campagne Mariette, t 04 94 85 93 93 (*expensive*). For something special, book a table at this old *mas*, where the chef does wonderful things with truffles. *Closed Sun eve and Mon*. There are also three luxurious rooms and one suite.

Tourtour ✉ 83690

★★★★**Bastide de Tourtour**, Montée St Denis, t 04 98 10 54 20, www.verdon.net (*luxury–expensive*). Modern Relais et Châteaux complex with pool, tennis and all the amenities, including a highly reputed restaurant with a blend of Provençal cooking and classic French. *Restaurant closed Mon–Fri lunch, exc July and Aug.*

★★★**Le Mas des Collines**, Route de Villecroze, t 04 94 70 59 30 (*expensive–moderate*). Charming and more affordable little hotel, offering tranquillity, air-conditioned rooms and a pretty pool overlooking the valley below Tourtour. *Restaurant closed Nov–Mar.*

★★★**Auberge St-Pierre**, 3km east at St-Pierre-de-Tourtour, Rte d'Ampus, t 04 94 70 57 17 (*moderate*). An up-to-date working farm built around a hotel; exceptional rooms in an 18th-century house and a fine restaurant, with authentic Provençal food – largely the farm's own produce. Also a pool, gym, tennis, archery and fishing. Beware of the hostess when she is tired. *Closed mid-Oct–Mar. Restaurant closed Wed.*

Salernes ✉ 83690

★**Allègre**, Cours Jean Bart, t 04 94 70 60 30 (*inexpensive*). An old establishment, with a bit of faded grandeur and some of its 1920s décor. *Closed mid-Nov–mid-Mar.*

La Fontaine, Place du 8 Mai 1945, t 04 94 70 64 51 (*moderate*). For a simple *magret* or stewed rabbit; outside tables too. *Closed Sun eve, Mon, and Jan.*

Sillans ✉ 83690

Restaurant des Pins, on the D32, t 04 94 04 63 26 (*moderate*). Very popular restaurant in an old stone house, serving grilled meats with shrimps for openers. Also a few rooms (*inexpensive*), but book early for summer. *Closed mid-Jan–Feb, and Wed eve and Thurs out of season.*

Thoronet (*open April–Sept Mon–Sat 9–7, Sun 9–12 and 2–7; Oct–Mar Mon–Sat 10–1 and 2–5, Sun 10–12 and 2–5; adm*), the first Cistercian foundation in Provence; the present buildings were begun about 1160. The mines themselves (nearby, but screened by trees) have caused some subsidence, and cracks are opening in the walls. Nevertheless, this purest and plainest of the Cistercian 'Three Sisters' of Provence (with Silvacane and Sénanque) is worth a detour. It displays sophisticated Romanesque architecture stripped to its bare essentials, with no worldly splendour to distract a monkish mind, only grace of form and proportion. Behind the blank façade is a marvellously elegant interior; note the slight point of the arches, a hint of the dawning Gothic. The **cloister** with its heavy arcades is equally good.

Its inhabitants might be unaware of it, but **Cotignac** is the cutest of the cute, a Provençal village where everything is just right. There are no sights, but one looming peculiarity: the tufa cliffs that hang dramatically over it. In former times these were hollowed out for wine cellars, stables or even habitations; today there are trails up to them for anyone who wants to explore. Westwards on the D13/D560, **Barjols** has little cuteness but much more character. This metropolis of 2,000 souls owes its existence to leather-tannin. It retains an urban and sombre air: elegant rectangular squares of the 18th century, and moss-covered fountains and *lavoirs* similar to the ones in Aix. At the tourist office you can get a '*circuit des fontaines*' to guide you round all 42 of them.

The Côte d'Azur: East to West

Just west of Italy begins that 20km swath of Mediterranean hyperbole that represents the favourite mental image of the French Riviera. Although first tamed by the Romans, this tasty morsel of the Côte d'Azur long remained a world apart, ruled until the mid-19th century by the Grimaldis of Monaco, when bad feelings over Napoleon brought the first English and Russians, with their titles and weak lungs, to winter here. The scenery is breathtaking, one mighty mountain after another plummeting drunkenly into the sea, traced by hairpinning corniche roads.

Where the shores of the eastern Riviera tend to be all shingle, the beaches of the western Côte d'Azur are mostly soft sand. The crowds, cars, art, yachts, boutiques and prices are less intense as well, with the outrageous exception of St-Tropez. And just behind these careless seaside pleasures bulge two of the world's most ancient chunks of land, the porphyry Esteral and the dark forested Maures.

Menton

The Côte d'Azur starts on the Italian frontier, where a wall of mountains blocks out the cold so that lemons can blossom all year. Menton declared its independence from the Grimaldis in 1848 and became part of France in 1860. Soon after, the town attracted a community of 5,000 Brits, led by Queen Victoria herself in 1883. Despite a poor beach and an elderly population, Menton is magnificently situated, sprinkled with some of the coast's finest gardens, and has a healthy attitude to relaxation compared to the hard-edged glamour-pusses to the west.

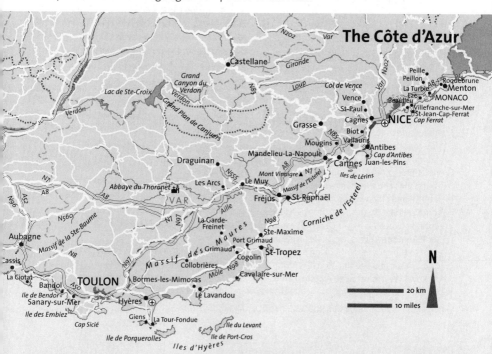

Getting Around

The *Métrazur* **trains** between St-Raphaël and Ventimiglia, and all others running between Nice and Italy, stop in Menton (Menton-Centre). There's also a stop – Menton-Garavan – behind the port.

Buses depart from the bus station on the Esplanade du Careï every 15mins to Nice, by way of Roquebrune-Cap-Martin and Monte-Carlo. There's a **taxi** rank outside the Menton-Centre station, or call **t** 04 92 10 47 00.

Tourist Information

Menton: Palais de l'Europe, 8 Av Boyer, **t** 04 92 41 76 76, *www.villedementon.com*.

Where to Stay

Menton ✉ 06500

Luxury–Expensive

****Hôtel des Ambassadeurs, 3 Rue Partouneaux, **t** 04 93 28 75 75, *www.ambassadeurs-menton.com*. The last *grande dame* of Menton, gracious, spacious, pink and balconied, and slap bang in the middle of town. There's nearly every luxury you'd expect for the price, but no pool. The restaurant, **Fiori**, is very popular.

Expensive

***Napoléon, 29 Porte de France, **t** 04 93 35 89 50, *www.napoleon-menton.com*. A delight; the rooms may be decorated in comfortable dark brown like a favourite great aunt's, but it has a pool, soundproofed, air-conditioned rooms, a private beach, and friendly staff. *Closed mid-Nov–mid-Dec.*

***L'Aiglon, 7 Av de la Madone, **t** 04 93 57 55 55, *www.hotelaiglon.net*. Belle Epoque, stylish and chic, with spindly antiques and high ceilings. By the pool, there is a lovely arbour. *Closed Nov–mid-Dec.* The restaurant, **Le Riaumont**, serves regional cuisine in a glassed-in terrace overlooking its pool. *Closed Sun, and Sat and Mon lunch, and Nov.*

***Royal Westminster, 28 Av Félix-Faure, **t** 04 93 28 69 69, *www.hotelmenton.com/hotel-royal-westminster*. Part of a smart hotel group with quiet rooms furnished in sea colours, views over the bay, huddles of elderly ladies on the terrace playing poker and Scrabble, and a *pétanque* court. *Closed Nov.*

Inexpensive

Hôtel de Londres, 15 Av Carnot, **t 04 93 35 74 62, *www.hotel-de-londres.com*. Nothing is too much trouble for the cheerful host, who will even lend you a mattress for the stony beach. Rooms are simply but attractively decorated, with air-conditioning, and some overlook the garden with its little bar and games area. *Closed Nov–Dec.*

Pension Beauregard, 10 Rue Albert Ier, **t** 04 93 28 63 63, *beauregard.menton@wanadoo.fr*. A good bargain below the station, a sweet place with a quiet garden. *Closed Nov.*

Eating Out

All along Rue St Michel masses of restaurants vie for your attention with tempting displays spilling out into the street that somehow miss the mark.

Pierrot-Pierrette, Place de l'Eglise, up at Monti, on the Rte de Sospel, **t** 04 93 35 79 76 (*moderate*). Complements the panoramic views with delicious fresh blue trout. *Closed Mon, and mid-Dec–mid-Jan.*

La Coquille d'Or, on the corner of Quai Bonaparte, **t** 04 93 35 80 67 (*moderate*). A bit of a tourist trap but, surprisingly, also packs in crowds of locals for the excellent *bouillabaisse* and paella. *Closed Wed and Nov.*

Le Nautic, 27 Quai de Monléon, **t** 04 93 35 78 74 (*moderate*). Serves up every possible fish dish, including *bouillabaisse*. *Closed Mon in Sept–June.*

A Braisade, 66 Rue Longue, **t** 04 93 35 65 65 (*moderate*). Tucked away in the old town, serving Provençal favourites.

Darkoum, 23 Rue St Michel 23, **t** 04 93 35 44 88 (*moderate–cheap*). Tasty Moroccan dishes. The house speciality is *pastilla*, a fragrant concoction with pigeon and almonds. *Closed Mon and Tues in winter.*

Menton is squeezed between the mountains and a pair of shingle-beached bays: the Baie de Garavan, on the Italian side, where villas and gardens overlook the yacht harbour, and the Baie du Soleil which stretches 3km west to Cap Martin. In between these two bays stands a little 17th-century harbour bastion that Jean Cocteau converted into the **Musée Cocteau** (*open daily 10–12 and 2–6; closed Tues; adm*) in the late 1950s, to hold his playful series of *Animaux fantastiques* and a tapestry of *Judith et Holopherne*, while the happier love affairs of the Mentonnais are portrayed in the *Innamorati* series. This theme of Menton's lovers was first explored by Cocteau in his decorations (1957) for the **Salle des Mariages** (*open Mon–Fri 8.30–12.30 and 2–5; adm*), in the Hôtel de Ville in Rue de la République.

At the western end of Menton, the frothy pink and white summer home of the princes of Monaco, the Palais Carnolès (1717), is now an art museum, the **Musée des Beaux-Arts Palais Carnolès**, 3 Av de la Madone (*bus 3; open daily 10–12 and 2–6; closed Tues; adm*). It holds Ludovico Bréa's luminous *Madonna and Child with St Francis*, several oil paintings attributed to Leonardo da Vinci, and all the previous winners from Menton's very own Biennale of painting. Other works were donated by the English landscape and portrait artist Graham Sutherland.

The tall, narrow 17th-century houses of Menton's Vieille Ville are knitted together by anti-earthquake arches that span stepped lanes named after old pirate captains and saints. It's hard to believe that the quiet main street, **Rue Longue** (the Roman Via Julia Augusta), was, until the 19th century, the main route between France and Italy.

From Rue Longue, the shallow stairs of the Rampes St-Michel lead up to the ice-cream-coloured church of **St-Michel** (1675), and the equally charming Baroque **Chapelle des Pénitents Blancs**, headquarters of one of the old Riviera's many religious confraternities. The Montée du Souvenir leads to the top of the Vieille Ville, where the citadel was replaced in the 19th century by the romantic, panoramic **Cimetière du Vieux Château** (*open summer daily 7–8; winter daily 7–6*). From the cemetery, Boulevard de Garavan leads to the **Jardin Exotique du Val Rahmeh** (*entrance on the Av St-Jacques; open summer Wed–Mon 10–12.30 and 3–6; winter Wed–Mon 10–12.30 and 2–5; closed Tues; adm*), planted with more than 700 tropical and subtropical species.

Roquebrune-Cap Martin

The medieval village of Roquebrune is all steep, winding, arcaded streets with a fair number of over-restored houses, galleries and ateliers, culminating at the top in the **château** (*open daily 10–12.30 and 2–6.30; July and Aug till 7.30; adm*), first erected in the 10th century. The view from the top floor is by far the best of the castle's attractions. Under the castle, Rue du Château, leads to Rue de la Fontaine and Chemin de St. Roch and a remarkable contemporary of the castle: a **1,000-year-old olive tree**.

In the 1890s a pair of empresses, Eugénie (widow of Napoléon III) and Elisabeth ('Sissi') of Austria, made Roquebrune's peninsula of **Cap Martin** an aristocratic enclave. Le Corbusier died here in 1965 while swimming off the white rocks beside what is now **Promenade Le Corbusier**. A spectacular path leads from Cap Martin to Monte-Carlo (a four-hour walk).

Where to Stay and Eat

Along the Corniches ✉ 06190

★★★★**Vista Palace, t** 04 92 10 40 00,
www.*vistapalace.com* (*luxury*).
The ultimate in luxury, hanging on a 1,000ft
cliff on the Grande Corniche, with a God's-
eye view over Monaco; also a heated pool,
squash, gym, and sauna. The hotel's cliff-
hanging restaurant, **Le Vistaero**, offers
some of the Côte's most talked-about
cuisinee. *Closed Feb, and Thurs in winter.*

★★**Westminster**, 14 Av L.-Laurens, **t** 04 93 35
00 68, *hotel@westminster. com* (*inexpensive*). Down on the poor sinners' level, with a
pretty garden terrace near the junction of
the lower two Corniches. *Closed Dec.*

Roquebrune ✉ 06190

Au Grand Inquisiteur, 18 Rue du Château,
Roquebrune, **t** 04 93 35 05 37 (*moderate*). In a
former sheepfold cut into the rock, serving
well-prepared Provençal dishes like *fleurs de
courgette farcies. Closed Mon and Tues lunch,
and mid-Nov–mid-Dec.*

Hôtel des Deux Frères, Place des Deux-Frères,
Roquebrune, **t** 04 93 28 99 00,
www.*lesdeuxfreres.com* (*moderate*).
Ethereally light and airy. The rooms are small
but white muslin canopies draped over the
beds, whitewashed walls and endless views
make up for the lack of space. Friendly,
knowledgeable staff serve excellent regional
dishes on the terrace. *Closed mid-Nov–mid-
Dec; restaurant closed Sun eve and Mon.*

Monaco

Big-time tax-dodgers agree: it's hard to beat the sanitized tax haven of Monaco for
comfort and convenience when the time comes to snuggle down with your piggy
chips. Rainier III, chairman of the board of Monaco Inc., will probably go down in
history as the Principality's greatest benefactor. Through landfill and burrowing he
has added a fifth to his realm and on it built more (but certainly not better) than any
of his predecessors, creating a Lilliputian Manhattan.

History

Lords of Monaco since 1308 and once rulers of a mini-empire including Antibes and
Menton, the Grimaldis today own 194 hectares of sea-hugging land. Here Rainier
presides as the living representative of the oldest ruling family in Europe, and
Europe's last constitutional autocrat. When the Grimaldis faced bankruptcy in the
mid-19th century, Prince Charles III looked for inspiration to the Duke of Baden-Baden,
whose casino lured Europe's big-spending aristocrats every summer. Monaco, Charles
decided, would be the winter Baden-Baden, and he founded the Société des Bains de
Mer (SBM) to operate a casino, with the Principality as chief shareholder. In 1870 the
coffers were so full that Charles abolished direct taxation in Monaco. In another dark,
bankrupt period, the 1950s, Rainier III gave his realm a fairytale cachet by wedding the
American film actress Grace Kelly, bringing in a much-needed injection of socialites.

Monte-Carlo

Set back in the sculpture-filled gardens of Place du Casino rises the most famous
building on the whole Côte d'Azur: the **Casino de Monte-Carlo** (1863), a fascinating
piece of Old World kitsch. Anyone over 21 with a passport can visit the *machines à sous*
section, with one-armed bandits and other mechanised games. To get past the
mastodons at the doorway to the glittering Salon of Europe, you have to fork out €10;

here, American roulette, craps and blackjack tables click and clatter away just as in Las Vegas or Atlantic City. €20 gets you into the *salons privés (open June–Oct from 4pm Mon–Fri to 3pm Sat and Sun; Nov–May daily from 3pm; adm exp)* – quieter, more intense – where oily croupiers under gilt rococo ceilings accept limitless bets on roulette and *chemin de fer*. The casino's bijou opera-theatre, the red and gold **Salle Garnier** (*open only for performances*), was designed by Charles Garnier, inaugurated

Getting There and Around

You can **drive** into Monaco along the Corniche Inférieure, or take the **helicopter** from Nice airport if you're in a hurry (7mins, from €60, Heli Air Monaco, t 92 05 00 50, Monacair t 97 97 39 00). **Buses** leave hourly from Nice Airport (terminal 2; 9am–9pm) or **taxi** (45mins); buses every 15mins between Menton and Nice stop at several points along the Corniche, including right outside the Monte-Carlo casino. The Monaco/Monte-Carlo **train** station is in Av Prince-Pierre.

Small as it is, Monaco is divided into several towns, Monte-Carlo to the east, Fontvieille by the port, Monaco-Ville on the rock, and La Condamine below; there's a **public bus** network to save you some legwork. More importantly, free **public lifts and escalators** operate between its tiers of streets. **Taxis** can be called (24hrs) on t 93 15 01 01.

Tourist Information

Monaco: 2a Bd des Moulins, Monaco, t 92 16 61 16, *www.monaco-tourisme.com*.
Note: In Monaco, if the telephone number has only 8 digits, you must dial t 00 377 before calling, even from France. If the number has 10 digits, it operates like a French number.
Money: the unit of currency is the euro; Monégasque coins with Prince Rainier's image are in circulation but are rarely accepted outside the Principality.

Where to Stay

Monaco ✉ 98030, t (00 377–)
Monte-Carlo
★★★★**Hôtel de Paris**, Place du Casino, t 92 16 30 00, *www.montecarloresort.com* (*luxury*). Opened in 1865 by the SBM for gambling tsars and duchesses, now with direct access to the modern-day Riviera prerequisite, a thalassotherapy centre. Also contains the famous Café de Paris.
★★★★**Hermitage**, Square Beaumarchais, t 92 16 40 00, *www.montecarloresort.com* (*luxury*). Also owned by the SBM, a beautiful Belle Epoque hotel perched high on its rock, with an Italian loggia and 'Winter Garden' designed by Gustave Eiffel.
★★★**Balmoral** 12 Av de la Costa, t 93 50 62 37, *www.hotel-balmoral.mc* (*expensive*). An old hotel next door, for a third of the price, with a view of the sea.
★★★**Hôtel Alexandra**, 35 Bd Princesse-Charlotte, t 93 50 63 13, *hotelalexandra@imcn.com* (*expensive*). More turn-of-the-last-century opulence, gilded and refurbished.
★★★**La Maison d'Or**, 21 Rue du Portier, t 93 50 66 66, *www.maisondor.com* (*expensive*). Pristine 20th-century copy of a 19th-century villa, with terraces looking out through the yacht masts to the sea.

Monaco-Ville
★★★**Terminus**, 9 Av Prince-Pierre, t 92 05 63 00, *www.terminus.monte-carlo.com* (*expensive*). A concrete high-rise block, but it has been refurbished.
★★**Le Versailles**, 4 Av Prince-Pierre, t 93 50 79 34, *hotelversailles@monte-carlo.mc* (*moderate*). Near the station, with a reasonable French-Italian restaurant
★★**Hôtel de France**, 6 Rue de la Turbie, t 93 30 24 64, *hotelfrance@monte-carlo.mc* (*moderate*). Staid, peachy building in a quiet street full of art galleries.
★★**Helvetia**, 1 bis Rue Grimaldi, t 93 30 21 71, *www.monte-carlo.mc/helvetia* (*moderate–inexpensive*). Old-fashioned, overlooking a pedestrianized shopping street lined with orange trees. The least expensive hotel in the Principality.

by Sarah Bernhardt in 1879 and backed by pots of SBM money. SBM's frothy **Hôtel de Paris** is next door to the casino.

La Condamine and Fontvieille

You can see the Prince's very own **Collection de Voitures Anciennes** (*open daily 10–6; adm*); or the **Musée Naval** (*open daily 10–6; adm*). More unusual are the prickly

Eating Out

Monaco t (00 377–)

Louis XV, in the Hôtel de Paris, **t** 92 16 20 76 (*luxury, see* above). In Monte-Carlo, those who make it big at the tables, or have simply made it big at life, dine in this incredible golden setting. Edward VII as Prince of Wales, while dining here with his mistress Suzette, was served a crêpe smothered in kirsch, curaçao and maraschino that its 14-year-old maker, Henri Charpentier, accidentally set alight, only to discover that the flambéeing improved it a hundredfold. The prince himself suggested that they name the new dessert after his companion. Under Alain Ducasse, the youngest chef ever to earn three Michelin stars, the cuisine is once again kingly. *Closed Tues and Wed, Dec, and mid-Feb–mid-Mar.*

Le Vistamar, at the Hermitage (*see* above), **t** 92 16 27 72 (*expensive*). Offers incredibly fresh fish dishes like the *pescadou à pesca du matin*, which brings the fish from the sea to your plate in under an hour at lunchtime.

L'Hirondelle, 2 Av Monte-Carlo, **t** 92 16 49 30 (*expensive*). Gourmets on a diet can take solace here, where lovely fresh and light dishes taste as good as they look, accompanied by swallow-eye views over the sea. *Closed eves.*

Le St Benoît, 10 ter Av de la Costa, just below the Hermitage (enter the car park and take the lift up), **t** 93 25 02 34 (*moderate*). Superb seafood to go with the views from the terrace, high above the port. *Closed Mon; July and Aug open Mon eve.*

Loga Café, 25 Bd des Moulins, **t** 93 30 87 72 (*moderate*). Dine sumptuously on Monégasque specialities like *barbagiuan* (a fried cheese- and leek-filled pie) or *stocafi* (stockfish stewed with tomatoes, herbs, wine and olives) on the terrace.

Le Texan, 4 Rue Suffren Reymond, **t** 93 30 34 54 (*cheap*), just up from the port. Vivacious, rowdy, Tex-Mex atmosphere. The place to rub shoulders with Crown Prince Albert and Boris Becker over a pizza.

Entertainment and Nightlife

Nightlife in Monaco is a glitzy, bejewelled fashion parade. January is the opera, theatre and ballet season. Call **t** 92 16 22 99 for information.

Monte-Carlo Sporting Club, Av Princesse-Grace, **t** 92 16 22 44. Summer discotheque, Las Vegas-style floor shows, dancing, restaurants and casino.

SBM/Loews Monte-Carlo, 12 Av des Spélugues. Similar offerings.

American Bar at the Hôtel de Paris. Similar offerings.

Jimmy'z, 26 Av Princesse-Grace, **t** 92 16 22 77. Monte-Carlo's number one, fantastical dance club where entrance is free but the drinks require a small bank loan. Now with Cuban cigar bar. Upstairs is the **Bar et Bœuf** (*expensive*), **t** 92 16 60 60, the Philippe Starck-designed Alain Ducasse restaurant and bar, open late. *Closed Nov–May.*

Le Stars N' Bars, 6 Quai Antoine 1er, **t** 97 97 95 95. Young people from all along the coast drive to this sports bar and club. *Closed Mon in winter.*

Flashman's, 7 Av Princesse-Alice, **t** 93 30 09 03. Beer-drinking in a Brit-run imitation pub. Open till the wee hours.

Ship and Castle, 42 Quai des Sanbarbani, **t** 92 05 76 72. Pub which also serves food.

Cinéma d'été, 26 Av Princesse-Grace, **t** 08 36 68 00 72. Open-air cinema which shows a different film in its original language every evening.

contents of another garden near the Moyenne Corniche, the **Jardin Exotique** (*bus 2; open mid-May–mid-Sept daily 9–7; winter daily 9–6 or nightfall; adm*), with 6,000 succulents planted in the rockface. The same ticket admits you to the adjacent **Grottes de l'Observatoire**, one of the few places in Provence inhabited in the Palaeolithic era.

Up on the Rock: Monaco-Ville

Monaco-Ville, as scrubbed and cute as any town in Legoland, offers the **Historial des Princes de Monaco**, 27 Rue Basse (*open Oct–Feb daily 11–5; Mar–Sept daily 9.30–6; adm*), with waxworks running the gamut from Francesco the Spiteful, founder of the Grimaldi clan, to Caroline and Stéphanie; and the Multi-vision **Monte-Carlo Story**, on Rue Emile-de-Loth (*showings winter hourly 2–5, summer 2–6; adm*). Monaco's most compelling attraction is nearby: the **Musée Océanographique de Monaco** in Avenue St-Martin (*open July and Aug daily 9–8; April–June and Sept 9–7; Oct–Mar 10–6; adm*), founded in 1910 by Prince Albert Ier, who sank all of his casino profits into a passion for deep-sea exploration. To house the treasures he accumulated in his 24 voyages, he built this museum in a cliff, filling it with instruments, shells, whale skeletons, and on the ground floor a fascinating aquarium with 90 tanks.

Monaco to Nice: Grande and Moyenne Corniches

From Monaco, the D53 ascends to the Grande Corniche, a road the Romans called Via Julia Augusta. The views are precipitous, and you can escape the crowds by venturing even further inland to the pretty villages of Peille and Peillon.

La Turbie and its Trophy

The old Via Julia Augusta (Rue Comte-de-Cessole) passes through town on its way to the **Trophy of the Alps**. This monument, built by the Romans to commemorate their victory over the Ligurians, originally stood 147ft high, supporting a series of Doric columns interspersed with statues of eminent generals, the whole surmounted by a colossal 20ft statue of Augustus flanked by two captives. The still formidable pile of rubble that remained in the 1930s – after it had been vandalized, ransacked for building materials and blown up over the centuries – was resurrected to 114ft.

Peillon and Peille

The two villages are tiny and lovely; balanced atop adjacent hilltops. **Peillon** is a bit posher, complete with a foyer – a cobbled square with a pretty fountain at the village entrance. Its big attraction is right at the entrance: the **Chapelle des Pénitents Blancs** (*ring the tourist office to arrange a visit, groups only*) adorned with a slightly faded cycle of Renaissance frescoes on the *Passion of Christ* by Giovanni Canavesio (*c.* 1485).

You can walk to **Peille**, following the Roman road for two hours. More isolated, Peille has more character, and its very own dialect, called Pelhasc. There's an ensemble of medieval streets like Peillon's and a church begun in the 12th century, with an interesting medieval portrait of Peille and its now ruined castle.

Getting Around

There are **buses** daily from Nice to La Turbie that continue up to Peille, but not on Sun; and several a day from Monaco. Buses leave less regularly from Nice to Peillon. Both Peillon and Peille have train stations several steep kilometres below their respective villages.

Métrazur **trains** stop at Eze's coastal outpost; a minibus (*navette*) will shuttle you up to the village in summer.

Some buses from Nice towards Peille stops at Eze-Grande Corniche. There are several buses from Nice for Eze-Village.

All the frequent buses on the Nice–Menton line stop at Eze-Bord-de-Mer; *navettes* leave regularly from the Basse Corniche for Eze-Village and Eze-Grande Corniche.

Where to Stay and Eat

Eze-Grande Corniche ✉ 06360

★★★★**Les Terrasses d'Eze**, Rte de la Turbie, t 04 92 41 55 55, *www.terrasses-eze.com* (*luxury–expensive*). Huge Best Western hotel complete with sauna and gym. The rooms are not quite big enough for the price, but the restaurant offers the best views of the coast to go with its rich Mediterranean cuisine. *Half-board only in summer.*

★★**L'Hermitage**, 2km from the village at Col d'Eze on the Grande Corniche, t 04 93 41 00 68 (*inexpensive*). Priceless views and traditional décor; an old-fashioned welcome and monstrous portions of startlingly good Provençal food (*moderate*). *Closed Dec–Jan.*

Eze-Village ✉ 06360

★★★★**Château Eza**, Rue de la Pise, t 04 93 41 12 24 (*luxury*). A former prince's residence, actually a collection of medieval houses linked together to form an eagle's nest, all sharing an extraordinary, perched terrace, with aromatic Niçois and other Provençal specialities to match. *Closed Nov–Mar.*

★★★★**Château de la Chèvre d'Or**, Rue du Barri, t 04 92 10 66 66, *www.chevredor.com* (*luxury*). In a medieval castle rebuilt in the 1920s, a romantic Relais et Châteaux with a small park rippling down the mountain-side, a pool, and more ravishing views; chef Jean-Marc Delacourt creates refined, light versions of the French classics, accompanied by one of the Riviera's best wine cellars. *Book well in advance. Closed Dec–Feb.*

★★**Le Golf**, Place de la Colette, t 04 93 41 18 50 (*inexpensive*). A more modest choice.

★★**Auberge des Deux Corniches**, t 04 93 41 19 54 (*inexpensive*). In the hills above Eze. *Closed mid-Nov–mid-Dec. Half-board only in summer.*

Le Troubadour, 4 Rue du Brec, t 04 93 41 19 03 (*expensive–moderate*). Turbot or *filet de bœuf aux cèpes* go down nicely. *Closed Sun, Mon lunch, and Nov–mid-Dec.*

Mas Provençal, Av de Verdun, just outside the tangle of medieval streets, t 04 93 41 19 53 (*expensive*). Completely covered in flowers and ivy, and ensconced in the 19th century; sink into plush red velvet chairs (with anti-macassars) and dine on milk-fed pig roasted on a spit, or *risotto aux cèpes*, before ordering the carriage home.

Eze-Bord-de-Mer ✉ 06360

★★★★**Le Cap Estel**, t 04 93 01 50 44, *www.webstore.fr/capestil* (*luxury*). Set in a 4-acre park, the luxurious sparkling white Riviera dream built for a Russian princess, has two heated pools and a flight of movie star steps down to the manicured gardens.

★★**Eric Rivot**, t 04 93 01 51 46, *www.auberge-ericrivot.com* (*inexpensive*). Family-run with well-priced rooms and gourmet dining. *Closed mid-Nov–mid-Dec; restaurant Wed.*

Eze

Between Monaco and Nice, the main reason for taking the middle road has long been the extraordinary village of Eze, the most perched, perhaps, of any *village perché* in France, squeezed on to a cone of a hill 430m over the sea. The tight little maze of stairs and alleys was built to confuse attackers, the better to ambush them or spill boiling oil on their heads. The **Jardin Exotique** (*open July and Aug 9–nightfall; Sept–June 9–12 and 2–6; adm*) is a spiky paradise created by municipal initiative in

1949. Eze's other non-commercial attraction, the cream and yellow **Chapelle des Pénitents Blancs**, built in 1766, has gathered an eccentric collection of scraps; an old ship's model is suspended from the ceiling, and a disembodied arm brandishes a 13th-century Catalan crucifix. Here too is a 14th-century *Madone des forêts*, where baby Jesus holds a pine cone. A scenic path to Eze-Bord-de-Mer is called the **Sentier Frédéric-Nietzsche** after the philosopher who walked up it. (It starts at the entrance to the old villlage, down a narrow, almost hidden, path on the left.)

The Corniche Inférieure

Beaulieu

'*O qual bel luogo!*' exclaimed Napoleon in his Corsican mother tongue, and the bland name stuck to this lush banana-growing town overlooking the Baie des Fourmis, 'the Bay of Ants', which is so called for the black boulders in the sea. Sheltered Beaulieu admits to a mere four days of frost a year. The highlight is the **Villa Kerylos** (*open July–Aug daily 10.30–7; Feb–Oct daily 10.30–6; Nov–Jan Mon–Fri 2–6, Sat and Sun 10–6; adm; bus stop Hôtel Métropole then a 5min walk*), a striking reproduction of a wealthy 5th-century BC Athenian's abode, furnishings and garden, built in 1908 by archaeologist Théodore Reinach; here this ultimate philhellene lived like an Athenian himself, holding symposia, exercising and bathing with his male buddies.

St-Jean-Cap-Ferrat

Another retro-repro fantasy, the **Villa Ephrussi de Rothschild** (*a 10min walk from the Corniche Inférieure, or catch the St-Jean bus which passes its entrance; open Nov–Jan state rooms and gardens only, Sat, Sun and hols 2–6; Feb–June and Sept–Oct daily 10–6; July and Aug daily 10–7; adm exp*), tops the narrow isthmus of bucolic Cap Ferrat. The flamboyant Béatrice de Rothschild was a compulsive art collector and lover of the 18th century, and, after marrying the banker Baron Ephrussi, had this Italianate villa specially built to house her treasures. To create the eclectic gardens, the isthmus was given a crew-cut, and terraced into different levels. **Cap Ferrat**, with its lush greenery, quiet yacht port of St-Jean, and little azure coves, is ripe territory for strolls or swims.

Villefranche-sur-Mer

In the 14th century, the deep, wooded bay between Cap Ferrat and Nice was a duty-free port, hence Villefranche's name. Tall, brightly coloured, piled-up houses line the narrow lanes and stairs; the fine shingle and sand beach with a shallow slope and calm bay is ideal for children. Villefranche's fishermen once stored their nets in the portside Romanesque **Chapelle St-Pierre**, Quai Courbet (*open winter daily 9.30–12 and 2–6; summer daily 10–12 and 4–8.30; closed Mon; adm*), and in 1957, after a protracted battle with the municipal authorities, Jean Cocteau won permission to restore and renovate it. He frescoed it in 'ghosts of colours' with scenes from the Life of St Peter, plus images of the fish-eyed fishergirls of Villefranche, the Gypsies at Stes-Maries-de-la-Mer, and angels from his own private heaven.

Where to Stay and Eat

Beaulieu-sur-Mer ✉ 06310

****La Réserve**, 5 Bd Général-Leclerc, t 04 93
01 00 01, *www.reservebeaulieu.com* (*luxury*).
In the 1870s, when James Gordon Bennett,
owner of the *New York Herald* and the man
who sent Stanley to find Livingstone, was
booted out of New York society for his scandalous behaviour, he came to the Riviera.
One of the most exclusive hotels on the
Riviera, with grand sea views, a beach and
marina, heated pool and more delights,
including an elegant neo-Renaissance
restaurant. *Closed Nov–mid-Dec.*

***Le Havre Bleu**, 29 Bd Maréchal-Joffre,
t 04 93 01 01 40, *www.hotel-lehavrebleu.fr*
(*inexpensive*). An attractive hotel with
pleasant rooms, many with terraces.

Le Riviera, 6 Rue Paul-Doumer, t 04 93 01 04
92, *www.hotel-riviera.fr* (*inexpensive*). With
pretty wrought-iron balconies just up from
the Basse Corniche. *Closed mid-Oct–Nov.*

Le Catalan, Bd Maréchal-Leclerc, t 04 93 01
02 78 (*moderate–cheap*). Wood-fired pizzas
and delicious pasta (*à la carte*). *Closed Sun,
and Mon lunch.*

La Casa, 4 Av Fernand Dunan, t 04 93 76 48 00
(*moderate–cheap*). Dance the night away
with the ageing but still game local retirees;
head for the Casino piano-bar and restaurant, with a Cuban orchestra, tapas, Havana
cocktails and enormous sizzling barbecues.

St-Jean-Cap-Ferrat ✉ 06230

****La Voile d'Or**, t 04 93 01 13 13, *reserva-
tion@lavoiledor.fr* (*luxury*). A charming,
voluptuous Italian villa, overlooking the
pleasure port. Once owned by film director
Michael Powell, the Voile d'Or is an ideal first
or second honeymoon hotel, with a laid-
back atmosphere, a garden hanging over the
port, a heated pool, and rooms with every
luxury. Its equally exceptional restaurant is
favoured by the languid yachting set.

****Grand Hôtel du Cap Ferrat**, 71 Bd Général
de Gaulle, t 04 93 76 50 50 (*luxury*). The
already luxurious Belle Epoque rooms have
been restored in a more airy Riviera style, all
set in acres of gardens, lawns, and palms. A
funicular lowers guests down to an
Olympic-size seawater pool just over the

Mediterranean. Its restaurant **Le Cap**, on a
palatial terrace shaded by parasol pines,
serves delicious meals decidedly unhealthy
for your wallet.

***Brise-Marine**, Av Jean-Mermoz, t 04 93 76
04 36, *www.hotel-brisemarine.fr* (*expensive*).
More down-to-earth, with a garden, and
large rooms, half with sea views. *Closed
Nov–Jan.*

Clair Logis, 12 Av Centrale, t 04 93 76 04 57,
www.hotel-clair-logis.fr (*expensive*). Near the
centre of the Cap, wonderful, and very
reasonable, welcoming villa set back in a
lush enclosed garden. *Closed Dec–Feb.*

*La Bastide, 3 Av Albert 1er, t 04 93 76 06 78
(*inexpensive*). Not luxurious, but it has a
good restaurant (*moderate*). *Closed Nov.*

Le Provençal, Place Clemenceau, t 04 93 76
03 97 (*expensive*). For a frisson of south coast
hauteur with your cuisine.

Skipper, Port de Plaisance, t 04 93 76 01 00
(*moderate*). Best for fish.

Villefranche-sur-Mer ✉ 06230

***Welcome**, Quai Amiral-Courbet, t 04 93 76
27 62, *resa@welcomehotel.fr* (*expensive*).
Legendary, although its wild days are over.
The refurbished rooms are air-conditioned;
those on the 5th floor are ravishing. *Closed
mid-Nov–mid-Dec.*

***Provençal**, 4 Av du Maréchal-Joffre, t 04 93
01 71 42, *provencal@riviera.fr* (*moderate*).
Unpretentious and family-run. *Closed
Nov–Xmas.*

Le Carpaccio, Promenade des Marinières,
t 04 93 01 72 97, *www.restaurant-
carpaccio.com* (*expensive*). Long a favourite
of the Rolls-Royce crowd from Monaco, yet
it remains affordable for a night-time
splurge or a pizza.

Michel's, Place Amélie Pollonnais, t 04 93 76
73 24 (*expensive–moderate*). Has a startling
(they are very proud of it) frieze depicting
Villefranche, with a lovely terrace looking
out over the bay and friendly staff. Light,
local specialities; the melt-in-the-mouth
house pâté and the aubergine and pepper
terrine are especially good. *Closed Tues.*

La Belle Epoque, Place de la Paix, t 04 93 01
96 22 (*cheap*). Extremely plesant lunch spot,
on a terrace in a quiet square up towards
the Corniche. Try the *plat du jour.*

Nice

The capital of the *département* of Alpes-Maritimes and France's fifth largest town, Nice is the Hexagon's most visited city after Paris. Agreeably named and superbly set on the Bay of Angels, Nice has a gleam and sparkle in its eye like no other city in France: only a sourpuss could resist its lively old town squeezed between promontory and sea, its markets blazing with colour, the glittering tiled domes and creamy *pâtisserie* 19th-century hotels and villas, the immaculate, exotic gardens, and the famous voluptuous curve of the beach and the palm-lined Promenade des Anglais.

History

Greeks from Marseille founded a commercial colony near the seaside *oppidum* that they named Nikaïa after an obscure military victory. Beset by Ligurian pirates, the Nikaïans asked the Romans for aid. The Romans duly came, and stayed, but preferred to live near the hilltop at Cemenelum (modern Cimiez) close to the Via Julia Augusta. In 1338 Nice allied herself with Savoy, who became firm allies with the English, and by 1755 the first trickle of milords began to discover the sunny charms of a Riviera winter and build the first villas. In 1860, Italy, in exchange for Napoléon III's aid against Austria, ceded Nice and Savoy to France. In recent years, Nice was the personal fiefdom of the right-wing Médecin family. Jean Médecin reigned from 1928 until 1965, and was succeeded by his flamboyant son Jacques, the man who twinned Nice with Cape Town when apartheid was still on the books. Jacques Médecin had an edifice complex nearly the size of Mitterrand's in Paris. In 1990 the slow, grinding wheels of French justice began to catch up with Médecin, when it was discovered, among other things, that money for the Nice Opera was being diverted into the mayor's bank account. He fled to Uruguay but was extradited to France in 1995 and died in 1998. Now, Jacques Peyrat, of Chirac's centre-right RPR party, holds the fort.

Vieux Nice

A dangerous slum in the 1970s, Nice's Vieille Ville, a piquant quarter east of Place Masséna, is busy becoming the trendiest part of the city. Old here means Genoese seaside Baroque – tall, steep *palazzi*, many with opulent 17th- and 18th-century portals and windows.

At its eastern end, the Vieille Ville is closed by the **Colline du Château**, the ancient acropolis of Nikaïa and site of the 10th- to 12th-century town and the cathedral of Ste-Marie. You can walk up the steps to the Château, take a mini-train (€6) from the Promenade des Anglais which tours around the Vieille Ville on the way, or pay a few sous to take the lift at the east end of the Quai des Etats-Unis near **Tour Bellanda**. If you descend by way of the Montée Eberlé and Rue Catherine-Ségurane, you'll end up in the wide, yellow, arcaded, 18th-century **Place Garibaldi**, named for Nice's most famous native son, who was born here when it was still called Nizza and who had a fit and a half when Napoléon III wheedled it off Italy.

South of Place Garibaldi off Rue Neuve is the old parish church, **St-Martin-St-Augustin**, where a monk named Martin Luther said a Mass during his momentous

Nice

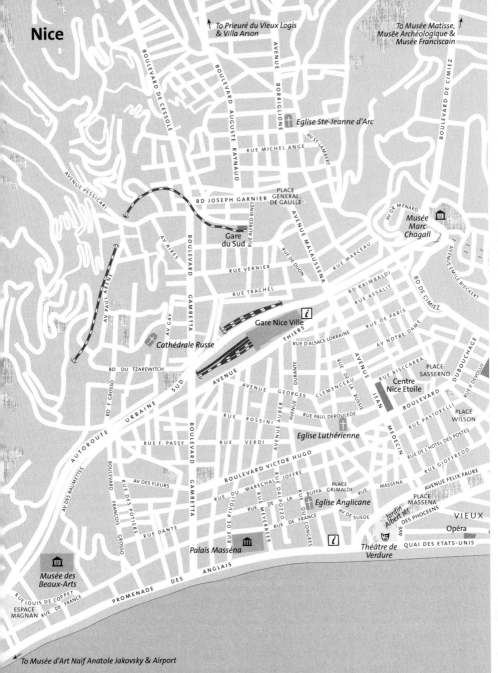

To Prieuré du Vieux Logis & Villa Arson

To Musée Matisse, Musée Archéologique & Musée Franciscain

BOULEVARD DE CESSOLE

BOULEVARD AUGUSTE RAYNAUD

AVENUE PESSICARI

AVENUE BORRIGLIONE

AV ST-LAMBERT

RUE MICHEL ANGE

† Eglise Ste-Jeanne d'Arc

BOULEVARD DE CIMIEZ

BD JOSEPH GARNIER

PLACE GENERAL DE GAULLE

RUE ALFRED BINET

AVENUE MALAUSSENA

AV DR MENARD

Musée Marc Chagall

AV AIRES

Gare du Sud

RUE VERNIER

RUE DE DIJON

RUE MARCEAU

AVENUE EMILE BIECKERT

BOULEVARD GAMBETTA

RUE TRACHEL

BD RAIMBALDI

BD DE CIMIEZ

AV PAUL ARÈNE

AV GAL

RUE ASSALIT

AV DE PARIS

i

BD DU TZAREWITCH

Gare Nice Ville

THIERS

RUE DE PARIS

AV NOTRE-DAME

BD F GROSSO

Cathédrale Russe

RUE D'ALSACE LORRAINE

RUE DE PARIS

DUBOUCHAGE

AVENUE

AVENUE SUD

DURANTE

RUE DE LA RUSSIE

AVENUE JEAN

RUE BISCARRA

PLACE SASSERNO

RUE DEVOLUY

URBAINE

AVENUE GEORGES CLEMENCEAU

AVENUE AUBER

Centre Nice Etoile

BOULEVARD

AUTOROUTE

RUE ROSSINI

RUE PAUL DEROULEDE

MEDECIN

RUE PASTORELLI

PLACE WILSON

RUE F. PASSY

RUE VERDI

Eglise Luthérienne

RUE DE L'HOTEL DES POSTES

AV DES BAUMETTES

BOULEVARD FRANCOIS GROSSO

RUE DES POTIERS

AV DES FLEURS

BOULEVARD GAMBETTA

BOULEVARD VICTOR HUGO

RUE JOFFRE

RUE GIOFFREDO

RUE DANTE

RUE DE RIVOLI

RUE DU MARECHAL

RUE DALPOZZO

LA BUFFA

PLACE GRIMALDI

MASSENA

AVENUE FELIX FAURE

RUE MEYERBEER

Eglise Anglicane

RUE DE FRANCE

AV DE SUEDE

PLACE MASSENA

VIEUX

Palais Masséna

🏛

AV DES FLEURS

RUE DE FRANCE

RUE DU CONGRES

i

Jardin Albert 1er

AV DES PHOCEENS

Opéra

ANGLAIS

Théâtre de Verdure

QUAI DES ETATS-UNIS

Musée des Beaux-Arts

🏛

RUE LOUIS DE COPPET

ESPACE MAGNAN

RUE DE FRANCE

PROMENADE DES ANGLAIS

To Musée d'Art Naïf Anatole Jakovsky & Airport

Baie des Anges

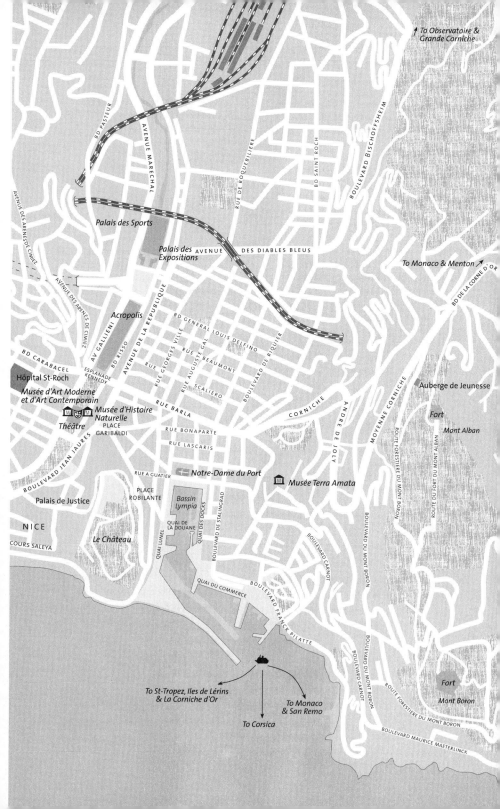

To Observatoire &
Grande Corniche

BD PASTEUR

AVENUE MARECHAL

RUE DE ROQUEBILIERE

BD SAINT ROCH

BOULEVARD BISCHOFFSHEIM

Palais des Sports

Palais des
Expositions

AVENUE   DES DIABLES BLEUS

To Monaco & Menton

BD DE LA CORNE D'OR

AVENUE DES ARENES CIMIEZ

AVENUE DES ARENES DE CIMIEZ

BD CARABACEL

ESPLANADE
KENNEDY

A GALLIENI

BD RISSO

AVENUE DE LA REPUBLIQUE

BD GENERAL LOUIS DELFINO

Acropolis

RUE GEORGES VILLE

RUE AUGUSTE GAL

RUE SCALIERO

RUE BEAUMONT

BOULEVARD DE RIQUIER

Hôpital St-Roch

Musée d'Art Moderne
et d'Art Contemporain

Musée d'Histoire
Naturelle

Théâtre   PLACE
GARIBALDI

RUE BARLA

RUE BONAPARTE

RUE LASCARIS

CORNICHE

MOYENNE CORNICHE

ANDRE DE JOLY

Auberge de Jeunesse

ROUTE FORESTIERE DU MONT BORON

Fort

Mont Alban

ROUTE DU FORT DU MONT ALBAN

BOULEVARD JEAN JAURES

RUE A GUATIER

Notre-Dame du Port

Musée Terra Amata

Palais de Justice

PLACE
ROBILANTE

Bassin
Lympia

QUAI DE
LA DOUANE

QUAI LUNEL

QUAI DES DOCKS

BOULEVARD DE STALINGRAD

BOULEVARD CARNOT

BOULEVARD DU MONT BORON

N I C E

COURS SALEYA

Le Château

QUAI DU COMMERCE

BOULEVARD FRANCK PILATTE

BOULEVARD DU MONT BORON

BOULEVARD CARNOT

ROUTE FORESTIERE DU MONT BORON

Fort

Mont Boron

To St-Tropez, Iles de Lérins
& La Corniche d'Or

To Monaco
& San Remo

To Corsica

BOULEVARD MAURICE MAETERLINCK

Getting There and Around

By Plane

The Aéroport Nice-Côte d'Azur is served by flights from around the world.

Buses run every 12 mins between the airport (terminal 2) and Nice coach station, while bus 23 and a another direct bus link with the train station every 30mins, t 04 93 56 35 40. The bus ticket to town will also give you a free onward connection on another city bus.

After 10pm the yellow airport bus will detour to the train station if you ask the driver, or else stops in Place Masséna, where the night buses depart. There are also several buses daily from the airport to Menton, Monaco, Cannes, Antibes, Grasse, St-Tropez, St-Raphaël and Marseille.

By Train

Nice's train station (t 08 92 353 353) is in Av Thiers, not far from the centre of town. Besides *Métrazur* trains between Ventimiglia and St-Raphaël, Nice has frequent connections to Marseille and is on the TGV route to Paris.

The Gare du Sud, 4 bis Rue Alfred-Binet, t 04 97 03 80 80, is served by the little *Train des Pignes*, with excursions to Provençal towns high up in the Var valley (*see* box, p.802).

By Coach

The coach station is on the Promenade du Paillon, t 04 93 85 61 81. There are frequent buses to Grasse, Vence, Cannes, Marseille, Aix-en-Provence, St-Raphaël, Cagnes, Antibes, Menton and Monte-Carlo. Bus 17 links the coach and train stations.

By Bus

Pick up a free *Guide Horaire du Réseau Bus* at the tourist office or from Sunbus's information centre, 10 Av Félix-Faure, t 04 93 13 53 13. Several tourist tickets, called 'Sun Pass', are available, offering limitless rides for one, five or seven days, including a trip to the airport. Buses stop around 9pm, and are replaced by four 'Noctambus' services from Pl Masséna.

Car Hire

Among the cheapest car hire places is **Rent-a-Car**, opposite the train station on Av Thiers,

t 04 93 88 69 69, or in the centre of town, t 04 93 37 42 22, or just by the airport at 61 Route de Grenoble, t 04 93 19 07 07.

Avis is at the train station, t 04 93 87 90 11, or at the airport, t 04 93 21 36 33, and **Hertz** is at the airport, t 08 25 342 343.

Taxis

Call t 04 93 13 78 78.

Tourist Information

Nice: Av Thiers, next to the train station, t 08 92 707 407, *www.nicetourism.com*. Also Terminal 1 at the airport, and at 5 Promenade des Anglais. A 1-, 3- or 7-day Carte Musées Côte d'Azur can be obtained for €8, €15 or €25 from any museum ticket desk or the tourist office, or FNAC bookshop. On the first and third Sunday of every month, all museums in Nice are free – so everyone goes.

Shopping

The pedestrian zone around Place Masséna has scores of designer clothes shops (mainly on Av Félix-Faure) and cheap boutiques (mainly on Rue Masséna). In Av Jean-Médecin you'll find Nice's biggest **department store**, Galeries Lafayette, and the Nice Etoile shopping centre.

Souvenirs are best found in the old town. Provençal fabrics can be found at 8 Av de Verdun. Not far away is a landmark, the fabulously rococo premises of **Auer**, 7 Rue St-François-de-Paule, which has been making the region's most celebrated confectionery, jams and fruits *confits* for almost two centuries, and **Boutique Alziari**, 14 Rue St-François-de-Paule, claimed by many Niçois to sell the world's best olive oil.

Where to Stay

Nice ✉ 06000

Nice is packed with hotels of all categories, and in the summer most are just as tightly packed inside. If you arrive without a reservation, the tourist office next to the station will book rooms. Get there by 10am in summer.

Luxury–Very Expensive

****Négresco**, 37 Promenade des Anglais, **t** 04 93 16 64 00, *direction@hotel-negresco.com* (*luxury*). For panache none can top this fabulous green-domed national historic monument, the one hotel in Nice where a Grand Duke would still feel at home, and the last independent luxury hotel on the coast. Its 150 chambers and apartments have all been redecorated with Edwardian furnishings and paintings by the likes of Picasso and Léger. Don't miss the *salon royal*, lit by a Baccarat chandelier made for the Tsar, and recently topped off with a contemporary sculpture by Nikki de Saint Phalle, *Nana jaune* (*Yellow Girl*).

****Palais Maeterlinck**, 30 Bd Maeterlinck, **t** 04 92 00 72 00, *www.palais-maeterlinck. com*. On the way to Villefranche, a fastidiously refurbished pink and white palace set in beautiful gardens, with a highly acclaimed restaurant, **Le Mélisande** (*expensive*), which serves wonderfully creative dishes on a precipitous terrace.

****Château des Ollières**, 39 Av des Baumettes, **t** 04 92 15 77 99, *chateaudesollieres@chateaudesollieres.com*. Flamboyant pink, orange and yellow crenellated folly which once belonged to a Russian prince. Eight heavenly rooms, with antique furnishings, eccentric stained glass and four-posters.

Hi Hôtel, 3 Av des Fleurs, **t** 04 97 07 26 26, *www.hi-hotel.net*. Nice's latest trend – a hip design hotel with no walls, 'concept' rooms and cool blues, greens and purples in the décor. Rooftop pool, hammam; at breakfast you make your own cappuccinos and squeeze your own juices. Vending machines on every floor sell champagne, not Coke.

Expensive

****Le Grimaldi**, 15 Rue Grimaldi, **t** 04 93 16 00 24, *www.le-grimaldi.com*. A delightful little hotel with a charge of Provençal colour.

****La Pérouse**, 11 Quai Rauba-Capeu, **t** 04 93 62 34 63, *lp@hroy.com*. Halfway up the Colline du Château, a lovely hotel with a pool and good restaurant high above the hubbub. *Restaurant closed Oct–April*.

***Windsor**, 11 Rue Dalpozzo (behind the Négresco), **t** 04 93 88 59 35, *contact@hotelwindsornice.com*. Best among the tri-star choices, an idiosyncratic hotel in the midst of a tropical garden, with a pool, an English-style pub, a Turkish hammam, a Thai sitting room and odd frescoes in the rooms.

***Vendôme**, 26 Rue Pastorelli, **t** 04 93 62 00 77, *contact@vendome-hotel-nice.com*. Prettily renovated, air-conditioned rooms, a superb stairway, and a garden.

*** **Hôtel du Petit Palais**, 17 Av Emile-Biekert, in Cimiez, **t** 04 93 62 19 11, *petitpalais@ provence-riviera.com*. A handsome white Belle Epoque mansion (Best Western). Rooms vary in size, but the best (at the back) look out over the rooftops of the old town to the sea.

Moderate

****Nouvel Hôtel**, 19bis Bd Victor-Hugo, **t** 04 93 87 15 00. More reasonable prices, a good location, bland but comfortable rooms.

Inexpensive

****Hôtel Trianon**, 15 Av Auber, **t** 04 93 88 30 69. A white grand piano serves as a reception desk, and the sweeping white staircase and little lift with an wrought-iron grille give it a comfortably old-fashioned feel.

***La Belle Meunière**, 21 Av Durante, **t** 04 93 88 66 15. Friendly hotel, a stone's throw from the station, and a long-time favourite of budget travellers – it even has parking and a little garden for breakfast.

Eating Out

Very Expensive

Le Chantecler, 37 Promenade des Anglais, **t** 04 93 16 64 00. Gastronomic Nice is dominated by the Belle Epoque magnificence of this restaurant snuggling into the opulent arms of the Négresco. Here, chef Alain Llorca has succeeded in seducing the Niçois with his own fabulous versions of Chantecler favourites like sea bass served with tomatoes and pesto, roast pigeon with *foie gras* ravioli and desserts like the exotic liquorice-flavoured meringue with raspberry sorbet. *Closed mid-Nov–mid-Dec*.

Expensive

Don Camillo, 5 Rue des Ponchettes, **t** 04 93 85 67 95. Run by a former pupil of Maximin and Paul Ducasse, already celebrated for its home-made ravioli filled with Swiss chard *en daube*, and fabulous desserts. *Closed Sun and Mon lunch*. Also has a less expensive café at 8 Place Guynemar, **t** 04 93 89 98 87.

Auberge de Théo, 52 Av Cap de Croix, **t** 04 93 81 26 19. One of the best is up in Cimiez, where you'll find genuine Italian pizzas, salads with *mesclun* (Nice's special mixed salad), and Venetian *tiramisù* for dessert. *Closed Sun eve in winter and Mon all year.*

Chez Simon, above Nice in St Antoine de Ginestière, **t** 04 93 86 51 62. Serving up local specialities – *beignets* stuffed with fresh sardines or courgettes, a melting fricassée of wild *cèpe* mushrooms in parsley – for four generations. Rustic wood carvings, and a lovely terrace in summer. *Closed Mon.*

Moderate

La Mérenda, 4 Rue de la Terrasse, no tel, near the Opera House and the Cours Saleya. Join the glitterati enjoying Dominique le Stanc's idiosyncratic Niçois cuisine. *Closed weekends and school hols*. No credit cards.

Villa d'Este, 6 Rue Masséna, **t** 04 93 82 47 77. The best Italian restaurant in Nice, over three floors with *trompe l'œil* Italianate décor in pretty pastel colours, attentive service and top-notch pasta. Try the plate of *antipasti* for a gastronomic feast.

Moderate–Cheap

Au Pizzaïolo, 4 bis Rue du Pont Vieux, **t** 04 93 92 24 79. Specialities include beef *carpaccio*, *farcis niçois* and local seafood. The surroundings may be humble, but the food ain't bad and the staff are good-natured. *Closed Tues.*

La Zucca Magica, 4bis Quai Papacino, **t** 04 93 56 25 27. The friendliest vegetarian restaurant in Nice, with imaginative dishes created by a troupe of genial chefs. Draws customers from all along the Riviera, so book ahead.

Cheap

Chez Fanny, 407 Rte de Bellet, **t** 04 93 37 87 07, above Nice. Fun, fresh cuisine. The lamb melts in the mouth, and the seafood is wonderfully fresh, but best of all is the virulent green *eau-de-vie* made from basil offered at the end. *Closed Mon and Tues.*

Café de Turin, 5 Place Garibaldi, **t** 04 93 85 30 87. Try this 19th-century café for a drink or snack or some of the best and cheapeast oysters in town.

Fenocchio, Place Rossetti and 6, Place de la Poissonerie. 99 varieties of ice cream. Lavender cream, jasmine sorbet and the bitterest chocolate imaginable.

Entertainment and Nightlife

You can find out what's happening in Nice in the daily *Nice-Matin*. Other sources covering the entire Côte are *7 jours/7 nuits*, distributed free in the tourist offices, the *Semaine des Spectacles* (Wed).

Opéra de Nice, 4–6 Rue St-François-de-Paule, **t** 04 93 13 98 53. Operas, concerts and recitals at various locations including the Acropolis; the Théâtre de Nice (Esplanade des Victoires); and the Théâtre de Verdure.

Théâtre de Verdure, Jardin Albert 1er. From April onwards rock, jazz, and other concerts take place in this outdoor theatre.

Nice's nightlife is divided between expensive clubs and bland piano bars, and the livelier bars and clubs of Vieux Nice, which come and go like ships in the night.

Wayne's, 15 Rue de la Préfecture. Noisiest of the jumping ex-pat joints, a British-owned pub and restaurant (*open noon–12.30am, reservations obligatory at weekends*).

De Klomp, 6 Rue Mascoïnat, near Place Rossetti. Funky Dutch hangout with live jazz, old whiskies and a hedonistic atmosphere (not for teetotallers or anti-smokers).

Hole in the Wall, 3 Rue de l'Abbaye. Small hole serving large beers, big fresh burgers, and live music on an unfeasibly small stage.

Jonathan's, 1 Rue de la Loge, in the north of Vieux Nice. Food, candles and the 1970s-inspired 'live' music hosted by Jonathan himself.

Le Klub, 6 Rue Halévy. Gay club, mostly techno.

Plasma Café, 11 Rue Offenbach, **t** 04 93 16 17 32. Juice bar and sushi bar, with internet access. *Open till 2.30am.*

pilgrimage to Rome in 1514. The dim interior was Baroqued in the 17th century; its treasures include a fine *Pietà* (*c.* 1500) attributed to Ludovico Bréa, and a tatty photo-copy of Garibaldi's baptismal certificate. The **Palais Lascaris** at 15 Rue Droite (*open daily 10–12 and 2–6; closed Tues and hols*) is a grand 1648 mansion. The ground floor contains a reconstructed pharmacy of 1738; a fantastically opulent staircase leads up to the *étage nobile*, saturated with elaborate Genoese *quadratura* (architectural *trompe-l'œil*) frescoes, Flemish tapestries, ornate woodwork, and a 1578 Italian precursor of the pianoforte.

Take Rue Rossetti west to the cafés of pretty Place Rossetti, dominated by Nice's 17th-century **Cathédrale Ste-Réparate**, designed by Jean-André Guibert and crowned with a joyful dome and lantern of glazed tiles in emerald bands.

Cours Saleya is an open, elongated little gem of urban planning, where bars and restaurants line up along the famous outdoor market and the **Chapelle de la Miséricorde**, designed in 1740 by Bernardo Vittone, a disciple of Turin's extraordinary Baroque architects Guarino Guarini and Juvarra, with a superb interior (ask at the tourist office about your chances of getting in).

Musée de Terra Amata

Overlooking the port is the **Musée de Terra Amata**, 25 Bd Carnot (*buses 32 and 1 from central Nice; open daily 10–12 and 2–6; closed Mon and hols*), incorporating a cave holding one of the world's oldest 'households', a pebble-walled wind-shelter built by elephant-hunters 400 millennia ago which was discovered in 1966. A fascinating set of models, bones and tools helps evoke life in Nice at the dawn of time.

Up the Paillon

In the old days Nice's laundresses plied their trade in the torrential waters of the Paillon, until the often dangerous river began to vanish under the pavements in the 1830s. Nearest the sea, Jardin Albert Ier is the site of the open-air **Théâtre de Verdure**, while upstream, as it were, vast terracotta-coloured **Place Masséna** is generously endowed with flower-beds and wisteria-shaded benches.

Further up loom a pair of dreadnoughts erected by ex-mayor Jacques Médecin. The first of these is the 282-million-franc **Théâtre de Nice** and the marble-coated **Musée d'Art Moderne et d'Art Contemporain** (*open daily 10–6; closed Mon and hols; adm*). The building – four concrete towers, linked by glass walkways – is an admirable setting for the works of Christo, Nikki de Saint-Phalle, Warhol, Dine, Oldenburg, Rauschenberg, Ben and other influential and irreverent figures of the 1960s and '70s.

The view up the Paillon is blocked by Médecin's 1985 congress and art centre and *cinémathèque* called **Acropolis**, 1 Esplanade Kennedy, a gruesome megalithic bunker of concrete slabs and smoked glass.

West of Place Masséna and the Promenade des Anglais

Important streets fan out from Place Masséna and the adjacent Jardin Albert Ier. Nice's main shopping street, **Av Jean-Médecin**, leads up to the train station; **Rue Masséna** is the centre of a lively pedestrian-only restaurant and shopping zone;

and the fabled, palm-lined sweep of the **Promenade des Anglais** around the Baie des Anges is still aglitter through the fumes of the traffic, which is usually as strangled as poor Isadora Duncan was when her scarf caught in the wheel of her Bugatti here in 1927. The long pebble beach is crowded day and night in the summer.

Visitors from the top end of the economic spectrum check into the fabled Belle Epoque **Hôtel Négresco** (No.37), vintage 1906. Next to it is the garden of the **Palais Masséna** (*closed for restoration, expected to reopen 2004*).

Fine Arts, and a Russian Cathedral

From the Masséna museum, a brisk 10-minute walk or bus 22 leads to the handsome 1876 villa that is home to the **Musée des Beaux Arts**, 33 Av des Baumettes (*open daily 10–12 and 2–6; closed Mon; adm*). With the Matisses and Chagalls in Nice's other museums, the Musée des Beaux Arts is left with the 'old masters of the 19th century'. A room dedicated to Kees Van Dongen includes his entertaining 1927 *Tango of the Archangel*, which superbly evokes the Roaring Twenties on the Riviera.

In 1865, the young Tsarevich Nicholas was brought to Nice, and, like so many consumptives who arrived in search of health, he quickly declined. The luxurious villa where he died was demolished to construct the **Cathédrale Orthodoxe Russe St-Nicolas**, located a few blocks from the west of the train station at 17 Bd du Tzarévitch, just off Bd Gambetta (*bus 7 and 15; open daily exc Sun am and services, summer 9–12 and 2.30–6; spring and autumn 9.15–12 and 2–5.30; winter 9.30–12 and 2.30–5; no shorts or sleeveless shirts; adm*). Paid for by Tsar Nicolas II and completed just before the Bolshevik Revolution, its onion domes glow with colourful glazed Niçois tiles; inside are frescoes, woodwork and icons.

Cimiez: Chagall, Matisse and Roman Ruins

On the low hills west of the Paillon, where wealthy Romans lived the good life in Cemenelum, modern Niçois do the same in Cimiez, a luxurious 19th-century suburb dotted with the grand hotels, now genteel apartment buildings. Bus 15 from the Gare SNCF will take you to the main attractions, beginning with the **Musée National Message Biblique Marc Chagall** on Av du Docteur Ménard (*open Oct–June daily 10–5; July–Sept daily 10–6; closed Tues; adm*), built to house Chagall's cycle of 17 paintings based on stories from the Old Testament. The paintings are divided into three sections: *Genesis, Exodus* and the *Songs of Solomon*; they have been hung, as Chagall requested, chromatically rather than chronologically and are paired to complement each others' rich glowing emeralds, cobalts and magentas.

Henri Matisse died in Cimiez in 1954 and left the city his works, displayed in the **Musée Matisse**, set in the olive-studded Parc des Arènes (*take bus 15, 17, 20 or 22 from the Promenade des Anglais or Av Jean-Médecin; open April–Sept daily 10–6; Oct–Mar daily 10–5; closed Tues and some hols; adm*). Matisse's last work, the gargantuan paper cut-out *Flowers and Fruit*, 1952–3, dominates one whole side of the entrance hall.

Adjacent to the Matisse Museum is the new **Musée Archéologique** (*open April–Sept daily 10–12 and 2–6; Oct–Mar daily 10–1 and 2–5; closed Tues and some hols; adm*), entered through the excavations of Roman Cemenelum. These include the baths, a marble swimming pool, and the amphitheatre, with seating for 4,000. The museum houses vases, coins, statues, jewels, and models of Cimiez 2,000 years ago.

From here, walk back past the Matisse museum and across the Jardin Public to the **Musée Franciscain, Eglise et Monastère de Cimiez** (*open Mon–Sat 1-–12 and 3–6*). The Franciscans have been here since the 1500s; their church was heavily restored in 1850, although it still has two beautiful altarpieces by Ludovico Bréa.

From Cagnes to Cannes

Cagnes

The bloated amoeba of Cagnes is divided into three cells – overbuilt Cros-de-Cagnes by the sea with a Hippodrome; Cagnes-sur-Mer, further up, ; and medieval Haut-de-Cagnes on the hill.

There is only one thing to do in sprawling **Cagnes-sur-Mer**: from central Place Général-de-Gaulle follow Av Auguste-Renoir up to Chemin des Colettes, to the **Musée Renoir** (*open Wed–Mon 10–12 and 2–5; May–Sept 10–12 and 2–6; closed Tues and Nov; adm*), where Renoir spent the last 12 years of his life. Stricken with rheumatoid arthritis, Renoir followed his doctor's advice to move to warmer climes,where he produced paintings even more sensuous and voluptuous than before. It was also in Cagnes that Renoir first experimented with sculpture, by proxy, dictating detailed instructions to a young sculptor.

Spared the worst of the tourist shops, intricate, medieval **Haut-de-Cagnes** has become instead the fiefdom of contemporary artists, thanks to the UNESCO-sponsored Festival International de la Peinture. The crenellated **Château-Musée Grimaldi** (*open winter daily 10–12 and 2–5; summer daily 10–12 and 2–6; closed Tues and 3 weeks Nov; adm*) was built by the first Rainier Grimaldi in the 1300s. This contains a **Musée de l'Olivier**, and the **Donation Suzy Solidor** – 40 paintings donated

Getting Around

There are **train** stations in both Cagnes-sur-Mer and Cros-de-Cagnes and a continuous service of minibuses from Cagnes-sur-Mer station up the steep hill to Haut-de-Cagnes.

Buses from Nice to Vence stop in Cagnes-sur-Mer.

Hire a **bike** at Cycles Marcel, 5 Rue Pasqualini, t 04 93 20 64 07.

Tourist Information

Cagnes-sur-Mer: 6 Bd Maréchal-Juin, **t** 04 93 20 61 64, *info@cagnes-tourisme.com*.
Haut-de-Cagnes: Espace Solidor, Place du Château, t 04 92 02 85 05.

Where to Stay and Eat

Haut-de-Cagnes ✉ 06800

★★★★**Le Cagnard**, Rue Sous-Barri, t 04 93 20 73 21, *www.le-cagnard.com* (*luxury*). Sumptuous comforts discreetly arranged to fit in with the 14th-century architecture. Nearly every room has a private terrace, but the largest and most magical belongs to the Michelin-starred restaurant, which also has a coffered Renaissance-style ceiling that opens up in summer. *Restaurant closed Nov–mid-Dec and Mon, Tues and Thurs lunch.*

Les Peintres, 71 Montée de la Bourgade, t 04 93 20 83 08 (*moderate*). The walls are covered with paintings and the tables with warm home-made bread and Provençal dishes. *Closed mid-Nov–mid-Dec, and Mon in winter.*

by the Paris cabaret star, all of herself and each by a different artist – Van Dongen, Dufy, Kisling, Friesz, Cocteau, and so on. On the next floor, the **Musée d'Art Moderne Méditerranéen** is dedicated to a rotating collection of works by painters who have worked along the coast.

St-Paul-de-Vence

Inland from Cagnes, formerly a '*ville fortifiée*' that still preserves a watchtower dating from the 12th century and ramparts built by François Ier, prettily cobbled St-Paul-de-Vence is now clogged with visitors and artsy trinket shops. In the square is the famed restaurant **La Colombe d'Or**, whose first owner fell in love with modern art and for 40 years accepted paintings in exchange for meals from the impoverished artists who flocked here after the First World War – including Picasso, Derain, Matisse, Braque, Vlaminck, Léger, Dufy, and Bonnard. By his death he had accumulated one of France's top private collections, strictly for viewing by those who can afford a meal.

Set back in the woods up on Route Passe-Prest, the **Fondation Maeght** (*open July–Sept daily 10–7; Oct–June daily 10–12.30 and 2.30–6; adm*) is the best reason of all for visiting St-Paul. Its fairy godparents, Aimé and Marguerite Maeght, art dealers and friends of Matisse and Bonnard, wanted to create an ideal environment for contemporary art, and they hired Catalan architect José-Luis Sert to design the perfect white luminous setting. The permanent collection, which includes around 6,000 pieces by nearly every major artist of the past century, is removed during the Foundation's frequent exhibitions and retrospectives, but you'll always be able to see the works that were incorporated into the walls and sculpture gardens. On the other side of the museum, opposite the entrance hall, is Giacometti's sculpture courtyard. The Foundation also has a cinema and a studio for making films, art workshops, and one of the world's most extensive art libraries.

Vence and Matisse's Chapelle du Rosaire

Vence lies 3km from St-Paul and 10km from the coast, sufficiently far to seem more like a town in Provence than a Riviera fleshpot. The Vieille Ville has kept most of its medieval integrity, partly because the citizens were granted permission to build their homes against the ramparts in the 15th century. Enter the walls by way of the west gate, the fortified Porte du Peyra, now yet another art gallery, the **Château de Villeneuve–Fondation Emile Hughes** (*open July–Sept Tues–Sun 9.30–12.30 and 1.30–6.30; Oct–June Tues–Sun 10–12.30 and 2–6; closed Mon; adm*) which displays a comprehensive collection covering the artist's fluttering career. Just inside the walls, the **Place du Peyra** was the Roman forum, and is still the site of the daily market. Roman tombstones are incorporated in the walls of the **Ancienne Cathédrale**, a rococo church full of treasures, the best of which are the stalls with lace-fine carvings satirizing Renaissance customs, sculpted by Jacques Bellot in the 1450s.

Matisse arrived in Vence in 1941 to escape the bombing along the coast, and fell seriously ill. The 'White' Dominican sisters nursed him back to health, and as a gift he built and decorated the simple **Chapelle du Rosaire** for them (*open Tues and Thurs 10–11.30 and 2–5.30, school hols also Mon, Wed and Sat 2–5.30; adm*). Matisse designed

Getting There

There are frequent buses from Cagnes-sur-Mer to La Colle-sur-Loup, St-Paul-de-Vence and Vence, and connections almost hourly from Nice. For bus times, call SAP, **t** 04 93 58 37 60.

Tourist Information

St-Paul-de-Vence: 2 Rue Grande, **t** 04 93 32 86 95, *artdevivre@wanadoo.fr*.

Vence: Place du Grand Jardin, **t** 04 93 58 06 38, *www.ville-vence.fr*.

Where to Stay and Eat

St-Paul-de-Vence ✉ 06570

★★★La Colombe d'Or, Place des Ormeaux, **t** 04 93 32 80 02, *www.la-columbe-dor.com* (*luxury*). Book early to sleep here among the 20th-century art. The rooms are full of character, the pool heated, the stone-arcaded terrace lovely. The restaurant (*expensive*), serves groaning platters of *hors-d'œuvres* and grilled meats. *Closed Nov–Dec.*

★★★★Le St Paul, 86 Rue Grande, **t** 04 93 32 65 25, *stpaul@relaischateaux.fr* (*luxury*). In the centre, in a 16th-century building: the interior designers let their hair down to create unusual but delightful juxtapositions of medieval, surreal, Egyptian and Art Deco elements. Its equally attractive restaurant (*expensive*) is in an ancient vault. *Closed Tues, and Wed lunch.*

★★★La Grande Bastide, 1350 Route de la Colle, **t** 04 93 32 50 30, *stpaullgb@lemail.fr* (*expensive*). Just outside the village, a stylishly renovated 16th-century manor with a pool and sun terrace, and welcoming *patronne*. *Closed Dec and Jan exc Xmas and New Year.*

★★★Le Hameau, 528 Rte de La Colle, **t** 04 93 32 80 24, *www.le-hameau.com* (*expensive*). Lovely, with wide views over the orange groves from its low-beamed rooms decked out in Provençal fabrics, and a small pool. *Closed mid-Nov–mid-Dec and Jan–mid-Feb.*

Le Ste Claire, Espace Ste-Claire, **t** 04 93 32 02 02, *www.sainte-claire.com* (*moderate–inexpensive*). Sturdy Provençal décor to match its cuisine, which is well-priced and served up on a terrace.

Vence ✉ 06140

★★★★Château St-Martin, 3km from Vence on Rte de Coursegoules, **t** 04 93 58 02 02, *www.chateau-st-martin.fr* (*luxury*). A set of villa-*bastides* built around a ruined Templar fortress. The 12-hectare park has facilities for riding, fishing, tennis and a heart-shaped pool installed at the request of Harry Truman. The restaurant is equally august, with prices to match. *Closed mid-Nov–Jan.*

★★★★Relais Cantemerle, 258 Chemin Cantemerle, **t** 04 93 58 08 18, *info@relais-cantemerle.com* (*expensive*). Decorated with Art Deco bits from the gutted Palais de la Méditerranée in Nice and set in its piney garden, with terraces and a pool. The Cantemerle's restaurant serves some of the finest food in Vence. *Closed Nov–mid-Mar.*

★★★Villa La Roseraie, 14 Av H.-Giraud, **t** 04 93 58 02 20 (*expensive–moderate*). In a garden of magnolias and cedars, with an enormous home-made breakfast, by an impeccable pool. Antiques, Salernes tiles a-plenty, and lovely ironwork, but beware the two topmost rooms, which are noisy and cramped. *Closed mid-Nov–Feb.*

★★Le Mas de Vence, 539 Av Emile Hughes, **t** 04 93 58 06 16, *www.azurline.com* (*moderate*). Be treated like one of the family; there is a decent pool and the restaurant is one of the best places to try real ravioli.

★La Closerie des Genêts, 4 Impasse Marcellin-Maurel, **t** 04 93 58 33 25 (*inexpensive*). Hidden in the centre of Vence, charming yet unpretentious, with quiet rooms and a shady garden where you can bring a picnic.

Auberge Les Templiers, 39 Av Joffre, **t** 04 93 58 06 05 (*expensive*). Traditional lamb, *foie gras* and fish dishes, served in Provençal surroundings and with warm service. *Closed Mon, Tues and Wed lunches, in summer all day Mon in winter.*

Le Vieux Couvent, 37 Rue Alphonse Toreille, **t** 04 93 58 78 58 (*expensive*). Hearty helpings of locally produced, well-prepared regional dishes. *Closed Wed, Thurs lunch, and mid-Jan–mid-Mar.*

Le Pêcheur du Soleil, on Place Godeau (behind the church), **t** 04 93 58 32 56 (*inexpensive*). Fine, as long as you won't be dazzled by the choice of 500 different pizza toppings. *Closed Sun and Mon, and mid-Oct–mid Jan.*

every aspect of the chapel, from the kaleidoscopic, geometrically patterned green and blue stained glass windows down to the priest's robes. He considered the result his masterpiece, an expression of the 'nearly religious feeling I have for life'.

Back towards the Coast: Biot, Antibes, Juan-les-Pins and Vallauris

Biot

Set in a couple of miles from the sea, Biot (rhymes with yacht) is a handsome village endowed with first-rate clay – in Roman times it specialized in large wine and oil jars. In 1955, Fernand Léger purchased some land here in order to construct a sculpture garden of monumental ceramics, then died 15 days later. In 1960 his widow used the land to build the superb **Musée National Fernand Léger** (*open Oct–June Wed–Mon 10–12.30 and 2–5.30; July–Sept 10.30–6; closed Tues; adm*), hard to mistake behind its giant ceramic-mosaic designed for the Olympic stadium of Hannover. Inside are the 348 paintings, tapestries, mosaics and ceramics that trace Léger's career from his first flirtations with Cubism back in 1909 – although even back then Léger was nicknamed the 'tubist' for his preference for fat noodly forms. After being gassed in the First World War, he recovered to flirt with the Purist movement founded by his buddies Le Corbusier and Amédée Ozenfant, a reaction to the 'decorative' tendencies of Cubism. After teaching at Yale during the Second World War, he returned to France with a keen interest in creating art for the working classes.

The presence of the museum has boosted the local ceramic and glass industry; across from the museum at the **Verrerie de Biot**, you can watch workers make glass suffused with tiny bubbles (*verre à bulles*). More ceramics and glass can be seen in the charming **Musée d'Histoire et de Céramique Biotoises** in the walled town (*open summer Wed–Sun 10–6; winter Wed–Sun 2–6; closed Tues; adm*). Guarded by 16th-century gates, Biot itself has retained much of its character, especially around central Place des Arcades, albeit crammed with art and pottery galleries.

Antibes and the Musée Picasso

Antibes still retains an authentic vivacity all its own, drawing in crowds of bright young things who disdain the hollower charms of Juan-les-Pins. A relic of Antibes' earlier incarnation as France's bulwark against Savoyard Nice are its sea-walls, especially the massive 16th-century **Fort Carré**. The handsome 17th- and 18th-century houses of Vieil Antibes look over their neighbours' shoulders towards the sea, obscuring it from **Cours Masséna**, the main street of Greek Antipolis, which holds a morning market.

The best sea views are monopolized by the **Château Grimaldi** – a seaside castle built by the same family who ran most of this coast at one time or another, including Antibes from 1385 to 1608. For six months in 1946, the owner, Romuald Dor, let Picasso use the second floor as a studio. Picasso, glad to have space to work in, quickly filled it up in a few months, only later discovering to his annoyance that all along Dor had intended to make his efforts into the **Musée Picasso** (*open summer Tues, Thurs, Sat and Sun 10–6, Wed and Fri 10–8; winter 10–12 and 2–6; closed Mon and*

Getting There and Around

Biot's **train** station is at La Brague, a steep 5km walk up to the village, although buses approximately every hour from Antibes stop at the station en route to Biot.

Antibes' **train** station is at Place P. Semard, about a 10-minute walk from the centre. The station in Juan-les-Pins is centrally located on the Av de l'Esterel.

There are frequent *Métrazur* and TGV trains from Antibes, Juan-les-Pins and Golfe-Juan to Nice and Cannes. **Buses** from Antibes (t 04 93 34 37 60) for Cannes, Nice, Nice airport, Cagnes-sur-Mer, and Juan-les-Pins depart from Place de Gaulle; others leave from Rue de la République.

Tourist Information

Antibes: 11 Place Charles de Gaulle, t 04 92 90 53 00, *www.antibes-juanlespins.com*.
Vallauris: Square du 8 Mai 1945, t 04 93 63 82 58.

Where to Stay and Eat

Biot ✉ 06410

★★Auberge du Jarrier, Passage de la Bourgade, t 04 93 65 11 68 (*expensive*). For a special feast, reserve a table at least a week in advance. In an old jar-works, with a magical terrace and a superb four-course seasonal menu that puts the Côte's *haute cuisine* budget-busters to shame. *Closed Mon and Tues out of season, Tues in season.*
★Hôtel des Arcades, 16 Place des Arcades, t 04 93 65 01 04 (*inexpensive*). A delightful old hotel in a 15th-century building,

furnished with antiques. The popular artsy restaurant below (*moderate*) does a genuine *soupe au pistou* and other Provençal favourites. *Closed Sun eve and Mon.*

Antibes ✉ 06600

★★★★Hôtel du Cap Eden Roc, Bd Kennedy, Cap d'Antibes, t 04 93 61 39 01, *www.edenroc-hotel.fr* (*luxury*). Still very much there, brilliantly white and set in an idyllic park overlooking the dreamy Iles de Lérins. No hotel on the Riviera has hosted more celebrities, film stars or plutocrats; you could easily drop €150 at the exalted restaurant, the **Pavillon Eden Roc**. *Closed mid-Oct–mid-April.*
★★★★Imperial Garoupe, 770 Chemin de la Garoupe, t 04 92 93 31 61, *www.imperial-garoupe.com* (*luxury*). Not quite in the same class but a sumptuous peachy villa with impeccable rooms and opulent marble bathrooms set in tranquil gardens above the sea and a private beach. Breakfast is served at your private terrace, or overlooking the pool. There is a restaurant. *Closed Nov–Mar.*
★★★Hôtel Garoupe-Gardiole, 74 Chemin de La Garoupe, t 04 93 61 35 03, *www.hotel-lagaroupe-gardiole.com* (*expensive*). In Cap d'Antibes, with large, luminous rooms set in a pine wood and a magnificent wisteria over the terrace. Rooms vary greatly in price. *Closed Nov–Mar.*
★★★Mas Djoliba, 29 Av de Provence, t 04 93 34 02 48, *www.hotel-djoliba.com* (*expensive*). A serendipitous *mas* in a small park with a heated pool. *Closed Nov–Jan.*
★Nouvel Hôtel, 1 Av du 24-Août, t 04 93 34 44 07 (*inexpensive*). Near the bus station, 20 soundproofed rooms which fill up rapidly.
De Bacon, Bd de Bacon, Cap d'Antibes, t 04 93 61 50 02 (*expensive*). As stylish and elegant

hols; adm). Because of the post-war lack of canvases and oil paint, Picasso used mostly fibro-cement and boat paint. You can't help but feel that he was exuberantly happy, inspired by the end of the war, his love of the time, Françoise Gillot, and the mythological roots of the Mediterranean.

Cap d'Antibes

Further south along the peninsula (follow the scenic coastal D2559) the delightful, free, sandy (and therefore packed) beach of **La Salis** marks the beginning of Cap

as its perfectly prepared seafood and *bouillabaisse*, at classy prices. *Closed Mon and Tues lunch and Nov–Jan.*

La Bonne Auberge, on the N7 near La Brague, **t** 04 93 33 36 65 (*expensive*). Renowned Chef Jo Rostang's son Philippe has inherited the kitchen, and has already made a name for his *salade de homard aux ravioles de Romans* and *millefeuille bonne auberge*. Reserve long in advance.

Les Vieux Murs, Promenade Amiral-de-Grasse, **t** 04 93 34 06 73 (*expensive*). Near the Picasso museum, cool and spacious, with wooden décor, and serves traditional food made modern.

Le Sucrier, 6 Rue des Bains, **t** 04 93 34 85 40 (*moderate*). The chef is proud to be the great-great-nephew of Guy de Maupassant and spirits up traditional French classics with an exotic twist in a cavernous stone setting. There is even a vegetarian menu. *Closed Tues and Jan.*

Chez Olive, 2 Bd Maréchal-Leclerc, **t** 04 93 34 42 32 (*cheap*). Good Provençal favourites and a truly succulent fresh ravioli. *Closed Mon out of season.*

Juan-les-Pins ✉ 06160

★★★★Juana, in a lovely garden on Av Georges Gallice La Pinède, **t** 04 93 61 08 70, *www.hotel-juana.com* (*luxury*). A grand survivor from the 1920s: a beautiful Art Deco hotel, a private beach and heated pool. *Closed Nov–mid-April.*

★★★★Belles Rives, Av Baudouin, **t** 04 93 61 02 79, *www.bellesrives.com* (*luxury*). De luxe rooms, vintage 1930, facing the sea. There's a private beach and jetty, and a good restaurant, with a view over the gulf, or you can eat on the beach. *Closed mid-Nov–mid-Mar.*

★★★Hôtel des Mimosas, in Rue Pauline, 500m from the sea, **t** 04 93 61 04 16, *www.hoteldes mimosas.fr.st* (*moderate*). The rooms have balconies overlooking the pool and garden.

★★★Welcome, 7 Av Docteur Hochet, **t** 04 93 61 26 12, *www.hotelwelcome.net* (*expensive*). Lives up to its name and has sunny terraces and a garden.

La Terrasse Morisset, **t** 04 93 61 20 37 (*expensive*). The resort's top restaurant, a luxurious place that boasts delicate dishes imbued with all the freshness and colour of Provence, and excellent wines to match from the region's best vineyards. *Closed Jan–Mar.*

Bijou-Plage, directly on the sea on Bd du Littoral, **t** 04 93 61 39 07 (*expensive*). An excellent array of sea and land dishes fill the menu; during the festival it's a good place to find the stars tucking into a *bouillabaise*.

Entertainment and Nightlife

In Antibes, the famous **La Siesta**, on the road to Nice, **t** 04 93 33 31 31, operates as a beach concession by day and at night turns into an over-the-top nightclub and casino where thousands of people flock every summer evening to five dance-floors, fountains, and fiery torches. The whole of Juan swings during the jazz festival.

Whisky à Gogo, La Pinède, Av Leonetti, **t** 04 93 61 26 40. *Closed Nov.*

Le Village, 1 Bd de la Pinède, **t** 04 92 93 90 00. Older shakers and movers.

Café Cosy, 3 Rue de Migrainier, **t** 04 93 34 81 55. A charming place to sip wine away from the hubbub.

d'Antibes, scented with roses, jasmine and the smell of money. The **Plateau de la Garoupe** is the highest point of the headland, with the ancient seamen's **Chapelle de la Garoupe**. Further west, a 12th-century tower holds the **Musée Napoléonien**, Av Kennedy (*open Mon–Fri 9.30–12 and 2.15–6, Sat 9.30–12; closed Oct*), with ships' models and items relating to Napoleon's connections with Antibes. The cape is practically synonymous with the **Grand Hôtel du Cap**, built in 1870, where the Murphys and F. Scott and Zelda Fitzgerald frolicked in the Roaring 20s, and played a major role in the creation of the Riviera's summer season.

Juan-les-Pins and Vallauris

On the other side of the Cap, created in the 1920s as a French-style Miami Beach, **Juan-les-Pins** flourished when it suddenly become desirable to bake brown on the beach. By 1930 it was the most popular and scandal-ridden resort on the Riviera, where women first dared to bathe in skirtless suits. The presence of Edith Piaf and Sidney Bechet boosted its popularity in the 1950s; all the young came here from Antibes and further. It's still going strong, not a beauty but a brash and sassy tart of a resort, with nightclubs, strings of minuscule private beaches, and a magnificent jazz festival in the last two weeks of July.

Two kilometres inland from Golfe-Juan, **Vallauris**, like Biot, was famous for pottery, but in this case useful household wares. Because of competition with aluminium, the industry was on its last legs in 1946 when Picasso rented a small villa in town and met Georges and Suzanne Ramié, owners of the Poterie Madoura. He gave the Ramiés the exclusive right to sell copies of his ceramics, and you can still buy them at **Madoura**, just off Rue du 19 Mars 1962. Thanks to Picasso, 200 potters now work in Vallauris, some talented, others trying. In 1951, the village asked Picasso if he would decorate a deconsecrated chapel next to the castle. The result is the famous plywood paintings of *La Guerre et la Paix*, now known as the **Musée National Picasso**, Place de la Libération (*open 10–12.15 and 2–5; closed Tues and hols; adm*).

Grasse

Grasse's most important industry throughout the Middle Ages was tanning imported sheep-skins and buffalo-hides, using aromatic herbs that grew nearby. From this, the Grassois moved on to making fine perfumed gloves at the request of Catherine de Médicis. When gloves fell out of fashion after the Revolution they became simply *parfumeurs*. Today, this picturesque but unglamorous hilltown, with approximately 30 *parfumeries*, leads the world in perfume-making.

The arcaded **Place aux Aires** near the top of the town in the Vieille Ville is the main meeting point for all and holds a morning food and flower market. From here Rue des Moulinets and Rue Mougins-Roquefort lead to the Romanesque **Cathédrale Notre-Dame-du-Puy**. The art is to the right: the *Crown of Thorns* and *Crucifixion* painted by Rubens at the age of 24, before he hit the big time; a rare religious subject by Fragonard, the *Washing of the Feet*; and, most sincere of all, a reredos by Ludovico Bréa. The Cannes road leads into Grasse's promenade, Place du Cours, with pretty views over the countryside. Close by, at 23 Bd Fragonard, is the **Musée Jean-Honoré Fragonard** (*open daily June–Sept 10–7; Oct–May Wed–Mon 10–1.30 and 2–5.30; closed Nov; adm*). Just north of the Cours, at 2 Rue Jean Ossola, the **Musée d'Art et d'Histoire de Provence** (*same hours as Musée Fragonard*) exhibits Gallo-Roman funerary objects, *santons* and furniture in all the Louis styles and an exceptional collection of faïence from Moustiers and Apt. At 8 Cours Honoré-Cresp, the **Musée International de la Parfumerie** (*same hours as Musée Fragonard*) displays lots of precious little bottles from Roman times to the present.

Getting There

There are no trains, but there are frequent **buses** from Cannes and Nice to Grasse.

The bus station (**t** 04 93 36 37 37) is on the north side of town, at the Parking Notre-Dame-des-Fleurs.

Leave your car here: Grasse's steep streets are narrow for motorists.

Tourist Information

Grasse: Palais des Congrès, **t** 04 93 36 66 66, *www.grasse-riviera.com*

Mougins: 15, Av Mallet, **t** 04 93 75 87 67.

Where to Stay and Eat

Grasse ✉ 06130

★★★**Hôtel Résidence des Parfums**, Rue Eugène-Charabot, **t** 04 92 42 35 35, *www.odalys-vacances.com* (*expensive*). Pretty views, a pool, sauna and Jacuzzi. It offers a 1hr 'Introduction to Perfume' that takes you into the secret heart of the smell biz, lending you a 'nose' to help create your own perfume.

★★★**Auberge du Colombier**, 15km east of Grasse at Roquefort-les-Pins, 2085 Rte Départementale, **t** 04 92 60 33 00, *www.auberge-du-colombier.com* (*expensive*). A delightful white *mas* with cheerfully decorated rooms, expansive gardens with a pool, and an extraordinary restaurant – try the ravioli stuffed with wild mushrooms and scattered with roasted hazelnuts. *Restaurant closed Tues.*

★★**Charm Hôtel du Patti**, in the medieval centre on Place du Patti, **t** 04 93 36 01 00 (*moderate*). Very comfortable rooms, all with air-conditioning and TV.

Bastide Saint-Antoine, 48 Rue Henri-Dunant, **t** 04 93 70 94 94, *www.jacques-chibois.com* (*very expensive*). For a sumptuous Tuscan feast in glorious al fresco surroundings.

Les Arcades, Place aux Aires, **t** 04 93 36 00 95 (*moderate*). For a reasonably priced lunch underneath the arches, with Provençal dishes and fishes.

Mougins ✉ 06250

★★★★**Les Muscadins**, 18 Bd Courteline, **t** 04 92 28 28 28, *www.lesmuscadins.com* (*luxury*). Individually decorated sumptuous bedrooms of charm and character. The nouvelle cuisine and chocolate desserts are excellent.

★★★★**Le Moulin de Mougins**, Notre-Dame-de-Vie, **t** 04 93 75 78 24, *www.moulin-mougins.com* (*expensive*). In 1969 chef Roger Vergé bought a 16th-century olive mill near Notre-Dame-de-Vie and made it into the internationally famous luxury restaurant, which also has three rooms and two apartments overlooking the sculpture gardens and wisteria-covered terraces. Of late, France's gourmet bibles have been sniffing that the mild-mannered celebrity chef has lost a bit of his touch – and little faults seem big when you shell out €150 for a meal. But it's still a once-in-a-lifetime experience for most, in the most enchanting setting on the Côte. *Closed Dec–mid-Jan.*

L'Amandier, Place des Patriotes, **t** 04 93 90 00 91 (*expensive*). If you can't get a table at Le Moulin, Vergé has a simpler restaurant, located up a winding staircase in a 14th-century olive-oil mill above his shop. The ivy-covered terrace is utterly romantic, and menus start at €25. In the shop, **Les Boutiques du Moulin**, you can stock up on a selection of the master's sauces and *compôtes*. For those that still haven't had enough Vergé, he has also opened a cookery school above L'Amandier; **t** 04 93 75 35 70.

Brasserie de la Méditerranée, Place du Cdt. Lamy, **t** 04 93 90 03 47 (*moderate*). Grilled *gambas* with ginger and other seafood delights accompanied by heavenly home-made bread. *Closed Tues out of season.*

Le Bistrot, **t** 04 93 75 78 34 (*moderate*). For traditional dishes like roast quail, beef stew and aubergine caviar, in a vaulted, wooden-beamed dining room. Don't miss the fig tart. *Closed Wed, Thurs and Sat lunches.*

Le Rendez-vous de Mougins, Place du Cdt. Lamy, **t** 04 93 75 87 47 (*moderate*). Long a local favourite, with aromatic dishes like beef with wild mushroom sauce and sea bass with truffles.

It's hard to miss the *parfumeries* in Grasse. The alchemical processes of extracting essences from freshly cut mimosa, jasmine, roses, bitter orange, etc. are explained – you learn that it takes 900,000 rosebuds to make a kilo of rose essence. Tours in English are offered by **Parfumerie Fragonard** at the 18th-century converted tannery at 20 Bd Fragonard, **t** 04 93 36 44 65, and at the spanking new factory at **Les 4 Chemins**, on the Route de Cannes.

Mougins

Cooking, that most ephemeral of arts, is the main reason most people make a pilgrimage to Mougins, a luxurious, fastidiously flawless village of *résidences secondaires*, with more gastronomy per square inch than any place in France, thanks to the magnetic presence of Roger Vergé (*see* 'Where to Eat').

Cannes

The English and Russians started arriving in Cannes in the mid-19th century. By the 1920s the byword was: 'Menton's dowdy. Monte's brass. Nice is rowdy. Cannes is class!' Less enthusiastic commentators mentioned the dust, the bad roads, the uncontrolled building, and turds bobbing in the sea. If nothing else, the French Riviera proper ends with a bang at Cannes. But besides ogling the shops, the shoppers and their dogs there isn't much to see. Characterless luxury apartment buildings and boutiques have replaced the gaudy Belle Epoque confections along the fabled promenade **La Croisette**. The shoreline is divided into 32 sections; one rare public beach is in front of the fan-shaped **Palais des Festivals**. The **Vieux Port**, with its bobbing fishing-boats and plush, luxury craft, is on the other side of the Palais des Festivals. Cannes' cramped old quarter, **Le Suquet**, rises up on the other side of the port, where the usual renovation

Birth of a Festival

In 1939 a film festival at Cannes was established to rival Mussolini's new Venice film festival. Cannes' historians cite 1954 as the year when everything coalesced, when the essential ingredients of sex and scandal were added to the glamour of film: the décolletage of newcomer Sophia Loren made a big impression, grabbing attention and headlines away from Gina Lollobrigida. Another well-endowed starlet (English this time) named Simone Silva went on to the Iles de Lérins for a photo session with Robert Mitchum and removed her brassiere. Two hours later she was told to leave Cannes and a few years later, no longer able to find work because of her precocious gesture, she committed suicide. Cannes should have made her an honorary citizen. Two years later, the new sensation was Brigitte Bardot, who coyly spun her skirts around to reveal her dainty *petites culottes*. Nowadays would-be starlets strip down completely and bump and grind on the Croisette hoping to attract attention. Although the big American studios have traditionally shunned the festival, the importance of the international entertainment market has brought a growing stream over from Hollywood and throughout Europe.

Getting There and Around

By train: The frequent *Métrazur* between St-Raphaël and Menton, and every other train whipping along the coast, calls into the station at Rue Jean-Jaurès.

By bus: There is a multiplicity of private bus companies, all arriving and departing from different places; though there is one central number: **t** 04 93 45 20 08.

By boat: Every hour in the summer, the glass-bottomed boat, *Nautilus*, at Jetée Albert-Edouard, departs for tours of the port; tickets 70F, call t 04 93 39 11 82.

Boat trips out to the Iles de Lérins, **t** 04 93 39 11 82, depart from the Gare Maritime, Allées de la Liberté, approximately every hour, and much less frequently between October and June. The general tour is a whirlwind trip; you're best off going to one island at a time.

By taxi: t 04 92 99 27 27.

Tourist Information

Cannes: Palais des Festivals, 1 La Croisette, **t** 04 93 39 01 01, *www.cannes.fr*; another office is in the Gare SNCF.

Where to Stay

Cannes ✉ 06400

Although there are sizeable discounts if you come in the off-season, you can't book too early for the film festival or for July and August. Cannes' two tourist offices offer a free reservation service, but they won't be much help at that time of year.

Luxury

★★★★**Carlton**, 58 La Croisette, **t** 04 93 06 40 06, *www.cannes-interconti.com*. A Riviera landmark, with its two black cupolas, said to be shaped like the breasts of the *grande horizontale* Belle Otero, the Andalusian flamenco dancer and courtesan of kings. Renovated by its new Japanese owners, the 7th floor has a pool, casino and beauty spa.

★★★★**Majestic**, 10 La Croisette, **t** 04 92 98 77 00, *www.lucienbarriere.com*. The movie stars' favourite with its classic French décor, heated pool, private beach, etc. *Closed mid-Nov–Dec.*

★★★★**Martinez**, 73 La Croisette, **t** 04 92 98 73 00, *martinez@concorde-hotels.com*. This has kept its Roaring 20s character, but now has all imaginable modern comforts, including tennis courts, a heated pool and, from the 7th floor, grand views over the city.

Expensive

★★★**Bleu Rivage**, 61 La Croisette, **t** 04 93 94 24 25, *bleu-rivage@wanadoo.fr*. A renovated older hotel amidst the big daddies on the beach, where rooms overlook the sea or the garden at the back.

★★★**Molière**, 5 Rue Molière, **t** 04 93 38 16 16, *www.hotel-moliere.com*. Sitting in the midst of a garden, with bright rooms and terraces. *Closed mid-Nov–mid-Dec.*

★★★ **Hôtel Vendôme**, 37 Bd d'Alsace, **t** 04 93 38 34 33, *hotel.vendome@wanadoo.fr*. This ice-cream-pink 19th-century villa has recently been attractively renovated and sits in a private garden in the heart of the town. *Closed mid-Nov–Xmas.*

Moderate–Inexpensive

If you aren't in Cannes on an MGM expense account, there are other alternatives.

★★**Select**, 16 Rue Hélène-Vagliano, **t** 04 93 99 51 00, *www.hotel-select-cannes.com*. A quiet, modern choice with air-conditioned rooms, all with bath.

and displacement of the not-so-rich is just beginning. At the city's highest point, the monks of St-Honorat built a square watchtower, the Tour du Mont Chevalier, in 1088; their priory is now the **Musée de la Castre** (*open April–May 10–12 and 2–6; June–Aug 10–12 and 3–7; Sept–Mar 10–12 and 2–5; closed Tues; adm*), with an archaeological and ethnographic collection, containing everything from Etruscan vases to pre-Columbian art and a 40-armed Buddha. A good way to see Cannes is by night. Climb up through Le Suquet to **La Tour**, and join the lovers to look beyond the white boats and lights.

Le Chanteclair, 12 Rue Forville, t 04 93 39 68 88. Good doubles with showers. *Closed Nov.*

t 04 93 48 13 00. Retains the ambience of the old village and has tasty daily specials like lamb with wild mushrooms.

Eating Out

Luxury–Expensive

La Palme d'Or, Martinez hotel (*see* above), t 04 92 98 74 14. The Alsatian chef, Christian Willer, prepares succulent dishes, served in a fabulous Art Deco dining room. *Closed mid-Nov–Dec, and Mon–Tues; open daily during Festival.*

La Belle Otero, on the 7th floor of the Carlton (*see* above), t 04 92 99 51 10. The seventh heaven of gastronomy – it shares two Michelin stars with the Palme d'Or. *Closed Sun, Mon, and Tues lunch out of season.*

Le Fouquet's, Hôtel Majestic (*see* above), t 04 92 98 77 41. Chef Bruno Oger presides over this sister restaurant to the acclaimed Paris original.

Moderate

Le Baoli, Port Canto, t 04 93 43 03 43. Indonesian décor, fusion food and glitterati, with a tree-shaded terrace.

Café Roma, 1 Square Mérimée, t 04 93 38 05 04. Decent Italian food served in a brasserie with terrace overlooking the Palais.

Lou Souléou, 16 Bd Jean-Hibert, t 04 93 39 85 55. For affordable seafood and fine views of its original habitat; try *bouillabaisse* and a pretty good *aïoli. Closed Mon and Nov.*

Le Coin de Clyve, 23 Bd Alexandre III, t 04 93 43 06 34, *www.ciel-bleu.com*. A homely, welcoming little place off the beaten track. *Closed Wed out of season.*

Moderate–Cheap

Hôtel Brasserie du Marché, 10 Rue Monseigneur-Jeancard, Cannes la Bocca,

Entertainment and Nightlife

Casino

The casinos draw in some of the highest rollers on the Riviera, although the adjoining casino discos are fairly staid:

Casino Croisette, Palais des Festivals, t 04 92 98 78 00.

Casino Club, Carlton Hotel, t 04 92 99 51 00.

Bars and Clubs

To get into the most fashionable clubs (those with no signs on the door), you need to look as if you've just stepped off a 100ft yacht to get past the sour-faced bouncers.

Jimmy's, at the Casino in the Palais des Festivals, t 04 93 68 00 07. A glitzy showcase billing itself '*La discothèque des stars*'; it's certainly for those with stars in their eyes – gamblers, their ladies and mainstream music (*11pm–dawn*).

La Chunga, 24 Rue Latour-Maubourg, t 04 93 94 11 29, t 04 93 94 11 29. There's usually live music to go with the food. *8.30pm–dawn.*

Le Whisky à Gogo, Ladybird, 115 Av de Lérins, t 04 93 43 20 63. A well-heeled crowd.

Brooms Bar, Hôtel Gray d'Albion. With a piano bar. It also has a disco on Sunday night – Jane's Club, t 04 92 99 79 59.

Zanzi-Bar, 85 Rue Félix-Faure, t 04 93 39 30 75. A gay bar of long standing (*6pm–6am*).

Disco 7, 7 Rue Rougière, t 04 93 39 10 36. Dancing and a transvestite show (€15 *cover charge*). *11.30pm–6am.*

Cat Corner, 22 Rue Macé, t 04 93 39 31 31. Dance until dawn at the hottest place in town.

The Iles de Lérins: St-Honorat and Ste-Marguerite

When Babylon begins to pall, you can take refuge on a delightful pair of green, wooded, traffic-free islets just off the coast (take water and a picnic) named after two saints who founded religious houses on them. **St Honorat** landed on the islet that bears his name in 375. The island became a beacon of light and learning in the Dark Ages, producing 20 saints, including Patrick. The 29 monks who live there now cultivate part of the island, producing a delicious golden liqueur called Lérina. Larger **Ile**

Ste-Marguerite has nicer beaches, especially on the south end of Chemin de la Chasse. On the north end stands the gloomy **Fort Royal** (*open Oct–Mar 10.30–1.15 and 2.15–4.45, April–Sept 10.30–1.15 and 2.15–5.45; closed Mon and hols; adm*), with a little aquarium and a **Musée de la Mer** which displays finds from submarine archaeological digs. The fort, built by Richelieu, served mainly as a prison, especially for the mysterious Man in the Iron Mask. Speculation about the man's identity continues: was he Louis XIV's twin, as Voltaire suggested, or, according to a recent theory, the gossiping son-in-law of the doctor who performed the autopsy on Louis XIII and discovered that the king was impotent?

St-Raphaël and Fréjus

Between the mountainous porphyry-red Esterel and the Massif des Maures are St-Raphaël and Fréjus: St-Raphaël has more beaches, holiday flats and yachts; its venerable neighbour Fréjus (*Forum Julii*) is a market town and naval port, founded by Julius Caesar to rival Marseille.

St-Raphaël

St-Raphaël's once glittering turn-of-the-last-century follies and medieval centre were bombed to smithereens in the war, all except the Victorian-Byzantine church of **Notre-Dame de Lépante** in Bd Felix-Martin, and the **Eglise des Templiers** or St-Pierre (1150), with its Templar watchtower, in Rue des Templiers. If the church is closed, pick up the key at the adjacent **Musée de Préhistoire et d'Archéologie Sous-marine** (*open June–Sept Tues–Sat 10–12 and 3–6.30; Oct–May Tues–Sat 10–12 and 2–5.30; adm*). This holds finds from a Roman shipwreck full of building materials, brought up by Jacques Cousteau. This is much the prettiest part of town.

Fréjus: the Roman Town

Founded in 49 BC, Forum Julii was the first Roman town of Gaul, but not the most successful; the site was malarial and hard to defend, and eventually the river Argens silted up, creating the vast sandy beach of Fréjus-Plage but leaving the Roman harbour high and dry a mile from the sea. The fragments of Forum Julii are a long hike across the modern town. Best preserved is the ungainly, greenish **Amphithéâtre Romain**, Rue Henri-Vadon (*open Nov–Mar Mon and Wed–Fri 10–12 and 1–5.30, Sat 9.30–12.30 and 1.30–5.30, Sun 8–5; April–Oct Mon and Wed–Sat 10–1 and 2.30–6.30, Sun 8–7; closed Tues; adm*). Arches from a 40km **aqueduct** still leapfrog by the road to Cannes; north, on Av du Théâtre Romain, the vaults of the **Théâtre Romain** (*same hours as amphitheatre; adm, free Sun*) survived, although seating had to be replaced.

When the Saracens had left and the coast was clear in the 12th century, the Fréjussiens rebuilt their **Cathédral St-Léonce** in Place Formigé, and in the 16th century gave it a superb pair of Renaissance doors. The cathedral was the centre of a mini **cité épiscopale** incorporating a defence tower, chapterhouse and bishop's palace (*opem mid-Aug–mid-May Tues–Sun 9–12 and 2–5; mid-May–mid-Aug daily 9–6.30; adm*), all built with the warm red stone of the Esterel. The tour includes the **baptistry**,

Getting There and Around

St-Raphaël is the terminus of the *Métrazur* **trains** that run along the coast to Menton. Other trains between Nice and Marseille call at both St-Raphaël and Fréjus stations, making it easy to hop between the two; St-Raphaël also has direct connections to Aix, Avignon, Nîmes, Montpellier and Carcassonne, and TGVs from Paris. Both towns have **buses** for Nice airport and Marseille (bus station, t 04 91 50 57 68) and for St-Tropez and Toulon (SODE-TRAV, t 04 94 95 24 82). Les Bateaux de St-Raphaël, t 04 94 95 17 46, **sail** to St-Tropez and Port Grimaud, and make day excursions to the Iles de Lérins and Ile de Port Cros (summer only), as well as jaunts around the Golfe de Fréjus and its *calanques* (creeks); reserve ahead in July and Aug. **Taxis** t 04 94 83 24 24.

Tourist Information

St-Raphaël: Rue Waldeck Rousseau, t 04 94 19 52 52, *www.saint-raphael.com*.
Fréjus: 325 Rue Jean-Jaurès, t 04 94 51 83 83, *www.ville-frejus.fr*.

Where to Stay and Eat

St-Raphaël ✉ 83700

★★★**Golf de Valescure**, Av Paul l'Hermite, t 04 94 52 85 00, *www.valescure.com* (*expensive*). In the same family for five generations, with tennis and a pool when you're not on the links. *Closed mid-Nov–Jan.*

★★★**San Pedro**, Av du Colonel Brooke, t 04 94 19 90 20, *www.hotel-sanpedro.com* (*moderate*). Reasonable option in the old artists' quarter.
★★**Les Pyramides**, 77 Av P. Doumer, t 04 98 11 10 10 (*inexpensive*). Budget choice with a little garden. *Closed Dec–Feb.*
L'Arbousier, 6 Av de Valescure, t 04 94 95 25 00 (*expensive*). The most genial place to eat, combines charm and aromatic gourmet food for half the price of elsewhere. *Closed Sun eve, Mon and Wed eve out of season.*
Pastorel, 54 Rue de la Liberté, t 04 94 95 02 36 (*moderate*). In the same family since 1922, with a pleasant no-nonsense proprietress and an attractive garden terrace. Friday special €26 aïoli menu. *Closed Sun eve, Mon and Tues, plus Nov and Feb.*

Fréjus ✉ 83600

★★★**Aréna**, 139 Rue du Gal. de Gaulle, t 04 94 17 09 40, *www.arena-hotel.com* (*expensive*). Colourful, air-conditioned rooms, a pool, and good food in old Fréjus. *Closed Dec, restaurant closed Sat, and Mon lunch.*
★**Le Bellevue**, by the cathedral in Place Paul-Vernet, t 04 94 17 27 05 (*inexpensive*). The best of the cheapies, and quiet.
Le Mérou Ardent, 157 Bd de la Libération, is t 04 94 17 30 58 (*moderate*). Overlooking the beach and boats, dine on monkfish with prawns and spices. *Closed Mon lunch and Thurs lunch in season, and mid-Nov–mid-Dec.*
Les Potiers, 135 Rue des Potiers, t 04 94 51 33 74 (*moderate*). Sparky nouvelle cuisine on a quiet back street in the old town. *Closed Tues, and Wed lunch.*

the 12th-century **cloister**, with marble columns and a 14th-century ceiling, coffered into 1,200 vignettes. Upstairs, the **Archaeology Museum** (*open Nov–Mar Mon and Wed–Fri 10–12 and 1.30–5.30, Sat 9.30–12.30 and 1.30–5.30; April–Oct Mon and Wed–Sat 10–1 and 2.30–6.30; adm*) has a collection of finds from *Forum Julii*.

Just off the N7, in the Tour de la Mare district, is **Notre-Dame de Jérusalem** (*open Nov–Mar Mon–Fri 2.30–6.30, Sat 10–1 and 2–6.30; April–Oct Mon–Fri 1.30–5.30, Sat 9.30–12.30 and 1.30–5.30; adm*), an octagonal chapel designed by Jean Cocteau in the 1960s. He died before its completion; his partner, artist Edouard Dermit, finally painted the chapel from Cocteau's plans. Inside is an anarchic flurry of colour and form.

Ste-Maxime and Port Grimaud

In the seaside conurbation spread between Fréjus and St-Tropez, the only place that may tempt a detour is **Ste-Maxime**, a modern resort town with a shady, older

Where to Stay and Eat

Ste-Maxime ✉ 83120

****Belle Aurore**. 4 Bd Jean-Moulin, t 04 94 96 02 45, www.belleaurore.com (*expensive*). Rooms with character and all the usual comforts, including parking, pool, private beach and a fine gastronomic restaurant. *Closed mid-Oct–April.*

***Parc Hôtel Jas Neuf**, t 04 94 55 07 30, www.hotel-jasneuf.com (*expensive*). A huddle of Provençal-style buildings around a swimming pool. *Closed mid-Oct–mid-Mar.*

*****Domaine du Calidianus**, Bd Jean Moulin, t 04 94 96 23 21 (*expensive*). Glam and newly refurbished. *Closed mid-Sept–mid-June.*

***Mas des Brugassières**, Pont-de-la-Tour, t 04 94 55 50 55, www.mas-des-brugassieres.com (*expensive*). Delightful farmhouse which doesn't require a king's ransom but makes you feel like royalty anyway. Some rooms open on to the gardens and pool. *Closed mid-Oct–Mar.*

Le Revest, 48 Bd Jean-Jaurès, t 04 94 96 19 60 (*inexpensive*). Central, with a rooftop pool. *Closed Nov–Mar.*

nucleus by the port and a beach of golden sand facing St-Tropez. It willingly takes the overflow of fashionable and bankable holidaymakers from the latter, linked by frequent boats; St-Tropez may not look far away but it's two hours' traffic jam in high season. Ten kilometres north towards Le Muy on the D25, the remarkable **Musée du Phonographe et de la Musique Mécanique** in the wooded Parc de St-Donat (*open Easter–Sept 10–12 and 3–6; closed Mon and Tues; adm*) has exhibits that include one of Edison's original phonographs of 1878, and an accordion-like 'Melophone' of 1780.

From Ste-Maxime, the road passes through **Port Grimaud**, a pleasure port designed in 1968 by Alsatian entrepreneur François Spoerry, inspired by the lagoon complexes around St Petersburg, Florida, where home-owners, like Venetians, can park their boats by the front doors of the traditionally styled, colourful houses.

St-Tropez

It made the headlines in France when St-Tropez's mayor forced the discos to close at 2am and declared the beaches off limits to dogs, inciting the fury of 'Most Famous Resident' Brigitte Bardot, that crusading Joan of Arc of animal rights who married a National Front politician and in a recent autobiography referred to her son as a 'tumour'. But then again BB has always been a bit ahead of the rest of us, ever since she came down here to star in Roger Vadim's *Et Dieu créa la femme* in 1956 and incidentally made this lovely fishing village into the national showcase of free-spirited fun, sun and sex. Pre-BB, St-Tropez was discovered by painters in the early 1900s. Writers, most famously Colette, joined the artists' 'Montparnasse on the Mediterranean' in the 1920s. The third wave of even more conspicuous invaders, Parisian existentialists and glitterati came in the 1950s, when Françoise '*Bonjour Tristesse*' Sagan and Bardot made St-Trop the pinnacle of chic. Joan Collins, George Michael and Elton John have houses here.

If everything about St-Tropez fills you with dismay, let the **Musée de l'Annonciade** (*open Oct–May 10–12 and 2–6, June–Sept 10–12 and 3–7, closed Tues, holidays and Nov; adm*) be your reason to visit. It concentrates on works by painters in Paul Signac's St-Tropez circle, post-Impressionists and Fauves – colour-saturated paintings that take on a life of their own. Just outside the museum, the port is edged with the colourful pastel houses that inspired the Fauves. The view is especially good from the Môle Jean Réveille, the narrow pier that encloses the yacht-filled port. Seek out **Place de l'Ormeau, Rue de la Ponche** and **Place aux Herbes**, poetic corners of old St-Tropez that have refused to shift into top gear. The rambling little **Quartier de la Ponche**, with several coolly chic restaurants and bars, folds itself around the shore and the tower of the now defunct Château de Suffren. Another essential ingredient of St-Tropez is the charming Place Carnot, better known by its old name of **Place des Lices**, an archetypal slice of Provence with its plane trees, market, cafés and eternal games of *pétanque*.

Getting There and Around

Toulon-Hyères **airport** is 50km away. Nice airport is 90km away.

SODETRAV **buses** (**t** 04 94 97 88 51) link St-Tropez to St-Raphaël, Grimaud, Cogolin and Hyères and to the nearest TGV stop at Les Arcs. There's also a regular bus from Toulon. You may be better off catching a **boat** to St-Tropez from St-Raphaël (**t** 04 94 95 17 46), or Ste-Maxime (MMG, **t** 04 94 96 51 00).

The ghastly traffic makes **bike and moped hire** an attractive alternative (M.A.S, 3 Rue Quaranta, near St-Tropez's Place Carnot, **t** 04 94 97 00 60).

Tourist Information

St-Tropez: Maison du Tourisme du Golfe de St-Tropez/Pays des Maures, **t** 04 94 55 22 00, *tourisme@golfe-infos.com, www.golfe-infos.com*, at the N98/D559 junction just before the traffic gridlock, and at Quai Jean-Jaurès, **t** 04 94 97 45 21.

Shopping

Although many boutiques are now owned by chains, a few exclusive shops remain.
Gas, Place Sibilli. Specializes in coral and turquoise jewellery.
Rondini, 16 Rue G. Clemenceau. For the famous *sandales tropéziennes*, invented in 1927.
Sugar, Rue Victor-Laugier. Cotton tops and shorts.
Galeries Tropéziennes, 55 Rue Gambetta. For fabrics, espadrilles, and everything else.

La Pause Douceur, 11 Rue Allard. De luxe chocolates.
Autour des Oliviers, 2 Place de l'Ormeau. For Provençal specialities.

Where to Stay and Eat

St-Tropez ✉ 83990

If you haven't already booked a hotel long ago, forget about arriving in St-Tropez on the off-chance between June and September. Prices are about 20 per cent higher than anywhere else on the coast. Beware that most hotels close in the winter.

★★★★**Le Byblos**, Av Paul Signac, **t** 04 94 56 68 00, *www.byblos.com* (*luxury*). Built by a Lebanese millionaire and designed like a *village perché*, with rambling corridors, patios and opulent rooms. In the middle there's a magnificent pool, and the nightclub is one of most desirable to be seen in. There is now a *nouvelle cuisine* restaurant, **Spoon**, **t** 04 94 56 68 20. *Closed mid-Oct–Easter*.

★★★★**Résidence La Pinède**, Plage de la Bouillabaisse, **t** 04 94 55 91 00, *www.residencepinede.com* (*luxury*). The *luxe, charme et volupté* of this Relais & Châteaux place has given it the current edge. Dining *à la carte* in its gourmet restaurant comes at an appropriate price. *Closed Oct–Mar*.

★★★★**La Bastide de Saint-Tropez**, Rte des Carles, **t** 04 94 55 82 55, *www.bastidesaint-tropez.com* (*luxury*). Similarly swish, but perched on a hill, this has an even better, Michelin-starred restaurant, **L'Olivier** (*expensive*). Served in a garden of oleander, figs, and parasol pines, the food is flamboyant,

Although the **beaches** begin even before you enter St-Tropez, those famous sandy strands where girls first dared to bathe topless (circumventing local indecency laws by placing Coke bottle tops over their nipples) skirt the outer rim of the peninsula. In the summer minibuses link them with Place Carnot, a good idea as beach parking is as expensive as the beaches themselves. **Plage de Pampelonne** is lined with restaurants and luxury concessions. On the other side of Cap Camarat, **Plage de l'Escalet** is hard to reach, but much less crowded and free (take the narrow road down from the D93); from L'Escalet you can pick up the coastal path and walk in an hour and a half to the best and most tranquil beach of all, **Plage de la Briande**.

generous and exceptionally delicious. *Closed Jan–mid-Feb.*

★★★★**Le Yaca**, 1 Bd d'Aumale, **t** 04 94 55 81 00, *www.hotel-le-yacas.fr.* Once home to Colette, and before her to Paul Signac. A rambling, but very very chic, fusion of three small cottages; most of the rooms look inwards to a courtyard bursting with flowers. *Closed Oct–Easter; restaurant closed Mon.*

★★★★**La Ponche**, 3 Rue des Remparts, **t** 04 94 97 02 53, *www.laponche.com* (*luxury*). Picasso's old watering hole, located in the old town – a romantic nook to entice your special darling. The rooms overlooking the street can be noisy, but there is double glazing and air-con. *Closed Nov–mid-Feb.*

★★★**Le Sube Continental**, 15 Quai Suffren, **t** 04 94 97 30 04 (*expensive*). The oldest hotel in town and an historic monument to boot, with views over the port. *Closed Jan–mid-Feb.*

★★**Les Lauriers**, Rue du Temple, behind Place des Lices **t** 04 94 97 04 88 (*moderate*). Modern, pleasant rooms with air-con, in a garden setting. *Closed Jan.*

Leï Mouscardins, Tour du Portalet, **t** 04 94 97 29 00 (*very expensive*). For pure atmosphere and the best creative food in town, book a table overlooking the harbour; it may be one of the high points of your holiday. *Closed Dec–Jan, and Tues and Wed, except summer. Closed lunch June–Sept.*

La Voile Rouge, Plage de Ramatuelle, **t** 04 94 79 84 34 (*expensive*). The current fashionable favourite.

Chez Maggi, 5 Rue Sibille, **t** 04 94 97 16 12 (*moderate*). A busy, fashionable, gay bar/restaurant serving up good and inexpensive Franco-Italian cuisine, such as

delicious *petits farcis provençaux*, to a youthful clientele in a small room adjoining the raucous bar area. *Dinner only in winter.*

Ramatuelle ✉ 83350

★★★★**Château de la Messardière**, Rte de Tahiti, **t** 04 94 56 76 00, *www.messardiere.com* (*luxury*). For self-indulgence, you can't beat this late 19th-century folly; ultra comfortable, with a superb panoramic restaurant and exquisite, exotic dishes you'll find nowhere else. *Closed mid-Oct–mid-Mar.*

★★★**La Figuière**, Rte de Tahiti, **t** 04 94 97 18 21 (*expensive*). Relaxing old farmhouse in a vineyard, tennis, and a pool. *Closed Oct–mid-April.*

Entertainment and Nightlife

The bars in Place des Lices provide an entertaining sideshow in which to pass the early part of the evening.

Café des Arts, Place des Lices, **t** 04 94 97 02 25. A quiet alternative on this popular square, with seafood specialities. *Open eves only. Closed mid-Oct–mid-April.*

Sénéquier, by the port, **t** 04 94 97 09 00. A St-Trop institution. *Closed Nov.*

La Bodega du Papagayo, Quai d'Epi, **t** 04 94 97 76 70. An attractive bar haunted by a younger clientele. *Closed Wed in season.*

Dancing and much besides goes on until dawn at St-Trop's clubs.

VIP Room, by the new port, **t** 04 94 97 14 70.
Les Caves du Roy, Hôtel Le Byblos (*see above*), **t** 04 94 56 68 00. Full of stars. *Closed winter.*

The Massif des Maures

Beckoning just a short drive from the coastal pandemonium are the quiet chestnut woodlands of the Massif des Maures, or at least what's left of them after a quarter of the forest burned in 1990; note that some of the roads that penetrate the mountain may be closed in dry summers.

Perhaps by now you've noticed signs advertising pipes from **Cogolin**; they've been making them for over two centuries (visits at Courrieu Pipes, 58 Av G.-Clemenceau, *open daily 9–12 and 2–6*). Other crafts particular to Cogolin are hand-knotted wool rugs, top-quality reeds for saxophones, and furniture. Unlike Cogolin, nearby **Grimaud** is all aesthetics and boutiques. A former Saracen and Templar stronghold, it can hold its own among the most perfect *villages perchés* on the coast, crowned by the ruined castle of the Grimaldis, after whom the village is named.

When Charles Martel defeated the Moorish invaders at Poitiers in 732 and pushed them back to Spain, a few managed to give the Franks the slip and escape into Provence. Their strongholds, or *fraxinets*, gave their name to **La Garde-Freinet**, a large village full of medieval charm and British expats. A path, past chestnuts said to be 1,000 years old, ascends to the site of a Saracen fortress (the standing walls are from the 15th century). Six kilometres off the D14 from Grimaud stands the moody, ruined **Chartreuse de la Verne** (*open summer 11–6, winter 11–5 , closed Tues and religious hols and Jan; adm*), founded in 1170 in one of the most romantically desolate corners of France – a vast and impressive Carthusian complex. The air is sweet in the biggest settlement of the western Maures, **Collobrières**, an attractive old village full of quirky fountains and scented with chestnuts being ground into paste and purée.

Getting Around

SODETRAV **buses (t** 04 94 97 88 51) link St-Tropez to Grimaud, Cogolin and Hyères and to the nearest TGV stop at Les Arcs. There's also a regular bus from Toulon.

Other villages in the Massif des Maures are much harder to reach by public transport: two buses a day go from Le Lavandou to La Garde-Freinet, and there's but one linking La Garde-Freinet and Grimaud to Toulon.

Where to Stay and Eat

Grimaud ✉ 83310

★★★**Hostellerie du Coteau Fleuri**, Place des Pénitents, **t** 04 94 43 20 17, *www.coteau fleuri.fr* (*moderate*). A comfortable stone inn, almost hidden by flowers and ivy, built in the 1930s on the quiet western outskirts of town, with grand views over the vineyards and the Maures; its restaurant (*expensive*) serves reliably good Provençal dishes. *Closed mid-Nov–mid-Dec, and Mon lunch, Tues, and Fri lunch.*

★★★**La Boulangerie**, Rte de Collobrières, **t** 04 94 43 23 16 (*expensive*). For more great views and silence. *Closed Oct–Easter.*

Le Verger, Route de la Collobrières, **t** 04 94 55 57 80 (*expensive*). A Provençal building a kilometre west of Grimaud. French windows lead out into the quiet gardens, and dinner is served by the pool. *Closed Nov–Easter.*

Les Santons, Rte Nationale, **t** 04 94 43 21 02 (*expensive*). Indulge in a gourmet spread of lobster salad, seafood or thyme-scented *selle d'agneau* in dining rooms full of santons. *Closed Nov–Mar.*

Café de France, Place Neuve, **t** 04 94 43 20 05 (*moderate*). Pennywise, the best bet for food, in an old stone house with a summer terrace. *Closed Nov–Feb and Sun eve in Mar.*

The Corniche des Maures

The bay on the underside of the St-Tropez peninsula, with its clear coves and large beaches of silken sand, has been given lock, stock and barrel to the property promoters. The longest beach, however, at **Cavalaire-sur-Mer**, remains more popular with families than movie stars. Near by, the **Domaine du Rayol**, Av des Belges (*open Feb–June and Sept–mid-Nov daily 9.30–12.30 and 2.30–6.30; mid-Nov–Jan by appointment; July and Aug Tues–Sun 9.30–12.30 and 4.30–8, Mon till 7; adm*) is well worth a stop for its Mediterranean gardens. Persevering west past Cap Nègre and the exclusive villages of Pramousquier and Cavalière you find the big boys on the Corniche-des-Maures, the fishing port and resort of **Le Lavandou** and **Bormes-les-Mimosas**, a cute hyper-restored medieval enclave that added the mimosas to tart up its name in 1968. Le Lavandou, where Bertolt Brecht and Kurt Weill wrote *The Threepenny Opera* in 1928, is a good place in which to empty your wallet on seafood, watersports, boutiques and nightclubs.

Hyères and its Golden Isles

Hyères claims to be the original resort of the Côte d'Azur, with a pedigree that goes back to Charles IX and Catherine de Médici,s who wintered here in 1564. In the early 19th century, people like Empress Josephine, Pauline Borghese, Victor Hugo, Tolstoy and Robert Louis Stevenson built villas here, before it faded genteelly from fashion in the 1880s. For despite its mild climate and lush gardens, Hyères was, unforgivably, three miles from the seaside.

Hyères and the Giens Peninsula

There isn't much to do in Hyères but take a brief wander into the **Vieille Ville**, beyond Place Massillon. Here stands the Tour des Templiers, a remnant from a Templar's lodge, and, on top of a monumental stair, the church of St-Paul (1599) with 400 ex votos dating back to the 1600s and a set of *santons* too large to move. The Renaissance house next to St-Paul doubles as a city gate, through which you can walk up to Parc St-Bernard. At the upper part of the park, the **Villa Noailles** (*open summer Wed–Sun 10–12 and 4–7; winter Wed–Sun 10–12 and 2–5*) was designed as a *château cubiste* for art patron Vicomte Charles de Noailles. Austere cement on the outside, furnished with pieces commissioned from Eileen Gray and designers from the Bauhaus, this vast villa was a busy hive of creativity between the wars; the garden has been recently linked to that of author Edith Wharton. Further up the hill are the hollow walls and towers of the **Vieux Château** with an overview of Hyères' peninsula. Originally the island of Giens, it has been anchored to the continent by two sand-bars whose arms embrace a salt marsh.

The Iles d'Hyères

Hyères' three islands are voluptuous little greenhouses that have seen more than their share of trouble. In the Middle Ages they belonged to St-Honorat by Cannes, and attracted pirates like moths to a flame. In the late 19th century, they were used to

Getting There and Around

By plane: Hyères-Toulon Airport is served mainly by Air France from Paris and Ryanair from London.

By train: Hyères is a dead end, linked to Toulon but nowhere else; the station is 1.5km south of town, but there are frequent buses into the town centre.

By bus: Buses can be tricky. Telephone first. SODETRAV, 47 Av Alphonse Denis, **t** 04 94 12 55 12, serves destinations west to Toulon and east to Le Lavandou. City buses (from the bus station in the town centre) link Hyères to Hyères-Plage and the Giens peninsula.

By boat: Boats for all three of Hyères' islands depart at least twice a day, year-round, from Port Saint-Pierre (Hyères) (**t** 04 94 12 54 40) and Le Lavandou (**t** 04 94 71 01 02), with additional sailings in the summer. There are more frequent connections from La Tour-Fondue, at the tip of the Giens peninsula, to Porquerolles (**t** 04 94 58 21 81), and in summer boats also sail from Toulon to Porquerolles. Be warned that inter-island connections are rare.

Tourist Information

Hyères ✉ 83400: 3 Av Ambroise Thomas, **t** 04 94 01 84 50, *www.ot-hyeres.fr*.

Where to Stay and Eat

Hyères Town ✉ 83400

★★Les Orangers, 64 Av Iles d'Or, **t** 04 94 00 55 11, *www.var-provence.com* (*inexpensive*). A sturdy Provençal-style building houses one of the prettiest and most comfortable hotels in town.

★Reine Jane, by the sea at Ayguade, **t** 04 94 66 32 64 (*inexpensive*). Good rooms and food at bargain prices.

Le Bistrot de Marius, 1 Place Massillon, **t** 04 94 35 88 38 (*moderate*). A tiny stone establishment with big platefuls of Provençal favourites, a very jolly host and tables out on the main square in summer. *Closed mid-Nov–mid–Dec and Jan.*

Les Jardins de Bacchus, 32 Av Gambetta, **t** 04 94 65 77 63 (*moderate*). Pulls out all the stops with its rich, flavoursome Provençal dishes and quietly elegant surroundings. *Closed Sun eve and Mon in winter; Sun lunch and Mon in summer and 1st two weeks Jan.*

Ile de Porquerolles ✉ 83400

★★★★Mas du Langoustier, **t** 04 94 58 30 09, *www.langoustier.com* (*luxury*). A romantic old inn between the woods and a long sandy beach, with lovely rooms and a superb restaurant (*expensive*), where the chef imaginatively combines the best ingredients of Provence. *Closed mid-Oct–April.*

★★Auberge Les Glycines, 22 Place d'Armes, **t** 04 94 58 30 36 (*expensive*). A small and charming inn, with rooms decorated in Provençal fabrics around a courtyard.

★★Relais de la Poste, Place d'Armes, **t** 04 98 04 62 62, *www.relais-de-la-poste.com* (*expensive*). This was the island's first hotel and has pleasant Provençal-style rooms with loggias and a simple *crêperie*. *Closed Oct–Mar.*

Il Pescatore, **t** 04 94 58 30 61 (*moderate*). For all things fish: not just the predictable *bouillabaisse*, but *carpaccio* and *sashimi*. Eat on the restful terrace overlooking the boats bobbing in the port. *Closed Nov–Feb.*

Port-Cros ✉ 83400

★★★Le Manoir d'Hélène, **t** 04 94 05 90 52 (*luxury–expensive*). An 18th-century mansion set among the eucalyptus groves, with an outdoor pool and a fine little restaurant (*expensive*). *Closed Oct–Mar.*

quarantine veterans of the colonial wars and as Dickensian orphanages. In 1892 the navy bought Le Levant and blew it to pieces as a firing range. In the 1890s fires burned most of the forests on Porquerolles and Port-Cros.

Largest of the islands, **Porquerolles** stretches 7km by 3km and has the largest permanent population, which in the summer explodes to 10,000. Its main village, also called Porquerolles, was founded in 1820 as a retirement village for Napoleon's finest soldiers and invalids. It still has a colonial air, especially around the central pine-planted Place d'Armes, the address of most of Porquerolles' restaurants, hotels and bicycle hire shops. Although barely measuring a square mile, **Port-Cros** is the most mountainous of the islands, and since 1963 it has been a national park, preserving not only its forests of pines and ilexes, but nearly a hundred species of birds; brochures will help you identify them as you walk along the mandatory trails. The surrounding waters, rich in fish and plant life, are also part of the park ; even divers have an under-water 'trail' to follow. The French navy still hogs almost all the flowering **Ile du Levant**, the third island, and uses it to test aircraft engines and rockets. The island's remaining quarter is occupied by Héliopolis, France's first nudist colony (1931).

Toulon

Thanks to an abundance of murex shells, Toulon was a centre for dyeing cloth from Phoenician times, until Louis XIV changed the town forever by making it the chief port of France's Mediterranean fleet. As such it has had more than its share of history. In 1793, when Toulon's royalists had confided the city to the English and their allies, they were driven out by a ragamuffin Revolutionary army led by a young Napoleon Bonaparte, beginning his meteoric career. In 1942, Vichy Admiral Laborde scuttled the entire Mediterranean fleet rather than let it fall into the hands of the Germans. In August 1944, after flattening the old port with aerial bombing raids, the Allies landed and the French army recaptured Toulon. The last decade has not been kind to Toulon, with the shipyards in La Seyne closing down and putting thousands out of work, as well as the notoriety of having elected a particularly xenophobic National Front mayor. Yet in the last few years, after electing one of Chirac's close allies to the mayoral office, the city's piquant charms are once again shining through.

From the train station, Avenue Vauban continues down to the large bleak square of Place d'Armes, decorated with ordnance from the adjacent arsenal, one of the biggest single employers in southeast France with some 10,000 workers. Alongside the arsenal in Place Monsenergue, the **Musée de la Marine** (*open April–Sept daily 2–6.30; Oct–Mar 1.30–6; adm*) displays models of the ships that it once made. Baroque sculptor Puget started out in Toulon carving figureheads for the ships, and the museum has works by his followers.

Off the Quai, Rue d'Alger, now a popular evening promenade, used to be the most notorious street in Toulon's Vieille Ville, or '*Le petit Chicago*', the pungent pocket of the pre-war town. Some of the narrow streets around 'the gut', as it's known, are still unsavoury after dark, even as the shifty bars and shabby flats give way to fashionable cafés and boutiques. One addition stands out: the **Maison de la Photographie** in Rue Nicholas Laugier on the Place du Globe (*t 04 94 93 05; open Tues–Sat 10–12.30 and 1.30–6*), with photos by the likes of Doisneau and Faucon in a beautifully lit gallery.

Toulon looks good from a distance. Bus 40 will take you to Bd Amiral-Vence in Super-Toulon, site of the terminus of the little blue **funicular** that runs (*Tues–Sun 9.30–12 and 2–6*) to the top of **Mont Faron**.

Getting There and Around

By plane: Toulon's airport, with flights to Paris, Corsica, and Brittany is out near Hyères (for information, **t** 04 94 00 83 83). British Airways flies from London.

By train: The train station is on the north side of Toulon in Place Albert 1er, with four daily TGVs to Nice and Marseille, four also direct to Paris (just over 4hrs), and frequent links along the coast and to Hyères.

By bus: For St-Tropez and the coast between Hyères and St-Raphaël, catch a SODETRAV bus in the bus station (next to the train station), **t** 04 94 12 55 12. Littoral buses (from Av Vauban, south from the station) go to Bandol.

By boat: Companies on Quai Cronstadt offer boat tours of Toulon's anchorages and battleships and the surrounding coasts and islands: Trans-med 2000, **t** 04 94 92 96 82 (daily commentated tours to the Ile de Porquerolles); Bateliers de la Rade, **t** 04 94 46 24 65 also has summer crossings to all three Iles d'Hyères.

Tourist Information

Place Raimu, **t** 04 94 18 53 00, *www.toulon-tourisme.com*.

Where to Stay

Toulon ✉ 83000

★★★La Corniche, 17 Littoral F.-Mistral, Mourillon, **t** 04 94 41 35 12, *www.corniche hotel.com* (*expensive*). Part of the Best Western chain, this cleverly designed modern Provençal hotel is near the beach. There is a restaurant built around the massive trunks of three maritime pines, serving refined seafood and meat dishes. *Restaurant closed Sun eve and Mon.*

La Résidence de Cap Brun, 192 Chemin de l'Aviateur Gayraud, off Corniche Gén. de Gaulle, **t** 04 94 41 29 46 (*expensive–moderate*). A magical old white villa set on a cliff top beyond the beaches of Mourillon. Surrounded by pine and plane trees and a world away from the urban hubbub of Toulon, it has a small swimming pool and a steep stone path to the shore. *No restaurant.*

★★Grand Hôtel du Dauphiné, 10 Rue Berthelot, **t** 04 94 92 20 28, *www.grandhoteldauphine. com* (*inexpensive*). In the pedestrian zone, not far from the opera, this is a comfortable, friendly older hotel, air-conditioned, with discounted parking.

★Le Jaurès, 11 Rue Jean-Jaurès, **t** 04 94 92 83 04 (*inexpensive*). The top bargain choice; the rooms all have baths.

Eating Out

Le Lingousto, Rte de Pierrefeu, Cuers, **t** 04 94 28 69 10 (*expensive*). Toulonnais in search of a special meal drive 20km northeast to Cuers to eat at Le Lingousto, located in an old *bastide*, where the freshest of fresh local ingredients are transformed into imaginative works of art. *Closed Sun eve and Mon, and Jan–Feb.*

Les Pins Penchées, Av de la Résistance, **t** 04 09 14 27 98 98 (*expensive*). A new gourmet restaurant with plenty of accolades and acres of gardens. *Closed Sun eve, Mon all day and Tues lunch in winter.*

Le Lido, Littoral Frédéric Mistral, **t** 04 94 03 38 18 (*moderate*). A restaurant with nice, nautical décor and a window onto the kitchen where you can watch your fish being prepared. *Closed Sun eve and Mon in winter.*

La Chamade, 25 Rue de la Comédie, **t** 04 94 92 28 58 (*moderate*). Serious fixed three-course menu by chef Francis Bonneau. *Closed Sun and first three weeks in August.*

West of Toulon: Bandol, La Ciotat and Cassis

Sheltered from the ravages of the mistral, **Bandol** is a typical, pretty Côte d'Azur town. But Bandol has something most of the Riviera hotspots lack – its own excellent wine and a little island, **Ile de Bendor**. A barren 6-hectare rock when Paul Ricard bought it with his pastis fortune in 1950, it is now a little adult playground. There's a

Getting Around

Bandol is on the Toulon–Marseille TGV rail line. SODETRAV buses run from Toulon to St-Tropez and St-Raphaël, and Littorals Cars, t 04 94 74 01 35, leave Toulon from Rue Vauban for Bandol. La Ciotat is a main stop for trains between Marseille and Toulon; regular buses cover the 3km from the station to the Vieux Port. Cassis' train station is just as far from the centre but has less frequent services; if you're coming from Marseille, take one of the frequent coaches instead.

Where to Stay and Eat

Bandol ✉ 83150

★★★**Master Ker Mocotte**, 103 Rue Raimu, t 04 94 29 46 53, *www.kermocotte.com* (*expensive–moderate*). This delightful hotel once belonged to the Toulon-born Raimu – the best actor in the world, according to Orson Welles. It has a seaside garden, private beach and pool, and offers facilities for water sports. The restaurant offers a summer grill in gardens above the Mediterranean. *Open all year*.

★★**Hôtel Bel Ombra**, 31 Rue de la Fontaine, t 04 94 29 40 90 (*inexpensive*). Quiet, friendly, unassuming. *Closed mid-Oct–Mar.*

L'Auberge du Port, 9 Allée J.-Moulin, t 04 94 29 42 63 (*expensive–moderate*). Bandol's gourmet rendezvous, specializing in seafood; go the whole hog with a *menu dégustation*.

Le Jérôme, on the waterfront, near the tourist office, t 04 94 32 55 85 (*moderate*). A cheerful restaurant and pizzeria serving huge portions at attractive prices.

Ile de Bendor ✉ 83150

★★★**Delos**, t 04 94 29 11 60, *www.hoteldelos. com* (*expensive*). Big, comfortable rooms

decorated in extravagant bad taste – but the views of the sea and the watersports make up for it. *Closed Jan–Feb.*

★★★**Hôtel Soukana**, t 04 94 25 06 06, *www. maeva.com* (*moderate*). This has lots of activities and an occasionally raucous but cheerful clientele and a restaurant. *Closed Oct–Easter.*

La Ciotat ✉ 13600

★★★**Miramar**, 3 Bd Beaurivage, t 04 42 83 09 54 (*moderate*). Classy, updated old hotel by the beach. Its restaurant, **L'Orchidée**, t 04 42 83 09 54, is the best in town.

République Indépendante de Figuerolles, a *chambre d'hôte* (*inexpensive*) on the beach at the Calanque de Figuerolles, t 04 42 08 41 71, *www.figuerolles.com*. The good restaurant (*moderate*) becomes Russian in Nov–May. *Closed Nov–mid-Dec.*

Cassis ✉ 13260

★★★★**Les Roches Blanches**, Av des Calanques, t 04 42 01 09 30, *www.roches-blanches-cassis.com* (*expensive*). Most spectacular, on the promontory overlooking the bay. Rooms are a tad small, but very comfortable; there's a private beach. *Closed mid-Nov–Feb.*

★★★**Les Jardins de Cassis**, Av Favier, t 04 42 01 84 85 (*expensive*). Set amid lemon groves and bougainvillaea, a lovely oasis, with a pool and restaurant.

★★**Grand Jardin**, 2 Rue Pierre Eydin, t 04 42 01 70 10 (*inexpensive*). Modern rooms with a terrace.

Chez César, 21 Quai des Baux, t 04 42 01 75 47 (*moderate*). On the waterfront with reasonably priced food served in Marcel Pagnol décor. *Closed Tues eve and Wed.*

Nino, 1 Quai Barthélemy, t 04 42 01 74 32 (*moderate*). Tasty fish soup and grilled prawns on a summery seaside terrace. *Closed Sun eve and Mon.*

diving and windsurfing school, a nautical club that organizes yacht races, an art school and gallery, a business centre, hotels, and the **Exposition Universelle des Vins et Spiritueux** (*open Easter–Sept 10–12 and 2–6, closed Wed*), with displays of 8,000 bottles and glasses from around the world. Apart from wine, Bandol offers its visitors pink flamingos, toucans, cockatoos, and Vietnamese pigs in a lovely exotic garden of tropical flora at the **Jardin Exotique et Zoo de Sanary-Bandol**, 3km east (*open winter daily 8–12 and 2–6, closed Sun am; summer daily 8–12 and 2–7; adm*).

La Ciotat has given the world two momentous pastimes. First, motion pictures, pioneered here in 1895, when Auguste and Louis Lumière filmed a train pulling into La Ciotat station (*L'Entrée d'un train en gare de La Ciotat*), a clip that made history's first film spectators jump out of their seats; the Eden Théâtre where it was shown, on 28 December 1895, is the oldest surviving cinema. And second, *pétanque*, that most Provençal of sports, which came into being here in 1907 when one old-timer's legs became paralysed and he could no longer take the regulation steps before a throw. Most visitors to La Ciotat keep to the beaches and pleasure port around La Ciotat-Plage, but it's the Vieux Port that affords the best loafing. Take bus no.3 to the cliff-top Parc du Mugel. Avenue de Figuerolles continues from here to the red pudding-stone walls and pebble beach of the Calanque de Figuerolles.

The old coral-fishing village of **Cassis**, with its fish-hook port, white cliffs, beaches and quaint houses spilling down steep alleyways, was a natural favourite of the Fauve painters. In the summer so many tourists descend on the now chic little port that it's often elbow room only here.

The sheer limestone cliffs that stand between Cassis and Marseille are pierced by startling tongues of lapis lazuli – mini-fjords known as *calanques*, or creeks. The nearest *calanque*, **Port-Miou**, is accessible by car or foot (a 30min walk): here the hard, white stone was cut for the Suez Canal. Another mile's hike will take you to **Port-Pin**, with a pretty beach, and another hour to **En-Vau**, the most beautiful of them all (you can also reach En-Vau with less toil from a car park on the Col de la Gardiole). Take a picnic and plenty of water. Note, however, that after being ravaged by forest fires in 1990 the paths to the *calanques* are strictly off limits from the beginning of July to the second Sat in Sept, when the only way to visit is by motor boat from Cassis port.

Corsica

During the long centuries that Paris spent 'perfecting' France's borders, it received a special offer from Genoa on an uppity piece of property outside the confines of the mystic Hexagon. The Corsicans, for their part, argued that Genoa had no right to sell what was no longer hers, because under Pascal Paoli they had declared themselves an independent republic. But the year was 1769, long before republics commanded much respect. The French defeated the politically precocious but defiant islanders and married Corsica to the mainland. A couple of months later, Mme Bonaparte gave birth to a bouncing baby boy named Napoleon – but then again, the island was always famous for its vendettas.

'I would recognize my island with my eyes closed, by nothing more than the smell of the maquis carried on waves,' Napoleon once remarked. For the most part, however, he turned his back on Corsica. Neglect, in fact, would characterize French policy until the 1980s, when Corsican separatist pressure (and violence) and a measure of common sense brought about change. Nowadays, not only has Corsica been granted

Getting There

You can fly from Nice, Paris or Marseille with:
Air Liberté, t 08 03 80 58 05, *www.airliberte.fr*.
Air France, t 08 02 80 28 02, *www.airfrance.fr*.
Air Littoral, t 08 25 83 48 34, *www.air-littoral.fr*.
Corse Méditerranée, t 08 36 67 95 20, *www.corsemed.com*.
Corseair, t 01 49 79 75 75, *www.corsair.fr*.
   Boats sail for Corsica from Marseille, Nice and Toulon to Ajaccio, Bastia, Calvi, Ile-Rousse, Propriano and Porto-Vecchio, but don't think you can just pop down on the spur of the moment in the summer, when cars especially have to be booked months in advance.
   Lines are **Corsica Ferries**, t 08 25 095 095, *www.corsicaferries.com*; and **SNCM Ferryterranée**, t 08 91 701 801, *www.sncm.fr*.
   Crossing times have been speeded up dramatically over the last few years and high-speed ferries (NGV – Navire à Grande Vitesse) from Nice to Calvi take just 2hrs 45mins, but they don't run in bad weather.

Getting Around

   A *micheline* **train** links Calvi, Bastia, Ajaccio and Corte, but faster **coaches** provide most of the somewhat infrequent public transport on the island. The trip from Ajaccio to Bastia is one of Europe's great train rides, with breath-taking views along the coast. There's no rail service in the south of the island.
   In summer, the mountains offer some of the most spectacular **walking** in France, especially along the legendary GR20 trail.

Tourist Information

Bastia ✉ **20200**: Place St-Nicolas, t 04 95 54 20 40, *www.bastia.tourisme.com*.
Calvi ✉ **20260**: Port de Plaisance, t 04 95 65 16 67.
Corte ✉ **20250**: La Citadelle, t 04 95 46 26 70, *www.corte-tourisme.com*.
Ajaccio ✉ **20000**: 3 Bd du Roi Jérôme. t 04 95 51 53 03, *www.tourisme.fr/ajaccio*.
Porto-Vecchio ✉ **20137**: Rue du Député de Rocca Serra, t 04 95 70 09 58, *www.accueil.portovecchio.com*.

Where to Stay and Eat

Bastia ✉ 20200
La Citadelle, 6 Rue du Dragon, t 04 95 31 44 70 (*expensive*). Near the top of Bastia and serving some of the best innovative and classic French dishes in Corsica in a vaulted old olive mill. *Closed Sat lunch and Sun.*

Erbalunga ✉ 20222
★★★**Castel' Brando**, t 04 95 30 10 30, *www.castelbrando.com* (*moderate; pricier in high season*). One of the nicest places to stay near Bastia is this 19th-century villa built by a Corsican who made good in Santo Domingo. The garden has a pool and old palm trees; rooms have many original furnishings and air conditioning; there's also a new annexe. *Open mid Mar–end Oct.*

Calvi ✉ 20260
★★★★**La Villa**, Chemin de Notre Dame de la Serra, t 04 95 65 10 50, *www.relaischateaux.*

an array of privileges, but the government has even put a modest degree of autonomy in the pipeline.
   Corsica is the fourth largest island in the Mediterranean, with the second highest mountains (after Etna in Sicily). A natural park encompasses a third of its deeply forested slopes, while the shore melts into sandy beaches or dive bombs to the sea in sheer cliffs. A central mountain chain, capped by 8,810ft Monte Cinto, divides Corsica into two: the north and east is *Diqua dei monti* ('this side of the mountains', now the *département* of Haute-Corse, or 2B); the south and west is *Dila dei monti* ('beyond the mountains', now the *département* of Corse du Sud, or 2A). The more fertile *Diqua dei monti* is historically the *Terra di commune*, a land of independent-minded peasantry whose frequent rebellions had a strong flavour of natural,

com/lavilla (*expensive*). A member of the Relais et Châteaux, in a hilltop garden; luminous and elegant rooms in an updated version of a Roman villa, with lovely views over the bay. Three pools, tennis, fitness centre, hammam and sailing on the beach a kilometre away; the hotel organizes four-wheel-drive excursions into the Balange. It has a good restaurant, too. *Closed Jan–Mar.*

Les Arbousiers, Rte de Pietramaggiore, **t 04 95 65 04 47 (*inexpensive*). A simple but pleasant beach hotel, 5 minutes' walk from the sea.

Corte ✉ 20250

La Restonica, Vallée de Restonica, **t** 04 95 45 25 25 (*moderate*). Very comfortable rooms by the river, all with TV; it also has a pool and a delightful restaurant, serving omelettes with *bruccio* (Corsican cheese) and fresh mint, and other delights in a magical setting. Half-board (*€114 for two*) is mandatory in season. *Closed Sun eve and Mon lunch.*

U Museu, Rampe Ribanelle, **t** 04 95 61 08 36 (*moderate; children's menu available*). Wonderful Corsican restaurant where each hearty dish is packed full of the island's flavours in every dish from soup to trout to boar *civet* with myrtle, served with a fine house wine. *Closed Sun out of season.*

Ajaccio ✉ 20000

***Fesch, 7 Rue Cardinal Fesch, **t** 04 95 51 62 62 (*moderate*). Traditional old hotel in the centre, recently refurbished; all rooms air-conditioned and with TVs.

***Hôtel du Golfe, 5 Bd Roi-Jérôme, **t** 04 95 21 47 64, *www.hoteldugolfe.com* (*moderate*). Modern, on the port, a short walk from the ferries and buses; soundproofed, air-conditioned rooms.

Da Mamma, Passage Guinguette, **t** 04 95 21 39 44 (*cheap*). Off Cours Napoléon and the best option in town for authentic Corsican cuisine. *Closed Sun lunch and Mon.*

Porto-Vecchio ✉ 20137

***Belvedere, Rte de Palombaggia, **t** 04 95 70 54 13, *www.hbcorsica.com* (*expensive–moderate*). Just what a seaside hotel should be, on the beach among the parasol pines, with 16 air-conditioned rooms and a lovely and excellent restaurant terrace (*very expensive–expensive*) with fossils embedded in the walls and dishes such as *aubergines confites* with *bruccio*.

Bonifacio ✉ 20169

***La Caravelle, 37 Quai Comparetti, **t** 04 95 73 00 03 (*luxury–expensive*). Occupies a handsome 19th-century house overlooking the marina. The restaurant, **t** 04 95 73 06 47 (*expensive*) in a 13th-century chapel, has a terrace under the palms and specializes in seafood prepared with a masterly touch. *Closed mid-Oct–Mar.*

U Castille, up in the Haute Ville on Rue Simon Varsi, **t** 04 95 73 04 99 (*moderate*). There's no view, so the cooking has to be good, served by the amiable Marcel in traditional old stone dining room. Try the delicious *soupe de poisson* if you're a fish-lover. *Closed 20 Dec–15 Feb.*

unideological socialism. *Dila dei monti*, the wild land of maquis, was the *Terra dei signori*, the battleground of feudal barons – sometimes patriots but more often petty gangsters on the make – warring against the Pisans, Genoese and French, but most of all against each other.

Corsica annually receives six tourists for each of its 250,000 inhabitants, yet remains remarkably unspoilt. Like many islands, it is a miniature continent, with its own traditions, language (close to medieval Tuscan), music, cuisine and granite architecture. It is a highly distinctive place, and intends to remain so; if all the trappings of globalization and homogenized corporate culture get you down, come here. Only avoid July and especially August, when it's packed to the gills.

Bastia and Diqua dei Monti

Bastia, the bustling main port of the north, was founded by the Genoese and looks it, with tall narrow houses and Baroque churches crowded over the old port; like Genoa itself it was heavily bombed in 1944 by the Americans, this time by mistake, a few days after Corsica became the first part of France to be liberated. Besides general atmosphere, the main things to soak up in town are the historical and geological collections in the **Musée d'Ethnographie Corse** (*closed for restoration at the time of writing*) in the 15th-century Palais des Gouverneurs. Bastia is also the gateway to Cap Corse, the narrow, steeply mountainous peninsula that seems to point so accusingly northwards to France. Its villages have always lived from the sea, and now from vineyards; much of the west coast plunges dramatically into the sea. **Erbalunga**, **Maciaggio** and **Centuri-Port** are among the few seaside hamlets along the Cap equipped to take more than a handful of visitors.

Just south and west of Bastia, the agricultural region of the **Nebbio** is rich in Pisan Romanesque churches, the architectural jewels of Corsica: the best is San Michele (1280), 1km from the village of **Murato**. Below the Nebbio, framed in a beautiful gulf, the chic resort and marina of **St-Florent** has another excellent Pisan church to go with its pretty beaches. The **Désert des Agriates**, just to the west, is an uninhabitable bulge of rock, light and maquis, although at the west end of it, above the port resort of **l'Ile Rousse**, you'll find the **Balagne**, known as the 'garden of Corsica', at least when there were enough men to cultivate its wheat fields and olive groves. Closing off the northeast corner of the island is the striking sun-bleached citadel of **Calvi**, with an almost feasible claim to being the birthplace of Christopher Columbus; a long sandy beach below has made the town a big holiday favourite.

Where the Balagne ends, the northern border of the **Parc Naturel Régional** begins, encompassing the spectacular coastline of the **Scandola Nature Reserve**, accessible only by boat from Calvi or **Porto**. Porto, set amid a fantastic tumble of red rocks, makes a fine base for visiting some of Corsica's renowned beauty spots. Just south, one of the most extraordinary roads in Europe weaves through the fantastical pinnacles and cliffs of the **Calanche** to **Piana** (in July and August, it becomes one of Europe's worst traffic jams), while inland you can explore the magnificent **Gorges de Spelunca** and the **Forêt d'Aitone**, where 500-year-old Laricio pines, once prized by the Genoese for masts, tickle the sky. Further up the road into the interior is the austere, fire-scarred mountain enclosure of the **Niolo**, where only goatherds can make a living; the Niolo's main village, **Calaccuia**, hosts the most traditional of Corsican festivals in early September, complete with singing and archaic poetry competitions.

In the centre, surrounded by magnificent mountain gorges, atmospheric grey granite **Corte** was chosen by patriot Pascal Paoli in the 18th century to be the capital of Corsica's short-lived republican government and (now revived) university. The new **Museu di a Corsica** (*t 04 95 45 25 45, open April–Oct Tues–Sun 10–6; July and Aug 10–8; winter Wed–Sat 10–6; adm*), at the top of the town, has excellent changing exhibitions on all aspects of the island, as well as an important ethnographic collection. A narrow road from Corte penetrates the magnificent **Gorges de la Restonica**, which rise towards glacial lakes and the island's second peak, **Monte Rotondo**.

Between Corte and the east coast are the picturesque mountain villages of the **Castagniccia**, where the Genoese established a thriving chestnut tree economy. After the mountains, the citrus and vine-covered **Eastern Plain** south of the Castagniccia is rather dull, but here you'll find **Aléria**, founded by the Greeks in 564 BC, who nick-named the island Kallisté, 'the most beautiful'. Later the island's Roman capital, the ruined city can be visited, but best of all is the nearby **Musée Jérôme Carcopino** (*open daily 8–12 and 2–5, to 7pm in summer*), filled with a prize collection of Greek vases found on the site.

Ajaccio and Dila dei Monti

Sunny **Ajaccio**, Corsica's little Paris, gave the world Napoleon Bonaparte, and has lain low ever since. The locals tend to view their ambitious famous son as a sell-out to the French, but he's what the punters come to see, so Ajaccio obliges with a plethora of embarassing statues, the shrine-like **Salon Napoléonien** in the Hôtel de Ville, and his birthplace, the **Maison Bonaparte** (stripped of most of its original furnishings). Best of all is the **Musée Fesch** (*open Tues–Sun 9.15–12.15 and 2.15–5.15; winter closed Sun and Mon*), housing the art collection accumulated by Cardinal Fesch, Madame Bonaparte's half-brother, who picked up plenty of masterpieces 'liberated' by his nephew's Grand Armée, including a Botticelli, a Veronese and a Titian. Sandy coves line the road from Ajaccio to the pretty **Iles Sanguinaires**; bigger beaches rim the gulf around **Porticcio**.

Corsica's most intriguing prehistoric site, **Filitosa** (*t 04 95 74 00 91; open April–Oct daily 8–8; adm*), is well signposted off the main N196 from Ajaccio to Propriano. Of all the Neolithic peoples in the Mediterranean, the Corsicans sculpted the most natura-listic human features on their statue-menhirs. But who do they represent? According to archaeologist Roger Grosjean, they are portraits of Corsica's Bronze Age invaders, the Torréens, who arrived *c.* 1700 BC. The Torréens later used these supposed portraits of themselves to build the walls of their citadel. The whole is shrouded in mystery, emphasized by the faces staring out of the night of time.

Nearby **Propriano** is a brash overbuilt resort by Corsican standards. In contrast, just south, the stalwart granite town of **Sartène** was labelled by Prosper Mérimée as 'the most Corsican of Corsican towns', where barons feuded and vendettas consumed the passions of generations; more benignly, it is now a key place in the revival of the island's ancient choral music, or polyphonies, sung by the Scola di cantu di Sarté, under Ghjuvan-Paulu Poletti. The Sartène region is also rich in Neolithic and Torréen sites, which you can learn about in the town's **Musée de la Préhistoire Corse** (*t 04 95 77 01 09; closed Sun; also Sat from Oct to May*). The most important of these is the 1500 BC Torréen site of **Pianu di Levie**, inland from Sartène (*t 04 95 78 48 21 for opening hours*). The spectacular mountain scenery in these parts culminates in the famous granite needles and wind-tormented pines of the **Col de Bavella**, along the D268.

On Corsica's southeast coast the big noise is **Porto-Vecchio**, a handsome medieval walled citadel town that over the past two decades has spread to become the most flagrant holiday target on the island, especially popular with Italians (Corsica, after all, is only 70km from Livorno, compared to 300km from Marseille); the gorgeous beaches to the south are only a short drive away. The south tip of Corsica – an hour's ferry ride from Sardinia – is guarded by **Bonifacio**, one of the most remarkable towns in France, where lofty medieval houses balance precariously on a narrow ridge over a fjord of white cliffs and sea caves, which you can visit by boat.

Languedoc-Roussillon

20

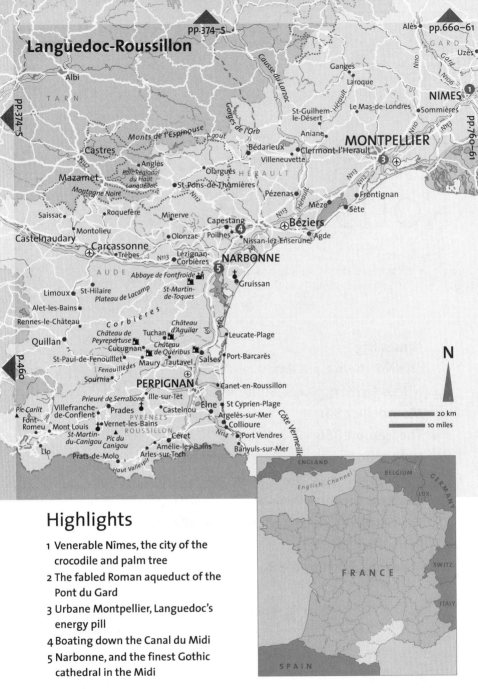

pp.374–5

Alès • pp.660–61

Languedoc-Roussillon

pp.374–5

pp.760–61

GARD

Uzès

Ganges

Laroque

NÎMES ❶

Albi

TARN

Causse du Larzac

St-Guilhem-le-Désert

Le Mas-de-Londres

Sommières

Gorges de l'Orb

Aniane

MONTPELLIER

Monts de l'Espinouse

Agout

Bédarieux

Clermont-l'Hérault

Castres

Anglès

Villeneuvette

❸

Parc Regional du Haut Languedoc

Olargues

HÉRAULT

Mazamet

St-Pons-de-Thomières

Montagne Noire

Pézenas

Frontignan

Saissac

Roquefère

Mèze

Sète

Minerve

Capestang

Béziers

Montolieu

Olonzac

Poilhes

❹

Castelnaudary

Carcassonne

Trèbes

Nissan-lez-Enserune

Agde

AUDE

Lézignan-Corbières

NARBONNE

Abbaye de Fontfroide

❺

Gruissan

Limoux

St-Hilaire

St-Martin-de-Toques

Plateau de Lacamp

Alet-les-Bains

Rennes-le-Château

Corbières

Château d'Aguilar

Château de Peyrepertuse

Tuchan

Leucate-Plage

Quillan

Cucugnan

Château de Quéribus

St-Paul-de-Fenouillet

Maury

Tautavel

Salses

Port-Barcarès

Fenouillèdes

Sournia

PERPIGNAN

Canet-en-Roussillon

Prieuré de Serrabone

Ille-sur-Têt

Pic Carlit

Villefranche-de-Conflent

Prades

Castelnou

Elne

St Cyprien-Plage

Font-Romeu

Mont Louis

Vernet-les-Bains

PYRÉNÉES

Argelès-sur-Mer

St-Martin-du-Canigou

Pic du Canigou

ROUSSILLON

Céret

Collioure

Côte Vermeille

Llo

Prats-de-Molo

Amélie-les-Bains

Arles-sur-Tech

Port Vendres

Banyuls-sur-Mer

Haut Vallespir

N

20 km

10 miles

p.460

ENGLAND

English Channel

BELGIUM

GERMANY

LUX.

FRANCE

SWITZ.

ITALY

SPAIN

Highlights

1 Venerable Nîmes, the city of the crocodile and palm tree
2 The fabled Roman aqueduct of the Pont du Gard
3 Urbane Montpellier, Languedoc's energy pill
4 Boating down the Canal du Midi
5 Narbonne, and the finest Gothic cathedral in the Midi

Languedoc-Roussillon is France's 'other' Mediterranean province, with rugged sun-baked scenery, long sandy beaches, and more vineyards producing more tons of wine than any other region in France. It flourished under the Romans and under the counts

Food and Wine

Castelnaudary's beans, combined with pork, sausage and *confits*, go into *cassoulet*, the totem dish of Languedoc; in second place comes *brandade de morue*, a salt cod purée with garlic. In the old days that was about it. Now arty influences from Provence and Catalan *nouvelle cuisine*, the rage in Barcelona, have met and collided in Languedoc, and you'll find no end of Mediterranean surprises. The biggest revolution of all has been in the wines: a fresh emphasis in quality rather than quantity has made the region one of the rising stars on the French wine charts: Corbières and Minervois are the two biggest regions, but don't neglect smaller regions like Fougères and La Clape, or Banyuls, France's answer to port.

of Toulouse, until the 13th-century Albigensian Crusaders destroyed its civilization (the name Languedoc comes from its language, Occitan, where *oc* meant yes). When the region began to revive in the 16th century, it embraced Protestantism. The subsequent Wars of Religion and Revocation of the Edict of Nantes were setbacks; in the 19th century phylloxera destroyed the wine industry and brought economic ruin. In 1959, Leo Larguier of the Académie Goncourt wrote of Languedoc, 'Talent has never flowered again, and the genius is forever dead.' But the dawn of the 21st century finds Montpellier one of the most dynamic and progressive cities in France, with Nîmes nipping at its heels. The handsome cities of Narbonne, Béziers and Perpignan have rubbed the sleep from their eyes. As Provence begins to seem all full up (and expensive), Languedoc-Roussillon is gaining a reputation as the great alternative.

Nîmes

Geography dealt Nîmes a pair of trump cards: first, a mighty spring, and second, a position on the road from Italy to Spain. The Romans paved it and called it the Via Domitia, and turned Celtic Nîmes into their Colonia Nemausensis. Augustus endowed Nîmes with the Maison Carrée, a sanctuary, an aqueduct (the Pont du Gard) to augment the water supply, and its walls.

Nîmes, like much of Languedoc, got into trouble with the Church in the early 13th century by taking up the Cathar heresy, although at the approach of the terrible Simon de Montfort the city surrendered without a fight. Catholicism never went down well in Nîmes, and when the Protestant alternative presented itself in the 16th century, three-quarters of the population switched. After nearly being ruined by the Revocation of the Edict of Nantes by Louis XIV, Nîmes went back to its second concern after religion: textiles. Its heavy-duty blue *serge de Nîmes* was reduced to the more familiar 'denim' in 1695, in London – where many of the Protestants went in exile – and it was exported widely. Some of it found its way to California, where in 1848 a certain Levi Strauss discovered it to be perfect for outfitting goldrushers.

Built of stone the colour of old piano keys, Nîmes disputes with Arles the title of the 'Rome of France'. With its new Carré d'Art designed by Sir Norman Foster, the city also vies for avant-garde cultural supremacy in this corner of France with

Nîmes

RUE MENARD

RUE DE LA LAMPEZE

RUE DE LA LAMPEZE

RUE BONFA

RUE DE LA GARRIGUE

AVENUE PELADIAN

RUE STEPH. MALLERME

Tour Magne

ROUGET DE L'ISLE

Castellum

RUE DE LA BAUME

RUE DE L'ENCLOS REY

D'AQUITAINE

Planétarium

RUE DE LA TOUR MAGNE

Mt Cavalier

PLACE DE LA REVOLUTION

CLERISEAU

Post Office

PLACE ST CHARLES

RUE DE BOURGOGNE

RUE VINCENT FAITA

Nymphée

Temple de Diane

RUE PASTEUR

RUE DU FORT

RUE BADUEL

BOULEVARD GAMBETTA

LES HALLES

R. DU MURIER D'ESPAGNE

RUE LITTRE

RUE DE L'AGAU

R.DU CDT COUSIN

PLACE DU CHATEAU

BD ET SAINTENAC

St-Baudile

Jardin de la Fontaine

PONT DE VIERNE

QUAI DE LA FONTAINE

SQUARE ANTONIN

RUE NATIONAL

PLACE BELE CROIX

Porte d'Auguste

PLACE D'AUGUSTE

RUE DE BEAUCAIRE

QUAI

DE

LA PLACE A. BRIAND

FONTAINE

BD A. DAUDET

PLACE D'ASSAS

RUE GENERAL PERRIER

Maison Carrée

Notre-Dame -et-St-Castor

RUE CURATERIE

RUE GRETRY

Carré d'Art

RUE DE L'HORLOGE

PLACE DE LA MAISON CARRÉE

Théâtre

PLACE AUX HERBES

R.LACROIX

RUE DU CHAPITRE

R. POISE

St-Ignace Musée Archéologique

RUE SEGUIER

RUE DES CHASSAINTES

Musée du Vieux Nîmes

RUE DOREE

RUE DES GREFFES

AMIRAL COURBET

RUE ROUSSY

RUE NOTRE-DAME

RUE FENELON

C.R.STANISLAS CLEMEN

St Paul

BD VICTOR HUGO

RUE DE L'ETOILE

RUE DE LA MADELEINE

Hôtel -de-Ville

PLACE DE LA SALAMANDRE

Ste-Perpétue

BD DE PRAGUE

RUE EMILE JAMAIS

C.R.DU CHATEAU FADAISE

RUE PORTE DE FRANCE

RUE D'ASPIC

Palais de Justice

BD DE LA LIBERATION

Synagogue

AVENUE CARNOT

PRADIER

ROUSSY

AVENUE GEORGES POMPIDOU

AVENUE JEAN JAURES

RUE DELON SOUBEYRAN

RUE BECDELIEVRE

RUE MATHIEU

RUE BIGOT

RUE DAGOBERT

Les Arènes

PLACE DES ARENES

BD DES ARENES

A. DUCROS

ESPL. CH. DE GAULLE

BD DE BRUXELES

Post Office

AVENUE FEUCHERES

RUE ERNEST RENAN

RUE LA PLACETTE

RUE EMILE ZOLA

RUE DE L'HOTEL DIEU

A. DUCROS

Chapelle

RUE DE LA CITE FOULC

RUE BRICONNET

RUE JEANNE D'ARC

POL Police

Gare

RUE DU MAIL

RUE MARC

PLACE MONTCALM

RUE BOURDALOUE

Musée des Beaux-Arts

FELICITE

Gare Routière

RUE DU CIRQUE ROMAIN

R. FRANÇOIS IER

St François- de-Salles

RUE DE L'AQUEDUC

PLACE DE LA REPUBLIQUE

RUE CHARLES MARTEL

RUE DE ST GILLES

RUE BOSSUET

SAINTE PERPETUE

RUE DE MARRONNIERSIE

PLACE SEVERINE

RUE HENRI IV

RUE ST REMY

LE PLANAS

CHARLEMAGNE

RUE DE LA TOUR DE LEVEQUE

RUE DU DR CALMETTE

RUE HENRI ESPERANDIEU

AVENUE JEAN JAURES

RUE DHUODA

SAINT

RUE DE GENERAC

RUE DE PLANAS

BOULEVARD SERGENT TRIAIRE

RUE PIERRE GAMEL

RUE ANDRE SIMON

N

300 metres
300 yards

To Aquatropique ↙

↓ To Airport

To L'Orangerie & Arles ↘

Getting There and Around

By air: Air France has 3–4 flights a day from Paris-Orly to Nîmes-Garons airport, **t** 04 66 70 49 49. Ryanair flies from London-Stansted to Nîmes once a day. Shuttle buses run 8km from between the airport and Nîmes (Palais de Justice).

By train: Nîmes' station, at the south end of Av Feuchères, has direct trains to Carcassonne, Montpellier, Arles, Orange and Marseille; and TGVs to Paris and Lille.

By bus: destinations include the Pont du Gard, Uzès, St-Gilles, Aigues-Mortes, Le Grau du Roi, La Grande Motte, Avignon, and Montpellier.

Tourist Information

Nîmes: 6 Rue Auguste, near the Maison Carrée, **t** 04 66 58 38 01, *www.ot-nimes.fr*.

Where to Stay

Nîmes ✉ **30000**

★★★★Impérator Concorde, Quai de la Fontaine, **t** 04 66 21 90 30, *www.hotel.imperator.com* (*expensive*). An old dowager with a recent facelift; a lovely garden, air-conditioning, TVs, and Nîmes' top restaurant, **L'Enclos de la Fontaine** (*expensive–moderate*) where the chef cooks up classics and imaginative dishes like veal with fresh fig *beignets*.

★★★L'Hacienda, Chemin du Mas de Brignon, Marguerittes ✉ 30320 (8km northeast on N86), **t** 04 66 75 02 25 (*expensive*). A large farmhouse in the *garrigue*, converted into a hotel with a spacious swimming pool, terraces and an excellent restaurant (*moderate; dinner only*).

★★★New Hotel La Baume, 21 Rue Nationale, **t** 04 66 76 28 42, *www.new-hotel.com* (*moderate*). Stylish modern rooms in a 17th-century mansion with a garden terrace.

★★Royal, 3 Bd Alphonse-Daudet, **t** 04 66 58 28 27 (*inexpensive*). A delightful Art Deco hotel with artistic rooms and a palm-fronded lobby and restaurant (*expensive–moderate*). Reserve early in the summer because it fills up fast. *Restaurant closed Sun and Mon.*

★★Kyriad, 10 Rue Roussy, **t** 04 66 76 16 20, *kyriad.nimescentre@wanadoo.fr* (*inexpensive*). An old house (with a private garage) converted into an air-conditioned hotel with attractive retro furnishings.

Montpellier. But what really makes the juices flow in Nîmes is bulls: its *ferias* feature top matadors from France, Spain and Portugal.

Les Arènes and the Maison Carrée

Twentieth in size, but the best-preserved of the 70 surviving amphitheatres of the Roman world, the **arena** at Nîmes (late 1st century AD) is just a bit smaller than its twin at Arles (*open 9–6.30; winter 9–12 and 2–5; closed public hols and concerts; adm*). It escaped being cannibalized for its stone by being put to constant use – as a castle for the Visigoths and the knightly militia of the Frankish viscounts, then after union with France, as a slum, housing some 2,000 people. When new, the arena could accommodate 24,000 people, who could reach or leave their seats in only a few minutes thanks to an ingenious system of five concentric galleries and 126 stairways. Near the top are holes pierced in the stone for the supports of the awning that sheltered the spectators from sun and rain – an idea revived in 1988, but with a mobile plexiglass and aluminium roof that allows it to host events year round. The event that has packed the crowds in since 1853 is the *corrida*.

To the north stands Nîmes' ragamuffin **Cathédrale Notre-Dame-et-St-Castor**, consecrated in 1096 but flattened by rampaging Huguenots in 1597 and 1622, who spared

**Hôtel de L'Amphithéâtre, 4 Rue des Arènes, t 04 66 67 28 51, *hotel-amphitheatre@ wanadoo.fr* (*inexpensive*). Sweetly restored 18th-century building in the old town, with antique furniture and nice big bathrooms. *Closed Jan.*

Eating Out

Magister, 5 Rue Nationale, t 04 66 76 11 00 (*expensive*). A smart restaurant with good service and highly professional cooking (*brandade* and *taureau* – bull's meat – *au pistou* especially recommended), as well as a good local wine list. *Closed Mon lunch, Sat lunch and Sun; also 2 weeks Feb.*

Aux Plaisirs des Halles, 4 Rue Littré, t 04 66 36 01 02 (*expensive–moderate*). Cosy little bistro near the market for *aïoli* with vegetables or *brandade* with truffles and black olives. *Closed Sun lunch, Mon lunch and Feb.*

Jardin d'Hadrien, 11 Rue de l'Enclos Rey, t 04 66 21 86 65 (*moderate*). A current favourite, with its beamed dining room and veranda; try the cod with olive oil, or courgette flowers with *brandade*. *Aug–July closed Sun and Mon, Tues lunch; Sept–June closed Sun lunch, Wed and Tues lunch.*

Nicolas, Rue Poise (off Bd Amiral Courbet), t 04 66 67 50 47 (*moderate–cheap*). One of the more affordable fine restaurants in town, and always busy. *Closed July.*

Au Flan Coco, 31 Rue du Mûrier d'Espagne, t 04 66 21 84 81 (*cheap*). A delightful tiny restaurant run by two *traiteurs* alongside their shop; the food comes fresh from the market and is whipped up before your eyes. *Lunch only, except Sat. Closed Sun and mid–end Aug.*

Entertainment and Nightlife

Opera, dance and concerts take place throughout July, August and September. For events at **Les Arènes** contact the Bureau de Location des Arènes, Rue Alexandre Ducros, t 04 66 02 80 90 or t 04 66 02 80 95.

Café Napoléon and **Café de la Petite Bourse**, both on Bd Victor Hugo. Popular late bars.

La Bodeguita, 3 Bd Alphonse Daudet, t 04 66 58 28 27. A *tapas* and music bar in the Royal Hotel, especially popular during *feria* time.

The Haddock Café, 13 Rue de l'Agau, t 04 66 67 86 57. Popular local club and café with food served late, music and philosophy evenings.

only the campanile to use as a watchtower. Across the façade runs a vigorous frieze of Old Testament scenes. There's another good Romanesque frieze nearby, in Place aux Herbes, this time adorning a rare, well-preserved 12th-century house (the **Maison Romane**).

Then there's the best-preserved Roman temple anywhere, the graceful little 1st-century BC **Maison Carrée** just off the Via Domitia (*open summer 9–6.30; winter 9–15*). Built by the great General Agrippa, who also built the Pantheon in Rome, the temple was dedicated to the imperial cult of Augustus' grandsons, Caius and Lucius. Known as 'Carrée' or square, because of its right angles and 'long' square shape (85 by 50ft), its *cella* (cult sanctuary) and the Corinthian columns of the porch are perfectly intact. Nîmes always found it useful for something, most notably as the meeting hall of the Consuls and least notably as a stable. It now houses a small museum which includes a 1st-century painting of *personnages grotesques* discovered in 1992.

The Maison Carrée is overlooked by Sir Norman Foster's **Carré d'Art** (*open 10–6, closed Mon, adm; guided tours Mon–Fri at 4.30, weekends and hols 3 and 4.30*). Inaugurated in May 1993, this palace of glass and steel houses a modern art museum, audiovisual centre and extensive library. The ancient columns of the Maison Carrée are reflected in Sir Norman's own slender columns of steel.

Jardin de la Fontaine and the Tour Magne

A short stroll to the west down Quai de la Fontaine is the great spring that origi-
nates in the karst caverns of the *garrigue* to gush out at the foot of Mont Cavalier. It
was domesticated in the 18th century as the lovely **Jardin de la Fontaine**, a kind of
neo-Roman nymphaeum; of the many Roman sanctuaries here only the ruins of a
temple of Diana survive. Paths wind up Mont Cavalier to the oldest Roman monument in Gaul, the octagonal 106ft **Tour Magne** (*open summer 9–7, winter 9–5; adm*).
No record of its origin has survived.

Museum-crawling

Two museums share the former Jesuit college at 13 bis Bd Amiral Courbet: the
Musée Archéologique, with a striking Celtic lintel found at Nages, and the old-fashioned **Musée d'Histoire Naturelle et de Préhistoire**, home to a collection of
two-headed lambs and so on, and those mysterious menhirs-with-personality, the
statue-steles (*both open 11–7, closed Mon; joint adm*). For the **Musée du Vieux Nîmes**,
with a collection of 19th-century textiles and 500 print designs from Nîmes' wool and
silk industries, follow Grand' Rue behind the museums, north to Rue Lacroix (*open
10–6, closed Mon; adm*). The **Musée des Beaux-Arts** is in Rue Cité-Foulc (*open 10–6,
closed Mon; adm*). The ground floor is dedicated to an enormous Roman mosaic, while
upstairs is a worthy provincial array of Venetian, Dutch and French paintings.

The Northern Gard

The Pont du Gard

By 19 BC, the spring of Nemausus could no longer slake Nîmes' thirst and a search
was on for a new source. The Romans were obsessed with the quality of their water,
and when they found a crystal-clear spring called the Eure near Uzès, the fact that it
was 50km away hardly mattered to antiquity's star engineers. The resulting aqueduct, built under Augustus' son-in-law Agrippa, was like a giant needle hemming the
landscape, piercing tunnels through hills and looping its arches over the open spaces
of the *garrigues*, all measured precisely to allow a slope of .07 centimetres per metre.

No matter how many photos you've seen before, the Pont du Gard's three tiers of
arches of golden stone without mortar makes a brave and lovely sight; since the
1920s the natural setting and river have been maintained as intact as possible. What
the photos never show are the two million people who come to pay it homage every
year, and you may well find it more evocative if you arrive very early in the morning or
about an hour before sunset. As you walk over it, note how it's slightly curved (the
better to stand up to floods) and how the Roman engineers left cavities and
protruding stones to support future scaffolding.

Uzès, the First Duchy of France

Few towns of 8,000 souls have so bold a skyline of towers, or so little truck with the
modern industrial world. Uzès seems to have been vacuum-packed when its wealthy

Getting Around

Uzès is linked by frequent buses to Nîmes, Bagnols-sur-Cèze, Avignon, Alès and the Pont du Gard, **t** 04 66 22 00 58, or STD Gard, **t** 04 66 29 27 29.

STDG (**t** 04 66 29 27 29) coaches from Nîmes, Uzès, and Avignon pass within a kilometre of the Pont du Gard 8 or 9 times a day. Canoe and kayak hire is available upstream at Collias: contact Kayak Vert, **t** 04 66 22 80 76.

Tourist Information

Uzès: Chapelle des Capucins, Place Albert 1er, **t** 04 66 22 68 88, *www.villle-uzes.fr.*
Remoulins: Pl des Grands Jours, **t** 04 66 37 22 34.

Where to Stay and Eat

Uzès ✉ 30700
★★★Hôtel d'Entraigues, Place de l'Evêché, **t** 04 66 22 32 68 (*moderate*). A fine old hotel fit for a duke in a 15th-century building opposite the cathedral, with a pool suspended over the dining room (*moderate*) and air-conditioning; try to get a room near the top for the view.
★★Le St Genies, Route de St-Ambroix, **t** 04 66 22 29 99, *saintgenies2@wanadoo.fr* (*inexpensive*). An oasis of tranquillity half a mile from the centre, with a charming pool. *Closed Dec–mid-Feb.*

★★La Taverne, 7 Rue Sigalon (just off Place Albert 1er), **t** 04 66 22 13 10 (*inexpensive*). Renovated rooms in the centre of town, and the chance to eat truffles in season on a garden terrace.
Les Jardins de Castille, **t** 04 66 22 32 68 (*inexpensive*). An elegant hotel-restaurant, with a classy lunch menu including regional dishes and *foie gras.*
Restaurant L'Ancienne Gare, outside of Uzès on the Remoulins road, **t** 04 66 03 19 15 (*moderate*). Opened in summer 1999 in a former train station; the delicious, refined cooking has kept it full of happy customers ever since. *Closed Sun lunch and Mon.*

Around Uzès ✉ 30700

★★★Hôtel Marie d'Agoult, 4km west of Uzès at Arpaillargues et Aureillac, **t** 04 66 22 14 48, *savrychateau30@aol.com* (*moderate*). Sleep in an antique bed (or just dine) at this 18th-century hotel. Marie d'Agoult was Liszt's muse and Wagner's mother-in-law, and a frequent guest at the château. There's a pool and tennis courts, and garden restaurant serving truffles in season. *Closed Nov–Mar.*
L'Auberge de St-Maximin, St-Maximin, 6km south of Uzès, **t** 04 66 22 26 41 (*expensive –moderate*). Some of the best food in the area is served on the garden terrace, where they do wonderful things with asparagus and other local products. *Closed Mon lunch and Tues lunch in summer, Mon and Tues in winter and Nov.*

Protestant merchants of cloth and silk packed their bags and left at the Revocation of the Edict of Nantes.'O little town of Uzès,' wrote André Gide, 'were you in Umbria, the Parisians would flock to visit you!' Now they do, more or less. Houses tumbling into ruin have been repaired, creating the perfect stage for films like *Cyrano de Bergerac*.

Uzès' café life engulfs most available space around Place Albert 1er, just under the **Duché** (*daily guided tours July–mid-Sept 10–1 and 2–7, mid-Sept–June 10–1 and 2–6; adm exp*), residence of the first dukes of France who picked up the title when the Duc de Montmorency lost his title and head in 1632. The rectangular donjon called the **Tour Bermonde** was built over a Roman tower in the 10th or 11th century. The Renaissance façade in the central courtyard was built in 1550 and bears the dukes' motto: *Ferro non auro* ('iron, not gold' – i.e. they were warriors, not financiers).

Uzès is a lot smaller than it seems, and a short wander will soon bring you to the delightfully irregular, arcaded **Place aux Herbes**, for centuries the centre of public life. Set apart from the rest of the old town on a terrace, the **Ancien Palais Episcopal** (1671) was the seat of the powerful bishops of Uzès. A restoration attempt in the 1970s caused the interior to cave in, although the right wing is in good enough nick to hold the eclectic collections of the **Musée Municipal** (*open 3–7, closed Mon and Jan*) with its fossils, ceramics, paintings, and memorabilia of the Gide family. Behind stretches the pleasant **Promenade des Marronniers**, while adjacent is the **Cathédrale St-Théodorit**, built in 1663. The quaint neo-Romanesque façade was tacked on in 1875, with the idea of making a better partner to the stunning 12th-century **Tour Fenestrelle**, spared by the Protestants only because they found it useful as a watchtower. Unique in France, the 137ft tower is encircled by six storeys of double-lit windows, inspired by the Romanesque campaniles of Ravenna and Lombardy. The cathedral's interior was severely damaged during the Revolution, when it was converted into a Temple of Reason, leaving only the peculiar upper gallery with its wrought-iron railing and the cathedral's pride and joy: a splendid **organ** of 1670 with original painted shutters.

Bagnols-sur-Cèze

North of Uzès, Bagnols-sur-Cèze is the traditional gateway to Languedoc, and although it's not much in itself, its **Musée de Peinture Albert André** (*open 10–12 and 2–6, summer 3–7; closed Mon, Feb and hols; adm*) was nothing less than the first provincial museum of contemporary art in France, thanks to André, a friend of Renoir's. In 1924, however, it all burned down during a firemen's ball. It was a blessing in disguise: André sent an SOS out to the French art world, and was able to cover his walls with works by Bonnard, Marquet, Matisse, Picacco, Renoir, Signac, and Gauguin.

Alès and the Parc National des Cévennes

The big town of the northern Gard, **Alès**, was known as the Ville Noire or 'Black Town' for its coal mines and industry; events here inspired Zola's *Germinal*. Since 1980, however, this little piece of Lorraine in the south has pretty much closed shop; for a vivid lesson in industrial archaeology, you can take a tour of the galleries of an abandoned mine at the **Mine Témoin**, just outside town at Rochebelle (*open April–Nov 9–12.30 and 2–5.30; June–Aug 9.30–7; arrive at least 90mins before close; adm*).

Today Alès would prefer to be known as the southern gateway to the Cévennes, the wild and mostly mountainous country of upper Languedoc. It prospered in past centuries, when the Crusaders brought back the secret of silk; mulberry trees were planted everywhere, and the industry reached its peak in the 19th century, then dwindled with the invention of synthetics. The last mill closed in 1965. In 1970 the **Parc National des Cévennes** was created to protect its rich range of flora and fauna, both

Getting Around

Alès' train and bus station are side by side; there are a dozen trains daily from Nîmes, and several buses a day to Anduze and St-Jean-du-Gard, **t** 04 66 85 30 21. There is one bus a day from Alès to Florac.

Tourist Information

Alès: Place Gabriel-Péri, **t** 04 66 52 32 15.
St-Jean-du-Gard: Place Rabaut-Saint-Etienne, **t** 04 66 85 32 11
Cévennes National Park Headquarters: Florac (at the beginning of the Gorges du Tarn in the Lozère), Av du Château, **t** 04 66 49 53 01.

The Camisards

Louis XIV may have been the Sun King, but nearly everything he did eclipsed the rest of France. One of his greatest blunders was the Revocation of the Edict of Nantes in 1685, undoing all the good work of his grandfather Henri IV, who declared for religious tolerance. As absolutist Louis saw it, French power depended on the country's universal Catholicism. As all the Protestants who could left for exile in Germany, England and Holland, greatly benefiting those countries, many parts of France, including Languedoc, faced bankruptcy. Those who remained in France faced severe repression. The shepherds of the Cévennes were fervent Huguenots who had nowhere else to go, were persecuted, and at the end of the 17th century, were swept by a religious revival that brought forth prophets, declaring that the dark days would soon come to an end. To speed up the process, they revolted in 1702, determined to destroy their Catholic oppressors. Known as the Camisards for the white shirts (*camisas*) they wore to identify themselves while fighting at night, they were led by a baker's apprentice, Jean Cavalier, a brilliant guerrilla leader, ambushing the king's armies and defeating his finest regiments. Louis responded with a policy of extermination. Cavalier's loss of his arsenal forced him to ask for a truce in 1704, but as the king still refused to let the Protestants worship in peace, his followers deserted him and he was forced to flee (he went on to become a brigadier general in the British Army). Without him, the revolt wound down, although resistance continued right up to the Edict of Tolerance in 1787.

The best places to learn about the Protestant resistance is the Musée du Désert at the Mas Soubeyran, 11km from St-Jean-de-Gard (*open Mar–Nov daily 9.30–12 and 2.30–6, July and Aug without break*).

in an inaccessible core area, but also in a wide peripheral area that encompasses much of the northern Gard and southern Lozère, including the Gorges du Tarn (*see pp.446–7*). One fun way to explore it is to follow the tracks of Robert Louis Stevenson, who was fascinated with the Camisards, and spent 12 days walking along a trail now named after him, with a donkey named Modestine: the origin of his *Travels with a Donkey in the Cévennes* (1879); contact the park office in **Florac** for details of donkey stables and maps.

Nîmes to Montpellier: Sommières

Between Nîmes and Montpellier, hidden under the cliffs of the river Vidourle, Sommières suffers only moderately from the usual plagues besetting picturesque southern villages. It even has to do without a famous writer, since longtime resident Lawrence Durrell died in 1990. Its streets and squares are well worn and well lived in, with faded shop signs, flowers under every window and huge plane trees.

Before Sommières, there was Sommières' **bridge**, built by Tiberius between AD 19 and 31. Oddly, almost half of the bridge is now hidden inside the town; medieval Sommières expanded into the dry parts of the riverbed, and eventually an

Tourist Information

Sommières: Rue Général-Bruyère, **t** 04 66 80 99 30, *www.ot-sommieres.fr*.

Where to Stay and Eat

Sommières ✉ 30250

Hôtel d'Orange, Chemin du Château Fort, **t** 04 66 77 79 94 (*moderate*). A 17th-century building, converted into a guesthouse, with a pool and garage but only six rooms, so book early; ask to see the *baume* (cave).

★★★**Auberge du Pont Romain**, 2 Av E. Jamais, **t** 04 66 80 00 58 (*inexpensive*). Lovely, spacious rooms in a 19th-century herbal distillery close to the river, with a pool and a gourmet restaurant (*expensive*). *Closed Nov and Mon lunch.*

L'Olivette, 11 Rue Abbé Fabre, **t** 04 66 80 97 71 (*moderate*). A local favourite in the centre, serving regional cuisine with an original twist, such as duck with balsamic vinegar and *œufs en meurette languedocienne* (eggs cooked in red wine). *Closed Tues in summer, Tues eve and Wed in winter.*

embankment was built. The **Tour de l'Horloge**, the entrance to the town, was built over the bridge's fifth arch in 1659. The other arches of the bridge lie under Rue Marx Dormoy, the street leading from the bridge to **Place des Docteurs Dax**, a lovely 12th-century market square that everyone in Sommières still calls by its old name, the **Marché-Bas**. The houses are all built on stone arcades: in the old days, the square would be underwater every spring, forcing the market up to the **Marché-Haut**.

Montpellier

Montpellier's reputation as a centre of medicine began in the 13th century with the formation of a *Universitas Medicorum*, and later a *studium* of law. In 1349 the Catalan Kings of Majorca sold Montpellier to France for 120,000 golden écus. A period of relative peace and prosperity followed until the 1560s, when the university academics and tradesmen embraced the Reformation. For the next 70 years much of what Montpellier had achieved was wiped out. In 1622 Louis XIII came in person to besiege the city and reassert royal authority.

Putting its merchant republic days behind it, Montpellier settled down to the life of a university town and regional capital of a wine region. The Revolution passed without kicking up much dust; a far bigger crisis for Montpellier occurred in the 1890s, when phylloxera knocked out the vineyards. Until 1977 and the election of the irrepressible Socialist Mayor Georges Frêche (now in his fifth term), Montpellier was a pleasant, sleepy university backwater of fawn-coloured stone. With his Paris-sized projects, notably the monumental new quarter called Antigone, Frêche has made Montpellier a European model for innovative and effective city government.

A Place Named Comédie

The various personalities of Montpellier all come together in the lively, café-lined **Place de la Comédie**, locally known as *l'Œuf*, or the Egg, due to the shape it had in the 18th century. Its ornaments include a *doppelgänger* of the Paris Opera, and various 19th-century larded bourgeois buildings with domes reminiscent of bathyspheres, while opposite looms a modern glass-and-steel semi-ziggurat, the **Polygone**,

Getting There and Around

By air: British Airways and Ryanair fly direct to Montpellier from London daily. Air Littoral serves Nice, Lyon, Strasbourg and Bordeaux, or take Air France from Paris.

By train: You can race here from Paris in 4hrs 40mins on the TGV, or catch direct trains to Avignon, Nîmes, Marseille, Nice, Perpignan, Béziers, Narbonne, Agde, Lunel, Sète, Carcassonne and Toulouse.

By bus: The coach station, next to the train station, t 04 67 92 01 43, has buses to Nîmes, La Grande Motte, Béziers, Aigues-Mortes, etc.; every 20mins bus no.17 trundles down to the sea at Palavas. In town, you may find the little Petibus vans useful to get around the pedestrian zones of the Ecusson and Antigone.

By tram: In summer 2000 Montpellier opened the first stage of its tram project. The first line crosses the city centre from southwest to northeast. Information from TAM, t 04 67 22 87 87, or the tourist office.

Car hire: The big firms are at the airport, or try Avis at 900 Av Prés-d'Arènes, t 04 67 92 51 92, or Hertz France, 18 Rue Jules-Ferry, t 04 67 58 65 18. For a less expensive car try A.D.A., 58 bis Av Clemenceau, t 04 67 58 34 35.

Tourist Information

Montpellier: Allée Jean de Lattre de Tassigny, Esplanade de la Comédie, t 04 67 60 60 60, *www.ot-montpellier.fr*. Also in the station, t 04 67 22 08 80, and at Antigone, at the motorway exit, t 04 67 22 06 16.

Shopping

At Espace Mosson (La Paillade), there is a **flower market** on Tuesday and a **flea market** on Sunday morning; free buses go every 20mins from Square Planchon. Daily **food** markets take place in Place J. Jaurès, Halles Castellanes, Halles Laissac, Plan Cabannes and La Comédie.

The tourist office has a large display of wine, *confits* and other regional products; antiques shops cluster around Place de la Canourgue. **Caves Notre Dame**, 1348 Av de la Mer, t 04 67 64 48 00. An excellent source of local wines and information, including tastings. *Open Mon–Fri 9–12 and 3–7.30.*

Where to Stay

Montpellier ✉ 30400

★★★★**Holiday Inn Métropole**, 3 Rue du Clos-René, t 04 67 12 32 32, *www.holidayinn.com* (*expensive*). Top of the line: antique-furnished, with a quiet garden courtyard, air-conditioning and restaurant (*moderate*), between the train station and Place de la Comédie. *Restaurant closed Sat and Sun.*

★★★**Demeure des Brousses**, Rte des Vauguières (4km east of town on the D24 and D127E towards the Château de la Mogère), t 04 67 65 77 66, *www.demeure-des-brousses.fr* (*moderate*). If you have a car, the most charming place to stay is this 18th-century ivy-covered *mas* in a vast park of shady trees, a few minutes from the city or the sea. Furnished with antiques; excellent restaurant (*expensive–moderate*).

★★★**La Maison Blanche**, 1796 Av de la Pompignane (off the route to Carnon), t 04 99 58 20 70, *www.hotel-maison-blanche.com* (*moderate*). Another gem requiring your own transport: 38 rooms in a big, balconied house that looks as if it has escaped from the French quarter of New Orleans, surrounded by a 5-hectare park.

★★**Hôtel du Parc**, 8 Rue Achille Bège, t 04 67 41 16 49, *www.hotelduparc-montpellier.com* (*inexpensive*). An 18th-century *hôtel particulier* fitted out with air-conditioning, TV, etc.

★**Les Fauvettes**, 8 Rue Bonnard, t 04 67 63 17 60 (*inexpensive*). Good value for money

a shopping mall and town hall complex. To the north of Place de la Comédie extends the **Esplanade Charles de Gaulle**, replacing the city walls demolished by Louis XIII after the siege of 1622. In the 18th century the Esplanade was planted with rows of trees and became Montpellier's chief promenade; along here is a rare survival of 1908, the **Cinématographe Pathé**, a little palace from the magical early days of

near the Jardin des Plantes, with quiet rooms overlooking interior courtyards. *Closed 20 Dec–3 Jan and 20 July–10 Aug.*

*Les Arceaux, 35 Bd Arceaux, **t** 04 67 92 03 03 (*inexpensive*). Clean and comfortable, with a small garden and terrace.

Eating Out

Le Jardin de Sens, 11 Av St-Lazare (off the N113 towards Nîmes; bus no.4), **t** 04 99 58 38 38 (*very expensive*). One of the most celebrated restaurants in the southwest. It is run by local twins Jacques and Laurent Pourcel. Try the squid stuffed with ratatouille and crayfish tails, *bourride* soup, fish soup and traditional *oreillette* pastries. The restaurant has an exquisite garden, and now has its own vineyard. A few rooms are also available. *Closed Wed lunch, Sun and Mon.*

Le Chandelier, 39 Place Zen, **t** 04 67 15 34 38 (*expensive*). Another established temple of fine cooking (complete with columns), featuring well-polished versions of the classic French repertoire. *Closed Sun all day, Mon lunch.*

Le Petit Jardin, 20 Rue J-J Rousseau, **t** 04 67 60 78 78 (*moderate*). Remarkably quiet restaurant in the centre of town, with a delightful large shady garden with a view of the cathedral. Good local fish, salads and fresh pasta with vegetables. *Closed Mon.*

L'Ollivier, 12 Rue Aristide Ollivier, **t** 04 67 92 86 28 (*moderate*). A popular family restaurant bang on the new tramway; smooth service, classic cuisine and the best local wine, of course. *Closed Mon and Aug.*

Le Vieil Ecu, 1 Place de la Chapelle Neuve, **t** 04 67 66 39 44 (*moderate*). Good French food, served in the old chapel or on the terrace. *Closed Sun lunch and Mon lunch in winter, Sun and Mon in summer.*

Lively Rue des Ecoles Laïques and Place de la Chapelle Neuve make up Montpellier's Latin Quarter, where the colours, smells and live music from the Turkish, Greek, Spanish and Tunisian restaurants collide in gleeful culinary discord.

Tripti-Kulai, 20 Rue Jacques Cœur, **t** 04 67 66 30 51 (*cheap*). A vegetarian restaurant and tea room near the Musée Languedocien that offers some exotic dishes: a good spot for a light lunch. *Closed Sun.*

Entertainment and Nightlife

Montpellier is a great town for **cinema**, both recent releases and classics, some in English; complete listings for these, as well as clubs, theatre and music, can be found in the city weekly *La Gazette*. FNAC, in the Polygone, has tickets for most events.

CORUM, **t** 04 67 61 67 61, *corum@enjoy-montpellier.com.* Home of L'Orchestre Philharmonique de Montpellier and Montpellier Danse.

Opéra Comédie, **t** 04 67 60 19 99. Opera and theatrical performances.

Most bars and clubs do not heat up until after 11pm, and the clubs rock until dawn.

Le Rockstore, down from Place de la Comédie on Rue de Verdun, **t** 04 67 06 80 00. By the beach, and still Montpellier's leading place to be. Entry is usually free on dance nights and drinks are inexpensive.

El Toto Loco, **t** 04 99 52 23 74, Rte de Carnon. A young, under-25 crowd.

On weekends and often weekdays there's live jazz, blues or world music at:

Sax'Aphone, 24 Rue Ernest-Michel, **t** 04 67 58 80 90.

L'Antrouille, 12 Rue Anatole-France, **t** 04 67 58 75 28.

Le Fil, 16 Rue du Pila St-Gély, **t** 04 67 66 20 67.

Brasserie Le Dôme, 2 Av Clemenceau, **t** 04 67 92 66 70. 'Philosophy café' with discussions Wed eve.

cinema (now the Rabelais Cultural Centre; it often shows foreign films). The north end of the Esplanade is flanked by **CORUM**, 'the House of Innovation' designed by Claude Vasconi, one of Georges Frêche's showcases, encompassing the Opéra Berlioz and two congress halls.

Antigone

East of Place de la Comédie lies another Frêche initiative: **Antigone**, a mostly moderate-income quarter with housing for 10,000 people, and shops and restaurants, all designed by trendy Barcelona architect Ricardo Bofill in 1979 and spread along a huge formal axis down to the river Lez. Bofill understood just what a Rome of Tomorrow needs: Mannerist neo-Roman arches, cornices, pilasters, and columns as big as California redwoods. On a bad day, Antigone looks like the surreal background to a De Chirico painting; on a good day, it seems like a delightful place to live, especially for kids, who can play football in the monumental Place du Millennium and still hear their parents call them in for lunch.

Musée Fabre

Open 9–5.30, until 5 Sat and Sun, closed Mon; adm.

On Boulevard Sarrail, between the Cinématographe and CORUM, the Musée Fabre was long the main reason for visiting Montpellier, with one of the most important collections of art in provincial France. The museum has six levels, with floors devoted to 17th-century painting, ceramics and painters from Montpellier. The superb collection on **Floor 5** was donated by the museum's great benefactor, Alfred Bruyas (1821–77). Born into a Montpellier banking family, Bruyas resolved the frustration of not being able to paint himself by befriending many of the artists of his day and asking them to paint him – there are 24 portraits of the red-bearded patron in this museum alone, including examples by Delacroix and Alexandre Cabanel of Montpellier (1823–89). Four are by Gustave Courbet (1819–77), Bruyas' friend.

Into the Ecusson

There is nothing as compelling as the Musée Fabre in Montpellier's historic centre, the Ecusson; much was lost in the Wars of Religion, and even the many 17th- and 18th-century *hôtels particuliers*, as stuccoed and ornate as many of them are inside, show mostly blank walls to the street. But few cities in the south of France manage to be as pleasant and lively. The entire Ecusson is a pedestrian zone, and it's a delightful place for walking. One of the major crossroads of the Ecusson is Place Notre-Dame, under the cool gaze of the neoclassical **Notre-Dame-des-Tables** (1748). At the Hôtel de Varennes in Place Pétrarque there's a pair of small museums devoted to the good old days. The **Musée du Fougau** (*open Mon–Sat 9–12.30 and 2–7*) preserves the arts and traditions of old Montpellier. The **Musée du Vieux Montpellier** (*open Tues–Sat 9.30–12 and 1.30–5; adm*) exhibits portraits of notables, and plans and views of the city from the 1500s on. At 7 Rue Jacques Cœur is the **Musée Languedocien** (*open Mon–Sat 2–5, July and Aug 3–6; guided tours on request; adm*), with Greek vases and prehistoric finds from the Hérault; Romanesque sculpture; three 12th-century Islamic funeral steles, and a major collection of 16th- to 18th-century faïence made in Montpellier.

Western Quarters: the Promenade du Peyrou

Since the late 17th century the lofty west edge of Montpellier has been devoted to tons of mouldy fol-de-rol glorifying Louis XIV, beginning with an **Arc de Triomphe**.

Beyond stretches the **Promenade du Peyrou**, a nice park spoiled by an equestrian statue of his megalomaniac majesty as big as the Trojan Horse. At the edge of the promontory stands the far more elegant **Château d'Eau**, a neoclassical temple designed to disguise the reservoir of the **Aqueduc St-Clément** (1771).

The waters feed the unicorn fountain in the nearby **Place de la Canourgue**, a charming 17th-century square. It looks down on the medieval monastery college of St-Benoît, built by papal architects from Avignon, used since 1795 as the **Faculté de Médecine**, housing an enormous medical library. Adjacent, the former monastic chapel has been Montpellier's **Cathédrale de St-Pierre** ever since the see was transferred here in 1563, although its status didn't spare it the usual depredations in the Wars of Religon and the Revolution. The cathedral's greatest distinction is its unusual porch, supported by two conical turrets. Beyond lies the lovely **Jardin des Plantes** (*open 10–7 in summer; 10–5 the rest of the year; closed Mon*), the oldest botanical garden in France, founded by a decree of Henri IV in 1593.

The Hérault

For devotees of rural France, this seemingly innocuous area may be the ultimate find. Just enough tourists come for there to be plenty of country inns and *fermes-auberges*, though in most villages foreigners are still a novelty. The food is good; and there's enough wine to make anyone happy; the Hérault is the most prolific wine-producing region in France – it's a perfect alternative to overcrowded Provence.

North of Montpellier: the Garrigue

On a map, you'll notice lots of blank space in this region, a *pays* without a name. It's a textbook example of *garrigue*, a dry limestone plateau with sparse vegetation, where even sheep only just get by. The few villages seem huddled, closed into themselves.

From Montpellier, the best approach is by way of the D17 to St Mathieu-de-Tréviers, where you can pick up the D1/D122 west, a scenic high road that passes below **Pic St-Loup**, a lone, striking 2,110ft exclamation point. The D122 passes through the typical *garrigue* village of **Le Mas de Londres** before arriving at **St-Martin-de-Londres** (25km direct on the D986 from Montpellier). St-Martin is a surprise package. Passing the tiny, densely built village on the road, you would never guess it conceals one of the most exquisite medieval squares anywhere, picturesquely asymmetrical and surrounded by houses that have not changed for centuries. The ensemble has a church to match, an architecturally sophisticated 11th-century building with a rare elliptical cupola.

South of St-Martin, in a military zone just off the D32, a 5,000-year-old settlement was discovered at **Cambous** in 1967 (*open weekends only Sept–June 2–6 pm, July–Sept Fri–Wed 2–6pm*). With considerable intelligence and dedication, the archaeologists have made the site into a veritable recreation of Neolithic life.

From St-Martin, the main D986 leads northwards towards the Cévennes. From the village of St-Bauzille-de-Putois there is a steep side road to the **Grotte des Demoiselles** (*open daily 9–12 and 2–6, July and Aug 9–6; adm*) with one of France's

Tourist Information

Ganges: Plan de l'Ormeau, **t** 04 67 73 00 56.

Where to Stay and Eat

St-Martin-de-Londres ✉ 34380

Auberge de Saugras, Argelliers, south of St-Martin-de-Londres, **t** 04 67 55 08 71 (*inexpensive*). A stone *mas* with several rooms and gourmet menus (*expensive–moderate*). Book ahead, and ask for directions! *Closed Tues and Wed, and Aug and Feb.*

★★Hostellerie Le Vieux Chêne, Causse de la Selle, west of Frouzet, **t** 04 67 73 11 00, *levieuxchene@wanadoo.fr* (*inexpensive*). Three luxurious double rooms and a good restaurant (*moderate*) serving French classics on a pretty terrace. *Closed mid-Nov–Feb.*

Les Muscardins, 19 Route des Cévennes, **t** 04 67 55 75 90 (*expensive*). Gourmets from Montpellier drive up especially to feast on the fancy terrines and pâté, game dishes, formidable desserts and a selection of the best regional wines on a choice of four menus. *Closed mid-Feb–mid-March and Mon and Tues.*

La Ferme des Moreaux, Causse de la Selle, **t** 04 67 73 12 11 (*expensive*). Attend a supper concert on the unique patios of 'Chapelle Musicale'. Madame Moreaux prepares a tasty meal based on medieval recipes and seasonal ingredients, while guests are regaled with everything from Gregorian chant to jazz with an electronic touch; dress up, bring a sweater, don't smoke and be quiet. *July–Aug nightly at 9pm, ring for* opening times in winter; reservations mandatory; no children or dogs are allowed.

Ganges ✉ 34190

★★Hôtel de la Poste, 8 Plan de l'Ormeau, **t** 04 67 73 85 88 (*inexpensive*). A prettily restored hotel.

Le Parc aux Cèdres, Laroques, south of Ganges, **t** 04 67 73 82 63 (*inexpensive*). With a garden, pool and restaurant (*moderate*). *Restaurant closed Wed in winter.*

Ferme-Auberge Domaine de Blancardy, Moules et Baucels, 7km east of Ganges on the D999, **t** 04 67 73 94 94 (*inexpensive*). Thirteen rooms in a distinctive old *mas* dating from the 12th century. *Closed end Dec–March and Wed.*

Joselyn Mélodie, Place Fabre d'Olivet, **t** 04 67 73 66 02 (*cheap*). An intimate restaurant in the old town, named after its two charming owners, who will fill you with good French cooking without breaking the bank. *Closed Wed and Christmas.*

Chez Maurice, Pont d'Hérault, 11km north of Ganges, **t** 04 67 82 40 02 (*expensive*). The best *cuisine de terroir* around. Book in advance. *Closed Sun eve and Mon lunch.*

Gorniès ✉ 34190

★★★★Château de Madières, 7km west of Gorniès, **t** 04 6773 84 03 (*expensive*). If you want to combine the austerity of the *garrigue* with style and creature comforts, this has 12 luxurious rooms in a 14th-century fort, with a park, pool, fitness centre and beautiful vaulted dining room (*expensive*). *Closed Nov–Mar.*

most spectacular displays of pipe-organ stalactites and stalagmites, in the staggeringly enormous 'Cathedral of the Abysses'. Visits are by subterranean funicular.

Ganges is the only real town around, and quite a pleasant one. In the 18th century, it was France's capital of silk stockings. Like most of the Cévennes, Ganges was and remains a mostly Protestant area; the old part of town is crisscrossed by *chemins de traverse*, labyrinthine passes laid out to confuse Catholic troops, and it has an imposing, peculiar seven-sided Protestant 'temple', built in 1850. Ganges makes a good base for exploring this pretty region between the *garrigue* and the Causse du Larzac. The **Gorges de la Vis** can be followed on the D25 west of town. The route through the gorges is 34km long (one-way only); if you go the whole route, there's a real curiosity to be seen at the end, the famous **Cirque de Navacelles**. It looks like a

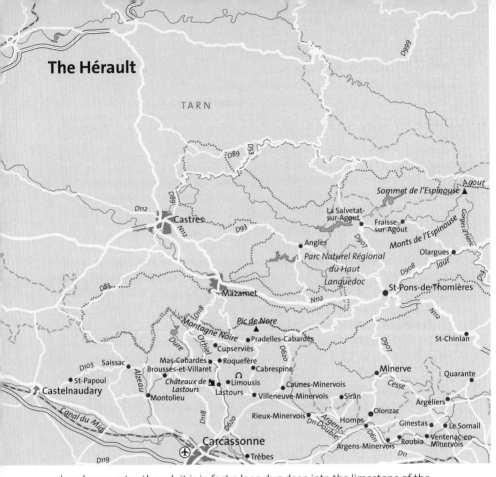

The Hérault

TARN

D999

Sommet de l'Espinouse ▲

Agout

La Salvetat-sur-Agout

Fraisse-sur-Agout

Castres

Anglès

Parc Naturel Régional du Haut Languedoc

Monts de l'Espinouse

Gorges d'Héric

Olargues

Jaur

Mazamet

St-Pons-de-Thomières

Pic de Nore ▲

Pradelles-Cabardès

Cupserviès

St-Chinian

Montagne Noire

Mas-Cabardès
Brousses-et-Villaret

Roquefère

Cabrespine

Minerve

Quarante

Saissac

Châteaux de Lastours

Limousis

Caunes-Minervois

Cesse

St-Papoul

Lastours

Villeneuve-Minervois

Siran

Argeliers

Castelnaudary

Montolieu

Rieux-Minervois

Olonzac

Le Somail

Homps

Ginestas

Ventenac-en-Minervois

Canal du Midi

Roubia

Carcassonne

Argens-Minervois

Trèbes

deep lunar crater, though it is in fact a loop dug deep into the limestone of the *garrigue* by the meandering river Vis long ago.

The Valley of the Hérault: the Haut Pays d'Oc

The Hérault slices dramatically through the *garrigue*, and the atmosphere is clear, luminous, otherworldly: the perfect landscape for saints and pilgrims, and wine.

'Desert', in French or English, originally meant deserted, and this is still as lonely a region as it was when the hermit St Guilhem came here, in the reign of Charlemagne. The little village of **St-Guilhem-le-Désert** northwest of Montpellier is stretched on the edge of a ravine and has changed little since medieval times. The abbey church (*open Mon–Sat 8–12 and 2–5.30, to 6.30 in summer; Sun 11–4, closed for Mass*) is a remarkably grand and lovely specimen of Lombard architecture. Some fragments of frescoes survive in the side chapels. The cloister is ruined, and most of its capitals have ended up at the Cloisters Museum in New York.

The steep **Gorges de l'Hérault** extend on both sides of the village, and can be followed on the D4. With all this eroded limestone about, you would expect caves, and there are several. The most impressive, 3km south, is the **Grotte de Clamouse** (*open summer 10–6; July and Aug 10–7; winter 10–5; adm*), one of the big tourist

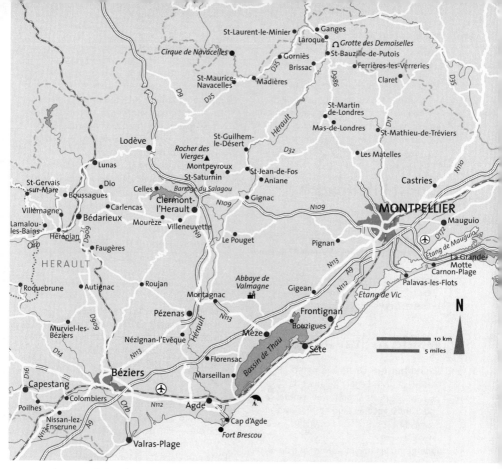

attractions of the Hérault, with its lovely aragonite crystals. Some 500 yards to the south, don't miss the massive stone bridge of 1030, the **Pont du Diable**.

Everyone who studies medieval history has trouble untangling the two Benedictine Benedicts. Benedict of Norcia founded the order. In the time of Charlemagne, Benedict of Aniane, St Guilhem's mentor, reformed it, forcing the poor Benedictines back to the original precepts of obedience, hard work and no fooling around. The abbey he built in **Aniane** was thoroughly wrecked by the Protestants and rebuilt in the 17th century. The church, St-Sauveur, was rebuilt under Louis XIV, and in drab little Aniane it comes as quite a shock, with its glorious Baroque façade framed in big volutes, one of the best in the south; the interior is typically divided into two parts: one for the monks and one for the villagers. South of Aniane on the D32, the market town of **Gignac** enjoyed prosperity in the 17th and 18th centuries; its best-known monument is outside town: the **Pont de Gignac**. This bridge, begun in 1776, is every inch a product of the Age of Enlightenment, strong and functional architecture without a trace of Bourbon curlicues.

Southeast of Gignac, off the main N109, the **Château d'Aumelas** occupies a romantically isolated hilltop. Built some time before 1036 by the Lords of Montpellier, it is on a dirt track and difficult to reach, but it's a wonderful place to explore; parts of the

Getting Around

Coach lines from the bus station in Montpellier have regular services to Gignac, Clermont-l'Hérault and Lodève; there are additional buses to some tourist attractions (like St-Guilhem-le-Désert) in the summer (t 04 67 06 03 67).

Tourist Information

St-Guilhem-le-Désert: At the *mairie*, Rue de la Font du Portal, t 04 67 57 44 33, *www.saint-guilhem-le-desert.com*.

Gignac: Hôtel des Laurès, Pl Général Claparède, t 04 67 57 58 83.

Clermont-l'Hérault: 9 Rue Doyen Réné Gosse, t 04 67 96 23 86.

Lodève: 7 Pl de la République, t 04 67 88 86 44.

Where to Stay and Eat

St-Guilhem-le-Désert ✉ 34150

**Hostellerie St-Benoit, Aniane, t 04 67 57 71 63 (*inexpensive*). A comfortable motel with a pool and a good restaurant (*moderate*) specializing in trout and crayfish. *Closed mid-Dec–Feb.*

Auberge sur le Chemin, 38 Rue Fond de Portal, t 04 67 57 75 05 (*inexpensive*). A medieval inn; tasty regional food (*moderate*).

Gignac ✉34150

**Les Liaisons Gourmandes de Capion, 3 Bd de l'Esplanade, t 04 67 57 50 83 (*inexpensive*).

Popular hotel restaurant with an outdoor terrace, worth a visit for inventive regional cooking such as chicken with truffles or marinated sardines. *Closed Sun in summer, Sat lunch, Sun eve and Mon in winter.*

Ferme-Auberge Le Pélican, Domaine du Pélican, t 04 67 57 68 92 (*inexpensive*). This place (which also has rooms) has wonderful dishes – *pintade* (guinea hen) stuffed with olives, duck in honey vinegar – and their own wines. *Booking essential. July–Aug open eves except Thurs and Sun; otherwise weekend eves only, except for parties of 10 and over.*

Clermont-l'Hérault ✉ 34800

**Sarac, Rte de Nebian, t 04 67 96 06 81, f 04 67 88 07 30 (*inexpensive*). A pleasant Logis de France overlooking the vineyards. *Closed Jan.*

**La Source, Place Louis XIV, Villeneuvette, 4km southwest, t 04 67 96 05 07, *www.hotel delasource.com* (*inexpensive*). Charming rural retreat with a pool and tennis, and a restaurant (*moderate*) serving salmon and truffles. *Closed Jan–mid-Feb; restaurant closed last 2 weeks Nov, Jan and Feb.*

**Les Hauts de Mourèze, 8km from Clermont, t 04 67 96 04 84 (*inexpensive*). Overlooking the *cirque*, with beautiful views. *Closed Nov–April.*

.L'Arlequin, Place St-Paul, in the medieval centre of town, t 04 67 96 37 47 (*moderate*). The best of the restaurants, serving smoked trout, *confits* and good Faugères wine in a refined candle-lit room. *Closed Sun eve, Mon, and Sat lunch.*

noble residence, chapels and other buildings are still substantially intact. South of the château, on a rocky track, is a beautiful and austere Romanesque church, **St-Martin-de-Cardonnet**, set amidst the ruins of the monastery. To the west, on the D139, the circular fortified village of **Le Pouget** is just north of the colossal **Dolmen Gallardet**.

Clermont-l'Hérault is a peacefully bovine and prosperous town, living off the wine and table grapes of this more fertile part of the Hérault valley. Its medieval centre, on a hilltop, is large and well preserved, including a tall, graceful Gothic church, **St-Paul**, begun in 1276, and the 10th–11th-century **castle** around which the town grew up.

To the south lie weirdly eroded rock formations in the **Cirque de Mourèze**, a long, stretched-out *cirque* with the dusty village of Mourèze and its ruined castle at the centre. Between the *cirque* and Clermont lies **Villeneuvette**, founded only in 1670 and a manufacturing centre for *londrins*, printed linen cloth. Though the works are now closed (since 1954), Villeneuvette is still the picture of a French paternalistic company town. The factories remain, behind the gate with the inscription *Honneur au Travail*.

North of Clermont, the N9 heads into the *causses* of deepest France, passing **Lodève**, a somewhat isolated town wedged between two rivers. Like Clermont-l'Hérault, Lodève has an impressive Gothic church with a lofty tower, St-Fulcran, begun in 1280, and turned into a fortress during the Hundred Years' War. Lodève's textile-manufacturing past is recalled in a local workshop of the famous Parisian tapestry factory, the **Atelier National de Tissage de Tapis de Lodève**, (*ring ahead to visit; t 04 67 96 40 40; open Tues, Wed, Thurs 2–5*). Lodève was a Roman town, and its **Musée Fleury**, in Rue de la République (*open 10–12 and 2–6, closed Mon*), has finds from that age.

The Northern Fringes: Monts de l'Espinouse

The natural beauty of the Espinouse – rough canyons, trout streams and chestnut groves – never did it much good; even forty years ago, this was a poor area. The creation of the **Parc Régional du Haut Languedoc** in the 1960s has made all the difference; *tourisme vert* – hiking, canoeing or just relaxing – increases every year.

Getting Around

Except along the coast, public transport is rudimentary; the coastal SNCF line runs from Montpellier through Frontignan, Sète, Agde and Béziers on its way to Narbonne and Perpignan, with as many as 22 trains a day. The only train service in the interior is from Béziers northwest to the Espinouse, taking a roundabout route through Bédarieux, Lamalou-les-Bains, Olargues and St-Pons on its way to Castres in the Tarn. St-Pons is also connected by bus to Béziers, via St-Chinian.

Tourist Information

Lamalou-les-Bains: 1 Av Capus, **t** 04 67 95 70 91, *www.ot-lamalouleslbains.fr.*
Olargues: Place de la Gare, **t** 04 67 97 71 26.
St-Pons-de-Thomières: Place du Foirail, **t** 04 67 97 06 65; Maison du Parc, 13 Rue du Cloître, **t** 04 67 97 38 22.

Where to Stay and Eat

Lamalou-les-Bains ✉ 34240

★★Belleville, 1 Av Charnot, **t** 04 67 95 57 00, *www.belleville.com* (*inexpensive*). Excellent value for relative luxury: some bathrooms come with Jacuzzi and there's a restaurant (*moderate*).

★★L'Arboisier, 18 Av Daudet, **t** 04 67 95 63 11 (*inexpensive*). This 100-year-old hotel has been prettily renovated; it serves old French favourites in the restaurant (*moderate*), with wine tastings in summer.

Olargues ✉ 34390

★★★Domaine de Rieumégé, 3km out on the St-Pons road, **t** 04 67 97 73 99, *www.tbs france.com/rieumege* (*moderate*). An enchanting 17th-century building set in an estate – peace and quiet guaranteed. Twelve nice rooms, pool and tennis, and a separate farmhouse with its own pool. If you don't stay, at least eat in the superb restaurant (*moderate*). Open April–Nov; restaurant open Mon–Fri eves only, weekend lunch.

St-Pons-de-Thomières ✉ 34220

★★Le Somail, 2 Av de Castres, **t** 04 67 97 00 12. A simple place in town.
La Route du Sel, 15 Grand'Rue, **t** 04 67 97 05 14. A little restaurant (*moderate*) specializing in original dishes such as *foie gras* with Jerusalem artichokes. *Closed Sun and Mon.*
Les Bergeries de Ponderach, about 1km outside St-Pons towards Narbonne, **t** 04 67 97 02 57, *www.bergeries-ponderach.com* (*moderate*). A haven of peace in the hills, with charming owner. There is a rustic restaurant, rooms with terraces and country views, summer concerts and even an art gallery.

The only big road in this region, the D908, runs west from Clermont-l'Hérault across the base of the mountains. The first town is **Bédarieux**, a humble enough market town. **Lamalou-les-Bains**, 10km further west, has been a thermal spa since the 1600s and made it big when the railway arrived in 1868. The prosperity of the next three decades – dukes and counts, famous actresses, even a sultan of Morocco checked in for the cure – brought Belle Epoque hotels and villas, cafés, a casino and a theatre. Either town is a good base for exploring the eastern half of the Espinouse: the **Gorges d'Heric**, a hiker's paradise, and the **Gorges de l'Orb**.

The loveliest village of the Espinouse, **Olargues**, has two medieval monuments, a striking 11th-century bell tower on a hill and a humpbacked bridge. Next, **St-Pons-de-Thomières** is the little capital of the Espinouse, surrounded by forests. Its landmarks are a cathedral, with a Romanesque portal and a tremendous 18th-century organ, and its **Musée Municipal de Préhistoire Régionale** (*open daily 10–12 and 2–5; adm*). North from St-Pons, the valley of the Agout spreads across the heart of the park; the D14 and D53 make a delightful tour, through villages like **La Salvetat-sur-Agout** and **Fraisse-sur-Agout**, which has a curious statue-menhir in situ, carved with a serpent and egg. The D53 continues towards the 3,651ft summit of the Espinouse.

The Hérault Coast

West of the Camargue, the lagoons continue for another 80km, dotting the coast like beads on a string. Unlike the Camargue, almost all of this coast is easily accessible by car; there are beaches and resorts in abundance.

Built in 1963, **La Grande Motte** looks like no other resort in the world, its hotels and apartments rising in colourful triangles and rollercoaster curves – but it is a great success as a resort, offering countless sports facilities and a casino. A more old-fashioned beach holiday can be spent at **Carnon-Plage** or **Palavas-les-Flots**, 15km down the dune-lined coast. Built around a narrow canal full of boats, Palavas is an endearingly humble resort with some 8km of good beaches.

Maguelone, 4km from Palavas, became a papal holding in the 12th century, valued for its salt pans. Though almost no trace of the town remains today, the impressive Cathedral St-Pierre was saved from ruin and restored in the 1870s (*open daily 9–7*).

Sète

Gritty, salty, workaday Sète is an attractive town, laced with canals, and livelier and more colourful than any place on the coast, save only Marseille. France's biggest Mediterranean fishing port, it also claims the Bassin de Thau, one of the largest lagoons along the Mediterranean, with salt-pans here, and now huge oyster and mussel farms. Businesslike freighters from Sète carry French sunflower and rape-seed oil to every corner of the globe. The bustling centre of Sète is its 'Grand Canal', the **Canal de Sète**, lined with quays where the ambience ranges from boat-yards and ship chandlers to banks and boutiques. At the southern end of the canal, the **Vieux Port** handles most of the fishing fleet, as well as offering tourist fishing boats and excursions around the Thau lagoon. From the Vieux Port it's a bit of a climb up to the **Cimetière Marin**, where the Sètois poet Paul Valéry was buried in 1945. The adjacent

Tourist Information

La Grande Motte: Allée des Parcs, **t** 04 67 56 42 00, *www.ot-lagrandemotte.fr.*
Palavas-les-Flots: Bd Joffre, **t** 04 67 07 73 34, *www.palavaslesflots.com.*
Sète: 60 Grand'Rue Mario Roustan, **t** 04 67 74 71 71, *www.ville-sete.fr.*
Agde: Place Molière, **t** 04 67 94 29 68.
Cap d'Agde: 11 Impasse du Hourier, **t** 04 67 01 04 04, *www.capagade.com.*

Where to Stay and Eat

La Grande Motte ✉ 34280

★★★Grand M'Hôtel, Quartier Point Zero, **t** 04 67 29 13 13 (*expensive*). The fanciest hotel, right on the front, with a thalassotherapy centre *www.thalass-grandemotte*) and balconied rooms with good sea views. *Centre closed mid-Dec–mid-Jan.*

★★★Mercure, Rue du Port, **t** 04 67 56 90 81 (*expensive–moderate*). The splashy status address on the Big Lump; rather charmless, but a chance to meet that segment of the fast crowd who choose to avoid the Riviera, and it does have a nice fish restaurant.

Alexandre, Esplanade de la Capitainerie, **t** 04 67 56 63 63 (*expensive*). A splurge for refined regional specialities in an especially elegant setting. *Closed 9 Jan–10 Feb, Sun eve and Mon.*

La Cuisine du Marché, 89 Rue Casino, **t** 04 67 29 90 11 (*moderate*). Good fresh fish served in classic style. It's small, so you'll need to book. *Closed Mon and Tues.*

Palavas-les-Flots ✉ 34250

★★Mas de Couran, Route de Fréjorgues, Lattes (✉ 34970), **t** 04 67 65 57 57, *www.mas-de-couran.com* (*moderate*). It's worth coming inland to Lattes for this special place, set in a beautiful park, with pool and restaurant. *Closed Sun eve, Mon, and Sat lunch.*

L'Escale, 5 Bd Sarrail, north of the canal on the seafront, **t** 04 67 68 24 17 (*expensive*). Here you can have *sèche à la rouille* for starters, or extravaganzas like the mixed shellfish plate they call *panaché de coquillages* – the bill can skyrocket before you recover your reason.

La Passerelle, Quai Paul-Cunq, **t** 04 67 68 55 80 (*moderate*). This couldn't be simpler, its menu limited to piles of fresh, inexpensive shellfish. *Closed Oct–April.*

Sète ✉ 34200

★★★Grand Hôtel, 17 Quai de Lattre de Tassigny, **t** 04 67 74 71 77, *www.sete-hotel.com* (*moderate*). Right on Sète's 'Grand Canal', it almost deserves its name, with plenty of original décor from the 1920s. The hotel's **Rotonde** restaurant (**t** 04 67 74 86 14, *expensive–moderate*) is refined and serves rewarding menus. *Closed Christmas.*

★★Les Abysses, 47 Grand'Rue Mario Roustan, **t** 04 67 74 37 73 (*inexpensive*). Small, central.

La Péniche, 1 Quai des Moulins, **t** 04 67 48 64 13 (*moderate*). For lunch with the dockhands try this place serving simple stuff on an old barge in the harbour. *Closed Sat lunch and Sun eve.*

La Palangrotte, Rampe Paul Valéry, **t** 04 67 74 80 35 (*moderate*). Quality seafood on the lower end of the Canal de Sète: grilled fish and several styles of fish stew, including the local *bourride sètoise. Closed Sun eve and Mon, except in July and Aug.*

Le Chalut, 38 Quai Maximin Licciardi, **t** 04 67 74 81 52 (*moderate*). The seafood, including many Sètois specialities, is as tasty as the décor. *Closed Wed out of season and Jan.*

Agde ✉ 34300

★★★La Tamarissière, 21 Quai Théophile Cornu (D32E), **t** 04 67 94 20 87 (*expensive*). A real charmer amid century-old parasol pines and roses 4km down the Hérault, with quiet, stylish, well-equipped rooms, a pool and the best restaurant in the area: fresh, colourful dishes such as St-Pierre baked with stuffed baby courgettes and saffron (*expensive–moderate*). *Closed Mon all day and Tues lunch in summer, Sun eve and Mon in winter.*

★★La Galiote, 5 Place Jean Jaurès, **t** 04 67 94 45 58, *www.lagaliote.fr* (*inexpensive*). Some of the rooms in this old bishops' palace overlook the river; there's a bar full of English beer, and an excellent restaurant (*expensive–moderate*): seafood or roast lamb with thyme, and alcoholic ices between courses.

★★Le Donjon, Place Jean Jaurès, **t** 04 67 94 12 32 (*inexpensive*). Old-fashioned rooms.

Musée Paul Valéry (*open Wed–Mon 10–12 and 2–6; closed Tues; adm*) contains exhibits on the poet, and on the history of Sète. Sète's other contribution to French culture, modern troubadour Georges Brassens (died 1981), is buried in the **Cimetière de Py**, under the Pierres Blanches, overlooking the Etang de Thau; the nearby **Espace Georges Brassens**, 67 Bd Camille-Blanc (*open 10–12 and 2–6, to 7pm July and Aug, closed Mon Oct–May; adm*) has photos and exhibits relating to his life.

Abbaye de Valmagne

Valmagne (*8km north of Mèze on the D161; guided tours; open June–Sept 10–12 and 2.30–6; Oct–May weekends only 2–5.30*) is not your typical austere Cistercian church. St Bernard would have frowned on architectural vanities like the porch, the bell towers and the sculpted decoration. Its size is astonishing: a 370ft nave, and great pointed arches almost as high as Narbonne cathedral's. Most of the work is 14th-century, in a straightforward but sophisticated late Gothic. The relatively few monks who lived here would hardly have needed such a church.

Agde, the 'Black Pearl of Languedoc'

If Sète is a brash young upstart, Agde, a lovely grey town, built almost entirely of volcanic basalt from nearby Mont St-Loup, has been watching the river Hérault flow down to the sea for some 2,500 years. Founded by Greeks from Phocis, in medieval times it was an important port, despite occasional visits by Arab sea-raiders. The stern basalt **Cathédrale St-Etienne** was begun about 1150. Its fortress-like appearance is no accident; Agde's battling bishops used it as their citadel. From the quay along the Hérault, Rue Chassefière leads into the *bourg*, or medieval addition to the city. On Rue de la Fraternité, the small, well arranged **Musée Agathois** (*open Wed–Sun 10–12 and 2–7; also Tues July and Aug; adm*, is one of the best of the south's town museums.

Cap d'Agde, 4km away, is the biggest beach playground in all Languedoc; the original 1960s plan even accommodated *naturistes*. One surprising attraction is a fine, small archaeological collection at the **Musée de l'Ephèbe** (*open daily exc Tues and Sun am out of season 9–12 and 2–6.30; adm*), the star of which is the *Ephèbe d'Agde*, a Hellenistic bronze of a boy, discovered in 1964.

Behind the Coast

Pézenas

If Carcassonne is Languedoc's medieval movie-set, Pézenas has often been used for dramas set in the time of Richelieu or Louis XIV. Few cities have a better ensemble of buildings from what the French (rather over-enthusiastically) used to call the 'Golden Age'. Roman *Piscenae* was known for wool, the best in Gaul. In the 1200s, it became a possession of the French crown. Later, the troubles of Béziers and Narbonne in the Albigensian Crusade and the Hundred Years' War would prove lucky for Pézenas and the town replaced Narbonne as seat of the Estates-General of Languedoc after 1456. The royal governors of the region followed, bringing in their wake a whole wave of wealthy nobles, clerics and jurists, who rebuilt Pézenas in their own image, with new

Getting Around

Béziers is on the main coastal rail line, and it's easy to get to Narbonne, Sète and Montpellier. The other line from the city heads north for Castres, passing through Bédarieux and St-Pons. The bus station has regular connections to Pézenas (and to everywhere the trains go), and less regular ones to villages of the eastern Hérault.

Tourist Information

Pézenas: Place Gambetta, **t** 04 67 98 36 40, *www.paysdepezenas.net*.
Béziers: Palais des Congrès, 29 Av St-Saëns, **t** 04 67 76 47 00, *www.ville-beziers.fr*.

Where to Stay and Eat

Pézenas ✉ 34120
★★★**Hostellerie de St-Alban**, 31 Rte d'Agde, Nézignan l'Evêque, just south of Pézenas, **t** 04 67 98 11 38 (*moderate*). A quiet 19th-century villa in the vines, with a pool, tennis and restaurant (*expensive*). *Closed Dec–Jan.*
★★**Genieys**, 9 Av Aristide Briand, **t** 04 67 98 13 99 (*inexpensive*). Outside the historic centre, but the only good hotel in town. *Half board only in July and Aug; restaurant closed Sun eve.*
Côté Sud, Place 14 Juillet, **t** 04 67 09 41 74 (*moderate*). For a shellfish feast. *Closed Dec and Mon in winter.*

Le Pré St-Jean, 18 Av du Maréchal-Leclerc, **t** 04 67 98 15 31 (*moderate*). Has a pretty terrace and serves classics like stuffed squid and *carré d'agneau en croûte*. *Closed Mon year round and Sun eve in winter.*

Béziers ✉ 34500
★★★**Imperator**, 28 Allées Paul Riquet, **t** 04 67 49 02 25, *www.hotel-imperator.fr* (*inexpensive*). This has the best location in town, and there's a garage, too.
★★**Champ de Mars**, 17 Rue Metz, **t** 04 67 28 35 53 (*inexpensive*). A good value place, nice and central but on a quiet street, with recently renovated rooms.
★**Paul Riquet**, 46 Allées Paul Riquet, **t** 04 67 76 44 37 (*inexpensive*). Small and pleasant.
L'Ambassade, 22 Bd de Verdun, **t** 04 67 76 06 24 (*expensive*). Elegant, with good-value menus. *Closed Sun and Mon.*
Le Jardin, 37 Av Jean Moulin, near Place 14 Juillet, **t** 04 67 36 41 31 (*expensive–moderate*). The finest local ingredients go into the wide-awake cuisine here. *Closed Sun eve and Wed and the last week in August–mid-Sept.*
Le Framboisier, 12 Rue Boieldieu, off Bd Paul Riquet, **t** 04 67 49 90 00 (*moderate–expensive*). Local gourmets favour this place, where the inventive chef serves up delicacies like fricassee of asparagus and eggs with truffles or *rouget* with tapenade.
Le Mondial, 2 Rue Solférino, **t** 04 67 28 22 15. Piano bar, packed most evenings, not so much for its food but for the music (*usually on Wed–Sat nights*). *Open eves Tues–Sat.*

churches, convents, government buildings and refined *hôtels particuliers*, with arcaded courtyards and external staircases. It all came to an end with the Revolution.

The tourist information office offers a brochure with a detailed walking tour of the town and its 70-odd listed historical buildings. Molière spent some seasons in Pézenas in the 1650s, when his troupe was employed by the governor, the Prince de Conti. On Rue Alliès, the **Musée de Vuillod-St-Germain** contains memorabilia of the playwright and his time here, along with collections of tapestries, faïence and paintings (*open 10–12 and 3–6, closed Sun am and Mon out of season; adm*).

Béziers

This city's history is succinct: a rude interruption and a second chance. In 1209, at the beginning of the Albigensian Crusade, a large number of Cathars took refuge in the city and were besieged. The troops stormed the city, and found that the entire population had taken refuge in the churches. The Abbot of Cîteaux, had ordered the massacre of the Cathars; asked how to distinguish them from the Catholics, he replied, 'Kill them all, God will know his own.' Not surprisingly, Béziers languished for centuries. The second chance came in the 1660s, with the building of the Canal du Midi. A new Béziers has grown up since, a busy industrial port.

Life in Béziers centres along the the **Allées Paul Riquet**, a promenade of plane trees named after the city's great benefactor, the builder of the Canal du Midi. Besides a statue of Riquet, there is a handsome 19th-century theatre, and a monument to Resistance hero Jean Moulin (another Bitérois) at the top of the romantic **Plateau des Poètes**. From the other end of the Allées Paul Riquet, any of the streets to the west will take you up to the medieval centre.

Someone must have been left in Béziers after 1209, for the city spent the next two centuries working on its grandiose **cathedral**, replacing the original that was wrecked in the sack. Behind the cathedral, the **Musée Fabregat** (*open Sept–June Tues–Sun 9–12 and 2–5; July and Aug 10–6; adm*) in Place de la Révolution, houses Béziers' fine arts museum, founded in 1859. Many of the fine modern works (de Chirico, Soutine, Friesz) were purchased by Jean Moulin, who posed as a designer and art dealer called Romanin. Just north, the **Musée Fayet** (*open Tues–Fri 9–12 and 2–6; same adm*), in a delightful 17th-century *hôtel particulier* at 9 Rue du Capus, contains several rooms of 18th- and 19th-century paintings and decorative arts. On a belvedere on the south side of Béziers is the **Musée du Biterrois** (or de St-Jacques) (*open daily summer 10–6, winter 9–12 and 2–6, closed Mon; adm*), with regional archaeological finds, medieval capitals and other bits, ethnography (especially wine-making), science and ceramics.

The Canal du Midi

The best thing to do in Béziers is go west for one of Languedoc's best-kept secrets. This canal, one of very few in the south, remains serene and relatively unburdened by

Getting Around

Forget about buses and trains; you'll need a car to get around here, or better a mountain bike (VTT in French); the shady towpaths are lovely for cycling. Best of all, hire a small boat (ask at any of the villages). The canal is open for navigation Mar–Nov.

Tourist Information

Nissan-lez-Ensérune. t 04 67 37 14 12.

Where to Stay and Eat

Nissan-lez-Ensérune ✉ 34440
**Résidence, 35 Av de la Cave, t 04 67 37 00 63, *www.hotel-residence.com* (*inexpensive*).

Antiquated charm, with a more modern annexe. *Closed mid-Dec–mid-Feb.*

Homps ✉ 11120
Auberge de l'Arbousier, 50 Av de Carcassonne, Le Somail, t 04 68 91 11 24 (*inexpensive*). A charming hotel-restaurant in an old *mas* on the banks of the Canal du Midi. *Closed Nov; restaurant closed Sun eve and Wed.*

Trèbes ✉ 11800
Château de Floure, 1 Allée Gaston Bonheur, Floure, t 04 68 79 11 29, *www.chateau-de-floure.com* (*expensive*). This ivy-covered chateau was a Romanesque abbey; now a Relais du Silence hotel, it has an elegant French garden, with pool and tennis, comfortable air-conditioned rooms and a restaurant (*expensive*). *Closed Nov–Mar.*

tourism, and is planted its entire length with parallel rows of great plane trees. Paul Riquet's canal is also an early monument of economic planning, from the days of Louis XIV's great minister Colbert. Riquet was a local baron and the state's Tax Farmer (*fermier-général*) for Languedoc. He conceived the idea for the 235km canal that would link the Mediterranean to the Atlantic by way of the Garonne and sold it to Colbert, then saw through its construction with remarkable single-mindedness, inventing ingenious tricks to get the canal over the highest stretches, paying a third of the expenses himself, and even sacrificing his daughters' dowries to the cause. From 1666, as many as 12,000 men worked on the project. It was completed 39 years later; Riquet died bankrupt a few months before the opening.

Oppidum d'Ensérune

Open April–Oct 9–12 and 2–6, July and Aug 9.30–7, otherwise 10–12 and 2–4; guided tours; adm.

Seven km southwest of Béziers on the N9 Narbonne road is one of the most important pre-Roman towns of southern Gaul. Initially settled in the 6th century BC, the Oppidum d'Ensérune began as a fortified trading village under Greek influence. It revived again under Roman rule but was largely abandoned by the 1st century AD. Not much remains of the town: the foundations of the wall, cisterns and so on, but there is an excellent **museum** in the centre of the excavations.

The Minervois

This is a *pays* with plenty of character, though not many people. The Minervois suffered grievously from poverty and rural depopulation throughout the 20th century – then, just when everyone was gone, vintners improved the quality of their Minervois wines, and the region's prosperity has returned. The country is ragged and wild, with outcrops of eroded limestone, and there is a sense of strange isolation.

West of Béziers, the narrow D10 will take you up into the heights of the Minervois, to **Minerve**, a town as old as any in Languedoc. The Celts and the Romans built the town, and in the Middle Ages it was a feudal stronghold with a Cathar slant. Minerve accepted refugees from the sack of Béziers in 1209; Simon de Montfort followed them, and took the town after a siege, followed by the usual butchery. All that is left of the château is a slender, octagonal tower; the Minervois call it the '*candela*'. There are narrow medieval alleys, gates and cisterns, and a simple 12th-century church with a white marble altar from 456, said to be the oldest in Europe. The real attractions are in the country. A short walk from town, there are '**natural bridges**' – really more like tunnels, eroded through the limestone by streams. To the west extends the narrow, blushing pink **Canyon de la Cesse**.

The seven-sided church of **Rieux-Minervois** is one of the most uncanny medieval monuments in France. The seven-pointed star is the recurring mystic symbol of the Midi. Just what it means has never been explained; neither has anyone ventured an explanation for the presence in this unremarkable Minervois village of what may be the only seven-sided church anywhere. Dedicated to the Virgin, the church was built some time in the late 12th century. The ambition of the builders of this church is seen in the sculptural detail inside, entrusted to the Master of Cabestany. Building in heptagons must have tried the patience and mathematical know-how of a 12th-century mason, especially the seven-sided belfry, directly over the altar, and the tricky toroid vaulting that connects the heptagon with the 14-sided exterior wall.

The Montagne Noire

Even wilder than the Minervois, if not as unusual, the bleak, brooding Black Mountain is a 30km-wide stretch of peaks, taller than their neighbours and difficult to access until modern times. All the routes into it follow narrow parallel valleys leading up from the river Aude. The **valley of the Orbiel** (D101) is the most populous of the region. It also contains the region's landmark, the **Châteaux de Lastours** (open daily Oct 10–5, April, May, June, Sept 10–6, July and Aug 9–8; Feb, Mar, Nov, Dec weekends only 10–5; closed Jan; adm) – not one, but four castles, in various states of picturesque ruin, all on the same hilltop to defend the Montagne Noire's mineral richness.

To the east of Lastours is a remarkable cave, the **Grotte de Limousis**, with unique formations of gleaming white aragonite crystals (open daily Mar–June and Sept 10–12 and 2–5.30; July and Aug 10–6; Oct–Mar 2–5; adm). Further up the valley are two of the most beautiful and unspoiled villages of the region: **Roquefère** and **Mas-Cabardès**. Mas-Cabardès has some half-timbered houses and a 16th-century church with a rugged belfry. In the village centre, note the typical carved stone **cross**.

In the valley furthest west, that of the Vernassonne, **Saissac** is another lovely village, built over a ravine and surrounded by forests. Saissac too has its romantically ruined, overgrown fortress, and a 10ft **menhir**, just to the north off the D4. To the south, **Montolieu**, balanced over the gorges of the the Alzeau and Dure, has become a centre of the local bookmaking trade: in the centre, the **Montolieu, Village du Livre** (open 10–12 and 2–6; adm), traces the history of bookbinding and printing.

Narbonne

The Roman colony of Colonia Narbo Martius, a good site for a trading port along the recently built Via Domitia, was founded in 118 BC. It rapidly became the most important city of southern Gaul, renowned for its beauty and wealth. In the 12th century, Narbonne entered its second golden age, which lasted until the 14th century when wars, plagues and the harbour silting up led to its ruin. By the end of the century, the city had shrunk to a mere market town. Now Languedoc's capital, Narbonne has a local economy largely fuelled on plonk – the bountiful vineyards of the Corbières and other nearby regions – and the city is also finding a new vocation as an industrial centre. With its impressive medieval monuments, boulevards and lively streets and the best cathedral in the south, it is quite a happy and contented place.

The City Centre

Follow Rue Jean Jaurès from near the train and bus stations and you'll be following the **Canal de la Robine** into the centre of the city, lined with a delightful park called the **Jardin Entre Deux Villes**. Narbonne's centre is the busy **Place de l'Hôtel de Ville**. Facing

Getting There and Around

Narbonne is on the main Bordeaux–Toulouse–Nice rail route across the Midi; there are frequent connections (about 12 a day) to Perpignan, Toulouse, and Béziers and the other coastal cities to the east. The bus station offers coach services that largely duplicate the trains; there will also be a bus or two a day to Gruissan and Leucate.

Tourist Information

Narbonne: Place Roger-Salengro, t 04 68 65 15 60, www.mairie-narbonne.fr.

Where to Stay

Narbonne ✉ 11100

***La Résidence**, 6 Rue du 1er Mai, t 04 68 32 19 41 (*inexpensive*). Near the cathedral in an old *hôtel particulier*, with calm, well-equipped rooms and a garage. *Closed mid-Jan–mid-Feb.*

*La Dorade**, 44 Rue Jean-Jaurès, t 04 68 32 65 95 (*inexpensive*). But for the lack of parking and a bit of street noise, this would be perfect. Narbonne's old 'Grand Hôtel', with marble telamones holding up the balcony, this establishment is still well kept,

centrally located overlooking the canal, and a good bargain.

Will's Hôtel, 23 Av Pierre Semard, t 04 68 90 44 50 (*inexpensive*). A comfortable and extremely friendly place.

Hôtel du Lion d'Or, Av Pierre Semard, t 04 68 32 06 92 *(inexpensive)*. Small family-run hotel with a good line in wine tastings.

*Hôtel de la Gare**, 7 Av Pierre Semard, t 04 68 32 10 54 (*cheap*). Very nice for its price.

Eating Out

Table St Crescent, Rte de Perpignan, t 04 68 41 37 37 (*expensive–moderate*). One of Narbonne's top restaurants is outside town at the Palais du Vin. A vine-covered terrace shelters a modern stylish establishment specializing, of course, in the best regional wines and dishes. *Closed Sun eve and Mon.*

Le Billot, 22 Rue de l'Ancienne Porte de Béziers, t 04 68 32 70 88 (*moderate*). East of the centre, near a delightful park called the Place Thérèse et Léon Blum. *Closed Aug.*

La Baie d'Along, Place Bistan, in old Narbonne, t 04 68 65 58 83 (*moderate*). For Chinese–Vietnamese cooking, very correct and tasty too, this is the best in town; there's a menu, though you may want to splurge for the elaborate starters. *Closed Wed.*

the square, the twin façades of the **Palais des Archevêques** were blessed with a romantic Gothic restoration by the master himself, Viollet-le-Duc, in the 1840s. The passage between the two buildings (the Palais Neuf on the left, and the Palais Vieux on the right) leads to a small courtyard, and the entrances to Narbonne's two excellent museums, the **Musée d'Art et d'Histoire** and the **Musée Archéologique** (*both open Oct–Mar Tues–Sun 10–12 and 2–5; April–Sept daily 9.30–12.15 and 2–6*). The Musée d'Art et d'Histoire's Grande Galerie contains some of the best paintings in the museum. In the Salle des Faïences are 18th-century painted ceramics. It is only luck that made Nîmes the 'French Rome', while only one of Narbonne's monuments has survived. There is, however, no shortage of remaining bits and pieces, and the best of them have been assembled in the Musée Archéologique.

Narbonne's one Roman monument is a warehouse or **Horreum**, on Rue Rouget de Lisle (*open 9–12.15 and 2–6, closed Mon Oct–mid-May; adm*). Typical of the state-run warehouses of any Roman city, this is the only complete one anywhere. Just a small part of the 500ft original structure has been excavated.

Cathédrale St-Just

This can be entered through the fine 14th-century **cloister**, a Gothic quadrangle with leering gargoyles. A better way, though, is to circumnavigate the huge bulk of the cathedral and palace complex towards the west front, and the **Cour St-Eutrope**, a spacious square that occupies the unfinished two-thirds of the cathedral itself.

This is the third church to occupy the site and was begun in 1272, at the height of the city's fortunes. To extend the new cathedral to its planned length, it would have been necessary to rebuild a section of the city wall, but a lawsuit between the city and the church brought construction to a halt. Just the same, this one-third of a cathedral is by any measure the finest on the Mediterranean. The short nave, in fact, heightens the exuberant verticality of the 131ft apse and choir, exceeded in height only by those of Amiens and Beauvais. Throughout, the structural lines are accented with ribbing or with protruding stone courses.

Inside, the best features are in the ambulatory and its chapels. Near the altar, facing the chapels, are two remarkable archepiscopal tombs. The **Tomb of Cardinal Briçonnet** (1514) has a mix of Renaissance refinement and ghoulish, grinning skeletons, typical of that age. The other, the **Tomb of Cardinal Pierre de Jugie**, is an exquisite Gothic work of 1376. The ambulatory chapels are illuminated by lovely 14th-century glass; the central **Chapelle de la Vierge** has a unique polychrome reliefs of the late 1300s. Ruined and covered in a Baroque remodelling of 1732, these were rediscovered in the last century, and are currently being restored. In the **cathedral treasury** (*open daily Oct–June Mon–Sat 2–6; July–Sept 11–6; closed Sun; adm*) are medieval reliquaries, a 10th-century carved ivory plaque, and two 16th-century Flemish tapestries.

The Bourg

This is Narbonne's medieval extension across the river (now the canal). Behind the city's popular covered **market**, the deconsecrated 13th-century church of Notre-Dame-de-Lamourguier now houses the **Musée Lapidaire**, a large collection of architectural fragments from ancient Narbonne (*open July and Aug 9.30–12.15 and 2–6; adm*). The **Basilique St-Paul-Serge** was first built in the 5th century and dedicated to the first bishop of Narbonne. The present imposing Gothic monument was begun in 1229.

Narbonne's Coast

The coastal road, more or less following the path of the Roman Via Domitia, cannot follow this complicated shoreline; some detours on the backroads will be necessary to see it. Beyond **Narbonne-Plage**, a bright, modern, characterless resort, the landscape rises into the **Montagne de la Clape**, once an island and still a world in itself. Parts are lush and pine-clad, others rugged and desolate. Near the top, the chapel of **Notre-Dame-des-Auzils** has a fascinating collection of sailors' ex votos – ship models, paintings and the like, many over a century old (*get the key from the tourist office at Gruissan*). Most of those sailors came from **Gruissan**, south of La Clape. One of Narbonne's ports in the Middle Ages, Gruissan today is surrounded by lagoons and salt-pans; the charming village is set in concentric rings around a ruined 13th-century castle, built to defend the approaches to Narbonne. Gruissan's other landmark (famous from the film *Betty Blue*) is the Plage des Pilotis, where beach cottages hang in the air; the sea regularly covers the sand here, and people began building their houses on stilts over a century ago.

Abbaye de Fontfroide

Down the D613 southwest of Narbonne, a marked side road leads to the **Abbaye de Fontfroide** (*t 04 68 45 11 08; open for guided tours only; call to confirm times; adm*). Fontfroide was founded in 1145, and until its suppression in 1791, it was one of the richest and most influential of all Cistercian houses in the south. The best part of the tour is the lovely 13th-century **cloister**, with its broad arches inset with smaller ones. The 12th-century **church** impresses with its proportions and Romanesque austerity. Fascinating abstract collages of old stained-glass fragments can be seen in the **dormitory**, brought here from northern French churches wrecked during the First World War.

Tourist Information

Gruissan: 1 Bd Pech-Maynaud, **t** 04 68 49 09 00.
Sigean: Place de la Libération, **t** 04 68 48 14 81, *www.sigean.org*.

Where to Stay and Eat

Narbonne-Plage ✉ 11100
Domaine d'Hospitalet, Rte de Narbonne Plage, **t** 04 68 45 34 47, *www.domaine-hospitalet* (*expensive–moderate*). A wine *domaine* on the Clape Massif, this incorporates an *auberge* with several pretty rooms, a restaurant, *caves* and wine tastings, a wine museum and other small museums devoted to the history of telephones, *La Poste* and old cars, all in an idyllic setting of vineyards overlooking the sea. *Closed Jan and Feb.*

Gruissan ✉ 11430
★★Hôtel Corail, Quai Ponant in Gruissan Port, **t** 04 68 49 04 43, *www.lecorail.com* (*inexpensive*). Has a fine restaurant specializing in *bouillabaisse. Closed Nov–Jan.*
L'Estagnol, t 04 68 49 01 26 (*moderate*). A popular converted fisherman's cottage at the entrance to the village, offering sumptuous seafood and fish. *Closed Oct–Mar.*

Carcassonne

After running north down from the Pyrenees, the river Aude makes a sharp right turn for the sea; the river's angle, a crossroads of France since prehistoric times, is an obvious site for a fortress; there seems to have been one since the 8th century BC. From 1084 to 1209 Carcassonne enjoyed a glorious period of wealth and culture under the Trencavels, a family who were also viscounts of Béziers and Nîmes, and very sympathetic to the Cathars. Under them the cathedral and the Château Comtal were begun. Simon de Montfort, realizing the importance of the town, made it one of his first stops in the Crusade of 1209. The last Viscount Trencavel was captured and probably poisoned by Montfort, who declared himself viscount and used Carcassonne as his base of operations until his death in 1218. When France gobbled up the province of Roussillon in 1659, this mighty bastion no longer had any military purpose, and it was allowed to fall into disrepair. Today's Carcassonne has a split personality. Up on its hill, the pink towers of the lovingly restored *cité* glitter like a dream; no longer impregnable, its 750 inhabitants are invaded by over 200,000 visitors each year. Down below, the workaday Ville Basse gets on with the job.

The Walls of the Cité

Most visitors arrive via the car parks and the bus stop, at the **Porte Narbonnaise**. Between the two walls of the *cité*, you can circumnavigate Carcassonne through the open space called **Les Lices**, the 'lists', where knights rained, and where tournaments were held. The **outer wall** is the work of Louis IX; note how it is completely open on the inside, so that attackers who stormed it would have no protection from the defenders on the **inner wall** – parts date back to the Romans.

To the right of the Porte Narbonnaise, the first large tower is the mighty **Tour du Trésau**. Beyond it, the northern side of the inner wall is almost completely Roman, with the characteristic rounded bastions used all over the Empire. The walls to the left of the Porte Narbonnaise were almost completely rebuilt under Philip III, a long stretch of impressive bastions culminating in the great **Tour St-Nazaire**. Atop both the inner and outer walls, almost everything you see today – the crenellations, wooden galleries (*hourds*) and pointed turrets – is the work of Viollet-le-Duc. As in all his other works, the pioneer of architectural restoration has been faulted for not adhering literally to original appearances. This is true, especially concerning the pointed turrets and northern slate roofs, but Viollet-le-Duc worked in a time before anyone could have imagined our own rigorous, antiseptic approach to recreating the old. His romantic, 19th-century appreciation of the Middle Ages made possible a restoration that was not only essentially correct, but creative and beautiful.

The defences are strongest on the western side because here, the *cité's* three lines of defence – the outer and inner walls and the citadel, the **Château Comtal** (*open Nov–Mar 9.30am–5pm; April, May and Oct 9.30am–6pm; June–Sept 9.30am–7.30pm; adm*) – are closely compressed. Probably the site of the Roman governors' palace, it was rebuilt by the Trencavels for their own palace, and expanded by King Louis IX. You have a choice of guided tours of the walls and towers which begin with a room-sized

Getting There and Around

Ryanair flies to Carcassonne from London; a shuttle bus goes from **airport** to station. There are **trains** to Toulouse and Narbonne (11 a day), and from there to all the coastal cities; also a few trains down the Aude valley to Limoux and Quillan. Several **buses** a day go to Narbonne and Castelnaudary, three to Toulouse, and a rare few to outlying towns like Limoux. Some buses to villages in the Montagne Noire and Minervois leave from the Café Bristol in front of the rail station. To get up to the *cité*, take the no.4 city bus (every 30 minutes) from the rail station or from Place Gambetta.

Tourist Information

Carcassonne: 15 Bd Camille Pelletan, opposite Place Gambetta, in the centre of the Ville Basse, **t** 04 68 10 24 30, *www.carcassonne-tourisme.com*. Also in the Porte Narbonnaise in the Cité, **t** 04 68 10 24 35.

Where to Stay

Carcassonne ✉ 11000
Stay in the *cité* if you can, but it's not cheap.
★★★★**Hôtel de la Cité**, Place St-Nazaire, **t** 04 68 71 98 71, *www.orient-express.com* (*luxury–expensive*). In a pretty garden right under the walls of the Cité, this hotel occupies the former episcopal palace, grandly restored in 1909, with marble baths, a pool, and three restaurants. *Closed Dec–mid-Jan.*
★★★★**Domaine d'Auriac**, Rte St-Hilaire, south of town, **t** 04 68 25 72 22, *www.relaischateaux.fr/auriac* (*luxury–expensive*). A luxury alternative to staying in the Cité is this Relais & Châteaux hotel, a stately, ivy-covered 18th-century mansion set in a large, immaculately kept park. There's a pool, tennis, and even a golf course close by. Also an elegant and highly rated restaurant, featuring some seafood but mostly traditional dishes of the Aude. *Hotel closed Jan; restaurant closed Mon, Wed, and Fri lunch May–Sept, Sun eve and Mon in winter.*

★★★**Bristol**, 7 Av Foch, **t** 04 68 25 07 24 (*moderate*). A grand 19th-century hotel near the station, with rooms overlooking the Canal du Midi. *Closed Sun eve and Mon.*
★★★**Hôtel du Donjon**, Rue du Comte Roger, **t** 04 68 11 23 00, *www.hotel-donjon.fr* (*moderate*). In a charming old mansion of the Cité, with a small garden and a fine restaurant.
★★★**Auberge du Château de Cavanac**, Cavanac, 4km south on the Rte St-Hilaire, **t** 04 68 79 61 04 (*moderate*). A big old farmhouse in a quiet garden, with an excellent restaurant in the former stables which serves a unique five-course menu with wine and all the works, starting with a kir and a choice of starters – *foie gras*, smoked salmon or lobster. *Closed Feb; restaurant closed Jan–Feb and Mon.*
★★★**Terminus**, 2 Av Maréchal Joffre, **t** 04 68 25 25 00 (*inexpensive*). For a touch of class at economy prices; it's been used as a set in French films. Get one of the rooms that have not been 'renovated'. *Closed Dec–Mar.*
★★**Hôtel du Pont Vieux**, 32 Rue Trivalle, **t** 04 68 25 24 99 (*inexpensive*). One of the closest hotels to the Cité, and one of the best.

Eating Out

Le Languedoc, Hôtel Montségur, 32 Allée Iéna, **t** 04 68 25 22 17 (*expensive–moderate*). A popular restaurant with a patio, serving regional cuisine but particularly famed for its *cassoulet* with *confit de canard* and salad of *foie gras*. *Closed Sun eve and Mon.*
Dame Carcas, 3 Place du Château, **t** 04 68 71 23 23 (*moderate*). Delicious wood-fired food. *Closed mid-Jan–mid-Feb, and Mon.*
L'Œil, 32 Rue de Lorraine, **t** 04 68 25 64 81 (*moderate*). Down in the Ville Basse, you can feast on smoked duck *magret* and other southwest fare. *Closed Sat lunch and Sun, and first 2 weeks Aug.*
Jardins de la Tour, 11 Rue Porte d'Aude, **t** 04 68 25 71 24 (*moderate–cheap*). A pretty, idiosyncratic restaurant with garden dining and authentic regional dishes and fish. *Booking advised in high season. Closed Nov–mid Dec and Sun and Mon.*

model and continue, in fascinating, excruciating detail, through an advanced course in medieval military architecture. Louis' builders laid many traps for invaders – for example the stairways where each riser is a different height. Your ticket also includes the **Musée Lapidaire**, which fills much of the palace. Old prints and paintings give an idea of the half-ruined state of the *cité* before Viollet-le-Duc went to work on it.

Erected in 1096, the cité's **Basilique St-Nazaire** (*open summer 9–11.45 and 2–6; winter 9.30–12 and 2–5*) took shape as an austere, typically southern Romanesque cathedral. The French conquerors had more ambitious plans, and in 1270 rebuilt the transepts and choir in glorious, perpendicular Gothic. The windows illuminate the interior with beautiful 16th- and 17th-century stained glass. In the right aisle, you can pay your respects to the devil himself, at the **Tomb of Simon de Montfort**.

The Corbières, Aude and Limouxin

The Aude's Northwest Corner: the Lauragais

West of Carcassonne and the Montagne Noire lies a region called the Lauragais, a mostly flat expanse of serious farming of the humbler sort: beans, barley and pigs. Windmills are a chief landmark, as is the shady blue and nearly straight ribbon of the Canal du Midi en route to Toulouse. Rugby makes the juices flow in these parts, but in the old days it was Catharism.

French cookery books claim that a *cassoulet* requires four things: 'white beans from Lavelanet, cooked in the pure water of **Castelnaudary**, in a casserole made of clay from the Issel, over a fire of furze from the Black Mountain'. Back in the 1570s, Castelnaudary's *cassoulet* was prescribed to Queen Margot as a cure for sterility, unfortunately without success. With *cassoulet*, the charms of Castelnaudary are nearly exhausted. There is the 14th-century church of **St-Michel**, with a steeple that dominates the city; also the **Moulin de Cugarel** (*open July and Aug only, Tues–Sat 10–12 and 3–6.30, Sun and Mon 3–6.30*), a restored 17th-century windmill, one of over 30 that once spun in the vicinity, and the port of the Canal du Midi.

The Corbières

Thanks to wine, the Corbières has finally found its vocation. This scrubby, mountainous area has been the odd region out since ancient times. As a refuge for disaffected Gauls, it was a headache to the Romans. In the Middle Ages, sitting astride the boundaries of France and Aragon, it was a permanent zone of combat. Local *seigneurs* littered the landscape with castles in incredible, impregnable mountain-top sites. Some of these became the last redoubts of the persecuted Cathars; nearly all of them are ruined today.

Castles, Gorges and the Fenouillèdes

The humble D611 and D14 were the main medieval routes through the Corbières, connecting with the passes over the Pyrenees to Spain, and castles occur with the frequency of petrol stations on a motorway. **Tuchan**, a typically stark and dusty

Getting Around

SNCF rail-lines make a neat square around the Corbières, but none of them ventures inside the region. The only useful one is from Carcassonne, stopping at Limoux, Alet-les-Bains, Couiza, Quillan and St-Paul-de-Fenouillet on its way to Perpignan. Don't count on buses either. There are some services from Perpignan's bus station up the Agly valley to Maury, St-Paul and Quillan, and one a day through the heart of the Fenouillèdes.

Tourist Information

Lézignan-Corbières: Cours de la République, t 04 68 27 05 42.
St-Paul-de-Fenouillet: 26 Bd Agly, t 04 68 59 07 57.
Quillan: Square André Tricoire, t 04 68 20 07 78, *www.ville-quillan.fr.*

Where to Stay and Eat

For tourism, the Corbières is virgin territory; accommodation is fairly scarce.

Maury ✉ 66460

★★Hôtel des Graves, 9 Bd Jean-Jaurès, Estagel, near Tautavel on the D117, t 04 68 29 00 84 (*inexpensive*). If you're passing by you can eat and/or sleep well and economically at this hotel owned by the local wine barons; Catalan specialities served with local wine.
L'Auberge du Grand Rocher, Rue Eloi Tresserres, Caramany, t 04 68 84 51 58 (*moderate*). This simply furnished restaurant in a pretty hill town is well worth the 20min drive from Maury; the terrace has lovely views over the valley. The husband-and-wife team prepare perfectly cooked local specialities such as

confit de canard with potatoes roasted in duck fat (the best in the region), or roast lamb with thyme. *July–Aug open every even, otherwise lunch and Fri and Sat eves only.*

Cucugnan ✉ 11350

★★Auberge du Vigneron, 1 Rue Achille-Mir, t 04 68 45 03 00 (*inexpensive*). The only hotel, but a good one, with cosy rustic rooms and a restaurant in a former wine cellar with simple but fragrant dishes. *Closed Mon, Sun eve and mid-Dec–mid-Feb.*

St-Paul-de-Fenouillet ✉ 66220

★★Le Châtelet, Rte de Caudies, t 04 68 59 01 20 (*inexpensive*). A Logis de France hotel, with a pool and restaurant. *Closed Dec–Mar; restaurant open eves only.*
★Relais des Corbières, 10 Av Jean Moulin, t 04 68 59 23 89 (*inexpensive*). Smaller, central and also Logis de France. *Closed Jan.*

Tautavel ✉ 66720

Le Petit Gris, Route d'Estagel, t 04 68 29 42 42 (*moderate*). A very popular family restaurant. There are great views of the plain from big windows, and they serve grilled dishes including an excellent Catalan *cargolade* of snails, pork, lamb and sausages cooked on your own personal grill. *Oct–May closed all day Mon, and Tues, Wed and Thurs eves.*

Quillan ✉ 11500

★★★La Chaumière, 25 Bd Charles de Gaulle, t 04 68 20 17 90 (*inexpensive*). Cosy rooms and gratifying mountain cooking featuring trout and salmon. *Closed mid-Nov–mid-Mar.*
★★Pierre Lys, Av de Carcassonne, t 04 68 20 08 65 (*inexpensive*). At the north end of town, this modern hotel offers comfort, quiet and the best meals in the town. *Closed mid-Nov–mid-Dec.*

Corbières village, has no fewer than three ruined castles; the best of them, the **Château d'Aguilar**, saw plenty of action: Simon de Montfort stormed it in 1210, but the French had to take it again from rebellious barons 30 years later, and over the next 200 years the Spaniards regularly knocked at the gate.

West of Tuchan the landscapes become higher and wilder. **Padern** has another castle, ruined despite rebuilding work in the 18th century; so does **Cucugnan**, a colourful little village. Both these towns offer scenic detours – from Padern, north through the **Gorges du Torgan**, and from Cucugnan, south through the spectacular

Grau de Maury, the Corbières' back door. Cucugnan's landmark is obvious from a distance, the picture-postcard **Château de Quéribus** (*open daily 10–6, July and Aug 10–8; Feb, Mar, Nov, and Dec weekends only 10–5, closed Jan; adm*), balancing nonchalantly on a slender peak, a half-mile in the air. The best-maintained of the Corbières castles, Quéribus was the last redoubt of the Cathars after Montségur (*see* p.523); a small band of bitter-enders held out for months here in 1255.

Castles atop mountains will be nothing new by now, but nowhere else, perhaps, is there a bigger castle atop a taller, steeper mountain than the **Château de Peyrepertuse** (*open April, May and Oct 9–7, June–Sept 8.30–8.30; Nov, Dec, Feb and Mar 10–5; closed Jan*). From Cucugnan it is an unforgettable sight, a white limestone cliff rising vertically in the clouds, crowned by a stretch of walls and towers over 777ft long. Close up, from the bottom of the cliff, you can't see it at all. Begun in the 10th century, Peyrepertuse was expanded by Saint Louis in the 1240s. As important to the defence of France's new southern border as Carcassonne, Peyrepertuse was intended as an unconquerable base; attacking the place would be madness. The vertiginous road to the castle starts from Duilhac; from the car park it's an exhausting 20-minute struggle up to the walls. The entrance leads into the Château Vieux, the original castle, rebuilt by Saint Louis. Nearly everything is in ruins; the keep is still in good shape, and a large cistern and the ruined chapel can be seen directly behind it. The Château St-Georges, with another keep and chapel, is on top.

There are no easy roads in any other direction from Peyrepertuse, but if you're heading west, rejoin the main route by way of the D7 and the white cliffs of the **Gorges de Galamus**, the most impressive natural wonder of the Corbières, a deep gorge with wonderful stone pools for swimming and canyoning.

Descending from Opoul to the southwest, the D9 passes through some romantically empty scenery towards **Tautavel**. Human bones have been found around here from as far back as 450–680,000 BC, making 'Tautavel Man' a contender for the honour of First European. Palaeolithic bones have become a cottage industry – over 430,000 have been found, especially in a cave called the **Caune de l'Arago** (*north of the village; open June–Aug for guided tours*) – the best being displayed in the village's **Musée de la Préhistoire** (*open daily April–June and Sept 10–12 and 1.30–7; July and Aug 10–8; Feb, Mar, Oct and Nov 1.30–5.30; Dec and Jan Sun only 10–12 and 1–5.30; adm*).

The Agly valley and the mountains around it make up the **Fenouillèdes**. Though equally mountainous, its scenery makes a contrast to the dry, windswept Corbières. Here, limestone gives way to granite, much of it covered by ancient virgin forest.

The Valley of the Upper Aude, and Rennes-le-Château

Near the castle of Puilaurens, the D117 joins the course of the Aude, passing northwards through a spectacular canyon, the **Défile de Pierre-Lys**. The *pays* that begins here is called the **Razès**, a sparse, scrubby, somewhat haunted region. **Quillan**, the first town after the Pierre-Lys canyon, makes its living from manufacturing shoes; it has an odd, perfectly square castle from the 1280s, and does its bit to cash in on the Cathars with models of the castles and exhibits at the **Espace Cathare,** by the tourist office in Place de la Gare (*open daily 10–12 and 2–6; adm*).

Whatever is haunting the Razès, it resides in **Rennes-le-Château,** a woebegone mountain-top village above Couiza. The fun began in the 1890s, when the young parish priest, Bérenger Saunière, began spending huge sums of money on himself and on embellishing his church. The story, and the speculation, hasn't stopped unfolding since. Rennes-le-Château's one permanent business is an occult bookshop, where you can pick up a copy of the 1970s bestseller *Holy Blood, Holy Grail* that attracted international attention to Rennes, describing Jesus' problematical but well-publicized European tour after a faked crucifixion. It has been a recurring theme in French and English legend from the beginning ('And did those feet in ancient time,' etc.). Here, the idea is that Jesus came to Gaul with his wife Mary Magdalene; both may have been buried in Rennes, and their descendants were the lazy 'do-nothing' Merovingian kings of France, deposed in the 8th century by a shady deal between the popes and Carolingians. Supposedly, the blood line has survived to this day.

Did Saunière discover proof of Jesus' tomb and make his fortune by blackmailing the Vatican? Or did he find the Holy Grail, or the treasure of the Visigoths, the Merovingians, or the Templars? The most fashionable theory these days leans towards the fabulous treasure of the Jews, stolen from Jerusalem by Titus in AD 10, and pillaged in turn by the Visigoths, before ending up in safekeeping in the impregnable fortress at Rennes. Saunière used his money to pave the road up to Rennes and redo the **church** (*open 10.45–6.45*). An adjacent **museum** (*open 10–6 in summer;, 10–5 in winter; adm*) dedicated (naturally) to Mary Magdalene, with unorthodox imagery relates some of this to the Cathars, who had a mysterious treasure of their own that they slipped out of Montségur and hid in parts unknown before the bitter end.

Into the Limouxin

Before its right turn at Carcassonne, the Aude traverses a lovely, modest stretch of open rolling country, the Limouxin. Most of the roads here are still graced with their long arcades of plane trees – there isn't enough traffic yet to threaten them.

Tourist Information

Alet-les-Bains: Av Nicolas Pavillon, t 04 68 69 93 56.
Limoux: Promenade du Tivoli, t 04 68 31 11 82.

Where to Stay and Eat

Alet-les-Bains ✉ 11580

**Hostellerie de l'Evêché, t 04 68 69 90 25 (*inexpensive*). The riverside former bishop's mansion; rather plain, bit with a huge garden with old cypresses. *Closed Oct–Mar.*

Limoux ✉ 11300

***Grand Hôtel Moderne et Pigeon, Place Général Leclerc, t 04 68 31 00 25 (*moderate–inexpensive*). The most luxurious choice. The restaurant (*expensive–moderate*) is good, appropriately serving *magret de pigeon*. *Closed Dec–mid-Jan; restaurant closed Sat lunch and Mon.*

**Hôtel des Arcades, 96 Rue St-Martin, just off Place de la République, t 04 68 31 02 57, f 04 68 31 66 42 (*inexpensive*). With seven comfortable rooms and a restaurant (*moderate*). *Restaurant closed Wed.*

Maison de la Blanquette, 46 Promenade du Tivoli, t 04 68 31 01 63 (*expensive–moderate*). Offering wine sampling and good home cooking, with an emphasis on local specialities like *fricassée* (Limoux even has an '*Association pour la Promotion de la Fricassée*').

On the Aude, **Alet-les-Bains** is one of the most beautiful and best-preserved medieval villages of Languedoc. A small spa since Roman times, Alet owes its prominence to the popes, who made it a bishopric in 1318. Its two jewels are the 14th-century church of **St-André** with frescoes and a fine west portal, and the nearby impressive Benedictine **abbey**, founded in the 9th century and wrecked in the Wars of Religion. Even before you notice the vineyards, the civilized landscapes suggest wine. **Limoux**, the capital, is an attractive town, with a medieval bridge across the Aude, the Pont Neuf; this meets the apse and steeple of St-Martin, a good piece of Gothic, if anachronistic – though the church was begun in the 1300s, most of the work is from three centuries later. The centre is the arcaded Place de la République.

To the east of Limoux, a pretty side road (the D104) takes you to **St-Hilaire d'Aude** (*open July–Sept for guided tours*), an abbey founded in the 8th century; its Benedictine monks invented the bubbly Blanquette de Limoux. A graceful, double-columned Gothic cloister survives, along with the Romanesque abbey church, containing the white marble sarcophagus of St Sernin (d. 250), the patron of Toulouse, sculpted by the Master of Cabestany – one of his masterpieces.

Roussillon

Heading for the southernmost angle of the French Hexagon, you'll begin to notice a certain non-Gallic whimsy in the names of the towns. The further south you go in Roussillon the stranger they become: Llivia, Llous and Llupia, Eus and Oms, Molitg, Politg and Py. Streets signs appear in two languages, and on your restaurant table impossibly sweet wines will appear. You are among the Catalans, in the corner of Catalunya that, for military considerations in the 17th century, was destined to become part of France.

Getting Around

The coastal railway from Narbonne to Spain passes through Leucate, Salses and Rivesaltes, dipping inland for Perpignan before returning to the coast; there are frequent services to Elne, and then Collioure and Cerbère.

There are buses from the station in Perpignan to resorts where the train doesn't go, such as Canet and Port-Barcarès, as well as frequent services to the Côte Vermeille. In the summer a Bus Inter-Plages stops at all ten resorts, from Barcarès and Cerbère.

Tourist Information

St-Cyprien: Quai A. Rimbaud, **t** 04 68 21 01 33, *www.st-cyprien.com*.

Elne: 2 Rue Docteur-Bolte, **t** 04 68 22 05 07.
Collioure: Place du 18 Juin, **t** 04 68 82 15 47, *www.collioure.com*.
Port-Vendres: Quai Forgas, **t** 04 68 82 07 54.
Banyuls-sur-Mer: Ave de la République, **t** 04 68 88 31 58, *www.banyuls-sur-mer.com*.

Where to Stay and Eat

St-Cyprien ✉ 66750
★★★★**L'Ile de la Lagune**, Bd de l'Almandin, **t** 04 68 21 01 02, *www.roussillhotel.com* (*expensive*). Air-conditioned rooms, tennis and pool, all on its own little island, L'Ile de la Lagune. The restaurant (*very expensive*) is considered one of the best on the coast, with stylish treatment of Catalan dishes, such as *carré d'agneau* with garlic *jus*.

The Roussillon Coast and the Côte Vermeille

A geographical oddity, the northern Roussillon coastline is nearly perfectly straight, and runs due north–south for 40km, from Port-Barcarès to Argelès. It isn't the most compelling landscape, but it is almost solid beach, and has been greatly developed since the 1940s. After Argelès, the shoreline, now called the Côte Vermeille, changes dramatically, climbing into the Pyrenees. Henri Matisse spent one summer here, at Collioure, and the result was a milestone in the artistic revolution called Fauvism.

The Roussillon Coast

New government-planned resorts at Leucate-Plage and Port-Leucate begin the least attractive stretch of Languedoc's coast, continuing for 8km down to **Port-Barcarès**. Inland behind the Etang de Salses appears the last, lowest, and least spectacular of this region's many castles – but the **Forteresse de Salses** (*open daily Nov–Mar 10–12 and 2–5; April, May and Oct 9.30–12.30 and 2–6; June–Sept 9.30–6.30; adm*) was the most important of them all. Built in 1497 by Ferdinand the Catholic, first king of united Spain, Salses was meant to guard Perpignan and the coast but did not have a chance to do so until 1639. The Spaniards, caught by surprise, had only a small garrison at Salses; nevertheless, it required 18,000 Frenchmen and a month's siege to take it. The same year, a Spanish army spent three months regaining it.

Back on the coast, **Canet-en-Roussillon** is the favourite resort of the Perpignanais. After taking a beating in the last war, it has been rebuilt without much distinction. South, past a long stretch of wild beach, you'll find **St-Cyprien-Plage**, which looks just like Canet, only more so. South again, **Argelès-Plage** makes some claim as the European Capital of Camping with 84 sites. Between these last two resorts, set a little way inland atop a steep hill, the citadel of **Elne** has guarded the Roussillon plain for at least 2,700 years. Through the Middle Ages, and until the 1500s, Elne remained the

---

Restaurant closed Mon and Tues from Oct–mid-April.
★★★**Mas d'Huston**, t 04 68 37 63 63 (*expensive*). Adjacent to the golf course; also with a pool and tennis, and two excellent restaurants: **Le Mas** (*expensive*) and **Les Parasols** (*expensive–moderate*).Closed Jan.

Elne ✉ 66201
★★**Le Weekend**, 29 Av Paul Roig, t 04 68 22 06 68 (*inexpensive*). A delightful place with only eight rooms and a garden terrace far from the crowds; good home cooking, too (*moderate*). Closed Nov–mid-Feb.

Argelès sur Mer ✉ 66700
Auberge de Roua, Chemin du Roua, t 04 68 95 85 85, *www.belle-demeure.com* (*moderate*). A little Catalan *auberge* with a terrace

restaurant. *Closed Nov–Mar; restaurant closed Mon lunch and Tues lunch.*

Collioure ✉ 66190
★★★**Casa Païral**, Impasse des Palmiers, t 04 68 82 05 81 (*moderate*). The best choice for an agreeable stay in the centre; a dignified, Mansard-roofed palace a few streets from the shore. There is a wide choice of rooms, from the simple to the luxurious and expensive; also a pool and enclosed garden. *No restaurant; closed Nov–April.*
★★★**La Frégate**, Av Camille Pelletan, t 04 68 82 06 05 (*moderate*). This pink and jolly place is on the busiest corner of Collioure, but has been soundproofed and air-conditioned; it has a good restaurant, serving mostly seafood. *Closed Nov–Mar.*

most important city in Roussillon and seat of the archbishops. Its cathedral, a fortified church begun in 1069 with a wonderful stage presence, has a crenellated roof-line and stout, arcaded tower. The cloister (*open daily exc services April–May 9.30–6; June–Sept 9.30–7; Oct–Mar 9.30–12 and 2–5; adm*), is perhaps the best in the Midi, and also the best-preserved. Capitals and pillars are decorated with exquisitely carved arabesques and floral patterns. The sides were completed at 50-year intervals.

The Côte Vermeille: Collioure and Beyond

It's hard to believe, looking at the map, but in the Middle Ages the village of **Collioure** was the port for Perpignan; with no good harbours on the dismal and (then) unhealthy coast to the north, Perpignan's fabrics and other goods had to come to the Pyrenees to go to sea. In the 14th century Collioure was one of the biggest trading centres of Aragon, but nearly the whole town was demolished by the French after they took possession in 1659. In 1905 it was discovered by Matisse and Derain. Many other artists followed, including Picasso. The village has created the *Chemin du fauvisme*, placing copies of their works on the spots where the two set up their easels. In a peaceful villa on the south edge of town over a lovely terraced olive grove, the **Musée d'Art Moderne** (*open daily 10–12 and 2–6; July and Aug till 7; closed Tues; adm*), has works by lesser-known artists in the Fauve style, and Moorish ceramics.

Collioure is a thoroughly Catalan town, and the red and yellow striped Catalan flag waves proudly over the **Château Royal** (*open daily 10–6 in summer, 9–5 in winter; adm*), dominating the harbour. First built by the Templars in the 13th century, it was expanded by various Aragonese kings. From the castle, cross the small stream called the Douy (usually dry and used as a car park) into the **Mouré**, the old quarter that is now the centre of Collioure. There is an amiable shorefront, with a small beach from which a few anchovy fishermen still ply their trade. At the far end you'll see Collioure's landmark, painted by Matisse and others: the church of **Notre-Dame-des-Anges**, built

**Les Templiers, Quai de l'Amirauté, t 04 68 98 31 10, *www.hotel-templiers.com* (*inexpensive*). Picasso, Matisse, Dufy and Dalí all stayed here, and owner Réné Pous was friend to them all. Each room has its own charm; reservations are imperative. The bar is a friendly local hang-out, and the restaurant (*moderate*) is excellent. *Closed Jan.*

Boramar, 19 Rue Jean-Bart, on the Plage du Faubourg, t 04 68 82 07 06 (*inexpensive*). A simple budget choice overlooking the busiest beach. *Closed Nov–Mar.*

Neptune, Rte Port-Vendres, t 04 68 82 02 27 (*expensive*). One of the best restaurants in town, with wonderful canopied sea views and the full *nouvelle* Catalan *cuisine* like lobster ravioli with cardamom vinaigrette. Ravishing desserts include poached figs and rosemary sorbet. *Closed Tues, Wed and Feb.*

La Marinade, Place 18 Juin, t 04 68 82 09 76 (*moderate*). Delectable seafood from simple sardines *en papillote* to an elaborate Catalan *bouillabaisse. Closed Dec–Jan.*

Banyuls-sur-Mer ✉ 66650

Les Elmes, Plages des Elmes, t 04 68 88 03 12, *www.hotel-des-elmes.com* (*moderate*). Pleasant seaside rooms and an excellent restaurant, **La Littorine, serving Catalan dishes with *savoir faire*; half board is excellent value. *Closed mid-Nov–Dec.*

**La Pergola, 5 Av Fontaulé, by the port, t 04 68 88 02 10 (*inexpensive*). Immaculate rooms and good fish. *Closed Dec and Jan.*

Chez Rosa, Rue St-Pierre, t 04 68 88 31 89 (*moderate*). A neighbourhood favourite for lunch: tasty dishes such as roast pork, couscous, chicken and mushrooms.

in the 1680s to replace the church destroyed by the French. The best thing about the church is that you can hear the waves of the sea from inside, a profound *basso continuo* that makes the celebration of Mass here a unique experience. The next best are the five retables (1699–1720) by Joseph Sunyer and others. The second of Collioure's beaches lies right behind the church; it connects the town with a former islet, the **Ilot St-Vincent**, crowned with a tiny medieval chapel. High above, you'll see **Fort Miradoux**, the Spanish King Philip II's addition.

Port-Vendres is a real port, modern-style, with none of the charm of Collioure. **Banyuls-sur-Mer** is the next town along the picturesque coastal N114, a sleepy resort with a beach and mini-golf right at the centre. The heart of the Banyuls wine region, it is also the home of the **Fondation Arago**, an oceanographic laboratory whose aquarium (*open daily 9–12 and 2–6.30, till 10 in July and Aug; adm*) of Mediterranean species was built in 1883. As for art, Banyuls has a good 11th-century Romanesque church, **La Rectorie**, on Av du Puig-del-Mas, and takes credit for Aristide Maillol, perhaps the best-known French sculptor of the 19th century after Rodin, born here in 1861. His tomb, documents tracing his life, and a few copies of works are in his old farm house, La Métairie, now the **Musée Aristide Maillol**, 4km up the Col de Banyuls road (*open 9–12 and 2–5, May–Oct till 7; closed Tues and hols; adm*).

If you don't care to go to Spain, there's an extremely scenic route through the mountains back to Collioure, along the steep and narrow D86. Several abandoned fortresses come into view. The **Tour Madeloc** is the highlight, a signal tower, part of a communications network for the medieval kings of Aragon.

Perpignan

Perpignan is named after Perperna, a lieutenant in the Roman army who murdered his boss, the great 1st-century BC populist general, Quintus Sertorius. The city enjoyed its most brilliant period in the 13th century when Jaime I, king of Aragon and conqueror of Majorca, created the Kingdom of Majorca and County of Roussillon for his younger son Jaime II. This little kingdom was absorbed by the Catalan kings of Aragon in the 14th century, but continued to prosper until 1463, when Louis XI's army came to claim Perpignan and Roussillon as payment for mercenaries sent to Aragon. Besieged, the Perpignanais ate rats rather than become French, until the king of Aragon himself ordered them to surrender. In 1493 Charles VIII, more interested in Italian conquests, gave Perpignan back to Spain. But in the 1640s, Richelieu pounced on the first available chance to grab it back, and, ever since, the forces of French centralization have attempted to suppress the Catalan exuberance of *Perpinyà*.

Le Castillet

When most of Perpignan's walls were destroyed in 1904, its easy-going river-cum-moat, La Basse, was planted with lawns, flower-beds, mimosas and Art Nouveau cafés. Only the fat brick towers and crenellated gate of **Le Castillet** were left upright; built in 1368 by Aragon to keep out the French, it became a prison once the French got

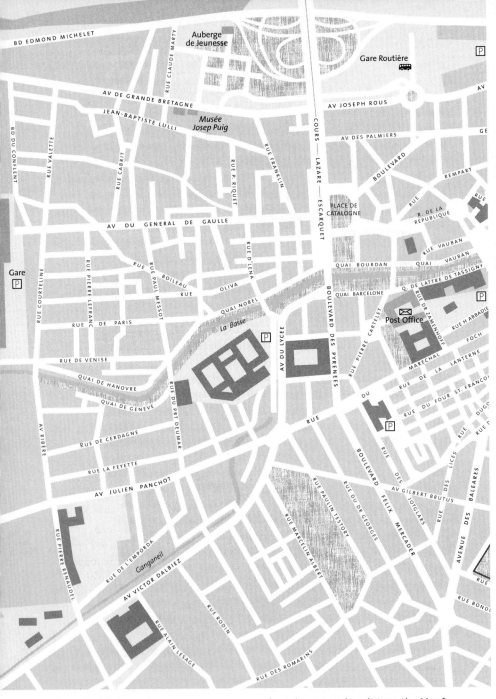

in. Le Castillet now houses a cosy museum of Catalan art and traditions, the **Musée Pairal** (*open Oct–April Wed–Mon 11–5.30; May–Sept Wed–Mon 10–7; adm*), with items ranging from casts of Pau (Pablo) Casals' hands to a kitchen from a Catalan *mas*. Place

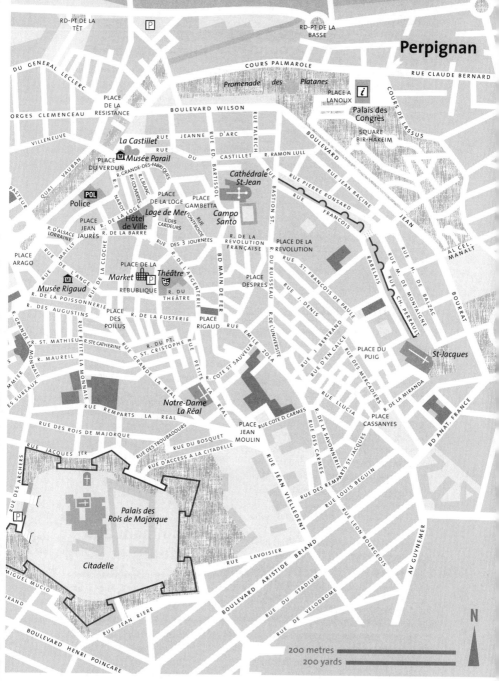

Perpignan

RD-PT DE LA TÊT

RD-PT DE LA BASSE

RUE CLAUDE BERNARD

COURS PALMAROLE

DU GENERAL LECLERC

Promenade des Platanes

PLACE A LANOUX

Palais des Congrès

PLACE DE LA RESISTANCE

ORGES CLEMENCEAU

BOULEVARD WILSON

SQUARE BIR-HAKEIM

VILLENEUVE

RUE JEANNE D'ARC

RUE ED. CASTILLET

R. RAMON LULL

BOULEVARD

COURS DE LASSUS

La Castillet

Musée Parail

PLACE DU VERDUN

RUE GRANDE-DES-FABRIQUES

Cathédrale St-Jean

RUE PIERRE RONSARD

RUE JEAN RACINE

QUAI VAUBAN

R. BLANC

R. COMBERTS

PLACE DE LA LOGE

PLACE GAMBETTA

Campo Santo

RUE BASTION ST.

RUE FRANCOIS

RUE M. DE MONTAIGNE

RABELAIS

JEAN

AL CEL MANALT

PASTEUR

POL Police

Loge de Mer

L DES CARDEURS

Hôtel de Ville

PLACE JEAN JAURÈS

R. DE LA LOGE

FONTFROIDE

R. DE LA REVOLUTION FRANÇAISE

PLACE DE LA REVOLUTION

RUE ST. FRANÇOIS DE PAULE

RUE CH. PERRAULT

BOURRAT

R. D'ALSACE LORRAINE

R. DE LA BARRE

RUE DES 3 JOURNEES

R. DU RUISSEAU

RUE J. DENIS

PLACE ARAGO

RUE DE LA CLOCHE

NABOT

RUE DE MAILLY

PLACE DE LA REBUBLIQUE

Market

Théâtre

R. DE L'ARGENTERIE

BD MAIN DE FER

PLACE DESPRES

PLACE DU PUIG

St-Jacques

Musée Rigaud

RUE DE L'ANGE

R. DU THEÂTRE

RUE J. BERTRAND

RUE D'EN CALCE

R. DE LA POISSONNERIE

PLACE DES POILUS

R. DE LA FUSTERIE

PLACE RIGAUD

RUE EMILE ZOLA

RUE DES MERCADIERS

R. DES AUGUSTINS

RUE EMILE ZOLA

R. DE LA MIRANDA

R. GRANDE LA MONNAIE

R. ST. MATHIEU

PETITE LA MONNAIE

R. STE CATHERINE

R. DU PT. ST. CRISTOPHE

R. COTE ST SAUVEUR LA

RUE LLUCIA

PLACE CASSANYES

R. MAUREIL

RUE GRANDE LA REAL

PETITE LA REAL

BD ANAT. FRANCE

ES SUREAUX

RUE REMPARTS LA REAL

Notre-Dame La Réal

PLACE JEAN MOULIN

RUE COTE D. CARMES

R. DE LA SAVONNERIE

RUE DES CARMES

RUE DES ROIS DE MAJORQUE

RUE DES TROUBADOURS

RUE DU BOSQUET

RUE REMPARTS ST-JACQUES

RUE LOUIS BEGUIN

RUE JACQUES 1er

RUE D'ACCESS A LA CITADELLE

RUE LEON BOURGEOIS

ES ARCHERS

Palais des Rois de Majorque

RUE JEAN VIELLEDENT

AV GUYNEMER

Citadelle

RUE LAVOISIER

BOULEVARD ARISTIDE BRIAND

MIGUEL MUCIO

RAND

RUE JEAN RIERE

RUE DU STADIUM

RUE DE VELODROME

BOULEVARD HENRI POINCARE

200 metres
200 yards

N

du Verdun, by Le Castillet, is one of Perpignan's liveliest squares, while, just outside the gate, the **Promenade des Platanes** is lined with magnificent plane trees.

Getting There and Around

By plane: Perpignan's airport is 7km northwest of the city and linked by *aerobus navettes* from the station an hour before each flight. There are connections with Paris Orly. Ryanair has a daily flight to Perpignan from London-Stansted.

By train: There are frequent trains down to the Spanish border at Port Bou and a new TGV that cuts the journey to Paris to 6 hours. An early morning bus from Perpignan's station links up with *Le Petit Train Jaune* into the Cerdagne, departing from Villefranche-Vernet-les-Bains (*see* pp.896–7); call **t** 04 68 96 22 96 for details.

By bus: The coach station is to the north, on Av Général Leclerc, **t** 04 68 35 29 02.

Tourist Information

Perpigan: **Palais des Congrès**, Place Armand-Lanoux, **t** 04 68 66 30 30, *www.perpignan tourisme.com*.

Where to Stay

Perpignan ✉ 66000

★★★**Le Park**, 18 Bd Jean-Bourrat, near the tourist office, **t** 04 68 35 14 14, *www.park hotel.fr* (*moderate*). Plush, air-conditioned, soundproofed rooms and restaurant (*expensive*) with an old Spanish feel and flair. *Closed Jan.*

★★**Hôtel de la Loge**, 1 Rue des Fabriques-Nabot, **t** 04 68 34 41 02 (*inexpensive*). Nicest in the centre, in a 16th-century building, this has pretty rooms, some with TV and air-conditioning, and a lovely inner courtyard.

★★**Le Maillol**, 14 Impasse des Cardeurs, **t** 04 68 51 10 20 (*inexpensive*). In a 17th-century building: not too noisy, and convenient for the sights.

★★**La Poste et Perdix**, 6 Rue des Fabriques-Nabot, **t** 04 68 34 42 53 (*inexpensive*). This charming place has kept much of its original 1832 décor. *Restaurant closed Mon and Feb.*

★★**Le Helder**, Av du Général de Gaulle, **t** 04 68 34 38 05 (*inexpensive*).

★**Le Berry**, 6 Av du Général de Gaulle, **t** 04 68 34 59 02 (*inexpensive*).

Eating Out

Le Chapon Fin, Le Park (*see above; expensive*), **t** 04 68 35 14 14. This has been Perpignan's finest restaurant for years, as well as one of the prettiest, with its Catalan ceramics. But it's the *tartare de saumon* and ravioli stuffed with scallops that keep its clients coming back for more, even all the way from Spain. *Closed Sun and first two weeks in Jan.*

Côté Théâtre, 7 Rue du Théâtre, **t** 04 68 34 60 00 (*expensive*). Elegantly converted restaurant in the old town, celebrated for its refined treatment of regional food, especially fish; the squid and artichoke salad is sensational. *Closed Sun, and Mon lunch.*

Casa Sansa, 3 Rue Fabriques Couvertes, near Le Castillet, **t** 04 68 34 21 84 (*moderate*). Lively, with excellent food served in a 14th-century cellar – with dishes ranging from Catalan *escargots* to rabbit with *aïoli*; occasional live music and wine-tasting; and more than its share of Catalan flair. *Book Fri and Sat nights. Closed Sun and Mon.*

Les Trois Soeurs, 2 Rue Fontfroide, **t** 04 68 51 22 33 (*moderate*). Fashionable new restaurant with stylish modern bar and terrace tables on the cathedral square. Serves Catalan cooking with a twist.

Brasserie L'Arago, Place Arago, **t** 04 68 51 81 96 (*cheap*). Packed day and night; good pizza.

Les Expéditeurs, 19 Av du Général Leclerc, **t** 04 68 35 15 80 (*cheap*). Catalan cooking and paella on Wed. *Closed Sat eve, Sun and 3 weeks in Aug.*

Entertainment and Nightlife

On evenings from June to September in Place de la Castillet, the Perpignanais come to dance *sardanas*, the Catalan circle dance.

Le Zinc, 8 Rue Grande-des-Fabriques, **t** 04 68 35 08 80. Jazz and cocktails; especially animated during the Perpignan Jazz Festival in October.

In September, Perpignan is host to **Visa pour Image**, the world festival of photo-journalism.

Le Drive-In-Ciné, Mas Sabole, 11km south. An American-style drive-in cinema (*first show at 9.45pm*).

Loge de Mer to the Musée Rigaud

In Place de la Loge stands Perpignan's most beautiful building, the Gothic **Loge de Mer**, or Llotja, built in 1397 by the king of Aragon. This proud and noble building of ochre stone, with its Venetian arches and loggia and ship-shaped weathercock, fell on hard times. But Perpignan takes good care of its monuments – the city rented it to a hamburger chain. The neighbouring 13th-century **Hôtel de Ville** has been spared the Llotja's humiliation, probably because it still serves its original purpose. To the right, the **Palais de la Députation Provinciale** (1447) is a masterpiece of Catalan Renaissance, formerly the seat of Roussillon's parliament and now housing dismal municipal offices. South of the Députation, in Rue de l'Ange the **Musée Rigaud** (*t 04 68 35 43 40; call for opening hours*) is named after Perpignan native Hyacinthe Rigaud (1659–1743), portrait painter to Louis XIV. Hyacinthe, master of raising the mediocre and unworthy to virtuoso heights of rosy-cheeked, debonair charm and sophistication, is well represented, as are works by Picasso, Dufy, Maillol and Miró.

Cathédrale St-Jean, the Dévôt Christ and the Quartier St-Jacques

Just east of Place de la Loge unfolds Place Gambetta, site of Perpignan's pebble-and-brick **cathedral**, topped by a lacy 19th-century wrought-iron campanile. Begun in 1324 but not ready for use until 1509, the interior is a success because the builders stuck to the design provided in the 1400s by Guillem Sagrera, architect of the great cathedral of Palma de Majorca. Typical of Catalan Gothic, it has a single nave, 157ft long, striking for its spacious width rather than its soaring height. The chapels, wedged between the huge piers, hold some unique treasures, the oldest of which is a marble **baptismal font** (first chapel on the left). The cathedral is proudest of its exquisite marble and painted wood retables. A door in the right aisle leads out to a 16th-century chapel constructed especially to house the extraordinary **Dévôt Christ**. Carved in the Cologne region in 1307, this wasted Christ, whose contorted bones, sinews and torn flesh are carved with a rare anatomical realism, is stretched to the limits of agony on the Cross.

The piquant neighbourhood south of the cathedral was once the Jewish quarter. After the Jews were exiled, the quarter was renamed St-Jacques, and inhabited by working men's families and Gypsies, and most recently by Algerians. The 12th–14th-century church of **St-Jacques** is opulent and rich inside: there's a 'Cross of Insults', a statue of St James in Compostela pilgrimage gear (1450) and more fine retables.

The Palace of the Kings of Majorca

Enclosed in a vast extent of walls, later enlarged by Vauban, Louis XIV's military genius, the **Palais des Rois de Majorque** (*Rue des Archers; open daily May–Sept 10–6, winter 9–5; adm*) is the oldest royal palace in France, begun in the 1270s by Jaime the Conqueror and occupied by his son Jaime II after 1283. Yet for all its grandeur, only three kings of Majorca were to reign here before Roussillon, Montpellier, the Cerdagne and the Balearic islands were reabsorbed by Aragon in 1349. The scale of magnificence they intended to become accustomed to survives, including a mastodonic but elegant Romanesque-Gothic courtyard, but not much else. The palace now hosts events.

West of Perpignan: Pyrenean Valleys

There are two major valleys: the **Conflent** (the valley of the river Têt) and the **Vallespir** (of the river Tech), sloping in parallel lines toward the Spanish border. In between the valleys stands snow-capped **Canigou**, not the highest (a mere 9,134ft) but certainly one of the most imposing peaks of the chain.

The Conflent (Têt Valley)

The narrow D48 wiggling west of **Castelnou**, a perfectly preserved medieval village, is unabashedly beautiful. At **Ille-sur-Têt**, an attractive old village at the gateway to the mountains, art from the 11th to 19th centuries from Roussillon's churches has been assembled in a 16th-century hospital, the **Centre d'Art Sacré** (*open Oct–mid-Jan Wed–Mon 2–6; June–Sept daily 10–12 and 2–7; adm*). The D2 northwest of Ille to Montalba-le-Château takes you to some surprising scenery: orange eroded 'fairy chimneys' called the **Orgues**, with a forgotten ruin of a 12th-century tower on top.

Seeing the finest medieval sculpture in Roussillon at the **Prieuré de Serrabonne** (*open daily 10–6; adm*) requires dedication: the most direct route requires 13km of hairpin turns, starting from the D618 at Bouleternère, just west of Ille, and ending in a remote spot on a mountain called Roque Rouge. The solemn, spare shape and dark schist of Serrabonne's church are not promising, making the surprise inside that much the greater. The best efforts of the 12th-century Catalan sculptors were concentrated in the single gallery of the cloister and the tribune, in rosy Canigou marble.

Prades, a typical stolid Catalan town, is known for its music festival (*late July–early Aug*) founded in 1951 by Pau Casals. A few km up through orchards is **St-Michel-de-Cuxa** (*open 9.30–11.50 and 2–6, to 5pm in winter, closed Sun am; adm*), one of the most important monasteries of medieval Catalunya. Even in its reduced, semi-ruined state, the scale is impressive; this was one of the great monastic centres from which medieval Europe was planned and built. St-Michel is occupied by a small community of Benedictine monks from Montserrat. The Romanesque architecture is Catalan as well, especially in the more-than-semicircular 'Visigothic' arches in the nave. Other notable features include the massive but elegant bell tower, and an unusual circular crypt, built in the 11th century.

Canigou, with its distinctive Phrygian cap of snow, is the 'fortunate mountain' of the Catalans. You can make two-thirds of the climb – 7,053ft – by car, on a forest road that begins at the east end of Prades. This leaves you at the **Chalet-Hôtel des Cortalets** refuge (*open May–Sept; call t 04 68 96 36 19 to book a bed; €12.50 a night, meals €13.50*). From here it's a fairly easy three- to four-hour walk to the summit.

Vernet-les-Bains, a bustling modern spa, has most of the accommodation in the area, and hot sulphuric waters that are good for your rheumatism and respiratory problems. From nearby Casteil, **St-Martin-du-Canigou** (*open daily in summer, closed Tues in winter, tours at 10, 11.45 (12 on Sun), 2, 3, 4 and 5 in summer, 10, 11.45, 2.30, 3.30 and 4.30 in winter; adm*) is a taxing though lovely 40-minute walk up. An innovative architect named Sclua designed this monastery complex in the early 11th century, making it a rustic acropolis, courtyards and terraces, spectacularly sited with views around

Getting Around

The coach and train service is good, but it won't help you see St-Michel or Serrabonne. From the bus station in Perpignan there are 10 or 12 buses to Prades and Villefranche-de-Conflent; a few go on to Font-Romeu. At Villefranche you can pick up *Le Petit Train Jaune*, a scenic narrow-gauge train into the Cerdagne. For the Vallespir, there are daily buses to Arles-sur-Tech and Amélie-les-Bains.

Tourist Information

Prades: 4 Rue Victor Hugo, t 04 68 05 41 02, *www.prades-tourisme.com.*
Villefranche-de-Conflent: 38 Rue St-Jacques, t 04 68 92 22 96.
Céret: Av Clemenceau, t 04 68 87 00 53.
Arles-sur-Tech: Rue Barjau, t 04 68 39 11 99.

Where to Stay and Eat

Prades ✉ 66500

Les Glycines, 12 Rue Général De Gaulle, t 04 68 96 51 65, *www.glycines.com* (*inexpensive*). In a quiet courtyard, with comfortable rooms and a decent restaurant. *Restaurant closed Sat lunch, Sun exc July–Aug, and first half Jan.*
Jardin de L'Aymeric, 3 Av du Général de Gaulle, t 04 68 96 53 38 (*moderate*). The best bet for stylish regional cooking, though the excess of neon detracts from the atmosphere.

Vernet-les-Bains ✉ 66820

★★★Le Mas Fleuri, 25 Bd Clemenceau (the road up to St-Martin), t 04 68 05 51 94, *www.hotel*

fleuri.fr (*moderate*). At the top of the list, this century-old hotel is set in a pretty park, with a pool (no restaurant). *Closed Dec–mid-April.*
★★★Comte Guilifred, t 04 68 05 51 37 (*inexpensive*). This modern place is the training ground for the local hotel school; ask for a room in the back overlooking the garden. *Closed Oct–Mar.*

Villefranche-de-Conflent ✉ 66500

★★Auberge du Cèdre, Domaine Ste-Eulalie, outside the walls, t 04 68 96 05 05 (*inexpensive*). Nine comfortable rooms, an adequate restaurant and two fat, friendly cats in the garden. *Restaurant only open to residents.*
Auberge St-Paul, Place de l'Eglise, t 04 68 96 30 95 (*expensive*). The chef at this lovely restaurant fetches from Canigou the basic ingredients for mountain surprises, like beef with morel mushrooms and boar (*sanglier*). *Closed Mon in summer, Sun eve, Mon and Tues in winter, and 3 weeks in Jan.*

Font-Romeu ✉ 66120

★★Clair Soleil, Rte Odeillo, t 04 68 30 13 65 (*inexpensive*). With a view, a swimming pool and a restaurant (*moderate*). *Closed last week April–1st week May and Nov–Dec.*

Céret ✉ 66400

★★★★Terrasse au Soleil, Route Fontfrède, t 04 68 87 01 94 (*expensive*). A restored, modernized *mas* on a hill above Céret, with a view, a heated pool and tennis court, and a restaurant, **Cerisaie**.
★★Les Arcades, 1 Place Picasso, t 04 68 87 12 30 (*inexpensive*). Artistically decorated, with balconies overlooking the market square.

Canigou and the peaks. The church, with its immense, fortress-like bell tower, has two levels, an upper church dedicated to St Martin, with medieval ribs, and a lower crypt for a certain obscure subterranean Virgin Mary: *Notre-Dame-sous-Terre*.

Villefranche-de-Conflent, the most logical place from which to defend the Têt valley, has had a castle at least since 1092. In the 17th century it took its present form, as a model Baroque fortress-town, rebuilt by Vauban. You can tour his **ramparts** with their walkway built through the wall (*daily June–Sept 10–7; April, May and Oct 10–12 and 2–6; Nov–Dec 2–7; Feb–Mar 2–5; closed Jan; adm*) and climb up the 1,000 subterranean rock-hewn steps to **Fort Liberia** (*open daily 9–8; 10–6 in winter; adm*). A survivor from the pre-Vauban Villefranche, the church of **St-Jacques** is a fine 12th-century building with capitals from the workshop of St-Michel-de-Cuxa; inside is another Sunyer retable .

The Cerdagne

The lofty plateau of the Cerdagne (*Cerdanya* in Catalan) was an isolated and effectively independent county in the Middle Ages, split between Spain and France in the 1659 Treaty of the Pyrenees. The building of the Little Yellow Train, in 1911, brought French Cerdagne into the modern world, and skiing has made it rather opulent today.

After Villefranche, the main N116 climbs dramatically into the mountains. Climb, climb, climb and at last you'll reach the gateway to the Cerdagne, **Mont-Louis**, another work of Vauban's and the highest fortress in France (5,250ft), named after Louis XIV. The army still resides here, though only to look after a pioneer **solar furnace** (*open 10–12.30 and 2–6; adm*), built in 1953. To the north, D118 takes you to the isolated plateau and hiker's wonderland of the **Capcir**. The best parts lie to the west, on the slopes of the **Pic Carlit**; there you will find the sources of both the Têt and the Aude.

The western road (D618) will take you through more pine forests to **Font-Romeu**, one of the biggest ski resorts in France with its satellites, Super-Bolquère and Pyrénées 2000. It has the **World's Largest Solar Furnace** (*open daily 10–6 in summer; 10–12.30 and 2–6 in winter; adm*), 'stronger than 10,000 suns!', the successor to the one in Mont-Louis. With its curved mirror, covering an entire side of the nine-storey laboratory building, it reflects the Pyrenees beautifully while helping scientists work out all sorts of high-temperature puzzles. South of Font-Romeu, along the N116, road signs startle with town names like Llo and Err; linguists say they're evidence that the Basques lived here in remote times. You can visit the **Musée de Cerdagne** (*open for guided tours July–Sept Thurs–Tues 11–5, closed Wed*) in a 17th-century farm.

The Vallespir

The valley of the Tech, the southernmost valley of Roussillon, known for its mineral waters since Roman times, now lives by tourism, with some euros on the side from cherries and cork oak. The D115 streaks up the valley from Le Boulou to the orchards surrounding **Céret**, a laid-back town under enormous plane trees, with perfect little squares (especially the Plaça dels Nou Raigs), medieval gates, a big Baroque church, a war memorial by Maillol, and an elegant 14th-century bridge over the Tech. Visit Céret before visiting the **Musée d'Art Moderne**, 8 Bd du Maréchal Joffre (*open 10–6, closed Tues Oct–April; adm*), and you'll be surprised at how many scenes you'll recognize. Céret found its artistic destiny at the start of the 20th century, thanks to Picasso, Braque, Gris, Matisse, Soutine, Kisling, Masson, Tzara, Lhote, Marquet and others.

Sulphurous waters, good for your rheumatism, have been the fortune of **Amélie-les-Bains** since ancient times; a Roman swimming-pool with a vaulted roof has been uncovered, and the spa, rising on either side of the river Tech, still does a grandstand business. Just west, **Arles-sur-Tech**, the ancient capital of the Vallespir, is a curious old village built on a narrow maze of lanes. Its 11th-century church of Ste-Marie was originally the centre of a monastery; its Dark Age anonymous saint – an empty 4th-century sarcophagus dripping holy water known as Sainte-Tombe – was once a major pilgrimage attraction and is outside the front door.

Language

Everywhere in France the same level of politeness expected: use *monsieur, madame* or *mademoiselle* when speaking to everyone (and never *garçon* in restaurants!), from your first *bonjour* to your last *au revoir*.

For food vocabulary, *see* pp.56–60.

Pronunciation

Vowels

a/à/â between *a* in 'bat' and 'part'
é/er/ez at end of word as *a* in 'plate' but a
　bit shorter
e/è/ê as *e* in 'bet'
e at end of word not pronounced
e at end of syllable or in one-syllable word
　pronounced weakly, like *er* in 'mother'
i as *ee* in 'bee'
o as *o* in 'pot'
ô as *o* in 'go'
u/û between *oo* in 'boot' and *ee* in 'bee'

Vowel Combinations

ai as *a* in 'plate'
aî as *e* in 'bet'
ail as *i* in 'kite'
au/eau as *o* in 'go'
ei as *e* in 'bet'
eu/œu as *er* in 'mother'
oi between *wa* in 'swam' and *wu* in 'swum'
oy as 'why'
ui as *wee* in 'twee'

Nasal Vowels

Vowels followed by an **n** or **m** have a nasal sound.
an/en as *o* in 'pot' + nasal sound
ain/ein/in as *a* in 'bat' + nasal sound
on as *aw* in 'paw' + nasal sound
un as *u* in 'nut' + nasal sound

Consonants

Many French consonants are pronounced as in English, but there are some exceptions:
c followed by *e, i* or *y*, and *ç* as *s* in 'sit'
c followed by *a, o, u* as *c* in 'cat'
g followed by *e, i* or *y* as *s* in 'pleasure'
g followed by *a, o, u* as *g* in 'good'
gn as *ni* in 'opinion'
j as *s* in 'pleasure'
ll as *y* in 'yes'
qu as *k* in 'kite'
s between vowels as *z* in 'zebra'
s otherwise as *s* in 'sit'
w except in English words as *v* in 'vest'
x at end of word as *s* in 'sit'
x otherwise as *x* in 'six'

Stress

The stress usually falls on the last syllable except when the word ends with an unaccented **e**.

Useful Phrases

hello *bonjour*
good evening *bonsoir*
good night *bonne nuit*
goodbye *au revoir*
please *s'il vous plaît*
thank you (very much) *merci (beaucoup)*
yes *oui*
no *non*
good *bon* (*bonne*)
bad *mauvais*
excuse me *pardon, excusez-moi*
Can you help me? *Pourriez-vous m'aider?*
My name is... *Je m'appelle...*
What is your name? *Comment t'appelles-tu?*
　(informal), *Comment vous appelez-vous?*
　(formal)
How are you? *Comment allez-vous?*
Fine *Ça va bien*

I don't understand *Je ne comprends pas*
I don't know *Je ne sais pas*
Speak more slowly *Pourriez-vous parler plus lentement?*
How do you say ... in French? *Comment dit-on ... en français?*
Help! *Au secours!*

WC *les toilettes*
men *hommes*
ladies *dames* or *femmes*

doctor *le médecin*
hospital *un hôpital*
emergency room *la salle des urgences*
police station *le commissariat de police*

No smoking *Défense de fumer*

Shopping and Sightseeing

Do you have...? *Est-ce que vous avez...?*
I would like... *J'aimerais...*
Where is/are...? *Où est/sont...*
How much is it? *C'est combien?*
It's too expensive *C'est trop cher*

entrance *l'entrée*
exit *la sortie*
open *ouvert*
closed *fermé*
push *poussez*
pull *tirez*

bank *une banque*
money *l'argent*
traveller's cheque *un chèque de voyage*
post office *la poste*
stamp *un timbre*
phone card *une télécarte*
postcard *une carte postale*
public phone *une cabine téléphonique*
Do you have any change? *Avez-vous de la monnaie?*

shop *un magasin*
central food market *les halles*
tobacconist *un tabac*
pharmacy *la pharmacie*
aspirin *l'aspirine*
condoms *les préservatifs*
insect repellent *un produit insectifuge*

sun cream *la crème solaire*
tampons *les tampons hygiéniques*

beach *la plage*
booking/box office *le bureau de location*
church *l'église*
museum *le musée*
sea *la mer*
theatre *le théâtre*

Accommodation

Do you have a room? *Avez-vous une chambre?*
Can I look at the room? *Puis-je voir la chambre?*
How much is the room per day/week? *C'est combien la chambre par jour/semaine?*
single room *une chambre pour une personne*
twin room *une chambre à deux lits*
double room *une chambre pour deux personnes*
... with a shower/bath *... avec douche/salle de bains*
... for one night/one week *... pour une nuit/une semaine*

bed *un lit*
blanket *une couverture*
cot (child's bed) *un lit d'enfant*
pillow *un oreiller*
soap *du savon*
towel *une serviette*

Transport

I want to go to... *Je voudrais aller à...*
How can I get to...? *Comment puis-je aller à..?*
When is the next...? *Quel est le prochain...?*
What time does it leave (arrive)? *A quelle heure part-il (arrive-t-il)?*
From where does it leave? *D'où part-il?*
Do you stop at...? *Passez-vous par...?*
How long does the trip take? *Combien de temps dure le voyage?*
A (single/return) ticket to... *un aller* or *aller simple/aller et retour) pour...*
How much is the fare? *Combien coûte le billet?*
Have a good trip! *Bon voyage!*

airport *l'aéroport*
aeroplane *l'avion*
berth *la couchette*

bicycle *la bicyclette/le vélo*
mountain bike *le vélo tout terrain, VTT*
bus *l'autobus*
bus stop *l'arrêt d'autobus*
car *la voiture*
coach *l'autocar*
coach station *la gare routière*
flight *le vol*
on foot *à pied*
port *le port*
railway station *la gare*
ship *le bateau*
subway *le métro*
taxi *le taxi*
train *le train*

delayed *en retard*
on time *à l'heure*
platform *le quai*
date-stamp machine *le composteur*
timetable *l'horaire*
left-luggage locker *la consigne automatique*
ticket office *le guichet*
ticket *le billet*
customs *la douane*
seat *la place*

Directions

Where is...? *Où se trouve...?*
left *à gauche*
right *à droite*
straight on *tout droit*
here *ici*
there *là*
close *proche*
far *loin*
forwards *en avant*
backwards *en arrière*
up *en haut*
down *en bas*
corner *le coin*
square *la place*
street *la rue*

Driving

breakdown *la panne*
car *la voiture*
danger *le danger*
driver *le chauffeur*

entrance *l'entrée*
exit *la sortie*
give way/yield *céder le passage*
hire *louer*
(international) driving licence *un permis de conduire (international)*

motorbike/moped *la moto/le vélomoteur*
no parking *stationnement interdit*
petrol (unleaded) *l'essence (sans plomb)*
road *la route*
roadworks *les travaux*
This doesn't work *Ça ne marche pas*
Is the road good? *Est-ce que la route est bonne?*

Numbers

one *un*
two *deux*
three *trois*
four *quatre*
five *cinq*
six *six*
seven *sept*
eight *huit*
nine *neuf*
ten *dix*
eleven *onze*
twelve *douze*
thirteen *treize*
fourteen *quatorze*
fifteen *quinze*
sixteen *seize*
seventeen *dix-sept*
eighteen *dix-huit*
nineteen *dix-neuf*
twenty *vingt*
twenty-one *vingt et un*
twenty-two *vingt-deux*
thirty *trente*
forty *quarante*
fifty *cinquante*
sixty *soixante*
seventy *soixante-dix*
seventy-one *soixante et onze*
eighty *quatre-vingts*
eighty-one *quatre-vingt-un*
ninety *quatre-vingt-dix*
one hundred *cent*
two hundred *deux cents*
one thousand *mille*

Months

January *janvier*
February *février*
March *mars*
April *avril*
May *mai*
June *juin*
July *juillet*
August *août*
September *septembre*
October *octobre*
November *novembre*
December *décembre*

Days

Monday *lundi*
Tuesday *mardi*
Wednesday *mercredi*
Thursday *jeudi*
Friday *vendredi*
Saturday *samedi*
Sunday *dimanche*

Time

What time is it? *Quelle heure est-il?*
It's 2 o'clock (am/pm) *Il est deux heures (du matin/de l'après-midi)*
... half past 2 *...deux heures et demie*
... a quarter past 2 *...deux heures et quart*
... a quarter to 3 *...trois heures moins le quart*
it is early *il est tôt*
it is late *il est tard*

month *un mois*
week *une semaine*
day *un jour/une journée*
morning *le matin*
afternoon *l'après-midi*
evening *le soir*
night *la nuit*
today *aujourd'hui*
yesterday *hier*
tomorrow *demain*
day before yesterday *avant-hier*
day after tomorrow *après-demain*
soon *bientôt*

Glossary

abbaye abbey
abside apse
arc-boutant flying-buttress
ardoise slate
arrondissement city district
auberge inn
autel altar
bas-côté aisle (which can also be a *collatéral*)
basse-cour (for château) outer courtyard; (for farm) farmyard
bastide a new town founded in the Middle Ages; usually rectangular, with a grid of streets and an arcaded central square; sometimes circular in plan
beffroi tower with a town's bell
bergère wing chair (more frequently means shepherdess, though)
bien national property of the state
boiserie(s) (en plis de serviette) (linenfold) wood panelling
cachot prison cell; dungeon
canonnière loophole for gun
castelnau a village, often planned, that grew up around a seigneur's castle (often the parish church will be on the edge of a castelnau instead of at its centre)
castrum a rectangular Roman army camp, which often grew into a permanent settlement (like Bordeaux and many others)
chaire pulpit
châtelain(e) lord of a château (lady of a château)
chemin path
chemin de ronde parapet walk, wall walk, rampart walk
chœur choir (architecturally speaking)
cintre arch (also coat-hanger)
clef (or clé) de voûte keystone or boss (architecturally speaking)
clocher-mur the west front of a church that rises high above the roofline for its entire width to make a bell tower; a common feature in medieval architecture in many parts of southwest France
col pass

colimaçon (escalier en) spiral (staircase)
collégiale collegiate church
colombage half-timbering (not to be confused with colombier)
colombier dovecot (not to be confused with colombage)
(les) combles attic, loft, garret; roof timbers
commanderie local headquarters of a knightly order (like the Templars or Knights Hospitallers), usually to look after the order's lands and properties in an area
commune in the Middle Ages, the government of a free town or city; today, the smallest unit of local government, encompassing a town or village
(les) communs outbuildings
corps de logis main building
côte coast; on wine labels *côte, coteaux* and *costières* mean 'hills' or 'slopes'
cour court; courtyard (a *cour d'honneur* is the principal courtyard of a château)
cours wide main street, like an elongated main square
couvent convent or monastery
croquant peasant guerilla in the anti-French revolts of the 17th and 18th centuries
cul-de-lampe sculpted pendant at the bottom of a rib or vault
domestique as an adjective, domestic, but just as commonly used as a noun meaning servant
donjon castle keep
douves (sèches) (dry) moat
ecluse canal lock
enceinte defensive enclosure (also means pregnant)
enfeu niche in a church's exterior or interior wall for a tomb
enfilade series of linked rooms
estampe engraving (*sur bois* = woodcut)
fabrique folly (more commonly manufacture or factory)
fenêtre à meneaux mullioned window
fossé ditch
fraise strawberry, but also ruff

fusain charcoal

géminé twin

gentilhommière a small country château, especially popular in Périgord in the 18th century

gisant a sculpted prone effigy on a tomb

gîte shelter

gîte d'étape basic shelter for walkers

Grande Randonnée (GR) long distance hiking path

grange farm

herse portcullis; (in agriculture) harrow

historié historiated (decorated with flowers or figures or animals, often telling a story in pictures)

hôtel originally the town residence of the nobility; by the 18th century became more generally used for any large, private residence; also a hotel

investir to invest, but also to besiege

lavoir communal fountain, usually covered, for the washing of clothes

lucarne dormer, attic or gable window

mairie town hall

la maison ordinary word for a house, but also a euphemism for a château, which it would be too vulgar to refer to directly

maquis Mediterranean scrub; also used as a term for the French Resistance during the Second World War

mascaron an ornamental mask, usually one carved on the keystone of an arch

mécène patron

modillon a stone projecting from the cornice of a church, carved with a face or animal figure

ogive diagonal rib (in architectural vaulting); an *arc en ogive* is a lancet arch; an *ogive nucléaire* is a modern instrument of the Apocalypse, a nuclear warhead

parlement a regional law court before the Revolution, with members appointed by the king; by the late Ancien Régime *parlements* exercised a great deal of influence over political affairs

particule (nom à) name with a handle (i.e. nobleman's name indicated by a 'de' or 'du' in front of the surname)

pech hill

pignon gable (*avoir pignon sur rue* = to be prosperous, or to have a shop in a prime position)

pleurant weeper, mourner

pont-levis drawbridge

porte cochère carriage entrance

poudre de succession 'powder of inheritance' (euphemism for poison)

poutre beam

presqu'île peninsula

primitif early master (in painting)

puy high point (also *pujol*)

retable a carved or painted altarpiece, often consisting of a number of scenes or sculptural ensembles

rez-de-chausée (rc) ground floor (US first floor)

rinceau(x) ornamental foliage, foliated scroll

romain Roman (note difference from *roman* in French; a *roman*, as a noun, is a novel)

sablière beam, stringer

sens de la visite generally not sense of the visit, but direction to follow on the visit

sens interdit no entry

sens unique one way

tomber en quenouille to pass into the female line or fall to the distaff

tourelle turret

transi in a tomb, a relief of the decomposing cadaver

travée bay (in church architecture); span (of bridge)

trumeau the column between twin doors of a church portal, often carved with reliefs

tympanum semicircular panel over a church door; often the occasion for the most ambitious ensembles of medieval sculpture

verdure tapestry representing trees or foliage as the main motif (more commonly means greenery or salad vegetables)

vieille ville historic, old quarter of town

village perché hilltop village

visite libre unaccompanied visit, not free visit (which would be *visite gratuite*)

vitrail (plural vitraux) stained glass window(s)

voûte vault or arch (*en anse de panier*: basket-handle arch; *d'arête*: groined vault; *en berceau*: barrel vault; *en éventail*: fan vault; *d'ogives*: ribbed vault; *en plein cintre*: semicircular arch)

Chronology

BC
c. 1,000,000: Arrival of first people in France
35,000–9,000: Palaeolithic cave painting
c. 4500: Beginnings of Neolithic civilization
c. 1000: Beginnings of Celtic migration
c. 600: Marseille founded as a Greek colony
121: Roman conquest of Provence
58: Julius Caesar begins the conquest of Gaul

AD
260–76: Incursions of Alemanni and Franks
c. 397: Death of St Martin of Tours
406: Germanic tribes breach the Rhine
c. 450: Celtic refugees from Britain begin to
settle in Brittany
455: Visigothic kingdom established in
Aquitaine, Franks occupy much of northern
Gaul, Burgundians the Rhône Valley
475: Formal end of the Western Roman Empire
Clovis (482–511) Merovingian
Frank rules most of Gaul
511: Division of Frankish kingdom between
Clovis' four sons
578: Gascons (Basques) begin to settle what
is now Gascony
687: Pépin of Herstal reunites the three
Merovingian kingdoms
732: Charles Martel stops the Arab invasion
at the Battle of Poitiers
Pépin the Short (751–68)
754–6: Frankish invasions of Italy in support
of the Pope
Charles Ier (Charlemagne, 768–814)
800: Charlemagne crowned Emperor in Rome
Louis Ier (the Pious, 814–40)
843: Treaty of Verdun, division of the
Carolingian Empire into three parts
845: First Viking raid on Paris
Charles II (the Bald, 843–77)
885: Count Eudes repels Vikings from Paris
Eudes (888–98)
896: Vikings begin to settle in Normandy
911: Duchy of Normandy created under
Norman Duke Rollo

Hugues Capet (987–96)
1066: Duke William of Normandy
conquers England
1095: First Crusade proclaimed at Clermont
1115: Foundation of the first Cistercian abbey at
Clairvaux, by St Bernard
Louis VII (1137–80)
1140: St-Denis begun, first Gothic church
1142: Death of Peter Abelard
1152: Louis divorces Eleanor of Aquitaine, who
in turn marries Henry II of England
Philippe II Auguste (1180–1223)
1190: Building of the original Louvre
1204–8: Philippe Auguste wrests control
of Normandy, Anjou and the Touraine
from the English
1209: Albigensian Crusade begins
1214: French victory at the Battle of Bouvines
1218: Death of Simon de Montfort at the Siege
of Toulouse
Louis VIII (1223–6)
Louis IX (St Louis, 1226–70)
1249: Louis's crusade to Egypt results in his
capture in battle
Philippe IV (the Fair, 1285–1314)
1302: First meeting of the Estates-General
1305: Papacy moves to Avignon
Louis X (1314–16)
Philippe V (1316–22)
Charles IV (the Fair, 1322–28)
Philippe VI (1328–50)
1328: Edward III of England proclaims himself
King of France; Hundred Years War begins
1346: Battle of Crécy
1347–9: The Black Plague
Jean II (the Good, 1350–64)
1358: Revolt of Etienne Marcel
Charles V (1364–80)
Charles VI (1380–1422)
1392: Beginnings of the factional strife of
Armagnacs and Bourguignons
1420: English occupy Paris
Charles VII (1422–61)

1438: Pragmatic Sanction places the French Church under royal control

1453: English chased out of France

Louis XI (1461–83)

1482: Burgundy becomes part of France

Charles VIII (1483–98)

1494: First invasion of Italy

Louis XII (1498–1515)

François Ier (1515–47)

1515–47: Wars in Italy

1525: François I captured in battle by imperial forces at Pavia

Henri II (1547–59)

1559: Treaty of Cateau-Cambrésis; end of French designs in Italy

François II (1559–60)

Charles IX (1560–74)

1562: Beginning of the Wars of Religion

1572: St Bartholomew's Day massacre of Protestants

Henri III (1574–89)

1589: Assassinations of the Duc de Guise and the King

Henri IV (1589–1610)

1594: Henri IV converts to Catholicism, enters Paris

1598: Edict of Nantes proclaimed; end of religious wars

Louis XIII (1610–43)

1610–24: Regency of Marie de' Medici

1624: Cardinal Richelieu becomes minister

1627–8: Siege of Huguenot La Rochelle

Louis XIV (1643–1715)

1643: Cardinal Mazarin becomes minister

1659: Treaty of the Pyrenees with Spain; France gains Roussillon

1682: King abandons Paris for newly built Palace of Versailles

1685: Revocation of the Edict of Nantes

1701–19: War of the Spanish Succession

Louis XV (1715–74)

1715–23: Regency of Philippe d'Orléans

1720: Bursting of John Law's 'Mississippi Bubble'

1756–63: Seven Years' War; France loses most of its American possessions to Britain

Louis XVI (1774–92)

1789: Beginning of Revolution; convocation of the Estates-General, storming of the Bastille

1791: Old provinces abolished; France divided into *départements*

1792: First Republic proclaimed

1793: The Terror; execution of Louis XVI

1795–9: Rule of the Directoire

1799: 'Coup of Brumaire'; Napoleon seizes power

Napoleon Ier (Emperor, 1804–15)

1814: Allies enter Paris; Napoleon sent to Elba

Louis XVIII (1814–24)

1815: The Hundred Days; Battle of Waterloo

Charles X (1824–30)

1830: Revolt of the 'Trois Glorieuses' overthrows Charles X

Louis-Philippe (1830–48)

1848: 'Revolution of contempt'; Second Republic formed

1851: Coup of Louis-Napoléon

Napoléon III (Emperor, 1852–70)

1870: Franco-Prussian War; disaster at Sedan, siege of Paris

1871: Paris Commune; Third Republic proclaimed at Versailles

1889: Paris Exposition, opening of Eiffel Tower

1894: 'Dreyfus Affair' begins

1914–18: First World War; France loses 10 per cent of its population

1919: Treaty of Versailles

1920: Newly elected President Paul Deschanel goes mad, falls off a train in the middle of the night and wanders through France in his pyjamas

1927: Construction starts on the Maginot Line

1934: Stavisky scandals: demonstrations and riots

1936: Election of Popular Front government

1940: Defeat by the Nazis; 'French State' government set up at Vichy in the unoccupied zone under Marshal Pétain

1943: Germans occupy all of France

1944: Normandy landings

1946: Fourth Republic; De Gaulle in power 1946–8

1954: Defeat in Vietnam at Dienbienphu

1958: Return of De Gaulle to power

1962: Retreat from Algeria, followed by the migration of a million *pied noirs* into France

1968: Students' revolt; De Gaulle resigns the following year

1968: Opening of space port at Kourou, French Guiana

1981: Election of first Socialist President, François Mitterrand

1995: Jacques Chirac elected president

1996: Death of François Mitterrand

Index

Main page references are in **bold**. Page references to maps are in *italics*.

Author's Acknowledgements

Philippe Barbour

I would like to dedicate this book to all my French family, who have made France such a very happy place for me.

My first enormous thank you goes to all the press officers of the French *départements* and to all the guides at the countless sights who have helped me with such bounding enthusiasm in the preparation and revision of this book. The complimentary ferry crossing from Condor Ferries was greatly appreciated too this time round.

A big thank you to Linda McQueen, my Cadogan editor and computer teacher, not just for her work, but also for her cheerfulness. Many thanks to Nick Rider for his contribution. A special thank you to Anselm Eustace for his sterling work updating the Travel and Practical chapters.

Lots of my friends supported me with wonderful visits during the preparation of the first edition of this book. John Lotherington was an angel during the revision. As ever, the biggest thanks of all go to my parents and to Ninan for providing me with love, encouragement and support, with the happiest of times in Brittany, and with one of the most beautiful offices in the world, in my parents' adoptive Drôme.

France
touring atlas

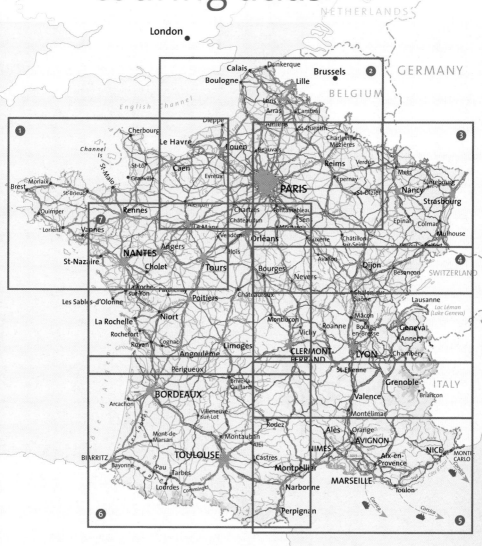

NETHERLANDS

Amsterdam

London

GERMANY

BELGIUM

English Channel

Calais
Dunkerque
Boulogne
Brussels
Lille
Lens
Arras
Cambrai
Amiens
St-Quentin
Charleville-
Mézières
Reims
Verdun
Metz
Sarrebourg
Nancy
Strasbourg
Épinal
Colmar
Mulhouse
Belfort
Châtillon-
sur-Seine
Auxerre
Dijon
Besançon
SWITZERLAND

Cherbourg
Le Havre
Rouen
Beauvais
PARIS
Épernay
St-Dizier
Channel Is
St-Lô
Granville
Caen
Évreux
Chartres
Fontainebleau
Sens
Montargis
St-Malo
St-Brieuc
Morlaix
Brest
Quimper
Lorient
Vannes
Rennes
Alençon
Le Mans
Vendôme
Blois
Orléans
Nevers
Avallon
Angers
NANTES
Cholet
Tours
Bourges
Châteauroux
Montluçon
Lausanne
Lac Léman
(Lake Geneva)
Mâcon
Bourg-
en-Bresse
Geneva
Annecy
Chambéry
Chalon-
sur-Saône
Roanne
Vichy
LYON
St-Nazaire
La Roche-
sur-Yon
Parthenay
Poitiers
Châtellerault
Niort
Les Sables-d'Olonne
La Rochelle
Rochefort
Royan
Cognac
Gironde
Angoulême
Limoges
CLERMONT-
FERRAND
St-Étienne
Grenoble
Briançon
ITALY
Valence
Montélimar
Périgueux
Brive-la-
Gaillarde
BORDEAUX
Arcachon
Villeneuve-
sur-Lot
Rodez
Alès
Orange
AVIGNON
NICE
MONTE-
CARLO
Mont-de-
Marsan
Montauban
Albi
NÎMES
Aix-en-
Provence
BIARRITZ
Bayonne
Pau
Tarbes
Lourdes
TOULOUSE
Castres
Montpellier
MARSEILLE
Toulon
Narbonne
Perpignan
Corsica
Corsica
Côte d'Argent

① ② ③ ④ ⑤ ⑥ ⑦

SPAIN

Madrid

N

100 km

50 miles

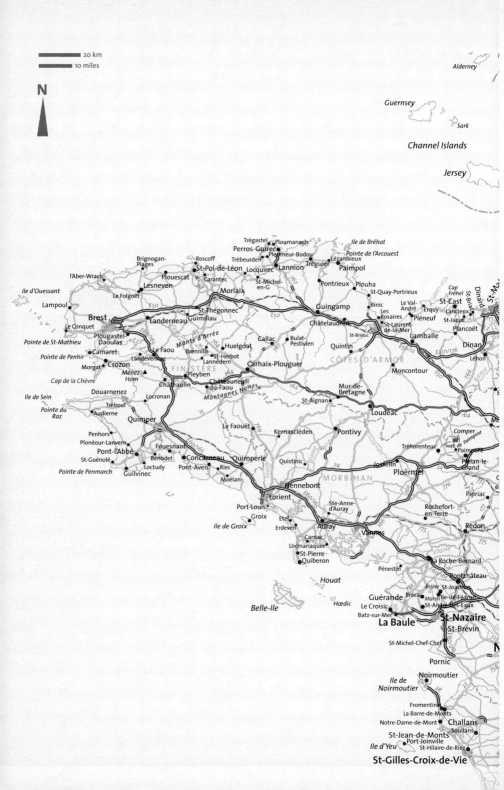

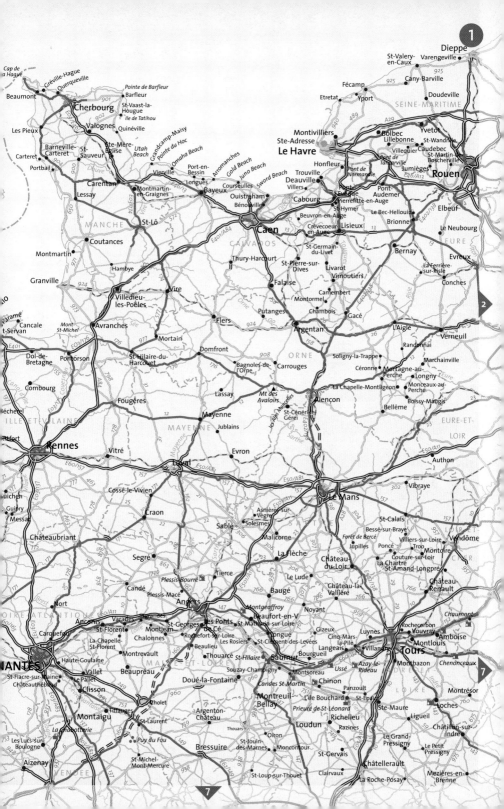

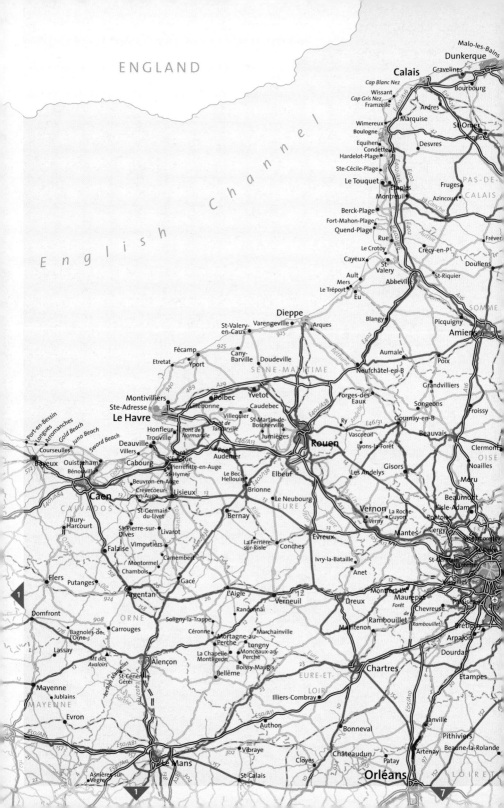

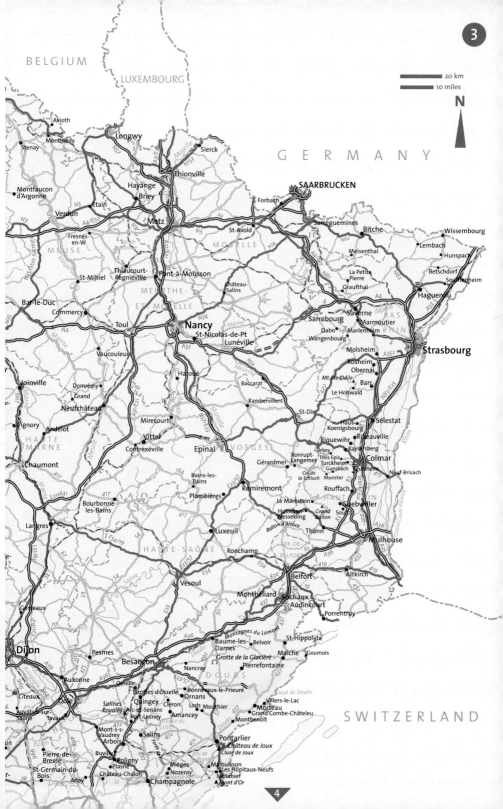

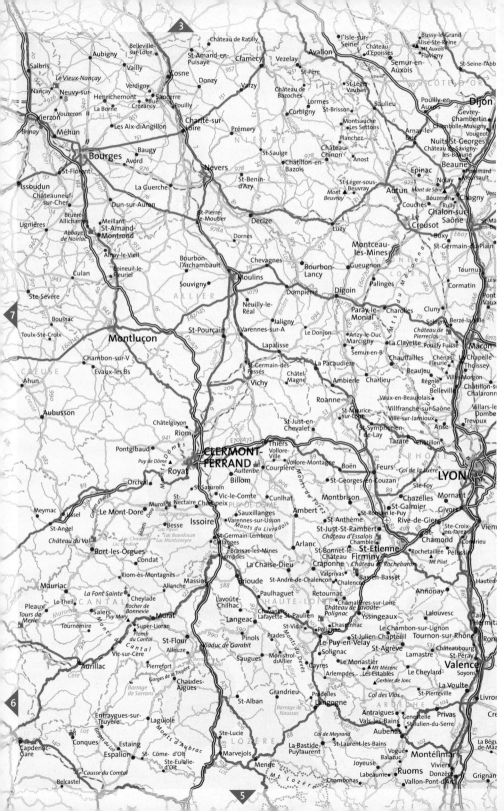

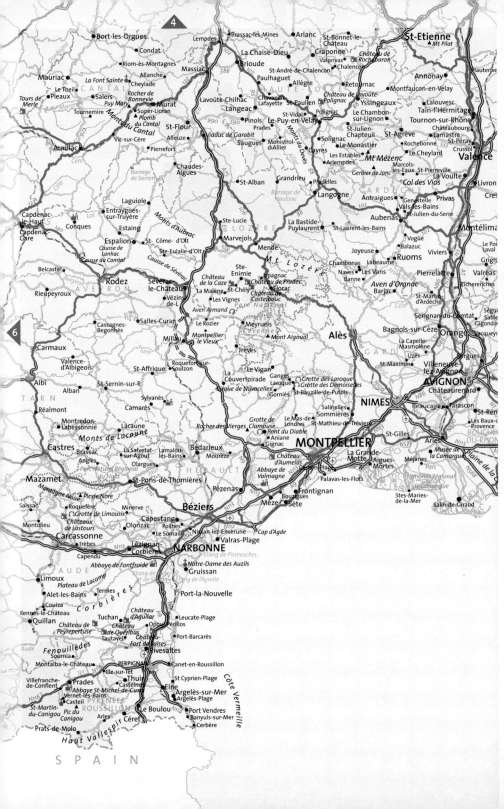

20 km
10 miles

N

ITALY

CÔTE D'AZUR

La Côte-St-André
Voiron
St-Laurent-du-P.
Allevard
Méribel
Pralognan-la-Vanoise
Parc National de la Vanoise
Bonneval
Bessans
St-Etienne-de-St-Geoirs
Tullins
St-Pierre-de-Chartreuse
Val-Thorens
Val-Thorens
Dent Parrachée
Aussois
Lanslebourg
Roybon
Le Pleyney
Pipay
Prapoutel
La Chambre
Avrieux
Modane
St-Antoine-l'Abbaye
Fort-du-St-Eynard
Valloire
St-Marcellin
Grenoble
Eybens
Chamrousse
Alpe-d'Huez
La Grave
Névache
Plampinet
Pont-en-Royans
Villard-de-Lans
Uriage
Vizille
Le Bourg-d'Oisans
Les Deux-Alpes
La Meije
Le Monetier
La Salle
Gorges de la Bourne
Venosc
La Meije
Chantemerle
Montgenèvre
Grands Goulets
La Ch-en-Vercors
St-Christophe-en-Oisans
Massif des Ecrins
Ecrins
Mt Pelvoux
Serre Chevalier
Briançon
Vassieux-en-Vercors
Vallouise
Col d'Izoard
Col de a Bataille
Vercors
Parc National des Ecrins
Parc Nat Reg du Queyras
Abriès
Aiguilles
Château-Queyras
St-Véran
L'Obiou
Vieux Chaillol
Mont-Dauphin
Ceillac
M Viso
Châtillon-en-Diois
Col du Festre
HAUTE-ALPES
Risoul
Guillestre
Vars
Col Bayard
St-André-d'Embrun
Embrun
Les Claux
Les Orres
Saillans
Die
Gap
St-Sauveur
Col de Vars
DRÔME
Bourdeaux
Col de Cabre
Barrage de Serre-Ponçon
Dieulefit
Valouse
Condorcet
Barcelonnette
Aubres
Les Pilles
Pra-Loup
Le Sauze
Nyons
Baronnies
Le Chapeau de Gendarme
Mérindol-les-Oliviers
Buis-les-Baronnies
St-Etienne-de-Tinée
Vaison-la-Romaine
Brantes
Montbrun-les-Bains
Sisteron
Malaucène
Aurel
Montagne de Lure
ALPES-DE-HAUT-PROVENCE
Montmirail
Sault
Volonne
Digne-les-Bains
Col de Tende
Notre-Dame-des-Fontaines
VAUCLUSE
Carpentras
Plateau de Vaucluse
Montagne de Lure
St-André-les-Alpes
St-Sauveur-sur-Tinée
Mont Bégo
Tende
St-Dalmas-de-Tende
Saorge
Alpes-les-Pilles-Fontaines
Abbaye de Sénanque
Roussillon
Rustrel
Apt
Plateau de Valensole
Castellane
Clans
Lantosque
L'Authion
Col de Turini
La Tour
Col du Pérus
Village des Bories
Lacoste
Montfuron
Manosque
Riez
Moustiers-Ste-Marie
Montagne du Cheiron
Levens
Peille
Sospel
Ménerbes
Bonnieux
Vitrolles
Col de Vence
Peillon
Menton
Lourmarin
Cucuron
Grambois
Comps-sur-Artuby
Vence
Cagnes-sur-Mer
Monte-Carlo
MONACO
Jonas
Cadenet
Ansouis
La Tour d'Aigues
Quinson
Aups
Grasse
Mougins
Blot
St-Jean-Cap-Ferrat
Abbaye de Silvacane
Pertuis
Montmeyan
La Verdière
Villecroze
Tourtour
Draguignan
Mandelieu-La-Napoule
Antibes
Juan-les-Pins
Salon-de-Provence
Barjols
Salernes
Cannes
St-Chamas
Vauvenargues
Cotignac
Entrecasteaux
Lorgues
Le Muy
Mont Vinaigre
Pic de l'Ours
Pic du Cap Roux
Le Tholonet
St-Maximin-la-Ste-Baume
Abbaye du Thoronet
Les Arcs
Fréjus
St-Raphaël
AIX-EN-PROVENCE
Brignoles
Etang de Berre
La Garde-Freinet
Ste-Maxime
Marignane
Massif de la Ste-Baume
Grimaud
Cap de St-Tropez
MARSEILLE
Aubagne
Cogolin
St-Tropez
Ile Pomègues
Le Gros Cerveau
Cavalaire-sur-Mer
Cap Croisette
Cassis
TOULON
Le Lavandou
Cap Nègre
La Ciotat
Bandol
Hyères
Les Calanques
Sanary-sur-Mer
La Seyne
L'Almanarre
Cap Blanc
Ile des Embiez
Cap Sicié
Giens
La Tour-Fondue
Ile du Levant
Porquerolles
Ile de Port-Cros
Ile de Porquerolles
Corsica
Corsica
Corsica
NICE
Ventimiglia
MARITIMES
St-Martin-Vésubie

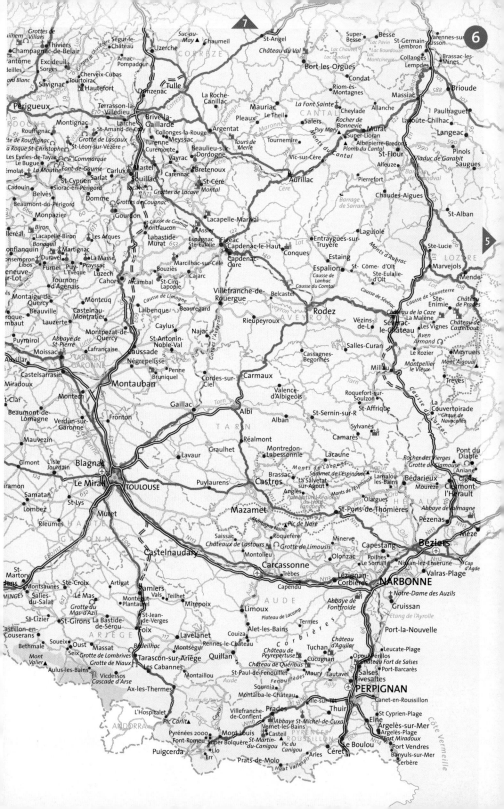